APPLIED CORPORATE FINANCE

THIRD EDITION

ASWATH DAMODARAN

STERN SCHOOL OF BUSINESS
NEW YORK UNIVERSITY

JOHN WILEY & SONS, INC.

WILEY

DEDICATION

To Michele, who keeps me sane,
and to my children, Ryan, Brendan, Kendra
and Kiran, for grounding me in reality.

VP and PUBLISHER: George Hoffman
PROJECT EDITOR: Jennifer Manias
EDITORIAL ASSISTANT: Emily McGee
PRODUCTION MANAGER: Janis Soo
ASSISTANT PRODUCTION EDITOR: Elaine S. Chew
ASSOCIATE DIRECTOR OF MARKETING: Amy Scholz
ASSISTANT MARKETING MANAGER: Diane Mars
MARKETING ASSISTANT: Laura Finley
MEDIA EDITOR: Greg Chaput
COVER DESIGNER: Wendy Lai
COVER CREDIT: © Vincent MacNamara/Alamy

This book was set in 10/12 Times Roman by Laserwords U.S. Inc. and printed and bound by Malloy Lithographers. The cover was printed by Malloy Lithographers.

This book is printed on acid-free paper. ∞

Library of Congress Cataloging-in-Publication Data
Damodaran, Aswath.
    Applied corporate finance / Aswath Damodaran.—3rd ed.
        p. cm.
    Includes index.
    ISBN 978-0-470-38464-0 (pbk.)
    1. Corporations—Finance. I. Title.

HG4011.D26 2011
658.15-dc22

                                          2009049434

Printed in the United States of America

10 9 8 7 6 5

About the Author

Aswath Damodaran is the Kerschner Family Professor of Finance at the Stern School of Business at New York University and teaches the corporate finance and equity valuation courses in the MBA program. He received his MBA and PhD from the University of California at Los Angeles. His research interests lie in valuation, portfolio management, and applied corporate finance. He has published in the *Journal of Financial and Quantitative Analysis*, the *Journal of Finance*, the *Journal of Financial Economics*, and the *Review of Financial Studies*.

He has written three books on equity valuation (*Damodaran on Valuation, Investment Valuation, The Dark Side of Valuation*) and two on corporate finance (*Corporate Finance: Theory and Practice, Applied Corporate Finance: A User's Manual*) and has coedited a book on investment management with Peter Bernstein (*Investment Management*) and a book on investment philosophies (*Investment Philosophies*). His book *Investment Fables* was released in 2004, and his book on risk management and measurement, *Strategic Risk Taking*, was published in 2006.

He was a visiting lecturer at the University of California, Berkeley, from 1984 to 1986, where he received the Earl Cheit Outstanding Teaching Award in 1985. He has been at NYU since 1986, received the Stern School of Business Excellence in Teaching Award (awarded by the graduating class) in 1988, 1991, 1992, 1999, 2001, 2006, 2007, and 2008, and was the youngest winner of the University-wide Distinguished Teaching Award (in 1990). He was profiled in *Business Week* as one of the top twelve business school professors in the United States in 1994.

PREFACE

Let me begin this preface with a confession of a few of my own biases. First, I believe that theory and the models that flow from it should provide the tools to understand, analyze, and solve problems. The test of a model or theory then should not be based on its elegance, but on its usefulness in problem solving. Second, there is little in corporate financial theory that is new and revolutionary. The core principles of corporate finance are grounded in common sense and have changed little over time. That should not be surprising. Corporate finance is only a few decades old, and people have been running businesses for thousands of years; it would be exceedingly presumptuous of us to believe that they were in the dark until corporate finance theorists came along and told them what to do. To be fair, it is true that corporate financial theory has made advances in taking commonsense principles and providing structure, but these advances have primarily had to do with the details. The storyline in corporate finance has remained remarkably consistent over time.

Talking about storylines allows me to set the first theme of this book. This book tells a story that essentially summarizes the corporate finance view of the world. It classifies all decisions made by any business into three groups—decisions of where to invest the resources or funds that the business has raised, either internally or externally (the investment decision); decisions of where and how to raise funds to finance these investments (the financing decision); and decisions of to what extent, and in what form, to return funds back to the owners (the dividend decision). As I see it, the first principles of corporate finance can be summarized in Figure 1, which also lays out a site map for the book. Every section of this book relates to some part of this picture, and each chapter is introduced with it, with emphasis on that portion that will be analyzed in that chapter. (Note the chapter numbers below each section.) Put another way, there are no sections of this book that are not traceable to this framework.

As you look at the chapter outline for the book, you are probably wondering where the chapters on present value, option pricing, and bond pricing are, as well as the chapters on short-term financial management, working capital, and international finance. The first set of chapters, which we can classify as "tools" chapters, are now contained in the appendices—and I relegated them there not because I think that they are unimportant, but because I want the focus to stay on the storyline. It is important that we understand the concept of time value of money, but only in the context of measuring returns on investments better and valuing business. Option pricing theory is elegant and provides impressive insights, but only in the context of looking at options embedded in projects and financing instruments like convertible bonds.

The second set of chapters I excluded for a very different reason. As I see it, the basic principles of whether and how much you should invest in inventory, or how generous your credit terms should be, are no different than the basic principles that apply if you are building a plant, buying equipment, or opening a new store. Put another way, there is no logical basis for the differentiation between investments in the latter (which in most corporate finance books is covered in the capital budgeting chapters) and the

Figure 1 Corporate Finance: First Principles

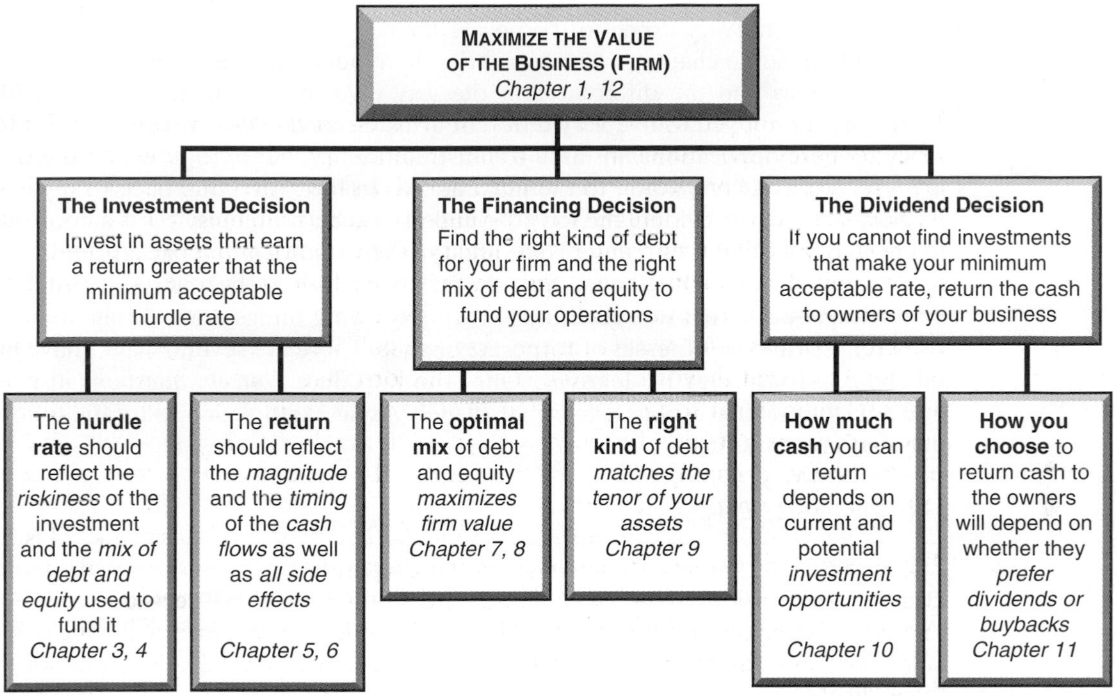

```
                    ┌─────────────────────────────┐
                    │   MAXIMIZE THE VALUE         │
                    │   OF THE BUSINESS (FIRM)     │
                    │      Chapter 1, 12           │
                    └─────────────────────────────┘
```

The Investment Decision	The Financing Decision	The Dividend Decision
Invest in assets that earn a return greater that the minimum acceptable hurdle rate	Find the right kind of debt for your firm and the right mix of debt and equity to fund your operations	If you cannot find investments that make your minimum acceptable rate, return the cash to owners of your business

The **hurdle rate** should reflect the *riskiness* of the investment and the *mix of debt and equity* used to fund it *Chapter 3, 4*	The **return** should reflect the *magnitude* and the *timing* of the *cash flows* as well as *all side effects* *Chapter 5, 6*	The **optimal mix** of debt and equity *maximizes firm value* *Chapter 7, 8*	The **right kind** of debt *matches the tenor of your assets* *Chapter 9*	**How much cash** you can return depends on current and potential *investment opportunities* *Chapter 10*	**How you choose** to return cash to the owners will depend on whether they *prefer dividends or buybacks* *Chapter 11*

The principles are universal

Big and small Firms
U.S. Firms
Foreign Firms
Private Firms
Public Firms

former (which are considered in the working capital chapters). You should invest in either if—and only if—the returns from the investment exceed the hurdle rate from the investment; the fact that one is short-term and the other is long-term is irrelevant. The same thing can be said about international finance. Should the investment or financing principles be different just because a company is considering an investment in Thailand and the cash flows are in Thai baht instead of in the United States, where the cash flows are in dollars? I do not believe so, and in my view separating the decisions only leaves readers with that impression. Finally, most corporate finance books that have chapters on small firm management and private firm management use them to illustrate the differences between these firms and the more conventional large publicly traded firms used in the other chapters. Although such differences exist, the commonalities between different types of firms vastly overwhelm the differences, providing a testimonial to the internal consistency of corporate finance. In summary, the second theme of this book is the emphasis on the *universality of corporate financial principles* across different firms, in different markets, and across different types of decisions.

The way I have tried to bring this universality to life is by using five firms through the book to illustrate each concept; they include a large, publicly traded U.S. corporation (Disney), a small, emerging market commodity company (Aracruz Celulose, a Brazilian paper and pulp company), an Indian manufacturing company that is part of a family group (Tata Chemicals), a financial service firm (Deutsche Bank), and a small private

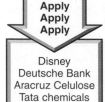

Apply
Apply
Apply

Disney
Deutsche Bank
Aracruz Celulose
Tata chemicals
Bookscape

business (Bookscape, an independent New York City bookstore). Although the notion of using real companies to illustrate theory is neither novel nor revolutionary, there are two key differences in the way they are used in this book. First, these companies are analyzed on every aspect of corporate finance introduced here, rather than just selectively in some chapters. Consequently, the reader can see for himself or herself the similarities and the differences in the way investment, financing, and dividend principles are applied to five very different firms. Second, I do not consider this to be a book where applications are used to illustrate theory, but a book where the theory is presented as a companion to the illustrations. In fact, reverting back to my earlier analogy of theory providing the tools for understanding problems, this is a book where the problem solving takes center stage and the theory stays in the background.

Reading through the theory and the applications can be instructive and even interesting, but there is no substitute for actually trying things out to bring home both the strengths and weaknesses of corporate finance. There are several ways I have made this book a tool for active learning. One is to introduce *concept questions* at regular intervals that invite responses from the reader. As an example, consider the following illustration from Chapter 7:

2.1   THE EFFECTS OF DIVERSIFICATION ON VENTURE CAPITALIST

You are comparing the required returns of two venture capitalists who are interested in investing in the same software firm. One has all of his capital invested in only software firms, whereas the other has invested her capital in small companies in a variety of businesses. Which of these two will have the higher required rate of return?
a.   The venture capitalist who is invested only in software companies.
b.   The venture capitalist who is invested in a variety of businesses.
c.   Cannot answer without more information.

Active
Learning

Concept
Questions

Live Case
Studies

This question is designed to check on a concept introduced in an earlier chapter on risk and return on the difference between risk that can be eliminated by holding a diversified portfolio and risk that cannot, then connecting it to the question of how a business seeking funds from a venture capitalist might be affected by this perception of risk. The answer to this question, in turn, will expose the reader to more questions about whether venture capital in the future will be provided by diversified funds, and what a specialized venture capitalist (who invests in one sector alone) might need to do to survive in such an environment. This will allow readers to see what—to me, at least—is one of the most exciting aspects of corporate finance: its capacity to provide a framework that can be used to make sense of the events that occur around us every day, and to make reasonable forecasts about future directions.

The second active experience in this book is found in the live case studies at the end of each chapter. These case studies essentially take the concepts introduced in the chapter and provide a framework for applying them to any company the reader chooses. Guidelines on where to get the information to answer the questions are also provided.

Although corporate finance provides an internally consistent and straightforward template for the analysis of any firm, information is clearly the lubricant that allows us to do the analysis. There are three steps in the information process—acquiring the

Links to the
Internet
Data sets on
the Web
Spreadsheets

information, filtering what is useful from what is not, and keeping the information updated. Accepting the limitations of the printed page on all of these aspects, I have put the power of online information to use in several ways.

1. The case studies that require the information are accompanied by links to Web sites that carry this information.

2. The data sets that are difficult to get from the Internet or that are specific to this book, such as the updated versions of the tables, are available on my own Web site (www.damodaran.com) and are integrated into the book. As an example, the table that contains the dividend yields and payout ratios by industry sectors for the most recent quarter is referenced in Chapter 9 as follows:

 There is a data set online that summarizes dividend yields and payout ratios for U.S. companies, categorized by sector.

You can get to this table by going to the website for the book (on damodaran.com) and checking for datasets under Chapter 9.

3. The spreadsheets used to analyze the firms in the book are also available on my Web site and are referenced in the book. For instance, the spreadsheet used to estimate the optimal debt ratio for Disney in Chapter 8 is referenced as follows:

 Capstru.xls: This spreadsheet allows you to compute the optimal debt ratio firm value for any firm, using the same information used for Disney. It has updated interest coverage ratios and spreads built in.

As with the dataset listing above, you can get this spreadsheet by going to the Web site for the book and checking under spreadsheets under Chapter 8.

For those of you between you and have: who have read the first two editions of this book, much of what I have said in this preface should be familiar. But there are two places where you will find this book to be different:

1. For better or insert between or and worse: for worse, the banking and market crisis of 2008 has left lasting wounds on our psyches as investors and shaken some of our core beliefs in how to estimate key numbers and approach fundamental tradeoffs. I have tried to adapt some of what I have learned about equity risk premiums and the distress costs of debt into the discussion.

2. I have always been skeptical about behavioral finance, but I think that the area has some very interesting insights on how managers behave that we ignore at our own peril. I have made my first foray into incorporating some of the work in behavioral financing into investing, financing, and dividend decisions.

As I set out to write this book, I had two objectives in mind. One was to write a book that not only reflects the way I teach corporate finance in a classroom but, more important, one that conveys the fascination and enjoyment I get out of the subject matter. The second was to write a book for practitioners that students would find useful, rather than the other way around. I do not know whether I have fully accomplished either objective, but I do know I had an immense amount of fun with this volume. I hope you do, too!

ACKNOWLEDGMENTS

I would like to acknowledge all of those students who have taken my corporate finance classes, patiently sitting through lectures, helping me fix my errors, providing invaluable suggestions, and helping me refine my message. In addition, I would like to thank all of the reviewers who have provided feedback over the three editions of this text: Sankar Acharya, University of Illinois at Chicago; Steven J. Ahn, University of Georgia; William H. Brent, Howard University; Miranda Lam Detzler, University of Massachusetts, Boston; Kathleen P. Fuller, University of Georgia; Robert T. Kleiman, Michael J. Lee, University of Maryland, Oakland University; James Nelson, Florida State University; Sarah Peck, Marquette University; Paul Pfleiderer, Stanford University; Sunder Raghavan, Embry-Riddle University; Assem Safieddine, Michigan State University; Peruvemba K. Satish, Washington State University; Hany A. Shawky, University at Albany; Paul A. Spindt, Tulane University; William Stahlin, Stevens Institute of Technology; Mark Stohs, California State University, Fullerton; Mahmoud Wahab, University of Hartford; and Jasmine Yur-Austin, California State University, Long Beach.

Contents

CHAPTER 12   VALUATION: PRINCIPLES AND PRACTICE   **596**

CHAPTER 1

THE FOUNDATIONS

It's all corporate finance.
MY UNBIASED VIEW OF THE WORLD

Every decision made in a business has financial implications, and any decision that involves the use of money is a corporate financial decision. Defined broadly, everything that a business does fits under the rubric of corporate finance. It is, in fact, unfortunate that we even call the subject corporate finance, because it suggests to many observers a focus on how large corporations make financial decisions and seems to exclude small and private businesses from its purview. A more appropriate title for this book would be *Business Finance*, because the basic principles remain the same, whether one looks at large, publicly traded firms or small, privately run businesses. All businesses have to invest their resources wisely, find the right kind and mix of financing to fund these investments, and return cash to the owners if there are not enough good investments.

In this chapter, we will lay the foundation for the rest of the book by listing the three fundamental principles that underlie corporate finance—the investment, financing, and dividend principles—and the objective of firm value maximization that is at the heart of corporate financial theory.

THE FIRM: STRUCTURAL SET-UP

In the chapters that follow, we will use **firm** generically to refer to any business, large or small, manufacturing or service, private or public. Thus, a corner grocery store and Microsoft are both firms.

The firm's investments are generically termed **assets**. Although assets are often categorized by accountants into fixed assets, which are long-term, and current assets, which are short-term, we prefer a different categorization. The assets that the firm has already invested in are called **assets in place**, whereas those assets that the firm is expected to invest in the future are called **growth assets**. Though it may seem strange that a firm can get value from investments it has not made yet, high-growth firms get the bulk of their value from these yet-to-be-made investments.

To finance these assets, the firm can raise money from two sources. It can raise funds from investors or financial institutions by promising investors a fixed claim (interest payments) on the cash flows generated by the assets, with a limited—or no—role in the day-to-day running of the business. We categorize this type of financing as **debt**.

Alternatively, it can offer a residual claim on the cash flows (i.e., investors can get what is left over after the interest payments have been made) and a much greater role in the operation of the business. We call this **equity**. Note that these definitions are general enough to cover both private firms, where debt may take the form of bank loans and equity is the owner's own money, as well as publicly traded companies, where the firm may issue bonds (to raise debt) and common stock (to raise equity).

Thus, at this stage, we can lay out the financial balance sheet of a firm as follows:

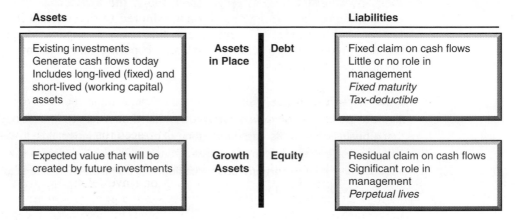

We will return to this framework repeatedly throughout this book.

FIRST PRINCIPLES

Every discipline has first principles that govern and guide everything that gets done within it. All of corporate finance is built on three principles, which we will call, rather unimaginatively, the investment principle, the financing principle, and the dividend principle. The investment principle determines where businesses invest their resources, the financing principle governs the mix of funding used to fund these investments, and the dividend principle answers the question of how much earnings should be reinvested back into the business and how much returned to the owners of the business. These core corporate finance principles can be stated as follows:

1. ***The Investment Principle*** Invest in assets and projects that *yield a return greater than the minimum acceptable hurdle rate*. The hurdle rate should be *higher for riskier projects* and should reflect the *financing mix* used—owners' funds (equity) or borrowed money (debt). Returns on projects should be measured based on *cash flows* generated and the *timing* of these cash flows; they should also consider both *positive and negative side effects* of these projects.

2. ***The Financing Principle*** Choose a *financing mix (debt and equity)* that maximizes the value of the investments made and *match the financing to the nature of the assets* being financed.

3. ***The Dividend Principle*** If there are not enough investments that earn the hurdle rate, *return the cash* to the owners of the business. In the case of a publicly traded firm, the *form of the return*—dividends or stock buybacks—will depend on what stockholders prefer.

When making investment, financing, and dividend decisions, corporate finance is single-minded about the ultimate objective, which is assumed to be maximizing the value of the business. These first principles provide the basis from which we will extract the numerous models and theories that comprise modern corporate finance, but they are also common sense principles. It is incredible conceit on our part to assume that until corporate finance was developed as a coherent discipline starting just a few decades ago, people who ran businesses made decisions randomly with no principles to govern their thinking. Good businesspeople through the ages have always recognized the importance of these first principles and adhered to them, albeit in intuitive ways. In fact, one of the ironies of recent times is that many managers at large and presumably sophisticated firms with access to the latest corporate finance technology have lost sight of these basic principles.

The Objective of the Firm

No discipline can develop cohesively over time without a unifying objective. The growth of corporate financial theory can be traced to its choice of a single objective and the development of models built around this objective. The objective in conventional corporate financial theory when making decisions is to maximize the value of the business or firm. Consequently, any decision (investment, financial, or dividend) that increases the value of a business is considered a good one, whereas one that reduces firm value is considered a poor one. Although the choice of a singular objective has provided corporate finance with a unifying theme and internal consistency, it comes at a cost. To the degree that one buys into this objective, much of what corporate financial theory posits makes sense. To the degree that this objective is flawed, however, it can be argued that the theory built on it is flawed as well. Many of the disagreements between corporate financial theorists and others (academics as well as practitioners) can be traced to fundamentally different views about the correct objective for a business. For instance, there are some critics of corporate finance who argue that firms should have multiple objectives where a variety of interests (stockholders, labor, customers) are met, and there are others who would have firms focus on what they view as simpler and more direct objectives, such as market share or profitability.

Given the significance of this objective for both the development and the applicability of corporate financial theory, it is important that we examine it much more carefully and address some of the very real concerns and criticisms it has garnered: it assumes that what stockholders do in their own self-interest is also in the best interests of the firm, it is sometimes dependent on the existence of efficient markets, and it is often blind to the social costs associated with value maximization. In the next chapter, we consider these and other issues and compare firm value maximization to alternative objectives.

The Investment Principle

Firms have scarce resources that must be allocated among competing needs. The first and foremost function of corporate financial theory is to provide a framework for firms to make this decision wisely. Accordingly, we define *investment decisions* to include not only those that create revenues and profits (such as introducing a new product line or expanding into a new market) but also those that save money (such as building a new and more efficient distribution system). Furthermore, we argue that decisions about how much and what inventory to maintain and whether and how much credit to grant to customers, which are traditionally categorized as working capital decisions, are ultimately investment decisions as well. At the other end of the spectrum, broad strategic decisions regarding which markets to enter and the acquisitions of other companies can also be considered investment decisions.

Corporate finance attempts to measure the return on a proposed investment decision and compare it to a minimum acceptable **hurdle rate** to decide whether the project is acceptable. The hurdle rate has to be set higher for riskier projects and has to reflect the financing mix used—i.e., the owner's funds (equity) or borrowed money (debt). In Chapter 3, we begin this process by defining risk and developing a procedure for measuring risk. In Chapter 4, we go about converting this risk measure into a hurdle rate—i.e., a minimum acceptable rate of return, both for entire businesses and for individual investments.

Having established the hurdle rate, we turn our attention to measuring the returns on an investment. In Chapter 5 we evaluate three alternative ways of measuring returns—conventional accounting earnings, cash flows, and time-weighted cash flows (where we consider both how large the cash flows are and when they are anticipated to come in). In Chapter 6 we consider some of the potential side costs that might not be captured in any of these measures (including costs that may be created for existing investments by taking a new investment) and side benefits (such as options to enter new markets and to expand product lines that may be embedded in new investments) and synergies, especially when the new investment is the acquisition of another firm.

The Financing Principle

Every business, no matter how large and complex, is ultimately funded with a mix of borrowed money (debt) and owner's funds (equity). With a publicly traded firm, debt may take the form of bonds and equity is usually common stock. In a private business, debt is more likely to be bank loans and an owner's savings represent equity. Though we consider the existing mix of debt and equity and its implications for the minimum acceptable hurdle rate as part of the investment principle, we throw open the question of whether the existing mix is the right one in the financing principle section. There might be regulatory and other real-world constraints on the financing mix that a business can use, but there is ample room for flexibility within these constraints. We begin this section in Chapter 7, by looking at the range of choices that exist for both private businesses and publicly traded firms between debt and equity. We then turn to the question of whether the existing mix of financing used by a business is optimal, given the objective function of maximizing firm value, in Chapter 8. Although the tradeoff between the benefits and costs of borrowing are established in qualitative terms first, we also look at quantitative approaches to arriving at the optimal mix in Chapter 8. In the first approach, we examine the specific conditions under which the optimal financing mix is the one that minimizes the minimum acceptable hurdle rate. In the second approach, we look at the effects on firm value of changing the financing mix.

When the optimal financing mix is different from the existing one, we map out the best ways of getting from where we are (the current mix) to where we would like to be (the optimal) in Chapter 9, keeping in mind the investment opportunities that the firm has and the need for timely responses, either because the firm is a takeover target or under threat of bankruptcy. Having outlined the optimal financing mix, we turn our attention to the type of financing a business should use, such as whether it should be long-term or short-term, whether the payments on the financing should be fixed or variable, and if variable, what it should be a function of. Using a basic proposition that a firm will minimize its risk from financing and maximize its capacity to use borrowed funds if it can match up the cash flows on the debt to the cash flows on the assets being financed, we design the perfect financing instrument for a firm. We then add additional considerations relating to taxes and external monitors (equity research analysts and ratings agencies) and arrive at strong conclusions about the design of the financing.

The Dividend Principle

Most businesses would undoubtedly like to have unlimited investment opportunities that yield returns exceeding their hurdle rates, but all businesses grow and mature. As a consequence, every business that thrives reaches a stage in its life when the cash flows generated by existing investments are greater than the funds needed to take on good investments. At that point, this business has to figure out ways to return the excess cash to owners. In private businesses, this may just involve the owner withdrawing a portion of his or her funds from the business. In a publicly traded corporation, this will involve either paying dividends or buying back stock. Note that firms that choose not to return cash to owners will accumulate cash balances that grow over time. Thus, analyzing whether and how much cash should be returned to the owners of a firm is the equivalent of asking (and answering) the question of how much cash accumulated in a firm is too much cash.

In Chapter 10, we introduce the basic tradeoff that determines whether cash should be left in a business or taken out of it. For stockholders in publicly traded firms, we note that this decision is fundamentally one of whether they trust the managers of the firms with their cash, and much of this trust is based on how well these managers have invested funds in the past. In Chapter 11, we consider the options available to a firm to return assets to its owners—dividends, stock buybacks, and spinoffs—and investigate how to pick between these options.

CORPORATE FINANCIAL DECISIONS, FIRM VALUE, AND EQUITY VALUE

If the objective function in corporate finance is to maximize firm value, it follows that firm value must be linked to the three corporate finance decisions outlined: investment, financing, and dividend decisions. The link between these decisions and firm value can be made by recognizing that *the value of a firm is the present value of its expected cash flows, discounted back at a rate that reflects both the riskiness of the projects of the firm and the financing mix used to finance them*. Investors form expectations about future cash flows based on observed current cash flows and expected future growth, which in turn depend on the quality of the firm's projects (its investment decisions) and the amount reinvested back into the business (its dividend decisions). The financing decisions affect the value of a firm through both the discount rate and potentially through the expected cash flows.

This neat formulation of value is put to the test by the interactions among the investment, financing, and dividend decisions and the conflicts of interest that arise between stockholders and lenders to the firm on the one hand and stockholders and managers on the other. We introduce the basic models available to value a firm and its equity in Chapter 12, and relate them back to management decisions on investment, financial, and dividend policy. In the process, we examine the determinants of value and how firms can increase their value.

A REAL-WORLD FOCUS

The proliferation of news and information on real-world businesses making decisions every day suggests that we do not need to use hypothetical examples to illustrate the principles of corporate finance. We will use five businesses through this book to make our points about corporate financial policy:

1. *Disney Corporation* Disney Corporation is a publicly traded firm with wide holdings in entertainment and media. Most people around the world recognize the Mickey Mouse logo and have heard about or visited a Disney theme park or seen some or all of the Disney animated classic movies, but it is a much more diversified corporation than most people realize. Disney's holdings include a cruise line, real estate (in the form of time shares and rental properties in Florida and South Carolina), television (Disney cable, ABC, and ESPN), publications, movie studios (Miramax, Pixar, and Disney) and consumer products. Disney will help illustrate the decisions that large multi-business and multinational corporations have to make as they are faced with the conventional corporate financial decisions: Where do we invest? How do we finance these investments? How much do we return to our stockholders?

2. *Bookscape Books* This company is a privately owned independent bookstore in New York City, one of the few left after the invasion of the bookstore chains such as Barnes and Noble and Borders. We will take Bookscape Books through the corporate financial decision-making process to illustrate some of the issues that come up when looking at small businesses with private owners.

3. *Aracruz Celulose* Aracruz Celulose is a Brazilian firm that produces eucalyptus pulp and operates its own pulp mills, electrochemical plants, and port terminals. Although it markets its products around the world for manufacturing high-grade paper, we use it to illustrate some of the questions that have to be dealt with when analyzing a company that is highly dependent upon commodity prices—paper and pulp, in this instance—and that operates in an environment where inflation is high and volatile and the economy itself is in transition.

4. *Deutsche Bank* Deutsche Bank is the leading commercial bank in Germany and is also a leading player in investment banking. We will use Deutsche Bank to illustrate some of the issues the come up when a financial service firm has to make investment, financing and dividend decisions. Since banks are highly regulated institutions, it will also serve to illustrate the constraints and opportunities created by the regulatory framework.

5. *Tata Chemicals* Tata Chemicals is a firm involved in the chemical and fertilizer business and is part of one of the largest Indian family group companies, the Tata Group, with holdings in technology, manufacturing, and service businesses.

In addition to allowing us to look at issues specific to manufacturing firms, Tata Chemicals will also give us an opportunity to examine how firms that are part of larger groups make corporate finance decisions.

We will look at every aspect of finance through the eyes of all five companies, sometimes to draw contrasts between the companies, but more often to show how much they share.

A RESOURCE GUIDE

To make the learning in this book as interactive and current as possible, we employ a variety of devices.

 This icon indicates that spreadsheet programs can be used to do some of the analysis that will be presented. For instance, there are spreadsheets that calculate the optimal financing mix for a firm as well as valuation spreadsheets.

 This symbol marks the second supporting device: updated data on some of the inputs that we need and use in our analysis that is available online for this book. Thus, when we estimate the risk parameters for firms, we will draw attention to the data set that is maintained online that reports average risk parameters by industry.

 At regular intervals, we will also ask readers to answer questions relating to a topic. These questions, which will generally be framed using real-world examples, will help emphasize the key points made in a chapter and will be marked with this icon.

 In each chapter, we will introduce a series of boxes titled "In Practice" that will look at issues that are likely to come up in practice and ways of addressing these issues.

 We examine how firms behave when it comes to assessing risk, evaluating investments and determining the mix off debt and equity, and dividend policy. To make this assessment, we will look at both surveys of decision makers (which chronicle behavior at firms) as well as the findings from studies in behavioral finance that try to explain patterns of management behavior.

SOME FUNDAMENTAL PROPOSITIONS ABOUT CORPORATE FINANCE

There are several fundamental arguments we will make repeatedly throughout this book.

- *Corporate finance has an internal consistency* that flows from its choice of maximizing firm value as the only objective function and its dependence on a few bedrock principles: risk has to be rewarded, cash flows matter more than accounting income, markets are not easily fooled, and every decision a firm makes has an effect on its value.

- *Corporate finance must be viewed as an integrated whole,* rather than a collection of decisions. Investment decisions generally affect financing decisions and vice versa; financing decisions often influence dividend decisions and vice versa. Although there are circumstances under which these decisions may be independent of each other, this is seldom the case in practice. Accordingly, it is unlikely that firms that deal with their problems on a piecemeal basis will ever resolve these problems. For instance, a firm that takes poor investments may soon find itself with a dividend problem (with insufficient funds to pay dividends) and a financing problem (because the drop in earnings may make it difficult for it to meet interest expenses).

- *Corporate finance matters to everybody* There is a corporate financial aspect to almost every decision made by a business; though not everyone will find a use for all the components of corporate finance, everyone will find a use for at least some *part* of it. Marketing managers, corporate strategists, human resource managers, and information technology managers all make corporate finance decisions every day and often don't realize it. An understanding of corporate finance will help them make better decisions.

- *Corporate finance is fun* This may seem to be the tallest claim of all. After all, most people associate corporate finance with numbers, accounting statements, and hardheaded analyses. Although corporate finance is quantitative in its focus, there is a significant component of creative thinking involved in coming up with solutions to the financial problems businesses do encounter. It is no coincidence that financial markets remain breeding grounds for innovation and change.

- *The best way to learn corporate finance is by applying its models and theories to real-world problems* Although the theory that has been developed over the past few decades is impressive, the ultimate test of any theory is application. As we show in this book, much (if not all) of the theory can be applied to real companies and not just to abstract examples, though we have to compromise and make assumptions in the process.

CONCLUSION

This chapter establishes the first principles that govern corporate finance. The investment principle specifies that businesses invest only in projects that yield a return that exceeds the hurdle rate. The financing principle suggests that the right financing mix for a firm is one that maximizes the value of the investments made. The dividend principle requires that cash generated in excess of good project needs be returned to the owners. These principles are the core for what follows in this book.

CHAPTER 2

THE OBJECTIVE IN DECISION MAKING

If you do not know where you are going, it does not matter how you get there.

ANONYMOUS

Corporate finance's greatest strength and greatest weakness is its focus on value maximization. By maintaining that focus, corporate finance preserves internal consistency and coherence and develops powerful models and theory about the right way to make investment, financing, and dividend decisions. It can be argued, however, that all of these conclusions are conditional on the acceptance of value maximization as the only objective in decision making.

In this chapter, we consider why we focus so strongly on value maximization and why, in practice, the focus shifts to stock price maximization. We also look at the

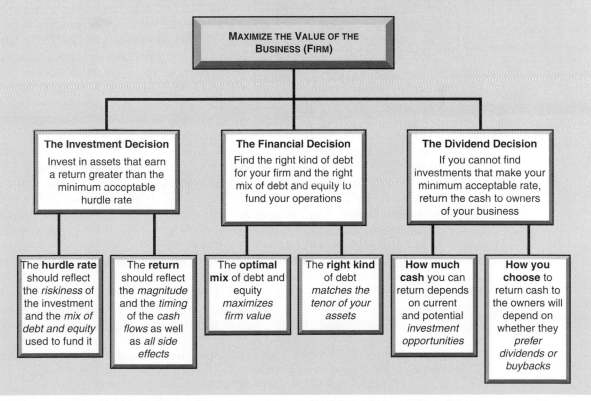

assumptions needed for stock price maximization to be the right objective, what can go wrong with firms that focus on it, and at least partial fixes to some of these problems. We will argue strongly that even though stock price maximization is a flawed objective, it offers far more promise than alternative objectives because it is self-correcting.

CHOOSING THE RIGHT OBJECTIVE

Let's start with a description of what an objective is and the purpose it serves in developing theory. An objective specifies what a decision maker is trying to accomplish and by so doing provides measures that can be used to choose between alternatives. In most firms, the managers of the firm, rather than the owners, make the decisions about where to invest or how to raise funds for an investment. Thus, if stock price maximization is the objective, a manager choosing between two alternatives will choose the one that increases stock price more. In most cases, the objective is stated in terms of maximizing some function or variable, such as profits or growth, or minimizing some function or variable, such as risk or costs.

So why do we need an objective? And if we do need one, why can't we have several? Let's start with the first question. If an objective is not chosen, there is no systematic way to make the decisions that every business will be confronted with at some point in time. For instance, without an objective, how can Disney's managers decide whether the investment in a new theme park is a good one? There would be a menu of approaches for picking projects, ranging from reasonable ones like maximizing return on investment to obscure ones like maximizing the size of the firm, and no statements could be made about their relative value. Consequently, three managers looking at the same project might well come to three separate conclusions.

If we choose multiple objectives, we are faced with a different problem. A theory developed around multiple objectives of equal weight will create quandaries when it comes to making decisions. For example, assume that a firm chooses as its objectives maximizing market share and maximizing current earnings. If a project increases market share and current earnings, the firm will face no problems, but what if the project under analysis increases market share while reducing current earnings? The firm should not invest in the project if the current earnings objective is considered, but it should invest in it based on the market share objective. If objectives are prioritized, we are faced with the same stark choices as in the choice of a single objective. Should the top priority be the maximization of current earnings, or should it be maximizing market share? Because there is no gain, therefore, from having multiple objectives, and developing theory becomes much more difficult, we argue that there should be only one objective.

There are a number of different objectives that a firm can choose between when it comes to decision making. How will we know whether the objective that we have chosen is the right objective? A good objective should have the following characteristics.

- It is *clear and unambiguous*. An ambiguous objective will lead to decision rules that vary from case to case and from decision maker to decision maker. Consider, for instance, a firm that specifies its objective to be increasing growth in the long term. This is an ambiguous objective, because it does not answer at least two questions.

The first is *growth in what variable?* Is it in revenue, operating earnings, net income, or earnings per share? The second is in the definition of the long term: is it three years, five years, or a longer period?

- It comes with a *timely measure* that can be used to evaluate the success or failure of decisions. Objectives that sound good but don't come with a measurement mechanism are likely to fail. For instance, consider a retail firm that defines its objective as maximizing customer satisfaction. How exactly is customer satisfaction defined, and how is it to be measured? If no good mechanism exists for measuring how satisfied customers are with their purchases, not only will managers be unable to make decisions based on this objective, but stockholders will also have no way of holding them accountable for any decisions they do make.

- It *does not create costs for other entities or groups* that erase firm-specific benefits and leave society worse off overall. As an example, assume that a tobacco company defines its objective to be revenue growth. Managers of this firm would then be inclined to increase advertising to teenagers, because it will increase sales. Doing so may create significant costs for society that overwhelm any benefits arising from the objective.

- Some may disagree with the inclusion of social costs and benefits and argue that a business only has a responsibility to its stockholders, not to society. This strikes us as short-sighted—the people who own and operate businesses are part of society!

THE CLASSICAL OBJECTIVE

There is general agreement, at least among corporate finance theorists, that the objective when making decisions in a business is to maximize value. There is some disagreement on whether the objective is to maximize the value of the stockholder's stake in the business or the value of the entire business (firm), which in addition to stockholders includes the other financial claim holders (debt holders, preferred stockholders, etc.). Furthermore, even among those who argue for stockholder wealth maximization, there is a question about whether this translates into maximizing the stock price. As we will see in this chapter, these objectives vary in terms of the assumptions needed to justify them. The least restrictive of the three objectives, in terms of assumptions needed, is to maximize the firm value, and the most restrictive is to maximize the stock price.

Multiple Stakeholders and Conflicts of Interest

In the modern corporation, stockholders hire managers to run the firm for them; these managers then borrow from banks and bondholders to finance the firm's operations. Investors in financial markets respond to information about the firm revealed to them by the managers, and firms have to operate in the context of a larger society. By focusing on maximizing stock price, corporate finance exposes itself to several risks. Each of these stakeholders has different objectives, and there is the distinct possibility that there will be conflicts of interest among them. What is good for managers may not necessarily be good for stockholders, and what is good for stockholders may not be in the best interests of bondholders—and what is beneficial to a firm may create large costs for society.

These conflicts of interest are exacerbated when we bring in two additional stakeholders in the firm. First, the employees of the firm may have little or no interest in stockholder wealth maximization and may have a much larger stake in improving wages, benefits, and job security. In some cases, these interests may be in direct conflict with stockholder wealth maximization. Second, the customers of the business will probably prefer that products and services be priced lower to maximize their utility, but, again, this may conflict with what stockholders would prefer.

Potential Side Costs of Value Maximization

As we noted at the beginning of this section, the objective in corporate finance can be stated broadly as maximizing the value of the entire business, more narrowly as maximizing the value of the equity stake in the business, and even more narrowly as maximizing the stock price for a publicly traded firm. The potential side costs increase as the objective is narrowed.

If the objective when making decisions is to maximize firm value, there is a possibility that what is good for the firm may not be good for society. In other words, decisions that are good for the firm, insofar as they increase value, may create social costs. If these costs are large, we can see society paying a high price for value maximization, and the objective will have to be modified to allow for these costs. To be fair, however, this is a problem that is likely to persist in any system of private enterprise; it is not peculiar to value maximization. The objective of value maximization may also face obstacles when there is separation of ownership and management, as there is in most large public corporations. When managers act as agents for the owners (stockholders), there is the potential for a conflict of interest between stockholder and managerial interests, which, in turn, can lead to decisions that make managers better off at the expense of stockholders.

When the objective is stated in terms of stockholder wealth, the conflicting interests of stockholders and bondholders have to be reconciled. Since stockholders are the decision makers and bondholders are often not completely protected from the side effects of stockholder decisions, one way of maximizing stockholder wealth is to take actions that expropriate wealth from the bondholders, even though such actions may reduce the wealth of the firm.

Finally, when the objective is narrowed further to one of maximizing stock price, inefficiencies in the financial markets may lead to misallocation of resources and to bad decisions. For instance, if stock prices do not reflect the long-term consequences of decisions, but respond, as some critics say, to short-term earnings effects, a decision that increases stockholder wealth (which reflects long-term earnings potential) may reduce the stock price. Conversely, a decision that reduces stockholder wealth but increases earnings in the near term may increase the stock price.

Why Corporate Finance Focuses on Stock Price Maximization

Much of corporate financial theory is centered on stock price maximization as the sole objective when making decisions. This may seem surprising given the potential side costs just discussed, but there are three reasons for the focus on stock price maximization in traditional corporate finance:

1. Stock prices are the *most observable* of all measures that can be used to judge the performance of a publicly traded firm. Unlike earnings or sales, which are updated once every quarter or once every year, stock prices are updated constantly to reflect new information coming out about the firm. Thus, managers receive instantaneous feedback from investors on every action that they take. A good illustration is the response of markets to a firm announcing that it plans to acquire another firm. Although managers consistently paint a rosy picture of every acquisition that they plan, the stock price of the acquiring firm drops at the time of the announcement of the deal in roughly half of all acquisitions, suggesting that markets are much more skeptical about managerial claims.

2. If investors are rational and markets are efficient, stock prices will reflect the long-term effects of decisions made by the firm. Unlike accounting measures like earnings or sales measures such as market share, which look at the effects on current operations of decisions made by a firm, the value of a stock is a function of the long-term health and prospects of the firm. In a rational market, the stock price is an attempt on the part of investors to measure this value. Even if they err in their estimates, it can be argued that an erroneous estimate of long-term value is better than a precise estimate of current earnings.

3. Finally, choosing stock price maximization as an objective allows us to make categorical statements about the best way to pick projects and finance them, and to test these statements with empirical observation.

2.1   WHICH OF THE FOLLOWING ASSUMPTIONS DO YOU NEED TO MAKE FOR STOCK PRICE MAXIMIZATION TO BE THE ONLY OBJECTIVE IN DECISION MAKING?

a. Managers act in the best interests of stockholders.
b. Lenders to the firm are fully protected from expropriation.
c. Financial markets are efficient.
d. There are no social costs.
e. All of the above.
f. None of the above.

IN PRACTICE: WHAT IS THE OBJECTIVE IN DECISION MAKING IN A PRIVATE FIRM OR A NONPROFIT ORGANIZATION?

The objective of maximizing stock prices is a relevant objective only for firms that are publicly traded. How, then, can corporate finance principles be adapted for private firms? For firms that are not publicly traded, the objective in decision making is the maximization of firm value. The investment, financing, and dividend principles we will develop in the chapters to come apply for both publicly traded firms (which focus on stock prices) and private businesses (which maximize firm value). Because firm value is not observable and has to be estimated, what private businesses will lack is the feedback—sometimes unwelcome—that publicly traded firms get from financial markets when they make major decisions.

It is, however, much more difficult to adapt corporate finance principles to a not-for-profit organization, because its objective is often to deliver a service in the most efficient way possible, rather than make profits. For instance, the objective of a hospital may be stated as delivering quality health care at the least cost. The problem, though, is that someone has to define the acceptable level of care, and the conflict between cost and quality will underlie all decisions made by the hospital. ■

MAXIMIZE STOCK PRICES: THE BEST-CASE SCENARIO

If corporate financial theory is based on the objective of maximizing stock prices, it is worth asking when it is reasonable to ask managers to focus on this objective to the exclusion of all others. There is a scenario in which managers can concentrate on maximizing stock prices to the exclusion of all other considerations and not worry about side costs. For this scenario to unfold, the following assumptions have to hold.

- *The managers of the firm put aside their own interests and focus on maximizing stockholder wealth.* This might occur either because they are terrified of the power stockholders have to replace them (through the annual meeting or via the board of directors) or because they own enough stock in the firm that maximizing stockholder wealth becomes their objective as well.

- *The lenders to the firm are fully protected from expropriation by stockholders.* This can occur for one of two reasons. The first is a reputation effect—i.e., that stockholders will not take any actions that hurt lenders now if they feel that doing so might hurt them when they try to borrow money in the future. The second is that lenders might be able to protect themselves fully by writing covenants proscribing the firm from taking any actions that hurt them.

- *The managers of the firm do not attempt to mislead or lie* to financial markets about the firm's future prospects, and there is sufficient information for markets to make judgments about the effects of actions on long-term cash flows and value. Markets are assumed to be *reasoned and rational* in their assessments of these actions and the consequent effects on value.

- *There are no social costs or social benefits.* All costs created by the firm in its pursuit of maximizing stockholder wealth can be traced and charged to the firm.

With these assumptions, there are no side costs to stock price maximization. Consequently, managers can concentrate on maximizing stock prices. In the process, stockholder wealth and firm value will be maximized, and society will be made better off. The assumptions needed for the classical objective are summarized in pictorial form in Figure 2.1.

MAXIMIZE STOCK PRICES: REAL-WORLD CONFLICTS OF INTEREST

Even a casual perusal of the assumptions needed for stock price maximization to be the only objective when making decisions suggests that there are potential shortcomings in each one. Managers might not always make decisions that are in the best interests of stockholders, stockholders do sometimes take actions that hurt lenders, the information delivered to markets is often erroneous and sometimes misleading, and there are social

Figure 2.1   Stock Price Maximization: The Costless Scenario

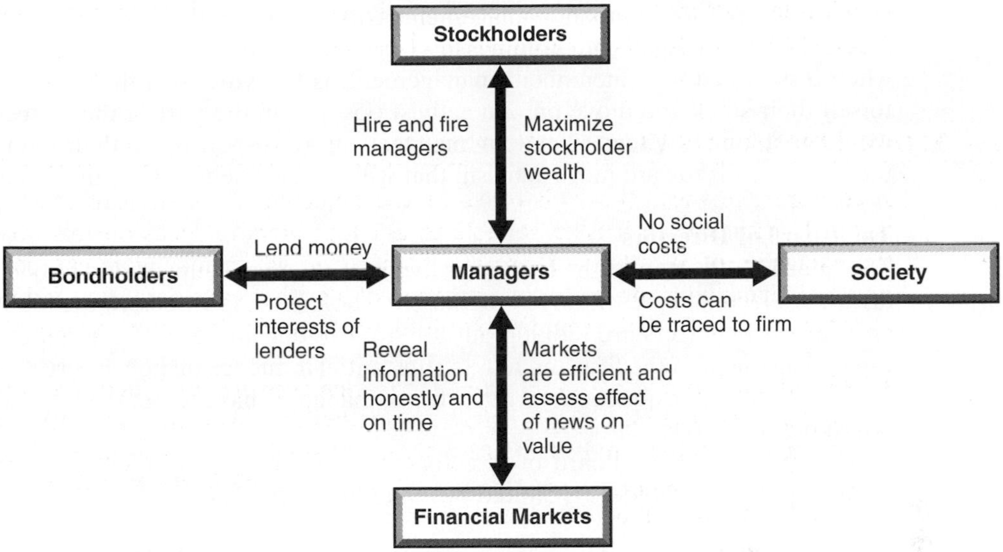

```
                        ┌──────────────────┐
                        │  Stockholders    │
                        └──────────────────┘
                              ▲
              Hire and fire   │   Maximize
              managers        │   stockholder
                              ▼   wealth

                        ┌──────────────────┐      No social
┌──────────────┐        │                  │      costs        ┌──────────────┐
│ Bondholders  │◄──────►│    Managers      │◄────────────────►│   Society    │
└──────────────┘        │                  │                  └──────────────┘
       Lend money       └──────────────────┘      Costs can
       Protect                  ▲                  be traced to firm
       interests of     Reveal  │  Markets
       lenders          information  are efficient and
                        honestly and assess effect
                        on time      of news on
                                     value
                        ┌──────────────────┐
                        │ Financial Markets│
                        └──────────────────┘
```

costs that cannot be captured in the financial statements of the company. In the section that follows, we consider some of the ways real-world problems might trigger a breakdown in the stock price maximization objective.

Stockholders and Managers

In classical corporate financial theory, stockholders are assumed to have the power to discipline and replace managers who do not maximize their wealth. The two mechanisms that exist for this power to be exercised are the annual meeting, wherein stockholders gather to evaluate management performance, and the board of directors, whose fiduciary duty it is to ensure that managers serve stockholders' interests. Although the legal backing for this assumption may be reasonable, the practical power of these institutions to enforce stockholder control is debatable. In this section, we will begin by looking at the limits on stockholder power and then examine the consequences for managerial decisions.

The Annual Meeting

Every publicly traded firm has an annual meeting of its stockholders, during which stockholders can both voice their views on management and vote on changes to the corporate charter. Most stockholders, however, do not go to the annual meetings, partly because they do not feel that they can make a difference, and partly because it would not make financial sense for them to do so.[1] It is true that investors can

---

[1] An investor who owns 100 shares of stock in, say, Coca-Cola will very quickly wipe out any potential returns he makes on his investment if he or she flies to Atlanta every year for the annual meeting.

exercise their power with proxies,[2] but incumbent management starts of with a clear advantage.[3] Many stockholders do not bother to fill out their proxies; among those who do, voting for incumbent management is often the default option. For institutional stockholders with significant holdings in a large number of securities, the easiest option, when dissatisfied with incumbent management, is to "vote with their feet," which is to sell their stock and move on. An activist posture on the part of these stockholders would go a long way toward making managers more responsive to their interests, and there are trends toward more activism that will be documented later in this chapter.

The Board of Directors

The board of directors is the body that oversees the management of a publicly traded firm. As elected representatives of the stockholders, the directors are obligated to ensure that managers are looking out for stockholder interests. They can change the top management of the firm and have a substantial influence on how it is run. On major decisions, such as acquisitions of other firms, managers have to get the approval of the board before acting.

The capacity of the board of directors to discipline management and keep them responsive to stockholders is diluted by a number of factors.

- Many individuals who serve as directors do not spend much time on their fiduciary duties, partly because of other commitments and partly because many of them serve on the boards of several corporations. Korn/Ferry,[4] an executive recruiter, publishes a periodical survey of directorial compensation, and time spent by directors on their work illustrates this very clearly. In their 1992 survey, they reported that the average director spent 92 hours a year on board meetings and preparation in 1992, down from 108 in 1988, and was paid $32,352, up from $19,544 in 1988.[5] As a result of scandals associated with lack of board oversight and the passage of Sarbanes–Oxley, directors have come under more pressure to take their jobs seriously. The Korn/Ferry survey for 2007 noted an increase in hours worked by the average director to 192 hours a year and a corresponding surge in compensation to $62,500 a year, an increase of 45% over the 2002 numbers.
- Even those directors who spend time trying to understand the internal workings of a firm are stymied by their lack of expertise on many issues, especially relating to accounting rules and tender offers, and rely instead on outside experts.
- In some firms, a significant percentage of the directors work for the firm, can be categorized as insiders, and are unlikely to challenge the chief executive office (CEO). Even when directors are outsiders, they are often not independent, insofar as

---

[2]A *proxy* enables stockholders to vote in absentia on boards of directors and on resolutions that will be coming to a vote at the meeting. It does not allow them to ask open-ended questions of management.

[3]This advantage is magnified if the corporate charter allows incumbent management to vote proxies that were never sent back to the firm. This is the equivalent of having an election in which the incumbent gets the votes of anybody who does not show up at the ballot box.

[4]Korn/Ferry surveys the boards of large corporations and provides insight into their composition.

[5]This understates the true benefits received by the average director in a firm, because it does not count benefits and perquisites—insurance and pension benefits being the largest component. Hewitt Associates, an executive search firm, reports that 67% of 100 firms surveyed offer retirement plans for their directors.

the company's CEO often has a major say in who serves on the board. Korn/Ferry's annual survey of boards also found in 1988 that 74% of the 426 companies it surveyed relied on recommendations by the CEO to come up with new directors, whereas only 16% used a search firm. In its 1998 survey, Korn/Ferry found a shift toward more independence on this issue, with almost three-quarters of firms reporting the existence of a nominating committee at least nominally independent of the CEO. The latest Korn/Ferry survey confirmed a continuation of this shift, with only 20% of directors being insiders and a surge in boards with nominating committees that are independent of the CEO.

- The CEOs of other companies are the favored choice for directors, leading to a potential conflict of interest when CEOs sit on each other's boards. In the Korn/Ferry survey, the former CEO of the company sits on the board at 30% of U.S. companies and 44% of French companies.

- Many directors hold only small or token stakes in the equity of their corporations. The remuneration they receive as directors vastly exceeds any returns that they make on their stockholdings, making it unlikely that they will feel any empathy for stockholders if stock prices drop.

- In many companies in the United States, the CEO chairs the board of directors, whereas in much of Europe, the chairman is an independent board member.

The net effect of these factors is that the board of directors often fails at its assigned role—protecting the interests of stockholders. The CEO sets the agenda, chairs the meeting, and controls the flow of information, and the search for consensus generally overwhelms any attempts at confrontation. Although there is an impetus toward reform, it has to be noted that these revolts were sparked not by board members but by large institutional investors.

The failure of the board of directors to protect stockholders can be illustrated with numerous examples from the United States, but this should not blind us to a more troubling fact. Stockholders exercise more power over management in the United States than in any other financial market. If the annual meeting and the board of directors are, for the most part, ineffective in the United States at exercising control over management, they are even more powerless in Europe and Asia as institutions that protect stockholders.

Ownership Structure

The power that stockholders have to influence management decisions either directly (at the annual meeting) or indirectly (through the board of directors) can be affected by how voting rights are apportioned across stockholders and by who owns the shares in the company.

- *Voting rights*   In the United States, the most common structure for voting rights in a publicly traded company is to have a single class of shares, with each share getting a vote. Increasingly, though, we are seeing companies like Google, News Corp, and Viacom, with two classes of shares, and with disproportionate voting rights assigned to one class. In much of Latin America, shares with different voting rights are more the rule than the exception, with almost every company having common shares (with voting rights) and preferred shares (without voting rights). While there may be good reasons for having share classes with different voting rights[6], they clearly tilt the scales in favor of incumbent managers (relative to stockholders), since insiders and incumbents tend to hold the high voting right shares.

- *Founder/owners* In young companies, it is not uncommon to find a significant portion of the stock held by the founders or original promoters of the firm. Thus, Larry Ellison, the founder of Oracle, continues to hold almost a quarter of the firm's stock and is also the company's CEO. As small stockholders, we can draw solace from the fact that the top manager in the firm is also its largest stockholder, but there is still the danger that what is good for an inside stockholder with all or most of his wealth invested in the company may not be in the best interests of outside stockholders, especially if the latter are diversified across multiple investments.

- *Passive versus active investors* As institutional investors increase their holdings of equity, classifying investors into individual and institutional becomes a less useful exercise at many firms. There are, however, big differences between institutional investors in terms of how much of a role they are willing to play in monitoring and disciplining errant managers. Most institutional investors, including the bulk of mutual and pension funds, are passive investors, insofar as their response to poor management is to vote with their feet by selling their stock. There are few institutional investors, such as hedge funds and private equity funds, that have a much more activist bent to their investing and seek to change the way companies are run. The presence of these investors should therefore increase the power of all stockholders relative to managers at companies.

- *Stockholders with competing interests* Not all stockholders are single-minded about maximizing stockholders wealth. For some stockholders, the pursuit of stockholder wealth may have to be balanced against their other interests in the firm, with the former being sacrificed for the latter. Consider two not uncommon examples. The first is employees of the firm investing in equity either directly or through their pension fund. They have to balance their interests as stockholders against their interests as employees. An employee layoff may help them as stockholders but work against their interests as employees. The second is that the government can be the largest equity investor, which is often the aftermath of the privatization of a government company. While governments want to see the values of their equity stakes grow, like all other equity investors, they also have to balance this interest against their other interests (as tax collectors and protectors of domestic interests). They are unlikely to welcome plans to reduce taxes paid or to move production to foreign locations.

- *Corporate cross-holdings* The largest stockholder in a company may be another company. In some cases, this investment may reflect strategic or operating considerations. In others, though, these cross-holdings are a device used by investors or managers to wield power often disproportionate to their ownership stake. Many Asian corporate groups are structured as pyramids, with an individual

---

[6]One argument is that stockholders in capital markets tend to be short-term, and that the investors who own the voting shares are long-term. Consequently, entrusting the latter with the power will lead to better decisions.

or family at the top of the pyramid controlling dozens of companies towards the bottom, using corporations to hold stock. In a slightly more benign version, groups of companies are held together by companies holding stock in each other and using these cross-holdings as a shield against stockholder challenges.

In summary, corporate governance is likely to be strongest in companies that have only one class of shares, limited cross-holdings, and a large activist investor holding, and weakest in companies that have shares with different voting rights, extensive cross-holdings, or a predominantly passive investor base.

IN PRACTICE: Corporate Governance at Companies

The modern publicly traded corporation is a case study in conflicts of interest, with major decisions being made by managers whose interests may diverge from those of stockholders. Put simply, corporate governance as a subarea in finance looks at the question of how best to monitor and motivate managers to behave in the best interests of the owners of the company (stockholders). In this context, a company where managers are entrenched and cannot be removed even if they make bad decisions (decisions that hurt stockholders) is one with poor corporate governance.

In the light of accounting scandals, and faced with opaque financial statements, it is clear investors today care more about corporate governance at companies and companies know that they do. In response to this concern, firms have expended resources and a large portion of their annual reports to conveying to investors their views on corporate governance (and the actions that they are taking to improve it). Many companies have made explicit the corporate governance principles that govern how they choose and remunerate directors. In the case of Disney, these principles, which were first initiated a few years ago, have been progressively strengthened over time, and the October 2008 version requires a substantial majority of the directors to be independent and own at least $100,000 worth of stock.

The demand from investors for unbiased and objective corporate governance scores has created a business for third parties that try to assess corporate governance at individual firms. In late 2002, Standard and Poor's introduced a corporate governance score that ranged from 1 (lowest) to 10 (highest) for individual companies, based upon weighting a number of factors, including board composition, ownership structure, and financial structure. The Corporate Library, an independent research group started by stockholder activists Neil Minow and Robert Monks, tracks and rates the effectiveness of boards. Institutional Shareholder Service (ISS), a proxy advisory firm, rates more than 8,000 companies on a number of proprietary dimensions and markets its corporate governance quotient (CGQ) to institutional investors. Other entities now offer corporate governance scores for European companies and Canadian companies. ■

The Consequences of Stockholder Powerlessness

If the two institutions of corporate governance—annual meetings and the board of directors—fail to keep management responsive to stockholders, as argued in the previous section, we cannot expect managers to maximize stockholder wealth, especially when their interests conflict with those of stockholders. Consider the following examples.

Fighting Hostile Acquisitions

When a firm is the target of a hostile takeover, managers are sometimes faced with an uncomfortable choice. Allowing the hostile acquisition to go through will allow stockholders to reap substantial financial gains but may result in the managers losing their jobs. Not surprisingly, managers often act to protect their own interests at the expense of stockholders:

- The managers of some firms that were targeted by acquirers (raiders) for hostile takeovers in the 1980s were able to avoid being acquired by buying out the acquirer's existing stake, generally at a price much greater than the price paid by the acquirer and by using stockholder cash. This process, called *greenmail*, usually causes stock prices to drop, but it does protect the jobs of incumbent managers. The irony of using money that belongs to stockholders to protect them against receiving a higher price on the stock they own seems to be lost on the perpetrators of greenmail.

- Another widely used antitakeover device is a *golden parachute*, a provision in an employment contract that allow for the payment of a lump sum, or cash flows over a period, if the manager covered by the contract loses his or her job in a takeover. Although there are economists who have justified the payment of golden parachutes as a way of reducing the conflict between stockholders and managers, it is still unseemly that managers should need large side payments to do what they are hired to do and are richly compensated for doing—maximize stockholder wealth

- Firms sometimes create *poison pills*, which are triggered by hostile takeovers. The objective is to make it difficult and costly to acquire control. A flipover right offers a simple example. In a flipover right, existing stockholders get the right to buy shares in the firm **at a price well above** the current stock price. As long as the existing management runs the firm, this right is not worth very much. If a hostile acquirer takes over the firm, though, stockholders are given the right to buy additional shares at a price much lower than the current stock price. The acquirer, having weighed in this additional cost, may very well decide against the acquisition.

Greenmail, golden parachutes, and poison pills generally do not require stockholder approval and are usually adopted by compliant boards of directors. In all three cases, it can be argued, managerial interests are being served at the expenses of stockholder interests.

Antitakeover Amendments

Antitakeover amendments have the same objective as greenmail and poison pills—dissuading hostile takeovers—but differ on one very important count. They require the assent of stockholders to be instituted. There are several types of antitakeover amendments, all designed with the objective of reducing the likelihood of a hostile takeover. Consider, for instance, a *supermajority amendment*: to take over a firm that adopts this amendment, an acquirer has to acquire more than the 51% that would normally be required to gain control. Antitakeover amendments do increase the bargaining power of managers when negotiating with acquirers and could work to the benefit of stockholders, but only if managers act in the best interests of stockholders.

2.2 ANTITAKEOVER AMENDMENTS AND MANAGEMENT TRUST

As a stockholder in a company, if you were asked to vote on an amendment to the corporate charter that would restrict hostile takeovers of your company and give your management more power, in which of the following types of companies would you be most likely to vote yes to the amendment?

a. Companies where the managers promise to use this power to extract a higher price for you from hostile bidders

b. Companies that have done badly (in earnings and stock price performance) in the past few years

c. Companies that have done well (in earnings and stock price performance) in the past few years

d. Never

Paying Too Much on Acquisitions

There are many ways in which managers can make their stockholders worse off—by investing in bad projects, by borrowing too much or too little, and by adopting defensive mechanisms against potentially value-increasing takeovers. The quickest and perhaps the most decisive way to impoverish stockholders is to overpay on a takeover, because the amounts paid on takeovers tend to dwarf those involved in the other decisions. Of course, the managers of the firms doing the acquiring will argue that they never overpay on takeovers,[7] and that the high premiums paid in acquisitions can be justified using any number of reasons—synergy, strategic considerations, the target firm is undervalued and badly managed, and so on. The stockholders in acquiring firms do not seem to share the enthusiasm for mergers and acquisitions that their managers have, because the stock prices of bidding firms decline on the takeover announcements—a significant proportion of the time.[8]

These illustrations are not meant to make the case that managers are venal and selfish, which would be an unfair charge, but they are manifestations of a much more fundamental problem: when there is conflict of interest between stockholders and managers, stockholder wealth maximization is likely to take second place to management objectives.

The Imperial CEO and Compliant Directors: A Behavioral Perspective

Many corporate fiascos would be avoided or at least made less damaging if independent directors asked tough questions and reined in top managers. Given this reality, an interesting question is why we do not see this defiance more often in practice. Some of the failures of boards to restrain CEOs can be attributed to institutional factors and board selection processes, but some can be attributed to human frailties.

---

[7]One explanation given for the phenomenon of overpaying on takeovers is that it is managerial hubris (pride) that drives the process.

[8]See G. A. Jarrell, J. A. Brickley, and J. M. Netter, "The Market for Corporate Control: The Empirical Evidence since 1980," *Journal of Economic Perspectives* 2:49–68. In an extensive study of returns to bidder firms, these authors note that excess returns on these firms' stocks around the announcement of takeovers have declined from an average of 4.95% in the 1960s to 2% in the 1970s to −1% in the 1980s. Studies of mergers also generally conclude that the stock prices of bidding firms decline in more than half of all acquisitions.

Studies of social psychology have noted that loyalty is hardwired into human behavior. While this loyalty is an important tool in building up organizations, it can also lead people to suppress internal ethical standards if they conflict with loyalty to an authority figure. In a famous experiment illustrating this phenomenon, Stanley Milgram, a psychology professor at Yale, asked students to electrocute complete strangers who gave incorrect answers to questions, with larger shocks for more subsequent erroneous answers. Milgram expected his students to stop when they observed the strangers (who were actually only acting) in pain, but he was horrified to find that students continued to shock subjects if ordered to do so by an authority figure. In the context of corporate governance, directors remain steadfastly loyal to the CEO, even in the face of poor performance or bad decisions—and this loyalty seems to outweigh their legal responsibilities to stockholders, who are not present in the room.

How can we break this genetic predisposition to loyalty? The same psychological studies that chronicle loyalty to authority figures also provide guidance on factors that weaken that loyalty. The first is the introduction of *dissenting peers*; if some people are observed voicing opposition to authority, it increases the propensity of others to do the same. The second is the existence of *discordant authority figures*, and disagreement among these figures; in the Milgram experiments, having two people dressed identically in lab coats disagreeing about directions reduced obedience significantly. If we take these findings to heart, we should not only aspire to increase the number of independent directors on boards, but also allow these directors to be nominated by the shareholders who disagree most with incumbent managers. In addition, the presence of a non-executive as chairman of the board, and lead independent directors, may allow for a counterweight to the CEO in board meetings.

Even with these reforms, we have to accept the reality that boards of directors will never be as independent, nor as probing, as we would like them to be, for two other reasons. The first is that people tend to go along with a *group consensus*, even if that consensus is wrong. To the extent that CEOs frame the issues at board meetings, this consensus is likely to work in their favor. The second comes from work done on *information cascades*, where people imitate someone they view to be an informed player, rather than pay to become informed themselves. If executive or inside directors are viewed as more informed about the issues facing the board, it is entirely likely that the outside directors, even if independent, will go along with their views. One solution, offered by Randall Morck, and modeled after the Catholic church, is to create a Devil's advocate—a powerful counterauthority to the CEO whose primary role is to oppose and critique proposed strategies and actions.[9]

ILLUSTRATION 2.1 **Assessing Disney's Corporate Governance**

To understand how corporate governance has evolved at Disney, we have to look at its history. For much of its early existence, Disney was a creation of its founder, Walt Disney. His vision and imagination were the genesis for the animated movies and theme parks that made the company's reputation. After Walt's demise in 1966, Disney went through a period of decline during which its movies failed at the box office

---

[9]R. Morck, "Behavioral Finance in Corporate Governance: Independent Directors, Non-Executive Chairs and the Importance of the Devil's Advocate," NBER working paper series, 2004.

and attendance at theme parks crested. In 1984, Michael Eisner, then an executive at Paramount, was hired as CEO for Disney. Over the next decade, Eisner succeeded in regenerating Disney, with his protégé, Jeffrey Katzenberg, at the head of the Disney movie division, producing blockbuster hits that included *The Little Mermaid, Beauty and the Beast*, and *The Lion King*.[10]

As Disney's earnings and stock price increased, Eisner's power also amplified, and by the mid-1990s, he had brought together a board of directors that genuflected to that power. In 1996, *Fortune* magazine ranked Disney as having the worst board of the Fortune 500 companies, and the sixteen members on its board and the members are listed in Table 2.1, categorized by whether they worked for Disney (insiders) or not (outsiders).

Note that eight of the sixteen members on the board were current or ex-Disney employees and that Eisner, in addition to being CEO, chaired the board. Of the eight outsiders, at least five had potential conflicts of interests because of their ties with either Disney or Eisner. The potential conflicts are listed in italics in Table 2.1. Given the composition of this board, it should come as no surprise that it failed to assert its

---

Table 2.1   Disney's Board of Directors 1996

Insiders	Outsiders
1. Michael D. Eisner: CEO	**1.** Reveta F. Bowers: Head of school for the Center for Early Education, *where Mr. Eisner's children attended class*
2. Roy E. Disney: Head of animation department	**2.** Ignacio E. Lozano Jr.: Chairman of Lozano Enterprises, publisher of *La Opinion* newspaper in Los Angeles
3. Sanford M. Litvack: Chief of corporate operations	**3.** George J. Mitchell: Washington, D.C., attorney, former U.S. senator. *Disney paid Mr. Mitchell $50,000 for his consulting on international business matters in 1996. His Washington law firm was paid an additional $122,764.*
4. Richard A. Nunis: Chairman of Walt Disney Attractions	
5. * Raymond L. Watson: Disney chairman in 1983 and 1984	**4.** Stanley P. Gold: President and chief executive of Shamrock Holdings, Inc., which *manages about $1 billion in investments for the Disney family.*
6. * E. Cardon Walker: Disney chairman and chief executive, 1980–83	**5.** The Rev. Leo J. O'Donovan: President of Georgetown University, where one of Mr. Eisner's children attended college. *Mr. Eisner sat on the Georgetown board and has contributed more than $1 million to the school.*
7. * Gary L. Wilson: Disney chief financial officer, 1985–89	
8. * Thomas S. Murphy: Former chairman and chief executive of Capital Cities/ABC Inc.	**6.** Irwin E. Russell: Beverly Hills, Calif., attorney, *whose clients included Mr. Eisner*
	7. * Sidney Poitier: Actor
	8. Robert A. M. Stern: New York architect *who has designed numerous Disney projects*. He received $168,278 for those services in fiscal year 1996.

*Former official of Disney

---

[10]For an exceptionally entertaining and enlightening read, we would suggest the book *Disney Wars*, authored by James Stewart. The book tracks Michael Eisner's tenure at Disney and how his strengths ultimately became his weakest links.

Table 2.2   DISNEY'S BOARD OF DIRECTORS 2008

Board Members	Occupation
John E. Pepper, Jr. (chairman)	Retired Chairman and CEO, Procter & Gamble Co.
Susan E. Arnold	President, Global Business Units, Procter & Gamble Co.
John E. Bryson	Retired Chairman and CEO, Edison International
John S. Chen	Chairman, CEO, and President, Sybase, Inc.
Judith L. Estrin	CEO, JLabs, LLC.
Robert A. Iger	CEO, Disney
Steven P. Jobs	CEO, Apple
Fred Langhammer	Chairman, Global Affairs, The Estée Lauder Companies
Aylwin B. Lewis	President and CEO, Potbelly Sandwich Works
Monica Lozano	Publisher and CEO, *La Opinion*
Robert W. Matschullat	Retired Vice Chairman and CFO, The Seagram Co.
Orin C. Smith	Retired President and CEO, Starbucks Corporation

power against incumbent management.[11] In 1997, CALPERS, the California Public Employees Retirement System, suggested a series of checks to see if a board was likely to be effective in acting as a counterweight to a powerful CEO, including

- Are a majority of the directors outside directors?
- Is the chairman of the board independent of the company (and not the CEO of the company)?
- Are the compensation and audit committees composed entirely of outsiders?

When CALPERS put the companies in the Standard & Poor's (S&P) 500 through these tests in 1997, Disney was the only company that failed all three tests, with insiders on every one of the key committees.

Disney came under pressure from stockholders to modify its corporate governance practices between 1997 and 2002 and made some changes to its corporate governance practices. By 2002, the number of insiders on the board had dropped to four, but it remained unwieldy (with sixteen board members) and had only limited effectiveness. In 2003, two board members, Roy Disney and Stanley Gold, resigned from the board, complaining that it was too willing to rubberstamp Michael Eisner's decisions. At the 2004 annual meeting, an unprecedented 43% of shareholders withheld their proxies when asked to reelect Eisner to the board. In response, Eisner stepped down as chairman of the board in 2004, and, finally, as CEO in March 2005. His replacement, Bob Iger, has shown more signs of being responsive to stockholders. At the end of 2008, Disney's board of directors had twelve members, only one of whom (Bob Iger) was an insider.

---

[11]One case that cost Disney dearly was when Eisner prevailed on the board to hire Michael Ovitz, a noted Hollywood agent, with a generous compensation. A few years later, Ovitz left the company after falling out with Eisner, creating a multimillion-dollar liability for Disney. A 2003 lawsuit against Disney's board members contended that they failed in their fiduciary duty by not checking the terms of the compensation agreement before assenting to the hiring.

At least in terms of appearances, this board looks more independent than the Disney boards of earlier years, with no obvious conflicts of interest. There are two other interesting shifts. The first is that there are only four board members from 2003 (the last Eisner board), who continue on this one, an indication that this is now Iger's board of directors. The other is the presence of Steve Jobs on the list. While his expertise in technology is undoubtedly welcome to the rest of the board members, he also happens to be Disney's largest stockholder, owning in excess of 7% of the company.[12] Disney stockholders may finally have someone who will advocate for their interests in board deliberations. External monitors who track corporate governance have noticed the improvement at Disney. At the start of 2009, ISS ranked Disney first among media companies on its corporate governance score (CGQ) and among the top ten firms in the S&P 500, a remarkable turnaround for a firm that was a poster child for bad corporate governance only a few years ago.

ILLUSTRATION 2.2   Corporate Governance at Aracruz: Voting and Nonvoting Shares

Aracruz Cellulose, like most Brazilian companies, had two classes of shares at the end of 2008. The common shares had all of the voting rights and were held by incumbent management, lenders to the company, and the Brazilian government. Outside investors held the nonvoting shares, which were called preferred shares,[13] and had no say in the election of the board of directors. At the end of 2008, Aracruz was managed by a board of seven directors, composed primarily of representatives of those who own the common (voting) shares and an executive board composed of three managers of the company.

Without analyzing the composition of the board of Aracruz, it is quite clear that there is the potential for a conflict of interest between voting shareholders who are fully represented on the board and preferred stockholders who are not. Although Brazilian law provides some protection for the latter, preferred stockholders have no power to change the existing management of the company and have little influence over major decisions that can affect their value.[14] As a more general proposition, the very existence of voting and nonvoting shares can be viewed as an indication of poor corporate governance, even at companies like Google that are viewed as well-managed companies.

ILLUSTRATION 2.3   Corporate Governance at Deutsche Bank: Two Boards?

Deutsche Bank follows the German tradition and legal requirement of having two boards. The board of managing directors, composed primarily of incumbent managers, develops the company's strategy, reviews it with the supervisory board, and ensures its implementation. The supervisory board appoints and recalls the members of the board of managing directors and, in cooperation with that board, arranges for long-term successor planning. It also advises the board of managing directors on the management of business and supervises it in its achievement of long-term goals.

---

[12]This holding can be traced back to the large ownership stake that Steve Jobs had in Pixar. When Pixar was acquired by Disney, Jobs received shares in Disney in exchange for this holding.

[13]This can create some confusion for investors in the United States, where preferred stock is stock with a fixed dividend and resembles bonds more than conventional common stock.

[14]This was brought home when Ambev, a large Brazilian beverage company, was acquired by Interbrand, a Belgian corporation. The deal enriched the common stockholders, but the preferred stockholders received little in terms of a premium and were largely bystanders.

A look at the supervisory board of directors at Deutsche Bank provides some insight into the differences between the U.S. and German corporate governance systems. The supervisory board at Deutsche Bank consists of twenty members, but eight are representatives of the employees. The remaining twelve are elected by shareholders, but employees clearly have a much bigger say in how companies are run in Germany and can sometimes exercise veto power over company decisions.

ILLUSTRATION 2.4   Corporate Governance at Tata Chemicals: Family Group Companies

As we noted in Chapter 1, Tata Chemicals is part of the Tata Group of companies, one of India's largest family group companies. In 2009, the company had eight directors, four of whom could be categorized as insiders and four as independent.[15] The chairman of the board, Ratan Tata, also operates as the chairman of the boards of twelve other Tata companies. In fact, many of the directors on the board of Tata Chemicals serve on the boards of other Tata companies as well. The intermingling of group and company interests is made even greater by the fact that other Tata group companies own 29.15% of the outstanding shares in Tata Chemicals and Tata Chemicals has significant investments in other Tata companies.

As stockholders in Tata Chemicals, there are two key implications for corporate governance:

1. *Limited power*   The large cross-holdings by group companies make it unlikely that individual investors (who are not members of the Tata family) will be able to exercise much power at any of these companies.

2. *Conflict of interest*   The conflict between what is good for the investors in the company (Tata Chemicals) and what is good for the group (Tata Group) will play out on almost every major corporate finance decision. For instance, when it comes to how much Tata Chemicals should pay in dividends, the key determinant may not be how much the company generates in excess cash but how much funding is needed by other companies in the group. Generalizing, decisions that are made with the best interests of the Tata Group may be hurtful or costly to investors in Tata Chemicals.

Note that this is not a critique directed specifically at the Tata Group. In fact, many investors who follow Indian companies view the Tata Group as one of the more enlightened family businesses in India. It is more of a general problem with investing in a company that belongs to a larger group, since group interests may render waste to the interests of investors in individual companies.

IN PRACTICE: IS THERE A PAYOFF TO BETTER CORPORATE GOVERNANCE?

We do not want to oversell the importance of strong corporate governance. It is not a magic bullet that will somehow make bad managers into good managers. In fact, we can visualize a well-managed company with poor corporate governance just as easily

---

[15]Two of the directors are categorized as promoters, a term that indicates that they are either founders or descendants of the founders of these firms.

as we can a poorly managed company with good corporate governance. The biggest payoff to good corporate governance is that it is far easier to replace bad managers at a firm, thus making long-term mismanagement less likely.

Academics and activist investors are understandably enthused by moves toward giving stockholders more power over managers, but a practical question that is often not answered is what the payoff to better corporate governance is. Are companies whose stockholders have more power over managers managed better and run more efficiently? If so, are they more valuable? Although no individual study can answer these significant questions, there are a number of different strands of research that offer some insight:

- In the most comprehensive study of the effect of corporate governance on value, a governance index was created for each of 1,500 firms based on twenty-four distinct corporate governance provisions.[16] Buying stocks that had the strongest investor protections while simultaneously selling shares with the weakest protections generated an annual excess return of 8.5%. Every 1-point increase in the index toward fewer investor protections decreased market value by 8.9% in 1999, and firms that scored high in investor protections also had higher profits, higher sales growth, and made fewer acquisitions. These findings are echoed in studies on firms in Korea and Germany.[17] The recent studies are more nuanced in their findings. While most continue to find a link between corporate governance scores and market pricing (such as price to book ratios), they find little relationship between operating performance measures (profit margins, returns on equity) and these scores.

- Actions that restrict hostile takeovers generally reduce stockholder power by taking away one of the most potent weapons available against indifferent management. In 1990, Pennsylvania passed a state law that would have protected incumbent managers against hostile takeovers by allowing them to override stockholder interests if other stakeholders were adversely impacted. In the months between the time the law was first proposed and the time it was passed, the stock prices of Pennsylvania companies declined by 6.9%.[18]

- There seems to be little evidence of a link between the composition of the board of directors and firm value. In other words, there is little to indicate that companies with boards that have more independent directors trade at higher prices than companies with insider-dominated boards.[19]

- Although this is anecdotal evidence, the wave of corporate scandals indicates a significant cost to having a compliant board. A common theme that emerges at

---

[16]P. A. Gompers, J. L. Ishii, and A. Metrick, "Corporate Governance and Equity Prices," *Quarterly Journal of Economics* 118:107–155. The data for the governance index was obtained from the Investor Responsibility Research Center, which tracks the corporate charter provisions for hundreds of firms.

[17]For Korea: B. S. Black, H. Jang, and W. Kim, "Does Corporate Governance Affect Firm Value? Evidence from Korea," Stanford Law School working paper, 2003. For Germany: W. Drobetz, "Corporate Governance: Legal Fiction or Economic Reality," working paper, University of Basel, 2003.

[18]J. M. Karpoff and P. H. Malatesta, "The Wealth Effects of Second-Generation State Takeover Legislation," *Journal of Financial Economics* 25:291–322.

[19]Sanjai Bhagat and Bernard Black, "The Uncertain Relationship between Board Composition and Firm Performance," *Business Lawyer* 54:921–963.

problem companies is an ineffective board that failed to ask tough questions of an imperial CEO. The banking crisis of 2008, for instance, revealed that the boards of directors at investment banks were not only unaware of the risks of the investments made at these banks, but had few tools for overseeing or managing those risks.

In closing, stronger corporate governance is not a panacea for all our troubles. However, it does offer the hope of change, especially when incumbent managers fail to do their jobs. ■

Stockholders and Bondholders

In a world where what is good for stockholders in a firm is also good for its bondholders (lenders), the latter might not have to worry about protecting themselves from expropriation. In the real world, however, there is a risk that bondholders who do not protect themselves may be taken advantage of in a variety of ways—by stockholders borrowing more money, paying more dividends, or undercutting the security of the assets on which the loans were based.

The Source of the Conflict

The source of the conflict of interest between stockholders and bondholders lies in the differences in the nature of the cash flow claims of the two groups. Bondholders generally have first claim on cash flows but receive fixed interest payments—assuming the firm makes enough income to meet its debt obligations. Equity investors have a claim on the cash flows that are left over but have the option in publicly traded firms of declaring bankruptcy if the firm has insufficient cash flows to meet its financial obligations. Bondholders do not get to participate on the upside if the projects succeed but bear a significant portion of the cost if they fail. As a consequence, bondholders tend to view the risk in investments much more negatively than stockholders. There are many issues on which stockholders and bondholders are likely to disagree.

Some Examples of the Conflict

Existing bondholders can be made worse off by increases in borrowing, especially if these increases are large and affect the default risk of the firm, and these bondholders are unprotected. The stockholders' wealth increases concurrently. This effect is dramatically illustrated in the case of acquisitions funded primarily with debt, where the debt ratio increases and the bond rating drops significantly. The prices of existing bonds fall to reflect the higher default risk.[20]

Dividend policy is another issue on which a conflict of interest may arise between stockholders and bondholders. The effect of higher dividends on stock prices can be debated in theory, with differences of opinion on whether it should increase or decrease prices, but the empirical evidence is clear. Increases in dividends, on average, lead to higher stock prices, whereas decreases in dividends lead to lower stock prices. Bond prices, on the other hand, react negatively to dividend increases and positively to dividend cuts. The reason is simple. Dividend payments reduce the cash available to a firm, making debt more risky.

---

[20]In the leveraged buyout of Nabisco, existing bonds dropped in price 19% on the day of the acquisition even as stock prices zoomed up.

The Consequences of Stockholder–Bondholder Conflicts

As these two illustrations make clear, stockholders and bondholders have different objectives, and some decisions can transfer wealth from one group (usually bondholders) to the other (usually stockholders). Focusing on maximizing stockholder wealth may result in stockholders' taking perverse actions that harm the overall firm but increase their wealth at the expense of bondholders.

It is possible that we are making too much of the expropriation possibility, for a couple of reasons. Bondholders are aware of the potential of stockholders to take actions that are inimical to their interests and generally protect themselves, either by writing in covenants or restrictions on what stockholders can do or by taking an equity interest in the firm. Furthermore, the need to return to the bond markets to raise further funds in the future will keep many firms honest, because the gains from any one-time wealth transfer are likely to be outweighed by the reputation loss associated with such actions. These issues will be considered in more detail later in this book.

The Firm and Financial Markets

There is an advantage to maintaining an objective that focuses on stockholder or firm wealth rather than stock prices or the market value of the firm, because it does not require any assumptions about the efficiency or otherwise of financial markets. The downside, however, is that stockholder or firm wealth is not easily measurable, making it difficult to establish clear standards for success and failure. It is true that there are valuation models—some of which we will examine in this book—that attempt to measure equity and firm value, but they are based on a large number of essentially subjective inputs on which people may disagree. Because an essential characteristic of a good objective is that it comes with a clear and unambiguous measurement mechanism, the advantages of shifting to an objective that focuses on market prices is obvious. The measure of success or failure is there for all to see. Successful managers raise their firms' stock prices; unsuccessful managers reduce them.

The trouble with market prices is that the investors who assess them can make serious mistakes. To the extent that financial markets are efficient and use the information that is available to make measured and unbiased estimates of future cash flows and risk, market prices will reflect true value. In such markets, both the measurers and the measured will accept the market price as the appropriate mechanism for judging success and failure.

There are two potential barriers to this. The first is that information is the lubricant that enables markets to be efficient. To the extent that this information is hidden, delayed, or misleading, market prices will deviate from true value, even in an otherwise efficient market. The second problem is that there are many, both in academia and in practice, who argue that markets are not efficient, even when information is freely available. In both cases, decisions that maximize stock prices may not be consistent with long-term value maximization.

2.3   THE CREDIBILITY OF FIRMS IN CONVEYING INFORMATION

Which do you think that the information revealed by companies about themselves is, usually?

a.   Timely and honest

b.   Biased

c.   Fraudulent

The Information Problem

Market prices are based on information, both public and private. In the world of classical theory, information about companies is revealed promptly and truthfully to financial markets. In the real world, there are a few impediments to this process. The first is that information is sometimes suppressed or delayed by firms, especially when it contains bad news. Although there is significant anecdotal evidence of this occurrence, the most direct evidence that firms do this comes from studies of earnings and dividend announcements. A study of earnings announcements noted that those announcements that had the worst news tended to be delayed the longest relative to the expected announcement date.[21] In a similar vein, a study of earnings and dividend announcements by day of the week for firms on the New York Stock Exchange between 1982 and 1986 found that the announcements made on Friday, especially after the close of trading, contained more bad news than announcements made on any other day of the week.[22] This suggests that managers try to release bad news when markets are least active or closed, because they fear that markets will overreact.

The second problem is more serious. In their zeal to keep investors happy and raise market prices, some firms release intentionally misleading information about current conditions and future prospects to financial markets. These misrepresentations can cause stock prices to deviate significantly from value. Consider the example of Bre-X, a Canadian gold mining company that claimed to have found one of the largest gold reserves in the world in Indonesia in the early 1990s. The stock was heavily touted by equity research analysts in the United States and Canada, but the entire claim was fraudulent. When the fraud came to light in 1997, the stock price tumbled, and analysts professed to be shocked that they had been misled by the firm. The implications of such fraudulent behavior for corporate finance can be profound because managers are often evaluated on the basis of stock price performance. Thus Bre-X managers with options or bonus plans tied to the stock price probably did very well before the fraud came to light. Repeated violations of investor trust by companies can also lead to a loss of faith in equity markets and a decline in stock prices for all firms. Again, the potential for information distortions is greater in emerging markets, where information disclosure laws and corporate governance are weaker. In 2008, the CEO and top management of Satyam Computers, a well-regarded Indian software company, stepped down after admitting to accounting fraud.[23]

2.4 REPUTATION AND MARKET ACCESS

Which of the following types of firms is more likely to mislead markets?

a.   Companies that access markets infrequently to raise funds for operations—they raise funds internally.

b.   Companies that access markets frequently to raise funds for operations.

Explain.

---

[21]S. H. Penman, "The Distribution of Earnings News over Time and Seasonalities in Aggregate Stock Returns," *Journal of Financial Economics* 18, no. 2:199–228.

[22]A. Damodaran, "The Weekend Effect in Information Releases: A Study of Earnings and Dividend Announcements," *Review of Financial Studies* 2, no. 4:607–623.

[23]To illustrate the pervasiveness of the misstatements in the financial statements, the cash balance that was reported on the balance sheet did not exist.

The Market Problem

The fear that managers have of markets overreacting or not assimilating information well into prices may be justified. Even if information flowed freely and with no distortion to financial markets, there is no guarantee that what emerges as the market price will be an unbiased estimate of true value. In fact, many would argue that the fault lies deeper, and that investors are much too irrational and unreliable to come up with a good estimate of the true value. Some of the criticisms that have been mounted against financial markets are legitimate, some are overblown, and some are simply wrong, but we will consider them all nonetheless.

- *Financial markets do not always reasonably and rationally assess the effects of new information on prices.* Critics using this argument note that markets can be volatile, reacting to no news at all in some cases; in any case, the volatility in market prices is usually much greater than the volatility in any of the underlying fundamentals. The argument that financial markets are much too volatile, given the underlying fundamentals, has some empirical support.[24] As for the irrationality of markets, the frequency with which you see bubbles in markets, from the tulip bulb mania of the 1600s in Holland to the dot-com debacle of the late 1990s, seems to be proof enough that emotions sometime get ahead of reason in markets.

- *Financial markets sometimes overreact to information.* Analysts with this point of view point to firms that reports earnings that are much higher or much lower than expected and argue that stock prices jump too much on good news and drop too much on bad news. The evidence on this proposition is mixed, though, because there are other cases in which markets seem to underreact to news about firms. Overall, the only conclusion that all these studies agree on is that markets make mistakes in assessing the effect of news on value.

- *There are cases in which insiders move markets to their benefit, often at the expense of outside investors.* This is especially true with illiquid stocks and is exacerbated in markets where trading is infrequent. Even with widely held and traded stocks, insiders sometimes use their superior access to information to get ahead of other investors.[25]

Notwithstanding these limitations, we cannot take away from the central contribution of financial markets. They assimilate and aggregate a remarkable amount of information on current conditions and future prospects into one measure—the price. No competing measure comes close to providing as timely or comprehensive a measure of a firm's standing. The value of having market prices is best illustrated when working with a private firm as opposed to a public firm. Although managers of the latter may resent the second-guessing of analysts and investors, there is a great deal of value to knowing how investors perceive the actions that the firm takes.

---

[24]R. J. Shiller, *Irrational Exuberance* (Princeton, NJ: Princeton University Press, 2000).

[25]This is true even in the presence of strong insider trading laws, as in the United States. Studies that look at insider trades registered with the Securities and Exchange Commission (SEC) seem to indicate that insider buying and selling does precede stock prices going up and down, respectively. The advantage is small, though.

Irrational Exuberance: A Behavioral Perspective on Markets

The belief in efficient markets, long an article of faith in academic finance, has come under assault from within the academy. The notion that markets make systematic mistakes and fail to reflect true value often is now not only backed up by evidence but also linked to well-documented quirks in human nature. In a survey article on the topic, Barberis and Thaler list the following characteristics that skew investor behavior:[26]

- *Overconfidence*   Investors are overconfident in their own judgments, as evidenced by their inability to estimate confidence intervals for quantities (such as the level of the Dow) and probabilities of event occurring.

- *Optimism and wishful thinking*   Individuals have unrealistically optimistic views of their own capabilities. For instance, 90% of people, when characterizing their own skills, describe themselves as above average.

- *Representativeness*   Individuals show systematic biases in how they classify data and evaluate. One manifestation of this bias is that they ignore sample sizes when judging likelihood, treating a 60% success rate in a sample of 10 and the same success rate in a sample of 1,000 equivalently, even though the latter should convey more information.

- *Conservatism and belief perseverance*   Individuals seem to attach to much weight to their prior beliefs about data and to not react sufficiently to new information. Once they form an opinion, they are reluctant to search for evidence that may contradict that opinion, and when faced with such evidence, they view it with excessive skepticism. In some cases, in what is called the confirmation bias, they actually look at contradictory evidence as supportive of their beliefs.

- *Anchoring*   When forming estimates, individuals start with an initial, often arbitrary, value and adjust this value insufficiently.

- *Availability biases*   When assessing the likelihood of an event, individuals looking for relevant information often overweight more recent events and events that affect them personally more than they should in making their judgments.

Given that these characteristics are widespread and perhaps universal, we should not be surprised that markets reflect them. The overconfidence and overoptimism feed into price bubbles in individual stocks as well as the entire market, and those who question the rationality of the bubbles are often ignored (belief perseverance). Anchoring and availability biases can skew how we value individual companies, again leading to significant differences between market prices and true values. In general, behavioral finance provides explanations for why stock prices may deviate from true value for extended periods.

2.5   ARE MARKETS SHORT-TERM?

Focusing on market prices will lead companies toward short-term decisions at the expense of long-term value.

a.   I agree.

b.   I do not agree.

---

[26]N. Barberis and R. Thaler, "A Survey of Behavioral Finance," NBER working paper, 2002.

Allowing managers to make decisions without having to worry about the effect on market prices will lead to better long-term decisions.

a. I agree.

b. I do not agree.

ILLUSTRATION 2.5   Interaction with Financial Markets: A Case Study with Disney

The complex interaction between firms and financial markets is best illustrated by what happens when firms make information announcements. Consider, for instance, Disney's earnings report for January–March 2009, which was released to financial markets on May 5, 2009. The report contained the news that net income at the company dropped 26% from the prior year's level, resulting in earnings per share of $0.43 a share. The stock price increased by about 2% on the announcement of this bad news, because the reported earnings per share was higher than the $0.40 per share expected by analysts.

There are several interesting points that are worth making here. The first relates to the role that analysts play in setting expectations. In May 2009, for example, there were twenty-five analysts working at brokerage houses and investment banks who provided estimates of earnings per share for Disney.[27] The lowest of the estimates was 33 cents per share, the highest was 48 cents per share, and the average (also called consensus) estimate was 40 cents per share. The second relates to the power of expectations. Any news that a company reports has to be measured relative to market expectations before it can be categorized as good or bad news. Thus, a report of a drop in earnings (as was the case with Disney in this example) can be good news because earnings did not drop as much as expected.

IN PRACTICE: ARE MARKETS SHORT-TERM?

There are many who believe that stock price maximization leads to a short-term focus for managers. The reasoning goes as follows: Stock prices are determined by traders, short-term investors, and analysts, all of whom hold the stock for short periods and spend their time trying to forecast the next quarter's earnings. Managers who concentrate on creating long-term value rather than short-term results will be penalized by markets. Most of the empirical evidence that exists suggests that markets are much more long-term than they are given credit for.

- There are hundreds of firms, especially small and startup firms that do not have any current earnings and cash flows and do not expect to have any in the near future but that are still able to raise substantial amounts of money on the basis of expectations of success in the future. If markets were in fact as short-term as critics suggest, these firms should be unable to raise funds in the first place.

- If the evidence suggests anything, it is that markets do not value current earnings and cash flows enough, and value future earnings and cash flows too much. Studies

---

[27]These analysts are called sell-side analysts, because their research is then offered to portfolio managers and other clients. The analysts who work for mutual funds are called buy-side analysts and toil in relative obscurity because their recommendations are for internal consumption at the mutual funds and are not publicized.

indicate that stocks with low price–earnings ratios and high current earnings have generally been underpriced relative to stocks with high price–earnings ratios.

- The market response to research and development (R&D) and investment expenditure is not uniformly negative, despite what the "short-term" critics would lead you to believe. Instead, the response is tempered, with stock prices rising on average on the announcement of R&D and capital expenditures.

Do some investors and analysts focus on short-term earnings and not on long-term value? Of course. In our view, financial managers cater far too much to these investors and skew their decisions to meet their approval, fleeting though it might be. ■

The Firm and Society

Most management decisions have social consequences, and the question of how best to deal with these consequences is not easily answered. An objective of maximizing firm or stockholder wealth implicitly assumes that the social side costs are either trivial enough that they can be ignored or that they can be priced and charged to the firm. In many cases, neither of these assumptions is justifiable.

There are some cases in which the social costs are considerable but cannot be traced to the firm. In these cases, the decision makers, though aware of the costs, may choose to ignore the costs and maximize firm wealth. The ethical and moral dilemmas of forcing managers to choose between their survival (which may require stockholder wealth maximization) and the broader interests of society can be debated, but there is no simple solution that can be offered in this book.

In the cases where substantial social costs exist, and firms are aware of these costs, ethicists might argue that wealth maximization has to be sublimated to the broader interests of society, but what about those cases where firms create substantial social costs without being aware of these costs? John Manville Corporation, for instance, produced asbestos in the 1950s and 1960s with the intention of making a profit and was unaware of the potential of the product to cause cancer and other illnesses. Thirty years later, the lawsuits from those afflicted with asbestos-related disease have driven the company to bankruptcy.

To be fair, conflicts between the interests of the firm and the interests of society are not restricted to the objective of maximizing stockholder wealth. They may be endemic to a system of private enterprise, and there will never be a solution to satisfy the purists who would like to see a complete congruence between the social and firm interests.

2.6 CAN LAWS MAKE COMPANIES GOOD CITIZENS?

It has often been argued that social costs occur because governments do not have adequate laws on the books to punish companies that create social costs. The follow-up is that passing such laws will eliminate social costs.

a. I agree.

b. I do not agree.

ILLUSTRATION 2.6 Assessing Social Costs

The ubiquity of social costs is made clear when we look at the companies we are analyzing—Disney, Aracruz, Tata Chemicals, and Deutsche Bank. These companies, in spite of their many differences, have social costs to consider.

- Disney was built and continues to market itself as the ultimate family-oriented company. When its only businesses were theme parks and animated movies, it faced relatively few conflicts. With its expansion into the movie business and TV broadcasting, Disney has exposed itself to new problems. To provide an illustration, the Southern Baptist Convention voted in 1997 to boycott Disney theme parks and movies in response to the airing of *Ellen*, a show on the ABC network starring Ellen DeGeneres as a gay bookstore owner. It is because of this fear of a backlash that Disney maintains separate movie studios—Miramax for edgier, more adult movies and Disney/Pixar Studios for animated and family-friendly movies.

- Aracruz is at the center of the controversy about the deforestation of the rain forests in South America. In the later 1990s, Aracruz was accused by environmental groups of replacing old-growth forests in Brazil with eucalyptus plantations and displacing native and indigenous peoples from these areas.[28]

- While Tata Chemicals has not been the focus of serious social backlash, the Tata Group has had its share of societal conflicts. Tata Motors, for instance, was forced to relocate a new plant that it was planning to build on former agricultural land in West Bengal in the face of protests from farmers and community activists.

- Deutsche Bank has been challenged for its role as banker for the Nazis during the Holocaust. Its acquisition of Bankers Trust in 2000 was almost derailed by accusations that it had helped fund the construction of the concentration camp at Auschwitz during World War II. Both Deutsche Bank and Dresdner Bank were sued by survivors of the Holocaust for profiting from gold and other assets stolen from concentration camp victims during World War II.[29] Finally, in the aftermath of the banking crisis of 2008, Deutsche Bank has been challenged both by regulators and activists for its role in creating the crisis.

For all these companies, these accusations are serious not only because they damage their reputations, but because they can also create serious economic costs. All of the firms aggressively defended themselves against the charges and spent a substantial number of pages in their annual reports detailing what they do to be good corporate citizens.

 IN PRACTICE: Stakeholder Wealth Maximization and Balanced Scorecards

Some theorists have suggested that the best way to consider the interests of all of the different stakeholders in a modern corporation is to replace stockholder wealth maximization with a broader objective of stakeholder wealth maximization wherein stakeholders include employees and society. Although it sounds wonderful as a concept, we believe that it is not a worthwhile alternative, for the following reasons:

- When you have multiple stakeholders with very different objectives, you will inevitably have to choose among them. For instance, laying off employees at a firm that is overstaffed will make stockholders and bondholders better off while

---

[28] In the 1990s, the Tupinikim and Guarani Indians launched an international campaign against Aracruz in the state of Espirito Santo to recover and expand their traditional territories

[29] A 1946 investigation by the U.S. military recommended that Deutsche Bank be liquidated and its top officials tried as war criminals.

creating costs to society as a whole. Stakeholder wealth maximization provides little direction on the proper way to balance these competing interests.

- Adding to the problem is the fact that not all of the costs and benefits to some stakeholders can be quantified. This is especially true of social costs and benefits, leaving the assessment to analysts who have their own biases.

- Most important, stakeholder wealth maximization makes managers accountable to no one by making them accountable to everyone. Managers can essentially go before each stakeholder and justify their failures by arguing that other stakeholder interests were being considered.

It may still be useful for firms to go beyond the proverbial bottom line, and a balanced scorecard attempts to do just that. As devised by Robert Kaplan, a Harvard strategy professor, balanced scorecards try to go beyond financial measures and look at customer satisfaction and internal business processes.[30] ∎

The Real World: A Pictorial Representation

We have spent the last few pages chronicling the problems in the real world with each of the linkages—managers and stockholders, stockholders and bondholders, firms and financial markets, and firms and society. Figure 2.2 summarizes the problems with each linkage in a pictorial representation:

Figure 2.2   Stock Price Maximization in the Real World

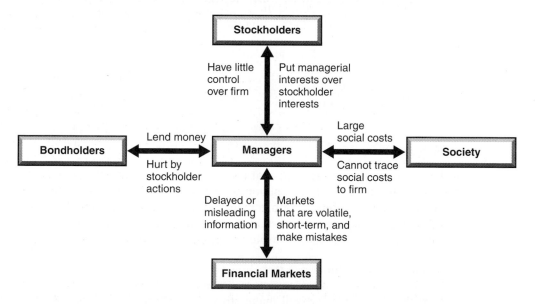

---

[30]Robert S. Kaplan and David P. Norton, *The Balanced Scorecard: Translating Strategy into Action* (Cambridge, MA: Harvard Business School Press, 1996).

ALTERNATIVES TO STOCK PRICE MAXIMIZATION

There are obvious problems associated with each of the linkages underlying wealth maximization. Stockholders often have little power over managers, and managers consequently put their own interests above those of stockholders. Lenders who do not protect their interests often end up paying a price when decisions made by firms transfer wealth to stockholders. Information delivered to financial markets is often erroneous, misleading, or delayed, and there are significant differences between price and market value. Finally, firms that maximize wealth may do so while creating large costs for society.

Given these problems, there are alternative courses of action that we can follow. One is to find a different system for keeping errant management in check. The second is to find an alternative objective for the firm. In this section, we will consider these alternatives.

A Different System for Disciplining Management (Corporate Governance)

In the system we have described thus far, stockholders bear the burden of replacing incompetent management; we can call this a market-based corporate governance system, where investors in financial markets govern how corporations are run. There are some who believe that this is too much of a responsibility to put on investors, who—as they see it—often operate with poor information and have short time horizons. Michael Porter, a leading thinker on corporate strategy, has argued that firms in the United States are hamstrung by the fact that investors are short-term and demand quick returns. He contrasts them with Japanese firms, which he argues can afford to adopt strategies that make sense in the long run, even though they might not maximize profits in the short term. He suggests that investors should form long-term relationships with firms and work with them to devise long-term strategies.[31] His view of the world is not unique and is shared by many corporate executives, even in the United States. These executives argue that there are alternatives to the market-based corporate governance systems, where stockholders act to discipline and replace errant managers and stock prices measure their success. In the German and Japanese systems of corporate governance,[32] firms own stakes in other firms and often make decisions in the best interests of the industrial group they belong to rather than in their own interests. In these systems, the argument goes, firms will keep an eye on each other, rather than ceding power to the stockholders. In addition to being undemocratic—the stockholders are, after all, the owners of the firm—these systems suggest a profound suspicion of how stockholders might use the power if they get it and is heavily skewed toward maintaining the power of incumbent managers.

Although this approach may protect the system against the waste that is a byproduct of stockholder activism and inefficient markets, it has its own disadvantages. Industrial

[31] There is some movement toward relationship investing in the United States, where funds such as Allied Partners (run by Dillon Read), Corporate Partners (run by Lazard Freres), and Lens (run by activist Robert Monks) have attempted to create long-term relationships with the managers of firms.
[32] There are subtle differences between the Japanese and the German systems. The Japanese industrial groups, called *keiretsus*, are based primarily on cross-holdings of companies and evolved from family-owned businesses. The German industrial groups revolve around leading commercial banks, like Deutsche Bank or Dresdner Bank, with the bank holding substantial stakes in a number of industrial concerns.

groups are inherently more conservative than investors in allocating resources and thus are much less likely to finance high-risk and venture capital investments by upstarts who do not belong to the group. The other problem is that entire groups can be dragged down by the bad decisions of individual firms.[33] In fact, the troubles that Japanese firms have had dealing with poor investments in the 1990s suggests to us that these alternative corporate governance systems, though efficient at dealing with individual firms that are poorly run, have a more difficult time adapting to and dealing with problems that are widespread. These problems, consequently, tend to fester and grow over time. For instance, while financial markets pushed corporate banks in the United States to confront their poor real estate loans in the late 1980s, Japanese banks spent much of the 1990s denying the existence of such loans on their books.[34]

In the wake of the success of Chinese companies in the last decade and the meltdown of global financial markets, there is another alternative being offered by those who dislike the market-based mechanism. Why not let the government be a larger player and decide where investments make the most sense? In the aftermath of a market meltdown in 2008, with subsequent government bailouts of banks and troubled companies, the number of advocates for an activist government role has increased even in the United Kingdom and United States, historically countries that have been friendly to market-based solutions. We remain skeptical for two reasons. The first is that history does not provide much encouragement for government-driven investment. When governments have tried to pick winners among companies, they have generally been unsuccessful. Not only did the Soviet and other socialist systems fail badly for decades after World War II at planning economic growth, but enlightened systems like the Japanese Ministry of Finance have not been able to forecast where growth will come from next. The second is that governments have other agendas besides economic growth, and there can be conflicts between these different interests. Thus, even if it is in the best long-term economic interests of taxpayers in the United States to let GM go under, it is unlikely that any government that has to face voters in Michigan (GM's home state) will be willing to let it happen. Finally, if the argument is that financial markets are hotbeds of investor irrationality, note that government agencies are also staffed with human beings, and there is no reason to believe that these decision makers will be immune from making the same mistakes.

Is there a way we can measure the effectiveness of alternative corporate governance systems? One suggestion is that corporate governance systems be measured on three dimensions—the capacity to restrict management's ability to obtain private benefits from control, easy access to financial markets for firms that want capital, and the ease with which inefficient management is replaced. It can be argued that a market-based

---

[33]Many Korean industrial groups (called *chaebols*), which were patterned after the Japanese *keiretsu*, were pushed to the verge of bankruptcy in 1990s because one or two errant firms in the group made bad real estate loans or borrowed too much.

[34]S. N. Kaplan, "Corporate Governance and Corporate Performance: A Comparison of German, Japan and the United States," *Journal of Applied Corporate Finance* 9, no. 4, 86–93. He compares the U.S., German, and Japanese corporate governance systems. He finds that the U.S. system provides better incentives for firms performing well, and that it is easier for companies in the United States to return cash to the stockholders.

corporate governance system does a better job than alternative systems on at least the last two counts.[35]

Choosing an Alternative Objective

Given its limitations, the easy answer would be to cast aside stock price maximization as an objective. The tough part is replacing it with another objective. It is not that there are no alternatives, but that the alternatives come with their own sets of problems—and it is not at all obvious that there is a benefit to switching. This is especially true when the alternative objective is evaluated on the three criteria used to evaluate the wealth maximization objective: (1) Is the objective clear and unambiguous? (2) Does it come with a timely measure that can be used to evaluate success and failure? (3) Does it create side costs that exceed the overall benefits? Let us consider three commonly offered alternatives to stock price maximization.

I. Maximize Market Share

In the 1980s, Japanese firms inundated global markets with their products and focused their attention on increasing market share. Their apparent success at converting this market share to profits led other firms, including some in the United States, to also target market share as an objective. In concrete terms, this meant that investments that increased market share more were viewed more favorably than investments that increased them less. Proponents of this objective note that market share is observable and measurable like market price and does not require any of the assumptions about efficient financial markets that are needed to justify the stock price maximization objective.

Underlying the market share maximization objective is the belief (often unstated) that higher market share will mean more pricing power and higher profits in the long run. If this is in fact true, maximizing market share is entirely consistent with the objective of maximizing firm value. However, if higher market share does not yield higher pricing power and the increase in market share is accompanied by lower or even negative earnings, firms that concentrate on increasing market share can be worse off as a consequence. In fact, many of the same Japanese firms that were used by corporate strategists as their examples for why the focus on market share was a good one discovered the harsh downside of this focus in the 1990s.

II. Profit Maximization Objectives

There are objectives that focus on profitability rather than value. The rationale for them is that profits can be measured more easily than value, and that higher profits translate into higher value in the long run. There are at least two problems with these objectives. First, the emphasis on current profitability may result in short-term decisions that maximize profits now at the expense of long-term profits and value. Second, the notion that profits can be measured more precisely than value may be incorrect, given the leeway that accountants have to shift profits across periods.

---

[35] J. R. Macey, "Measuring the Effectiveness of Different Corporate Governance Systems: Towards a More Scientific Approach," *Journal of Applied Corporate Finance* 10, no. 4:16–25.

In its more sophisticated forms, profit maximization is restated in terms of accounting returns (such as return on equity or capital) rather than dollar profits or even as excess returns (over a cost of capital). Although these variants may remove some of the problems associated with focusing on dollar profits next period, the problems with accounting measurements carry over into them as well.

III. Size/Revenue Objectives

There are a whole set of objectives that have little to do with stockholder wealth but focus instead on the size of the firm. In the 1970s, for instance, firms like Gulf & Western and ITT with strong CEOs at their helm were built up through acquisitions into giant conglomerates. There seemed to be no strategic imperative to these acquisitions, other than the desire on the part of the CEOs to increase the sizes of their corporate empires. Empire-building may no longer be in vogue, but there have been cases where corporations have made decisions that increase their size and perceived power at the expense of stockholder wealth and profitability.

MAXIMIZE STOCK PRICES: SALVAGING A FLAWED OBJECTIVE

The alternatives to stock price maximization—a corporate governance system build around self-governance or choosing a different objective like maximizing market share—have their own limitations. In this section, we consider the case for salvaging value maximization as an objective but consider ways we can reduce some of the problems highlighted in the earlier section. In particular, we consider ways we can reduce the conflicts of interest between stockholders, bondholders, and managers and the potential for market failures. We also present an argument for market-based mechanisms based on the market's capacity to correct systematic mistakes quickly and effectively.

Conflict Resolution: Reducing Agency Problems

If the conflicts between stockholders, managers, and bondholders lie at the heart of the problems with stock price maximization, reducing these conflicts should make it a more palatable objective. In this section, we examine the linkages between stockholders and managers, stockholders, and bondholders; firms and financial markets; and firms and society and look at how best we can reduce the side costs to maximizing stock prices.

Stockholders and Managers

There are clearly conflicts of interests between stockholders and managers, and the traditional mechanisms for stockholder control—annual meetings and boards of directors—often fail at their role of discipline management. This does not mean, however, that the chasm between the two groups is too wide to be bridged, either by closing the gap between their interests or by increasing stockholder power over managers.

Making Managers Think More Like Stockholders
As long as managers have interests that are distinct and different from the interests of the stockholders they serve, there is potential for conflict. One way to reduce this

conflict is to provide managers with an equity stake in the firms they manage, either by providing them with stock or warrants on the stock. If this is done, the benefits that accrue to management from higher stock prices may provide an inducement to maximize stock prices.

There is a downside to doing this, for although it reduces the conflict of interest between stockholders and managers, it may exacerbate the other conflicts of interest highlighted in the prior section. It may increase the potential for expropriation of wealth from bondholders and the probability that misleading information will be conveyed to financial markets.

There is a final distinction that we need to make between stock-based compensation and option-based compensation. As we will see in the coming chapters, options can sometimes become more valuable as businesses become more risky. Consequently, managers who have substantial option holdings and little in common stock may be tempted to take on far more risk than would be desired by other shareholders in the firm. It is for this reason that companies are increasingly turning away from option-based packages to restricted stock in compensating managers.

2.7 STOCKHOLDER INTERESTS, MANAGERIAL INTERESTS, AND MANAGEMENT BUYOUTS

In a management buyout, the managers of the firm buy out the existing stockholders and make the company a private firm. Is this a way of reducing the conflict of interests between stockholders and managers?

a. Yes

b. No

Explain.

More Effective Boards of Directors

In the past few years, there have been encouraging trends both in the composition and the behavior of boards, making them more effective advocates for stockholders. Korn/Ferry's survey of boards of directors at large global corporations in 2007 revealed the following.

- *Boards have become smaller over time.* The median size of a board of directors has decreased from a range of between sixteen and twenty in the 1970s to ten in 2007. The smaller boards are less unwieldy and more effective than larger boards.

- *There are fewer insiders on the board.* In contrast to the six or more insiders that many boards had in the 1970s, only two directors in most boards in 2007 were insiders.

- *Directors are increasingly compensated with equity in the company.* In 1973, only 4% of directors received compensation in the form of equity, whereas 86% did so in 2007. There has also been a shift away from options to restricted stock; 72% of firms used restricted stock, and only 14% used options. While the use of restricted stock in compensation has increased in Europe as well, it is still uncommon in Asia.

- *More directors are identified and selected by a nominating committee rather than chosen by the CEO of the firm.* In 2007, 97% of boards had nominating committees; the comparable statistic in 1973 was 2%.

- ***More firms restrict the number of outside directorships held by their directors.*** In 2001, only 23% of firms limited the number of other board memberships of their directors. In 2007, that number had risen to 62%. While many UK and European companies also restrict board memberships, such restrictions are less common in Asia.

- ***More firms have appointed lead directors to counter the CEO as chair.*** While it was unusual for boards to appoint lead directors twenty years ago, almost 84% of U.S. boards now have a lead director to serve as a counterweight to the CEO.

- ***More firms are evaluating CEOs on an annual basis.*** In 1999, 56% of U.S. corporate boards evaluated CEOs on an annual basis. That number had risen to 92% in 2007. In Asia, almost 95% of boards claim to evaluate CEOs on an annual basis.

While these are all positive trends, there are two precautionary notes that we add. The first is that the survey focused on large companies; board practices at smaller companies have been much slower to change. The second is that it is not clear how much of this change is window dressing—giving the appearance of active oversight to prevent lawsuits.

Is there a payoff to a more active board? MacAvoy and Millstein present evidence that companies with more activist boards, where activism was measured based upon indicators of board behavior, earned much higher returns on their capital than firms that had less active boards.[36] As hedge funds and activist investors have raised their profile in the last few years, there is evidence that directors that they place on the boards of challenged companies make a difference, at least in stock price performance. A study by the Investor Responsibility Research Center (IRRC) of 120 companies with hybrid boards—i.e., boards with directors elected by activist investors—found that their stock prices at these companies outperformed their peer group by almost 17% a year, with the bulk of the return occurring around the months that activists challenged the company. Interestingly, the performance of companies with a single dissident director elected was much better than those where three or more dissident directors were elected.

Increasing Stockholder Power

There are many ways in which stockholder power over management can be increased. The first is to provide stockholders with better and more updated information, so that they can make informed judgments on how well the management is doing. The second is to have a large stockholder become part of incumbent management and have a direct role in decisions that the firm makes. The third is to have more "activist" institutional stockholders who play a larger role in issues such as the composition of the board of directors, the question of whether to pass anti takeover amendments, and overall management policy. In recent years, some institutional investors have used their considerable power to pressure managers into becoming more responsive to their needs. Among

---

[36]See P. W. MacAvoy and I. M. Millstein, "The Active Board of Directors and Its Effect on the Performance of Large Publicly Traded Companies," *Columbia Law Review* 98:1283–1322.

the most aggressive of these investors has been the California State Pension fund (CALPERS), one of the largest institutional investors in the country. Unfortunately, the largest institutional investors—mutual funds and pension fund companies—have remained largely apathetic. In the last few years, hedge funds have stepped into the breach and have challenged even large companies to defend existing practices.

It is also critical that institutional constraints on stockholders exercising their power be reduced. All common shares should have the same voting rights, state restrictions on takeovers have to be eliminated, and shareholder voting should be simplified. The legal system should come down hard on managers (and boards of directors) who fail to perform their fiduciary duty. Ultimately, though, stockholders have to awaken to the reality that the responsibility for monitoring management falls to them. Like voters in a democracy, shareholders get the managers they deserve.

IN PRACTICE: THE LEGAL REMEDY

Can we legislate good corporate governance? Whether we can or not, legislators often try to fix what they see as significant corporate governance problems by passing laws. This is especially true in the aftermath of scandals, when stockholders, bondholders, and society bear the cost of managerial incompetence. As an example, after the accounting scandals in the United States in 2001 and 2002, the Sarbanes–Oxley Act was passed with the explicit intent of preventing future Enrons and Worldcoms. The act was far-reaching in its coverage, but large parts of it related to the composition of corporate boards and the responsibilities of boards. Without going into the provisions of the law, the objective was to create more transparency in the way boards were created and increase the independence of the directors from the CEO and the legal responsibilities of directors for managerial actions. Sarbanes–Oxley also substantially increased the information disclosure requirements for firms.

The other legal remedy that stockholders have is to sue the managers when they feel that they have been misled about future prospects. In recent years, class action lawsuits against companies whose stock prices have plummeted have multiplied, and the plaintiffs have won large awards in some of these suits. While the right to sue when wronged may seem fundamental, legal remedies are likely to be both imperfect and very expensive ways of bringing about better corporate governance. In fact, the cost of complying with Sarbanes–Oxley has been substantial, and the only group that consistently is enriched by lawsuits is trial lawyers. ■

2.8   INSIDE STOCKHOLDERS VERSUS OUTSIDE STOCKHOLDERS

There are companies like Microsoft where a large stockholder (Bill Gates) may be on the inside as the top manager of the concern. Is it possible that what is in Bill Gates's best interests as an "inside" stockholder may not be in the interests of a stockholder on the outside?

a.   Yes. Their interests may deviate.

b.   No. Their interests will not deviate.

If so, provide an example of an action that may benefit the inside stockholder but not the outside stockholder.

The Threat of a Takeover

The perceived excesses of many takeovers in the 1980s drew attention to the damage created to employees and society some of them. In movies and books, the raiders who were involved in these takeovers were portrayed as barbarians, while the firms being taken over were viewed as hapless victims. Although this may have been accurate in some cases, the reality was that most companies that were taken over deserved it. One analysis found that target firms in hostile takeovers in 1985 and 1986 were generally much less profitable than their competitors, had provided subpar returns to their stockholders, and had managers with significantly lower holdings of the equity. In short, badly managed firms were much more likely to become targets of hostile takeover bids.[37]

An implication of this finding is that takeovers operate as a disciplinary mechanism, keeping managers in check, by introducing a cost to bad management. Often, the very threat of a takeover is sufficient to make firms restructure their assets and become more responsive to stockholder concerns. It is not surprising, therefore, that legal attempts to regulate and restrict takeovers have had negative consequences for stock prices.

2.9 HOSTILE ACQUISITIONS: WHOM DO THEY HURT?

Given the information presented in this chapter, which of the following groups is likely to be the most likely to be protected by a law banning hostile takeovers?

a. Stockholders of target companies

b. Managers and employees of well-run target companies

c. Managers and employees of badly-run target companies

d. Society

ILLUSTRATION 2.7 Restive Stockholders and Responsive Managers: The Disney Case

In 1997, Disney was widely perceived as having an imperial CEO, in Michael Eisner, and a captive board of directors. After a series of missteps including the hiring and firing of Michael Ovitz and bloated pay packages, Disney stockholders were restive, but there were no signs of an impending revolt at that time. As Disney's stock price slid between 1997 and 2000, though, this changed as more institutional investors made their displeasure with the state of corporate governance at the company. As talk of hostile takeovers and proxy fights filled the air, Disney was forced to respond. In its 2002 annual report, Disney listed the following corporate governance changes:

- Required at least two executive sessions of the board, without the CEO or other members of management present, each year

- Created the position of management presiding director and appointed Senator George Mitchell to lead those executive sessions and assist in setting the work agenda of the board

- Adopted a new and more rigorous definition of director independence

---

[37] A. Bhide, "The Causes and Consequences of Hostile Takeovers," *Journal of Applied Corporate Finance* 2:36–59.

- Required that a substantial majority of the board be made up of directors meeting the new independence standards
- Provided for a reduction in committee size and the rotation of committee and chairmanship assignments among independent directors
- Added new provisions for management succession planning and evaluations of both management and board performance
- Provided for enhanced continuing education and training for board members

What changed between 1997 and 2002? Although we can point to an overall shift in the market toward stronger corporate governance, the biggest factor was Disney's poor stock price performance. The truth is that stockholders are often willing to overlook poor corporate governance and dictatorial CEOs if stock prices are going up but are less tolerant when stock prices decrease.

Toward the end of 2003, Roy Disney and Stanley Gold resigned from Disney's board of directors, complaining both about the failures of Eisner as a manager and about his autocratic style.[38] When the board of directors announced early in 2004 that Eisner would receive a $6.25 million bonus for his performance in 2003, some institutional investors voiced their opposition. Soon after, Comcast announced a hostile acquisition bid for Disney. At Disney's annual meeting in February 2004, Disney and Gold raised concerns about Eisner's management style and the still-captive board of directors; 43% of the stockholders voted against Eisner as director at the meeting. In a sense, the stars were lining up for the perfect corporate governance storm at Disney, with Eisner in the eye of the storm. Soon after the meeting, Disney announced that Eisner would step down as chairman of the board but would continue as CEO until his term expired in 2005.

IN PRACTICE: PROXY FIGHTS

In the section on annual meetings, we pointed out that many investors who are unable to come to annual meetings also fail to return their proxies, thus implicitly giving incumbent managers their votes. In a proxy fight, activist investors who want to challenge incumbent managers approach individual stockholders in the company and solicit their proxies, which they then can use in votes against the management slate.

In one very public and expensive proxy fight in 2002, David Hewlett, who was sitting on the board of Hewlett Packard (HP) at the time, tried to stop HP from buying Compaq by soliciting proxies from HP stockholders. After eight months of acrimony, HP finally won the fight with the bare minimum 51% of the votes. How did David Hewlett come so close to stopping the deal? One advantage he had was that the Hewlett and Packard families owned a combined 18% of the total number of shares outstanding. The other was that Hewlett's position on the board and his access to internal information gave him a great deal of credibility when it came to fighting for the votes of institutional investors. The fact that he failed, even with these advantages, shows how difficult it is to win at a proxy fight. Even a failed proxy fight, though, often has the salutary effect of awakening incumbent managers to the need to at least consider what shareholders want. ■

---

[38] You can read Roy Disney's letter of resignation on the Web site for the book.

Stockholders and Bondholders

The conflict of interests between stockholders and bondholders can lead to actions that transfer wealth to the former from the latter. There are ways bondholders can obtain at least partial protection against some of these actions.

The Effect of Covenants

The most direct way for bondholders to protect themselves is to write in covenants in their bond agreements specifically prohibiting or restricting actions that may make them worse off. Many bond (and bank loan) agreements have covenants that do the following:

- ***Restrict the firm's investment policy.*** Investing in riskier businesses than anticipated can lead to a transfer of wealth from bondholders to stockholders. Some bond agreements put restrictions on where firms can invest and how much risk they can take on in their new investments, specifically to provide bondholders with the power to veto actions that are not in their best interests.
- ***Restrict dividend policy.*** In general, increases in dividends increase stock prices while decreasing bond prices, because they reduce the cash available to the firm to meet debt payments. Many bond agreements restrict dividend policy by tying dividend payments to earnings.
- ***Restrict additional leverage.*** Some bond agreements require firms to get the consent of existing lenders before borrowing more money. This is done to protect the interests of existing secured bondholders.

Although covenants can be effective at protecting bondholders against some abuses, they do come with a price tag. In particular, firms may find themselves having to turn down profitable investments because of bondholder-imposed constraints and having to pay (indirectly, through higher interest rates) for the legal and monitoring costs associated with the constraints.

Taking an Equity Stake

Because the primary reason for the conflict of interests between stockholders and bondholders lies in the nature of their claims, another way that bondholders can reduce the conflict of interest is by owning an equity stake in the firm. This can take the form of buying equity in the firm at the same time as they lend money to it or can be accomplished by making bonds convertible into stock at the option of the bondholders. In either case, bondholders who feel that equity investors are enriching themselves at the lenders' expense can become stockholders and share in the spoils.

Bond Innovations

In the aftermath of several bond market debacles in the late 1980s, bondholders became increasingly creative in protecting themselves with new types of bonds. Although we will consider these innovations in more detail later in this book, consider the example of puttable bonds. Unlike a conventional bond, which constrains bondholders to hold the bond to maturity, the holders of a puttable bond can put the bond back to the issuing company and get the face value of the bond if the company violates the conditions of the bond. For instance, a sudden increase in borrowing by the company or a drop in its bond rating can trigger this action.

 IN PRACTICE: Hedge Funds and Corporate Governance

In the last few years, hedge funds have become key players in the corporate governance battle. They have accumulated large shares in many companies, including some large market cap firms, and have then used those shares to nominate directors and challenge management. While this may seem like an unmitigated good, at least from the perspective of corporate governance, there are four reasons for concern:

1. *Management shakedowns*   There have been cases where hedge funds have banded together, threatened management with dire consequences, and used that threat to extract side payments and special deals for themselves. In the process, other stockholders are made even worse off.

2. *Short-term objectives*   Some hedge funds have short-term objectives that may diverge from the long–term interests of the firm. Giving hedge funds more of a say in how companies are run can lead to decisions that feed into these short-term interests while damaging long-term firm value.

3. *Competing interests*   Since hedge funds can go long or short and invest in different markets (bonds and derivatives), it is conceivable for a hedge fund that owns equity in firm to also have other positions in the firm that may benefit when the value of equity drops. For instance, a hedge fund that owns stock in a company and has bet on the firm's demise in the derivatives market may use its voting power to drive the company into bankruptcy.

4. *Herd mentality*   While we assume that hedge fund managers are somehow smarter and more sophisticated than the rest of the market, they are not immune from the behavioral characteristics that bedevil other investors. In fact, the herd mentality seems to drive many hedge fund managers, who flock to the same companies at the same time—and their prescriptions for corporate renewal seem to follow the same script.

In spite of these concerns, we believe that the presence of hedge funds and activist investors in the mix of stockholders empowers other stockholders, for the most part, not because the changes they suggest are always wise or because management is always wrong, but because they force managers to explain their actions (on capital structure, asset deployment, and dividends) to stockholders. ■

Firms and Financial Markets

The information that firms convey to financial markets is often erroneous and sometimes misleading. The market price that emerges from financial markets can be wrong, partly because of inefficiencies in markets and partly because of the errors in the information. There are no easy or quick-fix solutions to these problems. In the long run, however, there are actions that will improve information quality and reduce deviations between price and value.

Improving the Quality of Information

Although regulatory bodies like the SEC can require firms to reveal more information and penalize those that provide misleading and fraudulent information, the quality of information cannot be improved with information disclosure laws alone. In particular, firms will always have a vested interest in what information they reveal to markets—and when. To provide balance, therefore, an active external market for information has to exist where analysts who are not hired or fired by the firms that they follow collect and disseminate information. These analysts are just as likely to make mistakes as the firm, but they presumably have a greater incentive to unearth bad news about the firm and disseminate that information to their clients. For this system to work, analysts have to be given free rein to search for good as well as bad news, and to make positive or negative judgments about a firm.

Making Markets More Efficient

Just as better information cannot be legislated into existence, markets cannot be made more efficient by edict. In fact, there is widespread disagreement on what is required to make markets more efficient. At minimum, these are necessary (though not sufficient) conditions for more efficient markets:

- Trading should be both inexpensive and easy. The higher transactions costs are, and the more difficult it is to execute a trade, the more likely it is that markets will be inefficient.
- There should be free and wide access to information about firms.
- Investors should be allowed to benefit when they pick the right stocks to invest in and to pay the price when they make mistakes.

Restrictions imposed on trading, although well intentioned, often lead to market inefficiencies. For instance, restricting short sales, where investors who don't own a stock can borrow and sell it if they feel it is overpriced, may seem like good public policy, but it can create a scenario in which negative information about stocks cannot be reflected adequately in prices.

Short Term versus Long Term

Even in liquid markets with significant information about companies, investors not only make mistakes, but make these mistakes systematically for extended periods, for the behavioral reasons that we noted earlier. In other words, there is no way to ensure that stock prices will not deviate from value for extended periods. As a consequence, even believers in stock price maximization need to pause and consider the possibility that doing what is right for a company's long-term value may result, at least in the short term, in lower stock prices. Conversely, actions that hurt the long-term interests of the firm may be accompanied by higher stock prices.

The lesson for corporate governance is a simple one. Managers should not be judged and compensated based upon stock price performance over short periods. If compensation is tied to stock prices, a portion of the compensation has to be held back to ensure that management actions are in the best long-term interests of the company. More companies now have claw-back provisions in compensation contracts, allowing them to reclaim compensation from earlier years in case stock prices come down after the initial blip, or require managers to wait to cash out their compensation. With restricted stock, for instance, managers often have to wait three or five years before the stock can be liquidated. Implicitly, we are assuming that stock prices ultimately will reflect the true value.

Firms and Society

There will always be social costs associated with actions taken by firms operating in their own best interests. The basic conundrum is as follows: social costs cannot be ignored in making decisions, but they are also too nebulous to be factored explicitly into analyses. One solution is for firms to maximize firm or stockholder value, subject to a good citizen constraint, where attempts are made to minimize or alleviate social costs, even though the firm may not be under any legal obligation to do so. The problem with this approach, of course, is that the definition of a good citizen is likely to vary from firm to firm and from manager to manager.

Ultimately, the most effective way to make companies more socially responsible is to make it in their best economic interests to behave well. This can occur in two ways. First, firms that are construed as socially irresponsible could lose customers and profits. This was the galvanizing factor behind a number of specialty retailers in the United States' disavowing the use of sweatshops and underage labor in other countries in making their products. Second, investors might avoid buying stock in these companies. As an example, many U.S. college and state pension plans have started reducing or eliminating their holding of tobacco stocks to reflect their concerns about the health effects of tobacco. In fact, investors now have access to "ethical mutual funds," which invest only in companies that meet a social consciousness threshold. Figure 2.3 summarizes the ways in which we can reduce potential side costs from stock price maximization.

Figure 2.3   Stock Price Maximization with Market Feedback

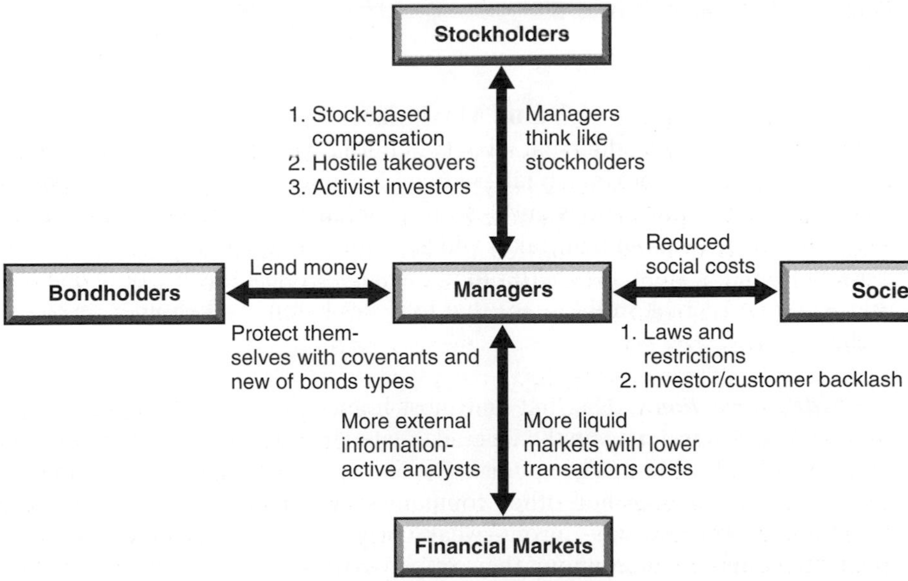

IN PRACTICE: CAN YOU ADD VALUE WHILE DOING GOOD?

Does doing social good hurt or help firms? On one side of this argument stand those who believe that firms that expend considerable resources to generate social good are misguided and are doing their stockholders a disservice. On the other side are those who believe that socially conscious firms are rewarded by consumers (with higher sales) and by investors (with higher values). The evidence is mixed and will undoubtedly disappoint both sides.

- Studies indicate that the returns earned by stockholders in socially conscious firms are no different than the returns earned by stockholders in the rest of the market. Studies of ethical mutual funds find that they neither lag nor lead other mutual funds.
- There is clearly a substantial economic cost borne by companies that are viewed by society as beyond the pale when it comes to creating social costs. Tobacco firms, for instance, have seen stock prices slide as investors avoid their shares and profits are hurt by legal costs.
- When firms are profitable and doing well, stockholders are usually willing to give managers the flexibility to use company money to do social good. Few Microsoft investors begrudged its 1998 decision to give free computers to public libraries around the country. In firms that are doing badly, stockholders tend to be much more resistant to spending company money in mending society's ills.

Summarizing this evidence, we can draw some conclusions. First, a firm's foremost obligation is to stay financially healthy and increase value; firms that are losing money cannot afford to be charitable. Second, firms that create large social costs pay a high price in the long run. Finally, managers should not keep stockholders in the dark about the cost of meeting social obligations; after all, it is the stockholders' money that is being used for the purpose. ■

A Compromise Solution: Value Maximization with Price Feedback

Let us start off by conceding that all of the alternatives—choosing a different corporate governance system, picking an alternative objective, and maximizing stock price with constraints—have limitations and lead to problems. The questions then become how each alternative deals with mistakes and how quickly errors get corrected. This is where a market-based system does better than the alternatives. It is the only one of the three that is self-correcting, in the sense that excesses by any stakeholder attract responses in three waves.

1. *Market reaction.* The first and most immediate reaction comes from financial markets. Consider again the turmoil created by well-publicized failures like Enron. Not only did the market punish Enron (by knocking its stock and bond prices down), but it punished other companies that it perceived as being exposed to the same problems as Enron—weak corporate governance and opaque financial statements—by discounting their values as well.

2. *Group activism.* Following on the heels of the market reaction to any excess is outrage on the part of those who feel that they have been victimized by it. In response to management excesses in the 1980s, we saw an increase in the number of activist investors and hostile acquisitions, reminding managers that there are limits to their power. In the aftermath of well-publicized scandals in the late 1980s where loopholes in lending agreements were exploited by firms, banks and bondholders began playing more active roles in management.

3. *Market innovations.* Markets often come up with innovative solutions to problems. In response to the corporate governance scandals in 2002 and 2003, Institutional Shareholder Services began scoring corporate boards on independence and effectiveness and offering these scores to investors. After the accounting scandals of the same period, the demand for forensic accounting, where accountants go over financial statements looking for clues of accounting malfeasance, increased dramatically. The bond market debacles of the 1980s gave birth to dozens of innovative bonds designed to protect bondholders. Even in the area of social costs, there are markets that have developed to quantify the cost.

Having made this argument for market-based mechanisms, we also need to be realistic. To the extent that market prices and value can deviate, tying corporate financial decisions to current stock prices can sometimes lead to bad decisions. As a blueprint for decision making, here is what we suggest:

- *Focus on long-term value* Managers should make decisions that maximize the long-term value of the firm. This, of course, will require that we be more explicit about the link between operating and financial decisions and value, and we will do so in the coming chapters.

- *Improve corporate governance* Having an independent and informed board of directors can help top managers by providing feedback on major decisions and by acting as a check on management ambitions. The quality of this feedback will improve if there are adversarial directors on the board. In fact, having an independent director take the role of devil's advocate may force managers to think through the consequences of their decisions.

- *Increase transparency* When managers make decisions that they believe to be in the best long-term interests of the firm, they should make every attempt to be transparent with financial markets about the motivation for and the consequences of these decisions. Too often, managers hold back critical information from markets or engage in obfuscation when dealing with markets.

- *Listen to the market* If the market reaction is not consistent with management expectations—i.e., the stock price goes down when markets receive news about a what managers believe to be a value-increasing decision—managers should consider the message in the market reaction. There are three possible explanations:

  1. The first is that the information provided about the decision is incomplete and or not convincing, in which case framing the decision better for betters may be all that is required (public relations response).

2. The second is that investors are being swayed by irrational factors and are responding in accordance. In this case, managers should consider modifying the decision to make it palatable to investors, so long as these modifications do not alter the value enhancement dynamic.

3. The third is that the market is right in its assessment that the decision will destroy and not increase value. In this case, managers should be willing to abandon decisions. While markets are not always right, they should never be ignored, and managers should consider modifying their decisions to reflect the market reaction.

- *Tie rewards to long-term value* Any management compensation and reward mechanisms in the firm should be tied to long-term value. Since market prices remain the only tangible manifestation of this value, this implies that any equity compensation (options or restricted stock) be tied to the long-term stock price performance of a firm, not the short-term.

Since this mechanism is central to how we will frame key corporate finance decisions, Figure 2.4 summarizes the process with the feedback loops.

Figure 2.4   Value Maximization with Feedback

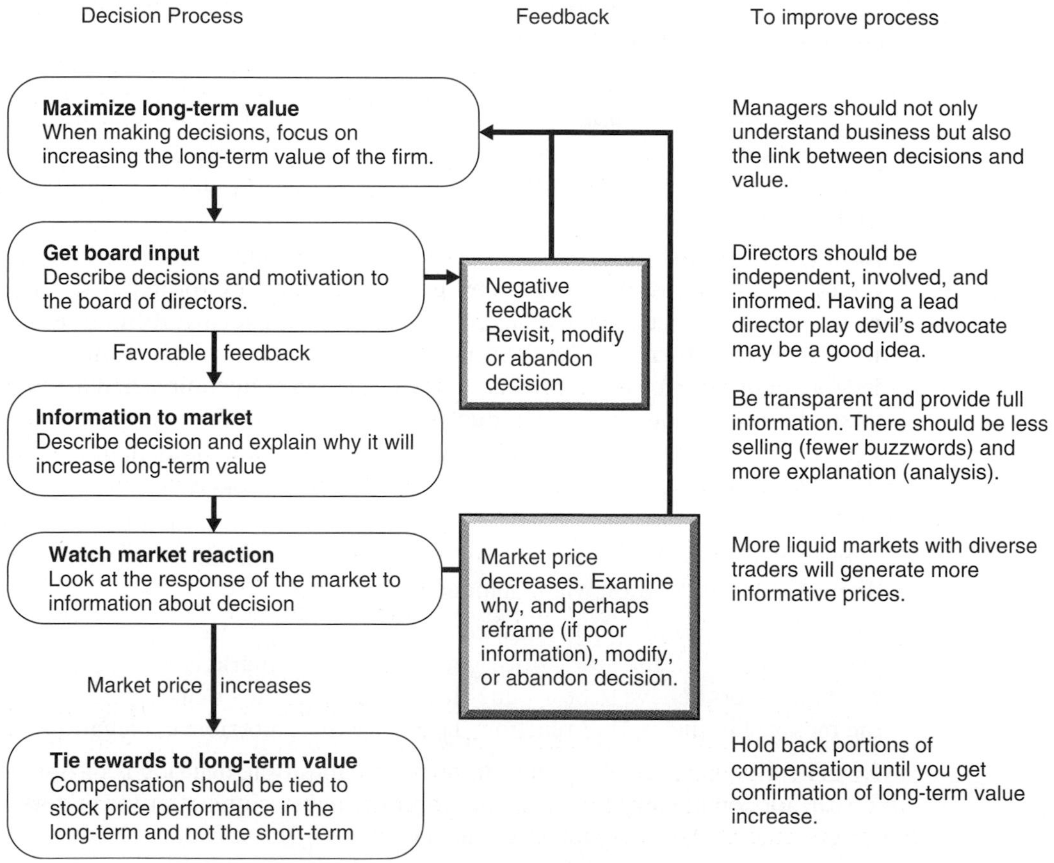

Decision Process	Feedback	To improve process
Maximize long-term value — When making decisions, focus on increasing the long-term value of the firm.		Managers should not only understand business but also the link between decisions and value.
Get board input — Describe decisions and motivation to the board of directors.	Negative feedback — Revisit, modify or abandon decision	Directors should be independent, involved, and informed. Having a lead director play devil's advocate may be a good idea.
Favorable feedback		Be transparent and provide full information. There should be less selling (fewer buzzwords) and more explanation (analysis).
Information to market — Describe decision and explain why it will increase long-term value	Market price decreases. Examine why, and perhaps reframe (if poor information), modify, or abandon decision.	More liquid markets with diverse traders will generate more informative prices.
Watch market reaction — Look at the response of the market to information about decision		
Market price increases		
Tie rewards to long-term value — Compensation should be tied to stock price performance in the long-term and not the short-term		Hold back portions of compensation until you get confirmation of long-term value increase.

A confession is in order here. In earlier editions of this book, we argued that the objective in corporate finance should be stock price maximization, notwithstanding the failures of financial markets. This is the first time that we have strayed from this classical objective, illustrating not only the effects of the market turmoil of 2008–2009 but also the collective evidence that has accumulated: that investors are not always rational in the way they price assets, at least in the short term.

We will stay with this framework as we make our way through each major corporate finance decision. With investment, financing, and dividend policies, we will begin by focusing on the link between policy and value and what we believe is the best approach for maximizing value. We will follow up by examining what information about these decisions has to be provided to financial markets, and why markets may provide dissonant feedback. Finally, we will consider how best to incorporate this market feedback into decisions (and the information we provide about these decisions) to increase the changes of aligning long-term value and stock prices.

A POSTSCRIPT: THE LIMITS OF CORPORATE FINANCE

Corporate finance has come in for more than its fair share of criticism in the past decade or so. There are many who argue that the failures of corporate America can be traced to its dependence on financial markets. Some of the criticism is justified, and is based on the limitations of a single-minded pursuit of stock price maximization. Some of it, however, is based on a misunderstanding of what corporate finance is about.

Economics was once branded the gospel of Mammon because of its emphasis on wealth. The descendants of those critics have labeled corporate finance as unethical, because of its emphasis on the bottom line and market prices. In restructuring and liquidations, it is true that value maximization for stockholders may mean that other stakeholders, such as customers and employees, lose out. In most cases, however, decisions that increase market value also make customers and employees better off. Furthermore, if the firm is really in trouble, either because it is being undersold by competitors or because its products are technologically obsolete, the choice is not between liquidation and survival but between a speedy resolution (which is what corporate financial theory would recommend) and a slow death (while the firm declines over time and costs society considerably more in the process).

The conflict between wealth maximization for the firm and social welfare is the genesis for the attention paid to ethics in business schools. There will never be an objective set of decision rules that perfectly factor in societal concerns, simply because many of these concerns are difficult to quantify, and are subjective. Thus corporate financial theory, in some sense, assumes that decision makers will not make decisions that create large social costs. This assumption that decision makers are for the most part ethical and will not create unreasonable costs for society or for other stakeholders is unstated but underlies corporate financial theory. When it is violated, it exposes corporate financial theory to ethical and moral criticism, although the criticism may be better directed at the violators.

2.10   WHAT DO YOU THINK THE OBJECTIVE OF THE FIRM SHOULD BE?

Having heard the pros and cons of the different objectives, the following statement best describes where I stand in terms of the right objective for decision making in a business:

a.   Maximize stock price or stockholder wealth, with no constraints

b.   Maximize stock price or stockholder wealth, with constraints on being a good social citizen

c.   Maximize profits or profitability

d.   Maximize market share.

e.   Maximize revenues

f.   Maximize social good

g.   None of the above

CONCLUSION

Although the objective in corporate finance is to maximize firm value, in practice we often adopt the narrower objective of maximizing a firm's stock price. As a measurable and unambiguous measure of a firm's success, stock price offers a clear target for managers in the course of their decision-making. Implicitly, we are assuming that the stock price is a reasonable and unbiased estimate of the true value of the company, and that any action that increases stock prices also increases value.

Stock price maximization as the only objective can be problematic when the different players in the firm—stockholders, managers, lenders, and society—all have different interests and work at cross purposes. These differences, which result in agency costs, can result in managers who put their interests over those of the stockholders who hired them, stockholders who try to take advantage of lenders, firms that try to mislead financial markets, and decisions that create large costs for society. In the presence of these agency problems, there are many who argue for an alternative to stock price maximization. Although this path is alluring, each of the alternatives, including using a different system of corporate governance or a different objective, comes with its own set of limitations. Stock price maximization also fails when markets do not operate efficiently and stock prices deviate from true value for extended periods—and there is mounting evidence that they do.

Given the limitations of the alternatives, we will split the difference. We believe that managers should make decisions that increase the long-term value of the firm and then try to provide as much information as they can about the consequences of these decisions to financial markets. If the market reaction is not positive, they should pay attention, since there is a message in the price reaction that may lead them to modify their decisions.

LIVE CASE STUDY

CORPORATE GOVERNANCE ANALYSIS

Objective: To analyze the corporate governance structure of the firm and assess where the power in the firm lies and the potential for conflicts of interest at the firm.

Key Questions

- Is this a company where there is a separation between management and ownership? If so, how responsive is management to stockholders?
- Is there a potential conflict between stockholders and lenders to the firm? If so, how is it managed?
- How does this firm interact with financial markets? How do markets get information about the firm?
- How does this firm view its social obligations and manage its image in society?

Framework for Analysis

1. *The Chief Executive Officer*

   - Who is the CEO of the company? How long has he or she been CEO?
   - If it is a "family-run" company, is the CEO part of the family? If not, what career path did the CEO take to get to the top? (Did he or she come from within the organization, or from outside?)
   - How much did the CEO make last year? What form did the compensation take (salary, bonus, option components)?
   - How much equity in the company does the CEO own, and in what form (stocks, or options)?

2. *The Board of Directors*

   - Who are on the board of directors of the company? How long have they served as directors?
   - How many of the directors are inside directors?
   - How many of the directors have other connections to the firm (as suppliers, clients, customers, etc.)?
   - How many of the directors are CEOs of other companies?
   - Do any of the directors have large stockholdings, or represent those who do?

3. *Bondholder Concerns*

   - Does the firm have any publicly traded debt?
   - Are there are bond covenants (that you can uncover) that have been imposed on the firm as part of the borrowing?
   - Do any of the bonds issued by the firm come with special protections against stockholder expropriation?

4. *Financial Market Considerations*
   - How widely held and traded is the stock? What proportion of its shares are widely traded (floats)?
   - How many analysts follow the firm?
   - How much trading volume is there on this stock?

5. *Societal Constraints*
   - What does the firm say about its social responsibilities?
   - Does the firm have a particularly good or bad reputation as a corporate citizen?
   - If it does, how has it earned this reputation?
   - If the firm has been a recent target of social criticism, how has it responded?

Information Sources

For firms that are incorporated in the United States, information on the CEO and the board of directors is primarily in the filings made by the firm with the SEC. In particular, the 14-DEF will list the directors in the firm, their relationship with the firm, and details on compensation for both directors and top managers. You can also get information on trading done by insiders from the SEC filings. For firms that are not listed in the United States, this information is much more difficult to obtain. However, the absence of readily accessible information on directors and top management is more revealing about the power that resides with incumbent managers.

Information on a firm's relationships with bondholders usually resides in the firm's bond agreements and loan covenants. Although this information may not always be available to the public, the presence of constraints shows up indirectly in the firm's bond ratings and when the firm issues new bonds.

The relationship between firms and financial markets is tougher to gauge. The list of analysts following a firm can be obtained from publications such as the *Nelson Directory of Securities Research*. For larger and more heavily followed firms, the archives of financial publications (e.g., the *Financial Times, The Wall Street Journal, Forbes, Barron's*) can be useful sources of information.

Finally, the reputation of a firm as a corporate citizen is the most difficult area to obtain clear information on, because it is only the outliers (the worst and the best corporate citizens) that make the news. The proliferation of socially responsible mutual funds, however, does give us a window on those firms that pass the tests (arbitrary though they sometimes are) imposed by these funds for a firm to be viewed as socially responsible.

PROBLEMS AND QUESTIONS

1. There is a conflict of interest between stockholders and managers. In theory, stockholders are expected to exercise control over managers through the annual meeting or the board of directors. In practice, why might these disciplinary mechanisms not work?

2. Stockholders can transfer wealth from bondholders through a variety of actions. How would the following actions by stockholders transfer wealth from bondholders?
   a. An increase in dividends
   b. A leveraged buyout
   c. Acquiring a risky business
   How would bondholders protect themselves against these actions?

3. Stock prices are much too volatile for financial markets to be efficient. Comment.

4. Maximizing stock prices does not make sense, because investors focus on short-term results and not on long-term consequences. Comment.

5. There are some corporate strategists who have suggested that firms focus on maximizing market share rather than market prices. When might this strategy work, and when might it fail?

6. Antitakeover amendments can be in the best interests of stockholders. Under what conditions is this likely to be true?

7. Companies outside the United States often have two classes of stock outstanding. One class of shares is voting and is held by the incumbent managers of the firm. The other class is nonvoting and represents the bulk of traded shares. What are the consequences for corporate governance?

8. In recent years, top managers have been given large packages of options, giving them the right to buy stock in the firm at a fixed price. Will these compensation schemes make managers more responsive to stockholders? Why, or why not? Are lenders to the firm affected by these compensation schemes?

9. *Reader's Digest* has voting and nonvoting shares. About 70% of the voting shares are held by charitable institutions, which are headed by the CEO of *Reader's Digest*. Assume that you are a large holder of the nonvoting shares. Would you be concerned about this setup? What are some of the actions you might push the firm to take to protect your interests?

10. In Germany, large banks are often large lenders and large equity investors in the same firm. For instance, Deutsche Bank is the largest stockholder in Daimler Chrysler, as well as its largest lender. What are some of the potential conflicts that you see in these dual holdings?

11. It is often argued that managers, when asked to maximize stock price, have to choose between being socially responsible and carrying out their fiduciary duty. Do you agree? Can you provide an example where social responsibility and firm value maximization go hand in hand?

12. Assume that you are advising a Turkish firm on corporate financial questions, and that you do not believe that the Turkish stock market is efficient. Would you recommend stock price maximization as the objective? If not, what would you recommend?

13. It has been argued by some that convertible bonds (i.e., bonds that are convertible into stock at the option of the bondholders) provide one form of protection against expropriation by stockholders. On what is this argument based?

14. Societies attempt to keep private interests in line by legislating against behavior that might create social costs (such as polluting the water). If the legislation is comprehensive enough, does the problem of social costs cease to exist? Why, or why not?

15. One of the arguments made for having legislation restricting hostile takeovers is that unscrupulous speculators may take over well-run firms and destroy them for personal gain. Allowing for the possibility that this could happen, do you think that this is sensible? If so, why? If not, why not?

Chapter 3

The Basics Of Risk

Risk, in traditional terms, is viewed as a negative and something to be avoided. Webster's dictionary, for instance, defines risk as "exposing to danger or hazard". The Chinese symbols for crisis, reproduced below, give a much better description of risk:

危机

The first symbol is the symbol for "danger", while the second is the symbol for "opportunity," making risk a mix of danger and opportunity. It illustrates very clearly the tradeoff that every investor and business has to make—between the "higher rewards"

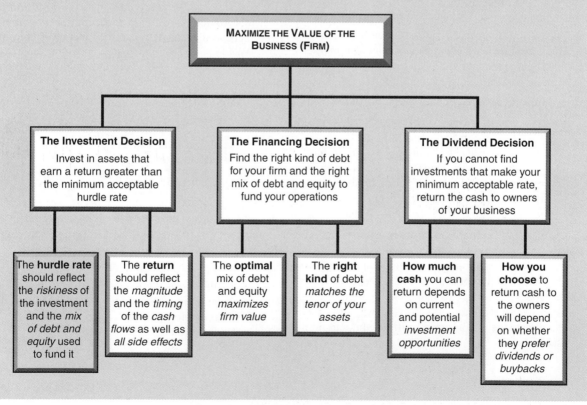

that potentially come with the opportunity and the "higher risk" that has to be borne as a consequence of the danger. The key test in finance is to ensure that when an investor is exposed to risk, he or she is "appropriately" rewarded for taking this risk.

In this chapter, we will lay the foundations for analyzing risk in corporate finance and present alternative models for measuring risk and converting these risk measures into "acceptable" hurdle rates.

MOTIVATION AND PERSPECTIVE IN ANALYZING RISK

Why do we need a model that measures risk and estimates expected return? A good model for risk and return provides us with the tools to measure the risk in any investment and uses that risk measure to come up with the appropriate expected return on that investment; this expected return provides us with the hurdle rate in project analysis.

What makes the measurement of risk and expected return so challenging is that it can vary depending upon whose perspective we adopt. When analyzing Disney's risk, for instance, we can measure it from the viewpoint of Disney's managers. Alternatively, we can argue that Disney's equity is owned by its stockholders, and that it is their perspective on risk that should matter. Disney's stockholders, many of whom hold the stock as one investment in a larger portfolio, might perceive the risk in Disney very differently from Disney's managers, who might have the bulk of their capital, human and financial, invested in the firm. In this chapter, we will argue that risk in an equity investment has to be perceived through the eyes of investors in the firm. Since firms like Disney have thousands of investors, often with very different perspectives, we will go further. We will assert that risk has to be measured from the perspective of not just any investor in the stock, but of the **marginal investor**, defined to be the investor most likely to be trading on the stock at any given point in time. The objective in corporate finance is the maximization of firm value and stock price. If we want to stay true to this objective, we have to consider the viewpoint of those who set the stock prices, and they are the marginal investors.

Finally, the risk in a company can be viewed very differently by investors in its stock (equity investors) and by lenders to the firm (bondholders and bankers). Equity investors who benefit from upside as well as downside tend to take a much more sanguine view of risk than lenders who have limited upside but potentially high downside. We will consider how to measure equity risk in the first part of the chapter and risk from the perspective of lenders in the latter half of the chapter.

We will be presenting a number of different risk and return models in this chapter. In order to evaluate the relative strengths of these models, it is worth reviewing the characteristics of a good risk and return model.

- It should come up with a measure of risk that applies to all assets and not be asset-specific.
- It should clearly delineate what types of risk are rewarded and what are not, and provide a rationale for the delineation.

- It should come up with standardized risk measures—i.e., an investor presented with a risk measure for an individual asset should be able to draw conclusions about whether the asset is above-average or below-average risk.
- It should translate the measure of risk into a rate of return that the investor should demand as compensation for bearing the risk.
- It should work well not only at explaining past returns, but also at predicting future expected returns.

Every risk and return model is flawed, and we should not let the perfect be the enemy of a good, or even adequate, model.

EQUITY RISK AND EXPECTED RETURNS

To understand how risk is viewed in corporate finance, we will present the analysis in three steps. First, we will define risk in terms of the distribution of actual returns around an expected return. Second, we will differentiate between risk that is specific to an investment or a few investments and risk that affects a much wider cross-section of investments. We will argue that when the marginal investor is well diversified, it is only the latter risk, called market risk that will be rewarded. Third, we will look at alternative models for measuring this market risk and the expected returns that go with this risk.

I. Measuring Risk

Investors who buy an asset expect to make a return over the time horizon that they will hold the asset. The actual return that they make over this holding period may be very different from the expected return, and this is where the risk comes in. Consider an investor with a one-year time horizon buying a one-year Treasury bill (or any other default-free one-year bond) with a 5% expected return. At the end of the one-year holding period, the actual return that this investor would have on this investment will always be 5%, which is equal to the expected return. The return distribution for this investment is shown in Figure 3.1.

Figure 3.1   Returns on a Risk-Free Investment

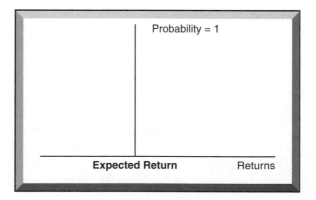

Figure 3.2   Probability Distribution for Risky Investment

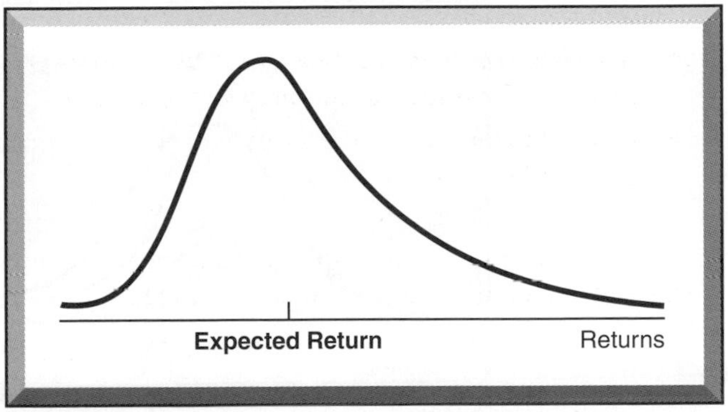

This is a riskless investment, at least in nominal terms.

To provide a contrast, consider an investor who invests in Disney. This investor, having done her research, may conclude that she can make an expected return of 30% on Disney over her one-year holding period. The actual return over this period will almost certainly not be equal to 30%; it might be much greater or much lower. The distribution of returns on this investment is illustrated in Figure 3.2.

In addition to the expected return, an investor now has to consider the following. First, the spread of the actual returns around the expected return is captured by the *variance* or *standard deviation* of the distribution; the greater the deviation of the actual returns from expected returns, the greater the variance. Second, the bias towards positive or negative returns is captured by the *skewness* of the distribution. The distribution above is positively skewed, since there is a greater likelihood of large positive returns than large negative returns. Third, the shape of the tails of the distribution is measured by the *kurtosis* of the distribution; fatter tails lead to higher kurtosis. In investment terms, this captures the tendency of the price of this investment to "jump" in either direction.

In the special case of the normal distribution, returns are symmetric and investors do not have to worry about skewness and kurtosis, since there is no skewness and a normal distribution is defined to have a kurtosis of 0. In that case, it can be argued that investments can be measured on only two dimensions: (1) the "expected return" on the investment comprises the reward and (2) the variance in anticipated returns comprises the risk on the investment. Figure 3.3 illustrates the return distributions on two investments with symmetric returns.

In this scenario, an investor faced with a choice between two investments with the same standard deviation but different expected returns will always pick the one with the higher expected return.

In the more general case, where distributions are neither symmetric nor normal, it is still conceivable, though unlikely, that investors still choose between investments on the basis of only the expected return and the variance, if they possess utility

Figure 3.3   Return Distribution Comparisons

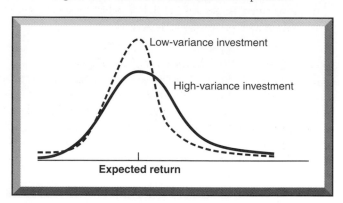

functions[1] that allow them to do so. It is far more likely, however, that they prefer positively skewed distributions to negatively skewed ones, and distributions with a lower likelihood of jumps (lower kurtosis) to those with a higher likelihood of jumps (higher kurtosis). In this world, investors will trade off the good (higher expected returns and more positive skewness) against the bad (higher variance and kurtosis) in making investments. Among the risk and return models that we will be examining, one (the capital asset pricing model or the CAPM) explicitly requires that choices be made only in terms of expected returns and variances. While it does ignore the skewness and kurtosis, it is not clear how much of a factor these additional moments of the distribution are in determining expected returns.

In closing, we should note that the return moments that we run into in practice are almost always estimated using past returns rather than future returns. The assumption we are making when we use historical variances is that past return distributions are good indicators of future return distributions. When this assumption is violated, as is the case when the asset's characteristics have changed significantly over time, the historical estimates may not be good measures of risk.

3.1   Do You Live in a Mean-Variance World?

Assume that you had to pick between two investments. They have the same expected return of 15% and the same standard deviation of 25%, but investment A offers a very small possibility that you could quadruple your money, whereas investment B's highest possible payoff is a 60% return. Which would you prefer?

---

[1] A utility function is a way of summarizing investor preferences into a generic term called "utility" on the basis of some choice variables. In this case, for instance, investor utility or satisfaction is stated as a function of wealth. By doing so, we effectively can answer various questions: Will an investor be twice as happy if he has twice as much wealth? Does each marginal increase in wealth lead to less additional utility than the prior marginal increase? In one specific form of this function, the quadratic utility function, the entire utility of an investor can be compressed into the expected wealth measure and the standard deviation in that wealth, which provides a justification for the use of a framework where only the expected return (mean) and its standard deviation (variance) matter.

a. Neither, since they have the same expected return and standard deviation
b. Investment A, because of the possibility of a high payoff
c. Investment B, because it is safer

 Risk Assessment: A Behavioral Perspective

The mean–variance framework for assessing risk is focused on measuring risk quantitatively, often with one number—a standard deviation. While this focus is understandable because it introduces discipline into the process and makes it easier for us to follow up and measure risk, it may not fully capture the complicated relationship that we, as human beings, have with risk. Behavioral finance scholars present three aspects of risk assessment that are at variance with the mean–variance school's view of risk:

1. ***Loss aversion*** In experiments with human subjects, there is evidence that individuals are affected far more negatively by a loss than they are helped by an equivalent gain, and that they generally measure losses in dollar terms rather than percentage terms. Put another way, investors are loss-averse rather than risk-averse. Consequently, investments where there is even a small chance of a significant loss in wealth will be viewed as risky, even if they have only a small standard deviation.

2. ***Familiarity bias*** Individuals seem to perceive less risk with investments that they are familiar with than with unfamiliar investments. Thus, they see less risk in a domestic company with a long provenance than they do in an emerging market firm. This may explain why there is a "home bias" in portfolios, where investors overinvest in investments in their domestic market and underinvest in foreign investments. In an extension of this bias, the risk that individuals perceive in an activity or investment is inversely proportional to the difficulty they face in understanding it.

3. ***Emotional factors*** There is an emotional component to risk that quantitative risk measures cannot capture. This component can have both a positive affect whereby gains accentuate positive affects (happiness and optimism) and losses feed into negative affects (worry and anxiety). More generally, investor moods can affect risk perceptions, with investments that are viewed as relatively safe in buoyant times becoming risky when investor moods shift.

In recent years, there have been attempts to build composite risk measures that bring these behavioral components into the analysis. While no consensus has emerged, it may explain why quantitative measures of risk (such as standard deviation) for a firm may deviate from the many qualitative risk measures that often exist for the same firm.

ILLUSTRATION 3.1 Calculation of Standard Deviation Using Historical Returns—Disney

We collected the data on the returns we would have made on a monthly basis for every month from January 2004 to December 2008 on an investment in Disney stock. To compute the returns, we looked at the price change in each month (with Price_t being the price at the end of month (t) and dividends, if any, during the month (Dividends_t):

$$\text{Return}_t = \frac{(\text{Price}_t - \text{Price}_{t-1} + \text{Dividends}_t)}{\text{Price}_{t-1}}$$

Figure 3.4 Returns on Disney Stock: 2004–2008

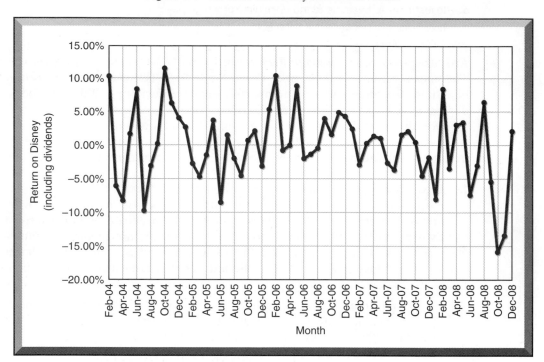

The monthly returns are graphed in Figure 3.4.

Disney's returns reflect the risk that an investor in the stock would have faced over the period, with October 2004 being the best month (with a return of 11.82%) and October 2008 representing the worst month (with a return of −15.58%).

Looking at the summary statistics, the average monthly return on Disney over the fifty-nine months was 0.18%. In fact, we started the period in January 2004 with a stock price of $23.68 and ended the period on December 31, 2008 with a stock price of $22.69. However, the stock did pay an annual dividend that increased from $0.24 in 2004 to $0.35 in 2008. To measure the volatility or risk in the stock, we estimated the standard deviation in monthly returns over this period to be 5.59%; the variance in monthly returns was 31.25%.[2] To convert monthly values to annualized ones,

$$\text{Annualized standard deviation} = 5.59\% * \sqrt{12} = 19.36\%$$
$$\text{Annualized variance} = 31.25\% * 12 = 374.98\%$$

Without making comparisons to the standard deviations in stock returns of other companies, we cannot really draw any conclusions about the relative risk of Disney by just looking at its standard deviation.

---

[2]The variance is percent squared. In other words, if you stated the standard deviation of 5.59% in decimal terms, it would be 0.0559, but the variance of 31.25% would be 0.003125 in decimal terms.

optvar.xls: This dataset on the Web summarizes average standard deviations of equity values by industry group in the United States.

3.2 UPSIDE AND DOWNSIDE RISK

You are looking at the historical standard deviations over the last five years on two investments. Both have standard deviations of 35% in returns during the period, but one had a return of −10% during the period, whereas the other had a return of +40% during the period. Would you view them as equally risky?

a. Yes

b. No

Why do we not differentiate between "upside risk" and "downside risk" in finance?

IN PRACTICE: ESTIMATING ONLY DOWNSIDE RISK

The variance of a return distribution measures the deviation of actual returns from the expected return. In estimating the variance, we consider not only actual returns that fall below the average return (downside risk) but also those that lie above it (upside risk). As investors, it is the downside that we generally consider as risk. There is an alternative measure called the semivariance that considers only downside risk. To estimate the semivariance, we calculate the deviations of actual returns from the average return only if the actual return is less than the expected return; we ignore actual returns that are higher than the average return.

$$\text{Semi-variance} = \sum_{t=1}^{t=n} \frac{(R_t - \text{Average return})^2}{n}$$

$n =$ Number of periods where actual return $<$ Average return

With a normal distribution, the semivariance will generate a value identical to the variance, but for any asymmetric distribution, the semivariance will yield different values than the variance. In general, a stock that generates small positive returns in most periods but very large negative returns in a few periods will have a semivariance that is much higher than the variance. ■

II. Rewarded and Unrewarded Risk

Risk, as we have defined it in the previous section, arises from the deviation of actual returns from expected returns. This deviation, however, can occur for any number of reasons, and these reasons can be classified into two categories: those that are specific to the investment being considered (called firm specific risks) and those that apply across most or all investments (market risks).

The Components of Risk

When a firm makes an investment in a new asset or a project, the return on that investment can be affected by several variables, most of which are not under the direct control of the firm. Some of the risk comes directly from the investment, a portion from competition, some from shifts in the industry, some from changes in exchange rates, and some from macroeconomic factors. A portion of this risk, however, will be eliminated by the firm itself over the course of multiple investments, and another portion by investors as they hold diversified portfolios.

The first source of risk is *project-specific*; an individual project may have higher or lower cash flows than expected, either because the firm misestimated the cash flows for that project or because of factors specific to that project. When firms take a large number of similar projects, it can be argued that much of this risk should be diversified away in the normal course of business. For instance, Disney, while considering making a new movie, exposes itself to estimation error: it may under- or overestimate the cost and time of making the movie and may also err in its estimates of revenues from both theatrical release and the sale of merchandise. Since Disney releases several movies a year, it can be argued that some or much of this risk should be diversifiable across movies produced during the course of the year.[3]

The second source of risk is *competitive risk*, whereby the earnings and cash flows on a project are affected (positively or negatively) by the actions of competitors. While a good project analysis will build in the expected reactions of competitors into estimates of profit margins and growth, the actual actions taken by competitors may differ from these expectations. In most cases, this component of risk will affect more than one project, making it more difficult to diversify away in the normal course of business by the firm. Disney, for instance, in its analysis of revenues from its theme parks division, may err in its assessments of the strength and strategies of competitors like Universal Studios. While Disney cannot diversify away its competitive risk, stockholders in Disney can, if they are willing to hold stock in the competitors.[4]

The third source of risk is *industry-specific risk*—those factors that impact the earnings and cash flows of a specific industry. There are three sources of industry-specific risk. The first is *technology risk*, which reflects the effects of technologies that change or evolve in ways different from those expected when a project was originally analyzed. The second source is *legal risk*, which reflects the effect of changing laws and regulations. The third is *commodity risk*, which reflects the effects of price changes in commodities and services that are used or produced disproportionately by a specific industry. Disney, for instance, in assessing the prospects of its broadcasting division (ABC) is likely to be exposed to all three risks: to technology risk as the lines between television entertainment and the Internet are increasing blurred by companies like Microsoft, to legal risk as the laws governing broadcasting change, and to commodity risk as the costs of making new television programs change over time. A firm cannot diversify away its industry-specific risk without diversifying across industries, either with new projects or through acquisitions. Stockholders in the firm should be able to diversify away industry-specific risk by holding portfolios of stocks from different industries.

The fourth source of risk is *international risk*. A firm faces this type of risk when it generates revenues or has costs outside its domestic market. In such cases, the earnings and cash flows will be affected by unexpected exchange rate movements or by political

---

[3]To provide an illustration: Disney released *Treasure Planet*, an animated movie, in 2002; it cost $140 million to make and resulted in a $98 million write-off. A few months later, *Finding Nemo*, another animated Disney movie, made hundreds of millions of dollars and became one of the biggest hits of 2003.

[4]Firms could conceivably diversify away competitive risk by acquiring their existing competitors. Doing so would expose them to legal challenge under the anti-trust law, however, and would not eliminate the risk from as-yet-unannounced competitors.

developments. Disney, for instance, is clearly exposed to this risk with its theme park in Hong Kong. Some of this risk may be diversified away by the firm in the normal course of business by investing in projects in different countries whose currencies may not all move in the same direction. McDonald's, for instance, operates in many different countries and should be able to diversify away some (though not all) of its exposure to international risk. Companies can also reduce their exposure to the exchange rate component of this risk by borrowing in the local currency to fund projects. Investors should be able to reduce their exposure to international risk by diversifying globally.

The final source of risk is *market risk*: macroeconomic factors that affect essentially all companies and all projects, to varying degrees. For example, changes in interest rates will affect the value of projects already taken and those yet to be taken, both directly (through the discount rates) and indirectly (through the cash flows). Other factors that affect all investments include the term structure (the difference between short- and long-term rates), the risk preferences of investors (as investors become more risk-averse, more risky investments will lose value), inflation, and economic growth. While expected values of all these variables enter into project analysis, unexpected changes in these variables will affect the values of these investments. Neither investors nor firms can diversify away this risk, since all risky investments bear some exposure to this risk.

3.3   RISK IS IN THE EYES OF THE BEHOLDER

A privately owned firm will generally end up with a higher discount rate for a project than would an otherwise similar publicly traded firm with diversified investors.

a.   True

b.   False

Does this provide a rationale for why a private firm may be acquired by a publicly traded firm?

Why Diversification Reduces or Eliminates Firm-Specific Risk

Why do we distinguish between the different types of risk? Risk that affect one of a few firms—i.e., firm-specific risk—can be reduced or even eliminated by investors as they hold more diverse portfolios, for two reasons.

1.   The first is that each investment in a diversified portfolio is a much smaller percentage of that portfolio. Thus, any risk that increases or reduces the value of only that investment or a small group of investments will have only a small impact on the overall portfolio.

2.   The second is that the effects of firm-specific actions on the prices of individual assets in a portfolio can be either positive or negative for each asset for any period. Thus, in large portfolios, it can be reasonably argued that this risk will average out to zero and thus not impact the overall value of the portfolio.

In contrast, risk that affects most of all assets in the market will continue to persist even in large and diversified portfolios. For instance, other things being equal, an increase in interest rates will lower the values of most assets in a portfolio. Figure 3.5 summarizes the different components of risk and the actions that can be taken by the firm and its investors to reduce or eliminate this risk.

Figure 3.5 A Breakdown of Risk

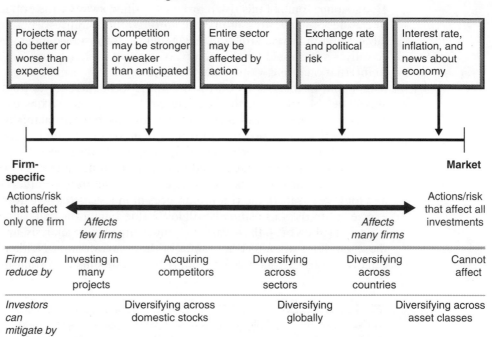

While the intuition for diversification reducing risk is simple, the benefits of diversification can also be shown statistically. In the last section, we introduced standard deviation as the measure of risk in an investment and calculated the standard deviation for an individual stock (Disney). When you combine two investments that do not move together in a portfolio, the standard deviation of that portfolio can be lower than the standard deviation of the individual stocks in the portfolio. To see how the magic of diversification works, consider a portfolio of two assets. Asset A has an expected return of μ_A and a variance in returns of σ_A^2, while Asset B has an expected return of μ_B and a variance in returns of σ_B^2. The correlation in returns between the two assets, which measures how the assets move together, is ρ_{AB}.[5] The expected returns and variance of a two-asset portfolio can be written as a function of these inputs and the proportion of the portfolio going to each asset.

$$\mu_{portfolio} = w_A\mu_A + (1 - w_A)\mu_B$$
$$\sigma_{portfolio}^2 = w_A^2\sigma_A^2 + (1 - w_A)^2\sigma_B^2 + 2w_A(1 - w_A)\rho_{AB}\sigma_A\sigma_B$$

where

$$w_A = \text{Proportion of the portfolio in Asset A}$$

The last term in the variance formulation is sometimes written in terms of the covariance in returns between the two assets, which is

$$\sigma_{AB} = \rho_{AB}\sigma_A\sigma_B$$

[5]The correlation is a number between −1 and +1. If the correlation is −1, the two stocks move in lockstep but in opposite directions. If the correlation is +1, the two stocks move together in sync.

The savings that accrue from diversification are a function of the correlation coefficient. Other things remaining equal, the higher the correlation in returns between the two assets, the smaller the potential benefits from diversification. The following example illustrates the savings from diversification.

 Underdiversification: A Behavioral Perspective
The argument that investors should diversify is impeccable, at least in a mean–variance world full of rational investors. The reality, though, is that most investors do not diversify. In one of the earliest studies of this phenomenon, Blume, Crockett, and Friend (1974) examined the portfolios of individual investors and reported that 34% of the investors held only one dividend-paying stock in their portfolios, 55% held between one and ten stocks, and only 11% held more than ten stocks.[6] While these investors could be granted the excuse that mutual funds were neither as prevalent nor as accessible as they are today, Goetzmann and Kumar looked at 60,000 investors at a discount brokerage house between 1991 and 1996 and concluded that there has been little improvement on the diversification front, and that the absence of diversification cannot be explained away easily with transactions costs.[7] While some researchers have tried to find explanations within the conventional finance framework, behavioral economists offer three possible reasons:

1. ***The gambling instinct***   One possible explanation is that investors construct their portfolios as layered pyramids, with the bottom layer designed for downside protection and the top layer for risk-seeking and upside potential. Investing in one or a few stocks in the top layer may not yield efficient risk-taking portfolios, but they offer more upside. In a sense, these investments are closer to lottery tickets than to financial investments.[8]

2. ***Overconfidence***   Goetzmann and Kumar note that investors who overweight specific industries or focus on stock characteristics such as volatility, when picking stocks, tend to be less diversified than investors who don't try to pick winners. They argue that this is consistent with investors being overconfident in their own abilities to find winners, and thus not diversifying.

3. ***Narrow framing and estimation biases***   Investors who frame their investment decisions narrowly (looking at pieces of their portfolio rather than the whole) or misestimate correlations (by assuming that individual stocks are more highly correlated with each other than they really are) will hold less diversified portfolios.

In summary, many individual investors and some institutional investors seem to ignore the lessons of diversification and choose to hold narrow portfolios. Their perspective on risk may vary from more diversified investors in the same companies.

[6]Blume, M., J. Crockett, and I. Friend, 1974. Stock ownership in the United States: characteristics and trends. Survey of Current Business 54, 16–40.
[7]W. N. Goetzmann and A. Kumar, "Equity Portfolio Diversification," *Review of Finance* 12:433–463. They find that 25% of investors hold only one stock and 50% of investors hold two or three stocks in their portfolios.
[8]H. Shefrin and M. Statman, "Behavioral Portfolio Theory," *Journal of Financial and Quantitative Analysis* 35:127–151.

ILLUSTRATION **3.2** Variance of a portfolio—Disney and Aracruz ADR

In Illustration 3.1, we computed the average return and standard deviation of returns on Disney between January 2004 and December 2008. While Aracruz is a Brazilian stock, it has been listed and traded as an American Depository Receipt (ADR) in the U.S. market over the same period.[9] Using the same sixty months of data on Aracruz, we computed the average return and standard deviation on its returns over the same period:

	Disney	**Aracruz ADR**
Average monthly return	0.18%	−0.74%
Standard deviation in monthly returns	5.59%	14.87%

Between 2004 and 2008, Disney generated higher returns than Aracruz with lower volatility. With the benefit of hindsight, Disney would have been a much better investment than Aracruz, at least over this period. There are two points worth making. The first is that Aracruz generated an average monthly return of 2.47% from January 2004 to April 2008; the stock price dropped from an all-time high of $90.74 to $8.39 between May and December of 2008. The second is that these returns were on the Aracruz ADR, and thus in dollar terms. These returns are therefore affected both by the stock price performance of Aracruz (in Brazilian Reals (R$)) and the $/R$ exchange rate. A contributing factor to decline in the ADR price in the latter part of 2008 was the precipitous fall in the value of the R$, relative to the dollar.

To examine how a combination of Disney and the Aracruz ADR would do as an investment, we computed the correlation between the two stocks over the sixty-month period to be 0.1807. Consider now a portfolio that is invested 90% in Disney and 10% in the Aracruz ADR. The variance and the standard deviation of the portfolio can be computed as follows:

$$\text{Variance of portfolio} = w_{Dis}^2 \sigma_{Dis}^2 + (1 - w_{Dis})^2 \sigma_{Ara}^2 + 2w_{Dis}w_{Ara}\rho_{Dis,Ara}\sigma_{Dis}\sigma_{Ara}$$
$$= (0.9)^2(0.0559)^2 + (0.1)^2(0.1487)^2$$
$$+ 2(0.9)(0.1)(0.1807)(0.0559)(0.1487)$$
$$= 0.003023$$
$$\text{Standard deviation of portfolio} = \sqrt{.003023} = 0.0550, \text{ or } 5.50$$

The portfolio is less risky than either of the two stocks that go into it. In Figure 3.6, we graph the standard deviation in the portfolio as a function of the proportion of the portfolio invested in Disney.

As the proportion of the portfolio invested in Aracruz shifts towards 100%, the standard deviation of the portfolio converges on the standard deviation of Aracruz.

Aracruz's travails between May and December of 2008 also provide some insight into the essence of firm specific and market risk. The company had reported healthy profits from 2004 through 2007, but some of those profits came from speculating with

---

[9]Like most foreign stocks, Aracruz has a listing for depository receipts or ADRs on the U.S. exchanges. Effectively, a bank buys shares of Aracruz in Brazil and issues dollar-denominated shares in the United States to interested investors. Aracruz's ADR price tracks the price of the local listing while reflecting exchange rate changes.

Figure 3.6 Standard Deviation of Portfolio: Disney and Aracruz ADR

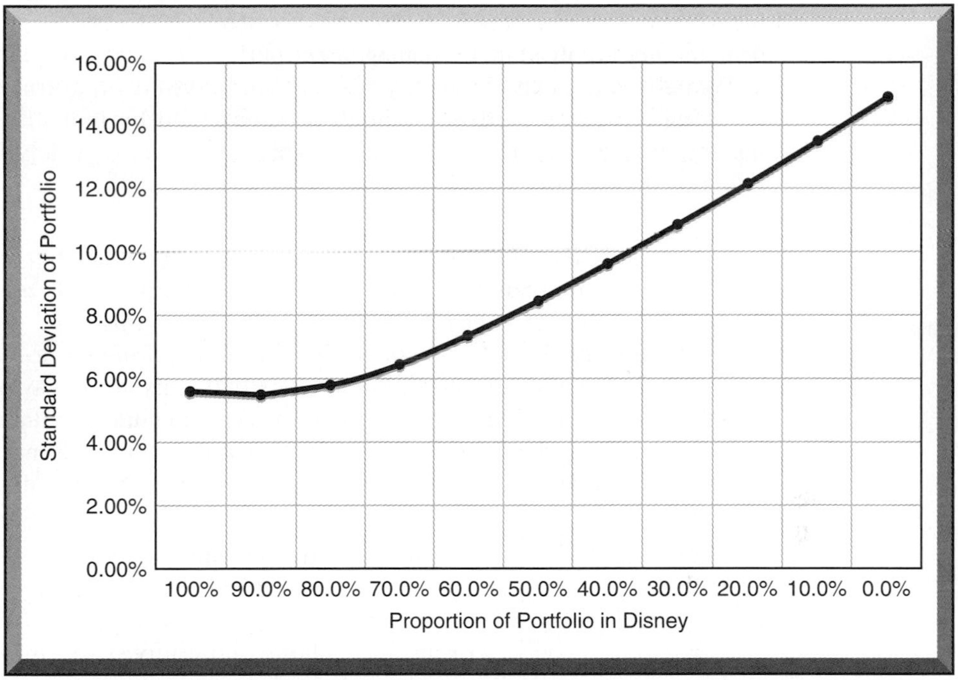

derivatives (options and futures) that the Brazilian Real would continue to strengthen against the U.S. dollar. When the tide turned in 2008 and the Brazilian Real started weakening, the derivative bets made by the firm generated losses in excess of $2 billion, which, in turn, caused the drop in the stock price. The global market collapse in the last three months of the year accelerated the fall. The speculative losses from exchange rate bets are clearly firm-specific risk, but the losses accruing from the global crisis can be attributed to market risk.

Identifying the Marginal Investor
The marginal investor in a firm is the investor who is most likely to be trading at the margin, and who therefore has the most influence on the pricing of its equity. With this definition, in mind, investors need to meet two criteria to qualify as marginal investors: own a significant portion of the equity in the company and trade on that equity. An investor who owns 1000 or 10,000 shares in a company like Disney will no have no impact on the stock price and neither will an investor who owns a million shares on the stock, but never trades.

With large and most midcap publicly traded firms, it is very likely, given the value of overall equity, that the marginal investor will be an institutional investor, but institutional investors themselves can differ in several ways. The institution may be a taxable mutual fund or a tax-exempt pension fund, may be domestically or internationally diversified, and may vary on investment philosophy. With smaller companies that are closely held, the marginal investors may be individuals, and here again there can be wide differences depending upon how diversified these individuals are and what their investment objectives may be. In still other cases, the marginal investors may be insiders in the firm who own a significant portion of the equity of the firm and are involved in the management of the firm.

While it is difficult to identify the marginal investor in a firm, we would begin by breaking down the percent of the firm's stock held by individuals, institutions, and insiders in the firm. This information, which is available widely for U.S. stocks, can then be analyzed to yield the following conclusions:

- If the firm has relatively small institutional holdings but substantial holdings by wealthy individual investors, the marginal investor is *an individual investor with a significant equity holding* in the firm. In this case, we have to consider how diversified that individual investor's portfolio is to assess project risk. If the individual investor is not diversified, this firm may have to be treated like a private firm, and the cost of equity has to include a premium for all risk rather than just nondiversifiable risk. If on the other hand, the individual investor is a wealthy individual with significant stakes in a large number of firms, a large portion of the risk may be diversifiable.

- If the firm has small institutional holdings and small insider holdings, its stock is held by large numbers of *individual investors with small equity holdings*. In this case, the marginal investor is an individual investor, with a portfolio that may be only partially diversified. For instance, phone and utility stocks in the United States, at least until recently, had holdings dispersed among thousands of individual investors, who held the stocks for their high dividends. This preference for dividends meant, however, that these investors held relatively few stocks and only in those sectors where firms paid high dividends.

- If the firm has significant institutional holdings and small insider holdings, the marginal investor is almost always a *diversified, institutional investor*. In fact, we can learn more about what kind of institutional investor holds stock by examining the top fifteen or twenty largest stockholders in the firms and then categorizing them by tax status (mutual funds versus pension funds), investment objective (growth or value), and globalization (domestic versus international).

- If the firm has significant institutional holdings and large insider holdings, the choice for marginal investor becomes a little more complicated. Often, in these scenarios, the large insider is the founder or original owner for the firm; often, this investor continues to be involved in the top management of firm. Microsoft and Dell are good examples, with Bill Gates and Michael Dell being the largest stockholders in the firms. In most of these cases, however, the insider owner trades only infrequently, and his or her wealth is determined by the level of the stock price, which is determined by institutional investors trading the stock. We would argue that the institutional investor is the marginal investor in these firms as well.

Thus, by examining the percent of stock held by different groups, and the largest investors in a firm, we should have a sense of who the marginal investor in the firm is, and how best to assess and risk in corporate financial analysis.

Why do we care about the marginal investor? Since the marginal investors are assumed to set prices, their assessments of risk should govern how the rest of us think about risk. Thus, if the marginal investors are diversified institutions, the only risk that they see in a company is the risk that they cannot diversify away, and managers at the firm should be considering only that risk when making investments. If the marginal investors are undiversified individuals, they will care about all risks in a company, and the firm should therefore consider all risks when making investments.

ILLUSTRATION 3.3   Identifying the Marginal Investor

Who are the marginal investors in Disney, Aracruz, Tata Chemicals, and Deutsche Bank? We begin to answer this question by examining whether insiders own a significant portion of the equity in the firm and are involved in the top management of the firm. Although no such investors exist at Deutsche Bank, there are significant insider holdings at the other three companies:

- While the shares held by the Disney family have dwindled to less than 1%, Disney's acquisition of Pixar has resulted in Steve Jobs becoming the largest single stockholder in the company, owning about 7% of the stock in the company.
- At Aracruz, the voting shares are held by the Votorantim Group (84%) and the Brazilian National Development Bank (BNDES), while the nonvoting shares are held by a mix of institutional and individual investors.
- At Tata Chemicals, the Tata family control (even if they might not hold) a significant portion of the stock through other Tata companies in the group.

However, we do not believe that insiders represent the marginal investors at any of these companies, because their holdings are static for two reasons. One is that their capacity to trade is restricted as insiders, especially in the case of Disney.[10] The other is that trading may result in loss of the control they exercise over the firm, at least for Tata Chemicals and Aracruz. Consequently, we examine the proportion of stock held in each of the firms by individuals, insiders, and institutions in Table 3.1.

All four companies are widely held by institutional investors, and foreign institutional investors hold significant portions of Aracruz and Tata Chemicals. In Table 3.2, we examine the ten largest investors in each firm at the end of 2008 in Table 8.5, with the percent of the firm's stock held by each (in brackets).

Table 3.1   INVESTORS IN DISNEY, ARACRUZ, DEUTSCHE BANK, AND TATA CHEMICALS

	Disney	**Deutsche Bank**	**Aracruz (nonvoting)**	**Tata Chemicals**
Institutions	72%	76%	32%	47%
Individuals	21%	23%	60%	24%
Insiders	7%	1%	8%	29%

Source: Value Line, Morningstar, Bloomberg.

---

[10]Insider trading laws in the United States restrict insiders from trading on material information and also require filings of any trades that are made.

Table 3.2   LARGEST STOCKHOLDERS IN DISNEY, DEUTSCHE BANK, AND TATA CHEMICALS

Disney	Deutsche Bank	Aracruz Preferred	Tata Chemicals
Steven Jobs (7.43%)	Deutsche Post (8.05%)	BB DTVM (0.89%)	Tata Sons (14.26%)
Fidelity (4.86%)	Allianz (6.81%)	Barclays (0.34%)	Life Insurance Co. (11.71%)
State Street (3.97%)	AXA (4.64%)	Banco Itau (0.32%)	Tata Investment (6.8%)
Barclays (3.79%)	Credit Suisse (3.55%)	Banco Barclays (0.19%)	Tata Tea (6.54%)
Vanguard Group (3.07%)	Deutsche Bank (3.52%)	Vanguard Group (0.18%)	New India Assur. (2.58%)
Southeastern Asset (2.40%)	Barclays (3.02%)	UBS Strategy (0.17%)	Hindustan Lever (2.14%)
State Farm Mutual (2.27%)	Blackrock (2.35%)	Banco Itau (0.17%)	General Insurance (2.12%)
AXA (2.13%)	UBS (1.65%)	Dimensional Fund (0.10%)	United India Insur. (1.13%)
Wellington Mgmt. (1.87%)	Deka (1.52%)	Banco Bradesco (0.09%)	National Insurance (1.01%)
Massachusetts Finl. (1.57%)	Dekabank (1.44%)	Landesbank (0.08%)	Templeton Funds (1.01%)

Source: Bloomberg.

Nine of the ten largest investors in Disney are institutional investors, suggesting that we are on safe grounds assuming that the marginal investor in Disney is likely to be both institutional and diversified. The two largest investors in Deutsche Bank are Allianz, the German insurance giant, and Deutsche Post, the privatized German postal company, reflecting again the cross-holding corporate governance structure favored by German corporations. However, the investors below Allianz are all institutional investors, and about half of them are non-German. Here again, we can safely assume that the marginal investor is likely to be institutional and broadly diversified across at least European equities rather than just German stocks. The common shares in Aracruz, where the voting rights reside, is held by a handful of controlling stockholders, but trading in this stock is light. The preferred shares are widely dispersed among a mix of domestic and international institutional investors. While there is a clear danger here that the company will be run for the benefit of the voting shareholders, the price of the voting stock is closely linked to the price of the preferred shares. Self-interest alone should induce the voting shareholders to consider the investors in the preferred shares as the marginal investors in the company. Finally, with Tata Chemicals, four of the ten largest investors are other Tata companies, and those holdings are seldom traded. All of the remaining large investors are institutional investors, with about 12% of the stock held by foreign institutional investors.

In summary, then, we are on very safe ground with Disney and Deutsche Bank when we assume that only the risk that cannot be diversified away should be considered when the company makes investments. We are on less secure ground with Aracruz and Tata Chemicals because of the heavy influence of insiders, but we feel that institutional investors exercise enough influence on how equity is priced at both firms for us to make the same assumption.

Why Is the Marginal Investor Assumed to Be Diversified?

The argument that investors can reduce their exposure to risk by diversifying can be easily made, but risk and return models in finance go further. They argue that the marginal investor, who sets prices for investments, is well diversified; thus, the only risk that will be priced is the risk as perceived by that investor. The justification that can be offered is a simple one. The risk in an investment will always be perceived to be higher for an undiversified investor than to a diversified one, since the latter does not consider any firm-specific risk, whereas the former does. If both investors have the same perceptions about future earnings and cash flows on an asset, the diversified investor will be willing to pay a higher price for that asset because of his or her risk perceptions. Consequently, the asset, over time, will end up being held by diversified investors.

While this argument is a powerful one for stocks and other assets, which are traded in small units and are liquid, it is less so for investments that are large and/or illiquid. Real estate in most countries is still held by investors who are undiversified and have the bulk of their wealth tied up in these investments. The benefits of diversification are strong enough, however, that securities such as real estate investment trusts and mortgage-backed bonds were created to allow investors to invest in real estate and stay diversified at the same time.

Note that diversification does not require investors to give up their pursuit of higher returns. Investors can be diversified and try to beat the market at the same time, For instance, investors who believe that they can do better than the market by buying stocks trading at low PE ratios can still diversify by holding low PE stocks in a number of different sectors at the same time.

3.4 MANAGEMENT QUALITY AND RISK

A well-managed firm is less risky than a firm that is badly managed.

a. True
b. False

IN PRACTICE: WHO SHOULD DIVERSIFY? THE FIRM OR INVESTORS?

As we noted in the last section, the exposure to each type of risk can be mitigated by either the firm or by investors in the firm. The question of who should do it can be answered fairly easily by comparing the costs faced by each. As a general rule, a firm should embark on actions that reduce risk only if it is cheaper for it to do so than it is for its investors to do it. With a publicly traded firm, it will usually be much cheaper for investors to diversify away risk than it is for the firm. Consider, for instance, risk that affects an entire sector. A firm can reduce its exposure to this risk by either acquiring other firms, paying large premiums over the market price, or investing large amounts in businesses where it does not have any expertise. Investors in the firm, on the other hand, can accomplish the same by expanding their portfolios to include stocks in other sectors or, even more simply, by holding diversified mutual funds. Since the cost of diversifying for investors is very low, firms should try to diversify away risk only if the cost is minimal or if the risk reduction is a side benefit from an action with a different objective. One example would be project risk. Since Disney is in the business of making movies, the risk reduction that comes from making lots of movies is essentially costless.

The choice is more complicated for privately owned (non-public) businesses. The owners of these businesses often have the bulk of their wealth invested in these businesses, and they can either try to take money out of the businesses and invest it elsewhere, or they can diversify their businesses. In fact, many family businesses in Latin America and Asia became conglomerates as they expanded, partly because they wanted to spread their risks. ■

III. Measuring Market Risk

While most risk and return models in use in corporate finance agree on the first two steps of this process—i.e., that risk comes from the distribution of actual returns around the expected return, and that risk should be measured from the perspective of a marginal investor who is well diversified—they part ways on how to measure the nondiversifiable or market risk. In this section, we will provide a sense of how each of the three basic models—the capital asset pricing model (CAPM), the arbitrage pricing model (APM), and the multifactor model—approaches the issue of measuring market risk. We will also consider a fourth model, where rather than measure risk directly, we use proxies for risk such as the market capitalization for the firm.

A. The Capital Asset Pricing Model

The risk and return model that has been in use the longest and that is still the standard in most real-world analyses is the capital asset pricing model (CAPM). While it has come in for its fair share of criticism over the years, it provides a useful starting point for our discussion of risk and return models.

1. Assumptions

While diversification has its attractions in terms of reducing the exposure of investors to firm specific risk, most investors limit their diversification to holding relatively few assets. Even large mutual funds are reluctant to hold more than a few hundred stocks, and many of them hold as few as ten to twenty stocks. There are two reasons for this reluctance. The first is that the marginal benefits of diversification become smaller as the portfolio gets more diversified—the twenty-first asset added will generally provide a much smaller reduction in firm specific risk than the fifth asset added, and may not cover the marginal costs of diversification, which include transactions and monitoring costs. The second is that many investors (and funds) believe that they can find undervalued assets and thus choose not to hold those assets that they believe to be correctly (or over-) valued.

The capital asset pricing model assumes that there are no transactions costs, that all assets are traded, and that investments are infinitely divisible (i.e., you can buy any fraction of a unit of the asset). It also assumes that there is no private information and that investors therefore cannot find under- or overvalued assets in the marketplace. By making these assumptions, it eliminates the factors that cause investors to stop diversifying. With these assumptions in place, the logical end of diversification is to hold every traded risky asset (stocks, bonds, and real assets included) in your portfolio in proportion to their market value.[11] This portfolio of every traded risky asset in the marketplace is called the *market portfolio*.

2. Implications for Investors

If every investor in the market holds the same market portfolio, how exactly do investors reflect their risk aversion in their investments? In the capital asset pricing

---

[11] If investments are not held in proportion to their market value, investors are still losing some diversification benefits. Since there is no gain from overweighting some sectors and underweighting others in a market place where the odds are random of finding undervalued and overvalued assets, investors will not do so.

model, investors adjust for their risk preferences in their allocation decisions, where they decide how much to invest in an asset with guaranteed returns—a riskless asset—and how much in risky assets (market portfolio). Investors who are risk-averse might choose to put much or even all of their wealth in the riskless asset. Investors who want to take more risk will invest the bulk, or even all, of their wealth in the market portfolio. Those investors who invest all their wealth in the market portfolio and are still desirous of taking on more risk would do so by borrowing at the riskless rate and investing in the same market portfolio as everyone else.

These results are predicated on two additional assumptions. First, there exists a riskless asset. Second, investors can lend and borrow at this riskless rate to arrive at their optimal allocations. There are variations of the CAPM that allow these assumptions to be relaxed and still arrive at conclusions that are consistent with the general model.

3.5 EFFICIENT RISK-TAKING

In the capital asset pricing model, the most efficient way to take a lot of risk is to

a. Buy a well-balanced portfolio of the riskiest stocks in the market

b. Buy risky stocks that are also undervalued

c. Borrow money and buy a well diversified portfolio

3. Measuring the Market Risk of an Individual Asset

The risk of any asset to an investor is the risk added by that asset to the investor's overall portfolio. In the CAPM world, where all investors hold the market portfolio, the risk of an individual asset to an investor will be the risk that this asset adds on to the market portfolio. Intuitively, assets that move more with the market portfolio will tend to be riskier than assets that move less, since the movements that are unrelated to the market portfolio will not affect the overall value of the portfolio when an asset is added on to the portfolio. Statistically, this added risk is measured by the *covariance* of the asset with the market portfolio.

The covariance is a nonstandardized measure of market risk; knowing that the covariance of Disney with the market portfolio is 55% does not provide a clue as to whether Disney is riskier or safer than the average asset. We therefore standardize the risk measure by dividing the covariance of each asset with the market portfolio by the variance of the market portfolio. This yields the beta of the asset:

$$\text{Beta of an asset } i = \frac{\text{Covariance of asset } i \text{ with market portfolio}}{\text{Variance of the market portfolio}}$$

Since the covariance of the market portfolio with itself is its variance, the beta of the market portfolio—and by extension, the average asset in it—is 1. Assets that are riskier than average (using this measure of risk) will have betas that exceed 1, and assets that are safer than average will have betas that are lower than 1. The riskless asset will have a beta of 0.

4. Getting Expected Returns

The fact that every investor holds some combination of the riskless asset and the market portfolio leads to the next conclusion: the expected return on an asset is linearly related to the beta of the asset. In particular, the expected return on an asset can be written as a function of the risk-free rate and the beta of that asset,

$$\text{Expected return on asset } i = R_f + \beta_i[E(R_m) - R_f]$$
$$= \text{Risk-free rate} + \text{Beta of asset } i * (\text{Risk premium on market portfolio})$$

where

$$E(R_i) = \text{Expected return on asset } i$$
$$R_f = \text{Risk-free rate}$$
$$E(R_m) = \text{Expected return on market portfolio}$$
$$\beta_i = \text{Beta of asset } i$$

To use the capital asset pricing model, we need three inputs. While we will look at the estimation process in far more detail in the next chapter, each of these inputs is estimated as follows:

- The riskless asset is defined to be an asset whose expected return the investor knows with certainty for the time horizon of the analysis. Consequently, the riskless rate used will vary depending upon whether the time period for the expected return is one, five, or ten years.

- The risk premium is the premium demanded by investors for investing in the market portfolio, which includes all risky assets in the market, instead of investing in a riskless asset. Thus, it does not relate to any individual risky asset but to risky assets as a class.

- The beta, which we defined to be the covariance of the asset divided by the market portfolio, is the only firm-specific input in this equation. In other words, the only reason two investments have different expected returns in the capital asset pricing model is because they have different betas.

In summary, in the capital asset pricing model all of the market risk is captured in one beta, measured relative to a market portfolio, which—at least, in theory—should include all traded assets in the market place held in proportion to their market value.

3.6 WHAT DO NEGATIVE BETAS MEAN?

In the capital asset pricing model, there are assets that can have betas that are less than 0. When this occurs, which of the following statements describes your investment?

a. This investment will have an expected return less than the riskless rate.
b. This investment insures your "diversified portfolio" against some type of market risk.
c. Holding this asset makes sense only if you are well diversified.
d. All of the above.

IN PRACTICE: INDEX FUNDS AND MARKET PORTFOLIOS

Many critics of the capital asset pricing model seize on its conclusion that all investors in the market will hold the market portfolio (which includes all assets in proportion to their market value) as evidence that it is an unrealistic model. But is it? It is true that not all assets in the world are traded, and that there are transactions costs.

It is also true that investors sometimes trade on inside information and often hold undiversified portfolios. However, we can create portfolios that closely resemble the market portfolio using index funds. An index fund replicates an index by buying all of the stocks in the index in the same proportions that they form of the index. The earliest and still the largest one is the Vanguard 500 Index fund, which replicates the S&P 500 index. Today, we have access to index funds that replicate smaller companies in the United States, European stocks, Latin American markets and Asian equities as well as bond and commodity markets An investor can create a portfolio composed of a mix of index funds—the weights on each fund should be based upon market values of the underlying markct—that resembles the market portfolio; the only asset class that is usually difficult to replicate is real estate. ■

B. The Arbitrage Pricing Model

The restrictive assumptions in the capital asset pricing model and its dependence upon the market portfolio have for long been viewed with skepticism by both academics and practitioners. In the late seventies, an alternative and more general model for measuring risk called the arbitrage pricing model was developed.[12]

1. Assumptions

The arbitrage pricing model is built on the simple premise that two investments with the same exposure to risk should be priced to earn the same expected returns. An alternate way of saying this is that if two portfolios have the same exposure to risk but offer different expected returns, investors can buy the portfolio that has the higher expected returns and sell the one with lower expected returns until the expected returns converge.

Like the capital asset pricing model, the arbitrage pricing model begins by breaking risk down into two components. The first is firm-specific and covers information that affects primarily the firm. The second is the market risk that affects all investment; this would include unanticipated changes in a number of economic variables, including gross national product, inflation, and interest rates. Incorporating this into the return model above,

$$R = E(R) + m + \varepsilon$$

where m is the marketwide component of unanticipated risk and ε is the firm-specific component.

2. The Sources of Marketwide Risk

While both the capital asset pricing model and the arbitrage pricing model make a distinction between firm-specific and marketwide risk, they part ways when it comes to measuring the market risk. The CAPM assumes that all of the market risk is captured in the market portfolio, whereas the arbitrage pricing model allows for multiple sources of marketwide risk and measures the sensitivity of investments to each source with

---

[12]Stephen A. Ross, "The Arbitrage Theory of Capital Asset Pricing," *Journal of Economic Theory* 13, no. 3:341–360.

a factor beta. In general, the market component of unanticipated returns can be decomposed into economic factors:

$$R = R + m + \varepsilon = R + (\beta_1 F_1 + \beta_2 F_2 + \ldots + \beta_n F_n) + \varepsilon$$

where

β_j = Sensitivity of investment to unanticipated changes in factor j

F_j = Unanticipated changes in factor j

3. The Effects of Diversification

The benefits of diversification have been discussed extensively in our treatment of the capital asset pricing model. The primary point of that discussion was that diversification of investments into portfolios eliminate firm-specific risk. The arbitrage pricing model makes the same point and concludes that the return on a portfolio will not have a firm-specific component of unanticipated returns. The return on a portfolio can then be written as the sum of two weighted averages: that of the anticipated returns in the portfolio, and that of the factor betas:

$$R_p = (w_1 R_1 + w_2 R_2 + \ldots + w_n R_n) + (w_1 \beta_{1,1} + w_2 \beta_{1,2} + \ldots + w_n \beta_{1,n}) F_1$$
$$+ (w_1 \beta_{2,1} + w_2 \beta_{2,2} + \ldots + w_n \beta_{2,n}) F_2 \ldots$$

where

w_j = Portfolio weight on asset j

R_j = Expected return on asset j

$\beta_{i,j}$ = Beta on factor i for asset j

Note that the firm-specific component of returns (ε) in the individual firm equation disappears in the portfolio as a result of diversification.

4. Expected Returns and Betas

The fact that the beta of a portfolio is the weighted average of the betas of the assets in the portfolio, in conjunction with the absence of arbitrage, leads to the conclusion that expected returns should be linearly related to betas. To see why, assume that there is only one factor and that there are three portfolios. Portfolio A has a beta of 2.0 and an expected return on 20%; Portfolio B has a beta of 1.0 and an expected return of 12%, and Portfolio C has a beta of 1.5 and an expected return on 14%. Note that the investor can put half of his wealth in Portfolio A and half in Portfolio B and end up with a portfolio with a beta of 1.5 and an expected return of 16%. Consequently, no investor will choose to hold Portfolio C until the prices of assets in that portfolio drop and the expected return increases to 16%. Alternatively, an investor can buy the combination of Portfolio A and B with an expected return of 16% and sell Portfolio C with an expected return of 15% and pure profit of 1% without taking any risk and investing any money. To prevent this "arbitrage" from occurring, the expected returns on every portfolio should be a linear function of the beta. This argument can be extended to multiple factors with the same results. Therefore, the expected return on an asset can be written as

$$E(R) = R_f + \beta_1 [E(R_1) - R_f] + \beta_2 [E(R_2) - R_f] \ldots + \beta_n [E(R_n) - R_f]$$

where

R_f = Expected return on a zero-beta portfolio

$E(R_j)$ = Expected return on a portfolio with a factor beta of 1 for factor j, and 0 for all other factors

The terms in the brackets can be considered to be risk premiums for each of the factors in the model.

Note that the capital asset pricing model can be considered to be a special case of the arbitrage pricing model, where there is only one economic factor driving marketwide returns, and the market portfolio is the factor.

$$E(R) = R_f + \beta_m(E(R_m) - R_f)$$

5. The APM in Practice

The arbitrage pricing model requires estimates of each of the factor betas and factor risk premiums in addition to the riskless rate. In practice, these are usually estimated using historical data on stocks and a statistical technique called factor analysis. Intuitively, a factor analysis examines the historical data looking for common patterns that affect broad groups of stocks (rather than just one sector or a few stocks). It provides two output measures:

1. It specifies the *number of common factors* that affected the historical data that it worked on.

2. It measures the *beta of each investment* relative to each of the common factors and provides an estimate of the actual risk premium earned by each factor.

The factor analysis does not, however, identify the factors in economic terms.

In summary, in the arbitrage-pricing model the market or nondiversifiable risk in an investment is measured relative to multiple unspecified macro economic factors, with the sensitivity of the investment relative to each factor being measured by a factor beta. The number of factors, the factor betas, and factor risk premiums can all be estimated using a factor analysis.

C. Multifactor Models for Risk and Return

The arbitrage pricing model's failure to specifically identify the factors in the model may be a strength from a statistical standpoint, but it is a clear weakness from an intuitive standpoint. The solution seems simple: replace the unidentified statistical factors with specified economic factors, and the resultant model should be intuitive while still retaining much of the strength of the arbitrage pricing model. That is precisely what multifactor models do.

Deriving a Multifactor Model

Multifactor models generally are not based on extensive economic rationale but are instead determined by the data. Once the number of factors has been identified in the arbitrage pricing model, the behavior of the factors over time can be extracted from the data. These factor time series can then be compared to the time series of macroeconomic variables to see if any of the variables are correlated over time with the identified factors.

For instance, a study from the 1980s suggested that the following macroeconomic variables were highly correlated with the factors that come out of factor analysis: industrial production, changes in the premium paid on corporate bonds over the riskless rate, shifts in the term structure, unanticipated inflation, and changes in the real rate of return.[13] These variables can then be correlated with returns to come up with a model of expected returns, with firm-specific betas calculated relative to each variable. The equation for expected returns will take the following form:

$$E(R) = R_f + \beta_{GNP}(E(R_{GNP}) - R_f) + \beta_i(E(R_i) - R_f) \ldots + \beta_\delta(E(R_\delta) - R_f)$$

where

$$\beta_{GNP} = \text{Beta relative to changes in industrial production}$$
$$E(R_{GNP}) = \text{Expected return on a portfolio with a beta of 1 on the industrial}$$
$$\text{production factor and 0 on all other factors}$$
$$\beta_i = \text{Beta relative to changes in inflation}$$
$$E(R_i) = \text{Expected return on a portfolio with a beta of 1 on the inflation}$$
$$\text{factor and 0 on all other factors}$$

The costs of going from the arbitrage pricing model to a macroeconomic multifactor model can be traced directly to the errors that can be made in identifying the factors. The economic factors in the model can change over time, as will the risk premium associated with each one. For instance, oil price changes were a significant economic factor driving expected returns in the 1970s but are not as significant in other time periods. Using the wrong factors or missing a significant factor in a multifactor model can lead to inferior estimates of cost of equity.

In summary, multifactor models, like the arbitrage pricing model, assume that market risk can be captured best using multiple macroeconomic factors and estimating betas relative to each. Unlike the arbitrage pricing model, multifactor models do attempt to identify the macroeconomic factors that drive market risk.

D. Proxy Models

All of the models described so far begin by thinking about market risk in economic terms and then developing models that might best explain this market risk. All of them, however, extract their risk parameters by looking at historical data. There is a final class of risk and return models that start with past returns on individual stocks, and then work backwards by trying to explain differences in returns across long time periods using firm characteristics. In other words, these models try to find common characteristics shared by firms that have historically earned higher returns and identify these characteristics as proxies for market risk.

Fama and French, in a highly influential study of the capital asset pricing model in the early 1990s, note that actual returns over long time periods have been highly correlated with price–book value ratios and market capitalization.[14] In particular, they note that firms with small market capitalization and low price–book ratios earned higher returns

---

[13]N. Chen, R. Roll, and S. A. Ross, "Economic Forces and the Stock Market," *Journal of Business* 59:383–404.
[14]E. F. Fama and K. R. French, "The Cross-Section of Expected Returns," *Journal of Finance* 47:427–466.

between 1963 and 1990. They suggest that these measures and similar ones developed from the data be used as proxies for risk and that the regression coefficients be used to estimate expected returns for investments. They report the following regression for monthly returns on stocks on the NYSE, using data from 1963 to 1990:

$$R_t = 1.77\% - 0.11 \ln(MV) + 0.35 \ln(BV/MV)$$

where

$$MV = \text{Market value of equity}$$
$$BV/MV = \text{Book value of equity/Market value of equity}$$

The values for market value of equity and book–price ratios for individual firms, when plugged into this regression, should yield expected monthly returns. For instance, a firm with a market value of $100 million and a book–market price ratio of 0.5 would have an expected monthly return of 1.02%.

$$R_t = 1.77\% - 0.11 \ln(100) + 0.35 \ln(0.5) = 1.02\%$$

As data on individual firms has become richer and more easily accessible in recent years, these proxy models have expanded to include additional variables. In particular, researchers have found that price momentum (the rate of increase in the stock price over recent months) also seems to help explain returns; stocks with high price momentum tend to have higher returns in following periods.

In summary, proxy models measure market risk using firm characteristics as proxies for market risk, rather than the macroeconomic variables used by conventional multifactor models.[15] The firm characteristics are identified by looking at differences in returns across investments over very long time periods and correlating with identifiable characteristics of these investments.

A Comparative Analysis of Risk and Return Models

All the risk and return models developed in this chapter have common ingredients. They all assume that only marketwide risk is rewarded, and they derive the expected return as a function of measures of this risk. Figure 3.7 presents a comparison of the different models.

The capital asset pricing model makes the most assumptions but arrives at the simplest model, with only one risk factor requiring estimation. The arbitrage pricing model makes fewer assumptions but arrives at a more complicated model, at least in terms of the parameters that require estimation. In general, the CAPM has the advantage of being a simpler model to estimate and to use, but it will underperform the richer multifactor models when the company is sensitive to economic factors not well represented in the market index. For instance, oil companies, which derive most of their risk from oil price movements, tend to have low CAPM betas. Using a multifactor model where one of the factors may be capturing oil and other commodity price movements will yield a better estimate of risk and higher cost of equity for these firms.[16]

---

[15]Adding to the confusion, researchers in recent years have taken to describing proxy models also as multifactor models.

[16]J. F. Weston and T. E. Copeland, Managerial Finance, Dryden Press, Chicago, 1992. They used both approaches to estimate the cost of equity for oil companies in 1989 and came up with 14.4% with the CAPM and 19.1% using the arbitrage pricing model.

Figure 3.7   Competing Models for Risk and Return in Finance

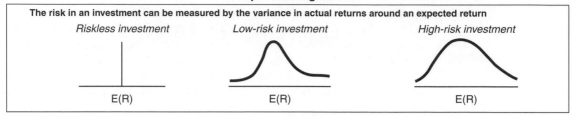

Step 1: Defining Risk

The risk in an investment can be measured by the variance in actual returns around an expected return

Riskless investment   Low-risk investment   High-risk investment

E(R)   E(R)   E(R)

Step 2: Differentiating between Rewarded and Unrewarded Risk

Risk that is specific to investment (firm-specific) Can be eliminated in a diversified portfolio 1. Each investment is a small proportion of portfolio 2. Risk averages out across investments in portfolio	*Risk that affects all investments (market risk)* Cannot be diversified away since most assets are affected by it

The marginal investor is assumed to hold a "diversified" portfolio. Thus, only market risk will be rewarded and priced.

Step 3: Measuring Market Risk

The CAPM	The APM	Multifactor Models	Proxy Models
If investors 1. have no private information 2. face no transaction cost the optimal diversified portfolio includes every traded asset in the market. Everyone will hold this market portfolio. **Market risk = Risk added by any investment to the market portfolio**	If there are no arbitrage opportunities, then the market risk of any asset must be captured by betas relative to factors that affect all investments. **Market risk = Risk exposures of any asset to market factors**	Since market risk affects most or all investments, it must come from macro-economic factors. **Market risk = Risk exposures of any asset to macro economic factors**	In an efficient market, differences in returns across long periods must be due to market risk differences. Looking for variables correlated with returns should then give us proxies for this risk. **Market risk = Captured by the proxy variable(s)**
Beta of asset relative to market portfolio (from a regression)	Betas of asset relative to unspecified market factors (from a factor analysis)	Betas of assets relative to specified macroeconomic factors (from a regression)	Equation relating returns to proxy variables (from a regression)

The biggest intuitive block in using the arbitrage pricing model is its failure to specifically identify the factors driving expected returns. While this may preserve the flexibility of the model and reduce statistical problems in testing, it does make it difficult to understand what the beta coefficients for a firm mean and how they will change as the firm changes (or restructures).

Does the CAPM work? Is beta a good proxy for risk, and is it correlated with expected returns? The answers to these questions have been debated widely in the last two decades. The first tests of the model suggested that betas and returns were positively related, though other measures of risk (such as variance) continued to explain differences in actual returns. This discrepancy was attributed to limitations in the testing techniques. In 1977, Roll, in a seminal critique of the model's tests, suggested that since the market portfolio (which should include every traded asset of the market) could never be observed, the CAPM could never be tested, and that all tests of the CAPM were therefore joint tests of both the model and the market portfolio used in the tests—i.e., all any test of the CAPM could show was that the model worked (or did not) given the proxy used for the market portfolio.[17] He argued that in any empirical test that claimed to reject the CAPM, the rejection could be of the proxy used for the market portfolio rather than of the model itself. Roll noted that there was no way to ever prove that the CAPM worked, and thus no empirical basis for using the model.

The study by Fama and French quoted in the last section examined the relationship between the betas of stocks and annual returns between 1963 and 1990 and concluded that there was little relationship between the two. They noted that market capitalization and book-to-market value explained differences in returns across firms much better than did beta and were better proxies for risk. These results have been contested on two fronts. First, Amihud, Christensen, and Mendelson used the same data, performed different statistical tests, and showed that betas did, in fact, explain returns during the time period.[18] Second, Chan and Lakonishok look at a much longer time series of returns from 1926 to 1991 and found that the positive relationship between betas and returns broke down only in the period after 1982.[19] They attribute this breakdown to indexing, which they argue has led the larger, lower-beta stocks in the S&P 500 to outperform smaller, higher-beta stocks. They also find that betas are a useful guide to risk in extreme market conditions, with the riskiest firms (the 10% with highest betas) performing far worse than the market as a whole. We illustrate this in Figure 3.8 by looking at the eleven worst months for the U.S. stock market in the last eighty years and contrasting the returns on high beta and low beta stocks.

Figure 3.8   Returns and Betas: Ten Worst Months between 1926 and 1991

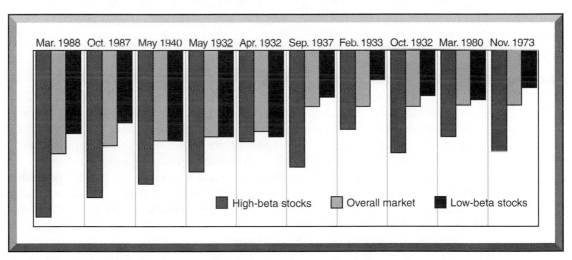

Source: Chan and Lakonsihok

[17]R. Roll, "A Critique of the Asset Pricing Theory's Tests: Part I: On Past and Potential Testability of Theory," *Journal of Financial Economics* 4:129–176.

[18]Y. Amihud, B. Christensen, and H. Mendelson, "Further Evidence on the Risk-Return Relationship," working paper, New York University, 1992.

[19]L. K. Chan and J. Lakonsihok, "Are the Reports of Beta's Death Premature?" *Journal of Portfolio Management* 19:51–62.

These results would suggest that while betas might not provide much explanatory power when markets are stable, they work much better during market crisis, which is when investors are most concerned about risk.

While the initial tests of the APM and the multifactor models suggested that they might provide more promise in terms of explaining differences in returns, a distinction has to be drawn between the use of these models to explain differences in past returns and their use to get expected returns for the future. The competitors to the CAPM clearly do a much better job at explaining past returns, since they do not constrain themselves to one factor as the CAPM does. This extension to multiple factors does become more of a problem when we try to project expected returns into the future, since the betas and premiums of each of these factors now have to be estimated. As the factor premiums and betas are themselves volatile, the estimation error may wipe out the benefits that could be gained by moving from the CAPM to more complex models. The regression models that were offered as an alternative are even more exposed to this problem, since the variables that work best as proxies for market risk in one period (such as size) may not be the ones that work in the next period. This may explain why multifactor models have been accepted more widely in evaluating portfolio performance evaluation than in corporate finance; the former is focused on past returns, whereas the latter is concerned with expected future returns.

Ultimately, the survival of the capital asset pricing model as the default model for risk in real-world application is a testament both to its intuitive appeal and the failure of more complex models to deliver significant improvement in terms of expected returns. We would argue that a judicious use of the capital asset pricing model without overreliance on historical data and in conjunction with the accumulated evidence[20] presented by those who have developed the alternatives to the CAPM is still the most effective way of dealing with risk in modern corporate finance.

 IN PRACTICE: Implied Costs of Equity and Capital

The controversy surrounding the assumptions made by each of the risk and return models outlined above and the errors that are associated with the estimates from each has led some analysts to use an alternate approach for companies that are publicly traded. With these companies, the market price represents the market's best estimate of the value of the company today. If you assume that the market is right, and you are willing to make assumptions about expected growth in the future, you can back out a cost of equity from the current market price. For example, assume that a stock is trading at $50 and that dividends next year are expected to be $2.50. Furthermore, assume that dividends will grow 4% a year in perpetuity. The cost of equity implied in the stock price can be estimated as follows:

Stock price = $50 = Expected dividends next year/(Cost of equity–Expected growth rate)

$$\$50 = 2.50/(r - 0.04)$$

---

[20]Barra, a leading beta estimation service, adjusts betas to reflect differences in fundamentals across firms (such as size and dividend yields). It is drawing on the regression studies that have found these to be good proxies for market risk.

Solving for r, $r = 9\%$. This approach can be extended to the entire firm, and to compute the cost of capital.

While this approach has the obvious benefit of being model-free, it has its limitations. In particular, our cost of equity will be a function of our estimates of growth and cash flows. If we use overly optimistic estimates of expected growth and cash flows, we will underestimate the cost of equity. It is also built on the presumption that the market price is right. ■

THE RISK IN BORROWING: DEFAULT RISK AND THE COST OF DEBT

When an investor lends to an individual or a firm, there is the possibility that the borrower may default on interest and principal payments on the borrowing. This possibility of default is called the default risk. Generally speaking, borrowers with higher default risk should pay higher interest rates on their borrowing than those with lower default risk. This section examines the measurement of default risk, and the relationship of default risk to interest rates on borrowing.

In contrast to the general risk and return models for equity, which evaluate the effects of market risk on expected returns, models of default risk measure the consequences of firm-specific default risk on promised returns. While diversification can be used to explain why firm-specific risk will not be priced into expected returns for equities, the same rationale cannot be applied to securities that have limited upside potential and much greater downside potential from firm-specific events. To see what we mean by limited upside potential, consider investing in a bond issued by a company. The coupons are fixed at the time of the issue, and these coupons represent the promised cash flow on the bond. The best-case scenario for you as an investor is that you receive the promised cash flows; you are not entitled to more than these cash flows even if the company is wildly successful. All other scenarios contain only bad news, though in varying degrees, with the delivered cash flows being less than the promised cash flows. Consequently, the expected return on a corporate bond is likely to reflect the firm-specific default risk of the firm issuing the bond.

The Determinants of Default Risk

The default risk of a firm is a function of its capacity to generate cash flows from operations and its financial obligations—including interest and principal payments.[21] It is also a function of the how liquid a firm's assets are, since firms with more liquid assets should have an easier time liquidating them in a crisis to meet debt obligations. Consequently, the following propositions relate to default risk:

- Firms that *generate high cash flows* relative to their financial obligations have lower default risk than do firms that generate low cash flows relative to obligations. Thus, firms with significant current investments that generate high cash flows will have lower default risk than will firms that do not.

---

[21] Financial obligation refers to any payment that the firm has legally obligated itself to make, such as interest and principal payments. It does not include discretionary cash flows, such as dividend payments or new capital expenditures, which can be deferred or delayed without legal consequences (though there may be economic consequences).

- The *more stable the cash flows*, the lower the default risk in the firm. Firms that operate in predictable and stable businesses will have lower default risk than will otherwise similar firms that operate in cyclical or volatile businesses, for the same level of indebtedness.

- The *more liquid a firm's assets* for any given level of operating cash flows and financial obligations, the less default risk in the firm.

For as long as there have been borrowers, lenders have had to assess default risk. Historically, assessments of default risk have been based on financial ratios to measure the cash flow coverage (i.e., the magnitude of cash flows relative to obligations) and control for industry effects to capture the variability in cash flows and the liquidity of assets.

Default Risk and Interest Rates

When banks did much of the lending to firms, it made sense for banks to expend the resources to make their own assessments of default risk, and they still do for most lenders. The advent of the corporate bond market created a demand for third-party assessments of default risk on the part of bondholders. This demand came from the need for economies of scale, since few individual bondholders had the resources to make the assessment themselves. In the United States, this led to the growth of ratings agencies like Standard and Poor's and Moody's, which made judgments of the default risk of corporations using a mix of private and public information, converted these judgments into measures of default risk (bond rating), and made these ratings public. Investors buying corporate bonds could therefore use the bond ratings as a shorthand measure of default risk.

The Ratings Process

The process of rating a bond starts when a company requests a rating from the ratings agency. This request is usually precipitated by a desire on the part of the company to issue bonds. While ratings are not a legal prerequisite for bond issues, it is unlikely that investors in the bond market will be willing to buy bonds issued by a company that is not well known and that has shown itself to be unwilling to put itself through the rigor of a bond rating process. It is not surprising, therefore, that the largest number of rated companies are in the United States, which has the most active corporate bond markets, and that there are relatively few rated companies in Europe, where bank lending remains the norm for all but the largest companies.

The ratings agency then collects information from both publicly available data, such as financial statements, and the company itself, and makes a decision on the rating. If the company disagrees with the rating, it is given the opportunity to present additional information. This process is presented schematically for one ratings agency, Standard and Poor's (S&P), in Figure 3.9.

The ratings assigned by these agencies are letter ratings. A rating of AAA from Standard and Poor's and Aaa from Moody's represents the highest rating granted to firms that are viewed as having the lowest default risk. As the default risk increases, the ratings decrease toward D for firms in default (Standard and Poor's). Table 3.3 provides a description of the bond ratings assigned by the two agencies.

Figure 3.9   The Ratings Process

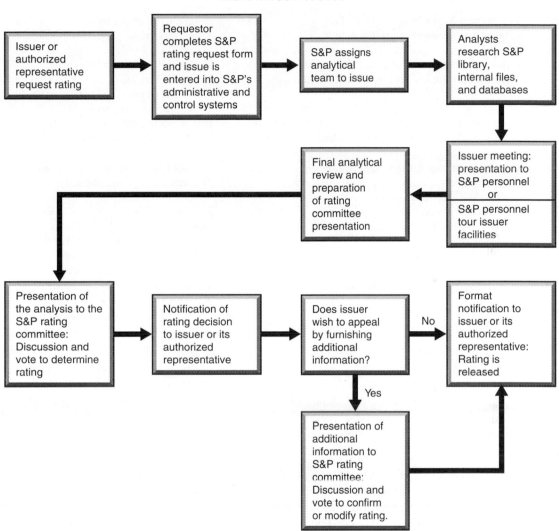

THE RATINGS PROCESS

IN PRACTICE: INVESTMENT GRADE AND JUNK BONDS

While ratings can range from AAA (safest) to D (in default), a rating at or above BBB by Standard and Poor's (Baa for Moody's) is categorized as investment-grade, reflecting the view of the ratings agency that there is relatively little default risk in investing in bonds issued by these firms. Bonds rated below BBB are generally categorized as junk bonds or as high-yield bonds. While it is an arbitrary dividing line, it is an important one for two reasons. First, many investment portfolios are restricted from investing in bonds below investment grade. Thus, the market for investment grade bonds tends to

Table 3.3 INDEX OF BOND RATINGS

Standard and Poor's		Moody's	
AAA	The highest debt rating assigned. The borrower's capacity to repay debt is extremely strong.	Aaa	Judged to be of the best quality with a small degree of risk.
AA	Capacity to repay is strong and differs from the highest quality only by a small amount.	Aa	High quality but rated lower than Aaa because margin of protection may not be as large or because there may be other elements of long-term risk.
A	Has strong capacity to repay; borrower is susceptible to adverse effects of changes in circumstances and economic conditions.	A	Bonds possess favorable investment attributes but may be susceptible to risk in the future.
BBB	Has adequate capacity to repay, but adverse economic conditions or circumstances are more likely to lead to risk.	Baa	Neither highly protected nor poorly secured; adequate payment capacity.
BB,B	Regarded as predominantly speculative,	Ba	Judged to have some speculative risk.
CCC	BB being the least speculative and	B	Generally lacking characteristics of a desirable investment; probability of payment small.
CC	CC the most.		
D	In default or with payments in arrears.	Caa	Poor standing and perhaps in default.
		Ca	Very speculative; often in default.
		C	Highly speculative; in default.

be wider and deeper than that for bonds below that grade. Second, firms that are not rated investment grade have a tougher time when they try to raise new funding and they also pay much higher issuance costs when they do. In fact, until the early 1980s, firms below investment grade often could not issue new bonds.[22] The perception that they are exposed to default risk also creates a host of other costs, including tighter supplier credit and debt covenants. ■

Determinants of Bond Ratings

The bond ratings assigned by ratings agencies are primarily based upon publicly available information, although private information conveyed by the firm to the rating agency does play a role. The rating that is assigned to a company's bonds will depend in large part on financial ratios that measure the capacity of the company to meet debt payments and generate stable and predictable cash flows. While a multitude of financial ratios exist, Table 3.4 summarizes some of the key ratios that are used to measure default risk.

There is a strong relationship between the bond rating a company receives and its performance on these financial ratios. Table 3.5 provides a summary of the median ratios from 2006 to 2008 for different S&P ratings classes for manufacturing firms.

---

[22] In the early 1980s, Michael Milken and Drexel Burnham created the junk bond market, allowing for original issuance of junk bonds. They did this primarily to facilitate hostile takeovers by the raiders of the era.

Table 3.4 FINANCIAL RATIOS USED TO MEASURE DEFAULT RISK

Ratio	Description
Pretax interest coverage	= (Pretax income from continuing operations + Interest expense)/Gross interest expense
EBITDA interest coverage	= EBITDA/Gross interest expense
Funds from operations/total debt	= (Net income from continuing operations + Depreciation)/Total debt
Free operating cash flow/total debt	= (Funds from operations − Capital expenditures − Change in working capital)/Total debt
Pretax return on permanent capital	= (Pretax income from continuing operations + Interest expense)/(Average of beginning of the year and end of the year of long- and short-term debt, minority interest, and shareholders equity)
Operating income/sales (%)	= (Sales − COGS [before depreciation] − Selling expenses − Administrative expenses − R&D Expenses)/Sales
Long-term debt/capital	= Long-term debt/(Long-term debt + Equity)
Total debt/capitalization	= Total debt/(Total debt + Equity)

Note that the pretax interest coverage ratio and the EBITDA interest coverage ratio are stated in terms of times interest earned, whereas the rest of the ratios are stated in percentage terms.

Not surprisingly, firms that generate income and cash flows that are significantly higher than debt payments that are profitable and that have low debt ratios are more likely to be highly rated than are firms that do not have these characteristics. There will be individual firms whose ratings are not consistent with their financial ratios, however, because the ratings agency does bring subjective judgments into the final mix. Thus, a firm that performs poorly on financial ratios but is expected to improve its performance dramatically over the next period may receive a higher rating than is justified by its current financials. For most firms, however, the financial ratios should provide a reasonable basis for guessing at the bond rating.

 There is a dataset on the Web that summarizes key financial ratios by bond rating class for the United States in the most recent period for which the data is available.

Table 3.5 FINANCIAL RATIOS BY BOND RATING: 2006–2008

	AAA	AA	A	BBB	BB	B	CCC
EBIT interest coverage	17.5	10.8	6.8	3.9	2.3	1.0	0.2
EBITDA interest coverage	21.8	14.6	9.6	6.1	3.8	2.0	1.4
Funds flow/total debt	105.8	55.8	46.1	30.5	19.2	9.4	5.8
Free operating cash flow/total debt (%)	55.4	24.6	15.6	6.6	1.9	−4.5	−14.0
Return on capital (%)	28.2	22.9	19.9	14.0	11.7	7.2	0.5
Operating income/sales (%)	29.2	21.3	18.3	15.3	15.4	11.2	13.6
Long-term debt/capital (%)	15.2	26.4	32.5	41.0	55.8	70.7	80.3
Total debt/capital (%)	26.9	35.6	40.1	47.4	61.3	74.6	89.4
Number of firms	10	34	150	234	276	240	23

Bond Ratings and Interest Rates

The interest rate on a corporate bond should be a function of its default risk. If the rating is a good measure of the default risk, higher-rated bonds should be priced to yield lower interest rates than would lower rated bonds. The difference between the interest rate on a bond with default risk and a default-free government bond is called the default spread. This default spread will vary by maturity of the bond and can also change from period to period depending on economic conditions. Table 3.6 summarizes default spreads in early 2009 for ten-year bonds in each ratings class (using S&P ratings) and the market interest rates on these bonds based upon a treasury bond rate of 3.5%.

Table 3.6 provides default spreads at a point in time, but default spreads not only vary across time but can vary for bonds with the same rating but different maturities. For the bonds with higher ratings, the default spread generally widens for the longer maturities. For bonds with lower ratings, the spreads may decrease as we go to longer maturities, reflecting the fact that short-term default risk is greater than long-term default risk. Historically, default spreads for every ratings class have increased during recessions and decreased during economic booms. In Figure 3.10, we take a look at the evolution of default spreads for different bond rating classes through 2008. (We also report the equity risk premium (ERP). We will explain the estimation process in chapter 4).

Note how much default spreads widened through 2008. The practical implication of this phenomenon is that default spreads for bonds have to be reestimated at regular intervals, especially if the economy shifts from low to high growth or vice versa.

A final point worth making here is that everything that has been said about the relationship between interest rates and bond ratings could be said more generally about interest rates and default risk. The existence of ratings is a convenience that makes the assessment of default risk a little easier for us when analyzing companies. In its absence, we would still have to assess default risk on our own and come up with estimates of the default spread we would charge if we were lending to a firm.

Table 3.6   DEFAULT SPREADS FOR RATINGS CLASSES: EARLY 2009

Rating	Default Spread	Interest Rate on Bond
AAA	1.25%	4.75%
AA	1.75%	5.25%
A+	2.25%	5.75%
A	2.50%	6.00%
A–	3.00%	6.50%
BBB	3.50%	7.00%
BB	4.25%	7.75%
B+	5.00%	8.50%
B	6.00%	9.50%
B–	7.25%	10.75%
CCC	8.50%	12.00%
CC	10.00%	13.50%
C	12.00%	15.50%
D	15.00%	18.50%

Source: bondsonline.com.

Figure 3.10   Default Spreads on Ratings Classes

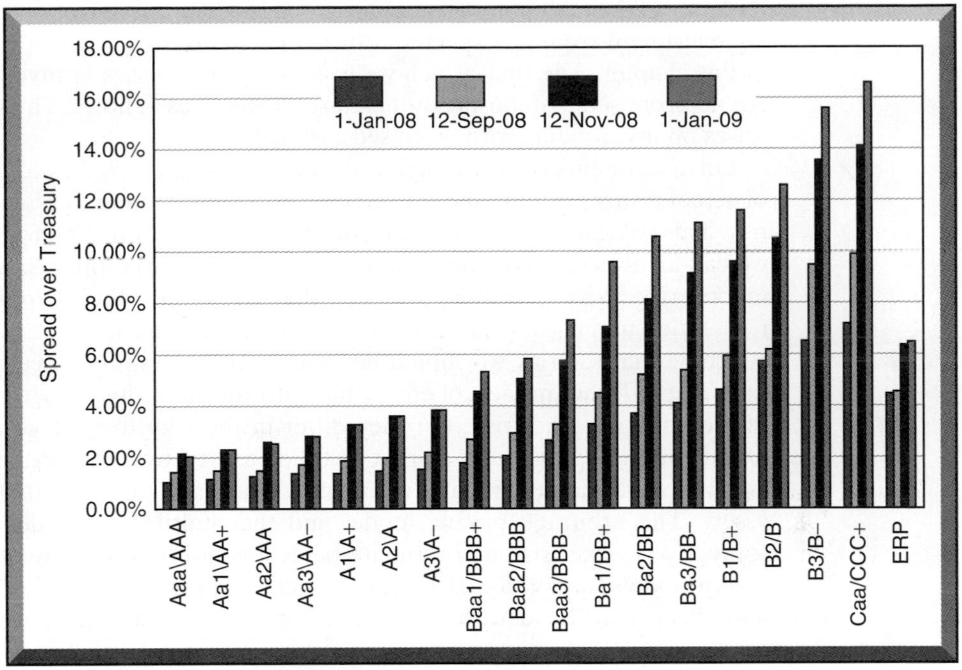

ratings.xls: There is a dataset on the Web that summarizes default spreads by bond rating class for the most recent period.

IN PRACTICE: RATINGS CHANGES AND INTEREST RATES

The rating assigned to a company can change at the discretion of the ratings agency. The change is usually triggered by a change in a firm's operating health, a new security issue by the firm, or new borrowing. Other things remaining equal, ratings will drop if the operating performance deteriorates or if the firm borrows substantially more and improve if it reports better earnings or raises new equity. In either case, though, the ratings agency is reacting to news that the rest of the market also receives. In fact, ratings agencies deliberate before making ratings changes, often putting a firm on a credit watch list before changing its ratings. Since markets can react instantaneously, it should come as no surprise that bond prices often decline before a ratings drop and increase before a ratings increase. In fact, studies indicate that much of the bond price reaction to deteriorating credit quality precedes a ratings drop.

This does not mean that there is no information in a ratings change. When ratings are changed, the market still reacts, but the reactions tend to be small. The biggest service provided by ratings agencies may be in providing a measure of default risk that is comparable across hundreds of rated firms, thus allowing bond investors a simple way of categorizing the risk in potential investments. ■

CONCLUSION

Risk, as we define it in finance, is measured based upon deviations of actual returns on an investment from its expected returns. There are two types of risk that we examine in this chapter. The first, which we call equity risk, arises in investments where there are no promised cash flows but there are expected cash flows. The second, default risk, arises on investments with promised cash flows.

On investments with equity risk, the risk is best measured by looking at the variance of actual returns around the expected returns, with greater variance indicating greater risk. This risk can be broken down into risk that affects one or a few investments, which we call firm-specific risk, and risk that affects many investments, which we refer to as market risk. When investors diversify, they can reduce their exposure to firm-specific risk. By assuming that the investors who trade at the margin are well diversified, we conclude that the risk we should be looking at with equity investments is the market risk. The different models of equity risk introduced in this chapter share this objective of measuring market risk, but they differ in the way they do it. In the capital asset pricing model, exposure to market risk is measured by a market beta, which estimates how much risk an individual investment will add to a portfolio that includes all traded assets. The arbitrage pricing model and the multifactor model allow for multiple sources of market risk and estimate betas for an investment relative to each source. Proxy models for risk look for firm characteristics (such as market capitalization) that have been correlated with high returns in the past, and they use these to measure market risk. In all these models, the risk measures are used to estimate the expected return on an equity investment. This expected return can be considered the cost of equity for a company.

On investments with default risk, risk is measured by the likelihood that the promised cash flows might not be delivered. Investments with higher default risk should have higher interest rates, and the premium that we demand over a riskless rate is the default premium. For many large U.S. companies, default risk is measured by rating agencies in the form of a company rating; these ratings determine, in large part, the interest rates at which these firms can borrow. Even in the absence of ratings, interest rates will include a default premium that reflects the lenders' assessments of default risk. These default-risk adjusted interest rates represent the cost of borrowing or debt for a business.

LIVE CASE STUDY

STOCKHOLDER ANALYSIS

Objective: To find out who the average and marginal investors in the company are. This is relevant because risk and return models in finance assume that the marginal investor is well diversified.

Key Questions

- Who is the average investor in this stock (individual or pension fund, taxable or tax-exempt, small or large, domestic or foreign)?
- Who is the marginal investor in this stock?

Framework for Analysis

1. **Who holds stock in this company?**
   - How many stockholders does the company have?
   - What percent of the stock is held by institutional investors?
   - Does the company have listings in foreign markets? (If you can, estimate the percent of the stock held by nondomestic investors.)

2. **Insider Holdings**
   - Who are the insiders in this company? (Besides the managers and directors, anyone holding more than 5% is treated as an insider.)
   - What role do the insiders play in running the company?
   - What percent of the stock is held by insiders in the company?
   - What percent of the stock is held by employees overall? (Include the holdings by employee pension plans.)
   - Have insiders been buying or selling stock in this company in the most recent year?

Getting Information on Stockholder Composition

Information about insider and institutional ownership of firms is widely available, since both groups have to file with the SEC. These SEC filings are used to develop rankings of the largest holders of stock in firms. Insider activity (buying and selling) is also recorded by the SEC, although the information is not available until a few weeks after the filing.

 Online Sources of Information
www.stern.nyu.edu/~adamodar/cfin2E/project/data.htm

PROBLEMS AND QUESTIONS

1. The following table lists the stock prices for Microsoft from 1989 to 1998. The company did not pay any dividends during the period.

	Price
1989	$1.20
1990	$2.09
1991	$4.64
1992	$5.34
1993	$5.05
1994	$7.64
1995	$10.97
1996	$20.66
1997	$32.31
1998	$69.34

a. Estimate the average annual return you would have made on your investment.

b. Estimate the standard deviation and variance in annual returns.

c. If you were investing in Microsoft today, would you expect the historical standard deviations and variances to continue to hold? Why, or why not?

2. Unicom is a regulated utility serving northern Illinois. The following table lists the stock prices and dividends on Unicom from 1989 to 1998.

	Price	Dividends
1989	$36.10	$3.00
1990	$33.60	$3.00
1991	$37.80	$3.00
1992	$30.90	$2.30
1993	$26.80	$1.60
1994	$24.80	$1.60
1995	$31.60	$1.60
1996	$28.50	$1.60
1997	$24.25	$1.60
1998	$35.60	$1.60

a. Estimate the average annual return you would have made on your investment.

b. Estimate the standard deviation and variance in annual returns.

c. If you were investing in Unicom today, would you expect the historical standard deviations and variances to continue to hold? Why, or why not?

3. The following table summarizes the annual returns you would have made on two companies—*Scientific Atlanta*, a satellite and data equipment manufacturer, and AT&T, the telecom giant, from 1988 to 1998.

	Scientific Atlanta	AT&T
1989	80.95%	58.26%
1990	−47.37%	−33.79%
1991	31.00%	29.88%
1992	132.44%	30.35%
1993	32.02%	2.94%
1994	25.37%	−4.29%
1995	−28.57%	28.86%
1996	0.00%	−6.36%
1997	11.67%	48.64%
1998	36.19%	23.55%

a. Estimate the average and standard deviation in annual returns in each company.

b. Estimate the covariance and correlation in returns between the two companies.

c. Estimate the variance of a portfolio composed, in equal parts, of the two investments.

4. You are in a world where there are only two assets—gold and stocks. You are interested in investing your money in one, the other, or both, so you collect the following data on the returns on the two assets over the last six years:

	Gold	Stock Market
Average return	8%	20%
Standard deviation	25%	22%
Correlation	−0.4	

a. If you were constrained to pick just one, which one would you choose?

b. A friend argues that basing a decision of whether to invest in gold on expected returns and standard deviations is wrong. He says that you are ignoring the big payoffs that you can get on gold. How would you go about alleviating his concern?

c. How would a portfolio composed of equal proportions in gold and stocks do in terms of mean and variance?

d. You now learn that GPEC (a cartel of gold-producing countries) is going to vary the amount of gold it produces with stock prices in the United States. (GPEC will produce less gold when stock markets are up and more when it is down.) What effect will this have on your portfolios? Explain.

5. You are interested in creating a portfolio of two stocks—Coca-Cola and Texas Utilities. Over the last decade, an investment in Coca-Cola stock would have earned an average annual return of 25%, with a standard deviation in returns of 36%. An investment in Texas Utilities stock would have earned an average annual return of 12%, with a standard deviation of 22%. The correlation in returns across the two stocks is 0.28.

a. Assuming that the average and standard deviation, estimated using past returns, will continue to hold in the future, estimate the average returns and standard deviation of a portfolio composed 60% of Coca-Cola and 40% of Texas Utilities stock.

b. Estimate the minimum variance portfolio.

c. Now assume that Coca-Cola's international diversification will reduce the correlation to 0.20 while increasing Coca-Cola's standard deviation in returns to 45%. Assuming all the other numbers remain unchanged, answer **a** and **b**.

6. Assume that you have half your money invested in Times Mirror, the media company, and the other half invested in Unilever, the consumer product giant. The expected returns and standard deviations on the two investments are summarized below:

	Times Mirror	Unilever
Expected return	14%	18%
Standard deviation	25%	40%

Estimate the variance of the portfolio as a function of the correlation coefficient. (Start with −1 and increase the correlation to +1 in 0.2 increments.)

7. You have been asked to analyze the standard deviation of a portfolio composed of the following three assets:

	Expected Return	Standard Deviation
Sony Corporation	11%	23%
Tesoro Petroleum	9%	27%
Storage Technology	16%	50%

You have also been provided with the correlations across these three investments:

	Sony	Tesoro	Storage Tech
Sony	1.00	−0.15	0.20
Tesoro	−0.15	1.00	−0.25
Storage Tech	0.20	−0.25	1.00

Estimate the variance of a portfolio equally weighted across all three assets.

8. You have been asked to estimate a Markowitz portfolio across a universe of 1,250 assets.

a. How many expected returns and variances would you need to compute?

b. How many covariances would you need to compute to obtain Markowitz portfolios?

9. Assume that the average variance of return for an individual security is 50 and that the average covariance is 10. What is the expected variance of a portfolio of 5, 10, 20, 50, and 100 securities? How many securities need to be held before the risk of a portfolio is only 10% more than the minimum?

10. Assume you have all your wealth ($1 million) invested in the Vanguard 500 index fund, and that you expect to earn an annual return of 12%, with a standard deviation in returns of 25%. Since you have become more risk-averse, you decide to shift $200,000 from the Vanguard 500 index fund to treasury bills. The T-bill rate is 5%. Estimate the expected return and standard deviation of your new portfolio.

11. Every investor in the capital asset pricing model owns a combination of the market portfolio and a riskless asset. Assume that the standard deviation of the market portfolio is 30%, and that the expected return on the portfolio is 15%. What proportion of the following investor's wealth would you suggest investing in the market portfolio and what proportion in the riskless asset? (The riskless asset has an expected return of 5%.)

    a. an investor who desires a portfolio with no standard deviation

    b. an investor who desires a portfolio with a standard deviation of 15%

    c. an investor who desires a portfolio with a standard deviation of 30%

    d. an investor who desires a portfolio with a standard deviation of 45%

    e. an investor who desires a portfolio with an expected return of 12%

12. The following table lists returns on the market portfolio and on *Scientific Atlanta* each year from 1989 to 1998:

	Scientific Atlanta	Market Portfolio
1989	80.95%	31.49%
1990	−47.37%	−3.17%
1991	31%	30.57%
1992	132.44%	7.58%
1993	32.02%	10.36%
1994	25.37%	2.55%
1995	−28.57%	37.57%
1996	0.00%	22.68%
1997	11.67%	33.10%
1998	36.19%	28.32%

    a. Estimate the covariance in returns between Microsoft and the market portfolio.

    b. Estimate the variances in returns on both investments.

    c. Estimate the beta for Microsoft.

13. United Airlines has a beta of 1.5. The standard deviation in the market portfolio is 22% and United Airlines has a standard deviation of 66%.

    a. Estimate the correlation between United Airlines and the market portfolio.

    b. What proportion of United Airlines' risk is market risk?

14. You are using the arbitrage pricing model to estimate the expected return on Bethlehem Steel and have derived the following estimates for the factor betas and risk premia:

Factor	Beta	Risk Premia
1	1.2	2.5%
2	0.6	1.5%
3	1.5	1.0%
4	2.2	0.8%
5	0.5	1.2%

    a. Which risk factor is Bethlehem Steel most exposed to? Is there any way, within the arbitrage pricing model, to identify the risk factor?

    b. If the riskfree rate is 5%, estimate the expected return on Bethlehem Steel.

    c. Now assume that the beta in the capital asset pricing model for Bethlehem Steel is 1.1 and that the risk premium for the market portfolio is 5%. Estimate the expected return, using the CAPM.

    d. Why are the expected returns different using the two models?

15. You are using the multifactor model to estimate the expected return on Emerson Electric and have derived the following estimates for the factor betas and risk premia:

Macro-economic Factor	Measure	Beta	Risk Premia $(R_{factor} - R_f)$
Level of interest rates	T-bond rate	0.5	1.8%
Term structure	T-bond rate–T-bill rate	1.4	0.6%
Inflation rate	CPI	1.2	1.5%
Economic growth	GNP growth rate	1.8	4.2%

    With a riskless rate of 6%, estimate the expected return on Emerson Electric.

16. The following equation is reproduced from the study by Fama and French of returns between 1963 and 1990.

$$R_t = 0.0177 - 0.11 \ln(MV) + 0.35 \ln(BV/MV)$$

where MV is the market value of equity in hundreds of millions of dollars and BV is the book value of equity in hundreds of millions of dollars. The return is a monthly return.

a. Estimate the expected annual return on Lucent Technologies. The market value of equity is $240 billion, and the book value of equity is $13.5 billion.

b. Lucent Technologies has a beta of 1.55. If the riskless rate is 6% and the risk premium for the market portfolio is 5.5%, estimate the expected return.

c. Why are the expected returns different under the two approaches?

CHAPTER 4

RISK MEASUREMENT AND HURDLE RATES IN PRACTICE

In the last chapter, we presented the argument that the expected return on an equity investment should be a function of the market or nondiversifiable risk embedded in that investment. Here we turn our attention to how best to estimate the parameters of market risk in each of the models described in the previous chapter—the capital asset pricing model, the arbitrage pricing model, and the multifactor model. We will present three alternative approaches for measuring the market risk in an investment; the first is to use historical data on market prices for the firm considering the project, the second is to use the market risk parameters estimated for other firms that are in

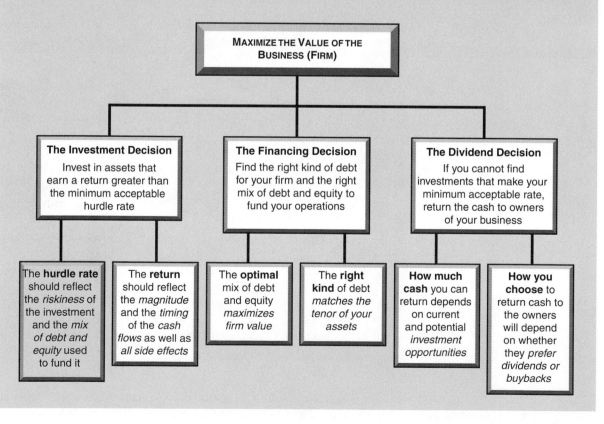

MAXIMIZE THE VALUE OF THE BUSINESS (FIRM)		
The Investment Decision Invest in assets that earn a return greater than the minimum acceptable hurdle rate	**The Financing Decision** Find the right kind of debt for your firm and the right mix of debt and equity to fund your operations	**The Dividend Decision** If you cannot find investments that make your minimum acceptable rate, return the cash to owners of your business

The **hurdle rate** should reflect the *riskiness* of the investment and the *mix of debt and equity* used to fund it	The **return** should reflect the *magnitude* and the *timing* of the *cash flows* as well as *all side effects*	The **optimal** mix of debt and equity *maximizes firm value*	The **right kind** of debt *matches the tenor of your assets*	**How much cash** you can return depends on current and potential *investment opportunities*	**How you choose** to return cash to the owners will depend on whether they *prefer dividends or buybacks*

the same business as the project being analyzed, and the third is to use accounting earnings or revenues to estimate the parameters.

In addition to assessing market risk exposure, we will also discuss how best to estimate a riskless rate and a risk premium (in the CAPM) or risk premiums (in the APM and multifactor models) to convert the risk measures into expected returns. We will present a similar argument for bringing default risk into a cost of debt and then bring the discussion to fruition by combining both the cost of equity and debt to estimate a cost of capital, which will become the minimum acceptable hurdle rate for an investment.

COST OF EQUITY

The *cost of equity* is the rate of return that investors require to invest in the equity of a firm. All of the risk and return models described in the previous chapter need a risk-free rate and a risk premium (in the CAPM) or premiums (in the APM and multifactor models). We begin by discussing those common inputs before turning attention to the estimation of risk parameters.

I. Risk-Free Rate

Most risk-and-return models in finance start off with an asset that is defined as risk-free and use the expected return on that asset as the risk-free rate. The expected returns on risky investments are then measured relative to the risk-free rate, with the risk creating an expected risk premium that is added on to the risk-free rate.

Requirements for an Asset to be Risk-Free

We defined a risk-free asset as one for which the investor knows the expected returns with certainty. Consequently, for an investment to be risk-free—that is, to have an actual return be equal to the expected return—two conditions have to be met:

1. There has to be *no default risk*, which generally implies that the security has to be issued by a government. Note, however, that not all governments are default-free, and the presence of government or sovereign default risk can make it very difficult to estimate risk-free rates in some currencies.

2. There can be *no uncertainty about reinvestment rates*, which implies that there are no intermediate cash flows. To illustrate this point, assume that you are trying to estimate the expected return over a five-year period and that you want a risk-free rate. A six-month Treasury bill rate, although default-free, will not be risk-free, because there is the reinvestment risk of not knowing what the bill rate will be in six months. Even a five-year Treasury bond is not risk-free, because the coupons on the bond will be reinvested at rates that cannot be predicted today. The risk-free rate for a five-year time horizon has to be the expected return on a default-free (government) five-year zero coupon bond.

This clearly has painful implications for anyone doing corporate financial analysis, where expected returns often have to be estimated for periods ranging over multiple years. A purist's view of risk-free rates would then require different risk-free rates for each period, and different expected returns. As a practical compromise, however, it is worth noting that the present value effect of using risk-free rates that vary from year to year tends to be small for most well-behaved term structures.[1] In these cases, we could use a duration matching strategy, where the duration of the default-free security used as the risk-free asset is matched up to the duration of the cash flows in the analysis.[2] If, however, there are very large differences in either direction between short-term and long-term rates, it does pay to use year-specific risk-free rates in computing expected returns.

Cash Flows and Risk-Free Rates: The Consistency Principle

The risk-free rate used to come up with expected returns should be measured in a way consistent with how the cash flows are measured. If the cash flows are nominal, the risk-free rate should be in the same currency in which the cash flows are estimated. This also implies that it is not where a project or firm is located that determines the choice of a risk-free rate, but the currency in which the cash flows on the project or firm are estimated. Thus Disney can analyze a proposed project in Mexico in dollars, using a dollar discount rate, or in pesos, using a peso discount rate. For the former, it would use the U.S. Treasury bond rate as the risk-free rate, but the latter would need a peso risk-free rate. Figure 4.1 compares risk-free rates in different currencies in early 2009.

Note that if these are truly default free rates, the key factor determining the differences across currencies is expected inflation. The risk-free rate in Australian dollars is higher than the risk-free rate in Swiss Francs, because expected inflation is higher in Australia than in Switzerland.

Under conditions of high and unstable inflation, valuation is often done in real terms. Effectively, this means that cash flows are estimated using real growth rates and without allowing for the growth that comes from price inflation. To be consistent, the discount rates used in these cases have to be real discount rates. To get a real expected rate of return, we need to start with a real risk-free rate. Although government bills and bonds offer returns that are risk-free in nominal terms, they are not risk-free in real terms, because inflation can be volatile. The standard approach of subtracting an expected inflation rate from the nominal interest rate to arrive at a real risk-free rate provides, at best, only an estimate of the real risk-free rate. Until recently, there were few traded default-free securities that could be used to estimate real risk-free rates; but the introduction of inflation-indexed Treasuries (called TIPs) has filled this void. An inflation-indexed Treasury security does not offer a guaranteed nominal return to buyers, but instead provides a guaranteed real return. In May 2009, for example, the inflation indexed U.S. ten-year Treasury bond rate was only 1.6%, much lower than the nominal ten-year bond rate of 3.5%.

---

[1] By "well-behaved term structures," I am assuming a normal upwardly sloping yield curve, where long-term rates are at most 2–3% higher than short-term rates.

[2] In investment analysis, where we look at projects, these durations are usually between three and ten years. In valuation, the durations tend to be much longer, because firms are assumed to have infinite lives. The duration in these cases is often well in excess of ten years and increases with the expected growth potential of the firm.

Figure 4.1 Risk-free Rates by Currency: January 2009

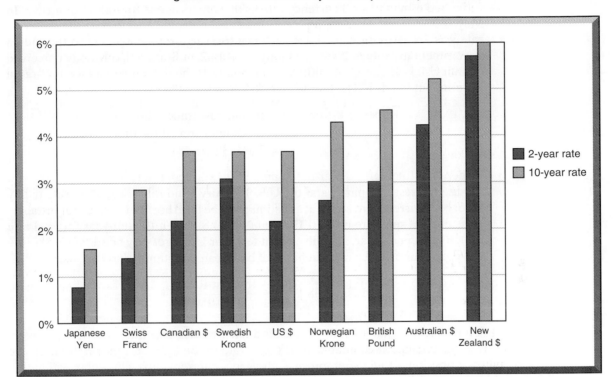

4.1 WHAT IS THE RIGHT RISK-FREE RATE?

The correct risk-free rate to use in the CAPM

a. Is the short-term government security rate
b. Is the long-term government security rate
c. Can be either the short-term or the long-term government security rate, depending on whether the prediction is short-term or long-term

IN PRACTICE: WHAT IF THERE IS NO DEFAULT-FREE RATE?

Our discussion to this point has been predicated on the assumption that governments do not default, at least on local borrowing. There are many emerging market economies where this assumption might not be reasonable. Governments in these markets are perceived as capable of defaulting even on local borrowing. When this is coupled with the fact that many governments do not borrow long-term in the local currency, there are scenarios in which obtaining a risk-free rate in that currency, especially for the long-term, becomes difficult. In these cases, there are compromises that give us reasonable estimates of the risk-free rate.

- If the government does issue long-term bonds in the local currency, you could adjust the government bond rate by the estimated default spread on the bond to arrive at a riskless local currency rate. The default spread on the government bond can be estimated using the local currency ratings that are available for many countries.[3] In May 2009, for instance, the ten-year rupee-denominated Indian government bond rate was 7%. However, the local currency sovereign rating assigned to the Indian government in January 2009 by Moody's was Ba2, indicating that Moody perceived default risk in Indian government rupee bonds. If the default spread for Ba2-rated government bonds is 3%, the rupee risk-free rate is 4%.[4]

$$\text{Rupee risk-free rate} = \text{Indian government bond rate} \\ - \text{Default spread for India} \\ = 7\% - 3\% = 4\%$$

- If there are long-term dollar-denominated forward contracts on the currency, you can use interest rate parity and the U.S. Treasury bond rate (or riskless rate in any other base currency) to arrive at an estimate of the local borrowing rate. For instance, if the current spot rate is 38.10 Thai baht per U.S. dollar, the ten-year forward rate is 61.36 baht per dollar, and the current ten-year U.S. Treasury bond rate is 5%, the ten-year Thai risk-free rate (in nominal baht) can be estimated as follows:

$$61.36 = (38.1) \left(\frac{1 + \text{Interest Rate}_{\text{Thai Baht}}}{1 + 0.05} \right)^{10}$$

Solving for the Thai interest rate yields a ten-year risk-free rate of 10.12%.

If every attempt at estimating a risk-free rate in the local currency falls short, the fallback position is to do your entire analysis in a different currency, where estimation poses fewer challenges. Thus, we can analyze a Russian company in euros or a Brazilian company in U.S. dollars. If we do so, though, we have to be consistent and estimate all of our cash flows in those currencies, which will require forecasting future exchange rates. We will come back to the question of how best to do this in the next chapter. ■

ILLUSTRATION 4.1   Estimating Risk-Free Rates

The companies that we are analyzing in this book include two U.S. companies, (Disney and Bookscape), a Brazilian company (Aracruz), an Indian company (Tata Chemicals), and a German bank (Deutsche Bank). We estimated risk-free rates in four currencies on May 23, 2009, and will use these numbers for the rest of the book:

- **Dollars**   The ten-year U.S. treasury bond rate at the time of the analysis was 3.5%. While concerns about the creditworthiness of the U.S. government have increased in the aftermath of the billions in financial commitments made after the banking crisis, we will use 3.5% as the risk-free rate in any dollar-based computation.

---

[3]Ratings agencies generally assign different ratings for local currency borrowings and dollar borrowings, with higher ratings for the former and lower ratings for the latter.

[4]The default spread for a sovereign rating is computed by comparing dollar- or euro-denominated sovereign bonds issued by emerging markets to the default free U.S. rate (treasury) or euro rate (the German ten-year bond).

- *Euros*   For a euro risk-free rate, we looked at ten-year euro-denominated government bonds and noted that at least twelve different European governments have such bonds outstanding, with wide differences in rates.[5] Since the only reason for differences in these government bond rates has to be default risk (since they are denominated in the same currency), we used the lowest of these rates, resulting in the German ten-year bond rate of 3.60% being used as the risk-free rate for euro-based computations.

- *Rupees*   On May 23, 2009, the ten-year rupee-denominated bond, issued by the Indian government, traded to yield 7%. Subtracting the default spread of 3% estimated for India, based upon its sovereign rating of Ba2, yields a risk-free rate of 4% for rupee-based computations:

$$\text{Risk-free rate in rupees} = \text{Ten-year rupee bond rate} - \text{Default spread}$$
$$= 7\% - 3\% = 4\%$$

- *Brazilian Reals*   On May 23, 2009, the ten-year Brazilian real (R\$)–denominated government rate was 11%. Subtracting the default spread of 2.5% estimated for Brazil, based upon its sovereign rating of Ba1, yields a risk-free rate of 8.5% for R\$-based computation.

- *Real terms*   For any computations done in real terms, we need a real risk-free rate. We will use the ten-year inflation-indexed treasury bond (TIPS) rate of 1.6% (as of May 23, 2009) as the risk-free rate for any computations done in real terms.

II. Risk Premium

The risk premium is clearly a significant input in all of the asset pricing models. In the following section, we will begin by examining the fundamental determinants of risk premiums and then look at practical approaches to estimating these premiums.

What Is the Risk Premium Supposed to Measure?

The risk premium in the CAPM measures the extra return that would be demanded by investors for shifting their money from a riskless investment to the market portfolio or risky investments, on average. It should be a function of two variables:

1. *Risk Aversion of Investors*   As investors become more risk-averse, they should demand a larger premium for shifting from the riskless asset. Although some of this risk aversion may be inherent, some of it is also a function of economic prosperity (when the economy is doing well, investors tend to be much more willing to take risks) and recent experiences in the market (risk premiums tend to surge after large market drops).

2. *Riskiness of the Average Risk Investment*   As the riskiness of the average risk investment increases, so should the premium. This will depend on what firms are

---

[5]On May 23, 2009, the German ten-year euro bond rate was 3.60%, the Italian ten-year euro bond was 4.46%, and the Greek ten-year euro bond rate was 5.26%.

actually traded in the market, as well as their economic fundamentals and how involved they are in managing risk.

Because each investor in a market is likely to have a different assessment of an acceptable equity risk premium, the premium will be a weighted average of these individual premiums, where the weights will be based on the wealth the investor brings to the market. Put more directly, what Warren Buffett, with his substantial wealth, thinks is an acceptable premium will be weighted in far more into market prices than might be the case with you or me.

In the APM and the multifactor models, the risk premiums used for individual factors are similar wealth-weighted averages of the premiums that individual investors would demand for each factor separately.

4.2 WHAT IS YOUR RISK PREMIUM?

Assume that stocks are the only risky assets and that you are offered two investment options:
☐ A riskless investment (say, a government security) on which you can make 4%
☐ A mutual fund of all stocks, on which the returns are uncertain

How much of an expected return would you demand to shift your money from the riskless asset to the mutual fund?

a. Less than 4%
b. 4–6%
c. 6–8%
d. 8–10%
e. 10–12%
f. More than 12%

Your answer to this question should provide you with a measure of your risk premium. (For instance, if your answer is 6%, your premium is 2%.)

Estimating Risk Premiums

There are three ways of estimating the risk premium in the CAPM: (1) large investors can be surveyed about their expectations for the future, (2) actual premiums earned over a past period can be obtained from historical data, and (3) the implied premium can be extracted from current market data. The premium can be estimated only from historical data in the APM and the multifactor models.

1. Survey Premiums

Because the premium is a weighted average of the premiums demanded by individual investors, one approach to estimating this premium is to survey investors about their expectations for the future. It is clearly impractical to survey all investors; therefore, most surveys focus on portfolio managers or chief financial officers (CFOs), who carry the most weight in the process. Table 4.1 summarizes the results of some of these surveys, along with the groups surveyed.

Table 4.1	EQUITY RISK PREMIUMS FROM SURVEYS	
Group Surveyed	**Survey Done By**	**Results (Year)**
Individual Investors	Securities Industry Association	8.3% (December 2004)
Institutional Investors	Merrill Lynch	3.8% (July 2008)
CFOs	Campbell and Harvey	4.2% (March 2008)
Finance academics	Pablo Fernandez	6.2% (March 2008)

Although numbers do emerge from these surveys, very few practitioners actually use these survey premiums. There are three reasons for this reticence:

1. There are no constraints on reasonability; individual money managers could provide expected returns that are lower than the risk-free rate, for instance.
2. Survey premiums are extremely volatile; the survey premiums can change dramatically, largely as a function of recent market movements.
3. Survey premiums tend to be short-term; even the longest surveys do not go beyond one year.

4.3 DO RISK PREMIUMS CHANGE?

In the previous question, you were asked how much of a premium you would demand for investing in a portfolio of stocks as opposed to a riskless asset. Assume that the market dropped by 20% last week, and you were asked the same question today. What would your premium be?

a. Higher
b. Lower
c. Unchanged

2. Historical Premiums

The most common approach to estimating the risk premium(s) used in financial asset pricing models is to base it on historical data. In the APM and multifactor models, the premiums are based on historical data on asset prices over very long time periods which are used to extract factor-specific risk premiums. In the CAPM, the premium is defined as the difference between average returns on stocks and average returns on risk-free securities over an extended period of history.

Basics In most cases, this approach is composed of the following steps. It begins by defining a time period for the estimation, which can range to as far back as 1871 for U.S. data. It then requires the calculation of the average returns on a stock index and average returns on a riskless security over the period. Finally, the difference between the average returns on stocks and the riskless return it is defined as the risk premium looking forward. In doing this, we implicitly assume that

- The risk aversion of investors has not changed in a systematic way across time. (The risk aversion may change from year to year, but it reverts back to historical averages.)

- The average riskiness of the "risky" portfolio (stock index) has not changed in a systematic way across time.

Estimation Issues Users of risk and return models may have developed a consensus that the historical premium is in fact the best estimate of the risk premium looking forward, but there are surprisingly large differences in the actual premiums used in practice. For instance, the risk premium estimated in the U.S. markets by different investment banks, consultants, and corporations range from 4% at the lower end to 12% at the upper end. Given that they almost all use the same database of historical returns, provided by Ibbotson Associates,[6] summarizing data from 1926, these differences may seem surprising. There are, however, three reasons for the divergence in risk premiums.

1. ***Time Period Used*** Although there are some who use all of the Ibbotson, which goes back to 1926, there are many using data over shorter time periods, such as fifty, twenty, or even ten years to come up with historical risk premiums. The rationale presented by those who use shorter periods is that the risk aversion of the average investor is likely to change over time, and using a shorter and more recent time period provides a more updated estimate. This has to be offset against a cost associated with using shorter time periods, which is the greater estimation error in the risk premium estimate. In fact, given the annual standard deviation in stock prices between 1928 and 2008 of 20%,[7] the standard error associated with the risk premium estimate can be estimated as follows for different estimation periods in Table 4.2.[8]

Table 4.2 STANDARD ERRORS IN RISK PREMIUM ESTIMATES

Estimation Period	Standard Error of Risk Premium Estimate
5 years	$20/\sqrt{5} = 8.94\%$
10 years	$20/\sqrt{10} = 6.32\%$
25 years	$20/\sqrt{25} = 4.00\%$
50 years	$20/\sqrt{50} = 2.83\%$

Note that to get reasonable standard errors, we need very long time periods of historical returns. Conversely, the standard errors from ten- and twenty-year estimates are likely to be almost as large as or larger than the actual risk premiums

[6]See *Stocks, Bonds, Bills and Inflation*, an annual publication that reports on the annual returns on stocks, Treasury bonds and bills, and inflation rates from 1926 to the present. Available online at www.ibbotson.com.
[7]For the historical data on stock returns, bond returns, and bill returns, check under Updated Data at www.damodaran.com.
[8]These estimates of the standard error are probably understated because they are based on the assumption that annual returns are uncorrelated over time. There is substantial empirical evidence that returns are correlated over time, which would make this standard error estimate much larger.

estimated. This cost of using shorter time periods seems, in our view, to overwhelm any advantages associated with getting a more updated premium.

2. *Choice of Risk-Free Security*   The Ibbotson database reports returns on both Treasury bills and bonds and the risk premium for stocks can be estimated relative to each. Given that short-term rates have been lower than long-term rates in the United States during most of the past seven decades, the risk premium is larger when estimated relative to shorter-term government securities (such as Treasury bills). The risk-free rate chosen in computing the premium has to be consistent with the risk-free rate used to compute expected returns. For the most part, in corporate finance and valuation, the risk-free rate will be a long-term government bond rate and not a short-term rate. Thus the risk premium used should be the premium earned by stocks over Treasury bonds.

3. *Arithmetic and Geometric Averages*   The final sticking point when it comes to estimating historical premiums relates to how the average returns on stocks and Treasury bonds and bills are computed. The arithmetic average return measures the simple mean of the series of annual returns, whereas the geometric average looks at the compounded return.[9] Conventional wisdom argues for the use of the arithmetic average. In fact, if annual returns are uncorrelated over time and our objective was to estimate the risk premium for the next year, the arithmetic average is the best unbiased estimate of the premium. In reality, however, there are strong arguments that can be made for the use of geometric averages. First, empirical studies seem to indicate that returns on stocks are negatively correlated over time.[10] Consequently, the arithmetic average return is likely to overstate the premium. Second, although asset pricing models may be single-period models, the use of these models to get expected returns over long periods (such as five or ten years) suggests that the analysis is more likely to be over multiple years than for just the next year. In this context, the argument for geometric average premiums becomes even stronger.

In summary, the risk premium estimates vary across users because of differences in time periods used, the choice of Treasury bills or bonds as the risk-free rate, and the use of arithmetic as opposed to geometric averages. The effect of these choices is summarized in Table 4.3, which uses returns from 1928 to 2008.[11]

Note that the premiums range from negative values (for the ten-year premiums) to values as high as 7.30% (which is the arithmetic average of the premium over

---

[9]The compounded return is computed by taking the value of the investment at the start of the period (Value_0) and the value at the end (Value_N) and then computing the following:

$$\text{Geometric average} = \left(\frac{\text{Value}_N}{\text{Value}_0} \right)^{1/N} - 1$$

[10]In other words, good years are more likely to be followed by poor years and vice versa. The evidence on negative serial correlation in stock returns over time is extensive and can be found in E. F. Fama and K. R. French, "Permanent and Temporary Components of Stock Prices," *Journal of Political Economy* 96:246–273. Although they find that the one-year correlations are low, the five-year serial correlations are strongly negative for all size classes.

[11]The raw data on Treasury bill rates, Treasury bond rates, and stock returns was obtained from the Federal Reserve data archives maintained by the Federal Reserve in St. Louis.

	Stocks–Treasury Bills		Stocks–Treasury Bonds	
	Arithmetic	**Geometric**	**Arithmetic**	**Geometric**
1928–2008	7.30%	5.65%	5.32%	3.88%
1959–2008	5.14%	3.33%	3.77%	2.29%
1999–2008	−2.53%	−6.26%	−4.53%	−7.96%

Table 4.3   HISTORICAL RISK PREMIUMS (%) FOR THE UNITED STATES, 1928–2008

Treasury bills). If we follow the propositions about picking a long-term geometric average premium over the long-term Treasury bond rate, the historical risk premium that makes the most sense is 3.88%.

Historical Premiums in Other Markets   Although historical data on stock returns is easily available and accessible in the United States, it is much more difficult to get for foreign markets. The most detailed look at these returns estimated the returns you would have earned on fourteen equity markets between 1900 and 2005 and compared these returns with those you would have earned investing in bonds.[12] Table 4.4 presents the risk premiums—that is, the additional returns—earned by investing in equity over short-term and long-term government bonds over that period in each of the fourteen markets.

Although equity returns were higher than what you would have earned investing in government bonds or bills in each of the countries examined, there are wide differences across countries. If you had invested in Spain, for instance, you would have earned only 3% over government bills and 2.3% over government bonds on an annual basis by investing in equities. In France, in contrast, the corresponding numbers would have been 6.8% and 3.9%. When looking at forty or fifty-year periods, therefore, it is entirely possible that equity returns can lag bond or bill returns, at least in some equity markets. In other words, the notion that stocks always win in the long run is not only dangerous but does not make sense. If stocks always beat riskless investments in the long run, they should be riskless to an investor with a long time horizon and the appropriate equity risk premium should be zero.

histretSP.xls: This data set has yearly data on Treasury bill rates, Treasury bond rates, and returns and stock returns going back to 1928.

A Modified Historical Risk Premium   In many emerging markets, there is very little historical data, and what does exist is too volatile to yield a meaningful estimate of the risk premium. To estimate the risk premium in these countries, let us start with the basic proposition that the risk premium in any equity market can be written as

Equity risk premium = Base premium for mature equity market
+ Country premium

---

[12]E. Dimson, P. Marsh, and M. Staunton, *Triumph of the Optimists: 101 Years of Global Investment Returns*, Princeton University Press, Princeton, 2002); and *Global Investment Returns Yearbook*, ABN AMRO/London Business School, 2006.

Table 4.4   HISTORICAL EQUITY RISK PREMIUMS BY COUNTRY

	Stocks Minus Short-Term Governments				Stocks Minus Long-Term Governments			
	Geometric Mean	Arithmetic Mean	Standard Error	Standard Deviation	Geometric Mean	Arithmetic Mean	Standard Error	Standard Deviation
Australia	7.08	8.49	1.65	17.00	6.22	7.81	1.83	18.80
Belgium	2.80	4.99	2.24	23.06	2.57	4.37	1.95	20.10
Canada	4.54	5.88	1.62	16.71	4.15	5.67	1.74	17.95
Denmark	2.87	4.51	1.93	19.85	2.07	3.27	1.57	16.18
France	6.79	9.27	2.35	24.19	3.86	6.03	2.16	22.29
Germany	3.83	9.07	3.28	33.49	5.28	8.35	2.69	27.41
Ireland	4.09	5.98	1.97	20.33	3.62	5.18	1.78	18.37
Italy	6.55	10.46	3.12	32.09	4.30	7.68	2.89	29.73
Japan	6.67	9.84	2.70	27.82	5.91	9.98	3.21	33.06
Netherlands	4.55	6.61	2.17	22.36	3.86	5.95	2.10	21.63
Norway	3.07	5.70	2.52	25.90	2.55	5.26	2.66	27.43
South Africa	6.20	8.25	2.15	22.09	5.35	7.03	1.88	19.32
Spain	3.40	5.46	2.08	21.45	2.32	4.21	1.96	20.20
Sweden	5.73	7.98	2.15	22.09	5.21	7.51	2.17	22.34
Switzerland	3.63	5.29	1.82	18.79	1.80	3.28	1.70	17.52
U.K.	4.43	6.14	1.93	19.84	4.06	5.29	1.61	16.60
U.S.	5.51	7.41	1.91	19.64	4.52	6.49	1.96	20.16
World, exc. U.S.	4.23	5.93	1.88	19.33	4.10	5.18	1.48	15.19
World	4.74	6.07	1.62	16.65	4.04	5.15	1.45	14.96

The differences in compounded annual returns between stocks and short-term governments/long-term governments are reported for each country.

The country premium could reflect the extra risk in a specific market. This boils down our estimation to answering two questions:

1. What should the base premium for a mature equity market be?

2. How do we estimate the additional risk premium for individual countries?

To answer the first question, we will make the argument that the U.S. equity market is mature and that there is sufficient historical data to make a reasonable estimate of the risk premium. In fact, reverting back to our discussion of historical premiums in the U.S. market, we will use the geometric average premium earned by stocks over Treasury bonds of 3.88% between 1928 and 2008. We chose the long time period to reduce the standard error in our estimate, the Treasury bond to be consistent with our choice of a risk-free rate, and geometric averages to reflect our desire for a risk premium that we can use for longer-term expected returns. There are three approaches that we can use to estimate the country risk premium.

1. ***Country Bond Default Spreads***   There are several measures of country risk, and one of the simplest and most easily accessible is the rating assigned to a country's debt by a ratings agency (S&P, Moody's, and IBCA all rate countries). These sovereign ratings measure default risk (rather than equity risk), but they are affected by many of the factors that drive equity risk—the stability of a country's

currency, its budget and trade balances, and its political stability, for instance.[13] The other advantage of ratings is that they come with default spreads over the U.S. Treasury bond. To illustrate, in May 2009, Moody's assigned ratings of Ba1 to Brazil and Ba2 to India; the typical default spread at the time was 2.5% for a Ba1-rated sovereign bond and 3% for a Ba2-rated sovereign bond.[14]

Analysts who use default spreads as measures of country risk typically add them onto both the cost of equity and debt of every company traded in that country. For instance, the cost of equity for a Brazilian company, estimated in U.S. dollars, will be 2.5% higher than the cost of equity of an otherwise similar U.S. company. If we assume that the risk premium for the United States and other mature equity markets is 3.88%, the cost of equity for a Brazilian company with a beta of 1.2 can be estimated as follows (with a U.S. Treasury bond rate of 3.5%).

$$
\begin{aligned}
\text{Cost of equity} &= \text{Risk-free rate} + \text{Beta} * (\text{U.S. Risk premium}) \\
&\quad + \text{Country bond default spread} \\
&= 3.5\% + 1.2(3.88\%) + 2.50\% = 10.65\%
\end{aligned}
$$

In some cases, analysts add the default spread to the U.S. risk premium and multiply it by the beta. This increases the cost of equity for high-beta companies and lowers them for low-beta firms.

2. ***Relative Standard Deviation*** There are some analysts who believe that the equity risk premiums of markets should reflect the differences in equity risk, as measured by the volatilities of these markets. A conventional measure of equity risk is the standard deviation in stock prices; higher standard deviations are generally associated with more risk. If you scale the standard deviation of one market against another, you obtain a measure of relative risk.

$$
\text{Relative standard deviation}_{\text{Country X}} = \frac{\text{Standard deviation}_{\text{Country X}}}{\text{Standard deviation}_{\text{US}}}
$$

This relative standard deviation, when multiplied by the premium used for U.S. stocks, should yield a measure of the total risk premium for any market.

$$
\begin{aligned}
&\text{Equity risk premium}_{\text{Country X}} \\
&\quad = \text{Risk premium}_{\text{U.S.}} * \text{Relative standard deviation}_{\text{Country X}}
\end{aligned}
$$

Assume for the moment that you are using a mature market premium for the United States of 3.88% and the annual standard deviation of U.S. stocks is 20%. The annualized standard deviation in the Brazilian equity index is 34%,[15] yielding

[13]The process by which country ratings are obtained is explained on the S&P Web site at www.ratings.standardpoor.com/criteria/index.htm.

[14]We estimated these spreads by looking at dollar- or euro-denominated bonds issued by governments with these ratings and comparing the rates on these bonds to the U.S. treasury (for dollar bonds) and the German euro bond (for euro bonds). We also looked at the Credit Default Swap (CDS) market, where we can observe day-to-day changes in the market's assessment of default spreads.

[15]Both the U.S. and Brazilian standard deviations were computed using weekly returns for two years from the beginning of 2007 to the end of 2008 and then annualizing the value. You could use daily returns to make the same judgments, but they tend to have much more estimation error in them.

a total risk premium for Brazil:

$$\text{Equity risk premium}_{\text{Brazil}} = 3.88\% * \frac{34\%}{20\%} = 6.60\%$$

The country risk premium can be isolated as follows:

$$\text{Country risk premium}_{\text{Brazil}} = 6.60\% - 3.88\% = 2.72\%$$

Using the 32% standard deviation in the Sensex (the Indian equity index) yields the equity risk premium for India:

$$\text{Equity risk premium}_{\text{India}} = 3.88\% * \frac{32\%}{20\%} = 6.21\%$$

$$\text{Country risk premium}_{\text{India}} = 6.21\% - 3.88\% = 2.33\%$$

Although this approach has intuitive appeal, there are problems with using standard deviations computed in markets with widely different market structures and liquidity. There are very risky emerging markets that have low standard deviations for their equity markets because the markets are illiquid. This approach will understate the equity risk premiums in those markets.

3. ***Default Spreads + Relative Standard Deviations***   The country default spreads that come with country ratings provide an important first step, but still only measure the premium for default risk. Intuitively, we would expect the country equity risk premium to be larger than the country default risk spread, since equities are riskier than bonds. To address the issue of how much higher, we look at the volatility of the equity market in a country relative to the volatility of the country bond used to estimate the default spread. This yields the following estimate for the country equity risk premium.

$$\text{Country risk premium} = \text{Country default spread} * \left(\frac{\sigma_{\text{Equity}}}{\sigma_{\text{Country Bond}}} \right)$$

To illustrate, consider the case of Brazil. As noted earlier, the dollar-denominated bonds issued by the Brazilian government trade with a default spread of 3% over the U.S. Treasury bond rate. The annualized standard deviation in the Brazilian equity index over the previous year is 34.0%, whereas the annualized standard deviation in the Brazilian C-bond is 21.5%.[16] The resulting additional country equity risk premium for Brazil is as follows:

$$\text{Brazil's country risk premium} = 2.50\% \left(\frac{34.0\%}{21.5\%} \right) = 3.95\%$$

Note that this country risk premium will increase if the country default spread widens or if the relative volatility of the equity market increases. It is also *in addition* to the equity risk premium for a mature market. Thus the total equity risk premium for a Brazilian company using the approach and a 3.88% premium

---

[16]The standard deviation in Brazilian dollar–denominated bond returns was computed using weekly returns over two years as well. Because these returns are in dollars and the returns on the Brazilian equity index are in real, there is an inconsistency here. We did estimate the standard deviation on the Brazilian equity index in dollars, but it made little difference to the overall calculation because the dollar standard deviation was close to our estimate.

for the United States would be 7.63%. Using the same approach for India, where the Indian government bond had a standard deviation of 21.3%, yields the country risk premium for India:

$$\text{India's country risk premium} = 3.00\% \left(\frac{32.0\%}{21.3\%}\right) = 4.51\%$$

$$\text{Total equity risk premium}_{\text{India}} = 3.88\% + 4.51\% = 8.39\%$$

Why should equity risk premiums have any relationship to country bond default spreads? A simple explanation is that an investor who can make spread 2.5% on a dollar-denominated Brazilian government bond would not settle for an expected equity risk premium of 5.2% (in dollar terms) on Brazilian equity. This approach and the previous one both use the standard deviation in equity of a market to make a judgment about country risk premium, but they measure it relative to different bases. This approach uses the country bond as a base, whereas the previous one uses the standard deviation in the U.S. market. This approach assumes that investors are more likely to choose between Brazilian government bonds and Brazilian equity, whereas the previous approach assumes that the choice is across equity markets.

The three approaches to estimating country risk premiums will generally give different estimates, with the bond default spread and relative equity standard deviation approaches yielding lower country risk premiums than the melded approach that uses both the country bond default spread and the equity and bond market standard deviations. Table 4.5 summarizes these estimates for India and Brazil.

Table 4.5 COUNTRY RISK PREMIUMS ESTIMATES FOR INDIA AND BRAZIL—MARCH 2009

	Sovereign Rating	Default Spread	Relative Equity Market Volatility	Composite Country Risk Premium
Brazil	Ba1	2.50%	$\frac{34\%}{20\%}(3.88\%) - 3.88\% = 2.72\%$	$\frac{34\%}{21.5\%}(2.5\%) = 3.95\%$
India	Ba2	3.00%	$\frac{32\%}{20\%}(3.88\%) - 3.88\% = 2.33\%$	$\frac{32\%}{21.3\%}(3\%) = 4.51\%$

We believe that the larger country risk premiums that emerge from the composite approach are the most realistic for the immediate future, but country risk premiums may decline over time. Just as companies mature and become less risky over time, countries can mature and become less risky as well.

IN PRACTICE: SHOULD THERE BE A COUNTRY RISK PREMIUM?

Is there more risk in investing in a Malaysian or Brazilian stock than there is in investing in the United States? The answer, to most, seems to be obviously affirmative. That, however, does not answer the question of whether there should be an additional risk premium charged when investing in those markets. Note that the only risk relevant for the purpose of estimating a cost of equity is market risk or risk that cannot be diversified away. The key question then becomes whether the risk in an emerging market is diversifiable or nondiversifiable risk. If, in fact, the additional risk of investing in Malaysia or Brazil can be diversified away, then there should be no additional risk premium charged. If it cannot, then it makes sense to think about estimating a country risk premium.

For purposes of analyzing country risk, we look at the marginal investor—the investor most likely to be trading on the equity. If that marginal investor is globally diversified, there is at least the potential for global diversification. If the marginal investor does not have a global portfolio, the likelihood of diversifying away country risk declines substantially. Even if the marginal investor is globally diversified, there is a second test that has to be met for country risk not to matter. All or much of country risk should be country-specific. In other words, there should be low correlation across markets. Only then will the risk be diversifiable in a globally diversified portfolio. If, on the other hand, stock markets across countries move together, country risk has a market risk component, is not diversifiable, and should command a premium. Whether returns across countries are positively correlated is an empirical question. Studies from the 1970s and 1980s suggested that the correlation was low, and this was an impetus for global diversification. Partly because of the success of that sales pitch, and partly because economies around the world have become increasingly intertwined over the past decade or so, more recent studies indicate that the correlation across markets has risen. This is borne out by the speed at which troubles in one market—say, Russia—can spread to a market with which it has little or no obvious relationship—say, Brazil.

So where do we stand? We believe that although the barriers to trading across markets have dropped, investors still have a home bias in their portfolios and that markets remain partially segmented. Globally diversified investors are playing an increasing role in the pricing of equities around the world, but the resulting increase in correlation across markets has resulted in a portion of country risk becoming nondiversifiable or market risk. Consequently, we should augment the cost of equity to reflect at least that portion of the country risk that is nondiversifiable. ■

 ctryprem.xls: There is a data set online that contains the updated ratings for countries and the risk premiums associated with each.

3. Implied Equity Premiums

There is an alternative to estimating risk premiums that does not require historical data or adjustments for country risk but does assume that the overall stock market is correctly priced. Consider, for instance, a very simple valuation model for stocks:

$$\text{Value} = \frac{\text{Expected dividends next period}}{(\text{Required return on equity} - \text{Expected growth rate in dividends})}$$

This is essentially the present value of dividends growing at a constant rate. Three of the four variables in this model can be obtained easily—the current level of the market (i.e., value), the expected dividends next period, and the expected growth rate in earnings and dividends in the long-term. The only unknown is then the required return on equity; when we solve for it, we get an implied expected return on stocks. Subtracting the risk-free rate will yield an implied equity risk premium.

To illustrate, assume that the current level of the S&P 500 Index is 900, the expected dividend yield on the index for the next period is 2%, and the expected growth rate in earnings and dividends in the long run is 7%. Solving for the required return on equity yields the following:

$$900 = \frac{900(0.02)}{r - 0.07}$$

Solving for r,

$$r - 0.07 = 0.02$$
$$r = 0.09 = 9\%$$

If the current risk-free rate is 6%, this will yield a premium of 3%.

This approach can be generalized to allow for high growth for a period and extended to cover cash flow–based rather than dividend-based models. To illustrate this, consider the S&P 500 Index on January 1, 2009. On December 31, 2008, the S&P 500 Index closed at 903.25, and the dividend yield on the index was roughly 3.12%. In addition, the consensus estimate of growth in earnings for companies in the index was approximately 4% for the next five years.[17] Since the companies in the index have bought back substantial amounts of their own stock over the last few years, we considered buybacks as part of the cash flows to equity investors. Table 4.6 summarizes dividends and stock buybacks on the index, going back to 2001.

In 2008, for instance, firms collectively returned 7.77% of the index in the form of dividends (3.15%) and stock buybacks (4.61%). Buybacks are volatile, and dropped about 40% in the last quarter of 2008, relative to the last quarter of 2007, in the face of a market crisis and a slowing economy. Since this slowdown is likely to continue into 2009, we reduced the buybacks in 2008 by 40% to compute a normalized cash yield of 5.82% for the year (resulting in a total cash to equity of 52.584 for the year). In Table 4.7, we estimate the cash flows to investors in the S&P 500 index from 2009 to 2014 by growing the normalized cash flow at 4% a year for the first five years and 2.21% (set equal to the risk-free rate) thereafter.

Table 4.6 DIVIDENDS AND STOCK BUYBACKS ON S&P 500 INDEX: 2001–2008

	Market Value of Index	Dividends	Buybacks	Cash to Equity	Dividend Yield	Buyback Yield	Total Yield
2001	1148.09	15.74	14.34	30.08	1.37%	1.25%	2.62%
2002	879.82	15.96	13.87	29.83	1.81%	1.58%	3.39%
2003	1111.91	17.88	13.70	31.58	1.61%	1.23%	2.84%
2004	1211.92	19.01	21.59	40.60	1.57%	1.78%	3.35%
2005	1248.29	22.34	38.82	61.17	1.79%	3.11%	4.90%
2006	1418.30	25.04	48.12	73.16	1.77%	3.39%	5.16%
2007	1468.36	28.14	67.22	95.36	1.92%	4.58%	6.49%
2008	903.25	28.47	40.25	68.72	3.15%	4.61%	7.77%
Normalized	903.25	28.47	24.11	52.584	3.15%	2.67%	5.82%

---

[17]We used the average of the analyst estimates for individual firms (bottom-up). Alternatively, we could have used the top-down estimate for the S&P 500 earnings.

Table 4.7 CASH FLOWS ON S&P 500 INDEX

	Expected Growth Rate	Dividends + Buybacks on Index
2008		52.584
2009	4.00%	54.69
2010	4.00%	56.87
2011	4.00%	59.15
2012	4.00%	61.52
2013	4.00%	63.98
2014	2.21%	65.39

Using these cash flows to compute the expected return on stocks, we derive the following:

$$903.25 = \frac{54.69}{(1+r)} + \frac{56.87}{(1+r)^2} + \frac{59.15}{(1+r)^3} + \frac{61.52}{(1+r)^4} + \frac{63.98}{(1+r)^5} + \frac{65.39}{(r-.0221)(1+r)^5}$$

Solving for the required return and the implied premium with the higher cash flows:

Required return on equity = 8.64%
Implied equity risk premium = Required return on equity − Risk-free rate
= 8.64% − 2.21% = 6.43%

We believe that this estimate of risk premium (6.43%) is a more realistic value for January 1, 2009, than the historical risk premium of 3.88%. The advantage of this approach is that it is market-driven and forward-looking and does not require any historical data. In addition, it will change in response to changes in market conditions. Note that the S&P 500 a year prior was trading at 1468.36, and the implied equity risk premium on January 1, 2008 was 4.37%. The unusual shift is best seen by graphing implied premiums from the S&P 500 from 1960 in Figure 4.2.

In terms of mechanics, we used analyst estimates of growth rates in earnings and dividends as our projected growth rates and a two-stage dividend discount model (similar to the one that we used to compute the implied premium in the last paragraph). Looking at these numbers, we would draw the following conclusions.

- *Implied versus Historical Risk Premiums*   For much of the last thirty years, the implied equity premium has been lower than the historical risk premium, reflecting the long-term upward movement in stock prices between 1981 and 2007. At the peak of dot-com boom at the end of 1999, the implied equity risk premium was 2% while the historical risk premium was about 6.5%. It was only in the last quarter of 2008 that implied premiums surged well above historical risk premiums.

- *Effects of inflation*   The implied equity premium did increase during the 1970s as inflation increased. This does have interesting implications for risk premium estimation. Instead of assuming that the risk premium is a constant and is unaffected by the level of inflation and interest rates, as we do with historical risk premiums, it may be more realistic to increase the risk premium as expected inflation and interest rates increase.

Figure 4.2   Implied Equity Premium for U.S. Equity Market: 1960–2008

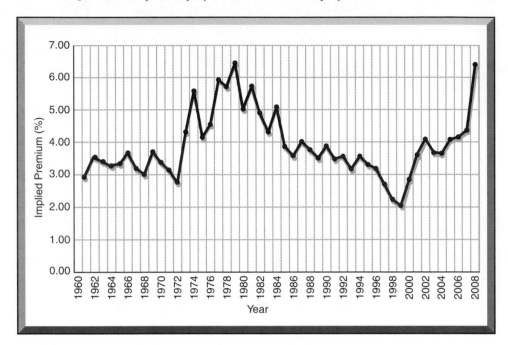

- ***Mean reversion***   While implied equity risk premiums have moved significantly over time, with a low of 2% in 1999 and a high of 6.43% at the end of 2008, there is evidence that they revert back to a historic norm of between 4% and 4.5%. That reversal, however, occurs over long time periods.

 histimpl.xls: This data set online shows the inputs used to calculate the premium in each year for the U.S. market.

 implprem.xls: This spreadsheet allows you to estimate the implied equity premium in a market.

Choosing an Equity Risk Premium   We have looked at three different approaches to estimating risk premiums: (1) the survey approach, where the answer seems to depend on who you ask and what you ask them, (2) the historical premium approach, with wildly different results depending on how you slice and dice historical data, and (3) the implied premium approach, for which the final number is a function of the model you use and the assumptions you make about the future. There are several reasons why the approaches yield different answers much of the time and why they converge sometimes.

1.   When stock prices enter an extended phase of upward (downward) movement, the historical risk premium will climb (drop) to reflect past returns. Implied premiums will tend to move in the opposite direction, since higher (lower) stock prices generally translate into lower (higher) premiums.

2. Survey premiums reflect historical data more than expectations. When stocks are going up, investors tend to become more optimistic about future returns and survey premiums reflect this optimism. In fact, the evidence that human beings overweight recent history (when making judgments) and overreact to information can lead to survey premiums overshooting historical premiums in both good and bad times. In good times, survey premiums are even higher than historical premiums, which, in turn, are higher than implied premiums; in bad times, the reverse occurs.

3. When the fundamentals of a market change, either because the economy becomes more volatile or because investors get more risk averse, historical risk premiums will not change, but implied premiums will. Shocks to the market are likely to cause the two numbers to deviate. After the terrorist attack of September 11, 2001, for instance, implied equity risk premiums jumped almost 0.50%, but historical premiums were unchanged.

In summary, we should not be surprised to see large differences in equity risk premiums as we move from one approach to another, and even within an approach, as we change estimation parameters.

If the approaches yield different numbers for the equity risk premium, and we have to choose one of these numbers, how do we decide which one is the "best" estimate? The answer to this question will depend upon several factors:

- *Predictive power* In corporate finance and valuation, what we ultimately care about is the equity risk premium for the future. Consequently, the approach that has the best predictive power (i.e. yields forecasts of the risk premium that are closer to realized premiums) should be given more weight. So, which of the approaches does best on this count? To answer this question, we used the implied equity risk premiums from 1960 to 2007 and considered three predictors of this premium: the historical risk premium through the end of the prior year, the implied equity risk premium at the end of the prior year, and the average implied equity risk premium over the previous five years. Since the survey data does not go back very far, we could not test the efficacy of the survey premium. Our results are summarized in Table 4.8.

  Over this period, the implied equity risk premium at the end of the prior period was the best predictor of the implied equity risk premium in the next period, whereas historical risk premiums did worst. The results, though, may be specific to one-year ahead forecasts and are skewed toward the implied premium forecasts. If we extend

Table 4.8   PREDICTIVE POWER OF DIFFERENT ESTIMATES

	Correlation with Implied Premium Next Year	Correlation with Actual Risk Premium Next Ten Years
Current implied premium	0.758	0.376
Average implied premium last five years	0.515	0.183
Historical premium	−0.288	−0.596

our analysis to make forecasts of the actual return premium earned by stocks over bonds for the next ten years, the current implied equity risk premium still yields the best forecast for the future. Historical risk premiums perform even worse as forecasts of actual risk premiums over the next ten years.

- **Beliefs about markets**   Implicit in the use of each approach are assumptions about market efficiency or lack thereof. If you believe that markets are efficient in the aggregate, or at least that you cannot forecast the direction of overall market movements, the current implied equity premium is the most logical choice, since it is estimated from the current level of the index. If you believe that markets, in the aggregate, can be significantly overvalued or undervalued, the historical risk premium or the average implied equity risk premium over long periods becomes a better choice. If you have absolutely no faith in markets, survey premiums will be the choice.

- **Purpose of the analysis**   Notwithstanding your beliefs about market efficiency, the task for which you are using equity risk premiums may determine the right risk premium to use. In acquisition valuations and equity research, for instance, you are asked to assess the value of an individual company and not take a view on the level of the overall market. This will require you to use the current implied equity risk premium, since using any other number will bring your market views into the valuation. In corporate finance, where the equity risk premium is used to come up with a cost of capital, which in turn determines the long-term investments of the company, it may be more prudent to build in a long-term average (historical or implied) premium.

In conclusion, there is no one approach to estimating equity risk premiums that will work for all analyses. If predictive power is critical or if market neutrality is a prerequisite, the current implied equity risk premium is the best choice. For those more skeptical about markets, the choices are broader, with the average implied equity risk premium over a long time period having the strongest predictive power. Historical risk premiums are very poor predictors of both short-term movements in implied premiums and long-term returns on stocks.

4.4   IMPLIED AND HISTORICAL PREMIUMS

Assume that the implied premium in the market is 3% and that you are using a historical premium of 7.5%. If you valued stocks using this historical premium, you are likely to find

a.   More undervalued stocks than overvalued ones

b.   More overvalued stocks than undervalued ones

c.   About as many undervalued as overvalued stocks

How would your answer change if the implied premium is 7% and the historical premium is 3%?

ILLUSTRATION 4.2   Estimating Equity Risk Premiums

In May 2009, the implied equity risk premium for the S&P 500 stood at 6.5%, well above the historical risk premium of 3.88%, computed from 1928 to 2008. Using the latter will generate hurdle rates that will be too low, given current market conditions. While we are mindful of the tendency of equity risk premiums to revert back to historic norms, we believe that memories of this crisis will linger for an extended period. Consequently, we will use an equity risk premium of 6% not only for the United States but also for other mature markets; for simplicity, we will assume that all countries with sovereign ratings of Aaa are mature. As a consequence, we will use the 6% equity risk premium for much of the European Union, the Scandinavian countries, Canada, and Australia.

For countries rated below Aaa, we will use the composite country risk premium approach, described in the earlier section. The country risk premium that we estimated using this approach was 3.95% for Brazil and 4.51% for India. Adding these premiums to the mature market premium of 6% yields the total risk premiums for the two countries:

$$\text{Total equity risk premium}_{\text{Brazil}} = 6\% + 3.95\% = 9.95\%$$
$$\text{Total equity risk premium}_{\text{India}} = 6\% + 4.51\% = 10.51\%$$

We will use this approach for computing equity risk premiums for any other risky markets that we encounter during the course of the book.

 Normal and Actual Values: A Behavioral Perspective
Risk-free rates and equity risk premiums vary over time, and managers often are confronted with numbers that they believe are "not normal." This was the case in early 2009, when managers saw the U.S. ten-year treasury bond rate at 2.2% and equity risk premiums at close to 7%. Faced with these unusual numbers, many analysts and corporate treasurers decided to override them and go with what they believed were more normal values.

While this push toward normalization has an empirical basis, there is also a behavioral spin that we can put on it. As we noted in Chapter 3, there is significant evidence that individuals anchor their estimates to arbitrary starting values. In the case of CFOs, those starting values may very well be the risk-free rates and equity risk premiums that they have become familiar with over their working lifetime, leading to very different definitions of what comprises normal. In addition, firms that have been using the same equity risk premiums for long periods find it hard to abandon these estimates, even in the face of substantial evidence to the contrary.

III. Risk Parameters
The final set of inputs we need to put risk and return models into practice are the risk parameters for individual assets and projects. In the CAPM, the beta of the asset has to be estimated relative to the market portfolio. In the APM and multifactor model, the betas of the asset relative to each factor have to be measured. There are three approaches available for estimating these parameters: (1) use historical data on market prices for individual assets, (2) estimate the betas from fundamentals, and (3) use accounting data. We use all three approaches in this section.

A. Historical Market Betas
This is the conventional approach for estimating betas used by most services and analysts. For firms that have been publicly traded for a length of time, it is relatively straightforward to estimate returns that an investor would have made investing in its

equity in intervals (such as a week or a month) over that period. These returns can then be related to returns on a equity market index to get a beta in the CAPM or to multiple macroeconomic factors to get betas in the multifactor models or can be put through a factor analysis to yield betas for the APM.

Standard Procedures for Estimating CAPM Parameters, Betas, and Alphas
To set up the standard process for estimating the beta in the CAPM, let us revisit the equation it provides for the expected return on an investment (R_j) as a function of the beta of the investment (β_j) risk-free rate (R_f) and the expected return on the market portfolio (R_m):

$$R_j = R_f + \beta_j (R_m - R_f)$$

This equation can be rewritten in one of two ways:

In terms of excess returns: $R_j - R_f = \beta_j (R_m - R_f)$
In terms of raw returns: $R_j = R_f(1 - \beta_j) + \beta_j R_m$

These equations provide the templates for the two standard procedures for estimating the beta of an investment, using past returns. In the first, we compute the returns earned by an investment and a specified market index over past time periods, in excess of the risk-free rates in each of the time periods, and regress the excess returns on the investment against the excess returns on the market:

$$(R_j - R_f) = \alpha + \beta_j (R_m - R_f)$$

In the second, we compute the raw returns (not adjusted for the risk-free rate) earned by an investment and the market index over past time period and regress the raw returns on the investment against the raw returns on the market:

$$R_j = \alpha + \beta_j R_m$$

In both regressions, the slope of the regression measures the beta of the stock and measures the riskiness of the stock. The intercept is a simple measure of stock price performance, relative to CAPM expectations, in each regression, but with slightly different interpretations. In the excess return regression, the intercept should be 0 if the stock did exactly as predicted by the CAPM; a positive (or negative) intercept can be viewed as a measure that the stock did better (or worse) than expected, at least during the period of the regression. In the raw return regression, the intercept has to be compared to the predicted intercept, $R_f(1 - \beta_j)$, in the CAPM equation:

If $\alpha > R_f(1 - \beta)$ then stock did better than expected during regression period
    $\alpha = R_f(1 - \beta)$ then stock did as well as expected during regression period
    $\alpha < R_f(1 - \beta)$ then stock did worse than expected during regression period

This measure of stock price performance (α in excess return regression, and $\alpha - R_f (1 - \beta)$ in the raw return regression) is called *Jensen's alpha* and provides a measure of whether the asset in question under- or outperformed the market, after adjusting for risk, during the period of the regression.

The third statistic that emerges from the regression is the *R squared* (R^2) of the regression. Although the statistical explanation of the R^2 is that it provides a measure of the goodness of fit of the regression, the financial rationale for the R^2 is that it provides an estimate of the proportion of the risk (variance) of a firm that can be attributed to market risk; the balance $(1 - R^2)$ can then be attributed to firm-specific risk.

The final statistic worth noting is the *standard error of the beta estimate*. The slope of the regression, like any statistical estimate, is estimated with error, and the standard error reveals just how noisy the estimate is. The standard error can also be used to arrive at confidence intervals for the "true" beta value from the slope estimate.

The two approaches should yield very similar estimates for all of the variables, but the excess return approach is slightly more precise, because it allows for the variation in risk-free rates from period to period. The raw return approach is easier to put into practice, precisely because we need only the average risk-free rate over the regression period.[18]

Estimation Issues
There are three decisions the analyst must make in setting up the regression described. The first concerns the *length of the estimation period*. The tradeoff is simple: A longer estimation period provides more data, but the firm itself might have changed in its risk characteristics over the time period. Disney and Deutsche Bank have changed substantially in terms of both business mix and financial leverage over the past few years, and any regression that we run using historical data will be affected by these changes.

The second estimation issue relates to the *return interval*. Returns on stocks are available on annual, monthly, weekly, daily, and even intraday bases. Using daily or intraday returns will increase the number of observations in the regression, but it exposes the estimation process to a significant bias in beta estimates related to nontrading.[19] For instance, the betas estimated for small firms, which are more likely to suffer from nontrading, are biased downward when daily returns are used. Using weekly or monthly returns can reduce the nontrading bias significantly.[20]

The third estimation issue relates to the choice of a *market index* to be used in the regression. Since we are estimating the betas for the capital asset pricing model, the index that we are using, at least in theory, should be the market portfolio, which includes all traded assets in the market, held in proportion to their market values. While such a market portfolio may not exist in practice, the closer the chosen index comes to this ideal, the more meaningful the beta estimate should be. Thus, we should steer away from narrow indices (Dow 30, Sector indices or the NASDAQ) toward broader indices, and away from equally weighted indices toward value weighted indices. It should be no surprise that the most widely used market index by beta estimation services in the United States is the S&P 500. It may include only 500 stocks, but since they represent the largest market capitalization companies in the market, held in proportion to their market value, it does represent a significant portion of the market portfolio (but only if

---

[18]With weekly or daily return regressions, the risk-free rate (weekly or daily) is close to 0. Consequently, many services estimate betas using raw returns rather than excess returns.
[19]The nontrading bias arises because the returns in nontrading periods is zero (even though the market may have moved up or down significantly in those periods). Using these nontrading period returns in the regression will reduce the correlation between stock returns and market returns and the beta of the stock.
[20]The bias can also be reduced using statistical techniques.

we define it narrowly as U.S. equities). As asset classes proliferate and global markets expand, we have to consider how best to broaden the index we use to reflect these excluded risky assets.

ILLUSTRATION 4.3 Estimating CAPM Risk Parameters for Disney

To evaluate how Disney performed as an investment between 2004 and 2008 and how risky it is, we regressed monthly raw returns on Disney against returns on the S&P 500 between January 2004 and December 2008. The returns on Disney and the S&P 500 index are computed as follows:

- The returns to a stockholder in Disney are computed month by month from January 2004 to December 2008. These returns include both dividends and price appreciation and are defined as follows:

$$\text{Return}_{\text{Disney},j} = (\text{Price}_{\text{Disney},j} - \text{Price}_{\text{Disney},j-1} + \text{Dividends}_{\text{Disney},j})/\text{Price}_{\text{Disney},j-1}$$

  where $\text{Price}_{\text{Disney},j}$ is the price of Disney stock at the end of month j and $\text{Dividends}_{\text{Disney},j}$ are dividends on Disney stock in month j. Note that Disney pays dividends only once a year and that dividends are added to the returns of the month in which the stock went ex-dividend.[21]

- The returns on the S&P 500 are computed for each month of the same time period, using the level of the index at the end of each month, and the monthly dividend yield on stocks in the index.

$$\text{Market return}_{\text{S\&P 500},j} = (\text{Index}_j - \text{Index}_{j-1} + \text{Dividends}_j)/\text{Index}_{j-1}$$

  where Index_j is the level of the index at the end of month j and Dividend_j is the dividends paid on stocks in the index in month j. Although the S&P 500 is the most widely used index for U.S. stocks, they are at best imperfect proxies for the market portfolio in the CAPM, which is supposed to include all traded assets.

  Figure 4.3 graphs monthly returns on Disney against returns on the S&P 500 index from January 2004 to December 2008.

  The regression statistics for Disney are as follows:[22]

- *Slope of the Regression = 0.95.* This is Disney's beta, based on returns from 2004 to 2008. Using a different time period for the regression or different return intervals (weekly or daily) for the same period can result in a different beta.

- *Intercept of the Regression = 0.47%.* This is a measure of Disney's performance, but only when it is compared with $R_f (1 - \beta)$.[23] Since we are looking at an investment made in the past, the monthly risk-free rate (because the returns used in the

---

[21] The ex-dividend day is the day by which the stock has to be bought for an investor to be entitled to the dividends on the stock.

[22] The regression statistics are computed in the conventional way. Appendix 1 explains the process in more detail.

[23] In practice, the intercept of the regression is often called the alpha and compared to 0. Thus a positive intercept is viewed as a sign that the stock did better than expected and a negative intercept as a sign that the stock did worse than expected. As noted earlier, this can be done only if the regression is run in terms of excess returns, that is, returns over and above the risk-free rate in each month for both the stock and the market index.

Figure 4.3   Disney versus S&P 500: 2004–2008

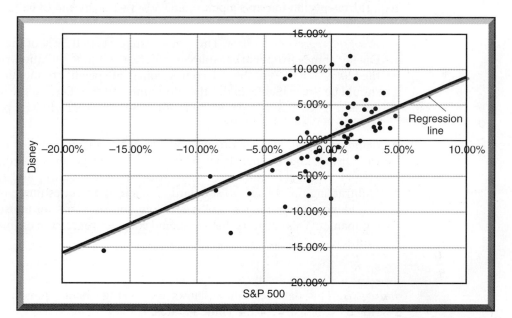

regression are monthly returns) between 2004 and 2008 averaged 0.272%, resulting in the following estimate for the performance:

$$R_f(1 - \beta) = 0.272\% (1 - 0.95) = 0.01\%$$
$$\text{Intercept} - R_f(1 - \beta) = 0.47\% - 0.01\% = 0.46\%$$

This analysis suggests that Disney's stock performed 0.46% better than expected, when expectations are based on the CAPM, on a monthly basis between January 2004 and December 2008. This results in an annualized excess return of approximately 5.62%.

$$\text{Annualized excess return} = (1 + \text{Monthly excess return})^{12} - 1$$
$$= (1 + 0.0046)^{12} - 1 = 0.0562 \text{ or } 5.62\%$$

By this measure of performance, Disney did better than expected during the period of the regression, given its beta and the market's performance over the period.

Note, however, that this does not imply that Disney would be a good investment looking forward. It also does not provide a breakdown of how much of this excess return can be attributed to industry-wide effects and how much is specific to the firm. To make that breakdown, the excess returns would have to be computed over the same period for other firms in the entertainment industry and compared with Disney's excess return. The difference would be then attributable to firm-specific actions. In this case, for instance, the average annualized excess return on other entertainment firms between 2004 and 2008 was −13.04%. This would imply that Disney stock outperformed its peer group by 18.66% between 2004 and 2008, after adjusting for risk. (Firm-specific Jensen's alpha = 5.62% − (−13.04%) = 18.66%)

- *R^2 of the regression = 39%*. This statistic suggests that 39% of the risk (variance) in Disney comes from market sources (interest rate risk, inflation risk, etc.) and that the balance of 61% of the risk comes from firm-specific components. The latter risk should be diversifiable, and is therefore unrewarded. Disney's R^2 is higher than the median R^2 of U.S. companies against the S&P 500, which was approximately 24% in 2008.
- *Standard Error of Beta Estimate = 0.15*. This statistic implies that the true beta for Disney could range from 0.80 to 1.10 (subtracting or adding one standard error to the beta estimate of 0.95) with 67% confidence, and from 0.65 to 1.25 (subtracting or adding two standard errors to the beta estimate of 0.95) with 95% confidence. These ranges may seem large, but they are not unusual for most U.S. companies. This suggests that we should consider regression estimates of betas with caution.

indreg.xls: This data set online shows the average betas, Jensen's alphas, and R^2, classified by industry for the United States.

4.5   THE RELEVANCE OF R^2 TO AN INVESTOR

Assume that having done the regression analysis, both Disney and Amgen (a biotechnology company) have betas of 0.95. Disney, however, has an R^2 of approximately 40%, while Amgen has an R^2 of only 20%. If you had to pick between these investments, which one would you choose?

a.   Disney, because its higher R^2 suggests that it is less risky.

b.   Amgen, because its lower R^2 suggests a greater potential for high returns.

c.   I would be indifferent, because they both have the same beta.

Would your answer be any different if you were running a well-diversified fund?

IN PRACTICE: USING A SERVICE BETA

Most analysts who use betas obtain them from an estimation service; Merrill Lynch, Barra, Value Line, S&P, Morningstar, and Bloomberg are some of the well-known services. All begin with regression betas and make what they feel are necessary changes to make them better estimates for the future. Although most of these services do not reveal the internal details of this estimation, Bloomberg is an honorable exception. The following is the beta calculation page from Bloomberg for Disney, using the same period as our regression (January 2004 to December 2008).

The regression is a raw return, rather than an excess return regression, and should thus be directly comparable to the regression in Figure 4.3. Although the time period used in the two regressions are identical, there are subtle differences. First, Bloomberg uses price appreciation in the stock and the market index in estimating betas and ignores dividends.[24] This does not make much of a difference for a Disney, but it could make a difference for a company that either pays no dividends or pays significantly higher dividends than the market. Second, Bloomberg also computes what it calls an adjusted beta, which is estimated as follows:

$$\text{Adjusted beta} = \text{Raw beta}\ (0.67) + 1(0.33)$$

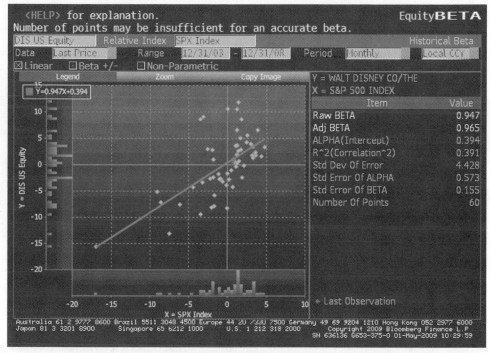

Source: Bloomberg

These weights do not vary across stocks, and this process pushes all estimated betas toward 1. Most services employ similar procedures to adjust betas toward 1. In doing so, they are drawing on empirical evidence that suggests that the betas for most companies over time tend to move toward the average beta, which is 1. This may be explained by the fact that firms get more diversified in their product mix and client base as they get larger.

Generally, betas reported by different services for the same firm can be very different because they use different time periods (some use two years and others five years), different return intervals (daily, weekly, or monthly), different market indices, and different post-regression adjustments. Although these beta differences may be troubling, the beta estimates delivered by each of these services comes with a standard error, and it is very likely that all of the betas reported for a firm fall within the range of the standard errors from the regressions. ■

---

[24]This is why the intercept in the Bloomberg graph (0.39%) is slightly different from the intercept estimated earlier in the chapter (0.47%). The beta and R^2 are identical.

ILLUSTRATION 4.4   **Estimating Historical Betas for Aracruz, Tata Chemicals, and Deutsche Bank**

Aracruz is a Brazilian company, and we can regress returns on the stock against a Brazilian index, the Bovespa, to obtain risk parameters. The stock also had an ADR listed on the U.S. exchanges, and we can regress returns on the ADR against a U.S. index to obtain parameters. Figure 4.4 presents both graphs for the January 2004–December 2008 time period.

Figure 4.4   Estimating Aracruz's Beta: Choice of Indices

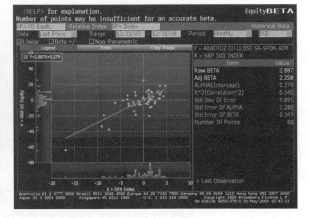

Source: Bloomberg

How different are the risk parameters that emerge from the two regressions? Aracruz has a beta of 2.89 when the ADR is regressed against the S&P 500, and a beta of only 0.89 when the local listing is regressed against the Bovespa.[25] Each regression has its own problems. The Bovespa is a narrow index dominated by a few liquid stocks and does not represent the broad spectrum of Brazilian equities. Although the S&P 500 is a broader index, the returns on the ADR have little relevance to a large number of non-U.S. investors who bought the local listing. While it may seem intuitive that an emerging market stock should have a higher beta to reflect its risk, the results are often unpredictable, with many emerging market ADRs having much lower betas than their domestic listings.

Deutsche Bank does not have an ADR listed in the United States, but we can regress returns against a multitude of indices. Table 4.9 presents comparisons of the results of the regressions of returns on Deutsche Bank against three indices—a German equity index (DAX), an index of large European companies (FTSE Euro 300), and a global equity index (Morgan Stanley Capital Index—MSCI).

---

[25]The returns in this regression are in the local currency for both the stock and the market.

Table 4.9   DEUTSCHE BANK RISK PARAMETERS: INDEX EFFECT

	DAX	FTSE euro 300	MSCI
Intercept	−1.63%	−1.05%	−0.48%
Beta	1.40	1.52	1.99
Standard error of beta	0.14	0.19	0.21
R^2	62%	54%	50%

Here again, the risk parameters estimated for Deutsche Bank are a function of the index used in the regression. The standard error is lowest (and the R^2 is highest) for the regression against the DAX; this is not surprising, because Deutsche Bank is a large component of the DAX. The standard error gets larger and the R^2 gets lower as the index is broadened to initially include other European stocks and then expanded to global stocks.

For Tata Chemicals, we regressed returns on the stock against returns on the Sensex, the most widely referenced Indian market index, using monthly returns from January 2004 to December 2008. Figure 4.5 contains the regression output.

As with the regression of Deutsche Bank against the DAX, the high R^2 is more indicative of the narrowness of the index rather than the quality of the regression.

Figure 4.5   Regression Output: Tata Chemicals versus Sensex

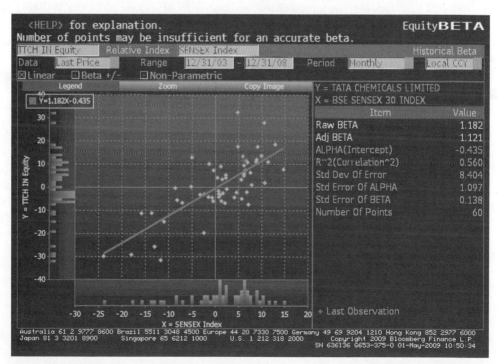

Source: Bloomberg

Table 4.10   JENSEN'S ALPHA, BETA AND R^2

	Beta (Std error)	Jensen's Alpha (Annualized)	R^2
Aracruz ADR	2.89 (0.35)	9.97%	55%
Aracruz	0.89 (0.16)	−15.51%	35%
Deutsche Bank	1.40 (0.14)	−16.89%	62%
Tata Chemicals	1.18 (0.14)	−4.29%	56%

Deconstructing the regression output for each of these companies, just as we did for Disney, does however does provide us with some information on the riskiness and performance of the stocks, at least relative to the indices used. Table 4.10 summarizes the estimates.

All three companies underperformed their domestic indices, after adjusting for risk and market performance. While the Aracruz ADR had a positive Jensen's alpha against the S&P 500, much of that positive performance was dissipated in the last few months of 2008.

IN PRACTICE: WHICH INDEX SHOULD WE USE TO ESTIMATE BETAS?

In most cases, analysts are faced with a mind-boggling array of choices among indices when it comes to estimating betas; there are more than twenty broad equity indices in the United States alone, ranging from the Dow 30 to the Wilshire 5000. One common practice is to use the index that is most appropriate for the investor who is looking at the stock. Thus, if the analysis is being done for a U.S. investor, the S&P 500 is used. This is generally not appropriate. By this rationale, an investor who owns only two stocks should use an index composed of only those stocks to estimate betas.

The right index to use in analysis should be determined by the holdings of the marginal investor in the company being analyzed. Consider Aracruz, Tata Chemicals, and Deutsche Bank in the earlier illustration. If the marginal investors in these companies are investors who hold only domestic stocks—only Brazilian stocks in the case of Aracruz, only Indian stocks in the case of Tata, or only German stocks in the case of Deutsche—we can use the regressions against the local indices. If the marginal investors are global investors, a more relevant measure of risk will emerge by using the global index. Over time, you would expect global investors to displace local investors as the marginal investors, because they will perceive far less of the risk as market risk and thus pay a higher price for the same security. Thus, one of the ironies of this notion of risk is that Aracruz will be less risky to an overseas investor who has a global portfolio than to a Brazilian investor with all of his or her wealth in Brazilian assets. ∎

Standard Procedures for Estimating Risk Parameters in the APM and Multifactor Model

Like the CAPM, the APM defines risk to be nondiversifiable risk, but unlike the CAPM, the APM allows for multiple economic factors in measuring this risk. Although the process of estimation of risk parameters is different for the APM, many of the issues raised relating to the determinants of risk in the CAPM continue to have relevance for the APM.

The parameters of the APM are estimated from a factor analysis on historical stock returns, which yields the number of common economic factors determining these returns, the risk premium for each factor, and the factor-specific betas for each firm.

Once the factor-specific betas are estimated for each firm and the factor premiums are measured, the APM can be used to estimate the expected returns on a stock.

$$\text{Cost of Equity} = R_f + \sum_{j=1}^{j=k} \beta_j (E(R_j) - R_f)$$

where

$$R_f = \text{Risk-free rate}$$
$$\beta_j = \text{Beta specific to factor } j$$
$$E(R_j) - R_f = \text{Risk premium per unit of factor } j \text{ risk}$$
$$k = \text{Number of factors}$$

In a multifactor model, the betas are estimated relative to the specified factors, using historical data for each firm.

B. Fundamental Betas

The beta for a firm may be estimated from a regression, but it is determined by fundamental decisions that the firm has made on what business to be in, how much operating leverage to use in the business, and the degree to which the firm uses financial leverage. In this section, we will examine an alternative way of estimating betas by which we are less reliant on historical betas and more cognizant of the intuitive underpinnings of betas.

Determinants of Betas

The beta of a firm is determined by three variables: (1) the type of business or businesses the firm is in, (2) the degree of operating leverage in the firm, and (3) the firm's financial leverage. Much of the discussion in this section will be couched in terms of CAPM betas, but the same analysis can be applied to the betas estimated in the APM and the multifactor model as well.

Type of Business

Because betas measure the risk of a firm relative to a market index, the more sensitive a business is to market conditions, the higher its beta. Thus, other things remaining equal, cyclical firms can be expected to have higher betas than noncyclical firms. Other things remaining equal, then, companies involved in housing and automobiles, two sectors of the economy that are very sensitive to economic conditions, will have higher betas than companies involved in food processing and tobacco, which are relatively insensitive to business cycles.

Building on this point, we would also argue that the degree to which a product's purchase is discretionary will affect the beta of the firm manufacturing the product. Thus, the betas of discount retailers, such as Wal-Mart, should be lower than the betas of high-end specialty retailers, such as Tiffany's or Gucci, because consumers can defer the purchase of the latters' products during bad economic times.

It is true that firms have only limited control over how discretionary a product or service is to their customers. There are firms, however, that have used this limited control to maximum effect to make their products less discretionary to buyers and by extension lowered their business risk. One approach is to make the product or service a much more integral and necessary part of everyday life, thus making its purchase more of a requirement. A second approach is to effectively use advertising and marketing to build brand loyalty. The objective in good advertising, as we see it, is to make discretionary products or services seem like necessities to the target audience. Thus corporate strategy, advertising, and marketing acumen can, at the margin, alter business risk and betas over time.

4.6   BETAS AND BUSINESS RISK

Polo Ralph Lauren, the upscale fashion designer, went public in 1997. Assume that you were asked to estimate its beta. Based on what you know about the firm's products, would you expect the beta to be?

a.   Greater than 1

b.   About 1

c.   Less than 1

Why?

Degree of Operating Leverage

The degree of operating leverage is a function of the cost structure of a firm and is usually defined in terms of the relationship between fixed costs and total costs. A firm that has high operating leverage (i.e., high fixed costs relative to total costs) will also have higher variability in operating income than would a firm producing a similar product with low operating leverage.[26] Other things remaining equal, the higher variance in operating income will lead to a higher beta for the firm with high operating leverage.

Although operating leverage affects betas, it is difficult to measure the operating leverage of a firm, at least from the outside, because fixed and variable costs are often aggregated in income statements. It is possible to get an approximate measure of the operating leverage of a firm by looking at changes in operating income as a function of changes in sales.

Degree of operating leverage = % change in operating profit/% change in sales

For firms with high operating leverage, operating income should change more than proportionately when sales change, increasing when sales increase and decreasing when sales decline.

---

[26]To see why, compare two firms with revenues of $100 million and operating income of $10 million, but assume that the first firm's costs are all fixed, whereas only half of the second firm's costs are fixed. If revenues increase at both firms by $10 million, the first firm will report a doubling of operating income (from $10 million to $20 million), whereas the second firm will report a rise of 55% in its operating income (because costs will rise by $4.5 million, 45% of the revenue increment).

Can firms change their operating leverage? Although some of a firm's cost structure is determined by the business it is in (an energy utility has to build costly power plants, and airlines have to lease expensive planes), firms in the United States have become increasingly inventive in lowering the fixed cost component in their total costs. Labor contracts that emphasize flexibility and allow the firm to make its labor costs more sensitive to its financial success, joint venture agreements in which fixed costs are borne by someone else, and subcontracting of manufacturing, which reduces the need for expensive plant and equipment, are only some of the manifestations of this phenomenon. The arguments for such actions may be couched in terms of competitive advantages and cost flexibility, but they do reduce the operating leverage of the firm and its exposure to market risk.

ILLUSTRATION 4.5 Measuring Operating Leverage for Disney

In Table 4.11, we estimate the degree of operating leverage for Disney from 1987 to 2008 using earnings before interest and taxes (EBIT) as the measure of operating income.

The degree of operating leverage changes dramatically from year to year, because of year-to-year swings in operating income. Using the average changes in sales and

Table 4.11 DEGREE OF OPERATING LEVERAGE — DISNEY

Year	Net Sales	% Change in Sales	EBIT	% Change in EBIT
1987	$2,877		$756	
1988	$3,438	19.50%	$848	12.17%
1989	$4,594	33.62%	$1,177	38.80%
1990	$5,844	27.21%	$1,368	16.23%
1991	$6,182	5.78%	$1,124	−17.84%
1992	$7,504	21.38%	$1,287	14.50%
1993	$8,529	13.66%	$1,560	21.21%
1994	$10,055	17.89%	$1,804	15.64%
1995	$12,112	20.46%	$2,262	25.39%
1996	$18,739	54.71%	$3,024	33.69%
1997	$22,473	19.93%	$3,945	30.46%
1998	$22,976	2.24%	$3,843	−2.59%
1999	$23,435	2.00%	$3,580	−6.84%
2000	$25,418	8.46%	$2,525	−29.47%
2001	$25,172	−0.97%	$2,832	12.16%
2002	$25,329	0.62%	$2,384	−15.82%
2003	$27,061	6.84%	$2,713	13.80%
2004	$30,752	13.64%	$4,048	49.21%
2005	$31,944	3.88%	$4,107	1.46%
2006	$33,747	5.64%	$5,355	30.39%
2007	$35,510	5.22%	$6,829	27.53%
2008	$37,843	6.57%	$7,404	8.42%
Average: 87–08		13.73%		13.26%
Average: 96–08		9.91%		11.72%

Source: Bloomberg

operating income over the period, we can compute the operating leverage at Disney:

$$\text{Operating leverage} = \% \text{ change in EBIT}/\% \text{ change in sales}$$
$$= 13.26\%/13.73\% = 0.97$$

There are two important observations that can be made about Disney over the period, though. First, the operating leverage for Disney is slightly lower than the operating leverage for other entertainment firms, which we computed to be 1.15.[27] This would suggest that Disney has lower fixed costs than its competitors and should therefore have a lower beta. Second, the acquisition of Capital Cities by Disney in 1996 may be affecting the operating leverage. Looking at the numbers since 1996, we get a higher estimate of operating leverage:

$$\text{Operating leverage}_{1996-03} = 11.71\%/9.91\% = 1.18$$

We would not read too much into these numbers because Disney has such a wide range of businesses. We would hypothesize that Disney's theme park business has higher fixed costs (and operating leverage) than its movie division.

4.7   SOCIAL POLICY AND OPERATING LEVERAGE

Assume that you are comparing a European automobile manufacturing firm with a U.S. automobile firm. European firms are generally much more constrained in terms of laying off employees if they get into financial trouble. What implications does this have for betas, if they are estimated relative to a common index?

a.   The European firm will have much a higher beta than the U.S. firm.

b.   The European firm will have a similar beta to the U.S. firm.

c.   The European firm will have a much lower beta than the U.S. firm.

IN PRACTICE: SHOULD SMALL OR HIGH-GROWTH FIRMS HAVE HIGHER BETAS THAN LARGER AND MORE MATURE FIRMS?

Though the answer may seem obvious at first sight—that smaller, higher-growth firms should are riskier than larger firms—it is not an easy question to answer. If the question were posed in terms of total risk, smaller and higher-growth firms will tend to be riskier simply because they have more volatile earnings streams (and their market prices reflect that). When it is framed in terms of betas or market risk, smaller- and higher-growth firms should have higher betas only if the products and services they offer are more discretionary to their customers or if they have higher operating leverage. It is possible that smaller firms operate in niche markets and sell products that customers can delay or defer buying and that the absence of economies of scales lead to higher fixed costs for these firms. These firms should have higher betas than their larger counterparts. It is also possible that neither condition holds for a particular small firm. The answer will therefore depend on both the company in question and the industry in which it operates.

In practice, analysts often add what is called a small firm premium to the cost of equity for smaller firms. This small firm premium is usually estimated from historical

---

[27]To compute this statistic, we looked at the aggregate revenues and operating income of entertainment companies each year from 1987 to 2008.

data and is the difference between the average annual returns on small market cap stocks and the rest of the market—about 3–3.4% when we look at the 1926–2008 period. This practice can be dangerous for three reasons. The first is that the small firm premium has been volatile, and even disappeared for an extended period in the 1980s. The second is that the definition of a small market cap stock varies across time, and that the historical small cap premium is largely attributable to the smallest (among the small cap) stocks. The third is that using a constant small stock premium adjustment removes any incentive that the analyst may have to examine the product characteristics and operating leverage of individual small market cap companies more closely. ∎

Degree of Financial Leverage

Other things remaining equal, an increase in financial leverage will increase the equity beta of a firm. Intuitively, we would expect the fixed interest payments on debt to increase earnings per share in good times and to push it down in bad times.[28] Higher leverage increases the variance in earnings per share and makes equity investment in the firm riskier. If all of the firm's risk is borne by the stockholders (i.e., the beta of debt is zero),[29] and debt creates a tax benefit to the firm, then

$$\beta_L = \beta_u(1 + (1 - t)(D/E))$$

where

$$\beta_L = \text{Levered beta for equity in the firm}$$
$$\beta_u = \text{Unlevered beta of the firm (i.e., the beta of the assets of the firm)}$$
$$t = \text{Marginal tax rate for the firm}$$
$$D/E = \text{Debt/equity ratio (in market value terms)}$$

The marginal tax rate is the tax rate on the last dollar of income earned by the firm and generally will not be equal to the effective or average rates; it is used because interest expenses save taxes on the marginal income. Intuitively, we expect that as leverage increases (as measured by the debt-to-equity ratio), equity investors bear increasing amounts of market risk in the firm, leading to higher betas. The tax factor in the equation captures the benefit created by the tax deductibility of interest payments.

The unlevered beta of a firm is determined by the types of the businesses in which it operates and its operating leverage. This unlevered beta is often also referred to as the *asset beta*, because its value is determined by the assets (or businesses) owned by the firm. Thus, the equity (or levered) beta of a company is determined both by the riskiness of the business it operates in as well as the amount of financial leverage risk it has taken on. Because financial leverage multiplies the underlying business risk, it stands to reason that firms that have high business risk should be reluctant to take on financial leverage. It also stands to reason that firms operating in relatively stable businesses should be much more willing to take on financial leverage. Utilities, for

---

[28] Interest expenses always lower net income, but the fact that the firm uses debt instead of equity implies that the number of shares will also be lower. Thus, the benefit of debt shows up in earnings per share.

[29] If we ignore the tax effects, we can compute the levered beta as $\beta_L = \beta_u (1 + D/E)$. If debt has market risk (i.e., its beta is greater than 0), the original formula can be modified to take it into account. If the beta of debt is β_D, the beta of equity can be written as $\beta_L = \beta_u (1 + (1 - t)(D/E)) - \beta_D (1 - t)D/E$.

instance, have historically had high debt ratios but not high betas, mostly because their underlying businesses have been stable and fairly predictable.

Breaking risk down into business and financial leverage components also provides some insight into why companies have high betas, because they can end up with high betas in one of two ways—they can operate in a risky business, or they can use very high financial leverage in a relatively stable business.

ILLUSTRATION 4.6   Effects of Financial Leverage on Betas—Disney

From the regression for the period 2004–2008, Disney had a beta of 0.95. To estimate the effects of financial leverage on Disney, we began by estimating the average debt-to-equity ratio between 2004 and 2008 using market values for debt and equity.

Average market debt/Equity ratio between 2004 and 2008 = 24.64%

The unlevered beta is estimated using a marginal corporate tax rate of 38%:[30]

$$\text{Unlevered beta} = \text{Current beta}/(1 + [1 - \text{tax rate}][\text{Average debt/Equity}])$$
$$= 0.95/(1 + [1 - 0.38][0.2464]) = 0.8241$$

The levered beta at different levels of debt can then be estimated:

$$\text{Levered beta} = \text{Unlevered beta} * [1 + (1 - \text{tax rate})(\text{Debt/Equity})]$$

For instance, if Disney were to increase its debt equity ratio to 10%, its equity beta will be

$$\text{Levered beta (@10\% D/E)} = 0.8241 * (1 + (1 - 0.38)(0.10)) = 0.88$$

If the debt equity ratio were raised to 25%, the equity beta would be

$$\text{Levered beta (@25\% D/E)} = 0.8215 * [1 + (1 - 0.38)(0.25)] = 0.95$$

Table 4.12 summarizes the beta estimates for different levels of financial leverage ranging from 0% to 90% debt.

Table 4.12   FINANCIAL LEVERAGE AND BETAS

Debt to Capital	Debt/Equity Ratio	Beta	Effect of Leverage
0.00%	0.00%	0.82	0.00
10.00%	11.11%	0.88	0.06
20.00%	25.00%	0.95	0.13
30.00%	42.86%	1.04	0.22
40.00%	66.67%	1.16	0.34
50.00%	100.00%	1.34	0.51
60.00%	150.00%	1.59	0.77
70.00%	233.33%	2.02	1.19
80.00%	400.00%	2.87	2.04
90.00%	900.00%	5.42	4.60

---

[30]The marginal federal corporate tax rate in the United States in 2008 was 35%. The marginal state and local tax rates, corrected for federal tax savings, is estimated by Disney in its annual report to be an additional 3%. Disney did report some offsetting tax benefits in 2008 that reduced its effective tax rate to 36.1%. We assumed that these offsetting tax benefits were temporary.

As Disney's financial leverage increases, the beta increases concurrently.

 levbeta.xls: This spreadsheet allows you to estimate the unlevered beta for a firm and compute the betas as a function of the leverage of the firm.

 ctrytaxrate.xls: This data set online has marginal tax rates for different countries.

 IN PRACTICE: DUELING TAX RATES

The marginal tax rate, which is the tax rate on marginal income (or the last dollar of income) is a key input not only for the levered beta calculation but also for the after-tax cost of debt, which we will be estimating later in this chapter. Estimating it can be problematic, because firms seldom report it in their financials. Most firms report an effective tax rate on taxable income in their annual reports and filings with the SEC. This rate is computed by dividing the taxes paid by the net taxable income, reported in the financial statement. The effective tax rate can be different from the marginal tax rate for several reasons.

- If it is a small firm and the tax rate is higher for higher income brackets, the average tax rate across all income will be lower than the tax rate on the last dollar of income. For larger firms, where most of the income is at the highest tax bracket, this is less of an issue.

- Publicly traded firms, at least in the United States, often maintain two sets of books, one for tax purposes and one for reporting purposes. They generally use different accounting rules for the two and report lower income to tax authorities and higher income in their annual reports. Because taxes paid are based on the tax books, the effective tax rate will usually be lower than the marginal tax rate.

- Actions that defer or delay the payment of taxes can also cause deviations between marginal and effective tax rates. In the period when taxes are deferred, the effective tax rate will lag the marginal tax rate. In the period when the deferred taxes are paid, the effective tax rate can be much higher than the marginal tax rate.

The best source of the marginal tax is the tax code of the country where the firm earns its operating income. If there are state and local taxes, they should be incorporated into the marginal tax rate as well. For companies in multiple tax locales, the marginal tax rate used should be the average of the different marginal tax rates, weighted by operating income by locale. ∎

Bottom-Up Betas
Breaking down betas into their business, operating leverage, and financial leverage components provides an alternative way of estimating betas such that we do not need past prices on an individual firm or asset to estimate its beta.

To develop this alternative approach, we need to introduce an additional feature that betas possess that proves invaluable. The beta of two assets put together is a weighted average of the individual asset betas, with the weights based on market value. Consequently, the beta for a firm is a weighted average of the betas of all of different businesses it is in. Thus, the bottom-up beta for a firm, asset, or project can be estimated as follows.

- Identify the business or businesses that make up the firm whose beta we are trying to estimate. Most firms provide a breakdown of their revenues and operating income by business in their annual reports and financial filings.

- Estimate the average unlevered betas of other publicly traded firms that are primarily or only in each of these businesses. In making this estimate, we have to consider the following estimation issues:

  - *Comparable firms*   In most businesses, there are at least a few comparable firms, and in some businesses, there can be hundreds. Begin with a narrow definition of comparable firms, and widen it if the number of comparable firms is too small.

  - *Beta estimation*   Once a list of comparable firms has been put together, we need to estimate the betas of each of these firms. Optimally, the beta for each firm will be estimated against a common index. If that proves impractical, we can use betas estimated against different indices.

  - *Unlever first or last*   We can compute an unlevered beta for each firm in the comparable firm list, using the debt-to-equity ratio, and tax rate for that firm, or we can compute the average beta, debt-to-equity ratio, and tax rate for the sector and unlever using the averages. Given the standard errors of the individual regression betas, we would suggest the latter approach.

  - *Averaging approach*   The average beta across the comparable firms can be either a simple average or a weighted average, with the weights based on market capitalization. Statistically, the savings in standard error are larger if a simple averaging process is used.

  - *Adjustment for cash*   Investments in cash and marketable securities have betas close to 0. Consequently, the unlevered beta that we obtain for a business by looking at comparable firms may be affected by the cash holdings of these firms. To obtain an unlevered beta cleansed of cash

$$\text{Unlevered beta corrected for cash} = \frac{\text{Unlevered beta}}{(1 - \text{Cash/Firm value})}$$

  The resulting number is sometimes called a pure play beta, indicating that it measures the risk of only the business and not of any other corporate holdings.

- To calculate the unlevered beta for the firm, we take a weighted average of the unlevered betas, using the proportion of firm value derived from each business as the weights. These firm values will have to be estimated, because divisions of a firm usually do not have market values available.[31] If these values cannot be estimated,

---

[31] The exception is when you have tracking stocks with each division traded separately in financial markets.

we can use operating income or revenues as weights. This weighted average is called the bottom-up unlevered beta. In general, it is good practice to estimate two unlevered betas for a firm: one for just the operating assets of the firm, and one with cash and marketable securities treated as a separate business, with a beta of 0.

- Calculate the current debt-to-equity ratio for the firm, using market values if available. Alternatively, use the target debt-to-equity ratio specified by the management of the firm or industry-typical debt ratios.
- Estimate the levered beta for the equity in the firm (and each of its businesses) using the unlevered beta from Step 3 and the debt-to-equity ratio from Step 4.

Clearly, this process rests on being able to identify the unlevered betas of individual businesses.

There are three advantages associated with using bottom-up betas, and they are significant:

1. We can estimate betas for firms that have no price history, because all we need is an identification of the business or businesses they operate in. In other words, we can estimate bottom-up betas for initial public offerings, private businesses, and divisions of companies.

2. Because the beta for the business is obtained by averaging across a large number of regression betas, it will be more precise than any individual firm's regression beta estimate. The standard error of the average beta estimate will be a function of the number of comparable firms used in Step 2 and can be approximated as follows:

$$\sigma_{\text{Average Beta}} = \frac{\text{Average } \sigma_{\text{Beta}}}{\sqrt{\text{Number of firms}}}$$

where σ_{Beta} is the standard error in individual regression betas and $\sigma_{Average\ Beta}$ is the standard error of the average beta across firms. Thus, the standard error of the average of the betas of 100 firms, each of which has a standard error of 0.25, will be only 0.025 ($0.25/\sqrt{100}$).

3. The bottom-up beta can reflect recent and even forthcoming changes to a firm's business mix and financial leverage, because we can change the mix of businesses and the weight on each business in making the beta estimate.

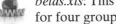

betas.xls: This data set online has updated betas and unlevered betas by business sector for four groupings: the United States, Europe, emerging markets, and Japan.

ILLUSTRATION 4.7   Bottom-Up Beta for Disney

Disney is an entertainment firm with diverse holdings. In addition to its theme parks, it has significant investments in broadcasting and movies. To estimate Disney's beta, we broke its business into four major components:

1. ***Studio entertainment***, which is the production and acquisition of motion pictures for distribution in theatrical, television, and home video markets, as well as TV programming for network and syndication markets. In addition to the television

and movie productions from Disney Studios, this segment also includes Pixar Studios and Miramax Studios, with the former specializing in computer-animated movies and the latter on movies for grown-ups.

2. *Media networks*, which includes the ABC Television and radio networks and reflects the acquisition made in 1995. In addition, Disney has an extensive exposure in the cable market through the Disney channel, A&E, and ESPN, among others.

3. *Park resorts*, which include Walt Disney World (in Orlando, Florida), Disneyland (in Anaheim, California) and the recently opened Hong Kong Disney. It also includes royalty holdings in Tokyo Disneyland and Euro Disney. The hotels at each of these theme parks are considered part of the parks, because they derive their revenue almost exclusively from visitors to these parks.

4. *Consumer products*, which includes a grab bag of businesses, including Disney's retail outlets, its licensing revenues, software, interactive products, and publishing.

This breakdown reflects Disney's reporting in its annual report. In reality, there are a number of smaller businesses that Disney is in that are embedded in these four businesses, including

- *Cruise lines*   Disney operates two ships—*Disney Magic* and *Disney Wonder*—that operate out of Florida and visit Caribbean ports.

- *Internet operations*   Disney made extensive investments in the GO network and other online operations. Much of this investment was written off by 2002, but still represents a potential source of future revenues. In recent years, Disney has ventured again online, and that portion of the business—while small—is growing.

- *Sports franchises*   Disney owns the National Hockey League franchise the Mighty Ducks of Anaheim; in 2002, it sold its stake in the Anaheim Angels, a Major League Baseball team.

Without detailed information on the operations of these businesses, we will assume that they represent too small a portion of Disney's overall revenues to make a significant difference in the risk calculation. For the four businesses for which we have detailed information, we estimated the unlevered beta by looking at comparable firms in each business.[32] Table 4.13 summarizes the comparables used and the unlevered beta for each of the businesses.

To obtain the beta for Disney, we have to estimate the weight that each business is of Disney as a company. The value for each of the divisions was estimated by applying the typical revenue multiple at which comparable firms trade to the revenue reported by Disney for that segment in 2008.[33] The unlevered beta for Disney as a company in 2008 is a value-weighted average of the betas of each of the different business areas. Table 4.14 summarizes this calculation.

---

[32]We used a 40% marginal tax rate for the comparable firms.

[33]We first estimated the enterprise value for each firm by adding the market value of equity to the book value of debt and subtracting cash. We divided the enterprise value by the revenues of each firm to obtain the EV/sales multiple and then used the median value of these estimates. We did not use the averages of these revenue multiples of the individual firms, because a few outliers skewed the results.

Business	**Comparable Firms**	**Number of Firms**	**Median Levered Beta**	**Median D/E**	**Unlevered Beta**	**Cash/ Firm**	**Beta Corrected**
Media Networks	Radio and TV broadcasting companies–US	19	0.83	38.71%	0.6735	4.54%	0.7056
Parks and Resorts	Theme park & Resort companies – Global	26	0.80	65.10%	0.5753	1.64%	0.5849
Studio Entertainment	Movie companies–US	19	1.57	53.89%	1.1864	8.93%	1.3027
Consumer Products	Toy companies–US	12	0.83	27.21%	0.7092	33.66%	1.690

Table 4.13 ESTIMATING UNLEVERED BETAS FOR DISNEY'S BUSINESS AREA

The equity beta can then be calculated using the current financial leverage for Disney as a firm. Combining the market value of equity of $45,193 million with an estimated market value of debt of $16,682 million,[34] we arrive at the levered (equity) beta for Disney's operating assets:

$$\text{Debt/Equity ratio for Disney} = \frac{\$16,682}{\$45,193} = 36.91\%$$

$$\text{Equity beta for Disney's operating assets} = 0.7333(1 + (1 - 0.38)(0.3691)) = 0.9011$$

These are the estimates of unlevered beta and equity beta that we will be using for the rest of the book, when analyzing operating assets.

We can also compute an unlevered beta for all of Disney's assets, including its cash holdings and the resulting equity beta:

$$\beta_{Disney} = \beta_{Operating\ Assets} \frac{Value_{Operating\ Assets}}{(Value_{Operating\ Assets} + Value_{Cash})}$$

$$+ \beta_{Cash} \frac{Value_{Cash}}{(Value_{Operating\ Assets} + Value_{Cash})}$$

$$= 0.7333 \left(\frac{58,525}{(58,525 + 3,795)} \right)$$

$$+ 0 \left(\frac{3,795}{(58,525 + 3,795)} \right) = 0.6885$$

$$\text{Equity beta}_{Disney\ as\ company} = 0.6885(1 + (1 - 0.38)(0.3691)) = 0.8460$$

This beta can be compared to the regression beta of 0.95. While it is lower, it is more precise (because of the averaging) and reflects Disney's current mix of businesses. There will be far less call for us to use these cash-adjusted beta values in analyses.[35]

The flexibility of this approach can be illustrated by looking at the effect of a news story that came out just as this book was going to print. Disney announced its acquisition

---

[34]The details of this calculation will be explored later in this chapter.

[35]The only setting where these betas will be used is if you are valuing the equity in Disney directly and basing your cash flows on net income (which includes the interest income from the cash). If you are computing a cost of capital to value the operating assets of the firm, you should stick with the betas of just the operating assets.

Table 4.14 ESTIMATING DISNEY'S UNLEVERED BETA

	Revenues in 2008	EV/Sales	Estimated Value	Firm Value Proportion	Unlevered Beta
Media networks	$16,116	2.13	$34,328	58.92%	0.7056
Parks and resorts	$11,504	1.51	$17,408	29.88%	0.5849
Studio entertainment	$7,348	0.78	$5,755	9.88%	1.3027
Consumer products	$2,875	0.27	$768	1.32%	1.0690
Disney operations	$37,843		$58,259	100.00%	0.7333

of Marvel for more than $4 billion. If called upon to do so, we could easily incorporate Marvel into the mix of businesses in Table 4.14 and reestimate Disney's beta.

IN PRACTICE: CAN'T FIND COMPARABLE FIRMS?

A problem faced by analysts using the bottom-up approach for some firms is a paucity of comparable firms, either because the company is unique in terms of the product it offers or because the bulk of the firms in the sector are private businesses. Rather than fall back on the regression approach, which is likely to yield a very wide range for the beta, we would suggest one of the following ways to expand the comparable firm sample.

- *Geographic expansion* When analyzing firms from smaller markets, such as Brazil or Greece, the number of comparable firms will be small if we restrict ourselves only to firms in the market. One way to increase sample size is to consider firms in the same business that are listed and traded in other markets—European markets for Greece and Latin American markets for Brazil. With commodity companies that trade in global markets, like paper and oil companies, we can consider a global sample.

- *Production chain* Another way to expand the sample is to look for firms that either provide supplies to the firm that you are analyzing or firms that feed off your firm. For instance, when analyzing book retailers, we can consider book publishers part of the sample, because the fortunes of the two are entwined. It is unlikely that one of these groups can have a good year without the other partaking in the success.

- *Customer specialization* Using the same rationale, the betas of firms that derive the bulk of their revenues from a sector is best estimated using firms in the sector. Thus, the beta of a law firm that derives all of its revenues from investment banks can be estimated by looking at the betas of investment banks. ■

ILLUSTRATION 4.8 **Bottom-Up Beta for Bookscape Books**

We cannot estimate a regression beta for Bookscape Books, the private firm, because it does not have a history of past prices. We can, however, estimate the beta for Bookscape Books using the bottom-up approach. Because we were able to find only three publicly traded book retailers in the United States, we expanded the sample to include book publishers. We list the betas of these firms as well as debt, cash, and equity values in Table 4.15.

Table 4.15   BETAS AND LEVERAGE OF PUBLICLY TRADED BOOK RETAILERS AND PUBLISHERS

	Industry Name	Beta	Debt-to-Equity Ratio	Unlevered Beta	Cash/Firm Value	Unlevered Beta Corrected for Cash
Courier Corp.	Publishing	0.98	12.33%	0.91	0.46%	0.92
Educational Devel.	Publishing	0.57	0.00%	0.57	15.38%	0.67
McGraw-Hill Ryerson Ltd.	Publishing	0.26	0.00%	0.26	46.97%	0.49
Meredith Corp.	Publishing	1.37	66.85%	0.98	3.11%	1.01
Presstek Inc.	Publishing	1.68	41.09%	1.35	10.83%	1.51
PRIMEDIA Inc	Publishing	1.65	340.84%	0.54	9.20%	0.60
Scholastic Corp.	Publishing	1.13	84.49%	0.75	13.36%	0.87
Torstar 'B'	Publishing	0.48	54.21%	0.36	4.93%	0.38
Wiley (John) & Sons	Publishing	1.03	52.73%	0.78	1.93%	0.80
Barnes & Noble	Retail (Special Lines)	1.34	0.00%	1.34	48.46%	2.60
Books-A-Million	Retail (Special Lines)	1.98	97.49%	1.25	7.90%	1.36
Borders Group	Retail (Special Lines)	2.44	240.87%	1.00	7.78%	1.08
Median		**1.235**	**53.47%**	**0.94**	**8.55%**	**1.02**

Although the firms in this sample are very different in terms of market capitalization, the betas are consistent. To estimate the unlevered beta for the sector, we first unlevered the beta for each firm and corrected each unlevered beta for the firm's cash holdings. The median value for the unlevered beta, corrected for cash holdings, is 1.02.[36]

Because the debt-to-equity ratios used in computing levered betas are market debt equity ratios, and the only debt equity ratio we can compute for Bookscape is a book value debt equity ratio, we have assumed that Bookscape is *close to the industry median* debt-to-equity ratio of 53.47%. Using a marginal tax rate of 40% for Bookscape, we get a levered beta of 1.35.

$$\text{Levered beta for Bookscape} = 1.02\,[1 + (1 - 0.40)(0.5347)] = 1.35$$

ILLUSTRATION 4.9   Bottom-Up Beta for Aracruz and Tata Chemicals

The bottom-up beta for Aracruz is difficult to estimate if we remain within its home market (Brazil), for two reasons. First, there are only three publicly traded firms within the market that are in the same line of business as Aracruz (i.e., paper and pulp production). Second, the betas for all Brazilian firms are unreliable because the index used to estimate these betas, the Bovespa, is a narrow one, dominated by a few large companies. There are three groups of comparable firms that we can use as comparable firms in the bottom-up beta estimate:

---

[36] Alternate approaches for estimating the beta yielded similar values, with aggregate values for debt, equity and cash generating an unlevered beta of 1.00 for the sector and simple averages for the beta, debt-to-equity ratio and cash to firm value across the firms provided an estimate of 0.97 for the beta.

1. ***Emerging market paper and pulp companies*** This is a much larger sample of firms. Although the individual firm betas may be skewed by the limitations of the local indices, the errors should average out over the sample.

2. ***U.S. paper and pulp companies*** The advantage gained is not just in terms of the number of firms but also in terms of reliable betas. The peril in this approach is that the risk in U.S. companies can be different from the risk in Brazilian because of regulatory differences.[37]

3. ***Global paper and pulp companies*** This is the largest group and includes a diverse group of companies in both emerging and developed markets. Because betas are measures of relative risk, we argue that barring significant differences in regulation and monopoly power across markets, it is reasonable to compare betas across markets.

The bottom-up betas estimated with each group are summarized in Table 4.16.

The tax rates used were 32% for emerging market companies, 40% for U.S. companies, and 35% for global companies, based on averaging the marginal tax rates in each group. The unlevered beta of emerging market companies is higher than the U.S. and global groupings. Although the average beta for U.S. companies is higher than the rest of the sample, this can be attributed to the higher debt-to-equity ratios of these companies. We will use an emerging market unlevered beta of 1.01 as the beta for the paper and pulp business in which Aracruz is involved.

When computing the levered beta for Aracruz's paper and pulp business, we used the gross debt outstanding of R\$9,805 million and the market value of equity of R\$8,907 million, in conjunction with the marginal tax rate of 34% for Brazil:

$$\text{Gross debt-to-equity ratio} = \text{Debt/Equity} = 9805/8907 = 110.08\%$$
$$\text{Levered beta for Aracruz paper business} = 1.01\,(1 + (1 - 0.34)(1.1008)) = 1.74$$

As with Disney, we can compute a beta for Aracruz as a company, including its cash balance, and estimate an equity beta based upon this computation. At the end of 2008, the firm had a negligible cash holding of R\$20 million, thus making almost no difference to the estimate.

				Table 4.16 BOTTOM-UP BETA—PAPER AND PULP BUSINESS		
Comparable firms	Number of Firms	Median Beta	Median D/E	Median Unlevered Beta	Cash/Value	Unlevered Beta Corrected for Cash
Emerging markets	46	1.03	4.47%	1.00	0.74%	1.01
U.S.	13	1.16	92.29%	0.75	2.87%	0.77
Global	111	0.91	9.82%	0.86	1.24%	0.87

---

[37] As a counterpoint, paper and pulp companies are commodity companies and are governed by the vagaries of the price of paper and pulp. In other words, there is a reasonable argument to be made that paper and pulp companies globally are governed by the same primary risk factors.

Business (# of comparables)	Revenues (millions)	EV/Sales (from comparable firms)	Estimated Value (millions)	Weights	Unlevered Beta	Debt-to-Equity Ratio	Levered Beta
Fertilizers (105)	Rs2,506	1.28	Rs3,208	62.18%	0.72	51.56%	0.965
Chemicals (31)	Rs1,586	1.23	Rs1,951	37.82%	0.68	51.56%	0.911
Tata Chemicals			Rs5,158		0.70	51.56%	0.945

TABLE 4.17   BETA FOR TATA CHEMICALS: DIVISIONS AND COMPANY

Tata Chemicals is in two businesses—diversified chemicals and fertilizers. To compute the bottom-up beta for Tata Chemicals, we faced a similar choice of using just Indian companies, emerging market companies, or globally listed companies. As with Aracruz, we decided to go with the emerging market companies as our comparable firms. Table 4.17 summarizes the revenues that Tata Chemicals generates from its two businesses, our estimates of value for each business (based upon the multiples of revenues that comparable companies trade at), and the unlevered beta for each business and for all of Tata Chemicals' operating assets.

We used the marginal tax rates of 33.99% for India in levering the betas.

IN PRACTICE: GROSS DEBT OR NET DEBT

Many analysts in Europe and Latin America prefer to subtract the cash from the gross debt to arrive at a net debt figure, which they then use in both levering betas and in computing cost of capital.

$$\text{Net debt} = \text{Gross debt} - \text{Cash and marketable securities}$$

The rationale for this netting is that the presence of cash reduces the effective debt burden of the firm.

We have no quarrel with that logic. In fact, there are two ways we can reflect the presence of cash in the levered beta of equity of a firm. In the gross debt approach, the unlevered beta for a firm (as opposed to just the operating assets of the firm) is a weighted average of the unlevered beta of its operations and the unlevered beta of its cash holdings. If we make the assumption that cash has a beta of 0, the unlevered beta for the firm is

$$\text{Unlevered beta}_{\text{Firm}} = 0 \, (\text{Cash/Firm value})$$
$$+ \text{Unlevered Beta}_{\text{Operations}} (1 - \text{Cash/Firm value})$$

We can then apply the gross debt-to-equity ratio to this unlevered beta to arrive at the levered beta of equity. In the net debt approach, we net cash from debt while computing the unlevered beta for the firm but then lever that beta using the net debt-to-equity ratio.

Consider a simple example of a chemical company with $80 million in operating assets and $20 million in cash, funded with $60 million in equity and $40 million in debt.

Assume that the unlevered beta of the chemical business is 1.20 and that the marginal tax rate is 40%. First, compute betas using the gross debt approach:

$$\text{Unlevered beta}_{\text{Company}} = 0(20/100) + 1.20(80/100) = 0.96$$

$$\text{Gross debt-to-equity ratio} = 40/60 = 0.6667$$

$$\text{Levered beta} = 0.96(1 + (1 - 0.40)(0.6667)) = 1.344$$

Now, let's try the net debt approach:

$$\text{Unlevered beta}_{\text{Company}} = 1.20$$

$$\text{Net debt-to-equity ratio} = (\text{Debt} - \text{Cash})/\text{Equity} = (40 - 20)/60 = 0.3333$$

$$\text{Levered beta} = 1.20(1 + (1 - 0.40)(0.3333)) = 1.44$$

Notice that the levered beta of 1.344, computed using the gross debt-to-equity ratio approach, does not match the computation using the net debt-to-equity ratio. The reason lies in an implicit assumption that we make when we net cash against debt. We assume that both debt and cash are riskless and that the tax benefit from debt is exactly offset by the tax paid on interest earned on cash. It is generally not a good idea to net debt if the debt is very risky or if the interest rate earned on cash is substantially lower than the interest rate paid on debt. With a net debt-to-equity ratio, there is one more potential complication. Any firm that has a cash balance that exceeds its debt will have negative net debt, and using this negative net debt-to-equity ratio will yield an unlevered beta that exceeds the levered beta. Although this may trouble some, it makes sense because the unlevered beta reflects the beta of the business that the firm operates in. Firms that have vast cash balances that exceed their borrowing can have levered betas that are lower than the unlevered betas of the businesses they operate in. ■

ILLUSTRATION 4.10   Bottom-Up Beta for Deutsche Bank

There are a few banks in Germany that can be viewed as competitors to Deutsche Bank, though none of them are as large as it is or have as large of a stake in investment banking. Because the rules and regulatory constraints governing banking in the United States are different from the rules governing banks in much of Europe, we will look at the betas of diversified European banks to estimate the beta for the commercial banking arm of Deutsche Bank. To estimate the beta of Deutsche Bank's investment banking arm, we use the betas of investment banking and brokerage firms, listed in the United States.[38] The results are presented in Table 4.18.

---

[38]In much of the rest of the world, investment banking is an arm of commercial banking rather than a standalone operation.

Table 4.18   BETA FOR DEUTSCHE BANK

Business	Comparable Firms	Number	Average Beta	Weights
Commercial banking	Diversified European banks	90	1.05	65%
Investment banking	U.S. investment banks	32	1.37	35%
Deutsche Bank			1.162	

Note that we do not adjust for differences in financial leverage, because regulatory constraints and the needs of the business keep the leverage of most commercial banks at similar levels.[39] The beta for Deutsche Bank as a firm can be estimated as a weighted average of these two betas, using estimated value weights of 65% for the commercial banking and 35% for the investment banking arms, based on the revenues that Deutsche Bank made from each in the most recent year.

Calculating Betas after a Major Restructuring

The bottom-up process of estimating betas provides a solution when firms go through a major restructuring, where they change both their business mix and leverage. In these cases, the regression betas are misleading because they do not fully reflect the effects of these changes. Disney's beta, estimated from the bottom-up approach, is likely to provide a more precise estimate than the beta from a regression, given Disney's changing business mix and its increase in financial leverage in recent years. In fact, a firm's beta can be estimated even before the restructuring becomes effective using this approach. In the illustration that follows, for instance, we estimate Disney's beta just before and after its acquisition of Capital Cities/ABC in 1995, allowing for the changes in both the business mix and the leverage.

ILLUSTRATION 4.11   Beta of a Firm after an Acquisition—Disney/Capital Cities

In 1995, Disney announced that it was acquiring Capital Cities, the owner of the ABC television and radio network, for approximately $120 per share, and that it would finance the acquisition partly through the issue of $10 billion in debt. At the time of the acquisition, Disney had a market value of equity of $31.1 billion, debt outstanding of $3.186 billion, and a levered beta of 1.15. Capital Cities, based on the $120 offering price, had a market value of equity of $18.5 billion, debt outstanding of $615 million, and a levered beta of 0.95.

To evaluate the effects of the acquisition on Disney's beta, we do the analysis in two parts. First, we examine the effects of the merger on the business risk of the combined firm by estimating the unlevered betas of the two companies and calculating the combined firm's unlevered beta (using a tax rate of 36% for both firms).

$$\text{Disney's unlevered beta} = 1.15/(1 + (1 - 0.36) * (3,186/31,100)) = 1.08$$
$$\text{Capital Cities' unlevered beta} = 0.95/(1 + (1 - 0.36) * (615/18,500)) = 0.93$$

---

[39] Regulators often specify capital ratios, specified in terms of book values of debt and equity that banks must meet to stay in business. Most banks stay close to these ratios, though some tend to be better capitalized than others.

The unlevered beta for the combined firm can be calculated as the weighted average of the two unlevered betas, with the weights being based upon the *market values of the two firms.*[40]

$$\text{Value of Disney} = \$31,100 + \$3,186 = \$34,286 \text{ million}$$
$$\text{Value of Capital Cities} = \$18,500 + \$615 = \$19,115 \text{ million}$$
$$\text{Unlevered beta for combined firm} = 1.08(34,286/53,401) + 0.93(19,115/53,401)$$
$$= 1.026$$

Then we examine the effects of the financing of the merger on the betas by calculating the debt-to-equity ratio for the combined firm after the acquisition. Because Disney is assuming the old debt of Capital Cities, we add that debt to Disney's existing debt and add the additional $10 billion in debt used to fund this acquisition:[41]

$$\text{Post-acquisition debt} = \text{Capital Cities' old debt} + \text{Disney's old debt} + \text{New debt}$$
$$= \$615 + \$3,186 + \$10,000 = \$13,801 \text{ million}$$
$$\text{Post-acquisition equity} = \text{Disney's old equity} + \text{New equity used for acquisition}$$
$$= \$31,100 + \$8,500 = \$39,600 \text{ million}$$

where

$$\text{New equity} = \text{Total cost of acquisition–New debt issued}$$
$$= \$18,500 – \$10,000 = \$8,500 \text{ million}$$

Notice that the equity in Capital Cities of $18,500 million disappears after the acquisition and is replaced with new debt of $10,000 million and new Disney equity of $8,500 million. The debt-to-equity ratio can then be computed as follows.

$$\text{Debt-to-equity ratio} = 13,801/39,600 = 34.82\%$$

This debt-to-equity ratio in conjunction with the new unlevered beta for the combined firm yields a new beta of

$$\text{New beta} = 1.026(1 + (1 - .36)(0.3482)) = 1.25$$

Based on this computation, we would expect Disney's beta to increase from 1.15 to 1.25 after the acquisition of Capital Cities.

C. Accounting Betas

A third approach is to estimate the beta of a firm or its equity from accounting earnings rather than from traded prices. Thus, changes in earnings at a division or a firm, on a quarterly or annual basis, can be regressed against changes in earnings for the market, in the same periods, to arrive at an estimate of a "market beta" to use in the CAPM. The approach has some intuitive appeal, but it suffers from three potential pitfalls. First, accounting earnings tend to be smoothed out relative to the underlying

---

[40]Unlevered betas should always be weighted based on firm values. With levered (equity) betas, the values of equity can be used as weights.

[41]If Disney had paid off Capital Cities' existing debt instead of assuming it, we could have ignored it in the debt calculation. However, Disney would then have had to raise an extra $615 million in financing to fund this acquisition.

value of the company, resulting in betas that are "biased down," especially for risky firms, or "biased up," for safer firms. In other words, betas are likely to be closer to 1 for all firms using accounting data. Second, accounting earnings can be influenced by nonoperating factors, such as changes in depreciation or inventory methods, and by allocations of corporate expenses at the division level. Finally, accounting earnings are measured, at most, once every quarter, and often only once every year, resulting in regressions with few observations and not much power.

ILLUSTRATION 4.12   Estimating Accounting Betas: Bookscape Books

Bookscape Books, even though it is a private business, has been in existence since 1980 and has accounting earnings going back to that year. Table 4.19 summarizes accounting earnings changes at Bookscape and for companies in the S&P 500 for each year since 1980.

Regressing the changes in profits at Bookscape against changes in profits for the S&P 500 yields the following:

$$\text{Bookscape earnings change} = 0.08 + 0.8211 \,(\text{S\&P 500 earnings change})$$

Based on this regression, the beta for Bookscape is 0.82. In calculating this beta, we used net income to arrive at an equity beta. Using operating earnings for both the firm and the S&P 500 should yield the equivalent of an unlevered beta.

Technically, there is no reason why we cannot estimate accounting betas for Disney, Aracruz Celulose, Tata Chemicals, and Deutsche Bank. In fact, for Disney, we could get net income numbers every quarter, which increases the data we have in the regression. We could even estimate accounting betas by division, because the divisional income is reported. We do not attempt to estimate accounting betas, for the following reasons:

Table 4.19   CHANGE IN NET INCOME (%) FOR BOOKSCAPE VERSUS S&P 500

Year	S&P 500	Bookscape	Year	S&P 500	Bookscape
1980	3.01%	3.55%	1995	18.74%	11.55%
1981	1.31%	4.05%	1996	7.77%	19.88%
1982	−8.95%	−14.33%	1997	8.52%	16.55%
1983	−3.84%	47.55%	1998	0.41%	7.10%
1984	26.69%	65.00%	1999	16.74%	14.40%
1985	−6.91%	5.05%	2000	8.61%	10.50%
1986	−7.93%	8.50%	2001	−30.79%	−8.15%
1987	11.10%	37.00%	2002	18.51%	4.05%
1988	50.42%	45.17%	2003	18.79%	12.56%
1989	0.83%	3.50%	2004	23.75%	14.50%
1990	−6.87%	−10.50%	2005	12.96%	8.35%
1991	−14.79%	−32.00%	2006	14.74%	16.74%
1992	8.13%	55.00%	2007	−5.91%	2.50%
1993	28.89%	31.00%	2008	−20.78%	−12.20%
1994	18.03%	21.06%			

- To get a sufficient number of observations in our regression, we would need to go back in time at least ten years, and perhaps more. The changes that many large companies undergo over time make this a hazardous exercise.
- Publicly traded firms smooth out accounting earnings changes even more than private firms do. This will bias the beta estimates downward.

 spearn.xls: This data set online has earnings changes, by year, for the S&P 500 going back to 1960.

Market, Fundamental, and Accounting Betas: Which One Do We Use?

For most publicly traded firms, betas can be estimated using accounting data, market data, or fundamentals. Because the betas will almost never be the same, the question then becomes one of choosing between them. We would almost never use accounting betas, for all of the reasons already specified. We are almost as reluctant to use historical market betas for individual firms because of the standard errors in beta estimates, the failures of the local indices, and the inability of these regressions to reflect the effects of major changes in the business and financial risk at the firm. Fundamental betas, in our view, provide the best beta estimates, because they not only are more precise (because of the averaging) but also allow us to reflect changes in business and financial mix. In summary, we will use the fundamental estimates of equity betas, based upon the operating assets, of 0.90 for Disney, 0.94 for Tata Chemicals, 1.35 for Bookscape, 1.74 for Aracruz, and 1.16 for Deutsche Bank.

IV. Estimating the Cost of Equity

Having estimated the risk-free rate, the risk premium(s), and the beta(s), we can now estimate the expected return from investing in equity at any firm. In the CAPM, this expected return can be written as

$$\text{Expected return} = \text{Risk-free rate} + \text{Beta} * \text{Expected risk premium}$$

where the risk-free rate would be the rate on a long-term government bond; the beta would be either the historical, fundamental, or accounting betas; and the risk premium would be either the historical premium or an implied premium.

In the APM and multifactor model, the expected return would be written as follows:

$$\text{Expected return} = \text{Risk-free rate} + \sum_{j-1}^{j=n} \beta_j * \text{Risk premium}_j$$

where the risk-free rate is the long-term government bond rate, β_j is the beta relative to factor j, estimated using historical data or fundamentals, and Risk premium$_j$ is the risk premium relative to factor j, estimated using historical data.

The expected return on an equity investment in a firm, given its risk, has key implications for both equity investors in the firm and the managers of the firm. For equity investors, it is the *rate they need to make* to be compensated for the risk that they have taken on investing in the equity of a firm. If after analyzing a stock, they conclude that they cannot make this return, they would not buy it; alternatively, if they decide they can make a higher return, they would make the investment. For managers

Table 4.20 ALLOCATING DEBT AND EQUITY TO DIVISIONS

Business	Estimated EV	Allocated Debt	Estimated Equity	Debt-to-Equity Ratio	Debt-to-Equity Ratio of Comps	Estimated Debt	Proportions
Media Networks	$34,328	$8,582	$25,746	33.33%	38.71%	$9,581	51.44%
Parks and Resorts	$17,408	$6,148	$11,260	54.61%	65.10%	$6,864	36.86%
Studio Entertainment	$5,755	$1,805	$3,950	45.70%	53.89%	$2,015	10.82%
Consumer Products	$768	$147	$621	23.70%	27.21%	$164	0.88%
						$18,624	100.00%

in the firm, the return that investors need to make to break even on their equity investments becomes the return that they have to try to deliver to keep these investors from becoming restive and rebellious. Thus, it becomes the rate that they have to beat in terms of returns on their equity investments in individual projects. In other words, this is the *cost of equity* to the firm.

ILLUSTRATION 4.13 Estimating the Cost of Equity

In Illustration 4.7, we estimated a bottom-up unlevered beta for Disney and each of its divisions. To estimate the levered beta for Disney, we estimated a debt-to-equity ratio of 36.91%, based upon the total market value of equity ($45,193 million) and debt ($16,682 million). To estimate the levered beta for each of the divisions, we face a challenge in determining the debt-to-equity ratio at the divisional level, since we do not have market equity values for the individual divisions, nor do we have full details on which divisions are responsible for the borrowing. We have two choices. One is to assume that Disney's debt-to-equity ratio applies to all of its individual divisions. The other is to try to make judgments about the debt-to-equity ratios for the individual divisions, based upon the information available. In Table 4.20, we tried to do the latter.

We started with the estimates of enterprise value that we obtained in Table 4.14, obtained by multiplying the revenues in each division by the median EV/sales ratio of comparable companies in the division. We then used the debt-to-equity ratios of these same comparable firms to estimate the debt in each division in the second to last column and used the proportions derived from these estimated debt numbers to allocate the existing debt ($16,682 million) across the divisions.[42] Finally, we estimated the value of equity in each division by subtracting the debt from the estimated enterprise value.

Using the U.S. dollar risk-free rate (from Illustration 4.1) and the equity risk premium estimated for mature markets (from Illustration 4.2), we estimate the cost of equity for Disney's operating assets and for each of its divisions, listed in Table 4.21.

The costs of equity vary across the remaining divisions, with studio entertainment having the highest beta (and cost of equity), and parks and resorts the lowest.

---

[42]Some analysts use the industry average debt-to-equity ratios to estimate levered betas by division. The problem with doing this is that the sum total of the debt that they estimate for the divisions may not match up to the actual debt of the company. In the case of Disney, for instance, the dollar debt that we would have obtained with this approach ($18,624 million) would have greater than the debt owed by the company ($16,682 million)

Table 4.21   LEVERED BETA AND COST OF EQUITY—DISNEY

Business	Unlevered Beta	Debt-to-Equity Ratio	Levered Beta	Cost of Equity
Media Networks	0.7056	33.33%	0.8514	8.61%
Parks and Resorts	0.5849	54.61%	0.7829	8.20%
Studio Entertainment	1.3027	45.70%	1.6718	13.53%
Consumer Products	1.0690	23.70%	1.2261	10.86%
Disney	0.7333	36.91%	0.9011	8.91%

To estimate the cost of equity for Deutsche Bank, we will use the same risk premium (6%) that we have used for the United States, because Deutsche Bank's business is still primarily in mature markets in Europe and the United States. Using the ten-year German euro bond rate of 3.60% as the euro risk-free rate (from Illustration 4.1) and Deutsche Bank's bottom-up beta of 1.16, the cost of equity for Deutsche Bank is shown in Table 4.22.

Note that the cost of equity for investment banking is significantly higher than the cost of equity for commercial banking, reflecting the higher risks.

For Aracruz, we will add the country risk premium estimated for Brazil of 3.95%, estimated earlier in the chapter, to the mature market premium, estimated from the United States, of 6% to arrive at a total risk premium of 9.95% (see Illustration 4.2). The cost of equity for Aracruz can then be computed in U.S. dollar terms using the bottom-up beta estimated in Illustration 4.9 and the U.S. treasury bond rate of 3.5%:

$$\text{Cost of equity}_{\text{US dollars}} = \text{Risk-free rate}_\$ + \text{Beta} * \text{Risk premium}$$
$$= 3.5\% + 1.74(9.95\%) = 20.82\%$$

Note that we can compute Aracruz's cost of equity in nominal Brazilian reals in one of two ways. The first is to replace the U.S. dollar risk-free rate with a nominal Brazilian real risk-free rate (estimated to be 8.5% in Illustration 4.1):

$$\text{Cost of equity}_{\text{Nominal R\$}} = \text{Risk-free rate}_{\text{R\$}} + \text{Beta} * \text{Risk premium}$$
$$= 8.5\% + 1.74(9.95\%) = 25.82\%$$

This approach assumes that the equity risk premium, which was computed using dollar-based securities, will stay constant even if we switch to a higher inflation currency. The second and more precise approach scales up the equity risk premium, when we switch to the higher inflation currency. If we assume that the expected inflation rate is

Table 4.22   COST OF EQUITY FOR DEUTSCHE BANK

Business	Beta	Cost of Equity
Commercial banking	1.05	3.6% + 1.05 (6%) = 9.90%
Investment banking	1.37	3.6% + 1.37 (6%) = 11.82%
Deutsche Bank	1.162	3.6% + 1.162 (6%) = 10.55%

7% in nominal R\$ and 2% in U.S. \$, we obtain:

$$\text{Cost of equity}_{\text{Nominal R\$}} = (1 + \text{Cost of equity}_{\text{US\$}}) \frac{(1 + \text{Expected inflation}_{\text{R\$}})}{(1 + \text{Expected inflation}_{\text{US\$}})} - 1$$

$$= (1.2082) \frac{(1.07)}{(1.02)} - 1 = 26.75\%$$

As an emerging market company with a high debt-to-equity ratio, Aracruz clearly faces a much higher cost of equity than its competitors in developed markets.

For Tata Chemicals, we estimate the cost of equity in Indian rupees, using the rupee risk-free rate of 4% (estimated in Illustration 4.1) and the equity risk premium for India of 10.51% (estimated in Illustration 4.2). Table 4.23 summarizes the cost of equity estimates for the fertilizer and chemical businesses separately, as well as for the entire company.

Finally, for Bookscape, we will use the beta of 1.35 estimated from Illustration 4.8 in conjunction with the risk-free rate and risk premium for the United States:

$$\text{Cost of equity} = 3.5\% + 1.35(6\%) = 11.60\%$$

Implicit in the use of beta as a measure of risk is the assumption that the marginal investor in equity is a well-diversified investor. Although this is a defensible assumption when analyzing publicly traded firms, it becomes much more difficult to sustain for private firms. The owner of a private firm generally has the bulk of his or her wealth invested in the business. Consequently, he or she cares about the total risk in the business rather than just the market risk. Thus, for a business like Bookscape, the beta that we have estimated of 1.35 (leading to a cost of equity of 11.60%) will understate the risk perceived by the owner. There are three solutions to this problem:

1. Assume that the business is run with the near-term objective of sale to a large publicly traded firm. In such a case, it is reasonable to use the market beta and cost of equity that comes from it.

2. Add a premium to the cost of equity to reflect the higher risk created by the owner's inability to diversify. This may help explain the high returns that some venture capitalists demand on their equity investments in fledgling businesses.

3. Adjust the beta to reflect total risk rather than market risk. This adjustment is relatively simple, because the R^2 of the regression measures the proportion of the variance that is market risk. Dividing the market beta by the square root of the R^2 (which yields the correlation coefficient) yields a total beta. In the Bookscape

Table 4.23	COST OF EQUITY BY DIVISION: TATA CHEMICALS	
Business	**Beta**	**Cost of equity**
Fertilizers	0.965	4% + 0.965 (10.51%) = 14.14%
Chemicals	0.911	4% + 0.911 (10.51%) = 13.58%
Tata Chemicals	0.945	4% + 0.945 (10.51%) = 13.93%

example, the regressions for the comparable firms against the market index have an average correlation with the market of 46.45% (the average R^2 was 21.58%). The total beta for Bookscape can then be computed as follows:

$$\text{Total beta} = (\text{Market beta})/\text{Correlation with the market} = 1.35/0.4645 = 2.91$$

Using this total beta would yield a much higher and more realistic estimate of the cost of equity.

$$\text{Cost of equity} = 3.5\% + 2.91(6\%) = 20.94\%$$

Thus, private businesses will generally have much higher costs of equity than their publicly traded counterparts, with diversified investors. Although many of them ultimately capitulate by selling to publicly traded competitors or going public, some firms choose to remain private and thrive. To do so, they have to diversify on their own (as many family-run businesses in Asia and Latin America did) or accept the lower value as a price paid for maintaining total control.

 IN PRACTICE: COMPANY EXPOSURE TO COUNTRY RISK

In our computations of cost of equity for companies, note that we attached country risk premiums to Aracruz (Brazil) and Tata Chemicals (India) and used only a mature market premium for Disney and Deutsche Bank. While we are following conventional practice in assessing country risk based upon where a company is incorporated, it can also lead to misleading values for companies that are incorporated in an emerging market (developed market) and have a significant portion of their operations in a developed market (emerging market). This would have been the case, for instance, if we had been analyzing Embraer, a Brazilian aerospace company with less than 10% of its revenues from Brazil and the rest from developed markets, or Infosys, an Indian technology company that derives more than half of its revenues in the United States.

There is a simple (perhaps even simplistic) way of adjusting for operating risk exposure.[43] Rather than use the risk premium of the country of incorporation, we can use a weighted average of the total risk premiums of the countries in which the company operates, using revenues as the basis for the weighting. Thus, the equity risk premium used for a company that derives half its revenues in India and half in the United States would be

$$\text{Equity risk premium} = (0.5)(6\%) + (0.5)(10.51\%) = 8.26\%$$

Thus, the costs of equity of companies like Nestle and Coca-Cola, which have substantial operations in emerging markets, will increase. We did break down Disney's revenues geographically and noted that while it does have significant non-U.S. operations, most are still centered in Western Europe and Japan and thus do not affect the risk premium. However, as its Hong Kong theme park's revenues increase, we may have to adjust the equity risk premium to reflect greater emerging market risk. Tata Chemicals gets almost 90% of its revenues from India, and the use of the

---

[43]For more comprehensive ways of estimating company risk exposure to country risk, see the working paper on my Web site: A. Damodaran, "Estimating Company Risk Exposure to Country Risk," 2003.

Indian total risk premium seems appropriate. We are a little more concerned about our equity risk premium assessments for Deutsche Bank (which we feel is exposed to more emerging market risk) and Aracruz (which has significant revenues outside Brazil). However, we made no adjustments because of the absence of a clear measure of emerging market operations for the former and the offsetting additional risk of being a natural resource company for the latter.[44] ∎

FROM COST OF EQUITY TO COST OF CAPITAL

Equity is undoubtedly an important and indispensable ingredient of the financing mix for every business, but it is only one ingredient. Most businesses finance some or much of their operations using debt or some hybrid of equity and debt. The costs of these sources of financing are generally very different from the cost of equity, and the minimum acceptable hurdle rate for a project will reflect their costs as well, in proportion to their use in the financing mix. Intuitively, the *cost of capital* is the weighted average of the costs of the different components of financing—including debt, equity, and hybrid securities—used by a firm to fund its financial requirements.

4.8 INTEREST RATES AND THE RELATIVE COSTS OF DEBT AND EQUITY

It is often argued that debt becomes a more attractive mode of financing than equity as interest rates go down and a less attractive mode when interest rates go up. Is this true?

a. Yes

b. No

Why or why not?

The Costs of Non-Equity Financing

To estimate the cost of the funding that a firm raises, we have to estimate the costs of all of the non-equity components. In this section, we consider the cost of debt first and then extend the analysis to consider hybrids, such as preferred stock and convertible bonds.

The Cost of Debt

The *cost of debt* measures the current cost to the firm of borrowing funds to finance projects. In general terms, it is determined by the following variables:

- *The current level of interest rates* As market interest rates rise, the cost of debt for all firms will also increase.
- *The default risk of the company* As the default risk of a firm increases, lenders will charge higher interest rates (a default spread) to compensate for the additional risk.

---

[44]Natural resource companies are particularly exposed to country risk, because they do not have the option of moving operations if the country in which their resources are is in trouble. Manufacturing companies can move their factories to more stable locations, but oil, mining, and forestry companies cannot.

- ***The tax advantage associated with debt*** Because interest is tax-deductible, the after-tax cost of debt is a function of the tax rate. The tax benefit that accrues from paying interest makes the after-tax cost of debt lower than the pretax cost. Furthermore, this benefit increases as the tax rate increases.

After-tax cost of debt = (Risk-free rate + Default spread)(1 − Marginal tax rate)

The challenge in estimating cost of debt is really one of estimating the correct default spread for a company.

4.9 COSTS OF DEBT AND EQUITY

Can the cost of equity ever be lower than the cost of debt for any firm at any stage in its life cycle?

☐ Yes

☐ No

Estimating the Default Risk and Default Spread of a Firm

The simplest scenario for estimating the cost of debt occurs when a firm has long-term bonds outstanding that are widely traded and that have no special features, such as convertibility or first claim on assets, to skew interest rates. The market price of the bond, in conjunction with its coupon and maturity, can serve to compute a yield we use as the cost of debt. For instance, this approach works for firms that have dozens of outstanding bonds that are liquid and trade frequently.

Many firms have bonds outstanding that do not trade on a regular basis. Because these firms are usually rated, we can estimate their costs of debt by using their ratings and associated default spreads. Thus, Disney, with an A rating, can be expected to have a cost of debt approximately 2.5% higher than the Treasury bond rate, in May 2009, because this was the spread typically paid by A-rated firms at the time.

Some companies choose not to get rated. Many smaller firms and most private businesses fall into this category. Ratings agencies have sprung up in many emerging markets, but there are still a number of markets in which companies are not rated on the basis of default risk. When there is no rating available to estimate the cost of debt, there are two alternatives:

1. ***Recent Borrowing History*** Many firms that are not rated still borrow money from banks and other financial institutions. By looking at the most recent borrowings made by a firm, we can get a sense of the types of default spreads being charged and use these spreads to come up with a cost of debt.

2. ***Estimate a Synthetic Rating and Default Spread*** An alternative is to play the role of a ratings agency and assign a rating to a firm based on its financial ratios; this rating is called a synthetic rating. To make this assessment, we begin with rated firms and examine the financial characteristics shared by firms within each ratings class. Consider a very simple version in which the ratio of operating income to interest expense, that is, the interest coverage ratio, is computed for each rated firm. In Table 4.24, we list the range of interest coverage ratios for manufacturing firms in each S&P ratings class, classified by market capitalization into large

Interest Coverage Ratio: Small Market Cap (< $5 billion)	Interest Coverage Ratio: Large Market Cap (> U.S. $5 billion)	Rating	Typical Default
>12.5	>8.5	AAA	1.25%
9.50–12.50	6.5–8.5	AA	1.75%
7.50–9.50	5.5–6.5	A+	2.25%
6.00–7.50	4.25–5.5	A	2.50%
4.50–6.00	3–4.25	A–	3.00%
4.00–4.50	2.5–3.0	BBB	3.50%
3.50–4.00	2.0–2.25	BB+	4.25%
3.00–3.50	2.0–2.25	BB	5.00%
2.50–3.00	1.75–2.0	B+	6.00%
2.00–2.50	1.5–1.75	B	7.25%
1.50–2.00	1.25–1.5	B–	8.50%
1.25–1.50	0.8–1.25	CCC	10.00%
0.80–1.25	0.65–0.8	CC	12.00%
0.50–0.80	0.2–0.65	C	15.00%
<0.65	<0.2	D	20.00%

Table 4.24   INTEREST COVERAGE RATIOS AND RATINGS

Source: Compustat and Bondsonline.com.

(>$5 billion) and small (<$5 billion).[45] We also report the typical default spreads for bonds in each ratings class in early 2009. [46]

Now consider a private firm with $10 million in earnings before interest and taxes and $3 million in interest expenses; it has an interest coverage ratio of 3.33. Based on this ratio and using the small cap ratios, we would assess a synthetic rating of BB for the firm and attach a default spread of 5.00% to the risk-free rate to come up with a pretax cost of debt. A large market cap firm with the same interest coverage ratio would be assigned a rating of A– and a default spread of 3.00%.

By basing the synthetic rating on the interest coverage ratio alone, we run two risks. One is that using last year's operating income as the basis for the rating may yield too low or too high a rating for a firm that had an exceptionally good or bad earnings years. We can counter that by using the average operating income over a period, say five years, to compute the coverage ratio. The other is that we risk missing the information that is available in the other financial ratios and qualitative information used by ratings agencies. The counter to that is to extend the approach to incorporate other ratios. The first step would be to develop a score based on multiple ratios. For instance, the Altman *z*-score, which is used as a proxy for default risk, is a function of five financial ratios that are weighted to generate a *z*-score. The ratios used and their relative weights are usually based on past history on defaulted firms. The second step is to relate the

---

[45]This table was first developed in early 2000 by listing all rated firms with market capitalization lower than $5 billion and their interest coverage ratios, and then sorting firms based on their bond ratings. The ranges were adjusted to eliminate outliers and to prevent overlapping ranges. It has been updated every two years since.

[46]These default spreads are obtained from an online site, found at www.bondsonline.com. You can find default spreads for industrial and financial service firms; these spreads are for industrial firms.

level of the score to a bond rating, much as we did in Table 4.24, with interest coverage ratios. In making this extension, though, note that complexity comes at a cost. Credit or z-scores may, in fact, yield better estimates of synthetic ratings than those based only on interest coverage ratios, but changes in ratings arising from these scores are much more opaque than those based on interest coverage ratios. That is the reason we prefer the flawed but more transparent ratings from interest coverage ratios.

ratings.xls: This spreadsheet allows you to estimate a synthetic rating for a firm.

IN PRACTICE: DEBT BETAS AND COSTS OF DEBT

Given our use of equity betas to compute the cost of equity, you may be wondering why we cannot use debt betas to compute the pre-tax cost of debt. In other words, instead of estimating a bond rating for a company and a default spread based upon the rating, why not estimate a beta for debt, by regressing bond returns against a market index, and use that beta in the capital asset pricing model to estimate the cost of debt. There are two reasons why we are reluctant to go down the road:

1. ***Non-traded debt*** Even at large publicly traded companies, a significant portion of the debt is not traded, making it impossible to regress returns against a market index.

2. ***Asymmetric payoffs*** Beta as a measure of risk draws on the mean-variance framework, which in turn assumes returns that are roughly symmetric, with upside risk offset by downside risk. When you lend to a firm, your risks tend to be asymmetric, with your best-case scenario being that you get your promised interest and principal payments and your worst-case scenarios containing far worse outcomes. That is why we focus on downside risk (i.e., default risk) when assessing the cost of debt for a firm.

It is conceivable that debt begins to have more symmetric payoffs as it gets riskier and that debt betas may therefore make sense, if we are looking at low-rated companies. It is unlikely that debt betas will be of much use in assessing the cost of debt for most other firms. ∎

Short-Term and Long-Term Debt

Most publicly traded firms have multiple borrowings—short-term and long-term bonds and bank debt with different terms and interest rates. Although some analysts create separate categories for each type of debt and attach a different cost to each category, this approach is both tedious and dangerous. Using it, we would conclude that short-term debt is cheaper than long-term debt, and that secured debt is cheaper than unsecured debt.

The solution is simple. Combine all debt—short- and long-term, bank debt and bonds—and attach the long-term cost of debt to it. In other words, add the default spread to the long-term risk-free rate and use that rate as the pretax cost of debt. Firms will undoubtedly complain, arguing that their effective cost of debt is lowered by using short-term debt. This is technically true, largely because short-term rates tend to be lower than long-term rates in most developed markets, but it misses the point of computing the cost of debt and capital. If this is the hurdle rate we want our long-term investments to beat, we want the rate to reflect the cost of long-term borrowing, not short-term borrowing. After all, a firm that funds long-term projects with short-term debt will have to return to the market to roll over this debt.

Operating Leases and Other Fixed Commitments

The essential characteristic of debt is that it gives rise to a tax-deductible *obligation that firms have to meet in both good times and bad—and failure to meet this obligation can result in bankruptcy or loss of equity control over the firm.* If we use this definition of debt, it is quite clear that what we see reported on the balance sheet as debt may not reflect the true borrowings of the firm. In particular, a firm that leases substantial assets and categorizes them as operating leases owes substantially more than is reported in the financial statements.[47] After all, a firm that signs a lease commits to making the lease payment in future periods and risks the loss of assets if it fails to make the commitment.

For corporate financial analysis, we should treat all lease payments as financial expenses and convert future lease commitments into debt by discounting them back the present, using the current pretax cost of borrowing for the firm as the discount rate. The resulting present value can be considered the debt value of operating leases and can be added on to the value of conventional debt to arrive at a total debt figure. To complete the adjustment, the operating income of the firm will also have to be restated:

Adjusted operating income = Stated operating income
+ Operating lease expense for the current year
− Depreciation on leased asset

To the extent that estimating depreciation on the leased asset can be tedious, an approximation can also be used:

Adjusted operating income = Stated operating income
+ PV of lease commitments ∗ Pretax cost of debt

In effect, we are computing the imputed interest expense on the lease debt and adding it back to the stated operating income, since it is income before interest expenses. In fact, this process can be used to convert any set of financial commitments into debt.

To convert leases to debt, we need a listing of all lease commitments into the future that *have already been made*; this is required already in the U.S. and is available for more and more non-U.S. firms. We also need a *pretax cost of debt* to do the discounting. While this may be simple if the firm has a bond rating, it becomes more complicated

---

[47] In an operating lease, the lessor (or owner) transfers only the right to use the property to the lessee. At the end of the lease period, the lessee returns the property to the lessor. Because the lessee does not assume the risk of ownership, the lease expense is treated as an operating expense in the income statement, and the lease does not affect the balance sheet. In a capital lease, the lessee assumes some of the risks of ownership and enjoys some of the benefits. Consequently, the lease, when signed, is recognized both as an asset and as a liability (for the lease payments) on the balance sheet. The firm gets to claim depreciation each year on the asset and also deducts the interest expense component of the lease payment each year. In general, capital leases recognize expenses sooner than equivalent operating leases.

if the firm is not rated. We can try to compute a synthetic rating, but we will run into a problem of circularity, since we need interest expenses to compute the rating but need the rating to compute the present value of debt and the potential interest expenses from that debt. There are three solutions. One is to use the unadjusted interest coverage ratio, based upon the stated operating income and interest expenses, but we will overrate companies if we do so. The second is to treat the entire current year's lease expense as an interest expense, and compute an interest coverage ratio by adding the lease expense to both the stated operating income and interests expenses. This will generally result in ratings that are too low and a cost of debt that is too high. The third, preferred solution is to use an iterative process whereby we compute the synthetic rating and the present value of debt simultaneously.[48]

 oplease.xls: This spreadsheet allows you to convert operating lease commitments into debt and to adjust operating income and interest expenses.

Book and Market Interest Rates

When firms borrow money, they often do so at fixed rates. When they issue bonds to investors, this rate that is fixed at the time of the issue is called the coupon rate. The cost of debt is not the coupon rate on outstanding bonds, nor is it the rate at which the company was able to borrow at in the past. Although these factors may help determine the interest cost the company will have to pay in the current year, they do not determine the pretax cost of debt in the cost of capital calculations. Thus, a company that has debt that it took on when interest rates were low cannot contend that it has a low cost of debt.

To see why, consider a firm that has $2 billion of debt on its books and assume that the interest expense on this debt is $80 million. The book interest rate on the debt is 4%. Assume also that the current risk-free rate is 6%. If we use the book interest rate of 4% in our cost of capital calculations, we require the projects we fund with the capital to earn more than 4% to be considered good investments. Because we can invest that money in Treasury bonds and earn 6%, without taking any risk, this is clearly not a high enough hurdle. To ensure that projects earn more than what we can make on alternative investments of equivalent risk today, the cost of debt has to be based on market interest rates today rather than book interest rates.

Assessing the Tax Advantage of Debt

Interest is tax-deductible, and the resulting tax savings reduce the cost of borrowing to firms. In assessing this tax advantage, we should keep the following things in mind.

- Interest expenses offset the marginal dollar of income and the tax advantage has to be therefore calculated using the marginal tax rate.

$$\text{After-tax cost of debt} = \text{Pretax cost of debt} (1 - \text{Marginal tax rate})$$

---

[48]This can be accomplished in Excel by checking the iteration box. The ratings spreadsheet that we referenced earlier does this.

- To obtain the tax advantages of borrowing, firms have to be profitable. In other words, there is no tax advantage from interest expenses to a firm that has operating losses. It is true that firms can carry losses forward and can offset them against profits in future periods. The most prudent assessment of the tax effects of debt will therefore provide for no tax advantages in the years of operating losses and will begin adjusting for tax benefits only in future years when the firm is expected to have operating profits.

$$\text{After-tax cost of debt} = \text{Pretax cost of debt if operating income} < 0$$
$$\text{Pretax cost of debt } (1 - t) \text{ if operating income} > 0$$

ILLUSTRATION 4.14 Estimating the Costs of Debt

Disney, Deutsche Bank, and Aracruz are all rated companies, and we will estimate their pretax costs of debt based on their ratings. To provide a contrast, we will also estimate synthetic ratings for Disney and Aracruz. For Tata Chemicals and Bookscape, we have to depend upon synthetic ratings for estimating the cost of debt.

- **Bond Ratings** S&P, Moody's, and Fitch rate three of the five companies, but the ratings are consistent, and we will use the S&P ratings and the associated default spreads (from Table 4.24) to estimate the costs of debt in Table 4.25.

  The marginal tax rates of the United States (Disney), Brazil (Aracruz), and Germany (Deutsche Bank) are used to compute the after-tax cost of debt. We will assume that all of Disney's divisions have the same cost of debt and marginal tax rate as the parent company. To estimate Aracruz's nominal R$ cost of debt, we use the same inflation adjustment that we used for the cost of equity on the pre-tax dollar cost of debt:

$$\text{Cost of debt}_{R\$} = (1 + \text{Cost of debt}_{US\$}) \frac{(1 + \text{Expected inflation}_{R\$})}{(1 + \text{Expected inflation}_{US\$})} - 1$$
$$= (1.085) \frac{(1.07)}{(1.02)} - 1 = 13.82\%$$

- **Synthetic Ratings** The synthetic ratings for the four nonfinancial service companies can be estimated using the interest coverage ratios and the look-up table (Table 4.26).

For Bookscape, the A rating yields a default spread of 2.50%, which when added to the U.S. dollar risk-free of 3.5% yields a pretax cost of debt of 6%. Allowing for the

		Table 4.25	COST OF DEBT (BASED ON ACTUAL RATING)			
	S&P Rating	**Risk-Free Rate**	**Default Spread**	**Cost of Debt**	**Tax Rate**	**After-Tax Cost of Debt**
Disney	A	3.50% (U.S.$)	2.50%	6.00%	38%	3.72%
Deutsche Bank	A+	3.60% (euros)	2.25%	5.85%	29.50%	4.12%
Aracruz	BB	3.50% (U.S.$)	5%	8.50%	34%	5.61%

Table 4.26 INTEREST COVERAGE RATIOS AND SYNTHETIC RATINGS

	Operating Income	Interest Expense	Interest Coverage Ratio	Synthetic Rating
Disney	$6,819	$821	8.31	AA
Aracruz	R$574	R$155	3.70	BB+
Tata Chemicals	Rs6,263	Rs1,215	5.15	A–
Bookscape	$3,575	$575	6.22	A

tax benefits, we estimate an after-tax cost of debt of 3.60% for Bookscape:

$$\text{After-tax cost of debt} = 6.0\% \ (1 - 0.40) = 3.60\%$$

For Tata Chemicals, things are a little more complicated. While the rating of A- for the company would result in a default spread of 3%, adding this default spread to the Indian rupee risk-free rate of 4% would miss a key component: the Indian government is perceived to be exposed to default risk and faces a default spread of 3% as a consequence. To estimate the pretax cost of debt for the firm, we will therefore add the default spreads for both the country and the company to the risk-free rate:

$$\text{Cost of debt}_{\text{Tata Chemcals}} = \text{Risk-free rate}_{\text{Rs}} + \text{Default spread}_{\text{India}}$$
$$+ \text{Default spread}_{\text{Tata}}$$
$$= 4.00\% + 3.00\% + 3.00\% = 10.00\%$$

For Disney, we used the large market capitalization categorizations, resulting in a AA rating for the company, higher than the synthetic rating.

IN PRACTICE: ACTUAL AND SYNTHETIC RATINGS

It is usually easy to estimate the cost of debt for firms that have bond ratings available for them. There are, however, a few potential problems that sometimes arise in practice.

- *Disagreement between ratings agencies*   Although the ratings are consistent across agencies for many firms, there are a few firms over which the ratings agencies disagree, with one agency assigning a much higher or lower rating to the firm than the others.

- *Multiple bond ratings for same firm*   Because ratings agencies rate bonds, the same firm can have many bond issues with different ratings depending on how the bond is structured and secured.

- *Lags or errors in the rating process*   Ratings agencies make mistakes, and there is evidence that ratings changes occur after the bond market has already recognized the change in the default risk.

It is a good idea to estimate synthetic ratings even for firms that have actual ratings. If there is disagreement between ratings agencies or a firm has multiple bond ratings, the synthetic rating can operate as a tiebreaker. If there is a significant difference between actual and synthetic ratings, and there is no fundamental reason that can be pinpointed for the difference, the synthetic rating may be providing an early signal of a ratings agency mistake.

Consider the synthetic and actual ratings for Disney and Aracruz in the last illustration. We estimated a synthetic rating of AA for Disney, whereas the ratings agency assigned it a rating of A. The discrepancy can be traced to our use of the 2008 operating income as the basis for the synthetic rating. The ratings agencies might be looking at Disney's volatile earnings history and drawing a more conservative conclusion. With Aracruz, the synthetic rating we derive of BB+ is higher than the actual rating of BB, but note that the latter is really a composite rating that incorporates both company and country risk. In effect, the ratings agencies are assigning Aracruz a lower rating because it is a Brazilian company.[49] With both companies, we will assume that the actual rating is a better estimate of default risk because it does draw on more information than the synthetic rating process. ∎

Calculating the Cost of Preferred Stock

Preferred stock shares some of the characteristics of debt (the preferred dividend is prespecified at the time of the issue and is paid out before common dividend) and some of the characteristics of equity (the payments of preferred dividends are not tax-deductible). If preferred stock is viewed as perpetual, the cost of preferred stock can be written as follows:

$$k_{ps} = \text{Preferred Dividend per Share/Market Price per Preferred Share}$$

This approach assumes that the dividend is constant in dollar terms forever and that the preferred stock has no special features (convertibility, callability, etc.). If such special features exist, they will have to be valued separately to come up with a good estimate of the cost of preferred stock. In terms of risk, preferred stock is safer than common equity but riskier than debt. Consequently, it should, on a pretax basis, command a higher cost than debt and a lower cost than equity.

ILLUSTRATION 4.15   Calculating the Cost of Preferred Stock—Disney and Deutsche Bank
None of the companies that we are analyzing have outstanding preferred stock in 2009. In 2004, however, both Disney and Deutsche Bank had preferred stock. The preferred dividend yields on the issues are computed in March 2004 in Table 4.27.

Table 4.27   COST OF PREFERRED STOCK

	Preferred Stock Price	Annual Dividends/Share	Dividend Yield
Disney	$26.74	$1.75	1.75/26.74 = 6.54%
Deutsche Bank	103.75 euros	6.60 euros	6.6/103.75 = 6.36%

[49]Ratings agencies used to be even more explicit about this linkage. In fact, the rating for a company was constrained to be less than or equal to the rating of the country in which it was incorporated for a long period.

Notice that the cost of preferred stock for Disney would have been higher than its pretax cost of debt of 5.25% in May 2004, and lower than its cost of equity of 10% at the time. For Deutsche Bank as well, the cost of preferred stock was higher than its pretax cost of debt (5.05%) and lower than its cost of equity of 8.76% in May 2004. For both firms, the market value of preferred stock was so small relative to the market values of debt and equity that it makes almost no impact on the overall cost of capital.

4.10   WHY DO COMPANIES ISSUE PREFERRED STOCK?

Which of the following are good reasons for a company issuing preferred stock?
a.   Preferred stock is cheaper than equity.
b.   Preferred stock is treated as equity by the ratings agencies and regulators.
c.   Preferred stock is cheaper than debt.
d.   Other:
Explain.

Calculating the Cost of Other Hybrid Securities

In general terms, *hybrid securities* share some of the characteristics of debt and some of the characteristics of equity. A good example is a convertible bond, which can be viewed as a combination of a straight bond (debt) and a conversion option (equity). Instead of trying to calculate the cost of these hybrid securities individually, they can be broken down into their debt and equity components and treated separately.

In general, it is not difficult to decompose a hybrid security that is publicly traded (and has a market price) into debt and equity components. In the case of a convertible bond, this can be accomplished in two ways:

1.   An option pricing model can be used to value the conversion option, and the remaining value of the bond can be attributed to debt.

2.   The convertible bond can be valued as if it were a straight bond, using the rate at which the firm can borrow in the market, given its default risk (pretax cost of debt) as the interest rate on the bond. The difference between the price of the convertible bond and the value of the straight bond can be viewed as the value of the conversion option.

If the convertible security is not traded, we have to value both the straight bond and the conversion options separately.

ILLUSTRATION 4.16 Breaking Down a Convertible Bond into Debt and Equity Components—Disney

While Disney has no convertible debt outstanding in 2008, in March 2004, it had convertible bonds outstanding with nineteen years left to maturity and a coupon rate of 2.125% trading at $1,064 a bond. Holders of this bond have the right to convert the bond into 33.9444 shares of stock any time over the bond's remaining life.[50] To break

---

[50] At this conversion ratio, the price that investors would be paying for Disney shares would be $29.46, much higher than the stock price of $20.46 prevailing at the time of the analysis.

the convertible bond into straight bond and conversion option components, we will value the bond using Disney's pretax cost of debt of 5.25% in 2004:[51]

Straight bond component
= Value of a 2.125% coupon bond due in 19 years with
a market interest rate of 5.25%
= PV of $21.25 in coupons each year for 19 years[52]
+ PV of $1000 at end of year 19

$$= 21.25 \left[\frac{1 - (1.0525)^{-19}}{.0525} \right] + \frac{1000}{(1.0525)^{19}} = \$629.91$$

Conversion option = Market value of convertible
− Value of straight bond
= $1064 − $629.91 = $434.09

The straight bond component of $630 would have been treated as debt, whereas the conversion option of $434 would have been treated as equity. Disney retired this bond in 2006 and the convertible debt is not a relevant value in the 2008 computations.

4.11   INCREASES IN STOCK PRICES AND CONVERTIBLE BONDS

As stock prices go up, which of the following is likely to happen to the convertible bond (you can choose more than one)?
a. The convertible bond will increase in value.
b. The straight bond component of the convertible bond will decrease in value.
c. The equity component of the convertible bond will increase as a percentage of the total value.
d. The straight bond component of the convertible bond will increase as a percentage of the total value.
Explain.

Calculating the Weights of Debt and Equity Components

Once we have costs for each of the different components of financing, all we need are weights on each component to arrive at a cost of capital. In this section, we consider the choices for weighting, the argument for using market value weights, and whether the weights can change over time.

Choices for Weighting

In computing weights for debt, equity, and preferred stock, we have two choices. We can take the accounting estimates of the value of each funding source from the balance sheet and compute book value weights. Alternatively, we can use or estimate market values for each component and compute weights based on relative market value. *As a general rule, the weights used in the cost of capital computation should be based on market*

---

[51]This rate was based on a ten-year Treasury bond rate. If the five-year Treasury bond rate had been substantially different, we would have recomputed a pretax cost of debt by adding the default spread to the five-year rate.
[52]The coupons are assumed to be annual. With semi-annual coupons, you would divide the coupon by two and apply a semi-annual rate to calculate the present value.

values. This is because the cost of capital is a forward-looking measure and captures the cost of raising new funds to finance projects. Because new debt and equity has to be raised in the market at prevailing prices, the market value weights are more relevant.

There are some analysts who continue to use book value weights and justify them using three arguments, none of which are convincing:

1. ***Book value is more reliable than market value because it is not as volatile.***   Although it is true that book value does not change as much as market value, this is more a reflection of weakness than strength, because the true value of the firm changes over time as new information comes out about the firm and the overall economy. We would argue that market value, with its volatility, is a much better reflection of true value than is book value.[53]

2. ***Using book value rather than market value is a more conservative approach to estimating debt ratios.***   The book value of equity in most firms in developed markets is well below the value attached by the market, whereas the book value of debt is usually close to the market value of debt. Because the cost of equity is much higher than the cost of debt, the cost of capital calculated using book value ratios will be lower than those calculated using market value ratios, making them less conservative estimates, not more so.[54]

3. ***Because accounting returns are computed based on book value, consistency requires the use of book value in computing cost of capital.***   Although it may seem consistent to use book values for both accounting return and cost of capital calculations, it does not make economic sense. The funds invested in these projects can be invested elsewhere, earning market rates, and the costs should therefore be computed at market rates and using market value weights.

Estimating Market Values

In a world in which all funding were raised in financial markets and securities were continuously traded, the market values of debt and equity would be easy to get. In practice, there are some financing components with no market values available, even for large publicly traded firms, and none of the financing components are traded in private firms.

The Market Value of Equity

The market value of equity is generally the number of shares outstanding times the current stock price. Because it measures the cost of raising funds today, it is not good practice to use average stock prices over time or some other normalized version of the price.

---

[53]There are some who argue that stock prices are much more volatile than the underlying true value. Even if this argument is justified (and it has not conclusively been shown to be so), the difference between market value and true value is likely to be much smaller than the difference between book value and true value.

[54]To illustrate this point, assume that the market value debt ratio is 10%, and the book value debt ratio 30%, for a firm with a cost of equity of 15% and an after-tax cost of debt of 5%. The cost of capital can be calculated as follows:

With market value debt ratios: 15% (0.9) + 5% (0.1) = 14%
With book value debt ratios: 15% (0.7) + 5% (0.3) = 12%

- *Multiple classes of shares*   If there is more than one class of shares outstanding, the market values of all of these securities should be aggregated and treated as equity. Even if some of the classes of shares are not traded, market values have to be estimated for nontraded shares and added to the aggregate equity value.

- *Equity options*   If there other equity claims in the firm—warrants and conversion options in other securities—these should also be valued and added on to the value of the equity in the firm. In the past decade, the use of options as management compensation has created complications, because the value of these options has to be estimated.

How do we estimate the value of equity for private businesses? We have two choices. One is to estimate the market value of equity by looking at the multiples of revenues and net income at which publicly traded firms trade. The other is to bypass the estimation process and use the market debt ratio of publicly traded firms as the debt ratio for private firms in the same business. This is the assumption we made for Bookscape, for whom we used the industry average debt-to-equity ratio for the book/publishing business as the debt-to-equity ratio for Bookscape.

The Market Value of Debt

The market value of debt is usually more difficult to obtain directly because very few firms have all of their debt in the form of bonds outstanding trading in the market. Many firms have nontraded debt, such as bank debt, which is specified in book value terms but not market value terms. To get around the problem, many analysts make the simplifying assumptions that the book value of debt is equal to its market value. Although this is not a bad assumption for mature companies in developed markets, it can be a mistake when interest rates and default spreads are volatile.

A simple way to convert book value debt into market value debt is to treat the entire debt on the books as a coupon bond, with a coupon set equal to the interest expenses on all of the debt and the maturity set equal to the face-value weighted average maturity of the debt, and to then value this coupon bond at the current cost of debt for the company. Thus, the market value of $1 billion in debt, with interest expenses of $60 million and a maturity of six years, when the current cost of debt is 7.5% can be estimated as follows:

$$\text{Estimated market value of debt} = 60 \left[\frac{1 - \dfrac{1}{(1.075)^6}}{0.075} \right] + \frac{1,000}{(1.075)^6} = \$930$$

This is an approximation; a more accurate computation would require valuing each debt issue separately using this process. As a final point, we should add the present value of operating lease commitments to this market value of debt to arrive at an aggregate value for debt in computing the cost of capital.

IN PRACTICE: CAN FINANCING WEIGHTS CHANGE OVER TIME?

Using the current market values to obtain weights will yield a cost of capital for the current year. But can the weights attached to debt and equity and the resulting cost of capital change from year to year? Absolutely, and especially in the following scenarios:

- *Young firms* Young firms often are all equity-funded largely, because they do not have the cash flows (or earnings) to sustain debt. As they become larger, increasing earnings and cash flow usually allow for more borrowing. When analyzing firms early in their life cycle, we should allow for the fact that the debt ratio of the firm will probably increase over time toward the industry average.

- *Target debt ratios and changing financing mix* Mature firms sometimes decide to change their financing strategies, pushing toward target debt ratios that are much higher or lower than current levels. When analyzing these firms, we should consider the expected changes as the firm moves from the current to the target debt ratio.

As a general rule, we should view the cost of capital as a year-specific number and change the inputs each year. Not only will the weights attached to debt and equity change over time, but so will the estimates of beta and the cost of debt. In fact, one of the advantages of using bottom-up betas is that the beta each year can be estimated as a function of the expected debt-to-equity ratio that year. ∎

ILLUSTRATION 4.17   Market Value and Book Value Debt Ratios—Disney and Aracruz

Disney has a number of debt issues on its books, with varying coupon rates and maturities. Table 4.28 summarizes Disney's outstanding debt, broken down by when the debt comes due; we treat the debt due in 2009 as due in one year, the debt due in 2010 as due in two years, and so on. The debt due after 2013 is given a maturity of ten years, based upon a perusal of the actual due dates on the long-term debt.

To convert the book value of debt to market value, we use the current pretax cost of debt for Disney of 6% estimated in Illustration 4.14, as the discount rate, the face

Table 4.28   DEBT AT DISNEY: MAY 2009

Due in	Maturity	Amount Due	% Due
2009	1	$3,513	24.33%
2010	2	$1,074	7.44%
2011	3	$1,205	8.35%
2012	4	$1,479	10.24%
2013	5	$1,842	12.76%
Thereafter	10	$5,324	36.88%
Weighted Average	5.38 years	$14,437	

value of debt ($16,003 million) in May 2009 as the book value of debt and the current year's interest expenses of $728 million as the coupon payment:

$$\text{Estimated MV of Disney debt} = 728 \left[\frac{1 - \dfrac{1}{(1.06)^{5.38}}}{0.06} \right]$$

$$+ \frac{16,003}{(1.06)^{5.38}} = \$14,962 \text{ million}$$

To this amount, we add the present value of Disney's operating lease commitments. This present value is computed by discounting the lease commitment each year at the pretax cost of debt for Disney (6%) in Table 4.29.[55]

Adding the debt value of operating leases to the market value of debt of $14,962 million yields a total market value for debt of $16,682 million at Disney.

For Aracruz and Tata Chemicals, we use the book value of debt as a proxy for the market value of debt. For the former, this is because a significant portion of its debt is recent (and should therefore reflect current market interest rates and prices.). For the latter, a large portion of the debt is short-term, which should ensure that the market value and book value of debt will converge. In Table 4.30 we contrast the book value debt ratios with the market value debt ratios for Disney, Aracruz, and Tata Chemicals. The market value of equity is estimated using the current market price and the number of shares outstanding.

For Disney, the market value debt ratio of 26.96%% is lower than the book value debt ratio of 32.89. That pattern is repeated for Aracruz and Tata Chemicals, with the difference being largest at Aracuz, where book value of equity recorded a significant write-down in 2008 (as a result of their trading losses in derivatives).

Table 4.29   PRESENT VALUE OF OPERATING LEASES AT DISNEY

Year	Commitment (in millions)	Present Value (in millions)
1	$392.00	$369.81
2	$351.00	$312.39
3	$305.00	$256.08
4	$265.00	$209.90
5	$198.00	$147.96
6–7	$309.50	$424.02
Debt value of leases =		$1,720.17

---

[55]Disney reports total commitments of $719 million beyond year six. Using the average commitment from years one through five as an indicator, we assumed that this total commitment would take the form of an annuity of $309.50 million a year for two years.

	Book D/E	Book Debt/Capital	Market D/E	Market Debt/Capital
Disney	49.01%	32.89%	36.91%	26.96%
Aracruz	1,012.22%	91.01%	110.41%	52.47%
Tata Chemicals	75.83%	43.13%	51.56%	34.02%

Table 4.30 BOOK VALUE VERSUS MARKET VALUE: DEBT RATIOS

Estimating and Using the Cost of Capital

With the estimates of the costs of the individual components—debt, equity and preferred stock (if any)—and the market value weights of each of the components, the cost of capital can be computed. Thus if E, D, and PS are the market values of equity, debt, and preferred stock respectively, the cost of capital can be written as follows:

$$\text{Cost of capital} = k_E[E/(D + E + PS)] + k_D$$
$$[D/(D + E + PS)] + k_{PS}[PS/(D + E + PS)]$$

The cost of capital is a measure of the composite cost of raising money that a firm faces. It will generally be lower than the cost of equity, which is the cost of just equity funding.

It is a source of confusion to many analysts that both the cost of equity and the cost of capital are used as hurdle rates in investment analysis. The way to resolve this confusion is to recognize when it is appropriate to use each one.

- If we want to adopt the perspective of just the equity investors in a business or a project and measure the returns earned just by these investors on their investment, the cost of equity is the correct hurdle rate to use. In measuring the returns to equity investors then, we have to consider only the income or cash flows left over after all other claimholders needs (interest payments on debt and preferred dividends, for instance) have been met.

- If the returns that we are measuring are composite returns to all claimholders, based on earnings before payments to debt and preferred stockholders, the comparison should be to the cost of capital.

Although these principles are abstract, we will consider them in more detail in the next chapter when we look at examples of projects.

 wacc.xls: This data set online has the average cost of capital, by industry (sector), for the United States.

 Hurdle Rates: A Behavioral Perspective
Our discussion of cost of equity and capital has centered on a critical premise that the right hurdle rate for a firm should reflect the weighted average of the cost of financing the firm today. As a consequence, we used the current costs of debt and equity, updated to reflect today's risk-free rates and risk premiums, and weighted them based upon market values. But do managers subscribe to this approach? There is

substantial evidence that some of them do not, and the reasons may have more to do with behavioral considerations than with financial arguments. Surveys of how firms set hurdle rates for investments indicate the following:

- *Book value versus market value*   Many firms continue to use book values for debt and equity to compute weights, rather than market values. One reason for this practice, stated or unstated, is that book debt ratios are more stable than market debt ratios. This is almost a given, since the market values (at least of equity) change continuously but the book values do not change until the next financial statement is put together. Intellectually, we can argue (as we have) that the stability of debt ratios is an illusion, but it is human nature to prefer stability to volatility.

- *Outsourcing risk premiums and betas*   In the earlier parts of this chapter, we noted that it is common practice for firms to purchase estimates of equity risk premiums and betas for external sources—Ibbotson Associates for the former, and Barra for the latter. While we believe that it is dangerous to outsource key components of the cost of capital to an outside source, it makes sense from a behavioral standpoint. Using external sources for data gives managers someone else to blame, if things go wrong, and thus deflects any criticism that they may have faced for bad decisions.

- *Hurdle rate not equal to cost of capital*   In many firms, the hurdle rate that is used for assessing investments is not based upon the cost of capital. Instead, it is set at a value above or below the cost of capital and often reflects what the firm has earned on projects it has invested in the past.[56] Thus, a firm that has generated a 15% return on capital on past investments will use a hurdle rate of 15% for future investments, rather than its computed cost of capital. From a behavioral finance perspective, this practice does make sense since it reflects both anchoring (where managers start with the familiar—i.e., past returns—as their anchors for estimates) and availability biases (where they overweight recent project return experience too much).

So how should managers set hurdle rates in a world that is composed of irrational investors? In a paper examining this question, Stein argues that firms that are focused on long-term value maximization should continue to use the conventional cost of capital as the hurdle rate, with the proviso that betas reflect the true economic risk of the enterprise rather than returns over short time periods. However, if the objective is to maximize the current stock price, the hurdle rate used should not be the cost of capital but should be adjusted for whatever errors investors are making in assessing stock price; he suggests using the price to book ratio as a proxy for this adjustment. This can lead to hurdle rates being lower than the cost of capital for some firms and higher for others.[57]

---

[56]C. Driver and P. Temple, 2009, "Why Do Hurdle Rates Differ from the Cost of Capital?" *Cambridge Journal of Economics, Advance Acesss* 1–23. They compare the costs of capital and hurdle rates for 3,000 business units at 450 companies that are part of the PIMS database and find that while 1,425 units use hurdle rates that are roughly equal to their costs of capital, 505 units use hurdle rates less than the cost of capital, and 452 use hurdle rates that are higher than their costs of capital.

[57]J. Stein, "Rational Capital Budgeting in an Irrational World," *Journal of Business* 69:429–455.

Table 4.31　Cost of Capital for Disney's Divisions

	Cost of Equity	After-Tax Cost of Debt	E/(D+E)	D/(D+E)	Cost of Capital
Media networks	8.61%	3.72%	75.00%	25.00%	7.39%
Parks and resorts	8.20%	3.72%	64.68%	35.32%	6.62%
Studio entertainment	13.53%	3.72%	68.64%	31.36%	10.45%
Consumer products	10.86%	3.72%	80.84%	19.16%	9.49%
Disney	8.91%	3.72%	73.04%	26.96%	7.51%

ILLUSTRATION 4.18　Estimating Cost of Capital

Culminating the analysis in this chapter, we first estimate the costs of capital for each of Disney's divisions. In making these estimates, we use the costs of equity that we obtained for the divisions in Illustration 4.13 and Disney's cost of debt from Illustration 4.14. We also use the debt ratios we estimated for each division in Illustration 4.13. Table 4.31 provides estimates of the costs of capital for the divisions.

The cost of capital for Disney's operating assets is 7.51%, but the costs of capital vary across divisions with a low of 6.62% for the parks and resorts division to a high of 10.45% for studio entertainment.

To estimate the cost of capital in U.S. dollars for Aracruz, we use the cost of equity of 20.82% (from Illustration 4.13), the after-tax cost of debt of 5.61% (from Illustration 4.14), and the debt-to-capital ratio of 52.47% (estimated based upon the current market values of debt and equity):

$$\text{Cost of capital}_\$ = 20.82\%(1 - 0.5247) + 5.61\% \ (0.5247) = 12.84\%$$

This dollar cost of capital can be converted into nominal R$ cost of capital or a real cost of capital, by adjusting for inflation:

$$\text{Cost of capital}_{R\$} = (1 + \text{Cost of capital}_\$) \ \frac{(1 + \text{Expected inflation}_{R\$})}{(1 + \text{Expected inflation}_{US\$})} - 1$$

$$= 1.1284 \frac{(1.07)}{(1.02)} - 1 = 18.37\%$$

$$\text{Cost of capital}_{Real} = (1 + \text{Cost of capital}_\$) \frac{1}{(1 + \text{Expected inflation}_{US\$})} - 1$$

$$= 1.1284 \frac{1}{(1.02)} - 1 = 10.63\%$$

Note again that the only reason for the differences across the estimates of cost of capital is different expectations for inflation: 0% for real, 2% for U.S. dollars and 7% for R$.

To estimate the cost of capital for Tata Chemicals, we look at its two businesses—fertilizers and chemicals—and use the estimates of cost of equity and debt obtained in earlier illustrations. Table 4.32 summarizes the estimates.

We stayed with the assumption that we made earlier that the debt ratios of the two divisions would the same as the overall company.

When estimating the cost of equity for Bookscape, we assumed that the company would be funded using the same market debt-to-equity ratio as the book/publishing

Table 4.32	COST OF CAPITAL—TATA CHEMICALS				
	Cost of Equity	Pretax Cost of Debt	After-Tax Cost of Debt	D/(D+E)	Cost of Capital
Fertilizers	14.14%	10.0%	6.60%	34.02%	11.58%
Chemicals	13.58%	10.0%	6.60%	34.02%	11.21%
Tata Chemicals	13.93%	10.0%	6.60%	34.02%	11.44%

Table 4.33	COST OF CAPITAL FOR BOOKSCAPE—MARKET AND TOTAL BETA				
	Cost of Equity	Pretax Cost of Debt	After-Tax Cost of Debt	D/(D+E)	Cost of Capital
Market beta	11.60%	6.00%	3.60%	34.84%	8.81%
Total beta	20.94%	6.00%	3.60%	34.84%	14.90%

industry. Staying consistent, we will use the market debt to capital ratio of the sector to compute the cost of capital for the firm. We will also present two estimates of the cost of capital—one using the market beta and the other using the total beta—in Table 4.33.

The cost of capital estimated using the total beta is a more realistic estimate, given that this is a private company, and we will use it as the cost of capital for Bookscape in the coming chapters.

 IN PRACTICE: EQUITY, DEBT, AND COST OF CAPITAL FOR BANKS

Note that we did not estimate a cost of capital for Deutsche Bank even though we have estimates of the costs of equity and debt for the firm. The reason is simple and goes to the heart of how firms view debt. For nonfinancial service firms, debt is a source of capital and is used to fund real projects—building a factory or making a movie. For banks, debt is raw material that is used to generate profits. Boiled down to its simplest elements, it is a bank's job to borrow money (debt) at a low rate and lend it out at a higher rate. It should come as no surprise that when banks (and their regulators) talk about capital, they mean equity capital.[58]

There is also a practical problem in computing the cost of capital for a bank. If we define debt as any fixed commitment where failure to meet the commitment can lead to loss of equity control, the deposits made by customers at bank branches qualify, and the debt ratio of a bank will very quickly converge on 100%. If we define it more narrowly, we still are faced with a problem of where to draw the line. A pragmatic compromise is to view only long-term bonds issued by a bank as debt, but even this is an artificial choice. Deutsche Bank, for instance, had long-term debt in December 2008 with a value of 143 billion euros and common equity with a market value of

---

[58] All of the capital ratios that govern banks are stated in terms of book value of equity, though equity is defined broadly to include preferred stock.

30 billion euros. Using the cost of equity of 10.55% (from Illustration 4.13) and the after-tax cost of debt of 3.13% (from Illustration 4.14), we obtain a cost of capital:

$$\text{Cost of capital} = 10.55\%(30/173) + 4.12\%(143/173) = 5.23\%$$

However, this number is tainted by the arbitrary definition of debt as only long-term debt. With Deutsche Bank, we will do almost all of our analyses in equity terms, using the cost of equity rather than the cost of capital. ■

CONCLUSION

This chapter explains the process of estimating discount rates, by relating them to the risk and return models described in the previous chapter:

- The cost of equity can be estimated using risk and return models—the CAPM, where risk is measured relative to a single market factor; the APM, where the cost of equity is determined by the sensitivity to multiple unspecified economic factors; or a multifactor model, where sensitivity to macroeconomic variables is used to measure risk.
  - In both these models, the key inputs are the risk-free rate, the risk premiums, and the beta (in the CAPM) or betas (in the APM). The last of these inputs is usually estimated using historical data on prices.
  - Although the betas are estimated using historical data, they are determined by the fundamental decisions that a firm makes on its business mix, operating, and financial leverage. Consequently, we can get much better estimates of betas by looking at sector averages and correcting for differences across firms.
- The cost of capital is a weighted average of the costs of the different components of financing, with the weights based on the market values of each component. The cost of debt is the market rate at which the firm can borrow long-term, adjusted for any tax advantages of borrowing. The cost of preferred stock, on the other hand, is the preferred dividend.
- The cost of capital is the minimum acceptable hurdle rate that will be used to determine whether to invest in a project.

While we will use the cost of capital as our hurdle rate, when assessing investments, in the next two chapters, we are also aware that many firms use hurdle rates that are different from their costs of capital.

LIVE CASE STUDY

RISK AND RETURN: ANALYSIS FOR THE FIRM

Objective: To develop a risk profile for your company, estimate its risk parameters, and use these parameters to estimate costs of equity and capital for the firm.

Key Questions

- What is the risk profile of your company? (How much overall risk is there in this firm? Where is this risk coming from [market, firm, industry, or currency]? How is the risk profile changing?)

- What is the performance profile of an investment in this company? What return would you have earned investing in this company's stock? Would you have under- or outperformed the market? How much of the performance can be attributed to management?

- How risky is this company's equity? Why? What is its cost of equity?

- How risky is this company's debt? What is its cost of debt?

- What is the mix of debt and equity used by this firm to fund its investments?

- What is this company's current cost of capital?

Framework for Analysis

1. ***Estimating Historical Risk Parameters (Top-Down Betas)***

   - Run a regression of returns on your firm's stock against returns on a market index, preferably using monthly data and five years of observations (or)

   - What is the intercept of the regression? What does it tell you about the performance of this company's stock during the period of the regression?

   - What is the slope of the regression?

     - What does it tell you about the risk of the stock?

     - How precise is this estimate of risk? (Provide a range for the estimate.)

   - What portion of this firm's risk can be attributed to market factors? What portion to firm-specific factors? Why is this important?

   - How much of the "risk" for this firm is due to business factors? How much of it is due to financial leverage?

2. ***Comparing to Sector Betas (Bottom-Up Betas)***

   - Break down your firm by business components, and estimate a business beta for each component.

   - Attach reasonable weights to each component and estimate a unlevered beta for the business.

   - Using the current leverage of the company, estimate a levered beta for each component.

3. ***Choosing between Betas***
   - Which of the betas that you have estimated for the firm (top-down or bottom-up) would you view as more reliable? Why?
   - Using the beta that you have chosen, estimate the expected return on an equity investment in this company to equity investors in the company?
   - As a manager in this firm, how would you use this expected return?

4. ***Estimating Default Risk and Cost of Debt***
   - If your company is rated,
     - What is the most recent rating for the firm?
     - What is the default spread and interest rate associated with this rating?
     - If your company has bonds outstanding, estimate the yield to maturity on a long-term bond? Why might this be different from the rate estimated in the last step?
     - What is the company's marginal tax rate?
   - If your company is not rated,
     - Does it have any recent borrowings? If so, what interest rate did the company pay on these borrowing?
     - Can you estimate a "synthetic" rating? If so, what interest rate would correspond to this rating?

5. ***Estimating Cost of Capital***
   - Weights for debt and equity:
     - What is the market value of equity?
     - Estimate a market value for debt. (To do this, you might have to collect information on the average maturity of the debt, the interest expenses in the most recent period, and the book value of the debt.)
     - What are the weights of debt and equity?
   - Cost of capital:
     - What is the cost of capital for the firm?

Getting Information on Risk and Return

If you want to run a regression of stock returns against a market index to estimate a beta, you will need to estimate past returns for both the stock and index. Several data services provide access to the data. If you want a beta estimate for your firm, you can find it online or obtain it from a data service. If you want to estimate bottom-up betas, based upon comparable firms, you will first have to identify the businesses that your firm operates in (which should be available in the firm's 10-K), find comparable firms in each business and then estimate the average beta and debt-to-equity ratio for these firms.

You can find the rating for your company from the S&P and Moody publications that list traded bonds and their ratings. Alternatively, you can estimate an interest coverage ratio and a synthetic rating.

Online Sources of Information
www.stern.nyu.edu/~adamodar/cfin2E/project/data.htm

PROBLEMS AND QUESTIONS (Use 5.5% as your equity risk premium, for T. Bonds, where none is given, and 8.5% as your short term ERP)

1. In December 1995, Boise Cascade's stock had a beta of 0.95. The Treasury bill rate at the time was 5.8%, and the Treasury bond rate was 6.4%. The firm had debt outstanding of $1.7 billion and a market value of equity of $1.5 billion; the corporate marginal tax rate was 36%.

   a. Estimate the expected return on the stock for a short-term investor in the company.

   b. Estimate the expected return on the stock for a long-term investor in the company.

   c. Estimate the cost of equity for the company.

2. Boise Cascade also had debt outstanding of $1.7 billion and a market value of equity of $1.5 billion; the corporate marginal tax rate was 36%.

   a. Assuming that the current beta of 0.95 for the stock is a reasonable one, estimate the unlevered beta for the company.

   b. How much of the risk in the company can be attributed to business risk and how much to financial leverage risk?

3. Biogen, a biotechnology firm, had a beta of 1.70 in 1995. It had no debt outstanding at the end of that year.

   a. Estimate the cost of equity for Biogen, if the Treasury bond rate is 6.4%.

   b. What effect will an increase in long-term bond rates to 7.5% have on Biogen's cost of equity?

   c. How much of Biogen's risk can be attributed to business risk?

4. Genting Berhad is a Malaysian conglomerate with holdings in plantations and tourist resorts. The beta estimated for the firm, relative to the Malaysian stock exchange, is 1.15, and the long-term government borrowing rate in Malaysia is 11.5%.

   a. Estimate the expected return on the stock.

   b. If you were an international investor, what concerns (if any) would you have about using the beta estimated relative to the Malaysian index? If you do, how would you modify the beta?

5. You have just done a regression of monthly stock returns of HeavyTech, a manufacturer of heavy machinery, on monthly market returns over the past five years and come up with the following regression:

$$R_{\text{HeavyTech}} = 0.5\% + 1.2 R_M$$

The variance of the stock is 50%, and the variance of the market is 20%. The current Treasure bill rate is 3% (it was 5% one year ago). The stock is currently selling for $50, down $4 over the past year, and has paid a dividend of $2 during the past year and expects to pay a dividend of $2.50 over the next year. The NYSE composite has gone down 8% over the past year, with a dividend yield of 3%. HeavyTech has a tax rate of 40%.

   a. What is the expected return on HeavyTech over the next year?

   b. What would you expect HeavyTech's price to be one year from today?

   c. What would you have expected HeavyTech's stock returns to be over the past year?

   d. What were the actual returns on HeavyTech over the past year?

   e. HeavyTech has $100 million in equity and $50 million in debt. It plans to issue $50 million in new equity and retire $50 million in debt. Estimate the new beta.

6. Safecorp, which owns and operates grocery stores across the United States, currently has $50 million in debt and $100 million in equity outstanding. Its stock has a beta of 1.2. It is planning a leveraged buyout, where it will increase its debt-to-equity ratio to 8. If the tax rate is 40%, what will the beta of the equity in the firm be after the leveraged buyout?

7. Novell, which had a market value of equity of $2 billion and a beta of 1.50, announced that it was acquiring WordPerfect, which had a market value of equity of $1 billion and a beta of 1.30. Neither firm had any debt in its financial structure at the time of the acquisition, and the corporate tax rate was 40%.

   a. Estimate the beta for Novell after the acquisition, assuming that the entire acquisition was financed with equity.

   b.   Assume that Novell had to borrow the $1 billion to acquire WordPerfect. Estimate the beta after the acquisition.

8. You are analyzing the beta for Hewlett Packard and have broken down the company into four broad business groups, with market values and betas for each group.

Business Group	Market Value of Equity	Beta
Mainframes	$2.0 billion	1.10
Personal computers	$2.0 billion	1.50
Software	$1.0 billion	2.00
Printers	$3.0 billion	1.00

   a.   Estimate the beta for Hewlett Packard as a company. Is this beta going to be equal to the beta estimated by regressing past returns on their stock against a market index. Why, or why not?

   b.   If the Treasury bond rate is 7.5%, estimate the cost of equity for Hewlett Packard. Estimate the cost of equity for each division. Which cost of equity would you use to value the printer division?

   c.   Assume that HP divests itself of the mainframe business and pays the cash out as a dividend. Estimate the beta for HP after the divestiture. (HP had $1 billion in debt outstanding.)

9. The following table summarizes the percentage changes in operating income, percentage changes in revenue, and betas for four pharmaceutical firms.

Firm	% Change in Revenue	% Change in Operating Income	Beta
PharmaCorp	27%	25%	1.00
SynerCorp	25%	32%	1.15
BioMed	23%	36%	1.30
Safemed	21%	40%	1.40

   a.   Calculate the degree of operating leverage for each of these firms.

   b.   Use the operating leverage to explain why these firms have different betas.

10. A prominent beta estimation service reports the beta of Comcast Corporation, a major cable TV operator, to be 1.45. The service claims to use weekly returns on the stock over the prior five years and the NYSE composite as the market index to estimate betas. You replicate the regression using weekly returns over the same period and arrive at a beta estimate of 1.60. How would you reconcile the two estimates?

11. Battle Mountain is a mining company that mines gold, silver, and copper in mines in South America, Africa, and Australia. The beta for the stock is estimated to be 0.30. Given the volatility in commodity prices, how would you explain the low beta?

12. You have collected returns on AnaDone, a large diversified manufacturing firm, and the NYSE index for five years:

Year	Returns (%) for AnaDone	Returns (%) for NYSE
1981	10%	5%
1982	5%	15%
1983	−5%	8%
1984	20%	12%
1985	−5%	−5%

   a.   Estimate the intercept (alpha) and slope (beta) of the regression.

   b.   If you bought stock in AnaDone today, how much would you expect to make as a return over the next year? (The six-month Treasury bill rate is 6%.)

   c.   Looking back over the past five years, how would you evaluate AnaDone's performance relative to the market?

   d.   Assume now that you are an undiversified investor and that you have all of your money invested in AnaDone. What would be a good measure of the risk that you are taking on? How much of this risk would you be able to eliminate if you *diversify*?

   e.   AnaDone is planning to sell off one of its divisions. The division under consideration has assets which comprise half of the book value of AnaDone and 20% of the market value. Its beta is twice the average beta for AnaDone (before divestment). What will the beta of AnaDone be after divesting this division?

13. You run a regression of monthly returns of Mapco, an oil- and gas-producing firm, on the S&P 500 Index and come up with the following output for the period 1991 to 1995.

Intercept of the regression $= 0.06\%$
X-Coefficient of the regression $= 0.46$
Standard error of X-Coefficient $= 0.20$
$$R^2 = 5\%$$

There are 20 million shares outstanding, and the current market price is $2. The firm has $20 million in debt outstanding. (The firm has a tax rate of 36%.)

a. What would an investor in Mapco's stock require as a return if the Treasure bond rate is 6%?

b. What proportion of this firm's risk is diversifiable?

c. Assume now that Mapco has three divisions, of equal size (in market value terms). It plans to divest itself of one of the divisions for $20 million in cash and acquire another for $50 million (it will borrow $30 million to complete this acquisition). The division it is divesting is in a business line where the average unlevered beta is 0.20, and the division it is acquiring is in a business line where the average unlevered beta is 0.80. What will the beta of Mapco be after this acquisition?

14. You have just run a regression of monthly returns of American Airlines (AMR) against the S&P 500 over the past five years. You have misplaced some of the output and are trying to derive it from what you have.

a. You know the R^2 of the regression is 0.36, and that your stock has a variance of 67%. The market variance is 12%. What is the beta of AMR?

b. You also remember that AMR was not a very good investment during the period of the regression and that it did worse than expected (after adjusting for risk) by 0.39% a month for the five years of the regression. During this period, the average risk-free rate was 4.84%. What was the intercept on the regression?

c. You are comparing AMR to another firm that also has an R^2 of 0.48. Will the two firms have the same beta? If not, why not?

15. You have run a regression of *monthly* returns on Amgen, a large biotechnology firm, against *monthly* returns on the S&P 500 Index, and come up with the following output:

$$R_{stock} = 3.28\% + 1.65 R_{Market} \quad R^2 = 0.20$$

The current one-year Treasury bill rate is 4.8% and the current thirty-year bond rate is 6.4%. The firm has 265 million shares outstanding, selling for $30 per share.

a. What is the expected return on this stock over the next year?

b. Would your expected return estimate change if the purpose was to get a discount rate to analyze a thirty-year capital budgeting project?

c. An analyst has estimated correctly that the stock did 51.1% better than expected annually during the period of the regression. Can you estimate the annualized risk-free rate that she used for her estimate?

d. The firm has a debt-to-equity ratio of 3% and faces a tax rate of 40%. It is planning to issue $2 billion in new debt and acquire a new business for that amount, with the same risk level as the firm's existing business. What will the beta be after the acquisition?

16. You have just run a regression of monthly returns on MAD, a newspaper and magazine publisher, against returns on the S&P 500, and arrived at the following result:

$$R_{MAD} = -0.05\% + 1.20 R_{S\&P}$$

The regression has an R^2 of 22%. The current Treasury bill rate is 5.5% and the current Treasury bond rate is 6.5%. The risk-free rate during the period of the regression was 6%. Answer the following questions relating to the regression:

a. Based on the intercept, you can conclude that the stock did

i. 0.05% worse than expected on a monthly basis, during the regression.

ii. 0.05% better than expected on a monthly basis during the period of the regression.

iii. 1.25% better than expected on a monthly basis during the period of the regression.

iv. 1.25% worse than expected on a monthly basis during the period of the regression.

v. None of the above.

b. You now realize that MAD went through a major restructuring at the end of last month (which was the last month of your regression), and made the following changes:

- The firm sold off its magazine division, which had an unlevered beta of 0.6, for $20 million.

- It borrowed an additional $20 million, and bought back stock worth $40 million. After the sale of the division and the share repurchase, MAD had $40 million in debt and $120 million in equity outstanding. If the firm's tax rate is 40%, reestimate the beta after these changes.

17. Time Warner, the entertainment conglomerate, has a beta of 1.61. Part of the reason for the high beta is the debt left over from the leveraged buyout of Time by Warner in 1989, which amounted to $10 billion in 1995. The market value of equity at Time Warner in 1995 was also $10 billion. The marginal tax rate was 40%.

a. Estimate the unlevered beta for Time Warner.

b. Estimate the effect of reducing the debt ratio by 10% each year for the next two years on the beta of the stock.

18. Chrysler, the automotive manufacturer, had a beta of 1.05 in 1995. It had $13 billion in debt outstanding in that year and 355 million shares trading at $50 per share. The firm had a cash balance of $8 billion at the end of 1995. The marginal tax rate was 36%.

a. Estimate the unlevered beta of the firm.

b. Estimate the effect of paying out a special dividend of $5 billion on this unlevered beta.

c. Estimate the beta for Chrysler after the special dividend.

19. You are trying to estimate the beta of a private firm that manufactures home appliances. You have managed to obtain betas for publicly traded firms that also manufacture home appliances.

	Beta	Debt (millions)	MV of Equity (millions)
Black & Decker	1.40	$2,500	$3,000
Fedders Corp.	1.20	$5	$200
Maytag Corp.	1.20	$540	$2,250
National Presto	0.70	$8	$300
Whirlpool	1.50	$2,900	$4,000

The private firm has a debt-to-equity ratio of 25% and faces a tax rate of 40%. The publicly traded firms all have marginal tax rates of 40%, as well.

a. Estimate the beta for the private firm.

b. What concerns, if any, would you have about using betas of comparable firms?

20. As the result of stockholder pressure, RJR Nabisco is considering spinning off its food division. You have been asked to estimate the beta for the division and decide to do so by obtaining the beta of comparable publicly traded firms. The average beta of comparable publicly traded firms is 0.95, and the average debt-to-equity ratio of these firms is 35%. The division is expected to have a debt ratio of 25%. The marginal corporate tax rate is 36%.

a. What is the beta for the division?

b. Would it make any difference if you knew that RJR Nabisco had a much higher fixed cost structure than the comparable firms used here?

21. Western Telecom, a phone company, is considering expanding its operations into the media business. The beta for the company at the end of the most recent year was 0.90, and the debt-to-equity ratio was 1. The media business is expected to be 30% of the overall firm value in five years, and the average beta of comparable firms is 1.20; the average debt-to-equity ratio for these firms is 50%. The marginal corporate tax rate is 36%.

a. Estimate the beta for Southwestern Bell in five years, assuming that it maintains its current debt-to-equity ratio.

b. Estimate the beta for Southwestern Bell in five years, assuming that it decides to finance its media operations with a debt-to-equity ratio of 50%.

22. The chief financial officer of Adobe Systems, a software manufacturing firm, has approached you for some advice regarding the beta of his company. He subscribes to a service that estimates Adobe System's beta each year, and he has noticed that the beta estimates have gone down every year since 1991—from 2.35 in 1991 to 1.40 in 1995. He would like the answers to the following questions:

a. Is this decline in beta unusual for a growing firm?

b. Why would the beta decline over time?

c. Is the beta likely to keep decreasing over time?

23. You are analyzing Tiffany's, an upscale retailer, and find that the regression estimate of the firm's beta is 0.75; the standard error for the beta estimate is 0.50. You also note that the average unlevered beta of comparable specialty retailing firms is 1.15.

a. If Tiffany's has a debt-to-equity ratio of 20%, estimate the beta for the company based on comparable firms. (The tax rate is 40%.)

b. Estimate a range for the beta from the regression.

c. How would you reconcile the two estimates? Which one would you use in your analysis?

CHAPTER 5

MEASURING RETURN ON INVESTMENTS

In Chapter 4, we developed a process for estimating costs of equity, debt, and capital and presented an argument that the cost of capital is the minimum acceptable hurdle rate when considering new investments. We also argued that an investment has to earn a return greater than this hurdle rate to create value for the owners of a business. In this chapter, we turn to the question of how best to measure the return on a project. In doing so, we will attempt to answer the following questions:

- What is a project? In particular, how general is the definition of an investment and what are the different types of investment decisions that firms have to make?

- In measuring the return on a project, should we look at the cash flows generated by the project or at the accounting earnings?

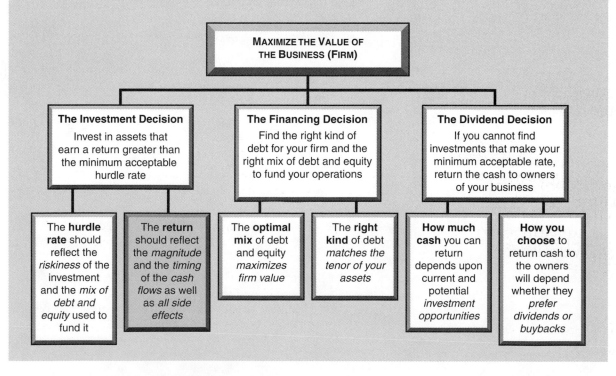

- If the returns on a project are unevenly spread over time, how do we consider (or should we not consider) differences in returns across time?

We will illustrate the basics of investment analysis using four hypothetical projects: an online book ordering service for Bookscape, a new theme park in Brazil for Disney, a plant to manufacture linerboard for Aracruz Celulose and an acquisition of a U.S. company by Tata Chemicals.

WHAT IS A PROJECT?

Investment analysis concerns which projects/investments a company should accept and which it should reject; accordingly, the question of what makes up a project or investment is central to this and the following chapters. The conventional project analyzed in capital budgeting has three criteria: (1) a large up-front cost, (2) cash flows for a specific time period, and (3) a salvage value at the end, which captures the value of the assets of the project when the project ends. Although such projects undoubtedly form a significant proportion of investment decisions, especially for manufacturing firms, it would be a mistake to assume that investment analysis stops there. If a project is defined more broadly to include any decision that relates to the use of the scarce resources of a business, then everything from strategic decisions and acquisitions to decisions about whether to outsource copying would fall within its reach.

Defined broadly then, any of the following decisions would qualify as projects:

- Major strategic decisions to enter new areas of business (such as Disney's foray into real estate or Deutsche Bank's into investment banking) or new markets (such as Disney Television's expansion into Latin America).

- Acquisitions of other firms are projects as well, notwithstanding attempts to create separate sets of rules for them. Thus, Disney's proposed acquisition of Marvel Entertainment in 2009 can be considered a very large project.

- Decisions on new ventures within existing businesses or markets, such as the one made by Disney to expand its Orlando theme park to include the Animal Kingdom or the decision to produce a new animated movie.

- Decisions that may change the way existing ventures and projects are run, such as programming schedules on the Disney channel or changing inventory policy at Bookscape.

- Decisions on how best to deliver a service that is necessary for the business to run smoothly. A good example would be Deutsche Bank's choice of what type of financial information system to acquire to allow traders and investment bankers to do their jobs. While the information system itself might not deliver revenues and profits, it is an indispensable component for other revenue generating projects.

Figure 5.1 The Project Continuum

Investment decisions can be categorized on a number of different dimensions. The first relates to how the project affects other projects the firm is considering and analyzing. Some projects are independent of other projects, and thus can be analyzed separately, whereas other projects are mutually exclusive—that is, taking one project will mean rejecting other projects. At the other extreme, some projects are prerequisites for other projects down the road, and others are complementary. In general, projects can be categorized as falling somewhere on the continuum between prerequisites and mutually exclusive, as depicted in Figure 5.1.

The second dimension that can be used to classify a project is its ability to generate revenues or reduce costs. The decision rules that analyze revenue-generating projects attempt to evaluate whether the earnings or cash flows from the projects justify the investment needed to implement them. When it comes to cost-reduction projects, the decision rules examine whether the reduction in costs justifies the up-front investment needed for the projects.

ILLUSTRATION 5.1 **Project Descriptions**
In this chapter and parts of the next, we will use four hypothetical projects to illustrate the basics of investment analysis.

1. The first project we will look at is a proposal by Bookscape to add an *online book ordering and information service.* Although the impetus for this proposal comes from the success of other online retailers like Amazon.com, Bookscape's service will be more focused on helping customers research books and find the ones they need rather than on price. Thus, if Bookscape decides to add this service, it will have to hire and train well-qualified individuals to answer customer queries, in addition to investing in the computer equipment and phone lines that the service will require. This project analysis will help illustrate some of the issues that come up when private businesses look at investments and also when businesses take on projects that have risk profiles different from their existing ones.

2. The second project we will analyze is a *proposed theme park for Disney in Rio De Janeiro, Brazil.* Rio Disneyworld, which will be patterned on Disneyland Paris and Walt Disney World in Florida, will require a huge investment in infrastructure and take several years to complete. This project analysis will bring several issues to the forefront, including questions of how to deal with projects when the cash flows are in a foreign currency and what to do when projects have very long lives.

3. The third project we will consider is a *plant in Brazil to manufacture linerboard* for Aracruz Celulose. Linerboard is a stiffened paper product that can be transformed into cardboard boxes. This investment is a more conventional one, with an initial investment, a fixed lifetime, and a salvage value at the end. We will, however, do the analysis for this project from an equity standpoint to illustrate the generality of investment analysis. In addition, we will do the analysis entirely in real terms.

4. The final project that we will examine is Tata Chemical's proposed acquisition of Sensient Technologies, a publicly traded U.S. firm that manufactures color, flavor, and fragrance additives for the food business. We will extend the same principles that we use to value internal investments to analyze how much Tata Chemicals can afford to pay for the U.S. company and the value of any potential synergies in the merger.

We should also note that while these projects are hypothetical, they are based upon real investments that these firms have taken in the past.

HURDLE RATES FOR FIRMS VERSUS HURDLE RATES FOR PROJECTS

In the previous chapter we developed a process for estimating the costs of equity and capital for firms. In this chapter, we will extend the discussion to hurdle rates in the context of new or individual investments.

Using the Firm's Hurdle Rate for Individual Projects

Can we use the costs of equity and capital that we have estimated for the firms for these projects? In some cases we can, but only if all investments made by a firm are similar in terms of their risk exposure. As a firm's investments become more diverse, the firm will no longer be able to use its cost of equity and capital to evaluate these projects. Projects that are riskier have to be assessed using a higher cost of equity and capital than projects that are safer. In this chapter, we consider how to estimate project costs of equity and capital.

Cost of Equity for Projects

In assessing the beta for a project, we will consider three possible scenarios. The first scenario is the one where all the projects considered by a firm are similar in their exposure to risk; this homogeneity makes risk assessment simple. The second scenario is one in which a firm is in multiple businesses with different exposures to risk, but projects within each business have the same risk exposure. The third scenario is the most complicated: each project considered by a firm has a different exposure to risk.

1. Single Business: Project Risk Similar within Business

When a firm operates in only one business and all projects within that business share the same risk profile, the firm can use its overall cost of equity as the cost of equity for each project. Because we estimated the cost of equity using a beta for the firm in Chapter 4, this would mean that we would use the same beta to estimate the cost of equity for each project that the firm analyzes. The advantage of this approach is that it does not require risk estimation prior to every project, providing managers with a fixed benchmark for their project investments. The approach is restricting, though, because it can be usefully applied only to companies that are in one line of business and take on homogeneous projects.

2. Multiple Businesses with Different Risk Profiles: Project Risk Similar within Each Business

When firms operate in more than one line of business, the risk profiles are likely to be different across different businesses. If we make the assumption that projects taken within each business have the same risk profile, we can estimate the cost of equity for each business separately and use that cost of equity for all projects within that business. Riskier businesses will have higher costs of equity than safer businesses, and projects taken by riskier businesses will have to cover these higher costs. Imposing the firm's cost of equity on all projects in all businesses will lead to overinvesting in risky businesses (because the cost of equity will be set too low) and underinvesting in safe businesses (because the cost of equity will be set too high).

How do we estimate the cost of equity for individual businesses? When the approach requires equity betas, we cannot fall back on the conventional regression approach (in the CAPM) or factor analysis (in the APM), because these approaches require past prices. Instead, we have to use one of the two approaches that we described in the last section as alternatives to regression betas—bottom-up betas based on other publicly traded firms in the same business, or accounting betas, estimated based on the accounting earnings for the division.

3. Projects with Different Risk Profiles

As a purist, you could argue that each project's risk profile is, in fact, unique and that it is inappropriate to use either the firm's cost of equity or divisional costs of equity to assess projects. Although this may be true, we have to consider the tradeoff. Given that small differences in the cost of equity should not make a significant difference in our investment decisions, we have to consider whether the added benefits of analyzing each project individually exceed the costs of doing so.

When would it make sense to assess a project's risk individually? If a project is large in terms of investment needs relative to the firm assessing it and has a very different risk profile from other investments in the firm, it would make sense to assess the cost of equity for the project independently. The only practical way of estimating betas and costs of equity for individual projects is the bottom-up beta approach.

Cost of Debt for Projects

In the previous chapter, we noted that the cost of debt for a firm should reflect its default risk. With individual projects, the assessment of default risk becomes much more difficult, because projects seldom borrow on their own; most firms borrow money for all the projects that they undertake. There are three approaches to estimating the cost of debt for a project:

1. One approach is based on the argument that because the borrowing is done by the firm rather than by individual projects, the cost of debt for a project should

be the cost of debt for the firm considering the project. This approach makes the most sense when the projects being assessed are small relative to the firm taking them and thus have little or no appreciable effect on the firm's default risk.

2. The second is to look at the project's capacity to generate cash flows relative to its financing costs and estimate default risk and cost of debt for the project. You can also estimate this default risk by looking at other firms that take similar projects and using the typical default risk and cost of debt for these firms. This approach generally makes sense when the project is large in terms of its capital needs relative to the firm and has different cash flow characteristics (both in terms of magnitude and volatility) from other investments taken by the firm and is capable of borrowing funds against its own cash flows.

3. The third approach applies when a project actually borrows its own funds, with lenders having no recourse against the parent firm, in case the project defaults. This is unusual, but it can occur when investments have significant tangible assets of their own and the investment is large relative to the firm considering it. In this case, the cost of debt for the project can be assessed using its capacity to generate cash flows relative to its financing obligations. In the last chapter, we used the bond rating of a firm to come up with the cost of debt for the firm. Although projects may not be rated, we can still estimate, an interest coverage ratio for the project and derive a synthetic rating, which can then be used to estimate a default spread and cost of debt.

Financing Mix and Cost of Capital for Projects

To get from the costs of debt and equity to the cost of capital, we have to weight each by their relative proportions. Again, the task is much easier at the firm level, where we use the current market values of debt and equity to arrive at these weights. We may borrow money to fund a project, but it is often not clear whether we are using the debt capacity of the project or the firm's debt capacity. The solution to this problem will again vary depending on the scenario we face.

*   When we are estimating the financing weights for small projects that do not affect a firm's debt capacity, the financing weights should be those estimated for of the firm before the project, using market value weights of debt and equity

*   When assessing the financing weights of large projects, with risk profiles different from that of the firm, we have to be more cautious. Using the firm's financing mix to compute the cost of capital for these projects can be misleading, because the project being analyzed may be riskier than the firm as a whole and thus incapable of carrying the firm's debt ratio. In this case, we would argue for the use of the average debt ratio of the other firms in the business in assessing the cost of capital of the project.

*   The financing weights for standalone projects that are large enough to issue their own debt should be based on the actual amounts borrowed by the projects. For firms with such projects, the financing weights can vary from project to projects, as will the cost of debt.

Table 5.1 COST OF DEBT AND DEBT RATIO: PROJECT ANALYSES

Project Characteristics	Cost of Debt	Debt Ratio
Project is small and has cash flow characteristics similar to the firm	Firm's cost of debt	Firm's debt ratio (actual or target)
Project is large and has cash flow characteristics different from the firm	Cost of debt of comparable firms (if nonrecourse debt) or the firm (if backed by the firm's creditworthiness)	Average debt ratio of comparable firms
Standalone project	Cost of debt for project (based on actual or synthetic ratings)	Debt ratio for project

In summary, the cost of debt and debt ratio for a project will reflect the size of the project relative to the firm, and its risk profile, again relative to the firm. Table 5.1 summarizes our analyses.

With stand-alone projects, there is one final point that is worth making. As the project ages, it is very likely that the debt used to fund the project will get paid off, thus reducing the debt ratio over time. While we can compute year-specific debt ratios and cost of capital, it makes more sense to compute an average debt ratio over the project life and estimate the cost of capital based upon that debt ratio.

ILLUSTRATION 5.2 Estimating Hurdle Rates for Individual Projects

Using the principles of estimation that we just laid out, we can estimate the hurdles rates for the projects that we are analyzing in this chapter.

- *Bookscape Online Information and Ordering Service* Because the beta and cost of equity that we estimated for Bookscape as a company reflect its status as a book store, we will re-estimate the beta for this online project by looking at publicly traded online retailers and examining the risk of an undiversified investor in this business. The unlevered total beta of internet retailers is 4.25,[1] and we assume that this project will be funded with the same mix of debt and equity (Debt/Equity = 53.47%, Debt/Capital = 34.84%) that Bookscape uses in the rest of the business. We will assume that Bookscape's tax rate (40%) and pretax cost of debt (6%) apply to this project. We chose to use the company's cost of debt and debt ratio rather than an industry average, because the project is a relatively small one.

$$\text{Levered beta}_{\text{Online service}} = 4.25[1 + (1 - 0.4)(0.5357)] = 5.61$$
$$\text{Cost of equity}_{\text{Online service}} = 3.5\% + 5.61(6\%) = 37.18\%$$
$$\text{Cost of capital}_{\text{Online service}} = 37.18\%(0.6516) + 6\%(1 - 0.4)(0.3484) = 25.48\%$$

This is much higher than the cost of capital we computed for Bookscape in Chapter 4, but it reflects the higher risk of the online retail venture.

- *Rio Disney* We did estimate a cost of equity of 8.20% for the Disney theme park business in the last chapter, using a bottom-up levered beta of 0.7829 for the

---

[1] The unlevered market beta for online retailers in early 2009 is 1.70, and the average correlation of these stocks with the market is 0.4. The unlevered total beta is therefore $1.7/0.4 = 4.25$.

business. The only concern we would have with using this cost of equity for this project is that it may not adequately reflect the additional risk associated with the theme park being in an emerging market (Brazil). To account for this risk, we compute the U.S.$ cost of equity for the theme park using a risk premium that includes a country risk premium for Brazil:[2]

$$\text{Cost of equity in U.S.\$} = 3.5\% + 0.7829(6\% + 3.95\%) = 11.29\%$$

Using this estimate of the cost of equity, Disney's theme park debt ratio of 35.32% and its after-tax cost of debt of 3.72% (see Chapter 4), we can estimate the cost of capital for the project:

$$\text{Cost of capital in U.S.\$} = 11.29\%(0.6468) + 3.72\%(0.3532) = 8.62\%$$

- *Aracruz Paper Plant* We estimated the cost of equity and capital for Aracruz's paper business in Chapter 4 in real, US$, and nominal R$ terms. We reproduce those estimates in Table 5.2:

Table 5.2   COSTS OF EQUITY AND CAPITAL: ARACRUZ

	Cost of Equity	Cost of Capital
US$	20.82%	12.84%
R$	26.75%	18.37%
Real	18.45%	10.63%

In analyzing projects, we will pick the appropriate discount rate based upon whether we are looking at cash flows prior to debt payments (cost of capital) or after debt payments (cost of equity) and the currency in which we are making our estimates.

- *Sensient Technologies Acquisition* The costs of capital that we estimated for Tata Chemicals and its divisions in Chapter 4 cannot be used in assessing the value of Sensient Technologies, for four reasons:
  1. *Currency* The cost of capital for Tata Chemicals was estimated in rupee terms, whereas our assessment of Sensient will be done in U.S. dollars.
  2. *Country risk* In estimating the cost of capital for Tata Chemicals, we incorporated an additional country risk premium for India, to reflect the fact that the operations are almost entirely in India. Sensient Technologies operates primarily in the United States and have very little emerging market exposure. Consequently, we should be using a mature market premium (of 6%) in estimating its cost of equity.
  3. *Business risk* To estimate the beta for Tata Chemicals, we looked at the betas of publicly traded emerging market companies in the diversified chemicals and fertilizers businesses. While Sensient Technologies is classified as a specialty

---

[2]We computed this country risk premium for Brazil in Chapter 4, in the context of computing the cost of capital for Aracruz. We multiplied the default spread for Brazil (2.50%) by the relative volatility of Brazil's equity index to the Brazilian government bond (34%/21.5%).
Country risk premium for Brazil = 2.50% (34/21.5) = 3.95%.

chemical company, its revenues are derived almost entirely from the food processing business. Consequently, we feel that the unlevered beta of food processing companies in the United States is a better measure of risk; in January 2009, we estimated an unlevered beta of 0.65 for this sector.

4. ***Cost of debt and debt ratio*** In this acquisition, Tata Chemicals plans to assume the existing debt of Sensient Technologies and to preserve Sensient's existing debt ratio. Sensient currently has a debt to capital ratio of 28.57% (translating into a debt to equity ratio of 40%) and faces a pretax cost of debt of 5.5%.

Using the U.S. corporate tax rate of 37% (to reflect the fact that Sensient's income will be taxed in the United States), we compute the cost of capital for Sensient in US$ terms:

$$\text{Levered beta} = 0.65\,(1 + (1 - 0.37)(0.40)) = 0.8138$$
$$\text{Cost of equity} = 3.5\% + 0.8138(6\%) = 8.38\%$$
$$\text{Cost of capital} = 8.38\%\,(1 - 0.2857) + 5.5\%\,(1 - 0.37)(0.2857) = 6.98\%$$

IN PRACTICE: EXCHANGE RATE RISK, POLITICAL RISK, AND FOREIGN PROJECTS

When computing the cost of capital for the Rio Disney project, we adjusted the cost of capital for the additional risk associated with investing in Brazil. Although it may seem obvious that a Brazilian investment is more risky to Disney than an investment in the United States, the question of whether discount rates should be adjusted for country risk is not an easy one to answer. It is true that a Brazilian investment will carry more risk for Disney than an investment in the United States, both because of exchange rate risk (the cash flows will be in Brazilian reals and not in U.S. dollars) and because of political risk (arising from Brazil's emerging market status). However, this risk should affect the discount rate only if it cannot be diversified away by the marginal investors in Disney.

To analyze whether the risk in Brazil is diversifiable to Disney, we went back to our assessment of the marginal investors in the company in Chapter 3, where we noted that they were primarily diversified institutional investors. Not only does exchange rate risk affect different companies in their portfolios very differently—some may be hurt by a strengthening dollar and others may be helped—but these investors can hedge exchange rate risk, if they so desire. If the only source of risk in the project were exchange rate, we would be inclined to treat it as diversifiable risk and not adjust the cost of capital. The issue of political risk is more confounding. To the extent that political risk is not only more difficult to hedge but is also more likely to carry a nondiversifiable component, especially when we are considering risky emerging markets, the cost of capital should be adjusted to reflect it.

In short, whether we adjust the cost of capital for foreign projects will depend both on the firm that is considering the project and the country in which the project is located. If the marginal investors in the firm are diversified and the project is in a country with relatively little or no political risk, we would be inclined not to add a risk premium on to the cost of capital. If the marginal investors in the firm are diversified and the project is in a country with significant political risk, we would add a political risk premium to the cost of capital. If the marginal investors in the firm are not diversified, we would adjust the discount rate for both exchange rate and political risk. ■

MEASURING RETURNS: THE CHOICES

On all of the investment decisions just described, we have to choose between alternative approaches to measuring returns on the investment made. We will present our argument for return measurement in three steps. First, we will contrast accounting earnings and cash flows and argue that cash flows are much better measures of true return on an investment. Second, we will note the differences between total and incremental cash flows and present the case for using incremental cash flows in measuring returns. Finally, we will argue that returns that occur earlier in a project life should be weighted more than returns that occur later in a project life and that the return on an investment should be measured using time-weighted returns.

A. Accounting Earnings versus Cash Flows

The first and most basic choice we have to make when it comes to measuring returns is the one between the accounting measure of income on a project—measured in accounting statements, using accounting principles and standards—and the cash flow generated by a project, measured as the difference between the cash inflows in each period and the cash outflows.

Why Are Accounting Earnings Different from Cash Flows?

Accountants have invested substantial time and resources in coming up with ways of measuring the income made by an investment. In doing so, they subscribe to some basic accounting principles. Generally accepted accounting principles in most markets require the recognition of revenues when the service for which the firm is getting paid has been performed in full or substantially and has received in return either cash or a receivable that is both observable and measurable. For expenses that are directly linked to the production of revenues (like labor and materials), expenses are recognized in the same period in which revenues are recognized. Any expenses that are not directly linked to the production of revenues are recognized in the period in which the firm consumes the services. Although the objective of distributing revenues and expenses fairly across time is worthy, the process of accrual accounting creates an accounting earnings number that can be very different from the cash flow generated by a project in any period. There are three significant factors that account for this difference.

1. Operating versus Capital Expenditure

Accountants draw a distinction between expenditures that yield benefits only in the immediate period or periods (such as labor and material for a manufacturing firm) and those that yield benefits over multiple periods (such as land, buildings, and long-lived equipment). The former are called *operating expenses* and are subtracted from revenues in computing the accounting income, whereas the latter are *capital expenditures* and are not subtracted from revenues in the period that they are made. Instead, the expenditure is spread over multiple periods and deducted as an expense in each period; these expenses are called depreciation (if the asset is a tangible asset like a building) or amortization (if the asset is an intangible asset, such as a patent or a trademark).

Although the capital expenditures made at the beginning of a project are often the largest part of investment, many projects require capital expenditures during their life-time. These capital expenditures will reduce the cash available in each of these periods.

5.1   WHAT ARE RESEARCH AND DEVELOPMENT EXPENSES?

Research and development (R&D) expenses are generally considered to be operating expenses by accountants. Based on our categorization of capital and operating expenses, would you consider R&D expenses to be

a. Operating expenses

b. Capital expenses

c. Operating or capital expenses, depending on the type of research being done

Why?

2. Noncash Charges

The distinction that accountants draw between operating and capital expenses leads to a number of accounting expenses, which are not cash expenses. These noncash expenses, though depressing accounting income, do not reduce cash flows. In fact, they can have a significant positive impact on cash flows if they reduce the tax paid by the firm since some noncash charges reduce taxable income and the taxes paid by a business. The most important of such charges is depreciation, which, although reducing taxable and net income, does not cause a cash outflow. In effect, depreciation and amortization is added back to net income to arrive at the cash flows on a project.

For projects that generate large depreciation charges, a significant portion of the cash flows can be attributed to the tax benefits of depreciation, which can be written as follows

$$\text{Tax benefit of depreciation} = \text{Depreciation} * \text{Marginal tax rate}$$

Although depreciation is similar to other tax-deductible expenses in terms of the tax benefit it generates, its impact is more positive because it does not generate a concurrent cash outflow.

Amortization is also a noncash charge, but the tax effects of amortization can vary depending on the nature of the amortization. Some amortization charges, such as the amortization of the price paid for a patent or a trademark, are tax-deductible and reduce both accounting income and taxes. Thus they provide tax benefits similar to depreciation. Other amortization, such as the amortization of the premium paid on an acquisition (called goodwill), reduces accounting income but not taxable income. This amortization does not provide a tax benefit.

Although there are a number of different depreciation methods used by firms, they can be classified broadly into two groups. The first is *straight-line depreciation*, whereby equal amounts of depreciation are claimed each period for the life of the project. The second group includes *accelerated depreciation methods*, such as double-declining balance depreciation, which result in more depreciation early in the project life and less in the later years.

3. Accrual versus Cash Revenues and Expenses

The accrual system of accounting leads to revenues being recognized when a sale is made, rather than when the customer pays for the good or service. Consequently, accrual revenues can be very different from cash revenues for three reasons. First, some customers, who bought their goods and services in prior periods, may pay in this period; second, some customers who buy their goods and services in this period (and are therefore shown as part of revenues in this period) may defer payment until the future. Finally, some customers who buy goods and services may never pay (bad debts). In some cases, customers may even pay in advance for products or services that will not be delivered until future periods.

A similar argument can be made on the expense side. Accrual expenses, relating to payments to third parties, will be different from cash expenses, because of payments made for material and services acquired in prior periods and because some materials and services acquired in current periods will not be paid for until future periods. Accrual taxes will be different from cash taxes for exactly the same reasons.

When material is used to produce a product or deliver a service, there is an added consideration. Some of the material used may have been acquired in previous periods and was brought in as inventory into this period, and some of the material that is acquired in this period may be taken into the next period as inventory.

Accountants define working capital as the difference between current assets (such as inventory and accounts receivable) and current liabilities (such as accounts payable and taxes payable). We will use a slight variant, and define noncash working capital as the difference between noncash current assets and nondebt current liabilities; debt is not considered part of working capital because it is viewed as a source of capital. The reason we leave cash out of the working capital computation is different. We view cash, for the most part, to be a nonwasting asset, insofar as firms earn a fair rate of return on the cash. Put another way, cash that is invested in commercial paper, treasury bills or other liquid, low risk financial assets is no longer a wasting asset and should not be considered part of working capital, even if it is viewed as an integral part of operations. Differences between accrual earnings and cash earnings, in the absence of noncash charges, can be captured by changes in the noncash working capital. A decrease in noncash working capital will increase cash flows, whereas an increase will decrease cash flows.

IN PRACTICE: The Payoff to Managing Working Capital

Firms that are more efficient in managing their working capital will see a direct payoff in terms of cash flows. Efficiency in working capital management implies that the firm has reduced its net working capital needs without adversely affecting its expected growth in revenues and earnings. Broadly defined, there are three ways net working capital can be reduced:

1. Firms need to maintain an inventory of both work in process and finished goods and to meet customer demand, but reducing this inventory while meeting the demand can produce a lower net working capital. In fact, recent advances in technology that use information systems for just-in-time production have helped U.S. firms reduce their inventory needs significantly.

2. Firms that sell goods and services on credit can reduce their net working capital needs by inducing customers to pay their bills faster and by improving their collection procedures.

3. Firms can also look for suppliers who offer more generous credit terms because accounts payable can be used to finance inventory and accounts receivable.

While lowering the amount invested in working capital will increase cash flows, that positive effect has to weighed off against any potential negative effects, including lost sales (because of insufficient inventory or more stringent credit terms) and higher costs (because suppliers may demand higher prices if you take longer to pay). ■

From Accounting Earnings to Cash Flows
The three factors outlined can cause accounting earnings to deviate significantly from the cash flows. To get from after-tax operating earnings, which measures the earnings to the firm, to cash flows to all investors in the firm, we have to

- *Add back all noncash charges*, such as depreciation and amortization, to the operating earnings.
- *Subtract* all cash outflows that represent *capital expenditures*.
- *Net out the effect of changes in noncash working capital*—that is, changes in accounts receivable, inventory, and accounts payable. If noncash working capital increased, the cash flows will be reduced by the change, whereas if it decreased, there is a cash inflow.

The first two adjustments adjust operating earnings to account for the distinction drawn by accountants between operating, and capital expenditures, whereas the last adjustment converts accrual revenues and expenses into cash revenues and expenses.

$$\text{Cash flow to firm} = \text{Earnings before interest and taxes}\,(1-t)$$
$$+ \text{Depreciation and amortization}$$
$$- \text{Change in noncash working capital} - \text{Capital expenditures}$$

The cash flow to the firm is a pre-debt, after-tax cash flow that measures the cash generated by a project for all claim holders in the firm after reinvestment needs have been met. This cash flow incorporates the tax benefits associated with depreciation but ignores those generated by interest expenses.

To get from net income, which measures the earnings of equity investors in the firm, to cash flows to equity investors requires the additional step of considering the net cash flow created by repaying old debt and taking on new debt. The difference between new debt issues and debt repayments is called the net debt, and it has to be added back to arrive at cash flows to equity. In addition, other cash flows to nonequity claim holders in the firm, such as preferred dividends, have to be netted from cash flows.

$$\text{Cash flow to equity} = \text{Net income} + \text{Depreciation and amortization}$$
$$- \text{Change in noncash working capital}$$
$$- \text{Capital expenditures}$$
$$+ (\text{New debt issues} - \text{Debt repayments})$$
$$- \text{Preferred dividends}$$

The cash flow to equity measures the cash flows generated by a project for equity investors in the firm, after taxes, debt payments, and reinvestment needs. Unlike cash flow to the firm, this cash flow incorporates the tax benefits from interest expenses.

5.2 EARNINGS AND CASH FLOWS

If the earnings for a firm are positive, the cash flows will also be positive.

a. True

b. False

Why or why not?

Earnings Management: A Behavioral Perspective

Accounting standards allow some leeway for firms to move earnings across periods by deferring revenues or expenses or by choosing a different accounting method for recording expenses. Publicly traded companies not only work at holding down expectations on the part of equity research analysts following them but also use their growth and accounting flexibility to move earnings across time to beat these expectations and to smooth out earning. It should come as no surprise that firms such as Microsoft and Intel consistently beat analyst estimates of earnings. Studies indicate that the tools for accounting earnings management range the spectrum and include choices on when revenues get recognized, how inventory gets valued, how leases and option expenses are treated, and how fair values get estimated for assets. Earnings can also be affected by decisions on when to invest in R&D and how acquisitions are structured.

In response to earnings management, FASB has created more stringent rules, but the reasons why companies manage earnings may have behavioral roots. One study, for instance, finds that the performance anxiety created among managers by frequent internal auditing can lead to more earnings management. Thus, more rules and regulations may have the perverse impact of increasing earnings management.

In addition, surveys indicate that managerial worries about personal reputation can induce them to try to meet earnings benchmarks set by external entities (such as equity research analysts) Finally, there is evidence that managers with "short horizons" are more likely to manage earnings with the intent of fooling investors.

The phenomenon of managing earnings has implications for a number of actions that firms may take, from how they sell their products and services to what kinds of projects they invest in or the firms they acquire and how they account for such investments. A survey of CFOs uncovers the troubling finding that more than 40% of them will reject an investment that will create value for a firm if the investment will result in the firm reporting earnings that fall below analyst estimates.

The Case for Cash Flows

When earnings and cash flows are different, as they are for many projects, we must examine which one provides a more reliable measure of performance. Accounting earnings, especially at the equity level (net income), can be manipulated at least for individual periods, through the use of creative accounting techniques. A book titled *Accounting for Growth*, which garnered national headlines in the United Kingdom and cost the author, Terry Smith, his job as an analyst at UBS Phillips & Drew, examined twelve legal accounting techniques commonly used to mislead investors about the profitability of individual firms. To show how creative accounting techniques can increase reported profits, Smith highlighted such companies as Maxwell Communications and Polly Peck, both of which eventually succumbed to bankruptcy.

The second reason for using cash flow is much more direct. No business that we know of accepts earnings as payment for goods and services delivered; all of them require cash. Thus, a project with positive earnings and negative cash flows will drain cash from the business undertaking it. Conversely, a project with negative earnings and positive cash flows might make the accounting bottom line look worse but will generate cash for the business undertaking it.

B. Total versus Incremental Cash Flows

The objective when analyzing a project is to answer the question: will investing in this project make the entire firm or business more valuable? Consequently, the cash flows we should look at in investment analysis are the cash flows the project creates for the firm or business considering it. We will call these incremental cash flows.

Differences between Incremental and Total Cash Flows

The total and the incremental cash flows on a project will generally be different for two reasons. First, some of the cash flows on an investment may have occurred already and therefore are unaffected by whether we take the investment or not. Such cash flows are called sunk costs and should be removed from the analysis. The second is that some of the projected cash flows on an investment will be generated by the firm, whether this investment is accepted or rejected. Allocations of fixed expenses, such as general and administrative costs, usually fall into this category. These cash flows are not incremental, and the analysis needs to be cleansed of their impact.

1. Sunk Costs

There are some expenses related to a project that are incurred before the project analysis is done. One example would be expenses associated with a test market done to assess the potential market for a product prior to conducting a full-blown investment analysis. Such expenses are called *sunk costs*. Because they will not be recovered if the project is rejected, sunk costs are not incremental and therefore should not be considered as part of the investment analysis. This contrasts with their treatment in accounting statements, which do not distinguish between expenses that have already been incurred and expenses that are still to be incurred.

One category of expenses that consistently falls into the sunk cost column in project analysis is research and development (R&D), which occurs well before a product is even considered for introduction. Firms that spend large amounts on R&D, have struggled to come to terms with the fact that the analysis of these expenses generally occur after the fact, when little can be done about them.

Although sunk costs should not be considered when analyzing investments, a firm does need to cover its sunk costs over time or it will cease to exist. Consider, for example, a firm like McDonald's, which expends considerable resources in test marketing products before introducing them. Assume, on the ill-fated McLean Deluxe (a low-fat hamburger introduced in 1990), that the test market expenses amounted to $30 million and that the net present value of the project, analyzed after the test market, amounted to $20 million. The project should be taken. If this is the pattern for every project McDonald's takes on, however, it will collapse under the weight of its test marketing expenses. To be successful, the *cumulative* net present value of its successful projects will have to exceed the *cumulative* test marketing expenses on both its successful and unsuccessful products.

The Psychology of Sunk Costs

While the argument that sunk costs should not alter decisions is unassailable, studies indicate that ignoring sunk costs does not come easily to managers. In an experiment, Arkes and Blumer presented forty-eight people with a hypothetical scenario: Assume that you are investing $10 million in research project to come up with a plane that cannot be detected by radar. When the project is 90% complete ($9 million spent), another firm begins marketing a plane that cannot be detected by radar and is faster and cheaper than the one you are working on. Would you invest the last 10% to complete the project? Of the group, forty individuals said they would go ahead. Another group of sixty was asked the question, with the same facts about the competing firm and its plane, but with the cost issue framed differently. Rather than mention that the firm had already spent $9 million, they were asked whether they would spend an extra million to continue with this investment. Almost none of this group would fund the investment.[3] Other studies confirm this finding, which has been labeled the *Concorde fallacy*.

Rather than view this behavior as irrational, we should recognize that lecturing managers to ignore sunk costs in their decisions will accomplish little. The findings in these studies indicate one possible way of bridging the gap. If we can frame investment analysis primarily around incremental earnings and cash flows, with little emphasis on past costs and decisions (even if that is provided for historical perspective), we are far more likely to see good decisions and far less likely to see good money thrown after bad. It can be argued that conventional accounting, which mixes sunk costs and incremental costs, acts as an impediment in this process.

2. Allocated Costs

An accounting device created to ensure that every part of a business bears its fair share of costs is *allocation*, whereby costs that are not directly traceable to revenues generated by individual products or divisions are allocated across these units, based on revenues, profits, or assets. Although the purpose of such allocations may be fairness, their effect on investment analyses have to be viewed in terms of whether they create incremental cash flows. An allocated cost that will exist with or without the project being analyzed does not belong in the investment analysis.

Any increase in administrative or staff costs that can be traced to the project is an incremental cost and belongs in the analysis. One way to estimate the incremental component of these costs is to break them down on the basis of whether they are

---

[3]H. R. Arkes and C. Blumer, "The Psychology of Sunk Cost." *Organizational Behavior and Human Decision Processes* 35:124–140.

fixed or variable, and if variable, what they are a function of. Thus, a portion of administrative costs may be related to revenue, and the revenue projections of a new project can be used to estimate the administrative costs to be assigned to it.

ILLUSTRATION 5.3   Dealing with Allocated Costs

Case 1:   Assume that you are analyzing a retail firm with general and administrative (G&A) costs currently of $600,000 a year. The firm currently has five stores and the G&A costs are allocated evenly across the stores; the allocation to each store is $120,000. The firm is considering opening a new store; with six stores, the allocation of G&A expenses to each store will be $100,000.

In this case, assigning a cost of $100,000 for G&A costs to the new store in the investment analysis would be a mistake, because it is not an incremental cost—the total G&A cost will be $600,000, whether the project is taken or not.

Case 2:   In the previous analysis, assume that all the facts remain unchanged except for one. The total G&A costs are expected to increase from $600,000 to $660,000 as a consequence of the new store. Each store is still allocated an equal amount; the new store will be allocated one-sixth of the total costs, or $110,000.

In this case, the allocated cost of $110,000 should not be considered in the investment analysis for the new store. The *incremental* cost of $60,000 ($660,000—$600,000), however, should be considered as part of the analysis.

IN PRACTICE: WHO WILL PAY FOR HEADQUARTERS?

As in the case of sunk costs, the right thing to do in project analysis (i.e., considering only direct incremental costs) may not add up to create a firm that is financially healthy. Thus, if a company like Disney does not require individual movies that it analyzes to cover the allocated costs of general administrative expenses of the movie division, it is difficult to see how these costs will be covered at the level of the firm.

In 2008, Disney's corporate shared costs amounted to $471 million. Assuming that these general administrative costs serve a purpose, which otherwise would have to be borne by each of Disney's business, and that there is a positive relationship between the magnitude of these costs and revenues, it seems reasonable to argue that the firm should estimate a fixed charge for these costs that every new investment has to cover, even though this cost may not occur immediately or as a direct consequence of the new investment. ■

The Argument for Incremental Cash Flows

When analyzing investments, it is easy to get tunnel vision and focus on the project or investment at hand, acting as if the objective of the exercise is to maximize the value of the individual investment. There is also the tendency, with perfect hindsight, to require projects to cover all costs that they have generated for the firm, even if such costs will not be recovered by rejecting the project at this stage. The objective in investment analysis is to maximize the value of the business or firm taking the investment. Consequently, it is the cash flows that an investment will add on in the future to the business, that is, the incremental cash flows, that we should focus on.

ILLUSTRATION 5.4   **Estimating Cash Flows for an Online Book Ordering Service: Bookscape**
As described in Illustration 5.1, Bookscape is considering investing in an online book ordering and information service, which will be staffed by two full-time employees. The following estimates relate to the costs of starting the service and the subsequent revenues from it.

1. The initial investment needed to start the service, including the installation of additional phone lines and computer equipment, will be $1 million. These investments are expected to have a life of four years, at which point they will have no salvage value. The investments will be depreciated straight-line over the four-year life.

2. The revenues in the first year are expected to be $1.5 million, growing 20% in year 2, and 10% in the two years following.

3. The salaries and other benefits for the employees are estimated to be $150,000 in year 1, and grow 10% a year for the following three years.

4. The cost of the books is assumed to be 60% of the revenues in each of the four years.

5. The working capital, which includes the inventory of books needed for the service and the accounts receivable (associated with selling books on credit) is expected to amount to 10% of the revenues; the investments in working capital have to be made at the beginning of each year. At the end of year 4, the entire working capital is assumed to be salvaged.

6. The tax rate on income is expected to be 40%, which is also the marginal tax rate for Bookscape.

Based on this information, we estimate the operating income for Bookscape Online in Table 5.3:

Table 5.3   EXPECTED OPERATING INCOME ON BOOKSCAPE ONLINE

	1	2	3	4
Revenues	$1,500,000	$1,800,000	$1,980,000	$2,178,000
Operating expenses				
Labor	$150,000	$165,000	$181,500	$199,650
Materials	$900,000	$1,080,000	$1,188,000	$1,306,800
Depreciation	$250,000	$250,000	$250,000	$250,000
Operating income	$200,000	$305,000	$360,500	$421,550
Taxes	$80,000	$122,000	$144,200	$168,620
After-tax operating income	$120,000	$183,000	$216,300	$252,930

To get from operating income to cash flows, we add back the depreciation charges and subtract the working capital requirements (which are the changes in working

	0 (Now)	1	2	3	4
Table 5.4 FROM OPERATING INCOME TO AFTER-TAX CASH FLOWS					
After-tax operating income		$120,000	$183,000	$216,300	$252,930
+ Depreciation		$250,000	$250,000	$250,000	$250,000
− Change in working capital	$150,000	$30,000	$18,000	$19,800	$0
− Capital Expenditures	$1,000,000				
+ Salvage value					$217,800
After-tax cash flows	−$1,150,000	$340,000	$415,000	$446,500	$720,730

capital from year to year) in Table 5.4. We also show the initial investment of $1 million as a cash outflow right now (year 0) and the salvage value of the entire working capital investment in year 4.

Note that there is an initial investment in working capital, which is 10% of the first year's revenues, invested at the beginning of the year. Each subsequent year has a change in working capital that represents 10% of the revenue change from that year to the next. In year 4, the cumulative investment in working capital over the four years ($217,800) is salvaged, resulting in a positive cash flow.[4]

5.3 THE EFFECTS OF WORKING CAPITAL

In the analysis, we assumed that Bookscape would have to maintain additional inventory for its online book service. If, instead, we had assumed that Bookscape could use its existing inventory (i.e., from its regular bookstore), the cash flows on this project will

a. Increase

b. Decrease

c. Remain unchanged

Explain.

ILLUSTRATION 5.5 Estimating Earnings, Incremental Earnings, and Incremental Cash Flows: Disney Theme Park

The theme parks to be built near Rio, modeled on Disneyland Paris, will include a Magic Kingdom to be constructed beginning immediately, and becoming operational at the beginning of the second year, and a second theme park modeled on Epcot at Orlando to be constructed in the second and third year and becoming operational at the beginning of the fourth year. The following is the set of assumptions that underlie the investment analysis.

• The cash flows will be estimated in nominal US dollars, even though the actual cash flows will be in Brazilian reals (R$).

---

[4]Salvaging working capital is essentially the equivalent of having a going-out-of-business sale, where all the inventory is sold at cost and all accounts receivable are collected.

- The cost of constructing Magic Kingdom will be $3 billion, with $2 billion to be spent right now and $1 billion to be spent a year from now. Disney has already spent $0.5 billion researching the proposal and getting the necessary licenses for the park; none of this investment can be recovered if the park is not built. This amount was capitalized and will be depreciated straight-line over the next ten years to a salvage value of zero.

- The cost of constructing Epcot II will be $1.5 billion, with $1 billion spent at the end of the second year and $0.5 billion at the end of the third year.

- The revenues at the two parks and the resort properties at the parks are assumed to be the following, based on projected attendance figures until the tenth year and an expected inflation rate of 2% (in U.S. dollars). Starting in year 10, the revenues are expected to grow at the inflation rate. Table 5.5 summarizes the revenue projections. Note that the revenues at the resort properties are set at 25% of the revenues at the theme parks.

- The direct operating expenses are assumed to be 60% of the revenues at the parks and 75% of revenues at the resort properties.

- The depreciation on fixed assets will be calculated as a percentage of the remaining book value of these assets at the end of the previous year. In addition, the parks will require capital maintenance investments each year, specified as a percentage of the depreciation that year. Table 5.6 lists both these statistics by year.[5]

The capital maintenance expenditures are low in the early years, when the parks are still new, but increase as the parks age since old attractions have to go through

Table 5.5	REVENUE PROJECTIONS—RIO DISNEY			
Year	**Magic Kingdom**	**Epcot II**	**Resort Properties**	**Total**
1	$0	$0	$0	$0
2	$1,000	$0	$250	$1,250
3	$1,400	$0	$350	$1,750
4	$1,700	$300	$500	$2,500
5	$2,000	$500	$625	$3,125
6	$2,200	$550	$688	$3,438
7	$2,420	$605	$756	$3,781
8	$2,662	$666	$832	$4,159
9	$2,928	$732	$915	$4,575
10	$2,987	$747	$933	$4,667
Beyond	Revenues grow 2% a year forever			

[5]Capital maintenance expenditures are capital expenditures to replace fixed assets that break down or become obsolete. This is in addition to the regular maintenance expenses that will be necessary to keep the parks going, which are included in operating expenses.

Year	Depreciation as % of Book Value	Capital Maintenance as % of Depreciation
	Table 5.6 DEPRECIATION AND CAPITAL MAINTENANCE PERCENTAGES	
1	0.00%	0.00%
2	12.50%	50.00%
3	11.00%	60.00%
4	9.50%	70.00%
5	8.00%	80.00%
6	8.00%	90.00%
7	8.00%	100.00%
8	8.00%	105.00%
9	8.00%	110.00%
10	8.00%	110.00%

either major renovations or be replaced with new attractions. After year 10, both depreciation and capital expenditures are assumed to grow at the inflation rate (2%) Note also that capital expenditures exceed depreciation after year 10, reflecting the fact that inflation will make the cost of replacement higher than the original cost.

- Disney will also allocate corporate G&A costs to this project, based on revenues; the G&A allocation will be 15% of the revenues each year. It is worth noting that a recent analysis of these expenses found that only one-third of these expenses are variable (and a function of total revenue) and that two-thirds are fixed. After year 10, these expenses are also assumed to grow at the inflation rate of 2%.

- Disney will have to maintain noncash working capital (primarily consisting of inventory at the theme parks and the resort properties, netted against accounts payable) of 5% of revenues, with the investments being made at the *end of each year*.

- The income from the investment will be taxed at Disney's marginal tax rate of 38%.
   The projected operating earnings at the theme parks, starting in the first year of operation (which is the second year) are summarized in Exhibit 5.1. Note that the project has no revenues until year 2, when the first park becomes operational and that the project is expected to have an operating loss of $150 million in that year. We have assumed that the firm will have enough income in its other businesses to claim the tax benefits from these losses (38% of the loss) in the same year. If this had been a standalone project, we would have had to carry the losses forward into future years and reduce taxes in those years.

The estimates of operating earnings in Exhibit 5.1 are distorted because they do mix together expenses that are incremental with expenses that are not. In particular, there are two points of contention:

1. ***Pre-project investment*** We included the depreciation on the pre-project investment of $500 million in the total depreciation for the project. This

depreciation, however, can be claimed by Disney, irrespective of whether it goes ahead with the new theme park investment.

2. ***Allocated G&A expenses*** While we considered the entire allocated expense in computing earnings, only one-third of this expense is incremental. Thus, we are understating the earnings on this project.

In Exhibit 5.2a, we compute the incremental earnings for Rio Disney, using only the incremental depreciation and G&A expenses. Note that the incremental earnings are more positive than the unadjusted earnings in Exhibit 5.1. In Exhibit 5.2a, we also estimate the incremental after-tax cash flow to Disney, prior to debt payments, by

- Adding back the incremental depreciation each year, because it is a noncash charge.

- Subtracting out the maintenance capital expenditures in addition to the primary capital expenditures, because these are cash outflows.

- Subtracting the incremental investment in working capital each year, which represents the change in working capital from the prior year. In this case, we have assumed that the working capital investments are made at the end of each year.

The investment of $3 billion in Rio Magic Kingdom is shown at time 0 (as $2 billion) and in year 1 (as $1 billion). The expenditure of $0.5 billion in pre-project investments is not considered because it has already been made (sunk cost). Note that we could have arrived at the same estimates of incremental cash flows, starting with the unadjusted operating income and correcting for the non-incremental items (adding back the fixed portion of G&A costs and subtracting the tax benefits from non-incremental depreciation). Exhibit 5.2b provides the proof.

5.4 DIFFERENT DEPRECIATION METHODS FOR TAX PURPOSES AND FOR REPORTING

The depreciation that we used for the project is assumed to be the same for both tax and reporting purposes. Assume now that Disney uses more accelerated depreciation methods for tax purposes and straight-line depreciation for reporting purposes. In estimating cash flows, we should use the depreciation numbers from the

a. Tax books
b. Reporting books

Explain.

Capbudg.xls: This spreadsheet allows you to estimate the cash flows to the firm on a project.

Exhibit 5.1   ESTIMATED OPERATING EARNINGS AT RIO DISNEY (IN US$ MILLIONS)

	0	1	2	3	4	5	6	7	8	9	10
Magic Kingdom: revenues		$0	$1,000	$1,400	$1,700	$2,000	$2,200	$2,420	$2,662	$2,928	$2,987
Epcot Rio: revenues		$0	$0	$0	$300	$500	$550	$605	$666	$732	$747
Resort and properties: revenues		$0	$250	$350	$500	$625	$688	$756	$832	$915	$933
Total Revenues			$1,250	$1,750	$2,500	$3,125	$3,438	$3,781	$4,159	$4,575	$4,667
Magic Kingdom: direct expenses		$0	$600	$840	$1,020	$1,200	$1,320	$1,452	$1,597	$1,757	$1,792
Epcot Rio: direct expenses		$0			$180	$300	$330	$363	$399	$439	$448
Resort & Property: direct expenses		$0	$188	$263	$375	$469	$516	$567	$624	$686	$700
Total direct expenses			$788	$1,103	$1,575	$1,969	$2,166	$2,382	$2,620	$2,882	$2,940
Depreciation and amortization		$50	$425	$469	$444	$372	$367	$364	$364	$366	$368
Allocated G&A costs		$0	$188	$263	$375	$469	$516	$567	$624	$686	$700
Operating income		–$50	–$150	–$84	$106	$315	$389	$467	$551	$641	$658
Taxes		–$19	–$57	–$32	$40	$120	$148	$178	$209	$244	$250
Operating income after taxes		–$31	–$93	–$52	$66	$196	$241	$290	$341	$397	$408
Capital expenditures											
Pre-project investments	$500										
Depreciation: pre-project		$50	$50	$50	$50	$50	$50	$50	$50	$50	$50
Magic Kingdom: construction	$2,000	$1,000									
Epcot Rio: construction	$0		$1,000	$500							
Capital maintenance			$188	$252	$276	$258	$285	$314	$330	$347	$350
Depreciation on fixed assets			$375	$419	$394	$322	$317	$314	$314	$316	$318
Book value of new fixed assets	$2,000	$3,000	$3,813	$4,145	$4,027	$3,962	$3,931	$3,931	$3,946	$3,978	$4,010
Book value of working capital			$63	$88	$125	$156	$172	$189	$208	$229	$233

Book value of fixed assets$_t$ = Book value of fixed assets$_{t-1}$ + New investment$_t$ + Capital maintenance$_t$ – Depreciation$_t$

Depreciation on fixed assets$_t$ = Book value of fixed assets$_{t-1}$ * Depreciation as % of prior year's book value of fixed assets

Depreciation and amortization$_t$ = Depreciation: pre-project investment$_t$ + Depreciation on fixed assets

Exhibit 5.2a   INCREMENTAL CASH FLOWS AT RIO DISNEY (IN US$ MILLIONS)

	0	1	2	3	4	5	6	7	8	9	10
Revenues		$0	$1,250	$1,750	$2,500	$3,125	$3,438	$3,781	$4,159	$4,575	$4,667
−Direct expenses		$0	$788	$1,103	$1,575	$1,969	$2,166	$2,382	$2,620	$2,882	$2,940
−Incremental depreciation		$0	$375	$419	$394	$322	$317	$314	$314	$316	$318
−Incremental G&A		$0	$63	$88	$125	$156	$172	$189	$208	$229	$233
Incremental operating income		$0	$25	$141	$406	$678	$783	$896	$1,017	$1,148	$1,175
−Taxes		$0	$10	$53	$154	$258	$298	$340	$386	$436	$447
Incremental after-tax operating income		$0	$16	$87	$252	$420	$485	$555	$630	$712	$729
+Incremental depreciation		$0	$375	$419	$394	$322	$317	$314	$314	$316	$318
−Capital expenditures	$2,000	$1,000	$1,188	$752	$276	$258	$285	$314	$330	$347	$350
−Change in noncash working capital		$0	$63	$25	$38	$31	$16	$17	$19	$21	$5
Cash flow to firm	−$2,000	−$1,000	−$860	−$270	$332	$453	$502	$538	$596	$660	$692

Exhibit 5.2b ANOTHER WAY OF COMPUTING INCREMENTAL CASH FLOWS AT RIO DISNEY

	0	1	2	3	4	5	6	7	8	9	10
Operating income (from Exhibit 5.1)		−$50	−$150	−$84	$106	$315	$389	$467	$551	$641	$658
− Taxes		−$19	−$57	−$32	$40	$120	$148	$178	$209	$244	$250
Operating income after taxes		−$31	−$93	−$52	$66	$196	$241	$290	$341	$397	$408
+ Depreciation and amortization		$50	$425	$469	$444	$372	$367	$364	$364	$366	$368
− Pre-project depreciation * tax rate		$19	$19	$19	$19	$19	$19	$19	$19	$19	$19
− Capital expenditures	$2,000	$1,000	$1,188	$752	$276	$258	$285	$314	$330	$347	$350
− Change in working capital	$0	$0	$63	$25	$38	$31	$16	$17	$19	$21	$5
+ Non-incremental allocated expense $(1 - t)$		$0	$78	$109	$155	$194	$213	$234	$258	$284	$289
Cash flow to firm	−$2,000	−$1,000	−$860	−$270	$332	$453	$502	$538	$596	$660	$692

ILLUSTRATION 5.6   Estimating Cash Flows to Equity for a New Plant: Aracruz

Aracruz Celulose is considering a plan to build a state-of-the-art plant to manufacture linerboard. The plant is expected to have a capacity of 750,000 tons and will have the following characteristics:

- It will require an initial investment of R$250 million. At the end of the fifth year, an additional investment of R$50 million will be needed to update the plant.

- Aracruz plans to borrow R$100 million at a real interest rate of 6.3725%, using a ten-year term loan (where the loan will be paid off in equal annual increments).

- The plant will have a life of ten years. During that period, the depreciable portion of the plant (and the additional investment in year five), not including salvage value, will be depreciated using double declining balance depreciation, with a life of ten years.[6] At the end of the tenth year, the plant is expected to be sold for its salvage value of R$75 million.

- The plant will be partly in commission in a couple of months but will have a capacity of only 650,000 tons in the first year and 700,000 tons in the second year before getting to its full capacity of 750,000 tons in the third year.

- The capacity utilization rate will be 90% for the first three years and rise to 95% after that.

- The price per ton of linerboard is currently $400 and is expected to keep pace with inflation for the life of the plant.

- The variable cost of production, primarily labor and material, is expected to be 45% of total revenues; there is a fixed cost of R$50 million, which will grow at the inflation rate.

- The working capital requirements are estimated to be 15% of total revenues, and the investments have to be made at the beginning of each year. At the end of the tenth year, it is anticipated that the entire working capital will be salvaged.

- Aracruz's corporate tax rate of 34% will apply to this project as well.

Before we estimate the net income on this project, we have to consider the debt payments each year and break them down into interest and principal payments. Table 5.7 summarizes the results.

Note that although the total payment remains the same each year, the breakdown into interest and principal payments changes from year to year.

Exhibit 5.3 summarizes the net income from plant investment to Aracruz each year for the next ten years. Note that all of the projections are in real cash flows. Consequently, the price of paper (which grows at the same rate as inflation) is kept constant in real terms, as is any other item having this characteristic.

---

[6]With double declining balance depreciation, we double the straight-line rate (which would be 10% a year, in this case with a ten-year life) and apply that rate to the remaining depreciable book value. We apply this rate to the investment in year 5 as well. We switch to straight-line depreciation in the sixth year because straight-line depreciation yields a higher value (and depreciates down to salvage value).

Table 5.7 DEBT PAYMENTS: ARACRUZ PAPER PLANT

Year	Beginning Debt	Interest Expense[a]	Principal Repaid	Total Payment	Ending Debt
1	R$ 100,000	R$ 6,373	R$ 7,455	R$ 13,828	R$ 92,545
2	R$ 92,545	R$ 5,897	R$ 7,930	R$ 13,828	R$ 84,615
3	R$ 84,615	R$ 5,392	R$ 8,436	R$ 13,828	R$ 76,179
4	R$ 76,179	R$ 4,855	R$ 8,973	R$ 13,828	R$ 67,206
5	R$ 67,206	R$ 4,283	R$ 9,545	R$ 13,828	R$ 57,661
6	R$ 57,661	R$ 3,674	R$ 10,153	R$ 13,828	R$ 47,508
7	R$ 47,508	R$ 3,027	R$ 10,800	R$ 13,828	R$ 36,708
8	R$ 36,708	R$ 2,339	R$ 11,488	R$ 13,828	R$ 25,220
9	R$ 25,220	R$ 1,607	R$ 12,220	R$ 13,828	R$ 12,999
10	R$ 12,999	R$ 828	R$ 12,999	R$ 13,828	R$ 0

[a]Interest expense = Beginning debt * Pretax interest rate on debt

In Exhibit 5.4, we estimate the cash flows to equity from the plant to Aracruz. To arrive at these cash flows, we do the following:

- Subtract the portion of the initial capital expenditures that comes from equity; of the initial investment of R$250,000, only R$150,000 comes from equity. In year five, there is an additional investment of R$50,000.

- Add back depreciation and amortization, because they are noncash charges.

- Subtract the changes in working capital; because investments in working capital are made at the beginning of each period, the initial investment in working capital of R$35.1 million is made at time 0 and is 15% of revenues in year 1. The changes in working capital in the years that follow are 15% of the changes in revenue in those years. At the end of year 10, the entire investment in working capital is recovered as salvage.

- Subtract the principal payments that are made to the bank in each period, because these are cash outflows to the nonequity claimholders in the firm.

- Add the salvage value of the plant in year 10 to the total cash flows, because this is a cash inflow to equity investors.

The cash flows to equity measure the cash flows that equity investors at Aracruz can expect to receive from investing in the plant.

5.5 THE EFFECTS OF DEBT FINANCING ON CASH FLOWS TO EQUITY

In the analysis, we assumed an additional capital expenditure of R$50 million in year 5, financed entirely with funds from equity; the cash flow to equity in year 5 (from Exhibit 5.4) is R$12.95 million. If, instead, we had assumed the R$50 million had come from new borrowing, the cash flow to equity in year 5 will

a. Increase by R$50 million

b. Decrease by R$50 million

c. Remain unchanged

Explain.

Capbudgeq.xls: This spreadsheet allows you to estimate the cash flows to equity on a project.

Exhibit: 5.3   ESTIMATED NET INCOME FROM PAPER PLANT INVESTMENT: ARACRUZ CELULOSE (IN THOUSANDS OF R$—REAL TERMS)

	1	2	3	4	5	6	7	8	9	10
Capacity (in thousands)	650	700	750	750	750	750	750	750	750	750
Utilization rate	90%	90%	90%	95%	95%	95%	95%	95%	95%	95%
Production rate (in thousands)	585	630	675	713	713	713	713	713	713	713
Price per ton	400	400	400	400	400	400	400	400	400	400
Revenues	234,000	252,000	270,000	285,000	285,000	285,000	285,000	285,000	285,000	285,000
−Direct expenses	155,300	163,400	171,500	178,250	178,250	178,250	178,250	178,250	178,250	178,250
−Depreciation	35,000	28,000	22,400	17,920	14,336	21,469	21,469	21,469	21,469	21,469
Operating income	43,700	60,600	76,100	88,830	92,414	85,281	85,281	85,281	85,281	85,281
−Interest expenses	6,373	5,897	5,392	4,855	4,283	3,674	3,027	2,339	1,607	828
Taxable income	37,327	54,703	70,708	83,975	88,131	81,607	82,254	82,942	83,674	84,453
−Taxes	12,691	18,599	24,041	28,552	29,965	27,746	27,966	28,200	28,449	28,714
Net income	24,636	36,104	46,667	55,424	58,167	53,860	54,287	54,742	55,225	55,739
Beginning book value: fixed assets	250,000	215,000	187,000	164,600	146,680	182,344	160,875	139,406	117,938	96,469
−Depreciation	35,000	28,000	22,400	17,920	14,336	21,469	21,469	21,469	21,469	21,469
+Capital exp.	0	0	0	0	50,000	0	0	0	0	0
Ending book value: fixed assets	215,000	187,000	164,600	146,680	182,344	160,875	139,406	117,938	96,469	75,000

Depreciation$_t$ = Higher of (20% (Beginning book value$_t$ − Salvage) or (Beginning book value − Salvage)/Remaining life). In year 1, for instance, 20% (250,000 − 75,000) = R$35,000, whereas (250,000 − 75,000)/10 = R$17,500. We use the former. We switch to straight-line in year 6, right after the additional investment of R$50 million.

Exhibit 5.4 CASH FLOWS TO EQUITY FROM PAPER PLANT: ARACRUZ CELULOSE (IN THOUSANDS OF REAL R$)

	0	1	2	3	4	5	6	7	8	9	10
Net Income		24,636	36,104	46,667	55,424	58,167	53,860	54,287	54,742	55,225	55,739
+ Depreciation amd amortization		35,000	28,000	22,400	17,920	14,336	21,469	21,469	21,469	21,469	21,469
–Capital expenditures	150,000	0	0	0	0	50,000	0	0	0	0	0
–Change in working capital	35,100	2,700	2,700	2,250	0	0	0	0	0	0	–42,750
–Principal repayments		7,455	7,930	8,436	8,973	9,545	10,153	10,800	11,488	12,220	12,999
+ Salvage value of plant											75,000
Cash flow to equity	–185,100	49,481	53,474	58,382	64,371	12,958	65,176	64,956	64,722	64,473	106,958

ILLUSTRATION 5.7 Estimating Cash Flows from an Acquisition: Sensient Technologies

To evaluate how much Tata Chemicals should pay for Sensient Technologies, we estimated the cash flows from the entire firm. As with the Disney analysis, we will estimate pre-debt cash flows—i.e., cash flow to the firm, using the same steps. We will begin with the after-tax operating income, add back depreciation and other noncash charges, and subtract changes in noncash working capital. There are two key differences between valuing a firm and valuing a project. The first is that a publicly traded firm, at least in theory, can have a perpetual life. Most projects have finite lives, although we will argue that projects such as theme parks may have lives so long that we could treat them as having infinite lives. The second is that a firm can be considered a portfolio of projects current and future. As a consequence, to value a firm, we have to make judgments about the quantity and quality of future projects.

For Sensient Technologies, we started with the 2008 financial statements and obtained the following inputs for cash flow in 2008:

- *Operating income*   The firm reported operating income of $162 million on revenues of $1.23 billion for the year. The firm paid 37% of its income as taxes in 2008, and we will use this as both the effective and marginal tax rate.
- *Capital expenditures and depreciation*   Depreciation in 2008 amounted to $44 million, whereas capital expenditures for the year were $54 million. Noncash working capital increased by approximately $16 million during the year.

The cash flow to the firm for Sensient Technologies in 2008 can be estimated as follows:

$$\text{Cash flow to the firm} = \text{After-tax operating income}$$
$$+ \text{Depreciation} - \text{Capital expenditures}$$
$$- \text{Change in noncash working capital}$$
$$= 162\,(1 - 0.37) + 44 - 54 - 16 = \$76.06 \text{ million}$$

We will assume that the firm is mature and that all of the inputs to this computation—earnings, capital expenditures, depreciation and working capital—will grow 2% a year in perpetuity.[7]

IN PRACTICE: ESTIMATING EXPECTED REVENUES AND CASH FLOWS

How do we estimate a project's expected revenues and expenses? The key word in this question is *estimate*. No one, no matter what his or her skill at forecasting and degree of preparation, can forecast with certainty how a risky project will do. There are generally three ways in which we can make these forecasts:

1. *Experience and history.*   The process of estimating project revenues and expenses is simplest for firms that consider the same kind of projects repeatedly.

---

[7]For the moment, this assumption seems to be an arbitrary one. Clearly, we need to give more thought to not only what a reasonable growth rate for a firm is but what may cause that growth rate to change. We will return to this issue in much more depth in Chapter 12 and use this simplified example for this chapter.

These firms can use their experience from similar projects that are already in operation to estimate expected values for new projects. Disney, for instance, can use its experiences with its existing theme parks in making its estimates for Rio Disney.

2. *Market testing.*   If the project being assessed is different from the firm's existing business, we may need a preliminary assessment of the market before actually investing in the project. In a market survey, potential customers are asked about the product or service being considered to gauge the interest they would have in acquiring it. The results usually are qualitative and indicate whether the interest is strong or weak, allowing the firm to decide whether to use optimistic forecasts for revenues (if the interest is strong) or pessimistic forecasts (if the interest is weak). Companies that need more information will often test market the concept on smaller markets, before introducing it on a larger scale. Test marketing not only allows firms to test out the product or service directly but also yields far more detailed information about the potential size of the market.

3. *Scenario analysis.*   There are cases in which a firm is considering introducing a product to a market it knows well, but there is considerable uncertainty introduced by external factors that the firm cannot control. In such cases, a firm may decide to consider different scenarios, and the revenues and expenses on the project under each scenario. We will return to this approach later in this chapter.

We have laid out three ways of estimating revenues and expenses for projects, but none of these approaches yields perfect estimates. Although some project risk may come from estimation error, a large portion of risk comes from real uncertainty about the future. Improving estimation techniques, using more market testing, and performing scenario analysis may reduce estimation error but cannot eliminate real uncertainty. This is why we incorporate a risk premium into the discount rate.   ■

C. Time-Weighted versus Nominal Cash Flows

Very few projects with long lifetimes generate earnings or cash flows evenly over their lives. In sectors with huge investments in infrastructure, such as telecommunications, the earnings and cash flows might be negative for an extended period (say, ten to twenty years) before they turn positive. In other sectors, the cash flows peak early and then gradually decrease over time. Whatever the reason for the unevenness of cash flows, a basic question that has to be addressed when measuring returns is whether they should reflect the timing of the earnings or cash flows. We will argue that they should, with earlier earnings and cash flows being weighted more when computing returns than earnings and cash flows later in a project life.

Why Cash Flows across Time Are Not Comparable

There are three reasons why cash flows across time are not comparable, and a cash flow in the future is worth less than a similar cash flow today:

1. *Individuals prefer present consumption to future consumption.* People would have to be offered more in the future to give up present consumption—this is called the

real rate of return. The greater the real rate of return, the greater the difference in value between a cash flow today and an equal cash flow in the future.

2. *When there is monetary inflation, the value of currency decreases over time.* The greater the inflation, the greater the difference in value between a cash flow today and an equal cash flow in the future.

3. *Any uncertainty (risk) associated with the cash flow in the future reduces the value of the cash flow.* The greater the uncertainty associated with the cash flow, the greater the difference between receiving the cash flow today and receiving an equal amount in the future.

The process by which future cash flows are adjusted to reflect these factors is called *discounting*, and the magnitude of these factors is reflected in the *discount rate*. Thus the present value of a cash flow (CF_t) at a point in time t in the future, when the discount rate is r, can be written as follows:

$$\text{Present value of cash flow} = CF_t \frac{1}{(1+r)^t}$$

Note that the second term in the brackets, $(1/[1 + r]^t)$, is called the discount factor and effectively weights the cash flow by when it occurs. The differences in weights across time will depend entirely on the level of the discount rate. Consequently, when discount rates are high, which could be due to high real rates, high inflation, or high uncertainty, returns that occur further in the future will be weighted less. Appendix 3 includes a more complete discussion of the mechanics of present value.

The Case for Time-Weighted Returns
If we accept the arguments that cash flows measure returns more accurately than earnings and that the incremental cash flows more precisely estimate returns than total cash flows, we should logically follow up by using discounted cash flows (i.e., time-weighted returns), rather than nominal cash flows, for two reasons:

1. Nominal cash flows at different points in time are not comparable and cannot be aggregated to arrive at returns. Discounted cash flows, on the other hand, convert all cash flows on a project to today's terms and allow us to compute returns more consistently.

2. If the objective in investment analysis is to maximize the value of the business taking the investments, we should be weighting cash flows that occur early more than cash flow that occur later, because investors in the business will also do so.

5.6 TIME HORIZONS AND TIME-WEIGHTING

Calculating present values for cash flows leads to a greater weighting for cash flows that occur sooner and a lower weighting for cash flows that occur later. Does it necessarily follow that using present value (as opposed to nominal value) makes managers more likely to take short-term projects over long-term projects?

a. Yes

b. No

Why, or why not?

Managerial Optimism and Cash Flow Estimation

There is substantial evidence that managers tend to be too optimistic when assessing outcomes from an investment, and systematically overestimate the cash flows on investments. From capital budgeting projects, where expected revenues are higher than expected and costs are lower than expected, to acquisitions, where the projected cash flows on target companies are much higher than actual cash flows, there is an "optimism bias" that leads firms to take many investments that should not be accepted.[8]

The literature on managerial optimism also has two key subfindings. The first is that people are more optimistic about outcomes that they believe that they can control. Thus, managers often overestimate their capacity to deliver market share and profit margins, in the face of competition. The second is that optimism tends to increase with commitment; the more committed a manager is to an investment, the more he or she is likely to over estimate the cash flows from that investment.

These findings suggests two possible solutions to the optimism bias. The first is to take away the project analysis duties away from the project advocates. In other words, managers should not be given the task of generating the expected cash flows from expansion opportunities that they have initiated. In the same vein, investment bankers touting potential target companies for acquisitions should not be generating the expected cash flows for the valuations of these companies. The second solution is a requirement that all investments, no matter what their pedigree and who advocates them, be put through stress tests, where key assumptions are questioned, changed and analyzed.

To those who believe that hiring more experienced or intelligent managers will solve this problem, there is substantial evidence that the optimism bias becomes worse as managers become more intelligent and experienced. In fact, it is to counter this bias that firms often set hurdle rates well above the cost of capital or require net present values to be much greater than 0 for a project to pass muster.

INVESTMENT DECISION RULES

Having estimated the accounting earnings, cash flows, and time-weighted cash flows on an investment, we are still faced with the crucial decision of whether we should take the investment. In this section, we will consider a series of investment decision rules and put them to the test.

What Is an Investment Decision Rule?

When faced with new investments and projects, firms have to decide whether to invest in them or not. We have been leading up to this decision over the last few chapters, but investment decision rules allow us to formalize the process and specify what conditions need to be met for a project to be acceptable. Although we will be looking at a variety of investment decision rules in this section, it is worth keeping in mind what characteristics we would like a good investment decision rule to have.

---

[8]J. B. Heaton, 2002 "Managerial Optimism and Corporate Finance." *Financial Management* v31:33–45.

- First, a good investment decision rule has to maintain a fair balance between allowing a manager analyzing a project to bring in his or her *subjective assessments* into the decision and ensuring that different projects are judged *consistently*. Thus, an investment decision rule that is too mechanical (by not allowing for subjective inputs) or too malleable (so much so that managers can bend the rule to match their biases) is not a good rule.

- Second, a good investment decision rule will allow the firm to further the stated objective in corporate finance, which is to *maximize the value of the firm*. Projects that are acceptable using the decision rule should increase the value of the firm accepting them, whereas projects that do not meet the requirements would destroy value if the firm invested in them.

- Third, a good investment decision rule should *work across a variety of investments*. Investments can be revenue-generating investments (such as Home Depot opening a new store) or they can be cost-saving investments (as would be the case if Boeing adopted a new system to manage inventory). Some projects have large up-front costs (as is the case with the Boeing Super Jumbo aircraft), whereas other projects may have costs spread out across time. A good investment rule will provide an answer on all of these different kinds of investments.

Does there have to be only one investment decision rule? Although many firms analyze projects using a number of different investment decision rules, one rule has to dominate. In other words, when the investment decision rules lead to different conclusions on whether the project should be accepted or rejected, one decision rule has to be the tie-breaker—it can be viewed as the primary rule.

Accounting Income-Based Decision Rules

Many of the oldest and most established investment decision rules have been drawn from the accounting statements and, in particular, from accounting measures of income. Some of these rules are based on income to equity investors (i.e., net income), and others are based on operating income.

Return on Capital

The return on capital on a project measures the returns earned by the firm on it is total investment in the project. Consequently, it is a return to all claimholders in the firm on their collective investment in a project. Defined generally,

$$\text{Return on capital (pretax)} = \frac{\text{Earnings before interest and taxes}}{\text{Average book value of capital invested in project}}$$

$$\text{Return on capital (after-tax)} = \frac{\text{Earnings before interest and taxes}(1 - \text{tax rate})}{\text{Average book value of capital invested in project}}$$

To illustrate, consider a one-year project with an initial investment of $1 million and earnings before interest and taxes (EBIT) of $300,000. Assume that the project has a salvage value at the end of the year of $800,000, and that the tax rate is 40%. In terms of a timeline, the project has the following parameters:

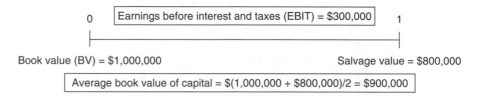

The pretax and after-tax returns on capital can be estimated as follows:

$$\text{Return on capital (pretax)} = \frac{\$300,000}{\$900,000} = 33.33\%$$

$$\text{Return on capital (after-tax)} = \frac{\$300,000\,(1 - 0.40)}{\$900,000} = 20\%$$

Although this calculation is rather straightforward for a one-year project, it becomes more involved for multiyear projects, where both the operating income and the book value of the investment change over time. In these cases, the return on capital can either be estimated each year and then averaged over time or the average operating income over the life of the project can be used in conjunction with the average investment during the period to estimate the average return on capital.

The after-tax return on capital on a project has to be compared to a hurdle rate that is defined consistently. The return on capital is estimated using the earnings before debt payments and the total capital invested in a project. Consequently, it can be viewed as return to the firm, rather than just to equity investors. Consequently, the cost of capital should be used as the hurdle rate.

If the after-tax return on capital > Cost of capital → Accept the project

If the after-tax return on capital < Cost of capital → Reject the project

For instance, if the company considering this project had a cost of capital of 10%, it would view the investment in the new project as a good one.

ILLUSTRATION 5.8   Estimating and Using Return on Capital in Decision Making—Disney and Bookscape Projects

In Illustrations 5.4 and 5.5, we estimated the operating income from two projects—an investment by Bookscape in an online book ordering service and an investment in a theme park in Brazil by Disney. We will estimate the return on capital on each of these investments using our earlier estimates of operating income. Table 5.8 summarizes the estimates of operating income and the book value of capital at Bookscape.

The book value of capital each year includes the investment in fixed assets and the noncash working capital. If we average the year-specific returns on capital, the average return on capital is 44.82%, but this number is pushed up by the extremely high return in year 4. A better estimate of the return on capital is obtained by dividing the average after-tax operating income ($193,058) over the four years by the average capital invested ($667,700) over this time, which yields a return on capital of 28.91%.

Table 5.8   RETURN ON CAPITAL ON BOOKSCAPE ONLINE

	1	2	3	4	Average
After-tax operating income	$120,000	$183,000	$216,300	$252,930	$193,058
BV of capital: beginning	$1,150,000	$930,000	$698,000	$467,800	
BV of capital: ending	$930,000	$698,000	$467,800	$0	
Average BV of capital	$1,040,000	$814,000	$582,900	$233,900	$667,700
Return on capital	11.54%	22.48%	37.11%	108.14%	28.91%

Because this number exceeds the cost of capital of 25.42% that we estimated in Illustration 5.2 for this project, the return on capital approach would suggest that this is a good project.

In Table 5.9, we estimate operating income, book value of capital, and return on capital (ROC) for Rio Disney. The operating income estimates are from Exhibit 5.1.

The book value of capital includes the investment in fixed assets (capital expenditures), net of depreciation, and the investment in working capital that year. It also includes the capitalized pre-project investment and the return on capital each year is computed based on the average book value of capital invested during the year. The average after-tax return on capital, computed using the average capital invested, over the ten-year period is 4.05%; it is slightly lower if we use capital at the end of the prior year. Here, the return on capital is lower than the cost of capital that we estimated in Illustration 5.2 to be 8.62%, and this suggests that Disney should not make this investment.

Table 5.9   RETURN ON CAPITAL FOR RIO DISNEY (INCOME AND CAPITAL IN MILLIONS)

Year	After-tax Operating Income	Book Value of				Average BV of Capital	ROC (a)	ROC (b)
		Pre-project Investment	Fixed Assets	Working Capital	Total Capital			
0		$500	$2,000	$0	$2,500		N/A	NA
1	−$31	$450	$3,000	$0	$3,450	$2,975	−1.04%	−1.24%
2	−$93	$400	$3,813	$63	$4,275	$3,863	−2.41%	−2.70%
3	−$52	$350	$4,145	$88	$4,582	$4,429	−1.18%	−1.22%
4	$66	$300	$4,027	$125	$4,452	$4,517	1.46%	1.44%
5	$196	$250	$3,962	$156	$4,368	$4,410	4.43%	4.39%
6	$241	$200	$3,931	$172	$4,302	$4,335	5.57%	5.52%
7	$290	$150	$3,931	$189	$4,270	$4,286	6.76%	6.74%
8	$341	$100	$3,946	$208	$4,254	$4,262	8.01%	8.00%
9	$397	$50	$3,978	$229	$4,257	$4,255	9.34%	9.34%
10	$408	$0	$4,010	$233	$4,243	$4,250	9.61%	9.59%
Average							4.05%	3.99%

Average BV of capital$_t$ = (Capital$_{t-1}$ + Capital$_t$)/2
ROC (a) = After-tax operating income/Average BV of capital
ROC (b) = After-tax operating income/BV of capital at end of prior year

Return on Equity

The return on equity looks at the return to equity investors, using the accounting net income as a measure of this return. Again, defined generally,

$$\text{Return on equity} = \frac{\text{Net income}}{\text{Average book value of equity investment in project}}$$

To illustrate, consider a four-year project with an initial equity investment of $800, and the following estimates of net income in each of the four years:

Net income		$140	$170	$210	$250
BV of equity	$800	$700	$600	$500	$400
Return on equity	18.67%	26.15%	38.18%	55.56%	

Like the return on capital, the return on equity tends to increase over the life of the project, as the book value of equity in the project is depreciated.

Just as the appropriate comparison for the return on capital is the cost of capital, the appropriate comparison for the return on equity is the *cost of equity*, which is the rate of return equity investors demand.

Decision Rule for ROE Measure for Independent Projects

If the return on equity > Cost of equity → Accept the project

If the return on equity < Cost of equity → Reject the project

---

The cost of equity should reflect the riskiness of the project being considered and the financial leverage taken on by the firm. When choosing between mutually exclusive projects of similar risk, the project with the higher return on equity will be viewed as the better project.

ILLUSTRATION 5.9   Estimating Return on Equity: Aracruz Celulose

Consider again the analysis of the paper plant for Aracruz Celulose that we started in Illustration 5.6. Table 5.10 summarizes the book value of equity and the estimated net income (from Exhibit 5.3) for each of the next ten years in thousands of real $R.

To compute the book value of equity in each year, we compute the book value of the fixed assets (plant and equipment), add to it the book value of the working capital in that year, and subtract the outstanding debt. The return on equity (ROE) each year is obtained by dividing the net income in that year by the average book value of equity invested in the plant in that year. The increase in the return on equity over time occurs because the net income rises while the book value of equity decreases. The average real return on equity of 36.19% on the paper plant project is compared to the real cost of equity for this plant, which is 18.45%, suggesting that this is a good investment.

Table 5.10   RETURN ON EQUITY: ARACRUZ PAPER PLANT

Year	Net Income	Beg. BV: Assets	Depreciation	Capital Exp.	Ending BV: Assets	BV of Working Capital	Debt	BV: Equity	Average BV: Equity	ROE
0		R$ 0	R$ 0	R$ 250,000	R$ 250,000	R$ 35,100	R$ 100,000	R$ 185,100		
1	R$ 24,636	R$ 250,000	R$ 35,000	R$ 0	R$ 215,000	R$ 37,800	R$ 92,545	R$ 160,255	R$ 172,678	14.27%
2	R$ 36,104	R$ 215,000	R$ 28,000	R$ 0	R$ 187,000	R$ 40,500	R$ 84,615	R$ 142,885	R$ 151,570	23.82%
3	R$ 46,667	R$ 187,000	R$ 22,400	R$ 0	R$ 164,600	R$ 42,750	R$ 76,179	R$ 131,171	R$ 137,028	34.06%
4	R$ 55,424	R$ 164,600	R$ 17,920	R$ 0	R$ 146,680	R$ 42,750	R$ 67,206	R$ 122,224	R$ 126,697	43.75%
5	R$ 58,167	R$ 146,680	R$ 14,336	R$ 50,000	R$ 182,344	R$ 42,750	R$ 57,661	R$ 167,433	R$ 144,828	40.16%
6	R$ 53,860	R$ 182,344	R$ 21,469	R$ 0	R$ 160,875	R$ 42,750	R$ 47,508	R$ 156,117	R$ 161,775	33.29%
7	R$ 54,287	R$ 160,875	R$ 21,469	R$ 0	R$ 139,406	R$ 42,750	R$ 36,708	R$ 145,448	R$ 150,783	36.00%
8	R$ 54,742	R$ 139,406	R$ 21,469	R$ 0	R$ 117,938	R$ 42,750	R$ 25,220	R$ 135,468	R$ 140,458	38.97%
9	R$ 55,225	R$ 117,938	R$ 21,469	R$ 0	R$ 96,469	R$ 42,750	R$ 12,999	R$ 126,220	R$ 130,844	42.21%
10	R$ 55,739	R$ 96,469	R$ 21,469	R$ 0	R$ 75,000	R$ 0	R$ 0	R$ 75,000	R$ 100,610	55.40%
									Average ROE =	36.19%

Ending BV = Beginning BV + Capital expenses—Depreciation

Assessing Accounting Return Approaches

How well do accounting returns measure up to the three criteria we listed for a good investment decision rule? In terms of maintaining balance between allowing managers to bring into the analysis their judgments about the project and ensuring consistency between analysis, the accounting returns approach falls short. It fails because it is significantly affected by accounting choices. For instance, changing from straight-line to accelerated depreciation affects both the earnings and the book value over time, thus altering returns. Unless these decisions are taken out of the hands of individual managers assessing projects, there will be no consistency in the way returns are measured on different projects.

Does investing in projects that earn accounting returns exceeding their hurdle rates lead to an increase in firm value? The value of a firm is the present value of expected cash flows on the firm over its lifetime. Because accounting returns are based on earnings rather than cash flows and ignore the time value of money, investing in projects that earn a return greater than the hurdle rates will not necessarily increase firm value. Conversely, some projects that are rejected because their accounting returns fall short of the hurdle rate may have increased firm value. This problem is compounded by the fact that the returns are based on the book value of investments, rather than the cash invested in the assets.

Finally, the accounting return works better for projects that have large up-front investments and generate level income over time. For projects that do not require a significant initial investment, the return on capital and equity has less meaning. For instance, a retail firm that leases store space for a new store will not have a significant initial investment and may have a very high return on capital as a consequence.

Note that all of the limitations of the accounting return measures are visible in the last two illustrations. First, the Disney example does not differentiate between money already spent and money still to be spent; rather, the sunk cost of $0.5 billion is shown in the initial investment of $3.5 billion. Second, in both the Bookscape and Aracruz analyses, as the book value of the assets decreases over time, largely as a consequence of depreciation, the operating income rises, leading to an increase in the return on capital. With the Disney analysis, there is one final and very important concern. The return on capital was estimated over ten years, but the project life is likely to be much longer. After all, Disney's existing theme parks in the United States are more than three decades old and generate substantial cash flows for the firm even today. Extending the project life will push up the return on capital and may make this project viable.

Notwithstanding these concerns, accounting measures of return endure in investment analysis. Although this fact can be partly attributed to the unwillingness of financial managers to abandon familiar measures, it also reflects the simplicity and intuitive appeal of these measures. More important, as long as accounting measures of return are used by investors and equity research analysts to assess to overall performance of firms, these same measures of return will be used in project analysis.

Cash Flow–Based Decision Rules

Measures of accounting return suffer from all of the problems that we noted with accounting profits. The simplest fix is to replace accounting earnings with cash flows. In this section, we will consider two simple variants: payback, where we examine the number of years it will take to get your money back on an investment, and cash flows return on capital, where we modify the conventional return on capital by replacing earnings with cash flows.

Payback

The **payback** on a project is a measure of how quickly the cash flows generated by the project cover the initial investment. Consider a project that has the following cash flows:

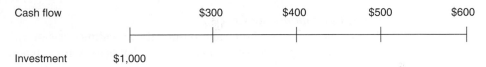

The payback on this project is between two and three years and can be approximated, based on the cash flows, to be 2.6 years. As with the other measures, the payback can be estimated either for all investors in the project or just for the equity investors. To estimate the payback for the entire firm, the free cash flows to the firm are added up until they cover the total initial investment. To estimate payback just for the equity investors, the free cash flows to equity are cumulated until they cover the initial equity investment in the project.

ILLUSTRATION 5.10   Estimating Payback for the Bookscape Online Service

This example estimates the payback from the viewpoint of the firm, using the Bookscape online service cash flows estimated in Illustration 5.4. Table 5.11 summarizes the annual cash flows and their cumulated value.

The initial investment of $1.15 million is covered sometime in the third year, leading to a payback of between two and three years. If we assume that cash flows occur uniformly over the course of the year:

$$\text{Payback for project} = 2 + (\$395,000/\$446,500) = 2.88 \text{ years}$$

Using Payback in Decision Making

Although it is uncommon for firms to make investment decisions based solely on the payback, surveys suggest that some businesses do in fact use payback as their primary decision mechanism. In those situations where payback is used as the primary criterion for accepting or rejecting projects, a maximum acceptable payback period is typically

Table 5.11   PAYBACK FOR BOOKSCAPE ONLINE

Year	Cash flow in year	Cumulated Cash flow
0	−$1,150,000	
1	$340,000	$810,000
2	$415,000	−$395,000
3	$446,500	$51,500
4	$720,730	$772,230

set. Projects that pay back their initial investment sooner than this maximum are accepted, and projects that do not are rejected.

Firms are much more likely to employ payback as a secondary investment decision rule and use it either as a constraint in decision making (e.g., accept projects that earn a return on capital of at least 15%, as long as the payback is less than ten years) or to choose between projects that score equally well on the primary decision rule (e.g., when two mutually exclusive projects have similar returns on equity, choose the one with the lower payback).

Biases, Limitations, and Caveats

The payback rule is a simple and intuitively appealing decision rule, but it does not use a significant proportion of the information that is available on a project.

- By restricting itself to answering the question, "When will this project make its initial investment?" it ignores what happens after the initial investment is recouped. This is a significant shortcoming when deciding between mutually exclusive projects. To provide a sense of the absurdities this can lead to, assume that you are picking between two mutually exclusive projects with the cash flows shown in Figure 5.2.

  On the basis of the payback alone, Project B is preferable to Project A because it has a shorter payback period. Most decision makers would pick Project A as the better project, however, because of the high cash flows that result after the initial investment is paid back.

- The payback rule is designed to cover the conventional project that involves a large up-front investment followed by positive operating cash flows. It breaks down, however, when the investment is spread over time or when there is no initial investment.

Figure 5.2   Using Payback for Mutually Exclusive Projects

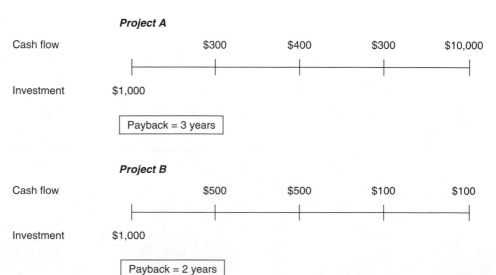

Table 5.12 MEASURES OF CASH FLOW RETURNS

Measure	Measurement Issues/Biases
$\dfrac{\text{EBITDA}}{\text{BV of capital invested}}$	Adding back depreciation without netting out capital expenditures and working capital changes will overstate returns, as will ignoring taxes.
$\dfrac{(\text{EBIT}(1-t)+\text{Depreciation})}{\text{BV of capital invested}}$ and $\dfrac{\text{Net income}+\text{Depreciation}}{\text{BV of equity}}$	Same issue with depreciation being added back and capital expenditures not being subtracted out.
$\dfrac{(\text{EBIT}(1-t)+\text{Depreciation})}{\text{Gross capital invested}}$	Gross capital invested is computed by adding back accumulated depreciation over time to the book value. It partially corrects for the failure to add back capital expenditures.

- The payback rule uses nominal cash flows and counts cash flows in the early years the same as cash flows in the later years. Because money has time value, however, recouping the nominal initial investment does not make the business whole again, because that amount could have been invested elsewhere and earned a significant return.

Cash Flow Returns
If the problem with the conventional return on capital and return on equity is the dependence on accounting earnings, there seems to be a simple fix in order. If we can replace earnings with cash flows, the return we estimate should be a cash flow returns. The modification, though, can be tricky, and many existing variants fail consistency tests. Table 5.12 summarizes some of the measures of cash flow returns in use and the measurement issues with each.

The full estimate of cash flows, described earlier in the chapter, requires subtracting capital expenditures and changes in noncash working capital but is far too volatile on a year-to-year basis to yield reliable measures of returns on equity or capital.

Discounted Cash Flow Measures
Investment decision rules based on discounted cash flows not only replace accounting income with cash flows but explicitly factor in the time value of money. The two most widely used discounted cash flows rules are *net present value* and the *internal rate of return*.

Net Present Value (NPV)
The *net present value* of a project is the sum of the present values of each of the cash flows—positive as well as negative—that occurs over the life of the project. The general formulation of the NPV rule is as follows:

$$\text{NPV of project} = \sum_{t=1}^{t=N} \frac{\text{CF}_t}{(1+\text{r})^t} - \text{Initial investment}$$

where

$$CF_t = \text{Cash flow in period } t$$
$$r = \text{Discount rate}$$
$$N = \text{Life of the project}$$

Consider a simple project, with an initial investment of $1 billion and expected cash flows of $300 million in year 1, $400 million in year 2, $500 million in year 3, and $600 million in year 4. Assuming a discount rate of 12%, the NPV of a project is depicted in Figure 5.3.

Once the NPV is computed, the decision rule is extremely simple because the hurdle rate is already factored in the present value.

Decision Rule for NPV for Independent Projects
If the NPV $> 0 \rightarrow$ Accept the project
If the NPV $< 0 \rightarrow$ Reject the project

Note that an NPV that is greater than 0 implies that the project makes a return greater than the hurdle rate.

5.7   THE SIGNIFICANCE OF A POSITIVE NPV

Assume that you have analyzed a $100 million project using a cost of capital of 15% and come up with an NPV of $1 million. The manager who has to decide on the project argues that this is too small an NPV for a project of this size and that this indicates a poor project. Is this true?

a.   Yes. The NPV is only 1% of the initial investment.
b.   No. A positive NPV indicates a good project.

Explain your answer.

Figure 5.3   NPV of a Project

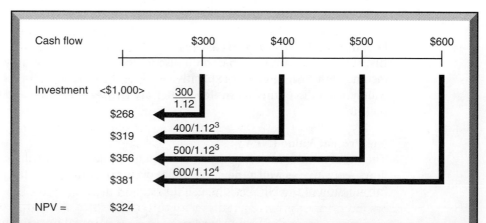

Table 5.13   CASH FLOW TO THE FIRM ON BOOKSCAPE ONLINE

Year	Cash Flow	PV of Cash Flows @ 25.48%
0	−$1,150,000	−$1,150,000
1	$340,000	$270,957
2	$415,000	$263,568
3	$446,500	$225,989
4	$720,730	$290,710
NPV		−$98,775

ILLUSTRATION 5.11   NPV from the Firm's Standpoint: Bookscape Online

Table 5.13 calculates the present value of the cash flows to Bookscape as a firm from the proposed online book ordering service using the cost of capital of 25.48% as the discount rate on the cash flows. (The cash flows are estimated in Illustration 5.4 and the cost of capital is estimated in Illustration 5.2.)

This project has a net present value of −$98,775, suggesting that it is a project that should not be accepted based on the projected cash flows and the cost of capital of 25.48%.

ILLUSTRATION 5.12   NPV from the Firm's Standpoint—Rio Disney

In estimating the cash flows to discount for Disney's theme park in Rio, the first point to note when computing the NPV of the proposed theme park is the fact that it has a life far longer than the ten years shown in Exhibit 5.2. To bring in the cash flows that occur after year 10, when cash flows start growing at 2%, the inflation rate forever, we draw on a present value formula for a growing perpetuity (See Appendix 3):

$$\text{Present value of cash flows after year 10}$$
$$= \frac{\text{Cash flow}_{11}}{(\text{Cost of capital} - \text{Perpetual growth rate})}$$
$$= \frac{\$692(1.02)}{(0.0862 - 0.02)} = \$10,669 \text{ million}$$

The cost of capital of 8.62% is the cost of capital for Rio Disney that we estimated in Illustration 5.2. This present value is called the *terminal value* and occurs at the end of year 10.

Table 5.14 presents the NPV of the proposed park estimated using the cash flows in millions of U.S. dollars from Exhibit 5.2 and Disney's cost of capital, in dollar terms, of 8.62%.

The NPV of this project is positive. This suggests that it is a good project that will earn $2.877 billion in surplus value for Disney.

NPV and Currency Choices

When analyzing a project, the cash flows and discount rates can often be estimated in one of several currencies. For a project like the Disney theme park, the obvious choices are the project's local currency (Brazilian reals—R$) and the company's home currency (U.S. dollars), but we can in fact use any currency to evaluate the project.

	Table 5.14	NPV OF RIO DISNEY	
Year	Annual Cash Flow	Terminal Value	Present Value
0	−$2,000		−$2,000
1	−$1,000		−$921
2	−$860		−$729
3	−$270		−$211
4	$332		$239
5	$453		$300
6	$502		$305
7	$538		$302
8	$596		$307
9	$660		$313
10	$692	$10,669	$4,970
Net Present Value =			$2,877

When switching from one currency to another, we have to go through the following steps:

1. ***Estimate the expected exchange rate for each period of the analysis.*** For some currencies (euro, yen, or British pound), we can estimates of expected exchange rates from the financial markets in the form of forward rates. For other currencies, we have to estimate the exchange rate, and the soundest way to do so is to use the expected inflation rates in the two currencies in question. For instance, we can estimate the expected R$/US$ exchange rate in n years:

$$\text{Expected rate(R\$/US\$)} = \$R/US\$ \text{ (Today)} * \left[\frac{(1 + \text{Expected inflation}_{\text{Brazil}})}{(1 + \text{Expected inflation}_{\text{US}})}\right]^n$$

We are assuming that inflation differences ultimately drives exchange rates—this is called purchasing power parity.

2. ***Convert the expected cash flows from one currency to another in future periods, using these exchange rates.*** Multiplying the expected cash flows in one currency by the expected exchange rates will accomplish this.

3. ***Convert the discount rate from one currency to another.*** We cannot discount cash flows in one currency using discount rates estimated in another. To convert a discount rate from one currency to another, we will again use expected inflation rates in the two currencies. A U.S. dollar cost of capital can be converted into R$ cost of capital as follows:

$$\text{Cost of capital(R\$)} = (1 + \text{Cost of capital(\$)}) * \frac{(1 + \text{Exp inflation}_{\text{Brazil}})}{(1 + \text{Exp inflation}_{\text{US}})} - 1$$

Compute the NPV by discounting the converted cash flows (from step 2) at the converted discount rate (from step 3). The NPV should be identical in both currencies, but only because the expected inflation rate was used to estimate the exchange rates. If the forecasted exchange rates diverge from purchasing power parity, we can get different NPVs, but our currency views are then contaminating our project analysis.

ILLUSTRATION 5.13   NPV in R$—Rio Disney

In Illustration 5.12, we computed the NPV for Rio Disney in dollar terms to be $2,877 million. The entire analysis could have been done in Brazilian real (R$) terms. To do this, the cash flows would have to be converted from dollars to R$, and the discount rate would then have been a R$ discount rate. To estimate the expected exchange rate, we will assume that the expected inflation rate will be 7% in Brazil and 2% in the United States and use the exchange rate is R$2.04 per U.S. dollar in May 2009 as the current exchange rate. The projected exchange rate in one year will be

$$\text{Expected exchange rate in year } 1 = \text{R\$}2.04 * (1.07/1.02) = \text{R\$}2.14/\$$$

Similar analyses will yield exchange rates for each of the next ten years.

The dollar cost of capital of 8.62%, estimated in Illustration 5.1, is converted to a R$ cost of capital using the expected inflation rates:

$$\text{Cost of capital(R\$)} = (1 + \text{Cost of capital(\$)}) * \frac{(1 + \text{Exp inflation}_{\text{Brazil}})}{(1 + \text{Exp inflation}_{\text{US}})} - 1$$
$$= (1.0862)(1.07/1.02) - 1 = 13.94\%$$

Table 5.15 summarizes exchange rates, cash flows, and the present value for the proposed Disney theme parks, with the analysis done entirely in Brazilian reals.

Note that the NPV of R$5,870 million is exactly equal to the dollar NPV computed in Illustration 5.12, converted at the current exchange rate of R$2.04 per dollar.

$$\text{NPV in dollars} = \text{NPV in R\$/Current exchange rate}$$
$$= 5,870/2.04 = \$2,877 \text{million}$$

	Table 5.15	EXPECTED CASH FLOWS FROM DISNEY THEME PARK IN R$		
Year	**Cash Flow ($)**	**R$/US$**	**Cash Flow (R$)**	**Present Value**
0	−$2,000.00	R$2.04	−R$4,080.00	−R$4,080.00
1	−$1,000.00	R$2.14	−R$2,140.00	−R$1,878.14
2	−$859.50	R$2.24	−R$1,929.49	−R$1,486.19
3	−$270.06	R$2.35	−R$635.98	−R$429.92
4	$332.50	R$2.47	R$821.40	R$487.32
5	$453.46	R$2.59	R$1,175.12	R$611.87
6	$501.55	R$2.72	R$1,363.46	R$623.06
7	$538.06	R$2.85	R$1,534.43	R$615.39
8	$595.64	R$2.99	R$1,781.89	R$627.19
9	$659.64	R$3.14	R$2,070.10	R$639.48
10	$11,360.86	R$3.29	R$37,400.49	R$10,139.72
				R$5,869.78

IN PRACTICE: TERMINAL VALUE, SALVAGE VALUE, AND NET PRESENT VALUE

When estimating cash flows for an individual project, practicality constrains us to estimate cash flows for a finite period—three, five, or ten years, for instance. At the end of that finite period, we can make one of three assumptions.

1. The most conservative one is that the project ceases to exist and its assets are worthless. In that case, the final year of operation will reflect only the operating cash flows from that year.

2. We can assume that the project will end at the end of the analysis period and that the assets will be sold for salvage. Although we can try to estimate salvage value directly, a common assumption that is made is that salvage value is equal to the book value of the assets. For fixed assets, this will be the undepreciated portion of the initial investment, whereas for working capital, it will be the aggregate value of the investments made in working capital over the course of the project life.

3. We can also assume that the project will not end at the end of the analysis period and try to estimate the value of the project on an ongoing basis—this is the terminal value. In the Disney theme park analysis, for instance, we assumed that the cash flows will continue forever and grow at the inflation rate each year. If that seems too optimistic, we can assume that the cash flows will continue with no growth for a finite period, or even that they will drop by a constant rate each year.

The right approach to use will depend on the project being analyzed. For projects that are not expected to last for long periods, we can use either of the first two approaches; a zero salvage value should be used if the project assets are likely to become obsolete by the end of the project life (e.g., computer hardware), and salvage can be set to book value if the assets are likely to retain significant value (e.g., buildings).

For projects with long lives, the terminal value approach is likely to yield more reasonable results but with one caveat. The investment and maintenance assumptions made in the analysis should reflect its long life. In particular, capital maintenance expenditures will be much higher for projects with terminal value because the assets have to retain their earning power. For the Disney theme park, the capital maintenance expenditures climb over time and become larger than depreciation as we approach the terminal year. ■

5.8 CURRENCY CHOICES AND NPV

A company in a high-inflation economy has asked for your advice regarding which currency to use for investment analysis. The company believes that using the local currency to estimate the NPV will yield too low a value because domestic interest rates are very high—this, in turn, would push up the discount rate. Is this true?

a. Yes. A higher discount rate will lead to lower NPV.

b. No.

Explain your answer.

NPV: Firm versus Equity Analysis

In the previous analysis, the cash flows we discounted were prior to interest and principal payments, and the discount rate we used was the weighted average cost of capital. In NPV parlance, we were discounting cash flows to the entire firm (rather than just its equity investors) at a discount rate that reflected the costs to different claimholders in the firm to arrive at an NPV. There is an alternative. We could have discounted the cash flows left over after debt payments for equity investors at the cost of equity and arrived at an NPV to equity investors.

Will the two approaches yield the same NPV? As a general rule, they will, but only if the following assumptions hold:

- The debt is correctly priced and the market interest rate to compute the cost of capital is the right one, given the default risk of the firm. If not, it is possible that equity investors can gain (if interest rates are set too low) or lose (if interest rates are set too high) to bondholders. This, in turn, can result in the NPV to equity being different from the NPV to the firm.

- The same assumptions are made about the financing mix used in both calculations. Note that the financing mix assumption affects the discount rate (cost of capital) in the firm approach and the cash flows (through the interest and principal payments) in the equity approach.

Given that the two approaches yield the same NPV, which one should we choose to use? Many practitioners prefer discounting cash flows to the firm at the cost of capital; it is easier to do, because the cash flows are before debt payments, and thus we do not have to estimate interest and principal payments explicitly. Cash flows to equity are more intuitive, though, because most of us think of cash flows left over after interest and principal payments as residual cash flows.

ILLUSTRATION 5.14   NPV from the Equity Investors' Standpoint: Paper Plant for Aracruz

The NPV is computed from the equity investors' standpoint for the proposed linerboard plant for Aracruz using real cash flows to equity, estimated in Exhibit 5.4, and a real cost of equity of 18.45% (estimated earlier in Illustration 5.2). Table 5.16 summarizes the cash flows and the present values.

The net present value of R$75.806 million suggests that this is a good project for Aracruz to invest in. The analysis was done entirely in real terms, but using nominal cash flows and discount rate would have had no impact on the NPV. The cash flows will be higher because of expected inflation, but the discount rate will increase by exactly the same magnitude, thus resulting in an identical NPV. The choice between nominal and real cash flows therefore boils down to one of convenience. When inflation rates are low, it is better to do the analysis in nominal terms because taxes are based on nominal income. When inflation rates are high and volatile, it is easier to do the analysis in real terms or in a different currency with a lower expected inflation rate.

Table 5.16   CASH FLOW TO EQUITY ON LINERBOARD PLANT
(IN THOUSANDS)

Year	Cash Flow to Equity	PV of Cash Flow @ 18.45%
0	−R$ 185,100	−R$ 185,100
1	R$ 49,481	R$ 41,773
2	R$ 53,474	R$ 38,110
3	R$ 58,382	R$ 35,126
4	R$ 64,371	R$ 32,696
5	R$ 12,958	R$ 5,556
6	R$ 65,176	R$ 23,594
7	R$ 64,956	R$ 19,851
8	R$ 64,722	R$ 16,698
9	R$ 64,473	R$ 14,043
10	R$ 181,958	R$ 33,458
Net Present Value =		R$ 75,806

5.9   EQUITY, DEBT, AND NPV

In the project just described, assume that Aracruz had used all equity to finance the project instead of its mix of debt and equity. Which of the following is likely to occur to the NPV?

a.   The NPV will go up, because the cash flows to equity will be much higher; there will be no interest and principal payments to make each year.

b.   The NPV will go down, because the initial investment in the project will much higher.

c.   The NPV will remain unchanged, because the financing mix should not affect the NPV.

d.   The NPV might go up or down, depending on . . .

Explain your answer.

ILLUSTRATION 5.15   Valuing a Company for an Acquisition: Sensient Technologies

Extending the net present value rule to cover an entire company is not complicated. Consider the proposed acquisition of Sensient Technologies by Tata Chemicals:

- In Illustration 5.2, we estimated the cost of capital of 6.98% as the right discount rate to apply in valuing Sensient Technologies. This cost is estimated in U.S. dollar terms and reflects the mature market exposure of the company.

- In Illustration 5.7, we estimated the cash flow to the firm of $76.06 million, in 2008, for Sensient Technologies. We also assumed that these cash flows would grow 2% a year in perpetuity.

We can estimate the value of the firm, based on these inputs:

$$\text{Value of operating assets} = \frac{\text{Expected cash flow to the firm next year}}{(\text{Cost of capital} - \text{Stable growth rate})}$$

$$= \frac{\$76.06(1.02)}{(0.0698 - 0.02)} = \$1,559 \text{ million}$$

Adding the cash balance of the firm ($8 million) and subtracting the existing debt ($460 million) yields the value of equity in the firm:

$$\text{Value of equity} = \text{Value of operating assets} + \text{Cash} - \text{Debt}$$
$$= 1{,}559 + \$8 - \$460 \, \text{million} = \$1{,}107 \, \text{million}$$

The market value of equity in Sensient Technologies in May 2009 was $1,150 million. To the extent that Tata Chemicals pays a premium over this market price, it has to generate other benefits from the merger that will cover the difference.

Properties of the NPV Rule

The NPV has several important properties that make it an attractive decision rule and the preferred rule, at least if a corporate finance theorist were doing the picking.

1. NPVs Are Additive   The NPVs of individual projects can be aggregated to arrive at a cumulative NPV for a business or a division. No other investment decision rule has this property. The property itself has a number of implications.

- The value of a firm can be written in terms of the present values of the cash flows of the projects it has already taken on, as well as the expected NPVs of prospective future projects:

$$\text{Value of firm} = \sum \text{Present value of projects in place}$$
$$+ \sum \text{NPV of future projects}$$

The first term in this equation captures the value of *assets in place*, whereas the second term measures the value of *expected future growth*. Note that the present value of projects in place is based on anticipated future cash flows on these projects.

- When a firm terminates an existing project that has a negative present value based on anticipated future cash flows, the value of the firm will increase by that amount. Similarly, when a firm invests in a new project, with an expected negative NPV, the value of the firm will decrease by that amount.

- When a firm divests itself of an existing asset, the price received for that asset will affect the value of the firm. If the price received exceeds the present value of the anticipated cash flows on that project to the firm, the value of the firm will increase with the divestiture; otherwise, it will decrease.

- When a firm invests in a new project with a positive NPV, the value of the firm will be affected depending on whether the NPV meets expectations. For example, a firm like Microsoft is expected to take on high positive NPV projects, and this expectation is built into value. Even if the new projects taken on by Microsoft have positive NPV, there may be a drop in value if the NPV does not meet the high expectations of financial markets.

- When a firm makes an acquisition and pays a price that exceeds the present value of the expected cash flows from the firm being acquired, it is the equivalent of taking on a negative NPV project and will lead to a drop in value.

5.10   FIRM VALUE AND OVERPAYMENT ON ACQUISITIONS

Megatech Corporation, a large software firm with a market value for its equity of $100 million, announces that it will be acquiring FastMail Corporation, a smaller software firm, for $15 million. On the announcement, Megatech's stock price drops by 3%. Based on these facts, estimate the amount the market thinks Megatech should have paid for FastMail.

a. $15 million

b. $3 million

c. $12 million

How does NPV additivity enter into your answer?

2. Intermediate Cash Flows Are Invested at the Hurdle Rate   Implicit in all present value calculations are assumptions about the rate at which intermediate cash flows get reinvested. The NPV rule assumes that intermediate cash flows on a projects—that is, cash flows that occur between the initiation and the end of the project—get reinvested at the **hurdle rate**, which is the cost of capital if the cash flows are to the firm and the cost of equity if the cash flows are to equity investors. Given that both the cost of equity and capital are based on the returns that can be made on alternative investments of equivalent risk, this assumption should be reasonable.

3. NPV Calculations Allow for Expected Term Structure and Interest Rate Shifts   In all the examples throughout in this chapter, we have assumed that the discount rate remains unchanged over time. This is not always the case, however; the NPV can be computed using time-varying discount rates. The general formulation for the NPV rule is as follows:

$$\text{NPV of project} = \sum_{t=1}^{t=N} \frac{CF_t}{(1 + r)^t} - \text{Initial investment}$$

where

$$CF_t = \text{Cash flow in period } t$$
$$r_t = \text{One-period discount rate that applies to period } t$$
$$N = \text{Life of the project}$$

The discount rates may change for three reasons:

1. The level of interest rates may change over time, and the term structure may provide some insight on expected rates in the future.

2. The risk characteristics of the project may be expected to change in a predictable way over time, resulting in changes in the discount rate.

3. The financing mix on the project may change over time, resulting in changes in both the cost of equity and the cost of capital.

ILLUSTRATION 5.16   NPV Calculation with Time-Varying Discount Rates

Assume that you are analyzing a four-year project investing in computer software development. Furthermore, assume that the technological uncertainty associated with the software industry leads to higher discount rates in future years.

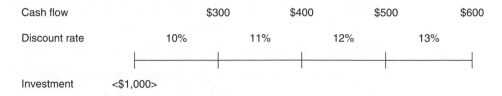

Cash flow		$300	$400	$500	$600
Discount rate		10%	11%	12%	13%
Investment	<$1,000>				

The present value of each of the cash flows can be computed as follows.

$$\text{PV of cash flow in year } 1 = \$300/1.10 = \$272.72$$
$$\text{PV of cash flow in year } 2 = \$400/(1.10 * 1.11) = \$327.60$$
$$\text{PV of cash flow in year } 3 = \$500/(1.10 * 1.11 * 1.12) = \$365.63$$
$$\text{PV of cash flow in year } 4 = \$600/(1.10 * 1.11 * 1.12 * 1.13) = \$388.27$$
$$\text{NPV of project} = \$272.72 + \$327.60 + \$365.63 + \$388.27 - \$1,000.00 = \$354.23$$

5.11   CHANGING DISCOUNT RATES AND NPV

In the analysis just done, assume that you had been asked to use one discount rate for all of the cash flows. Is there a discount rate that would yield the same NPV as the one above?

a.   Yes

b.   No

If so, how would you interpret this discount rate?

Biases, Limitations, and Caveats

In spite of its advantages and its linkage to the objective of value maximization, the NPV rule continues to have its detractors, who point out a couple of limitations:

- The NPV is stated in absolute rather than relative terms and does not therefore factor in the scale of the projects. Thus, Project A may have an NPV of $200, whereas Project B has an NPV of $100, but Project A may require an initial investment that is 10 or 100 times larger than Project B. Proponents of the NPV rule argue that it is surplus value, over and above the hurdle rate, no matter what the investment.

- The NPV rule does not control for the life of the project. Consequently, when comparing mutually exclusive projects with different lifetimes, the NPV rule is biased toward accepting longer-term projects.

Internal Rate of Return

The **internal rate of return (IRR)** is based on discounted cash flows. Unlike the NPV rule, however, it takes into account the project's scale. It is the discounted cash flow analog to the accounting rates of return. Again, in general terms, the IRR is that discount rate that makes the NPV of a project equal to 0. To illustrate, consider again the project described at the beginning of the NPV discussion.

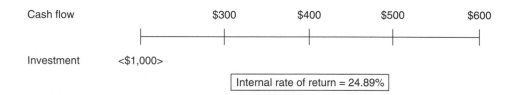

At the internal rate of return, the NPV of this project is 0. The linkage between the NPV and the IRR is most obvious when the NPV is graphed as a function of the discount rate in a **net present value profile**. An NPV profile for the project described is illustrated in Figure 5.4.

The NPV profile provides several insights on the project's viability. First, the internal rate of return is clear from the graph—it is the point at which the profile crosses the *x*-axis. Second, it provides a measure of how sensitive the NPV—and, by extension, the project decision—is to changes in the discount rate. The slope of the NPV profile is a

Figure 5.4   NPV Profile

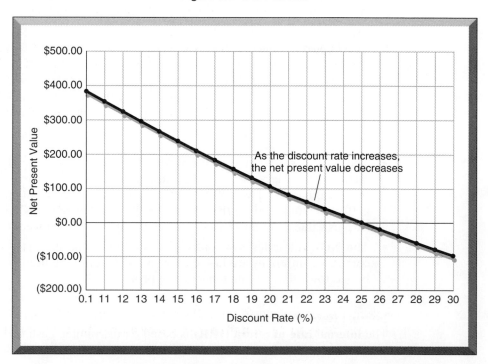

measure of the discount rate sensitivity of the project. Third, when mutually exclusive projects are being analyzed, graphing both NPV profiles together provides a measure of the break-even discount rate—the rate at which the decision maker will be indifferent between the two projects.

5.12 DISCOUNT RATES AND NPV

In the project just described, the NPV decreased as the discount rate was increased. Is this always the case?

a. Yes

b. No

If not, when might the NPV go up as the discount rate is increased?

Using the IRR

One advantage of the IRR is that it can be used even in cases where the discount rate is unknown. While this is true for the calculation of the IRR, it is *not* true when the decision maker has to use the IRR to decide whether to take a project. At that stage in the process, the IRR has to be compared to the discount rate—if the IRR is greater than the discount rate, the project is a good one; otherwise, the project should be rejected.

Like the NPV, the IRR can be computed in one of two ways:

1. The IRR can be calculated based on the free cash flows to the firm and the total investment in the project. In doing so, the IRR has to be compared to the cost of capital.

2. The IRR can be calculated based on the free cash flows to equity and the equity investment in the project. If it is estimated with these cash flows, it has to be compared to the cost of equity, which should reflect the riskiness of the project.

Decision Rule for IRR for Independent Projects

A. *IRR is computed on cash flows to the firm*

If the IRR > Cost of capital → Accept the project

If the IRR < Cost of capital → Reject the project

B. *IRR is computed on cash flows to equity*

If the IRR > Cost of equity → Accept the project

If the IRR < Cost of equity → Reject the project

When choosing between projects of equivalent risk, the project with the higher IRR is viewed as the better project.

ILLUSTRATION 5.17 Estimating the IRR Based on FCFF—Rio Disney

The cash flows to the firm from Rio Disney are used to arrive at a NPV profile for the project in Figure 5.5.

Figure 5.5 NPV Profile for Disney Theme Park

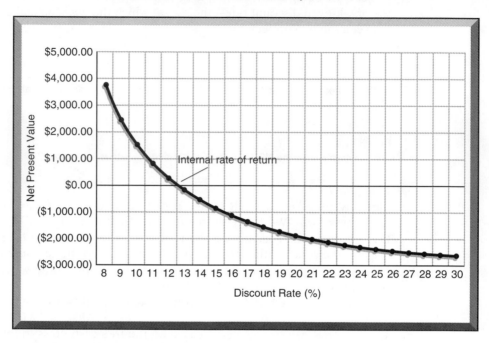

The IRR in dollar terms on this project is 12.35%, which is *higher* than the cost of capital of 8.62%. These results are consistent with the findings from the NPV rule, which also recommended investing in the theme parks.[9]

ILLUSTRATION 5.18 Estimating IRR Based Upon FCFE—Aracruz Celulose

The net present value profile depicted in Figure 5.6 is based upon the equity investment and the free cash flows to equity estimated for the paper plant for Aracruz.

The IRR (in real terms) on this project is 27.92%, which is *higher* than the real cost of equity of 18.45%. Again, these results are consistent with the findings from the NPV rule, which also recommended accepting this investment.

Biases, Limitations, and Caveats

The IRR is the most widely used discounted cash flow rule in investment analysis, but it does have some serious limitations.

- Because the IRR is a scaled measure, it tends to bias decision makers toward smaller projects, which are much more likely to yield high percentage returns, and away from larger ones.

---

[9]The terminal value of the project itself is a function of the discount rate used. That is why the IRR function in Excel will not yield the right answer. Instead, the NPV has to be recomputed at every discount rate and the IRR is the point at which the NPV equals 0.

Figure 5.6   NPV Profile on Equity Investment in Paper Plant: Aracruz

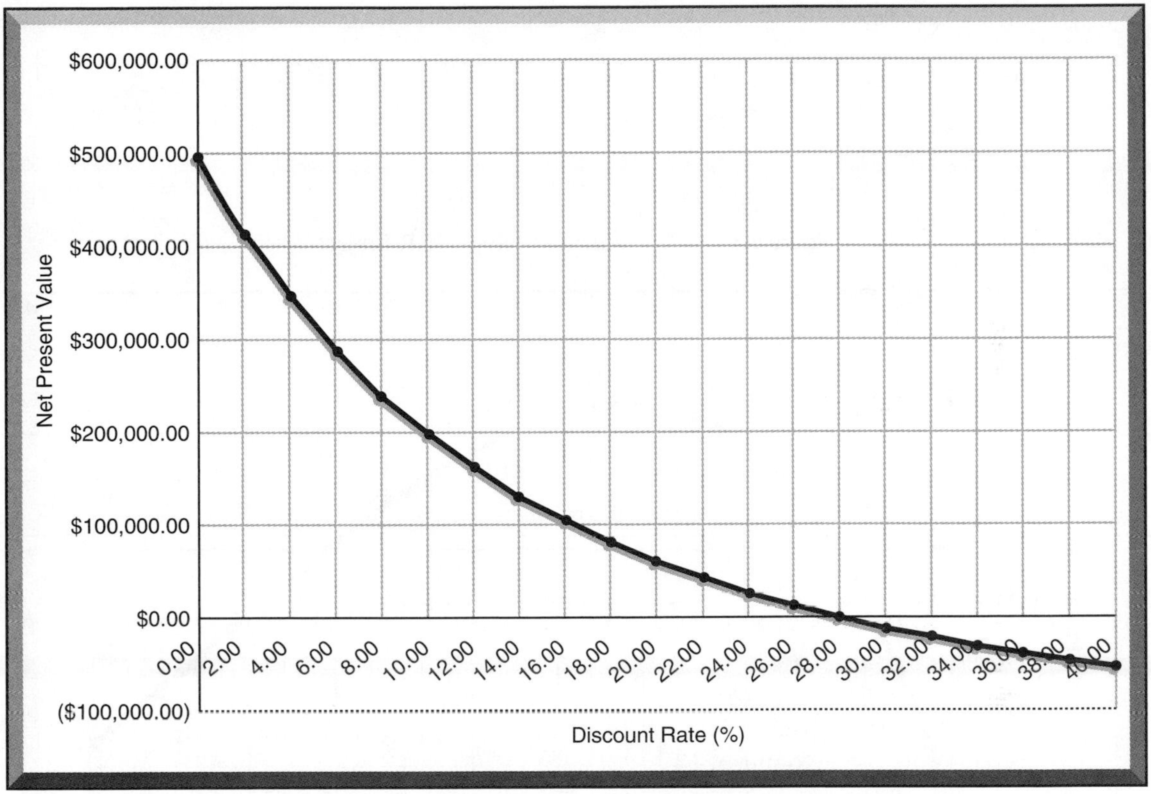

- There are a number of scenarios in which the IRR cannot be computed or is not meaningful as a decision tool. The first is when there is no—or only a very small—initial investment and the investment is spread over time. In such cases, the IRR cannot be computed or, if computed, is likely to be meaningless. The second is when there is more than one internal rate of return for a project, and it is not clear which one the decision maker should use.

ILLUSTRATION 5.19   Multiple IRR Projects

Consider a project to manufacture and sell a consumer product, with a hurdle rate of 12%, that has a four-year life and the following cash flows over those four years. The project, which requires the licensing of a trademark, requires a large payment at the end of the fourth year. Figure 5.7 shows the cash flows.

The NPV profile for this project, shown in Figure 5.8, reflects the problems that arise with the IRR measure.

As you can see, this project has two IRRs: 6.60% and 36.55%. Because the hurdle rate falls between these two IRRs, the decision on whether to take the project will

Figure 5.7 Cash Flows on Investment

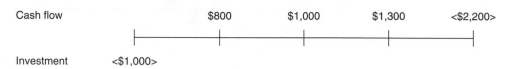

Figure 5.8 NPV Profile for Multiple IRR Project

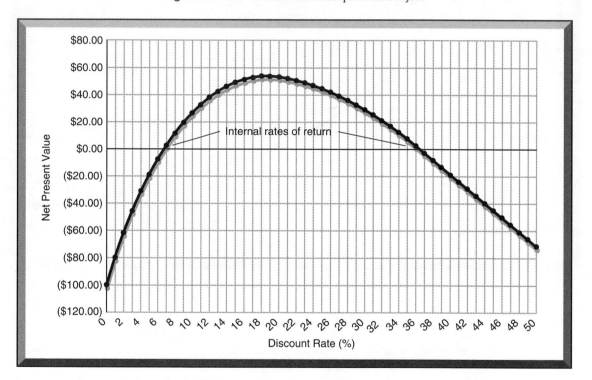

change depending on which IRR is used. To make the right decision in this case, the decision maker would have to look at the NPV profile. If, as in this case, the NPV is positive at the hurdle rate, the project should be accepted. If the NPV is negative at the hurdle rate, the project should be rejected.

IN PRACTICE: MULTIPLE IRRS: WHY THEY EXIST AND WHAT TO DO ABOUT THEM

The IRR can be viewed mathematically as a root to the present value equation for cash flows. In the conventional project, where there is an initial investment and positive cash flows thereafter, there is only one sign change in the cash flows, and one root—that is, there is a unique IRR. When there is more than one sign change in the cash flows, there will be more than one IRR.[10] In Figure 5.7, for example, the cash flow changes sign from negative to positive in year 1, and from positive to negative in year 4, leading to two IRRs.

Lest this be viewed as some strange artifact that is unlikely to happen in the real world, note that many long-term projects require substantial reinvestment at intermediate points in the project and that these reinvestments may cause the cash flows in those years to become negative. When this happens, the IRR approach may run into trouble.

There are a number of solutions suggested to the multiple IRR problems. One is to use the hurdle rate to bring the negative cash flows from intermediate periods back to the present. Another is to construct an NPV profile. In either case, it is probably much simpler to estimate and use the NPV. ∎

PROBABILISTIC APPROACHES TO INVESTMENT ANALYSIS

In all of the approaches that we described in the last section—accounting returns, payback, NPV and IRR—we used earnings or cash flows that were estimated for future years for the projects that we were analyzing. While we use expected values for revenues, margins and other key variables, the future is uncertain, and the estimates will reflect that uncertainty. While we cannot make this uncertainty disappear, we can consider ways in which we get a better handle on how a project's value will change as the inputs change. In this section, we will examine four approaches for dealing with uncertainty. The first and simplest is sensitivity analysis, where we ask what-if questions about key variables to estimate how much room for error we have on each one. The second is scenario analysis, where we develop a few possible scenarios, ranging from good to bad outcomes, and compute the value of the project under each one. The third approach is decision trees, designed for multi-stage investments, where we evaluate the probabilities of success and failure at each stage and the consequences for the final value. The last approach is simulations, where we estimate probability distributions for each input variable rather than expected values. As a consequence, we will generate a distribution of values for a project, rather than a single number.

Sensitivity Analysis

The simplest way to deal with uncertainty is to ask "what if?" questions about key inputs into the analysis, with two objectives in mind. One is to get a sense of how much the value of the project and your decision about investing in the project change as you modify key assumptions. The other is to get a measure of how much margin for error you have on your estimates. Put another way, sensitivity analysis can be used to analyze how much you can afford to be off in your estimates of revenue growth and margins without altering your decision to accept or reject the investment. There are some dangers to sensitivity analysis:

- *Overdoing what-if analyses* There are often dozens of inputs that go into a project analysis, and we could do sensitivity analyses on each and every one of these inputs.

---

[10]Athough the number of IRRs will be equal to the number of sign changes, some IRRs may be so far out of the realm of the ordinary (e.g. 10,000%) that they may not create the kinds of problems described here.

In the process, though, we mix the variables that matter with those that do not and risk obscuring the importance of the former.

- **Losing sight of the objective**   The ultimate objective of asking "what if?" is not to generate more tables, graphs, and numbers but to make better decisions in the face of uncertainty. To help in decision-making, sensitivity analysis should be focused on key variables and the findings should be presented in ways that help decision makers better a grip on how outcomes will change as assumptions change.

- *Not considering how variables move together*   In most sensitivity analysis, we change one input at a time, keeping all other inputs at their base case values. While this makes computation simpler, it may be unrealistic, since input variables are often correlated with each other. Thus, assuming that margins will increase while keeping revenue growth fixed or that interest rates will go down while inflation stays high may yield higher net present values for the project, but neither is actually likely to happen.

- *Double-counting risk*   In any sensitivity analysis, even good projects (with positive NPV and high IRR) will have negative net present values if key variables move adversely. Decision makers who use this as a rationale for rejecting these projects are potentially double-counting risk, since the cash flows were discounted back at a risk-adjusted rate to estimate the base case NPV.

In general, there are two good uses for sensitivity analysis. The first is that it can be used as a tie-breaker when firms have to choose between two projects that are roughly equivalent in terms of base case net present value or IRR; the project that is less sensitive to changes in the key variables should be picked. The second is to use the output from sensitivity analysis to better manage both the operations and the risks of an investment, in the post-acceptance phase. Thus, knowing that the net present value of an investment is sensitive to labor costs may lead to entering into labor contracts that keep these costs under control. Similarly, the finding that a project's value fluctuates as exchange rates move may result in the firm using currency options and futures to hedge risk.

ILLUSTRATION 5.20   Aracruz Paper Plant: Sensitivity Analysis and Break-Even

In Illustration 5.14, we estimated a NPV of R\$75.8 million for Aracruz's proposed paper plant. While that value suggests that the plant would be a good investment, the conclusion is heavily dependent upon two variables—the price of paper and pulp and the R\$/US\$ exchange rate. The pulp price affects revenues directly, and a significant drop in paper prices will make the project an unattractive one, so changing the assumption that the price per ton will remain at \$400 in real terms will affect the value of the project. The exchange rate matters because Aracruz sells a significant portion of its output into dollar-based markets but has most of its costs in Brazil (and in R\$). If the Brazilian real strengthens relative to the U.S. dollar, Aracruz will find itself squeezed, unable to raise prices but facing higher costs.

In the first part of the sensitivity analysis, we changed the price per ton, in real terms, of pulp from our base case value of \$400 and mapped out the effect on the NPV and IRR of the investment. Figure 5.9 presents the findings.

Note that the NPV for the project drops below 0 if paper prices drop below \$325/ton and the IRR drops below the real cost of equity of 18.45%. In making these computations, we held fixed costs constant and kept variable costs at 45% of revenues.

Figure 5.9   Aracruz Paper Plant: Effect of Changing Pulp Prices

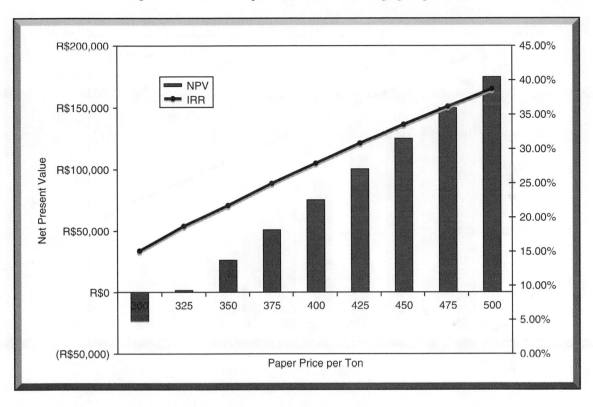

In the second part of the analysis, we assessed the impact of unexpected changes in the exchange rate. While we have built in an expected devaluation into the R$, based upon the inflation rates of 7% for Brazil and 2% for the United States, it is entirely possible that the R$ could become stronger or weaker relative to the U.S. dollar. Every 1% increase in the value of the R$/$, relative to our assessments, will increase the variable cost (which is entirely R$-based), as a proportion of revenues, by 1%. Thus, if the R$ is 5% stronger than expected, the variable costs will be 50% of revenues (instead of our base case estimate of 45%). Figure 5.10 presents the effects of exchange rate changes on NPV and IRR.

If the Brazilian real strengthens 10% of more, relative to our estimates, the associated jump in variable costs alters our assessment of the project, from positive to negative.

IN PRACTICE: SHOULD YOU HEDGE PROJECT RISK?

Looking at the sensitivity analysis for the Aracruz paper plant, it is quite clear that the value of the plant will change significantly if paper prices change or if there are unexpected changes in exchange rates. Since there are derivatives markets on both the commodity (paper) and exchange rates, an open question then becomes whether Aracruz should hedge against these risks using forwards, futures, or options.

Figure 5.10 Aracruz Paper Plant: Effect of Changing Exchange Rates

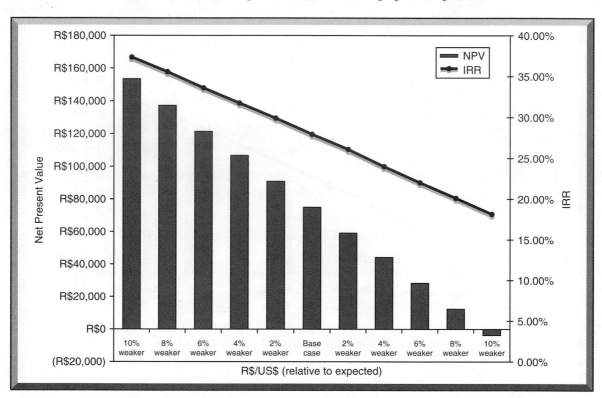

The answer is not clear-cut. While hedging risk makes the project's cash flows more predictable, there are two costs to consider. The first is that investors in the company may want to be exposed to the risk; investors in an oil, gold mining, or paper company may be investing in the company because they believe that these commodities will go up in price and hedging that risk will undercut their rationale. The second is that hedging can be costly and it may be more efficient and cheaper for investors to hedge risk in their portfolios than it is for individual companies to each hedge risks. Thus, an investor who holds a large number of stocks exposed to exchange rate risk in the R$/US$ rate may be able to diversify away a large component of that risk in his portfolio and then can choose to hedge or not hedge the remaining risk. These costs have to be weighed against two potential benefits. The first is that hedging against risks that can cause large losses, relative to the size of the firm, may reduce the chance of default, especially if a firm has significant debt obligations. The second is that hedging risk can sometimes yield tax benefits, both in the form of tax-deductible expenses for hedging and from smoothing out earnings.

Applying this tradeoff to Aracruz, we come to a mixed conclusion. The firm has significant debt obligations and cannot risk large losses. Consequently, we think it makes sense for the firm to hedge exchange rate risk, especially because it is relatively inexpensive to do so, using futures and forward contracts. Given that it is a commodity company, we are reluctant to suggest the same path for paper prices, since investors in the company may want that exposure. One compromise that will allow these investors to retain the upside, while protecting against very adverse moves in pulp prices, would be for Aracruz to buy put options on paper at a price of around $325 (the break-even point for NPV). Since the put options will be deep out of the money, the costs should be moderate and investors will still get most of the upside on paper prices. ■

Scenario Analysis

In sensitivity analysis, we change one input variable at a time and examine the effect on the output variables—NPV, IRR, and accounting returns. In scenario analysis, we outline scenarios that are different from the base case, where many or all of the inputs can have different values, and evaluate the project's value under these scenarios. In general, scenario analysis can take one of two forms: a best-case/worst-case analysis or an analysis of multiple possible scenarios.

Best-Case/Worst-Case

With risky projects, the actual cash flows can be very different from expectations. At the minimum, we can estimate the cash flows if everything works to perfection (a best-case scenario) and if nothing does (a worst-case scenario). In practice, there are two ways in which this analysis can be structured. In the first, each input into the project analysis is set to its best (or worst) possible outcome and the cash flows estimated with those values. Thus, when analyzing a project, you may set the revenue growth rate and operating margin at the highest possible level while setting the discount rate at its lowest level, and compute the value as the best-case scenario. The problem with this approach is that it may not be feasible; after all, to get the high revenue growth, the firm may have to lower prices and accept lower margins. In the second, the best possible scenario is defined in terms of what is feasible while allowing for the relationship between the inputs. Thus, instead of assuming that revenue growth and margins will both be maximized, we will choose that combination of growth and margin that is feasible and yields the maximum value. While this approach is more realistic, it does require more work to put into practice.

There are two ways in which the results from this analysis can help decision makers. First, the difference between the best-case and worst-case value can be used as a measure of risk on an asset; the range in value (scaled to size) should be higher for riskier investments. Second, firms that are concerned about the potential spillover effects on their operations of an investment going bad may be able to gauge the effects by looking at the worst-case outcome. Thus, a firm that has significant debt obligations may use the worst-case outcome to make a judgment as to whether an investment has the potential to push them into default. In general, though, best-case/worst-case analyses are not very informative. After all, there should be no surprise in knowing that an investment is worth a great deal in the best case and will do badly in the worst.

Multiple Scenario Analysis

Scenario analysis does not have to be restricted to the best and worst cases. In its most general form, the value of a risky investment can be computed under a number of different scenarios, varying the assumptions about both macroeconomic and asset-specific variables. While the concept of sensitivity analysis is a simple one, it has four critical components:

1. The first is the determination of which factors the scenarios will be built around. These factors can range from the state of the economy, for an automobile firm considering a new plant, to the response of competitors, for a consumer product firm introducing a new product, to the behavior of regulatory authorities, for a phone company considering a new phone service.

2. The second component is determining the number of scenarios to analyze for each factor. While more scenarios may be more realistic than fewer, it becomes more difficult to collect information and differentiate between the scenarios in terms of asset cash flows. The question of how many scenarios to consider will depend then upon how different the scenarios are and how well the analyst can forecast cash flows under each scenario.

3. The third component is the estimation of asset cash flows under each scenario. It is to ease the estimation at this step that we focus on only two or three critical factors and build relatively few scenarios for each factor.

4. The final component is the assignment of probabilities to each scenario. For some scenarios, involving macroeconomic factors such as exchange rates, interest rates, and overall economic growth, we can draw on the expertise of services that forecast these variables. For other scenarios involving either the sector or competitors, we have to draw on our knowledge about the industry.

The output from a scenario analysis can be presented as values under each scenario and as an expected value across scenarios (if the probabilities can be estimated in the fourth step).

In general, scenario analysis is best suited for risks that are either discrete or can be categorized into discrete groups. Thus, it is better suited to deal with the risk that a competitor will introduce a product similar to your product (the competitor either will or will not) than it is to deal with the risk that interest rates may change in future periods.

Decision Trees

In some projects, risk is not only discrete but is sequential. In other words, for an investment to succeed, it has to pass through a series of tests, with failure at any point potentially translating into a complete loss of value. This is the case, for instance, with a pharmaceutical drug that is just being tested on human beings. The three-stage FDA approval process lays out the hurdles that have to be passed for this drug to be commercially sold, and failure at any of the three stages dooms the drug's chances. Decision trees allow us to not only consider the risk in stages but also to devise the right response to outcomes at each stage.

Steps in Decision Tree Analysis

The first step in understanding decision trees is to distinguish between root nodes, decision nodes, event nodes, and end nodes.

- The root node represents the start of the decision tree, where a decision maker can be faced with a decision choice or an uncertain outcome. The objective of the exercise is to evaluate what a risky investment is worth at this node.
- Event nodes represent the possible outcomes on a risky gamble; whether a drug passes the first stage of the FDA approval process or not is a good example. We have to figure out the possible outcomes and the probabilities of the outcomes occurring, based upon the information we have available today.
- Decision nodes represent choices that can be made by the decision maker—to expand from a test market to a national market, after a test market's outcome is known.
- End nodes usually represent the final outcomes of earlier risky outcomes and decisions made in response.

Consider a very simple example. You are offered a choice where you can take $20 or partake in a gamble in which you have a fifty–fifty chance of winning $50 or winning $10. The decision tree for this offered gamble is shown in Figure 5.11:

Figure 5.11   Simple Decision Tree

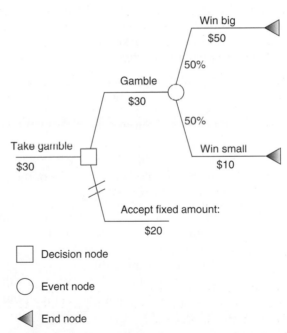

Note the key elements in the decision tree. First, only the event nodes represent uncertain outcomes and have probabilities attached to them. Second, the decision node represents a choice. On a pure expected value basis, the gamble is better (with an expected value of $30) than the guaranteed amount of $20; the double slash on the latter branch indicates that it would not be selected. While this example may be simplistic, the elements of building a decision tree are in it.

Step 1: **Divide analysis into risk phases**   The key to developing a decision tree is outlining the phases of risk that you will be exposed to in the future. In some cases, such as the FDA approval process, this will be easy to do since there are only two outcomes—the drug gets approved to move on to the next phase, or it does not. Other cases will be more difficult. For instance, a test market of a new consumer product can yield hundreds of potential outcomes; here, you will have to create discrete categories for the success of the test market.

Step 2: **In each phase, estimate the probabilities of the outcomes**   Once the phases of risk have been put down and the outcomes at each phase are defined, the probabilities of the outcomes have to be computed. In addition to the obvious requirement that the probabilities across outcomes has to sum up to one, the analyst will also have to consider whether the probabilities of outcomes in one phase can be affected by outcomes in earlier phases. For example, how does the probability of a successful national product introduction change when the test market outcome is only average?

Step 3: **Define decision points**   Embedded in the decision tree will be decision points where you will get to determine, based upon observing the outcomes at earlier stages, and expectations of what will occur in the future, what your best course of action will be. With the test market example, for instance, you will get to determine, at the end of the test market, whether you want to conduct a second test market, abandon the product or move directly to a national product introduction.

Step 4: **Compute cash flows/value at end nodes**   The next step in the decision tree process is estimating what the final cash flow and value outcomes will be at each end node. In some cases, such as abandonment of a test market product, this will be easy to do and will represent the money spent on the test marketing of the product. In other cases, such as a national launch of the same product, this will be more difficult to do since you will have to estimate expected cash flows over the life of the product and discount these cash flows to arrive at value.

Step 5: **Folding back the tree**   The last step in a decision tree analysis is termed "folding back" the tree; in it, the expected values are computed working backward through the tree. If the node is a chance node, the expected value is computed as the probability-weighted average of all of the possible outcomes. If it is a decision node, the expected value is computed for each branch, and the highest value is chosen (as the optimal decision). The process culminates in an expected value for the asset or investment today.[11]

There are two key pieces of output that emerge from a decision tree. The first is the expected value today of going through the entire decision tree. This expected value

---

[11]There is a significant body of literature examining the assumptions that have to hold for this folding back process to yield consistent values. In particular, if a decision tree is used to portray concurrent risks, the risks should be independent of each other. See R. Sarin and P. Wakker, "Folding Back in Decision Tree Analysis," *Management Science* 40:625–628.

will incorporate the potential upside and downside from risk and the actions that you will take along the way in response to this risk. In effect, this is analogous to the risk adjusted value that we talked about in the last chapter. The second is the range of values at the end nodes, which should encapsulate the potential risk in the investment.

Use in Decision Making

There are several benefits that accrue from using decision trees, and it is surprising that they are not used more often in analysis.

- *Dynamic response to risk*   By linking actions and choices to outcomes of uncertain events, decision trees encourage firms to consider how they should act under different circumstances. As a consequence, firms will be prepared for whatever outcome may arise rather than be surprised. In the example in the last section, for instance, the firm will be ready with a plan of action, no matter what the outcome of phase 3 happens to be.

- *Value of information*   Decision trees provide a useful perspective on the value of information in decision making. While it is not as obvious in the drug development example, it can be seen clearly when a firm considers whether to test market a product before commercially developing it. By test marketing a product, you acquire more information on the chances of eventual success. We can measure the expected value of this improved information in a decision tree and compare it to the test marketing cost.

- *Risk management*   Since decision trees provide a picture of how cash flows unfold over time, they are useful in deciding what risks should be protected against, and the benefits of doing so. Consider a decision tree on an asset, where the worst-case scenario unfolds if the dollar is weak against the euro. Since we can hedge against this risk, the cost of hedging the risk can be compared to the loss in cash flows in the worst-case scenario.

In summary, decision trees provide a flexible and powerful approach for dealing with risk that occurs in phases, with decisions in each phase depending upon outcomes in the previous one. In addition to providing us with measures of risk exposure, they also force to think through how we will react to both adverse and positive outcomes that may occur at each phase.

Issues

There are some types of risk that decision trees are capable of handling and others that they are not. In particular, decision trees are best suited for risk that is sequential; the FDA process where approval occurs in phases is a good example. Risks that affect an asset concurrently cannot be easily modeled in a decision tree.[12] As with scenario analysis, decision trees generally look at risk in terms of discrete outcomes. Again, this is not a problem with the FDA approval process where there are only two outcomes—success or failure. There is a much wider range of outcomes with most other

---

[12]If we choose to model such risks in a decision tree, they have to be independent of each other. In other words, the sequencing should not matter.

risks, and we have to create discrete categories for the outcomes to stay within the decision tree framework. For instance, when looking at a market test, we may conclude that selling more than 100,000 units in a test market qualifies as a great success, between 60,000 and 100,000 units as an average outcome, and below 60,000 as a failure.

Assuming risk is sequential and can be categorized into discrete boxes, we are faced with estimation questions to which there may be no easy answers. In particular, we have to estimate the cash flows under each outcome and the associated probability. With the drug development example, we had to estimate the cost and the probability of success of each phase. The advantage that we have when it comes to these estimates is that we can draw on empirical data on how frequently drugs that enter each phase make it to the next one and historical costs associated with drug testing. To the extent that there may be wide differences across different phase 1 drugs in terms of success—some may be longer shots than others—there can still be errors that creep into decision trees.

The expected value of a decision tree is heavily dependent upon the assumption that we will stay disciplined at the decision points in the tree. In other words, if the optimal decision is to abandon if a test market fails and the expected value is computed, based on this assumption, the integrity of the process and the expected value will quickly fall apart if managers decide to overlook the market testing failure and go with a full launch of the product anyway.

Simulations

If scenario analysis and decision trees are techniques that help us to assess the effects of discrete risk, simulations provide a way of examining the consequences of continuous risk. To the extent that most risks that we face in the real world can generate hundreds of possible outcomes, a simulation will give us a fuller picture of the risk in an asset or investment.

Steps in Simulation

Unlike scenario analysis, where we look at the values under discrete scenarios, simulations allow for more flexibility in how we deal with uncertainty. In its classic form, distributions of values are estimated for each parameter in the valuation (growth, market share, operating margin, beta, etc.). In each simulation, we draw one outcome from each distribution to generate a unique set of cash flows and value. Across a large number of simulations, we can derive a distribution for the value of investment or an asset that will reflect the underlying uncertainty we face in estimating the inputs to the valuation. The steps associated with running a simulation are as follows:

1. ***Determine "probabilistic" variables*** In any analysis, there are potentially dozens of inputs, some of which are predictable and some of which are not. Unlike scenario analysis and decision trees, where the number of variables that are changed and the potential outcomes have to be few in number, there is no constraint on how many variables can be allowed to vary in a simulation. At least in theory, we can define probability distributions for each and every input in a valuation. The reality, though, is that this will be time-consuming and may not provide much of a payoff, especially for inputs that have only marginal impact on value. Consequently, it makes sense to focus attention on a few variables that have a significant impact on value.

2. ***Define probability distributions for these variables***   This is a key and the most difficult step in the analysis. Generically, there are three ways in which we can go about defining probability distributions. One is to use historical data, especially for variables that have a long history and reliable data over that history. This approach works best for macroeconomic variables such as interest rates and inflation. The second is to use cross-sectional data, from investments similar to the one that is being analyzed. Thus, a retail store like Target can look at the distribution of profit margins across its existing stores when assessing what the margins will be on a new store. The third is to assume a reasonable statistical distribution for the variable, with parameters for that distribution.[13] Thus, we may conclude that operating margins will be distributed uniformly, with a minimum of 4% and a maximum of 8%, and that revenue growth is normally distributed, with an expected value of 8% and a standard deviation of 6%. The probability distributions can be discrete for some inputs and continuous for others, be based upon historical data for some and statistical distributions for others.

3. ***Check for correlation across variables***   While it is tempting to jump to running simulations right after the distributions have been specified, it is important that we check for correlations across variables. Assume, for instance, that you are developing probability distributions for both interest rates and inflation. While both inputs may be critical in determining value, they are likely to be correlated with each other; high inflation is usually accompanied by high interest rates. When there is strong correlation, positive or negative, across inputs, you have two choices. One is to pick only one of the two inputs to vary; it makes sense to focus on the input that has the bigger impact on value. The other is to build the correlation explicitly into the simulation; this does require more sophisticated simulation packages and adds more detail to the estimation process.

4. ***Run the simulation***   For the first simulation, you draw one outcome from each distribution and compute the value based upon those outcomes. This process can be repeated as many times as desired, though the marginal contribution of each simulation drops off as the number of simulations increases. The number of simulations you run should be determined by the following:

    *   ***Number of probabilistic inputs***   The larger the number of inputs that have probability distributions attached to them, the greater will be the required number of simulations.

    *   ***Characteristics of probability distributions***   The greater the diversity of distributions in an analysis, the larger will be the number of required simulations. Thus, the number of required simulations will be smaller in a simulation where all of the inputs have normal distributions than in one where some have normal distributions, some are based upon historical data distributions, and some are discrete.

    *   ***Range of outcomes***   The greater the potential range of outcomes on each input, the greater will be the number of simulations.

---

[13]For more details on the choices we face in terms of statistical distributions and how to pick the right one for a particular variable, see the paper I have on statistical distributions and simulations at www.damodaran.com/research/papers.)

Most simulation packages allow users to run thousands of simulations, with little or no cost attached to increasing that number. Given that reality, it is better to err on the side of too many simulations rather than too few.

There have generally been two impediments to good simulations. The first is informational: estimating distributions of values for each input into a valuation is difficult to do. In other words, it is far easier to estimate an expected growth rate of 8% in revenues for the next five years than it is to specify the distribution of expected growth rates—the type of distribution, parameters of that distribution—for revenues. The second is computational; until the advent of personal computers, simulations tended to be too time- and resource-intensive for the typical analyst. Both these constraints have eased in recent years, and simulations have become more feasible.

Use in Decision Making

A well-done simulation provides us with more than just an expected value for an asset or investment.

- ***Better input estimation***   In an ideal simulation, analysts will examine both the historical and cross sectional data on each input variable before making a judgment on what distribution to use and the parameters of the distribution. In the process, they may be able to avoid the sloppiness that is associated with the use of point estimates; many discounted cash flow valuations are based upon expected growth rates that are obtained from services such Zack's or IBES, which report analysts' consensus estimates.

- ***It yields a distribution for expected value rather than a point estimate***   Consider the valuation example that we completed in the last section. In addition to reporting an expected value of $11.67 million for the store, we also estimated a standard deviation of $5.96 million in that value and a breakdown of the values, by percentile. The distribution reinforces the obvious but important point that valuation models yield estimates of value for risky assets that are imprecise and explains why different analysts valuing the same asset may arrive at different estimates of value.

Note that there are two claims about simulations that we are unwilling to make. The first is that simulations yield better estimates of expected value than conventional risk adjusted value models. In fact, the expected values from simulations should be fairly close to the expected value that we would obtain using the expected values for each of the inputs (rather than the entire distribution). The second is that simulations, by providing estimates of the expected value and the distribution in that value, lead to better decisions. This may not always be the case, since the benefits that decision makers get by getting a fuller picture of the uncertainty in value in a risky asset may be more than offset by misuse of that risk measure. As we will argue later in this chapter, it is all too common for risk to be double-counted in simulations and for decisions to be based upon the wrong type of risk.

Illustration 5.21   Rio Disney—Simulation

In Illustration 5.12, we estimated a net present value of $2.877 billion for the Rio Disney theme park, suggesting that Disney should make the investment. The analysis,

Figure 5.12   Revenues as % of Predictions: Rio Disney

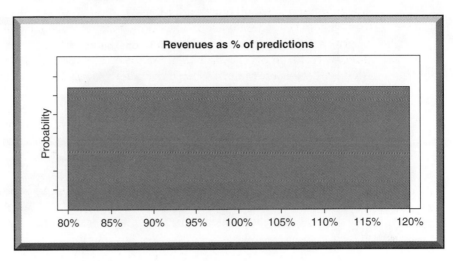

though, rested on a few key assumptions about revenues, expenses, and exchange rates that may put the value added to the test. We focused on four variables that we felt had the most uncertainty associated with them:

1. ***Revenues***   In our base case, Rio Magic Kingdom starts generating revenues of $1 billion in year 2, and revenues at that park grow to almost $3 billion in year 10. Rio Epcot is expected to generate revenues of $300 million in year 4 and grow to $750 million in year 10. We assume that the actual revenues will be within 20% of the estimate in either direction, with a uniform distribution (in Figure 5.12).

2. ***Direct expenses***   In the base case analysis, we assumed that the direct expenses would be 60% of revenues, but we based those estimates on Disney's existing theme parks. To the extent that we are entering a new market (Latin America) and may be faced with unexpected surprises, we assume that direct expenses will be normally distributed with an average of 60% and a standard deviation of 6% (as in Figure 5.13).

3. ***Country risk premium***   In our base case analysis, we used a country risk premium for Brazil of 3.95%, which when added to the mature market premium of 6% yielded a total risk premium of 9.95%. Given Brazil's volatile history, we examined the impact of changing this risk premium. Again, we assumed that the total equity risk premium would be normally distributed with an expected value of 9.95%, but with a standard deviation of 1% (as in Figure 5.14).

4. ***Correlation between assumptions***   We also recognize that our estimates of revenues will be tied to our assessments of country risk. In other words, if the risk in Brazil increases, it is likely to scare away potential visitors. To allow for this relationship, we assume that that the outcomes on revenues and total risk premium have a correlation of -0.40; revenues are low when the country risk premium is high and revenues are high when the country risk premium is low.

Figure 5.13 Operating Expenses as % of Revenues: Rio Disney

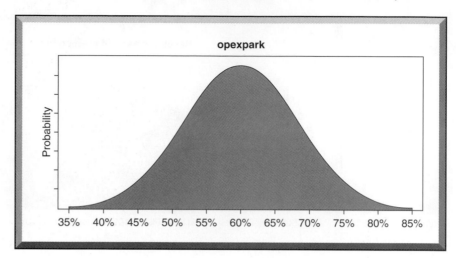

Figure 5.14 Equity Risk Premium: Rio Disney

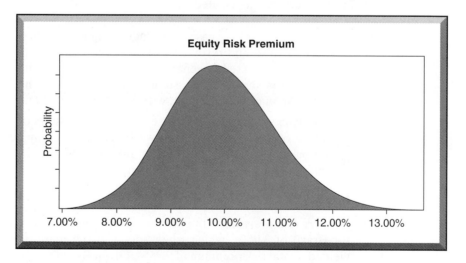

5. With these assumptions in place, we ran 10,000 simulations; the resulting NPVs are graphed in Figure 5.15.

There are three pieces of usable output. The first is that the average NPV across all 10,000 simulations is $2.95 billion and the median value is $2.73 billion, both close to our base case estimate of $2.877 billion. The second is that the NPV is negative in about 12% of all the simulations, indicating again why even the most lucrative investments come with risk premiums. The third is that net present values range from -$4 billion as the worst-case outcome to $14.6 billion as the best-case outcome.

Figure 5.15 NPV of Rio Disney: Results of Simulations

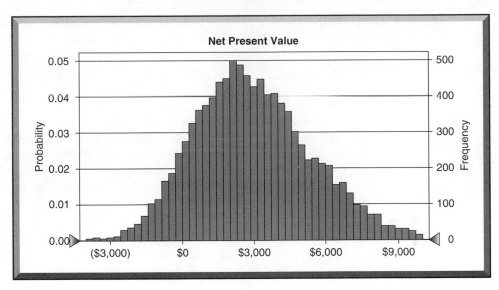

While this simulation does not change our overall assessment of the project, it does provide the decision makers at Disney with a fuller sense of what the new theme park will generate as value for the firm.

An Overall Assessment of Probabilistic Risk Assessment Approaches

Assuming that we decide to use a probabilistic approach to assess risk and could choose between scenario analysis, decision trees, and simulations, which one should we pick? The answer will depend upon how you plan to use the output and what types of risk you are facing:

- *Selective versus full risk analysis* In the best-case/worst-case scenario analysis, we look at only three scenarios (the best case, the most likely case, and the worst case) and ignore all other scenarios. Even when we consider multiple scenarios, we will not have a complete assessment of all possible outcomes from risky investments or assets. With decision trees and simulations, we attempt to consider all possible outcomes. In decision trees, we try to accomplish this by converting continuous risk into a manageable set of possible outcomes. With simulations, we can use distributions to capture all possible outcomes. Put in terms of probability, the sum of the probabilities of the scenarios we examine in scenario analysis can be less than 1, whereas the sum of the probabilities of outcomes in decision trees and simulations has to equal 1. As a consequence, we can compute expected values across outcomes in the latter, using the probabilities as weights, and these expected values are comparable to the single estimate risk adjusted values that we talked about in the last chapter.

Table 5.17   RISK TYPE AND PROBABILISTIC APPROACHES

Discrete/Continuous	Correlated/Independent	Sequential/Concurrent	Risk Approach
Discrete	Independent	Sequential	Decision tree
Discrete	Correlated	Concurrent	Scenario analysis
Continuous	Either	Either	Simulations

- *Discrete versus continuous risk*   As noted above, scenario analysis and decision trees are generally built around discrete outcomes in risky events, whereas simulations are better suited for continuous risks. Focusing on just scenario analysis and decision trees, the latter are better suited for sequential risks, since risk is considered in phases, whereas the former is easier to use when risks occur concurrently.

- *Correlation across risks*   If the various risks that an investment is exposed to are correlated, simulations allow for explicitly modeling these correlations (assuming that you can estimate and forecast them). In scenario analysis, we can deal with correlations subjectively by creating scenarios that allow for them; the high (low) interest rate scenario will also include slower (higher) economic growth. Correlated risks are difficult to model in decision trees.

Table 5.17 summarizes the relationship between risk type and the probabilistic approach used.

Finally, the quality of the information will be a factor in your choice of approach. Since simulations are heavily dependent upon being able to assess probability distributions and parameters, they work best in cases where there is substantial historical and cross-sectional data available that can be used to make these assessments. With decision trees, you need estimates of the probabilities of the outcomes at each chance node, making them best suited for risks where these risks can be assessed either using past data or population characteristics. Thus, it should come as no surprise that when confronted with new and unpredictable risks, analysts continue to fall back on scenario analysis, notwithstanding its slapdash and subjective ways of dealing with risk.

CONCLUSION

Investment analysis is arguably the most important part of corporate financial analysis. In this chapter we defined the scope of investment analysis and examined a range of investment analysis techniques, ranging from accounting rate of return measures, such as return of equity and return on assets, to discounted cash flow techniques, such as NPV and IRR. In general, it can be argued that

- Any decision that requires the use of resources is an investment decision; thus, investment decisions cover everything from broad strategic decisions at one extreme to narrower operating decisions such as how much inventory to carry at the other.

- There are two basic approaches to investment analysis; in the equity approach, the returns to equity investors from a project are measured against the cost of equity to decide on whether to take a project; in the firm approach, the returns to all investors in the firm are measured against the cost of capital to arrive at the same judgment.

- Accounting rate of return measures, such as return on equity or return on capital, generally work better for projects that have large initial investments, earnings that are roughly equal to the cash flows, and level earnings over time. For most projects, accounting returns will increase over time, as the book value of the assets is depreciated.

- Payback, which looks at how quickly a project returns its initial investment in nominal cash flow terms, is a useful secondary measure of project performance or a measure of risk, but it is not a very effective primary technique because it does not consider cash flows after the initial investment is recouped. Discounted cash flow methods provide the best measures of true returns on projects because they are based on cash flows and consider the time value of money.

- Among discounted cash flow methods, NPV provides an unscaled measure, whereas IRR provides a scaled measure of project performance. Both methods require the same information and, for the most part, provide the same conclusions when used to analyze independent projects.

- Uncertainty is a given when analyzing risky projects, and there are several techniques we can use to evaluate the consequences. In sensitivity analysis, we look at the consequences for value (and the investment decision) of changing one input at a time, holding all else constant. In scenario analysis, we examine the payoff to investing under the best and worst cases, as well as under specified scenarios. In decision trees, risk is assessed sequentially, where outcomes at one stage affect values at the next stage. Finally, in simulations, we use probability distributions for the inputs, rather than expected values, and derive probability distributions for the NPV and IRR (rather than one NPV and IRR).

LIVE CASE STUDY

ESTIMATING EARNINGS AND CASH FLOWS

Objective: To estimate earnings and cash flows on a typical project for the firm.

Key Questions

1. Does your firm have a typical investment?
2. If so, can you estimate the earnings and cash flows on a typical investment?

Framework for Analysis

1. ***Typical Investment***
   1.1 Does your firm take a few investments each year, or several?
   1.2 Do these investments have much in common?
   1.3 If so, what do they have in common, and what are the differences between them?

2. ***Earnings and Cash Flows***
   2.1 What is the typical life of an investment made by your firm?
   2.2 What is the pattern of earnings on such an investment?
   2.3 What is the pattern of cash flows on such an investment?
   2.4 Based upon the company's aggregate numbers, can you estimate the earnings and cash flows on a hypothetical investment?

Getting Information on Projects

Firms do describe their investments, though not in significant detail, in their annual reports. The statement of cash flows will provide some breakdown, as will the footnotes to the financial statements.

Online Sources of Information
www.stern.nyu.edu/~adamodar/cfin2E/project/data.htm

PROBLEMS AND QUESTIONS

1. You have been given the following information on a project.
   - It has a five-year lifetime.
   - The initial investment in the project will be $25 million, and the investment will be depreciated straight-line, down to a salvage value of $10 million at the end of the fifth year.
   - The revenues are expected to be $20 million next year and to grow 10% a year after that for the remaining four years.
   - The cost of goods sold, excluding depreciation, is expected to be 50% of revenues.
   - The tax rate is 40%.
   a. Estimate the pretax return on capital, by year and on average, for the project.
   b. Estimate the after-tax return on capital, by year and on average, for the project.
   c. If the firm faced a cost of capital of 12%, should it take this project?

2. Now assume that the facts in Problem 1 remain unchanged except for the depreciation method, which is switched to an accelerated method with the following depreciation schedule:

Year	% of Depreciable Asset
1	40%
2	24%
3	14.4%
4	13.3%
5	13.3%

   a. Estimate the pretax return on capital, by year and on average, for the project.
   b. Estimate the after-tax return on capital, by year and on average, for the project.
   c. If the firm faced a cost of capital of 12%, should it take this project?

3. Consider again the project described in Problem 1 (assume that the depreciation reverts to a straight line). Assume that 40% of the initial investment for the project will be financed with debt, with an annual interest rate of 10% and a balloon payment of the principal at the end of the fifth year.
   a. Estimate the return on equity, by year and on average, for this project.

   b. If the cost of equity is 15%, should the firm take this project?

4. Answer true or false to the following statements:
   a. The return on equity for a project will always be higher than the return on capital on the same project.
   b. If the return on capital is less than the cost of equity, the project should be rejected.
   c. Projects with high financial leverage will have higher interest expenses and lower net income than projects with low financial leverage and thus end up with a lower return on equity.
   d. Increasing the depreciation on an asset will increase the estimated return on capital and equity on the project.
   e. The average return on equity on a project over its lifetime will increase if we switch from straight-line to double declining balance depreciation.

5. Under what conditions will the return on equity on a project be equal to the IRR, estimated from cash flows to equity investors, on the same project?

6. You are provided with the projected income statements for a project:

Year	1	2	3	4
Revenues	$10,000	$11,000	$12,000	$13,000
−Cost of goods sold	$4,000	$4,400	$4,800	$5,200
−Depreciation	$4,000	$3,000	$2,000	$1,000
=EBIT	$2,000	$3,600	$5,200	$6,800

   - The tax rate is 40%.
   - The project required an initial investment of $15,000 and an additional investment of $2,000 at the end of year 2.
   - The working capital is anticipated to be 10% of revenues, and the working capital investment has to be made at the beginning of each period.
   a. Estimate the free cash flow to the firm for each of the four years.
   b. Estimate the payback period for investors in the firm.

c. Estimate the NPV to investors in the firm if the cost of capital is 12%. Would you accept the project?

d. Estimate the IRR to investors in the firm. Would you accept the project?

7. Consider the project described in Problem 6. Assume that the firm plans to finance 40% of its net capital expenditure and working capital needs with debt.

a. Estimate the free cash flow to equity for each of the four years.

b. Estimate the payback period for equity investors in the firm.

c. Estimate the NPV to equity investors if the cost of equity is 16%. Would you accept the project?

d. Estimate the IRR to equity investors in the firm. Would you accept the project?

8. You are provided with the following cash flows on a project:

Year	Cash Flow to Firm
0	$10,000,000
1	$4,000,000
2	$5,000,000
3	$6,000,000

Plot the net present valueNPV profile for this project. What is the IRR? If this firm had a cost of capital of 10% and a cost of equity of 15%, would you accept this project?

9. You have estimated the following cash flows on a project:

Year	Cash Flow to Equity ($)
0	−$5,000,000
1	$4,000,000
2	$4,000,000
3	−$3,000,000

Plot the NPV profile for this project. What is the IRR? If the cost of equity is 16%, would you accept this project?

10. Estimate the MIRR for the project described in Problem 8. Does it change your decision on accepting this project?

11. You are analyzing two mutually exclusive projects with the following cash flows:

Year	A	B
0	−$4,000,000	−$4,000,000
1	$2,000,000	$1,000,000
2	$1,500,000	$1,500,000
3	$1,250,000	$1,700,000
4	$1,000,000	$2,400,000

a. Estimate the NPV of each project, assuming a cost of capital of 10%. Which is the better project?

b. Estimate the IRR for each project. Which is the better project?

c. What reinvestment rate assumptions are made by each of these rules? Can you show the effect on future cash flows of these assumptions?

d. What is the MIRR on each of these projects?

12. You have a project that does not require an initial investment but has its expenses spread over the life of the project. Can the IRR be estimated for this project? Why, or why not?

13. Businesses with severe capital rationing constraints should use IRR more than NPV—do you agree? Explain.

14. You have to pick between three mutually exclusive projects with the following cash flows to the firm:

Year	Project A	Project B	Project C
0	−$10,000	$5,000	−$15,000
1	$8,000	$5,000	$10,000
2	$7,000	−$8,000	$10,000

The cost of capital is 12%.

a. Which project would you pick using the NPV rule?

b. Which project would you pick using the IRR rule?

c. How would you explain the differences between the two rules? Which one would you rely on to make your choice?

15. You are analyzing an investment decision, in which you will have to make an initial investment of $10 million and you will be generating annual cash flows to the firm of $2 million every year, growing at 5% a year, forever.
    a. Estimate the NPV of this project, if the cost of capital is 10%.
    b. Estimate the IRR of this project.

16. You are analyzing a project with a thirty-year lifetime, with the following characteristics:
- The project will require an initial investment of $20 million and additional investments of $5 million in year 10 and $5 million in year 20.
- The project will generate earnings before interest and taxes of $3 million each year. (The tax rate is 40%.)
- The depreciation will amount to $500,000 each year, and the salvage value of the equipment will be equal to the remaining book value at the end of year 30.
- The cost of capital is 12.5%.

    a. Estimate the NPV of this project.
    b. Estimate the IRR on this project. What might be some of the problems in estimating the IRR for this project?

17. You are trying to estimate the NPV of a three-year project in which the discount rate is expected to change over time.

Year	Cash Flow to Firm	Discount Rate
0	$15,000	9.5%
1	$5,000	10.5%
2	$5,000	11.5%
3	$10,000	12.5%

    a. Estimate the NPV of this project. Would you take this project?
    b. Estimate the IRR of this project. How would you use the IRR to decide whether to take this project?

18. Barring the case of multiple IRRs, is it possible for the NPV of a project to be positive while the IRR is less than the discount rate? Explain.

19. You are helping a manufacturing firm decide whether it should invest in a new plant. The initial investment is expected to be $50 million, and the plant is expected to generate after-tax cash flows of $5 million a year for the next twenty years. There will be an additional investment of $20 million needed to upgrade the plant in ten years. If the discount rate is 10%,
    a. Estimate the NPV of the project.
    b. Prepare an NPV Profile for this project.
    c. Estimate the IRR for this project. Is there any aspect of the cash flows that may prove to be a problem for calculating IRR?

20. You have been asked to analyze a project where the analyst has estimated the return on capital to be 37% over the ten-year lifetime of the project. The cost of capital is only 12%, but you have concerns about using the return on capital as an investment decision rule. Would it make a difference if you knew that the project was employing an accelerated depreciation method to compute depreciation? Why?

21. Accounting rates of return are based on accounting income and book value of investment, whereas internal rates of return are based on cash flows and take into account the time value of money. Under what conditions will the two approaches give you similar estimates?

CHAPTER 6

PROJECT INTERACTIONS, SIDE COSTS, AND SIDE BENEFITS

In much of our discussion so far, we have assessed projects independently of other projects that the firm already has or might have in the future. Disney, for instance, was able to look at Rio Disney standing alone and analyze whether it was a good or bad investment. In reality, projects at most firms have interdependencies with and consequences for other projects. Disney may be able to increase both movie and merchandise revenues because of the new theme park in Brazil and may face higher advertising expenditures because of its Latin American expansion.

In this chapter, we examine a number of scenarios in which the consideration of one project affects other projects. We start with the scenario in which a firm with capital constraints considers a new project. Accepting this project reduces the capital available for other projects that the firm considers later in the period and thus

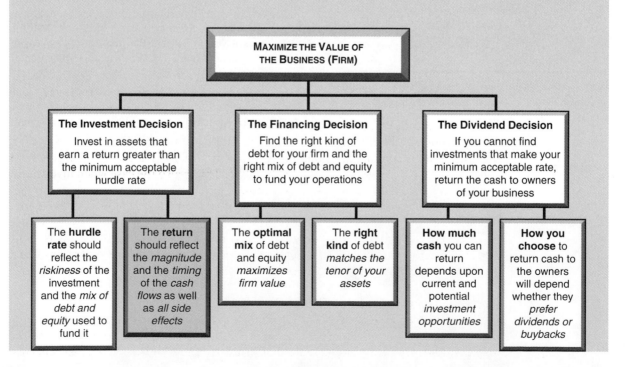

can affect their acceptance; this is the case of capital rationing. We then move to the more extreme case, whereby investing in one project leads to the rejection of one or more other projects; this is the case when firms have to choose between mutually exclusive investments.

In the third part of the chapter, we analyze side costs and side benefits that an investment can create for the rest of the firm. After all, projects can create costs for existing investments by using shared resources or excess capacity, and we consider these costs. In some cases, projects generate benefits for other investments, and we analyze how to bring these benefits into the analysis. In an extension of this principle, we introduce the notion that projects often have options embedded in them, and ignoring these options can result in poor project decisions.

In the final part of the chapter, we turn from looking at new investments to the existing investments of the company. We consider how we can extend the techniques used to analyze new investments to do postmortems of existing investments as well as to decide whether to continue or terminate an existing investment. We also look at how best to assess the portfolio of existing investments on a firm's books, using both cash flows and accounting earnings. Finally, we step away from investment and capital budgeting techniques and ask a more fundamental question. Where do good investments come from? Put another way, what are the qualities that a company or its management possess that allow it to generate value from its investments?

MUTUALLY EXCLUSIVE PROJECTS

Projects are mutually exclusive when accepting one investment means rejecting others, even though the latter standing alone may pass muster as good investments—i.e., have a positive NPV and a high IRR. There are two reasons for the loss of project independence. In the first, the firm may face a capital rationing constraint, such that not all good projects can be accepted and choices have to be made across good investments. In the second, projects may be mutually exclusive because they serve the same purpose and choosing one makes the other redundant. This is the case when the owner of a commercial building is choosing among a number of different air conditioning or heating systems for the building. This is also the case when investments provide alternative approaches to the future; a firm that has to choose between a "high-margin, low-volume" strategy and a "low-margin, high-volume" strategy for a product can choose only one of the two. We will begin this section by looking at why firms may face capital rationing and how to choose between investments, when faced with this constraint. We will then move on to look at projects that are mutually exclusive because they provide alternatives to the same ends.

Project Dependence from Capital Rationing

In Chapter 5, in our analysis of independent projects, we assumed that investing capital in a good project has no effect on other concurrent or subsequent projects that the firm may consider. Implicitly, we assume that firms with good investment prospects (with positive NPV) can raise capital at a fair price (from financial markets, banks or private sources), and without paying transaction costs. In reality, it is possible that the capital required to finance a project can cause managers to reject other good projects because the firm has limited access to capital. *Capital rationing* occurs when a firm is unable (or unwilling) to raise the capital or to invest in projects that earn returns greater than the hurdle rates.[1] Firms may face capital rationing constraints because they either do not have the capital on hand or do not have the capacity and willingness to raise the capital needed to finance these projects. This implies that the firm will have to reject some positive NPV projects and consequently needs a mechanism for choosing among these projects.

Reasons for Capital Rationing Constraints

In theory, there will be no capital rationing constraint as long as a firm can follow this series of steps in locating and financing investments:

1. The firm identifies an attractive investment opportunity.

2. The firm goes to capital providers (financial markets or financial institutions) with a description of the project to seek financing.

3. Capital providers believe the firm's description of the project.

4. The firm issues securities—that is, stocks and bonds—to raise the capital needed to finance the project at fair market prices. Implicit here is the assumption that markets are efficient and that expectations of future earnings and growth are built into these prices.

5. The cost associated with issuing these securities is minimal.

If this were the case, then every worthwhile project would be financed and no good project would ever be rejected for lack of funds; in other words, there would be no capital rationing constraint.

The sequence described depends on a several assumptions, some of which are clearly unrealistic, at least for some firms. Let's consider each step even more closely.

1. ***Project Discovery***   The implicit assumption that firms know when they have good projects on hand underestimates the uncertainty and the errors associated with project analysis. In very few cases can firms say with complete certainty that a prospective project will be a good one. It is possible that a firm may feel uncertain enough about its own project assessment (and the resulting positive NPV) and choose not to pursue that investment.

2. ***Credibility***   Financial markets and institutions tend to be skeptical when firms claim that they have good investments or projects. Because it is easy for any firm to contend that its future projects are good, regardless of whether this is true or not, more substantial backing for the viability of projects is usually required. Firms that are unable to provide this backing may not be able to convince capital providers that the investments that they are considering will create value.

---

[1]For discussions of the effect of capital rationing on the investment decision, see J. H. Lorie and L. J. Savage, "Three Problems in Rationing Capital," *Journal of Business* 28:229–239; H. M. Weingartner, "Capital Rationing: *n* Authors in Search of a Plot," *Journal of Finance* 32:1403–1432.

3. ***Market Efficiency***   If the securities issued by a firm are underpriced by markets, firms may be reluctant to issue stocks and bonds at these low prices to finance even good projects. In particular, the gains from investing in a project for existing stockholders may be overwhelmed by the loss from having to sell securities at or below their estimated true value. To illustrate, assume that a firm is considering a project that requires an initial investment of $100 million and has an NPV of $10 million. Also assume that the stock of this company, which management believes should be trading for $100 per share, is actually trading at $80 per share. If the company issues $100 million of new stock to take the new project, its existing stockholders will gain their share of the NPV of $10 million, but they will lose $20 million ($100 million − $80 million) to new investors in the company. There is an interesting converse to this problem. When securities are overpriced, there may be a temptation to overinvest, because existing stockholders gain from the very process of issuing equities to new investors.

4. ***Flotation Costs***   These are costs associated with raising funds in financial markets, and they can be substantial. If these costs are larger than the NPV of the projects considered, it would not make sense to raise these funds and finance the projects.

Sources of Capital Rationing

What are the sources of capital rationing? Going through the process described in the last section in Table 6.1, we can see the possible reasons for capital rationing at each step. The three primary sources of capital rationing constraints, therefore, are a

Table 6.1   CAPITAL RATIONING: THEORY VERSUS PRACTICE

	In Theory	**In Practice**	**Source of Rationing**
1. Project discovery	A business uncovers a good investment opportunity.	A business believes, given the underlying uncertainty, that it has a good project.	Uncertainty about true value of projects may cause rationing.
2. Information revelation	The business conveys information about the project to financial markets.	The business attempts to convey information to financial markets.	Difficulty in conveying information to markets may cause rationing.
3. Market response	Financial markets believe the firm— i.e., the information is conveyed credibly.	Financial markets may not believe the announcement.	The greater the credibility gap, the greater the rationing problem.
4. Market efficiency	The securities issued by the business (stocks and bonds) are fairly priced.	The securities issued by the business may not be correctly priced.	With underpriced securities, firms will be unwilling to raise funds for projects.
5. Flotation costs	There are no costs associated with raising funds for projects.	There are significant costs associated with raising funds for projects.	The greater the flotation costs, the larger will be the capital rationing problem.

Table 6.2   THE CAUSES OF CAPITAL RATIONING

Cause	Number of Firms	%
Debt limit imposed by outside agreement	10	10.7
Debt limit placed by management external to firm	3	3.2
Limit placed on borrowing by internal management	65	69.1
Restrictive policy imposed on retained earnings	1	2.1
Maintenance of target EPS or PE ratio	14	14.9

Source: Martin and Scott (1976)

firm's lack of credibility with financial markets, market underpricing of securities, and issuance costs.

Researchers have used surveys to determine whether firms face capital rationing constraints and, if so, to identify the sources of such constraints. One such survey was conducted by Scott and Martin and is summarized in Table 6.2.[2]

This survey suggests that although some firms face capital rationing constraints as a result of external factors largely beyond their control, such as issuance costs and credibility problems, many of the constraints are self-imposed. In some cases, managers are reluctant to issue additional equity, because they fear that doing so will dilute the control they have over the company. In others, firms hold back largely because they do not want to over extend their resource (people, infrastructure) constraints.

Looking at the sources of capital rationing, it seems clear that smaller firms with more limited access to capital markets are more likely to face capital rationing constraints than larger firms. Using similar reasoning, private businesses and emerging market companies are more likely to have limited capital than publicly traded and developed market companies.

Project Selection with Capital Rationing
Firms with capital rationing constraints have limited funds available for investment. Consequently, the standard advice of investing in all projects with positive NPV breaks down, because only a subset of these projects can be funded. Put another way, we have to devise ranking systems for good investments that will help us direct the limited capital to where it can generate the biggest payoff. We will begin this section by evaluating how and why the two discounted cash flow techniques that we introduced in Chapter 5—NPV and IRR—yield different rankings, and then consider modifying these techniques in the face of capital rationing.

Project Rankings: NPV and IRR
The NPV and the IRR are both time-weighted, cash flow–based measures of return for an investment and yield the same conclusion—accept or reject—for an independent, standalone investment. When comparing or ranking multiple projects, though, the two approaches can yield different rankings, either because of differences in scale or because of differences in the reinvestment rate assumption.

---

[2]J. D. Martin and D. F. Scott, "Debt Capacity and the Capital Budgeting Decision," *Financial Management* 5, no. 2:7–14.

Differences in Scale

The NPV of a project is stated in dollar terms and does not factor in the scale of the project. The IRR, by contrast, is a percentage rate of return, which is standardized for the scale of the project. Not surprisingly, rankings based upon the former will rank the biggest projects (with large cash flows) highest, whereas rankings based upon IRR will tilt towards projects that require smaller investments.

The scale differences can be illustrated using a simple example. Assume that you are a firm and that you are comparing two projects. The first project requires an initial investment of $1 million and produces the cash flows shown in Figure 6.1. The second project requires an investment of $10 million and is likely to produce the much higher cash flows (shown in Figure 6.1) as well. The cost of capital is 15% for both projects.

Both projects generate positive net present values and high IRRs but the two decision rules yield different rankings. The NPV rule, which is based on the magnitude of the cash flows, suggests that project B (which has the bigger investment and the larger cash flows) is the better project, whereas the IRR rule, which measures percentage or scaled returns, leans toward project A, with its smaller initial investment.

If a firm has easy access to capital markets, it would invest in both projects. However, if the firm has limited capital and has to apportion it across a number of good projects, investing in Project B may lead to the rejection of good projects later on. If the objective is maximize value created with limited capital, project A may be the better choice, since it requires a much smaller initial investment. It follows that the IRR rule will yield better choices for firms with significant capital rationing constraints.

Differences in Reinvestment Rate Assumptions

Although the differences between the NPV rule and the IRR rules due to scale are fairly obvious, there is a subtler and much more significant difference between them relating to the reinvestment of intermediate cash flows. The NPV rule assumes that intermediate cash flows are reinvested at the discount rate, whereas the IRR rule

Figure 6.1   NPV and IRR—Different Scale Projects

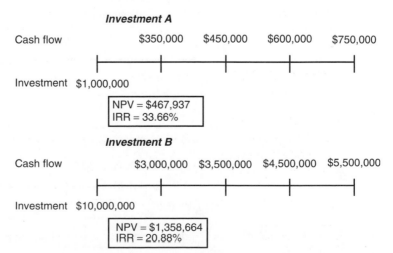

assumes that intermediate cash flows are reinvested at the IRR. As a consequence, the two rules can yield different conclusions, even for projects with the same scale, as illustrated in Figure 6.2.

In this case, the NPV rule ranks the second investment higher, whereas the IRR rule ranks the first investment as the better project. The differences arise because the NPV rule assumes that intermediate cash flows get invested at the hurdle rate, which is 15%. The IRR rule assumes that intermediate cash flows get reinvested at the IRR of that project. Although both projects are affected by this assumption, it has a much greater effect for project A, which has higher cash flows earlier on. The reinvestment assumption is made clearer if the expected end balance is estimated under each rule.

$$\text{End balance for Investment A with IRR of } 21.41\% = \$10,000,000 * 1.2141^4$$
$$= \$21,730,887$$
$$\text{End balance for Investment B with IRR of } 20.88\% = \$10,000,000 * 1.2088^4$$
$$= \$21,353,673$$

To arrive at these end balances, however, the cash flows in years 1, 2, and 3 will have to be reinvested at the IRR. If they are reinvested at a lower rate, the end balance on these projects will be lower, and the actual return earned will be lower than the IRR even though the cash flows on the project came in as anticipated.

The reinvestment rate assumption made by the IRR rule has more serious consequences the longer the term of the project and the higher the IRR, because it implicitly assumes that the firm has and will continue to have a fountain of projects yielding returns similar to that earned by the project under consideration.

Project Rankings: Modified Rules
The conventional discounted cash flow rules, NPV or IRR, have limitations when it comes to ranking projects, in the presence of capital rationing. The NPV rule is biased

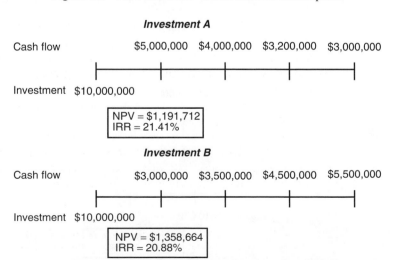

Figure 6.2 NPV and IRR—Reinvestment Assumption

Investment A

Cash flow $5,000,000 $4,000,000 $3,200,000 $3,000,000

Investment $10,000,000

NPV = $1,191,712
IRR = 21.41%

Investment B

Cash flow $3,000,000 $3,500,000 $4,500,000 $5,500,000

Investment $10,000,000

NPV = $1,358,664
IRR = 20.88%

towards larger investments and will not result in the best use of limited capital. The IRR rule is generally better suited for capital-rationed firms, but the assumption that intermediate cash flows get reinvested at the IRR can skew investment choices. We consider three modifications to traditional investment rules that yield better choices than the traditional rules: a scaled version of NPV called the profitability index, a modified internal rate of return with more reasonable reinvestment assumptions, and a more complex linear programming approach that allows capital constraints across many time periods (and not just in the current one).

Profitability Index
The profitability index is the simplest method of including capital rationing in investment analysis. It is particularly useful for firms that have a capital constraint for the current period only and relatively few projects. A scaled version of the NPV, the profitability index is computed by dividing the NPV of the project by the initial investment in the project.[3]

$$\text{Profitability index} = \frac{\text{Net present value of investment}}{\text{Initial investment needed for investment}}$$

The profitability index provides a rough measure of the NPV the firm gets for each dollar it invests. To use it in investment analysis, we first compute it for each investment the firm is considering and then rank (and pick) projects based on the profitability index, starting with the highest values and working down until we exhaust the capital available. When capital is limited and a firm cannot accept every positive NPV project, the profitability index identifies the highest cumulative NPV from the funds available for capital investment.

Although the profitability index is intuitively appealing, it has several limitations. First, it assumes that the capital rationing constraint applies to the current period only and does not consider investment requirements in future periods. Thus, a firm may choose projects with a total initial investment of less than the current period's capital constraint, but it may expose itself to capital rationing problems in future periods if these projects have outlays in those periods. A related problem is the classification of cash flows into an initial investment that occurs now and operating cash inflows that occur in future periods. If projects have investments spread over multiple periods and operating cash outflows, the profitability index may measure the project's contribution to value incorrectly. Finally, the profitability index does not guarantee that the total investment will add up to the capital rationing constraint. If it does not, we have to consider other combinations of projects, which may yield a higher NPV. Although this is feasible for firms with relatively few projects, it becomes increasing unwieldy as the number of projects increases.

ILLUSTRATION 6.1   Using the Profitability Index to Select Projects
Assume that Bookscape, as a private firm, has limited access to capital, and a capital budget of $100,000 in the current period. The projects available to the firm are listed in Table 6.3.

---

[3]There is another version of the profitability index, whereby the present value of all cash inflows is divided by the present value of cash outflows. The resulting ranking will be the same as with the profitability index as defined in this chapter.

Table 6.3   AVAILABLE PROJECTS

Project	Initial Investment (in 1,000s)	NPV (000s)
A	$25	$10
B	40	20
C	5	5
D	100	25
E	50	15
F	70	20
G	35	20

Note that all the projects have positive NPVs and would have been accepted by a firm not subject to a capital rationing constraint.

To choose among these projects, we compute the profitability index of each project in Table 6.4 and rank them on that basis.

The profitability index of 0.40 for Project A means that the project earns an NPV of forty cents for every dollar of initial investment. Based on the profitability index, we should accept Projects B, C, and G. This combination of projects would exhaust the capital budget of $100,000 while maximizing the cumulative NPV of the projects accepted. This analysis also highlights the cost of the capital rationing constraint for this firm; the NPV of the projects rejected as a consequence of the constraint is $70 million.

6.1   MUTUALLY EXCLUSIVE PROJECTS WITH DIFFERENT RISK LEVELS

Assume in this illustration that the initial investment required for Project B was $40,000. Which of the following would be your best combination of projects given your capital rationing constraint of $100,000?

a.   B, C, and G

b.   A, B, C, and G

c.   A, B, and G

d.   Other

Table 6.4   PROFITABILITY INDEX FOR PROJECTS

Project	Initial Investment (1,000s)	NPV (1,000s)	Profitability Index	Ranking
C	5	5	1.00	1
G	35	20	0.57	2
B	60	30	0.50	3
A	25	10	0.40	4
E	50	15	0.30	5
F	70	20	0.29	6
D	100	25	0.25	7

Modified Internal Rate of Return (MIRR)

We noted earlier that the IRR computation assumes that intermediate cash flows get reinvested at the computed IRR. One solution that has been suggested for the reinvestment rate assumption is to assume that intermediate cash flows get reinvested at the hurdle rate—the cost of equity if the cash flows are to equity investors and the cost of capital if they are to the firm—and to calculate the IRR from the initial investment and the terminal value. This approach yields what is called the **modified internal rate of return (MIRR)**.

Consider a four-year project with an initial investment of $1 billion and expected cash flows of $300 million in year 1, $400 million in year 2, $500 million in year 3, and $600 million in year 4. The conventional IRR of this investment is 24.89%, but that is based on the assumption that the cash flows in years 1, 2, and 3 are reinvested at that rate. If we assume a cost of capital of 15%, the modified internal rate of return computation is illustrated in Figure 6.3.

$$\text{MIRR} = (\$2{,}160/\$1{,}000)^{1/4} - 1 = 21.23\%$$

Thus, the $300 million in cash flows in year 1 is reinveseted at 15% for the remaining three years of the project to yield $456 million at the end of year 4. Using the cumulated end values of all of the cash flows ($2.16 billion) and the initial investment of $1 billion, we estimated a modified internal rate of return of 21.23%. The MIRR is lower than the IRR, because the intermediate cash flows are invested at the hurdle rate of 15% instead of the IRR of 24.89%.

There are many who believe that the MIRR is neither fish nor fowl, because it is a mix of the NPV rule and the IRR rule. From a practical standpoint, the MIRR

Figure 6.3   IRR versus Modified Internal Rate of Return

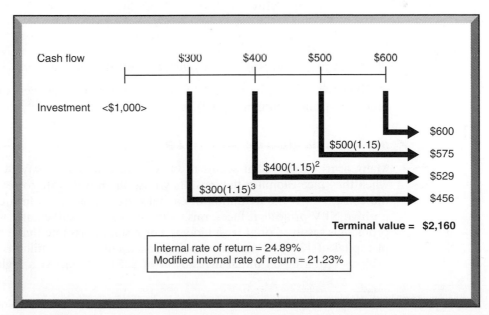

becomes a weighted average of the returns on an individual projects and the hurdle rates the firm uses, with the weights on each depending on the magnitude and timing of the cash flows—the larger and earlier the cash flows on the project, the greater the weight attached to the hurdle rate. Furthermore, the MIRR approach will yield the same choices as the NPV approach for projects of the same scale and lives.

Multiperiod Capital Rationing
The approaches that we have described so far are designed to deal with capital rationing in the current period. In most cases, capital rationing constraints apply not only to the current period but to future periods as well, with the amount of capital that is available for investment also varying across periods. If you combine these multiperiod constraints with projects that require investments in many periods (and not just in the current one), the capital rationing problem becomes much more complex and project rankings, based just on current investment, cannot provide an optimal solution.

One solution is to use linear programming techniques, developed in operations research. In a linear program, we begin by specifying an objective, subject to specified constraints. In the context of capital rationing, that objective is to maximize the value added by new investments, subject to the capital constraints in each period. For example, the linear program for a firm. with capital constraints of $1 billion for the current period, $1.2 billion for next year and $1.5 billion for year and trying to choose between k investments, can be written as follows:

$$\text{Maximize} \sum_{j=1}^{j=k} X_j \text{NPV}_j$$

where $X_j = 1$ if investment j is taken; 0 otherwise
Constraints:

$$\sum_{j=1}^{j=k} X_j \text{Inv}_{j,1} < \$1,000 \quad \sum_{j=1}^{j=k} X_j \text{Inv}_{j,2} < \$1,200 \quad \sum_{j=1}^{j=k} X_j \text{Inv}_{j,3} < \$1,500$$

where

$$\text{Inv}_{j,t} = \text{Investment (in millions) needed on investment } j \text{ in period } t$$

The approach can be modified to allow for partial investments in projects and for other constraints (human capital) as well.

IN PRACTICE: Using a Higher Hurdle Rate

Many firms choose what seems to be a more convenient way of selecting projects, when they face capital rationing—they raise the hurdle rate to reflect the severity of the constraint. If the definition of capital rationing is that a firm cannot take all the positive NPV projects it faces, raising the hurdle rate sufficiently will ensure that the problem is resolved or at least hidden. For instance, assume that a firm has a true cost of capital of 12%,[4] a capital rationing constraint of $100 million, and positive NPV projects requiring an initial investment of $250 million. At a higher cost of capital,

---
[4]By true cost of capital, we mean a cost of capital that reflects the riskiness of the firm and its financing mix.

fewer projects will have positive NPVs. At some cost of capital, say 18%, the positive NPV projects remaining will require an initial investment of $100 million or less.

There are problems that result from building the capital rationing constraint into the hurdle rate. First, once the adjustment has been made, the firm may fail to correct it for shifts in the severity of the constraint. Thus, a small firm may adjust its cost of capital from 12% to 18% to reflect a severe capital rationing constraint. As the firm gets larger, the constraint will generally become less restrictive, but the firm may not decrease its cost of capital accordingly. Second, increasing the discount rate will yield NPVs that do not convey the same information as those computed using the correct discount rates. The NPV of a project, estimated using the right hurdle rate, is the value added to the firm by investing in that project; the present value estimated using an adjusted discount rate cannot be read the same way. Finally, adjusting the hurdle rate penalizes all projects equally, whether or not they are capital-intensive.

We recommend that firms separate the capital rationing constraint from traditional investment analysis so that they can observe how much these constraints cost. In the simplest terms, the cost of a capital rationing constraint is the total NPV of the good projects that could not be taken for lack of funds, where than NPV is computed using the correct (rather than the artificially high) hurdle rate. There are two reasons why this knowledge is useful. First, if the firm is faced with the opportunity to relax these constraints, knowing how much these constraints cost is important. For instance, the firm may be able to enter into a strategic partnership with a larger firm with excess funds and use the cash to take the good projects that would otherwise have been rejected, sharing the NPV of these projects. Second, if the capital rationing is self-imposed, managers in the firm are forced to confront the cost of the constraint. In some cases, the sheer magnitude of this cost may be sufficient for them to drop or relax the constraint. ■

Project Dependence for Operating Reasons

Even without capital rationing, choosing one project may require that we reject other projects. This is the case, for instance, when a firm is considering alternative ways, with different costs and cash flows, of delivering a needed service such as distribution or information technology. In choosing among mutually exclusive projects, we continue to use the same rules we developed for analyzing independent projects. The firm should choose the project that adds the most to its value. Although this concept is relatively straightforward when the projects are expected to generate cash flows for the same number of periods (have the same project life), as you will see, it can become more complicated when the projects have different lives.

Projects with Equal Lives

When comparing alternative investments with the same lives, a business can make its decision in one of two ways. It can compute the net present value (NPV) of each project and choose the one with the highest positive NPV (if the projects generate revenue) or the one with the lowest negative NPV (if the projects minimize costs). Alternatively, it can compute the differential cash flow between two projects and base its decision on the NPV or the internal rate of return (IRR) of the differential cash flow.

Comparing NPVs

The simplest way of choosing among mutually exclusive projects with equal lives is to compute the NPVs of the projects and choose the one with the highest NPV. This decision rule is consistent with firm value maximization. If the investments all generate costs (and hence only cash outflows), which is often the case when a service is being delivered, we will choose that alternative that has the least negative NPV.

As an illustration, assume that Bookscape is choosing between alternative vendors who are offering telecommunications systems. Both systems have five-year lives, and the appropriate cost of capital is 10% for both projects. However, the choice is between a more expensive system with lower annual costs and a cheaper system with higher annual costs. Figure 6.4 summarizes the expected cash outflows on the two investments.

The more expensive system is also more efficient, resulting in lower annual costs. The NPVs of these two systems can be estimated as follows:

$$\text{NPV of less expensive system} = -\$20,000 - \$8,000 \frac{(1 - (1.10)^{-5})}{0.10}$$
$$= -\$50,326$$

$$\text{NPV of more expensive system} = -\$30,000 - \$3,000 \frac{(1 - (1.10)^{-5})}{0.10}$$
$$= -\$41,372$$

The NPV of all costs is much lower with the second system, making it the better choice.

 IN PRACTICE: NEGATIVE CASH FLOWS AND DISCOUNT RATES

In Chapter 4, we argued that discount rates should be increased when we are faced with more uncertain cash flows. But what if the cash flows are negative for the entire life of the investment (as in Figure 6.4) or even over a portion of the life (as is the case with many infrastructure investments, where the cash flows can be negative for an extended period before the positive cash flows begin)? Using a higher discount rate will make the present value of these negative cash flows lower, which operates to the benefit of the firm but is counter intuitive. After all, increasing risk should reduce value, not increase it.

Figure 6.4   Cash Flows on Telecommunication Systems

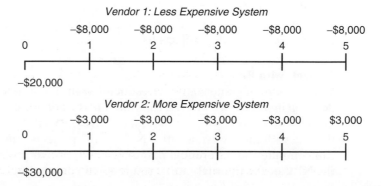

We are unwilling to abandon a basic principle—that discount rates have to reflect the uncertainty about cash flows—just because the cash flows are negative, but there are two factors that may help increase the comfort level for analysts.

1. If the negative cash flows are more certain (or predictable) than the rest of the project cash flows, it is perfectly appropriate to use a lower discount rate to discount these cash flows. To illustrate, assume that you are looking at a large infrastructure investments and that you have contracted to spend millions a year for the next five years on construction, after which operations will begin. Since the only uncertainty associated with the contracted payments is that the firm may default, it seems reasonable to use the after-tax cost of debt as the discount rate for these cash flows before reverting to an operating cost of capital for the cash flows thereafter.

2. If the negative cash flows are related to operating uncertainty—low revenues and high operating costs—in the first few years, we should continue to use the operating cost of capital. While making that cost of capital higher will reduce the present value of the negative cash flows in the early years, it will also reduce the present value of the positive cash flows in the years after.

In summary, it is dangerous to abandon first principles relating to risk on individual cash flows, just because the resulting values seems counterintuitive. Ultimately, the project will stand or fall based on the cumulative present value of the cash flows over its life. ■

Differential Cash Flows

An alternative approach for choosing between two mutually exclusive projects is to compute the difference in cash flows each period between the two investments. Using the telecommunications system from the last section as our illustrative example, we would compute the differential cash flow between the less expensive and the more expensive system in Figure 6.5.

In computing the differential cash flow, the project with the larger initial investment becomes the project against which the comparison is made. In practical terms, the differential cash flows can be read thus: the more expensive system costs $10,000 more up front, but saves $5,000 a year for the next five years.

The differential cash flows can be used to compute the NPV, and the decision rule can be summarized as follows:

$$\text{If} \quad \text{NPV}_{B-A} > 0: \quad \text{Project B is better than Project A}$$
$$\text{NPV}_{B-A} < 0: \quad \text{Project A is better than Project B}$$

Notice two points about the differential NPV. The first is that it provides the same result as would have been obtained if the business had computed NPVs of the individual projects and then taken the difference between them.

$$\text{NPV}_{B-A} = \text{NPV}_B - \text{NPV}_A$$

The second is that the differential cash flow approach works only when the two projects being compared have the same risk level and discount rates, because only one discount

Figure 6.5   Differential Cash Flows on Telecommunication Systems

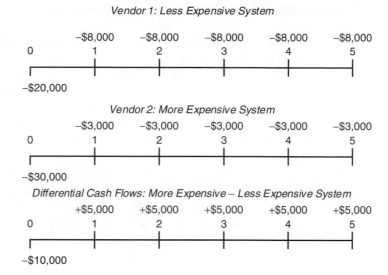

rate can be used on the differential cash flows. By contrast, computing project-specific NPVs allows for the use of different discount rates on each project. The differential cash flows can also be used to compute an IRR, which can guide us in selecting the better project.

If IRR_{B-A} > Hurdle Rate: Project B is better than Project A
    IRR_{B-A} < Hurdle Rate: Project A is better than Project B

Again, this approach works only if the projects are of equivalent risk. Illustrating this process with the telecommunications example in Figure 6.5, we estimate the NPV of the differential cash flows as follows:

$$\text{Net present value of differential cash flows} = -\$10,000 + \$5,000\frac{(1 - (1.10)^{-5})}{0.10}$$

$$= +\$8,954$$

This NPV is equal to the difference between the NPVs of the individual projects that we computed in the last section, and it indicates that the system that costs more up front is also the better system from the viewpoint of NPV. The IRR of the differential cash flows is 41.04%, which is higher than the discount rate of 10%, once again suggesting that the more expensive system is the better one from a financial standpoint.

6.2   MUTUALLY EXCLUSIVE PROJECTS WITH DIFFERENT RISK LEVELS

When comparing mutually exclusive projects with different risk levels and discount rates, what discount rate should we use to discount the differential cash flows?

a.   The higher of the two discount rates
b.   The lower of the two discount rates

c. An average of the two discount rates

d. None of the above

Explain your answer.

Projects with Different Lives

In many cases, firms have to choose among projects with different lives.[5] In doing so, they can no longer rely solely on the NPV. This is so because, as a nonscaled figure, the NPV is likely to be higher for longer-term projects; the NPV of a project with only two years of cash flows is likely to be lower than one with thirty years of cash flows.

Assume that you are choosing between two projects: a five-year project with an initial investment of $1 billion and annual cash flows of $400 million each year for the next five years, and a ten-year project with an initial investment of $1.5 billion and annual cash flows of $350 million for ten years. Figure 6.6 summarizes the cash flows; a discount rate of 12% applies for each.

The NPV of the first project is $442 million, whereas the NPV of the second project is $478 million. On the basis on NPV alone, the second project is better, but this analysis fails to factor in the additional NPV that could be made by the firm from years 6 to 10 in the project with a five-year life.

In comparing a project with a shorter life to one with a longer life, the firm must consider that it will be able to invest again with the shorter-term project. Two conventional approaches—project replication and equivalent annuities—assume that when the current project ends, the firm will be able to invest in the same project or one with identical cash flows and risk.

Project Replication

One way of tackling the problem of different lives is to assume that projects can be replicated until they have the same lives. Thus, instead of comparing a five-year to a ten-year project, we can compute the NPV of investing in the five-year project twice and comparing it to the NPV of the ten-year project. Figure 6.7 presents the resulting cash flows.

Figure 6.6   Cash Flows on Projects with Unequal Lives

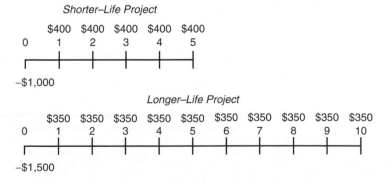

---

[5]G. W. Emery, "Some Guidelines for Evaluating Capital Investment Alternatives with Unequal Lives," *Financial Management* 11:14–19.

Figure 6.7 Cash Flows on Projects with Unequal Lives: Replicated with Poorer Project

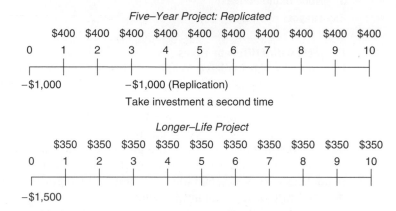

The NPV of investing in the five-year project twice is $693 million, whereas the net present value of the ten-year project remains at $478 million. These NPVs now can be compared because they correspond to two investment choices that have the same life.

This approach has limitations. On a practical level, it can become tedious to use when the number of projects increases and the lives do not fit neatly into multiples of each other. For example, an analyst using this approach to compare a seven-year, a nine-year, and a thirteen-year project would have to replicate these projects up to 819 years to arrive at an equivalent life for all three. It is also difficult to argue that a firm's project choice will essentially remain unchanged over time, especially if the projects being compared are very attractive in terms of NPV.

ILLUSTRATION 6.2 Project Replication to Compare Projects with Different Lives

Suppose you are deciding whether to buy a used car that is inexpensive but that does not give very good mileage or a new car that costs more but that gets better mileage. The two options are listed in Table 6.5.

Assume that you drive 5,000 miles a year and that your cost of capital is 15%. This choice can be analyzed with replication.

Step 1: Replicate the projects until they have the same lifetime; in this case, that would mean buying used cars five consecutive times and new cars four consecutive times.

Table 6.5 EXPECTED CASH FLOWS ON NEW VERSUS USED CAR

	Used Car	New Car
Initial cost	$3,000	$8,000
Maintenance costs/year	$1,500	$1,000
Fuel costs/mile	$0.20	$0.05
Lifetime	4 years	5 years

a. Buy a used car every four years for twenty years:

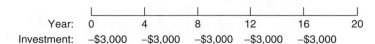

Year:	0	4	8	12	16	20
Investment:	−$3,000	−$3,000	−$3,000	−$3,000	−$3,000	

Maintenance costs: $1,500 every year for twenty years
Fuel costs: $1,000 every year for twenty years (5,000 miles at $0.20 per mile).

b. Buy a new car every five years for twenty years:

Year:	0	5	10	15	20
Investment:	−$8,000	−$8,000	−$8,000	−$8,000	

Maintenance costs: $1,000 every year for twenty years
Fuel costs: $250 every year for twenty years (5,000 miles at five cents a mile)

Step 2: Compute the NPV of each stream.

> NPV of replicating used cars for 20 years = −22,225.61
> NPV of replicating new cars for 20 years = −22,762.21

The NPV of the costs incurred by buying a used car every four years is less negative than the NPV of the costs incurred by buying a new car every five years, given that the cars will be driven 5,000 miles every year. As the mileage driven increases, however, the relative benefits of owning and driving the more efficient new car will also increase.

Equivalent Annuities
We can compare projects with different lives by converting their net present values into *equivalent annuities*. These equivalent annuities can be compared legitimately across projects with different lives. The NPV of any project can be converted into an annuity using the following calculation.

$$\text{Equivalent annuity} = \text{Net present value} * \frac{r}{(1 - (1+r)^{-n})}$$

where

$$r = \text{project discount rate,}$$
$$n = \text{project lifetime}$$

Note that the NPV of each project is converted into an annuity using that project's life and discount rate and that the second term in the equation is the annuity factor (see Appendix 3).[6] Thus, this approach is flexible enough to use on projects with different discount rates and lifetimes. Consider again the example of the five-year and ten-year

---

[6]This can be obtained just as easily using the present value functions in a financial calculator or a present value factor table.

projects from the previous section. The NPVs of these projects can be converted into annuities as follows:

$$\text{Equivalent annuity for five-year project} = \$442 * \frac{0.12}{(1 - (1.12)^{-5})} = \$122.62$$

$$\text{Equivalent annuity for ten-year project} = \$478 * \frac{0.12}{(1 - (1.12)^{-10})} = \$84.60$$

The NPV of the five-year project is lower than the NPV of the ten-year project, but using equivalent annuities, the five-year project yields $37.98 more per year than the ten-year project.

Although this approach does not explicitly make an assumption of project replication, it does so implicitly. Consequently, it will always lead to the same decision rules as the replication method. The advantage is that the equivalent annuity method is less tedious and will continue to work even in the presence of projects with infinite lives.

 eqann.xls: This spreadsheet allows you to compare projects with different lives using the equivalent annuity approach.

ILLUSTRATION 6.3   Equivalent Annuities to Choose between Projects with Different Lives
Consider again the choice between a new car and a used car described in Illustration 6.3. The equivalent annuities can be estimated for the two options as follows:

Step 1:   Compute the NPV of each project individually (without replication)

$$\text{NPV of buying a used car} = -\$3,000 - \$2,500 * \frac{(1 - (1.15)^{-4})}{0.15}$$

$$= -\$10,137$$

$$\text{NPV of buying a new car} = -\$8,000 - \$1,250 * \frac{(1 - (1.15)^{-5})}{0.15}$$

$$= -\$12,190$$

Step 2:   Convert the NPVs into equivalent annuities

$$\text{Equivalent annuity of buying a used car} = -\$10,137 * \frac{0.15}{(1 - (1.15)^{-4})}$$

$$= -\$3,551$$

$$\text{Equivalent annuity of buying a new car} = -\$12,190 * \frac{0.15}{(1 - (1.15)^{-5})}$$

$$= -\$3,637$$

Based on the equivalent annuities of the two options, buying a used car is more economical than buying a new car.

Calculating Break-Even
When an investment that costs more initially but that is more efficient and economical on an annual basis is compared with a less expensive and less efficient investment,

Figure 6.8   Equivalent Annual Costs as a Function of Miles Driven

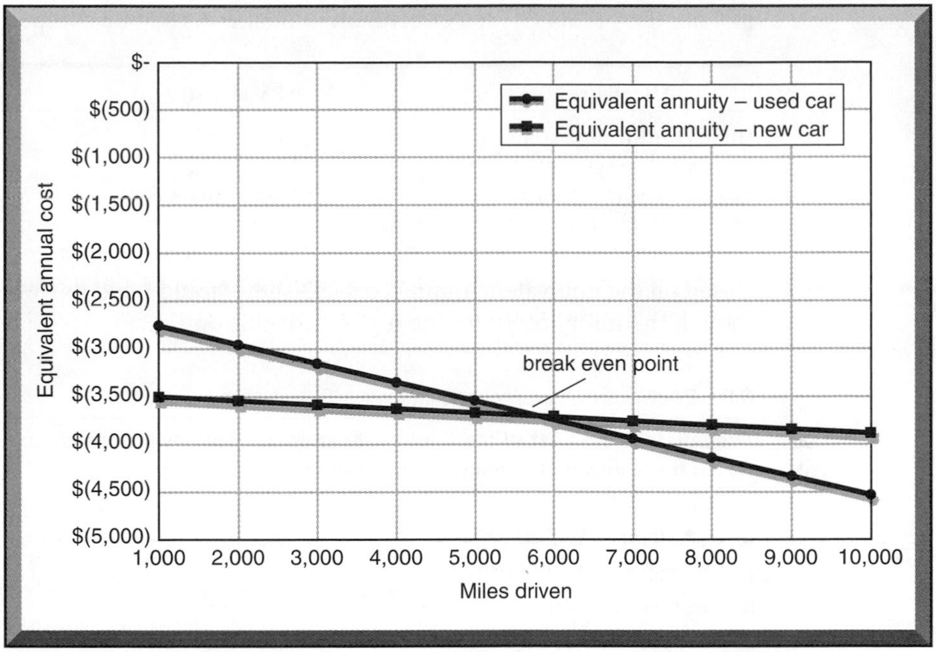

the choice between the two will depend on how much the investments get used. For instance, in Illustration 6.4, the less expensive used car is the more economical choice if the mileage driven is less than 5,000 miles in a year. The more efficient new car will be the better choice if the car is driven more than 5,000 miles. The *break-even* is the number of miles at which the two alternatives provide the same equivalent annual cost, as is illustrated in Figure 6.8.

The break-even point occurs at roughly 5,500 miles; if there is a reasonable chance that the mileage driven will exceed this, the new car becomes the better option.

ILLUSTRATION 6.4   **Using Equivalent Annuities as a General Approach for Multiple Projects**
The equivalent annuity approach can be used to compare multiple projects with different lifetimes. For instance, assume that Disney is considering three storage alternatives for its consumer products division:

Alternative	Initial Investment	Annual Cost	Project Life
Build own storage system	$10 million	$0.5 million	Infinite
Rent storage system	$2 million	$1.5 million	12 years
Use third-party storage	—	$2.0 million	1 year

These projects have different lives; the equivalent annual costs have to be computed for the comparison. Since the cost of capital computed for the consumer products business in Chapter 4 is 9.49%, the equivalent annual costs can be computed as follows:[7]

Alternative	NPV of costs	Equivalent Annual Cost
Build own storage system	$15.27 million	$1.45 million
Rent storage system	$12.48 million	$1.79 million
Use third-party storage	$2.00 million	$2.00 million

Based on the equivalent annual costs, Disney should build its own storage system, even though the initial costs are the highest for this option.

6.3 EQUIVALENT ANNUITY WITH GROWING PERPETUITY

Assume that the cost of the third-party storage option will increase 2.5% a year forever. What would the equivalent annuity for this option be?

a. $2.05 million

b. $2.50 million

c. $2 million

d.   None of the above

Explain your answer.

Project Comparison Generalized

To compare projects with different lives, we can make specific assumptions about the types of projects that will be available when the shorter-term projects end. To illustrate this point, we can assume that the firm will have no positive NPV projects when its current projects end; this will lead to a decision rule whereby the NPVs of projects can be compared, even if they have different lives. Alternatively, we can make specific assumptions about the availability and the attractiveness of projects in the future, leading to cash flow estimates and present value computations. Going back to the five-year and ten-year projects, assume that future projects will not be as attractive as current projects. More specifically, assume that the annual cash flows on the second five-year project that will be taken when the first five-year project ends will be $320 instead of $400. The NPVs of these two investment streams can be computed as shown in Figure 6.9.

The NPV of the first project, replicated to have a life of ten years, is $529. This is still higher than the NPV of $478 of the longer-life project. The firm will still pick the shorter-life project, though the margin in terms of NPV has shrunk.

This problem is not avoided by using IRRs. When the IRR of a short-term project is compared to the IRR of a long-term project, there is an implicit assumption that future projects will continue to have similar IRRs.

---

[7]The cost of the first system is based upon a perpetuity of $0.5 million a year. The net present value can be calculated as follows:

$$NPV = 10 + 0.5/0.0949 = \$15.27 \text{ million}$$

To convert it back to an annuity, all you need to do is multiply the NPV by the discount rate

$$\text{Equivalent annuity} = 15.27 * 0.0949 = \$1.45 \text{ million}$$

Figure 6.9 Cash Flows on Projects with Unequal Lives: Replicated with Poorer Project

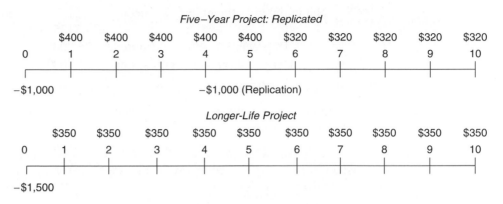

Five–Year Project: Replicated

	$400	$400	$400	$400	$400	$320	$320	$320	$320	$320
0	1	2	3	4	5	6	7	8	9	10

−$1,000   −$1,000 (Replication)

Longer-Life Project

	$350	$350	$350	$350	$350	$350	$350	$350	$350	$350
0	1	2	3	4	5	6	7	8	9	10

−$1,500

The Replacement Decision: A Special Case of Mutually Exclusive Projects

In a *replacement decision*, we evaluate the replacement of an existing investment with a new one, generally because the existing investment has aged and become less efficient. In a typical replacement decision,

- The replacement of old equipment with new equipment will require an initial cash outflow, because the money spent on the new equipment will exceed any proceeds obtained from the sale of the old equipment.
- There will be cash savings (inflows) during the life of the new investment as a consequence of either the lower operating costs arising from the newer equipment or the higher revenues flowing from the investment. These cash inflows will be augmented by the tax benefits accruing from the greater depreciation that will arise from the new investment.
- The salvage value at the end of the life of the new equipment will be the differential salvage value—that is, the excess of the salvage value on the new equipment over the salvage value that would have been obtained if the old equipment had been kept for the entire period and had not been replaced.

This approach has to be modified if the old equipment has a remaining life that is much shorter than the life of the new equipment replacing it.

 replace.xls: This spreadsheet allows you to analyze a replacement decision.

ILLUSTRATION 6.5 Analyzing a Replacement Decision

Bookscape would like to replace an antiquated packaging system with a new one. The old system has a book value of $50,000 and a remaining life of ten years and could be sold for $15,000, net of capital gains taxes right now. It would be replaced with a new machine that costs $150,000, has a depreciable life of ten years, and annual operating costs that are $40,000 lower than with the old machine. Assuming straight-line depreciation for both the old and the new systems, a 40% tax rate, and no salvage value on either machine in ten years, the replacement decision cash flows can be estimated as follows:

$$\text{Net initial investment in new machine} = -\$150,000 + \$15,000$$
$$= -\$135,000$$
$$\text{Depreciation on the old system} = \$5,000$$
$$\text{Depreciation on the new system} = \$15,000$$

Annual tax savings from additional depreciation on new machine

$$= (\text{Depreciation on old machine} - \text{Depreciation on new machine})(\text{Tax rate})$$
$$= (\$15,000 - \$5,000) * 0.4 = \$4,000$$
$$\text{Annual after-tax savings in operating costs} = \$40,000(1 - 0.4) = \$24,000$$

The cost of capital for the company is 14.90%%, resulting in an NPV from the replacement decision of

$$\text{NPV of replacement decision} = -\$135,000 + \$28,000 * \frac{(1 - (1.149)^{-10})}{0.149}$$
$$= \$6,063$$

This result would suggest that replacing the old packaging machine with a new one will increase the firm's value by $6,063 and would be a wise move to make.

SIDE COSTS FROM PROJECTS

In much of the project analyses that we have presented in this chapter, we have assumed that the resources needed for a project are newly acquired; this includes not only the building and the equipment but also the personnel needed to get the project going. For most businesses considering new projects, this is an unrealistic assumption, however, because many of the resources used on these projects are already part of the business and will just be transferred to the new project. When a business uses such resources, there is the potential for an **opportunity cost**—the cost created for the rest of the business as a consequence of this project. This opportunity cost may be a significant portion of the total investment needed on a project. Ignoring these costs because they are not explicit can lead to bad investments. In addition, a new product or service offered by a firm may hurt the profitability of its other products or services; this is generally termed **product cannibalization**, and we will examine and whether and how to deal with the resulting costs.

Opportunity Costs of Using Existing Resources

The opportunity cost for a resource is simplest to estimate when there is a current alternative use for the resource, and we can estimate the cash flows lost by using the resource on the project. It becomes more complicated when the resource does not have a current use but does have potential future uses. In that case, we have to estimate the cash flows forgone on those future uses to estimate the opportunity costs.

Resource with a Current Alternative Use

The general framework for analyzing opportunity costs begins by asking whether there is any other use for the resource right now. In other words, if the project that is considering using the resource is not accepted, what are the uses to which the resource will be put to and what cash flows will be generated as a result?

- The resource might be rented out, in which case the rental revenue lost is the opportunity cost of the resource. For example, if the project is considering the use of a vacant building already owned by the business, the potential revenue from renting out this building will be the opportunity cost.

- The resource could be sold, in which case the sales price, net of any tax liability, and lost depreciation tax benefits would be the opportunity cost for the resource.

- The resource might be used elsewhere in the firm, in which case the cost of replacing it is the opportunity cost. Thus, the transfer of experienced employees from established divisions to a new project creates a cost to these divisions, which has to be factored into the decision making.

Sometimes, decision makers have to decide whether the opportunity cost will be estimated based on the lost rental revenue, the foregone sales price, or the cost of replacing the resource. When such a choice has to be made, it is the highest of the costs—that is, the best alternative forgone—that should be considered as an opportunity cost.

6.4 Sunk Costs and Opportunity Costs

A colleague argues that resources that a firm owns already should not be considered in investment analysis because the cost is a sunk cost. Do you agree?

a. Yes

b. No

How would you reconcile the competing arguments of sunk and opportunity costs?

ILLUSTRATION 6.6   Estimating the Opportunity Cost for a Resource with a Current Alternative Use

Working again with the Bookscape Online example, assume that the following additional information is provided:

- Although Bookscape Online will employ only two full-time employees, it is estimated that the additional business associated with online ordering and the administration of the service itself will add to the workload for the current general manager of the bookstore. As a consequence, the salary of the general manager will be increased from $100,000 to $120,000 next year; it is expected to grow 5% a year after that for the remaining three years of the online venture. After the online venture is ended in the fourth year, the manager's salary will revert back to its old levels.

- It is also estimated that Bookscape Online will utilize an office that is currently used to store financial records. The records will be moved to a bank vault, which will cost $1,000 a year to rent.

The opportunity cost of the addition to the general manager's workload lies in the additional salary expenditure that will be incurred as a consequence. Taking the

Table 6.6   PRESENT VALUE OF ADDITIONAL SALARY EXPENSES

	1	2	3	4
Increase in salary	$20,000	$21,000	$22,050	$23,153
After-tax expense	$12,000	$12,600	$13,230	$13,892
Present value @25.48%	$9,563	$8,002	$6,696	$5,603

present value of the after-tax costs (using a 40% tax rate) over the next four years, using the cost of capital of 25.48% estimated in Illustration 5.2, yields the values in Table 6.6.

The cumulative present value of the costs is $29,865.

Turning to the second resource—a storage space originally used for the financial records—if this project is taken, the opportunity cost is the cost of the bank vault.

$$\text{Additional storage expenses per year} = \$1,000$$
$$\text{After-tax additional storage expenditure per year} = \$1,000(1 - 0.40) = \$600$$
$$\text{PV of after-tax storage expenditures for four years} = \$600 * \frac{(1 - (1.2548)^{-4})}{0.2548}$$
$$= \$1,404.92$$

The opportunity costs estimated for the general manager's added workload ($29,865) and the storage space ($1,405) are in present value terms and can be added on to −$98,775 that we computed as the NPV of Bookscape Online in Illustration 5.11. The NPV becomes more negative.

$$\text{NPV with opportunity costs} = \text{NPV without opportunity costs}$$
$$+ \text{PV of opportunity costs}$$
$$= -\$98,775 - \$29,865 - \$1,405$$
$$= -\$130,045$$

The cash flows associated with the opportunity costs could alternatively have been reflected in the years in which they occur. Thus, the additional salary and storage expenses could have been added to the operating expenses of the store in each of the four years. As Table 6.7 indicates, this approach would yield the same NPV and would have clearly been the appropriate approach if the IRR were to be calculated.

Note that this NPV is identical to our earlier computation—this project should not be taken.

Resources with No Current Alternative Use

In some cases, a resource being considered for use in a project will have no current alternative use, but the business will have to forgo alternative uses in the future. One example would be excess capacity on a machine or a computer. Most firms cannot lease or sell excess capacity, but using that capacity now for a new product may cause the

Table 6.7 NPV WITH OPPORTUNITY COSTS: ALTERNATE APPROACH

Year	Cash flows from Online Venture	Opportunity Costs	Cash flow with Opportunity Costs	Present Value @ 25.48%
0	−$1,150,000		−$1,150,000	−$1,150,000
1	$340,000	$12,600	$327,400	$260,916
2	$415,000	$13,200	$401,800	$255,184
3	$446,500	$13,830	$432,670	$218,989
4	$720,730	$14,492	$706,238	$284,865
				−$130,045

businesses to run out of capacity much earlier than they would otherwise, leading to one of two consequences:

1. A assume that excess capacity is free, because it is not being used currently and cannot be sold off or rented, in most cases.

2. A allocate a portion of the book value of the plant or resource to the project. Thus, if the plant has a book value of $100 million and the new project uses 40% of it, $40 million will be allocated to the project.

We will argue that neither of these approaches considers the opportunity cost of using excess capacity, because the opportunity cost comes usually comes from costs that the firm will face in the future as a consequence of using up excess capacity today. By using up excess capacity on a new project, the firm will run out of capacity sooner than if it did not take the project. When it does run out of capacity, it has to take one of two paths:

1. New capacity will have to be bought or built, in which case the opportunity cost will be the higher cost in present value terms of doing this earlier rather than later.

2. Production will have to be cut back on one of the product lines, leading to a loss in cash flows that would have been generated by the lost sales.

Again, this choice is not random, because the logical action to take is the one that leads to the lower cost, in present value terms, for the firm. Thus, if it is cheaper to lose sales rather than build new capacity, the opportunity cost for the project being considered should be based on the lost sales.

A general framework for pricing excess capacity for purposes of investment analysis asks three questions:

1. If the new project is not taken, when will the firm run out of capacity on the equipment or space that is being evaluated?

2. If the new project is taken, when will the firm run out of capacity on the equipment or space that is being evaluated? Presumably, with the new project using up some of the excess capacity, the firm will run out of capacity sooner than it would have otherwise.

3. What will the firm do when it does run out of capacity? The firm has two choices: It can cut back on production of the least profitable product line and make less profits than it would have without a capacity constraint. In this case, the opportunity cost is the present value of the cash flows lost as a consequence. Or, it can buy or build new capacity, in which case the opportunity cost is the difference in present value between investing earlier rather than later.

Product Cannibalization

Product cannibalization refers to the phenomenon whereby a new product introduced by a firm competes with and reduces sales of the firm's existing products. On one level, it can be argued that this is a negative incremental effect of the new product, and the lost cash flows or profits from the existing products should be treated as costs in analyzing whether to introduce the product. Doing so introduces the possibility that of the new product will be rejected, however. If this happens, and a competitor then exploits the opening to introduce a product that fills the niche that the new product would have and consequently erodes the sales of the firm's existing products, the worst of all scenarios is created—the firm loses sales to a competitor rather than to itself.

Thus, the decision on whether to build in the lost sales created by product cannibalization will depend on the potential for a competitor to introduce a close substitute to the new product being considered. Two extreme possibilities exist: the first is that close substitutes will be offered almost instantaneously by competitors; the second is that substitutes cannot be offered.

1. If the business in which the firm operates is extremely competitive and there are no barriers to entry, it can be assumed that the product cannibalization will occur anyway, and the costs associated with it have no place in an incremental cash flow analysis. For example, in considering whether to introduce a new brand of cereal, a company like Kellogg's can reasonably ignore the expected product cannibalization that will occur because of the competitive nature of the cereal business and the ease with which Post or General Mills could introduce a close substitute. Similarly, it would not make sense for Compaq to consider the product cannibalization that will occur as a consequence of introducing an updated notebook computer, because it can be reasonably assumed that a competitor, say, Lenovo or Dell, would create the lost sales anyway with their versions of the same product if Compaq does not introduce the product.

2. If a competitor cannot introduce a substitute—because of legal restrictions such as patents, for example—the cash flows lost as a consequence of product cannibalization belong in the investment analysis at least for the period of the patent protection. For example, a pharmaceutical company that has the only patented drug available to treat ulcers, may hold back on introducing a potentially better, new ulcer drug because of fears of product cannibalization.[8]

---

[8]Even the patent system does not offer complete protection against competition. It is entirely possible that another pharmaceutical company may come into the market with its own ulcer-treating drug and cause the lost sales anyway.

In most cases, there will be some barriers to entry, ensuring either that a competitor will introduce an imperfect substitute, leading to much smaller erosion in existing product sales, or not introduce a substitute for some period of time, leading to a much later erosion in existing product sales. In this case, an intermediate solution whereby some of the product cannibalization costs are considered may be appropriate. Note that brand name loyalty is one potential barrier to entry. Firms with stronger brand loyalty should therefore factor into their investment analysis more of the cost of lost sales from existing products as a consequence of a new product introduction.

6.5   PRODUCT CANNIBALIZATION AT DISNEY

In coming up with revenues on its proposed theme park in Brazil, Disney estimates that 15% of the revenues at these parks will be generated from people who would have gone to Disneyland in California if these parks did not exist. When analyzing the project in Thailand, would you use

a. The total revenues expected at the park?

b. Only 85% of the revenues, because 15% of the revenues would have come to Disney anyway?

c. A compromise estimated that lies between the first two numbers?

Explain.

SIDE BENEFITS FROM PROJECTS

A proposed investment may benefit other investments that a firm already has. In assessing this investment, we should therefore consider these side benefits. We will begin this section with a consideration of synergies between individual projects and then follow up by extending the discussion to cover acquisitions, in which synergy between two companies is often offered as the reason for large acquisition premiums.

Project Synergies

When a project under consideration creates positive benefits (in the form of cash flows) for other projects that a firm may have, **project synergies** are created. For instance, assume that you are a clothing retailer considering whether to open an upscale clothing store for children in the same shopping center where you already own a store that caters to an adult clientele. In addition to generating revenues and cash flows on its own, the children's store might increase the traffic to the adult store and increase profits there. That additional profit, and its ensuing cash flow, must be factored into the analysis of the new store.

Sometimes the project synergies are not with existing projects but with other projects being considered contemporaneously. In such cases, the best way to analyze the projects is jointly, because examining each separately will lead to a much lower NPV. Thus, a proposal to open a children's clothing store and an adult clothing store in the same shopping center will have to be treated as a joint investment analysis, and the NPV will have to be calculated for both stores together. A positive NPV would suggest opening both stores, whereas a negative NPV would indicate that neither should be opened.

ILLUSTRATION 6.7　Cash Flow Synergies with Existing Projects

Assume that Bookscape is considering adding a café to its bookstore. The café, it is hoped, will make the bookstore a more attractive destination for would-be shoppers. The following information relates to the proposed café:

- The initial cost of remodeling a portion of the store to make it a café, and of buying equipment, is expected to be $150,000. This investment is expected to have a life of five years, during which period it will be depreciated using straight-line depreciation. None of the cost is expected to be recoverable at the end of the five years.

- The revenues in the first year are expected to be $60,000, growing at 10% a year for the next four years.

- There will be one employee, and the total cost for this employee in year 1 is expected to be $30,000 growing at 5% a year for the next four years.

- The cost of the material (food, drinks, etc.) needed to run the café is expected to be 40% of revenues in each of the five years.

- An inventory amounting to 5% of the revenues has to be maintained; investments in the inventory are made at the beginning of each year.

- The tax rate for Bookscape as a business is 40%. ■

Based on this information, the estimated cash flows on the cafe are shown in Table 6.8.

Note that the working capital is fully salvaged at the end of year 5, resulting in a cash inflow of $4,392.

To compute the NPV, we will use Bookscape's cost of capital of 14.90% (from Chapter 4). In doing so, we recognize that it is the cost of capital for a bookstore and that this is an investment in a café. It is, however, a café whose good fortunes rest with how well the bookstore is doing and whose risk is therefore the risk associated with the bookstore. The present value of the cash inflows is reduced by the initial investment

Table 6.8　ESTIMATING CASH FLOWS FROM OPENING BOOKSCAPE CAFÉ						
Year	0	1	2	3	4	5
Investment	−$150,000					
Revenues		$60,000	$66,000	$72,600	$79,860	$87,846
Labor		$30,000	$31,500	$33,075	$34,729	$36,465
Materials		$24,000	$26,400	$29,040	$31,944	$35,138
Depreciation		$30,000	$30,000	$30,000	$30,000	$30,000
Operating income		−$24,000	−$21,900	−$19,515	−$16,813	−$13,758
Taxes		−$9,600	−$8,760	−$7,806	−$6,725	−$5,503
After-tax operating income		−$14,400	−$13,140	−$11,709	−$10,088	−$8,255
+ Depreciation		$30,000	$30,000	$30,000	$30,000	$30,000
− Change in working capital	$3,000	$300	$330	$363	$399	−$4,392
Cash flow to firm	−$153,000	$15,300	$16,530	$17,928	$19,513	$26,138
PV at 14.90%	−$153,000	$13,316	$12,521	$1,819	$1,195	$13,052
Total working capital		$3,000	$3,300	$3,630	$3,993	$4,392

of $150,000, resulting in an NPV of –$91,097. This suggests that this is not a good investment based on the cash flows it would generate.

Note, however, that this analysis is based on looking at the café as a standalone entity; one of the benefits of the café is that is that it might attract more customers to the store and get them to buy more books. For purposes of our analysis, assume that the café will increase revenues at the store by $500,000 in year 1, growing at 10% a year for the following four years. In addition, assume that the pretax operating margin on these sales is 10%. The incremental cash flows from the synergy are shown in Table 6.9.

The present value of the incremental cash flows generated for the bookstore as a consequence of the café is $115,882. Incorporating this into the present value analysis yields the following:

$$\text{NPV of café} = -\$91,097 + \$115,882 = \$24,785$$

By incorporating the cash flows from the synergy into the analysis, we can see that the café is a good investment for Bookscape.

6.6 SYNERGY BENEFITS

In the analysis, the cost of capital for both the café and the bookstore was identical at 14.90%. Assume that the cost of capital for the cafe had been 18%, whereas the cost of capital for the bookstore had stayed at 14.90%. Which discount rate would you use for estimating the present value of synergy benefits?

a.   18%

b.   14.90%

c.   An average of the two discount rates

d.   Either 14.90% or 18%, depending on . . .

Explain.

IN PRACTICE: THE VALUE OF SYNERGY: DISNEY'S ANIMATED MOVIES

Disney has a well-deserved reputation for finding synergy in its movie operations, especially its animated movies. Consider, for instance, some of the spin-offs from its recent movies:

- Plastic action figures and stuffed toys are produced and sold at the time the movies are released, producing profits for Disney both from its own stores and from royalties from sales of the merchandise at other stores.

Table 6.9   INCREMENTAL CASH FLOWS FROM SYNERGY

Year	1	2	3	4	5
Increased revenues	$500,000	$550,000	$605,000	$665,500	$732,050
Operating margin (%)	10.00%	10.00%	10.00%	10.00%	10.00%
Operating income	$50,000	$55,000	$60,500	$66,550	$73,205
Operating income after taxes	$29,000	$31,900	$35,090	$38,599	$42,459
PV of cash flows at 14.90%	$25,239	$24,163	$23,132	$22,146	$21,201

- Joint promotions of the movies with fast-food chains, such as McDonald's and Burger King, where the chains give away movie merchandise with their kids' meals and reduce Disney's own advertising costs for the movie by promoting it.

- With its acquisition of Capital Cities, Disney now has a broadcasting outlet for cartoons based on successful movies (*Aladdin*, *The Lion King*, *The Little Mermaid*), which generate production and advertising revenues for Disney.

- Disney has also made successful Broadway musicals of its hit movies *Beauty and the Beast*, *The Little Mermaid*, and *The Lion King* and plans to use the theater that it now owns on Broadway to produce more such shows.

- Disney's theme parks all over the world benefit indirectly as these movies attract more people to the parks.

- Disney produces computer software and video games based on its animated movie characters.

- Finally, Disney has been extremely successful in promoting the video and DVD releases of its movies as must-have items for video collections.

In fact, on its best-known classics *Snow White*, Disney released the movie in theaters dozens of times between the original release in 1937 and the eventual video release in 1985, making substantial profits each time. More recently, the company has released its masterworks on DVD, with special features added and a premium price. ■

Synergy in Acquisitions

Synergy is often a motive in acquisitions, but it is used as a way of justifying huge premiums and is seldom analyzed objectively. The framework we developed for valuing synergy in projects can be applied to valuing synergy in acquisitions. The key to the existence of synergy is that the target firm controls a specialized resource that becomes more valuable when combined with the bidding firm's resources. The specialized resource will vary depending on the merger. Horizontal mergers occur when two firms in the same line of business merge. In that case, the synergy must come from some form of economies of scale, which reduce costs, or from increased market power, which increases profit margins and sales. Vertical integration occurs when a firm acquires a supplier of inputs into its production process or a distributor or retailer for the product it produces. The primary source of synergy in this case comes from more complete control of the chain of production. This benefit has to be weighed against the loss of efficiency from having a captive supplier who does not have any incentive to keep costs low and compete with other suppliers.

When a firm with strengths in one functional area acquires another firm with strengths in a different functional area (functional integration), synergy may be gained by exploiting the strengths in these areas. Thus, when a firm with a good distribution network acquires a firm with a promising product line, value is gained by combining these two strengths. The argument is that both firms will be better off after the merger.

Most reasonable observers agree that there is a potential for operating synergy, in one form or the other, in many takeovers. Some disagreement exists, however, over whether synergy can be valued and, if so, how much that value should be. One school of thought argues that synergy is too nebulous to be valued and that any systematic attempt to do so requires so many assumptions that it is pointless. We disagree. It is true that valuing synergy requires assumptions about future cash flows and growth, but the lack of precision in the process does not mean that an unbiased estimate of value cannot be made. Thus we maintain that synergy can be valued by answering two fundamental questions:

1. *What form is the synergy expected to take?* The benefits of synergy have to show up in one of the inputs into value as higher revenues, a healthier operating margin, more investment opportunities, or higher growth in the future. To value synergy, we need to identify which of these inputs will most likely be affected and by how much.

2. *When can the synergy be expected to start affecting cash flows?* Even if there are good reasons for believing that synergy exists in a particular merger, it is unlikely that these benefits will accrue immediately after the merger is completed. It often takes time to integrate the operations of two firms, and the difficulty of doing so increases with the size of the firms. If we have to wait for the higher cash flows that arise as a result of synergy, the value of synergy decreases.

Once these questions are answered, the value of synergy can be estimated using an extension of investment analysis techniques. First, the firms involved in the merger are valued independently by discounting expected cash flows to each firm at the weighted average cost of capital for that firm. Second, the value of the combined firm, with no synergy, is obtained by adding the values obtained for each firm in the first step. Third, the effects of synergy are built into expected growth rates and cash flows, and the combined firm is revalued with synergy. The difference between the value of the combined firm with synergy and the value of the combined firm without synergy provides a value for synergy.

Illustration 6.8 Valuing Synergy in Tata-Sensient Merger

In Chapter 5, we valued Sensient Technologies for an acquisition by Tata Chemicals and estimated a value of $1,559 million for the operating assets and $1,107 million for the equity in the firm. In estimating this value, though, we treated Sensient Technologies as a standalone firm. Assume that Tata Chemicals foresees potential synergies in the combination of the two firms, primarily from using its distribution and marketing facilities in India to market Sensient's food additive products to India's rapidly growing processed food industry. To value this synergy, let us assume the following:

- It will take Tata Chemicals approximately three years to adapt Sensient's products to match the needs of the Indian processed food sector—more spice, less color.
- Tata Chemicals will be able to generate Rs1,500 million in after-tax operating income in year 4 from Sensient's Indian sales, growing at a rate of 4% a year after that in perpetuity from Sensient's products in India.

To value synergy, we first estimate the cost of capital that we should be using in this computation. In this case, there are two aspects to the synergy that focus our estimation. The first is that all the perceived synergies flow from Sensient's products, and the risks therefore relate to those products; we will begin with the levered beta of 0.8138 that we estimated for Sensient in Chapter 5 in estimating the cost of equity. The second is that the synergies are expected to come from India; consequently, we will add the country risk premium of 4.51% for India, estimated in Chapter 4 (for Tata Chemicals). Finally, we will assume that Sensient will maintain its existing debt to capital ratio of 28.57%, its current dollar cost of debt of 5.5% and its marginal tax rate of 37%.

$$\text{Cost of equity in U.S.\$} = 3.5\% + 0.8138(6\% + 4.51\%) = 12.05\%$$
$$\text{Cost of debt in U.S.\$} = 5.5\%(1 - 0.37) = 3.47\%$$
$$\text{Cost of capital in U.S.\$} = 12.05\%(1 - 0.2857) + 5.5\%(1 - 0.37)(0.2857) = 9.60\%$$

Since our cash flows are in rupees, we will convert this cost of capital to a rupee rate by using expected inflation rates of 3% for India and 2% for the United States.

$$\text{Cost of capital in Rs} = (1 + \text{Cost of capital}_{US\$})\frac{(1 + \text{Inflation rate}_{Rs})}{(1 + \text{Inflation rate}_{US\$})} - 1$$
$$= (1.096)\frac{(1.03)}{(1.02)} - 1 = 10.67\%$$

We can now discount the expected cash flows a this estimated cost of capital to value synergy, starting in year 4:

$$\text{Value of synergy}_{\text{Year 3}} = \frac{\text{Expected cash flow}_{\text{Year 4}}}{(\text{Cost of capital} - g)}$$
$$= \frac{1,500}{(0.1067 - 0.04)} = \text{Rs}22,476 \text{ million}$$
$$\text{Value of synergy today} = \frac{\text{Value of synergy}_{\text{year 3}}}{(1 + \text{Cost of capital})^3}$$
$$= \frac{22,476}{(1.1067)^3} = \text{Rs}16,580 \text{ million}$$

In Illustration 5.15, we estimated the value of equity in Sensient Technologies, with no synergy, to be $1,107 million. Converting the synergy value into dollar terms at the current exchange rate of Rs47.50/$, we can estimate a total value that Tata Chemicals can pay for Sensient's equity:

$$\text{Value of synergy in U.S.} = \text{Rs}16,580/47.50 = \$349 \text{ million}$$
$$\text{Value of Sensient Technologies} = \$1,107 \text{ million} + \$349 \text{ million} = \$1,456 \text{ million}$$

Since Sensient's equity trades at $1,150 million, Tata Chemicals can afford to pay a premium of up to $306 million and still gain in value from the acquisition.

Why Do Acquirers Pay Too Much? A Behavioral Perspective
There is substantial evidence that acquirers pay too much for target companies and that the value of synergy is overstated in the process. In addition to academic studies of mergers that indicate that acquiring firms' stock prices go down in a significant percentage of all acquisitions, on the announcement of the merger, both KPMG and McKinsey have studies that follow up acquisitions and indicate that there is little evidence of synergy gains in the years after.

The persistence and the magnitude of the overpayment suggest two problems. The first is that the process of analyzing acquisitions is flawed, with those that are richly compensated by the deal (investment bankers) also being responsible for analyzing whether the deal should be done. However, that does not mitigate the responsibility of the acquiring company's managers, who seem to be cavalier about spending stockholders' money; nor does it explain their behavior. There are three reasons that have been presented for this phenomenon:

1. *Hubris* Roll (1986) argues that it is managerial hubris that best explains acquisition overpayments. The managers in acquiring firms make mistakes in assessing target company values, and their pride prevents them from admitting these mistakes.[9]

2. *Overconfidence* The same overconfidence that leads managers to overestimate cash flows on conventional capital budgeting projects manifests itself in acquisitions, perhaps in a more virulent form.[10] Studies seem to indicate that the managers in acquiring firms are among the most overconfident of the entire group.

3. *Anchoring and framing* When negotiating a price for a target firm, both the acquiring firm's managers and the target firm's stockholders compare the price being offered to "reference points" often unrelated to intrinsic value. Wurgler, Pan, and Baker (2008) argue that while the current stock price is one reference point, the highest price over the previous fifty-two weeks seems to be an even stronger one.[11] In fact, they present evidence that the price paid on acquisitions has less to do with fair value and more to do with matching this fifty-two-week high.

How can we reduce the problem of overpayment? First, we need to reform the acquisition process and separate the deal making from the deal analysis. Second, we have to give stockholders a much bigger say in the process. If the board of directors cannot perform their oversight role, the largest investors in the acquiring company should be allowed representation during the negotiation, and the representative will be given the responsibility of questioning key assumptions and forecasts. Third, the managers who are most intent on pushing the acquisition through should be given the responsibility of delivering the projected cash flows.

OPTIONS EMBEDDED IN PROJECTS

In Chapter 5, we examined the process for analyzing a project and deciding whether to accept the project. In particular, we noted that a project should be accepted only if the returns on the project exceed the hurdle rate; in the context of cash flows and discount rates, this translates into projects with positive NPVs. The limitation with

[9]Richard Roll, "The Hubris Hypothesis of Corporate Takeovers," *Journal of Business* 59:197–216.

[10]J. Graham, C. Harvey, and M. Puri, "Managerial Attitudes and Corporate Actions," Duke University working paper, 2008.

[11]M. Baker, X. Pan, and J. Wurgler, "The Psychology of Pricing in Mergers and Acquisitions," working paper, ssrn.com, 2009.

traditional investment analysis, which analyzes projects on the basis of expected cash flows and discount rates, is that it fails to consider fully the myriad options that are usually associated with many projects.

In this section, we will begin by first describing what an option is and why they matter, and then we will analyze three options that are embedded in many capital budgeting projects. The first is the option to delay a project, especially when the firm has exclusive rights to the project. The second is the option to expand a project to cover new products or markets some time in the future. The third is the option to abandon a project if the cash flows do not measure up to expectations. These are generically called real options since the underlying asset is a real asset (a project) rather than a financial asset. With each of these options, we will present both the intuitive implications of valuing them as options as well as the details of using option pricing models to value them. Appendix 4 contains more detail on these models.

Options: Description and Determinants of Value

An option is an asset that derives its value from another asset, called an underlying asset, and that has a cash payoff that is contingent on what happens to the value of the underlying asset. There are two types of options. With a call option, you get the right to buy the underlying asset at a fixed price, called a strike price, whereas with put options, you get the right to sell the underlying asset at a fixed price. Since you have the right (but not obligation) as the holder of the option to buy or sell the underlying asset, you will exercise an option only if it makes sense for you to do so. With a call option, that will occur when the value of the underlying asset is greater than your strike price, whereas with a put, it is when the value is lower.

As explained in Appendix 4, the value of an option ultimately rests of six variables: the value, volatility and expected dividends of the underlying asset, the strike price, the life of the option, and the level of interest rates. Without delving into the minutiae of option pricing models, it is still worth noting the differences between valuing conventional assets or projects on the one hand and options on the other. The first is that conventional assets can be valued by discounting expected cash flows at a risk-adjusted discount rate, whereas options are valued at a premium over their exercise value. The premium can be attributed to the choice that the holder of the option as to when and whether to exercise. The second is that increasing risk and uncertainty reduce the value of conventional assets, but they increase the value of options. This is because the holders of options can never be forced to exercise an option, which protects them against downside risk but preserves upside potential.

It is because of these two differences that this section is necessitated. If an investment has options embedded in it, conventional net present value will miss the option premium and understate the value of the investment. In addition, the option portion of the investment may benefit as the investment becomes more risky, even as the rest of the investment becomes more valuable.

The Option to Delay a Project

Projects are typically analyzed based on their expected cash flows and discount rates at the time of the analysis; the NPV computed on that basis is a measure of its value and acceptability at that time. Expected cash flows and discount rates change over time, however, and so does the NPV. Thus, a project that has a negative NPV now may have a positive NPV in the future. In a competitive environment, in which individual firms have no special advantages over their competitors in taking projects, this may not seem significant. In an environment where a project can be taken by only one firm (because of legal restrictions or other barriers to entry to competitors), however, the changes in the project's value over time give it the characteristics of a call option.

Describing the Option to Delay

In the abstract, assume that a project requires an initial investment of X and that the present value of expected cash inflows computed right now is V. The NPV of this project is the difference between the two:

$$NPV = V - X$$

Now assume that the firm has exclusive rights to this project for the next n years, and that the present value of the cash inflows may change over that time because of changes in either the cash flows or the discount rate. Thus, the project may have a negative NPV right now, but it may still become a good project if the firm waits. Defining V as the present value of the cash flows, the firm's decision rule on this project can be summarized as follows:

$$\text{If} \quad V > X, \quad \text{project has positive NPV}$$
$$\text{If} \quad V < X, \quad \text{project has negative NPV}$$

This relationship can be presented in a payoff diagram of cash flows on this project, as shown in Figure 6.10, assuming that the firm holds out until the end of the period for which it has exclusive rights to the project.

Note that this payoff diagram is that of a call option—the underlying asset is the project, the strike price of the option is the investment needed to take the project, and the life of the option is the period for which the firm has rights to the project. The present value of the cash flows on this project and the expected variance in this present value represent the value and variance of the underlying asset.

Valuing the Option to Delay

On the surface, the inputs needed to apply option pricing models to valuing the option to delay are the same as those needed for any application: the value of the underlying asset, the variance in the value, the time to expiration on the option, the strike price, the riskless rate, and the equivalent of the dividend yield. Actually estimating these inputs for valuing real options can be difficult, however.

Value of the Underlying Asset
In the case of product options, the underlying asset is the project itself. The current value of this asset is the present value of expected cash flows from initiating the project now, which can be obtained by doing a standard capital budgeting analysis. There is likely to be a substantial amount of estimation error in the cash flow estimates and the present value, however. Rather than being viewed as a problem, this uncertainty should be viewed as the reason why the project delay option has value. If the expected

Figure 6.10   The Option to Delay a Project

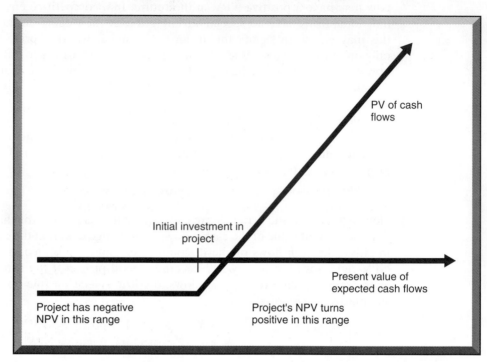

cash flows on the project were known with certainty and were not expected to change, there would be no need to adopt an option pricing framework, because there would be no value to the option.

Variance in the Value of the Asset
As noted in the previous section, there is likely to be considerable uncertainty associated with the cash flow estimates and the present value that measures the value of the asset now, partly because the potential market size for the product may be unknown and partly because technological shifts can change the cost structure and profitability of the product. The variance in the present value of cash flows from the project can be estimated in one of three ways. First, if similar projects have been introduced in the past, the variance in the cash flows from those projects can be used as an estimate. Second, probabilities can be assigned to various market scenarios, cash flows estimated under each scenario, and the variance estimated across present values. Finally, the average variance in firm value of publicly traded companies that are in the business in which the project will be can be used. Thus, the average variance in firm value of biotechnology companies can be used as the variance for the option to delay a biotechnology project.

The value of the option is largely derived from the variance in cash flows—the higher the variance, the higher the value of the project delay option. Thus, the value of an option to invest in a project in a stable business will be less than the value of one in an environment in which technology, competition, and markets are all changing rapidly.

There is a data set online that summarizes, by sector, the variances in firm value and equity value for companies in each sector in the United States.

Exercise Price on Option

A project delay option is exercised when the firm owning the rights to the project decides to invest in it. The cost of making this investment is equivalent to the exercise price of the option. For simplicity, it is best to assume that this cost remains constant (in present value dollars) and that any uncertainty associated with the product is reflected in the present value of cash flows on the product.

Expiration of the Option and the Riskless Rate

The project delay option expires when the rights to the project lapse; investments made after the project rights expire are assumed to deliver an NPV of 0 as competition drives returns down to the required rate. The riskless rate to use in pricing the option should be the rate that corresponds to the expiration of the option.

Dividend Yield

Once the NPV turns positive, there is a cost borne in delaying making an investment. Because the project rights expire after a fixed period, and excess profits (which are the source of positive present value) are assumed to disappear after that time as new competitors emerge, each year of delay translates into one less year of value-creating cash flows.[12] If the cash flows are evenly distributed over time, and the life of the option is n years, the cost of delay can be written as

$$\text{Annual cost of delay} = \frac{1}{n}$$

Thus, if the project rights are for twenty years, the annual cost of delay works out to 5% a year.

6.7 COST OF DELAY AND EARLY EXERCISE

For typical listed options on financial assets, it is argued that early exercise is almost never optimal. Is this true for real options as well? Explain.

a. Yes

b. No

ILLUSTRATION 6.9 Valuing a Patent

Assume that a pharmaceutical company has been approached by an entrepreneur who has patented a new drug to treat ulcers. The entrepreneur has obtained FDA approval and has the patent rights for the next seventeen years. Although the drug shows promise, it is still very expensive to manufacture and has a relatively small market. Assume that the initial investment to produce the drug is $500 million and that the present value of the cash flows from introducing the drug now is only $350 million.

---

[12] A value-creating cash flow is one that adds to the NPV because it is in excess of the required return for investments of equivalent risk.

The technology and the market is volatile, and the annualized standard deviation in the present value, estimated from a simulation, is 25%.[13]

Although the NPV of introducing the drug is negative, the rights to this drug may still be valuable because of the variance in the present value of the cash flow. In other words, it is entirely possible that this drug may not only be viable but extremely profitable a year or two from now. To value this right, we first define the inputs to the option pricing model:

$$\text{Value of the underlying asset } (S)$$
$$= \text{PV of cash flows from project if introduced now}$$
$$= \$350 \text{ million}$$
$$\text{Strike price } (K) = \text{Initial investment needed to introduce the product}$$
$$= \$500 \text{ million}$$

$$\text{Variance in underlying asset's value} = (0.25)^2 = 0.0625$$
$$\text{Time to expiration} = \text{Life of the patent} = 17 \text{ years}$$
$$\text{Cost of delay (Dividend yield in option model)} = 1/\text{Life of the patent}$$
$$= 1/17 = 5.88\%$$

Assume that the seventeen-year riskless rate is 4%. The value of the option can be estimated as follows:

$$\text{Call value} = 350 \exp^{(-0.0588)(17)}(0.5285) - 500 \exp^{(-0.04)(17)}(0.1219)$$
$$= \$37.12 \text{ million}$$

Thus, this ulcer drug, which has a negative NPV if introduced now, is still valuable to its owner.

6.8 HOW MUCH WOULD YOU PAY FOR THIS OPTION?

Assume that you are negotiating for a pharmaceutical company that is trying to buy this patent. What would you pay?

a. $37.12 million

b. More than $37.12 million

c. Less than $37.12 million

Explain.

Intuitive Implications

Several interesting implications emerge from the analysis of the option to delay a project. First, a project may have a negative NPV based on expected cash flows currently, but the rights to this project can still be valuable because of the option characteristics. Thus, although a negative NPV should encourage a firm to reject an investment or technology, it should not lead it to conclude that the rights to it are worthless. Second, a project may have a positive NPV but still not be accepted right away because the firm may gain by waiting and accepting the project in a future period, for the same reasons that investors do not always exercise an option just because they

---

[13]This simulation would yield an expected value for the project of $350 million and the standard deviation in that value of 25%.

have the money. This is more likely to happen if the firm has the rights to the project for a long time and the variance in project inflows is high. To illustrate, assume that a firm has the patent rights to produce a new type of disk drive for computer systems and that building a new plant will yield a positive NPV right now. If the technology for manufacturing the disk drive is in flux, however, the firm may delay taking the project in the hopes that the improved technology will increase the expected cash flows, and consequently the value of the project.

The Option to Expand a Project

In some cases, firms invest in projects because doing so allows them to either take on other investments or enter other markets in the future. In such cases, it can be argued that the initial projects yield expansion options for a firm, and that the firm should therefore be willing to pay a price for such options. It is easiest to understand this option if you consider the projects in sequence. The initial project is not an option and may very well have a negative net present value. However, investing in the initial investment gives the firm the opportunity to make a second investment—expanding into a new market or introducing a new product—later. The firm can choose to exploit this opportunity or ignore it, but the choice that it has gives the second investment the characteristics of an option.

Describing the Option to Expand

To examine the option to expand using the same framework developed earlier, assume that the present value of the expected cash flows from expanding into the new market or taking the new project is V, and the total investment needed to enter this market or take this project is X. Furthermore, assume that the firm has a fixed time horizon, at the end of which it has to make the final decision on whether to take advantage of this expansion opportunity. Finally, assume that the firm cannot move forward on this opportunity if it does not take the initial project. This scenario implies the option payoffs shown in Figure 6.11.

As you can see, at the expiration of the fixed time horizon, the firm will expand into the new market or take the new project if the present value of the expected cash flows at that point in time exceeds the cost of entering the market.

Valuing the Option to Expand

To understand how to estimate the value of the option to expand, let us begin by recognizing that there are two projects usually that drive this option. The first project generally has a negative net present value and is recognized as a poor investment, even by the firm investing in it. The second project is the potential to expand that comes with the first project. It is the second project that represents the underlying asset for the option. The inputs have to be defined accordingly.

- The present value of the cash flows that you would generate if you were to invest in the second project today (the expansion option) is the value of the underlying asset—S in the option pricing model.
- If there is substantial uncertainty about the expansion potential, the present value is likely to be volatile and change over time as circumstances change. It is the variance

Figure 6.11 The Option to Expand a Project

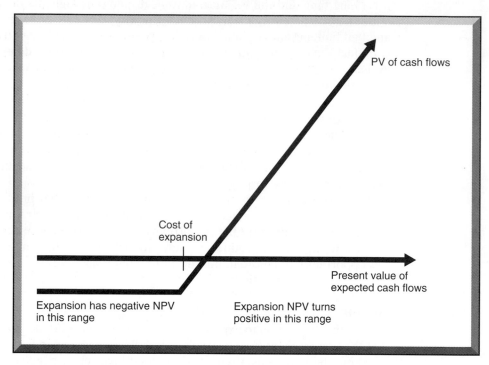

in this present value that you would want to use to value the expansion option. Since projects are not traded, you have to either estimate this variance from simulations or use the variance in values of publicly traded firms in the business.

- The cost that you would incur up front, if you invest in the expansion today, is the equivalent of the strike price.
- The life of the option is fairly difficult to define, since there is usually no externally imposed exercise period. When valuing the option to expand, the life of the option will be an internal constraint imposed by the firm on itself. For instance, a firm that invests on a small scale in China might impose a constraint that it either will expand within five years or pull out of the market. Why might it do so? There may be considerable costs associated with maintaining the small presence, or the firm may have scarce resources that have to be committed elsewhere.

As with other real options, there may be a cost to waiting, once the expansion option becomes viable. That cost may take the form of cash flows that will be lost on the expansion project if it is not taken or a cost imposed on the firm until it makes its final decision. For instance, the firm may have to pay a fee every year until it makes its final decision.

ILLUSTRATION 6.10 Valuing an Option to Expand—Disney Entertainment
Assume that Disney is considering investing $100 million to create a Spanish version of the Disney Channel to serve the growing Mexican market. Assume also that a financial

analysis of the cash flows from this investment suggests that the present value of the cash flows from this investment to Disney will be only $80 million. Thus, by itself, the new channel has a negative NPV of −$20 million.

One factor that does have to be considered in this analysis is that if the market in Mexico turns out to be more lucrative than currently anticipated, Disney could expand its reach to all of Latin America with an additional investment of $150 million any time over the next ten years. Although the current expectation is that the cash flows from having a Disney channel in Latin America will have a present value of only $100 million, there is considerable uncertainty about both the potential for such an channel and the shape of the market itself, leading to significant variance in this estimate.

The value of the option to expand can now be estimated, by defining the inputs to the option pricing model as follows:

$$\text{Value of the underlying asset } (S) = \text{PV of cash flows from}$$
$$\text{expansion to Latin America, if done now} = \$100 \text{ million}$$

$$\text{Strike price } (K) = \text{Cost of expansion into Latin America} = \$150 \text{ million}$$

We estimate the standard deviation in the estimate of the project value by using the annualized standard deviation in firm value of publicly traded entertainment firms in the Latin American markets, which is approximately 30%.

$$\text{Variance in underlying asset's value} = 0.30^2 = 0.09$$

$$\text{Time to expiration} = \text{Period for which expansion option applies} = 10 \text{ years}$$

Assume that the ten-year riskless rate is 4%. The value of the option can be estimated as follows:

$$\text{Call value} = 100(0.6803) - 150 \exp^{(-0.04)(10)}(0.3156) = \$36.30 \text{ million}$$

In other words, even though this expansion opportunity has a negative net present value today of −$50 million, the option to take it is worth $36.30 million. Since this option is dependent upon making the initial investment in the Spanish channel, this value can be added on to the NPV of −$20 million on the initial investment.

$$\text{NPV of Disney Channel in Mexico} = \$80 \text{ million} - \$100 \text{ million}$$
$$= -\$20 \text{ million}$$
$$\text{Value of option to expand} = \$36.30 \text{ million}$$
$$\text{NPV of project with option to expand} = -\$20 \text{ million} + \$36.3 \text{ million}$$
$$= \$16.3 \text{ million}$$

Considered as a package, Disney should invest in the Mexican project because the option to expand into the Latin American market more than compensates for the negative NPV of the Mexican project.

Tests for Expansion Option to Have Value

Not all investments have options embedded in them, and not all options, even if they do exist, have value. To assess whether an investment creates valuable options that need to be analyzed and valued, we need to understand three key questions.

1. ***Is the first investment a prerequisite for the later investment/expansion? If not, how necessary is the first investment for the later investment/expansion?*** Consider our earlier analysis of the value of a patent or the value of an undeveloped oil reserve as options. A firm cannot generate patents without investing in research or paying another firm for the patents, and it cannot get rights to an undeveloped oil reserve without bidding on it at a government auction or buying it from another oil company. Clearly, the initial investment here (spending on R&D, bidding at the auction) is required for the firm to have the second investment. Now consider the Disney investment in a Spanish-language channel, without which presumably it cannot expand into the larger Latin American market. Unlike the patent and undeveloped reserves examples, the initial investment is not a prerequisite for the second, though management might view it as such. The connection gets even weaker, and the option value lower, when we look at one firm acquiring another to have the option to be able to enter a large market. Acquiring an Internet service provider to have a foothold in the online retailing market or buying a Chinese brewery to preserve the option to enter the Chinese beer market would be examples of less valuable options.

2. ***Does the firm have an exclusive right to the later investment/expansion? If not, does the initial investment provide the firm with significant competitive advantages on subsequent investments?*** The value of the option ultimately derives not from the cash flows generated by the second and subsequent investments, but from the excess returns generated by these cash flows. The greater the potential for excess returns on the second investment, the greater the value of the expansion option. The potential for excess returns is closely tied to how much of a competitive advantage the first investment provides the firm when it takes subsequent investments. At one extreme, again, consider investing in R&D to acquire a patent. The patent gives the firm that owns it the exclusive rights to produce that product, and if the market potential is large, the right to the excess returns from the project. At the other extreme, the firm might get no competitive advantages on subsequent investments, in which case it is questionable whether there can be any excess returns on these investments. In reality, most investments will fall in the continuum between these two extremes, with greater competitive advantages being associated with higher excess returns and larger option values.

3. ***How sustainable are the competitive advantages?*** In a competitive marketplace, excess returns attract competitors, and competition drives out excess returns. The more sustainable the competitive advantages possessed by a firm, the greater the value of the options embedded in the initial investment. The sustainability of competitive advantages is a function of two forces. The first is the *nature of the competition*; other things remaining equal, competitive advantages fade much more quickly in sectors where there are aggressive competitors. The second is the *nature of the competitive advantage*. If the resource controlled by the firm is finite and scarce (as is the case with natural resource reserves and vacant land), the competitive advantage is likely to be sustainable for longer periods. Alternatively, if the competitive advantage comes from being the first mover in a market or from having technological expertise, it will come under assault far sooner. The most direct way of reflecting this competitive advantage in the value of the option is its

life; the life of the option can be set to the period of competitive advantage and only the excess returns earned over this period counts towards the value of the option.

Practical Considerations

The practical considerations associated with estimating the value of the option to expand are similar to those associated with valuing the option to delay. In most cases, firms with options to expand have no specific time horizon by which they have to make an expansion decision, making these open-ended options or, at best, options with arbitrary lives. Even in those cases where a life can be estimated for the option, neither the size nor the potential market for the product may be known, and estimating either can be problematic. To illustrate, consider the Disney expansion example. We adopted a period of ten years at the end of which Disney has to decide one way or another on its future expansion in Latin America, but it is entirely possible that this timeframe is not specified at the time the store is opened. Furthermore, we have assumed that both the cost and the present value of expansion are known initially. In reality, the firm may not have good estimates for either before starting its Spanish cable channel, because it does not have much information on the underlying market.

Intuitive Implications

The option to expand is implicitly used by firms to rationalize taking projects that may have negative NPV but provide significant opportunities to tap into new markets or sell new products. Although the option pricing approach adds rigor to this argument by estimating the value of this option, it also provides insight into those occasions when it is most valuable. In general, the option to expand is clearly more valuable for more volatile businesses with higher returns on projects (such as biotechnology or computer software) than in stable businesses with lower returns (such as housing, chemicals or automobiles).

It can also be argued that R&D provides one immediate application for this methodology. Investing in R&D is justified by noting that it provides the basis for new products for the future. In recent years, however, more firms have stopped accepting this explanation at face value as a rationale for spending more money on R&D and have started demanding better returns from their investments.

Firms that spend considerable amounts of money on R&D or test marketing are often stymied when they try to evaluate these expenses, because the payoffs are often in terms of future projects. At the same time, there is the very real possibility that after the money has been spent, the products or projects may turn out not to be viable; consequently, the expenditure is treated as a sunk cost. In fact, it can be argued that what emerges from R&D—patents or technological expertise—has the characteristics of a call option. If this is true, the amount spent on the R&D is the cost of the call option, and the patents that might emerge from the research provide the options.

Several logical implications emerge from this view of R&D. First, research expenditures should provide much higher value for firms that are in volatile technologies or businesses, because the higher variance in product or project cash flows creates more valuable call options. It follows then that R&D at pharmaceutical firms should be redirected to areas where little is known and there is substantial uncertainty—gene therapy, for example—and away from areas where there is more stability. Second, the value of research and the optimal amount to be spent on research will change over time as businesses mature. The best example is the pharmaceutical industry—drug companies spent most of the 1980s investing substantial amounts in research and earning high returns on new products as the health care business expanded. In the 1990s, however, as health care costs started leveling off and the business matured, many of these companies found that they were not getting the same payoffs on research and started cutting back.

6.9   R&D Expenditures and Option Pricing

If we perceive R&D expenses as the price of acquiring options (product patents), R&D expenditures will have most value if directed to

a. Areas where the technology is stable and the likelihood of success is high.

b. Areas where the technology is volatile, though the likelihood of success is low.

c. Neither

Explain.

IN PRACTICE: Are Strategic Considerations Really Options?

Many firms faced with projects that do not meet their financial benchmarks use the argument that these projects should be taken anyway because of strategic considerations. In other words, it is argued that these projects will accomplish other goals for the firm or allow the firm to enter into other markets. Although we are wary of how this argument is used to justify poor projects, there are cases where these strategic considerations are really referring to options embedded in projects—options to produce new products or expand into new markets.

Take the example of the Disney Channel expansion into Mexico and Latin America project. The project, based on conventional capital budgeting, has a negative NPV, but it should be taken nevertheless, because it gives Disney the option to enter a potentially lucrative market. Disney might well use the strategic considerations argument to accept the project anyway.

The differences between using option pricing and the strategic considerations argument are the following:

- Option pricing assigns value to only some of the strategic considerations that firms may have. For instance, the option to enter the Latin American market has value because of the variance in the estimates of the value of entering the market and the fact that Disney has to take the smaller project (the Mexican venture) first to get the option. However, strategic considerations that are not clearly defined and have little exclusivity, such as "corporate image" or "growth potential," may not have any value from an option pricing standpoint.

- Option pricing attempts to put a dollar value on the strategic consideration. As a consequence, the existence of strategic considerations does not guarantee that the project will be taken. In the Disney example, the Mexican venture should not be taken if the value of the option to enter the Latin American market is less than $20 million. ∎

The Option to Abandon a Project

The final option to consider here is the option to abandon a project when its cash flows do not measure up to expectations. Generally, the option to abandon a project later will make that project more attractive to investors now.

Describing the Option to Abandon

To illustrate the option to abandon, assume that you have invested in a project and that V is the remaining value on a project if you continue it to the end of its life. Now, assume that you can abandon the project today and that L is the liquidation or abandonment value for the same project. If the project has a life of n years, the value of continuing the project can be compared to the liquidation (abandonment) value—if it is higher, the project should be continued; if it is lower, the holder of the abandonment option could consider abandoning the project.

$$\text{Payoff from owning an abandonment option} = 0 \quad \text{if } V > L$$
$$= L - V \quad \text{if } V \leq L$$

These payoffs are graphed in Figure 6.12, as a function of the expected stock price.

Unlike in the prior two cases, the option to abandon takes on the characteristics of a put option.

ILLUSTRATION 6.11   Valuing Disney's Option to Abandon: A Real Estate Investment
Assume that Disney is considering taking a twenty-five-year project that requires an initial investment of $250 million in a real estate partnership to develop time-share

Figure 6.12   The Option to Abandon a Project

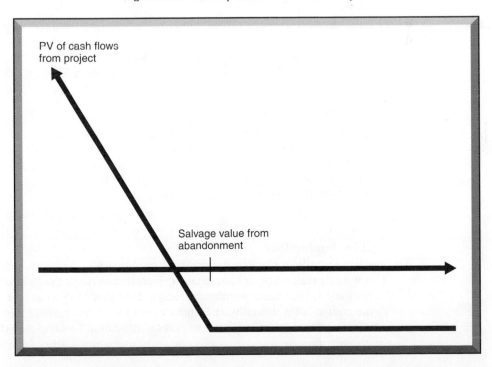

properties with a south Florida real estate developer and where the present value of expected cash flows is $254 million. Although the NPV of $4 million is small for a project of this size, assume that Disney has the option to abandon this project at any time by selling its share back to the developer in the next five years for $150 million. A simulation of the cash flows on this time-share investment yields a standard deviation in the present value of the cash flows from being in the partnership of 20%.

The value of the abandonment option can be estimated by determining the characteristics of the put option:

$$\text{Value of the underlying asset } (S) = \text{PV of cash flows from project}$$
$$= \$254 \text{ million}$$

$$\text{Strike price } (K) = \text{Salvage value from abandonment} = \$150 \text{ million}$$
$$\text{Variance in underlying asset's value} = 0.20^2 = 0.04$$

$$\text{Time to expiration} = \text{Life of the project} = 5 \text{ years}$$

$$\text{Dividend yield} = 1/\text{Life of the project}$$
$$= 1/25$$
$$= 0.04 \text{ (We are assuming that the project's present value}$$
$$\text{will drop by roughly } 1/n \text{ each year into the project.)}$$

Assume that the five-year riskless rate is 4%. The value of the put option can be estimated as follows:

$$\text{Call value} = 254 \exp^{(0.04)(5)}(0.9194) - 150 \exp^{(-0.04)(5)}(0.8300) = \$89.27 \text{ million}$$

$$\text{Put value} = \$89.27 - 254 \exp^{(0.04)(5)} + 150 \exp^{(-0.04)(5)} = \$4.13 \text{ million}$$

The value of this abandonment option has to be added on to the NPV of the project of $4 million, yielding a total NPV with the abandonment option of $8.13 million.

6.10 ABANDONMENT VALUE AND PROJECT LIFE

Consider the project just described. Assume that three years into the project, the cash flows are coming in 20% below expectations. What will happen to the value of the option to abandon?
a. It will increase.
b. It will decrease.
c. It may increase or decrease, depending on . . .
Explain.

Intuitive Implications

The fact that the option to abandon has value provides a rationale for firms to build the flexibility to scale back or terminate projects if they do not measure up to expectations. Firms can do this in a number of ways. The first and most direct way is to build in the option contractually with those parties that are involved in the project. Thus, contracts with suppliers may be written on an annual basis, rather than long-term, and employees may be hired on a temporary basis rather than permanently. The physical plant used for a project may be leased on a short-term basis rather than bought, and the financial investment may be made in stages rather than as an initial lump sum. Although there is a cost to building in this flexibility, the gains may be much larger, especially in volatile businesses. The option to abandon is particularly valuable for smaller companies investing in large projects, where the investment in the project may represent a significant percentage of the firm's capital.

MEASURING THE QUALITY OF EXISTING INVESTMENTS

A firm is composed of assets in place (i.e., investments already made) and growth assets (i.e., new investments). Much of the last two chapters has been spent talking about the latter, but the techniques we used to examine and analyze new investments can also be used to assess existing investments. In doing so, there is one area where we have to exercise care. Some of the cash flows on existing investments will be in the past, and some will be in the future. While we can use past cash flows to learn about these investments, they are sunk costs and should not drive decisions on whether to continue or abandon these investments. In this section, we will begin by looking at cash flow techniques for assessing existing investments and then move on to how accounting returns—return on equity and capital—can also be useful. We will close the section by linking returns on investments to the competitive advantages and the quality of management in a firm.

Analyzing a Past Investment

We could analyze a past project's performance by looking at the actual cash flows generated by the investment and measuring the return relative to the original investment in the project. We could measure the returns on the project on an accounting basis, or we could estimate a net present value and internal rate of return for this project.

While the way in which we estimate these measures is similar to what we would do for a new project, the numbers have to be interpreted differently. First, unlike the net present value on a new project, which measures the value that will be added to the firm by investing in the project today, the net present value on an old project is a historic number. It is, in a sense, a postmortem. If the net present value is negative, the firm cannot reverse its investment in the project, but it might be able to learn from its mistakes. If the net present value is positive, the project's effect on firm value is in the past. Second, unlike the net present value of a project that is based on expected numbers, the net present value on an existing project is based on actual numbers.

Analyzing an Ongoing Investment

An ongoing investment is one in which some of the cash flows on the investment have already occurred but some are still to come. Unlike an assessment of a past investment, which is postmortem, the assessment of an ongoing investment can help us answer the question of whether the investment should be continued or terminated. In making this assessment, the cash flows on an existing project have to be evaluated entirely on an incremental basis. Thus, if the firm is considering terminating the project, the incremental cash flow is the difference between the cash flow the firm can expect from continuing the project and the cash flow it could lose if the project is terminated. If the firm has already committed to the expenses on the project, for contractual or legal reasons, it may not save much by terminating the project.

If the incremental cash flows on the existing project are estimated and discounted at an appropriate rate, the firm is in a position to decide whether the project should be continued, liquidated or divested. For example, assume that you are analyzing a ten-year project two years into its life and that the cash flows are as shown in Figure 6.13.

In particular, the following general decision rules should apply:

- If the present value of the expected future cash flows is negative, and there are no offers from third parties to acquire the project, the project should be liquidated.

$$\sum_{t=0}^{t=n} \frac{NF_n}{(1+r)^n} < 0 \quad \text{Liquidate project}$$

where r is the discount rate that applies to the cash flows, based on perceived risk at the time of the analysis.

- If the present value of the expected future cash flows is positive but it is less than the salvage value that can be obtained by liquidating the project, the project should be liquidated.

$$\sum_{t=0}^{t=n} \frac{NF_n}{(1+r)^n} < \text{Salvage Value} \quad \text{Terminate project}$$

where r is the discount rate that applies to the cash flows, based on perceived risk at the time of the analysis.

- If the present value of the expected future cash flows is positive but there is an offer from a third party to buy the project for a higher price, the project should be divested.

$$\sum_{t=0}^{t=n} \frac{NF_n}{(1+r)^n} < \text{Divestiture Value} \quad \text{Divest project}$$

Figure 6.13   Analysis of Existing Project

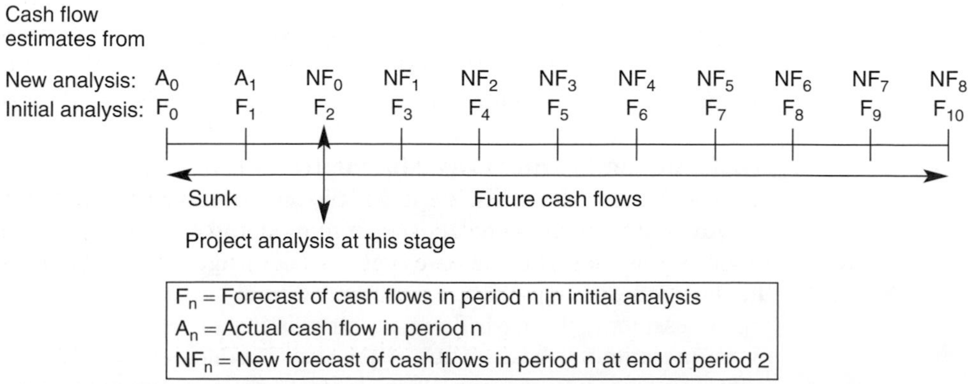

Cash flow
estimates from

| New analysis: | A_0 | A_1 | NF_0 | NF_1 | NF_2 | NF_3 | NF_4 | NF_5 | NF_6 | NF_7 | NF_8 |
| Initial analysis: | F_0 | F_1 | F_2 | F_3 | F_4 | F_5 | F_6 | F_7 | F_8 | F_9 | F_{10} |

Sunk   Future cash flows

Project analysis at this stage

F_n = Forecast of cash flows in period n in initial analysis
A_n = Actual cash flow in period n
NF_n = New forecast of cash flows in period n at end of period 2

- If the present value of the expected future cash flows is positive (even though it may be well below expectations and below the initial investment) and there are no better offers from third parties, the project should be continued.

$$\sum_{t=0}^{t=n} \frac{NF_n}{(1+r)^n} > 0 > \text{Divestiture Value} \quad \text{Continue project}$$

Firms should not liquidate or divest existing projects simply because the actual returns do not measure up to either the forecasts or the original investment. They should be liquidated or divested if, and only if, the present value of the forecasted incremental cash flows from continuing with the project is less than the salvage value or divestiture value.

ILLUSTRATION 6.12   Disney's California Adventure: Terminate, Continue, or Expand?

Disney opened the Disney California Adventure (DCA) Park in 2001, just across from Disneyland in Anaheim. The firm spent approximately $1.5 billion in creating the park, with a mix of roller coaster rides, California history, and movie nostalgia. Disney initially expected about 60% of its visitors to Disneyland to cross over to DCA and generate about $100 million in after-cash flows for the firm on an annual basis.

By 2008, it was clear that DCA had not performed to expectations. Of the 15 million people who came to Disneyland in 2007, only 6 million (about 40%) visited California Adventure, and the incremental after-tax cash flow averaged out to only $50 million between 2001 and 2007. In early 2008, Disney faced three choices:

1. Shut down California Adventure and try to recover whatever it can of its initial investment. It is estimated that Disney can, at best, recover about $500 million of its initial investment (either by selling the park or shutting it down).

2. Continue with the status quo, recognizing that future cash flows will be closer to the actual values ($50 million) than the original projections.

3. Expand and modify the park, with the intent of making it more attractive to visitors to Disneyland. Investing about $600 million more, with the intent of increasing the number of attractions for families with children, is expected to increase the percentage of Disneyland visitors who come to DCA from 40% to 60% and increase the annual after tax cash flow by 60% (from $50 million to $80 million) at the park.

The first step in assessing this investment is to estimate the cash flows from DCA as a continuing operation. To make this estimate, we assume that the current after-tax cash flow of $50 million will continue in perpetuity, growing at the inflation rate of 2%. Discounting back at the theme park cost of capital of 6.62% (from Chapter 4) yields a value for continuing with the status quo

$$\text{Value of DCA} = \frac{\text{Expected cash flow next year}}{(\text{Cost of capital} - g)} = \frac{50(1.02)}{(.0662 - .02)} = \$1.103 \text{ billion}$$

Note that this status quo value is well below the original investment of $1.5 billion, suggesting that Disney should never had opened this park, at least in hindsight. Abandoning this investment currently would do little to remedy this mistake, since Disney can recover only $500 million of its original investment. Since the value of the cash flows, disappointing though they might be, is still higher than the divestiture/salvage value, continuing with the park adds more value than shutting it down.

As a final piece, let us consider whether Disney should make the additional investment in the park. The up-front cost of $600 million will lead to more visitors in the park and an increase in the existing cash flows from $50 to $80 million. Using the same inflation rate and cost of capital, we can assess the present value of the cash flows from expansion:

$$\text{Value of CF from expansion} = \frac{\text{Increase in CF next year}}{(\text{Cost of capital} - g)} = \frac{30(1.02)}{(0.0662 - 0.02)}$$
$$= \$662 \text{ million}$$

Since the present value of the cash flows exceeds the cost of expansion, we would recommend that Disney not only continue with its investment in DCA, but expand it.

 Letting Go Is Hard to Do: A Behavioral Perspective
The principles of when to continue, expand and terminate projects are fairly simple, with all decisions based upon incremental cash flows. In practice, though, firms allow poor projects to continue far too long and often invest more to keep these projects going, behavior that has its roots in the human psyche. Statman and Caldwell provide three behavioral factors that explain why letting go of poor investments is so hard to do:

1. **Mental Accounting Versus Economic Accounting.** In economic accounting, we consider only incremental earnings and cash flows, thus following the conventional rule book in finance. In mental accounting, we keep track of sunk costs and investments already made in investment, making it difficult to let go of investments where substantial time and resources have been committed.

2. **Aversion to Regret.** Individuals distinguish between unrealized paper losses and realized losses and are much more averse to the latter. If terminating a bad project is the realization that a past investment was a mistake, the regret that is associated with this realization may be large enough that managers choose not to terminate. In fact, this resistance seems to increase with the degree of personal responsibility that the manager feels for the investment and with job insecurity.

3. **Procrastination.** When faced with unpleasant decisions, it is natural to procrastinate, hoping that time and chance will make the problem go away.

If it is human nature to be resistant to accepting mistakes, there are three things we can do to at least partially counter this tendency. The first is to require that all investment be reevaluated at regular intervals, say every two years. The second is to have hard and fast rules on termination such that projects that meet prespecified criteria (for example: actual revenues less than 70% of expectations, three years of losses) are shut down automatically. The third is to separate project assessment from those who initiated the project or currently manage the investment.

Analyzing a Firm's Project Portfolio

Analyzing projects individually becomes impractical when a firm has dozens or even hundreds of projects. Instead, we could consider whether the current portfolio of projects in which a firm has invested is earning a sufficient return relative to its required return. In this section, we will consider two approaches to analyzing a project portfolio: a cash-flow based approach, where we measure returns based upon cash flows, and an earnings-based approach, where we look at accounting returns.

Cash Flow Analysis

We could look at a firm's entire portfolio of existing investments and attempt to compute the amount invested in these investments, as well as the cash flows they generate. The problem with this approach is that different investments were made at different points in time, and given the time value of money, they cannot be easily aggregated. Instead, we will consider how to compute a cash flow return, taking into consideration both the investments in projects and the timing of the investments.

The cash flow return on investment (CFROI) for a firm measures the internal rate of return earned by the firm's existing projects. It is calculated using four inputs. The first is the *gross investment (GI)* that the firm has in its assets in place. This is computed by adding depreciation back to the book value of the assets (net asset value) to arrive at an estimate of the original investment in the asset. The gross investment, thus estimated, is converted into a current dollar value to reflect inflation that has occurred since the asset was purchased.

$$\text{Gross investment (GI)} = \text{Net asset value} + \text{Cumulated depreciation on asset}$$
$$+ \text{Current dollar adjustment}$$

The second input is the *gross cash flow (GCF)* earned in the current year on that asset. This is usually defined as the sum of the after-tax operating income of a firm and the noncash charges against earnings, such as depreciation and amortization. The operating income is adjusted for operating leases and any extraordinary or one-time charges.

$$\text{Gross cash flow (GCF)} = \text{Adjusted EBIT}(1 - t)$$
$$+ \text{Current year's depreciation and amortization}$$

The third input is the *expected life of the assets (n)* in place, at the time of the original investment, which can vary from business to business but reflects the earning life of the investments in question. The *expected value of the assets (SV)* at the end of this life, in current dollars, is the final input. This is usually assumed to be the portion of the initial investment, such as land and buildings, that is not depreciable, adjusted to current dollar terms.

Based on these inputs, the timeline for cash flows on the asset can be written as follows:

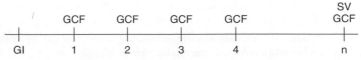

The gross investment in the asset is treated as the initial investment, the gross cash flow as an annuity for the life of the asset, and the expected value at the end of the asset's life as the salvage value. The CFROI is the internal rate of return of these cash flows—i.e, the discount rate that makes the net present value of the gross cash flows and salvage value equal to the gross investment. It can thus be viewed as a composite internal rate of return, in current dollar terms. This is compared to the firm's real cost of capital to pass judgment on whether assets in place are value creating or value destroying.

ILLUSTRATION 6.13 Estimating CFROI for Tata Chemicals

At the beginning of 2009, the book value of the Tata Chemical's assets was Rs25,149 million, including Rs15,126 million in net fixed assets and Rs10,023 million in noncash working capital. The accumulated depreciation on the fixed assets amounted to Rs18,424 million. The firm also earned Rs5,359 million in pre-tax operating income[14] and had a depreciation charge of Rs1,488 million in the most recent fiscal year. The average age of the investments that comprised Tata Chemical's existing assets was eight years, and the inflation rate during that eight-year period was approximately 3%. The operating assets are expected to have a remaining life of twelve years and have a salvage value of 20% of current asset value at the end of the investment period. The firm's marginal tax rate is 33.99%.

To estimate the CFROI, we first estimate the gross investment by adjusting the fixed asset value for inflation; we assume that the noncash working capital and capitalized leases are already at current value.

$$\text{Gross investment} = (\text{Rs}15,126 + \text{Rs}18,424)(1.03)^8 + \text{Rs}10,023 \text{ million}$$
$$= \text{Rs}52,523 \text{ million}$$

To estimate the gross cash flow, we add the noncash charges back to the after-tax operating income.

$$\text{Gross cash flow} = \text{Rs}5,359(1 - 0.3399) + \text{Rs}1,488 \text{ million} = \text{Rs}5,025 \text{ million}$$

The expected salvage value is assumed to be 20% of the gross investment:

$$\text{Expected salvage value} = \text{Gross investment } (0.2) = \text{Rs}52,523(0.2)$$
$$= \text{Rs}10,505 \text{ million}$$

To estimate the cash flow return on investment, we use the entire life of the asset obtained by adding together their existing age with the remaining life. The internal rate of return based upon these inputs is 7.78%, and it represents the CFROI.

$$\text{Rs}52,523 = \text{Rs}5,025(\text{PV of annuity, 20 years, CFROI}) + \text{Rs}10,505/(1 + \text{CFROI})^{20}$$

This can then be compared to the real cost of capital to evaluate whether the firm's asset are value-creating. Tata Chemicals's nominal cost of capital is currently 11.44%.

---

[14]Consistent with our treatment of operating leases as part of the assets, we adjust the operating income for the imputed interest expense on these leases.

With an expected inflation rate of 3%, the real cost of capital would be 8.19%.

Real cost of capital
$$= (1 + \text{Nominal cost of capital in Rs})/(1 + \text{Expected inflation rate in Rs})$$
$$= 1.1144/1.03 - 1 = 0.0819 \text{ or } 8.19\%$$

Based on this analysis, Tata Chemicals is earning about 0.41% (7.78% − 8.19%) less than its cost of capital on its existing investments.

 cfroi.xls: This spreadsheet allows you to estimate the CFROI for a firm.

Accounting Earnings Analysis

In Chapter 5, we introduced two measures of accounting return for investments: the return on capital and the return on equity. However, our entire discussion revolved around how to analyze individual projects. But it is possible to calculate the return on equity or capital for an entire firm based on its current earnings and book value. The computation parallels the estimation for individual projects but uses the values for the entire firm:

$$\text{Return on capital} = \frac{\text{EBIT}(1-t)}{(\text{Book value of debt} + \text{Book value of equity} - \text{Cash})}$$

$$\text{Return on equity} = \frac{\text{Net income}}{\text{Book value of equity}}$$

We use book value rather than market value because it represents the capital investment in existing investments and we deduct cash, in computing return on capital, because the income earned on cash balances is not included in operating income.[15] To preserve consistency, the book values used should reflect either the book values at the start of the period (over which the return is earned) or the average capital invested over the period. This return can be used as an approximate measure of the returns that the firm is making on its existing investments or assets, as long as the following assumptions hold:

- The income used (operating or net) is income derived from existing projects and is not skewed by expenditures designed to provide future growth (such as R&D expenses) or one-time gains or losses.

- More important, the book value of capital used measures the actual investment that the firm has in these assets. Here again, stock buybacks, one-time charges, and goodwill amortization can create serious distortions in the book value.[16]

---

[15]Extending the same principle to return on equity, we generally do not net cash out of book value of equity because net income includes the income from cash holdings. However, we can compute a noncash version of return on equity:

Noncash return on equity = (Net income − Interest income from cash(1 − t))/(BV of equity − Cash)

[16]Stock buybacks and large writeoffs will push down book capital and result in overstated accounting returns. Acquisitions that create large amounts of goodwill will push up book capital and result in understated returns on capital. Adjusting capital invested for these and other actions can be problematic and are examined in more detail in A. Damodaran, "Return on Capital, Return on Invested Capital and Return on Equity: Measurement and Implications," 2008, listed as a research paper on www.damodaran.com.

- The depreciation and other noncash charges that usually depress income are used to make capital expenditures that maintain the existing asset's income earning potential.

If these assumptions hold, the return on capital becomes a reasonable proxy for what the firm is making on its existing investments or projects, and the return on equity becomes a proxy for what the equity investors are making on their share of these investments.

With this reasoning, a firm that earns a return on capital that exceeds its cost of capital can be viewed as having, on average, good projects on its books. Conversely, a firm that earns a return on capital that is less than the cost of capital can be viewed as having, on average, bad projects on its books. From the equity standpoint, a firm that earns a return on equity that exceeds its cost of equity can be viewed as earning surplus returns for its stockholders, whereas a firm that does not accomplish this is taking on projects that destroy stockholder value.

ILLUSTRATION 6.14   **Evaluating Current Investments**
In Table 6.10, we summarize the current returns on capital and costs of capital for Disney, Aracruz, Tata Chemicals, and Bookscape. The book values of debt, equity and cash at the end of the previous financial year (2007) were used together to compute the book value of capital invested at the beginning of 2008, and the operating income for the most recent financial year (2008) is used to compute the return on capital.[17] Considering the issues associated with measuring debt and cost of capital for financial services firms, we have not computed the values for Deutsche Bank.

The marginal tax rates used in Chapter 4 are used here as well. This analysis suggests that Disney was the only company earning excess returns in 2008. Bookscape and Tata Chemicals were both close to breaking even, and Aracruz was underperforming. There are a few caveats that we would offer:

- The book value of capital is affected fairly dramatically by accounting decisions. The depreciation methods chosen and writeoffs taken during the year can affect book values and the measured returns.

Table 6.10   RETURN ON CAPITAL AND COST OF CAPITAL COMPARISON (VALUES IN MILLIONS)

	EBIT (1−t)	BV of Debt	BV of Equity	Cash	BV of Capital	Return on Capital	Cost of Capital	ROC–Cost of Capital
Disney	$4,359	$16,892	$30,753	$3,670	$43,975	9.91%	7.51%	2.40%
Aracruz	R$379	R$3,090	R$5,361	R$22	R$8,430	4.49%	10.63%	−6.14%
Bookscape	$2.15	$9.59	$6.00	$0.40	$15.59	13.76%	14.90%	−1.14%
Tata Chemicals	Rs4,134	Rs12,614	Rs23,928	Rs725	Rs36,542	11.31%	11.44%	−0.12%

---

[17]Some analysts use average capital invested over the year, obtained by averaging the book value of capital at the beginning and end of the year. By using the capital invested at the beginning of the year, we have assumed that capital invested during the course of year is unlikely to generate operating income during that year.

- We have used the operating income from the most recent year, notwithstanding the volatility in the income. To smooth out the volatility, we can compute the average operating income over the past three years and use it in computing the return on capital; this approach generates a "normalized" return on capital of 8.39% for Disney and 7.68% for Aracruz.

- In keeping with our treatment of operating leases as debt, we have included the present value of operating leases from the prior year in the debt for both Disney and Bookscape, and adjusted operating income accordingly.

- For Aracruz, we assume that because the book values are adjusted for inflation, the return on capital is a real return on capital and can be compared to the real cost of capital.[18]

The analysis can also be done purely in equity terms. To do this, we would first compute the return on equity for each company by dividing the net income for the most recent year by the book value of equity at the beginning of the year and compare it to the cost of equity. Table 6.11 summarizes these results.

Disney's excess equity returns are consistent with what the excess returns we estimated using return on capital and cost of capital. Aracruz and Deutsche reported large losses in 2008, leading to negative returns on equity and negative excess returns. In the case of Aracruz, the net loss stands in contrast to the positive operating income and can be explained by the multi-billion losses incurred on derivatives, which were classified as extraordinary expenses. Bookscape earns excess returns on an equity basis, whereas it broke even on a capital basis, and we would attribute this to the favorable terms it has on its current operating lease. With Tata Chemicals, the difference is stark, with equity excess returns being dramatically higher (26.37%) than capital excess returns. However, almost all of the excess returns can be attributed to an extraordinary gain of Rs6,077 million reported in 2008; if we eliminate this extraordinary gain, the return on equity drops to 15.46%, only 1.53% higher than the cost of equity.

Table 6.11   RETURN ON EQUITY AND COST OF EQUITY COMPARISONS (VALUES IN MILLIONS)

	Net Income	BV of Equity	ROE	Cost of Equity	ROE—Cost of Equity
Disney	$4,427	$30,753	14.40%	8.91%	5.49%
Aracruz	−R$4,213	R$5,361	−78.59%	18.45%	−97.05%
Bookscape	$1.50	$6.00	25.00%	20.94%	4.06%
Deutsche Bank	−€3,835.00	€38,466.00	−9.97%	10.72%	−20.69%
Tata Chemicals	Rs9,644	Rs23,928	40.30%	13.93%	26.37%
Tata Chemicals (w/o extraordinary item)	Rs3,700	Rs23,928	15.46%	13.93%	1.53%

[18]Brazilian accounting standards allow for the adjustment of book value for inflation.

This example brings home some of the reasons why excess returns can change when we move from capital to equity measures. First, the net income includes income (and losses) from nonoperating assets that can yield different results from looking at income from just operating assets. Second, firms that have been able to lock in debt at favorable terms (interest rates lower than what they should be paying, based upon their default risk) should have higher equity excess returns than excess returns on capital. In general, we believe that the excess returns computed from capital measures are more dependable measures than the equity excess returns.

There is a data set online that summarizes, by sector, returns on equity and capital as well as costs of equity and capital.

IN PRACTICE: ECONOMIC PROFIT OR ECONOMIC VALUE ADDED (EVA)

Economic value added is a value enhancement concept that has caught the attention both of firms interested in increasing their value and portfolio managers looking for good investments. Economic profit or economic value added is a measure of dollar surplus value created by a firm or project and is measured by doing the following:

$$\text{Economic value added (EVA)} = (\text{Return on capital} - \text{Cost of capital})(\text{Capital invested})$$

The return on capital is measured using "adjusted" operating income, where the adjustments eliminate items that are unrelated to existing investments,[19] and the capital investment is based on the book value of capital but is designed to measure the capital invested in existing assets. Firms that have positive EVA are firms that are creating surplus value, and firms with negative EVA are destroying value.

Although EVA is usually calculated using total capital, it can be easily modified to be an equity measure:

$$\text{Equity EVA} = (\text{Return on equity} - \text{Cost of equity})(\text{Equity invested in project or firm})$$

Again, a firm that earns a positive equity EVA is creating value for its stockholders, and a firm with a negative equity EVA is destroying value for its stockholders.

---

[19]Stern Stewart, which is the primary proponent of the EVA approach, claims to make as many as 168 adjustments to operating income to arrive at the true return on capital.

The measures of excess returns that we computed in the tables in the last section can be easily modified to become measures of EVA:

Company	ROC–Cost of Capital	BV of Capital	EVA	ROE–Cost of Equity	BV of Equity	Equity EVA
Disney	2.40%	$43,975	$1,057	5.49%	$30,753	$1,688
Aracruz	−6.14%	R$8,430	−R$517	−97.05%	R$ 5,361	−5203
Bookscape	−1.14%	$15.59	−$0.18	4.06%	$6.00	$0.24
Deutsche Bank	NMF	NMF	NMF	−20.69%	€38,466	−€7,959
Tata Chemicals	−0.12%	Rs36,542	−Rs45	1.53%	Rs23,928	Rs367

For Tata Chemicals, we used the net income prior to the extraordinary profits. There are no surprises here, since positive (negative) excess returns translate into positive (negative) economic profits or EVA. Note that while EVA converts the percentage excess returns in these tables to absolute excess returns, its measurement is affected by the same issues of earnings and book value measurement. Ultimately, it is only as good as the operating income and book value of capital numbers that feed into it. ∎

6.11   Stock Buybacks, Return on Capital, and EVA

When companies buy back stock, they are allowed to reduce the book value of their equity by the market value of the stocks bought back. When the market value of equity is well in excess of book value of equity, buying back stock will generally

a.   Increase the return on capital but not affect the EVA

b.   Increase the return on capital and increase the EVA

c.   Not affect the return on capital but increase the EVA

d.   None of the above

Explain.

There is a data set online that summarizes, by sector, the economic value added and the equity economic value added in each.

evacalc.xls: This spreadsheet allows you to estimate the economic value added for a firm.

Where Do Good Projects Come From?

In the process of analyzing new investments in the preceding chapters, we have contended that good projects have a positive NPV and earn an IRR greater than the hurdle rate. Although these criteria are certainly valid from a measurement standpoint, they do not address the deeper questions about good projects, including what economic conditions make for a good project and why it is that some firms have a more ready supply of good projects than others.

Competitive Advantages

Implicit in the definition of a good project is the existence of **excess returns** to the business considering the project. In a competitive market for real investments, the existence of these excess returns should act as a magnet, attracting competitors to take on similar investments. In the process, the excess returns should dissipate over time; how quickly they dissipate will depend on the ease with which competition can enter the market and provide close substitutes and on the magnitude of any differential advantages that the business with the good projects might possess. Consider an extreme scenario such that the business with the good projects has no differential advantage in cost or product quality over its competitors, and new competitors can enter the market easily and at low cost to provide substitutes. In this case, the excess returns on these projects should disappear very quickly.

An integral basis for the existence of a good project is the creation and maintenance of barriers to new or existing competitors taking on equivalent or similar projects. These barriers can take different forms, including

- *Economies of scale*   Some projects might earn high returns only if they are done on a large scale, thus restricting competition from smaller companies. In such cases, large companies in this line of business may be able to continue to earn supernormal returns on their projects because smaller competitors will not be able to replicate them.

- *Cost advantages*   A business might work at establishing a cost advantage over its competitors, either by being more efficient or by taking advantage of arrangements that its competitors cannot use. For example, in the late 1980s, Southwest Airlines was able to establish a cost advantage over its larger competitors, such as American Airlines and United, and the company exploited this cost advantage to earn much higher returns.

- *Capital requirements*   Entry into some businesses might require such large investments that it discourages competitors from entering, even though projects in those businesses may earn above-market returns. For example, assume that Boeing is faced with a large number of high-return projects in the aerospace business. Although this scenario would normally attract competitors, the huge initial investment needed to enter this business would enable Boeing to continue to earn these high returns.

- *Product differentiation*   Some businesses continue to earn excess returns by differentiating their products from those of their competitors, leading to either higher profit margins or higher sales. This differentiation can be created in a number of ways—through effective advertising and promotion (Coca-Cola), technical expertise (Sony), better service (Nordstrom), and responsiveness to customer needs.

- *Access to distribution channels*   Those firms that have much better access to the distribution channels for their products than their competitors are better able to earn excess returns. In some cases, the restricted access to outsiders is due to tradition or loyalty to existing competitors. In other cases, the firm may actually own the distribution channel, and competitors may not be able to develop their own distribution channels because the costs are prohibitive.

- ***Legal and government barriers*** In some cases, a firm may be able to exploit investment opportunities without worrying about competition because of restrictions on competitors from product patents the firm may own to government restrictions on competitive entry. These arise, for instance, when companies are allowed to patent products or services and gain the exclusive right to provide them over the patent life.

Quality of Management and Project Quality

In the preceding section we examined some of the factors that determine the attractiveness of the projects a firm will face. Some factors, such as government restrictions on entry, may largely be out of the control of incumbent management, but there are other factors that can clearly be influenced by management.[20] Considering each of the factors already discussed, for instance, we would argue that a good management team can increase both the number of and the excess returns earned on available projects by

- *Investing in projects that exploit any economies of scale that the firm may possess;* in addition, management can look for ways it can create economies of scale in the firm's existing operations.

- *Establishing and nurturing cost advantages over its competitors;* some cost advantages may arise from labor negotiations, and others may result from long-term strategic decisions made by the firm.

- *Taking actions that increase the initial cost for new entrants into the business;* one of the primary reasons Microsoft was able to dominate the computer software market in the early 1990s was its ability to increase the investment needed to develop and market new business software programs.

- *Nurturing markets in which the company's differential advantage is greatest, in terms of either cost of delivery or brand name value.* In some cases, this will involve expanding into foreign markets, as both Levi Strauss and McDonald's did in the 1980s to exploit their brand name recognition in those markets. In other cases, this may require concentrating on segments of an existing market, as Gap did when it opened its Old Navy stores to cater to more bargain-conscious consumers.

- *Improving the firm's reputation for customer service and product delivery;* this will enable the firm to increase both profits and returns. One of the primary factors behind Chrysler's financial recovery in the 1980s was the company's ability to establish a reputation for producing good-quality cars and minivans.

---

[20]When government policy is influenced by lobbying by firms, it can be argued that even these factors may be affected by the management of a firm.

- *Developing distribution channels that are unique and cannot be easily accessed by competitors.* Avon, for instance, employed a large sales force to go door-to-door to reach consumers who could not be reached by other distribution channels.

- *Obtaining patents on products or technologies that keep out the competition and earn high returns;* doing so may require large investments in R&D over time. It can be argued that success of pharmaceutical companies, small and large, can be traced to their capacity to patent blockbuster drugs.

Although the quality of management is typically related to the quality of projects a firm possesses, a good management team does not guarantee the existence of good projects. In fact, there is a rather large element of chance involved in the process; even the best-laid plans of the management team to create project opportunities may come to naught if circumstances conspire against them—a recession may upend a retailer, or an oil price shock may cause an airline to lose money.

ILLUSTRATION 6.15 Excess Returns and Competitive Advantages: an Assessment
In Illustration 6.14, we estimated the excess returns for each of the firms that we are analyzing. Of the four publicly traded firms, only Disney generated returns on capital and equity that exceeded its costs of capital and equity. Aracruz and Deutsche Bank generated negative excess returns, and Tata Chemicals roughly broke even on both capital and equity measures.

- *Disney* While most analysts would attribute Disney's excess returns to its brand name built up over decades, it is worth noting that Disney's excess returns have been volatile since Walt Disney's demise in 1966. After a long period of declining returns in the 1970s and early 1980s, Disney enjoyed a rebirth with its animated movie hits between 1986 and 1995. Those movies, which included *The Little Mermaid, Beauty and the Beast*, and *The Lion King*, created new franchises for Disney to exploit, as well as a new generation of young fans. That gain was put at risk by the Capital Cities acquisition in 1996, and Disney's excess returns dissipated over the next decade. In 2004, for instance, Disney was earning 4% less than its cost of capital. With Bob Iger at its helm, the company has seen a resurrection, and excess returns have become positive again. While some would read the ups and downs of Disney as just luck, we would read it differently. Disney has core advantages that are almost impossible for other firms to replicate, and the firm has done best when it has focused on those businesses where it can use these strengths. Using this template, the acquisition of Pixar and even the investment in the cruise line business (which uses Disney characters to appeal to families) make sense. Disney has faltered when it has strayed from this core mission, as was the case with its early investments in the Internet business (Go.com), sports (its investment in the California Angels, a major league baseball team), and its expensive entry into broadcasting (Capital Cities/ABC).

- *Aracruz* Aracruz's key advantage is its access to and ownership of the ample timber in the Brazilian rainforests. While the company remains dependent upon commodity prices for year-to-year profit swings, it should be able to use its cost advantages to generate at least moderate excess returns over time. While this was the template it followed over much of its lifetime, the ease with which money could be made speculating on exchange rates led the firm down that path from 2005 through 2007, generating large earnings for the firm in the process. Since Aracruz really has no core competence in the area of exchange rate forecasting, the huge losses in 2008 from its exchange rate bets were almost predictable. Looking forward, Aracruz has to refocus on the paper business and recognize that there are no easy pathways to profitability.

- ***Tata Chemicals*** Tata Chemicals looks like a mature firm in a mature business, with the excess returns (or lack thereof) to match. While managers should search for small competitive advantages in this market, coming perhaps from lower production costs in India and access to a large, vibrant economy, it is important that they show patience and not overreach. In particular, the allure of acquiring growth and entering other markets, especially through acquisitions, has to be resisted.

- ***Deutsche Bank*** The negative excess returns that Deutsche Bank posted in 2008 are not a surprise, given the turmoil in the financial services sector. These negative excess returns did follow an extended period of profitability for commercial and investment banks. Looking forward, we do know that substantial changes are coming to the banking business, both from a regulatory standpoint (capital ratios, controls on lending) and from the way the business is structured (risk controls, compensation). While these changes may suggest a cap on profitability, there is one factor working in Deutsche Bank's favor. As a relatively healthy survivor in a business with so many casualties, Deutsche Bank will find itself with less competition and can perhaps exploit this factor to generate higher profits.

CONCLUSION

Projects often create side costs and benefits that are not captured in the initial estimates of cash flows used to estimate returns. In this chapter, we examined some of these indirect costs and benefits:

- Investing in one project may prevent a firm from taking alternative investments if these are mutually exclusive. If projects have equal lives and there are no capital rationing constraints, we can pick the investment with the higher NPV. If this is not the case, we have to find ways of controlling for differences in project lives (by computing an equivalent annuity) and for differences in scale (by computing profitability indices).

- Opportunity costs measure the costs of resources that the company already owns that might be used for a new project. Although the business might not spend new money acquiring these resources, there are consequences in terms of the cash flows that have to be reflected in the returns.

- Projects may also provide synergistic benefits for other projects for a firm. These benefits, which also take the form of cash flows, should be reflected in the returns.

- Projects may also create options that are valuable—options to expand into new markets and produce new products. When such options exist, conventional discounted cash flow models will tend to understate the value of investments.

In summary, the project returns have to reflect all of the side costs and benefits.

In the final part of the chapter, we turned our attention from new investments to the existing investments of a firm. We started by looking at how we can extend the conventional tools of investment analysis (including NPV and IRR) to analyzing a past project and deciding whether to extend or terminate an existing one. We closed the section by evaluating the portfolio of existing projects of a firm by computing an overall return on capital invested in these projects and comparing that return to the cost of capital.

LIVE CASE STUDY

ESTIMATING EARNINGS AND CASH FLOWS

Objective: To analyze a firm's existing investments, and to identify differential advantages that explain excess returns on existing investments.

Key Questions

- What are the firm's competitive strengths and differential advantages, if any?
- Does this firm earn excess returns on its existing projects? If so, can it maintain the competitive strengths that allowed it to earn these excess returns? If not, what can it do to start earning excess returns on its projects?
- Does the firm have poor investments? If so, what might be the reasons for the poor returns?

Framework for Analysis

1. *Analyzing Existing Investments*
   - What is the accounting return that the firm earns on its existing investments? How does this compare with the cost of equity and capital?
   - What was the firm's economic value added in the most recent financial year? How does it compare with the previous year?
   - What, if anything, do the accounting returns and economic value added tell you about the quality of the firm's existing investments?

2. *Assessing Competitive Strengths*
   - Who are the primary competitors to this firm, and how does the firm compare to them in terms of both quantitative (size, profitability, risk) and qualitative measures (quality of management, service)?
   - Does the firm have any special strength that no other firm in the sector possesses?
   - Does the firm lag other firms in the sector on any of the measures?

3. *Evaluating Sustainability of Competitive Strengths*
   - Are the firm's competitors catching up with the firm on its strengths?
   - Are there new competitors either in the market or on the horizon who could compete with the firm on its strengths?

PROBLEMS AND QUESTIONS (If no tax rate is given, use 40%)

1. A small manufacturing firm that has limited access to capital has a capital rationing constraint of $150 million and is faced with the following investment projects (numbers in millions):

Project	Initial Investment	NPV
A	$25	$10
B	$30	$25
C	$40	$20
D	$10	$10
E	$15	$10
F	$60	$20
G	$20	$10
H	$25	$20
I	$35	$10
J	$15	$5

a. Which of these projects would you accept? Why?

b. What is the cost of the capital rationing constraint?

2. A closely held, publicly traded firm faces self-imposed capital rationing constraints of $100 million in this period and $75 million in the next period. It has to choose among the following projects (in millions):

Project	Current Period	Next Period	NPV
A	$20	$10	$20
B	$25	$15	$20
C	$30	$30	$15
D	$15	$15	$20
E	$40	$25	$30
F	$10	$10	$10
G	$20	$15	$20
H	$30	$25	$35
I	$35	$25	$25
J	$25	$15	$10

Set up the linear programming problem, assuming that fractions and multiples of projects cannot be taken.

3. You own a rental building in the city and are interested in replacing the heating system. You are faced with the following alternatives:

a. A solar heating system, which will cost $12,000 to install and $500 a year to run and will last forever (assume that your building does)

b. A gas heating system, which will cost $5,000 to install and $1,000 a year to run and will last twenty years

c. An oil heating system, which will cost $3,500 to install and $1,200 a year to run and will last fifteen years

If your opportunity cost is 10%, which of these three options is best for you?

4. You are trying to choose a new siding for your house. A salesman offers you two choices:

a. Wood siding, which will last ten years and cost $5,000 to install and $1,000 a year to maintain.

b. Aluminum siding, which will last forever, cost $15,000 to install, and will have a lower maintenance cost per year.

If your discount rate is 10%, how low would your maintenance costs have to be for you to choose the aluminum siding?

5. You have just been approached by a magazine with an offer for renewing your subscription. You can renew for one year at $20, two years for $36, or three years at $45. Assuming that you have an opportunity cost of 20% and the cost of a subscription will not change over time, which of these three options should you choose?

6. You have been hired as a capital budgeting analyst by a sporting goods firm that manufactures athletic shoes and that has captured 10% of the overall shoe market (the total market is worth $100 million a year). The fixed costs associated with manufacturing these shoes is $2 million a year, and variable costs are 40% of revenues. The company's tax rate is 40%. The firm believes that it can increase its market share to 20% by investing $10 million in a new distribution system (which can be depreciated over the system's life of ten years to a salvage value of zero) and spending $1 million a year in additional advertising. The company proposes to continue to maintain working capital at 10% of annual revenues. The discount rate to be used for this project is 8%.

a. What is the initial investment for this project?

b. What is the annual operating cash flow from this project?

c. What is the NPV of this project?

d. How much would the firm's market share have to increase for you to be indifferent to taking or rejecting this project?

7. You are considering the possibility of replacing an existing machine that has a book value of $500,000, a remaining depreciable life of five years, and a salvage value of $300,000. The replacement machine will cost $2 million and have a ten-year life. Assuming that you use straight-line depreciation and that neither machine will have any salvage value at the end of the next ten years, how much would you need to save each year to make the change (the tax rate is 40%)?

8. You are helping a bookstore decide whether it should open a coffee shop on the premises. The details of the investment are as follows:

   • The coffee shop will cost $50,000 to open; it will have a five-year life and be depreciated straight-line over the period to a salvage value of $10,000.

   • The sales at the shop are expected to be $15,000 in the first year and grow 5% a year for the following four years.

   • The operating expenses will be 50% of revenues.

   • The tax rate is 40%.

   • The coffee shop is expected to generate additional sales of $20,000 next year for the book shop, and the pretax operating margin is 40%. These sales will grow 10% a year for the following four years.

   a. Estimate the net present value of the coffee shop without the additional book sales.

   b. Estimate the present value of the cash flows accruing from the additional book sales.

   c. Would you open the coffee shop?

9. The lining of a plating tank must be replaced every three years at a cost of approximately $2,000. A new lining material has been developed that is more resistant to the corrosive effects of the plating liquid and will cost approximately $4,000. If the required rate of return is 20% and annual property taxes and insurance amount to about 4% of the initial

investment, how long must the new lining last to be more economical than the present one?

10. You are a small business owner considering two alternatives for your phone system:

	Plan A	Plan B
Initial cost	$50,000	$120,000
Annual maintenance cost	$9,000	$6,000
Salvage value	$10,000	$20,000
Life	20 years	40 years

The discount rate is 8%. Which alternative would you pick?

11. You have been asked to compare three alternative investments and make a recommendation.

   • Project A has an initial investment of $5 million and after-tax cash flows of $2.5 million a year for the next five years.

   • Project B has no initial investment, after-tax cash flows of $1 million a year for the next ten years, and a salvage value of $2 million (from working capital).

   • Project C has an initial investment of $10 million, another investment of $5 million in ten years, and after-tax cash flows of $2.5 million a year forever.

   The discount rate is 10% for all three projects. Which of the three projects would you pick? Why?

12. You are the manager of a pharmaceutical company and are considering what type of laptop computers to buy for your salespeople to take with them on their calls.

   • You can buy fairly inexpensive (and less powerful) older machines for about $2,000 each. These machines will be obsolete in three years and are expected to have an annual maintenance cost of $150.

   • You can buy newer and more powerful laptops for about $4,000 each. These machines will last five years and are expected to have an annual maintenance cost of $50.

   If your cost of capital is 12%, which option would you pick, and why?

13. You are the supervisor of a town where the roads are in need of repair. You have a limited budget and are considering two options:

- You can patch up the roads for $100,000, but you will have to repeat this expenditure every year to keep the roads in reasonable shape.

- You can spend $400,000 to repave and repair the roads, in which case your annual expenditures on maintenance will drop.

If your discount rate is 10%, how much would the annual expenditures have to drop in the second option for you to consider it?

14. You are the manager of a specialty retailing firm that is considering two strategies for getting into the Malaysian retail market. Under the first strategy, the firm will make an initial investment of $10 million and can expect to capture about 5% of the overall market share. Under the second strategy, the firm will make a much larger commitment of $40 million for advertising and promotion and can expect to capture about 10% of the market share. If the overall size of the market is $200 million, the firm's cost of capital is 12%, and the typical life of a project in the firm is fifteen years, what would the operating margin have to be for the firm to consider the second strategy? (You can assume that the firm leases its stores and has no depreciation or capital expenditures.)

15. You work for a firm that has limited access to capital markets. As a consequence, it has only $20 million available for new investments this year. The firm does have a ready supply of good projects, and you have listed all the projects.

Project	Initial Investment (million)	NPV (million)	IRR (%)
I	$10	$3.0	21%
II	$5	$2.5	28%
III	$15	$4.0	19%
IV	$10	$4.0	24%
V	$5	$2.0	20%

a. Based on the profitability index, which of these projects would you take?

b. Based on the IRR, which of these projects would you take?

c. Why might the two approaches give you different answers?

16. You are the owner of a small hardware store, and you are considering opening a gardening store in a vacant area in the back of your present store. You estimate that it will cost you $50,000 to set up the new store, and that you will generate $10,000 in after-tax cash flows from the store for the life of the store (which is expected to be ten years). The one concern you have is that you have limited parking; by opening the gardening store you run the risk of not having enough parking for customers who shop at your hardware store. You estimate that the lost sales from such occurrence would amount to $3,000 a year, and that your after-tax operating margin on sales at the hardware store is 40%. If your discount rate is 14%, would you open the gardening store?

17. You are the manager of a grocery store, and you are considering offering babysitting services to your customers. You estimate that the licensing and set up costs will amount to $150,000 initially and that you will be spending about $60,000 annually to provide the service. As a result of the service, you expect sales at the store, which is $5 million currently, to increase by 20%; your after-tax operating margin is 10%. If your cost of capital is 12% and you expect the store to remain open for ten years, would you offer the service?

18. You run a financial service firm where you replace your employee's computers every three years. You have 5000 employees, and each computer costs $2,500 currently—the old computers can be sold for $500 each. The new computers are generally depreciated straight-line over their three-year lives to a salvage value of $500. A computer-service firm offers to lease you the computers and replace them for you at no cost, if you will pay a leasing fee of $5 million a year (which is tax-deductible). If your tax rate is 40%, would you accept the offer?

19. You are examining the viability of a capital investment in which your firm is interested. The project will require an initial investment of $500,000 and the projected revenues are $400,000 a year for five years. The projected cost of goods sold is 40% of revenues and the tax rate is 40%. The initial investment is primarily in plant and equipment and can be depreciated straight-line over five years (the salvage value is zero). The project makes use of other resources that your firm already owns:

- Two employees of the firm, each with a salary of $40,000 a year, who are currently employed by another division, will be transferred to this project. The other division has no alternative use for them, but they are covered by a union contract that will prevent them from being fired

	Capacity Used (%)	Growth Rate (%)/Year Currently	Revenues Currently ($ million)	Fixed Cost ($ million) /Year	Variable Cost ($ million) /Year
Old product	50	5	100	25	50
New product	30	10	80	20	44

for three years (during which they would be paid their current salary).

- The project will use excess capacity in the current packaging plant. Although this excess capacity has no alternative use now, it is estimated that the firm will have to invest $250,000 in a new packaging plant in year 4 as a consequence of this project using up excess capacity (instead of year 8 as originally planned).

- The project will use a van currently owned by the firm. Although the van is not currently being used, it can be rented out for $3,000 a year for five years. The book value of the van is $10,000, and it is being depreciated straight-line (with five years remaining for depreciation).

- The discount rate to be used for this project is 10%.

a. What (if any) is the opportunity cost associated with using the two employees from another division?

b. What (if any) is the opportunity cost associated with the use of excess capacity of the packaging plant?

c. What (if any) is the opportunity cost associated with the use of the van?

d. What is the after-tax operating cash flow each year on this project?

e. What is the NPV of this project?

20. Your company is considering producing a new product. You have a production facility that is currently used to only 50% of capacity, and you plan to use some of the excess capacity for the new product. The

production facility cost $50 million five years ago when it was built and is being depreciated straight-line over twenty-five years (in real dollars, assume that this cost will stay constant over time).

The new product has a life of ten years, the tax rate is 40%, and the appropriate discount rate (real) is 10%.

a. If you take on this project, when would you run out of capacity?

b. When you run out of capacity, what would you lose if you chose to cut back on production (in present value after-tax dollars)? (You have to decide which product you are going to cut back on production.)

c. What would the opportunity cost to be assigned to this new product be if you chose to build a new facility when you run out of capacity instead of cutting back on production?

21. You are an analyst for a sporting goods corporation that is considering a new project that will take advantage of excess capacity in an existing plant. The plant has a capacity to produce 50,000 tennis racquets, but only 25,000 are being produced currently, although sales of the rackets are increasing 10% a year. You want to use some of the remaining capacity to manufacture 20,000 squash rackets each year for the next ten years (which will use up 40% of the total capacity), and this market is assumed to be stable (no growth). An average tennis racquet sells for $100 and costs $40 to make. The tax rate for the corporation is 40%, and the discount rate is 10%. Is there an opportunity cost involved? If so, how much is it?

CHAPTER 7

CAPITAL STRUCTURE: OVERVIEW OF THE FINANCING DECISION

In the past few chapters, we examined the investment principle and argued that projects that earn a return greater than the minimum acceptable hurdle rate are good projects. In coming up with the cost of capital, which we defined to be the minimum acceptable hurdle rate, however, we used the existing mix of debt and equity used by the firm.

In this chapter, we examine the choices that a firm has in terms of both debt and equity and how these choices change over a firm's life cycle. In particular, we look at how the choices change as a firm goes from being a small, private business to a large publicly traded corporation. We then evaluate the basic tradeoff between using debt and equity by weighing the benefits of borrowing against its costs. We close the chapter by examining when the costs of borrowing exactly offset its benefits, which essentially makes debt irrelevant, and the implications for corporate finance.

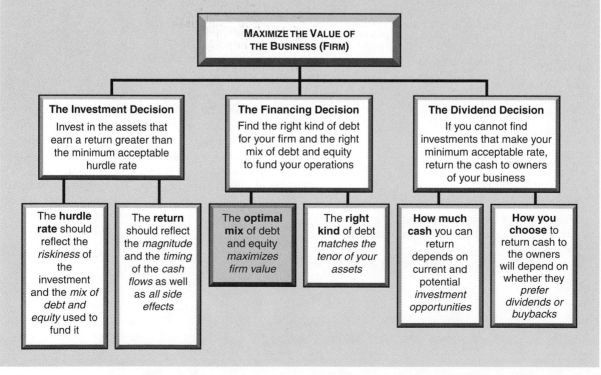

THE CHOICES: TYPES OF FINANCING

There are only two ways in which any business can raise money—debt or equity. This may seem simplistic, in light of the array of choices firms have in terms of financing vehicles. We will begin this section with a discussion of the characteristics of debt and equity and then look at a range of financing vehicles available within each of these categories. We will then examine of a range of securities that share some characteristics with debt and some with equity, and are therefore called **hybrid securities**.

The Continuum between Debt and Equity

Although the distinction between debt and equity is often made in terms of bonds and stocks, its roots lie in the nature of the cash flow claims of each type of financing. The first distinction is that a *debt claim* entitles the holder to a contractual set of cash flows (usually interest and principal payments), whereas an *equity claim* entitles the holder to any residual cash flows after meeting all other promised claims. This remains the fundamental difference, but other distinctions have arisen, partly as a result of the tax code and partly as a consequence of legal developments.

The second distinction, which is a logical outgrowth of the nature of cash flow claims (contractual versus residual), is that debt has a prior claim on both cash flows on a period-to-period basis (for interest and principal payments) and on the assets of the firm (in the case of liquidation). Third, the tax laws have generally treated interest expenses, which accrue to debt holders, very differently and often much more advantageously than dividends or other cash flows that accrue to equity. In the United States, for instance, interest expenses are tax-deductible to the entity paying them, and thus create tax savings, whereas dividend payments have to be made out of after-tax cash flows. Fourth, debt usually has a fixed maturity date, at which point the principal is due, whereas equity generally has an infinite life. Finally, equity investors, by virtue of their claim on the residual cash flows of the firm, are generally given the bulk of—or all—the control of the management of the firm. Debt investors, on the other hand, play a much more passive role in management, exercising at most veto power over significant financial decisions.[1] These differences are summarized in Figure 7.1.

To summarize, debt is defined as any financing vehicle that is a contractual claim on the firm (and not a function of its operating performance), creates tax-deductible payments, has a fixed life, and has a priority claim on cash flows both in operating periods and in bankruptcy. Conversely, equity is defined as any financing vehicle that is a residual claim on the firm, does not create a tax advantage from its payments, has an infinite life, does not have priority in bankruptcy, and provides management control to the owner. Any security that shares characteristics with both is a hybrid security. We will argue later in this chapter that the fixed versus perpetual life distinction is becoming less critical over time, as bond maturities lengthen and novel equity vehicles get created.

---

[1] Veto power is usually exercised through covenants or restrictions written into bond agreements.

Figure 7.1   Debt versus Equity

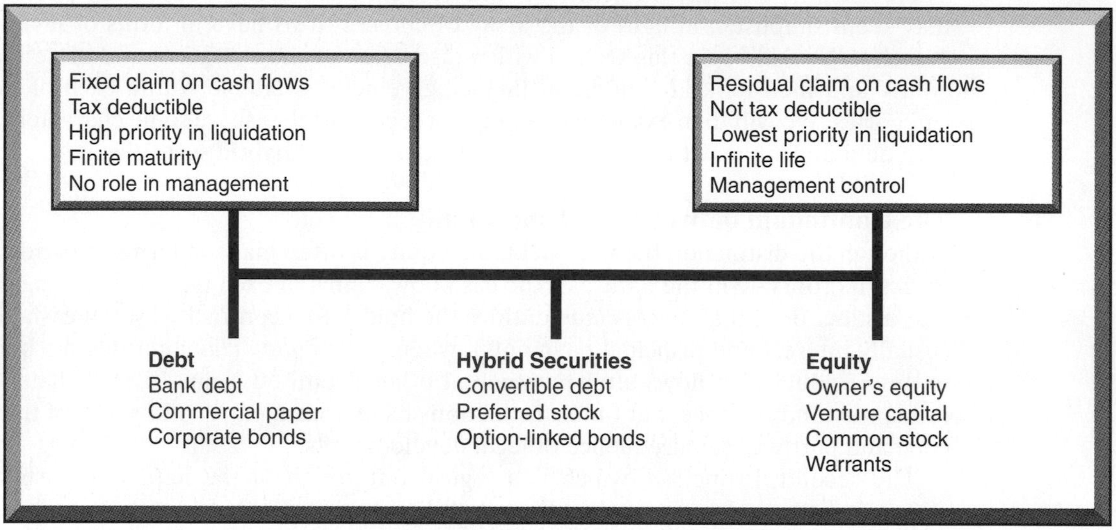

Fixed claim on cash flows
Tax deductible
High priority in liquidation
Finite maturity
No role in management

Residual claim on cash flows
Not tax deductible
Lowest priority in liquidation
Infinite life
Management control

Debt
Bank debt
Commercial paper
Corporate bonds

Hybrid Securities
Convertible debt
Preferred stock
Option-linked bonds

Equity
Owner's equity
Venture capital
Common stock
Warrants

 IN PRACTICE: A FINANCING CHECKLIST FOR CLASSIFYING SECURITIES

Some new securities at first sight are difficult to categorize as either debt or equity. To check where on the spectrum between straight debt and straight equity these securities fall, answer the following questions:

1. *Are the payments on the securities contractual or residual?*
    - If contractually set, it is closer to debt.
    - If residual, it is closer to equity.

2. *Are the payments tax-deductible?*
    - If so, it is closer to debt.
    - If not, if is closer to equity.

3. *Do the cash flows on the security have a high priority or a low priority if the firm is in financial trouble?*
    - If it has high priority, it is closer to debt.
    - If it has low priority, it is closer to equity.

4. *Does the security have a fixed life?*
    - If so, it is closer to debt.
    - If not, it is closer to equity.

5. *Does the owner of the security get a share of the control of management of the firm?*
    - If not, it is closer to debt.
    - If so, if is closer to equity. ∎

7.1 Is This Debt, or Is It Equity?

You have been asked to classify a security as debt or equity and have been provided the following characteristics for the security: It requires fixed monthly payments that are tax-deductible and it has an infinite life. Its claims on the cash flows of the firm, during operation, and on the assets, if the firm goes bankrupt, come after all debt holders' claims (including unsecured debt) are met.

a. It is debt.

b. It is equity.

c. It is a hybrid security.

A. Equity

Although most people think of equity in terms of common stock, the equity claim on a business can take a variety of forms, depending partly on whether the firm is privately owned or publicly traded and partly on the firm's growth and risk characteristics. Private firms have fewer choices available than do publicly traded firms, because they cannot issue securities to raise equity. Consequently, they have to depend either on the owner or a private entity, usually a venture capitalist, to bring in the equity needed to keep the business operating and expanding. Publicly traded firms have access to capital markets, giving them a wider array of choices.

1. Owner's Equity

Most firms, including some of the most successful companies of our time, such as Microsoft and Wal-Mart, started off as small businesses with one or a few individuals providing the seed money and plowing back the earnings of the firm into the businesses. These funds, brought in by the owners of the company, are referred to as the *owner's equity* and provide the basis for the growth and eventual success of the business.

2. Venture Capital and Private Equity

As small businesses succeed and grow, they typically run into a funding constraint wherein the funds that they have access to are insufficient to cover their investment and growth needs. A **venture capitalist** or private equity investor provides equity financing to small and often risky businesses in return for a share of the ownership of the firm.

Generally speaking, the capacity to raise funds from alternative sources or to go public will increase with the size of the firm and decrease with the uncertainty about its future prospects. Thus, smaller and riskier businesses are more likely to seek venture capital and are also more likely to be asked to give up a greater share of the value of the firm when receiving the venture capital.

7.2 The Effects of Diversification on Venture Capitalists

You are comparing the required returns of two venture capitalists who are interested in investing in the same software firm. One venture capitalist has all of his capital invested in only software firms, whereas the other has invested her capital in small companies in a variety of businesses. Which of these two will demand the higher required rate of return?

a. The venture capitalist who is invested only in software companies

b. The venture capitalist who is invested in a variety of businesses

c. More information is needed

If both venture capitalists had the same expected cash flow estimates for the business, which one would demand a larger share of the ownership for the same capital investment?

a. The venture capitalist with the higher required rate of return
b. The venture capitalist with the lower required rate of return

3. Common Stock

The conventional way for a publicly traded firm to raise equity is to issue common stock at a price the market is willing to pay. For a newly listed company, this price is estimated by the issuing entity (such as an investment banker) and is called the offering price. For an existing publicly traded company, the price at which additional equity is issued is usually based on the current market price. In some cases, the common stock issued by a company is uniform; that is, each share receives a proportional share of both the cash flows (such as dividends) and the voting rights. In other cases, different classes of common stock will provide different dividends and voting rights.

Common stock is a simple security, and it is relatively easy to understand and value. In fact, it can be argued that common stock makes feasible all other security choices for a publicly traded firm, because a firm without equity cannot issue debt or hybrid securities. The accounting treatment of common stock follows well-established precedent and can be presented easily within the conventional format of financial statements.

4. Warrants

In recent years, firms have started looking at equity alternatives to common stock. One alternative used successfully by Japanese companies in the late 1980s involved **warrants**, whereby the holders received the right to buy shares in the company at a fixed price sometime in the future in return for paying for the warrants up front. Because their value is derived from the price of the underlying common stock, warrants have to be treated as another form of equity.

Why might a firm use warrants rather than common stock to raise equity? We can think of several reasons. First, warrants are priced based on the implied volatility assigned to the underlying stock; the greater the volatility, the greater the value. To the degree that the market overestimates how risky a firm is, the firm may gain by using warrants and option-like securities. Second, warrants by themselves create no financial obligations at the time of the issue. Consequently, issuing warrants is a good way for a high-growth firm to raise funds, especially when current cash flows are low or negative. Third, for financial officers who are sensitive to the dilution created by issuing common stock, warrants seem to provide the best of both worlds—they do not create any new additional shares currently while they raise equity investment funds for current use.

7.3 STOCK PRICE VARIANCE AND THE USE OF WARRANTS

Companies with high variance in their stock prices should use warrants more than companies with low variance in their stock prices, because warrant prices increase with variance.

a. True
b. False

Explain.

IN PRACTICE: Valuing Warrants

Warrants are long-term call options, but standard option pricing models are based on the assumption that exercising an option does not affect the value of the underlying asset. This may be true for listed options on stocks, but it is not true for warrants, because their exercise increases the number of shares outstanding and brings fresh cash into the firm, both of which will affect the stock price. The expected negative impact (dilution) of their exercise will make warrants less valuable than otherwise similar call options. There are two significant differences between the inputs we use to value conventional options (see Appendix 4 for more on option pricing models) and the inputs used to value a dilution-adjusted option.

- The stock price is adjusted for the expected dilution from warrant exercise.

$$\text{Dilution-adjusted } S = (Sn_s + Wn_w)/(n_s + n_w)$$

where

$$S = \text{current value of the stock}$$
$$n_w = \text{number of warrants outstanding}$$
$$W = \text{market value of warrants outstanding}$$
$$n_s = \text{number of shares outstanding}$$

When the warrants are exercised, the number of shares outstanding will increase, reducing the stock price. The numerator reflects the market value of equity, including both stocks and warrants outstanding. Making this adjustment will lower the stock price used in the model and hence the value of the warrant. ■

5. Contingent Value Rights

Contingent value rights provide investors with the right to sell stocks for a fixed price and thus derive their value from the volatility of the stock and the desire on the part of investors to hedge away their losses. *Put options*, which are traded on the option exchanges, give their holders a similar right to sell the underlying stock at a fixed price. There are two primary differences between contingent value rights and put options. First, the proceeds from the contingent value rights sales go to the firm, whereas those from the sale of listed put options go to private parties. Second, contingent value rights tend to be much longer-term than typical listed put options.

There are several reasons why a firm may choose to issue contingent value rights. The most obvious is that the firm believes it is significantly undervalued by the market. In such a scenario, the firm may offer contingent value rights to take advantage of its belief and to provide a signal to the market of the undervaluation. Contingent value rights are also useful if the market is overestimating volatility and the put price reflects this misestimated volatility. Finally, the presence of contingent value rights as insurance may attract new investors to the market for the common stock.

B. Debt

The clear alternative to using equity, which is a residual claim, is to borrow money. This option both creates a fixed obligation to make cash flow payments and provides the lender with prior claims if the firm is in financial trouble.

1. Bank Debt

Historically, the primary source of borrowed money for all private firms and many publicly traded firms have been banks, with the interest rates on the debt based on the perceived risk of the borrower. Bank debt provides the borrower with several advantages. First, it can be used for borrowing relatively small amounts of money; in contrast, bond issues thrive on economies of scale, with larger issues having lower costs. Second, if the company is neither well known nor widely followed, bank debt provides a convenient mechanism to convey information to the lender that will help in both pricing and evaluating the loan; in other words, a borrower can provide internal information about projects and the firm to the lending bank. The presence of hundreds of investors in bond issues makes this both costly and not feasible if bonds are issued as the primary vehicle for debt. Finally, to issue bonds, firms have to submit to being rated by ratings agencies and provide sufficient information to make this rating. Dealing with a rating agency might be much more difficult and costly for many firms, especially smaller firms, than dealing with a lending bank.

Besides being a source of both long-term and short-term borrowing for firms, banks also often offer a flexible option to meet unanticipated or seasonal financing needs. This option is a *line of credit*, which the firm can draw on only if it needs financing. In most cases, a line of credit specifies an amount the firm can borrow and links the interest rate on the borrowing to a market rate, such as the prime rate or Treasury rates. The advantage of having a line of credit is that it provides the firm with access to the funds without having to pay interest costs if the funds remain unused. Thus, it is a useful type of financing for firms with volatile working capital needs. In many cases, however, the firm is required to maintain a compensating balance on which it earns either no interest or below-market rates. For instance, a firm that wants a $20 million line of credit from a bank might need to maintain a compensating balance of $2 million on which it earns no interest. The opportunity cost of having this compensating balance must be weighed against the higher interest costs that will be incurred by taking on a more conventional loan to cover working capital needs.

7.4   CORPORATE BONDS AND BANK DEBT

If a company can issue corporate bonds, it should not use bank debt.

a.   True

b.   False

Explain.

2. Bonds

For larger, publicly traded firms, an alternative to bank debt is to issue bonds. Generally speaking, bond issues have several advantages for these firms. The first is that bonds usually carry more favorable financing terms than equivalent bank debt, largely because risk is shared by a larger number of financial market investors. The second is that bond issues might provide a chance for the issuer to add on special features that could not be added on to bank debt. For instance, bonds can be convertible into common stock or be tied to commodity prices (commodity bonds). When borrowing money, firms have to make a variety of choices, including the maturity of the borrowing (short-term or long-term), whether the debt should have fixed interest payments or an interest rate tied to market rates (fixed and floating rates), the nature of the security offered to those buying the bonds (secured versus unsecured), and how the debt will be repaid over time. In Chapter 9, we will examine how best to make these choices.

3. Leases

A firm often borrows money to finance the acquisition of an asset needed for its operations. An alternative approach that might accomplish the same goal is to lease the asset. In a lease, the firm commits to making fixed payments to the owner of the asset for the rights to use the asset. These fixed payments are either fully or partially tax-deductible, depending on how the lease is categorized for accounting purposes. Failure to make lease payments initially results in the loss of the leased asset but can also result in bankruptcy, though the claims of the lessors (owners of the leased assets) may sometimes be subordinated to the claims of other lenders to the firm.

A lease agreement is usually categorized as either an operating lease or a capital lease. For *operating leases*, the term of the lease agreement is shorter than the life of the asset, and the present value of lease payments is generally much lower than the actual price of the asset. At the end of the life of the lease, the asset reverts back to the lessor, who will either offer to sell it to the lessee or lease it to somebody else. The lessee usually has the right to cancel the lease and return the asset to the lessor. Thus, the ownership of the asset in an operating lease clearly resides with the lessor, with the lessee bearing little or no risk if the asset becomes obsolete. Operating leases cover the store spaces leased out by specialty retailing firms like The Gap and Ann Taylor, for instance.

A *capital lease* generally lasts for the life of the asset, with the present value of lease payments covering the price of the asset. A capital lease generally cannot be canceled, and the lease can be renewed at the end of its life at a reduced rate or the asset acquired by the lessee at a favorable price. In many cases, the lessor is not obligated to pay insurance and taxes on the asset, leaving these obligations up to the lessee; the lessee consequently reduces the lease payments, leading to what are called *net leases*. A capital lease places substantial risk on the shoulders of the lessee if the asset loses value or becomes obsolete. Although the differences between operating and financial leases are obvious, some lease arrangements do not fit neatly into one or another of these extremes; rather, they share some features of both types of leases. These leases are called *combination leases*.

7.5 DEBT MATURITY AND INTEREST RATES

Assume that long-term interest rates are much higher than short-term rates (a steeply upward-sloping yield curve) and that your investment banker advises you to issue short-term debt because it is cheaper than long-term debt. Is this statement true?

a. Yes

b. False

Why, or why not?

IN PRACTICE: Leasing versus Borrowing

If borrowing money to buy an asset and leasing the asset are both variations on debt, why might a firm choose one over the other? We can think of several factors that may sway firms in this choice:

- **Service.** In some cases, the lessor of an asset will bundle service agreements with the lease agreement and offer to provide the lessee with service support during the life of the lease. If this service is unique—either because of the lessor's reputation or because the lessor is also the manufacturer of the asset—and if the cost of obtaining this service separately is high, the firm may choose to lease rather than buy the asset. IBM, for instance, has traditionally leased computers to users, with an offer to service them when needed.

- **Flexibility.** Some lease agreements provide the lessee with the option to exchange the asset for a different or upgraded version during the life of the lease. This flexibility is particularly valuable when the firm is unsure of its needs and when technology changes rapidly. Flexibility is also useful when the asset is required for a period much shorter than the life of the asset, because buying the asset and selling it again is expensive in terms of transaction time and cost.

- **Tax Reasons.** The classic reason provided for leasing is that different entities face different tax rates. An entity with a high tax rate buys an asset and leases it to one with no or a low tax rate. By doing so, the lessor obtains the tax benefits, which are greater because of its higher tax rate. The lessee, in turn, gets the use of the asset and also gains by sharing in some of the tax benefits.

In addition, if a lease qualifies as an operating lease, it essentially operates off-balance-sheet debt and may make firms that use it look safer to a careless analyst. If firms consider leasing as an alternative to borrowing, the choice becomes primarily financial. Operating leases create lease obligations to the firm, and these obligations are tax-deductible. The present value of these after-tax lease obligations has to be weighed against the present value of the after-tax cash flows that would have been generated if the firm had borrowed the money and bought the asset instead. The after-tax cash flows from borrowing and buying the asset have to include not only the interest and principal payments on the debt but also the tax benefits accruing from depreciation from owning the asset and the expected value of the asset at the end of operations. ■

C. Hybrid Securities

Summarizing our analysis thus far, equity represents a residual claim on the cash flows and assets of the firm and is generally associated with management control. Debt, on the other hand, represents a fixed claim on the cash flows and assets of the firm and is usually not associated with management control. There are a number of securities that do not fall neatly into either of these two categories; rather, they share some characteristics with equity and some with debt. These securities are called hybrid securities.

1. Convertible Bond

A **convertible bond** is a bond that can be converted into a predetermined number of shares at the discretion of the bondholder. Although it generally does not pay to convert at the time of the bond issue, conversion becomes a more attractive option as stock prices increase. Firms generally add conversions options to bonds to lower the interest rate paid on the bonds.

In a typical convertible bond, the bondholder is given the option to convert the bond into a specified number of shares of stock. The *conversion ratio* measures the number of shares of stock for which each bond may be exchanged. Stated differently, the *market conversion value* is the current value of the shares for which the bonds can be exchanged. The *conversion premium* is the excess of the bond value over the conversion value of the bond.

Thus, a convertible bond with a par value of $1,000, which is convertible into fifty shares of stock, has a conversion ratio of 50. The conversion ratio can also be used to compute a conversion price—the par value divided by the conversion ratio—yielding a conversion price of $20. If the current stock price is $25, the market conversion value is $1,250 (50 * $25). If the convertible bond is trading at $1,300, the conversion premium is $50.

IN PRACTICE: A Simple Approach to Decomposing Debt and Equity

The value of a convertible debt can be decomposed into straight debt and equity components using a simple approach. Because the price of a convertible bond is the sum of the straight debt and the conversion option components, the value of the straight bond component in conjunction with the market price of the convertible bond should be sufficient to estimate the conversion option component, which is also the equity component:

Value of equity component = Price of convertible bond
− Value of straight bond component

The value of the straight bond component can be estimated using the coupon payments on the convertible bond, the maturity of the bond, and the market interest rate the company would have to pay on a straight debt issue. This last input can be estimated directly if the company also trades straight bonds in the market place, or it can be based on the bond rating, if any, assigned to the company.

For instance, assume that you have a ten-year convertible bond, with a 5% coupon rate trading at $1,050, and that the company has a debt rating of BBB (with a market interest rate of 8%). The value of the straight bond, assuming annual coupons and equity components, can be estimated as follows:

Straight bond component = $50 (PVA, 10 years, 8%) + $1000/1.08^{10} = $799
Equity component = $1,050 − $799 = $251 ∎

7.6 Convertible Debt and Yields

The yields on convertible bonds are much lower than the yields on straight bonds issued by a company. Therefore, convertible debt is cheaper than straight debt.

a.   True
b.   False
Explain.

2. Preferred Stock

Preferred stock is another security that shares some characteristics with debt and some with equity. Like debt, preferred stock has a fixed dollar dividend; if the firm does not have the cash to pay the dividend, it is accumulated and paid in a period when there are sufficient earnings. Like debt, preferred stockholders do not have a share of control in the firm, and their voting privileges are strictly restricted to issues that might affect their claims on the firm's cash flows or assets. Like equity, payments to preferred stockholders are not tax-deductible and come out of after-tax cash. Also like equity, preferred stock does not have a maturity date when the face value is due. In terms of priority, in the case of bankruptcy, preferred stockholders have to wait until the debt holders' claims have been met before receiving any portion of the assets of the firm.

Although accountants and ratings agencies continue to treat preferred stock as equity, it can be argued that the fixed commitments that preferred stock create are like debt obligations and have to be dealt with likewise. The obligations created by preferred stock are generally less onerous than those created by debt; however, because they are generally cumulated, they cannot cause default and they do not have priority over debt claims in the case of bankruptcy.

Unlike convertible debt, which can be decomposed into equity and debt components, preferred stock is not easily classifiable. It cannot really be treated as debt, because preferred dividends are not tax-deductible and certainly cannot be viewed as the equivalent of equity because of the differences in cash flow claims and control. Consequently, preferred stock is treated as a third component of capital, in addition to debt and equity, for purposes of capital structure analysis and for estimating the cost of capital.

7.7 PREFERRED STOCK AND EQUITY

Many ratings agencies and regulators treat preferred stock as equity in computing debt ratios, because it does not have a finite maturity and firms cannot be forced into bankruptcy if they fail to pay preferred dividends. Do you agree with this categorization?

a.　Yes

b.　No

Explain.

3. Option-Linked Bonds

In recent years, firms have recognized the value of combining options with straight bonds to create bonds that more closely match the firm's specific needs. We considered one when with convertible bonds. Consider two other examples. In the first, commodity companies issued bonds linking the principal and even interest payments to the price of the commodity. Thus interest payments would rise if the price of the commodity increased, and vice versa. The benefit for the company was that it tailored the cash flows on the bond to the cash flows of the firm and reduced the likelihood of default. These **commodity-linked bonds** can be viewed as a combination of a straight security and a call option on the underlying commodity. In the second example, consider insurance companies that have issued bonds whereby the principal on the bond is reduced in the case of a specified catastrophe and remains unaffected in its absence. For instance, an insurance firm that has the bulk of its revenues coming from homeowners' insurance in California might attach a provision that reduces principal or interest in the case of a major earthquake. Again, the rationale is to provide the firm with some breathing room when it needs it the most—when a catastrophe creates huge cash outflows for the firm.

ILLUSTRATION 7.1   Financing Choices in 2008—Disney, Aracruz and Tata Chemicals

Disney, Aracruz, and Tata Chemicals all have debt on their books in 2008. We will begin by taking a look at both the amount of the debt and the composition of this debt in Table 7.1.

Looking at the breakdown of the debt, we can draw some preliminary conclusions:

- Disney used the corporate bond market much more extensively than Aracruz and Tata Chemicals in 2008, with 92% of its debt taking the form of bonds, reflecting both its standing as a large market capitalization company and its access to capital markets as a U.S.-based company.
- While Disney has the higher proportion of short-term debt of the three companies, it is the only one of the three companies with debt maturing in more than ten years.

Table 7.1   DEBT BREAKDOWN FOR DISNEY, ARACRUZ, AND TATA CHEMICALS

	Disney	**Aracruz**	**Tata Chemicals**
Debt due	$13.27 billion	R$24.20 billion	Rs42.22 billion
Loans vs. Bonds			
Maturity			
Leases	Has operating leases with a debt value of $1.72 billion (see Chapter 4)	No stated lease commitments	Small lease commitments.
Fixed vs. Floating	76% fixed rate 24% floating rate	100% fixed rate	100% fixed rate
Currency	90% U.S. dollar 10% Japanese yen	100% Brazilian R$	97% rupees 3% U.S. dollar
Other	43% of bonds are callable 10% of bonds are putable	Small portion of debt is convertible Bank debt is term loans	Bank debt is term loans

That may also be a reflection of its use of the bond market, since banks, especially in emerging markets, may be unwilling to commit to long-term loans.

- Disney is the only one of the three companies with a significant portion of floating rate debt for which interest rates will vary across time as a function of index rates (LIBOR, in the case of Disney).

- All three companies borrow predominantly in their domestic currencies. Disney does have some Japanese yen debt, and Tata Chemicals has two small U.S. dollar bond issues.

- Disney's corporate bonds follow the conventional form and have only coupon payments during their lifetime, with the face value due at the end (bullet payments). In contrast, the bank loans used by Aracruz and Tata Chemicals require that the principal be repaid over the course of the debt (term loans).

- A large portion of Disney's bonds can be called back by the firm if it chooses to do so, an option that will generally be exercised if interest rates drop significantly. A small portion of the bonds can be put back by the bondholders to the firm, a protection against actions that Disney may take that reduce the value of the bonds.

While we did not break out Bookscape's debt in Table 7.1, the only debt it has takes the form of an operating lease on its premises. As we noted in Chapter 4, the present value of the lease commitments (of $750,000 each year for the next 25 years) is $9.6 million.

FINANCING BEHAVIOR

We spent the last section looking at the different financing choices available to a firm. They all represent external financing—that is, funds raised from outside the firm. Many firms meet the bulk of their funding needs internally with cash flows from existing assets. In this section, we begin by presenting the distinction between internal and external financing and the factors that may affect how much firms draw on each source. We then turn our attention again to external financing. We consider how and why the financing choices may change as a firm goes through different stages of its life cycle, from startup to expansion to high growth to stable growth and on to decline. We will follow up by looking why some choices dominate in some stages and do not play a role in others.

Internal versus External Financing

Cash flows generated by the existing assets of a firm can be categorized as internal financing. Because these cash flows belong to the equity owners of the business, they are called *internal equity*. Cash flows raised outside the firm, whether from private sources or from financial markets, can be categorized as *external financing*. External financing can, of course, take the form of new debt, new equity, or hybrids.

A firm may prefer internal to external financing for several reasons. For private firms, external financing is typically difficult to raise, and even when it is available (from a venture capitalist, for instance) it is accompanied by a loss of control (the venture capitalist wants a share of control). For publicly traded firms, external financing may be easier to raise, but it is still expensive in terms of issuance costs (especially in the case of new equity). Internally generated cash flows, on the other hand, can be used to finance operations without incurring large transaction costs or losing control.

Despite these advantages, there are limits to the use of internal financing to fund projects. First, firms have to recognize that internal equity has the same cost as external equity, before the transaction cost differences are factored in. The cost of equity, computed using a risk and return model, such as the CAPM or APM, applies as much to internal as to external equity. Thus, Disney has a cost of equity of 8.91%, estimated as the cost of equity in Chapter 4, and this cost applies to both internal equity (or retained earnings) and external equity (new stock or equity option issues). After transactions costs are factored in, external equity will have a slightly higher cost. This equivalence implies that a project financed with internal equity should pass the same test as a project financed with external equity; Disney has to earn a return on equity that is greater than 8.91% on projects funded with either external equity or retained earnings. Second, internal equity is clearly limited to the cash flows generated by the firm on its operations. Even if the firm does not pay dividends, these cash flows may not be sufficient to finance the firm's projects. Depending entirely on internal equity can therefore result in project delays or the possible loss of these projects to competitors. Third, managers should not make the mistake of thinking that the stock price does not matter just because they use only internal equity for financing projects. Stockholders in firms whose stock prices have dropped are much less likely to trust their managers to reinvest their cash flows for them than are stockholders in firms with rising stock prices.

Growth, Risk, and Financing

As firms grow and mature, their cash flows and risk exposure follow fairly predictable patterns. Cash flows become larger relative to firm value, and risk approaches the average risk for all firms. The financing choices that a firm makes will reflect these changes. To understand these choices, let us consider five stages in a firm's life cycle:

1. *Startup.* This represents the initial stage after a business has been formed. Generally, this business will be a private business, funded by owner's equity and perhaps bank debt. It will also be restricted in its funding needs as it attempts to gain customers and get established.

2. *Expansion.* Once a firm succeeds in attracting customers and establishing a presence in the market, its funding needs increase as it looks to expand. Because this firm is unlikely to be generating high cash flows internally at this stage and investment needs will be high, the owners will generally look to private equity or venture capital initially to fill the gap. Some firms in this position will make the transition to publicly traded firms and raise the funds they need by issuing common stock.

3. *High growth.* With the transition to a publicly traded firm, financing choices increase. Although the firm's revenues are growing rapidly, earnings are likely to lag behind revenues and internal cash flows lag behind reinvestment needs. Generally, publicly traded firms at this stage will look to more equity issues, in the form of common stock, warrants, and other equity options. If they are using debt, convertible debt is most likely to be used to raise capital.

4. ***Mature growth.***   As growth starts leveling off, firms will generally find two phenomena occurring. The earnings and cash flows will continue to increase rapidly, reflecting past investments, and the need to invest in new projects will decline. The net effect will be an increase in the proportion of funding needs covered by internal financing and a change in the type of external financing used. These firms will be more likely to use debt in the form of bank debt or corporate bonds to finance their investment needs.

5. ***Decline.***   The last stage in this corporate life cycle is decline. Firms in this stage will find both revenues and earnings starting to decline as their businesses mature and new competitors overtake them. Existing investments are likely to continue to produce cash flows, albeit at a declining pace, and the firm has little need for new investments. Thus, internal financing is likely to exceed reinvestment needs. Firms are unlikely to be making fresh stock or bond issues but are more likely to be retiring existing debt and buying back stock. In a sense, the firm is gradually liquidating itself.

Figure 7.2 summarizes both the internal financing capabilities and external financing choices of firms at different stages in the growth life cycle.

Not all firms go through these five phases, and the choices are not the same for all of them. First, many firms never make it past the startup stage in this process. Of the tens of thousands of businesses that are started each year by entrepreneurs, many fail to survive, and even those that survive often continue as small businesses with little expansion potential. Second, not all successful private firms become publicly traded corporations. Some firms, like Cargill and Koch Industries, remain private and manage to raise enough capital to continue growing at healthy rates over long periods. Third, there are firms that seem to have no need for external financing even when they are in high growth, because internal funds prove more than sufficient to finance this growth. There are high-growth firms that issue debt, and low-growth firms that raise equity capital. In short, there are numerous exceptions, but the life cycle framework still provides a useful device to explain why different kinds of firms do what they do and what causes them to deviate from the prescribed financing choices.

Note that when we look at a firm's choices in terms of debt and equity at different stages in the growth life cycle, there are two things we do not do in this analysis. First, we do not explain in any detail why firms at each stage in the growth life cycle pick the types of financing that they do. Second, we do not consider what kind of debt is best for a firm—short-term or long-term, dollar or foreign currency, fixed rate or floating rate. The reason is that this choice has more to do with the types of assets the firm owns and the nature of the cash flows from these assets than with where in its life cycle a firm is in. We will return to examine this issue in more detail in Chapter 9.

How Firms Have Actually Raised Funds

In the first part of this chapter, we noted the range of choices in terms of both debt and equity that are available to firms to raise funds. Before we look at which of these choices should be used, it is worth noting how firms have historically raised funds

Figure 7.2 Life Cycle Analysis of Financing

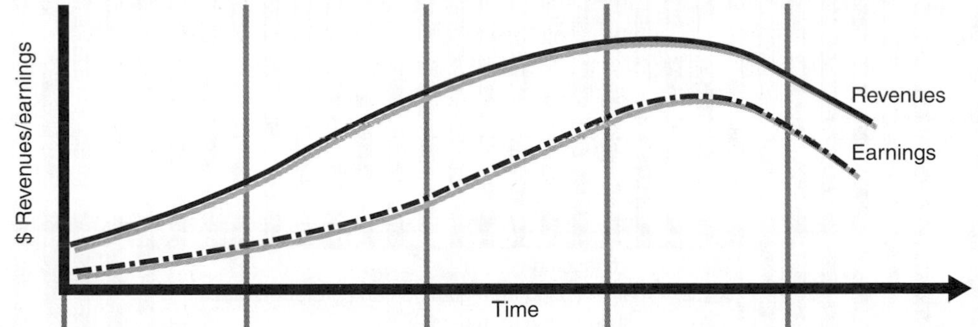

	Stage 1	Stage 2	Stage 3	Stage 4	Stage 5
External funding needs	High, but constrained by infrastructure	High, relative to firm value	Moderate, relative to firm value	Declining, as a percent of firm value	Low, as projects dry up
Internal financing	Negative or low	Negative or low	Low, relative to funding needs	High, relative to funding needs	More than funding needs
External financing	Owner's equity Bank debt	Venture capital Common stock	Common stock Warrants Convertibles	Debt	Retire debt Repurchase stock
Growth stage	Stage 1 Start-up	Stage 2 Rapid expansion	Stage 3 High growth	Stage 4 Mature growth	Stage 5 Decline
Financing transitions	**Accessing private equity**	**Initial public offering**	**Seasoned equity issue**	**Bond issues**	

for operations. Firms have used debt, equity, and hybrids to raise funds, but their dependence on each source has varied across time. In the United States, for instance, firms collectively have generally raised external financing through debt issues rather than equity issues, and have primarily raised equity funds internally from operations. Figure 7.3 illustrates the proportion of funds from new debt and equity issues, as well as from internal funds, for U.S. corporations between 1975 and 2007.

In every year, firms have relied more heavily on internal financing to meet capital needs than on external financing. Furthermore, when external financing is used, it is more likely to be new debt rather than new equity or preferred stock.

There are wide differences across firms in the United States in how much and what type of external financing is used. The evidence is largely consistent with the conclusions that emerge from looking at a firm's place in the growth cycle in Figure 7.2. Fluck, Holtz-Eakin, and Rosen looked at several thousand firms that were incorporated

Figure 7.3 External and Internal Financing at U.S. Firms

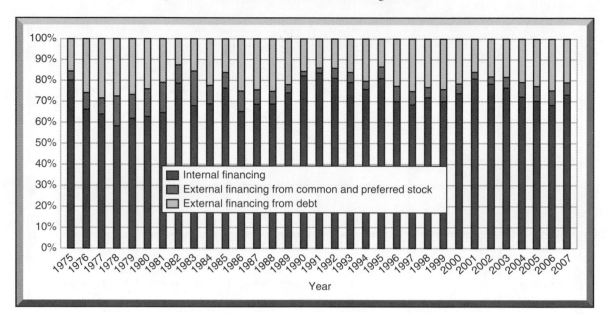

in Wisconsin; most of these firms were small, private businesses.[2] The authors find that these firms depend almost entirely on internal financing, owner's equity, and bank debt to cover capital needs. The proportion of funds provided by internal financing increases as the firms became older and more established. A small proportion of private businesses manage to raise capital from venture capitalists and private equity investors. Many of these firms ultimately plan on going public, and the returns to the private equity investors come at the time of the public offering. Bradford and Smith looked at sixty computer-related firms prior to their initial public offerings (IPOs) and noted that forty-one of these firms had private equity infusions before the public offering.[3] The median number of private equity investors in these firms was between two and three, and the median proportion of the firm owned by these investors was 43.8%; an average of 3.2 years elapsed between the private equity investment and the IPO at these firms. Although this is a small sample of firms in one sector, it does suggest that private equity plays a substantial role in allowing firms to bridge the gap between being small private businesses and becoming publicly traded firms.

[2]Z. Fluck, D. Holtz-Eakin, and H.S. Rosen, "Where Does the Money Come From? The Financing of Small Entrepreneurial Enterprises," working paper, NYU Salomon Center, 1998. This is a unique data set, because this information is usually either not collected or not available to researchers.
[3]T. Bradford and R. C. Smith, "Private Equity: Sources and Uses," *Journal of Applied Corporate Finance* 10, no. 1:89–97.

Figure 7.4   Financing Patterns for G-7 Countries: 1984–91

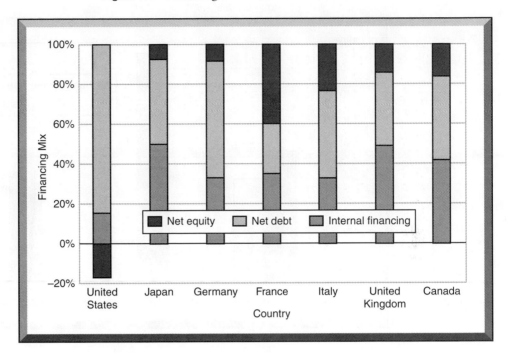

When we compare the financing patterns of U.S. companies to companies in other countries, we find some evidence that U.S. companies are much more heavily dependent on debt than equity for external financing than their counterparts in other countries. Figure 7.4 summarizes new security issues in the G-7 countries between 1984 to 1991.[4]

Net equity in Figure 7.4 refers to the difference between new equity issues and stock buybacks. Firms in the United States bought back more stock than they issued during the period of this comparison, leading to negative net equity. In addition, a comparison of financing patterns in the United States, Germany, and Japan reveals that German and Japanese firms are much more dependent on bank debt than firms in the United States, which are much likely to issue bonds.[5] Figure 7.5 provides a comparison of bank loans and corporate bonds as sources of debt for firms in the three countries, as reported in Hackethal and Schmidt.[6]

---

[4]See Raghuram G. Rajan and Luigi Zingales, "What Do We Know About Capital Structure? Some Evidence From International Data," *Journal of Finance* 50, no. 5:1421–1460. This is based on OECD data, summarized in the OECD publication *Financial Statements of Non-Financial Enterprises*. The G7 countries represent seven of the largest economies in the world. The leaders of these countries meet every year to discuss economic policy.

[5]A. Hackethal and R. H. Schmidt, "Financing Patterns: Measurement Concepts and Empirical Results," working paper, University of Frankfurt, 1999. They compare financing patterns in the three countries.

[6]A. Hackethal and R. H. Schmidt, "Financing Patterns: Measurement Concepts and Empirical Results," working paper, University of Frankfurt, 1999.

Figure 7.5 Bonds versus Bank Loans: 1990–96

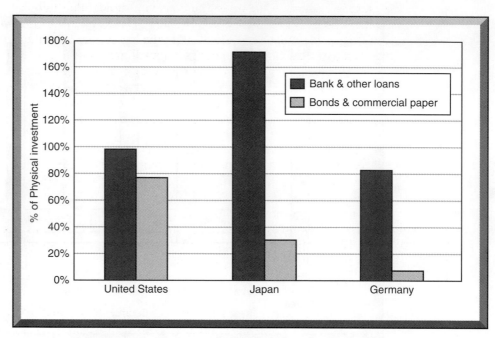

There is also some evidence that firms in some emerging markets, such as Brazil and India, use equity (internal and equity) much more than debt to finance their operations. Some of this dependence can be attributed to government regulation that discourages the use of debt, either directly, by requiring the debt ratios of firms to be below specified limits, or indirectly, by limiting the deductibility of interest expenses for tax purposes. One of the explanations for the greater dependence of U.S. corporations on debt issues relies on where they are in their growth life cycle. Firms in the United States, in contrast to firms in emerging markets, are much more likely to be in the mature growth stage of the life cycle. Consequently, firms in the United States should be less dependent on external equity. Another factor is that firms in the United States have far more access to corporate bond markets than do firms in other markets. Firms in Europe, for instance, often have to raise new debt from banks, rather than bond markets. This may constrain them in the use of new debt.

7.8 CORPORATE BOND MARKETS AND THE USE OF DEBT

Companies in Europe and emerging markets have historically depended on bank debt to borrow and have had limited access to corporate bond markets. In recent years, their access to corporate bond markets, both domestically and internationally, has increased. As a result, which of the following would you expect to happen to debt ratios in these countries?

a. Debt ratios should go up.

b. Debt ratios should go down.

c. Debt ratios should not change much.

Why Public Firms Are Reluctant to Issue New Shares: A Behavioral Perspective
If there is a common theme to the financing choices that publicly traded firms make, at least in the United States, it is that they are reluctant to issue new shares to raise funds, something that manifests itself in the low proportion of new funding that comes from equity (see Figure 7.3) and in an unwillingness to use rights issues, even though it is a less expensive way of raising equity than issuing new shares at the current stock price. Since the same firms are willing to use internal equity (retained earnings) to fund projects, we cannot attribute this behavior to an aversion to equity or a preference for debt. There are two behavioral explanations:

1. ***Anchoring/framing.*** A common theme in behavioral finance is that how individuals make decisions is a function of how they frame the outcomes and their choices of anchors. For better or worse, the number that equity research analysts seem to pay the most attention to when looking at corporate earnings is earnings per share. Any new equity issue, no matter what its justification, increases the number of shares outstanding and by doing so reduces earnings per share, at least in the near term. When firms do decide to raise external equity, rights issues, widely used by European companies to raise equity, are used infrequently by U.S. companies, primarily because it results in more shares being issued to raise the same funds.

2. ***Overconfidence.*** Malmendier, Tate and Yan (2007) note that the same overconfidence that leads managers to overestimate cash flows on investments also can lead them to believe that their stock is underpriced by the market, a perception that makes it less likely that they will issue shares at the price.[7]

It is interesting to note that the aversion to reducing earnings per share and issuing new equity is selective. The same firms that are reluctant to make rights issues are more than willing to split their stock and seem to put aside the unwillingness to issue new common stock when issuing convertible debt and preferred stock. Put another way, managers seem more averse to actions that increase the number of shares today than to actions that potentially could increase the number of shares in the future.

THE PROCESS OF RAISING CAPITAL

Looking back at Figure 7.2, we note four financing transitions, where the source of funding for a firm is changed by the introduction of a new financing choice. The first occurs when a private firm approaches a private equity investor or venture capitalist for new financing. The second occurs when a private firm decides to offer its equity to financial markets and become a publicly traded firm. The third takes place when a publicly traded firm decides to revisit equity markets to raise more equity. The fourth occurs when a publicly traded firm decides to raise debt from financial markets by issuing bonds. In this section, we examine the process of making each of these transitions. Because the processes for making seasoned equity and bond issues are very similar, we will consider them together.

---

[7]Malmendier, U., G. Tate and J. Yan, 2007, Corporate Finance Policies with Overconfident Managers, NBER working Paper 13570.

Private Firm Expansion: Raising Funds from Private Equity

Private firms that need more equity capital than can be provided by their owners can approach venture capitalists and private equity investors. Venture capital can prove useful at different stages of a private firm's existence. *Seed-money venture capital*, for instance, is provided to startup firms that want to test a concept or develop a new product, whereas *startup venture capital* allows firms that have established products and concepts to develop and market them. Additional rounds of venture capital allow private firms that have more established products and markets to expand. There are five steps associated with how venture capital gets to be provided to firms and how venture capitalists ultimately profit from these investments.

1. *Provoke Equity Investor's Interest.* The first step that a private firm wanting to raise private equity has to take is to get private equity investors interested in investing in it. There are a number of factors that help the private firm at this stage. One is the *type of business* that the private firm is in and how attractive this business is to private equity investors. The second factor is the track record of the top managers of the firm, who have a track record of converting private businesses into publicly traded firms and have an easier time raising private equity capital.

2. *Valuation and Return Assessment.* Once private equity investors become interested in investing in a firm, the value of the private firm has to be assessed by looking at both its current and expected prospects. This is usually done using the *venture capital method*, whereby the earnings of the private firm are forecast in a future year when the company is expected to go public (or be sold to a public acquirer). These earnings, in conjunction with a price-earnings multiple, estimated by looking at publicly traded firms in the same business, are used to assess the value of the firm at the time of the public sale, called the *exit or terminal value*.

    For instance, assume that Bookscape is expected to have an IPO in three years and that the net income in three years for the firm is expected to be $4 million. If the price-earnings ratio of publicly traded retail firms is 25, this would yield an estimated exit value of $100 million. This value is discounted back to the present at what venture capitalists call a *target rate of return*, which measures what venture capitalists believe is a justifiable return, given the risk to which they are exposed. This target rate of return is usually set at a much higher level than the traditional cost of equity for the firm.[8]

$$\text{Discounted terminal value} = \text{Estimated exit value}/(1 + \text{Target return})^n$$

    Using the Bookscape example again, if the venture capitalist requires a target return on 30% on his or her investment, the discounted terminal value for Bookscape would be

$$\text{Discounted terminal value for Bookscape} = \$100 \text{ million}/1.30^3$$
$$= \$45.52 \text{ million}$$

---

[8]For instance, the target rate of return for private equity investors can range from 30% for later stage financing to 50-60% for early stage financing. Some of this return is to cover survival risk, i.e., the risk that many small businesses will not make it to the exit point.

3. ***Structuring the Deal.*** In structuring the deal to bring private equity into the firm, the private equity investor and the firm have to negotiate two factors. First, the investor has to determine what proportion of the value of the firm he or she will demand in return for the private equity investment. The owners of the firm, on the other hand, have to determine how much of the firm they are willing to give up in return for the capital. In these assessments, the amount of new capital being brought into the firm has to be measured against the estimated firm value. In the Bookscape example, assuming that the venture capitalist is considering investing $12 million, he or she would want to own at least 20.86% of the firm.[9]

$$\text{Ownership proportion} = \text{Capital provided/Estimated value}$$
$$= \$12/(\$45.52 + \$12) = 20.86\%$$

Second, the private equity investor will impose constraints on new investments and fresh financing on the managers of the firm in which the investment is being made. This is to ensure that the private equity investors are protected and that they have a say in how the firm is run.

4. ***Post-deal management.*** Once the private equity investment has been made in a firm, the investor will often take an active role in the management of the firm. Private equity investors and venture capitalists bring not only a wealth of management experience to the process but also contacts that can be used to raise more capital and get fresh business for the firm.

5. ***Exit.*** Private equity investors and venture capitalists invest in private businesses because they are interested in earning a high return on these investments. How will these returns be manifested? There are three ways a private equity investor can profit from an investment in a business. The first and usually most lucrative alternative is an IPO made by the private firm. Although venture capitalists do not usually liquidate their investments at the time of the IPO, they can sell at least a portion of their holdings once they are traded.[10] The second alternative is to sell the private business to another firm; the acquiring firm might have strategic or financial reasons for the acquisition. The third alternative is to withdraw cash flows from the firm and liquidate the firm over time. This strategy would not be appropriate for a high-growth firm, but it may make sense if investments made by the firm no longer earn excess returns.

While there are well-known and publicized success stories of private businesses making it to prosperity, the reality is more sobering. Most private businesses do not make it. There are several studies that back up this statement, though they vary in the failure rates that they find. A study of 5,196 startups in Australia found that the annual failure rate was in excess of 9%, and that 64% of the businesses failed in a

---

[9]Many private equity investors draw a distinction between premoney valuation, or the value of the company without the cash inflow from the private equity investor ($45.52), and postmoney valuation ($57.52), which is the value of the company with the cash influx from the private equity investors.

[10]B. S. Black and R. J. Gilson, "Venture Capital and the Structure of Capital Markets: Banks versus Stock Markets," *Journal of Financial Economics* 47:243–277. They argue that one of the reasons why venture capital is much more active in the United States than in Japan or Germany is because the option to go public is much more easily exercised in the United States.

ten-year period.[11] Knaup and Piazza (2005, 2008) used data from the Bureau of Labor Statistics Quarterly Census of Employment and Wages (QCEW) to compute survival statistics across firms.[12] This census contains information on more than 8.9 million U.S. businesses in both the public and private sector. Using a seven-year database from 1998 to 2005, the authors concluded that only 44% of all businesses that were founded in 1998 survived at least four years, and only 31% made it through all seven years.

From Private to Publicly Traded Firm: The IPO

A private firm is restricted in its access to external financing, both for debt and equity. In our earlier discussion of equity choices, we pointed out the hard bargain venture capitalists extract for investing equity in a private business. As firms become larger and their capital needs increase, some of them decide to become publicly traded and to raise capital by issuing shares of their equity to financial markets.

Staying Private versus Going Public

When a private firm becomes publicly traded, the primary benefit is increased access to financial markets and capital for projects. This access to new capital is a significant gain for high-growth businesses with large and lucrative investment opportunities. A secondary benefit is that the owners of the private firm are able to cash in on their success by attaching a market value to their holdings. These benefits have to be weighed against the potential costs of being publicly traded. The most significant of these costs is the loss of control that may ensue from being a publicly traded firm. As firms get larger and the owners are tempted to sell some of their holdings over time, the owner's share of the outstanding shares will generally decline. If the stockholders in the firm come to believe that the owner's association with the firm is hurting rather than helping it, they may decide to put pressure for the owner's removal.

Other costs associated with being a publicly traded firm are the information disclosure requirements and the legal requirements.[13] A private firm experiencing challenging market conditions (declining sales, higher costs) may be able to hide its problems from competitors, whereas a publicly traded firm has no choice but to reveal the information. Yet another cost is that the firm has to spend a significant portion of its time on investor relations, a process in which equity research analysts following the firm are cultivated and provided with information about the firm's prospects.[14]

Overall, the net tradeoff to going public will generally be positive for firms with large growth opportunities and funding needs. It will be smaller for firms that have

---

[11] John Watson and Jim Everett, "Do Small Businesses Have High Failure Rates?" *Journal of Small Business Management* 34:45–63.

[12] Amy E. Knaup, "Survival and Longevity in the Business Employment Dynamics Data," *Monthly Labor Review* (May 2005): 50–56; Amy E. Knaup and M. C. Piazza, "Business Employment Dynamics Data: Survival and Longevity," *Monthly Labor Review* (September 2007): 3–10.

[13] The costs are twofold. One is the cost of producing and publicizing the information itself. The other is the loss of control over how much and when to reveal information about the firm to others.

[14] "Cultivated" may sound like an odd word choice, but it is accurate. Buy recommendations from equity research analysts following the firm provoke investor interest and can have a significant impact on the stock price; sell recommendations, on the other hand, can cause the stock price to drop. This is especially true for small, lightly followed firms.

smaller growth opportunities, substantial internal cash flows, and owners who value the complete control they have over the firms.

Steps in an IPO

Assuming that the benefits outweigh the costs, there are five steps involved in an IPO.

Step 1:   ***Choose an investment banker based on reputation and marketing skills.***   In most IPOs, this investment banker underwrites the issue and guarantees a specified price for the stock. This investment banker then puts together a group of several banks (called a syndicate) to spread the risk of the offering and to increase marketing reach.[15] Private firms tend to pick investment bankers based on reputation and expertise, rather than price. A good reputation provides the credibility and the comfort level needed for investors to buy the stock of the firm; expertise applies not only to the pricing of the issue and the process of going public but also to other financing decisions that might be made in the aftermath of a public issue. The investment banking agreement is then negotiated, rather than opened up for competition.

Step 2:   ***Assess the value of the company and set issue details.***   This valuation is generally done by the lead investment bank, with substantial information provided by the issuing firm. The value is sometimes estimated using discounted cash flow models. More often, though, the value is estimated by using a multiple, like a price–earnings ratio, and by looking at the pricing of comparable firms that are already publicly traded. Whichever approach is used, the absence of substantial historical information, in conjunction with the fact that these are small companies with high growth prospects, makes the estimation of value an uncertain one at best. Once the value for the company has been estimated, the value per share is obtained by dividing by the number of shares, which is determined by the price range the issuer would like to have on the issue. If the equity in the firm is valued at $50 million, for example, the number of shares would be set at 5 million to get a target price range of $10, or 1 million shares to get a target price range of $50, per share. The final step in this process is to set the offering price per share. Most investment banks set the offering price below the estimated value per share for two reasons. First, it reduces the bank's risk exposure. If the offering price is set too high and the investment bank is unable to sell all of the shares offered, it has to use its own funds to buy the shares at the offering price. Second, investors and investment banks view it as a good sign if the stock increases in price in the immediate aftermath of the issue. For the clients of the investment banker who get the shares at the offering price, there is an immediate payoff; for the issuing company, the ground has been prepared for future issues.

Step 3:   ***Gauge investor demand at the offering price.***   In setting the offering price, investment bankers have the advantage of first checking investor demand.

---

[15] In 2004, Google broke with precedent and decided to go public without an investment banking syndicate backing it. Using an auction process to set the stock price, it saved itself the normal costs associated with issuance fees. It remains to be seen whether Google is unique or at the vanguard of a new trend.

This process, which is called *building the book*, involves polling institutional investors prior to pricing an offering to gauge the extent of the demand for an issue. It is also at this stage in the process that the investment banker and issuing firm will present information to prospective investors in a series of presentations called *road shows*. In this process, if the demand seems very strong, the offering price will be increased; in contrast, if the demand seems weak, the offering price will be lowered. In some cases, a firm will withdraw an IPO at this stage if investors are not enthusiastic about it.[16]

Step 4: **Meet SEC filing requirements and issue a prospectus.** To make a public offering in the United States, a firm has to meet several requirements. First, it has to file a registration statement and prospectus with the SEC, providing information about its financial history, its forecasts for the future, and how it plans to use the funds it raises from the IPO. The prospectus provides information about the riskiness and prospects of the firm for prospective investors in its stock. The SEC reviews this information and either approves the registration or sends out a deficiency memorandum asking for more information. While the registration is being reviewed, the firm may not sell any securities, although it can issue a preliminary prospectus, called a *red herring*, for informational purposes only. Once the registration has been approved by the SEC, the firm can advertise its offering to the public; this usually takes the form of a tombstone advertisement, listing the investment banks involved in the deal.

Step 5: **Allocate stock to those who apply to buy it at offering price.** If the demand for the stock exceeds the supply (which will happen if the offering price is set too low), you will have to ration the stock. If the supply exceeds the demand, the investment banker will have to fulfill the underwriting guarantee and buy the remaining stock at the offering price.

On the offering date—the first date the shares can be traded—the market price is determined by supply and demand. If the offering price has been set too high, as is sometimes the case, the investment bankers will have to discount the offering to sell it and make up the difference to the issuer because of the underwriting agreement. If the offering price is set too low, as is often the case, the traded price on the offering date will be much higher than the offering price, thus enriching those who were allocated shares in the IPO.

The Costs of Going Public

There are three costs associated with an IPO. First, the firm must consider the legal and administrative cost of making a new issue, including the cost of preparing registration statements and filing fees. Second, the firm should examine the underwriting commission—the gross spread between the offering price and what the firm receives per share, which goes to cover the underwriting, management, and selling fees on

---

[16]One study of IPOs between 1979 and 1982 found that 29% of firms terminated their IPOs at this stage in the process.

Figure 7.6   Issuance Costs by Size of Issue

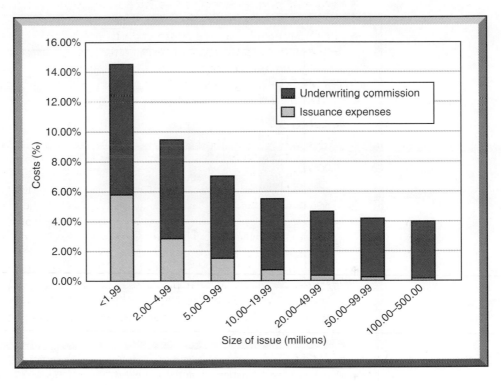

the issue. This commission can be substantial and decreases as the size of the issue increases. Figure 7.6 summarizes the average issuance and underwriting costs for issues of different sizes, reported by Ritter.[17]

The third cost is any underpricing on the issue, which provides a windfall to the investors who get the stock at the offering price and sell it at the much higher market price. Although precise estimates vary from year to year, the average IPO seems to be underpriced by 10–15%. Ibbotson, Sindelar, and Ritter in a study of the determinants of underpricing, estimate its extent as a function of the size of the issue.[18] Figure 7.7 summarizes the underpricing as a percentage of the price by size of issue.

Investment banks are fairly open about the fact that they underprice IPOs. This gives rise to two questions. First, why don't the offering firms express more outrage about the value left on the table by the underpricing? Second, can investors take advantage of the underpricing by subscribing to dozens of IPOs? There are answers to both questions. First, it is true that an underpriced IPO results in less proceeds going to the issuing firms. However, the loss of wealth is a function of how much of the equity of the firm is offered in the initial offering. If only 10% of the stock

---

[17]J. Ritter, "Initial Public Offerings," *Contemporary Finance Digest* 2:5–30.
[18]Roger G. Ibbotson, Jody L. Sindelar, and Jay R. Ritter, "The Market's Problems with the Pricing of Initial Public Offerings," *Journal of Applied Corporate Finance* 7, no. 1:66–74.

Figure 7.7 Underpricing as Percent of Price - by Issue Size

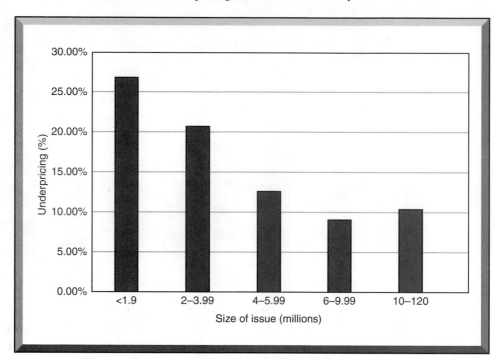

Source: Roger G. Ibbotson, Jody L. Sindelar, and Jay R. Ritter,. 1994, "The Market's Problems with the Pricing of Initial Public Offerings," *Journal of Applied Corporate Finance* v7, no. 1:66–74.

is being offered at the initial offering, we can see why many issuing firms go along with the underpricing. The favorable publicity associated with a strong opening day of trading may act as promotion for subsequent offerings that the firm plans to make in future months or even years. Second, it is not easy constructing an investment strategy that takes advantage of IPO mispricing. If an investor applies for shares in a number of offerings, he or she is likely to get all the shares requested in the offerings that are overpriced and only a fraction of the shares requested in the offerings that are underpriced (where there will be rationing because of excess demand). The resulting portfolio will be overweighted in overpriced public offerings and underweighted with the underpriced offerings, and the returns will not match up to those reported in IPO studies.

 The Underpricing of IPOs: A Behavioral Perspective
While conventional finance has viewed the underpricing of initial public offerings as a puzzle, there are two explanations that have their basis in behavioral finance.

1. ***Stable buyers.*** The investors who subscribe to an initial public offering provide a home and a stable price for the stock and by doing so allay the fears that other investors may have about investing in a young company. The initial discount is the

price that investment banks pay to the initial investors for voluntarily restricting their selling.[19]

2. ***The impresario hypothesis.***   The high initial return to investors in a public offering helps to create or sustain enthusiasm for initial public offerings in general. Since IPOs occur in waves and often are concentrated on specific sectors at any time (technology stocks in the late 1990s), investment bankers pricing offerings have to work at sustaining enthusiasm going by underpricing offerings. Implicit here is the assumption that waves of new offerings are in essence taking advantage of an underlying bubble in a sector or the market, and that the underpricing feeds that illusion.

Finally, there are two other characteristics that feed the underpricing. The first is that investment bankers who are "averse to losses" will underprice initial public offerings. The other is that the underpricing is compensation for the winner's curse in initial public offerings—i.e., that less informed investors oversubscribe to overpriced offerings and that the winners therefore have to offer their shares at a discount to keep these investors from dropping out of the game. As a consequence, informed investors in the IPO game will walk away with excess returns.

ILLUSTRATION 7.2   The IPO for United Parcel Service (UPS)

On July 21, 1999, UPS, the world's largest private package company, announced plans to sell its shares to the public. The company, which was wholly owned by its managers and employees, announced that it was going public to raise capital to make acquisitions in the future. UPS reported revenues of $24.8 billion and net income of $1.7 billion in 1998 and at that time employed about 330,000 people.

UPS followed the initial announcement by filing a prospectus with the SEC on the same day, announcing its intention of creating two classes of shares. Class A shares, with ten votes per share, would be held by the existing owners of UPS, and class B shares, having one vote per share, would be offered to the public.

The firm chose Morgan Stanley as its lead investment banker, and Morgan Stanley put together a syndicate that included Goldman Sachs and Merrill Lynch as senior comanagers. Other comanagers included Credit Suisse, Salomon Smith Barney, and Warburg Dillon Read. On October 20, 1999, UPS filed a statement with the SEC (called an S-1 registration statement) announcing that it planned to issue 109.4 million shares (about 10% of the 1.1 billion outstanding shares) at a price range of $36 to $42,[20] and that the IPO would occur sometime in early November.

Based on the strong demand from institutional investors, gauged in the process of building the book, the investment banking syndicate increased the offering price to $50 per share on November 8, 1999, and set the offering date at November 10, 1999. At that time, it was the largest IPO ever by a U.S. company.

---

[19]Since the restriction is voluntary, those investors who violate this implicit agreement will not be allocated stock in future initial public offerings.

[20]The process by which this price range was set was not made public. We would assume that it was partially based on how the market was pricing two other publicly traded rivals—FedEx and Airborne Freight.

On November 10, 1999, the stock went public. The stock price jumped to $70.1325 from the offering price of $50. At the end of the trading day, UPS shares were trading at $67.25. Based on this price and the total number of shares outstanding, the market value of UPS was assessed at $80.9 billion.

7.9   THE COST OF UNDERPRICING

Assume that the market is correct in its assessment of UPS value and that the investment bankers underpriced the issue. How much did the underpricing cost the owners of UPS?

a.   About $22 billion

b.   About $50 billion

c.   About $2.2 billion

d.   None of the above

The Choices for a Publicly Traded Firm

Once a firm is publicly traded, it can raise new financing by issuing more common stock, equity options, or corporate bonds. Additional equity offerings made by firms that are already publicly traded are called seasoned equity issues. In making stock and bond offerings, a publicly traded firm has several choices. It can sell these securities with underwritten general subscriptions, where stocks and bonds are offered to the public at an offering price guaranteed by the investment banker. It can also privately place both bonds and stocks with institutional investors or issue stocks and bonds directly to investors without any middlemen.

General Subscriptions

In a *general subscription*, the issue is open to any member of the general public to subscribe. In that sense, it is very similar to an IPO, though there are some basic differences:

- *Underwriting agreement.* The underwriting agreement of an IPO almost always involves a firm guarantee and is generally negotiated with the investment banker, whereas the underwriting agreements for seasoned issues take on a wider variety of forms. First, there is the potential for competitive bids to arise on seasoned issues, because investment bankers have the information to promise a fixed price.[21] There is evidence that competitive bids reduce the spread, though even seasoned firms continue to prefer negotiated offerings. Second, seasoned issues also offer a wider range of underwriting guarantees; some issues are backed up by a *best efforts guarantee*, which does not guarantee a fixed price; other issues come with *standby guarantees*, where the investment banker provides backup support, in case the actual price falls below the offering price. The payoff from relaxing the guarantee comes as lower underwriting commissions.

---

[21]The information takes two forms. The first are the filings that every publicly traded firm has to make with the SEC. The other, and more important, is the current stock price.

- *Pricing of issue.* The issuer of an IPO has to estimate the value of the firm and then the per-share value before pricing the issue, whereas the pricing of a seasoned issue starts with the current market price, simplifying the process. Often, the price of a seasoned issue will be set just below the current market price.

The overall evidence on the cost of public offerings indicates that it is still clearly much more expensive to issue stock rather than bonds, and the cost of the issue decreases with the size of the issue.

Private Placements

An alternative to a general subscription is a *private placement*, in which securities are sold directly to one or a few investors. The terms for the securities are negotiated between the two parties. The primary advantage of private placements over general subscriptions is the lower cost, because there are fewer intermediaries and no need for underwriting guarantees or marketing. There are also substantial savings in time and administrative costs, because the SEC registration requirements are bypassed. The other advantages are that the terms of the bond can be tailored to meet the specific needs of the buyer, and that the firm can convey proprietary information (presumably positive) to the potential investors.

The primary disadvantage of private placements is that there are relatively few potential investors, because large private placements may expose the investor to firm-specific risks. This is why private placements of corporate bonds are much more common than private placement of equity. In a typical private placement, the buyer tends to be a long-term institutional investor, such as a life insurance company or a pension fund. These investors tend to invest in these bonds and hold them until maturity. Private placements generally range from \$25 million to \$250 million in size and have more restrictions associated with them than typical corporate bond issues.

Rights Offerings

The third option available to seasoned issuers is a *rights offering*. In this case, instead of trying to sell new stock at the current market price to all investors, the existing investors in the firm are given the right to buy additional shares, in proportion to their current holdings, at a price much lower than the current market price.

A company that uses a rights offering generally issues one right for each outstanding common share, allowing each stockholder to use those rights to buy additional shares in the company at a *subscription price*, generally much lower than the market price. Rational stockholders will either exercise the right or sell it. Those investors who let a right expire without doing either will find that the market value of their remaining holding shrinks—the market price will almost certainly drop when the rights are exercised, because the subscription price is set much lower than the market price. In general, the value of a right should be equal to the difference between the stock price with the rights attached—the *rights-on price*—and the stock price without the rights attached—the *ex-rights price*. The reasoning is simple. If this were not true, there would be opportunities for easy profits on the part of investors, and the resulting price would not be stable. To illustrate, if the price of the right were greater than the difference between the rights-on price and the ex-rights price, every stockholder would be better off selling the right rather than exercising it. This, in turn, would push the price down toward the equilibrium price. If the price of the right were lower than the difference between the rights-on and the ex-right price, there would be an equally frenzied rush to buy the right and exercise it, which in turn would push the price up toward the equilibrium price. The value of a right can be estimated using the following equation:

$$\text{Price of a right} = (\text{Rights-on price} - \text{Subscription price})/(n + 1)$$

where n is the number of rights required for each new share.

Rights offerings are a much less expensive way of raising capital than public issues, for two reasons. First, the underwriting commissions are much lower, because a rights offering has little risk of not receiving subscriptions if the subscription price is set well below the market price. Second, the other transaction and administrative costs should also be lower, because there is a far smaller need for marketing and distribution.

What is the drawback of making a rights issue? The primary reservation seems to be that it increases the number of shares outstanding far more than a general subscription at the existing stock price. To illustrate, a firm that makes a rights issue at $5 per share when the stock price is $10 will have to issue 10 million shares to raise $50 million. In contrast, the same firm would have had to issue only 5 million shares if the issue had been at the existing stock price of $10. Some financial managers argue that this dilutes the shareholding and lowers the market price. Although this is true in a technical sense, the existing stockholders should not object, because they are the only ones who receive the rights. In other words, the stock price will drop, but everyone will own proportionately more shares in the firm. In general, firms in the United States have been much more reluctant to use rights issues than European firms, in spite of the significant cost savings that could accrue from them. Part of this reluctance can be attributed to the fear of dilution.

ILLUSTRATION 7.3 Valuing a Rights Offering: Tech Temp

Tech Temp has 10 million shares outstanding trading at $25 per share. It needs to raise $25 million in new equity and decides to make a rights offering. Each stockholder is provided with one right for every share owned, and five rights can be used to buy an additional share in the company at $12.50 per share. The value of a right can be calculated as follows:

	Before Rights Exercised	After Rights Exercised
Number of shares	10 million	12 million
Value of equity	$250 million	$275 million
Price per share	$25.00	$22.92

The rights-on price is $25.00 per share, and the ex-rights price is $22.92, leading to a per-right value of $2.08. This can be confirmed by using the equation

$$\text{Value per right} = (\text{Rights-on price} - \text{Subscription price})/(n + 1)$$
$$= (\$25 - \$12.50)/(5 + 1)$$
$$= \$12.50/6 = \$2.08$$

If the rights price were greater than this value, investors would want to sell their rights. Alternatively, if the rights could be acquired for less than $2.08, there would be an opportunity to gain by acquiring the rights at the lower price and exercising them.

rights.xls: This spreadsheet allows you to estimate the ex-rights price and the value per right in a rights issue.

7.10   RIGHTS ISSUES AND EXISTING STOCKHOLDERS

Assume that you own 1,000 shares in Tech Temp, trading at $25 a share, and that you receive the rights described in the last illustration. Assume also that due to an oversight, you neither exercise the right nor sell it. How much would you expect to lose as a result of the oversight?

a.   Nothing; you still own the shares.

b. $416.

c. $2,080.

d. $12,500.

Shelf Registrations

Firms that want to raise external financing have to disclose information and file the required statements with the SEC before they can issue securities. This registration process is costly and time-consuming and is one reason why some firms rely on internal financing. In response to this criticism, the SEC simplified its rules and allowed firms more flexibility in external financing. Rule 415, issued in 1982, allows firms to make a *shelf registration*, in which they can file a single prospectus for a series of issues they expect to make over the next two years.

Besides making the process less cumbersome, shelf registration also gives firms more flexibility in terms of timing, because stock and bond issues can be made when windows of opportunity open up. Thus, a firm might make a shelf registration for $200 million in bonds and make the bond issue when interest rates are at a low point. This flexibility in timing also allows firms to open up the process to aggressive bidding from investment banks, reducing transaction costs substantially. Some firms make the issues themselves rather than use investment bankers, because the process is simpler and faster.

Overall, the spreads on new issues, especially for bonds, have been under pressure since the passage of shelf registration. In spite of its benefits, however, shelf registration is more likely to be used by large firms making bond issues and less likely to be used by small firms making equity issues.

THE TRADEOFF OF DEBT

Now that we have defined debt and considered how financing choices change as a function of where a firm is in its life cycle, we can tackle a fundamental question. Why use debt instead of equity? In this section, we will first examine the benefits of using debt instead of equity and then follow up by looking at the costs.

The Benefits of Debt

In the broadest terms, debt provides two differential benefits over equity. The first is the *tax benefit*: interest payments on debt are tax-deductible, whereas cash flows on equity are not. The second is the *added discipline imposed on management* by having to make payments on debt. Both benefits can and should be quantified if firms want to make reasonable judgments on debt capacity.

1. Debt Has a Tax Advantage

The primary benefit of debt relative to equity is the tax advantage it confers on the borrower. In the United States, interest paid on debt is tax-deductible, whereas cash flows on equity (such as dividends) have to be paid out of after-tax cash flows. For the most part, this is true in other countries as well, though some countries try to provide partial protection against the **double taxation** of dividends by providing a tax credit to investors who receive the dividends for the corporate taxes paid (Britain) or by taxing retained earnings at a rate higher than dividends (Germany).

The tax benefits from debt can be presented in three ways. The first two measure the benefit in absolute terms, whereas the third measures it as a percentage cost.

1. In the first approach, the dollar tax savings in any financial year created by interest expenses can be computed by multiplying the interest expenses by the marginal tax rate of the firm. Consider a firm that borrows $B to finance it operations, on which it faces an interest rate of r percent, and assume that it faces a marginal tax rate of t on income. The annual tax savings from the interest tax deduction can be calculated as follows:

$$\text{Annual interest expense arising from the debt} = rB$$
$$\text{Annual tax savings arising from the interest payment} = trB$$

2. In the second approach, we can compute the present value of tax savings arising from interest payments over time. The present value of the annual tax savings can be computed by making three other assumptions. The first is that the debt is perpetual, which also means that the dollar savings are a perpetuity. The second is that the appropriate discount rate for this cash flow is the interest rate on the debt, because it reflects the riskiness of the debt. The third is that the expected tax rate for the firm will remain unchanged over time and that the firm is in a tax-paying position. With these three assumptions, the present value of the savings can be computed as follows:

$$\text{Present value of tax savings from debt} = trB/r = tB$$
$$= \text{Marginal tax rate} * \text{Debt}$$

Although the conventional view is to look at the tax savings as a perpetuity, the approach is general enough to be used to compute the tax savings over a shorter period (say, ten years.) Thus, a firm that borrows $100 million at 8% for ten years and has a tax rate of 40% can compute the present value of its tax savings as follows:

$$\text{Present value of interest tax savings} = \text{Annual tax savings (PV of annuity)}$$
$$= (0.08 * 0.4 * \$100 \text{ million}) \text{ (PV of annuity, 8\%, 10 years)}$$
$$= \$21.47 \text{ million}$$

When asked to analyze the effect of adding debt on value, some analysts use a shortcut and simply add the tax benefit from debt to the value of the firm with no debt:

$$\text{Value of levered firm with debt } B = \text{Value of unlevered firm} + tB$$

The limitation of this approach is that it considers only the tax benefit from borrowing and none of the additional costs. It also yields the unrealistic conclusion that firm value always increases as you borrow more money.

3. In the third approach, the tax benefit from debt is expressed in terms of the difference between the pretax and after-tax cost of debt. To illustrate, if r is the interest rate on debt, and t is the marginal tax rate, the after-tax cost of borrowing (k_d) can be written as follows:

$$\text{After-tax cost of debt } (k_d) = r(1 - t)$$

This is the familiar formula used for calculating the cost of debt in the cost of capital calculation. In this formula, the after-tax cost of debt is a decreasing function of the tax rate. A firm with a tax rate of 40%, which borrows at 8%, has an after-tax cost of debt of 4.8%. Another firm with a tax rate of 70%, which borrows at 8%, has an after-tax cost of debt of 2.4%.

Other things remaining equal, the benefits of debt are much greater when tax rates are higher. Consequently, there are three predictions that can be made about debt ratios across companies and across time.

1. The debt ratios of entities facing higher tax rates should be higher than the debt ratios of comparable entities facing lower tax rates. Other things remaining equal, you would expect German companies that face a 30% marginal corporate tax rate to borrow more money than Irish companies that face a 12.5% marginal corporate tax rate.

2. If tax rates increase over time in any given market, we would expect debt ratios to go up in that market over time as well, reflecting the higher tax benefits of debt.

There is a data set online that summarizes by sector the effective tax rates of firms.

7.11 NET OPERATING LOSS CARRYFORWARD AND TAX BENEFITS

You have been asked to assess the after-tax cost of debt for a firm that has $2 billion in net operating losses to carry forward, and operating income of roughly $2 billion this year. If the company can borrow at 8%, and the marginal corporate tax rate is 40%, the after-tax cost of debt this year is

a. 8%

b. 4.8%

What would your after-tax cost of debt be next year?

2. Debt May Make Managers More Disciplined

In the 1980s, in the midst of the leveraged buyout boom, a group of practitioners and academics led by Michael Jensen at Harvard developed and expounded a new rationale for borrowing based on improving firms' efficiency in the utilization of their free cash flows. **Free cash flows** represent cash flows made on operations over which managers have discretionary spending power—they may use them to take projects, pay them out to stockholders, or hold them as idle cash balances. The group argued that managers in firms that have substantial free cash flows and no or low debt have such a large cash cushion against mistakes that they have no incentive to be efficient in either project choice or project management. One way to introduce discipline into the process is to force these firms to borrow money, because borrowing creates the commitment to make interest and principal payments, increasing the risk of default on projects with substandard returns. It is this difference between the forgiving nature of the equity commitment and the inflexibility of the debt commitment that have led some to call equity a cushion and debt a sword.

The underlying assumptions in this argument are that there is a conflict of interest between managers and stockholders and that managers will not maximize shareholder wealth without a prod (debt). From our discussion in Chapter 2, it is clear that this assumption is grounded in fact. Most large U.S. corporations employ managers who own only a very small portion of the outstanding stock in the firm; they receive most of their income as managers rather than stockholders. Furthermore, evidence indicates that managers at least sometimes put their interests ahead those of stockholders.

The argument that debt adds discipline to the process also provides an interesting insight into management perspectives on debt. Based purely on managerial preferences, the optimal level of debt may be much lower than that estimated based on shareholder wealth maximization. Left to themselves, why would managers want to burden themselves with debt, knowing full well that they will have to become more efficient and pay a larger price for their mistakes? The corollary to this argument is that the debt ratios of firms in countries in which stockholder power to influence or remove managers is minimal will be much lower than optimal, because managers enjoy a more comfortable existence by carrying less debt than they can afford to. Conversely, as stockholders acquire power, they will push these firms to borrow more money and, in the process, increase their stock prices.

Do increases in debt lead to improved efficiency and higher returns on investments? The answer to this question should provide some insight into whether the argument for added discipline has some basis. A number of studies have attempted to answer this question, though most have done so indirectly.

- Firms that are acquired in hostile takeovers are generally characterized by poor performance in both accounting profitability and stock returns, prior to the takeovers. Bhide, for instance, noted that the return on equity of these firms is 2.2% below their peer group, whereas the stock returns are 4% below the peer group's returns.[22] Although this poor performance by itself does not constitute

---

[22] A. Bhide, "Reversing Corporate Diversification," in D. H. Chew Jr., ed., *The New Corporate Finance: Where Theory Meets Practice*, McGraw-Hill, New York, 1993), 526–537.

support for the free cash flow hypothesis, Palepu presented evidence that target firms in acquisitions carry less debt than similar firms that are not taken over.[23]

- There is evidence that increases in leverage are followed by improvements in operating efficiency, as measured by operating margins and returns on capital. Palepu presented evidence of modest improvements in operating efficiency at firms involved in leveraged buyouts.[24] Kaplan and Smith, in separate studies, also found that firms earn higher returns on capital following leveraged buyouts.[25] Denis and Denis presented more direct evidence on improvements in operating performance after **leveraged recapitalizations**.[26] In their study of twenty-nine firms that increased debt substantially, they report a median increase in the return on assets of 21.5%. Much of this gain seems to arise out of cutbacks in unproductive capital investments, because the median reduction in capital expenditures of these firms is 35.5%.

Of course, we must consider that the evidence presented is consistent with a number of different hypotheses. For instance, it is possible that the management itself changes at these firms and that the change of management rather than the additional debt leads to higher investment returns.

7.12   DEBT AS A DISCIPLINING MECHANISM

Assume that you buy into the argument that debt adds discipline to management. Which of the following types of companies will most benefit from debt adding this discipline?

a. Conservatively financed, privately owned businesses

b. Conservatively financed, publicly traded companies with a wide and diverse stock holding

c. Conservatively financed, publicly traded companies,with an activist and primarily institutional holding

(By "conservatively financed," we mean primarily with equity.)

The Costs of Debt

As any borrower will attest, debt certainly has disadvantages. In particular, borrowing money can expose the firm to default and eventual liquidation, increase the agency problems arising from the conflict between the interests of equity investors and lenders, and reduce the flexibility of the firm to take actions now or in the future.

1. Debt Increases Expected Bankruptcy Costs

The primary concern when borrowing money is the increase in expected bankruptcy costs that typically follows. The expected bankruptcy cost can be written as a product of the probability of bankruptcy and the direct and indirect costs of bankruptcy.

---

[23]Krishna G. Palepu, "Predicting Takeover Targets: A Methodological and Empirical Analysis," *Journal of Accounting and Economics* 8, no. 1:3–35.

[24]K. G. Palepu, "Consequences of Leveraged Buyouts," *Journal of Financial Economics* 26:247–262.

[25]See S. N. Kaplan, "Campeau's Acquisition of Federated: Value Destroyed or Value Added?" *Journal of Financial Economics* 25:191–212; A. J. Smith, "Corporate Ownership Structure and Performance: The Case of Management Buyouts," *Journal of Financial Economics* 27:143–164.

[26]David J. Denis and Diane K. Denis, "Leveraged Recaps in the Curbing of Corporate Overinvestment," *Journal of Applied Corporate Finance* 6, no. 1:60–71.

The Probability of Bankruptcy

The *probability of bankruptcy* is the likelihood that a firm's cash flows will be insufficient to meet its promised debt obligations (interest or principal). Although such a failure does not automatically imply bankruptcy, it does trigger default, with all its negative consequences. Using this definition, the probability of bankruptcy should be a function of both the size of the operating cash flows of the firm (larger cash flows should reduce the likelihood of default) and the volatility in these cash flows (more volatile cash flows should resulty in a higher probability of bankruptcy).

Accordingly, the probability of bankruptcy increases marginally for all firms as they borrow more money, irrespective of how large their cash flows might be, and the increase should be greater for firms in riskier businesses.

The Cost of Bankruptcy

The cost of going bankrupt is neither obvious nor easily quantified. It is true that bankruptcy is a disaster for all involved in the firm—lenders often get a fraction of what they are owed, and equity investors get nothing—but the overall cost of bankruptcy includes the indirect costs on operations of being perceived as having high default risk.

Direct Costs   The direct, or deadweight, cost of bankruptcy is that which is incurred in terms of cash outflows at the time of bankruptcy. These costs include the legal and administrative costs of a bankruptcy, as well as the present value effects of delays in paying out the cash flows. In a widely quoted study of railroad bankruptcies in the 1970s, Warner estimated the legal and administrative costs of eleven railroads to be on average 5.3% of the value of the assets at the time of the bankruptcy. He also estimated that it took, on average, thirteen years before the railroads were reorganized and released from the bankruptcy costs.[27] These costs, although certainly not negligible, are not overwhelming, especially in light of two additional factors. First, the direct cost as a percentage of the value of the assets decreases to 1.4% if the asset value is computed five years before the bankruptcy. Second, railroads in general are likely to have higher bankruptcy costs than other companies because of the nature of their assets (real estate and fixed equipment).

Indirect Costs   If the only costs of bankruptcy were the direct costs, the low leverage maintained by many firms would be puzzling. There are, however, much larger costs associated with taking on debt and increasing default risk, which arise prior to the bankruptcy, largely as a consequence of the perception that a firm is in financial trouble. The first is the perception on the part of the customers that the firm is in trouble. When this happens, customers may stop buying the product or service because of the fear that the company will go out of business. In 1980, for example, when car buyers believed that Chrysler was on the verge of bankruptcy, they chose to buy from Ford and GM, largely because they were concerned about receiving service and parts for their cars after their purchases. Similarly, in the late 1980s, when Continental Airlines found itself in financial trouble, business travelers switched to other airlines because they were unsure about

---

[27]J. N. Warner, "Bankruptcy Costs: Some Evidence," *Journal of Finance* 32:337–347.

whether they would be able to accumulate and use their frequent-flier miles on the airline. The second indirect cost is the stricter terms suppliers start demanding to protect themselves against the possibility of default, leading to an increase in working capital and a decrease in cash flows. The third cost is the difficulty the firm may experience trying to raise fresh capital for its projects—both debt and equity investors are reluctant to take the risk, leading to capital rationing constraints and the rejection of good projects.

Given this reasoning, the indirect costs of bankruptcy are likely to be higher for the following types of firms:[28]

- *Firms that sell durable products with long lives that require replacement parts.* Thus, an automobile manufacturer would have higher indirect costs associated with bankruptcy than would a grocery store.

- *Firms that provide goods or services for which quality is an important attribute though it is difficult to determine in advance.* Because the quality cannot be determined easily in advance, the reputation of the firm plays a significant role in whether the customer will buy the product in the first place.

- *Firms producing products whose value to customers depends on the services and complementary products supplied by independent companies.* Returning to the example of personal computers, a computer system is valuable only insofar as there is software available to run on it. If the firm manufacturing the computers is perceived to be in trouble, it is entirely possible that the independent suppliers that produce the software might stop providing it. Thus, if Apple Computers gets into financial trouble, many software manufacturers might stop producing software for its machines, leading to an erosion in its potential market.

- *Firms that sell products that require continuous service and support from the manufacturer.* A manufacturer of copying machines, for which constant service seems to be a operating characteristic, would be affected more adversely by the perception of default risk than would a furniture manufacturer, for example.

Implications for Optimal Capital Structure
If the expected bankruptcy cost is indeed the product of the probability of bankruptcy and the direct and indirect bankruptcy cost, interesting, testable implications emerge for capital structure decisions.

- Firms operating in businesses with volatile earnings and cash flows should use debt less than otherwise similar firms with stable cash flows. For instance, regulated utilities in the United States have high leverage because the regulation and the monopolistic nature of their businesses result in stable earnings and cash flows. At the other extreme, technology or commodity, can have large shifts in income from

---

[28]See A. Shapiro, *Modern Corporate Finance* (New York: Macmillan, 1989); also, S. Titman, "The Effect of Capital Structure on a Firm's Liquidation Decision," *Journal of Financial Economics* 13:1371–1351.

one year to.[29] These firms should use leverage far less in meeting their funding needs.

- If firms can structure their debt in such a way that the cash flows on the debt increase and decrease with their operating cash flows, they can afford to borrow more. Commodity companies, whose operating cash flows increase and decrease with commodity prices, may be able to use more debt if the debt payments are linked to commodity prices. Similarly, a company whose operating cash flows increase as interest rates (and inflation) go up and decrease when interest rates go down may be able to use more debt if the debt has a floating rate feature. We will discuss this point in more detail in chapter 9.

- If an external entity provides protection against bankruptcy, by providing either insurance or bailouts, firms will tend to borrow more. To illustrate, the deposit insurance offered by the FSLIC and the FDIC enables savings and loans and banks to maintain higher leverage than they otherwise could. Although one can argue for this insurance on the grounds of preserving the integrity of the financial system, undercharging for the insurance will induce high-risk firms to take on too much debt, letting taxpayers bear the cost. Similarly, governments that step in and regularly bail out firms on social grounds (e.g., to save jobs) will encourage all firms to overuse debt.

- Because the direct bankruptcy costs are higher, when the assets of the firm are not easily divisible and marketable, firms with assets that can be easily divided and sold should be able to borrow more than firms with assets that do not share these features. Thus, a firm whose value comes from its real estate holdings should be able to borrow more money than a firm which derives a great deal of its value from its brand name.

- Firms that produce products that require long-term servicing and support generally should have lower leverage than firms whose products do not share this feature, as discussed before.

 7.13   DEBT AND BANKRUPTCY

Rank the following companies on the magnitude of bankruptcy costs from most to least, taking into account both explicit and implicit costs:

a.   A grocery store
b.   An airplane manufacturer
c.   High-technology company

Explain.

 There is a data set online that summarizes variances in operating earnings by sector.

---

[29]The volatility in operating income at these companies comes from very different sources. For technology firms, the risk derives from the shifting nature of the market and competition. For commodity companies, it comes from volatile commodity prices.

2. Debt Creates Agency Costs

Equity investors, who receive a residual claim on the cash flows, tend to favor actions that increase the value of their holdings, even if that means increasing the risk that the bondholders (who have a fixed claim on the cash flows) will not receive their promised payments. Bondholders, on the other hand, want to preserve and increase the security of their claims. Because the equity investors generally control the firm's management and decision making, their interests will dominate bondholder interests unless bondholders take some protective action. By borrowing money, a firm exposes itself to this conflict and its negative consequences, and it pays the price, in terms of both higher interest rates and a loss of freedom in decision making.

The conflict between bondholder and stockholder interests appears in all three aspects of corporate finance: (1) deciding what projects to take (making investment decisions), (2) choosing how to finance these projects, and (3) determining how much to pay out as dividends:

1. *Risky projects.*   In the section on investment analysis, we argued that a project that earns a return that exceeds the hurdle rate, adjusted to reflect the risk of the project, should be accepted and will increase firm value. The caveat, however, is that bondholders may be hurt if the firm accepts some of these projects. Bondholders lend money to the firm with the expectation that the projects accepted will have a certain risk level, and they set the interest rate on the bonds accordingly. If the firm chooses projects that are riskier than expected, however, bondholders will lose on their existing holdings, because the price of the holdings will decrease to reflect the higher risk.

2. *Subsequent financing.*   The conflict between stockholder and bondholder interests also arises when new projects have to be financed. The equity investors in a firm may favor new debt, using the assets of the firm as security and giving the new lenders prior claims over existing lenders. Such actions will reduce the interest rate on the new debt. The existing lenders in a firm obviously do not want to give new lenders priority over their claims, because it makes the existing debt riskier (and less valuable).

3. *Dividends and stock repurchases.*   Dividend payments and equity repurchases also divide stockholders and bondholders. Consider a firm that has built up a large cash reserve but has very few good projects available. The stockholders in this firm may benefit if the cash is paid out as a dividend or used to repurchase stock. The bondholders, on the other hand, will prefer that the firm retain the cash, because it can be used to make payments on the debt, reducing default risk. It should come as no surprise that stockholders, if not constrained, will pay the dividends or buy back stock, overriding bondholder concerns. In some cases, the payments are large and can increase the default risk of the firm dramatically.

The potential for disagreement between stockholders and bondholders can show up in as real costs in two ways:

1. If bondholders believe there is a significant chance that stockholder actions might make them worse off, they will build this expectation into bond prices by demanding much higher interest rates on debt.

2. If bondholders can protect themselves against such actions by writing in restrictive covenants, two costs follow:

   a. The direct cost of monitoring the covenants, which increases as the covenants become more detailed and restrictive

   b. The indirect cost of lost investments, because the firm is not able to take certain projects, use certain types of financing, or change its payout (this cost will also increase as the covenants becomes more restrictive)

As firms borrow more and expose themselves to greater agency costs, these costs will also increase.

Because agency costs can be substantial, two implications relating to optimal capital structure follow. First, the agency cost arising from **risk shifting** is likely to be greatest in firms whose investments cannot be easily observed and monitored. For example, a lender to a firm that invests in real estate is less exposed to agency cost than is a lender to a firm that invests in people (consulting, for example) or intangible assets (as is the case with technology firms). Consequently, it is not surprising that manufacturing companies and railroads, which invest in substantial real assets, have much higher debt ratios than service companies. Second, the agency cost associated with monitoring management actions and second-guessing investment decisions is likely to be largest for firms whose projects are long-term, follow unpredictable paths, and may take years to come to fruition. Pharmaceutical companies in the United States, for example, which often take on research projects that may take years to yield commercial products, have historically maintained low debt ratios, even though their cash flows would support more debt.

7.14   RISK SHIFTING AND BONDHOLDERS

It is often argued that bondholders who plan to hold their bonds until maturity and collect the coupons and the face value are not affected by risk shifting that occurs after they buy the bonds, because the effect is only on market value. Do you agree?

a. Yes

b. No

Explain.

3. Using Up Excess Debt Capacity Reduces Financial Flexibility

As noted earlier, one of the byproducts of the conflict between stockholders and bondholders is the introduction of strict bond covenants that reduce the flexibility of firms to make investment, financing, or dividend decisions. It can be argued that this is part of a much greater loss of flexibility arising from taking on debt. One of the reasons firms do not use their available debt capacity is that they like to preserve it for a rainy day, when they might need the debt to meet funding needs or specific contingencies. Firms that borrow to capacity lose this flexibility and have no fallback funding if they get into trouble.

Firms value **financial flexibility** for two reasons. First, the value of the firm may be maximized by preserving some flexibility to take on future projects as they arise. Second, flexibility provides managers with more breathing room and more power, and it protects them from the monitoring that comes with debt. Thus, although the argument for maintaining flexibility in the interests of the firm is based on sound principles, it is sometimes used as camouflage by managers pursuing their own interests. There is also a tradeoff between not maintaining enough flexibility (because a firm has too much debt) and having too much flexibility (by not borrowing enough).

So, how best can we value financial flexibility? If flexibility is needed to allow firms to take advantage of unforeseen investment opportunities, its value should ultimately be derived from two variables. The first is access to capital markets. After all, large, developed market firms that have unfettered access to capital markets will not need to maintain excess debt capacity, because they can raise funds as needed for new investments. Smaller firms and firms in emerging markets, on the other hand, should value financial flexibility more. The second is the potential for excess returns on new investments. If a firm operates in a mature business where new investments, unpredictable though they might be, earn the cost of capital, there is no value to maintaining flexibility. Alternatively, a firm that operates in a volatile business with high excess returns should attach a much higher value to financial flexibility.

7.15 Value of Flexibility and Firm Characteristics

Both Ford and Microsoft have huge cash balances (as a percentage of firm value); assume that you are a stockholder in both firms. The management of both firms claims to hold the cash because they need the flexibility. Which of the two managements are you more likely to accept this argument from?

a. Microsoft's management

b. Ford's management

Explain.

The Tradeoff in a Balance Sheet Format

Bringing together the benefits and the costs of debt, we can present the tradeoff in a balance sheet format in Table 7.2.

Overall, if the marginal benefits of borrowing exceed the marginal costs, the firm should borrow money. Otherwise, it should use equity.

What do firms consider when they make capital structure decisions? To answer this question, Pinegar and Wilbricht surveyed financial managers at 176 firms in the United States.[30] They concluded that the financial principles listed in Table 7.3 determine capital structure decisions, in the order of importance in which they were given.

---

[30]J. Michael Pinegar and Lisa Wilbricht, "What Managers Think of Capital Structure Theory: A Survey," *Financial Management* 18, no. 4:82–91.

Table 7.2 TRADEOFF ON DEBT VERSUS EQUITY	
Advantages of Borrowing	**Disadvantages of Borrowing**
1. *Tax benefit:* Higher tax rates → higher tax benefit → higher debt ratio	1. *Bankruptcy cost:* Higher business risk and bankruptcy cost → higher cost → lower debt ratio
2. *Added discipline:* Greater the separation between managers and stockholders → greater the benefit	2. *Agency cost:* Assets that are more difficult to monitor → greater the separation between stockholders and lenders → higher cost → lower debt ratio
	3. *Loss of future financing flexibility:* Greater the uncertainty about future financing needs → higher cost → Lower debt ratio

Table 7.3   FINANCIAL PRINCIPLES DETERMINING CAPITAL STRUCTURE DECISIONS

Planning Principle by Order of Importance	Percentage of Responses within Each Rank						Mean
	Unimportant	2	3	4	Important	Not Ranked	
1. Maintaining financial flexibility	0.6	0.0	4.5	33.0	61.4	0.6	4.55
2. Ensuring long-term survivability	4.0	1.7	6.8	10.8	76.7	0.0	4.55
3. Maintaining a predictable source of funds	1.7	2.8	20.5	39.2	35.8	0.0	4.05
4. Maximizing security prices	3.4	4.5	19.3	33.5	37.5	1.7	3.00
5. Maintaining financial independence	3.4	4.5	22.2	27.3	40.9	1.7	3.99
6. Maintaining a high debt rating	2.3	9.1	32.4	43.2	13.1	0.0	3.56
7. Maintaining comparability with other firms in the industry	15.9	36.9	33.0	10.8	2.8	0.6	2.47

The foremost principles the survey participants identified were maintaining financial flexibility and ensuring long-term survivability (which can be construed as avoiding bankruptcy). Surprisingly, few managers attached much importance to maintaining comparability with other firms in their industries or maintaining a high debt rating.

ILLUSTRATION 7.4   Evaluating the Debt Tradeoff—Disney, Aracruz, Tata Chemicals, and Bookscape

In Table 7.4, we summarize our views on the potential benefits and costs to using debt, instead of equity, at Disney, Aracruz, and Tata Chemicals.

Table 7.4   THE DEBT EQUITY TRADEOFF—DISNEY, ARACRUZ, AND TATA CHEMICALS

	Disney	**Aracruz**	**Tata Chemicals**
Tax benefits	Significant. The firm has a marginal tax rate of 38%. It does have large depreciation tax shields.	Significant. The firm has a marginal tax rate of 34% as well. It does not have very much in noninterest tax shields.	Significant. The firm has a 33.99% tax rate. It does have significant noninterest tax shields in the form of depreciation.
Added discipline	Benefits will be high, because managers are not large stockholders.	Benefits are smaller, because the voting shares are closely held by insiders.	Since the Tata family controls the firm, the benefits from added discipline are small.
Bankruptcy costs	Movie and broadcasting businesses have volatile earnings. Direct costs of bankruptcy are likely to be small, but indirect costs can be significant.	Variability in paper prices makes earnings volatile. Direct and indirect costs of bankruptcy likely to be moderate, since assets are marketable (timber, real estate).	Firm is mature, with fairly stable earnings and cash flows from its chemicals and fertilizer business. Indirect bankruptcy costs should be low, since physical assets are marketable.
Agency costs	High. Although theme park assets are tangible and fairly liquid, it is much more difficult to monitor the movie and broadcasting businesses.	Low. Assets are tangible and liquid.	Biggest concern is that funds may be utilized in other (riskier) Tata companies.
Flexibility needs	Low in theme park business but high in media businesses, because technological change makes future investment uncertain.	Low. Business is mature and investment needs are well established.	Low. Tata Chemicals is a mature company with established reinvestment needs.

Based on this analysis, qualitative though it might be, we would argue that all three firms could benefit from borrowing, as long as the borrowing does not push them below an acceptable default risk threshold. For Aracruz and Tata Chemicals, the overlay of country risk (India and Brazil are both emerging markets, with substantial growth opportunities but significant risk) will be a factor that holds back additional debt, since a market shock can not only cause capital markets to shut down but also make earnings more volatile.

For Bookscape, the tradeoff is more personal, since the owner is fully invested in the company and is not diversified. Consequently, while the tax benefits of debt remain high, bankruptcy costs are likely to loom larger in the decision of whether to borrow money. If the firm defaults on its debt, the owner's entire wealth would be at risk, as would his reputation. While this will serve to keep debt in check, it has to be weighed off against the absence of alternative ways of raising funds. As a private business, Bookscape cannot easily raise fresh equity and may be entirely dependent on bank loans for external financing.

NO OPTIMAL CAPITAL STRUCTURE

We have just argued that debt has advantages relative to equity, as well as disadvantages. Will trading off the costs and benefits of debt yield an optimal mix of debt and equity for a firm? In this section, we will present arguments that it will not, and the resulting conclusion that there is no such optimal mix. The seeds of this argument were sown in one of the most influential papers ever written in corporate finance, containing one of corporate finance's best-known theorems, the *Modigliani-Miller theorem*.[31]

When they first looked at the question of whether there is an optimal capital structure, Modigliani-Miller drew their conclusions in a world void of taxes, transaction costs, and the possibility of default. Based on these assumptions, they concluded that the value of a firm was unaffected by its leverage and that investment and financing decisions could be separated. Their conclusion can be confirmed in several ways; we present two in this section. We will also present a more complex argument for why there should be no optimal capital structure even in a world with taxes, an argument made by Miller almost two decades later.

The Irrelevance of Debt in a Tax-Free World

In their initial work, Modigliani-Miller made three significant assumptions about the markets in which their firms operated. First, they assumed there were no taxes. Second, they assumed firms could raise external financing from debt or equity, with no issuance costs. Third, they assumed there were no costs—direct or indirect—associated with bankruptcy. Finally, they operated in an environment in which there were no agency costs; managers acted to maximize stockholder wealth, and bondholders did not have to worry about stockholders expropriating wealth with investment, financing, or dividend decisions.

In such an environment, reverting back to the tradeoff that we summarized in Table 7.2 it is quite clear that all the advantages and disadvantages disappear, leaving debt with no marginal benefits and no costs. In Table 7.5 we modify Table 7.2 to reflect

---

Table 7.5 THE TRADEOFF ON DEBT: NO TAXES, DEFAULT RISK, AND AGENCY COSTS	
Advantages of Debt	**Disadvantages of Debt**
1. Tax benefit: Zero, because there are no taxes.	**1.** Bankruptcy cost: Zero, because there are no bankruptcy costs.
2. Added discipline: Zero, because managers already maximize stockholder wealth.	**2.** Agency cost: Zero, because bondholders are fully protected from wealth transfer.
	3. Loss of future financing flexibility: Not costly, because firms can raise external financing costlessly.

---

[31]F. Modigliani and M. Miller, "The Cost of Capital, Corporation Finance and the Theory of Investment," *American Economic Review* 48:261–297.

Figure 7.8 Value of Levered Firm: Modigliani and Miller with Taxes

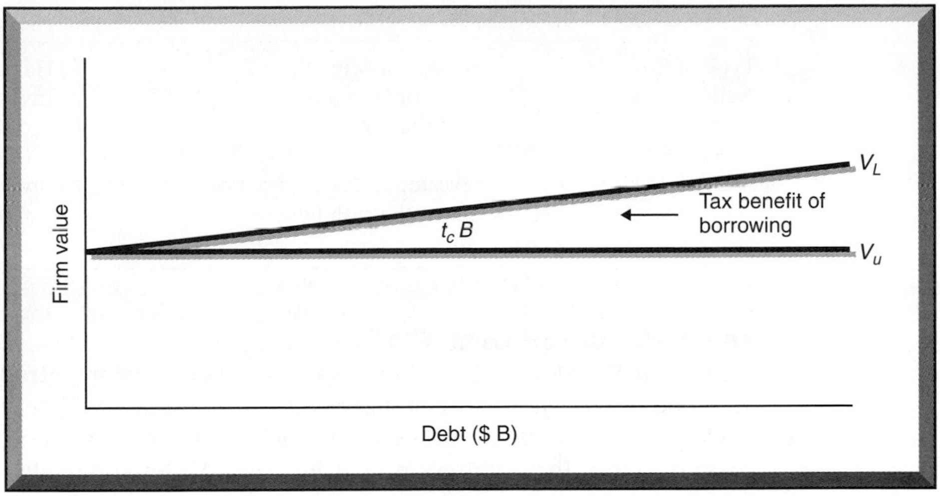

the assumptions just listed. Debt creates neither benefits nor costs and thus has a neutral effect on value. In such an environment, the capital structure decision becomes irrelevant.

In a later study, Modigliani-Miller preserved this environment but made one change, allowing for a tax benefit for debt. In this scenario, where debt continues to have no costs, the optimal debt ratio for a firm is 100% debt. In fact, in such an environment the value of the firm increases by the present value of the tax savings for interest payments.

$$\text{Value of levered firm} = \text{Value of unlevered firm} + t_c B$$

where t_c is the corporate tax rate and B is the dollar borrowing. Note that the second term in this valuation is the present value of the interest tax savings from debt, treated as a perpetuity. Figure 7.8 graphs the value of a firm with just the tax benefit from debt.

Modigliani-Miller presented an alternative proof of the irrelevance of leverage, based on the idea that debt does not affect the underlying operating cash flows of the firm in the absence of taxes. Consider two firms that have the same cash flow (X) from operations. Firm A is an all-equity firm, whereas Firm B has both equity and debt. The interest rate on debt is r. Assume you are an investor and you buy a fraction (α) of the equity in Firm A, and the same fraction of both the equity and debt of Firm B. Table 7.6 summarizes the cash flows that you will receive in the next period.

Because you receive the same total cash flow in both firms, the price you will pay for either firm has to be the same. This equivalence in values of the two firms implies that leverage does not affect the value of a firm. Note that this proof works only if the firm does not receive a tax benefit from debt; a tax benefit would give Firm B a higher cash flow than Firm A.

Table 7.6 CASH FLOWS TO INVESTOR FROM LEVERED AND ALL-EQUITY FIRM

	Firm A	Firm B
Type of firm	All-equity firm ($V_u = E$)	Has some equity and debt
Actions now	Investor buys a fraction α of the firm (αV_u)	Investor buys a fraction a of both equity and debt of the firm; $\alpha E_L + \alpha D_L$
Next period	Investor receives a fraction α of the cash flow (αX)	Investor receives the following: $\alpha(X - rD_L) + \alpha rD_L = \alpha X$

The Irrelevance of Debt with Taxes

It is clear in the Modigliani-Miller model that when taxes are introduced into the model, debt does affect value. In fact, introducing both taxes and bankruptcy costs into the model creates a tradeoff, where the financing mix of a firm affects value, and there is an optimal mix. In an address in 1979, however, Miller argued that the debt irrelevance theorem could apply even in the presence of corporate taxes if taxes on the equity and interest income individuals receive from firms were included in the analysis.[32]

To demonstrate the Miller proof of irrelevance, assume that investors face a tax rate of t_d on interest income and a tax rate of t_e on equity income. Assume also that the firm pays an interest rate of r on debt and faces a corporate tax rate of t_c. The after-tax return to the investor from owning debt can then be written as

$$\text{After-tax return from owning debt} = r(1 - t_d)$$

The after-tax return to the investor from owning equity can also be estimated. Because cash flows to equity have to be paid out of after-tax cash flows, equity income is taxed twice—once at the corporate level and once at the equity level:

$$\text{After-tax return from owning equity} = k_e(1 - t_c)(1 - t_e)$$

The returns to equity can take two forms—dividends or capital gains; the equity tax rate is a blend of the tax rates on both. In such a scenario, Miller noted that the tax benefit of debt relative to equity becomes smaller, because both debt and equity now get taxed, at least at the level of the individual investor.

$$\text{Tax benefit of debt relative to equity} = [1 - (1 - t_c)(1 - t_e)]/(1 - t_d)$$

With this relative tax benefit, the value of the firm with leverage can be written as

$$V_L = V_u + [1 - (1 - t_c)(1 - t_e)/(1 - t_d)]B$$

where

> V_L is the value of the firm with leverage
> V_U is the value of the firm without leverage
> B is the dollar debt

---

[32]M. Miller, "Debt and Taxes," *Journal of Finance* 32:261–275.

With this expanded equation, which includes both personal and corporate taxes, there are several possible scenarios:

- *Personal tax rates on both equity and dividend income are zero.* If we ignore personal taxes, this equation compresses to the original equation for the value of a levered firm, in a world with taxes but no bankruptcy costs:

$$V_L = V_u + t_c B$$

- *The personal tax rate on equity is the same as the tax rate on debt.* If this were the case, the result is the same as the original one—the value of the firm increases with more debt:

$$V_L = V_u + t_c B$$

- *The tax rate on debt is higher than the tax rate on equity.* in such a case, the differences in the individual investor tax rates may more than compensate for the double taxation of equity cash flows. To illustrate, assume that the tax rate on ordinary income is 70%, the tax rate on capital gains on stock is 28%, and the tax rate on corporations is 35%. In such a case, the tax liabilities for debt and equity can be calculated for a firm that pays no dividend as follows:

    Tax rate on debt income = 70%
    Tax rate on equity income = $1 - (1 - 0.35)(1 - 0.28) = 0.532$, or 53.2%

    This is a plausible scenario, especially considering tax law in the United States until the early 1980s. In this scenario, debt creates a tax disadvantage for investors.

- *The tax rate on equity income is just low enough to compensate for the double taxation.* in this case, we are back to the original debt irrelevance theorem.

$$(1 - t_d) = (1 - t_c)(1 - t_e) \ldots \text{Debt is irrelevant}$$

Miller's analysis brought investor tax rates into the analysis for the first time and provided some insight into the role of investor tax preferences on a firm's capital structure. As Miller himself notes, however, this analysis does not reestablish the irrelevance of debt under all circumstances, but rather opens up the possibility that debt could still be irrelevant despite its tax advantages.

The Consequences of Debt Irrelevance

If the financing decision is irrelevant, as proposed by Modigliani-Miller, corporate financial analysis is simplified in a number of ways. The cost of capital, which is the weighted average of the cost of debt and the cost of equity, is unaffected by changes in the proportions of debt and equity. This might seem unreasonable, especially because the cost of debt is much lower than the cost of equity. In the Modigliani-Miller world, however, any benefits incurred by substituting cheaper debt for more expensive equity are offset by increases in both their costs, as shown in Figure 7.9.

The value of the firm is also unaffected by the amount of leverage it has. Thus, if the firm is valued as an all-equity entity, its value will remain unchanged if it is valued with

Figure 7.9   Cost of Capital in the MM World

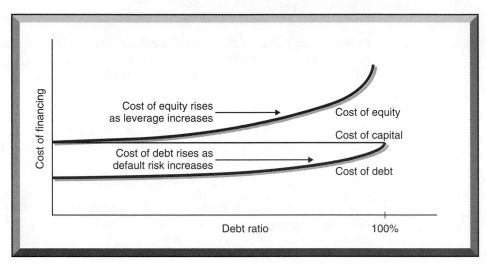

any other debt ratio. (This actually follows from the implication that the cost of capital is unaffected by changes in leverage and from the assumption that the operating cash flows are determined by investment decisions rather than financing decisions.)

Finally, the investment decision can be made independently of the financing decision. In other words, if a project is a bad project when evaluated as an all-equity project, it will remain so using any other financing mix.

The Contribution of the Modigliani-Miller Theorem

It is unlikely that capital structure is irrelevant in the real world, given the tax preferences for debt and existence of default risk. In spite of this, Modigliani-Miller were pioneers in moving capital structure analysis from an environment in which firms picked their debt ratios based on comparable firms and management preferences to one that recognized the tradeoffs. They also drew attention to the impact of good investment decisions on firm value. To be more precise, a firm that invests in poor projects cannot hope to recoup the lost value by making better financing decisions; a firm that takes good projects will succeed in creating value, even if it uses the wrong financing mix. Finally, although the concept of a world with no taxes, default risk, or agency problems may seem a little far-fetched, there are some environments in which the description might hold. Assume, for instance, that the U.S. government decides to encourage small businesses to invest in urban areas by relieving them of their tax burden and providing a backup guarantee on loans (default protection). Firms that respond to these initiatives might find that their capital structure decisions do not affect their value.

Finally, surveys of financial managers indicate that in practice, they do not attach as much weight to the costs and benefits of debt as we do in theory. In the survey quoted earlier by Pinegar and Wilbricht, managers were asked to cite the most important

Table 7.7 INPUTS INTO CAPITAL STRUCTURE DECISIONS

| Inputs/assumptions by order of importance | Percentage of Responses within Each Rank | | | | | | |
| | Least Important | | Most Important | | | | |
	1	2	3	4	5	Not Ranked	Mean
1. Projected cash flow from asset to be financed	1.7%	1.1%	9.7%	29.5%	58.0%	0.0%	4.41
2. Avoiding dilution of common equity's claims	2.8%	6.3%	18.2%	39.8%	33.0%	0.0%	3.94
3. Risk of asset to be financed	2.8%	6.3%	20.5%	36.9%	33.0%	0.6%	3.91
4. Restrictive covenants on senior securities	9.1%	9.7%	18.7%	35.2%	27.3%	0.0%	3.62
5. Avoiding mispricing of securities to be issued	3.4%	10.8%	27.3%	39.8%	18.7%	0.0%	3.60
6. Corporate tax rate	4.0%	9.7%	29.5%	42.6%	13.1%	1.1%	3.52
7. Voting control	17.6%	10.8%	21.0%	31.2%	19.3%	0.0%	3.24
8. Depreciation and other tax shields	8.5%	17.6%	40.9%	24.4%	7.4%	1.1%	3.05
9. Correcting mispricing of securities	14.8%	27.8%	36.4%	14.2%	5.1%	1.7%	2.66
10. Personal tax rates of debt and equity holders	31.2%	34.1%	25.6%	8.0%	1.1%	0.0%	2.14
11. Bankruptcy costs	69.3%	13.1%	6.8%	4.0%	4.5%	2.3%	1.58

inputs governing their financial decisions. Their responses are ranked in the order of the importance managers attached to them in Table 7.7.

Financial managers seem to weigh financial flexibility and potential dilution much more heavily than bankruptcy costs and taxes in their capital structure decisions.

IN PRACTICE: THE DILUTION BOGEY

The dilution effect refers to the possible decrease in earnings per share from any action that might lead to an increase in the number of shares outstanding. As evidenced in Table 7.7, managers (especially in the United States) weigh these potential dilution effects heavily in decisions on what type of financing to use and how to fund projects. Consider, for instance, the choice between raising equity using a rights issue, where the stock is issued at a price below the current market price, and a public issue of stock at the market price. The latter is a much more expensive option, from the perspective of investment banking fees and other costs, but is chosen nevertheless because it results in fewer shares being issued (to raise the same amount of funds). The fear of dilution is misplaced for the following reasons:

- Investors measure their returns in terms of total return and not just in terms of stock price. Although the stock price will go down more after a rights issue, each investor will be compensated adequately for the price drop (by either receiving more shares or by being able to sell their rights to other investors). In fact, if the transactions costs are considered, stockholders will be better off after a rights issue than after an equivalent public issue of stock.

- Although the earnings per share will always drop in the immediate aftermath of a new stock issue, the market value of equity will not necessarily follow suit. In particular, if the stock issue is used to finance a good project (i.e., a project with a positive net present value), the increase in value should be greater than the increase in the number of shares, leading to a higher stock price.

Ultimately, the measure of whether a company should issue stock to finance a project should depend on the quality of the investment. Firms that dilute their stockholdings to take good investments are choosing the right course for their stockholders. ■

There Is an Optimal Capital Structure

The counter to the Modigliani-Miller proposition is that the tradeoffs on debt may work in favor of the firm (at least initially) and that borrowing money may lower the cost of capital and increase firm value. We will examine the mechanics of putting this argument into practice in the next chapter; here, we make a case for the existence of an optimal capital structure and look at some of the empirical evidence for and against it.

The Case for an Optimal Capital Structure
If the debt decision involves a tradeoff between the benefits of debt (tax benefits and added discipline) and the costs of debt (bankruptcy costs, agency costs, and lost flexibility), it can be argued that the marginal benefits will be offset by the marginal costs *only in exceptional cases* and not always then (as argued by Modigliani-Miller). In fact, under most circumstances, the marginal benefits will either exceed the marginal costs (in which case debt is good and will increase firm value) or fall short of marginal costs (in which case equity is better). Accordingly, there is an optimal capital structure for most firms at which firm value is maximized.

Of course, it is always possible that managers may be operating under an illusion: that capital structure decisions matter, when the reality might be otherwise. Consequently, we examine some of the empirical evidence to see if it is consistent with the theory of an optimal mix of debt and equity.

Empirical Evidence
The question of whether there is an optimal capital structure can be answered in a number of ways. The first is to see if differences in capital structure across firms can be explained systematically by differences in the variables driving the tradeoffs. Other things remaining equal, we would expect to see relationships listed in Table 7.8.

This may seem like a relatively simple test to run, but keeping all other things equal in the real world is often close to impossible. In spite of this limitation, attempts to see if the direction of the relationship is consistent with the theory have produced mixed results.

Table 7.8 DEBT RATIOS AND FUNDAMENTALS

Variable	Effect on Debt Ratios
Marginal tax rate	As marginal tax rates increase, debt ratios increase.
Separation of ownership and management	The greater the separation of ownership and management, the higher the debt ratio.
Variability in operating cash flows	As operating cash flows become more variable, the bankruptcy risk increases, resulting in lower debt ratios.
Debt holders' difficulty in monitoring firm actions, investments, and performance	The more difficult it is to monitor the actions taken by a firm, the lower the optimal debt ratio.
Need for flexibility	The greater the need for decision-making flexibility in future periods, the lower the optimal debt ratio.

Bradley, Jarrell, and Kim analyzed whether differences in debt ratios can be explained by proxies for the variables involved in the capital structure tradeoff.[33] They noted that the debt ratio is

- *Negatively correlated with the volatility in annual operating earnings*, as predicted by the bankruptcy cost component of the optimal capital structure tradeoff
- *Positively related to the level of nondebt tax shields*, which is counter to the tax hypothesis, which argues that firms with large nondebt tax shields should be less inclined to use debt
- *Negatively related to advertising and R&D expenses used as a proxy for agency costs*; which is consistent with optimal capital structure theory

Others who have attempted to examine whether cross-sectional differences in capital structure are consistent with the theory have come to contradictory conclusions.

An alternate test of the optimal capital structure hypothesis is to examine the stock price reaction to actions taken by firms either to increase or decrease leverage. In evaluating the price response, we have to make some assumptions about the motivation of the firms making these changes. If we assume that firms are rational and that they make these changes to get closer to their optimal, both leverage-increasing and leverage-decreasing actions should be accompanied by positive excess returns, at least on average. Smith noted that the evidence is *not* consistent with an optimal capital structure hypothesis, however, because leverage-increasing actions seem to be accompanied by positive excess returns, whereas leverage-reducing actions seem to be

---

[33]M. Bradley, G. Jarrell, and E. H. Kim, "On the Existence of an Optimal Capital Structure: Theory and Evidence," *Journal of Finance* 39:857–878.

followed by negative returns.[34] The only way to reconcile this tendency with an optimal capital structure argument is by assuming that managerial incentives (desire for stability and flexibility) keep leverage below optimal for most firms and that actions by firms to reduce leverage are seen as serving managerial interests rather than stockholder interests.

The Debt Equity Tradeoff: A Behavioral Perspective

The tradeoff between the benefits of debt (tax advantages and added discipline) and the costs of debt (expected bankruptcy costs and agency costs) is not always made rationally. Managers bring to this tradeoff all of the behavioral characteristics that influence other corporate finance decisions. Several papers note that managers who are overconfident in their abilities to deliver cash flows (and thus take negative NPV investments) also tend to borrow too much. Put in another way, they underestimate the bankruptcy costs of debt and overestimate its benefits.[35] The same overconfidence, though, can reduce agency costs, since overconfident managers are less likely to divert funds away from the stated investments.[36]

How do we counter the tendency of firms with optimistic, overconfident managers to borrow too much? The first line of defense has to be lenders. Historically, banks have played the role of the realistic pessimist, who sees the potential downside to the management's upside, restraining borrowing. However, the shift to corporate bonds has weakened this constraint. The second line of defense are the bond ratings agencies, especially for firms that borrow through corporate bonds. It is the role of ratings agencies to look past the hype and the sales pitches made by managers and to assess default risk realistically.

There are periods in history when both lines of defense crumble and lenders do not operate as restraints on managers. It is in these environments that we see firms collectively borrow too much at interest rates that do not adequately reflect the underlying default risk. Eventually, though, the bubble bursts, leaving bondholders, banks, and the borrowing firms feeling the pain.

There is a data set online that summarizes debt ratios and averages by sector for the fundamental variables that should determine debt ratios.

HOW FIRMS CHOOSE THEIR CAPITAL STRUCTURES

We have argued that firms should choose the mix of debt and equity by trading off the benefit of borrowing against the costs. There are, however, three alternative views of how firms choose a financing mix. The first is that the choice between debt and equity is determined by where a firm is in the growth life cycle. High-growth firms will tend to use debt less than more mature firms. The second is that firms choose their financing

---

[34]C. W. Smith, "Investment Banking and the Capital Acquisition Process," *Journal of Financial Economics* 15:3–29.

[35]R. Fairchild, "The Effect of Managerial Overconfidence, Asymmetric Information, and Moral Hazard on Capital Structure Decisions," *ICFAI Journal of Behavioral Finance* 2, no. 4:46–68.

[36]D. Hackbart, "Managerial Trails and Capital Structure Decisions," working paper, ssrn.com, 2007.

mix by looking at other firms in their business. The third view is that firms have strong preferences in for the kinds of financing they prefer to use—a financing hierarchy—and that they deviate from these preferences only when they have no choice. We will argue that in each of these approaches, firms still implicitly make the tradeoff between costs and benefits, though the assumptions needed for each approach to work are different.

Financing Mix and a Firm's Life Cycle

Earlier in this chapter, we looked at how a firm's financing choices might change as it makes the transition from a startup firm to a mature firm to final decline. We can also look at how a firm's financing mix changes over the same life cycle. Typically, startup firms and firms in rapid expansion use debt sparingly; in some cases, they use no debt at all. As the growth eases and as cash flows from existing investments become larger and more predictable, we see firms beginning to use debt. Debt ratios typically peak when firms are in mature growth.

How does this empirical observation relate to our earlier discussion of the benefits and costs of debt? We argue that the behavior of firms at each stage in the life cycle is entirely consistent with making this tradeoff. In the startup and high-growth phases, the tax benefits to firms from using debt tend to be small or nonexistent, because earnings from existing investments are low or negative. The owners of these firms are usually actively involved in the management of these firms, reducing the need for debt as a disciplinary mechanism.

On the other side of the ledger, the low and volatile earnings increase the expected bankruptcy costs. The absence of significant existing investments or assets and the magnitude of new investments makes lenders much more cautious about lending to the firm, increasing the agency costs; these costs show up as more stringent covenants or in higher interest rates on borrowing. As growth eases, the tradeoff shifts in favor of debt. The tax benefits increase and expected bankruptcy costs decrease as earnings from existing investments become larger and more predictable. The firm develops both an asset base and a track record on earnings, which allows lenders to feel more protected when lending to the firm. As firms get larger, the separation between owners (stockholders) and managers tends to grow, and the benefits of using debt as a disciplinary mechanism increase. We have summarized the tradeoff at each stage in the life cycle in Figure 7.10.

As with our earlier discussion of financing choices, there will be variations between firms in different businesses at each stage in the life cycle. For instance, a mature steel company may use far more debt than a mature pharmaceutical company because lenders feel more comfortable lending on a steel company's assets (which are tangible and easy to liquidate) than on a pharmaceutical company's assets (which might be patents and other assets that are difficult to liquidate). Similarly, we would expect a company like IBM to have a higher debt ratio than a firm like Microsoft at the same stage in the life cycle, because Microsoft has large insider holdings, making the benefit of discipline that comes from debt much smaller.

Financing Mix Based on Comparable Firms

Firms often try to use a financing mix similar to that used by other firms in their business. With this approach, Bookscape would use a low debt-to-capital ratio, because

Figure 7.10   The Debt-Equity Trade off and Life Cycle

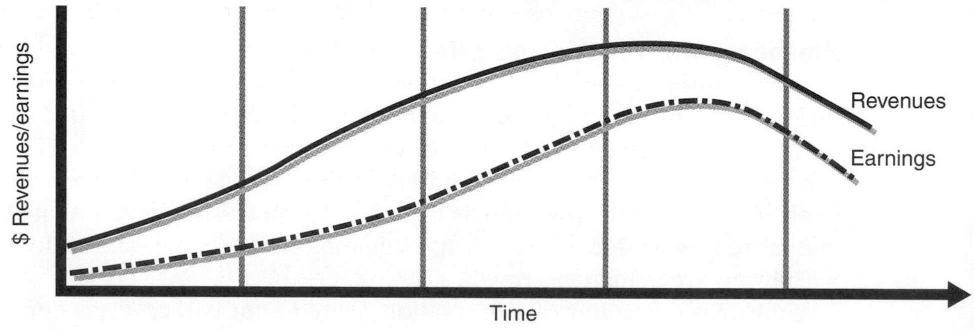

	Stage 1 Start-up	Stage 2 Rapid expansion	Stage 3 High growth	Stage 4 Mature growth	Stage 5 Decline
					Revenues Earnings
Tax benefits	Zero, if losing money	Low, as earnings are limited	Increase, with earnings	High	High, but declining
Added discipline of debt	Low, as owners run the firm	Low. Even if public, firm is closely held	Increasing, as managers own less of firm	High, managers are separated from owners	Declining, as firm does not take many new investments
Bankruptcy cost	Very high, as firm has no or negative earnings	Very high. Earnings are low and volatile	High. Earnings are increasing but still volatile	Declining, as earnings from existing assets increase	Low, but increases as existing projects end
Agency costs	Very high, as firm has almost no assets	High. New investments are difficult to monitor	High. Lots of new investments and unstable risk	Declining, as assets in place become a larger portion of firm	Low. Firm takes few new investments
Need for flexibility	Very high, as firm looks for ways to establish itself	High. Expansion needs are large and unpredictable	High. Expansion needs remain unpredictable	Low. Firm has low and more predictable investment needs	Nonexistent. Firm has no new investment needs
Net tradeoff	Costs exceed benefits. Minimal debt	Costs still likely to exceed benefits. Mostly equity	Debt starts yielding net benefits to the firm. Increasing debt ratio	Debt becomes a more attractive option. High debt ratio	Debt will provide benefits. High debt ratio

The y-axis of the graph is labeled "$ Revenues/earnings" and the x-axis is labeled "Time".

other book retailers have low debt ratios. Verizon, on the other hand, would use a high debt-to-capital ratio because other phone companies have high debt-to-capital ratios.

The empirical evidence about the way firms choose their debt ratios strongly supports the hypothesis that they tend not to stray too far from their sector averages. In fact, when we look at the determinants of the debt ratios of individual firms, the strongest determinant is the average debt ratio of the industries to which these firms belong. Some would view this approach to financing as contrary to the approach where we trade off the benefits of debt against the cost of debt, but we do not view it thus.

If firms within a business or sector share common characteristics, it should not be surprising if they choose similar financing mixes. For instance, software firms have volatile earnings and high growth potential and choose low debt ratios. In contrast, phone companies have significant assets in place and high and stable earnings; they tend to use more debt in their financing. Thus, choosing a debt ratio similar to that of the industry in which you operate is appropriate when firms in the industry are at the same stage in the life cycle and, on average, choose the right financing mix for that stage.

It can be dangerous to choose a debt ratio based on comparable firms under two scenarios. The first occurs when there are wide variations in growth potential and risk across companies within a sector. In this case, we would expect debt ratios to be different across firms. The second occurs when firms on average have too much or too little debt given their characteristics. This can happen when an entire sector changes. For instance, phone companies have historically had stable and large earnings, because they have had monopoly power. As technology and deregulation breaks down this power, it is entirely possible that earnings will become more volatile and that these firms should carry a lot less debt than they do currently.

Following a Financing Hierarchy

There is evidence that firms follow a *financing hierarchy*: retained earnings are the most preferred choice for financing, followed by debt, new equity, common, and preferred; convertible preferred is the least preferable choice. Going back again to the survey by Pinegar and Wilbricht (Table 7.9), managers were asked to rank six different sources of financing—internal equity, external equity, external debt, preferred stock, and hybrids (convertible debt and preferred stock)—from most preferred to least.[37]

One reason for this hierarchy is that managers value *flexibility and control*. To the extent that external financing reduces flexibility for future financing (especially if it is debt) and control (bonds have covenants; new equity attracts new stockholders into the company and may reduce insider holdings as a percentage of total holding), managers prefer retained earnings as a source of capital. Another reason is it costs nothing in terms of issuance costs to use retained earnings, whereas *it costs more* to use external debt, and even more to use external equity.

Table 7.9   SURVEY RESULTS ON PLANNING PRINCIPLES

Ranking	Source	Planning Principle Cited
1	Retained earnings	None
2	Straight debt	Maximize security prices
3	Convertible debt	Cash flow and survivability
4	Common stock	Avoiding dilution
5	Straight preferred stock	Comparability
6	Convertible preferred stock	None

[37]J. Michael Pinegar and Lisa Wilbricht, "What Managers Think of Capital Structure Theory: A Survey," *Financial Management* 18, no. 4:82–91.

Figure 7.11   External Financing Breakdown

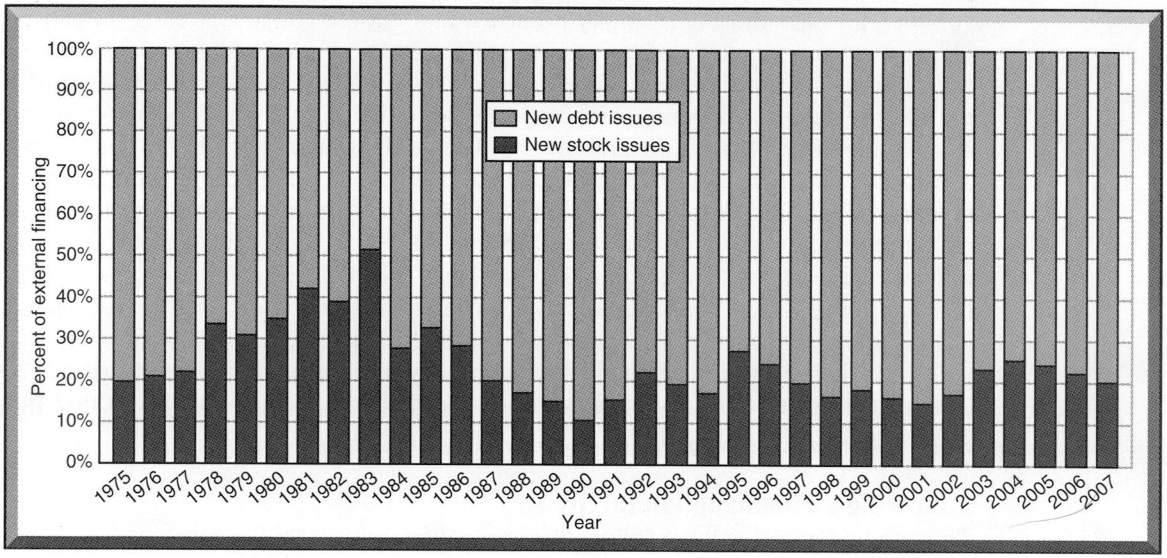

Source: Compustat.

The survey yielded some other interesting conclusions as well. External debt is strongly preferred over external equity as a way of raising funds. The percentages of external financing from debt and external equity between 1975 and 2007 issued by U.S. corporations are shown in Figure 7.11 and bear out this preference.

Given a choice, firms had much rather use straight debt than convertible debt, even though the interest rate on convertible debt is much lower. Managers perhaps have a much better sense of the value of the conversion option than is recognized.

A firm's choices may say a great deal about its financial strength. Thus, the 1993 decisions by RJR Nabisco and GM to raise new funds through convertible preferred stock were seen by markets as an admission of their financial weakness. Not surprisingly, the financial market response to the issue of securities listed in Table 7.9 mirrors the preferences: the most negative responses are reserved for securities near the bottom of the list, and the most positive (or, at least, the least negative) for those at the top of the list.

Why do firms have a financing hierarchy? In the discussion of financing choices so far, we have steered away from questions about how firms convey information to financial markets with their financing choices and how well the securities that the firms issue are priced. Firms know more about their future prospects than do the financial markets that they deal with; markets may under- or overprice securities issued by firms. Myers and Majluf note that in the presence of this asymmetric information, firms that believe their securities are underpriced, given their future prospects, may be inclined to reject good projects rather than raise external financing. Alternatively, firms that believe their securities are overpriced are more likely to issue these securities, even if they have no projects available.[38] In this environment, the following implications emerge:

- Managers prefer retained earnings to external financing, because it allows them to consider projects on their merits rather than depending on whether markets are pricing their securities correctly. It follows then that firms will be more inclined to retain earnings over and above their current investment requirements to finance future projects.

- When firms issue securities, markets will consider the issue a signal that these securities are overvalued. This signal is likely to be more negative for securities, such as stocks, where the asymmetry of information is greater, and smaller for securities, such as straight bonds, where the asymmetry is smaller. This would explain both the rankings in the financial hierarchy and the market reaction to these security issues.

7.16   VALUE OF FLEXIBILITY AND FIRM CHARACTERISTICS

You are reading *The Wall Street Journal* and notice a tombstone ad for a company offering to sell convertible preferred stock. What would you hypothesize about the health of the company issuing these securities?

a.   Nothing

b.   Healthier than the average firm

c.   In much more financial trouble than the average firm

CONCLUSION

In this chapter, we laid the groundwork for analyzing a firm's optimal mix of debt and equity by laying out the benefits and the costs of borrowing money. In particular, we made the following points:

- We differentiated between debt and equity at a generic level by pointing out that any financing approach that results in contractual cash flows and has prior claims in the case of default, fixed maturity, and no voting rights is debt, whereas a financing approach that provides for residual cash flows and has low or no priority in claims in the case of default, infinite life, and a lion's share of the control is equity.

- Although all firms, private as well as public, use both debt and equity, the choices in terms of financing and the type of financing used change as a firm progresses

---

[38]S. C. Myers and N. S. Majluf, "Corporate Financing and Investment Decisions When Firms Have Information That Investors Do Not Have," *Journal of Financial Economics* 13:187–221.

through the life cycle, with equity dominating at the earlier stages and debt as the firm matures.

- The primary benefit of debt is a tax benefit: interest expenses are tax-deductible and cash flows to equity (dividends) are not. This benefit increases with the tax rate of the entity taking on the debt. A secondary benefit of debt is that it forces managers to be more disciplined in their choice of projects by increasing the costs of failure; a series of bad projects may create the possibility of defaulting on interest and principal payments.

- The primary cost of borrowing is an increase in the expected bankruptcy cost—the product of the probability of default and the cost of bankruptcy. The probability of default is greater for firms that have volatile cash flows. The cost of bankruptcy includes both the direct costs (legal and time value) of bankruptcy and the indirect costs (lost sales, tighter credit, and less access to capital). Borrowing money exposes the firm to the possibility of conflicts between stock and bondholders over investment, financing, and dividend decisions. The covenants that bondholders write into bond agreements to protect themselves against expropriation cost the firm in both monitoring costs and lost flexibility. The loss of financial flexibility that arises from borrowing money is more likely to be a problem for firms with substantial and unpredictable investment opportunities.

- In the special case where there are no tax benefits, default risk, or agency problems, the financing decision is irrelevant. This is known as the Modigliani-Miller theorem. In most cases, however, the tradeoff between the benefits and costs of debt will result in an optimal capital structure whereby the value of the firm is maximized.

- Firms generally choose their financing mix in one of three ways—based on where they are in the life cycle, by looking at comparable firms, or by following a financing hierarchy where retained earnings is the most preferred option and convertible preferred stock the least.

ANALYZING A FIRM'S CURRENT FINANCING CHOICES

Objective: To examine a firm's current financing choices and to categorize them into debt (borrowings) and equity and to examine the tradeoff between debt and equity for your firm.

Key Questions

- Where and how does the firm get its current financing?
- Would these financing choices be classified as debt, equity, or hybrid securities?
- How large, in qualitative or quantitative terms, are the advantages to this company from using debt?
- How large, in qualitative or quantitative terms, are the disadvantages to this company from using debt?
- From the qualitative tradeoff, does this firm look like it has too much or too little debt?

Framework for Analysis

1. **Assessing Current Financing**

    1.1. How does the firm raise equity?

    a. If it is a publicly traded firm, it can raise equity from common stock and warrants or options.

    b. If is a private firm, the equity can come from personal savings and venture capital.

    1.2. How (if at all) does the firm borrow money?

    a. Does it use bank loans or corporate bonds?

    b. What is the maturity structure for the debt?

    c. What type of debt does the firm have (currency mix, fixed versus floating)?

    1.3. Does the firm use any hybrid approaches to raising financing that combine some of the features of debt and equity?
    Examples would include preferred stock, convertible bonds, and bonds with warrants attached to them.

2. **Detailed Description of Current Financing**

    2.1. If the firm raises equity from warrants or convertibles, what are the characteristics of the options (exercise price, maturity, etc.)?

    2.2. If the firm has borrowed money, what are the characteristics of the debt (maturity, coupon or stated interest rate, call features, fixed or floating rate, secured or unsecured, and currency)?

    2.3. If the firm has hybrid securities, what are the features of the hybrid securities?

3. **Breakdown into Debt and Equity**

   3.1. If the firm has financing with debt and equity components (such as convertible bonds), how much of the value can be attributed to debt and how much to equity?

   3.2. Given the coupon or stated interest rate and maturity of the nontraded debt, what is the current estimated market value of the debt?

   3.3. What is the market value of equity that the firm has outstanding?

4. **Tradeoff on Debt versus Equity**

   Benefits of Debt

   - What marginal tax rate does this firm face, and how does this measure up to the marginal tax rates of other firms? Are there other tax deductions that this company has (like depreciation) to reduce the tax bite?

   - Does this company have high free cash flows (for example, EBITDA/firm value)? Has it taken, and does it continue to have, good investment projects? How responsive are managers to stockholders? (Will there be an advantage to using debt in this firm as a way of keeping managers in line or do other [cheaper] mechanisms exist?)

   Costs of Debt

   - How high are the current cash flows of the firm (to service the debt), and how stable are these cash flows? (Look at the variability in the operating income over time.)

   - How easy is it for bondholders to observe what equity investors are doing? Are the assets tangible or intangible? If not, what are the costs in terms of monitoring stockholders or in terms of bond covenants?

   - How well can this firm forecast its future investment opportunities and needs?

Getting Information about Current Financing Choices

The information about current financing choices can almost all be extracted from the financial statements. The balance sheet should provide a summary of the book values of the various financing choices made by the firm, though hybrids are usually categorized into debt (if they are debt hybrids) and equity (if they are equity hybrids). The description of warrants outstanding as well as the details of the borrowing that the firm has should be available in the footnotes to the balance sheets. In particular, the maturity dates for different components of borrowing, the coupon rates and information on any other special features should be available in the notes.

 Online Sources of Information
www.stern.nyu.edu/~adamodar/cfin2E/project/data.htm

PROBLEMS AND QUESTIONS

1. An income bondholder receives interest payments only if the firm makes income. If the firm does not make interest payments in a year, the interest is cumulated and paid in the first year the firm makes income. A preferred stock receives preferred dividends only if the firm makes income. If a firm does not make preferred dividend payments in a year, the dividend is cumulated and paid in the first year the firm makes income. Are income bonds really preferred stock? What are the differences? For purposes of calculating debt, how would you differentiate between income bonds and regular bonds?

2. A commodity bond links interest and principal payments to the price of a commodity. Differentiate a commodity bond from a straight bond, and then from equity. How would you factor these differences into your analysis of the debt ratio of a company that has issued exclusively commodity bonds?

3. You are analyzing a new security that has been promoted as equity, with the following features:
   - The dividend on the security is fixed in dollar terms for the life of the security, which is twenty years.
   - The dividend is not tax-deductible.
   - In the case of default, the holders of this security will receive cash only after all debt holders, secured as well as unsecured, are paid.
   - The holders of this security will have no voting rights.

   Based on the description of debt and equity in the chapter, how would you classify this security? If you were asked to calculate the debt ratio for this firm, how would you categorize this security?

4. You are analyzing a convertible preferred stock with the following characteristics for the security:
   - There are 50,000 preferred shares outstanding, with a face value of $100 and a 6% preferred dividend rate.
   - The firm has straight preferred stock outstanding, with a preferred dividend rate of 9%.
   - The preferred stock is trading at $105.

   Estimate the preferred stock and equity components of this preferred stock.

5. You have been asked to calculate the debt ratio for a firm that has the following components to its financing mix:
   - The firm has 1 million shares outstanding, trading at $50 per share.
   - The firm has $25 million in straight debt, carrying a market interest rate of 8%.
   - The firm has 20,000 convertible bonds outstanding, with a face value of $1,000, a market value of $1,100, and a coupon rate of 5%.

   Estimate the debt ratio for this firm.

6. You have been asked to estimate the debt ratio for a firm with the following financing details:
   - The firm has two classes of shares outstanding: 50,000 shares of class A stock, with two voting rights per share, trading at $100 per share, and 100,000 shares of class B stock, with half a voting right per share, trading at $90 per share.
   - The firm has $5 million in bank debt, and the debt was taken on recently.

   Estimate the debt ratio. Why does it matter when the bank debt was taken on?

7. Zycor Corporation obtains most of its funding internally. Assume that the stock has a beta of 1.2, the riskless rate is 6.5%, and the market risk premium is 6%.
   a. Estimate the cost of internal equity.
   b. Now assume that the cost of issuing new stock is 5% of the proceeds. Estimate the cost of external equity.

8. Office Helpers is a private firm that manufactures and sells office supplies. The firm has limited capital and is estimated to have a value of $80 million with the capital constraints. A venture capitalist is willing to contribute $20 million to the firm in exchange for 30% of the value of the firm. With this additional capital, the firm will be worth $120 million.
   a. Should the firm accept the venture capital?
   b. At what percentage of firm value would you (as the owner of the private firm) break even on the venture capital financing?

9. Assume now that Office Helpers decides to go public and would like to have its shares trade at a target price of $10 per share. If the IPO is likely to

be underpriced by 20%, how many shares should the firm have?

10. You are a venture capitalist and have been approached by Cirrus Electronics, a private firm. The firm has no debt outstanding and does not have earnings now but is expected to be earning $15 million in four years, when you also expect it to go public. The average price–earnings ratio of other firms in this business is 50.

   a. Estimate the exit value of Cirrus Electronics.

   b. If your target rate of return is 35%, estimate the discounted terminal value of Cirrus Electronics.

   c. If you are contributing $75 million of venture capital to Cirrus Electronics, at minimum, what percentage of the firm value would you demand in return?

11. The unlevered beta of electronics firms, on average, is 1.1. The riskless rate is 6.5% and the market risk premium is 6%.

   a. Estimate the expected return, using the CAPM.

   b. If you are a venture capitalist, why might you have a target rate of return much higher than this expected return?

12. Sunshine Media has just completed an IPO, where 50 million shares of the 125 million shares outstanding were issued to the public at an offering price of $22 per share. On the offering date, the stock price zoomed to $40 per share. Who gains from this increase in the price? Who loses, and how much?

13. IPOs are difficult to value, because firms going public tend to be small and little information is available about them; thus investment bankers have to underprice IPOs because they bear substantial pricing risk—do you agree with this statement? How would you test it empirically?

14. You are the owner of a small and successful firm with an estimated market value of $50 million. You are considering going public.

   a. What considerations would you have in choosing an investment banker?

   b. You want to raise $20 million in new financing, which you plan to reinvest back in the firm. (The estimated market value of $50 million is based on the assumption that this $20 million is reinvested.) What proportion of the firm

would you have to sell in the IPO to raise $20 million?

   c. How would your answer to **b** change if the investment banker plans to underprice your offering by 10%?

   d. If you wanted your stock to trade in the $20–25 range, how many shares would you have to create? How many shares would you have to issue?

15. You have been asked for advice on a rights offering by a firm with 10 million shares outstanding trading at $50 per share. The firm needs to raise $100 million in new equity. Assuming that the rights subscription price is $25, answer the following questions.

   a. How many rights would be needed to buy one share at the subscription price?

   b. Assuming that all rights are subscribed to, what will the ex-rights price be?

   c. Estimate the value per right.

   d. If the price of a right were different (higher or lower) than the value estimated in **c**, how would you exploit the difference?

16. You are stockholder in a SmallTech, a company that is planning to raise new equity. The stock is trading at $15 per share, and there are 1 million shares outstanding. The firm issues 500,000 rights to buy additional shares at $10 per share to its existing stockholders.

   a. What is the expected stock price after the rights are exercised?

   b. If the rights are traded, what is the price per right?

   c. As a stockholder, would you be concerned about the dilution effect lowering your stock price? Why, or why not?

17. Assume that SmallTech has net income of $1 million and that the earnings will increase in proportion with the additional capital raised.

   a. Estimate the earning per share that SmallTech will have after the rights issue described in the last problem.

   b. Assume that SmallTech could have raised the capital by issuing 333,333 shares at the prevailing market price of $15 per share (thus raising the same amount of equity as was raised in the rights issue) to the public. Estimate the earnings per share that SmallTech would have had with this alternative.

c. As a stockholder, are you concerned about the fact that the rights issue results in lower earnings per share than the general subscription offering (described in **b**)?

18. MVP, a manufacturing firm with no debt outstanding and a market value of $100 million, is considering borrowing $40 million and buying back stock. Assuming that the interest rate on the debt is 9% and that the firm faces a tax rate of 35%, answer the following questions:

a. Estimate the annual interest tax savings each year from the debt.

b. Estimate the present value of interest tax savings, assuming that the debt change is permanent.

c. Estimate the present value of interest tax savings, assuming that the debt will be taken on for ten years only.

d. What will happen to the present value of interest tax savings if interest rates drop tomorrow to 7% but the debt itself is fixed rate debt?

19. A business in the 45% tax bracket is considering borrowing money at 10%.

a. What is the after-tax interest rate on the debt?

b. What is the after-tax interest rate if only half of the interest expense is allowed as a tax deduction?

c. Would your answer change if the firm is losing money now and does not expect to have taxable income for three years?

20. WestingHome is a manufacturing company that has accumulated a net operating loss of $2 billion over time. It is considering borrowing $5 billion to acquire another company.

a. Based on the corporate tax rate of 36%, estimate the present value of the tax savings that could accrue to the company.

b. Does the existence of a net operating loss carryforward affect your analysis? (Will the tax benefits be diminished as a consequence?)

21. Answer true or false to the following questions relating to the free cash flow hypothesis (as developed by Jensen).

a. Companies with high operating earnings have high free cash flows.

b. Companies with large capital expenditures relative to earnings have low free cash flows.

c. Companies that commit to paying a large portion of their free cash flow as dividends do not need debt to add discipline.

d. The free cash flow hypothesis for borrowing money makes more sense for firms in which there is a separation of ownership and management.

e. Firms with high free cash flows are inefficiently run.

22. Assess the likelihood that the following firms will be taken over, based on your understanding of the free cash flow hypothesis. You can assume that earnings and free cash flows are highly correlated.

a. A firm with high growth prospects, good projects, low leverage, and high earnings

b. A firm with low growth prospects, poor projects, low leverage, and poor earnings

c. A firm with high growth prospects, good projects, high leverage, and low earnings

d. A firm with low growth prospects, poor projects, high leverage, and good earnings

e. A firm with low growth prospects, poor projects, low leverage, and good earnings

23. Nadir, an unlevered firm, has expected earnings before interest and taxes of $2 million per year. Nadir's tax rate is 40%, and the market value is $V = E = \$12$ million. The stock has a beta of 1, and the risk-free rate is 9%. (Assume that $E(R_m) - R_f = 6\%$.) Management is considering the use of debt; debt would be issued and used to buy back stock, and the size of the firm would remain constant. The default free interest rate on debt is 12%. Because interest expense is tax-deductible, the value of the firm would tend to increase as debt is added to the capital structure, but there would be an offset in the form of the rising cost of bankruptcy. The firm's analysts have estimated approximately that the present value of any bankruptcy cost is $8 million and the probability of bankruptcy will increase with leverage according to the following schedule:

Value of Debt	Probability of Failure
$2,500,000	0.00%
$5,000,000	8.00%
$7,500,000	20.5%
$8,000,000	30.0%
$9,000,000	45.0%
$10,000,000	52.5%
$12,500,000	70.0%

    a. What is the cost of equity and cost of capital at this time?

    b. What is the optimal capital structure when bankruptcy costs are considered?

    c. What will the value of the firm be at this optimal capital structure?

24. A firm that has no debt has a market value of $100 million and a cost of equity of 11%. In the Modigliani-Miller world,

    a. What happens to the value of the firm as the leverage is changed (assume no taxes)?

    b. What happens to the cost of capital as the leverage is changed (assume no taxes)?

    c. How would your answers to **a** and **b** change if there are taxes?

25. Assume that personal investors pay a 40% tax rate on interest income and only a 20% tax rate on equity income. If the corporate tax rate is 30%, estimate whether debt has a tax benefit relative to equity. If a firm with no debt and $100 million in market value borrows money in this world, estimate what the value of the firm will be if the firm borrows $50 million.

26. In the illustration in Problem 25, what would the tax rate on equity income need to be for debt to have no effect on value?

27. XYZ Pharma is a pharmaceutical company that traditionally has not used debt to finance its projects. Over the past ten years, it has also reported high returns on its projects and growth and made substantial research and development expenses over the time period. The health care business overall is growing much slower now, and the projects that the firm is considering have lower expected returns.

    a. How would you justify the firm's past policy of not using debt?

    b. Do you think the policy should be changed now? Why, or why not?

28. Unitrode, which makes analog/linear integrated circuits for power management, is a firm that has not used debt in the financing of its projects. The managers of the firm contend that they do not borrow money because they want to maintain financial flexibility.

    a. How does not borrowing money increase financial flexibility?

    b. What is the tradeoff you would be making if you have excess debt capacity and you choose not to use it because you want financial flexibility?

29. Consolidated Power is a regulated electric utility that has equity with a market value of $1.5 billion and debt outstanding of $3 billion. A consultant notes that this is a high debt ratio relative to the average across all firms, which is 27%, and suggests that the firm is overlevered.

    a. Why would you expect a electric utility to be able to maintain a higher debt ratio than the average company?

    b. Does the fact that the company is a regulated monopoly affect its capacity to carry debt?

CHAPTER 8

CAPITAL STRUCTURE: THE OPTIMAL FINANCIAL MIX

What is the optimal mix of debt and equity for a firm? In the last chapter we looked at the qualitative tradeoff between debt and equity, but we did not develop the tools we need to analyze whether debt should be 0%, 20%, 40%, or 60% of capital. Debt is always cheaper than equity, but using debt increases risk in terms of default risk to lenders and higher earnings volatility for equity investors. Thus, using more debt can increase value for some firms and decrease value for others, and even for the same firm, debt can be beneficial up to a point but destroy value beyond that point. We have to consider ways of going beyond the generalities in the last chapter to specific ways of identifying the right mix of debt and equity.

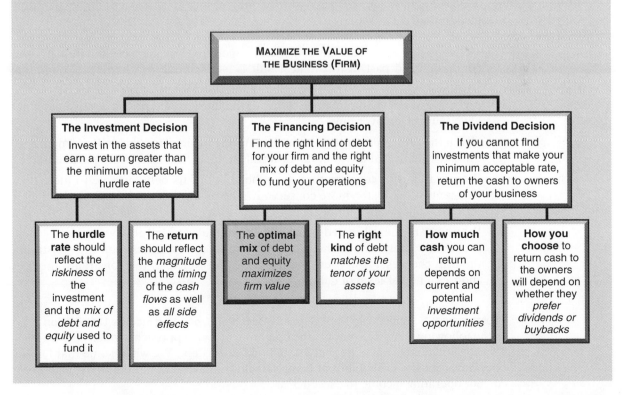

MAXIMIZE THE VALUE OF THE BUSINESS (FIRM)

The Investment Decision
Invest in the assets that earn a return greater than the minimum acceptable hurdle rate

The Financing Decision
Find the right kind of debt for your firm and the right mix of debt and equity to fund your operations

The Dividend Decision
If you cannot find investments that make your minimum acceptable rate, return the cash to owners of your business

The **hurdle rate** should reflect the *riskiness* of the investment and the *mix of debt and equity* used to fund it

The **return** should reflect the *magnitude* and the *timing* of the *cash flows* as well as *all side effects*

The **optimal mix** of debt and equity *maximizes firm value*

The **right kind** of debt *matches the tenor of your assets*

How much cash you can return depends on current and potential *investment opportunities*

How you choose to return cash to the owners will depend on whether they *prefer dividends or buybacks*

In this chapter, we explore four ways to find an optimal mix. The first approach begins with a distribution of future operating income; we can then decide how much debt to carry by defining the maximum possibility of default we are willing to bear. The second approach is to choose the debt ratio that minimizes the cost of capital. We review the role of cost of capital in valuation and discuss its relationship to the optimal debt ratio. The third approach, like the second, also attempts to maximize firm value, but it does so by adding the value of the unlevered firm to the present value of tax benefits from debt and then netting out the expected bankruptcy costs. The final approach is to base the financing mix on the way comparable firms finance their operations.

OPERATING INCOME APPROACH

The *operating income approach* is the simplest, and one of the most intuitive, ways of determining how much a firm can afford to borrow. We determine a firm's maximum acceptable probability of default as our starting point and, based on the distribution of operating income and cash flows, estimate how much debt the firm can carry.

Steps in Applying Operating Income Approach

We begin with an analysis of a firm's operating income and cash flows, and we consider how much debt it can afford to carry based on its cash flows. The steps in the operating income approach are as follows:

1. We assess the firm's capacity to generate operating income based on both current conditions and past history. The result is a distribution for expected operating income, with probabilities attached to different levels of income.

2. For any given level of debt, we estimate the interest and principal payments that have to be made over time.

3. Given the probability distribution of operating income and the debt payments, we estimate the probability that the firm will be unable to make those payments.

4. We set a limit or constraint on the probability of its being unable to meet debt payments. Clearly, the more conservative the management of the firm, the tighter this probability constraint will be.

5. We compare the estimated probability of default at a given level of debt to the probability constraint. If the probability of default is higher than the constraint, the firm chooses a lower level of debt; if it is lower than the constraint, the firm chooses a higher level of debt.

ILLUSTRATION 8.1 Estimating Debt Capacity Based on Operating Income Distribution
In the following analysis, we apply the operating income approach to analyzing whether Disney should issue an additional $10 billion in new debt. We will assume that Disney does not want the probability of being unable to make its total debt payments from current operating income to exceed 5%.

Step 1:   We derive a probability distribution for expected operating income from Disney's historical earnings and estimate percentage differences in operating income from 1988 to 2008 and present it in Figure 8.1.

The average change in operating income on an annual basis over the period was 13.26%, and the standard deviation in the annual changes is 19.80%. If we assume that the changes are normally distributed, these statistics are sufficient for us to compute the approximate probability of being unable to meet the specified debt payments.[1]

Step 2:   We estimate the interest and principal payments on a proposed bond issue of $10 billion by assuming that the *debt will be rated BBB*, lower than Disney's current bond rating of A. Based on this rating, we estimated an interest rate of 7% on the debt. In addition, we assume that the sinking fund payment set aside to repay the bonds is 10% of the bond issue.[2] This

Figure 8.1   Disney's Operating Income Changes: 1988–2008

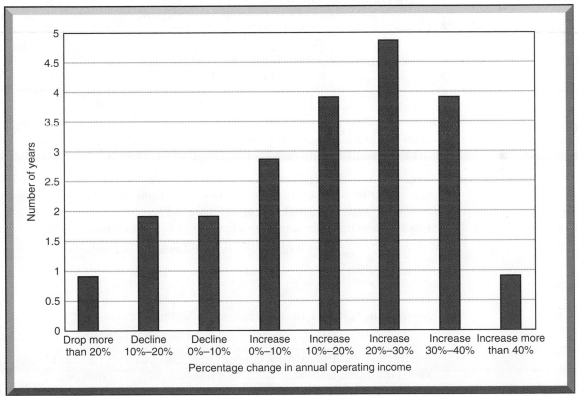

---

[1]Assuming income changes are normally distributed is undoubtedly a stretch. You can try alternative distributions that better fit the actual data.

[2]A sinking fund payment allows a firm to set aside money to pay off a bond when it comes due at maturity in annual installments.

results in an annual debt payment of $1,700 million:

$$\text{Additional debt payment} = \text{Interest expense} + \text{Sinking fund payment}$$
$$= 0.07 * \$10,000 + 0.10 * \$10,000$$
$$= \$1,700 \text{ million}$$

The total debt payment then can be computed by adding the interest payment of $728 million on existing debt and the operating lease expenses of $550 million (from the current year) to the additional debt payment that will be created by taking on $10 billion in additional debt.

$$\text{Total debt payment} = \text{Interest on existing debt}$$
$$+ \text{Operating lease expense}$$
$$+ \text{Additional debt payment}$$
$$= \$728 \text{ million} + \$550 \text{ million} + \$1,700 \text{ million}$$
$$= \$2,978 \text{ million}$$

Step 3:   We can now estimate the probability of default[3] from the distribution of operating income. The simplest computation is to assume that the percentage changes in operating income are normally distributed, with the operating income of $6,726 million that Disney earned the last four quarters as the base year income and the standard deviation of 19.8% from the historical data as the expected future standard deviation. The resulting t statistic is 2.81:

$$t\text{-statistic}$$
$$= (\text{Current EBIT} - \text{Debt payment})/\sigma_{OI}(\text{Current operating income})$$
$$= (\$6,726 - \$2,978)/(0.1980 * \$6,726) = 2.81$$

Based on the t-statistic, the probability that Disney will be unable to meet its debt payments in the next year is 0.24%.[4]

Step 4:   Because the estimated probability of default is indeed less than 5%, Disney can afford to borrow more than $10 billion. If the distribution of operating income changes is normal, we can estimate the level of debt payments Disney can afford to make for a probability of default of 5%.

$$t\text{-statistic for 5\% probability level} = 1.645$$

Consequently, the debt payment can be estimated as

$$(\$6,726 - X)/(0.1980 * \$6,726) = 1.645$$

Solving for X, we estimate a break-even debt payment of

$$\text{Break-even debt payment} = \$4,535 \text{ million}$$

Subtracting out the existing interest and lease payments from this amount yields the break-even additional debt payment of $3,257 million.

$$\text{Break-even additional debt payment} = \$4,535 - 728 - 550$$
$$= \$3,257 \text{ million}$$

---

[3]This is the probability of defaulting on interest payments in one period. The cumulative probability of default over time will be much higher.

[4]This is likely to be a conservative estimate, because it does not allow for the fact that Disney has a cash balance of $3,795 million that can be used to service debt, if the operating income falls short.

If we assume that the interest rate remains unchanged at 7% and the sinking fund will remain at 10% of the outstanding debt, this yields an optimal additional debt of $19,161 million.

Optimal additional debt
= Break-even additional debt payment/(Interest rate
+ Sinking fund rate) = $3,257/(0.07 + 0.10) = $19,161 million

Based on this analysis, Disney should be able to more than double its existing debt ($16,682 million) and stay within its constraint of keeping the probability of default to less than 5%.

Limitations of the Operating Income Approach

Although this approach may be intuitive and simple, it has key drawbacks. First, estimating a distribution for operating income is not as easy as it sounds, especially for firms in businesses that are changing and volatile. The operating income of firms can vary widely from year to year, depending on the success or failure of individual products. Second, even when we can estimate a distribution, the distribution may not fit the parameters of a normal distribution, and the annual changes in operating income may not reflect the risk of consecutive bad years. The latter problem can be remedied by calculating the statistics based on multiple years of data but the former has more serious statistical implicatioins. For Disney, if operating income is computed over rolling two-year periods,[5] the standard deviation will increase and the optimal debt ratio will decrease.

This approach is also an extremely conservative way of setting debt policy, because it assumes that principal payments have to be made out of a firm's operating income and that the firm has no access to financial markets or pre-existing cash balances. Finally, the probability constraint set by management is subjective and may reflect management concerns more than stockholder interests—for instance, management may decide that it wants no chance of default and refuse to borrow money as a consequence.

Refinements on the Operating Income Approach

The operating income approach described in this section is simplistic because it is based on historical data and the assumption that operating income changes are normally distributed. We can make it more sophisticated and robust by making relatively small changes.

- We can look at simulations of different possible outcomes for operating income, rather than looking at historical data; the distributions of the outcomes can be based both on past data and on expectations for the future.
- Instead of evaluating just the risk of defaulting on debt, we can consider the indirect bankruptcy costs that can accrue to a firm if operating income drops below a specified level.
- We can compute the present value of the tax benefits from the interest payments on the debt across simulations and thus compare the expected cost of bankruptcy to the expected tax benefits from borrowing.

---

[5]By rolling two-year periods, we mean 1988–1989, 1989–1990, and so on for the rest of the data.

With these changes, we can look at different financing mixes for a firm and estimate the optimal debt ratio as that mix that maximizes the firm's value.[6]

COST OF CAPITAL APPROACH

In Chapter 4, we estimated the minimum acceptable hurdle rates for equity investors (the cost of equity), and for all investors in the firm (the cost of capital). We defined the *cost of capital* to be the weighted average of the costs of the different components of financing—including debt, equity, and hybrid securities—used by a firm to fund its investments. By altering the weights of the different components, firms might be able to change their cost of capital.[7] In the cost of capital approach, we estimate the costs of debt and equity at different debt ratios, use these costs to compute the costs of capital, and look for the mix of debt and equity that yields the lowest cost of capital for the firm. At this cost of capital, we will argue that firm value is maximized.

Cost of Capital and Maximizing Firm Value

In Chapters 3 and 4, we laid the foundations for estimating the cost of capital for a firm. We argued that the cost of equity should reflect the risk as perceived by the marginal investors in the firm. If those marginal investors are diversified, the only risk that should be priced in should be the risk that cannot be diversified away, captured in a beta (in the CAPM) or betas (in multifactor models). If the marginal investors are not diversified, the cost of equity may reflect some or all of the firm-specific risk in the firm. The cost of debt is a function of the default risk of the firm and reflects the current cost of long term borrowing to the firm. Since interest is tax-deductible, we adjust the cost of debt for the tax savings, using the marginal tax rate, to estimate an after-tax cost. In summary, the cost of capital is a weighted average of the costs of equity and debt, with the weights based upon market values:

$$\text{Cost of capital} = \text{Cost of equity} \frac{\text{Equity}}{(\text{Debt} + \text{Equity})}$$
$$+ \text{Cost of debt}(1 - t) \frac{\text{Debt}}{(\text{Debt} + \text{Equity})}$$

To understand the relationship between the cost of capital and optimal capital structure, we first have to establish the relationship between firm value and the cost of capital. In Chapter 5, we noted that the value of a project to a firm could be computed by discounting the expected cash flows on it at a rate that reflected the riskiness of the cash flows, and that the analysis could be done either from the viewpoint of equity investors alone or from the viewpoint of the entire firm. In the latter approach, we discounted the cash flows to the firm on the project—that is, the project cash flows prior to debt payments but after taxes, at the project's cost of capital.

Extending this principle, the value of the entire firm can be estimated by discounting the aggregate expected cash flows to the firm over time at the firm's cost of capital. The firm's aggregate cash flows can be estimated as cash flows after operating expenses,

---

[6]T. Opler, M. Saron, and S. Titman, "Designing Capital Structure to Create Stockholder Value," *Journal of Applied Corporate Finance* 10:21–32.

[7]If capital structure is irrelevant, the cost of capital will be unchanged as the capital structure is altered.

taxes, and any capital investments needed to create future growth in both fixed assets and working capital, but before debt payments.

$$\text{Cash flow to firm} = \text{EBIT}(1 - t) - (\text{Capital expenditures} - \text{Depreciation})$$
$$- \text{Change in noncash working capital}$$

The value of the firm can then be written as

$$\text{Value of firm} = \sum_{t=1}^{t=\infty} \frac{\text{CF to firm}_t}{(1 + \text{Cost of capital})^t}$$

The value of a firm is therefore a function of its cash flows and its cost of capital. In the special case where the cash flows to the firm remain constant as the debt/equity mix is changed, the value of the firm will increase as the cost of capital decreases. If the objective in choosing the financing mix for the firm is the maximization of firm value, this can be accomplished, in this case, by *minimizing the cost of capital*. In the more general case where the cash flows to the firm themselves change as the debt ratio changes, the optimal financing mix is the one *that maximizes firm value*.

The Cost of Capital Approach—Basics

To use the cost of capital approach in its simplest form, where the cash flows are fixed and only the cost of capital changes, we need estimates of the cost of capital at every debt ratio. In making these estimates, the one thing we cannot do is keep the costs of debt and equity fixed while changing the debt ratio. In addition to being unrealistic in its assessment of risk as the debt ratio changes, this analysis will yield the unsurprising conclusion that the cost of capital is minimized at a 100% debt ratio, since the after-tax cost of debt is usually much lower than the cost of equity.

As the debt ratio increases, each of the components in the cost of capital will change. Let us start with the equity component. Equity investors are entitled to the residual earnings and cash flows in a firm, after interest and principal payments have been made. As that firm borrows more money to fund a given level of assets, debt payments will increase, and equity earnings will become more volatile. This higher earnings volatility, in turn, will translate into a higher cost of equity. In the language of the CAPM and multifactor models, the beta or betas we use for equity should increase as the debt ratio goes up. The debt holders will also see their risk increase as the firm borrows more. Holding operating income constant, a firm that contracts to pay more to debt holders has a greater chance of defaulting, which will result in a higher cost of debt. As an added complication, the tax benefits of interest expenses can be put at risk, if these expenses become greater than the earnings.

The key to using the cost of capital approach is coming up with realistic estimates of the cost of equity and debt at different debt ratios. The optimal financing mix for a firm is trivial to compute if one is provided with a schedule that relates the costs of equity and debt to the debt ratio of the firm. Computing the optimal debt ratio then becomes purely mechanical. To illustrate, assume that you are given the costs of equity and debt at different debt levels for a hypothetical firm and that the after-tax cash flow to this firm is currently $200 million. Assume also that these cash flows are expected to grow at 3% a year forever and are unaffected by the debt ratio of the firm. The cost of capital schedule is provided in Table 8.1, along with the value of the firm at each level of debt.

Table 8.1   WACC, FIRM VALUE, AND DEBT RATIOS

D/(D + E)	Cost of Equity	After-Tax Cost of Debt	Cost of Capital	Firm Value
0%	10.50%	4.80%	10.50%	$2,747
10%	11.00%	5.10%	10.41%	$2,780
20%	11.60%	5.40%	10.36%	$2,799
30%	12.30%	5.52%	10.27%	$2,835
40%	13.10%	5.70%	10.14%	$2,885
50%	14.00%	6.10%	10.05%	$2,922
60%	15.00%	7.20%	10.32%	$2,814
70%	16.10%	8.10%	10.50%	$2,747
80%	17.20%	9.00%	10.64%	$2,696
90%	18.40%	10.20%	11.02%	$2,569
100%	19.70%	11.40%	11.40%	$2,452

$$\text{Value of firm} = \frac{\text{Expected cash flow to firm next year}}{(\text{Cost of capital} - g)} = \frac{200(1.03)}{(\text{Cost of capital} - .03)}$$

The value of the firm increases (decreases) as the WACC decreases (increases), as illustrated in Figure 8.2:

Figure 8.2   Cost of Capital and Firm Value as a Function of Leverage

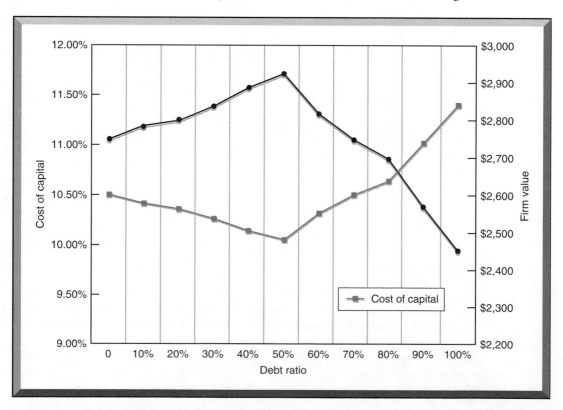

This illustration makes the choice of an optimal financing mix seem trivial and it obscures some real problems that may arise in its applications. First, we typically do not have the benefit of having the entire schedule of costs of financing prior to an analysis. In most cases, the only level of debt about which there is any certainty about the cost of financing is the current level. Second, the analysis assumes implicitly that the level of cash flows to the firm is unaffected by the financing mix of the firm, and, consequently, by the default risk (or bond rating) for the firm. Although this may be reasonable in some cases, it might not in others. For instance, a firm that manufactures consumer durables (cars, televisions, etc.) might find that its sales and operating income drop if its default risk increases, because investors are reluctant to buy its products. We will deal with the computational component of estimating costs of debt, equity, and capital first in the standard cost of capital approach and then follow up by examining how to bring in changes in expected cash flows into the analysis in the enhanced cost of capital approach.

8.1   MINIMIZING COST OF CAPITAL AND MAXIMIZING FIRM VALUE

A lower cost of capital will lead to a higher firm value only if

a.   The operating income does not change as the cost of capital declines

b.   The operating income goes up as the cost of capital goes down

c.   Any decline in operating income is offset by the lower cost of capital

The Standard Cost of Capital Approach

In the standard cost of capital approach, we keep the operating income and cash flows fixed while changing the cost of capital. Not surprisingly, the optimal debt ratio is the one that minimizes the cost of capital. While the assumptions seem heroic, it is a good starting point for the discussion.

Steps in Computing Cost of Capital

We need three basic inputs to compute the cost of capital—the cost of equity, the after-tax cost of debt, and the weights on debt and equity. The costs of equity and debt change as the debt ratio changes, and the primary challenge of this approach is in estimating each of these inputs.

Let us begin with the cost of equity. In Chapter 4, we argued that the beta of equity will change as the debt ratio changes. In fact, we estimated the levered beta as a function of the debt to equity ratio of a firm, the unlevered beta, and the firm's marginal tax rate:

$$\beta_{levered} = \beta_{unlevered}[1 + (1 - t)\text{Debt/Equity}]$$

Thus, if we can estimate the unlevered beta for a firm, we can use it to computed the levered beta of the firm at every debt ratio. This levered beta can then be used to compute the cost of equity at each debt ratio.

$$\text{Cost of equity} = \text{Risk-free rate} + \beta_{levered}(\text{Risk premium})$$

The cost of debt for a firm is a function of the firm's default risk. As firms borrow more, their default risk will increase, and so will the cost of debt. If we use bond ratings as the measure of default risk, we can estimate the cost of debt in three steps. First, we estimate a firm's dollar debt and interest expenses at each debt ratio; as firms increase their debt ratio, both dollar debt and interest expenses will rise. Second, at each debt level, we compute a financial ratio or ratios that measure default risk and use the ratio(s) to estimate a rating for the firm; again, as firms borrow more, this rating will decline. Third, a default spread, based on the estimated rating, is added on to the risk-free rate to arrive at the pretax cost of debt. Applying the marginal tax rate to this pretax cost yields an after-tax cost of debt.

Once we estimate the costs of equity and debt at each debt level, we weight them based on the proportions used of each to estimate the cost of capital. Although we have not explicitly allowed for a preferred stock component in this process, we can have preferred stock as a part of capital. However, we have to keep the preferred stock portion fixed while changing the weights on debt and equity. The debt ratio at which the cost of capital is minimized is the optimal debt ratio.

In this approach, the effect of changing the capital structure, on firm value, is isolated by keeping the operating income fixed, and varying only the cost of capital. In practical terms, this requires us to make two assumptions. First, the debt ratio is decreased by raising new equity and retiring debt; conversely, the debt ratio is increased by borrowing money and buying back stock. This process is called *recapitalization*. Second, the pretax operating income is assumed to be unaffected by the firm's financing mix and, by extension, its bond rating. If the operating income changes with a firm's default risk, the basic analysis will not change, but minimizing the cost of capital may not be the optimal course of action, because the value of the firm is determined by both the cash flows and the cost of capital. The value of the firm will have to be computed at each debt level and the optimal debt ratio will be that which maximizes firm value.

ILLUSTRATION 8.2   Analyzing the Capital Structure for Disney: May 2009

The cost of capital approach can be used to find the optimal capital structure for a firm, as we will for Disney in May 2009. Disney had $16,003 million in interest-bearing debt on its books, and we estimated the market value of this debt to be $14,962 million in Chapter 4. Adding the present value of operating leases of $1,720 million (also estimated in Chapter 4) to this value, we arrive at a total market value for the debt of $16,682 million. The market value of equity at the same time was $45,193 million; the market price per share was $24.34, and there were 1,856.752 million shares outstanding. Proportionally, 26.96% of the overall financing mix was debt, and the remaining 73.04% was equity.

The beta for Disney's stock in May 2009, as estimated in Chapter 4, was 0.9011. The Treasury bond rate at that time was 3.5%. Using an estimated equity risk premium of 6%, we estimated the cost of equity for Disney to be 8.91%:

$$\text{Cost of equity} = \text{Risk-free rate} + \text{Beta} * (\text{Market premium})$$
$$= 3.5\% + 0.9011(6\%) = 8.91\%$$

Disney's bond rating in May 2009 was A, and based on this rating, the estimated pretax cost of debt for Disney is 6%. Using a marginal tax rate of 38%, we estimate the after-tax cost of debt for Disney to be 3.72%.

$$\text{After-tax cost of debt} = \text{Pretax interest rate}(1 - \text{Tax rate})$$
$$= 6.00\%(1 - 0.38) = 3.72\%$$

The cost of capital was calculated using these costs and the weights based on market value:

$$\text{Cost of capital} = \text{Cost of equity}\frac{\text{Equity}}{(\text{Debt} + \text{Equity})}$$
$$+ \text{Cost of debt}(1 - t)\frac{\text{Debt}}{(\text{Debt} + \text{Equity})}$$
$$= 8.91\%\frac{45,193}{(16,682 + 45,193)} + 3.72\%\frac{16,682}{(16,682 + 45,193)} = 7.51\%$$

8.2 MARKET VALUE, BOOK VALUE, AND COST OF CAPITAL

Disney had a book value of equity of approximately $32.7 billion and a book value of debt of $16 billion. If you held the cost of equity and debt constant and replaced the market value weights in the cost of capital with book value weights, you will end up with

a. A lower cost of capital

b. A higher cost of capital

c. The same cost of capital

What are the implications for valuation?

I. Disney's Cost of Equity and Leverage

The cost of equity for Disney at different debt ratios can be computed using the unlevered beta of the firm, and the debt equity ratio at each level of debt. We use the levered betas that emerge to estimate the cost of equity. The first step in this process is to compute the firm's current unlevered beta, using the current market debt to equity ratio and a tax rate of 38%.

$$\text{Unlevered beta} = \frac{\text{Levered beta}}{\left(1 + (1 - t)\frac{\text{Debt}}{\text{Equity}}\right)} = \frac{0.9011}{\left(1 + (1 - 0.38)\frac{16,682}{45,193}\right)} = 0.7333$$

Note that this is the bottom-up unlevered beta that we estimated for Disney in Chapter 4, based on its business mix, which should come as no surprise since we computed the levered beta from that value. We compute the levered beta at each debt ratio, using this unlevered beta and Disney's marginal tax rate of 38%:

$$\text{Levered beta} = 0.7333 \left[1 + (1 - 0.38)(\text{Debt/Equity})\right]$$

We continued to use the Treasury bond rate of 3.5% and the market premium of 6% to compute the cost of equity at each level of debt. If we keep the tax rate constant at 38%, we obtain the levered betas for Disney in Table 8.2.

In calculating the levered beta in this table, we assumed that all market risk is borne by the equity investors (although this may be unrealistic, especially at higher levels of debt) and that the firm will be able to get the full tax benefits of interest expenses even

Table 8.2 LEVERED BETA AND COST OF EQUITY—DISNEY			
Debt-to-Capital Ratio	D/E Ratio	Levered Beta	Cost of Equity
0%	0.00%	0.7333	7.90%
10%	11.11%	0.7838	8.20%
20%	25.00%	0.8470	8.58%
30%	42.86%	0.9281	9.07%
40%	66.67%	1.0364	9.72%
50%	100.00%	1.1879	10.63%
60%	150.00%	1.4153	11.99%
70%	233.33%	1.7941	14.26%
80%	400.00%	2.5519	18.81%
90%	900.00%	4.8251	32.45%

at very high debt ratios. We will also consider an alternative estimate of levered betas that apportions some of the market risk to the debt:

$$\beta_{levered} = \beta_u[1 + (1 - t)D/E] - \beta_{debt}(1 - t)D/E$$

The beta of debt can be based on the rating of the bond, estimated by regressing past returns on bonds in each rating class against returns on a market index or backed out of the default spread. The levered betas estimated using this approach will generally be lower than those estimated with the conventional model.[8] We will also examine whether the full benefits of interest expenses will accrue at higher debt ratios.

II. Disney's Cost of Debt and Leverage

There are several financial ratios that are correlated with bond ratings, and we face two choices. One is to build a model that includes several financial ratios to estimate the synthetic ratings at each debt ratio. In addition to being more labor and data intensive, the approach will make the ratings process less transparent and more difficult to decipher. The other is to stick with the simplistic approach that we developed in Chapter 4, of linking the rating to the interest coverage ratio, with the ratio defined as:

$$\text{Interest coverage ratio} = \frac{\text{Earnings before interest and taxes}}{\text{Interest expenses}}$$

We will stick with the simpler approach for three reasons. First, we are not aiming for precision in the cost of debt, but an approximation. Given that the more complex approaches also give you approximations, we will tilt in favor of transparency. Second, there is significant correlation not only between the interest coverage ratio and bond

---

[8]Consider, for instance, a debt ratio of 40%. At this level, the firm's debt will take on some of the characteristics of equity. Assume that the beta of debt at a 40% debt ratio is 0.1. The equity beta at that debt ratio can be computed as follows:

Levered beta = 0.7333 [1 + (1 − 0.38)(40/60) − 0.10 (1 − 0.38)(40/60)] = 0.99

In the unadjusted approach, the levered beta would have been 1.0364.

ratings, but also between the interest coverage ratio and other ratios used in analysis, such as the debt coverage ratio and the funds flow ratios. In other words, we may be adding little by adding other ratios that are correlated with interest coverage ratios, including EBITDA/Fixed charges, to the mix. Third, the interest coverage ratio changes as a firm changes is financing mix and decreases as the debt ratio increases, a key requirement since we need the cost of debt to change as the debt ratio changes.

To make our estimates of the synthetic rating, we will use the lookup table that we introduced in Chapter 4, for large market capitalization firms (since Disney's market capitalization is greater than $5 billion) and continue to use the default spreads that we used in that chapter to estimate the pretax cost of debt. Table 8.3 reproduces those numbers.

Using this table as a guideline, a firm with an interest coverage ratio of 2.75 would have a rating of BBB and a default spread of 3.5% over the risk-free rate.

Because Disney's capacity to borrow is determined by its earnings power, we will begin by looking at key numbers from the company's income statements for the most recent fiscal year (July 2007–June 2008) and for the last four quarters (calendar year 2008) in Table 8.4.

Note that converting leases to debt affects both the operating income and the interest expense; the imputed interest expense on the lease debt is added to both the operating income and interest expense numbers.[9] Since the trailing twelve-month

Table 8.3   INTEREST COVERAGE RATIOS, RATINGS AND DEFAULT SPREADS

Interest Coverage Ratio	Rating	Typical Default
>8.5	AAA	1.25%
6.5–8.5	AA	1.75%
5.5–6.5	A+	2.25%
4.25–5.5	A	2.50%
3.0–4.25	A−	3.00%
2.5–3.0	BBB	3.50%
2.25–2.5	BB+	4.25%
2.0–2.25	BB	5.00%
1.75–2.0	B+	6.00%
1.5–1.75	B	7.25%
1.25–1.5	B−	8.50%
0.8–1.25	CCC	10.00%
0.65–0.8	CC	12.00%
0.2–0.65	C	15.00%
<0.2	D	20.00%

[9]The present value of operating leases ($1,720 million) was multiplied by the pretax cost of debt of 6% to arrive at an interest expense of $103 million, which is added to both operating income and interest expense. Multiplying the pretax cost of debt by the present value of operating leases yields an approximation. The full adjustment would require us to add back the entire operating lease expense and to subtract the depreciation on the leased asset.

Table 8.4   DISNEY'S KEY OPERATING NUMBERS

	Last Fiscal Year	Trailing 12 Months
Revenues	$37,843	$36,990
EBITDA	$8,986	$8,319
Depreciation and amortization	$1,582	$1,593
EBIT	$7,404	$6,726
Interest expenses	$712	$728
EBITDA (adjusted for leases)	$9,989	$8,422
EBIT (adjusted for leases)	$7,708	$6,829
Interest expenses (adjusted for leases)	$815	$831

Source: Capital IQ and Bondsonline.com.

figures represent more recent information, we will use those numbers in assessing Disney's optimal debt ratio. Based on the EBIT (adjusted for leases) of $6,829 million and interest expenses of $831 million, Disney has an interest coverage ratio of 8.22 and should command a rating of AA, two notches above its actual rating of A.

To compute Disney's ratings at different debt levels, we start by assessing the dollar debt that Disney will need to issue to get to the specified debt ratio. This can be accomplished by multiplying the total market value of the firm today by the desired debt to capital ratio. To illustrate, Disney's dollar debt at a 10% debt ratio will be $6,188 million, computed thus:

$$\text{Value of Disney} = \text{Current market value of equity} + \text{Current market value of debt}$$
$$= 45,193 + \$16,682 = \$61,875 \text{ million}$$

$$\$\text{Debt at 10\% debt-to-capital ratio} = 10\% \text{ of } \$61,875 = \$6,188 \text{ million}$$

The second step in the process is to compute the interest expense that Disney will have at this debt level, by multiplying the dollar debt by the pretax cost of borrowing at that debt ratio. The interest expense is then used to compute an interest coverage ratio which is employed to compute a synthetic rating. The resulting default spread, based on the rating, can be obtained from Table 8.3, and adding the default spread to the risk-free rate yields a pretax cost of borrowing. Table 8.5 estimates the interest expenses, interest coverage ratios, and bond ratings for Disney at 0% and 10% debt ratios, at the existing level of operating income.

Note that the EBITDA and EBIT remain fixed as the debt ratio changes. We ensure this by using the proceeds from the debt to buy back stock, thus leaving operating assets untouched and isolating the effect of changing the debt ratio.

There is circular reasoning involved in estimating the interest expense. The interest rate is needed to calculate the interest coverage ratio, and the coverage ratio is necessary to compute the interest rate. To get around the problem, we began our analysis by assuming that Disney could borrow $6,188 billion at the AAA rate of 4.75%; we then compute an interest expense and interest coverage ratio using that rate. At the 10% debt ratio, our life was simplified by the fact that the rating remained

D/(D + E)	0.00%	10.00%
Table 8.5	EFFECT OF MOVING TO HIGHER DEBT RATIOS—DISNEY	
D/E	0.00%	11.11%
$ Debt	$0	$6,188
EBITDA	$8,422	$8,422
Depreciation	$1,593	$1,593
EBIT	$6,829	$6,829
Interest	$0	$294
Pretax int. cov	∞	23.24
Likely rating	AAA	AAA
Pretax cost of debt	4.75%	4.75%

unchanged at AAA. To illustrate a more difficult step up in debt, consider the change in the debt ratio from 20% to 30%:

		Iteration 1 (Debt @AAA rate)	Iteration 2 (Debt @AA rate)
D/(D + E)	20.00%	30.00%	30.00%
D/E	25.00%	42.86%	42.86%
$ Debt	$12,375	$18,563	$18,563
EBITDA	$8,422	$8,422	$8,422
Depreciation	$1,593	$1,593	$1,593
EBIT	$6,829	$6,829	$6,829
Interest	$588	18,563 * 0.0475 = $881	18,563 * 0.0525 = $974
pretax int. cov	11.62	7.74	7.01
Likely rating	AAA	AA	AA
pretax cost of debt	4.75%	5.25%	5.25%

While the initial estimate of the interest expenses at the 30% debt ratio reflects the AAA rating and 4.75% interest rate) that the firm enjoyed at the 20% debt ratio, the resulting interest coverage ratio of 7.74 pushes the rating down to AA and the interest rate to 5.25%. Consequently, we have to recompute the interest expenses at the higher rate (in iteration 2) and reach steady state: the interest rate that we use matches up to the estimated interest rate.[10] This process is repeated for each level of debt from 10% to 90%, and the iterated after-tax costs of debt are obtained at each level of debt in Table 8.6.

Note that the interest expenses increase more than proportionately as the debt increases, since the cost of debt rises with the debt ratio. There are three points to make about these computations.

1. At each debt ratio, we compute the dollar value of debt by multiplying the debt ratio by the existing market value of the firm ($61,875 million). In reality, the

---

[10]Because the interest expense rises, it is possible for the rating to drop again. Thus, a third iteration might be necessary in some cases.

Table 8.6 DISNEY: COST OF DEBT AND DEBT RATIOS

Debt Ratio	$ Debt	Interest Expense	Interest Coverage Ratio	Bond Rating	Interest Rate on Debt	Tax Rate	After-Tax Cost of Debt
0%	$0	$0	∞	AAA	4.75%	38.00%	2.95%
10%	$6,188	$294	23.24	AAA	4.75%	38.00%	2.95%
20%	$12,375	$588	11.62	AAA	4.75%	38.00%	2.95%
30%	$18,563	$975	7.01	AA	5.25%	38.00%	3.26%
40%	$24,750	$1,485	4.60	A	6.00%	38.00%	3.72%
50%	$30,938	$2,011	3.40	A−	6.50%	38.00%	4.03%
60%	$37,125	$2,599	2.63	BBB	7.00%	38.00%	4.34%
70%	$43,313	$5,198	1.31	B−	12.00%	38.00%	7.44%
80%	$49,500	$6,683	1.02	CCC	13.50%	38.00%	8.37%
90%	$55,688	$7,518	0.91	CCC	13.50%	34.52%	8.84%

value of the firm will change as the cost of capital changes and the dollar debt that we will need to get to a specified debt ratio, say 30%, will be different from the values that we have estimated. The reason that we have not tried to incorporate this effect is that it leads more circularity in our computations, since the value at each debt ratio is a function of the savings from the interest expenses at that debt ratio, which, in turn, will depend upon the value.

2. We assume that at every debt level, all existing debt will be refinanced at the new interest rate that will prevail after the capital structure change. For instance, Disney's existing debt, which has a A rating, is assumed to be refinanced at the interest rate corresponding to a A− rating when Disney moves to a 50% debt ratio. This is done for two reasons. The first is that existing debt holders might have protective puts that enable them to put their bonds back to the firm and receive face value.[11] The second is that the refinancing eliminates "wealth expropriation" effects—the effects of stockholders expropriating wealth from bondholders when debt is increased, and vice versa when debt is reduced. If firms can retain old debt at lower rates while borrowing more and becoming riskier, the lenders of the old debt will lose value. If we lock in current rates on existing bonds and recalculate the optimal debt ratio, we will allow for this wealth transfer.[12]

3. Although it is conventional to leave the marginal tax rate unchanged as the debt ratio is increased, we adjust the tax rate to reflect the potential loss of the tax benefits of debt at higher debt ratios, where the interest expenses exceed the EBIT. To illustrate this point, note that the EBIT at Disney is $6,829 million. As long as interest expenses are less than $6,829 million, interest expenses remain fully tax-deductible and earn the 38% tax benefit. For instance, even at an 80% debt

---

[11] If they do not have protective puts, it is in the best interests of the stockholders not to refinance the debt if debt ratios are increased.

[12] This will have the effect of reducing interest cost, when debt is increased, and thus interest coverage ratios. This will lead to higher ratings, at least in the short term, and a higher optimal debt ratio.

ratio, the interest expenses are $6,683 million and the tax benefit is therefore 38% of this amount. At a 90% debt ratio, however, the interest expenses balloon to $7,518 million, which is greater than the EBIT of $6,829 million. We consider the tax benefit on the interest expenses up to this amount:

$$\text{Maximum tax benefit} = \text{EBIT} * \text{Marginal tax rate} = \$6,829 \text{ million} * 0.38$$
$$= \$2,595 \text{ million}$$

As a proportion of the total interest expenses, the tax benefit is now only 34.52%:

$$\text{Adjusted marginal tax rate} = \text{Maximum tax benefit/interest expenses}$$
$$= \$2,595/\$7,518 = 34.52\%$$

This in turn raises the after-tax cost of debt. This is a conservative approach, because losses can be carried forward. Given that this is a permanent shift in leverage, it does make sense to be conservative. We used this tax rate to recompute the levered beta at a 90% debt ratio, to reflect the fact that tax savings from interest are depleted.

III. Leverage and Cost of Capital

Now that we have estimated the cost of equity and the cost of debt at each debt level, we can compute Disney's cost of capital. This is done for each debt level in Table 8.7. The cost of capital, which is 7.90% when the firm is unlevered, decreases as the firm initially adds debt, reaches a minimum of 7.32% at a 40% debt ratio, and then starts to increase again. (See Table 8.10 for the full details of the numbers in this table.)

Note that we are moving in 10% increments and that the cost of capital flattens out between 30% and 50%. We can get a more precise reading of the optimal by looking at how the cost of capital moves between 30% and 50%, but in smaller increments. Using 1% increments, the optimal debt ratio that we compute for Disney is 43%, with a cost of capital of 7.28%. The optimal cost of capital is shown graphically in Figure 8.3. We will stick with the approximate optimal of 40% for the rest of this chapter.

To illustrate the robustness of this solution to alternative measures of levered betas, we reestimate the costs of debt, equity, and capital under the assumption that debt bears some market risk; the results are summarized in Table 8.8.

		Table 8.7	COST OF EQUITY, DEBT, AND CAPITAL—DISNEY	
Debt Ratio	**Beta**	**Cost of Equity**	**Cost of Debt (after-tax)**	**Cost of Capital**
0%	0.73	7.90%	2.95%	7.90%
10%	0.78	8.20%	2.95%	7.68%
20%	0.85	8.58%	2.95%	7.45%
30%	0.93	9.07%	3.26%	7.32%
40%	1.04	9.72%	3.72%	7.32%
50%	1.19	10.63%	4.03%	7.33%
60%	1.42	11.99%	4.34%	7.40%
70%	1.79	14.26%	7.44%	9.49%
80%	2.55	18.81%	8.37%	10.46%
90%	5.05	33.83%	8.84%	11.34%

Figure 8.3   Disney's Costs of Debt, Equity and Capital

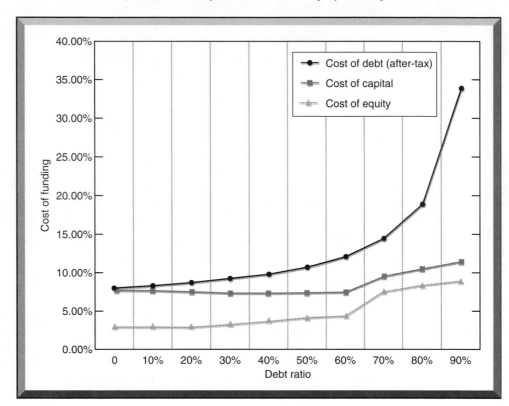

If the debt holders bear some market risk, the cost of equity is lower at higher levels of debt, and Disney's optimal debt ratio increases to 60%, higher than the optimal debt ratio of 40% that we computed using the conventional beta measure.[13]

IV. Firm Value and Cost of Capital

The reason for minimizing the cost of capital is that it maximizes the value of the firm. To illustrate the effects of moving to the optimal on Disney's firm value, we start off with a simple valuation model, designed to value a firm in stable growth.

$$\text{Firm value} = \frac{\text{Expected cash flow to firm}_{\text{Next year}}}{(\text{Cost of capital} - g)}$$

---

[13]To estimate the beta of debt, we used the default spread at each level of debt, and assumed that 25% of this risk is market risk. Thus, at an A− rating, the default spread is 3%. Based on the market risk premium of 6% that we used elsewhere, we cestimated the beta at a A rating to be

$$\text{Imputed debt beta at a C rating} = (3\%/6\%) * 0.25 = 0.125$$

Table 8.8   COSTS OF EQUITY, DEBT, AND CAPITAL WITH DEBT CARRYING MARKET RISK—DISNEY

Debt Ratio	Beta of Equity	Beta of Debt	Cost of Equity	Cost of Debt (after-tax)	Cost of Capital
0%	0.73	0.05	7.90%	2.95%	7.90%
10%	0.78	0.05	8.18%	2.95%	7.66%
20%	0.84	0.05	8.53%	2.95%	7.42%
30%	0.91	0.07	8.95%	3.26%	7.24%
40%	0.99	0.10	9.46%	3.72%	7.16%
50%	1.11	0.13	10.16%	4.03%	7.10%
60%	1.28	0.00	11.18%	4.34%	7.08%
70%	1.28	0.35	11.19%	7.44%	8.57%
80%	1.52	0.42	12.61%	8.37%	9.22%
90%	2.60	0.42	19.10%	8.84%	9.87%

where g is the growth rate in the cash flow to the firm (in perpetuity). We begin by computing Disney's current free cash flow using its current earnings before interest and taxes of $6,829 million, its tax rate of 38%, and its reinvestment in 2008 in long-term assets (ignoring working capital):[14]

EBIT (1 − Tax rate) = 6,829 (1 − 0.38) =	$4,234
+ Depreciation and amortization =	$1,593
− Capital expenditures =	$1,628
− Change in noncash working capital	$0
Free cash flow to the firm =	$4,199

The market value of the firm at the time of this analysis was obtained by adding up the estimated market values of debt and equity:

Market value of equity =	$45,193
+ Market value of debt =	$16,682
= Value of the firm	$61,875

If we assume that the market is correctly pricing the firm, we can back out an implied growth rate from the value and the current cost of capital of 7.51%:

$$\text{Value of firm} = \$61,875 = \frac{\text{FCFF}_0(1 + g)}{(\text{Cost of capital} - g)} = \frac{4,199(1 + g)}{(0.0751 - g)}$$

Growth rate

$$= (\text{Firm value} * \text{Cost of capital} - \text{CF to firm})/(\text{Firm value} + \text{CF to firm})$$
$$= (61,875 * 0.0751 - 4199)/(61,875 + 4,199) = 0.0068, \text{ or } 0.68\%$$

---

[14]We will return to do a more careful computation of this cash flow in Chapter 12. In this chapter, we are just attempting for an approximation of the value.

Table 8.9 COST OF CAPITAL WORKSHEET FOR DISNEY

D/(D + E)	0.00%	10.00%	20.00%	30.00%	40.00%	50.00%	60.00%	70.00%	80.00%	90.00%
D/E	0.00%	11.11%	25.00%	42.86%	66.67%	100.00%	150.00%	233.33%	400.00%	900.00%
$ Debt	$0	$6,188	$12,375	$18,563	$24,750	$30,938	$37,125	$43,313	$49,500	$55,688
Beta	0.73	0.78	0.85	0.93	1.04	1.19	1.42	1.79	2.55	5.05
Cost of equity	7.90%	8.20%	8.58%	9.07%	9.72%	10.63%	11.99%	14.26%	18.81%	33.83%
EBITDA	$8,422	$8,422	$8,422	$8,422	$8,422	$8,422	$8,422	$8,422	$8,422	$8,422
Depreciation	$1,593	$1,593	$1,593	$1,593	$1,593	$1,593	$1,593	$1,593	$1,593	$1,593
EBIT	$6,829	$6,829	$6,829	$6,829	$6,829	$6,829	$6,829	$6,829	$6,829	$6,829
Interest	$0	$294	$588	$975	$1,485	$2,011	$2,599	$5,198	$6,683	$7,518
Interest coverage ratio	∞	23.24	11.62	7.01	4.60	3.40	2.63	1.31	1.02	0.91
Likely rating	AAA	AAA	AAA	AA	A	A−	BBB	B−	CCC	CCC
Pretax cost of debt	4.75%	4.75%	4.75%	5.25%	6.00%	6.50%	7.00%	12.00%	13.50%	13.50%
Eff. tax rate	38.00%	38.00%	38.00%	38.00%	38.00%	38.00%	38.00%	38.00%	38.00%	34.52%

COST OF CAPITAL CALCULATIONS

D/(D + E)	0.00%	10.00%	20.00%	30.00%	40.00%	50.00%	60.00%	70.00%	80.00%	90.00%
D/E	0.00%	11.11%	25.00%	42.86%	66.67%	100.00%	150.00%	233.33%	400.00%	900.00%
$ Debt	$0	$6,188	$12,375	$18,563	$24,750	$30,938	$37,125	$43,313	$49,500	$55,688
Cost of equity	7.90%	8.20%	8.58%	9.07%	9.72%	10.63%	11.99%	14.26%	18.81%	33.83%
Cost of debt	2.95%	2.95%	2.95%	3.26%	3.72%	4.03%	4.34%	7.44%	8.37%	8.84%
Cost of capital	7.90%	7.68%	7.45%	7.32%	7.32%	7.33%	7.40%	9.49%	10.46%	11.34%

Now assume that Disney shifts to 40% debt and a cost of capital of 7.32%. The firm can now be valued using the following parameters:

$$\text{Cash flow to firm} = \$4,199 \text{ million}$$
$$\text{WACC} = 7.32\%$$
$$\text{Growth rate in cash flows to firm} = 0.68\%$$
$$\text{Firm value} = \frac{\text{FCFF}_0(1 + g)}{(\text{Cost of capital} - g)} = \frac{4,199(1.0068)}{(0.0732 - 0.0068)}$$
$$= \$63,665 \text{ million}$$

The value of the firm will increase from $61,875 million to $63,665 million if the firm moves to the optimal debt ratio:

$$\text{Increase in firm value} = \$63,665 \text{ million} - \$61,875 \text{ million} = \$1,790 \text{ million}$$

The limitation of this approach is that the growth rate is heavily dependent on both our estimate of the cash flow in the most recent year and the assumption that the firm is in stable growth.[15] We can use an alternate approach to estimate the change in firm value. Consider first the change in the cost of capital from 7.51% to 7.32%, a drop of

---

[15]No company can grow at a rate higher than the long-term nominal growth rate of the economy. The risk-free rate is a reasonable proxy for the long-term nominal growth rate in the economy, because it is composed of two components—the expected inflation rate and the expected real rate of return. The latter has to equate to real growth in the long term.

0.19%. This change in the cost of capital should result in the firm saving on its annual cost of financing its business:

Cost of financing Disney at existing debt ratio = 61,875 * 0.0751 = $4,646.82 million
Cost of financing Disney at optimal debt ratio = 61,875 * 0.0732 = $4,529.68 million
Annual savings in cost of financing = $4,646.82 million − $4,529.68 million
= $117.14 million

Note that most of these savings are implicit rather than explicit and represent the savings next year.[16] The present value of these savings over time can now be estimated using the new cost of capital of 7.32% and the capped growth rate of 0.68% (based on the implied growth rate):

$$PV \text{ of savings} = \frac{\text{Annual savings next year}}{(\text{Cost of capital} - g)} = \frac{\$117.14}{(0.0732 - 0.0068)} = \$1,763 \text{ million}$$

Value of the firm after recapitalization = Existing firm value + PV of savings
= $61,875 + $1,763 = $63,638 million

Using this approach, we estimated the firm value at different debt ratios in Figure 8.4.

Figure 8.4   Firm Value and Debt Ratios

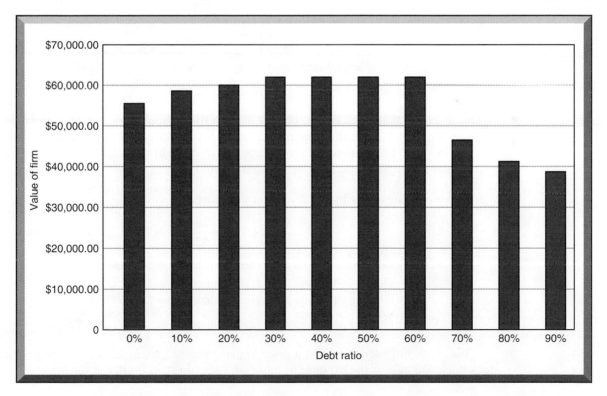

---

[16]The cost of equity is an implicit cost and does not show up in the income statement of the firm. The savings in the cost of capital are therefore unlikely to show up as higher aggregate earnings. In fact, as the firm's debt ratio increases, the earnings will decrease, but the per share earnings will increase.

There are two ways of getting from firm value to the value per share. Because the increase in value accrues entirely to stockholders, we can estimate the increase in value per share by dividing by the *total number of shares outstanding*:

$$\text{Increase in value per share} = \$1,763/1856.732 = \$0.95$$
$$\text{New stock price} = \$24.34 + \$0.95 = \$25.29$$

Since the change in cost of capital is being accomplished by borrowing $8,068 million (to get from the existing debt of $16,682 million to the debt of $24,750 million at the optimal) and buying back shares, it may seem surprising that we are using the shares outstanding before the buyback. Implicit in this computation is the assumption that the increase in firm value will be spread evenly across both the stockholders who sell their stock back to the firm and those who do not, which is why we term this the "rational" solution, since it leaves investors indifferent between selling back their shares and holding on to them. The alternative approach to arriving at the value per share is to compute the number of shares outstanding after the buyback:

$$\text{Number of shares after buyback} = \text{\# Shares before} - \frac{\text{Increase in debt}}{\text{Share price}}$$

$$= 1,856.732 - \frac{\$8,068}{\$25.29} = 1,537.713 \text{ million shares}$$

$$\text{Value of firm after recapitalization} = \$63,638 \text{ million}$$
$$\text{Debt outstanding after recapitalization} = \$24,750 \text{ million}$$
$$\text{Value of equity after recapitalization} = \$38,888 \text{ million}$$
$$\text{Value of equity per share after recapitalization} = \frac{38,888}{1,537.713} = \$25.29$$

To the extent that stock can be bought back at the current price of $24.34 or some value lower than $25.29, the remaining stockholders will get a bigger share of the increase in value. For instance, if Disney could have bought stock back at the existing price of $24.34, the increase in value per share would be 1.16.[17]

$$\text{Number of shares after buyback} = \text{\#Shares before} - \frac{\text{Increase in debt}}{\text{Share price}}$$

$$= 1,856.732 - \frac{\$8,068}{\$24.34} = 1,525.26 \text{ million shares}$$

$$\text{Value of firm after recapitalization} = \$63,638 \text{ million}$$
$$\text{Debt outstanding after recapitalization} = \$24,750 \text{ million}$$
$$\text{Value of equity after recapitalization} = \$38,888 \text{ million}$$
$$\text{Value of equity per share after recapitalization} = \frac{38,888}{1,525.26} = \$25.50$$

If the stock buyback occurs at a price higher than $25.29, investors who sell their stock back will gain at the expense of those who remain stockholder in the firm.

---

[17]This would clearly require stockholders who are selling their shares back to be oblivious to the gigantic stock buyback and its effect on value.

8.3   Rationality and Stock Price Effects

Assume that Disney does make a tender offer for its shares but pays $27 per share. What will happen to the value per share for the shareholders who do not sell back?

a.   The share price will drop below the pre-announcement price of $24.34.

b.   The share price will be between $24.34 and the estimated value (above) or $25.30.

c.   The share price will be higher than $25.30.

capstru.xls: This spreadsheet allows you to compute the optimal debt ratio firm value for any firm, using the same information used for Disney. It has updated interest coverage ratios and spreads built in.

Capital Structure and Market Timing: A Behavioral Perspective

Inherent in the cost of capital approach is the notion of a tradeoff, where managers measure the tax benefits of debt against the potential bankruptcy costs. But do managers make financing decisions based on this tradeoff? Baker and Wurgler argue that whether managers use debt or equity to fund investments has less to do with the costs and benefits of debt and more to do with market timing.[18] If managers perceive their stock to be overvalued, they are more likely to use equity, and if they perceive stock to by undervalued, they tend to use debt. The observed debt ratio for a firm is therefore the cumulative result of attempts by managers to time equity and bond markets.

The "market timing" view of capital structure is backed up by surveys that have been done over the last decade by Graham and Harvey, who report that two-thirds of CFOs surveyed consider how much their stock is under or over valued, when issuing equity and are more likely to borrow money, when they feel "interest rates are low."[19] There is also evidence that initial public offerings and equity issues spike when stock prices in a sector surge.

While the evidence offered by behavioral economists for the market-timing hypothesis is strong, it is not inconsistent with a tradeoff hypothesis. In its most benign form, managers choose a long-term target for the debt ratio, but how they get there will be a function of the timing decisions made along the way. In its more damaging form, market timing can also explain why firms end up with actual debt ratios very different from their target debt ratios. If a sector or a firm goes through an extended period where managers think stock prices are "low" and that interest rates are also "low," they will defer issuing equity and continue borrowing money for that period, thus ending up with debt ratios that are far too high, relative to their targets.

Given the pull of market timing, telling managers to ignore the market is not only impractical but may also potentially cost stockholders money in the long term. One solution is for firms to compute their optimal debt ratios and then allow managers to make judgments on the timing of debt and equity issues based on their views on the

---

[18]Malcolm Baker and Jeffrey Wurgler, "Market Timing and Capital Structure," *Journal of Finance* 57:1–32.

[19]John R. Graham and Campbell R. Harvey, "The Theory and Practice of Corporate Finance: Evidence from the Field," *Journal of Financial Economics* 60:187–243.

pricing of the stock and interest rates. If the market timing does not work, the costs should be small because the firm will converge on the optimal at some point in time. If the market timing works, stockholders will gain from the timing.

Constrained Versions

The cost of capital approach that we have described is unconstrained, because our only objective is to minimize the cost of capital. There are several reasons why a firm may choose not to view the debt ratio that emerges from this analysis as optimal. First, the firm's default risk at the point at which the cost of capital is minimized may be high enough to put the firm's survival at jeopardy. Stated in terms of bond ratings, the firm may have a below–investment grade rating. Second, the optimal debt ratio was computed using the operating income from the most recent financial year. To the extent that operating income is volatile and can decline, firms may want to curtail their borrowing. In this section, we consider ways we can bring each of these considerations into the cost of capital analysis.

Bond Rating Constraint

One way of using the cost of capital approach without putting firms into financial jeopardy is to impose a bond rating constraint on the cost of capital analysis. Once this constraint has been imposed, the optimal debt ratio is the one that has the lowest cost of capital, subject to the constraint that the bond rating meets or exceeds a certain level.

Although this approach is simple, it is essentially subjective and is therefore open to manipulation. For instance, the management at Disney could insist on preserving a AA rating and use this constraint to justify reducing its debt ratio. One way to make managers more accountable in this regard is to measure the cost of a rating constraint.

$$\text{Cost of rating constraint} = \text{Maximum firm value without constraints} - \text{Maximum firm value with constraints}$$

If Disney insisted on maintaining a AA rating, its constrained optimal debt ratio would be 30%. The cost of preserving the constraint can then be measured as the difference between firm value at 40% (the unconstrained optimal) and at 30% (the constrained optimal).

$$\text{Cost of AA rating constraint} = \text{Value at 40\% debt} - \text{Value at 30\% debt}$$
$$= \$63{,}651 - \$63{,}596$$
$$= \$55 \text{ million}$$

In this case, the rating constraint has a very small cost. The loss in value that can accrue from having an unrealistically high rating constraint can be viewed as the cost of being too conservative when it comes to debt policy. A AAA rating constraint at Disney would restrict them at 20% debt ratio and the concurrent cost would be higher:

$$\text{Cost of AAA rating constraint} = \text{Value at 40\% debt} - \text{Value at 20\% debt}$$
$$= \$63{,}651 - \$62{,}371$$
$$= \$1{,}280 \text{ million}$$

Disney's management would then have to weigh off this lost value against what they perceive to be the benefits of a AAA rating.

8.4 AGENCY COSTS AND FINANCIAL FLEXIBILITY

In the last chapter, we consider agency costs and lost flexibility as potential costs of using debt. Where in the cost of capital approach do we consider these costs?

a. These costs are not considered in the cost of capital approach.

b. These costs are fully captured in the cost of capital through the costs of equity and debt, which increase as you borrow more money.

c. These costs are partially captured in the cost of capital through the costs of equity and debt, which increase as you borrow more money.

Sensitivity Analysis

The optimal debt ratio we estimate for a firm is a function of all the inputs that go into the cost of capital computation—the beta of the firm, the risk-free rate, the risk premium, and the default spread. It is also indirectly a function of the firm's operating income, because interest coverage ratios are based on this income, and these ratios are used to compute ratings and interest rates.

The determinants of the optimal debt ratio for a firm can be divided into variables specific to the firm, and macroeconomic variables. Among the variables specific to the firm that affect its optimal debt ratio are the tax rate, the firm's capacity to generate operating income, and its cash flows. In general, the tax benefits from debt increase as the tax rate goes up. In relative terms, firms with higher tax rates will have higher optimal debt ratios than will firms with lower tax rates, all else being equal. It also follows that a firm's optimal debt ratio will increase as its tax rate increases. Firms that generate higher operating income and cash flows as a percent of firm market value can also sustain much more debt as a proportion of the market value of the firm, because debt payments can be covered much more easily by prevailing cash flows.

The macroeconomic determinants of optimal debt ratios include the level of interest rates and default spreads. As interest rates rise, the costs of debt and equity both increase. However, optimal debt ratios tend to be lower when interest rates are higher, perhaps because interest coverage ratios drop off steeply. The default spreads commanded by different ratings classes tend to increase during recessions and decrease during recoveries. Keeping other things constant, as the spreads increase, optimal debt ratios decrease for the simple reason that higher default spreads result in higher costs of debt.

How does sensitivity analysis allow a firm to choose an optimal debt ratio? After computing the optimal debt ratio with existing inputs, firms may put it to the test by changing both firm-specific inputs (such as operating income) and macroeconomic inputs (such as default spreads). The debt ratio the firm chooses as its optimal then reflects the volatility of the underlying variables and the risk aversion of the firm's management.

ILLUSTRATION 8.3 Sensitivity Analysis on Disney's Optimal Debt Ratio

In the base case, in Illustration 8.3, we used Disney's operating income in 2008 to find the optimal debt ratio. We could argue that Disney's operating income is subject to large swings, depending on the vagaries of the economy and the fortunes of the entertainment business, as shown in Table 8.10.

	EBIT	% Change in EBIT
Table 8.10	DISNEY'S OPERATING INCOME HISTORY: 1987–2008	
1987	$756	
1988	$848	12.17%
1989	$1,177	38.80%
1990	$1,368	16.23%
1991	$1,124	−17.84%
1992	$1,287	14.50%
1993	$1,560	21.21%
1994	$1,804	15.64%
1995	$2,262	25.39%
1996	$3,024	33.69%
1997	$3,945	30.46%
1998	$3,843	−2.59%
1999	$3,580	−6.84%
2000	$2,525	−29.47%
2001	$2,832	12.16%
2002	$2,384	−15.82%
2003	$2,713	13.80%
2004	$4,048	49.21%
2005	$4,107	1.46%
2006	$5,355	30.39%
2007	$6,829	27.53%
2008	$7,404	8.42%

There are several ways of using the information in such historical data to modify the analysis. One approach is to look at the firm's performance during previous downturns. In Disney's case, the operating income in 2002 dropped by 15.82% as the firm struggled with the aftermath of the terrorist attacks of September 11, 2001, and the resultant downturn in leisure travel. In 2000, Disney's self-inflicted wounds from overinvestment in the Internet business and poor movies caused operating income to plummet almost 30%. A second approach is to obtain a statistical measure of the volatility in operating income so that we can be more conservative in choosing debt levels for firms with more volatile earnings. In Disney's case, the standard deviation in percentage changes in operating income is 19.80%. Table 8.11 illustrates the impact of lower operating income on the optimal debt level.

The optimal debt ratio stays at 40% until EBITDA declines by 20%, matching Disney's worst year on record. This would suggest that Disney has excess debt capacity, even with conservative estimates of operating income.

IN PRACTICE: EBIT VERSUS EBITDA

In recent years, analysts have increasingly turned to using EBITDA as a measure of operating cash flows for a firm. It may therefore seem surprising that we focus on operating income, or EBIT, far more than EBITDA when computing the optimal

Table 8.11 EFFECTS OF OPERATING INCOME ON OPTIMAL DEBT RATIO

EBITDA Drops By	EBITDA	Optimal Debt Ratio
0%	$8,319	40%
5%	$7,903	40%
10%	$7,487	40%
15%	$7,071	40%
20%	$6,655	30%

capital structure. The interest coverage ratios, for instance, are based on operating income, not EBITDA. Although it is true that depreciation and amortization are noncash expenses and should be added back to cash flows, it is dangerous for a firm with ongoing operations to depend on the cash flows generated by these items to service debt payments. After all, firms with high depreciation and amortization expenses usually have high ongoing capital expenditures. If the cash inflows from depreciation and amortization are redirected to make debt payments, the reinvestment made by firms will be insufficient to generate future growth or to maintain existing assets.

In summary, then, a firm with high EBITDA and low EBIT that borrows money based on the former can find itself in trouble one way or the other. If it uses the cash flows from depreciation to pay interest expenses rather than make capital expenditures, it will put its growth prospects at risk. If it continues to make capital expenditures, it will find itself dependent upon new financing to cover its debt costs. ■

Enhanced Cost of Capital Approach

A key limitation of the standard cost of capital approach is that it keeps operating income fixed, while bond ratings vary. In effect, we are ignoring indirect bankruptcy costs when computing the optimal debt ratio. In the enhanced cost of capital approach, we bring these indirect bankruptcy costs into the expected operating income. As the rating of the company declines, the operating income is adjusted to reflect the loss in operating income that will occur when customers, suppliers, and investors react.

To quantify the distress costs, we have tie the operating income to a company's bond rating. Put another way, we have to quantify how much we would expect the operating income to decline if a firm's bond rating drops from AA to A or from A to BBB. This will clearly vary across sectors and across time.

- Across sectors, the different effects of distress on operating income will reflect how much customers, suppliers, and employees in that sector react to the perception of default risk in a company. As we noted in Chapter 7, indirect bankruptcy costs are likely to be highest for firms that produce long-lived assets, where customers are dependent upon the firm for parts and service.

- Across time, the indirect costs of distress will vary depending how easy it is to access financial markets and sell assets. In buoyant markets (e.g., 1999 and 2006), the effect of a ratings downgrade on operating income are likely to be much smaller than in a market in crisis.

While getting agreement on these broad principles is easy, we are still faced with the practical question of how best to estimate the impact of declining ratings on operating income. We would suggest looking at the track record of other firms in the same sector that have been downgraded by ratings agencies in the past, and the effects that the downgrading has had on operating income in subsequent years.

Once we link operating income to the bond rating, we can then modify the cost of capital approach to deliver the optimal debt ratio. Rather than look for the debt ratio that delivers the lowest cost of capital (the decision rule in the standard approach), we look for the debt ratio that delivers the highest firm value, through a combination of high earnings and low cost of capital.

ILLUSTRATION 8.4   Disney—Enhanced Cost of Capital Approach

In Illustration 8.3, we estimated an optimal debt ratio of 40% for Disney in the standard cost of capital approach. In making this estimate, we kept Disney's operating income fixed at $6,829 million as Disney's ratings moved from AAA (at a 20% debt ratio) to well below investment grade. In Table 8.12, we take a more realistic view: once Disney's rating drops below A (that is, below investment grade), distress costs occur in the form of a percentage decrease in operating earnings.

The result of this enhancement to the cost of capital approach can be seen in Table 8.13, where we compute the costs of capital, operating income, and firm values at different debt ratios for Disney.

As long as the bond ratings remain investment grade, Disney's value remains intact. Its value, in fact, achieves its highest level at an A+ rating and a debt ratio of 30%. But as soon as the rating drops below investment grade, the distress costs begin to take effect, and Disney's value drops precipitously. Thus, the debt ratio of 40% that seemed optimal under the unmodified cost of capital approach now appears to be imprudent. The optimal debt ratio is now 30%, which means that Disney can borrow an additional $1.9 billion (to get from its existing dollar debt of $16,682 million to its optimal debt of $18,563 million).

Table 8.12   OPERATING INCOME AND BOND RATING

Rating	Drop in EBITDA
A or higher	No effect
A−	2.00%
BBB	10.00%
BB+ to B	20.00%
B−	25.00%
C to CCC	40.00%
D	50.00%

Table 8.13 FIRM VALUE, COST OF CAPITAL, AND DEBT RATIOS: ENHANCED COST OF CAPITAL

Debt Ratio	Bond Rating	Cost of Capital	Firm Value (G)
0%	AAA	7.90%	$58,522
10%	AAA	7.68%	$60,384
20%	AAA	7.45%	$62,368
30%	A+	7.42%	$62,707
40%	CCC	9.18%	$24,987
50%	C	12.77%	$17,569
60%	C	14.27%	$15,630
70%	C	15.77%	$14,077
80%	C	17.27%	$12,804
90%	C	18.77%	$11,743

 capstruEnh.xls: This spreadsheet allows you to compute the optimal debt ratio firm value for any firm using the same information used for Disney. It has updated interest coverage ratios and spreads built in.

Extensions of the Cost of Capital Approach

The cost of capital approach, which works so well for manufacturing firms that are publicly traded, can be adapted to compute optimal debt ratios for cyclical firms, family group companies, private firms, or even financial service firms such as banks and insurance companies.

Cyclical and Commodity Firms

A key input that drives the optimal capital structure is the current operating income. If this income is depressed, either because the firm is a cyclical firm or because there are firm-specific factors that are expected to be temporary, the optimal debt ratio that will emerge from the analysis will be much lower than the firm's true optimal. For example, automobile manufacturing firms will have very low debt ratios if the optimal debt ratios had been computed based on the operating income in 2008, which was a recession year for these firms, and oil companies would have had very high optimal debt ratios with 2008 earnings, because high oil prices during the year inflated earnings.

When evaluating a firm with depressed current operating income, we must first decide whether the drop in income is temporary or permanent. If the drop is temporary, we must estimate the **normalized operating income** for the firm—i.e., the income that the firm would generate in a normal year, rather than what it made in the most recent years. Most analysts normalize earnings by taking the average earnings over a period of time (usually five years). Because this holds the scale of the firm fixed, it may not be appropriate for firms that have changed in size over time. The right way to normalize income will vary across firms:

- For *cyclical firms*, whose current operating income may be overstated (if the economy is booming) or understated (if the economy is in recession), the operating income can be estimated using the average operating margin over an entire economic cycle (usually five to ten years).

$$\text{Normalized operating income} = \text{Average operating margin (Cycle)}$$
$$* \text{ Current sales}$$

- For *commodity firms*, we can also estimate the normalized operating income by making an assumption about the normalized price of the commodity. With an oil company, for instance, this would translate into making a judgment about the normal oil price per barrel. This normalized commodity price can then be used, in conjunction with production, to generate normalized revenues and earnings.

- For *firms that have had a bad year* in terms of operating income due to firm-specific factors (such as the loss of a contract), the operating margin for the industry in which the firm operates can be used to calculate the normalized operating income:

$$\text{Normalized operating income} = \text{Average operating margin (Industry)}$$
$$* \text{ Current sales}$$

The normalized operating income can also be estimated using returns on capital across an economic cycle (for cyclical firms) or an industry (for firms with firm-specific problems), but returns on capital are much more likely to be skewed by mismeasurement of capital than operating margins.

ILLUSTRATION 8.5 Applying the Cost of Capital Approach with Normalized Operating Income to Aracruz Celulose

Aracruz Celulose, the Brazilian pulp and paper manufacturing firm, reported operating income of R$574 million on revenues of R$3,696 million in 2008. This was significantly lower than its operating income of R$1,011 million in 2007 and R$1,074 million in 2006. We estimated the optimal debt ratio for Aracruz based on the following information:

- In 2008, Aracruz had depreciation of R$973 million and capital expenditures amounted to R$1,502 million.

- Aracruz had debt outstanding of R$9,834 million with a dollar cost of debt of 8.50%.

- The corporate tax rate in Brazil is estimated to be 34%.

- Aracruz had 588.29 million shares outstanding, trading at R$15.14 per share. The beta of the stock, estimated from the beta of the sector and Aracruz's debt ratio, is 1.74.

In Chapter 4, we estimated Aracruz's current U.S. dollar cost of capital to be 12.84%, using an equity risk premium of 9.95% for Brazil and Aracruz's current debt ratio of 52.47%:

$$\text{Current \$ cost of equity} = 3.5\% + 1.74(9.95\%) = 20.82\%$$
$$\text{Current \$ cost of debt} = 8.5\% \, (1 - 0.34) = 5.61\%$$
$$\text{Current \$ cost of capital} = 20.82\% \, (1 - 0.5247) + 5.61\% * 0.5247 = 12.84\%$$

We made three significant changes in applying the cost of capital approach to Aracruz as opposed to Disney:

1. The operating income at Aracruz is a function of the price of paper and pulp in global markets. We computed Aracruz's average pretax operating margin between 2004 and 2008 to be 27.24%. Applying this average margin to 2008 revenues of R$. 3,697 million generates a normalized operating income of R$1,007 million. We will compute the optimal debt ratio using this normalized value.

2. In Chapter 4, we noted that Aracruz's synthetic rating of BB+, based on the interest coverage ratio, is higher than its actual rating of BB and attributed the difference to Aracruz being a Brazilian company, exposed to country risk. Because we compute the cost of debt at each level of debt using synthetic ratings for the company, we run the risk of understating the cost of debt, because we ignore the overlay of country risk. To account for Brazilian country risk, we add the country default spread for Brazil (2.50%) to Aracruz's company default spread in assessing the dollar cost of debt:

$$\text{R\$ Cost of debt} = \text{U.S. T-bond rate} + \text{Default spread}_{Country} + \text{Default spread}_{Company}$$

3. Aracruz has a market value of equity of about $4.4 billion (R$8.9 billion). We used the interest coverage ratio/rating relationship for smaller companies to estimate synthetic ratings at each level of debt. In practical terms, the rating that we assign to Aracruz for any given interest coverage ratio will generally be lower than the rating that Disney, a much larger company, would have had with the same ratio.

Using the normalized operating income, we estimated the costs of equity, debt, and capital in Table 8.14 for Aracruz at different debt ratios.

The optimal debt ratio for Aracruz using the normalized operating income is 10%, well below its current debt ratio of 52.48%. However, the cost of capital at the optimal is higher than its current cost of capital, at first sight, a puzzling result. The reason for the divergence is that the interest expenses that we compute for Aracruz, using the estimated interest rates are dramatically higher than the current interest expenses. For

Table 8.14   COST OF CAPITAL, FIRM VALUE, AND DEBT RATIOS: ARACRUZ CELULOSE

Debt Ratio	Beta	Cost of Equity	Bond Rating	Interest Rate on Debt	Tax Rate	Cost of Debt (after-tax)	WACC	Firm Value (G)
0%	1.01	13.52%	AAA	7.25%	34.00%	4.79%	13.52%	R$17,424
10%	1.08	14.26%	A−	9.00%	34.00%	5.94%	13.42%	R$17,600
20%	1.17	15.17%	B−	14.50%	34.00%	9.57%	14.05%	R$16,511
30%	1.29	16.36%	CC	18.00%	33.83%	11.91%	15.03%	R$15,062
40%	1.53	18.75%	C	21.00%	21.75%	16.43%	17.82%	R$11,994
50%	1.87	22.13%	D	26.00%	14.05%	22.35%	22.24%	R$9,012
60%	2.34	26.79%	D	26.00%	11.71%	22.95%	24.49%	R$7,975
70%	3.12	34.55%	D	26.00%	10.04%	23.39%	26.74%	R$7,140
80%	4.68	50.08%	D	26.00%	8.78%	23.72%	28.99%	R$6,452
90%	9.36	96.66%	D	26.00%	7.81%	23.97%	31.24%	R$5,875

instance, at a 50% debt ratio (roughly equal to their current debt ratio), the interest expenses of R$1,968 million are more than twelve times higher than the current interest expense of R$155 million and are more than double the normalized operating income. The only explanation that we can provide for this phenomenon is that a great deal of the debt on Aracruz's books is recent debt and that the current interest expenses therefore do not reflect the debt on its books. Given how much Aracruz owes currently (almost R$10 billion), we do not see how interest expenses can stay at levels resembling the current numbers.

The conclusion that we would draw about Aracruz is that it is dangerously over levered, at its existing debt ratio. The interest expenses on the current debt will be too high to be serviced from operations, even if operating income reverts back to normalized levels. If operating income does not bounce back quickly, the situation becomes even more dire.

 There is a data set online that summarizes operating margins and returns on capital by industry group in the United States for the most recent quarter.

Companies That Are Part of a Group

When a company is part of a family group, the logic of minimizing cost of capital does not change but the mechanics can be skewed by two factors.

1. The first is that the cost of debt may be more reflective of the credit standing of the group to which the firm belongs, rather than its own financial strength. Put another way, a distressed company that is part of a healthy family group of companies may be able to borrow more money at a lower rate than an otherwise similar standalone company. This can—at least artificially—increase its optimal debt ratio. Conversely, a healthy company that is part of a distressed group may find its cost of debt and capital affected by perceptions about the group; in this case, the optimal debt ratio will be lower for this company than for an independent company.

2. The second is that rather than optimizing the mix of debt and equity for individual companies, the controllers of the family group of companies may view their objective as finding a mix of debt and equity that maximizes the value of the group of companies. Thus, our assessments of the capital structures of individual companies may not be particularly meaningful.

There is one final factor to consider. The consolidated operating income of the entire family group should be more stable than the earnings of the individual companies that comprise the group, reflecting diversification over multiple businesses. Consequently, the optimal debt computed for the family group will be higher than the aggregate of the optimal debt computed for individual companies in the group.

ILLUSTRATION 8.6   Applying the Cost of Capital Approach to Tata Chemicals

As we noted in earlier chapters, Tata Chemicals is part of the Tata Group, a family controlled group with diverse holdings across the spectrum. To assess the optimal capital structure for Tata Chemicals, we started with the current mix of debt and equity and cost of capital in rupees.

- Cost of equity = Risk-free rate + Beta (equity risk premium for India)
$$= 4\% + 0.945(10.51\%) = 13.93\%$$

- Pretax cost of debt = Risk-free rate + Default spread$_{India}$
$$+ \text{Default spread}_{Tata\ Chemicals}$$
$$= 4\% + 3\% + 3\% = 10\%$$

Debt ratio for the firm −34%
Marginal tax rate = 33.99%

- Cost of capital = $13.93\%(1 - 0.34) + 10\%(1 - 0.3399)(0.34) = 11.44\%$

In 2008, Tata Chemicals generated operating income (EBIT) of Rs6,268 million after depreciation charges of Rs1,582 million. We estimated the costs of equity, debt, and capital at debt ratios ranging from 0% to 90% in Table 8.15.

Note that we have made allowances for the fact that Tata Chemicals is an Indian company in our computations. When computing the cost of equity, we added the country risk premium for India to the mature market premium to arrive at a total equity risk premium of 10.51%. For the cost of debt at each debt ratio, we added the default spread for Tata Chemicals at that debt ratio to the default spread for India (3%) to arrive at the total cost of debt.

The optimal debt ratio, based on this calculation, is 10% debt and the cost of capital at that ratio is 11.35%. At its existing debt ratio of 34%, Tata Chemicals looks overlevered even though its current cost of capital is only slightly higher at 11.44%. However, it is not clear how much of the additional debt can be attributed to the reputation effects of being part of a well-regarded and profitable family group of companies.

Table 8.15   COSTS OF DEBT, EQUITY, AND CAPITAL: TATA CHEMICALS

Debt Ratio	Beta	Cost of Equity	Bond Rating	Interest Rate on Debt	Tax Rate	Cost of Debt (after-tax)	WACC	Firm Value (G)
0%	0.70	11.39%	AAA	8.25%	33.99%	5.45%	11.39%	Rs79,626
10%	0.75	11.93%	A+	9.25%	33.99%	6.11%	11.35%	Rs80,084
20%	0.82	12.61%	BB	12.00%	33.99%	7.92%	11.67%	Rs76,586
30%	0.90	13.48%	B−	15.50%	33.99%	10.23%	12.51%	Rs68,768
40%	1.01	14.64%	CC	19.00%	33.99%	12.54%	13.80%	Rs59,257
50%	1.23	16.98%	C	22.00%	24.43%	16.63%	16.80%	Rs44,637
60%	1.58	20.64%	D	27.00%	16.59%	22.52%	21.77%	Rs31,272
70%	2.11	26.19%	D	27.00%	14.22%	23.16%	24.07%	Rs27,325
80%	3.17	37.28%	D	27.00%	12.44%	23.64%	26.37%	Rs24,189
90%	6.33	70.56%	D	27.00%	11.06%	24.01%	28.67%	Rs21,638

Private Firms

There are three major differences between public and private firms in terms of analyzing optimal debt ratios. One is that unlike the case for publicly traded firms, we do not have a direct estimate of the market value of a private firm. Consequently, we have to estimate firm value before we move to subsequent stages in the analysis. The second difference relates to the cost of equity and how we arrive at that cost. Although we use betas to estimate the cost of equity for a public firm, that usage might not be appropriate when we are computing the optimal debt ratio for a private firm, since the owner may not be well diversified. Finally, whereas publicly traded firms tend to think of their cost of debt in terms of bond ratings and default spreads, private firms tend to borrow from banks. Banks assess default risk and charge the appropriate interest rates.

To analyze the optimal debt ratio for a private firm, we make the following adjustments. First, we estimate the value of the private firm by looking at how publicly traded firms in the same business are priced by the market. Thus, if publicly traded firms in the business have market values that are roughly three times revenues, we would multiply the revenues of the private firm by this number to arrive at an estimated value. Second, we continue to estimate the costs of debt for a private firm using a synthetic bond rating, based on interest coverage ratios, but we will require much higher interest coverage ratios to arrive at the same rating, to reflect the fact that banks are likely to be more conservative in assessing default risk at small, private firms. Finally, we will use total betas to capture total risk, rather than just market risk, to estimate the cost of equity.

ILLUSTRATION 8.7   Applying the Cost of Capital Approach to a Private Firm—Bookscape

Bookscape, a private firm, has neither a market value for its equity nor a rating for its debt. In Chapter 4, we assumed that Bookscape would have a debt-to-capital ratio of 34.84%, similar to that of publicly traded book companies, and that the tax rate for the firm is 40%. We computed a cost of capital based on that assumption. We also used a total beta of 2.91 to measure the additional risk that the owner of Bookscape is exposed to because of his lack of diversification.

$$\text{Cost of equity} = \text{Risk-free rate} + \text{Total beta} * \text{Risk premium}$$
$$= 3.5\% + 2.91 * 6\% = 20.94\%$$
$$\text{Pretax cost of debt} = 6\% \text{(based on synthetic rating of A)}$$
$$\text{Cost of capital} = 20.94\%(0.6516) + 6\%(1 - 0.40)(0.3484) = 14.90\%$$

To estimate the optimal capital structure for Bookscape, we made the following assumptions:

- Although Bookscape has no conventional debt outstanding, it does have one large operating lease commitment. Given that the operating lease has twenty-five years to run and that the lease commitment is $750,000 for each year, the present value of the operating lease commitments is computed using Bookscape's pretax cost of debt of 6%:

$$\text{Present value of operating lease commitments (in thousands)}$$
$$= \$750 \text{ (PV of annuity, 6\%, 25 years)} = \$9,587$$

Note that Bookscape's pretax cost of debt is based on their synthetic rating of A, which we estimated in Chapter 4.

- Bookscape had operating income before taxes of $3 million in the most recent financial year, after depreciation charges of $400,000 and operating lease expenses of $750,000. Because we consider the present value of operating lease expenses to be debt, we add back the imputed interest expense on the present value of lease expenses to the EBIT to arrive at an adjusted EBIT. For the rest of the analysis, operating lease commitments are treated as debt and the interest expense estimated on the present value of operating leases is treated as the interest expense:

$$\text{Adjusted EBIT (in thousands)} = \text{EBIT} + \text{Pretax cost of debt}$$
$$* \text{PV of operating lease expenses}$$
$$= \$3,000 + 0.06 * \$9,587 = \$3,575$$

- To estimate the market value of equity, we looked at publicly traded book retailers and computed an average price to earnings ratio of 10 for these firms. Applying this multiple of earnings to Bookscape's net income of $1.5 million in 2008 yielded an estimate of Bookscape's market value of equity.

$$\text{Estimated market value of equity (in thousands)} = \text{Net income for Bookscape}$$
$$* \text{Average PE for publicly traded book retailers} = 1,500 * 10 = \$15,000$$

This estimate of the market value of equity result in a debt ratio of 38.99%:

$$\text{Debt ratio} = \frac{\text{Debt}}{\text{Debt} + \text{Equity}} = \frac{\$9,587}{\$9,587 + \$15,000} = 38.99\%$$

- The interest rates at different levels of debt will be estimated based on a synthetic bond rating. This rating will be assessed using Table 8.16, which summarizes ratings

Table 8.16   INTEREST COVERAGE RATIOS, RATING, AND DEFAULT SPREADS—SMALL FIRMS

Interest Coverage Ratio: Small Market Cap (< $5 billion)	Rating	Typical Default Spread
>12.5	AAA	1.25%
9.50–12.50	AA	1.75%
7.50–9.50	A+	2.25%
6.00–7.50	A	2.50%
4.50–6.00	A−	3.00%
4.00–4.50	BBB	3.50%
3.50–4.00	BB+	4.25%
3.00–3.50	BB	5.00%
2.50–3.00	B+	6.00%
2.00–2.50	B	7.25%
1.50–2.00	B−	8.50%
1.25–1.50	CCC	10.00%
0.80–1.25	CC	12.00%
0.50–0.80	C	15.00%
<0.65	D	20.00%

and default spreads over the long-term bond rate as a function of interest coverage ratios for small firms that are rated by S&P as of January 2009.
Note that smaller firms need higher coverage ratios than the larger firms to get the same rating.

- The tax rate used in the analysis is 40%, and the long-term bond rate at the time of this analysis was 3.5% and the equity risk premium is 6%.

Based on this information and using the same approach used for Disney, the cost of capital and firm value are estimated for Bookscape at different debt ratios. The information is summarized in Table 8.17.

The firm value is maximized (and the cost of capital is minimized) at a debt ratio of 40%. At its existing debt ratio of 38.99%, Bookscape is at its optimal. (Note that we estimate the cost of capital in 10% increments. Hence, an optimal of 40% indicates that the optimal debt ratio lies between 35 and 45%.

IN PRACTICE: OPTIMAL DEBT RATIOS FOR PRIVATE FIRMS

Although the tradeoff between the costs and benefits of borrowing remains the same for private and publicly traded firms, there are differences between the two kinds of firms that may result in private firms borrowing less money:

- Increasing debt increases default risk, and expected bankruptcy costs much substantially more for small private firms than for larger publicly traded firms. This is partly because the owners of private firms may be exposed to unlimited liability, and partly because the perception of financial trouble on the part of customers and suppliers can be much more damaging to small, private firms.

- Increasing debt yields a much smaller advantage in terms of disciplining managers in the case of privately run firms, because the owners of the firm tend to be the top managers as well.

- Increasing debt generally exposes small private firms to far more restrictive bond covenants and higher agency costs than it does large publicly traded firms.

Table 8.17   COSTS OF CAPITAL AND FIRM VALUE FOR BOOKSCAPE

Debt Ratio	Beta	Cost of Equity	Bond Rating	Interest Rate on Debt	Tax Rate	Cost of Debt (after-tax)	Cost of Capital	Firm Value (G)
0%	1.98	15.38%	AAA	4.75%	40.00%	2.85%	15.38%	$20,701.79
10%	2.11	16.18%	AAA	4.75%	40.00%	2.85%	14.84%	$21,728.94
20%	2.28	17.17%	AAA	4.75%	40.00%	2.85%	14.30%	$22,858.84
30%	2.49	18.44%	A	6.00%	40.00%	3.60%	13.99%	$23,572.02
40%	2.77	20.14%	A−	6.50%	40.00%	3.90%	13.64%	$24,403.93
50%	3.17	22.51%	BB	8.50%	40.00%	5.10%	13.81%	$24,000.23
60%	3.76	26.08%	B	10.75%	40.00%	6.45%	14.30%	$22,861.61
70%	4.75	32.02%	B−	12.00%	40.00%	7.20%	14.65%	$22,128.00
80%	6.73	43.90%	CC	15.50%	40.00%	9.30%	16.22%	$19,282.19
90%	13.20	82.73%	CC	15.50%	37.03%	9.76%	17.06%	$18,039.01

- The loss of flexibility associated with using excess debt capacity is likely to weigh much more heavily on small, private firms than on large, publicly traded firms due to the former's lack of access to public markets.

All these factors would lead us to expect much lower debt ratios at small private firms. ∎

8.5 GOING PUBLIC: EFFECT ON OPTIMAL DEBT RATIO

Assume that Bookscape is planning to make an IPO in six months. How would this information change your assessment of the optimal debt ratio?

a. It will increase the optimal debt ratio, because publicly traded firms should be able to borrow more than private businesses.

b. It will reduce the optimal debt ratio, because only market risk counts for a publicly traded firm.

c. It may increase or decrease the optimal debt ratio, depending on which effect dominates.

Financial Service Firms

There are several problems in applying the cost of capital approach to financial service firms, such as banks and insurance companies. The first is that the interest coverage ratio spreads, which are critical in determining the bond ratings, have to be estimated separately for financial service firms; applying manufacturing company spreads will result in absurdly low ratings for even the safest banks and very low optimal debt ratios. Furthermore, the relationship between interest coverage ratios and ratings tend to be much weaker for financial service firms than it is for manufacturing firms. The second is a measurement problem that arises partly from the difficulty in estimating the debt on a financial service company's balance sheet. Given the mix of deposits, repurchase agreements, short-term financing, and other liabilities that may appear on a financial service firm's balance sheet, one solution is to focus only on long-term debt, defined tightly, and to use interest coverage ratios defined using only long-term interest expenses. The third problem is that financial service firms are regulated and have to meet capital ratios that are defined in terms of book value. If these firms violate the book capital ratios in the process of moving to an optimal market value debt ratio, they could put themselves in jeopardy.

While we could try to adapt the cost of capital approach to come up with optimal debt ratios for banks and other financial service companies, the results are very sensitive to how we define debt and the relationship we assume between bond ratings and operating income. An alternative and more effective approach is to use the regulatory capital ratios, usually determined in terms of book equity, as the basis for determining how much equity a financial service firm needs to raise to not only continue operating, but to do so without putting itself at peril. As a simple example, consider a bank with $100 million in loans outstanding and a book value of equity of $6 million. Furthermore, assume that the regulatory requirement is that equity capital be maintained at 5% of loans outstanding. Finally, assume that this bank wants to increase its loan base by $50 million (to $150 million) and to augment its equity capital ratio to 7% of loans outstanding. The amount of equity that the bank will have to raise to fund its expansion is computed below:

$$\text{Loans outstanding after expansion} = \$150 \text{ million}$$
$$\text{Equity/capital ratio desired} = 7\%$$
$$\text{Equity after expansion} = \$10.5 \text{ million}$$
$$\text{Existing equity} = \$6.0 \text{ million}$$
$$\text{New equity needed} = \$4.5 \text{ million}$$

As we look at more complex financial service firms that operate in multiple businesses with different risk levels, there are two challenges that we will face in putting this approach into practice:

1. *Different regulatory capital requirements for different businesses*   When a firm operates in different businesses, the regulatory capital restrictions can vary across businesses. In general, the capital requirements will be higher in riskier businesses and lower in safer businesses. Hence, the equity that a firm has to raise to fund expansion will depend in large part of which businesses are being expanded.

2. *Regulatory versus risk-based capital ratios*   The regulatory capital ratios represent a floor on what a firm has to invest in equity, to keep its operations going and not a ceiling. It is possible that the firm's own assessment of risk in a business can lead it to hold more equity than required by the regulatory authorities.

As a final twist, it is worth nothing that banking regulators consider preferred stock as part of equity, when computing regulatory ratios.

In general, there are three strategies that a financial service firm can follow when it comes to the use of leverage:

1. *The regulatory minimum strategy*   In this strategy, financial service firms try to stay with the bare minimum equity capital, as required by the regulatory ratios. In the most aggressive versions of this strategy, firms exploit loopholes in the regulatory framework to invest in those businesses where regulatory capital ratios are set too low (relative to the risk of these businesses). The upside of this strategy is that the returns on equity in good times will exceptionally high, since the equity capital is kept low. The downside of this strategy is that the risk in the investments ultimately will manifest itself, and the absence of equity to cover losses will put the firm's existence in jeopardy.

2. *The self-regulatory strategy*   The objective for a bank raising equity is not to meet regulatory capital ratios, but to ensure that losses from the business can be covered by the existing equity. In effect, financial service firms can assess how much equity they need to hold by evaluating the riskiness of their businesses and the potential for losses. Having done so, they can then check to also make sure that they meet the regulatory requirements for capital. The upside of this strategy is that it forces the firm both to assess risk in its businesses and to make the tradeoff between risk and return when entering new businesses. The downside is that it is more data-intensive, and errors in assessing risk will affect the firm's value.

3. *Combination strategy* In this strategy, the regulatory capital ratios operate as a floor for established businesses, with the firm adding buffers for safety where needed. In new or evolving businesses, the firm makes its own assessments of risk that may be very different from those made by the regulatory authorities.

We would argue that the responsibility for maintaining enough equity has to rest ultimately with the management of the firm and not with the regulatory authorities. A bank that blames the laxness of regulatory oversight for its failures is not a well-managed bank.

ILLUSTRATION 8.8 Deutsche Bank's Capital Mix

The financial crisis of 2008 centered on financial service firms and can at least partially be traced to the inadequacy of equity capital at these firms relative to the riskiness of the investments. Thus, investment banks, insurance companies, and banks that had vast holdings of risky securities, some based on real estate and some on leveraged loans, had too little equity capital to cover the losses from these investments.

While many U.S. banks, including Wells Fargo, JP Morgan, and Bank of America, were tagged as undercapitalized and had to raise billions in fresh equity to bridge the gap, Deutsche Bank has generally been much more conservative in its use of equity capital. In October 2008, it raised its Tier 1 Capital Ratio to 10%, well above the Basel 1 regulatory requirement of 6%. While its loss of 4.8 billion euros in the last quarter of 2008 did reduce equity capital, Deutsche Bank was confident (at least as of the first part of 2009) that it could survive without fresh equity infusions or government bailouts. In fact, Deutsche Bank reported net income of 1.2 billion euros for the first quarter of 2009 and a Tier 1 capital ratio of 10.2%.

While Deutsche Bank looks safe for the moment in terms of having adequate equity, it is possible that significant losses on its leveraged loans and securities can create a deficit. In 2009, U.S. banking regulators applied an "extreme stress test" to U.S. banks, where they assumed a significant economic downturn and continued losses in the housing market. Deutsche Bank emerged intact from the stress test, with no need for additional equity even under dire circumstances. In contrast, Commerzbank, another German bank, faced an equity shortfall of 4.28 billion euros to get back to a 4% Tier 1 ratio under this dire scenario.

IN PRACTICE: VALUE AT RISK—A RISK MANAGEMENT TOOL?

In its most general form, the value at risk (VaR) measures the potential loss in value of a risky asset or portfolio over a defined period for a given confidence interval. Thus, if the VaR on an asset is $100 million at a one-week 95% confidence level, there is a only a 5% chance that the value of the asset will drop more than $100 million over any given week. In its adapted form, the measure is sometimes defined more narrowly as the possible loss in value from "normal market risk" as opposed to all risk, requiring that we draw distinctions between normal and abnormal risk as well as between market and nonmarket risk. While value at risk can be used by any entity to measure its risk exposure, it is used most often by commercial and investment banks to capture the potential loss in value of their traded portfolios from adverse market movements over a specified period; this can then be compared to their available capital and cash reserves to ensure that the losses can be covered without putting the firms at risk.

Taking a closer look at value at risk, there are three key aspects to using it as a risk measure:

1. To estimate the probability of the loss with a confidence interval, we need to define the probability distributions of individual risks, the correlation across these risks and the effect of such risks on value. In fact, simulations are widely used to measure the VaR for asset portfolio.

2. The focus in VaR is clearly on downside risk and potential losses. Its use in banks reflects their fear of a liquidity crisis in which a low-probability catastrophic occurrence creates a loss that wipes out the capital and creates a client exodus.

3. There are three key elements of VaR: a specified level of loss in value, a fixed time period over which risk is assessed, and a confidence interval. The VaR can be specified for an individual asset, a portfolio of assets or for an entire firm.

While the use of VAR has increased in the last decade, its weakness is its dependence upon historical data and, at least in some forms, its assumption that returns are normally distributed. As a consequence, it has been argued that unusual events of large magnitude—exactly the risks that banks should be worrying about—are not factored in adequately into capital ratios. ∎

8.6   BANKRUPTCY COSTS AND DEBT RATIOS

The optimal debt ratio obtained by minimizing the cost of capital is too high because it does not consider bankruptcy costs.
a. True
b. False
Explain.

Determinants of Optimal Debt Ratio

The preceding analysis highlights some of the determinants of the optimal debt ratio. We can then divide these determinants into firm-specific and macroeconomic factors.

Firm-Specific Factors

The optimal debt ratios that we compute will vary across firms. There are three firm specific factors that contribute to these differences: the tax rate of the firm, its capacity to generate cash flows to cover debt payments, and uncertainty about future income.

Firm's Tax Rate

In general, the tax benefits from debt increase as the tax rate goes up. In relative terms, firms with higher tax rates will have higher optimal debt ratios than do firms with lower tax rates, other things being equal. It also follows that a firm's optimal debt ratio will increase as its tax rate increases. We can illustrate this by computing the optimal debt ratios for Disney, Aracruz, Tata Chemicals, and Bookscape, holding all else constant and simply changing the tax rate in Table 8.18.

| | Table 8.18 | Tax Rates and Optimal Debt Ratios | | |

Tax Rate	Disney	Aracruz	Tata Chemicals	Bookscape
0%	0%	0%	0%	0%
10%	0%	0%	0%	20%
20%	20%	0%	0%	20%
30%	30%	10%	0%	40%
40%	50%	10%	10%	40%
50%	60%	20%	20%	50%

At a 0% tax rate, the optimal debt ratio is 0 for all four firms. Without the benefits that accrue from taxes, the rationale for using debt disappears. As the tax rate increases, the optimal debt ratios increase for all three firms but at different rates. For Disney, the optimal debt ratio climbs to 60% if the tax rate increases to 50%. The effect of changing tax rates is more muted for Aracruz and Tata Chemicals, but the optimal debt ratio is higher at higher tax rates. For Bookscape, however, the optimal continues to increase and reaches 50% when the tax rate is 50%.

pretax Returns on the Firm (in Cash Flow Terms)
The most significant determinant of the optimal debt ratio is a firm's earnings capacity. In fact, the operating income as a percentage of the market value of the firm (debt plus equity) is usually good indicator of the optimal debt ratio. When this number is high (or low), the optimal debt ratio will also be high (or low). A firm with higher pretax earnings can sustain much more debt as a proportion of the market value of the firm, because debt payments can be met much more easily from prevailing earnings. Disney, for example, has operating income of $6,829 million, which is 11% of the market value of the firm of $61,875 million in the base case, and an optimal debt ratio of 40%. Increasing the operating income to 15% of the firm value will increase the optimal debt ratio to 60%. In contrast, the normalized operating income (R$1,007 million) at Aracruz is 5.37% of the value of the firm (R$18,741 million), leading to a much lower optimal debt ratio of 10% for the firm.

Variance in Operating Income
The variance in operating income enters the base case analysis in two ways. First, it plays a role in determining the current beta: Firms with high (or low) variance in operating income tend to have high (or low) betas. Second, the volatility in operating income can be one of the factors determining bond ratings at different levels of debt: Ratings drop off much more dramatically for higher variance firms as debt levels are increased. It follows that firms with higher (or lower) variance in operating income will have lower (or higher) optimal debt ratios. The variance in operating income also plays a role in the constrained analysis, because higher-variance firms are much more likely to register significant drops in operating income. Consequently, the decision to increase debt should be made much more cautiously for these firms.

Macroeconomic Factors

Should macroeconomic conditions affect optimal debt ratios? In purely mechanical terms, the answer is yes. In good economic times, firms will generate higher earnings and be able to service more debt. In recessions, earnings will decline, and with them the capacity to service debt. That is why prudent firms borrow based on normalized earnings rather than current earnings. Holding operating income constant, macroeconomic variables can still affect optimal debt ratios. In fact, both the level of risk-free rate and the magnitude of default spreads can affect optimal debt ratios.

Level of Rates

As interest rates decline, the conventional wisdom is that debt should become cheaper and more attractive for firms. Though this may seem intuitive, the effect is muted by the fact that lower interest rates also reduce the cost of equity. In fact, changing the risk-free rate has a surprisingly small effect on the optimal debt ratio as long as interest rates move within a normal range.[20] When interest rates exceed normal levels, optimal debt ratios do decline, partly because we keep operating income fixed. The higher interest payments at every debt ratio reduce bond ratings and affect the capacity of firms to borrow more.

Default Spreads

The default spreads for different ratings classes tend to increase during recessions and decrease during economic booms. Keeping other things constant, as the spreads increase (or decrease) optimal debt ratios decrease (or increase), for the simple reason that higher spreads penalize firms that borrow more money and have lower ratings. In fact, the default spreads on corporate bonds declined between 2002 and 2007, leading to higher optimal debt ratios for all firms. In 2008, as the economy slowed and the market entered crisis mode, default spreads widened again, leading to lower optimal debt ratios.

There is another factor to consider. The same factors that cause default spreads to increase and decrease also play a role in determining equity risk premiums. Hence, the question of how much changing default spreads affect optimal debt ratios cannot be answered without looking at how much equity risk premiums also change. If equity risk premiums increase more than default spreads do, debt will become a more attractive choice relative to equity.

Adjusted Present Value Approach

In the adjusted present value (APV) approach, we begin with the value of the firm without debt. As we add debt to the firm, we consider the net effect on value by considering both the benefits and the costs of borrowing. The value of the levered firm can then be estimated at different levels of the debt, and the debt level that maximizes firm value is the optimal debt ratio.

---

[20]The normal range for long-term interest rates in the United States for the past forty years has been between 4% and 8%. There was a short period between 1978 and 1982 when long-term interest rates were much higher and a short period in the last couple of years when long term rates dropped below 3%.

Steps in the APV Approach

In the APV approach, we assume that the primary benefit of borrowing is a tax benefit and that the most significant cost of borrowing is the added risk of bankruptcy. To estimate the value of the firm with these assumptions, we proceed in three steps. We begin by estimating the value of the firm with no leverage. We then consider the present value of the interest tax savings generated by borrowing a given amount of money. Finally, we evaluate the effect of borrowing the amount on the probability that the firm will go bankrupt and the expected cost of bankruptcy.

Step 1: *Estimate the value of the firm with no debt.* The first step in this approach is the estimation of the value of the unlevered firm. This can be accomplished by valuing the firm as if it had no debt—that is, by discounting the expected after-tax operating cash flows at the unlevered cost of equity. In the special case where cash flows grow at a constant rate in perpetuity,

$$\text{Value of unlevered firm} = FCFF_1/(\rho_u - g)$$

where $FCFF_1$ is the expected after-tax operating cash flow to the firm in the next period, ρ_u is the unlevered cost of equity, and g is the expected growth rate. The inputs needed for this valuation are the expected cash flows, growth rates, and the unlevered cost of equity. To estimate the latter, we can draw on our earlier analysis and compute the unlevered beta of the firm:

$$\beta_{\text{unlevered}} = \frac{\beta_{Current}}{\left(1 + (1-t)\frac{Debt}{Equity}\right)}$$

where $\beta_{\text{unlevered}}$ = unlevered beta of the firm, β_{current} = current equity beta of the firm, t = tax rate for the firm, and D/E = current debt–equity ratio. This unlevered beta can then be used to arrive at the unlevered cost of equity. Alternatively, we can take the current market value of the firm as a given and back out the value of the unlevered firm by subtracting out the tax benefits and adding back the expected bankruptcy cost from the existing debt.

$$\text{Current firm value} = \text{Value of unlevered firm} + \text{PV of tax benefits}$$
$$- \text{Expected bankruptcy costs}$$
$$\text{Value of unlevered firm} = \text{Current firm value} - \text{PV of tax benefits}$$
$$+ \text{Expected bankruptcy costs}$$

Step 2: *Estimate the present value of tax benefits from debt.* The second step in this approach is the calculation of the expected tax benefit from a given level of debt. This tax benefit is a function of the tax rate of the firm and is discounted at the cost of debt to reflect the riskiness of this cash flow. If the tax savings are viewed as a perpetuity,

$$\text{Value of tax benefits} = [\text{Tax rate} * \text{Cost of debt} * \text{Debt}]/\text{Cost of debt}$$
$$= \text{Tax rate} * \text{Debt}$$
$$= t_c D$$

The tax rate used here is the firm's marginal tax rate, and it is assumed to stay constant over time. If we anticipate the tax rate changing over time, we can still compute the present value of tax benefits over time, but we cannot use the perpetual growth equation.

Step 3:   *Estimate the expected bankruptcy costs as a result of the debt.* The third step is to evaluate the effect of the given level of debt on the default risk of the firm and on expected **bankruptcy costs**. In theory, at least, this requires the estimation of the probability of default with the additional debt and the direct and indirect cost of bankruptcy. If π_a is the probability of default after the additional debt and BC is the present value of the bankruptcy cost, the present value of expected bankruptcy cost can be estimated.

$$
\begin{aligned}
\text{PV of expected bankruptcy cost} &= \text{Probability of bankruptcy} \\
&\quad * \text{PV of bankruptcy cost} \\
&= \pi_a BC
\end{aligned}
$$

This step of the APV approach poses the most significant estimation problem, because neither the probability of bankruptcy nor the bankruptcy cost can be estimated directly. There are two ways the probability of bankruptcy can be estimated indirectly. One is to estimate a bond rating, as we did in the cost of capital approach, at each level of debt and use the empirical estimates of default probabilities for each rating. For instance, Table 8.19, extracted from an annually updated study by Altman, summarizes the probability of default over ten years by bond rating class.[21]

Table 8.19	DEFAULT RATES BY BOND RATING CLASSES
Rating	**Likelihood of Default**
AAA	0.07%
AA	0.51%
A+	0.60%
A	0.66%
A−	2.50%
BBB	7.54%
BB	16.63%
B+	25.00%
B	36.80%
B−	45.00%
CCC	59.01%
CC	70.00%
C	85.00%
D	100.00%

[21] E. I. Altman, "The Default Experience of U.S. Bonds," working paper, Salomon Center, New York University, 2008. This study estimated default rates over ten years only for some of the ratings classes. We extrapolated the rest of the ratings.

The other is to use a statistical approach, such as a probit to estimate the probability of default, based on the firm's observable characteristics, at each level of debt.

The bankruptcy cost can be estimated, albeit with considerable error, from studies that have looked at the magnitude of this cost in actual bankruptcies. Studies that have looked at the direct cost of bankruptcy conclude that they are small relative to firm value.[22] The indirect costs of bankruptcy can be substantial, but the costs vary widely across firms. Shapiro and Titman speculate that the indirect costs could be as large as 25% to 30% of firm value but provide no direct evidence of the costs.[23]

The net effect of adding debt can be calculated by aggregating the costs and the benefits at each level of debt.

$$\text{Value of levered firm} = FCFF_1/(\rho_u - g) + t_c D - \pi_a BC$$

We compute the value of the levered firm at different levels of debt. The debt level that maximizes the value of the levered firm is the optimal debt ratio.

IN PRACTICE: USING A PROBIT TO ESTIMATE THE PROBABILITY OF BANKRUPTCY

It is possible to estimate the probability of default using statistical techniques when sufficient data is available. For instance, if we have a database that lists all firms that went bankrupt during a period of time, as well as firms that did not go bankrupt during the same period, together with descriptive characteristics on these firms, a probit analysis can be used to estimate the likelihood of bankruptcy as a function of these characteristics. The steps involved in a probit analysis are as follows:

1. Identify the event of interest. Probits work best when the event either occurs or it does not. For bankruptcy, the event might be the filing for bankruptcy protection under the law.

2. Over a specified time period, collect information on all the firms that were exposed to the event. In the bankruptcy case, this would imply collecting information on which firms that filed for bankruptcy over a certain period (say, five years).

3. Based on your knowledge of the event and other research on it, specify measurable and observable variables that are likely to be good predictors of that event. In the case of bankruptcy, these might include excessive debt ratios, declining income, poor project returns, and small market capitalization.

4. Collect information on these variables for the firms that filed for bankruptcy at the time of the filing. Collect the same information for all other firms that were in existence at the same time and that have data available on them on these variables. (If this is too data-intensive, a random sampling of the firms that were not exposed to the event can be used.) In the bankruptcy analysis, this would imply

---

[22] J. N. Warner, "Bankruptcy Costs: Some Evidence," *Journal of Finance* 32:337–347. In this study of railroad bankruptcies, the direct cost of bankruptcy seems to be about 5%.

[23] A. Shapiro, *Modern Corporate Finance* (New York: Macmillan, 1989); S. Titman, "The Effect of Capital Structure on a Firm's Liquidation Decision," *Journal of Financial Economics* 13:1371–1351.

collecting information on debt ratios, income trends, project returns, and market capitalization on the firms that filed for bankruptcy at the time of the filing, and all other firms across the period.

5. In a probit, the dependent variable is the occurrence of the specified event (1 if it occurs, 0 if it does not) and the independent variables are the variables specified in Step 3. The output from the probit looks very much like the output from a multiple regression, with statistical significance attached to each of the independent variables. (In the bankruptcy analysis, firms filing for bankruptcy would be tagged with a 1 and firms that survive would be categorized as 0.)

Once the probit has been done, the probability of a firm defaulting can be estimated by plugging in that firm's values for the independent variables into the model. The predicted value that emerges from the probit is the probability of default. ■

ILLUSTRATION 8.9   **Using the APV Approach to Calculate Optimal Debt Ratio for Disney in Early 2009**

The APV approach can be applied to estimating the optimal capital structure for Disney. The first step is to estimate the value of the unlevered firm. To do so, we start with the firm value of Disney in 2009 and net out the effect of the tax savings and bankruptcy costs arising from the existing debt.

$$\text{Current market value of Disney} = \text{Value of equity} + \text{Value of debt}$$
$$= \$45,193 + \$16,682 = \$61,875 \text{ million}$$

We first compute the present value of the tax savings from the existing debt, assuming that the interest payment on the debt constitutes a perpetuity, using a marginal tax rate for Disney of 38%.

$$\text{PV of tax savings from existing debt} = \text{Existing debt} * \text{Tax rate}$$
$$= \$16,682 * 0.38 = \$6,339 \text{ million}$$

Based on Disney's current rating of A, we estimate a probability of bankruptcy of 0.66% from Table 8.19. The bankruptcy cost is assumed to be 25% of the firm value, prior to the tax savings. Allowing for a range of 10–40% for bankruptcy costs, we have put Disney's exposure to expected bankruptcy costs in the middle of the range. There are some businesses that Disney is in where the perception of distress can be damaging—theme parks, for instance—but the movie and broadcasting businesses are less likely to be affected, because projects tend be shorter-term and on a smaller scale.

$$\text{PV of expected bankruptcy cost} = \text{Probability of default} * \text{Bankruptcy cost}$$
$$= 0.66\% * (0.25 * 61,875) = \$102 \text{ million}$$

We then compute the value of Disney as an unlevered firm.

$$\text{Value of Disney as an unlevered firm}$$
$$= \text{Current market value} - \text{PV of tax savings}$$
$$+ \text{Expected bankruptcy costs}$$
$$= \$61,875 - \$6,339 + \$102 = \$55,638 \text{ million}$$

Table 8.20 TAX SAVINGS FROM DEBT $(t_c D)$ — DISNEY

Debt Ratio	$ Debt	Tax Rate	Tax Benefits
0%	$0	38.00%	$0
10%	$6,188	38.00%	$2,351
20%	$12,375	38.00%	$4,703
30%	$18,563	38.00%	$7,054
40%	$24,750	38.00%	$9,405
50%	$30,938	38.00%	$11,756
60%	$37,125	38.00%	$14,108
70%	$43,313	38.00%	$16,459
80%	$49,500	38.00%	$18,810
90%	$55,688	34.52%	$19,223

The next step in the process is to estimate the tax savings in Table 8.20 at different levels of debt. Although we use the standard approach of assuming that the present value is calculated as a perpetuity, we reduce the tax rate used in the calculation, if interest expenses exceed the EBIT. The adjustment to the tax rate was described earlier in the cost of capital approach.

The final step in the process is to estimate the expected bankruptcy cost, based on the bond ratings, the probabilities of default, and the assumption that the bankruptcy cost is 25% of firm value. Table 8.21 summarizes these probabilities and the expected bankruptcy cost, computed based on the levered firm value.

The expected bankruptcy cost at a 40% debt ratio is computed thus:

$$\text{Expected bankruptcy cost}$$
$$= (\text{Unlevered firm value} + \text{Tax savings})(0.25)(0.0066)$$
$$= (55,638 + \$9,405)(0.25)(0.0066)$$
$$= \$107 \text{ million}$$

The value of the levered firm is estimated in Table 8.22 by aggregating the effects of the tax savings and the expected bankruptcy costs.

Table 8.21 EXPECTED BANKRUPTCY COST — DISNEY

Debt Ratio	Bond Rating	Probability of Default	Expected Bankruptcy Cost
0%	AAA	0.07%	$10
10%	AAA	0.07%	$10
20%	AAA	0.07%	$11
30%	A+	0.60%	$94
40%	A	0.66%	$107
50%	A−	2.50%	$421
60%	B	36.80%	$6,417
70%	CCC	59.01%	$10,636
80%	CCC	59.01%	$10,983
90%	CCC	59.01%	$11,044

Table 8.22   VALUE OF DISNEY WITH LEVERAGE

Debt Ratio	$ Debt	Tax Rate	Unlevered Firm Value	Tax Benefits	Expected Bankruptcy Cost	Value of Levered Firm
0%	$0	38.00%	$55,638	$0	$10	$55,629
10%	$6,188	38.00%	$55,638	$2,351	$10	$57,979
20%	$12,375	38.00%	$55,638	$4,703	$11	$60,330
30%	$18,563	38.00%	$55,638	$7,054	$94	$62,598
40%	$24,750	38.00%	$55,638	$9,405	$107	$64,936
50%	$30,938	38.00%	$55,638	$11,756	$421	$66,973
60%	$37,125	38.00%	$55,638	$14,108	$6,417	$63,329
70%	$43,313	38.00%	$55,638	$16,459	$10,636	$61,461
80%	$49,500	38.00%	$55,638	$18,810	$10,983	$63,466
90%	$55,688	34.52%	$55,638	$19,223	$11,044	$63,817

The firm value is maximized at about 50% debt, slightly higher than the optimal computed using the cost of capital approach. These results are, however, very sensitive to both the estimate of bankruptcy cost as a percent of firm value and the probabilities of default.

Benefits and Limitations of the APV Approach

The advantage of the APV approach is that it separates the effects of debt into different components and allows an analyst to use different discount rates for each component. In this approach, we do not assume that the debt ratio stays unchanged forever, which is an implicit assumption in the cost of capital approach. Instead, we have the flexibility to keep the dollar value of debt fixed and to calculate the benefits and costs of the fixed dollar debt.

These advantages have to be weighed against the difficulty of estimating probabilities of default and the cost of bankruptcy. In fact, many analyses that use the APV approach ignore the expected bankruptcy costs, leading them to the conclusion that firm value increases as firms borrow money. Not surprisingly, they conclude that the optimal debt ratio for a firm is 100% debt.

In general, with the same assumptions, the APV and the cost of capital conclusions give identical answers. However, the APV approach is more practical when firms are evaluating the feasibility of adding a dollar amount of debt, whereas the cost of capital approach is easier when firms are analyzing debt proportions.[24]

 apv.xls: This spreadsheet allows you to compute the value of a firm, with leverage, using the adjusted present value approach.

---

[24]I. Inselbag and H. Kaufold, "Two DCF Approaches and Valuing Companies under Alternative Financing Strategies," *Journal of Applied Corporate Finance* 10, no. 1:115–122.

COMPARATIVE ANALYSIS

The most common approach to analyzing the debt ratio of a firm is to compare its leverage to that of similar firms. A simple way to perform this analysis is to compare a firm's debt ratio to the average debt ratio for the industry in which the firm operates. A more complete analysis would consider the differences between a firm and the rest of the industry when determining debt ratios. We will consider both ways below.

Comparing to Industry Average

Firms sometimes choose their financing mixes by looking at the average debt ratio of other firms in the industry in which they operate. For instance, Table 8.23 compares the debt ratios at Disney, Aracruz, and Tata Chemicals to other firms in their industries. We define these comparable firms as U.S. entertainment companies (Disney), emerging market paper companies (Aracruz), and emerging market chemical companies (Tata Chemicals).

Based on this comparison, Disney is operating at a debt ratio lower than those of other firms in the industry in both market and book value terms, whereas Aracruz and Tata Chemicals have debt ratios much higher than the averages for their sector.

The underlying assumptions in this comparison are that firms within the same industry are **comparable** and that on average, these firms are operating at or close to their optimal. Both assumptions can be questioned, however. Firms within the same industry can have different product mixes, different amounts of operating risk, different tax rates, and different project returns. In fact, most do. For instance, Disney is considered part of the entertainment industry, but its mix of businesses is very different from that of Lion's Gate, which is primarily a movie company, or Liberty Media, which is primarily a cable broadcasting company. Furthermore, Disney's size and risk characteristics are very different from that of Westwood One, which is also considered part of the same industry group. The other problem is that, as we noted in Chapter 4, Disney is a multibusiness company, and picking a sector to compare it to is difficult to do.

Table 8.23 COMPARISON TO INDUSTRY AVERAGES

	Book Debt Ratio	Market Debt Ratio	Comparable Group	Book Debt Ratio Average	Book Debt Ratio Median	Market Debt Ratio Average	Market Debt Ratio Median
Disney	32.89%	26.96%	U.S. entertainment companies	47.76%	43.59%	36.90%	37.83%
Aracruz	91.01%	52.47%	Emerging market paper companies	38.11%	40.74%	33.75%	34.22%
Tata Chemicals	42.95%	34.02%	Emerging market chemical companies	33.88%	34.76%	25.56%	21.34%

Source: Value Line and Capital IQ.

There is a data set online that summarizes market value and book value debt ratios, by industry, in addition to other relevant characteristics.

Controlling for Differences between Firms

Firms within the same industry can exhibit wide differences on tax rates, capacity to generate operating income and cash flows, and variance in operating income. Consequently, it can be dangerous to compare a firm's debt ratio to the industry and draw conclusions about the optimal financing mix. The simplest way to control for differences across firms while using the maximum information available in the market is to run a regression, regressing debt ratios against these variables, across the firms in a industry:

$$\text{Debt ratio} = \alpha_0 + \alpha_1 \text{ Tax rate} + \alpha_2 \text{ Pretax returns}$$
$$+ \alpha_3 \text{ Variance in operating income}$$

There are several advantages to the cross-sectional approach. Once the regression has been run and the basic relationship established (i.e., the intercept and coefficients have been estimated), the predicted debt ratio for any firm can be computed quickly using the measures of the independent variables for this firm. If a task involves calculating the optimal debt ratio for a large number of firms in a short period, this may be the only practical way of approaching the problem, because the other approaches described in this chapter are time-intensive.

There are also limitations to this approach. The coefficients tend to shift over time. Besides some standard statistical problems and errors in measuring the variables, these regressions also tend to explain only a portion of the differences in debt ratios between firms. However, the regressions provide significantly more information than a naive comparison of a firm's debt ratio to the industry average.

 Sticking with Industry Averages: A Behavioral Perspective
The pull of industry averages on the debt ratios of individual firms in the industry is too strong to be ignored. While it may make little sense from a fundamental standpoint to mimic the behavior of other firms in the sector, there are two reasons that have been offered for why it appeals to managers.

1. ***Herd migration*** Patel, Zeckhauser, and Hendricks use the behavior of birds and wildebeest to explain why companies stick close to industry averages.[25] They note that the same "safety in numbers" that induces animals to travel in groups also influences managers when they make financing choices. Put another way, a manager who chooses to take on a significant amount of debt simply because other firms in the sector have also done so is unlikely to be fired even if that debt turns out to be too high in hindsight. In fact, if analysts follow the same herd mentality, they are likely to punish firms that deviate from the herd, even if that deviation can be justified on intrinsic grounds. Looking across 182 firms in ten sectors, they find evidence of herd behavior in seven of the ten sectors.

[25]J. Patel, R. Zeckhauser, and D. Hendricks, 1991, "The Rationality Struggle: Illustrations from Financial Markets," *American Economic Review Papers and Proceedings*, v81, 232–236.

2. *Following the leader* A variant of this theme with its roots in the natural sciences as well is that firms in a business tend to follow the leader. In this model, success and reputation lead to a firm being anointed the leader for a sector. When this firm chooses a financing mix, presumably based upon its fundamentals, other firms in that sector then imitate the leader, hoping to imitate its success

Whatever the reasons may be, there is no denying the fact that managers look at industry averages and practices on capital structure for guidance. Consequently, it does make sense to check the optimal debt ratios that emerge from the cost of capital and APV approaches against industry averages, and to adjust them towards peer group ratios.

ILLUSTRATION 8.10   Estimating Disney's Debt Ratio Using the Cross-Sectional Approach
This approach can be applied to look at differences within an industry or across the entire market. We can illustrate looking at the Disney against firms in the entertainment sector first and then against the entire market.

To look at the determinants of debt ratios within the entertainment industry, we regressed debt ratios of the eighty firms in the industry against two variables—the effective tax rate and the EBITDA as a percent of the market value of the firm. Based on our earlier discussion of the determinants of capital structure, we would expect firms with higher operating cash flows (EBITDA) as a percent of firm value to borrow more money. We would also expect higher tax rates to lead to more benefits from debt and higher debt ratios. The results of the regression are reported, with t-statistics in brackets below the coefficients:

Debt to capital
$$= 0.049 + 0.543 \text{ (Effective tax rate)} + 0.692 \text{ (EBITDA/Firm value)}$$
$$(1.07) \quad (4.10^{a}) \qquad\qquad\qquad (4.08)^{a}$$

The dependent variable is the market debt-to-capital ratio, and the regression has an R^2 of 40%. Although there is statistical significance, it is worth noting that the predicted debt ratios will have substantial standard errors associated with them. Even so, if we use the current values for these variables for Disney in this regression, we get a predicted debt ratio:

$$DFR_{\text{Disney}} = 0.049 + 0.543\,(0.372) + 0.692\,(0.1735) = 0.3710, \text{ or } 37.10\%$$

At its existing debt ratio of 27%, Disney is significantly underlevered. Thus, relative to the industry in which it operates and its specific characteristics, Disney could potentially borrow more.

One of the limitations of this analysis is that there are only a few firms within each industry. This analysis can be extended to all firms in the market. Although firms in different businesses differ in terms of risk and cash flows and these differences can translate into differences in debt ratios, we can control for the differences in the regression. To illustrate, we regressed debt ratios of all listed firms in the United States against four variables:

1. The expected growth rate in EPS (G_{EPS}) as a proxy for growth assets. Firms with a higher percentage of value from growth assets should have less debt.

2. Closely held shares as a percent of shares outstanding (CLSH) as a measure of how much separation there is between managers and stockholders (and hence as a proxy for debt as a disciplinary mechanism). We would expect the debt ratio to be lower for firms with significant insider holdings.

3. EBITDA as a percent of enterprise value (E/V) as a measure of the cash flow generating capacity of a firm; we would anticipate debt ratios will increase as E/V increases.

4. Intangible assets as a percentage of total assets (Intangible %); firms that derive more of their value from intangible assets face bigger agency costs (with lenders) and should borrow less.

The results of the regression from early 2009 are presented below.[26]

$$DFR = 0.327 - 0.064 \text{ Intangible\%} - 0.138 \text{ CLSH} + 0.026 \text{ E/V} - 0.878 \text{ G}_{EPS}$$
$$(25.45^a)\ (2.16^a) \qquad\qquad (2.88^a) \qquad (1.25) \qquad (12.6)^a$$

where *DFR* is debt as a percentage of the market value of the firm (debt + equity). While the signs on the coefficients are all consistent with our hypotheses, the R^2 for this regression is only 13%. If we plug in the values for Disney in 2009 into this regression, we get a predicted debt ratio:

$$DFR_{Disney} = 0.327 - 0.064(0.24) - 0.138(0.077) + 0.0.26(0.1735) - 0.878(0.065)$$
$$= 0.2891, \text{ or } 28.91\%$$

Based on the debt ratios of other firms in the market and Disney's financial characteristics, we would expect Disney to have a debt ratio of 28.91%. Because its actual debt ratio is 27%, Disney is slightly underlevered.

8.7 OPTIMAL DEBT RATIOS BASED ON COMPARABLE FIRMS

The predicted debt ratio from the regression shown above will generally yield

a. A debt ratio similar to the optimal debt ratio from the cost of capital approach

b. A debt ratio higher than the optimal debt ratio from the cost of capital approach

c. A debt ratio lower than the optimal debt ratio from the cost of capital approach

d. Any of the above, depending on . . .

Explain.

There is a data set online that summarizes the latest debt ratio regression across the entire market.

SELECTING THE OPTIMAL DEBT RATIO

Using the different approaches for estimating optimal debt ratios, we come up with different estimates of the right financing mix for Disney, Aracruz, and Tata Chemicals. Table 8.24 summarizes our estimates.

---

[26]This regression has about 2,000 publicly traded companies in the United States, with information available on both debt ratios and the independent variables.

Table 8.24   SUMMARY OF PREDICTED DEBT RATIOS

	Disney	Aracruz	Tata Chemicals
Actual debt ratio	27%	52.58%	34.02%
Optimal			
I. Operating income	50.00%	–	–
II. Standard cost of capital	40.00%	10.00%	10.00%
III. Enhanced cost of capital	30.00%	10.00%	10.00%
IV. APV	50.00%	20.00%	10.00%
V. Comparable			
To industry	37.10%	34.22%	21.34%
To market	28.91%	–	–

Although there are differences in the estimates across the different approaches, a few consistent conclusions emerge: Disney, at its existing debt ratio, is underlevered relative to every estimate of the optimal debt ratio, though it looks less underlevered relative to the rest of the market, than it does relative to its own fundamentals or to the sector. Aracruz and Tata Chemicals are overlevered relative to every estimate of the optimal debt ratio.

With Bookscape, we will stick with the conclusion that we drew earlier, based upon the cost of capital approach. The firm at its existing debt ratio is very close to its optimal and has the right amount of debt.

CONCLUSION

This chapter has provided background on four tools that can be used to analyze capital structure.

1. The first approach is based on operating income. Using historical data or forecasts, we develop a distribution of operating income across both good and bad scenarios. We then use a predefined acceptably probability of default to specify the maximum borrowing capacity.

2. The second approach is the cost of capital—the weighted average of the costs of equity, debt, and preferred stock, where the weights are market value weights and the costs of financing are current costs. The objective is to minimize the cost of capital, which also maximizes the value of the firm. We also considered an enhanced version of this approach, where the operating cash flows also change as the debt ratio changes, and the optimal debt ratio is the one that delivers the highest firm value, rather than the lowest cost of capital.

3. The APV approach estimates the value of the firm at different levels of debt by adding the present value of the tax benefits from debt to the unlevered firm's value and then subtracting the present value of expected bankruptcy costs. The optimal debt ratio is the one that maximizes firm value.

4. The final approach is to compare a firm's debt ratio to similar firms. Although comparisons of firm debt ratios to an industry average are commonly made, they are generally not very useful in the presence of large differences among firms within the same industry. A cross-sectional regression of debt ratios against underlying financial variables brings in more information from the general population of firms and can be used to predict debt ratios for a large number of firms.

The objective in all of these analyses is to come up with a mix of debt and equity that will maximize the value of the firm.

LIVE CASE STUDY

THE OPTIMAL FINANCING MIX

Objective: To estimate the optimal mix of debt and equity for your firm and to evaluate the effect on firm value of moving to that mix.

Key Questions

- Based on the cost of capital approach, what is the optimal debt ratio for your firm? Bringing in reasonable constraints into the decision process, what would your recommended debt ratio be for this firm?
- Does your firm have too much or too little debt
  - Relative to the industry in which they operate?
  - Relative to the market?

Framework for Analysis

1. ***Cost of Capital Approach***
   - What is the current cost of capital for the firm?
   - What happens to the cost of capital as the debt ratio is changed?
   - At what debt ratio is the cost of capital minimized and firm value maximized? (If they are different, explain.)
   - What will happen to the firm value if the firm moves to its optimal?
   - What will happen to the stock price if the firm moves to the optimal and stockholders are rational?

2. ***Building Constraints into the Process***
   - What rating does the company have at the optimal debt ratio? If you were to impose a rating constraint, what would it be? Why? What is the optimal debt ratio with this rating constraint?
   - How volatile is the operating income? What is the "normalized" operating income of this firm, and what is the optimal debt ratio of the firm at this level of income?

3. ***Relative Analysis***
   - Relative to the industry to which this firm belongs, does it have too much or too little in debt? (Do a regression, if necessary.)
   - Relative to the rest of the firms in the market, does it have too much or too little in debt? (Use the market regression, if necessary.)

Getting Information about Optimal Capital Structure

To get the inputs needed to estimate the optimal capital structure, examine regulatory filings and the annual report. The ratings and interest coverage ratios can be obtained from the ratings agencies (S&P, Moody's), and default spreads can be estimated by finding traded bonds in each ratings class.

 Online Sources of Information
www.stern.nyu.edu/~adamodar/cfin2E/project/data.htm

PROBLEMS AND QUESTIONS (Use a risk premium of 5.5% where none is given)

1. Plastico, a manufacturer of consumer plastic products, is evaluating its capital structure. The balance sheet of the company is as follows (in millions):

Assets		Liabilities	
Fixed assets	$4,000	Debt	$2,500
Current assets	$1,000	Equity	$2,500

In addition, you are provided the following information:
- The debt is in the form of long-term bonds, with a coupon rate of 10%. The bonds are currently rated AA and are selling at a yield of 12% (the market value of the bonds is 80% of the face value).
- The firm currently has 50 million shares outstanding, and the current market price is $80 per share. The firm pays a dividend of $4 per share and has a price–earnings ratio of 10.
- The stock currently has a beta of 1.2. The Treasury bond rate is 8%.
- The tax rate for this firm is 40%.

a. What is the debt–equity ratio for this firm in book value terms? In market value terms?

b. What is the debt/(debt + equity) ratio for this firm in book value terms? In market value terms?

c. What is the firm's after-tax cost of debt?

d. What is the firm's cost of equity?

e. What is the firm's current cost of capital?

2. Now assume that Plastico is considering a project that requires an initial investment of $100 million and has the following projected income statement (depreciation for the project is expected to be $5 million a year forever):

EBIT	$20 million
– Interest	$4 million
EBT	$16 million
Taxes	$6.40 million
Net income	$9.60 million

This project is going to be financed at the same debt–equity ratio as the overall firm and is expected to last forever. Assume that there are no principal repayments on the debt (it, too, is perpetual).

a. Evaluate this project from the equity investors' standpoint. Does it make sense?

b. Evaluate this project from the firm's standpoint. Does it make sense?

c. In general, when would you use the cost of equity as your discount rate/benchmark?

d. In general, when would you use the cost of capital as your benchmark?

e. Assume, for economies of scale, that this project is going to be financed entirely with debt. What would you use as your cost of capital for evaluating this project?

3. Plastico is considering a major change in its capital structure. It has three options:
- *Option 1*   Issue $1 billion in new stock and repurchase half of its outstanding debt. This will make it an AAA-rated firm (AAA rated debt is yielding 11% in the marketplace).
- *Option 2*   Issue $1 billion in new debt and buy back stock. This will drop its rating to A–. (A– rated debt is yielding 13% in the marketplace.)
- *Option 3*   Issue $3 billion in new debt and buy back stock. This will drop its rating to CCC (CCC-rated debt is yielding 18% in the marketplace).

a. What is the cost of equity under each option?

b. What is the after-tax cost of debt under each option?

c. What is the cost of capital under each option?

d. What would happen to (1) the value of the firm, (2) the value of debt and equity, and (3) the stock price under each option if you assume rational stockholders?

e. From a cost of capital standpoint, which of the three options would you pick—or would you stay at your current capital structure?

f. What role (if any) would the variability in Plastico's income play in your decision?

g. How would your analysis change (if at all) if the money under the three options were used to take new investments (instead of repurchasing debt or equity)?

h. What other considerations (besides minimizing the cost of capital) would you bring to bear on your decision?

i. Intuitively, why doesn't the higher rating in option 1 translate into a lower cost of capital?

4. Plastico is interested in how it compares with its competitors in the same industry.

	Plastico	Competitors
Debt–equity ratio	50%	25%
Variance in EBITDA	20%	40%
EBITDA/MV of firm	25%	15%
Tax rate	40%	30%
R&D/sales	2%	5%

a. Taking each of these variables, explain at an intuitive level whether you would expect Plastico to have more or less debt than its competitors and why.

b. You have also run a regression of debt–equity ratios against these variables for all the firms on the NYSE and have come up with the following regression equation:

$$D/E = 0.10 - 0.5(\text{Variance in EBITDA})$$
$$+ 2.0(\text{EBITDA/MV})$$
$$+ 0.4(\text{Tax rate})$$
$$+ 2.5(\text{R\&D/Sales})$$

(All inputs to the regression were in decimals—i.e., 20% was input as 0.20.) Given this cross-sectional relationship, what would you expect Plastico's debt–equity ratio to be?

5. As CEO of a major corporation, you have to make a decision on how much you can afford to borrow. You currently have 10 million shares outstanding, and the market price per share is $50. You also currently have about $200 million in debt outstanding (market value). You are rated as a BBB corporation now.

- Your stock has a beta of 1.5 and the Treasury bond rate is 8%.

- Your marginal tax rate is 46%.

- You estimate that your rating will change to a B if you borrow $100 million. The BBB rate now is 11%. The B rate is 12.5%.

a. Given the marginal costs and benefits of borrowing the $100 million, should you go ahead with it?

b. What is your best estimate of the weighted average cost of capital with and without the $100 million in borrowing?

c. If you borrow the $100 million, what will the price per share be after the borrowing?

d. Assume that you have a project that requires an investment of $100 million. It has expected before-tax revenues of $50 million and costs of $30 million a year in perpetuity. Is this a desirable project by your criteria? Why, or why not?

e. Does it make a difference in your decision if you were told that the cash flows from the project in **d** are certain?

6. You have been hired as a management consultant by AD Corporation to evaluate whether it has an appropriate amount of debt (the company is worried about a leveraged buyout). You have collected the following information on AD's current position:

- There are 100,000 shares outstanding at $20/share. The stock has a beta of 1.15.

- The company has $500,000 in long-term debt outstanding and is currently rated BBB. The current market interest rate is 10% on BBB bonds and 6% on T-bonds.

- The company's marginal tax rate is 40%.
  You proceed to collect the data on what increasing debt will do to the company's ratings:

Additional Debt	New Rating	Interest Rate
$500,000	BB	10.5
$1,000,000	B	11.5
$1,500,000	B–	13.5
$2,000,000	C	15

a. How much additional debt should the company take on?

b. What will the price per share be after the company takes on new debt?

c. What is the WACC before and after the additional debt?

d. Assume that you are considering a project that has the earnings in table (below part b) in perpetuity and is of comparable risk to existing projects.

Revenues/year	$1,000,000
Cost of goods sold	$400,000 (includes depreciation of $100,000)
EBIT	$600,000
Debt payments	$100,000 (all interest payments)
Taxable income	$500,000
Tax	$200,000
After-tax profit	$300,000

If this project requires an investment of $3,000,000, what is its NPV?

7. UB is examining its capital structure with the intent of arriving at an optimal debt ratio. It currently has no debt and has a beta of 1.5. The riskless interest rate is 9%. Your research indicates that the debt rating will be as follows at different debt levels:

D/(D + E)	Rating	Interest Rate
0%	AAA	10%
10%	AA	10.5%
20%	A	11%
30%	BBB	12%
40%	BB	13%
50%	B	14%
60%	CCC	16%
70%	CC	18%
80%	C	20%
90%	D	25%

The firm currently has 1 million shares outstanding at $20 per share (tax rate = 40%).

a. What is the firm's optimal debt ratio?

b. Assuming that the firm restructures by repurchasing stock with debt, what will the value of the stock be after the restructuring?

8. GenCorp, an automotive parts manufacturer, currently has $25 million in outstanding debt and has 10 million shares outstanding. The book value per share is $10, and the market value is $25. The company is currently rated A, its bonds have a yield to maturity of 10%, and the current beta of the stock is 1.06. The riskfree rate is 8% now, and the company's tax is 40%.

a. What is the company's current weighted average cost of capital?

b. The company is considering a repurchase of 4 million shares at $25 per share with new debt. It is estimated that this will push the company's rating down to a B (with a yield to maturity of 13%). What will the company's WACC be after the stock repurchase?

9. You have been called in as a consultant for Herbert's, a sporting goods retail firm, which is examining its debt policy. The firm currently has a balance sheet as follows:

Liability		Assets	
LT bonds	$100	Fixed assets	$300
Equity	$300	Current assets	$100
Total	$400	Total	$400

The firm's income statement is as follows:

Revenues	$250
Cost of goods sold (cogs)	$175
Depreciation	$25
EBIT	$50
Long-term interest	$10
EBT	$40
Taxes	$16
Net income	$24

The firm currently has 100 shares outstanding, selling at a market price of $5 per share and the bonds are selling at par. The firm's current beta is 1.12, and the riskfree rate is 7%.

a. What is the firm's current cost of equity?

b. What is the firm's current cost of debt?

c. What is the firm's current weighted average cost of capital?

d. Assume that management of Herbert's is considering doing a debt–equity swap (i.e., borrowing enough money to buy back seventy shares of stock at $5 per share). It is believed that this swap will lower the firm's rating to C and raise the interest rate on the company's debt to 15%.

e. What is the firm's new cost of equity?

f. What is the effective tax rate (for calculating the after-tax cost of debt) after the swap?

g. What is the firm's new cost of capital?

10. Terck, a leading pharmaceutical company, currently has a balance sheet that is as follows:

Liability		Assets	
Long-term bonds	$1,000	Fixed assets	$1,700
Equity	$1,000	Current assets	$300
Total	$1,000	Total	$1,000

The firm's income statement looks as follows:

Revenues	$1,000
Cost of goods sold (COGS)	$400
Depreciation	$100
EBIT	$500
Long-term interest expense	$100
EBT	$400
Taxes	$200
Net income	$200

The firm's bonds are all twenty-year bonds with a coupon rate of 10% that are selling at 90% of face value (the yield to maturity on these bonds is 11%). The stocks are selling at a P/E ratio of 9 and have a beta of 1.25. The riskfree rate is 6%.

a. What is the firm's current cost of equity?

b. What is the firm's current after-tax cost of debt?

c. What is the firm's current weighted average cost of capital?

   Assume that management of Terck, which is very conservative, is considering doing an equity-for-debt swap (i.e., issuing $200 more of equity to retire $200 of debt). This action is expected to lower the firm's interest rate by 1%.

d. What is the firm's new cost of equity?

e. What is the new WACC?

f. What will the value of the firm be after the swap?

11. You have been asked to analyze the capital structure of DASA, an environmental waste disposal firm, and make recommendations on a future course of action. DASA has 40 million shares outstanding, selling at $20 per share, and a debt–equity ratio (in market value terms) of 0.25. The beta of the stock is 1.15, and the firm currently has a AA rating, with

a corresponding market interest rate of 10%. The firm's income statement is as follows:

EBIT	$150 million
Interest expenses	$20 million
Taxable income	$130 million
Taxes	$52 million
Net income	$78 million

The current T-bond rate is 8%.

a. What is the firm's current WACC?

b. The firm is proposing borrowing an additional $200 million in debt and repurchasing stock. If it does so, its rating will decline to A, with a market interest rate of 11%. What will the WACC be if it makes this move?

c. What will the new stock price be if the firm borrows $200 million and repurchases stock (assuming rational investors)?

d. Now assume that the firm has another option to raise its debt–equity ratio (instead of borrowing money and repurchasing stock). It has considerable capital expenditures planned for the next year ($150 million). The company also currently pays $1 in dividends per share. If the company finances all its capital expenditures with debt and doubles its *dividend yield* from the current level for the next year, what would you expect the debt–equity ratio to be at the end of the next year?

12. You have been asked by JJ Corporation, a California-based firm that manufacturers and services digital satellite TV systems, to evaluate its capital structure. It currently has 70 million shares outstanding trading at $10 per share. In addition, the company has 500,000 convertible bonds, with a coupon rate of 8%, trading at $1,000 per bond. JJ is rated BBB, and the interest rate on BBB straight bonds is currently 10%. The beta for the company is 1.2, and the current risk-free rate is 6%. The tax rate is 40%.

a. What is the firm's current debt–equity ratio?

b. What is the firm's current weighted average cost of capital?

JJ Corporation is proposing to borrow $250 million and use it for the following purposes:

• Buy back $100 million worth of stock.

• Pay $100 million in dividends.

- Invest $50 million in a project with a NPV of $25 million.

The effect of this additional borrowing will be a drop in the bond rating to B, which currently carries an interest rate of 11%.

c.   What will the firm's cost of equity be after this additional borrowing?

d.   What will the firm's weighted average cost of capital be after this additional borrowing?

e.   What will the value of the firm be after this additional borrowing?

13. Pfizer, one of the largest pharmaceutical companies in the United States, is considering what its debt capacity is. In March 1995, Pfizer had an outstanding market value of equity of $24.27 billion, debt of $2.8 billion, and a AAA rating. Its beta was 1.47, and it faced a marginal corporate tax rate of 40%. The Treasury bond rate at the time of the analysis was 6.50%, and AAA bonds trade at a spread of 0.30% over the Treasury rate.

a.   Estimate the current cost of capital for Pfizer.

b.   It is estimated that Pfizer will have a BBB rating if it moves to a 30% debt ratio and that BBB bonds have a spread of 2% over the Treasury rate. Estimate the cost of capital if Pfizer moves to its optimal.

c.   Assuming a constant growth rate of 6% in the firm value, how much will firm value change if Pfizer moves its optimal? What will the effect be on the stock price?

d.   Pfizer has considerable R&D expenses. Will this fact affect whether Pfizer takes on the additional debt?

14. Upjohn, another major pharmaceutical company, is also considering whether it should borrow more. It has $664 million in book value of debt outstanding and 173 million shares outstanding at $30.75 per share. The company has a beta of 1.17, and faces a tax rate of 36%. The Treasury bond rate is 6.50%.

a.   If the interest expense on the debt is $55 million, the debt has an average maturity of ten years, and the company is currently rated AA− (with a market interest rate of 7.50%), estimate the market value of the debt.

b.   Estimate the current cost of capital.

c.   It is estimated that if Upjohn moves to its optimal debt ratio, and no growth in firm value is

assumed, the value per share will increase by $1.25. Estimate the cost of capital at the optimal debt ratio.

15. Bethlehem Steel, one of the oldest and largest steel companies in the United States, is considering the question of whether it has any excess debt capacity. The firm has $527 million in market value of debt outstanding and $1.76 billion in market value of equity. The firm has earnings before interest and taxes of $131 million and faces a corporate tax rate of 36%. The company's bonds are rated BBB, and the cost of debt is 8%. At this rating, the firm has a probability of default of 2.30%, and the cost of bankruptcy is expected to be 30% of firm value.

a.   Estimate the unlevered value of the firm.

b.   Estimate the levered value of the firm, using the APV approach, at a debt ratio of 50%. At that debt ratio, the firm's bond rating will be CCC, and the probability of default will increase to 46.61%.

16. Kansas City Southern, a railroad company, had debt outstanding of $985 million and 40 million shares trading at $46.25 per share in March 1995. It earned $203 million in EBIT, and faced a marginal tax rate of 36.56%. The firm was interested in estimating its optimal leverage using the APV approach. The following table summarizes the estimated bond ratings and probabilities of default at each level of debt from 0% to 90%.

Debt Ratio	Bond Rating	Probability of Default
0%	AAA	0.28%
10%	AAA	0.28%
20%	A−	1.41%
30%	BB	12.20%
40%	B−	32.50%
50%	CCC	46.61%
60%	CC	65.00%
70%	C	80.00%
80%	C	80.00%
90%	D	100.00%

The direct and indirect bankruptcy costs are estimated to be 25% of the firm value. Estimate the optimal debt ratio of the firm based on levered firm value.

17. In 1995, an analysis of the capital structure of Reebok provided the following results on the cost of capital and firm value.

	Actual	Optimal	Change
Debt ratio	4.42%	60.00%	55.58%
Beta for the stock	1.95	3.69	1.74
Cost of equity	18.61%	28.16%	9.56%
Bond rating	A−	B+	
After-tax cost of debt	5.92%	6.87%	0.95%
Cost of capital	18.04%	15.38%	−2.66%
Firm value (with no growth)	$3,343 million	$3,921 million	$578 million
Stock price	$39.50	$46.64	$7.14

This analysis was based on the 1995 EBIT of $420 million and a tax rate of 36.90%.

a. Why is the optimal debt ratio for Reebok so high?

b. What might be some of your concerns in moving to this optimal?

18. You are trying to evaluate whether United Airlines (UAL) has any excess debt capacity. In 1995, UAL had 12.2 million shares outstanding at $210 per share and debt outstanding of approximately $3 billion (book as well as market value). The debt had a rating of B, and carried a market interest rate of 10.12%. In addition, the firm had leases outstanding, with annual lease payments anticipated to by $150 million. The beta of the stock is 1.26, and the firm faces a tax rate of 35%. The treasury bond rate is 6.12%.

a. Estimate the current debt ratio for UAL.

b. Estimate the current cost of capital.

c. Based on 1995 operating income, the optimal debt ratio is computed to be 30%, at which point the rating will be BBB, and the market interest rate is 8.12%.

d. Would the fact that 1995 operating income for airlines was depressed alter your analysis in any way? Explain why.

19. Intel has an EBIT of $3.4 billion and faces a marginal tax rate of 36.50%. It currently has $1.5 billion in debt outstanding, and a market value of equity of $51 billion. The beta for the stock is 1.35, and the pretax cost of debt is 6.80%. The Treasury bond rate is 6%. Assume that the firm is considering a massive increase in leverage to a 70% debt ratio, at which level the bond rating will be C (with a pretax interest rate of 16%).

a. Estimate the current cost of capital.

b. Assuming that all debt gets refinanced at the new market interest rate, what would your interest expenses be at 70% debt? Would you be able to get the entire tax benefit? Why, or why not?

c. Estimate the beta of the stock at 70% debt, using the conventional levered beta calculation. Reestimate the beta, on the assumption that C-rated debt has a beta of 0.60. Which one would you use in your cost of capital calculation?

d. Estimate the cost of capital at 70% debt.

e. What will happen to firm value if Intel moves to a 70% debt ratio?

f. What general lessons on capital structure would you draw for other growth firms?

20. NYNEX, the phone utility for the New York City area, has approached you for advice on its capital structure. In 1995, NYNEX had debt outstanding of $12.14 billion and equity outstanding of $20.55 billion. The firm had an EBIT of $1.7 billion and faced a corporate tax rate of 36%. The beta for the stock is 0.84, and the bonds are rated A− (with a market interest rate of 7.5%). The probability of default for A− rated bonds is 1.41%, and the bankruptcy cost is estimated to be 30% of firm value.

a. Estimate the unlevered value of the firm.

b. Value the firm if it increases its leverage to 50%. At that debt ratio, its bond rating would be BBB and the probability of default would be 2.3%.

c. Assume now that NYNEX is considering a move into entertainment, which is likely to be both more profitable and riskier than the phone business. What changes would you expect in the optimal leverage?

21. A small, private firm has approached you for advice on its capital structure decision. It is in the specialty retailing business, and it had an EBIT last year of $500,000.

- The book value of equity is $1.5 million, but the estimated market value is $6 million.

- The firm has $1 million in debt outstanding and paid an interest expense of $80,000 on the debt last year. (Based on the interest coverage ratio, the firm would be rated AA and would be facing an interest rate of 8.25%.)

- The equity is not traded, but the average beta for comparable traded firms is 1.05, and their average debt–equity ratio is 25%.

a. Estimate the current cost of capital for this firm.

b. Assume now that this firm doubles it debt from $1 million to $2 million and that the interest rate at which it can borrow increases to 9%. Estimate the new cost of capital and the effect on firm value.

c. You also have a regression that you have run of debt ratios of publicly traded firms against firm characteristics:

$$\text{DBTFR} = 0.15 + 1.05(\text{EBIT/Firm value}) - 0.10(\text{Beta})$$

Estimate the debt ratio for the private firm based on this regression.

d. What are some of the concerns you might have in extending the approaches used by large publicly traded firms to estimate optimal leverage to smaller firms?

e. XCV Inc., which manufactures automobile parts for assembly, is considering the costs and the benefits of leverage. The CFO notes that the return on equity of the firm, which is only 12.75% now based on the current policy of no leverage, could be increased substantially by borrowing money. Is this true? Does it follow that the value of the firm will increase with leverage? Why, or why not?

CHAPTER 9

CAPITAL STRUCTURE: THE FINANCING DETAILS

In Chapter 7, we looked at the wide range of choices available to firms to raise capital. In Chapter 8, we developed the tools needed to estimate the optimal debt ratio for a firm. Here we discuss how firms can use this information to choose the mix of debt and equity they use to finance investments, and the financing instruments they can employ to reach that mix.

We begin by examining whether having identified an optimal debt ratio, firms should move to that debt ratio from current levels. A variety of concerns may lead a firm not to use its excess debt capacity if it is underlevered, or to lower its debt, if it is overlevered. A firm that decides to move from its current debt level to its optimal financing mix has two decisions to make. First, it has to consider how quickly it wants

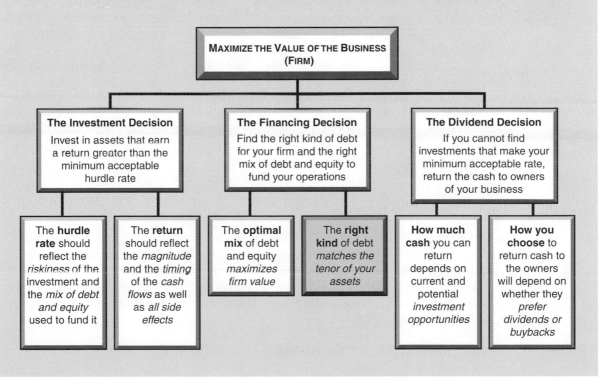

455

to move. The degree of urgency will vary widely across firms, depending on how much of a threat it perceives from being under- or overlevered. The second decision is whether to increase (or decrease) the debt ratio by recapitalizing investments, divesting assets and using the cash to reduce debt or equity, investing in new projects with debt or equity, or changing dividend policy.

In the second part of this chapter, we will consider how firms should choose the right financing vehicle for raising capital for their investments. We argue that a firm's choice of financing should be determined largely by the nature of the cash flows on its assets. Matching financing choices to asset characteristics decreases default risk for any given level of debt and allows the firm to borrow more. We then consider a number of real-world concerns, including tax law, the views of ratings agencies, and information effects that might lead firms to modify their financing choices.

A FRAMEWORK FOR CAPITAL STRUCTURE CHANGES

A firm whose actual debt ratio is very different from its optimal has several choices to make. First, it has to decide *whether to move toward the optimal or to preserve the status quo*. Second, once it decides to move toward the optimal, the firm has to choose *between changing its leverage quickly or moving more deliberately*. This decision may also be governed by pressure from external sources, such as impatient stockholders or bond ratings agency concerns. Third, if the firm decides to move gradually to the optimal, it has to decide whether to use new financing *to invest in new projects*, or to shift its *financing mix on existing projects*.

In the previous chapter, we presented the rationale for moving toward the optimal in terms of the value that could be gained for stockholders by doing so. Conversely, the cost of preserving the status quo is that this potential value increment is lost. Although managers nominally make this decision of whether to move towards their optimal debt ratios, they will often find themselves under some pressure from stockholders if they are underlevered, or under threat of bankruptcy if they are overlevered, to move toward their optimal debt ratios.

IMMEDIATE, GRADUAL OR NO CHANGE

In Chapter 7, we discussed the trade off between using debt and using equity. In Chapter 8, we developed a number of approaches used to determine the optimal financing mix for a firm. The next logical step, it would seem, is for firms to move to this optimal mix. In this section, we will first consider what might lead some firms not to make this move; we follow up by looking at some of the subsequent decisions firms that changing the mix requires.

No Change, Gradual Change, or Immediate Change
We have hitherto implicitly assumed that firms that have debt ratios different from their optimal debt ratios, once made aware of this gap, will want to move to the optimal

ratios. That does not always turn out to be the case. There are a number of firms that look underlevered using any of the approaches described in the last section but choose not to use their excess debt capacity. Conversely, there are a number of firms with too much debt that choose not to pay it down. At the other extreme are firms that shift their financing mix overnight to reflect the optimal mix. In this section, we look at the factors a firm might have to consider in deciding whether to leave its debt ratio unchanged, change gradually, or change immediately to the optimal mix.

To Change or Not to Change

Firms that are under- or overlevered might choose not to move to their optimal debt ratios for a number of reasons. Given our identification of the optimal debt ratio as the mix at which firm value is maximized, this inaction may seem not only irrational but also value-destroying for stockholders. In some cases, it is. In some cases, however, not moving to the optimal may be consistent with value maximization.

Let's consider underlevered firms first. The first reason a firm may choose not to move to its optimal debt ratio is that it does not view its objective as maximizing firm value. If the objective of a firm is to maximize net income or maintain a high bond rating, having less debt is more desirable than having more. Stockholders should clearly take issue with managers who avoid borrowing because they have an alternative objective and force them to justify their use of the objective.

Even when firms agree on firm value maximization as the objective, there are a number of reasons why underlevered firms may choose not to use their excess debt capacity.

- When firms borrow, the debt usually comes with covenants that restrict what the firm can do in the future. Firms that value flexibility may choose not to use their excess debt capacity.

- The flexibility argument can also be extended to cover future financing requirements. Firms that are uncertain about future financing needs may want to preserve excess debt capacity to cover these needs.

- In closely held or private firms, the likelihood of bankruptcy that comes with debt may be weighted disproportionately in making the decision to borrow.[1]

These are all viable reasons for not using excess debt capacity, and they may be consistent with value maximization. We should, however, put these reasons to the financial test. For instance, we estimated in Illustration 8.2 that the value of Disney as a firm will increase almost $1.8 billion if it moves to its optimal debt ratio. If the reason given by the firm's management for not using excess debt capacity is the need for financing flexibility, the value of this flexibility has to be greater than $1.8 billion.

Firms that have too much debt relative to their optimal level should have a fairly strong incentive to try reducing debt. Here again, there might be reasons why a firm

---

[1] We do consider the likelihood of default in all the approaches described in the last chapter. However, this consideration does not allow for the fact that cost of bankruptcy may vary widely across firms. The manager of a publicly traded firm may lose only his or her job in the event of default, whereas the owner of a private or closely held business may lose both wealth and reputation if he or she goes bankrupt.

may choose not to take this path. The primary fear of overlevered firms is bankruptcy. If the government makes a practice of shielding firms from the costs associated with default by either bailing out those that default on their debt or backing up the loans made to them by banks, firms may choose to remain overlevered. This would explain why Korean firms, which looked overlevered using any financial yardstick in the 1990s, did nothing to reduce their debt ratios until the government guarantee collapsed.

 IN PRACTICE: VALUING FINANCIAL FLEXIBILITY AS AN OPTION

If we assume unlimited and costless access to capital markets, a firm will always be able to fund a good project by raising new capital. If, on the other hand, we assume that there are internal or external constraints on raising new capital, financial flexibility can be valuable. To value this flexibility as an option, assume that a firm has expectations about how much it will need to reinvest in future periods based on its own past history and current conditions in the industry, but is uncertain about these investment needs. Assume also that a firm knows how much it can raise from internal funds and its normal access to capital markets in future periods. The advantage (and value) of having excess debt capacity or large cash balances is that the firm can meet any reinvestment needs, in excess of funds available, using its debt capacity. The payoff from these projects, however, comes from the excess returns the firm expects to make on them.

With this framework, we can specify the types of firms that will value financial flexibility the most.

- *Access to capital markets.* Firms with limited access to capital markets—private business, emerging market companies, and small market cap companies—should value financial flexibility more that those with wider access to capital.
- *Project quality.* The value of financial flexibility accrues not just from the fact that excess debt capacity can be used to fund projects but from the excess returns that these projects earn. Firms in mature and competitive businesses, where excess returns are close to zero, should value financial flexibility less than firms with substantial competitive advantages and high excess returns.
- *Uncertainty about future investment needs.* Firms that can forecast their reinvestment needs with certainty do not need to maintain excess debt capacity, because they can plan to raise capital well in advance. Firms in volatile businesses in which investment needs can shift dramatically from period to period will value financial flexibility more.

The bottom line is that firms that value financial flexibility more should be given more leeway to operate with debt ratios below their theoretical optimal debt ratios (where the cost of capital is minimized). This may explain why many mature technology firms such as Microsoft and Intel may choose not to remain underlevered. It can also explain why emerging market firms, with limited access to capital markets, not only use less debt but often accumulate large cash balances. Using the same logic, firms should value financial flexibility more in periods of market crisis than when markets are functioning well. One lesson from the banking and financial crisis of 2008 is that capital access, even in developed markets, can be restricted in some environments; the logical outcome will be that firms should borrow less than they did prior to the crisis and accumulate more cash. ■

Gradual versus Immediate Change

Many firms attempt to move to their optimal debt ratios, either gradually over time or immediately. The advantage of an abrupt shift to the optimal debt ratio is that the firm immediately receives the benefits of the optimal leverage, which include a lower cost of capital and a higher value. The disadvantage of a sudden change in leverage is that it alters both the way managers make decisions and the environment in which these decisions are made. If the optimal debt ratio has been incorrectly estimated, a sudden change may also increase the risk that the firm will have to backtrack and reverse its financing decisions. To illustrate, assume that a firm's optimal debt ratio has been calculated to be 40%, and that the firm moves to this optimum from its current debt ratio of 10%. A few months later, the firm discovers that its optimal debt ratio is really 30%. It will then have to repay some of the debt it has taken on to get back to optimal leverage.

Gradual versus Immediate Change for Underlevered Firms

For underlevered firms, the decision to increase the debt ratio to the optimal either quickly or gradually is determined by four factors:

1. ***Degree of Confidence in the Optimal Leverage Estimate.*** The greater the possible error in the estimate of optimal financial leverage, the more likely the firm will choose to move gradually to the optimal. Since, this error can be traced back to uncertainty about the key inouts into the optimal debt ratio computation—the estimated operating income, the tax rate and risk premiums for both equity and debt, firms that are in more volatile businesses will be more likely to pick the path of gradual change.

2. ***Comparability to Industry.*** When the optimal debt ratio for a firm differs markedly from that of the industry to which the firm belongs, analysts and ratings agencies might not look favorably on the change, and the firm is much less likely to shift to the optimal quickly.

3. ***Likelihood of a Takeover.*** Empirical studies of the characteristics of target firms in acquisitions have noted that underlevered firms are much more likely to be acquired than overlevered firms are.[2] Often, the acquisition is financed at least partially by the target firm's unused debt capacity. Consequently, firms with excess debt capacity that delay increasing debt run the risk of being taken over. The greater this risk, the more likely the firm will choose to take on additional debt quickly. Several additional factors may determine the likelihood of a takeover. One is the prevalence of antitakeover laws (at the state level) and amendments in the corporate charter designed specifically to prevent hostile acquisitions; the

---

[2] K. Palepu, "Predicting Takeover Targets: A Methodological and Empirical Analysis," *Journal of Accounting and Economics* 5:3–35. He notes that one of the variables that seems to predict a takeover is a low debt ratio in conjunction with poor operating performance.

more restrictive these provisions, the less the firm has to worry about being taken over. Another is the size of the firm. Because raising financing for an acquisition is far more difficult when acquiring a $100 billion firm than when acquiring a $1 billion firm, larger firms will feel more protected from the threat of hostile takeovers. The third factor is the extent of holdings by insiders and managers in the company. Insiders and managers with substantial stakes may be able to prevent hostile acquisitions. The final factor is the stock price performance of the firm; stockholders in firms where stock prices have dropped significantly over time tend to be much more receptive to the entreaties of hostile acquirers.

4. ***Need for Financial Flexibility.***   On occasion, firms may preserve excess debt capacity to meet unanticipated needs for funds, either to maintain existing projects or to invest in new ones. Firms that need and value this flexibility will be less likely to shift quickly to their optimal debt ratios and use up their excess debt capacity.

9.1   INSIDER HOLDINGS AND LEVERAGE

Closely held firms (where managers and insiders hold a substantial portion of the outstanding stock) are less likely to increase leverage quickly than firms with widely dispersed stockholdings.

a.   True

b.   False

Explain.

ILLUSTRATION 9.1   Debt Capacity and Takeovers

The Disney acquisition of Capital Cities in 1996, although a friendly acquisition, illustrates some of advantages to a firm of acquiring an underlevered firm. At the time of the acquisition, Capital Cities had $657 million in debt and 154.06 million shares outstanding, trading at $100 per share. Its market value debt-to-capital ratio was only 4.07%. With a beta of 0.95, a borrowing rate of 7.7%, and a corporate tax rate of 43.5%, this yielded a cost of capital of 11.9%. (The Treasury bond rate at the time of the analysis was 7%.)

$$\text{Cost of capital}$$
$$= \text{Cost of equity}[\text{Equity}/(\text{Debt} + \text{Equity})]$$
$$+ \text{Cost of debt}[\text{Debt}/(\text{Debt} + \text{Equity})]$$

$$= 12.23\%[15{,}406/(15{,}406+657)] + 7.7\%(1 - 0.435)[657/(15{,}406 + 657)]$$
$$= 11.9\%$$

Table 9.1 summarizes the costs of equity, debt, and capital, as well as the estimated firm values and stock prices at different debt ratios for Capital Cities.

Note that the firm value is maximized at a debt ratio of 30%, leading to an increase in the stock price of $23.69 over the prevailing market price of $100.

Although debt capacity was never stated as a reason for the acquisition of Capital Cities, Disney borrowed about $10 billion for this acquisition and paid $125 per share. Capital Cities' stockholders could well have achieved the same premium if management had borrowed the money and repurchased stock. To the extent that there were other

Table 9.1   COSTS OF FINANCING, FIRM VALUE, AND DEBT RATIOS: CAPITAL CITIES

Debt Ratio	Beta	Cost of Equity	Interest Coverage Ratio	Bond Rating	Interest Rate	Cost of Debt	Cost of Capital	Firm Value (in millions)	Stock Price
0.00%	0.93	12.10%	∞	AAA	7.30%	4.12%	12.10%	$15,507	$96.41
10.00%	0.99	12.42%	10.73	AAA	7.30%	4.12%	11.59%	$17,007	$106.15
20.00%	1.06	12.82%	4.75	A	8.25%	4.66%	11.19%	$18,399	$115.19
30.00%	1.15	13.34%	2.90	BBB	9.00%	5.09%	10.86%	$19,708	$123.69
40.00%	1.28	14.02%	1.78	B	11.00%	6.22%	10.90%	$19,546	$122.63
50.00%	1.45	14.99%	1.21	CCC	13.00%	7.35%	11.17%	$18,496	$115.81
60.00%	1.71	16.43%	1.00	CCC	13.00%	7.35%	10.98%	$19,228	$120.57
70.00%	2.37	20.01%	0.77	CC	14.50%	9.63%	12.74%	$13,939	$86.23
80.00%	3.65	27.08%	0.61	C	16.00%	11.74%	14.81%	$10,449	$63.58
90.00%	7.30	47.16%	0.54	C	16.00%	12.21%	15.71%	$9,391	$56.71

potential benefits accruing to Disney from this merger from synergy, it is possible that Capital Cities stockholders did not get their full share of the benefits.

Gradual versus Immediate Change for Overlevered Firms

Firms that are overlevered also have to decide whether they should shift gradually or immediately to an optimal debt ratio. As in the case of underlevered firms, the precision of the estimate of the optimal leverage will play a role, with more precise estimates leading to quicker adjustments. So will comparability to other firms in the sector. When most or all of the firms in a sector become overlevered, as was the case with the telecommunications sector in the late 1990s, firms seem to feel little urgency to reduce their debt ratios, even though they might be struggling to make their payments. In contrast, the pressure to reduce debt is much greater when a firm has a high debt ratio in a sector where most firms have lower debt ratios.

The other factor, in the case of overlevered firms, is the possibility of default. Too much debt also results in higher interest rates and lower ratings on the debt. Thus, the greater the chance of bankruptcy, the more likely the firm is to move quickly to reduce debt and move to its optimal. How can we assess the probability of default? If firms are rated, their bond ratings offer a noisy but simple measure of default risk. A firm with a below investment grade rating (below BBB) has a significant probability of default. Even if firms are not rated, we can use their synthetic ratings (based on interest coverage ratios) to come to the same conclusion.

9.2   INDIRECT BANKRUPTCY COSTS AND LEVERAGE

In Chapter 7, we talked about indirect bankruptcy costs, where the perception of default risk affected sales and profits. Assume that a firm with substantial indirect bankruptcy costs has too much debt. Is the urgency to get back to an optimal debt ratio for this firm greater or less than it is for a firm without such costs?

a.   Greater

b.   Lesser

Explain.

Implementing Changes in Financial Mix

A firm that decides to change its financing mix has several alternatives. In this section, we begin by considering the details of each of these alternatives to changing the financing mix, and we conclude by looking at how firms can choose the right approach for themselves.

Ways of Changing the Financing Mix

There are four basic paths available to a firm that wants to change its financing mix. One is to change the current financing mix using new equity to retire debt or new debt to reduce equity; this is called *recapitalization*. The second path is to sell assets and use the proceeds to pay off debt (if the objective is to reduce the debt ratio), or to buy back stock or pay dividends to reduce equity (if the objective is to increase the debt ratio). The third is to use a disproportionately high debt or equity ratio, relative to the firm's current ratios, to finance new investments over time. The value of the firm increases, but the debt ratio will also change in the process. The fourth option is to change the proportion of earnings that a firm returns to its stockholders in the form of dividends or by buying back stock. As this proportion changes, the debt ratio will also change over time.

Recapitalization

The simplest, and often the quickest, way to change a firm's financial mix is to change the way existing investments are financed. Thus, an underlevered firm can increase its debt ratio by borrowing money and buying back stock or replacing equity with debt of equal market value.

- *Borrowing money and buying back stock (or paying a large dividend)* increases the debt ratio because the borrowing increases the debt, whereas the equity repurchase or dividend payment concurrently reduces the equity; the former accomplishes this by reducing the number of shares outstanding, and the latter by lowering the stock price. Many companies have used this approach to increase leverage quickly, largely in response to takeover attempts. For example, in 1985, to stave off a hostile takeover, Atlantic Richfield borrowed $4 billion and repurchased stock to increase its debt-to-capital ratio from 12% to 34%.[3]

- In a **debt-for-equity swap**, a firm replaces equity with debt of equivalent market value by swapping the two securities. Here again, the simultaneous increase in debt, and the decrease in equity causes the debt ratio to increase substantially. In many cases, firms offer equity investors a combination of cash and debt in lieu of equity. In 1986, for example, Owens Corning gave its stockholders $52 in cash and debt with a face value of $35 for each outstanding share, thereby increasing its debt and reducing equity.

In each of these cases, the firm may be restricted by bond covenants that explicitly prohibit these actions or that impose large penalties on the firm. The firm will have to weigh these restrictions against the benefits of the higher leverage and the increased value that flows from it. A recapitalization designed to increase the debt ratio

---

[3]The stock buyback increased the stock price and took away a significant rationale for the acquisition.

substantially is called a *leveraged recapitalization*, and many of these recapitalizations are motivated by a desire to prevent a hostile takeover.[4]

Firms that want to lower their debt ratios can adopt a similar strategy. An overlevered firm can attempt to *renegotiate debt agreements* and try to convince some of the lenders to take equity stakes in the firm in lieu of some or all of their debt in the firm. It can also try to get lenders to offer more generous terms, including longer maturities and lower interest rates for existing debt. Finally, the firm can issue new equity and use it pay off some of the outstanding debt. The best bargaining chip such a firm possesses is the possibility of default, because default creates substantial losses for lenders. In the late 1980s, for example, many U.S. banks were forced to trade in their Latin American debt for equity stakes or else receive little or nothing on their loans.

Divestiture and Use of Proceeds

Firms can also change their debt ratios by selling assets and using the cash they receive from the divestiture to reduce debt or equity. Thus an underlevered firm can sell some of its assets and use the proceeds to repurchase stock or pay a large dividend. This action reduces the equity outstanding at the firm and will increase the debt ratio of the firm, but only if the firm already has some debt outstanding. An overlevered firm may choose to sell assets and use the proceeds to retire some of the outstanding debt and reduce its debt ratio.

If a firm chooses this path, the choice of which assets to divest is critical. Firms usually want to divest themselves of investments that are doing poorly, i.e, earning less than their required returns, but that cannot be the overriding consideration in this decision. The key question is whether there are potential buyers for the asset who are willing to pay fair value or more for it, where the fair value measures how much the asset is worth to the firm, based on its expected cash flows. In fact, one peril faced by overlevered firms that try to divest assets is that their bargaining position is weakened by their desperate need for cash and that potential buyers for the assets recognize this weakness (and adjust their bids accordingly).

9.3 ASSET SALES TO REDUCE LEVERAGE

Assume that a firm has decided to sell assets to pay off its debt. In deciding which assets to sell, the firm should

a. Sell its worst performing assets to raise the cash
b. Sell its best performing assets to raise the cash
c. Sell its most liquid assets to raise the cash
d. None of the above (specify the alternative)

Explain.

Financing New Investments

Firms can also change their debt ratios by financing new investments disproportionately with debt or equity. If they use a much higher proportion of debt in financing

---

[4]A study of leveraged recapitalizations between 1985 and 1988 indicates that all but five were motivated by the threat of hostile takeovers.

new investments than their current debt ratio, they will increase their debt ratios. Conversely, if they use a much higher proportion of equity in financing new investments than their existing equity ratio, they will decrease their debt ratios.

There are two key differences between this approach and the previous two. First, because new investments are spread out over time, the debt ratio will adjust gradually over the period. Second, the process of investing in new assets will increase both the firm value and the dollar debt that goes with any debt ratio. For instance, if Disney decides to increase its debt ratio to 30% and proposes to do so by investing in a new theme park, the value of the firm will increase from the existing level to reflect the new assets created by the investment.

Changing Dividend Payout

We will not be considering dividend policy in detail until the next chapter, but we will mention here that a firm can change its debt ratio over time by changing the proportion of its earnings that it returns to stockholders in each period. Increasing the proportion of earnings paid out in dividends (the dividend payout ratio) or buying back stock each period will increase the debt ratio for two reasons. First, the payment of the dividend or buying back stock will reduce the equity in the firm;[5] holding debt constant, this will increase the debt ratio. Second, paying out more of the earnings to stockholders increases the need for external financing to fund new investments; if firms fill this need with new debt, the debt ratio will be increased even further. (Decreasing the proportion of earnings returned to stockholders will have the opposite effects.)

Firms that choose this route have to recognize that debt ratios will increase gradually over time. In fact, the value of equity in a firm can be expected to increase each period by the expected price appreciation rate. This rate can be obtained from the cost of equity, after netting out the expected portion of the return that will come from dividends. This portion is estimated with the dividend yield, which measures the expected dollar dividend as a percent of the current stock price:

$$\text{Expected price appreciation} = \text{Cost of equity} - \text{Expected dividend yield}$$

To illustrate, in 2009 Disney had a cost of equity of 8.91% and an expected dollar dividend per share of $0.35. Based on the stock price of $24.34, the expected price appreciation can be computed:

$$\text{Expected price appreciation}_{\text{Disney}} = 8.91\% - (\$0.35/\$24.34) = 7.47\%$$

Disney's market value of equity can be expected to increase 7.47% next period. The dollar debt would have to increase by more than that amount for the debt ratio to increase.

9.4 DOLLAR DEBT VERSUS DEBT RATIO

Assume that a firm worth $1 billion has no debt and needs to get to a 20% debt ratio. How much would the firm need to borrow if it wants to buy back stock?

a. $200 million

b. $250 million

---

c. $260 million

d. $160 million

How much would it need to borrow if it were planning to invest in new projects (with zero net present value)? What if the projects had an NPV of $50 million?

Choosing between the Alternatives

Given the choice between recapitalizing, divesting, financing new investments, and changing dividend payout, how can a firm choose the right way to change debt ratios? The choice will be determined by three factors. The first is the *urgency with which the firm is trying to move to its optimal debt ratio*. Recapitalizations and divestitures can be accomplished in a few weeks and can change debt ratios significantly. Financing new investments or changing dividend payout, on the other hand, is a long-term strategy to change debt ratios. Thus, a firm that needs to change its debt ratio quickly—because it is either under threat of a hostile takeover or faces imminent default—is more likely to use recapitalizations than to finance new investments.

The second factor is the *quality of new investments*. In the earlier chapters on investment analysis, we defined a good investment as one that earns a positive NPV and a return greater than its hurdle rate. Firms with good investments will gain more by financing these new investments with new debt if the firm is underlevered, or with new equity if the firm is overlevered. Not only will the firm value increase by the value gain we computed in Chapter 8, based on the change in the cost of capital, but the positive NPV of the project will also accrue to the firm. On the other hand, using excess debt capacity or new equity to invest in poor projects is a bad strategy, because the projects will destroy value.

The final consideration is the *marketability of existing investments*. Two considerations go into marketability. One is whether existing investments earn excess returns; firms are often more willing to divest themselves of assets that are earning less than the required return. The other (and, in our view, the more important) consideration is whether divesting these assets will generate a price high enough to compensate the firm for the cash flows lost by selling them. Ironically, firms often find that their best investments are more likely to meet the second criterion than their worst investments are.

We summarize our conclusions about the right route to follow to the optimal, based on all these determinants, in Table 9.2.

We also summarize our discussion of whether a firm should shift to its financing mix quickly or gradually, as well as the question of how to make this shift, in Figure 9.1.

Although we have presented this choice in stark terms, whereby firms decide to use one or another of the four alternatives described, a combination of actions may be what is needed to get a firm to its desired debt ratio. This is especially likely when the firm is large and the change in debt ratio is significant. In the illustrations following this section, we consider four companies. The first, Nichols Research, is a small firm that gets to its optimal debt ratio by borrowing money and buying back stock. The other two, Disney and Tata Chemicals, choose a combination of new investments and recapitalization—Disney to increase its debt ratio and Time Warner to decrease its

Table 9.2 OPTIMAL ROUTE TO FINANCING MIX

Desired Speed of Adjustment	Marketability of Existing Investments	Quality of New Investments	Optimal Route to Increasing Debt Ratio	Optimal Route to Decreasing Debt Ratio
Urgent	Poor	Poor	Recapitalize; borrow money and buy back stock.	Recapitalize: issue equity and pay off debt.
Urgent	Good	Good	Divest assets and buy back stock; finance new investments with debt.	Divest assets and retire debt; finance new investments with equity.
Urgent	Good	Poor	Divest and buy back stock.	Divest and retire debt.
Gradual	Neutral or poor	Neutral or poor	Increase payout to stockholders.	Retire debt each year using earnings.
Gradual	Good	Neutral or poor	Divest and increase payout to stockholders.	Divest and retire debt over time.
Gradual	Neutral or poor	Good	Finance new investments with debt.	Finance new investments with equity.

debt ratio. The fourth, Aracruz Celulose, raises equity to reduce its debt ratio, since the firm faces some urgency and its investments are earning less than the cost of capital.

ILLUSTRATION 9.2 Increasing Financial Leverage Quickly—Nichols Research

In 1994, Nichols Research, a firm that provides technical services to the defense industry, had debt outstanding of $6.8 million and market value of equity of $120 million. Based on its EBITDA of $12 million, Nichols had an optimal debt ratio of 30%, which would lower the cost of capital to 12.07% (from the current cost of capital of 13%) and increase the firm value to $146 million (from $126.8 million). There are a number of reasons for arguing that Nichols should increase its leverage quickly:

- Its small size, in conjunction with its low leverage and large cash balance ($25.3 million), make it a prime target for an acquisition.
- Although 17.6% of the shares are held by owners and directors, this amount is unlikely to hold off a hostile acquisition, because institutions own 60% of the outstanding stock.
- The firm has been reporting steadily decreasing returns on its projects, due to the shrinkage in the defense budget. In 1994, the return on capital was only 10%, which was lower than the cost of capital.

If Nichols decides to increase leverage, it can do so in a number of ways:

- It can borrow enough money to get to 30% of its overall firm value ($146 million at the optimal debt ratio) and buy back stock. This would require $37 million in new debt to get to a total dollar debt level of $44 million.
- It can borrow $37 million and pay a special dividend of that amount.

Figure 9.1   A Framework for Changing Debt Ratios

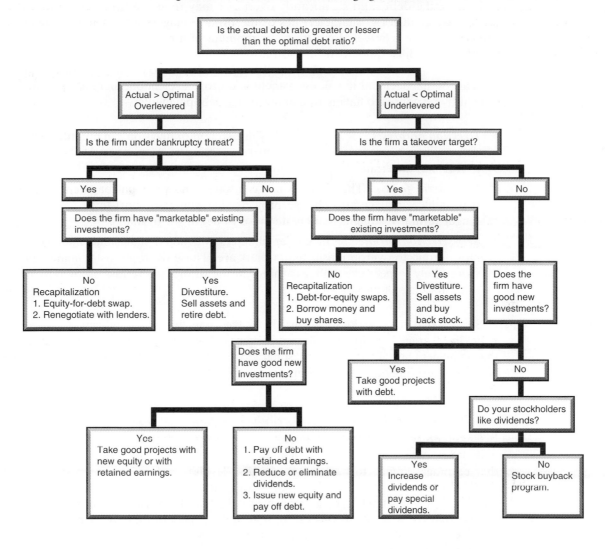

- It can use the cash balance of $25 million to buy back stock or pay dividends, and increase debt to 30% of the remaining firm value (30% of $121 million).[6] This would require approximately $29.5 million in new debt, which can be used to buy back stock.[7]

The Shock of Debt: A Behavioral Perspective
Increasing the debt ratio significantly overnight may reduce a firm's cost of capital, but it does change the characteristics of the firm. Managers who are accustomed to operating in the relatively low-stress environment of a predominantly equity-funded firm have to adjust quickly to the cash flow demands of a highly levered firm. While the argument posed by Jensen and others is that this will lead to the more discipline on the part of management in risk assessment and project selection, there are potentially unhealthy responses to having to making larger debt payments:

- *Decision paralysis.*   Since every risky investment or decision can potentially cause default, managers may hold back on committing to new investments that they perceive as uncertain.

- *Short-term focus.*   The need to make interest and principal payments on debt may induce managers to choose projects that generate short-term payoffs over longer-term investments that create more value for the business.

- *Self-selection problem.*   In earlier chapters, we noted that some managers are more prone to overoptimism than others are. These overoptimistic managers are more likely to perceive higher earnings in the future and follow up by borrowing large amounts of money.

Studies that have looked at firms that have gone through significant increases in debt (in leveraged recapitalization and leveraged buyouts) find, at least on average, that managers are able to cope reasonably well with the demands of debt payments and that operating performance improves after the leverage increase.

ILLUSTRATION 9.3   Decreasing Leverage Quickly—Aractruz Celulose

In Chapter 8, we noted the perilous state of Aracruz Celulose, a firm with R$9.8 billion in debt and a debt ratio of 52% and an optimal debt ratio of 10% (even if we assume that earnings bounce to back to normalized levels). In fact, the interest expenses that will accrue from the existing debt will be higher than the normalized operating income, which puts the firm on a pathway to default and bankruptcy. Consequently, we believe that the firm needs to act quickly to reduce its debt ratio and list the possible options:

- *Equity-for-debt swap.*   The first and least painful option is to get lenders to the firm to agree to exchange their debt for equity in the firm. While this will increase the number of shares outstanding and reduce the control that the existing inside stockholders have over the firm, it is the option least likely to disrupt operations and most in tune with current financial conditions.

- *Issue new equity and retire debt.*   While Aracruz's stock price plummeted during the last nine months of 2008, it has shown signs of recovery in the last few months. If that recovery continues, aided and abetted by an increase in commodity prices, Aracruz may be able to issue new stock and use the proceeds to retire a significant portion of the debt.

- ***Sell assets to pay down debt.***   This is the least desirable scenario, since it indicates that the firm has run out of options. However, if debt holders do not agree to swaps and issuing new equity becomes a nonviable option, the firm may be forced to sell some or a large portion of its assets, perhaps at bargain basement prices, and use the proceeds to pay down debt.

Given the need to retire debt, it is clear that Aracruz is in no position to pay dividends to stockholders. Consequently, we believe that Aracruz should suspend paying dividends, even if this gives control rights to preferred stockholders. Desperate times call for desperate measures.

ILLUSTRATION 9.4   Charting a Framework for Increasing Leverage—Disney

Reviewing the capital structure analysis done for Disney in Chapter 8, we see that it had a debt ratio of approximately 27% in early 2009, with $16.7 billion in debt (estimated market value) and $45.2 billion in equity. Its optimal debt ratio, based on minimizing cost of capital, was 40%. Table 9.3 summarizes the debt ratios, costs of capital, and firm value at debt ratios ranging from 0% to 90%.

In early 2009, Disney looked like it was not under any immediate pressure to increase its leverage, partly because of its size ($61.9 billion) and partly because its stock price and earnings had recovered from their lows of 2003.[8] Let us assume, therefore, that Disney decides to increase its leverage over time toward its optimal level.

The question of how to increase leverage over time can be best answered by looking at the quality of the projects that Disney had available to achieve it in 2008. In Chapter 5, we compute the return on capital that Disney earned in 2008 as 9.29%, higher than its current cost of capital of 7.51% and much higher than the cost of capital of 7.32% at

Table 9.3   DEBT RATIO, COST OF CAPITAL, AND FIRM VALUE: DISNEY

Debt Ratio	Cost of Capital	Firm Value (G)
0%	7.90%	$58,499.82
10%	7.68%	$60,373.92
20%	7.45%	$62,371.16
30%	7.32%	$63,595.96
40%	7.32%	$63,650.81
50%	7.33%	$63,556.35
60%	7.40%	$62,873.20
70%	9.49%	$47,883.80
80%	10.46%	$43,090.17
90%	11.34%	$39,497.05

---

[8]See Jensen's alpha calculation in Chapter 4. Over the past five years, Disney has earned an excess return of 5.62% a year.

the optimal debt ratio.[9] If we assume that these positive excess returns are likely to continue into the future, the path to a higher optimal debt ratio is to invest in more projects, using disproportionately more debt in these investments.

To make forecasts of changes in leverage over time, we made the following assumptions:

- Revenues, operating earnings, capital expenditures, and depreciation are expected to grow 5% a year from 2009 to 2013 (based on analyst estimates of growth). The current value for each of these items is provided in Table 9.4.
- In 2008, noncash working capital was 2.28% of revenues, and that ratio is expected to be unchanged over the next five years.
- The interest rate on new debt is expected to be 6%, which is Disney's pretax cost of debt. The bottom-up unlevered beta is 0.7333 and the current levered beta is 0.90, as estimated in Chapter 4.
- The dividend payout ratio in 2008 was 15.36%.
- The Treasury bond rate is 3.5%, and the risk premium is assumed to be 6%.

Table 9.4 ESTIMATED DEBT RATIOS WITH EXISTING PAYOUT RATIOS: DISNEY (CASH OUTFLOWS ARE SHOWN AS POSITIVE, AND CASH INFLOWS AS NEGATIVE)

	Current Year	1	2	3	4	5
Equity	$45,193	$48,521	$52,014	$55,677	$59,517	$63,537
Debt	$16,682	$14,768	$12,697	$10,458	$8,036	$5,417
Debt/(Debt + Equity)	26.96%	23.33%	19.62%	15.81%	11.90%	7.86%
Revenues	$36,990	$38,840	$40,781	$42,821	$44,962	$47,210
Noncash working capital	$844	$886	$931	$977	$1,026	$1,077
Capital expenditures	$3,389	$3,559	$3,737	$3,924	$4,120	$4,326
+ Chg in work. cap	$40	$42	$44	$47	$49	$51
− Depreciation	$1,593	$1,673	$1,756	$1,844	$1,936	$2,033
− Net income	$4,324	$4,540	$4,838	$5,157	$5,499	$5,864
+ Dividends	$664	$697	$743	$792	$844	$900
= Debt issued (repaid)	($1,823)	($1,915)	($2,071)	($2,239)	($2,422)	($2,619)
Beta	0.90	0.87	0.84	0.82	0.79	0.77
Cost of equity	8.91%	8.73%	8.57%	8.41%	8.27%	8.13%
Growth rate		5.00%	5.00%	5.00%	5.00%	5.00%
Dividend payout ratio	15.36%	15.36%	15.36%	15.36%	15.36%	15.36%

[a]Net income$_t$ = Net income$_{t-1}$ $(1 + g)$ − Interest rate $(1 - t)$ * (Debt$_t$−Debt$_{t-1}$)

---

[9]The correct comparison should be to the cost of capital that Disney will have at its optimal debt ratio. It is, however, even better if the return on capital also exceeds the current cost of capital, because it will take time to get to the optimal.

To estimate the expected market value of equity in future periods, we will use the cost of equity computed from the beta in conjunction with dividends. The estimated values of debt and equity, over time, are estimated as follows.

$$\text{Equity}_t = \text{Equity}_{t-1}(1 + \text{Cost of equity}_{t-1}) - \text{Dividends}_t - \text{Stock Buybacks}_t$$

The rationale is simple: the cost of equity measures the expected return on the stock, inclusive of price appreciation and the dividend yield, and the payment of dividends or stock buybacks reduces the value of equity outstanding at the end of the year.[10] The value of debt is estimated by adding the new debt taken on to the debt outstanding at the end of the previous year.

We begin this analysis by looking at what would happen to the debt ratio if Disney maintains its existing payout ratio of 15.36%, does not buy back stock, and applies excess funds to pay off debt. Table 9.4 uses the expected capital expenditures and noncash working capital needs over the next five years, in conjunction with external financing needs, to estimate the debt ratio in each year.

There are two points to note in these forecasts. The first is that the net income is adjusted for the change in interest expenses that will occur as a result of the debt being paid off. The second is that the beta is adjusted to reflect the changing debt to equity ratio from year to year. Disney produces a cash surplus every year, because internal cash flows (net income + depreciation) are well in excess of capital expenditures and working capital needs. If this is applied to paying off debt, the increase in the market value of equity over time will cause the debt ratio to drop from 27% to 7.86% by the end of year 5.

If Disney wants to increase its debt ratio to 35%, it will need to do one or a combination of the following:

1. ***Increase its dividend payout ratio.***   The higher dividend increases the debt ratio in two ways. It increases the need for debt financing in each year, and it reduces the expected price appreciation on the equity. In Table 9.5, for instance, increasing the dividend payout ratio to 75% results in a debt ratio of 30.85% at the end of the fifth year.

   In other words, the dividend payout ratio would have to be increased fivefold for Disney's debt ratio to rise to 31% over the next five years, and even more so if the objective were to increase the debt ratio to 35% or higher.

2. ***Repurchase stock each year.***   This affects the debt ratio in much the same way as increasing dividends, because it increases debt requirements and reduces equity. If Disney bought back 7.5% of the stock outstanding each year, the debt ratio at the end of year 5 would rise to almost 36%, as shown in Table 9.6.[11]

   In this scenario, Disney will need to borrow money each year to cover its stock buybacks and the debt ratio increases to 35.98% by the end of year 5.

---

[10]The effect of dividends on the market value of equity can best be captured by noting the effect the payment on dividends has on stock prices on the ex-dividend day. Stock prices tend to drop on ex-dividend day by about the same amount as the dividend paid.

[11]Stock buyback in year t = (Market value of equity$_{t-1}$ (1 + Cost of equity)$_{t-1}$ − Dividends$_t$) (Buyback %).

Table 9.5   ESTIMATED DEBT RATIO WITH HIGHER DIVIDEND PAYOUT RATIO (CASH OUTFLOWS ARE SHOWN AS POSITIVE, AND CASH INFLOWS AS NEGATIVE)

	Current Year	1	2	3	4	5
Equity	$45,193	$45,813	$46,356	$46,810	$47,164	$47,404
Debt	$16,682	$17,475	$18,316	$19,206	$20,149	$21,148
Debt/(Debt + Equity)	26.96%	27.61%	28.32%	29.09%	29.93%	30.85%
Revenues	$36,990	$38,840	$40,781	$42,821	$44,962	$47,210
Capital expenditures	$3,389	$3,559	$3,737	$3,924	$4,120	$4,326
+ Chg in work. cap	$40	$42	$44	$47	$49	$51
− Depreciation	$1,593	$1,673	$1,756	$1,844	$1,936	$2,033
− Net income	$4,324	$4,540	$4,738	$4,943	$5,157	$5,380
+ Dividends	$664	$3,405	$3,553	$3,707	$3,868	$4,035
= Debt issued (repaid)	($1,823)	$793	$840	$890	$943	$999
Beta	0.90	0.91	0.91	0.92	0.93	0.94
Cost of equity	8.91%	8.94%	8.98%	9.02%	9.07%	9.12%
Growth rate		5.00%	5.00%	5.00%	5.00%	5.00%
Dividend payout ratio	15.36%	75.00%	75.00%	75.00%	75.00%	75.00%

Table 9.6   ESTIMATED DEBT RATIO WITH EQUITY BUYBACK OF 7.5% A YEAR

	Current Year	1	2	3	4	5
Equity	$45,193	$44,882	$44,592	$44,320	$44,062	$43,815
Debt	$16,682	$18,407	$20,066	$21,658	$23,179	$24,625
Debt/(Debt + Equity)	26.96%	29.08%	31.03%	32.83%	34.47%	35.98%
Revenues	$36,990	$38,840	$40,781	$42,821	$44,962	$47,210
Capital expenditures	$3,389	$3,559	$3,737	$3,924	$4,120	$4,326
+ Chg in work. cap	$40	$42	$44	$47	$49	$51
− Depreciation	$1,593	$1,673	$1,756	$1,844	$1,936	$2,033
− Net income	$4,324	$4,540	$4,703	$4,876	$5,061	$5,258
+ Dividends	$664	$697	$722	$749	$777	$807
+ Stock buybacks		$3,639	$3,616	$3,593	$3,573	$3,553
= Debt issued (repaid)	($1,823)	$1,724	$1,660	$1,592	$1,521	$1,446
Beta	0.90	0.92	0.94	0.96	0.97	0.99
Cost of equity	8.91%	9.02%	9.13%	9.23%	9.33%	9.43%
Growth rate		5.00%	5.00%	5.00%	5.00%	5.00%
Dividend payout ratio	15.36%	15.36%	15.36%	15.36%	15.36%	15.36%

3. *Increase capital expenditures each year.* The first two approaches increase the debt ratio by shrinking the equity, whereas the third approach increases the scale of the firm. It does so by increasing the capital expenditures, which, incidentally, includes acquisitions of other firms, and financing these expenditures with debt. Disney could increase its debt ratio fairly significantly by increasing capital expenditures. In Table 9.7, we estimate the debt ratio for Disney if it doubles its capital expenditures (relative to the estimates in the earlier tables) and meets its external financing needs with debt.

With the higher capital expenditures, and maintaining the existing dividend payout ratio of 15.36%, the debt ratio is 29.14% by the end of year 5. This is the riskiest strategy of the three, because it presupposes the existence of enough good investments (or acquisitions) to cover $25 billion in new investments over the next five years. It may, however, be the strategy that seems most attractive to management intent on building a global entertainment empire. In the process of expanding, though, Disney will have to figure out ways of keeping its return on capital above its cost of capital.

9.5 CASH BALANCES AND CHANGING LEVERAGE

Companies with excess debt capacity often also have large cash balances. Which of the following actions by a company with a large cash balance will increase its debt ratio?

a. Using the cash to acquire another company

b. Paying a large special dividend

c. Paying off debt

d. Buying back stock

Explain.

Table 9.7 ESTIMATED DEBT RATIO WITH 100% HIGHER CAPITAL EXPENDITURES

	Current Year	1	2	3	4	5
Equity	$45,193	$48,521	$52,111	$55,985	$60,166	$64,681
Debt	$16,682	$18,326	$20,125	$22,092	$24,244	$26,597
Debt/(Debt + Equity)	26.96%	27.42%	27.86%	28.30%	28.72%	29.14%
Revenues	$36,990	$38,840	$40,781	$42,821	$44,962	$47,210
Capital expenditures	$3,389	$7,118	$7,474	$7,847	$8,240	$8,652
+ Chg in work. cap	$40	$42	$44	$47	$49	$51
− Depreciation	$1,593	$1,673	$1,756	$1,844	$1,936	$2,033
− Net income	$4,324	$4,540	$4,706	$4,874	$5,045	$5,217
+ Dividends	$664	$697	$743	$792	$844	$900
+ Stock buybacks		$0	$0	$0	$0	$0
= Debt issued (repaid)	($1,823)	$1,644	$1,799	$1,967	$2,152	$2,353
Beta	0.90	0.91	0.91	0.91	0.92	0.92
Cost of equity	8.91%	8.93%	8.95%	8.98%	9.00%	9.02%
Growth rate		5.00%	5.00%	5.00%	5.00%	5.00%
Dividend payout ratio	15.36%	15.36%	15.36%	15.36%	15.36%	15.36%

ILLUSTRATION 9.5   Decreasing Leverage Gradually—Tata Chemicals

In 2009, Tata Chemicals had Rs 26.9 billion rupees in debt outstanding, representing a debt ratio of 34.02%. In Chapter 8, we computed the optimal debt ratio for the firm to be about 10% but there is little threat of bankruptcy, partly because the firm has enough operating income to cover its interest expenses comfortably and partly because it has the backing of the Tata Group's ample financial resources. Table 9.8 examines the effect on leverage of cutting dividends to zero and using operating cash flows to invest in new projects and repay debt.

Allowing for a growth rate of 8% in operating income, Tata Chemicals repays Rs 1.7 billion of its outstanding debt in the first year. By the end of the fifth year, the growth in equity and the reduction in debt combine to lower the debt ratio to 9.21%.

Chgcapstru.xls: This spreadsheet allows you to estimate the effects of changing dividend policy or capital expenditures on debt ratios over time.

9.6   INVESTING IN OTHER BUSINESS LINES

In the analysis above, we have argued that firms should invest in projects as long as the return on equity is greater than the cost of equity. Assume that a firm is considering acquiring another firm with its debt capacity. In analyzing the return on equity the acquiring firm can make on this investment, we should compare the return on equity to

a.   The cost of equity of the acquiring firm

b.   The cost of equity of the target firm

c.   A blended cost of equity of the target and acquiring firm

d.   None of the above

Explain.

	Current Year	1	2	3	4	5
Equity	Rs52,160	Rs59,187	Rs67,129	Rs75,832	Rs85,364	Rs95,794
Debt	Rs26,892	Rs24,324	Rs21,381	Rs18,008	Rs14,143	Rs9,714
Debt/(Debt + Equity)	34.02%	29.13%	24.16%	19.19%	14.21%	9.21%
Revenues	Rs59,757	Rs64,538	Rs69,701	Rs75,277	Rs81,299	Rs87,803
Capital expenditures	Rs2,162	Rs2,335	Rs2,522	Rs2,723	Rs2,941	Rs3,177
+ Chg in work. cap	Rs742	Rs802	Rs866	Rs935	Rs1,010	Rs1,091
− Depreciation	Rs1,582	Rs1,709	Rs1,845	Rs1,993	Rs2,152	Rs2,324
− Net income	Rs3,700	Rs3,996	Rs4,485	Rs5,039	Rs5,664	Rs6,373
+ Dividends	Rs664	Rs0	Rs0	Rs0	Rs0	Rs0
= Debt issued (repaid)	(Rs1,714)	(Rs2,568)	(Rs2,943)	(Rs3,373)	(Rs3,865)	(Rs4,429)
Beta	0.90	0.90	0.85	0.82	0.78	0.75
Cost of equity	13.47%	13.42%	12.97%	12.57%	12.22%	11.90%
Growth rate		8.00%	8.00%	8.00%	8.00%	8.00%
Dividend payout ratio	17.94%	0.00%	0.00%	0.00%	0.00%	0.00%

Table 9.8   ESTIMATED DEBT RATIOS: TATA CHEMICALS

IN PRACTICE: SECURITY INNOVATION AND CHANGING CAPITAL STRUCTURE

The changes in leverage discussed so far in this chapter have been accomplished using traditional securities, such as straight debt and equity, but firms that have specific objectives on leverage may find certain products that are designed to meet those objectives. Consider a few examples:

- Hybrid securities (such as convertible bonds) are combinations of debt and equity that change over time as the firm changes. To be more precise, if the firm prospers and its equity value increases, the conversion option in the convertible bond will become more valuable, thus increasing the equity component of the convertible bond and decreasing the debt component (as a percent of the value of the bond). If the firm does badly and its stock price slides, the conversion option (and the equity component) will become less valuable, and the debt ratio of the firm will increase.

- An alternative available to a firm that wants to increase leverage over time is a forward contract to buy a specified number of shares of equity in the future. These contracts lock the firms into reducing their equity over time and may carry a more positive signal to financial markets than would an announcement of plans to repurchase stock, because firms are not obligated to carry through on these announcements.

- A firm with high leverage, faced with a resistance from financial markets to common stock issues, may consider more inventive ways of raising equity, such as using warrants and contingent value rights. Warrants represent call options on the firm's equity, whereas contingent value rights are put options on the firm's stock. The former have appeal to those who are optimistic about the future of the company, and the latter make sense for risk-averse investors who are concerned about the future. ■

CHOOSING THE RIGHT FINANCING INSTRUMENTS

In Chapter 7, we presented a variety of ways in which firms can raise debt and equity. Debt can be bank debt or corporate bonds, can vary in maturity from short- to long-term, can have fixed or floating-rates, and can be in different currencies. In the case of equity, there are fewer choices, but firms can still raise equity from common stock, warrants, and contingent value rights. Although we suggested broad guidelines that could be used to determine when firms should consider each type of financing, we did not develop a methodology by which a specific firm can pick the right kind of financing.

In this section, we lay out a sequence of steps by which a firm can choose the right financing instruments. This analysis is useful not only in determining what kind of securities should be issued to finance new investments, but also in highlighting limitations in a firm's existing financing choices. The first step in the analysis is an examination of the cash flow characteristics of the assets or projects that will be financed; the objective is to try matching the cash flows on the liability stream as closely as possible to the cash flows on the asset stream. We then superimpose a series of considerations that may lead the firm to deviate from or modify these financing choices.

First, we consider the tax savings that may accrue from using different financing vehicles and weigh the tax benefits against the costs of deviating from the optimal choices. Next, we examine the influence that equity research analysts and ratings agency views have on the choice of financing vehicles; instruments that are looked on favorably by either or (better still) both groups will clearly be preferred to those that evoke strong negative responses from one or both groups. We also factor in the difficulty that some firms might have in conveying information to markets; in the presence of asymmetric information, firms may have to make financing choices that do not reflect their asset mix. Finally, we allow for the possibility that firms may want to structure their financing to reduce agency conflicts between stockholders and bondholders.

I. Matching Financing Cash Flows with Asset Cash Flows

The first and most important characteristic a firm has to consider in choosing the financing instrument it will use to raise funds is the cash flow patterns of the assets to be financed.

Why Match Asset Cash Flows to Cash Flows on Liabilities?

We begin with the premise that the cash flows of a firm's liability stream should match the cash flows of the assets that they finance. Let us begin by defining firm value as the present value of the cash flows generated by the assets owned by the firm. This firm value will vary over time, not only as a function of firm-specific factors (such as project success) but also as a function of broader macroeconomic variables, such as interest rates, inflation rates, economic cycles, and exchange rates. Figure 9.2 represents the time series of firm value for a hypothetical firm, where all the changes in firm value are assumed to result from changes in macroeconomic variables.

This firm can choose to finance these assets with any financing mix it wants. The value of equity at any point in time is the difference between the value of the firm and

Figure 9.2   Firm Value Over Time with Short-Term Debt

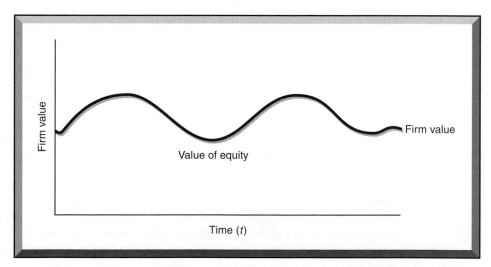

Figure 9.3   Firm Value Over Time with Long-Term Debt

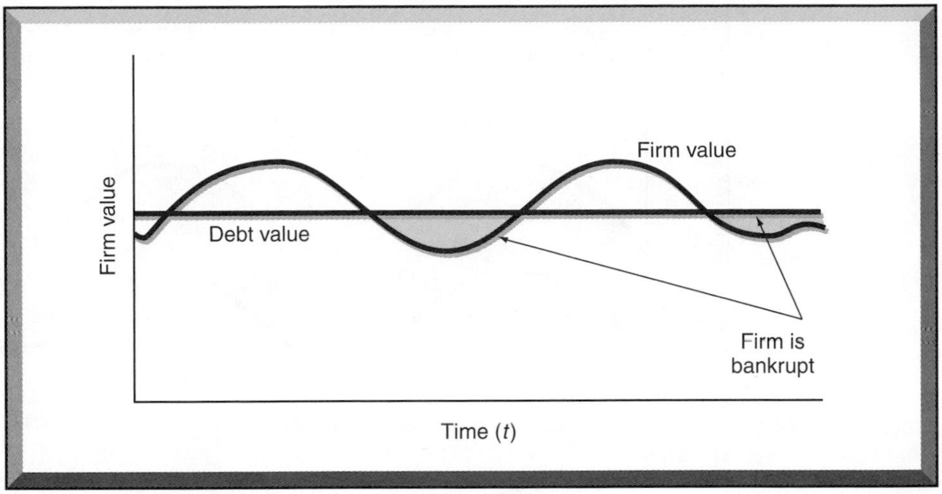

the value of outstanding debt. Assume, for instance, that the firm chooses to finance the assets shown in Figure 9.2 using very short-term debt, and that the value of this debt is unaffected by changes in macroeconomic variables. Figure 9.3 provides the firm value, debt value, and equity value over time for the firm.

Note that there are periods when the firm value drops below the debt value, which would suggest that the firm is technically bankrupt in those periods. Firms that weigh this possibility into their financing decision will therefore borrow less.

Now consider a firm that finances the assets described in Figure 9.2 with debt that matches the assets exactly in terms of cash flows and also in terms of the sensitivity of debt value to changes in macroeconomic variables. Figure 9.4 provides the firm value, debt value, and equity value for this firm.

Because debt value and firm value move together, the possibility of default is eliminated. This, in turn, will allow the firm to carry much more debt, and the added debt should provide tax benefits that make the firm more valuable. Thus, matching liability cash flows to asset cash flows allows firms to have higher optimal debt ratios.

9.7   THE RATIONALE FOR ASSET AND LIABILITY MATCHING

In Chapter 4, we argued that firms should focus on only market risk, because firm-specific risk can be diversified away. By the same token, it should not matter if firms use short-term debt to finance long-term assets, because investors in these firms can diversify away this risk anyway.

a.   True

b.   False

Comment.

Matching Liabilities to Assets
The first step every firm should take toward making the right financing choices is to understand how cash flows on its assets vary over time. In this section, we consider five

Figure 9.4 Firm Value Over Time with Long-Term Debt

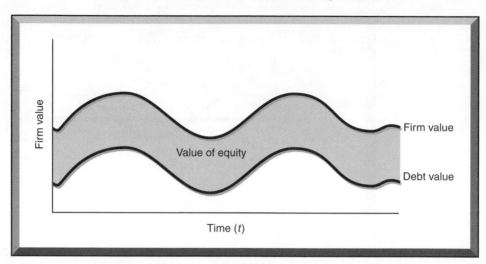

aspects of financing choices and how they are guided by the nature of the cash flows generated by assets. We begin by looking at the question of financing maturity—that is, the choice between long-term, medium-term, and short-term debt—and we argue that this choice will be determined by how long-term asset cash flows are. Next, we examine the choice between fixed and floating-rate debt and how this choice will be affected by the way inflation affects the cash flows on the assets financed by the debt. Third, we look at the currency in which the debt is to be denominated and link it to the currency in which asset cash flows are generated. Fourth, we evaluate when firms should use convertible debt instead of straight rate debt, and how this determination should be linked to how much growth there is in asset cash flows. Finally, we analyze other features that can be attached to debt, and how these features can be used to insulate a firm against specific factors that affect cash flows on assets, either positively or negatively.

A. Financing Maturity

Firms can issue debt of varying maturities, ranging from very short-term to very long-term. In making this choice, they should first be guided by how long-term the cash flows on their assets are. For instance, firms should not finance assets that generate cash flows over the short term (say, two to three years) using twenty-year debt. In this section, we begin by examining how best to assess the life of assets and liabilities, and then we consider alternative strategies to matching financing with asset cash flows.

Measuring the Cash Flow Lives of Liabilities and Assets When we talk about projects as having a ten-year life or a bond as having a thirty-year maturity, we are referring to the time when the project ends or the bond comes due. The cash flows on the project, however, occur over the ten-year period, and there are usually interest payments on the bond every six months until maturity. The *duration* of an asset or liability is a weighted maturity of all the cash flows on that asset or liability, where the weights are based on both the timing and the magnitude of the cash flows. In general, larger and earlier cash flows are weighted more than smaller and later cash flows. The duration of a thirty-year bond with coupons every six months will be lower than thirty years, and the duration of a ten-year project with cash flows each year will generally be lower than ten years.

A simple measure of duration for a bond, for instance, can be computed as follows:[12]

$$\text{Duration of bond} = \frac{dP/dr}{(1+r)} = \frac{\left[\sum_{t=1}^{t=N} \dfrac{t * \text{Coupon}_t}{(1+r)^t} + \dfrac{N * \text{Face value}}{(1+r)^N}\right]}{\left[\sum_{t=1}^{t=N} \dfrac{\text{Coupon}_t}{(1+r)^t} + \dfrac{\text{Face value}}{(1+r)^N}\right]}$$

where N is the maturity of the bond, and t is when each coupon comes due. Holding other factors constant, the duration of a bond will increase with the maturity of the bond and decrease with the coupon rate on the bond. For example, the duration of a 7%, thirty-year coupon bond, when interest rates are 8% and coupons are paid each year, can be written as follows:

$$\text{Duration of thirty-year bond} = \frac{dP/dr}{(1+r)} = \frac{\left[\sum_{t=1}^{t=30} \dfrac{t * \$70}{(1.08)^t} + \dfrac{30 * \$1,000}{(1.08)^{30}}\right]}{\left[\sum_{t=1}^{t=30} \dfrac{\$70}{(1.08)^t} + \dfrac{\$1,000}{(1.08)^N}\right]} = 12.41$$

What does the duration tell us? First, it provides a measure of when, on average, the cash flows on this bond come due, factoring in both the magnitude of the cash flows and the present value effects. This thirty-year bond, for instance, has cash flows that come due in about 12.41 years, after considering both the coupons and the face value. Second, it is an approximate measure of how much the bond price will change for small changes in interest rates. For instance, this thirty-year bond will drop in value by approximately 12.41% for a 1% increase in interest rates. Note that the duration is lower than the maturity. This will generally be true for coupon-bearing bonds, though special features in the bond may sometimes increase duration.[13] For zero-coupon bonds, the duration is equal to the maturity.

This measure of duration can be extended to any asset with expected cash flows. Thus, the duration of a project or asset can be estimated in terms of its predebt operating cash flows:

$$\text{Duration of project/Asset} = dPV/dr = \frac{\left[\sum_{t=1}^{t=N} \dfrac{t * \text{CF}_t}{(1+r)^t} + \dfrac{N * \text{Terminal value}}{(1+r)^N}\right]}{\left[\sum_{t=1}^{t=N} \dfrac{\text{CF}_t}{(1+r)^t} + \dfrac{\text{Terminal value}}{(1+r)^N}\right]}$$

---

[12]This measure of duration is called *Macaulay duration*, and it makes some strong assumptions about the yield curve; specifically, the yield curve is assumed to be flat and move in parallel shifts. Other duration measures change these assumptions. For purposes of our analysis, however, a rough measure of duration will suffice.

[13]For instance, making the coupon rate floating, rather than fixed, will reduce the duration of a bond. Similarly, adding a call feature to a bond will decrease duration, whereas making bonds extendible will increase duration.

where CF_t is the after-tax cash flow on the project in year t and the terminal value is a measure of how much the project is worth at the end of its lifetime of N years. The duration of an asset measures both when, on average, the cash flows on that asset come due and how much the value of the asset changes for a 1% change in interest rates.

One limitation of this analysis of duration is that it keeps cash flows fixed while interest rates change. On real projects, the cash flows will be adversely affected by increases in interest rates, and the degree of the effect will vary from business to business—more for cyclical firms (automobiles, housing) and less for noncyclical firms (food processing). Thus the actual duration of most projects will be higher than the estimates obtained by keeping cash flows constant. One way of estimating duration without depending on the traditional bond duration measures is to use historical data. If the duration is, in fact, a measure of how sensitive asset values are to interest rate changes, and a time series of data of asset value and interest rate changes is available, a regression of the former on the latter should yield a measure of duration:

$$\Delta \text{ Asset value}_t = a + b\Delta \text{ Interest rate}_t$$

In this regression, the coefficient b on interest rate changes should be a measure of the duration of the assets. For firms with publicly traded stocks and bonds, the asset value is the sum of the market values of the two. For a private company or for a public company with a short history, the regression can be run using changes in operating income as the dependent variable:

$$\Delta \text{ Operating income}_t = a + b\Delta \text{ Interest rate}_t$$

Here again, the coefficient b is a measure of the duration of the assets.

ILLUSTRATION 9.6 Calculating Duration for Rio Disney

In this application, we will calculate duration using the traditional measures for Rio Disney, which we analyzed in Chapter 5. The cash flows for the project are summarized in Table 9.9, together with the present value estimates, calculated using the cost of capital for this project of 8.62%.

$$\text{Duration of the Project} = 58{,}375/2{,}877 = 20.29 \text{ years}$$

This would suggest that the cash flows on this project come due, on average, in about twenty years. The duration is longer than the ten years because the cash flows in the first few years are negative and the terminal value assumes cash flows continue forever.

9.8 PROJECT LIFE AND DURATION

In investment analyses, analysts often cut off project lives at an arbitrary point and estimate a salvage or a terminal value. If these cash flows are used to estimate project duration, we will tend to

a. Understate duration.

b. Overstate duration.

c. Not affect the duration estimate.

Explain.

Year (t)	Annual Cash Flow	Terminal Value	Present Value @ 8.62%	Present Value * t
0	−$2,000		−$2,000	$0
1	−$1,000		−$921	−$921
2	−$860		−$729	−$1,457
3	−$270		−$211	−$632
4	$332		$239	$956
5	$453		$300	$1,500
6	$502		$305	$1,833
7	$538		$302	$2,112
8	$596		$307	$2,460
9	$660		$313	$2,821
10	$692	$10,669	$4,970	$49,704
			$2,877	$58,375

Table 9.9 CALCULATING A PROJECT'S DURATION: RIO DISNEY

Duration Matching Strategies   We just considered ways of estimating the duration of assets and liabilities. The basic idea is to match the duration of a firm's assets to the duration of its liabilities. This can be accomplished in two ways: by matching individual assets and liabilities, or by matching the assets of the firm with its collective liabilities. In the first approach, the Disney Rio project would be financed with bonds with duration of approximately twenty years. Although this approach provides a precise matching of each asset's characteristics to those of the financing used for it, it has several limitations. First, it is expensive to arrange separate financing for each project, given the issuance costs associated with raising funds. Second, this approach ignores interactions and correlations between projects that might make project-specific financing suboptimal for the firm. Consequently, this approach works only for companies that have very large, independent projects.

It is far more straightforward, and often cheaper, to match the duration of a firm's collective assets to the duration of its collective liabilities. If there is a significant difference, the firm might have to consider changing the duration of its liabilities. For instance, if Disney's assets have a duration of fifteen years, and its liabilities have a duration of only five years, the firm should try to extend the duration of its liabilities. It can do so in one of three ways. First, it can finance its new investments with debt of much longer duration; thus, using 100-year bonds to finance the new theme park will increase the weighted average duration of all its debt. Second, it can repay some of its short-term debt and replace it with long-term debt. Third, it can exchange or swap short-term debt for long-term debt.

9.9   PROJECT AND FIRM DURATION

Which of the following types of firms should be most likely to use project-specific financing (as opposed to financing the portfolio of projects)?

a.   Firms with a few large homogeneous projects

b.   Firms with a large number of small homogeneous projects

c. Firms with a few large heterogeneous projects

d. Firms with a large number of small heterogeneous projects

Explain.

B. The Fixed/Floating Rate Choice

One of the most common choices firms face is whether to make the coupon rate on bonds (and the interest rate on bank loans) a fixed rate or a floating-rate, pegged to an index rate such as the LIBOR, the ten-year Treasury bond rate or even the prime reate. In making this decision, we once again examine the characteristics of the projects being financed with the debt. In particular, we argue that the use of **floating-rate debt** should be more prevalent for firms that are uncertain about the duration of future projects and that have cash flows that move with the inflation rate.

Uncertainty about Future Projects The duration of assets and liabilities can be synchronized if assets and projects are well identified, interest rate sensitivity can be estimated, and the appropriate maturity for financing can be ascertained. For some firms, this estimation may be difficult to do, however. The firm might be changing its business mix by divesting itself of some assets and acquiring new ones. Alternatively, the industry to which the firm belongs might be changing. In such cases, the firm may use short-term or floating-rate loans[14] until it feels more certain about its future investment plans.

Cash Flows and Inflation Floating-rate loans have interest payments that increase as market interest rates rise and fall as rates fall. If a firm has assets whose earnings increase as interest rates go up and decrease as interest rates go down, it should finance those assets with floating-rate loans. The expected inflation rate is a key ingredient in determining interest rates. On floating-rate loans, this rate will lead to high interest payments in periods when inflation is high and low interest payments in periods when inflation is low. Firms whose earnings increase in periods of high inflation and decrease in periods with low inflation should therefore also be more likely to use floating-rate loans.

A number of factors determine whether a firm's earnings move with inflation. One critical ingredient is the degree of pricing power the firm possesses. Firms that have significant pricing power, either because they produce a unique product or because they are price leaders in their industries, have a much higher chance of being able to increase their earnings as inflation increases. Consequently, these firms should gain more by using floating-rate debt. Firms that do not have pricing power are much more likely to be see cash flows decline with unexpected inflation, and they should be more cautious about using floating-rate debt.

---

[14]The presence of derivatives provides an alternative for firms that are faced with this uncertainty. They can use the financing mix that is most appropriate given their current asset mix and use derivatives to manage the intermediate risk.

C. The Currency Choice

Many of the points we have made about interest rate risk exposure also apply to currency risk exposure. If any of a firm's assets or projects creates cash flows denominated in a currency other than the one in which the equity is denominated, currency risk exists. The debt of a firm can be issued in these currencies to reduce the currency risk. A firm that expects 20% of its cash flows to be in euros, for example, would attempt to issue euro-denominated debt in the same proportion to mitigate the currency risk. If the euro weakens and the assets become less valuable, the value of the debt will decline proportionately.

In recent years, firms have used more sophisticated variations on traditional bonds to manage foreign exchange risk on investments. For instance, Philip Morris issued a dual-currency bond in 1985—coupon payments were made in Swiss francs, and the principal payment was in U.S. dollars. In 1987, Westinghouse issued **principal exchange rate–linked securities** (**PERLSs**), in which the principal payment was the U.S. dollar value of 70.13 New Zealand dollars. Finally, firms have issued bonds embedded with foreign currency options called indexed currency option notes (ICONs), which combine a fixed rate bond with an option on a foreign currency. This approach is likely to work only for firms that have fairly predictable currency flows, however. For firms that do not have predictable currency flows, currency options or futures may be a cheaper way to manage currency risk, because the currency exposure changes from period to period.

D. The Choice between Straight and Convertible Bonds

Firms vary in terms of how much of their value comes from projects or assets they already own and how much comes from future growth. Firms that derive the bulk of their value from future growth should use different types of financing and design their financing differently than those that derive most of their value from assets in place. This is so because the current cash flows on high-growth firms will be low relative to the market value. These cash flows can be expected to grow substantially over time as the firm invests in new projects. Accordingly, the financing approach should not create large cash outflows early; it can create substantial cash outflows later, however, reflecting the cash flow patterns of the firm. In addition, the financing should exploit the value that the perception of high growth adds to securities, and it should put relatively few constraints on investment policies.

Straight bonds do not quite fit the bill, because they create large interest payments and do not gain much value from the high-growth perceptions. Furthermore, they are likely to include covenants designed to protect the bondholders, which restrict investment and future financing policy. Convertible bonds, by contrast, create much lower interest payments, impose fewer constraints, and gain value from higher growth perceptions. They might be converted into common stock, but only if the firm is successful. In 1999, for instance, Amazon.com, the online retailer, raised $1.25 billion from a convertible bond issue with a coupon rate of 3.5%. The firm benefited in two ways. First, the low coupon rate allowed the firm, which faced significant cash flow constraints at that point, to make its interest payments. Second, the value of the conversion option on the bond was increased by the perceived uncertainty about the firm's future cash flows and expectations of future growth.

E. Special Financing Features

Every firm is exposed to risk, coming from macroeconomic sources (such as recessions), acts of God (such as weather events), acts of competitors, or technological shifts. If a firm's exposure to any or all these sources of risk is substantial, it may choose to refrain from borrowing rather than risk default. One way firms can partially protect themselves against this default risk is to incorporate special features into bonds or debt shielding themselves against the most serious risk or risks. Two examples of bonds provide good illustrations:

- Insurance companies, for instance, have issued bonds whose payments can be drastically curtailed if there is a catastrophe that creates a substantial liability for the insurance company. By doing so, they reduce their debt payments in those periods when their overall cash flows are most negative, thereby reducing their likelihood of default.[15]

- Companies in commodity businesses have issued bonds whose principal and interest payments are tied to the price of the commodity. Because the operating cash flows in these firms are also positively correlated with commodity prices, adding this feature to debt decreases the likelihood of default and allows the firm to use more debt. In 1980, for instance, Sunshine Mining issued fifteen-year silver-linked bond issues, which combined a debt issue with an option on silver prices. As silver prices increased, the coupon rate on the bond increased; as silver prices decreased, the coupon rate on the bond decreased as well.

 IN PRACTICE: CUSTOMIZED BONDS

In keeping with the notion of customizing bonds to match asset cash flows, firms have come up with increasingly creative solutions in recent years. In this endeavor, they have been assisted by two developments. The first is that investors in bond markets are more open to both pricing and buying complex bonds than they were in the 1970s and even the 1980s. The second is that advancements in option pricing allow us to value complicated securities with multiple options embedded in them. Consider a few examples:

- In the early 1990s, David Bowie acquired the rights to all of his songs, bundled them, and sold bonds backed by sales of his recording. What made the bonds unique was the fact that the interest rate on the bonds was tied to the sales of his recordings—higher (lower) rates with higher (lower) sales.

---

[15]As an example of a catastrophe bond issue, consider the bond issue made by USAA Insurance Company. The company privately placed $477 million of these bonds, backed up by reinsurance premiums, in June 1997. The company was protected in the event of any hurricane that created more that $1 billion in damage to the East Coast any time before June 1998. The bonds came in two classes; in the first class, called principal-at-risk, the company could reduce the principal on the bond in the event of a hurricane; in the second class, which was less risky to investors, the coupon payments would be suspended in the event of a hurricane, but the principal would be protected. In return, in October 1997 the investors in these bonds were earnings an extra yield of almost 1.5% on the principal-at-risk bonds and almost 0.5% on the principal-protected bonds.

- In 2001, an Italian soccer team issued bonds to fund the construction of a stadium but tied the interest rate on the bond to the success of the team. Specifically, the interest rate on the bond would rise if the team stayed in the first division (and drew larger crowds and revenues) and drop if the team dropped to the second division. ■

9.10 SPECIAL FEATURES AND INTEREST RATES

Adding special features to bonds, such as linking coupon payments to commodity prices or catastrophes, will reduce their attractiveness to investors and make the interest rates paid on them higher. It follows then that

a. Companies should not add these special features to bonds.

b. Adding these special features cannot create value for the firm if the bonds are fairly priced.

c. Adding special features can still create value even if the bonds are fairly priced.

Explain.

Market Timing, Interest Rate Illusions, and Mismatched Debt: A Behavioral Perspective
The argument that we should match the cash flow on debt to the cash flow on assets is based on the premise that managers are not very good at timing markets or assessing what types of debt are cheap or expensive. That premise may not be wrong, but that does not stop managers from trying to use what they perceive to be "cheap" debt, even if it results in mismatching debt to assets.

- *Playing the term structure.*   In the last chapter, we presented evidence that managers try to time markets with equity and bond issues, issuing more equity when they feel that their stock is underpriced and less equity when they feel that it is overpriced. There is also evidenc that the managers are more likely to use short-term debt when the yield curve is "too steep" and more long-term debt when it is "too flat."

- *The convertible option.*   The use of convertible securities—convertible bonds and preferred stock—increases when managers perceive their stock to be overpriced and decreases when it is considered underpriced.

- *The interest rate illusion.*   When comparing different types of borrowing, some managers find themselves comparing the interest rates on the debt issues, with the view that lower interest rates represent cheaper financing. It is this rationale that allows some managers to think of short-term debt as cheaper than long term debt and of convertible debt as less expensive than straight debt. In emerging markets, borrowing in the local currency (with higher expected inflation) looks more expensive than borrowing in a foreign currency.

As a consequence of these factors, the debt used by a firm can be at variance with the assets funded with this debt. While it may be impractical and perhaps even unwise to ask managers to stop trying to pick the cheapest debt, there are two things we can do to minimize potential damage:

1. We can impose constraints that prevent the mismatch from becoming too severe. For instance, a firm whose assets are 20% short-term and 80% long-term may specify that short-term debt cannot exceed 40% of overall debt.

2. We can use the derivatives and swaps markets to hedge some of the mismatch risk, at least at the aggregate level. Thus, a firm that chooses to use Japanese yen to fund euro assets because managers believe that yen debt is cheaper than euro debt can use currency futures to hedge some of its yen/euro risk exposure.

II. Tax Implications

As firms become more creative with their financing choices, structuring debt that behaves more like equity, there is a danger that the tax authorities might decide to treat the financing as equity and prevent the firm from deducting interest payments. Because the primary benefit of borrowing is a tax benefit, it is important that firms preserve—and, if possible, increase—this tax benefit.

It is also conceivable that the favorable tax treatment of some financing choices may encourage firms to use them more than others, even if it means deviating from the choices that would be dictated by the asset characteristics. Thus, a firm that has assets that generate cash flows in Japanese yen may decide to issue dollar-denominated bonds to finance these assets if it derives a larger tax benefit from issuing dollar debt than yen debt.

The danger of structuring financing with the intention of saving on taxes is that changes in the tax law can very quickly render the benefit moot and leave the firm with a financing mix unsuited to its asset mix.

III. Views of Ratings Agencies, Equity Research Analysts, and Regulatory Authorities

Firms are rightfully concerned about the views of equity research analysts and ratings agencies regarding their actions, but in our view, they often overestimate the influence of both groups. Analysts represent stockholders, and ratings agencies represent bondholders; consequently, they take very different views of the same actions. For instance, analysts may view a stock repurchase by a company with limited project opportunities as a positive action, whereas ratings agencies may view it as negative, and lower ratings in response. Analysts and ratings agencies also measure the impact of financing choices made by a firm using very different criteria. In general, analysts view a firm's actions through the prism of higher earnings per share and by looking at the firm relative to comparable firms, using multiples such as price earnings or price–to–book value ratios. Ratings agencies, on the other hand, measure the effect of actions on the financial ratios, such as debt ratios and coverage ratios, which they then use to assess default risk and assign ratings.

Given the weight attached to the views of both these groups, firms sometimes design securities with the intent of satisfying both. In some cases, they find ways of raising funds that seem to make both groups happy, at least on the surface. To illustrate, consider the use of leasing, before generally accepted accounting principles required capitalizing of leases. Leasing increased the real financial leverage of the company, and thus, the earnings per share, but it did not affect the measured leverage of the company because it was not viewed as debt. To the degree that analysts and ratings agencies rely on quantitative measures and do not properly factor in the effects of these actions, firms can exploit their limitations. In fact, they still do with operating leases. In a more recent example, a security labeled as trust-preferred stock has become popular largely because of the different ways in which it is viewed by various entities. It is viewed as debt by the equity research analysts and tax authorities, with the preferred dividend being tax-deductible. Trust preferred is viewed as equity by ratings agencies, allowing the firms issuing it to retain high ratings.[16]

When securities are designed in such a way, the real question is whether the markets are fooled—and if so, for how long. A firm that substitutes leases and trust-preferred stock for debt may fool the ratings agencies and even the debt markets for some time, but it cannot evade the reality that it is much more levered, and hence much riskier.

This balancing act becomes even more precarious for regulated firms such as banks and insurance companies. These firms also have to make sure that any financing actions they take are viewed favorably by regulatory authorities. For instance, financial service firms have to maintain equity–capital ratios that exceed regulatory minimums. However, regulatory authorities use a different definition of equity capital than ratings agencies and equity research analysts, and firms can exploit these differences. For instance, banks are among the heaviest users of conventional preferred stock, because preferred stock is treated as equity by bank regulators. In the past few years, insurance companies in the United States have issued surplus notes,[17] which are considered debt for tax purposes and equity under insurance accounting rules, enabling them to have the best of both worlds—they can issue debt, while counting it as equity.[18]

IV. The Effects of Asymmetric Information

Firms generally have more information about their future prospects than do financial markets. This asymmetry in information creates friction when firms try to raise funds. In particular, firms with good prospects try to distinguish themselves from firms without such prospects by taking actions that are costly and difficult to imitate. Firms also try to design securities to reduce the effect of uncertainty in future cash flows on bondholders. In the process, they may issue securities that are not optimal from the standpoint of matching their asset cash flows but that are specifically designed to convey information to financial markets and reduce the effects of uncertain cash flows on value.

A number of researchers have used this information asymmetry argument to draw very different conclusions about the debt structure firms should use. Myers (1977) argued that firms tend to under invest as a consequence of the asymmetry of information. One proposed solution to the problem is to issue short-term debt, even if the assets being financed are long-term assets.[19] Flannery (1986) and Kale and Noe (1990) note that although both short-tem and long-term debt will be mispriced in the presence of asymmetric information, long-term debt will be mispriced more.[20] Consequently, they

---

[16]Ratings agencies initially treated trust-preferred stock as equity. Over time, they have become more cautious. By the late 1990s, firms were being given credit for only a portion of the trust-preferred stock (about 40%).

[17]Surplus notes are bonds where the interest payments need to be made only if the firm is profitable. If it is not, the interest payments are cumulated and paid in subsequent periods.

[18]In recent years, insurance companies have issued billions of dollars of surplus notes in the private placement market.

[19]S. C. Myers, "Determinants of Corporate Borrowing," *Journal of Financial Economics* 5, no. 2:147–175.

[20]M. J. Flannery, "Asymmetric Information and Risky Debt Maturity Choice," *Journal of Finance* 41, no. 1:19–38; J. R. Kale and T. H. Noe, "Risky Debt Maturity Choice in a Sequential Game Equilibrium," *Journal of Financial Research* 8:155–165.

argue that high-quality firms will issue short-term debt, and low-quality firms will issue long-term debt. Goswami, Noe, and Rebello (1995) analyze the design of securities and relate it to uncertainty about future cash flows.[21] They conclude that if the asymmetry of information concerns uncertainty about long-term cash flows, firms should issue coupon-bearing long-term debt with restrictions on dividends. In contrast, firms with uncertainty about near-term cash flows and significant refinancing risk should issue long-term debt, without restrictions on dividend payments. When uncertainty about information is uniformly distributed across time, firms should finance with short-term debt.

V. Implications for Agency Costs

The final consideration in designing securities is the provision of features intended to reduce the agency conflicts between stockholders and bondholders. As we noted in Chapter 7, differences between bondholders and stockholders on investment, financing, and dividend policy decisions can influence financing decisions by increasing either the costs of borrowing or the constraints associated with borrowing. In some cases, firms design securities with the specific intent of reducing this conflict and its associated costs.

- We explained that convertible bonds are a good choice for growth companies because of their cash flow characteristics. By allowing bondholders to become stockholders if the stock price increases enough, convertible bonds can also reduce the anxiety of bondholders about equity investors investing in riskier projects and expropriating wealth

- More corporate bonds include embedded put options that allow bondholders to put the bonds back at face value if the firm takes a specified action (such as increasing leverage) or if its rating drops. In a variation, in 1988, Manufacturer Hanover issued rating-sensitive notes promising bondholders higher coupons if the firm's rating deteriorated over time. Thus, bond investors would be protected in the event of a downgrade.

- In the same time period, Merrill Lynch introduced liquid yield option notes (LYONs), which incorporated put and conversion features to protect against both the risk shifting and claim substitution to which bondholders are exposed.

Barclay and Smith (1996) examined debt issues by U.S. companies between 1981 and 1993 and concluded that high-growth firms are more likely to issue short-term debt with higher priority.[22] This finding is consistent with both the information asymmetry argument and the agency cost argument, because lenders are more exposed to both costs with high-growth firms.

In Summary

In choosing the right financing vehicles to use, firms should begin by examining the characteristics of the assets they are financing and try to match the maturity, interest

---

[21]G. Goswami, T. Noe, and M. Rebello, "Debt Financing under Asymmetric Information," *Journal of Finance* 50, no. 2:633–659.
[22]M. J. Barclay and C. W. Smith, "On Financial Architecture: Leverage, Maturity and Priority," *Journal of Applied Corporate Finance* 8, no. 4:4–17.

Figure 9.5 The Design of Debt: An Overview of the Process

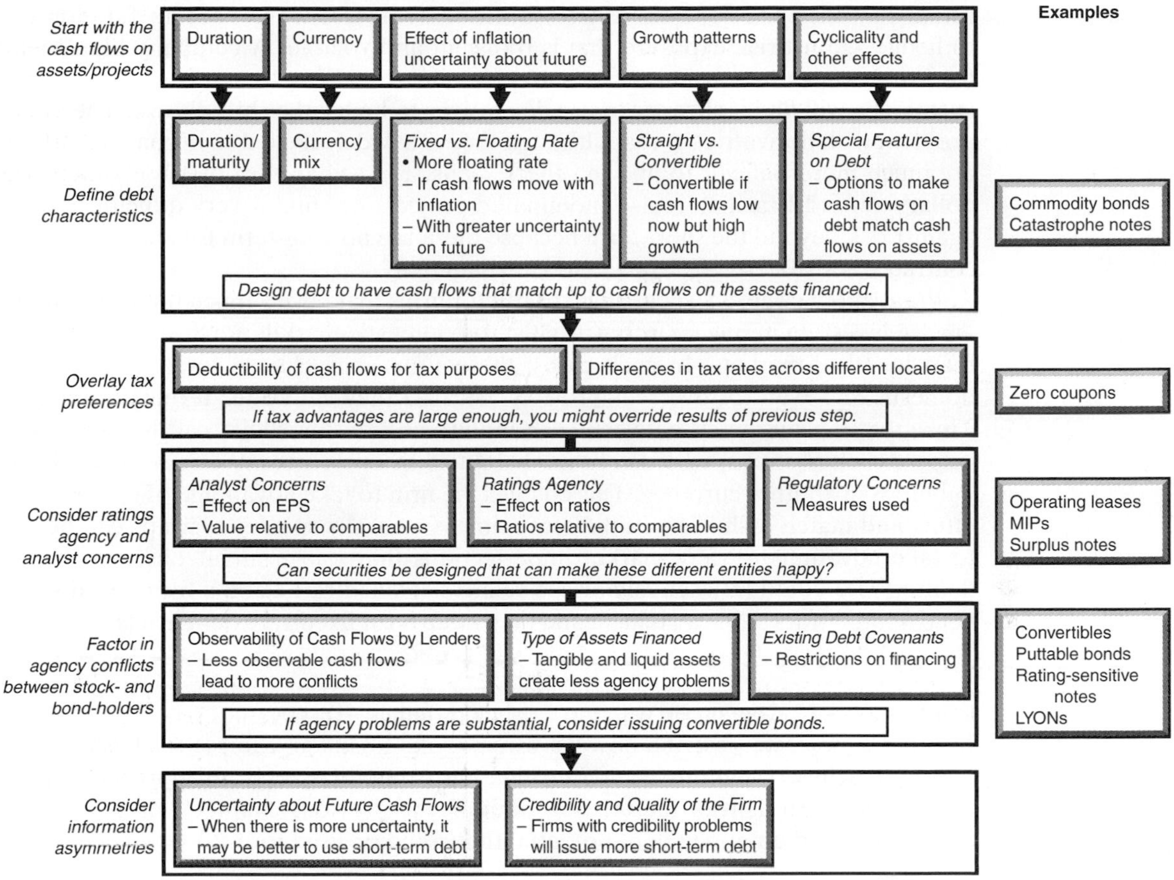

					Examples

Start with the cash flows on assets/projects

Duration	Currency	Effect of inflation uncertainty about future	Growth patterns	Cyclicality and other effects

Define debt characteristics

Duration/ maturity	Currency mix	**Fixed vs. Floating Rate** • More floating rate – If cash flows move with inflation – With greater uncertainty on future	**Straight vs. Convertible** – Convertible if cash flows low now but high growth	**Special Features on Debt** – Options to make cash flows on debt match cash flows on assets

Design debt to have cash flows that match up to cash flows on the assets financed.

Examples: Commodity bonds / Catastrophe notes

Overlay tax preferences

Deductibility of cash flows for tax purposes	Differences in tax rates across different locales

If tax advantages are large enough, you might override results of previous step.

Examples: Zero coupons

Consider ratings agency and analyst concerns

Analyst Concerns – Effect on EPS – Value relative to comparables	**Ratings Agency** – Effect on ratios – Ratios relative to comparables	**Regulatory Concerns** – Measures used

Can securities be designed that can make these different entities happy?

Examples: Operating leases / MIPs / Surplus notes

Factor in agency conflicts between stock- and bond-holders

Observability of Cash Flows by Lenders – Less observable cash flows lead to more conflicts	**Type of Assets Financed** – Tangible and liquid assets create less agency problems	**Existing Debt Covenants** – Restrictions on financing

If agency problems are substantial, consider issuing convertible bonds.

Examples: Convertibles / Puttable bonds / Rating-sensitive notes / LYONs

Consider information asymmetries

Uncertainty about Future Cash Flows – When there is more uncertainty, it may be better to use short-term debt	**Credibility and Quality of the Firm** – Firms with credibility problems will issue more short-term debt

rate, currency mix, and special features of their financing to these characteristics. They can then superimpose tax considerations, the views of analysts and ratings agencies, agency costs, and the effects of asymmetric information to modify this financing mix. Figure 9.5 summarizes the discussion.

 IN PRACTICE: THE ROLE OF DERIVATIVES AND SWAPS

In the past thirty years, the futures and options markets have developed to the point that firms can hedge exchange rate, interest rate, commodity price, and other risks using derivatives. In fact, firms can use derivatives to protect themselves against risk exposures generated by mismatching debt and assets. Thus, a firm that borrows in dollars to fund projects denominated in yen can use dollar/yen forward, futures, and options contracts to reduce or even eliminate the resulting risk. Given the existence of these derivatives, you may wonder why it is even necessary to go through the process we have just described to arrive at the perfect debt. We suggest two reasons. The first is that the use of derivatives can be costly if used recurrently. Thus a firm with a stable portion of its revenues coming from yen will find it cheaper to use yen debt rather than derivatives to correct mismatched debt. Derivatives are useful, however, to hedge against risk exposure that is transient and volatile. A company like Boeing, for instance, whose currency exposure can shift from year to year depending on its customers, will find it cheaper to use derivatives to hedge the shifting risk. The second problem with derivatives is that although they are widely available in some cases, they are much more difficult to find in others. Thus, a Brazilian firm that borrows in U.S. dollars to fund Brazilian real–denominated projects will find it very difficult to hedge against risk beyond the short term because there are no long-term forward and futures contracts available for dollars versus Brazilian real.

What about swaps? Swaps can be useful for firms that have a much better reputation among investors in one country (usually, the domestic market in which they operate) than in other markets. In such cases, these firms may choose to raise their funds domestically, even for overseas projects, because they get better terms on financing. This creates a mismatch between cash inflows and outflows that can be resolved by using currency swaps, where a firm's liabilities in one currency can be swapped for liabilities in another currency. This enables the firm to take advantage of its reputation effect and match cash flows at the same time. Generally speaking, swaps can be used to take advantage of any market imperfections that a firm might observe. Thus, if floating-rate debt is attractively priced relative to fixed-rate debt, a firm that does not need floating-rate debt can issue it and then swap it for fixed-rate debt at a later date. ■

ILLUSTRATION 9.7 Coming Up with the Financing Details—Disney

In this example, we describe how we would make financing choices for Disney, using two approaches: one intuitive and the other more quantitative. Both approaches should be considered in light of the analysis done in the previous chapter, which suggested that Disney had untapped debt potential that could be used for future projects.

Intuitive Approach

The intuitive approach begins with an analysis of the characteristics of a typical project and uses it to make recommendations for the firm's financing. For Disney, the analysis is complicated by the fact that as a diverse entertainment business with theme park holdings, its typical project varies by type of business. In Chapter 4, we broke down Disney into four businesses—studio entertainment, media networks, park resorts, and consumer products. In Table 9.10 we consider the typical project in each business and the appropriate debt for each.

A Quantitative Approach

A quantitative approach estimates Disney's sensitivity to changes in a number of macro economic variables using two measures: Disney's firm value (the market value of debt and equity) and its operating income.

Value Sensitivity to Factors: Past Data

The value of a firm is the obvious choice when it comes to measuring the firm's sensitivity to changes in interest rates, inflation rates, or currency rates, because firm

Table 9.10   DESIGNING DISNEY'S PERFECT DEBT: INTUITIVE ANALYSIS

	Project Cash Flow Characteristics	**Type of Financing**
Studio entertainment	Movie projects are likely to 1. Be short-term 2. Have cash outflows primarily in dollars (because Disney makes most of its movies in the United States), but cash inflows could have a substantial foreign currency component (because of overseas revenues) 3. Have net cash flows that are heavily driven by whether the movie is a hit, something often difficult to predict	Debt should be • Short-term • Primarily dollar debt • If possible, tied to the success of movies (*The Lion King* or *Mulan* bonds)
Media networks	Projects are likely to be 1. Short-term 2. Primarily in dollars (although foreign component is growing) 3. Driven by advertising revenues and show success (Nielsen ratings)	Debt should be • Short-term • Primarily dollar debt • If possible, linked to network ratings
Park resorts	Projects are likely to be 1. Very long-term 2. Primarily in dollars, but a significant proportion of revenues come from foreign tourists, who are likely to stay away if the dollar strengthens 3. Affected by success of studio entertainment and media networks divisions	Debt should be • Long-term • A mix of currencies, based on tourist makeup
Consumer products	Projects are likely to be short- to medium-term and linked to the success of the movie division; most of Disney's product offerings are derived from its movie productions	Debt should be • Medium-term • Dollar debt

value reflects the effect of these variables on current and future cash flows as well as on discount rates. We begin by collecting past data on firm value, operating income, and the macroeconomic variables against which we want to measure its sensitivity. In the case of Disney, we choose four broad measures (see Table 9.11):

- ***Long-term Treasury bond rate,*** because the sensitivity of firm value to changes in interest rates provides a measure of the duration of the projects. It also provides insight into whether the firm should use fixed- or floating-rate debt; a firm whose

Table 9.11   DISNEY'S FIRM VALUE AND MACROECONOMIC VARIABLES

	Operating Income (OI)	Firm Value (V)	% Chg in OI	% Chg in V	Chg in T-Bond Rate	% Chg in GDP	% Chg in CPI	% Chg in US$
2008	$7,404	$72,357	8.42%	−6.55%	−1.44%	−1.18%	−4.26%	10.88%
2007	$6,829	$77,428	27.53%	−2.13%	−0.65%	2.93%	2.19%	−11.30%
2006	$5,355	$79,116	30.39%	35.81%	0.30%	3.40%	−1.84%	−2.28%
2005	$4,107	$58,256	1.46%	3.09%	0.16%	3.68%	0.66%	3.98%
2004	$4,048	$56,510	49.21%	8.41%	0.13%	3.72%	1.34%	−3.92%
2003	$2,713	$52,125	13.80%	19.03%	0.05%	4.32%	−0.65%	−14.59%
2002	$2,384	$43,792	−15.82%	−7.02%	−0.97%	2.80%	1.44%	−11.17%
2001	$2,832	$47,099	12.16%	−46.31%	−0.18%	−0.04%	−2.50%	7.45%
2000	$2,525	$87,716	−22.64%	34.80%	−0.98%	2.24%	0.96%	7.73%
1999	$3,264	$65,073	−15.07%	1.50%	1.56%	4.70%	1.04%	1.68%
1998	$3,843	$64,110	−2.59%	−1.63%	−1.03%	4.51%	0.11%	−4.08%
1997	$3,945	$65,173	30.46%	19.16%	−0.63%	4.33%	−1.43%	9.40%
1996	$3,024	$54,695	33.68%	70.95%	0.80%	4.43%	0.31%	4.14%
1995	$2,262	$31,995	25.43%	38.75%	−2.09%	2.01%	−0.08%	−0.71%
1994	$1,804	$23,059	15.59%	3.69%	1.92%	4.12%	0.27%	−5.37%
1993	$1,560	$22,238	21.23%	8.65%	−0.83%	2.50%	−0.72%	0.56%
1992	$1,287	$20,467	28.18%	26.57%	−0.02%	4.15%	0.64%	6.89%
1991	$1,004	$16,171	−21.98%	27.90%	−1.26%	1.09%	−2.89%	0.69%
1990	$1,287	$12,643	16.01%	−24.90%	0.12%	0.65%	0.43%	−8.00%
1989	$1,109	$16,834	40.64%	−2.64%	−1.11%	2.66%	0.51%	2.04%
1988	$789	$17,290	11.65%	65.50%	0.26%	3.66%	0.60%	1.05%
1987	$707	$10,447	53.02%	85.24%	1.53%	4.49%	2.54%	−12.01%
1986	$462	$5,640	25.15%	61.24%	−1.61%	2.83%	−2.33%	−15.26%
1985	$369	$3,498	157.99%	24.37%	−2.27%	4.19%	3.89%	−13.51%

operating income increases or decreases with interest rates should consider using floating-rate loans.

- **_Real GDP (gross domestic product),_** because the sensitivity of firm value to this variable provides a measure of the cyclicality of the firm.

- **_Exchange rates,_** because the sensitivity of firm value to currency movements provides a measure of the exposure to currency rate risk and thus helps determine what the currency mix for the debt should be.

- **_Inflation rate,_** because the sensitivity of firm value to the inflation rate helps determine whether the interest rate on the debt should be fixed- or floating-rate debt.

$$\text{Enterprise value} = \text{Market value of equity} + \text{Book value of debt} - \text{Cash}$$
$$\text{CPI} = \text{Consumer Price Index}$$

Once these data have been collected, we can estimate the sensitivity of firm value to changes in the macroeconomic variables by regressing changes in firm value each year against changes in each of the individual variables.

I. Sensitivity to Changes in Interest Rates

As discussed earlier, the duration of a firm's projects provides useful information for determining the maturity of its debt. Although bond-based duration measures may provide some answers, they will understate the duration of assets or projects if the cash flows on these assets or projects themselves vary with interest rates. Regressing changes in firm value at Disney against changes in interest rates over this period yields the following result (with *t*-statistics parenthesized):[23]

$$\text{Change in firm value} = 0.1949 + 2.9439 \text{ (Change in interest rates)}$$
$$\quad (2.89) \quad (0.50)$$

Based on this regression, Disney's firm value increase as interest rates go up, indicating that its assets have very short duration. However, the standard error on the coefficient is so large that we are reluctant to draw strong conclusions based on this regression.

II. Sensitivity to Changes in the Economy

Is Disney a cyclical firm? One way to answer this question is to measure the sensitivity of firm value to changes in economic growth. Regressing changes in firm value against changes in the real GDP over this period yields the following result:

$$\text{Change in firm value} = -0.0826 + 8.89 \text{ (GDP Growth)}$$
$$\quad (0.65) \quad (2.36^{a})$$

Disney's value as a firm has been affected significantly by economic growth. Again, to the extent that we trust the coefficients from this regression, this would suggest that Disney is a cyclical firm whose value increases in good times and decreases in bad times.

III. Sensitivity to Changes in the Inflation Rates

We earlier made the argument, based on asset/liability matching, that firms whose values tend to move with inflation should be more likely to issue floating-rate debt. To examine whether Disney fits this pattern, we regressed changes in firm value against changes in the inflation rate over this period with the following result:

$$\text{Change in firm value} = 0.18 + 2.71 \text{ (Change in inflation rate)}$$
$$\quad (2.90) \quad (0.80)$$

Disney's firm value is unaffected by changes in inflation because the coefficient on inflation is not statistically different from 0. Interest payments have to be made out of operating cash flows, so we will also have to look at how operating income changes with inflation before we can make a final decision on this issue.

IV. Sensitivity to Changes in the Dollar

We can answer the question of how sensitive Disney's value is to changes in currency rates by looking at how the firm's value changes as a function of changes in currency

---

[23]To ensure that the coefficient on this regression is a measure of duration, we compute the change in the interest rate as follows: $(r_t - r_{t-1})/(1 + r_{t-1})$. Thus, if the long-term bond rate goes from 8% to 9%, we compute the change to be $(0.09 - 0.08)/1.08$.

rates. Regressing changes in firm value against changes in the dollar over this period yields the following regression:

$$\text{Change in firm value} = 0.17 - 0.65 \text{ (Change in dollar)}$$
$$(2.63) \quad (0.80)$$

At least in general terms. Disney's firm value decreases as the dollar strengthens. However, the relationship between value and exchange rates is weak, indicating that there are aspects of Disney's business that are helped by a stronger dollar.

Cash Flow Sensitivity to Factors: Past Data
In some cases, it is more reasonable to estimate the sensitivity of operating cash flows directly against changes in interest rates, inflation, and other variables. This is particularly true when we are designing interest payments on debt, because these payments are to be made out of operating income. For instance, although our regression of firm value against inflation rates showed a negative relationship and led to the conclusion that Disney should not issue floating-rate debt, we might reverse our view if operating income were positively correlated with inflation rates. For Disney, we repeated the analysis using operating income as the dependent variable, rather than firm value. Because the procedure for the analysis is similar, we summarize the conclusions here.

- Regressing changes in operating cash flow against changes in interest rates over this period yields the following result:

$$\text{Change in operating income} = 0.1958 + 6.5439 \text{ (Change in interest rates)}$$
$$(2.56) \quad (0.97)$$

  Disney's operating income, unlike its firm value, has moved with interest rates, albeit in the opposite directions. Again, this result has to be considered with caution in light of the low *t*-statistics on the coefficients.

- Regressing changes in operating cash flow against changes in real GDP over this period yields the following regression:

$$\text{Change in operating income} = 0.04 + 6.06 \text{ (GDP growth)}$$
$$(0.22) \quad (1.30)$$

  Disney's operating income, like its firm value, does increase with operating income, confirming the conclusion that Disney is a cyclical firm.

- Regressing changes in operating cash flow against changes in the dollar over this period yields the following regression:

$$\text{Change in operating income} = 0.19 - 1.57 \text{ (Change in dollar)}$$
$$(2.63) \quad (1.73^b)$$

  Disney's operating income, like its firm value, is negatively affected by a stronger dollar, but the relationship is much stronger.

- Regressing changes in operating cash flow against changes in inflation over this period yields the following result:

$$\text{Change in operating income} = 0.22 + 8.79 \text{ (Change in inflation rate)}$$
$$(3.28) \quad (2.40)$$

Unlike firm value, which sees only minor effects from changes in inflation, Disney's operating income moves strongly with inflation, rising as inflation increases. This suggests that Disney has substantial pricing power, allowing it to transmit inflation increases into its prices and operating income. This makes a strong case for the use of floating-rate debt.

The question of what to do when operating income and firm value have different results can be resolved fairly simply. For issues relating to the overall design of the debt, the firm value regression should be relied on more; for issues relating to the design of interest payments on the debt, the operating income regression should be used more. Thus, for the duration measure, the regression of firm value on interest rates should generally give a more precise estimate. For the inflation rate sensitivity, because it affects the choice of interest payments (fixed or floating), the operating income regression should be relied on more.

Bottom-Up Estimates for Debt Design
While this type of analysis yields quantitative results, those results should be taken with a grain of salt. They make sense only if the firm has been in its current business for a long time and expects to remain in it for the foreseeable future. In today's environment, in which firms find their business mixes changing dramatically from period to period as they divest some businesses and acquire new ones, it is unwise to base too many conclusions on a historical analysis. In such cases, we might want to look at the characteristics of the industry in which a firm plans to expand, rather than using past earnings or firm value as a basis for the analysis. Furthermore, the small sample sizes used tend to yield regression estimates that are not statistically significant (as is the case with the duration estimate that we obtained for Disney from the firm value regression).

To illustrate, we looked at the sector estimates for each of the sensitivity measures for the entertainment, theme park, and consumer product businesses:[24]

	Interest Rates	**GDP Growth**	**Inflation**	**Currency**	**Weights**
Studio entertainment	−3.70	0.56	1.41	−1.23	9.88%
Media networks	−4.50	0.70	−3.05	−1.58	58.92%
Park resorts	−6.47	0.22	−1.45	−3.21	29.88%
Consumer products	−4.88	0.13	−5.51	−3.01	1.32%
Disney	*−5.01*	*0.54*	*−2.16*	*−2.05*	

---

[24]These sector estimates were obtained by aggregating the firm values of all firms in a sector on a quarter-by-quarter basis going back twelve years, and then regressing changes in this aggregate firm value against changes in the macroeconomic variable each quarter.

These bottom-up estimates, akin to bottom-up betas, suggest that Disney should be issuing long-term fixed-rate debt with a duration of 5.01 years and that firms in this sector are relatively unaffected by movements in the overall economy. Like Disney, firms in these businesses tend to be hurt by a stronger dollar, but unlike Disney, they do not have much pricing power (note the negative coefficient on inflation). The sector averages also have the advantage of being more precise than the firm-specific estimates and can be relied on more.

Overall Recommendations

Based on the analyses of firm value and operating income, as well as the sector averages, our recommendations would essentially match those of the intuitive approach, but they would have more depth to them because of the additional information we have acquired from the quantitative analysis:

- The debt issued should be long-term and should have duration of approximately five years.
- A significant portion of the debt should be floating-rate debt, reflecting Disney's capacity to pass inflation through to its customers, and operating income's tendency to increase as interest rates increase.
- Given Disney's sensitivity to a stronger dollar, a significant portion of the debt should be in foreign currencies. The specific currency used and the magnitude of the foreign currency debt should reflect where Disney generates its revenues. Based on 2009 numbers, this would indicate that about 20% of the debt should be in euros and about 10% of the debt in yen, reflecting Disney's larger exposures in Europe and Japan. As its businesses expand into Latin America (ESPN and broadcasting) and emerging Asia (Hong Kong Disney), it may want to consider using debt in other currencies as well.

These conclusions can be used to both design the new debt issues that the firm will be making going forward, and to evaluate the existing debt on the firm's books to see if there is a mismatching of assets and financing in the current firm. Examining Disney's debt at the end of 2008, we note the following:

- Disney has $16 billion in debt with a face-value weighted average maturity of 5.38 years. Allowing for the fact that the maturity of debt is higher than the duration, this would indicate that Disney's debt is of the right maturity.
- Of the debt, about 10% is yen-denominated debt but the rest is in U.S. dollars. Based on our analysis, we would suggest that Disney increase its proportion of debt in other currencies to about 20% in euros and about 5% in Chinese yuan.
- Disney has no convertible debt, and about 24% of its debt is floating-rate debt, which is appropriate given its status as a mature company with significant pricing power. In fact, we would argue for increasing the floating-rate portion of the debt to about 40%.

If Disney accepts the recommendation that its debt should be more more foreign currency and more floating-rate debt, it can get there in two ways:

1. It can swap some of its existing fixed-rate dollar debt for floating-rate foreign-currency debt. Given Disney's standing in financial markets and its large market capitalization, this should not be difficult to do.

2. If Disney is planning new debt issues, either to get to a higher debt ratio or to fund new investments, it can use primarily floating-rate foreign currency debt to fund these new investments. Although it may be mismatching the funding on these investments, its debt matching will become better at the company level.

macrodur.xls: This spreadsheet allows you to estimate the sensitivity of firm value and operating income to changes in macroeconomic variables.

There is a data set online that summarizes the results of regressing firm value against macroeconomic variables, by sector, for U.S. companies.

ILLUSTRATION 9.8 **Estimating the Right Financing Mix for Bookscape, Aracruz, Tata Chemicals, and Deutsche Bank**

Although we will not examine the right financing type for Bookscape, Aracruz, and Deutsche Bank to the same level of detail that we did Disney, we will summarize, based on our understanding of their businesses, what we think will be the best kind of financing for each of these firms:

- *Bookscape.* Given Bookscape's dependence on revenues at its New York bookstore, we would design the debt to be
  - Long-term, because the store is a long-term investment
  - Dollar-denominated, because all the cash flows are in dollars
  - Fixed-rate debt, because Bookscape's lack of pricing power makes it unlikely that it can keep pace with inflation

  It is worth noting that operating leases fulfill all of these conditions, making it the appropriate debt for Bookscape. Because that is the only debt that Bookscape carries currently, we would suggest no changes.

- *Aracruz.* Aracruz operates most of its paper plants in Brazil but gets a significant proportion of its products overseas. A significant portion of its revenues in 2008 were from other countries, and the bulk of these revenues were dollar-denominated, while its operating expenses are in R$. Given this structure, we would design debt to be
  - Long-term, because a typical paper plant has a life in excess of twenty years
  - Dollar-denominated, because the cash inflows are primarily in dollars
  - Of an interest rate linked to pulp prices if possible, given the volatility of paper prices

The existing debt at Aracruz is primarily R$ debt with an average maturity of 3.2 years. Although this may reflect the difficulties that Brazilian firms have faced in borrowing long-term historically, the constraints on borrowing long-term are easing for many emerging market companies that derive the bulk of their revenues in dollars.

- **Tata Chemicals.** As a manufacturing firm with the bulk of its revenues in India, Tata Chemicals should stick with debt that has the following characteristics:

  - Medium- to long-term debt, reflecting the life of the plant and equipment used to produce its fertilizer and chemical products

  - Fixed-rate debt, since the company is unlikely to have much pricing power in this business

  - Rupee-denominated debt, since almost 90% of Tata Chemical's revenues come from India

  The existing debt at Tata Chemicals matches this ideal debt for the most part (since it is fixed-rate and rupee-based), though the average maturity of the existing debt, at about three years, is lower than what we would expect for the firm. While part of the reason for this mismatch is that banks in India may be unwilling to lend for longer periods, the expansion of corporate bond markets in India should increase access to longer-term borrowing.

- **Deutsche Bank.** In the case of Deutsche Bank, we will steer away from explicit recommendations of what type of debt should be used, for two reasons. The first is that the maturity structure for a bank's assets, especially its investments in securities, can be volatile, and the bank's borrowing should reflect this volatility. The second is that banks can legitimately claim that their expertise lies in detecting what types of borrowing are cheapest at any point in time, and that they can exploit mismatches to their benefit.

CONCLUSION

In this chapter, we examine how firms move toward their optimal debt ratios, and how they choose the right financing vehicles to use, to finance both existing assets and new investments.

Some firms that are under- or overlevered may choose to not change their debt ratios to the optimal level. This may arise either because they do not share the objective of maximizing firm value that underlies optimal debt ratios, or because they feel that the costs of moving to the optimal outweigh the benefits. Firms that do decide to change their financing mixes can change either gradually or quickly. Firms are much more likely to change their financing mixes quickly if external pressure is brought to bear on the firm. For underlevered firms, the pressure takes the form of hostile acquisitions, whereas for overlevered firms, the threat is default and bankruptcy. Firms that are not under external pressure for change have the luxury of changing toward their optimal debt ratios gradually.

Firms can change their debt ratios in four ways. They can recapitalize existing investments, using new debt to reduce equity or new equity to retire debt. They can divest existing assets and use the cash to reduce equity or retire debt. They can invest in new projects and finance them disproportionately with debt or equity. Finally, they can increase or decrease the proportion of their earnings that are returned to stockholders in the form of dividends or stock buybacks. To decide between these alternatives, firms have to consider how quickly they need to change their debt ratios, the quality of the new investments they have, and the marketability of existing investments.

In the final section, we examined how firms choose between financing vehicles. Matching cash flows on financing to the cash flows on assets reduces default risk and increases the debt capacity of firms. Applying this principle, long-term assets should be financed with long-term debt, assets with cash flows that move with inflation should be financed with floating-rate debt, assets with cash flows in a foreign currency should be financed with debt in the same currency, and assets with growing cash flows should be financed with convertible debt. This matching can be done intuitively, by looking at a typical project, or based on historical data. Changes in operating income and value can be regressed against changes in macroeconomic variables to measure the sensitivity of the firm to these variables. The results can then be used to design the optimal financing vehicle for the firm.

LIVE CASE STUDY

MECHANICS OF MOVING TO THE OPTIMAL

Objective: To determine whether your firm should move to its optimal mix (and if so, how) and to analyze the right type of debt for your firm.

Key Questions

- If your firm's actual debt ratio is different from its "recommended" debt ratio, how should it get from the actual to the optimal? In particular,

  a. Should it do it gradually over time, or right now?

  b. Should it alter its existing mix (by buying back stock or retiring debt), should it invest in new projects with debt or equity, or should it change how much it returns to stockholders?

- What type of financing should this firm use? In particular,

  a. Should the financing be short-term, or long-term?

  b. What currency should it be in?

  c. What special features should the financing have?

Framework for Analysis

1. ***The Immediacy Question***

   - If the firm is underlevered, does it have the characteristics of a firm that is a likely takeover target? (Target firms in hostile takeovers tend to be smaller, have poorer project and stock price performance than their peer groups, and have lower insider holdings.)

   - If the firm is overlevered, is it in danger of bankruptcy? (Look at the bond rating if the company is rated. A junk bond rating suggests high bankruptcy risk.)

2. ***Alter Financing Mix or Take Projects***

   - What kind of projects does this firm expect to have? Can it expect to make excess returns on these projects? (Past project returns is a reasonable place to start—see the section under investment returns.)

   - What type of stockholders does this firm have? If cash had to be returned to them, would they prefer dividends, or stock buybacks? (Again, look at the past. If the company has paid high dividends historically, it will end up with investors who like dividends.)

3. ***Financing Type***

   - How sensitive has this firm's value been to changes in macroeconomic variables such as interest rates, currency movements, inflation, and the economy?

   - How sensitive has this firm's operating income been to changes in the same variables?

   - How sensitive are the sector's value and operating income to the same variables?

- What do the answers to the last three questions tell you about the kind of financing that this firm should use?

Getting Information on Mechanics of Capital Structure

To get the inputs needed to estimate the capital structure mechanics, you can get the information on macroeconomic variables such as interest rates, inflation, gross national product growth and exchange rates from my Web site. You can get historical information on your own firm by looking at the Value Line page for your firm, which has information for the last fifteen years on revenues and operating income.

Online sources of information
www.stern.nyu.edu/~adamodar/cfin2E/project/data.htm.

PROBLEMS AND QUESTIONS

(In the problems below, you can use a risk premium of 5.5% and a tax rate of 40% if either is not specified.)

1. BMD is a firm with no debt currently on its books and a market value of equity of $2 billion. Based on its EBITDA of $200 million, it can afford to have a debt ratio of 50%, at which level the firm value should be $300 million higher.

   a. Assuming that the firm plans to increase its leverage instantaneously, what are some of the approaches it could use to get to 50%?

   b. Is there a difference between repurchasing stock and paying a special dividend? Why, or why not?

   c. If BMD has a cash balance of $250 million at this time, would that change any of your analysis?

2. MiniSink is a manufacturing company that has $100 million in debt outstanding and 9 million shares trading at $100 per share. The current beta is 1.1, and the interest rate on the debt is 8%. In the latest year, MiniSink reported a net income of $7.50 per share, and analysts expect earnings growth to be 10% a year for the next five years. The firm faces a tax rate of 40% and pays out 20% of its earnings as dividends (the Treasury bond rate is 7%).

   a. Estimate the debt ratio each year for the next five years, assuming that the firm maintains its current payout ratio.

   b. Estimate the debt ratio each year for the next five years, assuming that the firm doubles its dividends and repurchases 5% of the outstanding stock every year.

3. IOU has $5 billion in debt outstanding (carrying an interest rate of 9%), and 10 million shares trading at $50 per share. Based on its current EBIT of $200 million, its optimal debt ratio is only 30%. The firm has a beta of 1.2, and the current Treasury bond rate is 7%. Assuming that the operating income will increase 10% a year for the next five years, and that the firm's depreciation and capital expenditures both amount to $100 million annually for each of the five years, estimate the debt ratio for IOU if it

   a. Maintains its existing policy of paying $50 million a year in dividends for the next five years

   b. Eliminates dividends

4. DGF Corporation has come to you for some advice on how best to increase its leverage over time. In the most recent year, DGF had an EBITDA of $300 million, owed $1 billion in both book value and market value terms, and had a net worth of $2 billion (the market value was twice the book value). It had a beta of 1.3, and the interest rate on its debt is 8% (the Treasury bond rate is 7%). If it moves to its optimal debt ratio of 40%, the cost of capital is expected to drop by 1%.

   a. How should the firm move to its optimal? In particular, should it borrow money and take on projects or should it pay dividends/repurchase stock?

   b. Are there any other considerations that may affect your decision?

5. STL has asked you for advice on putting together the details of the new debt issues it is planning to make. What information would you need to obtain to provide this advice?

6. Assume now that you have uncovered the following facts about the types of projects STL takes:

   • The projects are primarily infrastructure projects, requiring large initial investments and long gestation periods.

   • Most of the new projects will be in emerging markets, and the cash flows are expected to be in the local currencies when they do occur.

   • The magnitude of the cash flows will largely depend on how quickly the economies of the emerging markets grow in the long run.

   How would you use this information in the design of the projects?

7. You are attempting to structure a debt issue for Eaton Corporation, a manufacturer of automotive components. You have collected the following information on the market values of debt and equity for the past ten years:

	Market Value of Equity (in US$ millions)	Debt (in US$ millions)
1985	1,824.9	436
1986	2,260.6	632
1987	2,389.6	795
1988	1,960.8	655
1989	2,226.0	836
1990	1,875.9	755
1991	2,009.7	795
1992	2,589.3	833
1993	3,210.0	649
1994	3,962.7	1,053

In addition, you have the following information on the changes in long-term interest rates, inflation rates, gross national product (GNP), and exchange rates over the same period.

	Long Bond Rate	GNP Growth	Weighted Dollar	Inflation Rate
1985	11.40%	6.44%	125.95	3.50%
1986	9.00%	5.40%	112.89	1.90%
1987	9.40%	6.90%	95.88	3.70%
1988	9.70%	7.89%	95.32	4.10%
1989	9.30%	7.23%	102.26	4.80%
1990	9.30%	5.35%	96.25	5.40%
1991	8.80%	2.88%	98.82	4.20%
1992	8.10%	6.22%	104.58	3.00%
1993	7.20%	5.34%	105.22	3.00%
1994	8.00%	5.97%	98.6	2.60%

Using this information,

a. Estimate the duration of this firm's projects. How would you use this information in designing the debt issue?

b. How cyclical is this company? How would that affect your debt issue?

c. Estimate the sensitivity of firm value to exchange rates. How would you use this information in designing the debt issue?

d. How sensitive is firm value to inflation rates? How would you use this information in designing the debt issue?

e. What factors might lead you to override the results of this analysis?

8. Repeat the analysis in Problem 7 for a private firm that has provided you with the following estimates of operating income for the ten years, for which you have the macroeconomic data:

	Operating Income (in US$ thousands)
1985	463.050
1986	411.696
1987	483.252
1988	544.633
1989	550.650
1990	454.875
1991	341.481
1992	413.983
1993	567.729
1994	810.968

9. Assuming that you do the analysis in Problem 8 with both firm value and operating income, what are the reasons for the differences you might find in the results, using each? When would you use one over the other?

10. Pfizer, a major pharmaceutical company, has a debt ratio of 10.3% and is considering increasing its debt ratio to 30%. Its cost of capital is expected to drop from 14.51% to 13.45%. Pfizer had an EBIT of $2 billion in 1995, and a book value of capital (debt + equity) of approximately $8 billion. It also faced a tax rate of 40% on its income. The stock in the firm is widely held, but the corporate charter includes significant antitakeover restrictions.

a. Should Pfizer move to its desired debt ratio quickly, or gradually? Explain.

b. Given your choice in part **a**, explain how you would move to the optimal.

c. Pfizer is consider using the excess debt capacity for an acquisition. What are some of the concerns it should have?

11. Upjohn, also a major pharmaceutical company, is considering increasing its debt ratio from 11% to 40%, its optimal debt ratio. Its beta is 1.17, and the current Treasury bond rate is 6.5%. The return on equity was 14.5% in the most recent year, but it is dropping as health care matures as a business. The company has also been mentioned as a possible takeover target and is widely held.

a. Would you suggest that Upjohn move to the optimal ratio immediately? Explain.

b. How would you recommend that Upjohn increase its debt ratio?

12. U.S. steel companies have generally been considered mature in terms of growth and often take on high leverage to finance plants and equipment. Steel companies in some emerging markets often have high growth rates and good growth prospects. Would you expect these companies to also have high leverage? Why, or why not?

13. You are trying to decide whether the debt structure that Bethlehem Steel has currently is appropriate, given its assets. You regress changes in firm value against changes in interest rates, and arrive at the following equation

$$\text{Change in firm value} = 0.2\% - 6.33 \, (\text{Change in interest rates})$$

a. If Bethlehem Steel has primarily short-term debt outstanding, with a maturity of one year, would you deem the debt structure appropriate?

b. Why might Bethlehem Steel be inclined to use short-term debt to finance longer-term assets?

14. Railroad companies in the United States tend to have long-term, fixed-rate, dollar-denominated debt. Explain why.

15. The following table summarizes the results of regressing changes in firm value against changes in interest rates for six major footwear companies:

$$\text{Change in firm value} = a + b \, (\text{Change in long-term interest rates})$$

	Intercept (*a*)	Slope Coefficient (*b*)
LA Gear	−0.07	−4.74
Nike	0.05	−11.03
Stride Rite	0.01	−8.08
Timberland	0.06	−22.50
Reebok	0.04	−4.79
Wolverine	0.06	−2.42

a. How would you use these results to design debt for each of these companies?

b. How would you explain the wide variation across companies? Would you use the average across the companies in any way?

16. You have run a series of regressions of firm value changes at Motorola, the semiconductor company, against changes in a number of macroeconomic variables. The results are summarized here:

$$\text{Change in firm value} = 0.05 - 3.87 \, (\text{Change in long-term interest rate})$$

$$\text{Change in firm value} = 0.02 + 5.76 \, (\text{Change in real GNP})$$

$$\text{Change in firm value} = 0.04 - 2.59 \, (\text{Inflation rate})$$

$$\text{Change in firm value} = 0.05 - 3.40 \, (\$/\text{DM})$$

a. Based on these regressions, how would you design Motorola's financing?

b. Motorola, like all semiconductor companies, is sensitive to the health of high-technology companies. Is there any special feature you can add to the debt to reflect this dependence?

CHAPTER 10

DIVIDEND POLICY

At the end of each year, every publicly traded company has to decide whether to return cash to its stockholders and, if so, how much in the form of dividends. The owner of a private company has to make a similar decision about how much cash he or she plans to withdraw from the business and how much to reinvest. This is the dividend decision, and we begin this chapter by providing some background on three aspects of dividend policy. One is a purely procedural question about how dividends are set and paid out to stockholders. The second is an examination of widely used measures of how much a firm pays in the dividends. The third is an empirical examination of some patterns that firms follow in dividend policy.

Having laid this groundwork, we look at three schools of thought on dividend policy. The dividend irrelevance school believes that dividends do not really matter because they do not affect firm value. This argument is based on two assumptions.

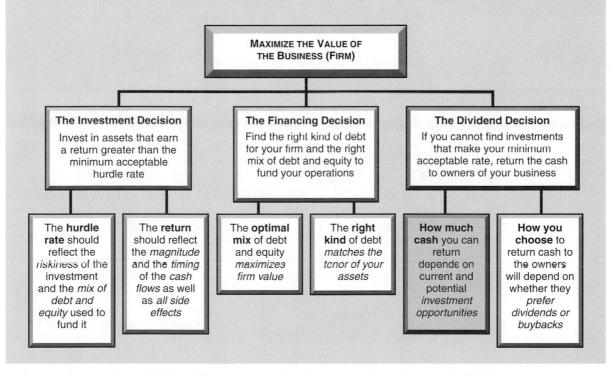

The first is that there is no tax disadvantage to an investor to receiving dividends instead of price appreciation, and the second is that firms can raise funds in capital markets for new investments without bearing significant issuance costs. The proponents of the second school feel that dividends are bad for the average stockholder because of the tax disadvantage they create, which results in lower value. Finally, there are those in a third group who argue that dividends are clearly good because stockholders (at least some of them) like them and react accordingly when dividends are increased.

Although dividends have traditionally been considered the primary approach for publicly traded firms to return cash or assets to their stockholders, they comprise only one of many ways available to the firm to accomplish this objective. In particular, firms can return cash to stockholders through equity repurchases, where the cash is used to buy back outstanding stock in the firm and reduce the number of shares outstanding. In addition, firms can return some of their assets to their stockholders in the form of spin-offs and split-offs. This chapter will focus on dividends specifically, but the next chapter will examine the other alternatives available to firms and how to choose between dividends and these alternatives.

BACKGROUND ON DIVIDEND POLICY

In this section, we consider three issues. First, how do firms decide how much to pay in dividends, and how do those dividends actually get paid to the stockholders? We then consider two widely used measures of how much a firm pays in dividends, the dividend payout ratio and the dividend yield. We follow up by looking at some empirical evidence on firm behavior in setting and changing dividends.

The Dividend Process

Firms in the United States generally pay dividends every quarter, whereas firms in other countries typically pay dividends on a semi-annual or annual basis. Let us look at the time line associated with dividend payment and define different types of dividends.

The Dividend Payment Timeline

Dividends in publicly traded firms are usually set by the board of directors and paid out to stockholders a few weeks later. There are several key dates between the time the board declares the dividend and the time the dividend is actually paid.

- The first date of note is the *dividend declaration date*, the date on which the board of directors declares the dollar dividend that will be paid for that quarter (or period). This date is important because by announcing its intent to increase, decrease, or maintain dividend, the firm conveys information to financial markets. Thus, if the firm changes its dividends, this is the date on which the market reaction to the change is most likely to occur.

- The next date of note is the *ex-dividend date*, at which time investors must have bought the stock to receive the dividend. Because the dividend is not received by

Figure 10.1   The Dividend Timeline

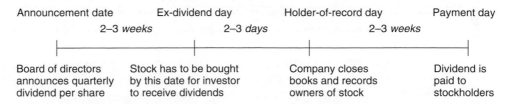

investors buying stock after the ex-dividend date, the stock price will generally fall on that day to reflect that loss.

- At the close of the business or a few days after the ex-dividend date, the company closes its stock transfer books and makes up a list of the shareholders to date on the *holder-of-record date*. These shareholders will receive the dividends. There should be generally be no price effect on this date.

- The final step involves mailing out the dividend checks on the *dividend payment date*. In most cases, the payment date is two to three weeks after the holder-of-record date. Although stockholders may view this as an important day, there should be no price impact on this day either.

Figure 10.1 presents these key dates on a timeline.

Types of Dividends

There are several ways to classify dividends. First, dividends can be paid in cash or as additional stock. *Stock dividends* increase the number of shares outstanding and generally reduce the price per share. Second, the dividend can be a *regular dividend*, paid at regular intervals (quarterly, semiannually, or annually), or a *special dividend*, paid in addition to the regular dividend. Most U.S. firms pay regular dividends every quarter; special dividends are paid at irregular intervals. Finally, firms sometimes pay dividends that are in excess of the retained earnings they show on their books. These are called *liquidating dividends* and are viewed by the Internal Revenue Service as return on capital rather than ordinary income. As a result, they can have different tax consequences for investors.

Measures of Dividend Policy

We generally measure the dividends paid by a firm using one of two measures. The first is the **dividend yield**, which relates the dividend paid to the price of the stock:

$$\text{Dividend yield} = \text{Annual dividends per share/price per share}$$

The dividend yield is significant because it provides a measure of that component of the total return that comes from dividends, with the balance coming from price appreciation.

$$\text{Expected return on stock} = \text{Dividend yield} + \text{Price appreciation}$$

Some investors also use the dividend yield as a measure of risk and as an investment screen; that is, they invest in stocks with high dividend yields. Studies indicate that

Figure 10.2 Dividend Yields for U.S. Stocks—Jan. 2008 vs. Jan. 2009

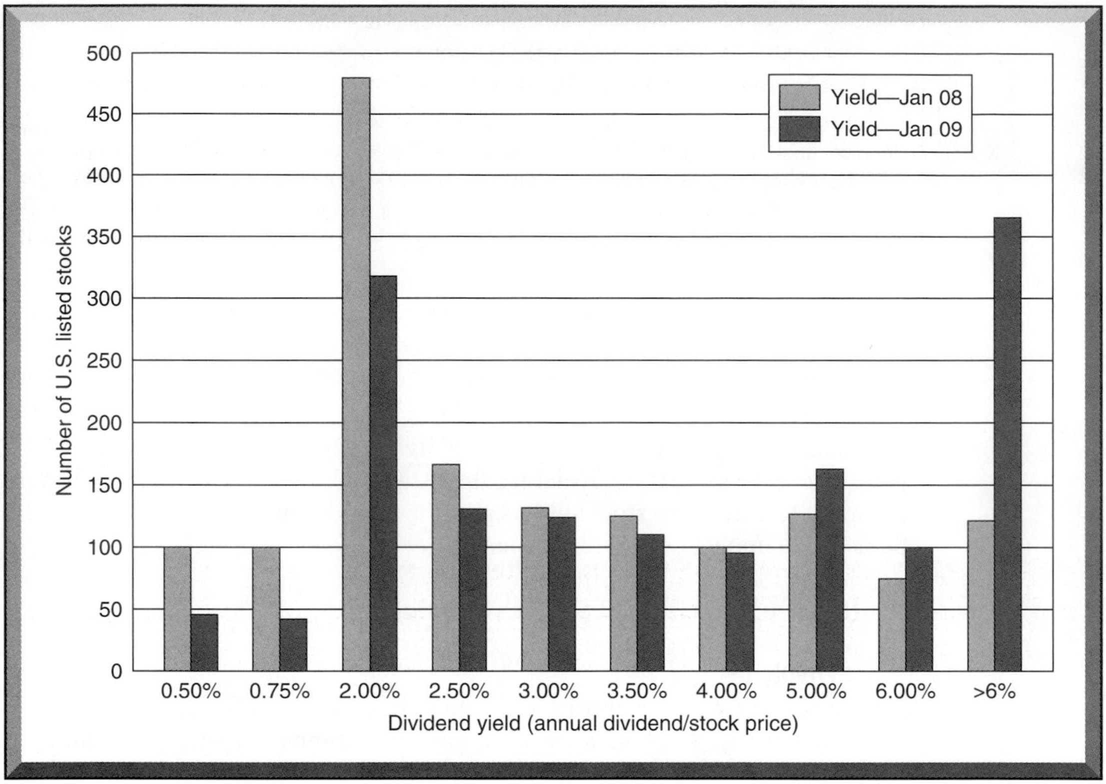

Source: Estimated using Value Line Data on Companies in January 2009.

stocks with high dividend yields, after adjusting for market performance and risk, earn excess returns.

Figure 10.2 tracks dividend yields on the 2,700 listed stocks in the United States that paid dividends on the major exchanges in January 2009 and contrasts them with the yields a year earlier. The median dividend yield among dividend paying stocks in January 2009 was about 3%, significantly higher than the median dividend yield of 2% in January 2008. The reason for the increase, though, was not higher dividends in 2008 but lower stock prices, as a consequence of the market collapse in the last quarter of 2008. In both time periods, it is worth noting that almost 65% of the overall sample of 7,200 companies paid no dividends, making 0% the median dividend yield across all companies.

The second widely used measure of dividend policy is the **dividend payout** ratio, which relates dividends paid to the earnings of the firm.

$$\text{Dividend payout ratio} = \text{Dividends/earnings}$$

The payout ratio is used in a number of different settings. It is used in valuation as a way of estimating dividends in future periods, because most analysts estimate growth in earnings rather than dividends. Second, the retention ratio—the proportion of the earnings reinvested in the firm (retention ratio = 1 − dividend payout ratio)—is useful in estimating future growth in earnings; firms with high retention ratios (low payout ratios) generally have higher growth rates in earnings than firms with lower retention ratios (higher payout ratios). Third, the dividend payout ratio tends to follow the life cycle of the firm, starting at zero when the firm is in high growth and gradually increasing as the firm matures and its growth prospects decrease. Figure 10.3 graphs the dividend payout ratios of U.S. firms that paid dividends in January 2009.

The payout ratios greater than 100% represent firms that paid out more than their earnings as dividends; approximately 150 firms fall into this group. In 2008, about 120 firms paid out dividends, even though they reported losses for the year. The median dividend payout ratio in January 2009 among dividend-paying stocks was about 35%, whereas the average payout ratio was approximately 40%.

Finally, we look at how current dividend yields and payout ratios measure up against historical numbers by looking at the average dividend yield and payout ratio for stocks in the S&P 500 from 1960 to 2008 in Figure 10.4. Note that the dividend yield went through an extended period of decline from 1980, when it was about 5.5%, to less than

Figure 10.3   Dividend Payout Ratios for U.S. Companies—January 2009

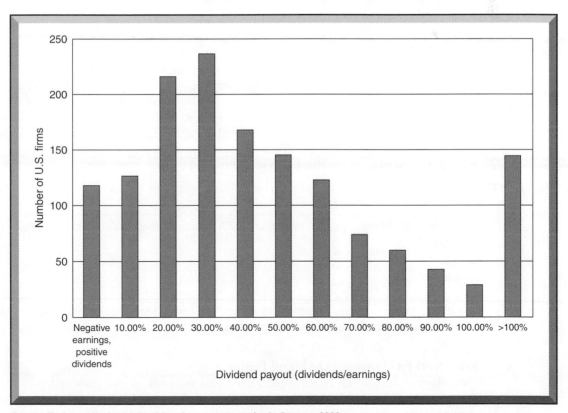

Source: Estimated using Value Line data on companies in January 2009.

Figure 10.4   Dividend Yield and Payout on S&P 500: 1960–2008

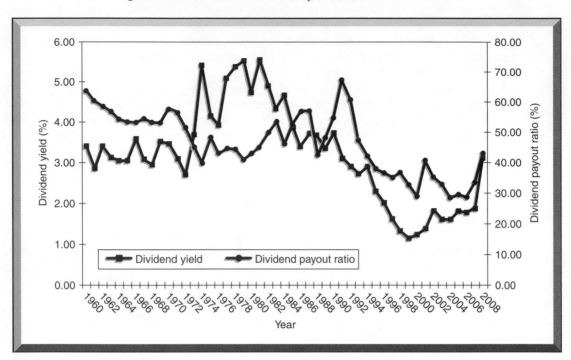

2% for much of the last decade, before bouncing back in 2008. The dividend payout ratio has also declined for much of the last decade, but the drop has been less dramatic. While some of the decline in both measures can be attributed to rising values for the denominators—stock prices for dividend yields and earnings for payout ratios—some of it can also be accounted for by a increased number of growth (technology) firms in the S&P 500 index and a move from dividends to stock buybacks across companies. We will return to examine this trend in Chapter 11.

10.1   Dividends That Exceed Earnings

Companies should never pay out more than 100% of their earnings as dividends.

a.   True

b.   False

Explain.

divUS.xls: There is a data set online that summarizes dividend yields and payout ratios for U.S. companies from 1960 to the present.

Empirical Evidence on Dividend Policy

We observe several interesting patterns when we look at the dividend policies of firms in the United States in the past fifty years. First, dividends tend to lag behind earnings; that is, increases in earnings are followed in subsequent years by increases

Figure 10.5 Dividends and Earnings—S&P 500

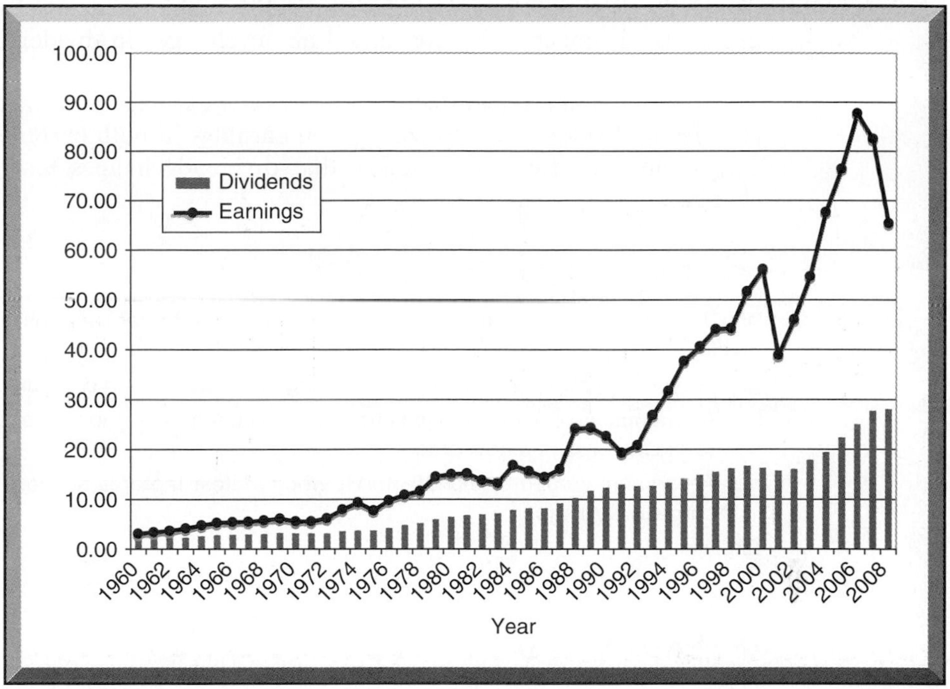

Source: Standard & Poor's

in dividends, and decreases in earnings sometimes by dividend cuts in the following years. Second, dividends are "sticky," because firms are typically reluctant to cut dividends even when earnings drop; this reluctance also makes them less willing to increase dividends, out of the fear that they will not be able to sustain the increase. Third, dividends tend to follow a much smoother path than do earnings. Finally, there are distinct differences in dividend policy over the life cycle of a firm, resulting from changes in growth rates, cash flows, and project availability.

Dividends Tend to Follow Earnings

It should not come as a surprise that earnings and dividends are positively correlated over time, because dividends are paid out of earnings. Figure 10.5 shows the movement in both earnings and dividends between 1960 and 2008 for companies in the S&P 500.

Take note of two trends in this graph: (1) dividend changes trail earnings changes over time, and (2) the dividend series is much smoother than the earnings series is. In the 1950s, John Lintner studied the way firms set dividends and noted three consistent patterns.[1] First, firms set **target dividend payout ratios**, by deciding on the fraction of earnings they are willing to pay out as dividends in the long

---

[1] J. Lintner, "Distribution of Income of Corporations among Dividends, Retained Earnings and Taxes," *American Economic Review* 46:97–113.

term. Second, they change dividends to match long-term and sustainable shifts in earnings, but they increase dividends only if they feel they can maintain these higher dividends. Because firms avoid cutting dividends, dividends lag earnings. Finally, managers are much more concerned about changes in dividends than about levels of dividends.

Fama and Babiak identified a lag between earnings and dividends by regressing changes in dividends against changes in earnings in both current and prior periods.[2] They confirmed Lintner's findings that dividend changes tend to follow earnings changes.

10.2 DETERMINANTS OF DIVIDEND LAG

Which of the following types of firms is likely to wait *least* after earnings go up before increasing dividends?

a. A cyclical firm, whose earnings have surged because of an economic boom
b. A pharmaceutical firm whose earnings have increased steadily over the past five years due to the success of a new drug
c. A personal computer manufacturer, whose latest laptop's success has translated into a surge in earnings

Explain.

Dividends Are Sticky

Many firms do not change their dollar dividends frequently. This reluctance to change dividends, which results in sticky dividends, is rooted in several factors. One is the firm's concern about its capability to maintain higher dividends in future periods. Another is that markets tend to take a dim view of dividend decreases, and the stock price drops to reflect that. Figure 10.6 provides a summary of the percentages of all U.S. firms that increased, decreased, or left unchanged their annual dividends per share from 1989 to 2008.

As you can see, in most years the number of firms that do not change their dollar dividends far exceeds the number that do. Among the firms that change dividends, a much higher percentage, on average, increase dividends than decrease them. Even in 2008, a crisis year by any year, the number of firms that increased dividends outnumbered the firm that cut dividends.[3]

 Sticky Dividends: A Behavioral Perspective

John Lintner's study of how firms decide how much to pay in dividends was done more than fifty years ago, but its findings have had had remarkable durability. His basic conclusions—that firms set target payout ratios, that dividends lag earnings, and that dividend changes are infrequent—still characterize how most companies set dividends.

---

[2]E. F. Fama and H. Babiak, "Dividend Policy: An Empirical Analysis," *Journal of the American Statistical Association* 63, no. 324:1132–1161.
[3]In the last quarter of 2008, in the midst of the biggest financial market crisis of the last fifty years, twenty-seven firms in the S&P 500 cut dividends (the highest number during one quarter in history) but thirty-two firms increased dividends.

Figure 10.6   Dividend Changes by Year: U.S. Companies

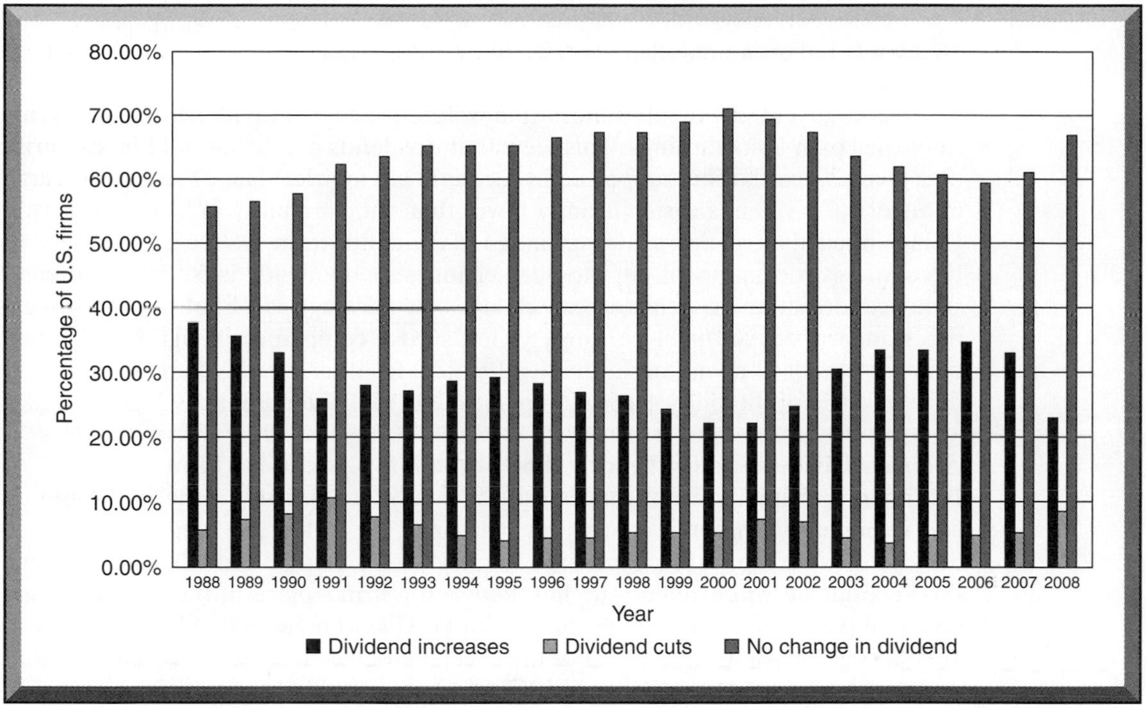

Source: Standard & Poor's.

Given the increased volatility in earnings and cash flows at firms, it seems surprising that dividends do not reflect that volatility and that firms do not actively reassess how much they should pay in dividends.

Cyert and March provide an explanation for the Lintner findings, grounded in what they call "uncertainty avoidance."[4] They argue that managers attempt to avoid anticipating or forecasting future events by using decision rules that emphasize short-term feedback from the economic environment. Put another way, firms adopt standardized rules that do not eliminate uncertainty but that make dealing with it more tractable. In the context of dividend policy, their model predicts that managers will

- Set a level of dividends (payout ratios) by looking at industry norms
- Focus on changes in dividends in response to changes in earnings
- Use simple rules of thumb on how to adjust dividends, such as raising dividends only if earnings increase 30% or more
- Avoid adjusting dividends in response to changes in stockholder attitudes, if these changes are viewed as short-term changes

---

[4]Cyert, R. and J. March, *A Behavioral Theory of the Firm* (Englewood Cliffs, NJ: Prentice-Hall, 1993).

These predictions are well in line with the findings in the Lintner study.

Dividends Follow a Smoother Path Than Earnings

As a result of the reluctance to raise dividends until the firm feels able to maintain them and to cut dividends unless it absolutely has to, dividends follow a much smoother path than earnings. This view that dividends are not as volatile as earnings on a year-to-year basis is supported by a couple of empirical facts. First, the variability in historical dividends is significantly lower than the variability in historical earnings. Using annual data on aggregate earnings and dividends from 1960 to 2008, for instance, the standard deviation of year-to-year changes in dividends is 5.17%, whereas the standard deviation in year-to-year changes in earnings is about 14.69%. Second, the standard deviation in earnings yields across companies is significantly higher than the standard deviation in dividend yields. In other words, there are far greater differences in profitability across companies than in dividend policy.

A Firm's Dividend Policy Tends to Follow the Life Cycle of the Firm

In previous chapters, we introduced the link between a firm's place in the life cycle and its financing mix and choices. In particular, we noted five stages in the growth life cycle—start up, rapid expansion, high growth, mature growth, and decline. In this section, we will examine the link between a firm's place in the life cycle and its dividend policy. Not surprisingly, firms adopt dividend policies that best fit where they are currently in their life cycles. For instance, high-growth firms with great investment opportunities do not usually pay dividends, whereas stable firms with larger cash flows and fewer projects tend to pay more of their earnings out as dividends. Figure 10.7 looks at the typical path that dividend payout follows over a firm's life cycle.

This intuitive relationship between dividend policy and growth is emphasized when we look at the relationship between a firm's payout ratio and its expected growth rate. For instance, we classified firms on the New York Stock Exchange in January 2009 into six groups based on analyst estimates of expected growth rates in earnings per share for the next five years and estimated the dividend payout ratios and dividend yields for each class; these are reported in Figure 10.8.

The firms with the highest expected growth rates pay the lowest dividends, both as a percent of earnings (payout ratio) and as a percent of price (dividend yield).[5]

10.3 DIVIDEND POLICY AT GROWTH FIRMS

Assume that you are following a growth firm whose growth rate has begun easing. Which of the following would you most likely observe in terms of dividend policy at the firm?

a. An immediate increase of dividends to reflect the lower reinvestment needs

b. No change in dividend policy, and an increase in the cash balance

c. No change in dividend policy, and an increase in acquisitions of other firms

Explain.

---

[5]These are growth rates in earnings for the next five years projected by Value Line for firms in January 2009.

Figure 10.7   Life Cycle Analysis of Dividend Policy

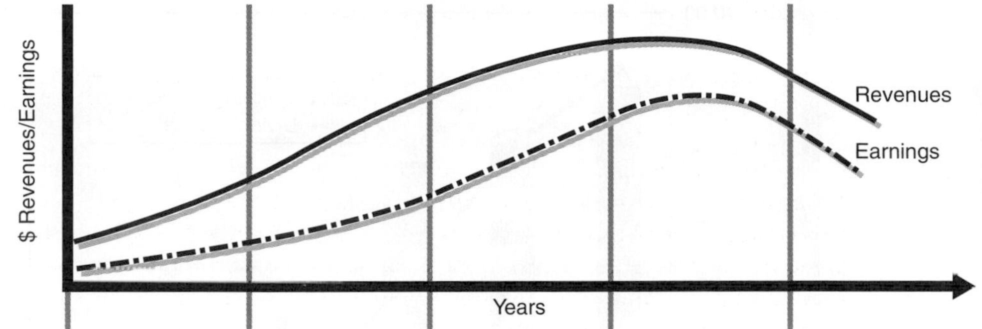

	High, but constrained by infrastructure	High relative to firm value	Moderate relative to firm value	Low, as projects dry up	Low, as projects dry up
External funding needs	High, but constrained by infrastructure	High relative to firm value	Moderate relative to firm value	Low, as projects dry up	Low, as projects dry up
Internal financing	Negative or low	Negative or low	Low relative to funding needs	High relative to funding needs	More than funding needs
Capacity to pay dividends	None	None	Low	Increasing	High
Growth stage	Stage 1 Start-up	Stage 2 Rapid expansion	Stage 3 High growth	Stage 4 Mature growth	Stage 5 Decline

Differences in Dividend Policy across Countries

Figures 10.5 to 10.8 showed several trends and patterns in dividend policies at U.S. companies. While they share some common features with firms in other countries, there are some differences. As in the United States, dividends in other countries are sticky and follow earnings. However, there are differences in the magnitude of dividend payout ratios across countries. Figure 10.9 shows the proportion of earnings paid out in dividends in the G-7 countries in 1982–1984 and again in 1989–1991, with an update for 2009 values.[6]

The differences in dividend payout can be attributed to

- *Differences in stage of growth.* Just as higher-growth companies tend to pay out less of their earnings in dividends (see Figure 10.8), countries with higher growth

---

[6]R. Rajan and L. Zingales, "What Do We Know about Capital Structure? Some Evidence from International Data," *Journal of Finance* 50:1421–1460. The 1982–1984 and 1989–1991 data come from this paper. The update for 2009 is estimated using Capital IQ data from 2009; we added Russia to the group to reflect its new standing as the G-8.

Figure 10.8   Dividend Yield and Payout Ratio–Growth Class

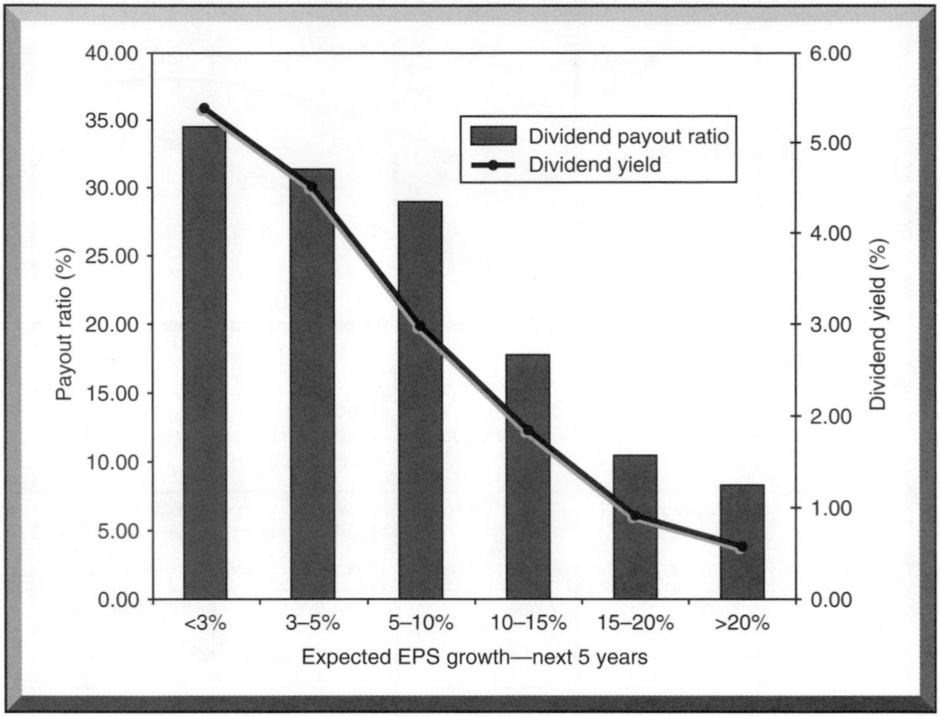

Source: Value Line Database in January 2009.

pay out less in dividends. For instance, Japan had much higher expected growth in 1982–1984 than the other G-7 countries and paid out a much smaller percentage of its earnings as dividends. As Japan's growth has declined, its payout ratio has risen.

- ***Differences in tax treatment.***   Unlike the United States, where dividends are doubly taxed, some countries provide at least partial protection against the double taxation of dividends. For instance, Germany taxed corporate retained earnings at a higher rate than corporate dividends during much of this period, and the United Kingdom allowed investors to offset corporate taxes against taxes due on dividends, thus reducing the effective tax rate on dividends.

- ***Differences in corporate control.***   When there is a separation between ownership and management, as there is in many large publicly traded firms, and where stockholders have little control over managers, the dividends paid by firms will be lower. Managers, left to their own devices, have an incentive to accumulate cash. Russia, with its abysmal corporate governance system, has a dividend payout ratio of less than 10% in 2009.

Not surprisingly, the dividend payout ratios of companies in most emerging markets are much lower than the dividend payout ratios in the G-7 countries. The higher growth

Figure 10.9 Dividend Payout Ratios—G-7 Countries

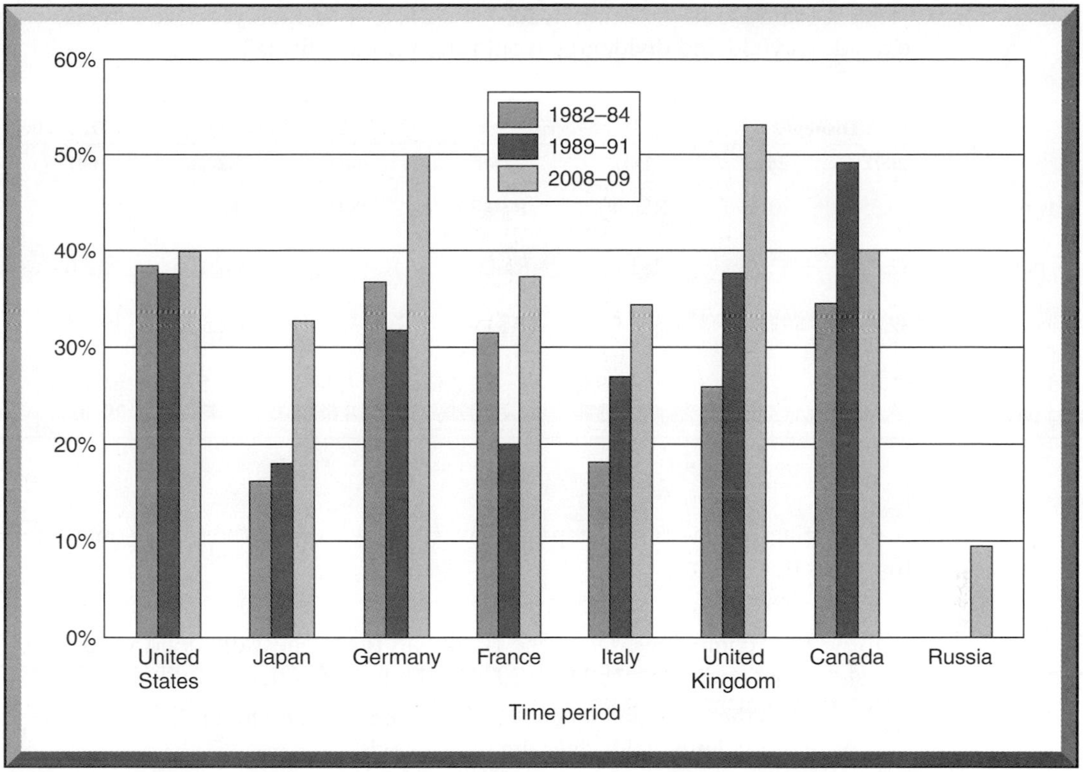

Source: R. Rajan and L. Zingales, "What Do We Know about Capital Structure? Some Evidence from International Data," *Journal of Finance* 50:1421–1460. The 2009 numbers represent an update and include Russia, which was not part of the G-7 in earlier periods.

and relative power of incumbent management in these countries contribute to keeping these payout ratios low.

10.4 DIVIDEND POLICIES AND STOCK BUYBACK RESTRICTIONS

Some countries do not allow firms to buy back stock from their stockholders. Which of the following would you expect of dividend policies in these countries (relative to countries that don't restrict stock buybacks)?

a. Higher portion of earnings paid out in dividends; more volatile dividends

b. Lower portion of earnings paid out in dividends; more volatile dividends

c. Higher portion of earnings paid out in dividends; less volatile dividends

d. Lower portion of earnings paid out in dividends; less volatile dividends

Explain.

countrystats.xls: There is a data set online that summarizes dividend yields and payout ratios for different markets globally.

ILLUSTRATION 10.1 Dividends, Dividend Yields, and Payout Ratios

In this illustration, we will examine the dollar dividends paid at Disney, Aracruz, Tata Chemicals, and Deutsche Bank in 2007 and 2008.[7] For each year, we will also compute the dividend yield and dividend payout ratio for each firm.

	Disney		Aracruz		Tata Chemicals		Deutsche Bank	
	2007	2008	2007	2008	2007	2008	2007	2008
Dividends per share	$0.35	$0.35	R$0.43	R$0.33	Rs8.00	Rs9.00	€4.00	€0.50
Earnings per share	$2.25	$2.28	R$1.01	−R$4.09	Rs42.82	Rs20.65	€13.65	−€7.61
Stock price at end of year	$32.28	$22.69	R$15.97	R$3.98	Rs413.05	Rs165.25	€89.47	€27.83
Dividend yield	1.08%	1.54%	2.69%	8.19%	1.94%	5.45%	4.47%	1.8%
Dividend payout	15.56%	15.35%	42.43%	−7.97%	18.68%	43.58%	29.30%	−6.57%

Looking across the four companies over the two years, there are some interesting differences that emerge:

- Of the four companies, Deutsche Bank had the highest dividend yield in 2007 but slashed dividends drastically for 2008 as the market crisis unfolded.

- Disney paid the same dividends per share each year and had relatively stable payout ratios and dividend yields over the two periods.

- The dividend yield and payout ratio for Tata Chemicals jumped in 2008, mostly because the stock price and earnings dropped by more than 50% during the year.

- Both Deutsche and Aracruz paid dividends in 2008, in spite of negative earnings—a testimonial to the stickiness of dividends.

Aracruz, in particular, will have trouble maintaining its existing dividends, but it is faced with a dilemma that pits control interests against cash flow constraints. As noted earlier in the book, Aracruz, like most Brazilian companies, maintains two classes of shares—voting shares (called common shares, and held by insiders) and nonvoting shares (called preferred shares, and held by outside investors). The dividend policies are different for the two classes, with preferred shares getting higher dividends. In fact, the failure to pay a mandated dividend to preferred stockholders can result in preferred stockholders getting some voting control of the firm. Effectively, this puts a floor on the dividend payout ratio unless the voting shareholders are willing to cede control and give voting rights to the preferred shareholders in return for cutting dividends.

---

[7]The dividends for these years are actually paid in the subsequent years by these companies. Deutsche Bank's dividend of 0.5 euros per share for 2008 was paid out in May 2009.

WHEN ARE DIVIDENDS IRRELEVANT?

There is a school of thought that argues that what a firm pays in dividends is irrelevant and that stockholders are indifferent about receiving dividends. Like the capital structure irrelevance proposition, the dividend irrelevance argument has its roots in a paper crafted by Miller and Modigliani.[8]

The Underlying Assumptions

The underlying intuition for the dividend irrelevance proposition is simple. Firms that pay more dividends offer less price appreciation but must provide the same total return to stockholders, given their risk characteristics and the cash flows from their investment decisions. Thus, if there are no taxes, or if dividends and capital gains are taxed at the same rate, investors should be indifferent to receiving their returns in dividends or price appreciation.

For this argument to work, in addition to assuming that there is no tax advantage or disadvantage associated with dividends, we also have to assume the following:

- There are no transaction costs associated with converting price appreciation into cash, by selling stock. If this were *not* true, investors who need cash urgently might prefer to receive dividends.

- Firms that pay too much in dividends can issue stock—again, with no issuance or transaction costs—and use the proceeds to invest in good projects. Thus, a firm that pays too much in dividends can always issue new equity to fund its investments. Managers of firms that pay too little in dividends do not waste the cash pursuing their own interests (i.e., managers with large surplus cash flows do not use them to invest in bad projects). Consequently, the investment decisions of the firm are unaffected by its dividend decisions, and the firm's operating cash flows are the same no matter which dividend policy is adopted.

- There is also an implicit assumption that this stock is fairly priced.

Under these assumptions, neither the firms paying the dividends nor the stockholders receiving them will be adversely affected by firms paying either too little or too much in dividends.

10.5 DIVIDEND IRRELEVANCE

Based on the Miller–Modigliani assumptions, dividends are least likely to affect value for what types of firms?

a. Small companies with substantial investment needs

b. Large companies with significant insider holdings

c. Large companies with significant holdings by pension funds (which are tax-exempt) and minimal investment needs

Explain.

---

[8]M. Miller and F. Modigliani, "Dividend Policy, Growth and the Valuation of Shares," *Journal of Business* 34:411–433.

A Proof of Dividend Irrelevance

To provide a formal proof of irrelevance, assume that LongLast Corporation, an unlevered furniture manufacturing firm, has operating income after taxes of $100 million, is growing at 5% a year, and has a cost of capital of 10%. Furthermore, assume that this firm has reinvestment needs of $50 million, also growing at 5% a year, and there are 105 million shares outstanding. Finally, assume that this firm pays out residual cash flows as dividends each year. The value of LongLast can be estimated as follows:

$$\text{Free cash flow to the firm} = \text{EBIT}(1 - \text{Tax rate}) - \text{Reinvestment needs}$$
$$= \$100 \text{ million} - \$50 \text{ million} = \$50 \text{ million}$$
$$\text{Value of the firm} = \frac{\text{FCFF}_0(1 + g)}{(\text{Cost of capital} - g)}$$
$$= \frac{50(1.05)}{(0.10 - 0.05)} = \$1,050 \text{ million}$$
$$\text{Price per share} = \$1,050 \text{ million}/105 \text{ million} = \$10.00$$

Based on its cash flows, this firm could pay out $50 million in dividends.

$$\text{Dividend per share} = \$50 \text{ million}/105 \text{ million} = \$0.476$$
$$\text{Total value per share} = \$10.00 + \$0.476 = \$10.476$$

The total value per share measures what stockholders get in price and dividends from their stock holdings.

Scenario 1: LongLast Doubles Dividends

To examine how the dividend policy affects firm value, assume that LongLast is told by an investment banker that its stockholders would gain if the firm paid out $100 million in dividends instead of $50 million. It now has to raise $50 million in new financing to cover its reinvestment needs. Assume that LongLast can issue new stock with *no issuance cost* to raise these funds. If it does so, the firm value will remain unchanged, because the value is determined not by the dividend paid but by the cash flows generated on the projects. Because the growth rate and the cost of capital are unaffected, we get

$$\text{Value of the firm} = \frac{\text{FCFF}_0(1 + g)}{(\text{Cost of capital} - g)} = \frac{50(1.05)}{(0.10 - 0.05)} = \$1,050 \text{ million}$$

The existing stockholders will receive a much larger dividend per share, because dividends have been doubled:

$$\text{Dividends per share} = \$100 \text{ million}/105 \text{ million shares} = \$0.953$$

To estimate the price per share at which the new stock will be issued, note that after the new stock issue of $50 million, the old stockholders in the firm will own only $1,000 million of the total firm value of $1,050 million.

$$\text{Value of the firm for existing stockholders}$$
$$\text{after dividend payment} = \$1,000 \text{ million}$$
$$\text{Price per share} = \$1,000 \text{ million}/105 \text{ million} = \$9.523$$

The price per share is now lower than it was before the dividend increase, but it is exactly offset by the increase in dividends.

$$\text{Value accruing to stockholder} = \$9.523 + \$0.953 = \$10.476$$

Thus, if the operating cash flows are unaffected by dividend policy, we can show that the firm value will be unaffected by dividend policy and that the average stockholder will be indifferent to dividend policy, because he or she receives the same total value (price + dividends) under any dividend payment.

Scenario 2: LongLast Stops Paying Dividends

To consider an alternate scenario, assume that LongLast pays out no dividends and retains the residual $50 million as a cash balance. The value of the firm to existing stockholders can then be computed as follows:

$$\text{Value of firm} = \text{Present value of after-tax operating CF} + \text{Cash balance}$$
$$= \frac{50(1.05)}{(0.10 - 0.05)} + \$50 \text{ million} = \$1,100 \text{ million}$$
$$\text{Value per share} = \$1,100 \text{ million}/105 \text{ million shares} = \$10.476$$

Note that the total value per share remains at $10.476. In fact, as shown in Table 10.1, the value per share remains $10.476 no matter how much the firm pays in dividends.

When LongLast pays less than $50 million in dividends, the cash accrues in the firm and adds to its value. The increase in the stock price again is offset by the loss of cash flows from dividends. When it pays out more, the price decreases, reflecting the issuance of new shares, but is exactly offset by the increase in dividends per share.

Note, however, that the value per share remains unchanged because we assume that there are no tax differences to investors between receiving dividends and capital gains, that firms can raise new capital with no issuance costs, and that firms do not change their investment policy even when they have excess cash. These assumptions eliminate the costs associated with paying too much or too little in dividends.

Table 10.1   VALUE PER SHARE TO EXISTING STOCKHOLDERS FROM DIFFERENT DIVIDEND POLICIES

Value of Firm (Operating CF)	Dividends	Value to Existing Stockholders	Price per Share	Dividends per Share	Total Value per Share
$1,050	–	$1,100	$10.476	–	$10.476
$1,050	$10.00	$1,090	$10.381	$0.095	$10.476
$1,050	$20.00	$1,080	$10.286	$0.190	$10.476
$1,050	$30.00	$1,070	$10.190	$0.286	$10.476
$1,050	$40.00	$1,060	$10.095	$0.381	$10.476
$1,050	$50.00	$1,050	$10.000	$0.476	$10.476
$1,050	$60.00	$1,040	$9.905	$0.571	$10.476
$1,050	$70.00	$1,030	$9.810	$0.667	$10.476
$1,050	$80.00	$1,020	$9.714	$0.762	$10.476
$1,050	$90.00	$1,010	$9.619	$0.857	$10.476
$1,050	$100.00	$1,000	$9.524	$0.952	$10.476

Implications of Dividend Irrelevance

If dividends are, in fact, irrelevant, firms are spending a great deal of time pondering an issue about which their stockholders are indifferent. A number of strong implications emerge from this proposition. Among them, the value of aggregate equity in a firm should not change as its dividend policy changes. This does not imply that the price per share will be unaffected, however, because larger dividends should result in lower stock prices and more shares outstanding. In addition, in the long run, there should be no correlation between dividend policy and stock returns. Later in this chapter, we will examine some studies that have attempted to examine whether dividend policy is actually irrelevant in practice.

The assumptions needed to arrive at the dividend irrelevance proposition may seem so onerous that many reject it without testing it. That would be a mistake, however, because the argument does contain a valuable message: a firm that has invested in bad projects cannot hope to resurrect its image with stockholders by offering them higher dividends. Conversely, a firm that has a history of making good investments will be forgiven by stockholders, even if it chooses not to pay out what it can afford to in dividends. This may yield some insight into why investors are much more sanguine about cash being accumulated in some companies than in others.

THE "DIVIDENDS ARE BAD" SCHOOL

In the United States, dividends have historically been taxed at much higher rates than capital gains. Based on this tax disadvantage, the second school of thought on dividends argued that dividend payments reduce the returns to stockholders after personal taxes. Stockholders, they posited, would respond by reducing the stock prices of the firms making these payments, relative to firms that do not pay dividends. Consequently, firms would be better off either retaining the money they would have paid out as dividends or repurchasing stock. In 2003, the basis for this argument was largely eliminated when the tax rate on dividends was reduced to match the tax rate on capital gains. In this section, we will consider both the history of tax-disadvantaged dividends and the potential effects of the tax law changes.[9]

The History of Dividend Taxation

The tax treatment of dividends varies widely depending on who receives the dividend. Individual investors were taxed at ordinary tax rates until 2003, corporations are sheltered from paying taxes on at least a portion of the dividends they receive, and pension funds are not taxed at all.

Individuals

Since the inception of income taxes in the early twentieth century in the United States, dividends received on investments have been treated as ordinary income when received by individuals, and taxed at ordinary tax rates. In contrast, the price appreciation on an

---

[9]Adding to the uncertainty is the fact that the tax changes of 2003 are not permanent and are designed to sunset (disappear) in 2010. It is unclear whether the tax disadvantages of dividends have disappeared for the long term, or only until 2010.

Figure 10.10   Marginal Tax Rates on Dividends and Capital Gains

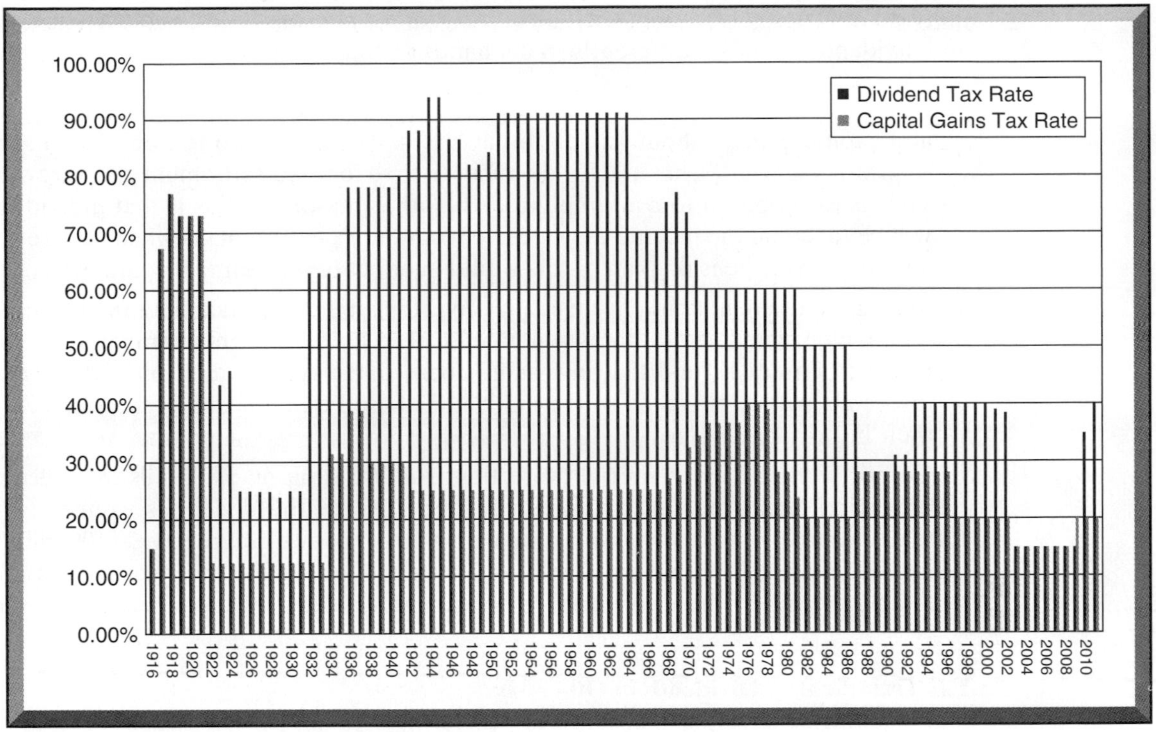

investment has been treated as capital gains and taxed at a different, much lower rate. Figure 10.10 graphs the highest marginal tax rate on dividends in the United States and the highest marginal capital gains tax rate since 1954 (when capital gains taxes were introduced).

Barring the very early part of the last century and a brief period after the 1986 tax reform act, when dividends and capital gains were both taxed at 28%, the capital gains tax rate has been significantly lower than the ordinary tax rate in the United States. In 2003, the tax rate on dividends was dropped to 15% to match the tax rate on capital gains, thus nullifying the tax disadvantage of dividends. However, that change in the tax law is expected to lapse in 2010, returning the tax rates to pre-2001 numbers.

There are two points worth making about this chart. The first is that these are the highest marginal tax rates, and that most individuals are taxed at lower rates. In fact, some older and poorer investors may pay no taxes on income if it falls below the threshold for taxes. The second and related issue is that the capital gains taxes can be higher for some of these individuals than the ordinary tax rate they pay on dividends. Overall, however, wealthier individuals have more invested in equities than poorer individuals, and it seems fair to conclude that individuals have collectively paid significantly more taxes on the income that they have received in dividends than on capital gains profits over the past few decades.

Institutional Investors

About two-thirds of all traded equities are held by institutional investors rather than individuals. These institutions include mutual funds, pension funds, and corporations, and dividends get taxed differently in the hands of each.

- Pension funds are tax-exempt. They are allowed to accumulate both dividends and capital gains without having to pay taxes. There are two reasons for this tax treatment. One is to encourage individuals to save for their retirement and to reward savings (as opposed to consumption). The other reason for this is that individuals will be taxed on the income they receive from their pension plans when they retire, and that taxing pension plan profits would in effect tax the same income twice.

- Mutual funds are not directly taxed, but investors in them are taxed for their share of the dividends and capital gains generated by the funds. If high–tax rate individuals invest in a mutual fund that invests in stocks that pay high dividends, these high dividends will be allocated to the individuals based on their holdings and taxed at their individual tax rates.

- Corporations are given special protection from taxation on dividends they receive on their holdings in other companies, with 70% of the dividends exempt from taxes.[10] In other words, a corporation with a 40% tax rate that receives $100 million in dividends will pay only $12 million in taxes. Here again, the reasoning is that dividends paid by these corporations to their stockholders will ultimately be taxed.

Tax Treatment of Dividends in Other Markets

Many countries have plans in place to protect investors from the double taxation of dividends. There are two ways in which they can do this. One is to allow corporations to claim a full or partial tax deduction for dividends paid in computing corporate taxes. The other is to give partial or full tax relief to individuals who receive dividends for taxes paid by corporations on their income.

Corporate Tax Relief

In some countries, corporations are allowed to claim a partial or full deduction for dividends paid. This brings their treatment into parity with the treatment of the interest paid on debt, which is entitled to a full deduction in most countries. Among the Organisation for Economic Cooperation and Development (OECD) countries, the Czech Republic and Iceland offer partial deductions for dividend payments made by companies, but no country allows a full deduction. In a variation, Germany until recently applied a higher tax rate to income that was retained by firms than to income that was paid out in dividends. In effect, this gives a partial tax deduction to dividends.

Why don't more countries offer tax relief to corporations? There are two factors. One is the presence of foreign investors in the stock, who now also share in the tax windfall. The other is that investors in the stock may be tax-exempt or pay no taxes, which effectively reduces the overall taxes paid on dividends to the treasury to zero.

---

[10]The exemption increases as the proportion of the stock held increases. Thus, a corporation that owns 10% of another company's stock has 70% of dividends exempted. This rises to 80% if the company owns between 20% and 80% of the stock and to 100% if the company holds more than 80% of the outstanding stock.

Individual Tax Relief

There are far more countries that offer tax relief to individuals than to corporations. This tax relief can take several forms:

- ***Tax credit for taxes paid by corporation.*** Individuals can be allowed to claim the taxes paid by the corporation as a credit when computing their own taxes. In the example earlier, in which a company paid 30% of its income of $100 million as taxes and then paid its entire income as dividends to individuals with 40% tax rates, the individuals would be allowed to claim a tax credit of $30 million against the taxes owed, thus reducing taxes paid to $10 million. In effect, this will mean that only individuals with marginal tax rates that exceed the corporate tax rate will be taxed on dividends. Australia, Finland, Mexico, and New Zealand allow individuals to get a full credit for corporate taxes paid. Canada, France, the United Kingdom, and Turkey allow for partial tax credits.

- ***Lower tax rate on dividends.*** Dividends get taxed at a lower rate than other income to reflect the fact that it is paid out of after-tax income. In some countries, the tax rate on dividends is set equal to the capital gains tax rate. South Korea, for instance, has a flat tax rate of 16.5% for dividend income. This is the path that the United States chose in 2003 to grant relief from double taxation to stock investors.

In summary, it is far more common for countries to provide tax relief to investors than to corporations. By focusing on individuals, you can direct the tax relief only toward domestic investors and only to those investors who pay taxes in the first place.

Timing of Tax Payments

When the 1986 tax reform was signed into law, equalizing tax rates on ordinary income and capital gains, some believed that all the tax disadvantages of dividends had disappeared. Others noted that even with the same tax rates, dividends carried a tax disadvantage because the investor had no choice as to when to report the dividend as income; taxes were due when the firm paid out the dividends. In contrast, investors retained discretionary power over when to recognize and pay taxes on capital gains, because such taxes were not due until the stock was sold. This timing option allowed the investor to reduce the tax liability in one of two ways. First, by taking capital gains in periods of low income or capital losses to offset against the gain, the investor could reduce the taxes paid. Second, deferring a stock sale until an investor's death could result in tax savings, especially if the investor was not subject to estate taxes.

Assessing Investor Tax Preferences for Dividends

As you can see from the foregoing discussion, the tax rate on dividends can vary widely for different investors—individual, pension fund, mutual fund, or corporation—receiving the dividends, and even for the same investor on different investments. It is thus difficult to look at a company's investor base and determine their preferences for dividends and capital gains. A simple way to measure the tax disadvantage associated with dividends is to measure the price change on the ex-dividend date and compare it to the actual dividend paid. The stock price on the ex-dividend day should drop to reflect the loss in dividends to those buying the stock after that day. It is not clear, however, whether the price drop will be equal to the dividends if dividends and capital gains are taxed at different rates.

To see the relationship between the price drop and the tax rates of the marginal investor, assume that investors in a firm acquired stock at some point in time at a price P, and that they are approaching an ex-dividend day, in which the dividend is known to be D. Assume that each investor in this firm can either sell the stock before the ex-dividend day at a price P_B or wait and sell it after the stock goes ex-dividend at a price P_A. Finally, assume that the tax rate on dividends is t_o and that the tax rate on capital gains is t_{cg}. The cash flows the investor will receive from selling *before* the stock goes ex-dividend is

$$CF_B = P_B - (P_B - P)t_{cg}$$

In this case, by selling before the ex-dividend day, the investor receives no dividend. If the sale occurs *after* the ex-dividend day, the cash flow is

$$CF_A = P_A - (P_A - P)t_{cg} + D(1 - t_o)$$

If the cash flow from selling before the ex-dividend day were greater than the cash flow from selling after for all investors, they would all sell before, resulting in a drop in the stock price. Similarly, if the cash flows from selling after the ex-dividend day were greater than the cash flows from selling before for all investors, they would all sell after, resulting in a price drop after the ex-dividend day. To prevent either scenario, the marginal investors in the stock have to be indifferent between selling before and after the ex-dividend day. This will occur only if the cash flows from selling before are equal to the cash flows from selling after:

$$P_B - (P_B - P)t_{cg} = P_A - (P_A - P)t_{cg} + D(1 - t_o)$$

This can be simplified to yield the following ex-dividend day equality:

$$\frac{P_B - P_A}{D} = \frac{(1 - t_o)}{(1 - t_{cg})}$$

Thus, a necessary condition for the marginal investor to be indifferent between selling before and after the ex-dividend day is that the price drop on the ex-dividend day must reflect the investor's tax differential between dividends and capital gains.

By turning this equation around, we would argue that by observing a firm's stock price behavior on the ex-dividend day and relating it to the dividends paid by the firm, we can, in the long run, form some conclusions about the tax disadvantage the firm's marginal stockholders attach to dividends. In particular,

If	Tax Treatment of Dividends and Capital Gains
$P_B - P_A = D$	Marginal investor is indifferent between dividends and capital gains.
$P_B - P_A < D$	Marginal investor is taxed more heavily on dividends.
$P_B - P_A > D$	Marginal investor is taxed more heavily on capital gains.

Although there are obvious measurement problems associated with this measure, it does provide some interesting insight into how investors view dividends.

The first study of ex-dividend day price behavior was completed by Elton and Gruber in 1970.[11] They examined the behavior of stock prices on ex-dividend days for stocks listed on the NYSE between 1966 and 1969. Based on their finding that the price drop was only 78% of the dividends paid, Elton and Gruber concluded that dividends are taxed more heavily than capital gains. They also estimated the price change as a proportion of the dividend paid for firms in different dividend yield classes and reported that price drop is larger, relative to the dividend paid, for firms in the highest dividend–yield classes than for firms in lower dividend–yield classes. This difference in price drops, they argued, reflected the fact that investors in these firms are in lower tax brackets. Their conclusions were challenged, however, by some who argued, justifiably, that the investors trading on the stock on ex-dividend days are not the normal investors in the firm; rather, they are short-term, tax-exempt investors interested in capturing the difference between dividends and the price drops.

In the years since this study, several variables have changed. First, the highest marginal tax rate on dividends dropped, especially in the aftermath of the changes to the tax law in 1981 and again in 1986. Second, the composition of investors buying stocks has changed—a greater proportion of stocks are now held by institutional investors and, in particular, tax-exempt institutional investors than in the 1960s. Consequently, we would expect the implicit tax differential, reflected in the proportional price drop, to decrease substantially over time and there is evidence that it has.[12]

Implications

It is clear that dividends have historically been treated less favorably than capital gains by the tax authorities. In the United States, the double taxation of dividends, at least at the level of individual investors, should have created a strong disincentive to pay or to increase dividends. Other implications of the tax disadvantage argument include the following:

- Firms with investor bases composed primarily of individuals typically should have paid lower dividends than do firms with investor bases predominantly made up of tax-exempt institutions.

- The higher the income level (and hence the tax rates) of the investors holding stock in a firm, the lower the dividend paid out by the firm.

- As the tax disadvantage associated with dividends increased, the aggregate amount paid in dividends should have decreased. Conversely, if the tax disadvantage associated with dividends decreased, the aggregate amount paid in dividends should have increased.

The tax law changes of 2003 changed the terms of this debate, at least for the short term. By reducing the tax rate on dividends, they made dividends more attractive at least

---

[11] E. J. Elton and M. J. Gruber, "Marginal Stockholder Rates and the Clientele Effect," *Review of Economics and Statistics* 52:68–74.

[12] Elton, E. J., M. J. Gruber and J. Rentzler, 1984, The Ex-Dividend Day Behavior Of Stock Prices; A Reexamination Of The Clientele Effect: A Comment, Journal of Finance, v39(2), 551–556; Michaely, R. and J. Vila, 1995, Investors Heterogeneity, Prices and Volume around the Ex-Dividend Day, Journal of Financial and Quantitative Analysis, v30, 171–198.

to individual investors than they were prior to the change. We would expect companies to pay more dividends in response, and there is some evidence that companies changed dividend policy in response to the tax law change. Technology companies like Microsoft that had never paid dividends before have initiated dividends. In Figure 10.11, we look at the percent of S&P 500 companies that pay dividends by year, and at the market capitalization of dividend payers as a percent of the market capitalization of the S&P 500 from 1960 to 2008.

There was an uptick in both the number of companies paying dividends in 2003 and the dividends paid, reversing a long decline in both statistics. However, dividends leveled off after 2004, and companies continued the trend of shifting toward stock buybacks; the market crisis of 2008 resulted in a reversal of much of the post-2003 gain in dividends.

Figure 10.11   Dividend on S&P 500 Companies

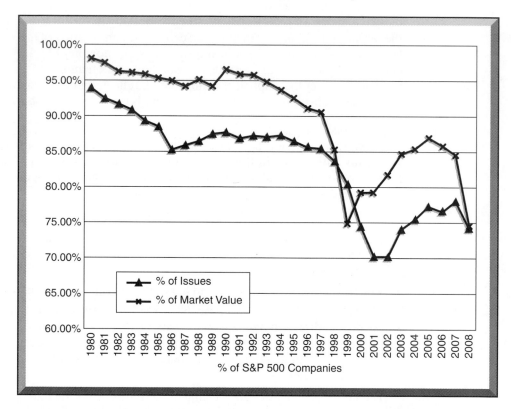

 IN PRACTICE: FROM STICKY TO FLEXIBLE DIVIDEND PAYOUTS

When firms increase dividends, the biggest peril that they face is being unable to sustain these dividends, given volatile earnings. In other words, the inability to cut dividends acts as an impediment to initiating and increasing dividends in the first place. There are two ways that firms can alleviate the problem of "sticky dividends":

1. One is to shift to a policy of *residual dividends*, where dividends paid are a function of the earnings in the year rather than a function of dividends the year before. Note that the sticky dividend phenomenon in the United States, where companies are reluctant to change their dollar dividends, is not universal. In countries like Brazil, companies target dividend payout ratios rather than dollar dividends and there is no reason why U.S. companies cannot adopt a similar practice. A firm that targets a constant dividend payout ratio will pay more dividends when its earnings are high and less when its earnings are low, and the signaling effect of lower dividends will be mitigated if the payout policy is clearly stated up-front.

2. The other option is to adopt a policy of regular dividends that will be based on sustainable and predictable earnings and to supplement these with special dividends when earnings are high. In this form, the special dividends will take the place of stock buybacks.

In summary, we should expect to see more creative dividend policies, in the face of increased uncertainty about future earnings and cash flows. In 2004, British Petroleum provided a preview of innovations to come by announcing that it would supplement its regular dividends with any extra cash flows generated if the oil price stayed above $30 a barrel, thus creating dividends tied more closely to its cash flows. ■

10.6 CORPORATE TAX STATUS AND DIVIDEND POLICY

Corporations are exempt from paying taxes on 70% of the dividends they receive from their stock holdings in other companies, whereas they face a capital gains tax rate of 20%. If all the stock in your company is held by other companies, and the ordinary tax rate for companies is 36%,

a. Dividends have a tax advantage relative to capital gains
b. Capital gains have a tax advantage relative to dividends
c. Dividends and capital gains are taxed at the same rate

Explain.

THE "DIVIDENDS ARE GOOD" SCHOOL

Notwithstanding the tax disadvantages, firms continue to pay dividends, and many investors view such payments positively. A third school of thought argues that dividends are good, and that they can increase firm value. Some of the arguments used are questionable, but some have a reasonable basis in fact. We consider both in this section.

Some Reasons for Paying Dividends That Do Not Measure Up

Some firms pay and increase dividends for the wrong reasons. We will consider two of those reasons in this section.

The Bird-in-the-Hand Fallacy

One reason given for the view that investors prefer dividends to capital gains is that dividends are certain, whereas capital gains are uncertain. Proponents of this view of dividend policy feel that risk-averse investors will therefore prefer the former. This argument is flawed. The simplest response is to point out that the choice is not between certain dividends today and uncertain capital gains at some unspecified point in the future, but between dividends today and an almost equivalent amount in price appreciation today. This comparison follows from our earlier discussion, where we noted that the stock price dropped by slightly less than the dividend on the ex-dividend day. By paying the dividend, the firm causes its stock price to drop today.

Another response to this argument is that a firm's value is determined by the cash flows from its projects. If a firm increases its dividends but its investment policy remains unchanged, it will have to replace the dividends with new stock issues. The investor who receives the higher dividend will therefore find himself or herself losing, in present value terms, an equivalent amount in price appreciation.

Temporary Excess Cash

In some cases, firms are tempted to pay or initiate dividends in years in which their operations generate excess cash. Although it is perfectly legitimate to return excess cash to stockholders, firms should also consider their own long-term investment needs. If the excess cash is a temporary phenomenon resulting from having an unusually good year or a nonrecurring action (such as the sale of an asset) and the firm expects cash shortfalls in future years, it may be better off retaining the cash to cover some or all these shortfalls. Another option is to pay the excess cash as a dividend in the current year and issue new stock when the cash shortfall occurs, but the substantial expense associated with new security issues makes this a costly strategy in the long run. Figure 10.12 summarizes the cost of issuing bonds and common stock by size of issue in the United States.[13]

Because issuance costs increase as the size of the issue decreases and for common stock issues, small firms should be especially cautious about paying out temporary excess cash as dividends. This said, it is important to note that some companies do pay dividends and issue stock during the course of the same period, mostly out of a desire to maintain their dividends. Figure 10.13 reports new stock issues by firms as a percentage of firm value, classified by their dividend yields, between 2005 and 2007.

Although it is not surprising that stocks that pay no dividends are most likely to issue stock, it is disconcerting that firms in the highest dividend yield class also issue significant proportions of new stock (approximately half of all the firms in this class also make new stock issues). This suggests that many of these firms are paying dividends on the one hand and issuing stock on the other, creating significant issuance costs for their stockholders in the process.

Some Good Reasons for Paying Dividends

Although the tax disadvantages of dividends were clear before 2003, especially for individual investors, there were some good reasons why firms that were paying dividends during the prior years did not suspend them. First, some investors liked to receive dividends and did not care about the tax disadvantage, either because they

---

[13]R. G. Ibbotson, J. L. Sindelar, and J. R. Ritter, "Initial Public Offerings," *Journal of Applied Corporate Finance* 1, no. 2:37–45.

Figure 10.12 Issuance Costs for Stocks and Bonds

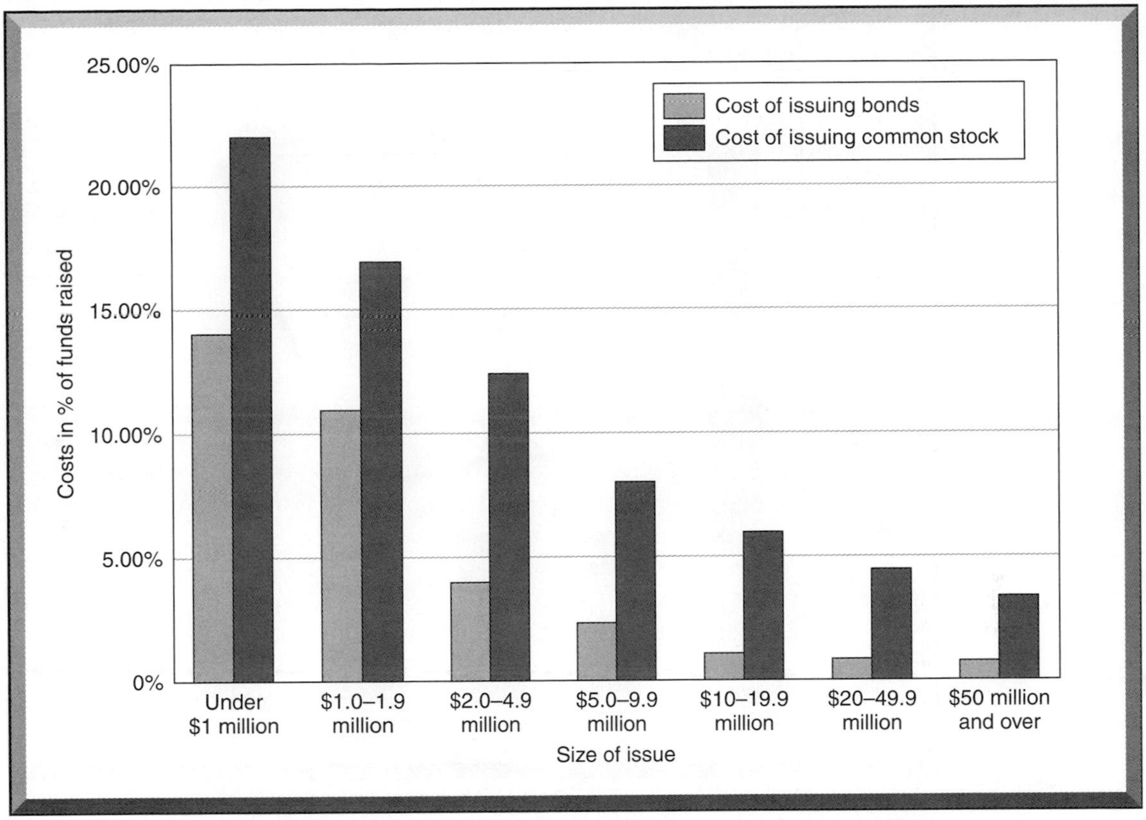

Source: R. G. Ibbotson, J. L. Sindelar, and J. R. Ritter, "Initial Public Offerings," *Journal of Applied Corporate Finance* 1, no. 2:37–45.

paid no or very low taxes or because they needed the regular cash flows. Firms that had paid dividends over long periods were likely to have accumulated investors with these characteristics, and cutting or eliminating dividends would not have been viewed favorably by this group.

Second, changes in dividends allow firms to signal to financial markets how confident they feel about future cash flows. Firms that are more confident about their future are therefore more likely to raise dividends; stock prices often increase in response. Cutting dividends is viewed by markets as a negative signal about future cash flows, and stock prices often decline in response. Third, as we noted in chapter 9, firms can use dividends as a tool for altering their financing mix and moving closer to an optimal debt ratio. Finally, the commitment to pay dividends can help reduce the conflicts between stockholders and managers by reducing the cash flows available to managers.

Some Investors Like Dividends

Prior to the tax law change in 2003, many in the "dividends are bad" school of thought argued that rational investors should have rejected dividends due to their tax

Figure 10.13 Equity Issues by Dividend Class, United States: 2005–2007

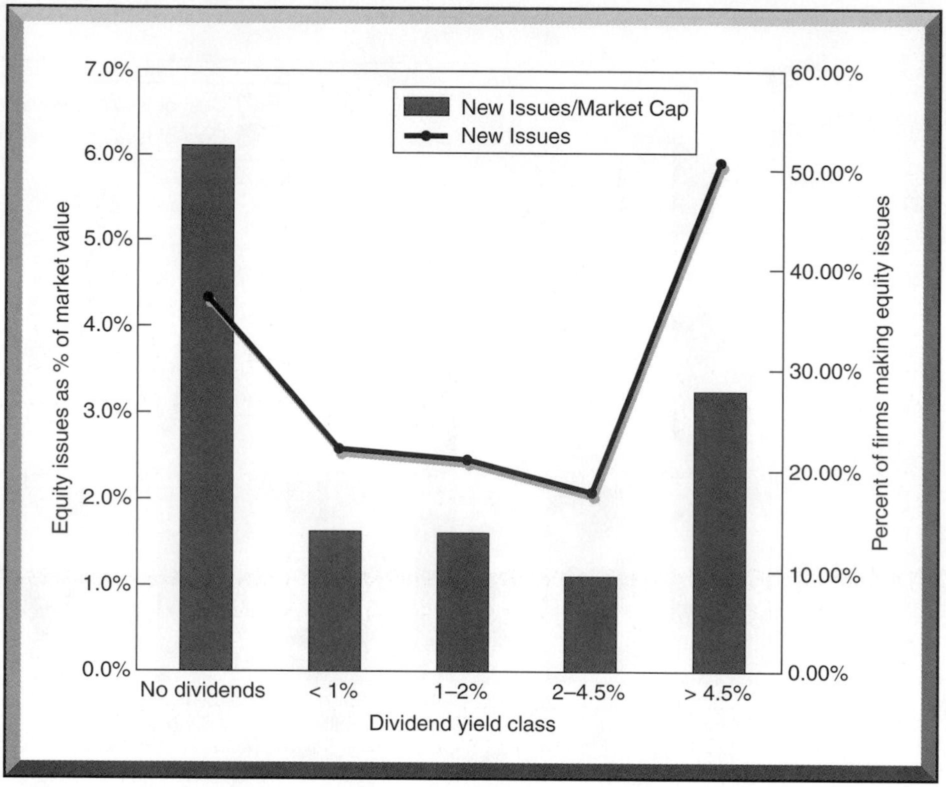

Source: Compustat database, 1998.

disadvantage. Whatever you might have thought of the merits of that argument, some investors had a strong preference for dividends and viewed large dividends positively. The most striking empirical evidence for this came from studies of companies that had two classes of shares: one that paid cash dividends, and another that paid an equivalent amount of stock dividends; thus, investors are given a choice between dividends and capital gains.

In 1978, John Long studied the price differential on Class A and B shares traded on Citizens Utility.[14] Class A shares paid a cash dividend, and Class B shares paid an equivalent stock dividend. Moreover, Class B shares could be converted at little or no cost to Class A shares at the option of its stockholders. Thus, an investor could choose to buy Class A shares to get cash dividends or Class B shares to get an equivalent capital gain. During the period of this study, the tax advantage was clearly on the side of capital gains; thus, we would expect to find Class A shares selling at a discount on Class B shares. The study found, surprisingly, that the Class A shares sold at a premium

---

[14]John B. Long Jr., "The Market Valuation of Cash Dividends: A Case to Consider," *Journal of Financial Economics* 6, nos. 2/3:235–264.

Figure 10.14   Price Differential on Citizens Utility Stock

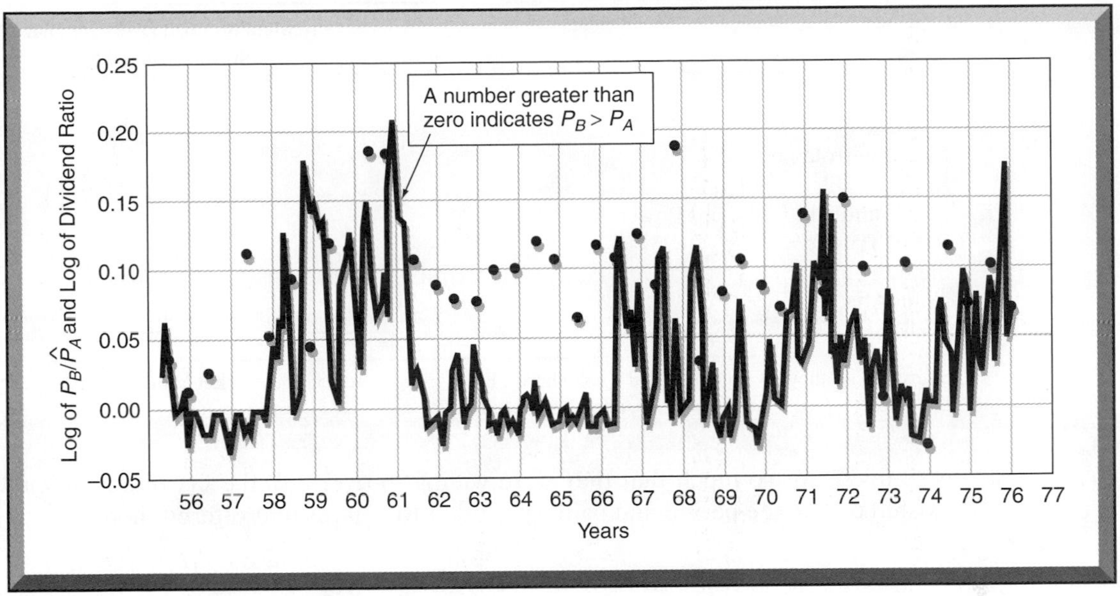

Source: John B. Long Jr., "The Market Valuation of Cash Dividends: A Case to Consider," *Journal of Financial Economics* 6, nos. 2/3:235–264.

over Class B shares. Figure 10.14 reports the price differential between the two share classes over the period of the analysis; note that when the price of class B shares is greater (lower) than the price of class A shares, $\ln(P_B/P_A)$ is greater (less) than zero.

Although it may be tempting to attribute this phenomenon to the irrational behavior of investors, that may not be the case. The investors in Citizen's Utility may not have been paying much in taxes and consequently did not care about the tax disadvantage associated with dividends. Alternatively, they might have needed and valued the predictable cash flow generated by the dividend payment. Why, you might ask, did they not sell stock to raise the cash flow they needed? The transaction costs and the difficulty of breaking up small holdings and selling unit shares may have made selling small amounts of stock infeasible.[15]

Bailey extended Long's study to examine Canadian utility companies, which also offered dividend and capital gains shares, and reported similar findings.[16] Table 10.2 summarizes the price premium at which the dividend shares sold. Note once again that on average, the cash dividend shares sell at a premium of 7.5% over the stock dividend shares. We caution that although these findings do not indicate that *all* stockholders like dividends, they do indicate that the stockholders in these specific companies liked

[15] Consider a stockholder who owns 100 shares trading at $20 per share, on which she receives a dividend of $0.50 per share. If the firm did not pay a dividend, the stockholder would have to sell 2.5 shares of stock to raise the $5 that would have come from the dividend.

[16] W. Bailey, "Canada's Dual Class Shares: Further Evidence on the Market Value of Cash Dividends," *Journal of Finance* 43, no. 5:1143–1160.

Table 10.2 Price Differential between Cash and Stock Dividend Shares	
	Premium on Cash Dividend Shares over Stock Dividend Shares
Consolidated Bathurst	19.30%
Donfasco	13.30%
Dome Petroleum	0.30%
Imperial Oil	12.10%
Newfoundland Light and Power	1.80%
Royal Trustco	17.30%
Stelco	2.70%
TransAlta	1.10%
Average	*7.54%*

Source: W. Bailey, "Canada's Dual Class Shares: Further Evidence on the Market Value of Cash Dividends," *Journal of Finance* 43, no. 5:1143–1160.

cash dividends so much that they were willing to overlook the tax disadvantage that existed during the period and paid a premium for shares that offered them.

 Why Do Some Investors Like Dividends? A Behavioral Perspective
Until the tax law was changed in 2003, dividends were taxed at much higher tax rates than capital gains. In fact, in most corporate finance books written in the 1970s and 1980s, the chapter on dividend policy was titled "The Dividend Puzzle." Rational investors, it was argued, would prefer that firms buy back stock (rather than pay dividends), and rational managers would oblige by eliminating dividends. Notwithstanding this argument, firms that had paid dividends in the past continued to do so, with little or no opposition from their stockholders. With the rise of behavioral finance, there have been attempts to explain the "irrational" liking for dividends manifested by some investors. Shefrin and Statman provide three possible explanations for why investors may like dividends:[17]

1. ***Absence of self control.*** To the extent that investors have trouble controlling consumption and resisting temptation, they look for simple rules that prevent them from indulgence. One simple rule with stocks that protects investors from overspending may be to consume the dividend but leave the principal untouched.

2. ***Mental accounting.*** The utility gained by investors from a gain that is broken down into dividends and capital gains may be greater than the utility from the same gain if delivered entirely as a capital gain. For instance, investors may get more utility when they receive $1 in dividends and $4 in capital gains than from a capital gain of $5.

3. ***Regret avoidance.*** Investors regret mistakes, but they regret errors of commission more than errors of omission. An investor who buys a nondividend stock that goes

---

[17]H. Shefrin and M. Statman, "Explaining Investor Preference for Cash Dividends," *Journal of Financial Economics* 13:253–282.

down may be forced to sell the stock to generate cash, and is thus forced to confront his or her error. In contrast, an investor who buys a dividend-paying stock that goes down may be able to get by without selling the stock, thus feeling less regret.

Shefrin and Statman are not claiming that all investors are susceptible to these phenomena, but even if a subset of investors are, they will like dividends, tax disadvantages notwithstanding.

The Clientele Effect

Stockholders examined in the studies just described clearly like cash dividends. At the other extreme are companies that pay no dividends, whose stockholders seem perfectly content with that policy. Given the vast diversity of stockholders, it is not surprising that over time, investors tend to invest in firms whose dividend policies match their preferences. Stockholders in high tax brackets who do not need the cash flow from dividend payments tend to invest in companies that pay low or no dividends. By contrast, those in low tax brackets who need the cash from dividend payments, as well as tax-exempt institutions that need current cash flows, invest in companies with high dividends. This clustering of stockholders in companies with dividend policies that match their preferences is called the *clientele effect*.

The existence of a clientele effect is supported by empirical evidence. One study looked at the portfolios of 914 investors to see whether they were affected by their tax brackets. The study found that older and poorer investors were more likely to hold high dividend–paying stocks than were younger and wealthier investors.

In another study, dividend yields were regressed against the characteristics of the investor base of a company (including age, income, and differential tax rates).[18]

$$\text{Dividend yield}_t = a + b\,\beta_t + c\,\text{Age}_t + d\,\text{Income}_t + e\,\text{Differential tax rate}_t + \varepsilon_t$$

	Coefficient	Implies
Constant	4.22%	
Beta coefficient	−2.145	Higher beta stocks pay lower dividends.
Age/100	3.131	Firms with older investors pay higher dividends.
Income/1,000	−3.726	Firms with wealthier investors pay lower dividends.
Differential tax rate	−2.849	If ordinary income is taxed at a higher rate than capital gains, the firm pays less dividends.

Source: R. R. Pettit, "Taxes, Transactions Costs and the Clientele Effect of Dividends," *Journal of Financial Economics* 5:419–436.

Not surprisingly, this study found that mature companies, with older and poorer investors, tended to pay more in dividends than companies with wealthier and younger

---

[18]R. R. Pettit, "Taxes, Transactions Costs and the Clientele Effect of Dividends," *Journal of Financial Economics* 5:419–436.

investors. Overall, dividend yields decreased as the tax disadvantage of dividends increased.

 10.7 DIVIDEND CLIENTELE AND TAX-EXEMPT INVESTORS

Pension funds are exempt from paying taxes on either ordinary income or capital gains and also have substantial ongoing cash flow needs. What types of stocks would you expect these funds to buy?

a. Stocks that pay high dividends

b. Stocks that pay no or low dividends

Explain.

Consequences of the Clientele Effect

The existence of a clientele effect has some important implications. First, it suggests that firms get the investors they deserve, because the dividend policy of a firm attracts investors who like that policy. Second, it means that firms will have a difficult time changing an established dividend policy, even if it makes sense to do so. For instance, U.S. telephone companies have traditionally paid high dividends and acquired an investor base that liked these dividends. In the 1990s, many of these firms entered new businesses (entertainment, multimedia, etc.) with much larger reinvestment needs and less stable cash flows. Although the need to cut dividends in the face of the changing business mix might seem obvious, it was nevertheless a hard sell to stockholders, who had become used to the dividends.

The clientele effect also provides an alternative argument for the irrelevance of dividend policy, at least when it comes to valuation. In summary, if investors migrate to firms that pay the dividends that most closely match their needs, no firm's value should be affected by its dividend policy. Thus, a firm that pays no or low dividends should not be penalized for doing so, because its investors *do not want* dividends. Conversely, a firm that pays high dividends should not have a lower value, because its investors like dividends. This argument assumes that there are enough investors in each dividend clientele to allow firms to be fairly valued, no matter what their dividend policy.

Empirical Evidence on the Clientele Effect

If there is a strong enough clientele effect, the returns on stocks should not be affected over long periods by the dividend policies of the underlying firms. If there is a tax disadvantage associated with dividends, the returns on stocks that pay high dividends should be higher than the returns on stocks that pay low dividends to compensate for the tax differences. Finally, if there is an overwhelming preference for dividends, these patterns should be reversed.

In their study of the clientele effect, Black and Scholes created twenty-five portfolios of NYSE stocks, classifying firms into five quintiles based on dividend yield, and then subdivided each group into five additional groups based on risk (beta) each year for thirty-five years, from 1931 to 1966.[19] When they regressed total returns on these portfolios against the dividend yields, the authors found no statistically significant relationship between them. These findings were contested in a study in 1979 by

---

[19]F. Black and M. Scholes, "The Effects of Dividend Yield and Dividend Policy on Common Stock Prices and Returns," *Journal of Financial Economics* 1:1–22.

Litzenberger and Ramaswamy, who used updated dividend yields every month and examined whether the total returns in ex-dividend months were correlated with dividend yields.[20] They found a strong *positive* relationship between total returns and dividend yields, supporting the hypothesis that investors are averse to dividends. They also estimated that the implied tax differential between capital gains and dividends was approximately 23%. Miller and Scholes countered by arguing that this finding was contaminated by the stock price effects of dividend increases and decreases.[21] In response, Litzenberger and Ramaswamy removed from the sample all cases in which the dividends were declared and paid in the same month and concluded that the implied tax differential was only 4%, which was not significantly different from zero.

Most studies of the clientele effect have concluded that total returns and dividend yields are positively correlated. Although many of them contend that this occurs because the implied tax differential between dividends and capital gains is significantly different from zero, there are alternative explanations for the phenomena. In particular, although one may disagree with Miller and Scholes's conclusions, their argument—that the higher returns on stocks that pay high dividends might have nothing to do with the tax disadvantages associated with dividends but may instead be a reflection of the price increases associated with unexpected dividend increases—has both a theoretical and an empirical basis.

10.8   DIVIDEND CLIENTELE AND CHANGING DIVIDEND POLICY

Phone companies in the United States have for long had the following features been regulated, had stable earnings and low reinvestment needs, and paid high dividends. Many of these phone companies are now considering entering the multimedia age and becoming entertainment companies, which requires more reinvestment and creates more volatility in earnings. If you were the CEO of the phone company, would you

a.   Announce an immediate cut in dividends as part of a major capital investment plan?

b.   Continue to pay high dividends, and use new stock issues to finance the expansion?

c.   Do something else?

Explain.

Dividends Operate as an Information Signal

Financial markets examine every action a firm takes for implications for future cash flows and firm value. When firms announce changes in dividend policy, they are conveying information to markets, whether or not they intend to do so.

Financial markets tend to view announcements made by firms about their future prospects with a great deal of skepticism, because firms routinely make exaggerated claims. At the same time, some firms with good investment prospects are undervalued by markets. How do such firms convey that information credibly to markets? Signaling theory suggests that these firms need to take actions that cannot be easily imitated by firms without good projects. Increasing dividends is viewed as one such action. By increasing dividends, firms create a cost to themselves, because they commit to paying

---

[20]R. H. Litzenberger and K. Ramaswamy, "The Effect of Personal Taxes and Dividends on Capital Asset Prices: Theory and Empirical Evidence," *Journal of Financial Economics* 7:163–196.

[21]M. H. Miller and M. S. Scholes, "Dividends and Taxes," *Journal of Financial Economics* 6, no. 4:333–364.

these dividends in the long run. Their willingness to make this commitment indicates to investors that they believe they have the capacity to generate these cash flows in the long run. This positive signal should therefore lead investors to reevaluate the cash flows and firm values and increase the stock price.

Decreasing dividends is a negative signal, largely because firms are reluctant to cut dividends. Thus, when a firm take this action, markets see it as an indication that this firm is in substantial, long-term financial trouble. Consequently, such actions lead to a drop in stock prices.

The empirical evidence concerning price reactions to dividend increases and decreases is consistent, at least on average, with this signaling theory. Figure 10.15 summarizes the average excess returns around dividend changes for firms.[22]

Figure 10.15 Excess Returns around Announcements of Dividend Changes

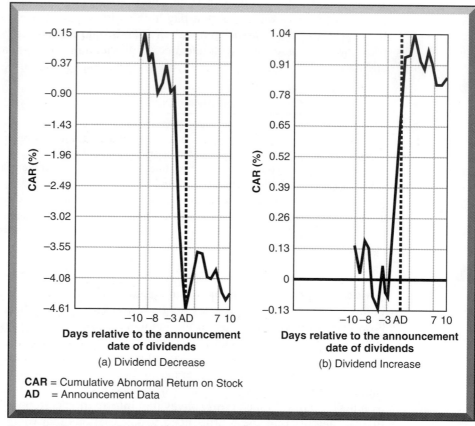

CAR = Cumulative Abnormal Return on Stock
AD = Announcement Data

Source: J. Aharony and I. Swary, "Quarterly Dividends and Earnings Announcements and Stockholders' Returns: An Empirical Analysis," *Journal of Finance* 36:1–12

---

[22]J. Aharony and I. Swary, "Quarterly Dividends and Earnings Announcements and Stockholders' Returns: An Empirical Analysis," *Journal of Finance* 36:1–12.

On average, stock prices increase about 1% on the announcement of dividend increases and drop about 4.6% on the announcement of dividend decreases. The more negative reaction to dividend decreases reflects their infrequency and also can be taken as an indication that dividend decreases are more potent negative signals than dividend increases are positive signals. We should view the signaling explanation for dividend increases and decreases cautiously, however. Although it is true that firms with good projects may use dividend increases to convey information to financial markets, is it the most efficient way? For smaller firms, which have relatively few conduits to convey information to the market, the answer might be yes. For larger firms, which have many ways of conveying information to markets, dividend increases might not be the least expensive or most effective signals. For instance, information may be more effectively and economically conveyed through an analyst report on the company.

There is another reason for skepticism. An equally plausible story can be told about how an increase in dividends sends a negative signal to financial markets. Consider a firm that has never paid dividends in the past but has registered extraordinary growth and high returns on its projects. When this firm first starts paying dividends, its stockholders may consider this an indication that the firm's projects are neither as plentiful nor as lucrative as they used to be. However, Palepu and Healy found that the initiation of dividends did not signal a decline in earnings growth in a study of 151 firms from 1970 to 1979.[23]

10.9   DIVIDENDS AS SIGNALS

Silicon Electronics, a company with a history of not paying dividends, high earnings growth, and reinvestment back into the company, announces that it will be initiating dividends. You would expect the stock price to

a.   go up

b.   go down

c.   remain unchanged

Explain.

Dividend Policy Is a Tool for Changing Financing Mix

Dividend policy cannot be analyzed in a vacuum. Firms can use dividend policy as a tool to change their debt ratios. We previously examined how firms that want to increase or decrease leverage can do so by changing their dividend policy: increasing dividends increases financial leverage over time, and decreasing dividends reduces leverage. Thus, an under levered firm may choose to increase or initiate dividends to increase its debt ratio over time and an overlevered firm may reduce or terminate dividends to reduce its financial leverage.

There is another dynamic at play, as well. When dividends increase, stockholders sometimes get a bonus in the form of a wealth transfer from lenders to the firm. Lenders would rather have firms accumulate cash than pay it out as dividends. The payment of dividends takes cash out of the firm, and this cash could have been used to cover

---

[23]K. Palepu and P. Healy, "Earnings Information Conveyed by Dividend Initiations and Omissions," *Journal of Financial Economics* 21:149–175.

outstanding interest or principal payments. Not surprisingly, bond prices decline on the announcement of large increases in dividends. It is equity investors who gain from the loss in market value faced by bondholders. Bondholders, of course, try to protect themselves against this loss by restricting how much firms can pay out in dividends.

 A Catering Explanation for Dividends: A Behavioral Perspective
In conventional corporate finance, firms trade off the costs of paying dividends (the differential tax costs to their investors, the issuance costs of new financing) against the benefits of dividends (signaling benefits and reduced agency costs) to determine whether they should pay dividends. Baker and Wurgler offer an alternative explanation where firms cater to the investor desire for dividends. Looking at the time period between 1963 and 2000, they use the difference between the market to book ratios of dividend paying firms and dividend nonpayers as a measure of investor demand for dividends; when investors, in the aggregate, like dividends, dividend payers trade at a premium over nonpayers, and when investors do not want dividends, dividend payers trade at a discount. They find that the dividends paid by firms can be better explained by investor demand for dividends, with more firms paying dividends when dividend payers trade at a premium, and fewer firms paying dividends when dividend payers trade at a discount.

The catering rationale for dividends is more an explanation for how firms set dividends in the aggregate and less about dividend policy in individual firms, but it does point to an important reality. Investor preferences for dividends shift over time, and firms have to respond to changes in these preferences. Managers, when setting dividend policy, have to be aware not only of what investors, in the aggregate, think about dividends, but also of what investors in their firm think about dividends. It would seem to us that the catering explanation is a dynamic version of the clientele story, where the preferences for dividends on the part of investors in a firm can change over time, and dividend policy has to change with it.

MANAGERIAL INTERESTS AND DIVIDEND POLICY

We have considered dividend policy almost entirely from the perspective of equity investors in the firm. In reality, though, managers set dividend policy, and it should come as no surprise that there may be potential for a conflict of interests between stockholders and managers.

The Source of the Conflict
When examining debt policy, we noted that one reason for taking on more debt was to induce managers to be more disciplined in their project choices. Implicit in this free cash flow argument is the assumption that accumulated cash, if left to the discretion of the managers of the firm, would be wasted on poor projects. If this is true, we can argue that forcing a firm to make a commitment to pay dividends provides an alternative way of forcing managers to be disciplined in project choice by reducing the cash that is available for discretionary uses.

If this is the reason stockholders want managers to commit to paying larger dividends, firms in which there is a clear separation between ownership and management should pay larger dividends than firms with substantial insider ownership and involvement in managerial decisions.

What Do Managers Believe about Dividend Policy?

Given the pros and cons for paying dividends and the lack of a consensus on the effect of dividends on value, it is worth considering what managers factor in when they make dividend decisions. Baker, Farrelly, and Edelman surveyed managers on their views on dividend policy and reported the level of agreement with a series of statements.[24] Table 10.3 summarizes their findings.

It is quite clear from this survey that, rightly or wrongly, managers believe that their dividend payout ratios affect firm value and operate as signals of future prospects. They also operate under the presumption that investors choose firms with dividend policies that match their preferences and that management should be responsive to their needs.

In an updated and comprehensive survey of dividend policy published in 2004,[25] Brav, Graham, Harvey, and Michaely conclude that management's focus is not on the level of dividends but on changes in these dividends. Indicating a shift from views in prior studies, many managers in this survey saw little gain from increasing dividends, even in response to higher earnings and preferred stock buybacks instead. In fact, many managers in companies that paid dividends regret the level of dividends paid by their

Table 10.3 MANAGEMENT BELIEFS ABOUT DIVIDEND POLICY			
	Agree	**No Opinion**	**Disagree**
1. A firm's dividend payout ratio affects the price of the stock.	61%	33%	6%
2. Dividend payments provide a signaling device of future prospects.	52%	41%	7%
3. The market uses divided announcements as information for assessing firm value.	43%	51%	6%
4. Investors have different perceptions of the relative riskiness of dividends and retained earnings.	56%	42%	2%
5. Investors arc basically indifferent with regard to returns from dividends and capital gains.	6%	30%	64%
6. A stockholder is attracted to firms that have dividend policies appropriate to the stockholder's tax environment.	44%	49%	7%
7. Management should be responsive to shareholders' preferences regarding dividends.	41%	49%	10%

[24] H. Kent Baker, Gail E. Farrelly, and Richard B. Edelman, "A Survey of Management Views on Dividend Policy," *Financial Management* 14, no. 3:78–84.
[25] A. Brav, J. R. Graham, C. R. Harvey, and R. Michaely, "Payout Policy in the 21st Century," working paper, Duke University, Durham, NC, 2004.

firms, indicating that they would have set the dividend at a much lower level if they had the choice. In contrast to the survey quoted in the last paragraph, managers also rejected the idea that dividends operate as useful financial signals. From the survey, the authors conclude that the rules of the game for dividends are the following: do not cut dividends, have a dividend policy similar to your peer group, preserve a good credit rating, maintain flexibility, and do not take actions that reduce earnings per share.

10.10   CORPORATE GOVERNANCE AND DIVIDEND POLICY

In countries where stockholders have little or no control over incumbent managers, you would expect dividends paid by companies to be

a.   Lower than dividends paid in other countries

b.   Higher than dividends paid in other countries

c.   About the same as dividends paid in other countries

Managerial Traits and Dividends: A Behavioral Perspective
Managers have the discretion to determine how much a firm pays as dividends. Not surprisingly, managerial traits play a role in how much dividends get paid in the first place and, by extension, how much cash is accumulated. In particular, studies indicate that the following factors affect dividend policy:

- *Managerial overconfidence.*   A common theme across all aspects of corporate finance is that the decisions made by managers can be affected by their confidence. In addition to borrowing too much money, issuing too little new equity, overestimating the cash flows and benefits from acquisitions, and investing in too many projects, overconfident managers also tend to pay too little in dividends. Dividend payout ratios at firms run by overconfident CEOs are lower than otherwise similar firms run by less confident CEOs.

- *Conservative vs. aggressive managers.*   To examine how managerial style affects corporate finance decisions, Schoar and Bertrand tracked 500 top managers as they moved across firms to see how much their styles affected policy. They find that management predispositions follow them from firm to firm. In other words, CEOs that were acquirers at one firm brought that acquisitive streak to the next firm that they moved on to. Looking at dividend policy, they noted that conservative managers tended to pay less dividends and accumulate more cash than aggressive managers at firms with similar characteristics. As an aside, they find that managers with earlier birth cohorts are more conservative than other managers and that executives with MBAs are more aggressive than executives without.

The bottom line is that dividend policy is set by managers, some of whom are more willing to pay out dividends than others.

CONCLUSION

There are three schools of thought on dividend policy. The first is that dividends are neutral and neither increase nor decrease value. Stockholders are therefore indifferent between receiving dividends and enjoying price appreciation. This view is based on the assumptions that there are no tax disadvantages to investors associated with receiving dividends, relative to capital gains, and that firms can raise external capital for new investments without issuance costs.

The second view is that dividends destroy value for stockholders because they are taxed at much higher rates than capital gains. Until the tax code was changed in 2003, the evidence for this tax disadvantage was strong both in the tax code and in markets, when we examine stock price changes on ex-dividend days. On average, stock prices decline by less than the amount of the dividend, suggesting that stockholders in most firms consider dividends to be less attractive than equivalent capital gains.

The third school of thought argues that dividends can be value-increasing, at least for some firms. In particular, firms that have accumulated stockholders who prefer dividends to capital gains should continue to pay large, increasing dividends to keep their investor clientele happy. Furthermore, increasing dividends can operate as a positive signal to financial markets and allow a firm to change its financing mix over time. Finally, forcing firms to pay out dividends reduces the cash available to managers for new investments. If managers are not investing with the objective of maximizing stockholder wealth, this can make stockholders better off.

LIVE CASE STUDY

THE TRADEOFF ON DIVIDEND POLICY

Objective: To examine how much cash your firm has returned to its stockholders and in what form (dividends or stock buybacks) and to evaluate whether the tradeoff favors returning more or less.

Key Questions

- Has this firm ever paid out dividends? If so, is there a pattern to the dividends over time?

- Given this firm's characteristics today, do you think that this firm should be paying more dividends, less dividends, or no dividends at all?

Framework for Analysis

1. ***Historical Dividend Policy***

   - How much has this company paid in dividends over the past few years?

   - How have these dividends related to earnings in these years?

2. ***Firm Characteristics***

   - How easily can the firm convey information to financial markets? In other words, how necessary is it for it to use dividend policy as a signal?

   - Who are the marginal stockholders in this firm? Do they like dividends, or would they prefer stock buybacks?

   - How well can this firm forecast its future financing needs? How valuable is preserving flexibility to this firm?

   - Are there any significant bond covenants that you know of that restrict the firm's dividend policy?

   - How does this firm compare with other firms in the sector in terms of dividend policy?

Getting Information on Dividend Policy

You can get information about dividends paid back over time from the financial statements of the firm. (The statement of changes in cash flows is usually the best source.) To find typical dividend payout ratios and yields for the sector in which this firm operates, examine the data set on industry averages on my Web site.

 Online Sources of Information
www.stern.nyu.edu/~adamodar/cfin2E/roject/data.htm.

PROBLEMS AND QUESTIONS

(In the problems below, you can use a risk premium of 5.5% and a tax rate of 40% if either is not specified.)

1. If Consolidated Power is priced at $50.00 with dividend, and its price falls to $46.50 when a dividend of $5.00 is paid, what is the implied marginal rate of personal taxes for its stockholders? Assume that the tax on capital gains is 40% of the personal income tax.

2. You are comparing the dividend policies of three dividend-paying utilities. You have collected the following information on the ex-dividend behavior of these firms.

	NE Gas	SE Bell	Western Electric
Price before	50	70	100
Price after	48	67	95
Dividends/share	4	4	5

If you were a tax-exempt investor, which company would you use to make "dividend arbitrage" profits? How would you go about doing so?

3. Southern Rail has just declared a dividend of $1. The average investor in Southern Rail faces an ordinary tax rate of 50%. Although the capital gains rate is also 50%, it is believed that the investor gets the advantage of deferring this tax until future years (the effective capital gains rate will therefore be 50% discounted back to the present). If the price of the stock before the ex-dividend day is $10 and it drops to $9.20 by the end of the ex-dividend day, how many years is the average investor deferring capital gains taxes? (Assume that the opportunity cost used by the investor in evaluating future cash flows is 10%.)

4. LMN Corporation, a real estate company, is planning to pay a dividend of $0.50 per share. Most of the investors in LMN are other corporations that pay 40% of their ordinary income and 28% of their capital gains as taxes. However, they are allowed to exempt 85% of the dividends they receive from taxes. If the shares are selling at $10 per share, how much would you expect the stock price to drop on the ex-dividend day?

5. UJ Gas is a utility that has followed a policy of increasing dividends every quarter by 5% over dividends in the prior year. The company announces that it will increase quarterly dividends from $1.00 to $1.02 next quarter. What price reaction would you expect to the announcement? Why?

6. Microsoft, which has had a history of high growth and pays no dividends, announces that it will start paying dividends next quarter. How would you expect its stock price to react to the announcement? Why?

7. JC Automobiles is a small auto parts manufacturing firm that has paid $1.00 in annual dividends each year for the past five years. It announces that dividends will increase to $1.25 next year. What would you expect the price reaction to be? Why? If your answer is different from the previous problem, explain the reasons for the difference.

8. Would your answer be different for the previous problem if JC Automobiles were a large firm followed by thirty-five analysts? Why, or why not?

9. WeeMart, a retailer of children's clothes, announces a cut in dividends following a year in which both revenues and earning dropped significantly. How would you expect its stock price to react? Explain.

10. RJR Nabisco, in response to stockholder pressure in 1996, announced a significant increase in dividends paid to stockholders financed by the sale of some of its assets. What would you expect the stock price to do? Why?

11. RJR Nabisco also had $10 billion in bonds outstanding at the time of the dividend increase in Problem 10. How would you expect the bonds to react to the announcement? Why?

12. When firms increase dividends, stock prices tend to increase. One reason given for this price reaction is that dividends operate as a positive signal. What is the increase in dividends signaling to markets? Will markets always believe the signal? Why, or why not?

CHAPTER 11

ANALYZING CASH RETURNED TO STOCKHOLDERS

Companies have always returned cash to stockholders in the form of dividends, but over the past few years, they have used stock buybacks as an alternative. How much have companies returned to their stockholders, and how much could they have returned? As stockholders in these firms, would we want them to change their policies and return more or less than they are currently? In this chapter, we expand our definition of cash returned to stockholders to include stock buybacks. As we will document, firms in the United States have been buying back stock to either augment regular dividends or, in some cases, substitute for cash dividends.

Using this expanded measure of actual cash flows returned to stockholders, we consider two ways to analyze whether firms are returning too little or too much to

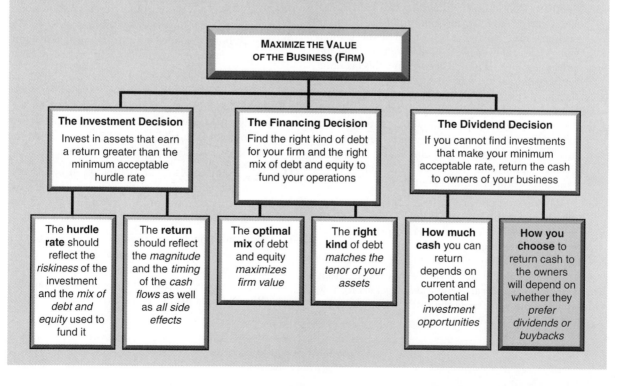

MAXIMIZE THE VALUE OF THE BUSINESS (FIRM)

The Investment Decision
Invest in assets that earn a return greater than the minimum acceptable hurdle rate

The Financing Decision
Find the right kind of debt for your firm and the right mix of debt and equity to fund your operations

The Dividend Decision
If you cannot find investments that make your minimum acceptable rate, return the cash to owners of your business

The **hurdle rate** should reflect the *riskiness* of the investment and the *mix of debt and equity* used to fund it

The **return** should reflect the *magnitude* and the *timing* of the *cash flows* as well as *all side effects*

The **optimal mix** of debt and equity *maximizes firm value*

The **right kind** of debt *matches the tenor of your assets*

How much cash you can return depends on current and potential *investment opportunities*

How you choose to return cash to the owners will depend on whether they *prefer dividends or buybacks*

stockholders. First, we examine how much cash is left over after reinvestment needs have been met and debt payments made. We consider this cash flow to be the cash available for return to stockholders and compare it to the actual amount returned. We categorize firms into firms that return more to stockholders than they have available in this cash flow, firms that return what they have available, and those that return less than they have available. We then examine the firms that consistently return more or less cash than they have available and the consequences of these policies. For this part of the analysis, we bring in two factors—the quality of the firm's investments and the firm's plans to change its financing mix. We argue that stockholders are more willing to trust management with excess cash if the firm has a track record of good investments. Also, firms that return more cash than they have available are on firm ground if they are trying to increase their debt ratios.

In the second approach to analyzing dividend policy, we consider how much comparable firms in the industry pay as dividends. Many firms set their dividend policies by looking at their peer groups. We discuss this practice and suggest some refinements in it to allow for the vast differences that often exist between firms in the same sector.

In the last part of this chapter, we look at how firms that decide they are paying too much or too little in dividends can change their dividend policies. Because firms tend to attract stockholders who like their existing dividend policies, and because dividends convey information to financial markets, changing dividends can have unintended and negative consequences. We suggest ways firms can manage a transition from a high dividend payout to a low dividend payout or vice versa.

CASH RETURNED TO STOCKHOLDERS

In the previous chapter, we considered the decision about how much to pay in dividends and discussed three schools of thought about whether dividend policy affected firm value. Until the middle of the 1980s, dividends remained the primary mechanism for firms to return cash to stockholders. Starting in that period, we have seen firms increasingly turn to buying back their own stock, using either cash on hand or borrowed money, as a mechanism for returning cash to their stockholders.

The Effects of Buying Back Stock

First let's consider the effect of a stock buyback on the firm doing the buyback. A stock buyback requires cash, just as a dividend would, and thus has the same effect on the assets of the firm—a reduction in the cash balance. Just as a dividend reduces the book value of the equity in the firm, a stock buyback reduces the book value of equity. Thus, if a firm with a book value of equity of $1 billion buys back $400 million in equity,[1] the

---

[1]The stock buyback is at market value. Thus, when the market value is significantly higher than the book value of equity, a buyback of stock will reduce the book value of equity disproportionately. For example, if the market value is five times the book value of equity, buying back 10% of the stock will reduce the book value of equity by 50%.

book value of equity will drop to $600 million. Both a dividend payment and a stock buyback reduce the overall market value of equity in the firm, but the way they affect the market value is different. The dividend reduces the market price on the ex-dividend day and does not change the number of shares outstanding. A stock buyback reduces the number of shares outstanding and may be accompanied by a stock price increase. For instance, if a firm with 100 million shares outstanding trading at $10 per share buys back 10 million shares, the number of shares will decline to 90 million, but the stock price may increase to $10.50. The total market value of equity after the buyback will be $945 million, a drop in value of 5.5%.

Unlike a dividend, which returns cash to all stockholders in a firm, a stock buyback returns cash selectively to those stockholders who choose to sell their stock to the firm. The remaining stockholders get no cash; they gain indirectly from the stock buyback if the stock price increases. In the example above, stockholders in the firm will find the value of their holdings increasing by 5% after the stock buyback.

IN PRACTICE: How Do You Buy Back Stock?

The process of repurchasing equity will depend largely on whether the firm intends to repurchase stock in the open market at the prevailing market price or to make a more formal tender offer for its shares. There are three widely used approaches to buying back equity:

1. ***Repurchase tender offers*** In a repurchase tender offer, a firm specifies a price at which it will buy back shares, the number of shares it intends to repurchase, and the period of time for which it will keep the offer open; it then invites stockholders to submit their shares for the repurchase. In many cases, firms retain the flexibility to withdraw the offer if an insufficient number of shares are submitted or to extend the offer beyond the originally specified time period. This approach is used primarily for large equity repurchases.

2. ***Open market repurchases*** In the case of open market repurchases, firms buy shares in the market at the prevailing market price. Although firms do not have to publicly disclose their intent to buy back shares in the market, they do have to comply with SEC requirements preventing price manipulation or insider trading. Finally, open market purchases can be spread out over much longer time periods than tender offers and are more widely used for smaller repurchases. In terms of flexibility, an open market repurchase affords the firm much more freedom in deciding when to buy back shares and how many shares to repurchase.

3. ***Privately negotiated repurchases*** In privately negotiated repurchases, firms buy back shares from a large stockholder in the company at a negotiated price. This method is not as widely used as the first two and may be employed by managers or owners as a way of consolidating control and eliminating a troublesome stockholder. ■

The Magnitude of Stock Buybacks

In the past decade, more firms have used equity repurchases as an alternative to paying dividends. Figure 11.1 summarizes dividends paid and equity repurchases at U.S. corporations between 1989 and 2008.

It is worth noting that although aggregate dividends at all U.S. firms have grown at a rate of about 1.18% a year over this period, stock buybacks have grown 9.83% a year. In another interesting shift, the proportion of cash returned to stockholders in the form of stock buybacks has climbed from 32% in 1989 to more than 60% in recent years. In 1999, for the first time in U.S. corporate history, stock buybacks in aggregate exceeded dividends in aggregate. Although the slowdown in the economy and the market crisis resulted in both dividends and stock buybacks decreasing in 2008, buybacks still exceeded dividends for the year.

This shift has been much less dramatic outside the United States. Firms in other countries have been less likely to use stock buybacks to return cash to stockholders for a number of reasons.[2] First, until 2003, dividends in the United States faced a much higher tax burden, relative to capital gains, than dividends paid in other countries. Many European countries, for instance, allow investors to claim a tax credit on dividends to

Figure 11.1   Stock Buybacks and Dividends: Aggregate for US Firms: 1989–2008

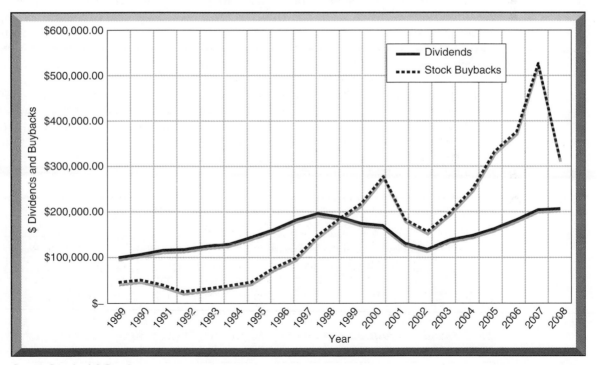

Source: Standard & Poor's.

---

[2]This may be changing as well. In 2003, large European companies bought back more stock than their U.S. counterparts.

compensate for taxes paid by the firms paying them. Stock buybacks thus provided a much greater tax benefit to investors in the United States than they did to investors outside the United States, by shifting income from dividends to capital gains. Second, stock buybacks were prohibited or tightly constrained in many countries, at least until very recently. Third, a strong reason for the increase in stock buybacks in the United States was pressure from stockholders on managers to pay out idle cash. This pressure was far less in the weaker corporate governance systems that exist outside the United States.

For the rest of this section, we will be using the phrase "dividend policy" to mean not just what gets paid out in dividends but also the cash returned to stockholders in the form of stock buybacks.

ILLUSTRATION 11.1   Dividends and Stock Buybacks: Disney, Aracruz, and Deutsche Bank
In Table 11.1, we consider how much Disney, Aracruz, Tata Chemicals and Deutsche Bank have returned to stockholders in dividends and how much stock they have bought back each year between 2004 and 2008. (Aracruz and Disney's numbers are in millions of US dollars, whereas Tata Chemicals and Deutsche Bank are reported in their local currencies in millions.)

All four companies paid dividends over the five-year period, but there are interesting differences between the companies. Disney, and Tata Chemicals increased dividends in each of the five years, but Aracruz had more volatile dividends over the period, with dividends dropping significantly in 2007. This reflects the convention of focusing on absolute dividends in the United States and India, but the practice of maintaining payout ratios in Brazil. Deutsche Bank had a precipitous drop in dividends in 2008, reflecting the effects of the market crisis and the desire to maintain regulatory capital ratios.

Looking at stock buybacks, Disney has been the most active player buying stock in all five years, with buybacks exceeding $6 billion each year in 2006 and 2007. None of the other companies have bought back stock.[3] These differences reflect the markets in which these firms operate. As noted earlier, companies in the United States have generally bought back more stock than their counterparts in other markets.

Table 11.1   CASH RETURNED TO STOCKHOLDERS: DISNEY, ARACRUZ, AND DEUTSCHE BANK (IN MILLIONS)

	Disney		Aracruz		Tata Chemicals		Deutsche Bank	
	Dividends	**Buybacks**	**Dividends**	**Buybacks**	**Dividends**	**Buybacks**	**Dividends**	**Buybacks**
2004	$430	$335	$74	$0	Rs1,307	$0	€924	€0
2005	$490	$2,420	$109	$0	Rs1,338	$0	€1,386	€0
2006	$519	$6,898	$199	$0	Rs1,589	$0	€1,995	€0
2007	$637	$6,923	$139	$0	Rs1,716	$0	€2,255	€0
2008	$664	$4,453	$252	$0	Rs2,010	$0	€285	€0

---

[3]The key difference with treasury stock that stays on the books is that the number of shares in the company remains unchanged. In the United States, companies are not allowed to keep treasury stock on their books for extended periods.

Reasons for Stock Buybacks

Firms that want to return substantial amounts of cash to their stockholders can either pay large special dividends or buy back stock. There are several advantages to both the firm and its stockholders that came by using stock buybacks as an alternative to dividend payments.

1. Unlike regular dividends, which typically commit the firm to continue payment in future periods, equity repurchases are one-time returns of cash. Consequently, firms with excess cash that are uncertain about their ability to continue generating these cash flows in future periods should repurchase stocks rather than pay dividends. (They could also choose to pay special dividends, which do not commit the firm to making similar payments in the future.)

2. The decision to repurchase stock affords a firm much more flexibility to reverse itself and spread the repurchases over a longer period than does a decision to pay an equivalent special dividend. In fact, there is substantial evidence that many firms that announce ambitious stock repurchases do reverse themselves and do not carry the plans through to completion.

3. Equity repurchases may provide a way of increasing insider control in firms, because they reduce the number of shares outstanding. If the insiders do not tender their shares back, they will end up holding a larger proportion of the firm and, consequently, greater control. From the perspective of insiders (who make the buyback decision), this is an advantage.

4. Finally, equity repurchases may provide firms with a way of supporting their stock prices when they are declining.[4] For instance, in the aftermath of the stock market crash of 1987, many firms initiated stock buyback plans to keep prices from falling further with partial success.

There are two potential benefits that stockholders might perceive in stock buybacks:

1. Equity repurchases may offer tax advantages to stockholders. This was clearly true before 2003, because dividends were taxed at ordinary tax rates, whereas the price appreciation that results from equity repurchases was taxed at capital gains rates. Even when dividends and capital gains are taxed at the same rate, stockholders have the option not to sell their shares back to the firm and therefore do not have to realize the capital gains at the time of the equity repurchases, whereas they have no such choice with dividends.

2. Equity repurchases are much more selective in terms of paying out cash only to those stockholders who need it. This benefit flows from the voluntary nature of stock buybacks: those who need the cash can tender their shares back to the firm, and those who do not can continue to hold onto them.

In summary, equity repurchases allow firms to return cash to stockholders and still maintain flexibility for future periods.

---

[4]This will be true only if the price decline is not supported by a change in the fundamentals—drop in earnings, declining growth, and so on. If the price drop is justified, a stock buyback program can, at best, provide only temporary respite.

Table 11.2 Returns Around Stock Repurchase Tender Offers			
	1962–79	**1980–86**	**1962–86**
Number of buybacks	131	90	221
Percentage of shares purchased	15.45%	16.82%	16.41%
Abnormal return to all stockholders	16.19%	11.52%	14.29%

Intuitively, we would expect stock prices to increase when companies announce that they will be buying back stock. The announcement, after all, can be viewed as an indication that these compainies believe that their stock is under valued. Studies have looked at the effect on stock price of the announcement that a firm plans to buy back stock. There is strong evidence that stock prices increase in response. Lakonishok and Vermaelen examined a sample of 221 repurchase tender offers that occurred between 1962 and 1986 and at stock price changes in the fifteen days around the announcement.[5] Table 11.2 summarizes the fraction of shares bought back in these tender offers and the change in stock price for two subperiods: 1962–1979 and 1980–1986. The abnormal return represents the return earned by these stocks over and above what you would have expected them to earn, given their risk and the market performance over the period. On average, across the entire period, the announcement of a stock buyback increased stock value by 14.29%.

IN PRACTICE: Equity Repurchase and the Dilution Illusion

Some equity repurchases are motivated by the desire to reduce the number of shares outstanding and therefore increase the earnings per share. If we assume that the firm's price–earnings ratio will remain unchanged, reducing the number of shares will usually lead to higher earnings per share and a higher price. This provides a simple rationale for many companies embarking on equity repurchases.

There is a problem with this reasoning, however. Although the reduction in the number of shares might increase earnings per share, the increase is usually accompanied by higher debt ratios. This increase in debt ratios will increase the riskiness of equity and lower the price–earnings ratio. The trade off between higher earnings per share and higher equity risk will determine the stock price effect. Whether a stock buyback will increase or decrease the price per share will depend on whether the firm is moving to its optimal debt ratio by repurchasing stock (in which case the price will increase) or moving away from it (in which case the price will decrease).

To illustrate, assume that a completely equity-financed firm in the specialty retailing business, with 100 shares outstanding, has $100 in earnings after taxes and a market value of $1,500. Assume that this firm borrows $300 and uses the proceeds to buy back twenty shares. As long as the after-tax interest expense on the borrowing is less than $20, this firm will report higher earnings per share after the repurchase. If the firm's tax rate is 50%, for instance, the effect on earnings per share is summarized in the table

---

[5] J. Lakonishok and T. Vermaelen, "Anomalous Price Behavior around Repurchase Tender Offers," *Journal of Finance* 45:455–478.

below for two scenarios: one in which the interest expense is $30 and one in which the interest expense is $55. As long as the interest expense is less than $40 ($20 after taxes), the firm will report higher earnings per share after the repurchase.

	Before Repurchase	After Repurchase	
EFFECT OF STOCK REPURCHASE ON EARNINGS PER SHARE			
		Interest Expense = $30	Interest Expense = $55
EBIT	$200	$200	$200
− Interest	$0	$30	$55
= Taxable income	$200	$170	$145
− Taxes	$100	$85	$72.50
= Net income	$100	$85	$72.50
# Shares	100	80	80
Earnings per share	$1.00	$1.125	$0.91

If we assume that the price–earnings ratio remains at 15, the price per share will change in proportion to the earnings per share. Realistically, however, we should expect to see a drop in the price–earnings ratio as the increase in debt makes the equity in the firm riskier. In the scenario where interest expenses are $30, the price per share will increase only if the PE ratio stays above 13.33. If it drops below that value, the price per share will drop, even though EPS is higher. ■

Choosing between Dividends and Equity Repurchases

Firms that plan to return cash to their stockholders can either pay them dividends or buy back stock. The choice they make will depend on the following factors:

- *Sustainability and stability of excess cash flow* Both equity repurchases and increased dividends are triggered by a firm's excess cash flows. If the excess cash flows are temporary or unstable, firms should repurchase stock or pay a special dividend; if they are stable and predictable, paying regular dividends provides a stronger signal of future project quality.

- *Stockholder tax preferences* If stockholders are taxed at much higher rates on dividends than capital gains, they will be better off if the firm repurchases stock. If, on the other hand, stockholders are taxed less on dividends, they will gain if the firm pays a special dividend.

- *Predictability of future investment needs* Firms that are uncertain about the magnitude of future investment opportunities should use equity repurchases as a way of returning cash to stockholders. The flexibility that is gained by avoiding what may be perceived as a fixed obligation will be useful if they need cash flows in future periods to fund new investments.

- *Undervaluation of the stock* An equity repurchase makes even more sense when managers believe their stock is undervalued, for two reasons. First, if the stock remains undervalued, the remaining stockholders will benefit if managers buy back stock at less than true value. The difference between the true value and the market price paid on the buyback will be accrue to those stockholders who do not sell their stock back. Second, the stock buyback may send a signal to financial markets that the stock is undervalued, and the market may react accordingly by pushing up the price.

- *Management compensation* Managers often receive options as part of compensation packages. The prevalence and magnitude of such option-based compensation can affect whether firms use dividends or buy back stock. The payment of dividends reduces stock prices while leaving the number of shares unchanged. The buying back of stock reduces the number of shares, and the share price usually increases on the buyback. Because options become less valuable as the stock price decreases and more valuable as the stock price increases, managers with significant option positions may be more likely to buy back stock than pay dividends.

Bartov, Krinsky, and Lee examined three of these determinants—undervaluation, management compensation, and institutional investor holdings (as a proxy for stockholder tax preferences)—of whether firms buy back stock or pay dividends.[6] They looked at 150 firms announcing stock buyback programs between 1986 and 1992 and compared these firms to others in their industries that chose to increase dividends instead. Table 11.3 reports on the characteristics of the two groups.

Although the option holdings of managers seemed to have had no statistical impact on whether firms bought back stock or increased dividends, firms buying back stock had higher book-to-market ratios than firms increasing dividends, as well as more institutional stockholders. The higher book-to-price ratio can be viewed as an indication that these firms are more likely to view themselves as undervalued. The larger institutional holding might suggest a greater sensitivity to the tax advantage of stock buybacks.

Stock Buybacks: A Behavioral Perspective

The explosive growth in stock buybacks in the United States in the last two decades can only partially be explained by financial rationale. In fact, many of the stories offered for stock buybacks—the tax disadvantages associated with dividends, their impact on earnings per share—have always been in existence and cannot be used to rationalize behavior just in the last twenty years. There are three behavioral rationale that have been offered for the growth of buybacks:

Table 11.3 CHARACTERISTICS OF FIRMS BUYING BACK STOCK VERSUS THOSE INCREASING DIVIDENDS

	Firms Buying Back Stock	Firms Increasing Dividends	Difference Is Significant
Book/market	56.90%	51.70%	Yes
Options/shares	7.20%	6.30%	No
Number of institutional holders	219.4	180	Yes

[6]E. Bartov, I. Krinsky, and J. Lee, "Some Evidence on How Companies Choose between Dividends and Stock Repurchases," *Journal of Applied Corporate Finance* 11:89–96.

1. *Herd behavior*   In the chapter on capital structure, we noted the pull that industry averages and peer group behavior have on debt policy. The same phenomenon applies in dividend policy, as firms attempt not only to keep their dividends in line with the rest of the sector but also to buy back stock to match other firms that may have done so. The fact that stock buybacks often tend to be clustered in sectors can be viewed as evidence of this phenomenon.

2. *Framing and anchoring*   Earlier in this chapter, we pointed to the dividend illusion and noted that the increases in earnings per share that follow stock buybacks will not always translate into higher price per share, since the price earnings ratio will decrease to reflect the higher risk in the firm. To the extent that managers think in per share terms and have in mind a "right PE ratio" for their firms, they may believe that stock buybacks always lead to higher earnings per share and stock prices. If investors share these same views, stock prices will increase in the aftermath of buybacks, at least for the short term.

3. *Overoptimism*   More optimistic managers believe that their stocks are undervalued and are therefore more likely to initiate and carry through stock buybacks than their less optimistic brethren. Consequently, the same market timing imperatives that drive financing choices (debt versus equity) affect stock buyback decisions.

In summary, it can be argued that once some firms started buying back stock in the 1980s and were successful with that tactic (in terms of higher stock prices), other firms imitated them, creating a trend that has continued for more than two decades.

11.1   STOCK BUYBACKS AND STOCK PRICE EFFECTS

For which of the following types of firms would a stock buyback be most likely to lead to a drop in the stock price?

a.   Companies with a history of poor project choice

b.   Companies that borrow money to buy back stock

c.   Companies that are perceived to have great investment opportunities

Explain.

A CASH FLOW APPROACH TO ANALYZING DIVIDEND POLICY

Given what firms are returning to their stockholders in the form of dividends or stock buybacks, how do we decide whether they are returning too much or too little? In the cash flow approach, we follow four steps. We first measure how much cash is available to be paid out to stockholders after meeting debt service and reinvestment needs and compare this amount to the amount actually returned to stockholders. Next, we the quality of investment opportunities in the firm. Third, based on the cash payout and project quality, we consider whether firms should be accumulating more cash or less. Finally, we look at the relationship between dividend policy and debt policy.

Step 1: Measuring Cash Available to be Returned to Stockholders

To estimate how much cash a firm can afford to return to its stockholders, we begin with the net income—the accounting measure of the equity earnings during the period—and convert it to a cash flow by subtracting out a firm's reinvestment needs, broken up into two components:

1. ***Investments in long-term assets***   Any capital expenditures, defined broadly to include acquisitions, are subtracted from the net income, because they represent cash outflows. Depreciation and amortization, on the other hand, are added back in, because they are noncash charges. The difference between capital expenditures and depreciation is referred to as *net capital expenditures* and is usually a function of the growth characteristics of the firm. High-growth firms tend to have high net capital expenditures relative to earnings, whereas low-growth firms may have low (and sometimes even negative) net capital expenditures.

2. ***Investments in short-term assets***   Increases in working capital, i.e., inventory and accounts receivable, drain a firm's cash flows, whereas decreases in working capital increase the cash flows available to equity investors. Firms that are growing fast, in industries with high working capital requirements (retailing, for instance), typically have large increases in working capital. Because we are interested in the cash flow effects, we consider only changes in *noncash working capital* in this analysis.

Finally, equity investors also have to consider the effect of changes in the levels of debt on their cash flows. Repaying the principal due on existing debt represents a cash outflow, but the debt repayment may be fully or partially financed by the issue of new debt, which is a cash inflow. Again, netting the repayment of old debt against the new debt issues provides a measure of the cash flow effects of changes in debt.

Allowing for the cash flow effects of net capital expenditures, changes in working capital, and net changes in debt on equity investors, we can define the cash flows left over after these changes as the *free cash flow to equity* (FCFE):

$$\begin{aligned}
\text{Free cash flow to equity (FCFE)} = &\ \text{Net income} \\
&- (\text{Capital expenditures} - \text{Depreciation}) \\
&- (\text{Change in noncash working capital}) \\
&+ (\text{New debt issued} - \text{Debt repayments})
\end{aligned}$$

This is the cash flow available to be paid out as dividends.

This calculation can be simplified if we assume that firm is at its desired debt mix and that the net capital expenditures and working capital changes are financed using that mix of debt and equity.[7] If δ is the proportion of the net capital expenditures and working capital changes raised from debt financing, the effect on cash flows to equity of these items can be represented as follows:

$$\begin{aligned}
&\text{Equity reinvestment associated with capital expenditure needs} \\
&\quad = (\text{Capital expenditures} - \text{Depreciation})(1 - \delta) \\
&\text{Equity reinvestment associated with working capital needs} \\
&\quad = (\Delta \text{Noncash working capital})(1 - \delta)
\end{aligned}$$

[7]The mix has to be fixed in book value terms.

Accordingly, the cash flow available for equity investors after meeting capital expenditure and working capital needs is

$$\text{Free cash flow to equity} = \text{Net income}$$
$$- (\text{Capital expenditures} - \text{Depreciation})(1 - \delta)$$
$$- (\Delta\text{Noncash working capital})(1 - \delta)$$

Note that the net debt payment item is eliminated, because debt repayments are financed with new debt issues to keep the debt ratio fixed. The key to this simplified approach for estimating FCFE is coming up with a debt ratio and there are two choices. One is to use the optimal debt ratio that we computed in chapter 8 as the desired debt ratio for the future. The other is to use the average debt ratio used by the firm in the past.

IN PRACTICE: Estimating the FCFE at a Financial Service Firm

Estimating FCFE is straightforward for most manufacturing firms, because the net capital expenditures, noncash working capital needs, and debt ratio can be obtained from the financial statements. In contrast, the estimation of FCFE is problematic for financial service firms for several reasons. First, estimating net capital expenditures and noncash working capital for a bank or insurance company is complicated by the fact that all the assets and liabilities are in the form of financial claims. Second, it is difficult to define short-term debt for financial service firms—again, because of the complexity of their balance sheets.

To estimate the FCFE for a bank, we redefine reinvestment as investment in regulatory capital, which is usually defined in terms of the book value of equity. After all, a financial service firm can grow its business only to the extent that its has the book value of equity to back up that growth and maintain regulatory capital ratios (including any safety buffers that it may have built in). In Chapter 8, we looked at regulatory capital ratios and how they affect financing choices at banks and insurance companies. Since any dividends paid deplete book equity capital and retained earnings increase that capital, the free cash flow to equity for a financial service firm can be written as follows:

$$\text{FCFE}_{\text{Bank}} = \text{Net income} - \text{Increase in regulatory capital base (Book equity)}$$

As a simple example, consider a bank with $10 billion in loans outstanding and book equity (Tier 1 capital) of $750 million. Assume that the bank wants to maintain its existing capital ratio of 7.5%, intends to grow its loan base by 10% (to $11 billion), and expects to generate $150 million in net income next year. We can estimate the FCFE next year:

$$\text{FCFE} = \$150 \text{ million} - (11{,}000 - 10{,}000) * (0.075) = \$75 \text{ million}$$

As a follow-up, assume that this bank wants to increase its regulatory capital ratio to 8% (for precautionary purposes) while increasing its loan base to $11 billion. The total book equity next year will have to rise to $880 million (8% of $11 billion) and the FCFE will be lower:

$$\text{FCFE} = \$150 \text{ million} - (\$880 - \$750) = \$20 \text{ million}$$

This computation obviously becomes more complex if a firm is involved in multiple businesses, with different regulatory capital requirements on each. To estimate FCFE, we have to estimate growth and capital requirements in each business separately.

Putting together the pieces, the FCFE (and potential dividends) at a financial service firm will be a function of the following:

- **Growth in asset base**   Since the regulatory capital is tied to the size of the asset base, the higher the growth rate in the asset base, the greater the investment in regulatory capital will be. Holding all else constant, higher-growth firms should have lower FCFE and dividends than more mature firms.

- **Desired capital ratio**   The reinvestment in regulatory capital for a given growth rate in the asset base will depend upon the equity capital ratio that the firm wants to maintain on that asset base. While regulatory requirements play a key role in determining this ratio, it will also depend upon the safety buffer the firm desires to build into its capital. Put more simply, conservative financial service firms will have higher target capital ratios and reinvest more than more aggressive firms, for a given growth rate, leading to lower FCFE for the former.

- **Profitability**   Ultimately, dividends have to be paid out of net income. Other things remaining equal, the more profits that a firm can generate on a given asset and book equity base, the more it will be able to generate in FCFE. The return on equity, which scales profits to book equity capital, therefore becomes a key factor in how much a firm can generate in FCFE. Firms that generate higher returns on equity for a given growth rate and desired capital ratio will generate more in FCFE (and thus be able to pay more in dividends). ■

DividendsBank.xls: This spreadsheet allows you to estimate the free cash flow to equity for a financial service firm for the future.

ILLUSTRATION 11.2   **Estimating FCFE: Disney, Aracruz, Tata Chemicals and Deutsche Bank**
In Table 11.4, we estimate the FCFE for Disney from 1999 to 2008, using historical information from its financial statements. The depreciation numbers also include amortization and the capital expenditures include cash acquisitions. Increases in noncash working capital, shown as positive numbers, represent a drain on the cash, whereas decreases in noncash working capital, shown as negative numbers, represent positive cash flows. In 1999, for example, noncash working capital decreased by $363 million, increasing the cash available for stockholders in that year by the same amount. Finally, the net cash flow from debt is the cash generated by the issuance of new debt, netted out against the cash outflow from the repayment of old debt. Again, using 1999 as an example, Disney issued $176 million more in new debt than it paid off on old debt, and this represents a positive cash flow in that year. We have computed two

measures of FCFE: one before the net debt cash flow and one after. Using 1999 as an illustration, we compute each as follows:

$$\text{FCFE}_{\text{Before--debt CF}} = \text{Net income} + \text{Depreciation} - \text{Capital expenditures}$$
$$- \text{Change in noncash working capital}$$
$$= 1{,}300 + 3{,}779 - 6{,}113 - (-363)$$
$$= -\$671 \text{ million}$$
$$\text{FCFE}_{\text{After--debt CF}} = \text{FCFE}_{\text{Before--debt CF}} + \text{Net debt CF}$$
$$= -\$671 + \$176 = -\$495 \text{ million}$$

As Table 11.4 indicates, Disney had negative free cash flows to equity in three of the ten years. The average annual FCFE before net debt issues over the period was $1,897 million, and the average net debt issued over the period was $21 million, resulting in an average annual FCFE after net debt issues of $1,918 million. We can compute Disney's FCFE each year using the approximation that we described in the last section. To do this, we first have to compute the net debt cash flows as percent of reinvestment needs over this period. Using the aggregate values from Table 11.4 for debt cash flows, capital expenditures, depreciation, and changes in noncash working capital between 1999 and 2008, we estimate the average debt ratio:

$$\text{Average debt ratio} = \frac{\text{Net debt issued}}{(\text{Cap ex} - \text{Depreciation} + \text{Chg in WC})}$$
$$= \frac{207}{(20{,}693 - 16{,}906 - 825)} = 6.99\%$$

The FCFE each year can then be estimated using the average debt ratio, instead of the actual net debt cash flows. Table 11.5 contains the estimates of FCFE each year using this approach for Disney.

Note that the average FCFE between 1999 and 2008 remains unchanged at $1,918 million a year when we use the approximation. However, the FCFE in each year is

	Net Income	Capital Expenditures	Depreciation	Chg in WC	Change in Net Debt	FCFE
1999	$1,300	$6,113	$3,779	−$363	$176	−$495
2000	$920	$1,091	$2,195	−$1,184	$2,118	$5,326
2001	−$158	$2,015	$1,754	$244	−$77	−$740
2002	$1,236	$3,176	$1,042	$27	−$1,892	−$2,817
2003	$1,267	$1,034	$1,077	−$264	$1,145	$2,719
2004	$2,345	$1,484	$1,210	$51	$2,203	$4,223
2005	$2,533	$1,691	$1,339	$270	$699	$2,610
2006	$3,374	$1,300	$1,437	−$136	−$941	$2,706
2007	$4,687	$627	$1,491	$45	−$2,696	$2,810
2008	$4,427	$2,162	$1,582	$485	−$528	$2,834
Aggregate	$21,931	$20,693	$16,906	−$825	$207	$19,176
Average	$2,193	$2,069	$1,691	$83	$21	$1,918

Table 11.4   ESTIMATES OF FCFE FOR DISNEY: 1999–2008 (IN MILLIONS)

Table 11.5   APPROXIMATE FCFE FOR DISNEY FROM 1999 TO 2008 (IN MILLIONS)

	Net Income	(Cap Ex − Depreciation) (1 − DR)	Chg in WC (1 − DR)	FCFE
1999	$1,300	$2,171	−$338	−$533
2000	$920	−$1,027	−$1,101	$3,048
2001	−$158	$243	$227	−$628
2002	$1,236	$1,985	$25	−$774
2003	$1,267	−$40	−$246	$1,553
2004	$2,345	$255	$47	$2,043
2005	$2,533	$327	$251	$1,954
2006	$3,374	−$127	−$126	$3,628
2007	$4,687	−$804	$42	$5,449
2008	$4,427	$539	$451	$3,436
Aggregate	$21,931	$3,522	−$767	$19,176
Average				$1,918

different from the estimates in Table 11.5, because we are smoothing out the effects of the cash flows from debt.

A similar estimation of FCFE was done for Aracruz from 2002 to 2008 in Table 11.6, again using historical information. Since the cash flow statement in U.S. dollars, filed in the United States, is more complete than the R$ counterpart, we will report all the values in U.S. dollars.

Between 2002 and 2007, Aracruz reported an almost fourfold increase in net income, but aggregate free cash flows to equity averaged only $79.65 million a year over the period. In 2008, Aracruz reported a net loss of $1.239 billion, largely because of misguided bets on currency derivatives, but the FCFE for 2008 was positive, as the firm borrowed more than $3 billion to cover its losses. The average FCFE over the 2002–2008 time period is $229.41 million with the cash flows from debt counted in, but −$271.70 million without debt cash flows.

Table 11.6   FCFE FOR ARACRUZ IN US$ FROM 2002 TO 2008 (IN MILLIONS)

	Net Income	Capital Expenditures	Depreciation	Change in WC	Change in Net Debt	FCFE
2002	$111.91	$260.66	$171.53	$53.53	$36.34	$5.59
2003	$148.09	$791.87	$191.51	$79.85	$530.69	−$1.43
2004	$227.24	$193.54	$206.95	$31.80	−$13.53	$195.32
2005	$341.10	$216.98	$211.62	$75.55	−$93.40	$166.79
2006	$455.32	$325.51	$217.84	$72.20	−$89.60	$185.85
2007	$422.07	$712.48	$217.64	$113.71	$112.28	−$74.20
2008	−$1,239.00	$814.60	$218.05	$61.50	$3,025.00	$1,127.95
Aggregate	$466.73	$3,315.64	$1,435.14	$488.14	$3,507.78	$1,605.87
				Average FCFE: 2002–2008		$229.41
				Average FCFE: 2002–2007		$79.65
				Average FCFE without debt cash flows		−$271.70

	Net Income	Capital Expenditures	Depreciation	Change in WC	Change in Net Debt	FCFE
2003–2004	Rs3,418	Rs357	Rs1,442	−Rs557	−Rs2,771	Rs2,289
2004–2005	Rs4,550	Rs692	Rs1,377	−Rs493	Rs5,448	Rs11,176
2005–2006	Rs5,156	Rs11,730	Rs1,389	Rs2,823	Rs867	−Rs7,141
2006–2007	Rs6,338	Rs1,196	Rs1,504	−Rs1,662	−Rs4,411	Rs3,896
2007–2008	Rs11,571	Rs28,956	Rs1,488	Rs88	Rs17,054	Rs1,069
Aggregate	Rs31,033	Rs42,930	Rs7,199	Rs200	Rs16,187	Rs11,290
Average						Rs2,258

Table 11.7   FCFE FOR TATA CHEMICALS FROM 2003 TO 2008 (IN MILLIONS)

Using the same procedure, we estimate the FCFE for Tata Chemicals from 2004 to 2008 in Table 11.7.

While the net income for Tata Chemicals increased every year between 2003 and 2008, the FCFE follow a rockier path, with big swings in the cash flows for three reasons. The first is that noncash working capital is volatile, with big increases in some years and large decreases in others. The second is that there are spikes in the capital expenditures in 2005–2006 and 2007–2008, reflecting large investments in subsidiaries in those years. Finally, the cash flow from net debt is negative in two of the five years and is a very large positive number in 2007–2008, reflecting the fact that Tata funded its large capital expenditures that year—primarily with debt. Over the five-year period, the average FCFE was Rs2.258 billion.

To estimate the FCFE for Deutsche Bank, we use the approach described in the last section, where we define reinvestment in regulatory capital as reinvestment. Rather than look backward, we decided to focus on estimating future FCFE. We begin with the current values for the asset base and regulatory capital at the end of 2008:

Current value of asset base (end of 2008) = 312,885 billion euros
Current value of regulatory capital (book equity) = 31,914 billion euros

While Deutsche Bank reported a loss of 4.12 billion Euros in 2008, much of the loss can be attributed to writeoffs of investments in the aftermath of the market crisis in the last quarter of 2008. Though it is unlikely that Deutsche Bank will revert back to the 6 billion euros in profits it reported in 2007, we assume that the normalized net income for 2008 will be 3 billion euros.[8] With these estimates, we obtain a current regulatory capital ratio of 10.2% and a current return on equity of 9.40%:

$$\text{Current regulatory capital ratio} = \frac{\text{Regulatory capital}}{\text{Asset base}} = \frac{31,914}{312,885} = 10.2\%$$

$$\text{Current return on equity} = \frac{\text{Net income}}{\text{Regulatory capital (Book equity)}} = \frac{3,000}{31,914} = 9.40\%$$

---

[8]To normalize the net income, we looked at profits prior to writeoffs. In the first quarter of 2009, Deutsche Bank reported a bounce back to profitability, generating 1.2 billion in euros in profits. Analysts estimate that Deutsche will generate profits in excess of 4 billion euros for the year, but we have chosen to be conservative in our estimates.

	Current	2009	2010	2011	2012	2013	Steady state (2014)
Table 11.8 EXPECTED FCFE—DEUTSCHE BANK (IN MILLIONS OF EUROS)							
Asset base	€312,882	€325,398	€338,414	€351,950	€366,028	€380,669	€392,089
Capital ratio	10.20%	10.16%	10.12%	10.08%	10.04%	10.00%	10.00%
Regulatory capital	€31,914	€33,060	€34,247	€35,477	€36,749	€38,067	€39,209
Change in regulatory capital		€1,146	€1,187	€1,229	€1,273	€1,318	€1,142
ROE	9.40%	9.52%	9.64%	9.76%	9.88%	10.00%	10.00%
Net income	€3,000	€3,147	€3,302	€3,463	€3,631	€3,807	€3,921
−Investment in regulatory capital		€1,146	€1,187	€1,229	€1,273	€1,318	€1,142
FCFE		€2,001	€2,114	€2,233	€2,358	€2,489	€2,779

As a final piece for the estimation of FCFE, we estimate three values. First, we assume that the expected growth in the asset base will be 4% a year for the next five years and 3% thereafter. Second, we assume a target regulatory capital ratio of 10% in year 5, based on Deutsche Bank's own statements in early 2009; note that this value is well above the regulatory requirement of 6–7% and reflects Deutsche Bank's conservative outlook. Third, we assume only a modest improvement in the return on equity from the current value of 9.4% to 10% in year 5 and beyond.

To estimate the regulatory capital and net income in each of the next five years, we assume that the improvements will occur in equal annual increments over each of the years. Table 11.8 summarizes the estimates of regulatory capital, net income, and FCFE for the next six years.

Based on our estimates, Deutsche Bank should be able to return about 2 billion euros in dividends in 2009 to its equity investors. Note, though, that the regulatory definition of equity includes both preferred and common stockholders, and that preferred stockholders have fixed and prior claims to the dividends; the dividends to common stockholders represent the residual FCFE. Just as an illustration, assume that Deutsche Bank's existing capital base includes 5 billion euros in preferred stock with a dividend set at 8% of face value. The FCFE available for common stockholders in 2009 can then be computed as follows:

$$\text{Total FCFE in 2009} = 2{,}001 \text{ million euros}$$
$$\text{Preferred dividends} = 0.08\ (5{,}000)$$
$$= 400 \text{ million euros}$$
$$\text{FCFE for common equity} = 1{,}601 \text{ million euros}$$

This can be repeated for subsequent years.

11.2   DEFINING FCFE

The reason that the net income is not the amount that a company can afford to pay out in dividends is because

a.   Earnings are not cash flows.

b.   Some of the earnings have to be reinvested back in the firm to create growth.

c. There may be cash inflows or outflows associated with the use of debt.

d. All of the above.

Explain.

Measuring the Payout Ratio

The conventional measure of dividend policy—the dividend payout ratio—gives us the value of dividends as a proportion of earnings. In contrast, our approach measures the total cash returned to stockholders as a proportion of FCFE:

$$\text{Dividend payout ratio} = \text{Dividends/Earnings}$$

$$\text{Cash to stockholders–to–FCFE ratio} = (\text{Dividends} + \text{Equity repurchases})/\text{FCFE}$$

The ratio of cash returned to stockholders to FCFE shows how much of the cash available to be paid out to stockholders is actually returned to them in the form of dividends and stock buybacks. If this ratio over time is equal or close to 100%, the firm is paying out all that it can to its stockholders. If it is significantly less than 100%, the firm is paying out less than it can afford and is using the difference to increase its cash balance or to invest in marketable securities. If it is significantly over 100%, the firm is paying out more than it can afford and is either drawing on an existing cash balance or issuing new securities (stocks or bonds).

ILLUSTRATION 11.3   Comparing Dividend Payout Ratios to FCFE Payout Ratios—Disney and Tata Chemicals

In the following analysis, we compare the dividend payout ratios to the cash to stockholders (dividends and stock buybacks) as a percent of FCFE for Disney and Tata Chemicals. Table 11.9 shows both numbers for Disney from 1999 to 2008.

As you can see, Disney paid out 20.38% of its aggregate earnings as dividends over this period.[9] Over the same period, it returned 139.53% of its FCFE to its

Table 11.9   DISNEY: DIVIDENDS AS PERCENTAGE OF EARNINGS AND CASH RETURNED AS PERCENTAGE OF FCFE

	Dividends	Earnings	Payout Ratio	Cash Returned	FCFE	Cash/FCFE
1999	$0.00	$1,300.00	0.00%	$19.00	−$495.00	−3.84%
2000	$434.00	$920.00	47.17%	$600.00	$5,326.00	11.27%
2001	$438.00	−$158.00	−277.22%	$1,511.00	−$740.00	−204.19%
2002	$428.00	$1,236.00	34.63%	$428.00	−$2,817.00	−15.19%
2003	$429.00	$1,267.00	33.86%	$429.00	$2,719.00	15.78%
2004	$430.00	$2,345.00	18.34%	$765.00	$4,223.00	18.12%
2005	$490.00	$2,533.00	19.34%	$2,910.00	$2,610.00	111.49%
2006	$519.00	$3,374.00	15.38%	$7,417.00	$2,706.00	274.09%
2007	$637.00	$4,687.00	13.59%	$7,560.00	$2,810.00	269.04%
2008	$664.00	$4,427.00	15.00%	$5,117.00	$2,834.00	180.56%
Aggregate	$4,469.00	$21,931.00	20.38%	$26,756.00	$19,176.00	139.53%

---

[9]To compute the payout ratio over the entire period, we first aggregated earnings and dividends over the entire period and then divided the aggregate dividends by the aggregate earnings. This avoids the problems created by averaging ratios where outliers are common.

Table 11.10   TATA CHEMICALS: DIVIDENDS AS PERCENTAGE OF EARNINGS AND CASH RETURNED AS PERCENT OF FCFE (IN MILLIONS)

	Dividends	Net Income	Payout ratio	Cash returned	FCFE	Cash/FCFE
2003–2004	Rs1,306.50	Rs3,418.40	38.22%	Rs1,306.50	Rs2,289.10	57.07%
2004–2005	Rs1,338.20	Rs4,550.00	29.41%	Rs1,338.20	Rs11,176.40	11.97%
2005–2006	Rs1,589.30	Rs5,155.60	30.83%	Rs1,589.30	−Rs7,140.90	−22.26%
2006–2007	Rs1,715.70	Rs6,338.40	27.07%	Rs1,715.70	Rs3,896.30	44.03%
2007–2008	Rs2,009.60	Rs11,571.00	17.37%	Rs2,009.60	Rs1,068.60	188.06%
Aggregate	Rs7,959.30	Rs31,033.40	25.65%	Rs7,959.30	Rs11,289.50	70.50%

stockholders in the form of dividends and stock buybacks. Although the payout ratio suggests that the firm is retaining a significant portion of its earnings, the cash returned as a percent of FCFE suggests that Disney has paid out far more than it had available to pay during the period.

Table 11.10 shows dividend payout ratios and cash returned to stockholders as a percent of FCFE for Tata Chemicals from 2002 to 2008. Tata paid out about 25.7% of its earnings as dividends and returned about 70.5% of its FCFE to its stockholders. The remaining cash (the 29.5% of FCFE that did not get paid out) was held back by the firm and reinvested in other firms in the Tata group.

With Aracruz, the comparison is moot, since we know that the aggregate FCFE would have been negative between 2002 and 2008 without the significant borrowings in 2008 (see Table 11.6). Since Aracruz paid out significant dividends over this period, it is quite clear that these dividends are not being funded from operations. We will return to examine both why Aracruz is in this bind and ways that it may be able to release itself from the cash flow constraint in future years.

 Dividends.xls: This spreadsheet allows you to estimate the free cash flow to equity and the cash returned to stockholders for a period of up to ten years.

 There is a data set online that summarizes dividends, cash returned to stockholders, and FCFE by sector in the United States.

Why Firms May Not Pay Out What Is Available

Many firms pay out less to stockholders, in the form of dividends and stock buybacks, than they have available in free cash flows to equity. The reasons vary from firm to firm, and we list some here.

- The managers of a firm may gain by retaining cash rather than paying it out as a dividend. The desire for empire building makes increasing the size of the firm an objective on its own. Alternatively, management may feel the need to build up a cash cushion to tide them over periods when earnings may dip; in such periods, the cash cushion may help buffer the earnings drop and may allow managers to remain in control.

- The firm may be unsure about its future financing needs and may choose to retain some cash to take on unexpected investments or meet unanticipated needs.
- The firm may have volatile earnings and may retain cash to help smooth out dividends over time.
- Bondholders may impose restrictions on cash payments to stockholders, which may prevent the firm from returning available cash flows to its stockholders.

At the other end of the spectrum, there are firms that pay out more cash than they generate in FCFE (though this is a less common phenomenon). Here again, there are several possible reasons.

- When earnings are volatile and swing from period to period, firms may choose to pay more than their FCFE in down periods and hope to make up for it when earnings recover.
- Firms that have historically paid high dividends often are under pressure to maintain those dividends even when earnings drop, for fear of sending a bad signal to the market.
- Firms that are underlevered can use a policy of returning more cash to their stockholders as a way of reducing equity and increasing debt ratios

Finally, firms that are part of larger corporate groups—such as Tata Chemicals—can hold back cash to invest in other companies in the group.

11.3   WHAT HAPPENS TO THE FCFE THAT ARE NOT PAID OUT?

In 2003, Microsoft had FCFE of roughly $9 billion, paid no dividends, and bought back no stock. Where would you expect to see the difference of $9 billion show up in Microsoft's financial statements?

a.   It will be invested in new projects.

b.   It will be in retained earnings, increasing the book value of equity.

c.   It will increase the cash balance of the company.

d.   None of the above.

Explain.

Evidence on Dividends and FCFE

We can observe the tendency of firms to pay out less to stockholders than they have available in FCFE by examining cash returned to stockholders paid as a percentage of FCFE. In 2008, for instance, the median cash returned to FCFE ratio across dividend paying firms listed in the United States was about 55%. However, there were scores of firms that paid out more in dividends than they have available in FCFE. Figure 11.2 provides a breakdown of U.S. firms in 2008, based upon how much they paid in dividends, relative to what they had available in FCFE.

Note that there are 755 firms that pay less in dividends than they have available in FCFE, and they have to finance these dividend payments either out of existing cash

Figure 11.2 Dividends versus FCFE: U.S. Firms in 2008

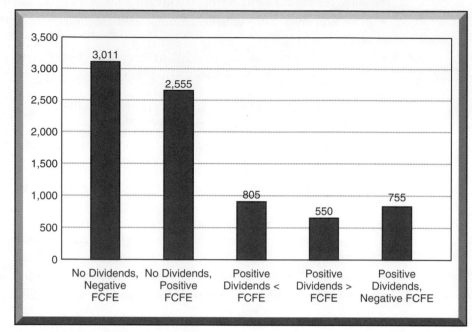

Source: Value Line, 2008.

balances or by making new stock and debt issues. Note also that there are 550 firms in this period that paid dividends even though they had negative FCFE. These firms will have to come up with enough funds, either from existing cash balances or new stock issues, to cover both the dividends and the cash deficit. A large number of firms (3,011) pay no dividends, but that makes sense, given the fact that they have negative FCFE. That still leaves us with 2,555 firms that pay out no dividends, even though they have positive FCFE, and about 805 firms that pay out less in dividends than they have available in FCFE. However, that does not necessarily mean that these firms are accumulating cash, since some of them buy back their own stock in large quantities. With the rest of the firms, the cash that is not paid out is accumulated as a balance, and it does help explain how some firms end up with outsized cash balances, relative to value.

 Dividends.xls: This spreadsheet allows you to estimate the FCFE for a firm over a period for up to ten years, comparing it to dividends paid.

Step 2: Assessing Project Quality

The alternative to returning cash to stockholders is reinvestment. Consequently, a firm's investment opportunities influence its dividend policy. Other things remaining equal, a firm with better projects to invest in typically has more flexibility in setting dividend policy and defending it against stockholder pressure for higher dividends. But how do we define a good project?

Drawing on our analysis of investment decisions, a good project is one that earns more than the hurdle rate, which is the cost of equity if cash flows are estimated on an equity basis, or the cost of capital if cash flows are measured on a predebt basis. To analyze a firm's potential investments, we could estimate the expected cash flows on every project available to the firm and calculate the internal rates of return (IRR) or net present value (NPV) of each project to evaluate project quality. There are several practical problems with this, however. First, we have to be able to obtain the detailed cash flow estimates and hurdle rates for all available projects, which can be daunting if the firm has dozens (much less hundreds) of projects. The second problem is that even if these cash flows are available for existing projects, they will not be available for future projects.

As an alternative approach to measuring project quality, we can use one or more of the measures we developed in Chapter 6 to evaluate a firm's current project portfolio:

- Accounting return differentials, where we compare the accounting return on equity to the cost of equity and the accounting return on capital to the cost of capital
- Economic value added (EVA), which measures the excess return earned on capital invested in existing investments and can be computed either on an equity or capital basis

We did note the limitations of each of these approaches in Chapter 6, but they still provide a measure of the quality of a firm's existing investments.

Using past project returns as a measure of future project quality can result in errors if a firm is making a transition from one stage in its growth cycle to the next or if it is in the process of restructuring. In such situations, it is entirely possible that the expected returns on new projects will differ from past project returns. Consequently, it may be worthwhile scrutinizing past returns for trends that may carry over into the future. The average return on equity or capital for a firm will not reveal these trends very well, because these numbers are slow to reflect the effects of new projects, especially for large firms. An alternative accounting return measure, which better captures year-to-year shifts, is the *marginal return on equity or capital*, defined as follows:

$$\text{Marginal return on equity}_t = \frac{\text{Net income}_t - \text{Net income}_{t-1}}{\text{Book value of equity}_{t-1} - \text{Book value of equity}_{t-2}}$$

$$\text{Marginal return on capital} = \frac{\text{EBIT}(1-t)_t - \text{EBIT}(1-t)_{t-1}}{\text{Book value of capital}_{t-1} - \text{Book value of capital}_{t-2}}$$

Although the marginal return on equity (capital) and the average return on equity (capital) will move in the same direction, the marginal returns typically will change much more than do the average returns, with the difference a function of the size of the firm. These marginal returns can be used to compute the quality of the new projects.

The alternative to using accounting returns to measure the quality of a firm's projects is to look at how well or badly a firm's stock has done in financial markets. In Chapter 4, we compared the returns earned by a stock to the returns earned on the market after adjusting for risk (Jensen's Alpha). The risk-adjusted excess return that we estimated becomes a measure of whether a stock has under- or outperformed the market. A positive excess return would then be viewed as an indication that a firm has done better than expected, whereas a negative excess return would indicate that a firm has done worse than anticipated.

Finally, accounting income and stock returns may vary year to year, not only because of changes in project quality but also because of fluctuations in the business cycles and interest rates. Consequently, the comparisons between returns and hurdle rates should be made over long enough periods—say, five to ten years—to average out these other effects.

ILLUSTRATION 11.4 Evaluating Project Quality at Disney, Aracruz, and Tata Chemicals

In Illustration 6.10, we examined the quality of existing investments at Disney, Aracruz, and Tata Chemicals, using both accounting returns and EVA; stock price performance at each of these companies was evaluated using Jensen's alpha in Chapter 4. Table 11.11 summarizes our findings.

In summary, we concluded that Disney earns positive excess returns on its projects, Tata Chemicals breaks even, and Aracruz earns negative excess returns, the stock price performance at Disney is consistent with its positive project choices but Aracruz has a positive jensen's alpha and Tata Chemicals a negative one.

In the following analysis, we revisit both accounting and market measures of return at Disney, Aracruz, and Tata Chemicals over recent time periods and compare them to the appropriate hurdle rates to evaluate the quality of the projects taken at each firm during the period. In this analysis, though, we could be faulted for focusing on performance over short periods and failing to adjust the cost of equity for actual market performance. We will try to remedy both defects in this illustration.

We begin with an analysis of Disney's accounting return on equity, the return from holding the stock, and the required return (given the beta and market performance during each year) from 1999 to 2008 as shown in Table 11.12.[10]

As you can see, the trend lines favor Disney, with negative accounting and market returns in the early years followed by positive excess returns on both dimensions in recent years. To provide some history on these measures, the return on equity for the firm, which exceeded 20% in the years prior to the acquisition of Capital Cities/ABC in 1996, plummeted in the years after to single digits, and the excess returns were negative

---

Table 11.11 PROJECT RETURNS AND STOCK PRICE PERFORMANCE

	ROC	Cost of Capital	ROC − Cost of Capital	ROE	Cost of Equity	ROE − Cost of Equity	Jensen's Alpha
Disney	9.29%	7.51%	1.78%	14.40%	8.91%	5.49%	5.62%
Aracruz	4.49%	10.63%	−6.14%	−78.59%	18.45%	−97.05%	9.97%
Tata Chemicals	11.31%	11.44%	−0.12%	15.46%	13.93%	1.53%	−4.29%

---

[10]For instance, to estimate the expected return in 1999, we use the following: Expected return in 1999 = Risk-free rate at beginning of 1999 + Beta (Return on market in 1999 – Risk-free rate at beginning of 1999). An average beta of 0.9011 was used over the entire period for Disney.

Table 11.12 RETURN ON EQUITY, RETURN ON STOCK, AND COST OF EQUITY—DISNEY

	ROE	Return on Stock	Cost of Equity	Accounting Excess Return	Market Excess Return
1999	6.71%	−1.80%	19.27%	−12.56%	−21.07%
2000	4.39%	−0.36%	−7.57%	11.96%	7.21%
2001	−0.66%	−27.68%	−10.31%	9.66%	−17.37%
2002	5.45%	−20.27%	−19.64%	25.09%	−0.63%
2003	5.40%	44.36%	25.70%	−20.30%	18.65%
2004	9.86%	20.19%	9.77%	0.09%	10.42%
2005	9.71%	−12.81%	4.67%	5.05%	−17.48%
2006	12.87%	44.25%	14.54%	12.87%	29.71%
2007	14.73%	−3.49%	5.40%	9.33%	−8.89%
2008	14.40%	−28.62%	−32.81%	47.20%	4.18%

*Cost of equity = Risk-free rate at start of year + Beta (Return on S&P 500 for year − Risk-free rate)

for much of 1997–2004. Since Bob Iger replaced Michael Eisner as CEO in 2005, the company has done better, and its performance may have earned it a reprieve when it comes to dividend policy.

Repeating this analysis for Aracruz for 2002 to 2008 yields a different conclusion. Table 11.13 summarizes returns on equity, returns on the stock, and the required return at the firm for each year between 2002 and 2008.

For much of this period, Aracruz performed well, earning high returns on equity on its projects and earning excess returns for its stockholders. However, 2008 was a devastating year, as losses on derivatives wiped out profits from prior years and the stock price plummeted. While much of the volatility in earnings and returns from year to year, in prior years, can be attributed to commodity price variation, the losses in 2008 can be attributed mostly to failures on the part of management.

Finally, we look at Tata Chemicals and estimate the accounting and market-based excess returns from 2003–2008 in Table 11.14.

Across the five-year period, Tata Chemicals delivered a stock return and return on equity that roughly matched up to the cost of equity over the period. In effect, the firm's performance has been neutral over the period.

Table 11.13 RETURN ON EQUITY, RETURN ON STOCK, AND COST OF EQUITY—ARACRUZ

	ROE	Return on Stock	Cost of Equity	Accounting Excess Return	Market Excess Return
2002	13.90%	6.11%	−39.49%	53.39%	45.59%
2003	17.40%	94.57%	48.70%	−31.30%	45.87%
2004	25.49%	13.56%	17.73%	7.76%	−4.17%
2005	37.70%	11.40%	6.21%	31.49%	5.19%
2006	43.15%	58.50%	23.74%	19.41%	34.76%
2007	32.64%	25.49%	6.10%	26.53%	19.39%
2008	−51.91%	−81.91%	−64.86%	12.95%	−17.05%

Table 11.14   ROE, STOCK RETURNS, AND COST OF EQUITY—TATA CHEMICALS

	ROE	Return on Stock	Cost of Equity	Accounting Excess Return	Market Excess Return
2003–2004	16.80%	11.53%	14.30%	2.50%	−2.77%
2004–2005	22.78%	46.14%	42.02%	−19.25%	4.12%
2005–2006	13.07%	−5.28%	45.91%	−32.84%	−51.19%
2006–2007	17.01%	95.29%	45.79%	−28.78%	49.50%
2007–2008	18.68%	−57.81%	−48.60%	67.28%	−9.21%
Average	17.34%	17.97%	19.89%	−2.22%	−1.91%

Dividends.xls: This spreadsheet allows you to estimate the average return on equity and cost of equity for a firm for a period of up to ten years.

11.4   HISTORICAL, AVERAGE, AND PROJECTED RETURNS ON CAPITAL

You have been asked to judge the quality of the projects available at Super Meats, a meat processing company. It has earned an average return on capital of 10% over the previous five years, but its marginal return on capital last year was 14%. The industry average return on capital is 12%, and it is expected that Super Meats will earn this return on its projects over the next five years. If the cost of capital is 12.5%, which of the following conclusions would you draw about Super Meat's projects?

a.   It invested in good projects over the last five years.

b.   It invested in good projects last year.

c.   It can expect to invest in good projects over the next five years.

In terms of setting dividend policy, which of these conclusions matters most?

IN PRACTICE: DEALING WITH ACCOUNTING RETURNS

Accounting rates of return, such as return on equity and capital, are subject to abuse and manipulation. For instance, decisions on how to account for acquisitions (purchase or pooling), choice of depreciation methods (accelerated versus straight line), and whether to expense or capitalize an item (R&D) can all affect reported income and book value. In addition, in any specific year, the return on equity and capital can be biased upward or downward, depending on whether the firm had an unusually good or bad year. To estimate a fairer measure of returns on existing projects, we recommend the following:

- Normalize the income before computing returns on equity or capital. For Aracruz, using the average income over the past three years instead of the depressed income in 1996 provides returns on equity or capital that are much closer to the required returns.

- Back out cosmetic earnings effects caused by accounting decisions, such as the one on pooling versus purchase. This is precisely why we should consider Disney's income prior to the amortization of the Capital Cities acquisition in computing returns on equity and capital.

- If there are operating expenses designed to create future growth, rather than current income, capitalize those expenses and treat them as part of book value while computing operating income prior to those expenses. This is what we did with Bookscape when we capitalized operating leases and treated them as part of the capital base, using the adjusted values in computing return on capital. ∎

Step 3: Evaluating Dividend Policy

Once we have measured a firm's capacity to pay dividends and assessed its project quality, we can decide whether the firm should continue its existing policy of returning cash to stockholders, return more cash, or return less. The assessment will depend on how much of the FCFE is returned to stockholders each period, and how good the firm's project opportunities are. There are four possible scenarios:

1. *A firm may have good projects and may be paying out more (in dividends and stock buybacks) than its FCFE.*   In this case, the firm is losing value in two ways. First, by paying too much in dividends, it creates a cash shortfall that has to be met by issuing more securities. Second, the cash shortfall often creates capital rationing constraints; as a result, the firm may reject good projects it otherwise would have taken.

2. *A firm may have good projects and may be paying out less than its FCFE as a dividend.*   Although it will accumulate cash as a consequence, the firm can legitimately argue that it will have good projects in the future in which it can invest the cash, though investors may wonder why it did not take the projects in the current period.

3. *A firm may have poor projects and may be paying out less than its FCFE as a dividend.*   This firm will also accumulate cash, but it will find itself under pressure from stockholders to distribute the cash because of their concern that the cash will be used to finance poor projects.

4. *A firm may have poor projects and may be paying out more than its FCFE as a dividend.*   This firm first has to deal with its poor project choices, possibly by cutting back on those investments that make returns below the hurdle rate. Because the reduced capital expenditure will increase the FCFE, this may take care of the dividend problem. If it does not, the firm will have to cut dividends as well.

Figure 11.3 illustrates the possible combinations of cash payout and project quality. In this matrix, Disney, with its combination of good investments (at least in recent years) and too much cash returned to its stockholders, falls into the quadrant where reducing the payout makes sense. Since much of the cash payout is in the form of stock buybacks, this would suggest that Disney reduce its buybacks. Tata Chemicals, with its combination of neutral investments and cash build-up, could be targeted for more dividends if the quality of its projects deteriorates. Finally, Aracruz poses the toughest challenge, since it clearly is paying out too much in dividends, relative to cash available, but also has the worst track record of the three companies in terms of project returns

Figure 11.3   Analyzing Dividend Policy

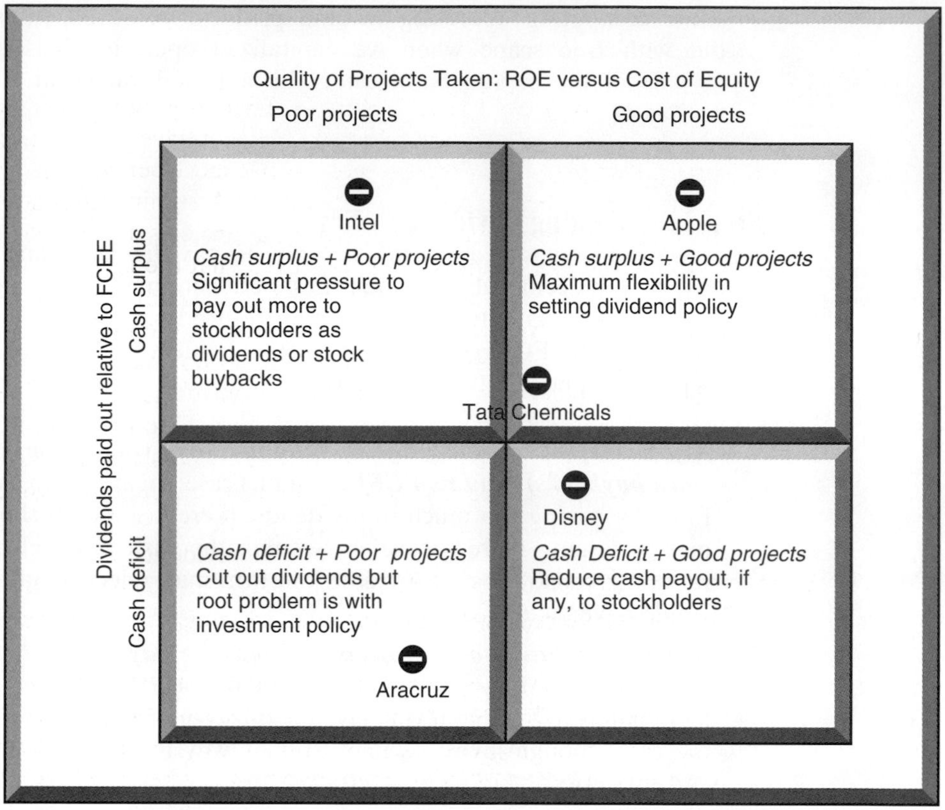

and stock price performance. Reducing dividends is part of the solution, but it has to be combined with more discipline in investment analysis and better risk controls.

Note, however, that the pressure to pay dividends comes from the lack of trust in management rather than greed on the part of stockholders. For a contrast, consider Apple and Google, two companies that generated billions in FCFE in 2008 and returned little to their stockholders while accumulating large cash balances. The high returns earned on projects and superior stock price performance at both companies earned them the flexibility to pay out far less in cash than they generated, with little protest from stockholders. In contrast, Intel has struggled to convince stockholders to allow it to retain a large cash balance, largely because its project and stock returns have lagged in recent years.

Consequences of Payout Not Matching FCFE

The consequences of the cash payout to stockholders not matching the FCFE can vary depending on the quality of a firm's projects. In this section, we examine the consequences of paying out too little or too much for firms with good projects and for firms with bad projects. We also look at how managers in these firms may justify their payout policy and how stockholders are likely to react to the justification.

A. Poor Projects and Low Payout

There are firms that invest in poor projects and accumulate cash by not returning any to stockholders. We discuss stockholder reaction and management response to the dividend policy.

Consequences of Low Payout When a firm pays out less than it can afford to in dividends, it accumulates cash. If a firm does not have good projects in which to invest this cash, it faces several possibilities. In the most benign case, the cash accumulates in the firm and is invested in financial assets. Assuming that these financial assets are fairly priced, the investments are zero-NPV projects and should not negatively affect firm value. There is the possibility, however, that the firm may find itself the target of an acquisition, financed in part by its large holdings of liquid assets.

In the more damaging scenario, as the cash in the firm accumulates, the managers may be tempted to invest in projects that do not meet their hurdle rates, either to reduce the likelihood of a takeover or to earn higher returns than they would on financial assets.[11] These actions will lower the value of the firm. Another possibility is that the management may decide to use the cash to finance an acquisition. This hurts stockholders in the firm, because some of their wealth is transferred to the stockholders of the acquired firms. The managers will claim that such acquisitions have strategic and synergistic benefits. The evidence indicates, however, that most firms that have financed takeovers with large cash balances, acquired over years of paying low dividends while generating a high FCFE, have reduced stockholder value.

Stockholder Reaction Because of the negative consequences of building large cash balances, stockholders of firms that pay insufficient dividends and do not have "good" projects pressure managers to return more of the cash. This is the basis for the free cash flow hypothesis, where dividends serve to reduce free cash flows available to managers and, by doing so, reduce the losses management actions can create for stockholders.

Management's Defense Not surprisingly, managers of firms that pay out less in dividends than they can afford view this policy as being in the best long-term interests of the firm. They maintain that although the current project returns may be poor, future projects will both be more plentiful and have higher returns. Such arguments may be believable initially, but they become more difficult to sustain if the firm continues to earn poor returns on its projects. Managers may also claim that the cash accumulation is needed to meet demands arising from future contingencies. For instance, cyclical firms will often state that large cash balances are needed to tide them over the next recession. Again, although there is some truth to this view, whether the cash balance that is accumulated is reasonable has to be assessed by looking at the experience of the firm in prior recessions.

Finally, in some cases, managers will justify a firm's cash accumulation and low dividend payout based on the behavior of comparable firms. Thus, a firm may claim

---

[11]This is especially likely if the cash is invested in Treasury bills or other low-risk, low-return investments. On the surface, it may seem better for the firm to take on risky projects that earn, say 7%, than for it to invest in Treasury bills and make 3%, though this clearly does not make sense after adjusting for the risk.

that it is essentially matching the dividend policy of its closest competitors and that it has to continue to do so to remain competitive. The argument that "every one else does it" cannot be used to justify a bad dividend policy, however.

Although all these justifications seem consistent with stockholder wealth maximization or the best long-term interests of the firm, they may really be smoke screens designed to hide the fact that this dividend policy serves managerial rather than stockholder interests. Maintaining large cash balances and low dividends provides managers with two advantages: it increases the funds that are directly under their control and thus increases their power to direct future investments, and it increases their margin for safety by stabilizing earnings and thus protecting their jobs.

B. Good Projects and Low Payout

Although the outcomes for stockholders in firms with poor projects and low dividend payout ratios range from neutral to terrible, the results may be more positive for firms that have a better selection of projects and whose management have had a history of earning high returns for stockholders.

Consequences of Low Payout   The immediate consequence of paying out less in dividends than is available in FCFE is the same for firms with good projects as it is for firms with poor projects: the cash balance of the firm increases to reflect the cash surplus. The long-term effects of cash accumulation are generally much less negative for these firms, however, for the following reasons:

- These firms have projects that earn returns greater than the hurdle rate, and it is likely that the cash will be used productively in the long run.
- The high returns earned on internal projects reduce both the pressure and the incentive to invest the cash in poor projects or in acquisitions.
- Firms that earn high returns on their projects are much less likely to be targets of takeovers, reducing the threat of hostile acquisitions.

To summarize, firms that have a history of investing in good projects and expect to continue to have such projects in the future may be able to sustain a policy of retaining cash rather than paying out dividends. In fact, they can actually create value in the long run by using this cash productively.

Stockholder Reaction   Stockholders are much less likely to feel a threat to their wealth in firms that have historically shown good judgment in picking projects. Consequently, they are more likely to agree when managers in those firms withhold cash rather than pay it out. Although there is a solid basis for arguing that managers cannot be trusted with large cash balances, this proposition does not apply equally across all firms. The managers of some firms earn the trust of their stockholders because of their capacity to deliver extraordinary returns on both their projects and their stock over long periods of time. These managers will be generally have much more flexibility in determining dividend policy.

The notion that greedy stockholders force firms with great investments to return too much cash too quickly is not based in fact. Rather, stockholder pressure for dividends or stock repurchases is greatest in firms whose projects yield marginal or poor returns and least in firms whose projects have high returns.

Management Responses   Managers in firms that have posted stellar records in project and stock returns clearly have a much easier time convincing stockholders of the desirability of withholding cash rather than paying it out. The most convincing argument for retaining funds for reinvestment is that the cash will be used productively in the future and earn excess returns for the stockholders. Not all stockholders will agree with this view, especially if they feel that future projects will be less attractive than past projects—which might be the case if the industry in which the firm operates is maturing. For example, many specialty retail firms, such as The Limited, found themselves under pressure to return more cash to stockholders in the early 1990s as margins and growth rates in the business declined.

C. Poor Projects and High Payout

In many ways, the most troublesome combination of circumstances occurs when firms pay out much more in dividends than they can afford and at the same time earn disappointing returns on their projects. These firms have problems with both their investment and their dividend policies, and the latter cannot be solved adequately without addressing the former.

Consequences of High Payout   When a firm pays out more in dividends than it has available in FCFE, it is creating a cash deficit that has to be funded by drawing on the firm's cash balance, by issuing stock to cover the shortfall, or by borrowing money to fund its dividends. If the firm uses its cash reserves, it will reduce equity and raise its debt ratio. If it issues new equity, the drawback is the issuance cost of the stock. By borrowing money, the firm increases its debt while reducing equity and increasing its debt ratio.

Because the FCFE is after capital expenditures, this firm's real problem is not that it pays out too much in dividends, but that it invests in bad projects. Cutting back on these projects would therefore increase the FCFE and might eliminate the cash shortfall created by paying dividends.

Stockholder Reaction   The stockholders of a firm that pays more in dividends than it has available in FCFE faces a dilemma. On the one hand, they may want the firm to reduce its dividends to eliminate the need for additional borrowing or equity issues each year. On the other hand, the management's record in picking projects does not evoke much trust that the firm is using funds wisely, and it is likely that the funds saved by not paying the dividends will be used on other poor projects. Consequently, these firms will first have to solve their investment problems by cutting back on poor projects, which, in turn, will increase the FCFE. If the cash shortfall persists, the firm should then cut back on dividends.

It is therefore entirely possible, especially if the firm is underleveraged to begin with, that the stockholders will not push for lower dividends but will instead try to convince managers to improve project choice. It is also possible that they will encourage the firm to eliminate enough poor projects that the FCFE covers the expected dividend payment.

Management Responses   The managers of firms with poor projects and dividends that exceed FCFE may not think that they have investment problems rather than dividend problems. They may also disagree that the most efficient way of dealing with these problems is to eliminate some of the capital expenditures. In general, their views will be the same as managers who have a poor investment track record. They will claim the period used to analyze project returns was not representative, but was an industry-wide problem that will pass, or that the projects have long gestation periods.

Overall, it is unlikely that these managers will convince the stockholders of their good intentions on future projects. Consequently, there will be a strong push toward cutbacks in capital expenditures, especially if the firm is borrowing money to finance the dividends and does not have much excess debt capacity.

11.5 STOCKHOLDER PRESSURE AND DIVIDEND POLICY

Which of the following companies would you expect to see under greatest pressure from its stockholders to buy back stock or pay large dividends? (All of the companies have costs of capital of 12%.)

a.   A company with a historical return on capital of 25%, and a small cash balance

b.   A company with a historical return on capital of 6%, and a small cash balance

c.   A company with a historical return on capital of 25%, and a large cash balance

d.   A company with a historical return on capital of 6%, and a large cash balance

The managers at the company argue that they need the cash for acquisitions. Would this make it more or less likely that stockholders will push for stock buybacks?

a.   More likely

b.   Less likely

D. Good Projects and High Payout

The costs of trying to maintain unsustainable dividends are most evident in firms that have a selection of good projects to choose from. The cash that is paid out as dividends could well have been used to invest in some of these projects, leading to a much higher return for stockholders and higher stock prices for the firm.

Consequences of High Payout   When a firm pays out more in dividends than it has available in FCFE, it creates a cash shortfall. If this firm also has good projects available but cannot invest in them because of capital rationing constraints, the firm is paying a hefty price for its dividend policy. Even if the projects are passed up for other reasons, the cash this firm is paying out as dividends would earn much better returns if left to accumulate in the firm.

Dividend payments also create a cash deficit that now has to be met by issuing new securities. Issuing new stock carries a potentially large issuance cost, which reduces firm value. But if the firm issues new debt, it might become overleveraged, and this may reduce value.

Stockholder Reaction   The best course of action for stockholders is to insist that the firm pay out less in dividends and invest in better projects. If the firm has paid high dividends for an extended period of time and has acquired stockholders who value high dividends even more than they value the firm's long-term health, reducing dividends may be difficult. Even so, stockholders may be much more amenable to cutting dividends and reinvesting in the firm if the firm has a ready supply of good projects at hand.

Management Responses   The managers of firms that have good projects while paying out too much in dividends have to figure out a way to cut dividends while differentiating themselves from those firms that are cutting dividends due to declining earnings. The initial suspicion with which markets view dividend cuts can be overcome (at least partially) by providing markets with information about project quality at the time of the dividend cut. If the dividends have been paid for a long time, however, the firm may have stockholders who like the high dividends and may not particularly be interested in the projects that the firm has available. If this is the case, the initial reaction to the dividend cut, no matter how carefully packaged, will be negative. However, as disgruntled stockholders sell their holdings, the firm will acquire new stockholders who may be more willing to accept the lower dividend and higher investment policy.

In Summary

Looking across the four scenarios, it is quite clear that investor assessments of dividend policy and reactions to cash accumulation cannot be separated from evaluations of investment policy. Firms are judged based upon their track records, and investors are more likely to trust successful firms with their cash than firms that have a history of poor investments and bad management. Figure 11.4 provides a summary of the four scenarios described above.

11.6   DIVIDEND POLICY AND HIGH-GROWTH FIRMS

High-growth firms are often encouraged to start paying dividends to expand their stockholder base, because there are stockholders who will not or cannot hold stock that do not pay dividends. Do you agree with this rationale?

a.   Yes.

b.   No.

Explain.

Step 4: Interaction between Dividend Policy and Financing Policy

The analysis of dividend policy is further enriched—and complicated—if we bring in the firm's financing decisions as well. In Chapter 9, we noted that one of the ways a firm can increase leverage over time is by increasing dividends or repurchasing stock; at the same time, it can decrease leverage by cutting or not paying dividends. Thus we cannot decide how much a firm should pay in dividends without determining whether it is under- or overlevered and whether or not it intends to close this leverage gap.

An underlevered firm may be able to pay more than its FCFE as dividend and may do so intentionally to increase its debt ratio. An overlevered firm, on the other hand, may have to pay less than its FCFE as dividends because of its desire to reduce leverage. In some of the scenarios already described, leverage can be used to strengthen the suggested recommendations. For instance, an underlevered firm with poor projects and

Figure 11.4   A Framework for Analyzing Dividend Policy

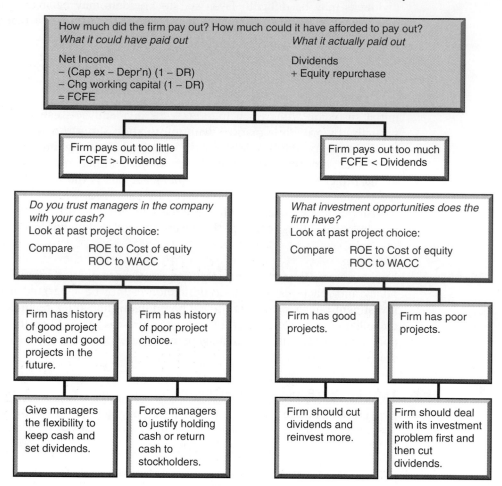

a cash flow surplus has an added incentive to raise dividends and reevaluate investment policy, because it will be able to increase its leverage by doing so. In some cases, however, the imperatives of moving to an optimal debt ratio may act as a barrier to carrying out changes in dividend policy. Thus, an overlevered firm with poor projects and a cash flow surplus may find the cash better spent reducing debt rather than paying out dividends.

ILLUSTRATION 11.5   **Analyzing the Dividend Policy of Disney, Aracruz, Tata Chemicals, and Deutsche Bank**

Using the cash flow approach, we are now in a position to analyze Disney's dividend policy. To do so, we will draw on three findings:

1. While Disney has a payout ratio of 20%, it has returned almost 140% of its FCFE over the last decade to stockholders, primarily through stock buybacks.

2. While Disney's project returns and stock price performance lagged in the early part of the last decade (1999–2008), it has improved significantly on both measures in the last four years and now delivers excess returns on both dimensions.

3. Finally, in our analysis in Chapter 8, we noted that Disney was slightly underlevered, with an actual debt ratio of 27% and an optimal debt ratio of between 30% and 40%, depending upon assumptions about operating income.

Given this combination of findings, we would recommend that Disney reduce its stock buybacks for the near term, in the face of a slowing economy and potentially lower earnings. If earnings stay healthy, Disney can go back to using buybacks as a way of moving towards it optimal debt ratio. In Table 11.15, we forecast the FCFE for the next five years, assuming that Disney funds 40% of its reinvestment needs with debt each year.

Note that we have assumed that revenues, net income, dividends, capital expenditures, and depreciation are expected to grow 5% a year for the next five years, and that working capital remains at its existing percentage (2.28%) of revenues. Based on these forecasts, and assuming that Disney maintains its existing dividend, Disney should have about $14,842 million in excess cash that it can return to its stockholders in stock buybacks over the period.

Turning our attention to Aracruz, we review our findings on the company in both this chapter and prior ones:

- Aracruz has paid out far more in dividends than it has available in FCFE and has funded the deficit primarily with new debt.

- As a result of the borrowing, Aracruz is significantly overlevered, with a debt-to-capital ratio in excess of 50% and an optimal debt ratio, computed in Chapter 8, of about 10%.

- While Aracruz delivered high returns between 2002 and 2007, we suspect that some or much of these returns were the result of speculation on currency derivatives during that period. The unraveling of this strategy in 2008 generated billions of dollars in losses and makes us wary about management capabilities in the firm to manage risk and deliver performance.

Table 11.15 FORECASTED FCFE AND CASH AVAILABLE FOR STOCK BUYBACKS—DISNEY (IN MILLIONS)

	Current	2009	2010	2011	2012	2013
Net income	$4,324	$4,540	$4,767	$5,006	$5,256	$5,519
−(Cap ex − Depreciation) (1 − 0.40)	$1,078	$1,132	$1,188	$1,248	$1,310	$1,376
−Change in working capital (1 − 0.40)		$25	$27	$28	$29	$31
FCFE		$3,383	$3,552	$3,730	$3,916	$4,112
Expected dividends		$697	$732	$769	$807	$847
Cash available for stock buybacks		$2,686	$2,820	$2,961	$3,109	$3,265

Taken as a whole, we see few alternatives for Aracruz other than cutting or even eliminating dividends and using the cash to pay down debt.

With Tata Chemicals, our analysis so far has led us to the following conclusions about the firm:

- Tata Chemicals has paid out about 70% of its FCFE as dividends each year and has redirected the withheld cash to other companies in the Tata Group.

- While Tata Chemical's stock price performance looks good in absolute terms, much of that performance can be attributed to the performance of the Indian stock market. On a risk-adjusted basis, Tata Chemicals has delivered excess returns close to zero on both its projects and the stock.

- Tata Chemicals is overlevered with a debt-to-capital ratio of 34% and an optimal debt ratio of 10%, though it is not clear how much of this debt is being subsidized by the Tata Group.

Unlike Aracruz, Tata Chemicals is not in financial distress and has some leeway to use its dividend policy to adjust its capital structure over time. We would recommend that Tata Chemicals continue its existing dividend policy, and that it redirect some of its excess cash to paying down debt.

Finally, with Deutsche Bank, we draw on the estimates of expected future FCFE that we made in Table 11.8. Recapping, we assumed a target regulatory capital ratio of 10% and estimated the reinvestment that would be needed in future years to sustain a modest growth rate of 4% for the next five years. In Table 11.16, we reproduce the expected FCFE and net income and compute an aggregate dividend payout ratio that would be appropriate for Deutsche Bank for the future.

Based upon these estimates, Deutsche Bank can afford to pay out about 66% of its earnings as dividends:

$$\text{Potential payout ratio} = \frac{\text{FCFE}}{\text{Earnings}} = \frac{11,486}{17,349} = 66\%$$

Given the uncertainties in the banking sector about potential losses on securities and regulatory changes, we would hold off on making major changes in dividend policy until some of the uncertainty is resolved.

Table 11.16	Expected FCFE and Net Income—Deutsche Bank	
	FCFE	**Net Income**
2009	€2,001	€3,147
2010	€2,114	€3,302
2011	€2,233	€3,463
2012	€2,358	€3,631
2013	€2,779	€3,807
Aggregate	€11,486	€17,349

A Comparable Firm Approach to Analyzing Dividend Policy

So far, we have examined the dividend policy of a firm by looking at its cash flows and the quality of its investments. There are managers who believe that their dividend policies are judged relative to those of their competitors. This comparable-firm approach to analyzing dividend policy is often used narrowly, by looking at only firms that are in the same industry group or sector. As we will illustrate, it can be used more broadly, by looking at the determinants of dividend policy across all firms in the market.

Using Firms in the Industry

In the simplest form of this approach, a firm's dividend yield and payout are compared to those of firms in its industry and accordingly judged to be adequate, excessive, or inadequate. Thus, a utility stock with a dividend yield of 3.5% may be criticized for paying out an inadequate dividend if utility stocks, on average, have a much higher dividend yield. In contrast, a computer software firm that has a dividend yield of 1.0% may be viewed as paying too high a dividend if software firms pay a much lower dividend on average.

Although comparing a firm to comparable firms on dividend yield and payout may have some intuitive appeal, it can be misleading. First, it assumes that all firms within the same industry group have the same net capital expenditure and working capital needs. These assumptions may not be true if firms are in different stages of the life cycle. Second, even if the firms are at the same stage in their life cycles, the entire industry may have a dividend policy that is unsustainable or suboptimal. Third, it does not consider stock buybacks as an alternative to dividends. The third criticism can be mitigated when the approach is extended to compare cash returned to stockholders, rather than just dividends.

 There is a data set online that summarizes the dividend yields and payout ratios by sector for U.S. companies.

ILLUSTRATION 11.6   Analyzing Disney's Dividend Payout Using Comparable Firms

In comparing Disney's dividend policy to its peer group, we analyze the dividend yields and payout ratios of comparable firms in 2008, as shown in Table 11.17. We defined comparable firms as entertainment companies with a market capitalization in excess of $500 million.

Of the seventeen companies in this group, only seven paid dividends. Relative to the other dividend-paying companies in this sector, Disney pays low dividends. The interesting question, though, is whether Disney should be setting dividend policy based on entertainment firms, most of which are smaller, riskier, and much less diversified than Disney, or on large firms in other businesses that resemble it in terms of cash flows and risk.

For Deutsche Bank, we used large money center European banks as comparable firms. Table 11.18 provides the listing of the firms, as well as their dividend yields and payout ratios. On both dividend yield and payout ratios, Deutsche Bank pays a much higher dividend than the typical European bank, if we use dividends paid in May 2008.

Table 11.17   PAYOUT RATIOS AND DIVIDEND YIELDS—ENTERTAINMENT COMPANIES

	Market Cap	Payout Ratio	Dividend Yield
Astral Media Inc. "A"	$1,221.70	0.00%	0.00%
CBS Corp. "B"	$5,103.70	53.52%	14.22%
Central European Media Enterps	$827.70	0.00%	0.00%
Corus Entertainment Inc	$806.50	0.00%	0.00%
CTC Media Inc	$715.10	0.00%	0.00%
Discovery Communications Inc	$3,860.60	NA	0.00%
Disney (Walt)	$41,114.70	17.11%	1.67%
DreamWorks Animation	$2,074.30	0.00%	0.00%
Hearst-Argyle Television Inc	$589.10	40.59%	4.46%
IAC/InterActiveCorp	$2,215.30	NA	0.00%
Lions Gate Entertainment Corp	$705.60	NA	0.00%
News Corp.	$23,245.30	9.07%	1.35%
Regal Entertainment Group	$1,447.60	176.09%	12.70%
Scripps Networks	$3,422.30	NA	0.00%
Time Warner	$34,112.40	22.17%	2.63%
Viacom Inc. "B"	$10,669.30	0.00%	0.00%
World Wrestling Ent.	$749.50	198.45%	13.79%
Average		39.77%	2.99%

Source: Value Line Database.

However, Deutsche Bank had cut the dividends it will be paying in May 2009 by almost 90%, reducing both its dividend yield and payout ratio well below the industry average.

For Aracruz and Tata Chemicals, we looked at the average dividend yield and payout ratios of three sets of comparable firms in their businesses—emerging market companies, U.S. companies and all companies listed globally. Table 11.19 summarizes these statistics. Aracruz has a higher dividend yield than comparable companies, but that statistic reflects the collapse of its stock price, and Aracruz's payout ratio cannot be computed because it lost money in 2008. In summary, this does back up our earlier contention that Aracruz is paying out too much in dividends and has to cut dividends. Tata Chemicals pays more in dividends than comparable companies on both a yield and payout basis.

With all four companies, the dangers of basing dividend policy based on comparable firms are clear. The "right" amount to pay in dividends will depend heavily on what we define "comparable" to be. If managers are allowed to pick their peer group, it is easy to justify even the most irrational dividend policy.

11.7   PEER GROUP ANALYSIS

Assume that you are advising a small, high-growth bank that is concerned about the fact that its dividend payout and yield are much lower than other banks. The CEO of the bank is concerned that investors will punish the bank for its dividend policy. What do you think?

a.   I think that the bank will be punished for its errant dividend policy.

b.   I think that investors are sophisticated enough for the bank to be treated fairly.

c.   I think that the bank will not be punished for its low dividends as long as it tries to convey information to its investors about the quality of its projects and growth prospects.

Table 11.18   PAYOUT RATIOS AND DIVIDEND YIELDS—EUROPEAN BANKS (BASED ON DIVIDENDS PAID IN 2008)

	Dividend Yield	Dividend Payout
HSBC Holdings plc (LSE:HSBA)	0.00%	0.00%
Banco Santander, S.A. (CATS:SAN)	0.00%	0.00%
Intesa Sanpaolo SpA (CM:ISP)	0.00%	0.00%
Banco Bilbao Vizcaya Argentaria (CATS:BBVA)	0.00%	0.00%
BNP Paribas (ENXTPA:BNP)	0.00%	0.00%
UBS AG (VIRTX:UBSN)	0.00%	0.00%
UniCredito Italiano S.p.A. (CM:UCG)	0.00%	0.00%
Royal Bank of Scotland Group plc (LSE:RBS)	22.06%	98.61%
Credit Suisse Group (VIRTX:CSGN)	8.68%	0.00%
Societe Generale Group (ENXTPA:GLE)	0.00%	0.00%
Standard Chartered PLC (LSE:STAN)	2.84%	22.98%
Credit Agricole SA (ENXTPA:ACA)	0.00%	0.00%
Barclays plc (LSE:BARC)	0.00%	0.00%
Nordea Bank AB (OM:NDA SEK)	9.00%	45.03%
Deutsche Bank AG (DB:DBK)	15.80%	119.37%
Banca Monte dei Paschi di Siena SpA (CM:BMPS)	0.00%	0.00%
Lloyds TSB Group plc (LSE:LLOY)	35.76%	87.14%
Banco Popular Espanol SA (CATS:POP)	0.00%	0.00%
KBC Group NV (ENXTBR:KBC)	17.04%	152.94%
Svenska Handelsbanken AB (OM:SHB A)	11.54%	60.24%
National Bank of Greece SA (ATSE:ETE)	2.64%	12.49%
Unione di Banche Italiane Scpa (CM:UBI)	8.89%	64.61%
Average	6.10%	30.16%

Source: Capital IQ.

Using the Market

The alternative to using only comparable firms in the same industry is to study the entire population of firms, trying to estimate the variables that cause differences in dividend payout across firms. We outlined some of the determinants of dividend policy in the last chapter, and we could try to arrive at more specific measures of each of these determinants. For instance,

- *Growth opportunities* Firms with greater growth opportunities should pay out less in dividends than firms without these opportunities. Consequently, dividend

Table 11.19   DIVIDEND YIELD AND PAYOUT RATIOS FOR COMPARABLE COMPANIES—ARACRUZ AND TATA CHEMICALS

	Aracruz	Paper and Pulp			Tata Chemicals	Diversified Chemicals		
		Emerging	U.S.	Global		Emerging	U.S.	Global
Dividend Yield	8.19%	3.15%	2.08%	2.81%	5.45%	3.87%	2.54%	3.18%
Payout	N/A	43.93%	28.92%	35.55%	43.58%	34.33%	19.75%	26.20%

payout ratios (yields) and expected growth rates in earnings should be negatively correlated with each other.

- **Investment needs** Firms with larger investment needs (capital expenditures and working capital) should pay out less in dividends than firms without these needs. Dividend payout ratios and yields should be lower for firms with significant capital expenditure needs.

- **Insider holdings** As noted earlier in the chapter, firms where stockholders have less power are more likely to hold on to cash and not pay out dividends. Hence, dividend payout ratios and insider holdings should be negatively correlated with each other.

- **Financial leverage** Firms with high debt ratios should pay lower dividends, because they have already precommitted their cash flows to make debt payments. Therefore, dividend payout ratios and debt ratios should be negatively correlated with each other.

Because multiple measures can be used for each of these variables, we chose specific proxies—analyst estimates of growth in earnings per share for growth opportunities (EGR), percent of stock held by insiders for insider holdings (INS), and the standard deviation in stock prices (STD) as measures of equity risk. Using data from 2008, we regressed dividend yields and payout ratios against all of these variables and arrived at the following regression equations (t-statistics are in brackets below coefficients):

$$PYT = 0.683 - 0.185 \, ROE - 1.07 \, STD - 0.313 \, EGR$$
$$\quad (27.41) \quad (3.06) \qquad (10.85) \qquad (2.60)$$

$$R^2 = 13.3\%$$

$$YLD = 0.039 - 0.039 \, STD - 0.010 \, INS - 0.093 \, EGR$$
$$\quad (37.38) \quad (9.39) \qquad (2.62) \qquad (16.23)$$

$$R^2 = 32.2\%$$

The regressions explain about 32% of the differences in dividend yields and 13% of the differences in payout ratios across firms in the United States. The two strongest factors are earnings growth and equity risk, with higher-growth, higher-risk firms paying out less of their earnings as dividends and having lower dividend yields. In addition, firms with high insider holdings tend to pay out less in dividends than do firms with low insider holdings, and firms with high capital expenditures needs seem to pay less in dividends than firms without these needs.

 There is a data set online that summarizes the results of regressing dividend yield and payout ratio against fundamentals for U.S. companies.

ILLUSTRATION 11.7 **Analyzing Dividend Payout Using the Cross-Sectional Regression**
To illustrate the applicability of the market regression in analyzing the dividend policy of Disney, we estimate the values of the independent variables in the regressions for the firm.

Insider holdings at Disney (as % of outstanding stock) = 7.7%
Standard deviation in Disney stock prices = 19.3%
Disney's ROE = 13.05%
Expected growth in earnings per share (analyst estimates) = 14.5%

Substituting into the regression equations for the dividend payout ratio and dividend yield, we estimate a predicted payout ratio:

$$\text{Predicted payout} = 0.683 - 0.185(0.1305) - 1.07(0.1930) - 0.313(0.145) = 0.4069$$
$$\text{Predicted yield} = 0.039 - 0.039(0.1930) - 0.010(0.077) - 0.093(0.145) = 0.0172$$

Based on this analysis, Disney, with its dividend yield of 1.67% and a payout ratio of approximately 20%, is paying too little in dividends. This analysis, however, fails to factor in the huge stock buybacks made by Disney over the last few years.

MANAGING CHANGES IN DIVIDEND POLICY

In Chapter 10, we noted the tendency on the part of investors to buy stocks with dividend policies that meet their specific needs. Thus, at least prior to 2003, investors who wanted high current cash flows and did not care much about the tax consequences migrated to firms that paid high dividends; those who wanted price appreciation and were concerned about the tax differential held stock in firms that paid low or no dividends. One consequence of this clientele effect is that changes in dividends, even if entirely justified by the cash flows, may not be well received by stockholders. In particular, a firm with high dividends that cuts them drastically may find itself facing unhappy stockholders. At the other extreme, a firm with a history of not paying dividends that suddenly institutes a large dividend may find that its stockholders also are displeased.

Is there a way in which firms can announce changes in dividend policy that minimizes the negative fallout that is likely to occur? In this section, we will examine dividend changes and the market reaction to them and draw broader lessons for all firms that may plan to make such changes.

Empirical Evidence

Firms may cut dividends for several reasons; some clearly have negative implications for future cash flows and the current value of the firm, whereas others have more positive implications. In particular, the value of firms that cut dividends because of poor earnings and cash flows should drop, whereas the value of firms that cut dividends because of a dramatic improvement in project choice should increase. At the same time, financial markets tend to be skeptical of the latter claims, especially if the firm making the claims reports lower earnings and has a history of poor project returns. Thus, there is value to examining closely timed earnings and dividend cut announcements, to see whether the market reaction changes as a consequence.

Woolridge and Ghosh looked at 408 firms that cut dividends, and at the actions taken or information provided by these firms in conjunction with the dividend

| | Periods around Announcement Date | | |
	Prior Quarter	Announcement Period	Quarter After
Table 11.20 EXCESS RETURNS AROUND DIVIDEND CUT ANNOUNCEMENTS			
Simultaneous announcement of earnings decline/loss ($N = 176$)	−7.23%	−8.17%	+1.80%
Prior announcement of earnings decline or loss ($N = 208$)	−7.58%	−5.52%	+1.07%
Simultaneous announcement of investment or growth opportunities ($N = 16$)	−7.69%	−5.16%	+8.79%

cuts.[12] In particular, they examined three groups of companies: The first group announced an earnings decline or loss with the dividend cut, the second had made a prior announcement of earnings decline or loss, and the third made a simultaneous announcement of growth opportunities or higher earnings. The results are summarized in Table 11.20.

We can draw several conclusions from this study. First, more firms announcing dividend cuts did so in response to earnings declines (384) rather than in conjunction with investment or growth opportunities (16). The market seems to react negatively to all of them, however, suggesting that it does not attach much credibility to the firm's statements. The negative reaction to the dividend cut seems to persist in the case of the firms with the earnings declines, whereas it is reversed in the case of the firms with earnings increases or better investment opportunities.

Woolridge and Ghosh also found that firms that announced stock dividends or stock repurchases in conjunction with the dividend cuts fared much better than firms that did not. Finally, they noted the tendency across the entire sample for prices to correct themselves, at least partially, in the year following the dividend cut. This would suggest that markets tend to overreact to the initial dividend cut, and the price recovery can be attributed to the subsequent correction.

In an interesting case study, Soter, Brigham, and Evanson looked at Florida Power & Light's dividend cut in 1994.[13] FPL was the first healthy utility in the United States to cut dividends by a significant amount (32%). At the same time as it cut dividends, FPL announced that it was buying back 10 million shares over the next three years and emphasized that dividends would be linked more directly to earnings. On the day of the announcement, the stock price dropped 14% but recovered this amount in the month after the announcement and earned a return of 23.8% in the year after, significantly more than the S&P 500 (11.2%) and other utilities (14.2%) over the period.

---

[12]J. R. Woolridge and C. Ghosh, "Dividend Cuts: Do They Always Signal Bad News?" *Midland Corporate Finance Journal* v3, 20–31.

[13]D. Soter, E. Brigham, and P. Evanson, "The Dividend Cut 'Heard 'Round the World': The Case of FPL," *Journal of Applied Corporate Finance* 9:4–15. This is also a Harvard Business School case study authored by Ben Esty.

Lessons for Firms

There are several lessons for a firm that plans to change its dividend policy. First, no matter how good the rationale may be for cutting dividends, it should be expected that markets will react negatively to the initial announcement, for two reasons. The first reason is the well-founded skepticism with which markets greet any statement by the firm about dividend cuts. A second is that large dividend changes typically make the existing investor clientele unhappy. Although other stockholders may be happy with the new dividend policy, the transition will take time, during which stock prices fall. Second, if a firm has good reasons for cutting dividends, such as an increase in project availability, it will gain at least partial protection by providing information to markets about these projects.

Dividend Cuts and Investor Reaction: A Behavioral Perspective
There are few corporate finance actions that managers dread more than cutting dividends, which may explain why they happen so infrequently. When firms are paying too much, either because earnings have dropped or investment opportunities have increased, the rationale for cutting dividends may seem simple, but there are reasons why these firms choose to put off making this decision:

- *Indiscriminate investors* There is evidence that the stock prices of firms that cut dividends drop, at the time of the announcement, no matter what the reasons for the action. In other words, investors seem to treat firms that cut dividends because of operating problems (declining earnings and losses) the same way that they treat firms that cut dividends to invest in potentially lucrative investments.

- *Stock price drift* Michaely, Thaler, and Womack looked at 887 dividend omissions between 1964 and 1987 and found evidence that stock prices continue to drift downwards in the weeks after a dividend decrease.[14] While some of this downward drift can be attributed to higher risk, it is possible that some of it is due to herd behavior on the part of investors. Boehme and Sorescu contest this conclusion by noting that the price drift is isolated to smaller firms.[15]

There is, however, some good news for firms that do need to reduce dividends. Firms that can frame dividend decreases in terms that appeal to investors may be able to overcome the generally negative reaction from investors, at least over longer periods. Bulan, Subramaniam and Talan divide dividend omissions into good and bad omissions based upon two factors.[16] They find that firms that confront and deal with dividend problems early and use the cash from dividend omissions to retire debt see their stock prices recover more quickly than firms that allow the pain to linger and misuse the cash from dividend omissions.

---

[14]Roni Michaely, Richard H. Thaler, and Kent L. Womack, "Price Reactions to Dividend Initiations and Oomissions: Overreaction or Drift?" *Journal of Finance* 50:573–608.

[15]Rodney D. Boehme and Sorin M Sorescu, "The Long-Run Performance Following Dividend Initiations and Resumptions: Underreaction or Product of Chance?" *Journal of Finance* 57:871–900.

[16]L. Bulan, N. Subramaniam, and L. Tanlu, "When Are Dividend Omissions Good News?" working paper, 2005, ssrn.com.

CONCLUSION

We began this chapter by expanding our definition of cash returned to stockholder to include stock buybacks with dividends. Firms in the United States in particular have turned to buying back stock and returning cash selectively to those investors who need it.

With this expanded definition, we first used a cash flow–based approach to decide whether a firm is paying too much or too little to its stockholders. To form this judgment, we first estimate what the firm has available to pay out to its stockholders; we measure this cash flow by looking at the cash left over after reinvestment needs have been covered and debt has been serviced and call it the free cash flow to equity. We then looked at the quality of the firm's projects; firms with better projects get more leeway from equity investors to accumulate cash than firms with poor projects. We next considered the effect of wanting to increase or decrease the debt ratio on the amount of cash that is returned to stockholders. Finally, we considered all three factors—the cash flow available for stockholders, the returns on existing investments, and the need to increase or decrease debt ratios—in coming up with broad conclusions about dividend policy. Firms with a good track record in investing can pay out less in dividends than is available in cash flows and not face significant pressure from stockholders to pay out more. When the managers of firms are not trusted by their stockholders to invest wisely, firms are much more likely to face pressure to return excess cash to stockholders.

We also analyzed a firm's dividend policy by looking at the dividend policies of comparable firms in the business. In this approach, a firm paying out less in dividends than comparable firms would be viewed as paying too little, and one that is paying out more would be viewed as paying too much. We used both a narrow definition of comparable firms (firms in the same line of business) and a broader definition (all firms). We controlled for differences in risk and growth across firms using a multiple regression.

We closed the chapter by looking at how firms that intend to change their dividend policy can minimize the side costs of doing so. This is especially true when firms have to reduce their dividends to meet legitimate reinvestment needs. Although the initial reaction to the announcement of a dividend cut is likely to be negative, firms can buffer some of the impact by providing information to markets about the investments that they plan to accept with the funds.

Given the tax law changes in the United States in 2003, it may be time to revisit the whole basis for dividend policy. Historically, in the United States and Western Europe, firms have locked themselves into a dance with investors wherein they institute dividends and are then committed to maintaining these dividends in good times and in bad. In fact, much of what we observe in dividend policy—from sticky dividends to reluctance to increase dividends in the face of good news and to cut dividends in the face of bad news—can be traced to this commitment. This commitment has also led companies to increasingly shift to stock buybacks as an alternative to dividends. If dividends no longer have a tax disadvantage, it is time for firms to shift to a more flexible dividend payout policy whereby dividends reflect what they can afford to pay rather than their historical dividends.

LIVE CASE STUDY

A FRAMEWORK FOR ANALYZING DIVIDENDS

Objective: To determine whether your firm should change its dividend policy, based on an analysis of its investment opportunities and comparable firms.

Key Questions

- How much could this firm have returned to its stockholders over the past few years? How much did it actually return?
- Given this dividend policy and the current cash balance of this firm, would you push the firm to change its dividend policy (return more or less cash to its owners)?
- How does this firm's dividend policy compare to those of its peer group and to the rest of the market?

Framework for Analysis

1. *Cash Return to Stockholders*
   - How much has the firm paid out in dividends each year for the past few years?
   - How much stock has it bought back each year for the past few years?
   - Cumulatively, how much cash has been returned to stockholders each year for the past few years?

2. *Affordable Dividends*
   - What was this firm's FCFE over the last few years?
   - What is this firm's current cash balance?

3. *Management Trust*
   - How well have the managers of the firm picked investments, historically? (Look at the investment return section.)
   - Is there any reason to believe that future investments of this firm will be different from the historical record?

4. *Changing Dividend Policy*
   - Given the relationship between dividends and FCFE and the trust you have in the management of this firm, would you change this firm's dividend policy?

5. *Comparing to Sector and Market*
   - Relative to the sector to which this firm belongs, does it pay too much or too little in dividends? (Do a regression, if necessary.)
   - Relative to the rest of the firms in the market, does it pay too much or too little in dividends? (Use the market regression, if necessary.)

Getting Information on Analyzing Dividend Policy

You can get the information that you need to estimate FCFE and returns on equity from past financials. You will also need a beta (see risk and return section) and a debt ratio (see risk and return section) to estimate the free cash flows to equity. Finally, you will need stock returns for your stock and the returns on a market index over the period of your analysis.

 Online Sources of Information
www.stern.nyu.edu/~adamodar/cfin2E/project/data.htm

PROBLEMS AND QUESTIONS

(In the problems below, you can use a risk premium of 5.5% and a tax rate of 40% if either is not specified)

1. Stock buybacks really do not return cash to stockholders, because only those who sell back stock receive the cash. Is this statement true, or false? Explain.

2. Between 1988 and 2008, we saw a decrease in the percent of cash returned to stockholders in the form of dividends. Why?

3. Lube Oil, a chain of automobile service stations, reports net income of $100 million after depreciation of $50 million. The firm has capital expenditures of $80 million, and the noncash working capital increased from $25 to $40 million. Estimate the firm's FCFE, assuming that the firm is completely equity-financed.

4. Lube Oil (Question 3) paid a dividend of $20 million and bought back $25 million in stock. Estimate how much the cash balance of the firm changed during the year.

5. How would your answers to the last two questions change if you were told that Lube Oil started the year with $120 million in debt and ended the year with $135 million?

6. Now assume that Lube Oil has a return on equity of 5% and a cost of equity of 10%. As a stockholder in Lube Oil, would you want the firm to change its dividend policy? Why, or why not?

7. Tech Products reported a net loss of $80 million for the latest financial year. In addition, the firm reported a net capital expenditure of $70 million and an increase in noncash working capital of $10 million. Finally, the firm had $10 million in debt at the start of the year that it paid off during the year. Estimate the FCFE.

8. Tech Products (Question 7) pays a dividend of $40 million. Assuming that the firm started the period with no cash, how did it raise the funding for the dividend payment?

9. New Age Telecomm is a young, high-growth telecommunications firm. It pays no dividends, even though the average dividend payout for other firms in the telecommunications sector is 40%. Is New Age paying too little in dividends? Why, or why not?

10. The following is a regression of dividend payout ratios on the risk and ln(market capitalization: in millions) of chemical firms:

    Dividend payout ratio $= 0.14 + 0.05$
    [ln(Market capitalization in millions)] $- 0.1$(Beta)

    Harman Chemicals has a market capitalization of $1.5 billion and a beta of 1.2. It pays out 22% of its earnings as dividends. How does this dividend payout compare to the industry?

11. JLChem Corporation, a chemical manufacturing firm with changing investment opportunities, is considering a major change in dividend policy. It currently has 50 million shares outstanding and pays an annual dividend of $2 per share. The firm current and projected income statement are provided below (in millions):

	Current	Projected for Next Year
EBITDA	$1,200	$1,350
− Depreciation	$200	$250
EBIT	$1,000	$1,100
− Interest expense	$200	$200
EBT	$800	$900
− Taxes	$320	$360
Net income	$480	$540

The firm's current capital expenditure is $500 million. It is considering five projects for the next year:

Project	Investment	Beta	IRR (Using Cash Flows to Equity)
A	$190 million	0.6	12.0%
B	$200 million	0.8	12.0%
C	$200 million	1.0	14.5%
D	$200 million	1.2	15.0%
E	$100 million	1.5	20.0%

The firm's current beta is 1.0, and the current Treasury bill rate is 5.5%. The firm expects working capital to increase $50 million both this year and next. The firm plans to finance its net capital expenditures and working capital needs with 30% debt.

Project	Initial Investment	Annual EBIT	Salvage	Lifetime	Depreciation
1	$10 million	$1 million	$500,000	5 years	$2.5 million
2	$40 million	$5 million	$1 million	10 years	$10 million
3	$50 million	$5 million	$1 million	10 years	$10 million

a. What is the firm's current payout ratio?

b. What proportion of its current FCFE is it paying out as dividends?

c. What would your projected capital expenditure be for next year (i.e., which of the five projects would you accept, and why)?

d. How much cash will the company have available to pay out as dividends next year (i.e., what is the maximum amount the company can pay out as dividends)?

e. Would you pay out this maximum amount as dividends? Why, or why not? What other considerations would you bring to this decision?

f. JKL Corporation currently has a cash balance of $100 million (after paying the current year's dividends). If it pays out $125 million as dividends next year, what will its projected cash balance be at the end of the next year?

12. GL Corporation, a retail firm, is making a decision on how much it should pay out to its stockholders. It has $100 million in investible funds. The following information is provided about the firm:

- It has 100 million shares outstanding, each share selling for $15. The beta of the stock is 1.25, and the risk-free rate is 8%. The expected return on the market is 16%.

- The firm has $500 million of debt outstanding. The marginal interest rate on the debt is 12%.

- The corporate tax rate is 50%.

- The firm has the following investment projects:

Project	Investment Requirement	After-Tax Return on Capital
A	$15 million	27%
B	$10 million	20%
C	$25 million	16%
D	$20 million	14%
E	$30 million	12%

The firm plans to finance all its investment needs at its current debt ratio.

a. Should the company return money to its stockholders?

b. If so, how much should be returned to stockholders?

13. InTech, a computer software firm that has never paid dividends before, is considering whether it should start doing so. This firm has a cost of equity of 22% and a cost of debt of 10% (the tax rate is 40%). The firm has $100 million in debt outstanding and 50 million shares outstanding, selling for $10 per share. The firm currently has net income of $90 million and depreciation charges of $10 million. It also has the following projects available: (see table on top of next page)

The firm plans to finances its future capital investment needs using 20% debt.

a. Which of these projects should the firm accept?

b. How much (if anything) should the firm pay out as dividends?

14. LimeAde, a large soft drink manufacturing firm, is faced with the decision of how much to pay out as dividends to its stockholders. It expects to have a net income of $1,000 (after depreciation of $500), and it has the following projects:

Project	Initial Investment	Beta	IRR (to Equity Investors)
A	$500	2.0	21%
B	$600	1.5	20%
C	$500	1.0	12%

The firm's beta is 1.5, and the current risk-free rate is 6%. The firm plans to finance net capital expenditures (Cap ex − Depreciation) and working capital with 20% debt. The firm also has current revenues of $5,000, which it expects to grow at 8%. Working capital will be maintained at 25% of revenues. How much should the firm return to its stockholders as a dividend?

15. NoLone, an all-equity manufacturing firm, has net income of $100 million currently and expects this number to grow at 10% a year for the next three years. The firm's working capital increased by $10 million this year and is expected to increase by the same dollar amount each of the next three years. The depreciation is $50 million and is expected to grow 8% a year for the next three years. Finally, the firm plans to invest $60 million in capital expenditure for each of the next three years. The firm pays 60% of its earnings as dividends each year. NoLone has a cash balance currently of $50 million. Assuming that the cash does not earn any interest, how much would you expect to have as a cash balance at the end of the third year?

16. Boston Turkey is a publicly traded firm, with the following income statement and balance sheet from its most recent financial year:

Income Statement

Revenues	$1,000,000
− Expenses	$400,000
− Depreciation	$100,000
EBIT	$500,000
− Interest Expense	$100,000
Taxable Income	$400,000
− Tax	$160,000
Net Income	$240,000

Balance Sheet

Assets		Liabilities	
Property, plant, and equipment	$1,500,000	Accounts payable	$500,000
Land and buildings	$500,000	Long-term debt	$1,000,000
Current assets	$1,000,000	Equity (100,000 shares)	$1,500,000
Total	$3,000,000	Total	$3,000,000

Boston Turkey expects its revenues to grow 10% next year and its expenses to remain at 40% of revenues. The depreciation and interest expenses will remain unchanged at $100,000 next year. The working capital, as a percentage of revenue, will also remain unchanged next year.
The managers of Boston Turkey claim to have several projects available to choose from next year, in which they plan to invest the funds from operations, and they suggest that the firm really should not be paying dividends. The projects have the following characteristics:

Project	Equity Investment	Expected Annual Cash Flow to Equity	Beta
A	$100,000	12,500	1.00
B	$100,000	14,000	1.50
C	$50,000	8,000	1.80
D	$50,000	12,000	2.00

The Treasury bill rate is 3%, and the Treasury bond rate is 6.25%. The firm plans to finance 40% of its future net capital expenditures (Cap ex—Depreciation) and working capital needs with debt.

a. How much can the company afford to pay in dividends next year?

b. Now assume that the firm actually pays out $1.00 per share in dividends next year. The current cash balance of the firm is $150,000. How much will the cash balance of the firm be at the end of next year, after the payment of the dividend?

17. Z-Tec, a firm providing Internet services, reported net income of $10 million in the most recent year while making $25 million in capital expenditures (depreciation was $5 million). The firm had no working capital needs and uses no debt.

a. Can the firm afford to pay out dividends right now? Why, or why not?

b. Assuming that net income grows 40% a year and that net capital expenditures grow 10% a year, when will the firm be in a position to pay dividends?

18. You are analyzing the dividend policy of Conrail, a major railroad, and you have collected the information from the past five years. (Table at bottom of page)
The average debt ratio during this period was 40%, and the total noncash working capital at the end of 1990 was $10 million.

a. Estimate how much Conrail could have paid in dividends during this period.

b. If the average return on equity during the period was 13.5% and Conrail had a beta of 1.25, what conclusions would you draw about its dividend policy? (The average Treasury bond rate during the period was 7%, and the average return on the market was 12.5%.)

	Net Income (millions)	Capital Expenditure (millions)	Depreciation (millions)	Noncash Working Capital (millions)	Dividends (millions)
1991	$240	$314	$307	$35	$70
1992	$282	$466	$295	$(110)	$80
1993	$320	$566	$284	$215	$95
1994	$375	$490	$278	$175	$110
1995	$441	$494	$293	$250	$124

19. Assume now that you have been asked to forecast cash flows that you will have available to repurchase stock and pay dividends during the next five years for Conrail (Problem 18). In making these forecasts, you can assume the following:
    • Net income is anticipated to grow 10% a year from 1995 levels for the next five years.
    • Capital expenditures and depreciation are expected to grow 8% a year from 1995 levels.
    • The revenues in 1995 were $3.75 billion and are expected to grow 5% each year for the next five years. The working capital as a percent of revenues is expected to remain at 1995 levels.
    • The proportion of net capital expenditures and depreciation that will be financed with debt will drop to 30%.
    a. Estimate how much cash Conrail will have available to pay dividends or repurchase stocks over the next five years.
    b. How will the perceived uncertainty associated with these cash flows affect your decision on dividends and equity repurchases?

20. Cracker Barrel, which operates restaurants and gift stores, is reexamining its policy of paying minimal dividends. In 1995, Cracker Barrel reported net income of $66 million; it had capital expenditures of $150 million in that year and claimed depreciation of only $50 million. The working capital in 1995 was $43 million on sales of $783 million. Looking forward, Cracker Barrel expects the following:
    • Net income is expected to grow 17% a year for the next five years.
    • During the five years, capital expenditures are expected to grow 10% a year, and depreciation is expected to grow 15% a year.
    • The working capital as a percent of revenues is expected to remain at 1995 levels, and revenues are expected to grow 10% a year during the period.

    • The company has not used debt to finance its net capital expenditures, and does not plan to use any for the next five years.
    a. Estimate how much cash Cracker Barrel would have available to pay out to its stockholders over the next five years.
    b. How would your answer change if the firm plans to increase its leverage by borrowing 25% of its net capital expenditure and working capital needs?

21. Assume that Cracker Barrel (Problem 20) wants to continue with its policy of not paying dividends. You are the CEO of Cracker Barrel and have been confronted by dissident stockholders demanding to know why you are not paying out your FCFE (estimated in the previous problem) to your stockholders. How would you defend your decision? How receptive will stockholders be to your defense? Would it make any difference that Cracker Barrel has earned a return on equity of 25% over the previous five years and that its beta is only 1.2?

22. Manpower, which provides nongovernment employment services in the United States, reported net income of $128 million in 1995. It had capital expenditures of $50 million and depreciation of $24 million in 1995, and its working capital was $500 million (on revenues of $5 billion). The firm has a debt ratio of 10% and plans to maintain this debt ratio.
    a. Estimate how much Manpower will have available to pay out as dividends next year.
    b. The current cash balance is $143 million. If Manpower is expected to pay $12 million in dividends next year and repurchase no stock, estimate the expected cash balance at the end of the next year.

23. How would your answers to the previous problem change if Manpower in plans to pay off its outstanding debt of $100 million next year and become a debt-free company?

24. You are an institutional investor and have the collected the following information on five maritime firms to assess their dividend policies.

	FCFE	Dividends Paid	ROE	Beta
Alexander & Brown	$55	$35	8.0%	0.80
American President	$60	$12	14.5%	1.30
OMI	−$15	$5	4.0%	1.25
Overseas Shipholding	$20	$12	1.5%	0.90
Sea Containers	−$5	$8	14.0%	1.05

The average risk-free rate during the period was 7%, and the average return on the market was 12%.

a. Assess which of these firms you would pressure to pay more in dividends.

b. Which of the firms would you encourage to pay less in dividends?

c. How would you modify this analysis to reflect your expectations about the future of the entire sector?

25. You are analyzing the dividend policy of Black & Decker, a manufacturer of tools and appliances. The following table summarizes the dividend payout ratios, yields, and expected growth rates of other firms in the waste disposal business.

	Payout Ratio	Dividend Yield	Ex. Growth
Fedders	11%	1.2%	11.0%
Maytag	37%	2.8%	23.0%
National Presto	67%	4.9%	13.5%
Toro	15%	1.5%	16.5%
Whirlpool	30%	2.5%	20.5%
Black & Decker	24%	1.3%	23.0%

a. Compare Black & Decker's dividend policy to those of its peers, using the average dividend payout ratios and yields.

b. Do the same comparison, controlling for differences in expected growth.

26. The following regression was run using all NYSE firms in 1995

$$\text{YIELD} = 0.0478 - 0.0157 \text{ BETA}$$
$$+ 0.0000008 \text{ MKTCAP}$$
$$+ 0.006797 \text{ DBTRATIO}$$
$$+ 0.0002 \text{ ROE}$$
$$- 0.09 \text{ NCEX/TA} \quad R^2 = 12.88\%$$

where

$$\text{BETA} = \text{beta of the stock}$$
$$\text{MKTCAP} = \text{market value of equity} + \text{book value of debt}$$
$$\text{DBTRATIO} = \text{book value of debt/MKTCAP}$$
$$\text{ROE} = \text{return on equity in 1994}$$
$$\text{NCEX/TA} = (\text{Capital expenditures} - \text{Depreciation})/\text{Total assets}$$

The corresponding values for Black & Decker, in 1995, were as follows:

$$\text{Beta} = 1.30$$
$$\text{MKTCAP} = \$5,500 \text{ million}$$
$$\text{DBTRATIO} = 35\%$$
$$\text{ROE} = 14.5\%$$
$$\text{NCEX/TA} = 4.00\%$$

Black & Decker had a dividend yield of 1.3% and a dividend payout ratio of 24% in 1995.

a. Estimate the dividend yield for Black & Decker, based on the regression.

b. Why might your answer be different using this approach than the answer to the prior question, in which you used only the comparable firms?

27. Handy and Harman, a leading fabricator of precious metal alloys, pays out only 23% of its earnings as dividends. The average dividend payout ratio for metal fabricating firms is 45%. The average growth rate in earnings for the entire sector is 10% (Handy and Harman is expected to grow 23%). Should Handy and Harman pay more in dividends just to get closer to the average payout ratio? Why, or why not?

CHAPTER 12

VALUATION: PRINCIPLES AND PRACTICE

In this chapter, we look at how to value a firm and its equity, given what we now know about investment, financing, and dividend decisions. We will consider three approaches to valuation. The first and most fundamental approach to valuing a firm is *discounted cash flow valuation*, which extends the present value principles that we developed to analyze projects to value a firm. The value of any firm is determined by four factors—its capacity to generate cash flows from assets in place, the expected growth rate of these cash flows, the length of time it will take for the firm to reach stable growth, and the cost of capital. Consequently, to increase the value of a firm, we have to change one or more of these variables.

The second way of valuing a firm or its equity is to base the value on how the market is valuing similar or comparable firms; this approach is called *relative valuation*. This

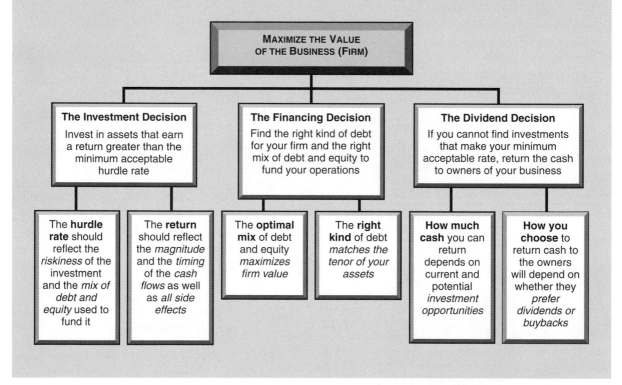

approach can yield values that are different from a discounted cash flow valuation, and we will look at some of the reasons these differences occur.

The third approach to valuing a firm applies for highly levered firms, where the equity acquires the characteristics of a *call option*. In this special case, equity becomes more valuable, as debt maturity increases and the volatility in asset value goes up. Equity investors, in effect, derive their value from the expectation (or hope) that asset value will increase over time.

In a departure from previous chapters, we will take the perspective of investors in financial markets in estimating value. Investors assess the value of a firm's stock to decide whether to buy the stock or, if they already own it, whether to continue holding it.

DISCOUNTED CASH FLOW VALUATION

In discounted cash flow valuation, we estimate the value of any asset by discounting the expected cash flows on that asset at a rate that reflects their riskiness. In a sense, we measure the intrinsic value of an asset. The value of any asset is a function of the cash flows generated by that asset, the life of the asset, the expected growth in the cash flows, and the riskiness associated with these cash flows. In other words, it is the present value of the expected cash flows on that asset.

$$\text{Value of asset} = \sum_{t=1}^{t=N} \frac{E(\text{Cash flow}_t)}{(1+r)^t}$$

where the asset has a life of N years and r is the discount rate that reflects both the riskiness of the cash flows and the financing mix used to acquire the asset. If we view a firm as a portfolio of assets, this equation can be extended to value a firm, using cash flows to the firm over its life and a discount rate that reflects the collective risk of the firm's assets.

This process is complicated by the fact that although some of the assets of a firm have already been created, and thus are assets-in-place, a significant component of firm value reflects expectations about future investments. Thus we not only need to measure the cash flows from current investments but also must estimate the expected value from future investments. In the sections that follow, we will introduce the discounted cash flow model in steps. We begin by discussing two different ways of approaching valuation—equity and firm valuation—and then move on to consider how best to estimate the inputs into valuation models. We then consider how to go from the value of a firm to the value of equity per share.

Equity Valuation versus Firm Valuation

There are two paths to discounted cash flow valuation—the first is to value just the equity stake in the business, and the second is to value the entire firm, including equity and any other claims in the firm (from bondholders, preferred stockholders, etc.). Although both approaches discount expected cash flows, the relevant cash flows and discount rates are different for each.

The **value of equity** is obtained by discounting expected cash flows to equity—that is, the residual cash flows after meeting all operating expenses, reinvestment needs, tax obligations, and debt payments—at the cost of equity: that is, the rate of return required by equity investors in the firm.

$$\text{Value of Equity} = \sum_{t=1}^{t=n} \frac{\text{CF to Equity}_t}{(1 + k_e)^t}$$

where CF to equity$_t$ = expected cash flow to equity in period t, and k_e = cost of equity. The dividend discount model is a special case of equity valuation, where the value of a stock is the present value of expected future dividends.

The **value of the firm** is obtained by discounting expected cash flows to the firm—that is, residual cash flows after meeting all operating expenses, taxes, and reinvestment needs, but prior to debt payments—at the weighted average cost of capital (WACC)—that is, the cost of the different components of financing used by the firm, weighted by their proportions.

$$\text{Value of firm} = \sum_{t=1}^{t=n} \frac{\text{CF to firm}_t}{(1 + \text{WACC})^t}$$

where CF to firm$_t$ = expected cash flow to firm in period t, and WACC = weighted average cost of capital. Subtracting out the value of non-equity claims from the value of the firm yields the value of equity. Although the two approaches use different definitions of cash flow and discount rates, they will yield consistent estimates of the value of equity so long as the same set of assumptions is applied for both. It is important to avoid mismatching cash flows and discount rates, because discounting cash flows to equity at the weighted average cost of capital will lead to an upwardly biased estimate of the value of equity, whereas discounting cash flows to the firm at the cost of equity will yield a downwardly biased estimate of the value of the firm.

12.1 FIRM VALUATION AND LEVERAGE

It is often argued that equity valuation requires more assumptions than firm valuation, because cash flows to equity require explicit assumptions about changes in leverage, whereas cash flows to the firm are predebt cash flows and do not require assumptions about leverage. Is this true?

a. Yes

b. No

Explain.

Choosing the Right Valuation Model

All discounted cash flow models ultimately boil down to estimating four inputs— cash flows from exising assets, an expected growth rate in such cash flows, a point in time in the future when the firm will be growing at a rate it can sustain forever, and a discount rate to use in discounting such cash flows. In this section, we will examine the choices available in terms of each of these inputs.

In terms of cash flows, there are three choices—dividends or free cash flows to equity (FCFE) for equity valuation models, and free cash flows to the firm (FCFF) for firm valuation models. Discounting dividends usually provides the most conservative estimate of value for the equity in any firm, because most firms pay less in dividends than they can afford to. In the dividend policy section, we noted that the FCFE—that is, the cash flow left over after meeting all investment needs and making debt payments—is the amount that a firm can pay in dividends. The value of equity, based on the FCFE, will therefore yield a more realistic estimate of value for equity, especially in the context of a takeover, since the acquirer can lay claim to the entire FCFE rather than just the dividends. Even if a firm is not the target of a takeover, it can be argued that the value of equity has to reflect the possibility of a takeover, and hence the expected FCFE. The choice between FCFE and FCFF is really a choice between equity and firm valuation. Done consistently, both approaches should yield the same values for the equity in a business. As a practical concern, however, cash flows to equity are after net debt issues or payments and become much more difficult to estimate when financial leverage is changing over time, whereas cash flows to the firm are predebt cash flows and are unaffected by changes in financial leverage. Consequently, firm valuation will be more straightforward when debt ratios are expected to change over time.

Although we can estimate cash flows for the past from the most recent financial statements, the challenge in valuation is in estimating them in future years. In most valuations, this takes the form of an *expected growth rate in earnings* that is then used to forecast earnings and cash flows in future periods. The growth rates estimated should be consistent with our definition of cash flows. When forecasting cash flows to equity, we will generally forecast growth in net income or earnings per share that are measures of equity earnings. When forecasting cash flows to the firm, the growth rate that matters is the growth rate in operating earnings.[1]

The choice of *discount rates* will be dictated by the choice in cash flows. If the cash flow being discounted is dividends or FCFE, the appropriate discount rate is the cost of equity. If the cash flow being discounted is the cash flow to the firm, the discount rate has to be the cost of capital.

The final choice that all discounted cash flow models have to make relates to *expected growth patterns*. Because publicly traded firms have infinite lives, at least in theory, the way we apply closure to our estimates of cash flows is to estimate a terminal value at a point in time and dispense with estimating cash flows beyond that point. To do this in the context of discounted cash flow valuation, we have to assume that the growth rate in cash flows beyond this point in time are constant forever, an assumption of stable growth. If we do this, the present value of these cash flows can be estimated as the present value of a growing perpetuity. Thus, there are three questions that every valuation then has to answer:

1. How long into the future will a company be able to grow at a rate higher than the stable growth rate?

2. How high will the growth rate be during the high-growth period, and what pattern will it follow?

---

[1]We should generally become much more conservative in our growth estimates as we move up the income statements. Generally, growth in earnings per share will be lower than the growth in net income, and growth in net income will be lower than the growth in operating income.

3. What will happen to the firm's fundamentals (risk, cash flow patterns, etc.) as the expected growth rate changes?

At the risk of being simplistic, we can broadly classify growth patterns into three categories—firms that are in stable growth already, firms that expect to maintain a constant high growth rate for a period and then drop abruptly to stable growth, and firms that will have high growth for a specified period and then grow through a transition phase to reach stable growth at some point in the future. As a practical point, it is important that as the growth rate changes, the firm's risk and cash flow characteristics change as well. In general, as expected growth declines toward stable growth, firms should see their risk approach the average, and their reinvestment needs decline. These choices are summarized in Figure 12.1:

Figure 12.1 The Ingredients in a Valuation

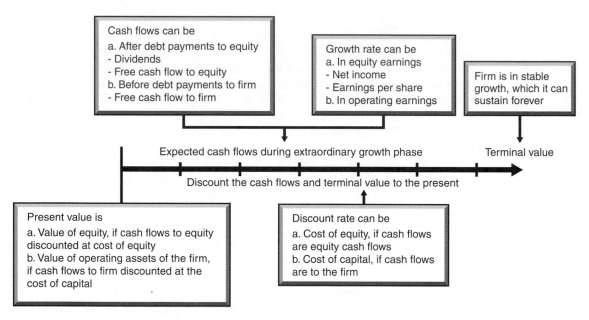

We will examine each of these valuation models in more detail in the next section.

model.xls: This spreadsheet allows you to pick the right discounted cash flow valuation model for your needs, given the characteristics of the business you are valuing.

IN PRACTICE: WHAT IS A STABLE GROWTH RATE?

Determining when your firm will be in stable growth is difficult to do without first defining what we mean by a *stable growth rate*. There are two insights to keep in mind when estimating a stable growth rate. First, because the growth rate in the firm's cash flows is expected to last forever, the firm's other measures of performance (including revenues, earnings, and reinvestment) can be expected to grow at the same rate. Consider the long-term consequences of a firm whose earnings grow 6% a year forever while its dividends grow at 8%. Over time, the dividends will exceed earnings. Similarly, if a firm's earnings grow at a faster rate than its dividends in the long run, the payout ratio will converge toward 0, which also is not a steady state. The second issue relates to what growth rate is reasonable as a stable growth rate. Again, the assumption that this growth rate will last forever establishes rigorous constraints on reasonableness. In the long run, a firm cannot grow at a rate significantly greater than the growth rate in the economy in which it operates. Thus, a firm that grows at 8% forever in an economy growing at 4% will eventually become larger than the economy. In practical terms, if the valuation is done in nominal (real) terms, the stable growth rate cannot be larger than the nominal (real) growth rate in the economy in which the firm operates.

Can a stable growth rate be much lower than the growth rate in the economy? There are no logical or mathematical limits on the downside. Firms that have stable growth rates much lower than the growth rate in the economy will become smaller in proportion to the economy over time. Because there is no economic basis for arguing that this cannot happen, there is no reason why we cannot use a stable growth rate much lower than the nominal growth rate in the economy. In fact, the stable growth rate can be a negative number. Using a negative stable growth rate will ensure that your firm peaks in the last year of high growth and becomes smaller each year after that.

There is a rule of thumb that works well in setting a cap on the stable growth rate. The stable growth rate should not exceed the risk-free rate used in a valuation. Why should the two be related? The risk-free rate can be decomposed into an expected inflation rate and an expected real interest rate. If we assume that the real growth rate of an economy will be equal to the real interest rate in the long run, the risk-free rate becomes a proxy for the nominal growth rate in the economy.

$$\text{Risk free Rate} = \text{Expected Inflation} + \text{Expected Real Interest Rate}$$
$$\text{Growth}_{\text{Nominal GDP}} = \text{Expected Inflation} + \text{Expected Real Growth Rae}$$

In the long term, Expected Real Interest Rate = Expected Real Growth Rate

Therefore, Risk free Rate = Growth$_{\text{Nominal GDP}}$ ∎

12.2   CYCLICAL FIRMS AND CONSTANT GROWTH RATES

Models built on the assumption of an expected constant growth rate over time cannot be used for cyclical firms, whose earnings growth is likely to be very volatile over time—high during economic booms, and very low or negative during recessions.

a.   True

b.   False

Explain.

Estimation in Discounted Cash Flow Models

Although all discounted cash flow models require the same four ingredients—cash flows, a discount rate, a period of high growth, and a growth rate during the period—there are different estimation challenges we face with each model. In this section, we will begin by estimating these inputs to the simplest of the three models, the dividend discount model, and then extend the discussion to cash flow to equity and firm valuation models.

I. Dividend Discount Models

When an investor buys stock, he or she generally expects to get two types of cash flows—dividends during the holding period, and an expected price at the end of the holding period. Because this expected price is itself determined by future dividends, the value of a stock is the present value of just expected dividends. The dividend discount model is therefore the most direct, and most conservative, way of valuing a stock because it counts only those cash flows that are actually paid out to stockholders.

Setting Up the Model

In its most general form, the value of a stock in the dividend discount model is the present value of the expected dividends on the stock in perpetuity.

$$\text{Value per share of stock} = \sum_{t=1}^{t=\infty} \frac{\text{Expected dividends in period t}}{(1 + \text{Cost of equity})^t}$$

Because we cannot estimate dividends in perpetuity, we generally allow for a period during which dividends can grow at extraordinary rates (much higher or lower than the stable growth rate), but we allow for closure in the model by assuming that the growth rate will shift to a rate that can be sustained forever at some point in the future. By assuming stable growth at some point in the future, we can stop estimating annual dividends and estimate what we think the stock will be worth at the end of the extraordinary growth period.

$$\text{Value}_0 = \sum_{t=1}^{t=n} \frac{E(\text{Dividends})_t}{(1+r)^t} + \frac{\text{Terminal value}_n}{(1+r)^n}$$

$$\text{where Terminal value}_n = \frac{E(\text{Dividends})_{n+1}}{(r_n - g_n)}$$

where r is the cost of equity and g_n is the expected growth rate in dividends in perpetuity after year n.[2] Note that it is possible for a firm to already be in stable growth, in which case this model collapses into its simplest form:

Value of a stock in stable growth = Expected dividends next year$/(r_n - g_n)$

This model is called the Gordon growth model and is a special case of the dividend discount model. It can be used only for firms that are already in stable growth.[3]

Estimating Model Inputs

By breaking down the general version of the dividend discount model, we find four basic components. The first is the length of the high-growth period, during which the firm can sustain extraordinary growth. The second is the expected dividends each year during the high-growth period. The third is the cost of equity that stockholders will demand for holding the stock, based on their assessments of equity risk. The final input is the expected price at the end of the high-growth period—the **terminal value**.

---

[2]The cost of equity can be different for the high-growth and stable growth periods. Hence, r_n is the cost of equity for the stable growth period.

[3]When the Gordon growth model is used to value high-growth companies, it is entirely possible that $g >$ r and the model will yield a negative value. If this occurs, the problem is not with the model but in its misapplication to a high-growth firm.

In this section, we will consider the challenges associated with estimating each of these components.

a. Length of High-Growth Period   The question of how long a firm will be able to sustain high growth is perhaps the most difficult to answer in a valuation, but two points are worth keeping in mind. One is that it is not a question of whether but when; all firms will ultimately become stable growth firms, because high growth makes firms larger, and the firm's size will eventually become a barrier to further high growth. The second is that high growth in valuation—at least, high growth that creates value—comes from firms earning excess returns on their marginal investments. Using the terminology that we have used before in investment analysis, it comes from firms having a return on equity (capital) that is well in excess of the cost of equity (capital). Thus, when we assume that a firm will experience high growth for the next five or ten years, we also implicitly assume that it will earn excess returns (over and above the cost of equity or capital) during that period. In a competitive market, these excess returns will eventually draw in new competitors, and the excess returns will disappear.

We should look at three factors when considering how long a firm will be able to maintain high growth.

1. ***Size of the firm in relation to the market***   Smaller firms are much more likely to earn excess returns and maintain high growth than otherwise similar larger firms. This is so because they have more room to grow, and a larger potential market. When looking at the size of the firm, we should look not only at its current market share but also the potential growth in the total market for its products or services. Thus, Microsoft may have a large market share of the computer software market, but it may be able to grow in spite of it because the entire software market is growing. On the other hand, Boeing dominates the market for commercial aircraft, but we do not expect the overall market for aircraft to increase substantially. Boeing, therefore, is far more constrained in terms of future growth.

2. ***Existing growth rate and excess returns***   Although the returns we would like to estimate are the marginal returns on new investments, there is a high correlation between the returns generated on current investments and these marginal returns. Thus, a firm earning excess returns of 20% on its current investments is far more likely to have large positive excess returns on its marginal investments, and a long growth period, than a firm currently earning excess returns of 2%. There are cases where this rule will not work, such as in industries going through major restructuring.

3. ***Magnitude and sustainability of competitive advantages***   This is perhaps the most critical determinant of the length of the high-growth period. If there are significant barriers to entry and sustainable competitive advantages, firms can maintain high growth for longer periods. On the other hand, if there are no or only minor barriers to entry, or if the firm's existing competitive advantages are fading, we should be far more conservative about allowing for long growth periods. The quality of existing management also influences our choices on growth. The essence of good management is the capacity to make the strategic choices that increase competitive advantages and create new ones.[4]

---

[4]Jack Welch at GE and Robert Goizueta at Coca-Cola are good examples of CEOs who made a difference in the growth of their firms and the market assessment of their values.

Again, the sensitivity of value to changes in the length of the high-growth period can always be estimated. Some analysts use growth periods greater than ten years, but the combination of high-growth rates and long growth periods creates a potent mix in terms of increasing the size of the firm, in many cases well beyond the realm of what is reasonable. Looking back, there are very few firms that have been able to grow at high rates for more than ten years.

ILLUSTRATION 12.1 Length of High-Growth Period

To assess how long high growth will last at Disney, Aracruz, and Tata Chemicals, we assessed their standings on each of the above characteristics in Table 12.1.

Using the same template for Deutsche Bank, its size and maturity work against high growth in its asset base, but in the current banking turmoil, Deutsche Bank's biggest competitive advantage is its safety and stability, as competitors are forced to raise fresh capital to meet regulatory requirements. As a consequence, we expect Deutsche Bank's income to rebound from current levels over the next five years. What about

Table 12.1 ASSESSMENT OF LENGTH OF HIGH-GROWTH PERIOD

	Disney	Aracruz	Tata Chemicals
Firm size/market size	Firm is one of the largest players in the entertainment and theme park businesses, but the businesses are being redefined and are expanding.	Firm has a small market share of the paper/pulp business, but the sector is mature.	Firm has a large market share of Indian (domestic) market, but is small by global standards. Domestic market is also growing.
Current excess returns	Firm is making a return on capitlal slightly higher than its cost of capital, a reversal from negative excess returns in recent years.	Returns on capital are largely a function of paper/pulp prices, but on average have been less than the cost of capital.	Firm has a return on capital that is roughly equal to its cost of capital.
Competitive advantages	Owns some of the most recognized animated characters in the world. Knows more about operating theme parks than any other firm in the world. Has skilled animation studio staff.	Cost advantages because of access to Brazilian forests. Has invested in newer, updated plants and has skilled workforce.	Has cost advantages, because of lower labor and production costs in India.
Length of high-growth period	Ten years, entirely because of its strong competitive advantages, but the excess returns are likely to be small, because of the firm's size and the competitive nature of market.	Five years, largely due to access to cheap raw material.	Five years, primarily because of high real growth in India.

Bookscape? The single biggest competitive advantage possessed by this firm is its long-term lease at favorable terms in a superb location in New York City. It is unlikely that the firm will be able to replicate this advantage elsewhere. In addition, this is a private firm, which leads us to conclude that there will be no high-growth period.

12.3 LENGTH OF HIGH-GROWTH PERIOD AND BARRIERS TO ENTRY

Assume that you are analyzing two firms, both of which are enjoying high growth. The first firm is Earthlink Network, an Internet service provider, which operates in an environment with few barriers to entry and extraordinary competition. The second firm is Biogen, a biotechnology firm that is enjoying growth from two drugs for which it owns patents for the next decade. Assuming that both firms are well managed, which of the two firms would you expect to have a longer high-growth period?

a. Earthlink Network

b. Biogen

c. Both are well managed and should have the same high-growth period

b. Expected Dividends during High-Growth Period The first step in estimating expected dividends during the high-growth period is to estimate the expected earnings for each year. This can be done in one of two ways—you can apply an expected growth rate to current earnings, or you can begin by estimating future revenues first and then estimate net profit margins in each year. The first approach is easier, but the second provides for more flexibility because margins can change over time. The resulting expected earnings are paired with estimated dividend payout ratios in each period, which may change over the high-growth period. This may seem like an awkward procedure, because expected dividends could well be estimated using the current dividends and applying a dividend growth rate, but we use it for two reasons. First, most projections for growth, either from analysts or management, are stated in terms of revenues or earnings rather than dividends. Second, separating earnings forecasts from dividend payout provides more flexibility in terms of changing dividend payout ratios as earnings growth rates change. In particular, it allows us to raise dividend payout ratios as earnings growth rates decline.

The growth rate in earnings can be estimated using one of three approaches. The first is to look at the past and measure the historical growth rate in earnings over previous years. When measuring earnings growth, we have to consider how far back to go in time and whether to use arithmetic average or geometric average growth rates.[5] In general, geometric growth rates yield more meaningful values than arithmetic average growth rates. The second is to look at estimates made by others following the same stock. In fact, growth estimates made by equity research analysts following a stock are public information, and easily accessible.[6] The third is to consider the determinants

---

[5]Arithmetic average growth rates represent simple averages of growth rates over multiple years. The geometric average growth rate is a compounded growth rate.

[6]I/B/E/S, First Call, and Zacks are services that track equity research analyst forecasts continuously, and the consensus estimate across all analysts is publicly available.

of growth and to estimate a growth rate based on a firm's investment choices. In particular, the growth in earnings per share of a firm can be written as the product of two variables—the percentage of the net income retained in the firm to generate future growth (retention ratio) and the return earned on equity in these new investments:

Expected growth rate in Earnings per Share = Retention ratio * Return on equity

Thus, a firm with a return on equity of 20% and a retention ratio of 70% should have earnings per share growth of 14% a year. Reverting back to the discussion of dividend policy in Chapter 10, note that the retention ratio and the payout ratio are two sides of the same coin:

Retention ratio = 1 − Payout ratio

Because the retention ratio cannot exceed 100%, the expected growth in earnings per share in the long run for a firm cannot exceed its return on equity.

Assuming that we can obtain all three estimates of the growth rate in earnings for a firm, which one should we use in valuing a company? Past growth should be weighted least, because earnings are volatile and past growth has generally not been highly correlated with future growth.[7] Analyst estimates are useful signposts of what the investment community thinks about a company and could include information that is not in the financial statements. In particular, it could reflect changes in both the company's management and strategic plans. However, trusting analysts (no matter how well informed they may be) to come up with the most important input in a valuation is not prudent. Ultimately, the fundamental growth equation offers the most promise, because it relates growth back to what the firm does and also constrains us to pay for growth (by requiring firms to reinvest) as we estimate value.

12.4 DIFFERENCES IN GROWTH RATES

The growth rates from historical earnings, analyst projections, and fundamentals can often be very different. These differences can be best explained by which of the following statements?

a. The past is not always a good indicator of the future.

b. Analysts are biased toward making optimistic estimates of growth.

c. The inputs used to estimate fundamental growth reflect what happened last year rather than what we expect will happen in the future.

d. All of the above.

ILLUSTRATION 12.2   Growth in Earnings per Share—Deutsche Bank in Early 2008

In early 2008, in calmer times, we estimated the earnings growth for Deutsche Bank using fundamentals. In 2007, Deutsche Bank reported net income of 6.51 billion euros on a book value of equity of 33.475 billion euros at the start of the year (end of 2006). The resulting return on equity is 19.45%:

$$\text{Return on equity} = \frac{\text{Net income}_{2007}}{\text{Book value of equity}_{2006}} = \frac{6,510}{33,475} = 19.45\%$$

[7]One of the most famous studies of growth was titled "Higgledy Piggledy Growth" (I. M. D. Little, 1962, *Higgledy Piggledy Growth*, Oxford: Institute of Statistics), precisely because earnings growth was so difficult to predict based on history.

In 2007, Deutsche Bank paid out 2.146 billion euros to equity investors. The resulting retention ratio is 67.03%.

$$\text{Retention ratio} = 1 - \frac{\text{Dividends}}{\text{Net income}} = 1 - \frac{2,146}{6,510} = 67.03\%$$

If Deutsche Bank maintains the return on equity (ROE) and retention ratio that it delivered in 2007 for the long run, its expected growth rate in earnings will be strong.

$$\text{Expected growth rate}_{\text{Existing fundamentals}} = \text{Retention ratio}^* \text{ROE}$$
$$= 0.6703 * 0.1945 = 13.04\%$$

The danger with this estimate is that it is based upon 2007, a very profitable year for Deutsche Bank. If we replace the net income in 2007 with average net income from 2003 to 2007, while keeping book equity at 2006 levels, we arrive at lower estimates of ROE and expected growth rate:

$$\text{Normalized return on equity} = \frac{\text{Average net income}_{2003-07}}{\text{Book value of equity}_{2006}}$$
$$= \frac{3,954}{33,475} = 11.81\%$$
$$\text{Normalized retention ratio} = 1 - \frac{\text{Dividends}}{\text{Net income}}$$
$$= 1 - \frac{2,146}{3,954} = 45.72\%$$
$$\text{Expected growth rate}_{\text{Normalized fundamentals}} = \text{Retention ratio} * \text{ROE}$$
$$= 0.4572 * 0.1181 = 5.40\%$$

How does this contrast and compare to the historical growth in net income at Deutsche Bank? Deutsche Bank's net income grew from 1.365 billion euros in 2003 to 6.510 billion euros in 2007, resulting in a compounded earnings growth rate of 47.78%:

$$\text{Compounded earnings growth rate} = \left(\frac{\text{Net Income}_{2007}}{\text{Net Income}_{2003}}\right)^{1/4} - 1$$
$$= \left(\frac{6,510}{1,365}\right)^{1/4} - 1 = 47.78\%$$

This high growth rate, however, reflects the facts that the net income at Deutsche Bank was depressed between 2001 and 2003 and that much of this growth reflect a recovery back to more normal earnings levels.

In hindsight, all of these estimates of earnings growth would have been wrong, since the financial crisis in 2008 caused billions of dollars in writeoffs at Deutsche Bank, and the firm reported a loss of 3.896 billion euros for the year. In the first quarter of 2009, Deutsche Bank reported a return to profitability and net income in excess of 1 billion euros.

c. Cost of Equity　The dividends and terminal price should be discounted back at a rate that reflects the risk in the investment to stockholders to arrive at the current value. In Chapter 4, we argued that the only risk that diversified investors see in a stock is market risk, which can be measured with a beta (in the capital asset pricing model) or multiple betas (in the arbitrage pricing or multifactor models). The same reasoning applies here. In fact, the costs of equity that we estimated for Disney, Deutsche Bank, and Aracruz in Chapter 4 will be the costs of equity that will be used if we were valuing stock in these companies using a dividend discount model. The only point that relates specifically to valuation is that high-growth firms tend to have higher betas than low-growth firms. Building on this premise, it is important that as we change growth rates over time we also adjust risk accordingly. Thus, when a firm goes from high-growth to low-growth, its beta should be moved toward one to reflect the lower growth.

d. Terminal Value　The last component of the model is the value attached to the equity at the end of a period of high growth. This value is estimated from expected dividends in the first time period following the high-growth period, the cost of equity in the stable phase, and the expected stable growth rate in dividends as follows:

$$\text{Value of equity in year } n = \frac{\text{Expected dividends}_{n+1}}{r_n - g_n}$$

where r_n is the cost of equity in the stable-growth period and g_n is the expected growth rate in dividends beyond year n (forever).

Before you estimate terminal value, you need to map out a path for the earnings growth during the high-growth phase to move toward the stable-growth rate. The simplest assumption to make is that your earnings growth rate is constant for the high-growth period, after which the growth rate drops to the stable level, as shown in Figure 12.2.

This is a two-stage model, and its limitation is obvious. It assumes that the growth rate is high during the initial period and that it is transformed overnight to a lower, stable rate at the end of the period. Although these sudden transformations in growth can happen, it is much more realistic to assume that the shift from high growth to stable growth happens gradually, over time. The assumption that the growth rate drops precipitously from its level in the initial phase to a stable rate also implies that this model is more appropriate for firms with modest growth rates in the initial phase. For instance, it is more reasonable to assume that a firm growing at 8% in the high-growth period will see its growth rate drop to 4% than it is to assume that the same will happen for a firm growing at 40% in the high-growth period. If we assume that the growth rate (g), cost of equity (r) and payout ratio are fixed for the

Figure 12.2 Two-Stage Growth Model

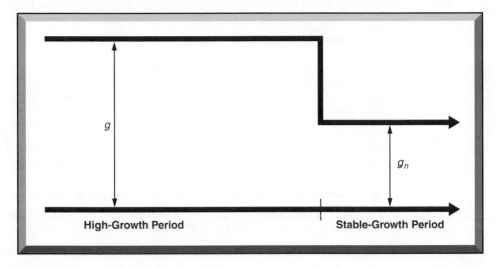

High-Growth Period **Stable-Growth Period**

high-growth period, the present value of the dividends during the high-growth period can be estimated as follows:[8]

$$\text{PV of high-growth dividends}_0 = \frac{\text{Dividends}_0 * (1 + g) * \left(1 - \frac{(1+g)^n}{(1+r)^n}\right)}{r - g}$$

A more general formulation would allow for growth during the high-growth period, followed by a gradual reduction to stable growth over a transition period, as illustrated in Figure 12.3. This model allows for growth rates and payout ratios to change gradually during the transition period.

No matter what path you devise to get your firm to stable growth, it is not just the growth rate that should change in stable growth. The other characteristics of the firm should also change to reflect the stable-growth rates.

- The cost of equity should be more reflective of that of a mature firm. If it is being estimated using a beta, that beta should be closer to 1 in stable growth, even though it can take on very high or very low values in high growth.
- The dividend payout ratio, usually low or zero for high-growth firms, should increase as the firm becomes a stable-growth firm. In fact, drawing on the fundamental growth equation from the last section, we can estimate the payout ratio in stable growth:

$$\text{Dividend payout ratio} = 1 - \text{Retention ratio} = 1 - \frac{g_{\text{Stable}}}{\text{ROE}_{\text{Stable}}}$$

---

[8]Unlike the stable growth model equation, this one can be used even if the expected growth rate exceeds the discount rate. Although this makes the denominator negative, it will also result in a negative numerator, and the net effect will be positive. The only condition when it will not work is if $g = r$, but the PV of dividends in that case will just be the product of the number of years of growth and dividends today, because the growth and the discounting effects each year will cancel out.

Figure 12.3 High Growth Followed by Transition

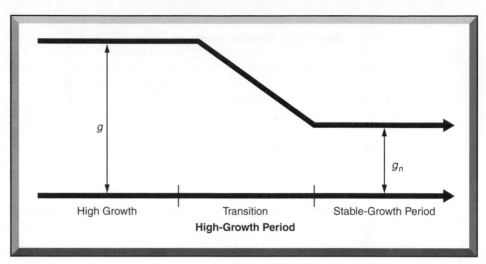

If we expect the stable growth rate to be 4% and the return on equity in stable growth to be 12%, the payout ratio in stable growth will be 66.67% (1 − 4/12).

- The return on equity in stable growth, if used to estimate the payout ratio, should be also reflective of a stable-growth firm. The most conservative estimate to make in stable growth is that the return on equity will be equal to the cost of equity, thus denying the firm the possibility of excess returns in perpetuity. If this is too rigid a framework, you can assume that the return on equity will converge on an industry average in the stable-growth phase, as long as that industry average is within a reasonable range (4-5% higher than the cost of equity).

If there is a transition period for growth, as in Figure 12.3, the betas and payout ratios should adjust in the transition period, as the growth rate changes.

12.5 TERMINAL VALUE AND PRESENT VALUE

The bulk of the present value in most discounted cash flow valuations comes from the terminal value, so it is reasonable to conclude that the assumptions about growth during the high-growth period do not affect value as much as assumptions about the terminal value do.

a. True

b. False

Explain.

Closing Thoughts on the Dividend Discount Model
Many analysts view the dividend discount model as outmoded, but it is a useful starting point in valuing all companies and may be the only choice in valuing companies

where estimating cash flows is not feasible. As noted in Chapter 11, estimating free cash flows for financial service companies is often difficult both because the line between operating and capital expenses is fuzzy and because working capital, defined broadly, could include just about all of the balance sheet. Although we can arrive at approximations of cash flows by making assumptions about regulatory capital, we are often left in the uncomfortable position of assuming that dividends represent FCFE for these firms. Even for firms for which we can estimate FCFE with reasonable precision, the dividend discount model allows us to estimate a "floor value," in most cases, because firms tend to pay out less in dividends than they have available in FCFE.

It is often argued that the dividend discount model cannot be used to value high-growth companies that pay no dividends. That is true only if we use the inflexible version of the model, whereby future dividends are estimated by growing current dividends. In the more flexible version, in which both payout ratios and earnings growth can change over time, the dividend discount model can be extended to cover all types of firms.

There is one final point worth making in this section. We can estimate the value of equity on a per-share basis by using dividends per share, or we can obtain the aggregate value of equity using total dividends paid. The two approaches will yield the same results if there are no management options, warrants, or convertible bonds outstanding. If there are management or conversion options outstanding, it is safest to value the equity on an aggregate basis. We will consider how best to deal with equity options in arriving at a value per share later in this chapter.

12.6 PAYOUT RATIOS AND EXPECTED GROWTH

The dividend discount model cannot be used to value stock in a company with high growth that does not pay dividends.

a. True

b. False

Explain.

Valndata.xls: This file online contains the industry averages by sector for returns on capital, retention ratios, debt equity ratios, and interest rates.

ILLUSTRATION 12.3 **Valuing Equity Using the Dividend Discount Model—Deutsche Bank in early 2008**

In Illustration 12.2, we estimated the annual growth rate of 5.40% for the next five years at Deutsche Bank at the start of 2008, using normalized earnings from 2003 to 2007 to compute the return on equity, retention ratio and expected growth rate.

$$\text{Normalized growth rate in net income} = 5.40\%$$
$$\text{Normalized dividend payout ratio} = 54.28\%$$

In the analysis that follows, we will value Deutsche Bank at the start of 2008, using this growth rate. In 2007, Deutsche Bank paid out dividends of 2,146 million euros on normalized net income of 3,954 million euros. In Chapter 4, we estimated a beta of 1.162 for Deutsche Bank, which, used in conjunction with the euro risk-free rate of 4% (in early 2008) and a risk premium of 4.50% (the mature market risk premium in early 2008), yielded a cost of equity of 9.23%.[9]

$$\text{Cost of equity}_{\text{January 2008}} = \text{Risk-free rate}_{\text{January 2008}}$$
$$+ \text{Beta} * \text{Mature market risk premium}$$
$$= 4.00\% + 1.162 (4.5\%) = 9.23\%$$

Based on these inputs, we estimate the expected net income and dividends for the next five years, and the present value of these dividends, in Table 12.2.

Note that we could have arrived at the same present value using the shortcut described earlier (because the payout ratio and the cost of equity remain unchanged for the high-growth period):

$$\text{PV of high-growth dividends}_0 = \frac{2{,}146 * (1.054) * \left(1 - \frac{(1.054)^5}{(1.0923)^5}\right)}{0.0923 - 0.054}$$
$$= 9{,}653 \text{ million euros}$$

At the end of year 5, we will assume that Deutsche Bank's earnings growth will drop to 3%, and stay at that level in perpetuity. In keeping with the assumption of stable growth, we will also assume that

- The beta will drop marginally to 1, resulting in a slightly lower cost of equity of 8.50%.

$$\text{Cost of equity} = \text{Risk-free rate} + \text{Beta} * \text{Risk premium}$$
$$= 4\% + 4.50\% = 8.50\%$$

- The return on equity will drop to the cost of equity of 8.50%, thus preventing excess returns from being earned in perpetuity.

- The payout ratio will adjust to reflect the stable period growth rate and return on equity.

$$\text{Stable period payout ratio} = 1 - g/\text{ROE} = 1 - 0.03/0.085 = 0.6471, \text{ or } 64.71\%$$

Table 12.2 PRESENT VALUE OF EXPECTED DIVIDENDS FOR HIGH-GROWTH PERIOD

	Net Income	Payout Ratio	Dividends	PV @ 9.23%
2008	€4,167	54.28%	€2,262	€2,071
2009	€4,392	54.28%	€2,384	€1,998
2010	€4,629	54.28%	€2,513	€1,928
2011	€4,879	54.28%	€2,648	€1,861
2012	€5,143	54.28%	€2,791	€1,795
				€9,653

[9]In truth, we should be estimating a beta at the start of 2008, instead of using the beta that we estimated at the start of 2009. However, the difference should be small enough to not affect value by much.

The expected dividends in year six is calculated using this payout ratio:

$$\text{Expected dividends in year 6} = \text{Expected net income}_5$$
$$* (1 + g_{\text{Stable}}) * \text{Stable payout ratio}$$
$$= \text{\euro}5{,}143(1.03) * 0.6471 = \text{\euro}3{,}427 \text{ million}$$

The value of equity at the end of the fifth year can be estimated using these inputs:

$$\text{Terminal value} = \frac{\text{Expected dividends}_6}{(\text{Cost of equity} - g)} = \frac{3{,}247}{(0.085 - 0.03)} = 62{,}318 \text{ million euros}$$

The present value of the terminal value is computed using the high-growth period cost of equity:

$$\text{PV of terminal value} = \frac{\text{Terminal value}_n}{(1 + \text{Cost of equity}_{\text{High growth}})^n}$$
$$= \frac{62{,}318}{(1.0923)^5} = 40{,}079 \text{ million euros}$$

The total value of equity is the sum of this value and the present value of the expected dividends in the high-growth period:

$$\text{Value of Equity} = \text{PV of expected dividends in high growth}$$
$$+ \text{PV of terminal value}$$
$$= \text{\euro}9{,}653 + \text{\euro}40{,}079 = \text{\euro}49{,}732 \text{ million euros}$$

Dividing this value by the number of shares outstanding at the start of 2008 yields the value of equity per share:

$$\text{Value of equity per share} = \frac{\text{Value of equity}}{\text{\# Shares}} = \frac{49{,}732}{474.2} = 104.88 \text{ euros/share}$$

The market price of Deutsche Bank at the time of this valuation was 89 euros per share. Based on our assumptions, Deutsche Bank looked undervalued at the start of 2008.

ILLUSTRATION 12.4 Valuing Equity in More Unsettled Times—Deutsche Bank in 2009

In the last illustration, we estimated a value of 105 euros/share for Deutsche Bank at the beginning of 2008, and concluded that it was undervalued at its then prevailing stock price of 89 euros/share. During 2008, the landscape for financial service firms changed, as banks entered crisis mode and financial markets collapsed. After taking billions of dollars of writeoffs, Deutsche Bank reported a loss of 3,835 million euros for 2008 and cut dividends to 285 million euros. While neither of these numbers represents a stable starting point, we made the following assumptions to value Deutsche Bank:

- ***Net income bounceback*** We will assume that net income will bounce back to 3.147 billion euros in 2009, basing this assumption on the improved earnings for the first quarter of 2009 reported by Deutsche Bank (1.12 billion euros in quarterly profits) and the average net income between 2003 and 2007 (approximately 3.95 billion euros).

- *Asset base and target ROE* We will assume that the current asset base for the firm (312,882 million euros) will grow 4% a year for the next five years, and that the return on equity will improve to 10% over this period. The net income each year is obtained by multiplying the regulatory capital (equity) by the ROE each year.

- *Potential dividends* Rather than focus on current dividends, which have been cut drastically, we estimate the potential dividends, based upon the assumption that the firm will move towards a target regulatory capital ratio of 10%. (We are replicating the analysis we did in Chapter 11 to estimate FCFE.)

- *Cost of equity* To arrive at the cost of equity, we use the beta of 1.162 that we estimated in Chapter 4, in conjunction with the euro risk-free rate of 3.6% at the start of 2009 and the updated equity risk premium of 6% for mature markets:

$$\text{Cost of equity} = \text{Risk-free rate} + \text{Beta (Equity risk premium)}$$
$$= 3.6\% + 1.162(6\%) = 10.572\%$$

Table 12.3 summarizes the estimates of net income, potential dividends, and the present value of these dividends over the next five years:

At the end of year 5, we assume that the firm will be in stable growth, growing 3% a year in perpetuity. In addition, we will also assume that

- The beta will decrease to 1, resulting in a drop of cost of equity to 9.60%.

$$\text{Cost of equity} = \text{Risk-free rate} + \text{Beta} * \text{Equity risk premium}$$
$$= 3.6\% + 1(6\%) = 9.60\%$$

- The return on equity after year 5 will be equal to the stable period cost of equity of 9.60%.

Table 12.3	EXPECTED POTENTIAL DIVIDENDS OVER NEXT FIVE YEARS—DEUTSCHE BANK IN 2009						
	Current	1	2	3	4	5	Sum
Asset base	€312,882	€325,398	€338,414	€351,950	€366,028	€380,669	
Capital ratio	10.20%	10.16%	10.12%	10.08%	10.04%	10.00%	
Regulatory capital	€31,914	€33,060	€34,247	€35,477	€36,749	€38,067	
Change in regulatory capital		€1,146	€1,187	€1,229	€1,273	€1,318	
ROE	9.40%	9.52%	9.64%	9.76%	9.88%	10.00%	
Net income	€3,000	€3,147	€3,302	€3,463	€3,631	€3,807	
– Investment in regulatory capital		€1,146	€1,187	€1,229	€1,273	€1,318	
FCFE (potential dividend)		€2,001	€2,114	€2,233	€2,358	€2,489	
Present value @ 10.572%		€1,810	€1,729	€1,652	€1,578	€1,506	€8,275

- Given the expected growth rate of 3% after year 5 and the stable ROE of 9.60%, the payout ratio in stable growth is 68.75%

$$\text{Stable payout ratio} = 1 - \frac{\text{Stable growth rate}}{\text{Stable ROE}} = 1 - \frac{0.03}{0.096} = 68.75\%$$

The value of equity at the end of year 5 can be estimated as follows:

$$\text{Terminal value} = \frac{\text{Expected dividends}_6}{(\text{Cost of equity} - g)} = \frac{3,807(1.03)(0.6875)}{(0.096 - 0.03)}$$
$$= 39,728 \text{ million euros}$$

Discounting the terminal value back at the cost of equity for the high growth period:

$$\text{PV of terminal value} = \frac{\text{Terminal value}_n}{(1 + \text{Cost of equity}_{\text{High growth}})^n}$$
$$= \frac{39,728}{(1.10572)^5} = 24,036 \text{ million euros}$$

Adding the present value of dividends to this number yields the value of equity for Deutsche Bank in early 2009:

$$\text{Value of equity} = €8,275 \text{ million} + €24,036 \text{ million} = €32,311 \text{ million}$$

Dividing by the number of shares outstanding at the start of 2009 (581.85 million), we can obtain the value of equity per share:

$$\text{Value of equity per share} = \frac{\text{Value of equity}}{\# \text{Shares}} = \frac{32,311}{581.85} = 55.53 \text{ euros/share}$$

In June 2009, Deutsche Bank was trading at 48.06 euros per share and thus remains undervalued.

Valuation Biases: A Behavioral Perspective

In theory, we start with the financial fundamentals and move "objectively" from the numbers to the value of the firm, making reasonable assumptions along the way. In practice, though, valuations are not just subjective but are contaminated by biases that analysts bring to the process. In fact, there are at least three sources of bias.

1. ***Anchoring bias*** When valuing a company, we generally look for a number to use as a basis or comparison, and that number then affects the valuation. With publicly traded companies, for instance, the market price becomes a logical anchor to compare our estimates of value to. In fact, it is not uncommon to see analysts change their assumptions to move their valuations closer to the stock price.

2. ***Recency bias*** There is evidence that when data is presented sequentially, the most recent data is weighted too much (relative to its importance) and less recent data too little. In the context of valuing companies, this often manifests itself as too great a dependence on how these companies have done in the most recent year and too little attention paid to historical data. As a consequence, we tend to overvalue companies after good years and undervalue companies after bad years.

3. *Confirmation bias*   There is some evidence that analysts who form a perception of what the fair value is early in the process tend to then model the data to confirm that perception.

As a result of these biases, we would argue that in many valuations, the value gets set first and the valuation follows.

As a confession, the valuations of Deutsche Bank in 2008 and 2009 in this chapter reflect some of these biases. While some of the drop in value per share (from 105 euros/share to 56 euros/share can be attributed to changing fundamentals, some of it also reflects the effect of not only the market crisis, but also seeing the drop in Deutsche Bank's stock price from 89 euros to 48 euros between the two valuations. Put another way, it is entirely possible that I am overreacting to recent events (by raising the equity risk premium from 4.5% to 6%) and undervaluing Deutsche Bank as a consequence.

II. FCFE Models

In Chapter 11, while developing a framework for analyzing dividend policy, we estimated the free cash flow to equity as the cash flow that the firm can afford to pay out as dividends and contrasted it with the actual dividends. We noted that many firms do not pay out their FCFE as dividends; thus, the dividend discount model may not capture their true capacity to generate cash flows for stockholders. A more appropriate model is the *FCFE model*.

Setting Up the Model

The FCFE is the residual cash flow left over after meeting interest and principal payments and providing for reinvestment to maintain existing assets and create new assets for future growth. The FCFE is measured as follows:

$$\text{FCFE} = \text{Net income} + \text{Depreciation} - \text{Capital expenditures}$$
$$- \Delta\text{Working Capital} - \text{Principal repayments} + \text{New debt issues}$$

where ΔWorking capital is the change in noncash working capital.

In the special case where the capital expenditures and the working capital are financed at the target debt ratio δ, and principal repayments are made from new debt issues, the FCFE is measured as follows:

$$\text{FCFE} = \text{Net income} - (1 - \delta)(\text{Capital expenditures} - \text{Depreciation})$$
$$- (1 - \delta)\Delta\text{Working capital}$$

There is one more way in which we can present the FCFE. If we define the portion of the net income that equity investors reinvest back into the firm as the equity reinvestment rate, we can state the FCFE as a function of this rate.

$$\text{Equity reinvestment rate}$$
$$= \frac{(\text{Capital Expenditures} - \text{Depreciation} + \Delta\text{Working capital})(1 - \delta)}{\text{Net income}}$$
$$\text{FCFE} = \text{Net income}(1 - \text{Equity reinvestment rate})$$

Once we estimate the FCFE, the general version of the FCFE model resembles the dividend discount model, with FCFE replacing dividends in the equation:

$$\text{Value of the stock} = \text{PV of FCFE during high growth} + \text{PV of terminal price}$$

$$\text{Value}_0 = \sum_{t=1}^{t=n} \frac{E(\text{FCFE})_t}{(1+r)^t} + \frac{\text{Terminal value}_n}{(1+r)^n}$$

where

$$\text{Terminal value}_n = \frac{E(\text{FCFE})_{n+1}}{(r_n - g_n)}$$

where the expected FCFEs are estimated each year for the high growth period, r is the cost of equity, and g_n is the stable growth rate.

There is one key difference between the two models, though. Although the dividends can never be less than zero, the FCFE can. This can occur even if earnings are positive, if the firm has substantial working capital and capital expenditure needs. In fact, the expected FCFE for many small, high-growth firms will be negative at least in the early years, when reinvestment needs are high, but will become positive as the growth rates and reinvestment needs decrease.

IN PRACTICE: Estimating Capital Expenditure and Working Capital Needs

Two components go into estimating reinvestment. The first is net capital expenditures, which is the difference between capital expenditures and depreciation. Although both numbers can easily be obtained for the current year for any firm in the United States, they should be used with the following caveats:[10]

- Firms seldom have smooth capital expenditure streams. They can go through periods when capital expenditures are very high, followed by periods of relatively light expenditures. Consequently, when estimating the capital expenditures to use for forecasting future cash flows, we should look at capital expenditures over time and normalize them by taking an average, or we should look at industry norms.

- If we define capital expenditures as expenses designed to generate benefits over many years, expenses such as research and development (R&D) expenses (for technology firms), exploration costs (for natural resource company) and training and recruiting costs (for human capital firms) should be treated as capital expenditures (rather than as operating expenses). Consequently, these expenses need to be capitalized, and the asset that is created as a consequence needs to be amortized, with the amortization showing up as part of depreciation.[11]

---

[10]It is surprisingly difficult to obtain the capital expenditure numbers even for large, publicly traded firms in some markets outside the United States. Accounting standards in these markets often allow firms to lump investments together and report them in the aggregate. One solution is to back out the net capital expenditures from the balance sheet, by looking at the change in net fixed assets from period to period.

[11]Capitalizing R&D is a three-step process. First, you need to specify, on average, how long it takes for research to pay off (amortizable life). Second, you have to collect R&D expenses from the past for an equivalent period. Third, the past R&D expenses have to be written off (straight-line) over the amortizable life.

- Finally, when estimating capital expenditures, we should not distinguish between internal investments (which are usually categorized as capital expenditures in cash flow statements) and external investments (which are acquisitions). The capital expenditures of a firm therefore need to include acquisitions, whether they are funded with stock or cash. Because firms seldom make acquisitions every year, and each acquisition has a different price tag, the point about normalizing capital expenditures applies even more strongly to this item.

The second component of reinvestment is the cash that needs to be set aside for working capital needs. As in the chapters on investment analysis, we define working capital needs as noncash working capital, i.e., the difference between non-cash current assets and non-debt current liabilities, and the cash flow effect is the period-to-period change in this number. Again, although we can estimate this change for any year using financial statements, it has to be used with caution. Changes in noncash working capital are volatile, with big increases in some years followed by big decreases in the following years. To ensure that the projections are not the result of an unusual base year, we tie the changes in working capital to expected changes in revenues or costs of goods sold at the firm over time. For instance, we use the noncash working capital as a percent of revenues, in conjunction with expected revenue changes each period, to estimate projected changes in noncash working capital. As a final point, noncash working capital can be negative, which can translate into positive cash flows from working capital as revenue increases. It is prudent, when this occurs, to set noncash working capital needs to zero.[12] ■

Estimating Model Inputs
Just as in the dividend discount model, there are four basic inputs needed for this model to be usable. First, the *length of the high-growth period* is defined. Second, the *FCFE* each period during the growth period is computed; this means that net capital expenditures, changes in non-cash working capital, and the debt financing mix are all estimated for the high-growth period. Third, the *rate of return* that stockholders will demand for holding the stock is estimated. Fourth, the *terminal value of equity at the end of the high-growth period* is calculated, based on estimates of stable growth, the FCFE, and required return after the high-growth ends. Of the four inputs, the length of the high-growth period and the rate of return required by stockholders are the same for the dividend discount and FCFE valuation models. On the other two, the differences are minor but still worth emphasizing.

a. Estimating FCFE during High-Growth Period   As in the dividend discount model, we start with the earnings per share and estimate expected growth in earnings. Thus the entire discussion about earnings growth in the dividend discount model applies here as well. The only difference is in the estimation of fundamental growth. When estimating fundamental growth in the dividend discount model, we used the retention ratio and the return on equity to estimate the expected growth in earnings. When estimating fundamental growth in the FCFE valuation model, it is more consistent to

---

[12]Although it is entirely possible that firms can generate positive cash flows from working capital decreasing for short periods, it is dangerous to assume that this can occur forever.

use the equity reinvestment rate defined in the last section and the return on equity to estimate expected growth:

Expected growth in net income = Equity reinvestment rate * Return on equity

Unlike the retention ratio, which cannot exceed 100% or drop below 0%, the equity reinvestment rate can be negative (if capital expenditures drop below depreciation) or greater than 100%. If the equity reinvestment rate is negative and is expected to remain so for the foreseeable future, the expected growth in earnings can be negative. If the equity reinvestment rate is greater than 100%, the net income can grow at a rate higher than the return on equity, though the firm will have to issue new stock to fund the reinvestment.[13]

Once the earnings are estimated, the net capital expenditures, working capital needs, and debt financing needs have to be specified to arrive at the FCFE. Just as the dividend payout ratio was adjusted to reflect changes in expected growth, the net capital expenditure and working capital needs should change as the growth rate changes. In particular, high growth companies will have relatively higher net capital expenditures and working capital needs. In other words, the equity reinvestment rate will generally be high in high growth and decline as the growth rate declines. A similar point can be made about leverage. High-growth, high-risk firms generally do not use much leverage to finance investment needs; as the growth tapers off, however, the firm will be much more willing to use debt, suggesting that debt ratios will increase as growth rates drop.

There is one final point worth making about equity valuations. Because the net income includes both income from operations and income from cash and marketable securities, we have two choices when it comes to deal with these assets. The first and easier (albeit less precise) option is to discount the total FCFE (including the income from cash holdings) at a cost of equity that is adjusted to reflect the cash holdings.[14] The present value of equity will then incorporate the cash holdings of the company. The second, more precise way is to discount the net income, without including the interest income from cash, at a cost of equity that reflects only the operations of the firm, and then to add the cash and marketable securities on to this present value at the end.

 Capex.xls: This file online contains the industry averages by sector for net capital expenditures and working capital as a percent of revenues.

ILLUSTRATION 12.5 Estimating Growth Rate in Net Income- Tata Chemicals

Like many manufacturing firms, Tata Chemicals has volatile reinvestment outlays and the cash flows from debt swing wildly from year to year. In Table 12.4, we report net income and equity reinvestment (Capital expenditures − Depreciation + Change in noncash working capital − Net cash flow from debt) each year from 2004 to 2008.

---

[13]If the equity reinvestment rate exceeds 100%, the net income of the firm is insufficient to cover the equity reinvestment needs of the firm. Fresh equity will have to be issued to fund the difference.

[14]The beta for equity will be based on an unlevered beta, adjusted for the cash holdings of the company. In other words, if the company is 20% cash and 80% operations, the unlevered beta will be estimated attaching a 20% weight to cash and a beta of 0 for cash and a 80% weight for the unlevered beta of the operating business.

Table 12.4 EQUITY REINVESTMENT AND NET INCOME AT TATA CHEMICALS, 2004–2008

	Net Income	Cap Ex	Depreciation	Change in WC	Change in Debt	Equity Reinvestment	Equity Reinvestment Rate
2003–2004	$3,418	$357	$1,442	−$557	−$2,771	$1,129	33.04%
2004–2005	$4,550	$692	$1,377	−$493	$5,448	−$6,626	−145.64%
2005–2006	$5,156	$11,730	$1,389	$2,823	$867	$12,297	238.51%
2006–2007	$6,338	$1,196	$1,504	−$1,662	−$4,411	$2,442	38.53%
2007–2008	$11,571	$28,956	$1,488	$88	$17,054	$10,502	90.76%
Aggregate	$31,033	$42,930	$7,199	$200	$16,187	$19,744	63.62%

Rather than base the equity reinvestment rate on the most recent year's numbers, we will use the aggregate values for each of the variables over the entire period to compute a normalized equity reinvestment rate:

$$\text{Equity reinvestment rate} = \frac{\text{Equity reinvestment}_{\text{Total 2004–08}}}{\text{Net income}_{\text{Total 2004–08}}} = \frac{19,744}{31,033} = 63.62\%$$

To estimate the return on equity, we look at the same time period and look at the net income and the book value of equity each year from 2004 to 2008 in Table 12.5.

The normalized return on equity over the period is computed using the aggregated values of net income and book value of equity:

$$\text{Return on equity} = \frac{\text{Net income}_{\text{Total 2004–08}}}{\text{Book value of equity}_{\text{Total 2004–2008}}} = \frac{31,033}{178,992} = 17.34\%$$

The expected growth in net income can be computed as the product of the ROE and the equity reinvestment rate.

$$\text{Expected growth in net income} = \text{Equity reinvestment rate} * \text{ROE}$$
$$= 63.62\% * 17.34\% = 11.03\%$$

Based on fundamentals, we would expect Tata Chemical's net income to grow 11.03% a year.

Table 12.5 NET INCOME AND ROE, 2003–2008

	Net Income	BV of Equity at start of year	ROE
2003–2004	$3,418	$20,353	16.80%
2004–2005	$4,550	$19,978	22.78%
2005–2006	$5,156	$39,451	13.07%
2006–2007	$6,338	$37,258	17.01%
2007–2008	$11,571	$61,952	18.68%
Aggregate	$31,033	$178,992	17.34%

IN PRACTICE: PATHS TO A HIGHER ROE

The expected growth rate in earnings per share and net income are dependent on the return on equity that a firm makes on its new investments. The higher the return on equity, the higher the expected growth rate in earnings. But how do firms generate higher returns on equity? Algebraically, the return on equity can be decomposed into a return on capital and a leverage effect:

$$\text{ROE} = \text{Return on capital} + \frac{\text{Debt}}{\text{Equity}}(\text{Return on capital} - \text{After-tax cost of debt})$$

The second term in the equation reflects the influence of debt. To the extent that a firm can earn a return on capital that exceeds the after-tax cost of debt, its return on equity will increase as it uses more debt. A firm with a return on capital of 12%, a debt to equity ratio of 0.5, and an after-tax cost of debt of 4% will have a return on equity of 16%. Lest firms view this as a free lunch, we hasten to point out that using more debt will also increase the firm's beta and cost of equity, and the value of equity may very well decrease with higher borrowing, even though the return on equity and expected growth rate may be higher. ■

b. Estimating Terminal Value As with the dividend discount model, the terminal value in the FCFE model is determined by the stable growth rate and cost of equity. The difference between this model and the dividend discount model lies primarily in the cash flow used to calculate the terminal price: the latter uses expected dividends in the period after high growth, whereas the former uses the FCFE in that period:

$$\text{Terminal value of equity}_n = \frac{\text{FCFE}_{n+1}}{r - g_n}$$

In estimating that cash flow, the net capital expenditures change in non-cash working capital should be consistent with the definition of stability. The simplest way to ensure this is to estimate an equity reinvestment rate from the stable period return on equity:

$$\text{Equity reinvestment rate in stable growth} = 1 - \frac{g_{\text{Stable}}}{\text{ROE}_{\text{Stable}}}$$

This is exactly the same equation we used to compute the retention ratio in stable growth in the dividend discount model.

Some analysts assume that stable-growth firms have capital expenditures that offset depreciation, and no working capital requirements. This will yield a equity reinvestment rate of 0, which is consistent only with a stable growth rate of zero. Using a stable growth rate of 3% or 4% while allowing for no reinvestment essentially allows your firm to grow without paying for the growth and will yield too high a value for the firm.

Reconciling FCFE and Dividend Discount Model Valuations
The FCFE discounted cash flow model can be viewed as an alternative to the dividend discount model. Because the two approaches sometimes provide different estimates of value, however, it is worth examining why this occurs.

There are two conditions under which the value obtained from using the FCFE in discounted cash flow valuation will be the same as the value obtained from using the dividend discount model. The first is obvious: When the dividends are equal to the FCFE, the value will be the same. The second is more subtle: When the FCFE is greater than dividends, but the excess cash (FCFE − Dividends) is invested in projects with a net present value of zero, the values will also be similar. For instance, investing in financial assets that are fairly priced should yield an NPV of zero.[15]

More often, the two models will provide different estimates of value. First, when the FCFE is greater than the dividend and the excess cash either earns below-market returns or is invested (or expected to be invested) in negative NPV projects, the value from the FCFE model will be greater than the value from the dividend discount model. This is not uncommon. There are numerous case studies of firms having accumulated large cash balances by paying out low dividends relative to FCFE that have chosen to use this cash to finance unwise takeovers (the price paid is greater than the value received). Second, the payment of smaller dividends than the firm can afford to pay (FCFE) lowers debt-equity ratios; accordingly, the firm may become underlevered, reducing its value.

In those cases where dividends are greater than FCFE, the firm will have to issue new shares or borrow money to pay these dividends, leading to at least one of three possible negative consequences. One is the issuance cost on these security issues, which can be substantial for equity issues. Second, if the firm borrows the money to pay the dividends, the firm may become overlevered (relative to the optimal), leading to a loss in value. Finally, paying too much in dividends can lead to capital rationing constraints, whereby good projects are rejected, resulting in a loss of wealth.

When the two models yield different values, two questions remain: (1) what does the difference between the two models tell us, and (2) which of the two models is appropriate to use in evaluating the market price? In most cases, the value from the FCFE model will exceed the value from the dividend discount model. The difference between the value obtained from the FCFE model and that obtained from the dividend discount model can be considered one component of the value of controlling a firm—that is, it measures the value of controlling dividend policy. In a hostile takeover, the bidder can expect to control the firm and change the dividend policy (to reflect FCFE), thus capturing the higher FCFE value. In the more infrequent case—the value from the dividend discount model exceeds the value from the FCFE—the difference has less economic meaning but can be considered a warning on the sustainability of expected dividends.

As for which of the two values is more appropriate for evaluating the market price, the answer lies in the openness of the market for corporate control. If there is a significant probability that a firm can be taken over or its management changed, the market price will reflect that likelihood; in that case, the value from the FCFE model would be a more appropriate benchmark. As changes in corporate control become more difficult, either because of a firm's size or because of legal or market restrictions on takeovers, the value from the dividend discount model will provide a more appropriate benchmark for comparison.

---

[15] Mechanically, this will work out only if you keep track of the cash build-up in the dividend discount model and add it to the terminal value. If you do not do this, you will undervalue your firm with the dividend discount model.

12.7   FCFE AND DISCOUNT DIVIDEND VALUE

Most firms can be valued using FCFE and discount dividend valuation models. Which of the following statements would you most agree with on the relationship between these two values?

a.   The FCFE value will always be higher than the discount dividend value.

b.   The FCFE value will usually be higher than the discount dividend value.

c.   The discount dividend value will usually be higher than the FCFE value.

d.   The discount dividend value will generally be equal to the FCFE value.

ILLUSTRATION 12.6   FCFE Valuation—Tata Chemicals

To value Tata Chemicals using the FCFE model, we will use the expected growth in net income that we estimated in Illustration 12.4 and value the equity in operating assets first and then add on the value of cash and other non-operating assets. Summarizing the basic information that we will be using:

- Rather than use the net income from 2007–2008 as the base year income, we used the normalized return on equity of 17.34% (from Illustration 11.5) and the current book value of equity (Rs35,717 million) to estimate the base year net income:

$$\text{Normalized net income} = \text{Current book value of equity} * \text{Normalized ROE}$$
$$= 35,717 * 0.1734 = \text{Rs6,193 million}$$

- We will use the average equity reinvestment rate of 63.62%, based on the average values from 2004–2008, that we computed in Illustration 12.5 as the equity reinvestment rate for the next five years. In conjunction with the normalized return on equity of 17.34% that we computed in that illustration, we estimate an expected growth rate of 11.03% a year for the next five years.

- In Illustration 4.9, we estimated a beta for equity of 0.945 for Tata Chemical's operating assets.[16] With a nominal rupee risk-free rate of 4% and an equity risk premium of 10.51% for India (also estimated in Chapter 4), we arrive at a cost of equity of 13.93%.

$$\text{Cost of equity} = 4\% + 0.945(10.51\%) = 13.93\%$$

After year 5, we will assume that the beta will increase to 1, and that the equity risk premium will decline to 7.5%.[17] The resulting cost of equity is 11.5%.

$$\text{Cost of equity in stable growth} = 4\% + 1(7.5\%) = 11.5\%$$

- After year 5, we will assume that the growth in net income will drop to 4% and that the return on equity will rise to 11.5% (which is also the cost of equity). The equity

---

[16]We used the equity beta of just the operating asssets in this valuation. If we had chosen to include the cash from financial holdings as part of net income, we would have adjusted the beta for Tata Chemical's cross holdings.

[17]We reduced the country risk premium from 4.51% to 1.5%. We assume that as India grows, it will become a less risky country in which to invest.

	2009	2010	2011	2012	2013	Sum
Table 12.6 EXPECTED FCFE AT TATA CHEMICALS, 2009–2013						
Net income	Rs6,876	Rs7,634	Rs8,476	Rs9,411	Rs10,449	
Equity reinvestment rate	63.62%	63.62%	63.62%	63.62%	63.62%	
FCFE	Rs2,501	Rs2,777	Rs3,084	Rs3,423	Rs3,801	
Cost of equity	13.93%	13.93%	13.93%	13.93%	13.93%	
Present value	Rs2,195	Rs2,160	Rs2,085	Rs2,032	Rs1,980	Rs10,433

FCFE = Net Income (1 − Reinvestment Rate).

reinvestment rate in stable growth can then be estimated as follows:

$$\text{Equity reinvestment rate}_{\text{Stable growth}} = \text{Expected growth rate/Return on equity}$$
$$= 4\%/11.5\% = 34.78\%$$

To value the equity in Tata Chemicals, we begin by estimating the FCFE from operations in Table 12.6.

To estimate the terminal value of equity, we first estimate the FCFE in year 6:

$$\text{FCFE in year 6} = \text{Net income in year 6 } (1 - \text{Equity reinvestment rate}_{\text{Stable growth}})$$
$$= \text{Rs10,449}(1.04)(1 - 0.3478) = \text{Rs7,087 million}$$

The terminal value is then computed using the stable period cost of equity of 11.5%:

$$\text{Terminal value of equity} = 7,087/(0.115 - 0.04) = \text{Rs94,497 million}$$

The current value of equity is the sum of the present values of the expected cash flows in Table 12.3, the present value of the terminal value of equity, and the value of cash and non-operating assets today:

$$\text{Present value of FCFEs in high-growth phase} = \text{Rs10,433}$$
$$+ \text{Present value of terminal equity value} = 94,497/1.1393^5 = \text{Rs49,231}$$
$$= \text{Value of equity in operating assets} = \text{Rs59,664}$$
$$+ \text{Value of cash and marketable securities} = \text{Rs1,759}$$
$$\text{Value of equity in firm} = \text{Rs61,423}$$

Dividing by the 235.17 million shares outstanding yields a value per share of Rs261, about 20% higher than the stock price of Rs222 at the time of the valuation (June 2009).

IN PRACTICE: RECONCILING VALUE WITH THE MARKET PRICE

When you value a company and arrive at a number very different from the market price, there are three possible explanations. The first is that we are mistaken in our assumptions and that our valuations are wrong while the market is right. Without resorting to the dogma of efficient markets, this is a reasonable place to start because this is the most likely scenario. The second is that the market is wrong and we are right, in which case we have to decide whether we have enough confidence in our valuations to act on them. If we find a company to be undervalued, this would require buying and holding the stock. If the stock is overvalued, we would have to sell short. The problem, though, is that there is no guarantee that markets, even if they are wrong, will correct their mistakes in the near future. In other words, a stock that is overvalued can become even more overvalued, and a stock that is undervalued may stay that way for years, wreaking havoc on our portfolio. This also makes selling short a much riskier strategy, because we generally can do so only for a limited period.

One way to measure market expectations is to solve for a growth rate that will yield the market price. In the Tata Chemicals valuation, for instance, we would need an expected growth rate of 7% in earnings over the next five years to justify the current market price. This is called an implied growth rate and can be compared to the estimate of growth we used in the valuation of 11.03%. ∎

III. Free Cash Flow to the Firm Models

The dividend discount and FCFE models are models for valuing the equity in a firm directly. The alternative is to value the entire business, and then to use this value to arrive at a value for the equity. That is precisely what we try to do in firm valuation models, where we focus on the operating assets of the firm and the cash flows they generate.

Setting Up the Model
The cash flow to the firm can be measured in two ways. One is to add up the cash flows to all of the different claim holders in the firm. Thus, the cash flows to equity investors (which take the form of dividends or stock buybacks) are added to the cash flows to debt holders (interest and net debt payments) to arrive at the cash flow to the firm. The other approach to estimating cash flow to the firm, which should yield equivalent results, is to estimate the cash flows to the firm prior to debt payments but after reinvestment needs have been met:

$$\text{EBIT}(1 - \text{Tax Rate})$$
$$- (\text{Capital expenditures} - \text{Depreciation})$$
$$- \text{Change in noncash working capital}$$
$$= \text{Free cash flow to the firm}$$

The difference between capital expenditures and depreciation (net capital expenditures) and the increase in noncash working capital represents the reinvestment made by the firm to generate future growth. Another way of presenting the same equation is to add the net capital expenditures and the change in working capital and state that value as a percentage of the after-tax operating income. This ratio of reinvestment to after-tax operating income is called the *reinvestment rate*, and the FCFF can be written as

$$\text{Reinvestment rate} = \frac{(\text{Capital expenditures} - \text{depreciation} + \Delta\text{Working capital})}{\text{EBIT}(1 - \text{tax rate})}$$

$$\text{Free cash flow to the firm} = \text{EBIT}(1 - t)(1 - \text{Reinvestment rate})$$

Note that the reinvestment rate can exceed 100% if the firm has substantial reinvestment needs.[18] If that occurs, the FCFF will be negative even though after-tax operating income is positive. The cash flow to the firm is often called an unlevered cash flow, because it is unaffected by debt payments or the tax benefits flowing from these payments.[19]

As with the dividends and the FCFE, the value of the operating assets of a firm can be written as the present value of the expected cash flows during the high-growth period (which lasts n years) and a terminal value at the end of the period:

$$\text{Value}_0 = \sum_{t=1}^{t=n} \frac{E(\text{FCFF})_t}{(1+r)^t} + \frac{\text{Terminal value}_n}{(1+r)^n} \text{ where Terminal value}_n = \frac{E(\text{FCFF})_{n+1}}{(r-g_n)}$$

where r is the cost of capital and g_n is the expected growth rate in perpetuity after year n.

Estimating Model Inputs

As with the dividend discount and the FCFE discount models, there are four basic components that go into the value of the operating assets of the firm—a period of high growth, the FCFF during that period, the cost of capital to use as a discount rate, and the terminal value for the operating assets of the firm. We have additional steps to take to get to the value of equity per share. In particular, we have to incorporate the value of nonoperating assets, subtract debt, and then consider the effect of options outstanding on the equity of the firm.

a. Estimating FCFF during High-Growth Period   We base our estimate of a firm's value on expected future cash flows, not current cash flows. The forecasts of earnings, net capital expenditures, and working capital will yield these expected cash flows. One of the key inputs into any valuation is the expected growth rate in operating income. As with the growth rates we estimated for dividends and net income, the variables that determine expected growth are simple. The expected growth in operating income is a product of a firm's reinvestment rate—that is, the proportion of the after-tax operating income that is invested in net capital expenditures and noncash working capital, and the quality of these reinvestments, measured as the after-tax return on the capital invested.

$$\text{Expected growth}_{\text{EBIT}} = \text{Reinvestment rate} * \text{Return on capital}$$

where

$$\text{Reinvestment rate} = \frac{\text{Capital expenditure} - \text{Depreciation} + \Delta\text{Noncash WC}}{\text{EBIT}(1 - \text{Tax rate})}$$

$$\text{Return on capital} = \frac{\text{EBIT}(1 - t)}{(\text{BV of equity} + \text{BV of debt} - \text{Cash})}$$

---

[18]In practical terms, this firm will need external financing, either from debt or equity or both, to cover the excess reinvestment.

[19]The tax benefits from interest payments, which are real cash benefits, show up in the discount rate when we compute the after-tax cost of debt. If we add this tax benefit as a cash flow to the FCFF, we double-count the tax benefit.

Both measures should be forward-looking, and the return on capital should represent the expected return on capital on future investments.

The reinvestment rate is often measured using a firm's past history on reinvestment. Although this is a good place to start, it is not necessarily the best estimate of the future reinvestment rate. A firm's reinvestment rate can ebb and flow, especially in firms that invest in relatively few large projects or acquisitions. For these firms, looking at an average reinvestment rate over time may be a better measure of the future. In addition, as firms grow and mature, their reinvestment needs (and rates) tend to decrease. For firms that have expanded significantly over the past few years, the historical reinvestment rate is likely to be higher than the expected future reinvestment rate. For these firms, industry averages for reinvestment rates may provide a better indication of the future than using numbers from the past. Finally, it is important that we continue treating R&D expenses and operating lease expenses consistently. The R&D expenses in particular need to be categorized as part of capital expenditures for purposes of measuring the reinvestment rate.

The return on capital is often based on the firm's return on capital on existing investments, where the book value of capital is assumed to measure the capital invested in these investments. Implicitly, we assume that the current accounting return on capital is a good measure of the true returns earned on existing investments, and that this return is a good proxy for returns that will be made on future investments. This assumption, of course, is open to question if the book value of capital is not a good measure of the capital invested in existing projects, or if the operating income is mismeasured or volatile. Given these concerns, we should consider not only a firm's current return on capital, but also any trends in this return, as well as the industry average return on capital. If the current return on capital for a firm is significantly higher than the industry average, the forecasted return on capital should be set lower than the current return to reflect the erosion that is likely to occur as competition responds.

Finally, any firm that earns a return on capital greater than its cost of capital is earning an excess return. These excess returns are the result of a firm's competitive advantages or barriers to entry into the industry. High excess returns locked in for very long periods imply that a firm has a permanent competitive advantage.

IN PRACTICE: AFTER-TAX OPERATING INCOME

The income statement for a firm provides a measure of the operating income of the firm in the form of the EBIT and a tax rate in the form of an effective tax rate. Because the operating income we would like to estimate is before capital and financing expenses, we have to make at least two adjustments to the accounting operating income:

1.   The first adjustment is for financing expenses that accountants treat as operating expenses. The most significant example is operating leases. Because these lease payments constitute firm commitments into the future, they are tax-deductible, and the failure to make lease payments can result in bankruptcy, so we treat these

expenses as financial expenses. The adjustment, which we describe in detail in Chapter 4, generally results in an increase in both the operating income and the debt outstanding at the firm.

2. The second adjustment is to correct for the incidence of one-time or irregular income and expenses. Any expense (or income) that is truly a one-time expense (or income) should be removed from the operating income and not used in forecasting future operating income. Although this would seem to indicate that all extraordinary charges should be expunged from operating income, there are some extraordinary charges that seem to occur at regular intervals—say, once every four or five years. Such expenses should be viewed as irregular rather than extraordinary expenses and should be built into forecasts. The easiest way to do this is to annualize the expense. Put simply, this would mean taking one-fifth of any expense that occurs once every five years, and computing the income based on this apportioned expense.

As for the tax rate, the effective tax rates reported by most firms are much lower than the marginal tax rates. As with the operating income, we should look at the reasons for the difference and see if these firms can maintain their lower tax rates. If they cannot, it is prudent to shift to marginal tax rates in computing future after-tax operating income. ∎

ILLUSTRATION 12.7 **Estimating Growth Rate in Operating Income—Disney**
We begin by estimating the reinvestment rate and return on capital for Disney in 2008 using the numbers from the latest financial statements. We converted operating leases into debt and adjusted the operating income and capital expenditure accordingly.[20]

$$\text{Reinvestment rate}_{2008} = \frac{(\text{Cap ex} - \text{Depreciation} + \text{Chg in WC})}{\text{EBIT}(1 - t)}$$
$$= \frac{(2,752 - 1,839 + 241)}{7,030\,(1 - 0.38)} = 26.48\%$$

We include $516 million in acquisitions made during 2008 in capital expenditures, but this is a volatile item. Disney does not make large acquisitions every year, but it does so infrequently —$7.5 billion to buy Pixar in 2006, and $11.5 billion to buy Capital Cities in 1996. Averaging acquisitions from 1994–2008, we estimate an average annual value of $1,761 million for acquisitions over this period. Replacing the current year's acquisition with this normalized value yields a higher reinvestment rate:

$$\text{Reinvestment rate}_{2008} = \frac{(3,939 - 1,839 + 241)}{7,030(1 - 0.38)} = 53.72\%$$

---

[20]The book value of debt is augmented by the $1,720 million in present value of operating lease commitments. The unadjusted operating income for Disney was $6,726 million. The operating lease adjustment adds the current year's operating lease expense to capital expenditures ($550 million) and subtracts the depreciation on the leased asset to depreciation ($246 million) to arrive at an adjusted operating income of $7,030 million.

We compute the return on capital, using operating income in 2008 and capital invested at the start of 2008 (end of 2007):

$$\text{Return on capital}_{2008} =$$
$$\frac{\text{EBIT}(1-t)}{(\text{BV of equity} + \text{BV of debt} - \text{Cash})} = \frac{7{,}030(1-0.38)}{(30{,}753 + 16{,}892 - 3{,}670)} = 9.91\%$$

Note that Disney's effective and marginal tax rates are very similar; we have used the marginal tax rate of 38% in estimating after-tax income. If Disney maintains its 2008 reinvestment rate and return on capital for the next few years, its growth rate will be 5.32%.

Expected growth rate from existing fundamentals $= 53.72\% \, ^* \, 9.91\% = 5.32\%$

Valuing Growth Companies: A Behavioral Perspective
In theory, we should expect to see larger valuation errors when valuing growth companies than mature companies, because there is more firm-specific uncertainty that we face in valuing growth companies; we have to estimate how long growth will last, and how high growth will be during the period. In practice, we generally find support for this hypothesis, but there seems to be more bias in the valuation of growth companies. In particular, there is evidence to suggest that high-growth (and high-PE) stocks tend to earn returns that are too low and are thus priced too high relative to low-growth stocks. There are three reasons why this may occur:

1. ***Overconfidence*** Through this book, we have chronicled the effects of overconfidence on corporate finance decisions. Overconfident managers tend to take too many investments, overpay on acquisitions, and borrow too much. Overconfident investors tend to underestimate the likelihood that firms will fail and overestimate future potential growth. While all valuations are affected by this overconfidence, the effects on value are much greater with growth companies, where failure is much more likely and growth potential accounts for a much larger proportion of value.

2. ***Scaling biases*** For better or for worse, analysts tend to look at growth rates in recent periods and extrapolate that growth into future periods. Again, while this practice may affect all valuations, it has a much bigger effect when valuing small companies that have been able to post very high growth rates (reflecting their small size) in recent time periods.

3. ***Selection Biases*** There is a final factor that may be at play here. The analysts, managers, and appraisers who are attracted to the sectors with high growth (technology, for instance) may represent the most overoptimistic individuals in the overall population, and their valuations will reflect that selection bias.

fundgrEB.xls: There is a data set online that summarizes reinvestment rates and return on capital by industry group in the United States for the most recent quarter.

b. Estimating Cost of Capital Unlike equity valuation models, where the cost of equity is used to discount cash flows to equity, the cost of capital is used to discount cash flows to the firm. The cost of capital is a composite cost of financing that includes the costs of both debt and equity and their relative weights in the financing structure:

$$\text{Cost of capital} = k_{\text{equity}}(\text{Equity}/[\text{Debt} + \text{Equity}]) + k_{\text{debt}}(\text{Debt}/[\text{Debt} + \text{Equity}])$$

where the cost of equity represents the rate of return required by equity investors in the firm and the cost of debt measures the current cost of borrowing, adjusted for the tax benefits of borrowing. The weights on debt and equity have to be market value weights. We discussed the cost of capital estimation extensively earlier in this book, in the context of both investment analysis and capital structure. We will consider each of the inputs in the model in the context of valuing a firm.

The cost of equity, as we have defined it through this book, is a function of the nondiversifiable risk in an investment, which in turn is measured by a beta (in the single factor model) or betas (in the multiple factor models). We argued that the beta(s) are better measured by looking at the average beta(s) of other firms in the business—that is, bottom-up estimates, which reflect a firm's current business mix and leverage. This argument is augmented when we value companies by the fact that a firm's expected business mix and financial leverage can change over time, and its beta will change as a consequence. As the beta changes, the cost of equity will also change from year to year.

Just as the cost of equity can change over time as a firm's exposure to market risk changes, so can the cost of debt as its exposure to default risk changes. The default risk of a firm can be expected to change, for two reasons. One is that the firm's size will change as we project earnings further into the future; the volatility in these earnings is also likely to change over time. The second reason is that changes may occur in financial leverage. If we expect a firm's debt ratio to change over time, it will affect its capacity to service debt, and hence its cost of borrowing. The after-tax cost of debt can also change as a consequence of expected changes in the tax rate over time.

As a firm changes its leverage, the weights attached to equity and debt in the cost of capital computation will change. Should a firm's leverage be changed over the forecast period? The answer to this depends on two factors. The first is whether the firm is initially under- or overlevered. If it is at its appropriate leverage, there is a far smaller need to change leverage in the future. The second is the views of the firm's management, and the degree to which they are responsive to the firm's stockholders. Thus, if the management of a firm is firmly entrenched and steadfast in its opposition to debt, an underlevered firm will stay that way over time. In an environment where stockholders have more power, there will eventually be pressure on this firm to increase its leverage toward its optimal level.

ILLUSTRATION 12.8 Cost of Capital—Disney

Recapping the inputs we used to estimate the cost of capital in Disney, we will make the following assumptions:

- The beta for the first five years will be the bottom-up beta of 0.9011 that we estimated in Illustration 4.7. In conjunction with a risk-free rate of 3.5% and market risk premium of 6%, this yields a cost of equity of 8.91%.

$$\text{Cost of equity} = \text{Risk-free rate} + \text{Beta} * \text{Risk premium}$$
$$= 3.5\% + 0.9011(6\%) = 8.91\%$$

- The cost of debt for Disney for the first five years, based on its rating of A, is 6%. Using Disney's tax rate of 38% gives an after-tax cost of debt of 3.29%:

$$\text{After-tax cost of debt} = 6\%(1 - 0.38) = 3.72\%$$

- The current market debt ratio of 26.7% debt will be used as the debt ratio for the first five years of the valuation. Keep in mind that this debt ratio is computed using the market value of debt (inclusive of operating leases) of $16,682 million and a market value of equity of $46,045 million.

The cost of capital for Disney, at least for the first five years of the valuation, is 7.52%.

$$\text{Cost of capital} = \text{Cost of equity}(E/[D + E]) + \text{After-tax cost of debt}(D/[D + E])$$
$$= 8.91\%(0.763) + 3.72\%(0.267) = 7.52\%$$

12.8 FIRM VALUATION AND LEVERAGE

A standard critique of the use of cost of capital in firm valuation is that it assumes that leverage stays stable over time (through the weights in the cost of capital). Is this true?
a. Yes
b. No

wacc.xls: There is a data set online that summarizes the costs of capital for firms in the United States by industry group.

c. Estimating Terminal Value   The approach most consistent with a discounted cash flow model assumes that cash flows beyond the terminal year will grow at a constant rate forever, in which case the terminal value can be estimated as follows:

$$\text{Terminal value}_n = \text{Free cash flow to firm}_{n+1}/(\text{Cost of capital}_{n+1} - g_n)$$

where the cost of capital and the growth rate in the model are sustainable forever. We can use the relationship between growth and reinvestment rates that we noted earlier to estimate the reinvestment rate in stable growth:

$$\text{Reinvestment rate in stable growth} = \text{Stable growth rate}/\text{ROC}_n$$

where the ROC_n is the return on capital that the firm can sustain in stable growth. This reinvestment rate can then be used to generate the FCFF in the first year of stable growth:

$$\text{Terminal value} = \frac{\text{EBIT}_{n+1}(1 - t)\left(1 - \dfrac{g_n}{\text{ROC}_n}\right)}{(\text{Cost of capital}_n - g_n)}$$

In the special case where ROC is equal to the cost of capital, this estimate simplifies to become the following:

$$\text{Terminal value}_{\text{ROC} = \text{WACC}} = \frac{\text{EBIT}_{n+1}(1 - t)}{\text{Cost of capital}_n}$$

In other words, growth becomes irrelevant when a firm earns zero excess returns. Thus, in every discounted cash flow valuation, there are two critical assumptions we need to make on stable growth. The first relates to when the firm we are valuing will become a stable-growth firm, if it is not one already. The second relates to what the characteristics of the firm will be in stable growth, in terms of return on capital and cost of capital. We examined the first question earlier in this chapter when we looked at the dividend discount model. Let us consider the second question now.

As firms move from high growth to stable growth, we need to give them the characteristics of stable-growth firms. A firm in stable growth will be different from that same firm in high growth on a number of dimensions. For instance,

- As we noted with equity valuation models, high-growth firms tend to be *more exposed to market risk* (and have higher betas) than stable-growth firms. Thus, although it might be reasonable to assume a beta of 1.8 in high growth, it is important that the beta be lowered, if not to 1 at least toward stable growth.[21]

- High-growth firms tend to have *high returns on capital and earn excess returns*. In stable growth, it becomes more difficult to sustain excess returns. There are some who believe that the only assumption sustainable in stable growth is a zero excess return assumption; the return on capital is set equal to the cost of capital. Although we agree, in principle, with this view, it is difficult in practice to assume that all investments, including those in existing assets, will suddenly lose the capacity to earn excess returns. Because it is possible for entire industries to earn excess returns over long periods, we believe that assuming a firm's return on capital will move toward its industry average sometimes yields more reasonable estimates of value.

- Finally, high-growth firms tend to *use less debt* than stable-growth firms. As firms mature, their debt capacity increases. The question of whether the debt ratio for a firm should be moved toward its optimal cannot be answered without looking at the incumbent managers' power relative to their stockholders, and their views about debt. If managers are willing to change their debt ratios and stockholders retain some power, it is reasonable to assume that the debt ratio will move to the optimal level in stable growth; if not, it is safer to leave the debt ratio at existing levels.

12.9 NET CAPITAL EXPENDITURES, FCFE, AND STABLE GROWTH

Assume that you are valuing a high-growth firm with high risk (beta) and large reinvestment needs (high reinvestment rate). You assume the firm will be in stable growth after five years, but you leave the risk and reinvestment rate at high-growth levels. Will you undervalue or overvalue this firm?

a. Undervalue the firm

b. Overvalue the firm

---

[21] As a rule of thumb, betas outside the range of 0.8 to 1.2 are inconsistent with stable-growth firms. Two-thirds of all U.S. firms have betas that fall within this range.

ILLUSTRATION 12.9   Stable Growth Inputs and Transition Period: Disney

We will assume that Disney will be in stable growth after year 10. In its stable growth phase, we will assume the following:

- The beta for the stock will increase to 1, reflecting Disney's status as a mature company. This will lower the cost of equity for the firm to 9.5%.

  Cost of equity = Risk-free rate + Beta * Risk premium = 3.5% + 6% = 9.50%

- The debt ratio for Disney will stay at 26.73%. This is at the lower end of the range for the optimal we computed for Disney in Chapter 8, but we see no signs that the firm will increase its debt ratio. Because we assume that the cost of debt remains unchanged at 6%, this will result in a cost of capital of 7.95%.

  Cost of capital = 9.5%(0.7327) + 6%(1 − 0.38)(0.2673) = 7.95%

- The return on capital for Disney will drop from its high-growth period level of 9.91% to a stable-growth level of 9%. This is still higher than the cost of capital of 7.91%, but Disney's competitive advantages are unlikely to dissipate completely by the end of the tenth year.

- The expected growth rate in stable growth will be 3%. In conjunction with the return on capital of 9%, this yields a stable period reinvestment rate of 33.33%:

  Reinvestment rate = Growth rate/Return on capital = 3%/9% = 33.33%

The values of all of these inputs adjust gradually during the transition period, from years 6 to 10, from high-growth levels to stable-growth values.

a. From Operating Asset Value to Firm Value   The operating income is the income from operating assets, and the cost of capital measures the cost of financing these assets. When the operating cash flows are discounted to the present, we value the operating assets of the firm. Firms, however, often have significant amounts of cash and marketable securities on their books. The value of these assets should be added to the value of the operating assets to arrive at firm value.

Cash and marketable securities can easily be incorporated into firm value, whereas other nonoperating assets are more difficult to value. Consider, for instance, minority holdings in other firms and subsidiaries.[22] If we consider only the reported income from these holdings, we will miss a significant portion of the value of the holdings.[23] The most accurate way to incorporate these holdings into firm value is to value each subsidiary or firm in which there are holdings and assign a proportional share of this value to the firm. If a firm owns more than 50% of a subsidiary, accounting standards in the United States require that the firm fully consolidate the income and assets of the subsidiary into its own, and the portion of the equity that does not belong to the firm

---

[22] When income statements are consolidated, the entire operating income of the subsidiary is shown in the income statement of the parent firm. Firms do not have to consolidate financial statements if they hold minority stakes in firms and take a passive role in their management.

[23] When firms hold minority, passive interests in other firms, they report only the portion of the dividends they receive from these investments. With minority, active holdings, they report the portion of the net income that is attributable to them, but not as part of operating income.

is shown as minority interest on the balance sheet. If the cash flows are estimated from the consolidated statements of a firm, the estimated value of minority interests should be subtracted to get to the value of the equity in the firm.[24]

There is one final asset to consider. Firms with defined pension liabilities sometimes accumulate pension fund assets in excess of these liabilities. Although the excess does belong to the owners of the firm, they face a tax liability if they claim it. The conservative rule would be to assume that the social and tax costs of reclaiming the excess pension funds are so large that few firms would ever even attempt to do so.

ILLUSTRATION 12.10   Value of Nonoperating Assets at Disney

At the end of 2008, Disney reported holding $3,795 million in cash and marketable securities. In addition, Disney reported a book value of $1.763 billion for minority investments in other companies, primarily in foreign Disney theme parks.[25] In the absence of detailed financial statements for these investments, we will assume that the book value is roughly equal to the market value; an alternative solution would have been to estimate the price to book ratio of publicly traded theme park companies and to apply this multiple to the book value. Note that we consider the rest of the assets on Disney's balance sheet including the $5.4 billion it shows in capitalized TV and film costs and $22.2 billion it shows in goodwill and intangibles to be operating assets that we have already captured in the cash flows.[26]

Finally, Disney consolidates its holdings in a few subsidiaries in which it owns less than 100%. The portion of the equity in these subsidiaries that does not belong to Disney is shown on the balance sheet as a liability (minority interests) of $1,344 million. As with its holdings in other companies, we assume that this is also the estimated market value and subtract it from firm value to arrive at the value of equity in Disney.

 cash.xls: There is a data set online that summarizes the value of cash and marketable securities by industry group in the United States for the most recent quarter.

b. From Firm Value to Equity Value   The general rule that we should use is that the debt you subtract from the value of the firm should be at least equal to the debt that you use to compute the cost of capital. Thus, if we decide to convert operating leases to debt to compute the cost of capital, we should subtract the debt value of operating leases from the value of operating assets to estimate the value of equity. If the firm we are valuing has preferred stock, we would use the market value of the stock (if it is traded) or estimate a market value (if it is not) and deduct it from firm value to get to the value of common equity.[27]

---

[24]Optimally, we would like to subtract out the market value of the minority interests rather than the book value, which is reported in the balance sheet.

[25]Disney owns 39% of Euro Disney and 43% of the Hong Kong Disney park. It also owns 37.5% of the A&E network and 39.6% of E! Television.

[26]Adding these on to the present value of the cash flows would represent double-counting.

[27]Estimating market value for preferred stock is relatively simple. Preferred stock generally is perpetual, and the estimated market value of the preferred stock is therefore

$$\text{Cost of preferred stock} = \text{Preferred dividend/Cost of preferred stock}$$

The cost of preferred stock should be higher than the pretax cost of debt, because debt has a prior claim on the cash flows and assets of the firm.

There may be other claims on the firm that do not show up in debt for purposes of computing cost of capital but that should be subtracted from firm value to get the value of equity.

- ***Expected liabilities on lawsuits***   When analyzing a firm that is the defendant in a lawsuit where it potentially could have to pay tens of millions of dollars in damages, we should estimate the probability that this will occur and use this probability to estimate the expected liability. Thus, if there is a 10% chance that the firm could lose a case and the expected damage award is $1 billion, we would reduce the value of the equity in the firm by $100 million (Probability * Expected damages). If the expected liability is not expected to occur until several years from now, we would compute the present value of the payment.

- ***Unfunded pension and health care obligations***   If a firm has significantly underfunded a pension or a health plan, it will need to set aside cash in future years to meet these obligations. Although it would not be considered debt for cost of capital purposes, it should be subtracted from firm value to arrive at equity value.

- ***Deferred tax liability***   The deferred tax liability that shows up on the financial statements of many firms reflects the fact that firms often use strategies that reduce their taxes in the current year while increasing their taxes in future years. Of the three items listed here, this one is the least clearly defined, because it is not clear when or even whether the obligation will come due. Ignoring it, though, may be foolhardy, because the firm could find itself making these tax payments in the future. The most sensible way of dealing with this item is to consider it an obligation, but one that will come due only when the firm's growth rate moderates. Thus, if we expect your firm to be in stable growth in ten years, you would discount the deferred tax liability back ten years and deduct this amount from the firm value to get to equity value.

e. From Equity Value to Equity Value per Share   Once the value of the firm, inclusive of nonoperating assets, has been estimated, we generally subtract the value of the outstanding debt to arrive at the value of equity and then divide the value of equity by the number of shares outstanding to estimate the value per share. This approach works only when common stock is the only equity outstanding. When there are warrants and employee options outstanding, the estimated value of these options has to be subtracted from the value of the equity before we divide by the number of shares outstanding. The same procedure applies when the firm has convertible bonds outstanding, because these conversion options represent claims on equity as well.

For those unwilling to use option pricing models, there are two shortcuts available. One is to divide the value of equity by the fully diluted number of shares outstanding, rather than by the actual number.[28] This approach will underestimate the value of the equity, because it fails to consider the cash proceeds from option exercise. The other shortcut, called the *treasury stock approach*, adds the expected proceeds from the exercise of the options (exercise price multiplied by the number of options outstanding)

---

[28]We assume that all options will be exercised and compute the number of shares that will be outstanding in that event.

to the numerator before dividing by the number of shares outstanding. Although this approach will yield a more reasonable estimate than the first one, it does not include the time premium of the options outstanding. Thus, it tends to overstate the value of the common stock.

 warrants.xls: This spreadsheet allows you to value the options outstanding in a firm, allowing for the dilution effect.

ILLUSTRATION 12.11   Value of Equity Options

Disney has granted considerable numbers of options to its managers. At the end of 2008, there were 171 million options outstanding, with a weighted average exercise price of $28.37 and weighted average life of six years. Using the current stock price of $24.34, an estimated standard deviation of 29%,[29] a dividend yield of 1.54%, and an option pricing model, we estimate the value of these equity options to $851 million.[30] The value we have estimated for the options above are probably too high, because we assume that all the options are exercisable. In fact, a significant proportion of these options (about 30%) are not vested yet,[31] and this fact will reduce their estimated value. We also assume that these options, when exercised, will generate a tax benefit to the firm equal to 38% of their value:

$$\text{After-tax value of equity options} = 851(1 - 0.38) = \$528 \text{ million}$$

To get to the value of equity in common stock, we will reduce the overall value of equity by this after-tax value of options. Dividing the value of equity in common stock by the actual number of shares outstanding should yield a value of equity value per share.

Reconciling Equity and Firm Valuations

The FCFF model, unlike the dividend discount model or the FCFE model, values the operating assets of the firm rather than equity. The value of equity, however, can be extracted from the value of the firm by adding non-operating assets and subtracting out the market value of outstanding debt. Because this model can be viewed as an alternative way of valuing equity, two questions arise: Why value the firm rather than equity? Will the values for equity obtained from the firm valuation approach be consistent with the values obtained from the equity valuation approaches described in the previous section?

The advantage of using the firm valuation approach is that cash flows relating to debt do not have to be considered explicitly, because the FCFF is a predebt cash flow, whereas they do have to be taken into account in estimating FCFE. In cases where the leverage is expected to change significantly over time, this is a significant saving, because estimating new debt issues and debt repayments when leverage is changing can become increasingly messy the further into the future you go. The firm valuation

---

[29] We used the historical standard deviation in Disney's stock price to estimate this number.

[30] The option pricing model used is the Black–Scholes model, adjusted for potential dilution. It is explained in Appendix 4.

[31] When options are not vested, they cannot be exercised. When providing options to their employees, firms often require that they continue as employees for a set period (vesting period) before they can exercise these options.

approach does, however, require information about debt ratios and interest rates to estimate the cost of capital.

The value for equity obtained from the firm valuation and equity valuation approaches will be the same if you make consistent assumptions about financial leverage. Getting them to converge in practice is much more difficult. Let us begin with the simplest case—a no-growth, perpetual firm. Assume that the firm has $166.67 million in EBIT and a tax rate of 40%. Assume that the firm has equity with a market value of $600 million, with a cost of equity of 13.87%, and debt of $400 million, with a pretax cost of debt of 7%. The firm's cost of capital can be estimated:

$$\text{Cost of capital} = (13.87\%)\left(\frac{600}{1,000}\right) + (7\%)(1-0.4)\left(\frac{400}{1,000}\right) = 10\%$$

$$\text{Value of the firm} = \frac{\text{EBIT}(1-t)}{\text{Cost of capital}} = \frac{166.67(1-0.4)}{0.10} = \$1,000$$

Note that the firm has no reinvestment and no growth. We can value equity in this firm by subtracting out the value of debt.

$$\text{Value of equity} = \text{Value of firm} - \text{Value of debt} = \$1,000 - \$400 = \$600 \text{ million}$$

Now let us value the equity directly by estimating the net income:

$$\text{Net income} = (\text{EBIT} - \text{Pretax cost of debt} * \text{Debt})(1-t)$$
$$= (166.67 - 0.07 * 400)(1 - 0.6) = \$83.202 \text{ million}$$

The value of equity can be obtained by discounting this net income at the cost of equity:

$$\text{Value of equity} = \frac{\text{Net income}}{\text{Cost of equity}} = \frac{83.202}{0.1387} = \$600 \text{ million}$$

Even this simple example works because of the following assumptions that we made implicitly or explicitly during the valuation.

- The values for debt and equity used to compute the cost of capital were equal to the values that we obtained in the valuation. Notwithstanding the circularity in reasoning—you need the cost of capital to obtain the values in the first place—it indicates that a cost of capital based on market value weights will not yield the same value for equity as an equity valuation model if the firm is not correctly priced in the first place.

- There are no extraordinary or nonoperating items that affect net income but not operating income. Thus, to get from operating to net income, all we do is subtract out interest expenses and taxes.

- The interest expenses are equal to the pretax cost of debt (used in the cost of capital) multiplied by the market value of debt. If a firm has old or short term debt on its books, with interest expenses that are different from this value, the two approaches will diverge.

If there is expected growth, the potential for inconsistency multiplies. We have to ensure that we borrow enough money to fund new investments each period to keep our debt ratio at a level consistent with what we are assuming when we compute the cost of capital.

fcffvsfcfe.xls: This spreadsheet allows you to compare the equity values obtained using FCFF and FCFE models.

ILLUSTRATION 12.12   FCFF Valuation—Disney

To value Disney, we will consider all of the numbers that we have estimated already in this section. Recapping those estimates:

- The operating income in 2008, before taxes and adjusted for operating leases, is $7,030 million. Based upon the capital invested at the start of 2008, we estimate a return on capital is 9.91%.

- For years 1 through 5, we will assume that Disney will maintain its return on capital on new investments at 9.91%, and that the reinvestment rate will be 53.72% (see Illustration 12.7). This will result in an expected growth rate of 5.32% a year.

- For years 1 through 5, we will assume that Disney will maintain its existing debt ratio of 26.73% and its current cost of capital of 7.52% (see Illustration 12.8).

- The assumptions for stable growth (after year 10) and for the transition period are listed in Illustration 12.9.

In Table 12.7, we estimate the after-tax operating income, reinvestment, and free cash flow to the firm each year for the next ten years.

In Table 12.8, we estimate the present value of the FCFF using the cost of capital. Because the beta and debt ratio change each year from year 6 to 10, the cost of capital also changes each year.

To compute the present value of the cash flows in years 6 through 10, we have to use the compounded cost of capital over the previous years. To illustrate, the present value of $3,761 million in cash flows in 2016 is

$$\text{PV of cash flow in 2009} = \frac{3,761}{(1.0752)^5(1.0761)(1.0769)(1.0778)} = \$2,095 \text{ million}$$

The final piece of the valuation is the terminal value. To estimate the terminal value, at the end of year 10, we estimate the free cash flow to the firm in year 11, using the

Table 12.7   ESTIMATED FCFF, DISNEY

	Expected Growth Rate	EBIT $(1 - t)$	Reinvestment Rate	Reinvestment	FCFF
2009	5.32%	$4,591	53.72%	$2,466	$2,125
2010	5.32%	$4,835	53.72%	$2,598	$2,238
2011	5.32%	$5,093	53.72%	$2,736	$2,357
2012	5.32%	$5,364	53.72%	$2,882	$2,482
2013	5.32%	$5,650	53.72%	$3,035	$2,615
2014	4.86%	$5,924	49.64%	$2,941	$2,983
2015	4.39%	$6,185	45.57%	$2,818	$3,366
2016	3.93%	$6,428	41.49%	$2,667	$3,761
2017	3.46%	$6,650	37.41%	$2,488	$4,162
2018	3.00%	$6,850	33.33%	$2,283	$4,567

Table 12.8   PRESENT VALUE OF FREE CASH FLOWS TO FIRM—DISNEY

	FCFF	Cost of Capital	Cumulated Cost of Capital	PV of Cash Flow
2009	$2,125	7.52%	1.0752	$1,976
2010	$2,238	7.52%	1.1561	$1,936
2011	$2,357	7.52%	1.2430	$1,896
2012	$2,482	7.52%	1.3365	$1,857
2013	$2,615	7.52%	1.4370	$1,819
2014	$2,983	7.61%	1.5463	$1,929
2015	$3,366	7.69%	1.6653	$2,022
2016	$3,761	7.78%	1.7948	$2,095
2017	$4,162	7.87%	1.9361	$2,150
2018	$4,567	7.95%	2.0901	$2,185

reinvestment rate of 33.33% and the stable period cost of capital of 7.95% that we estimated in Illustration 12.9:

$$FCFF_{11} = EBIT_{10}(1 - t)(1 + g_n)(1 - \text{Reinvestment rate}_{\text{Stable-growth}})$$
$$= 6{,}850(1.03)(1 - 0.333) = \$4{,}704 \text{ million}$$
$$\text{Terminal value} = FCFF_{11}/(\text{Cost of capital}_{\text{Stable-growth}} - g)$$
$$= 4704/(0.0795 - 0.03) = \$94{,}928 \text{ million}$$

The value of the firm is the sum of the present values of the cash flows during the high-growth period, the present value of the terminal value, and the value of the nonoperating assets that we estimated in Illustration 12.10.

$$\text{PV of cash flows during the high growth phase} = \$19{,}865 \text{ million}$$
PV of terminal value
$$= \frac{\$94{,}928}{(1.0752)^5(1.0761)(1.0769)(1.0778)(1.0787)(1.0795)} = \$45{,}419$$
$$+ \text{ Cash and marketable securities} = \$3{,}795$$
$$+ \text{ Nonoperating assets (holdings in other companies)} = \$1{,}763$$
$$\text{Value of the firm} = \$70{,}842$$

Subtracting out the market value of debt (including operating leases) of $16,682 million the value of minority interests ($1,344 million) and the value of the equity options (estimated to be worth $528 million in Illustration 12.11) yields the value of the common stock:

Value of equity in common stock
$$= \text{Value of firm} - \text{Debt} - \text{Minority interests} - \text{Equity options}$$
$$= \$70{,}842 - \$16{,}682 - \$1{,}344 - \$528 = \$52{,}288$$

Dividing by the number of shares outstanding (1,856.75 million), we arrive at a value per share of $28.16, about 17% above the market price of $24.34 at the time of this valuation. Figure 12.4 summarizes the valuation.

Figure 12.4 Valuation Summary

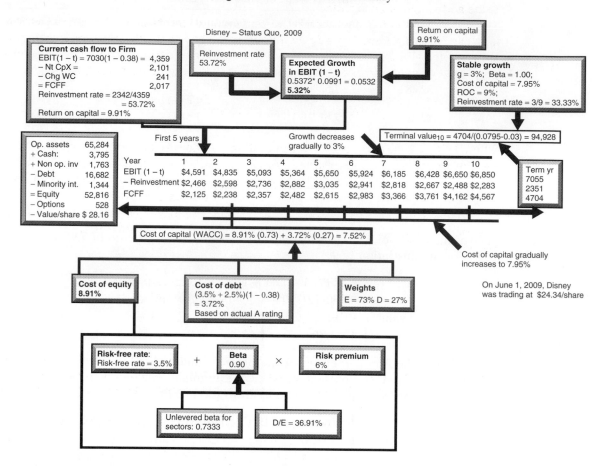

Disney – Status Quo, 2009

Current cash flow to Firm
EBIT(1 − t) = 7030(1 − 0.38) = 4,359
− Nt CpX = 2,101
− Chg WC 241
= FCFF 2,017
Reinvestment rate = 2342/4359
= 53.72%
Return on capital = 9.91%

Reinvestment rate
53.72%

Return on capital
9.91%

Expected Growth
in EBIT (1 − t)
0.5372* 0.0991 = 0.0532
5.32%

Stable growth
g = 3%; Beta = 1.00;
Cost of capital = 7.95%;
ROC = 9%;
Reinvestment rate = 3/9 = 33.33%

Op. assets 65,284
+ Cash: 3,795
+ Non op. inv 1,763
− Debt 16,682
− Minority int. 1,344
= Equity 52,816
− Options 528
− Value/share $ 28.16

First 5 years

Growth decreases
gradually to 3%

Terminal value$_{10}$ = 4704/(0.0795-0.03) = 94,928

Year	1	2	3	4	5	6	7	8	9	10
EBIT (1 − t)	$4,591	$4,835	$5,093	$5,364	$5,650	$5,924	$6,185	$6,428	$6,650	$6,850
− Reinvestment	$2,466	$2,598	$2,736	$2,882	$3,035	$2,941	$2,818	$2,667	$2,488	$2,283
FCFF	$2,125	$2,238	$2,357	$2,482	$2,615	$2,983	$3,366	$3,761	$4,162	$4,567

Term yr
7055
2351
4704

Cost of capital (WACC) = 8.91% (0.73) + 3.72% (0.27) = 7.52%

Cost of capital gradually
increases to 7.95%

Cost of equity
8.91%

Cost of debt
(3.5% + 2.5%)(1 − 0.38)
= 3.72%
Based on actual A rating

Weights
E = 73% D = 27%

On June 1, 2009, Disney
was trading at $24.34/share

Risk-free rate:
Risk-free rate = 3.5%

+

Beta
0.90

×

Risk premium
6%

Unlevered beta for
sectors: 0.7333

D/E = 36.91%

 12.10 NET CAPITAL EXPENDITURES AND VALUE

In the valuation above, we assumed that the reinvestment rate would be 33.33% in perpetuity to sustain the 3% stable growth rate. What would the terminal value have been if instead we had assumed that the reinvestment rate was zero while continuing to use a stable growth rate of 3%?

a. Higher than $94.9 billion (estimated in Illustration 12.12)

b. Lower than $94.9 billion

 IN PRACTICE: ADJUSTED PRESENT VALUE

In Chapter 8, we presented the adjusted present value (APV) approach to estimate the optimal debt ratio for a firm. In that approach, we begin with the value of the firm without debt. As we add debt to the firm, we consider the net effect on value by considering both the benefits and the costs of borrowing. To do this, we assume that the primary advantage of borrowing is a tax benefit, and that the most significant cost is the added risk of bankruptcy.

The first step in this approach is the estimation of the value of the unlevered firm. This can be accomplished by valuing the firm as if it had no debt—that is, by discounting the expected FCFF at the unlevered cost of equity. In a special case in which cash flows grow at a constant rate in perpetuity, the value of the firm is easily computed:

$$\text{Value of unlevered firm} = \frac{\text{FCFF}_0(1 + g)}{\rho_u - g}$$

where FCFF_o is the current after-tax operating cash flow to the firm, ρ_u is the unlevered cost of equity, and g is the expected growth rate. In more general cases, you can value the firm using any set of growth assumptions you believe are reasonable for the firm.

The second step is the calculation of the expected tax benefit from a given level of debt. This tax benefit is a function of the tax rate of the firm and is discounted at the cost of debt to reflect the riskiness of this cash flow. If the tax savings are viewed as a perpetuity,

$$\text{Value of tax benefits} = \frac{(\text{Tax Rate})(\text{Cost of Debt})(\text{Debt})}{\text{Cost of Debt}}$$
$$= (\text{Tax rate})(\text{Debt})$$
$$= t_c D$$

The tax rate used here is the firm's marginal tax rate, and it is assumed to stay constant over time. If we anticipate that the tax rate will change over time, we can still compute the present value of tax benefits over time, but we cannot use the perpetual growth equation.

The third step is to evaluate the effect of the given level of debt on the default risk of the firm and on expected bankruptcy costs. In theory, at least, this requires the estimation of the probability of default with the additional debt and the direct and indirect cost of bankruptcy. If π_a is the probability of default after the additional debt and BC is the present value of the bankruptcy cost, the present value of expected bankruptcy cost can be estimated.

$$\text{PV of expected bankruptcy cost}$$
$$= (\text{Probability of bankruptcy})(\text{PV of bankruptcy cost})$$
$$= \pi_a BC$$

This step of the APV approach poses the most significant estimation problems, because neither the probability of bankruptcy nor the bankruptcy cost can be estimated directly.

In theory, both the APV and the cost of capital approach will yield the same values for a firm if consistent assumptions are made about financial leverage. The difficulties associated with estimating the expected bankruptcy cost, though, often lead many to use an abbreviated version of the APV model, in which the tax benefits are added to the unlevered firm value and bankruptcy costs are ignored. This approach will overvalue firms. ∎

Valuing Private Businesses

All of the principles that we have developed for valuation apply to private companies as well. In other words, the value of a private company is the present value of the expected cash flows that you would expect that company to generate over time, discounted back at a rate that reflects the riskiness of the cash flows. The differences that exist are primarily in the estimation of the cash flows and the discount rates:

- When estimating cash flows, keep in mind that although accounting standards are, for the most part, standardized in publicly traded firms, they can diverge dramatically in private firms. In small, private businesses, we should reconstruct financial statements rather than trust the earnings numbers that are reported. There are also two common problems that arise in private firm accounting that we have to correct for. The first is the failure on the part of many owners to attach a cost to the time that they spend running their businesses. Thus the owner of a store who spends most of every day stocking the store shelves, staffing the cash register, and completing the accounting will often not show a salary associated with these activities in his or her income statement, resulting in overstated earnings. The second is the intermingling of personal and business expenses that is endemic in many private businesses. When reestimating earnings, we have to strip the personal expenses out of the analysis.

- When estimating discount rates for publicly traded firms, we hewed to two basic principles. With equity, we argued that the only risk that matters is the risk that cannot be diversified away by marginal investors, who we assumed were well diversified. With debt, the cost of debt was based on a bond rating and the default spread associated with that rating. With private firms, both these assumptions will come under assault. First, the owner of a private business is almost never diversified and often has his or her entire wealth tied up in the firm's assets. That is why we developed the concept of a total beta for private firms in Chapter 4, where we scaled the beta of the firm up to reflect all risk and not just nondiversifiable risk. Second, private businesses usually have to borrow from the local bank and do not have the luxury of accessing the bond market. Consequently, they may well find themselves facing a higher cost of debt than otherwise similar publicly traded firms.

- The final issue relates back to terminal value. With publicly traded firms, we assume that firms have infinite lives and use this assumption, in conjunction with stable growth, to estimate a terminal value. Private businesses, especially smaller ones, often have finite lives since they are much more dependent on the owner/founder for their existence.

With more conservative estimates of cash flows, higher discount rates to reflect the exposure to total risk and finite life assumptions, it should come as no surprise that the values we attach to private firms are lower than those that we would attach to otherwise similar publicly traded firms. This also suggests that private firms that have the option of becoming publicly traded will generally opt to do so even though the owners might not like the oversight and loss of control that comes with this transition.

ILLUSTRATION 12.13   Valuing a Private Business: Bookscape

To value Bookscape, we will use the pretax operating income of $3 million that the firm had in its most recent year as a starting point. Adjusting for the operating lease commitments that the firm has, we arrive at an adjusted pretax operating income of $3,575 million.[32] To estimate the cost of capital, we draw on the estimates of total beta and the assumption that the firm's debt to capital ratio would resemble the industry average of 34.84% that we made in Chapter 4:

$$\text{Cost of capital} = \text{Cost of equity}(D/[D+E]) + \text{After-tax cost of debt}(D/[D+E])$$
$$= 20.94\%(0.6516) + 6\%(1-0.4)(0.3484) = 0.149, \text{ or } 14.9\%$$

The total beta for Bookscape is 2.91, and we will continue to use the 40% tax rate for the firm, as long as the firm has taxable income.

In Chapter 6, we estimated a return on capital for Bookscape of 13.76%, and we will assume that the firm will continue to generate this return on capital for the foreseeable future, while growing its earnings at 2% a year. The resulting reinvestment rate is 14.53%:

$$\text{Reinvestment rate} = \text{Growth rate}/\text{Return on capital} = 2\%/13.76\% = 14.53\%$$

The present value of the cash flows, assuming perpetual growth, can be computed as follows:

$$\text{Value of operating assets} = \frac{\text{EBIT}(1-t)(1-\text{Reinvestment rate})(1+g)}{(\text{Cost of capital} - g)}$$
$$= \frac{3.575(1-0.4)(1-0.1453)(1.02)}{(0.149-0.02)} = \$14.497 \text{ million}$$

To get to the value of equity, we add back the cash holdings ($500,000) and subtract out the debt ($9.588 million).

$$\text{Value of equity} = \text{Value of operating assets} + \text{Cash} - \text{Debt}$$
$$= 14.497 + 0.5 - 9.588 = \$5.409 \text{ million}$$

Note that this valuation of equity is conditioned on two assumptions: that the firm will continue operating in perpetuity, and that the buyer is an undiversified individual.

To see the effect on value of altering the assumption of perpetual life, we assumed instead that the business would continue for only as long as the lease (twenty-five years), with cash flows growing at 2% a year for that period, and that there is no residual value at the end of twenty-five years. With this assumption, the value of the business drops to $13.576 million and the value of equity to $4.67 million:

---

[32] In Illustration 4.15, we estimated the present value of the operating lease commitments at Bookscape to be $9.588 million. To adjust the operating income, we add back the imputed interest expense on this debt, obtained by multiplying the pretax cost of borrowing by the present value of the operating leases (6% of $9.588 million).

$$\text{Value of operating assets} = \text{EBIT}(1-t)(1-\text{Reinvestment rate})\frac{1-\dfrac{(1+g)^n}{(1+r)^n}}{(r-g)}$$

$$= 3.575(1-0.4)(1-0.1453)\frac{1-\dfrac{(1.02)^{25}}{(1.149)^{25}}}{(0.149-0.02)}$$

$$= 13.576 \text{ million}$$

$$\text{Value of equity} = \text{Value of operating assets} + \text{Cash} - \text{Debt}$$

$$= 13.576 + 0.5 - 9.588 = \$4.67 \text{ million}$$

Finally, we also consider the value of the firm to a diversified investor or a publicly traded company by reverting back to a perpetual life and using the cost of capital of 8.81% that we estimated for Bookscape, using a market beta (see Illustration 4.18):

$$\text{Value of operating assets} = \frac{\text{EBIT}(1-t)(1-\text{Reinvestment rate})(1+g)}{(\text{Cost of capital}-g)}$$

$$= \frac{3.575(1-0.4)(1-0.1453)(1.02)}{(0.0881-0.02)} = \$27.442 \text{ million}$$

$$\text{Value of equity} = \text{Value of operating assets} + \text{Cash} - \text{Debt}$$

$$= 27.442 + 0.5 - 9.588 = \$18.35 \text{ million}$$

The gap between the value of equity to a private buyer ($5.4 million) and to a public buyer ($18.35 million) yields some interesting implications:

- *Diversification discount.* The only reason for the difference in values lies in the fact that the private owner is not diversified and thus sees more risk (and demands a higher return to compensate) than a public buyer, looking at the same business.

- *A rationale for acquisitions.* The different perspectives on risk and value on the part of private and public buyers also offers a rationale for acquisitions of private businesses by publicly traded companies, where both sides see themselves as winners. Thus, if a public company (say, Barnes and Noble) offers $8 million for the equity in Bookscape, the owner of the company is being offered more than what he thinks the business is worth ($5.4 million) and the public company gets a bargain (since the equity is worth $18.35 million to it).

- *Intermediate solutions.* Venture capital and private equity investors fall between the two extremes, since they are more diversified than the private owner but less so than public investors. Consequently, they will arrive at values between $5.4 million and $18.35 million and derive their payoff from nurturing the business for an initial public offering or sale or public company.

The fact that some public companies go private is often viewed as inconsistent with our analyses here. After all, why would investors in a firm accept a huge drop in value by taking a company off the market? Note that when private equity investors such as KKR or Blackstone take a company private, their intent is not to keep them private, but to fix what they see as potential problems and take the company back public sooner rather than later. Since the endgame remains the public market, they continue to run these businesses as if they were publicly held.

IN PRACTICE: ILLIQUIDITY DISCOUNTS IN PRIVATE FIRM VALUATION

If you buy stock in a publicly traded firm and then change your mind and decide to sell, you face modest transaction costs. If you buy a private business and change your mind, it is far more difficult to reverse your decision. As a consequence, many analysts valuing private businesses apply an illiquidity discount that ranges from 20% to 40% of the value to arrive at a final value. Although the size of the discount is large, there is surprisingly little thought that goes into the magnitude of the discount. In fact, it is almost entirely based on studies of restricted stock issued by publicly traded firms. These stock are placed with investors who are restricted from trading on the stock for two years after the issue, and the price on the issue can be compared to the market price of the traded shares of the company to get a sense of the discount that investors demand for the enforced illiquidity. Because there are relatively few restricted stock issues, the sample sizes tend to be small and involve companies that may have other problems raising new funds.

Although we concede the necessity of illiquidity discounts in the valuation of private businesses, the discount should be adjusted to reflect the characteristics of the firm in question. Other things remaining equal, we would expect smaller firms with less liquid assets and in poorer financial health to have much larger illiquidity discounts attached to their values. One way to make this adjustment is to take a deeper look at the restricted stock issues for which we have data and look at reasons for the differences in discounts across stocks.[33] Another way is to view the bid–ask spread as the illiquidity discount on publicly traded companies and extend an analysis of the determinants of these spreads to come up with a reasonable measure of it or illiquidity discount of a private business.[34] ■

Value Enhancement

In a discounted cash flow valuation, the value of a firm is the function of four key inputs—the cash flows from existing investments, the expected growth rate in these cash flows for the high-growth period, the length of time before the company becomes a stable-growth company, and the cost of capital. Put simply, to enhance the value of a firm, we have to change one or more of these inputs:

- *Increase cash flows from existing assets*   There are a number of ways we can increase cash flows from assets. First, we can use assets more efficiently, cutting costs and improving productivity. If we succeed, we should see higher operating margins and profits. Second, we can, within the bounds of the law, reduce the taxes we pay on operating income through good tax planning. Third, we can reduce maintenance capital expenditures and investments in working capital—inventory and accounts receivable—thus increasing the cash left over after these outflows.

- *Increase the growth rate during the high-growth period*   Within the structure that we used in the last section, there are only two ways of increasing growth. We can

---

[33]Silber did this in a 1989 study, where he found that the discount tended to be larger for companies with smaller revenues and negative earnings. See W. L. Silber, "Discounts on Restricted Stock: The Impact of Illiquidity on Stock Prices," *Financial Analysts Journal* v47,:60–64.

[34]See Aswatch Damodaran, *Investment Valuation*, 2nd ed. (John Wiley and Sons, 2001) for more details.

reinvest more in internal investments and acquisitions, or we can try to earn higher returns on the capital that we invest in new investments. To the extent that we can do both, we can increase the expected growth rate. One point to keep in mind, though, is that increasing the reinvestment rate will almost always increase the growth rate, but it will not increase value if the return on capital on new investments lags the cost of capital.

- *Increase the length of the high-growth period* It is not growth, per se, that creates value, but rather excess returns. Because excess returns and the capacity to continue earning them comes from the competitive advantages possessed by a firm, a firm has to either create new competitive advantages—brand name, economies of scale, and legal restrictions on competition all come to mind—or augment existing ones.

- *Reduce the cost of capital* In Chapter 8, we considered how changing the mix of debt and equity may reduce the cost of capital, and in Chapter 9, we considered how matching your debt to your assets can reduce your default risk and reduce your overall cost of financing. Holding all else constant, reducing the cost of capital will increase firm value.

Figure 12.5 summarizes the ways in which value can be enhanced at a public company.

Which one of these four approaches you choose will depend on where the firm you are analyzing or advising is in its growth cycle. For large mature firms with little or no

Figure 12.5 Ways of Enhancing Value

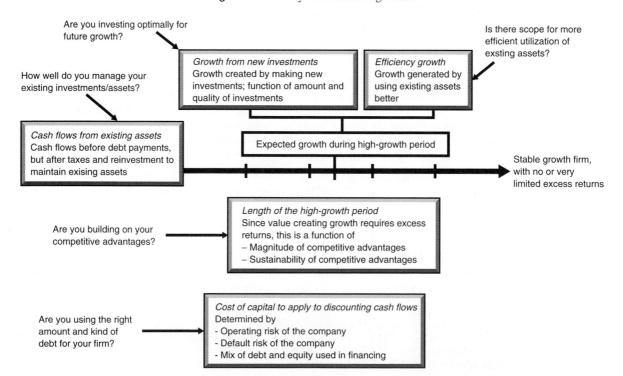

growth potential, cash flows from existing assets and the cost of capital offer the most promise for value enhancement. For smaller, risky, high-growth firms, it is likely to be changing the growth rate and the growth period that generate the biggest increases in value.

ILLUSTRATION 12.14   Value Enhancement at Disney

In Illustration 12.12, we valued Disney at $28.16 a share. In the process, though, we assumed that there would be no significant improvement in the return on capital that Disney earns on its existing assets (which at 9.91% is still well below the return on capital that Disney earned until 1996), and that the debt ratio would remain unchanged at the existing level of 27%. To examine how much the value per share could be enhanced at Disney if it were run differently, we made the following changes:

- We assumed that there is little scope left for operating efficiencies on existing investments, and that the return on capital on these investments will remain at its existing level of 9.91%.

- We assumed that the return on capital on new investments would increase to 12%, higher than the 9.91% that we used in the status quo valuation. This is closer to the return that Disney used to make prior to its acquisition of Capital Cities. We kept the reinvestment rate unchanged at 53.72%. The resulting growth rate in operating income (for the first five years) is 6.45% a year.

- We assumed that the firm would increase its debt ratio immediately to 40%, which is its current optimal debt ratio (from Chapter 8). Though the beta will increase to 1.04 as a consequence, the cost of capital will drop to 7.33%. Keeping this debt ratio in stable growth—assuming that the beta moves to 1—results in a cost of capital in stable growth of 7.19%.

Keeping the assumptions about stable growth unchanged, we estimate significantly higher cash flows for the firm for the high-growth period in Table 12.9.

	Expected Growth Rate	EBIT $(1 - t)$	Reinvestment Rate	Reinvestment	FCFF	Cost of Capital	Cumulated Cost of Capital	PV
				Table 12.9 EXPECTED FCFF, DISNEY				
2009	6.45%	$4,640	53.72%	$2,492	$2,147	7.33%	1.0733	$2,001
2010	6.45%	$4,939	53.72%	$2,653	$2,286	7.33%	1.1520	$1,984
2011	6.45%	$5,257	53.72%	$2,824	$2,433	7.33%	1.2365	$1,968
2012	6.45%	$5,596	53.72%	$3,006	$2,590	7.33%	1.3271	$1,951
2013	6.45%	$5,957	53.72%	$3,200	$2,757	7.33%	1.4244	$1,935
2014	5.76%	$6,300	49.64%	$3,127	$3,172	7.30%	1.5285	$2,076
2015	5.07%	$6,619	45.57%	$3,016	$3,603	7.27%	1.6397	$2,197
2016	4.38%	$6,909	41.49%	$2,866	$4,043	7.25%	1.7585	$2,299
2017	3.69%	$7,164	37.41%	$2,680	$4,484	7.22%	1.8854	$2,378
2018	3.00%	$7,379	33.33%	$2,460	$4,919	7.19%	2.0209	$2,434

The terminal value is also pushed up as a result of the higher growth in the high growth period:

$$\text{Terminal value} = \text{FCFF}_{11}/(\text{Cost of capital} - g)$$
$$= 4,919(1.03)/(0.0719 - 0.03) = \$120,982 \text{ million}$$

The value of the firm and the value per share can now be estimated:

$$\text{Present value of FCFF in high-growth phase} = 21,233$$
$$+ \text{Present value of terminal value of firm} = \$59,866$$
$$+ \text{Value of cash and marketable securities} = \$3,795$$
$$+ \text{Value of minority holdings in other companies} = 1,763$$
$$\text{Value of firm} = \$86,647$$
$$-\text{Market value of outstanding debt} = \$16,682$$
$$-\text{Minority interests} = \$1,344$$
$$-\text{Value of equity in options} = \$528$$
$$\text{Value of equity in common stock} = \$68,093$$
$$\text{Market value of equity/Share} = \$36.67$$

Figure 12.6 Value of Control

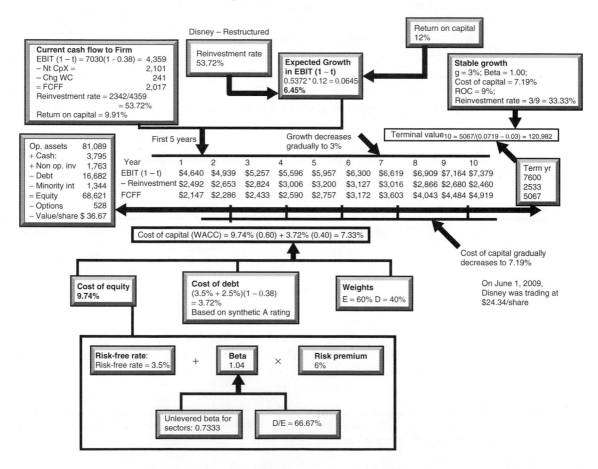

Disney's value per share increases from \$28.16 per share in Illustration 12.12 to \$36.67 a share when we make the changes to the way it is managed.[35] Figure 12.6 presents the restructured valuation.

IN PRACTICE: THE VALUE OF CONTROL

The notion that control is worth 15% or 20% or some fixed percent of every firm's value is deeply embedded in valuation practice—and it is not true. The value of control is the difference between two values—the value of the firm run by its existing management (status quo) and the value of the same firm run optimally.

$$\text{Value of control} = \text{Optimal value for firm} - \text{Status quo value}$$

Thus, a firm that takes poor investments and funds them with a suboptimal mix of debt and equity will be worth more if it takes better investments and funds them with the right mix of debt and equity. In general, the worse a firm is managed, the greater the value of control is. This view of the world has wide ramifications in corporate finance and valuation:

- In a hostile acquisition, which is usually motivated by the desire to change the way that a firm is run, you should be willing to pay a premium that, at best, is equal to the value of control. You would prefer to pay less to preserve some of the benefits for yourself (rather than give them to target company stockholders).
- In companies with voting and nonvoting shares, the difference in value between the two classes should be a function of the value of control. If the value of control is high and there is a high likelihood of control changing, the value of the voting shares will increase relative to nonvoting shares.

In the Disney valuation, the value of control can be estimated by comparing the value of Disney run optimally with the status quo valuation done earlier in the chapter.

$$\text{Value of control}_{\text{Disney}} = \text{Optimal value} - \text{Status quo value}$$

$$= \$36.67 - \$28.16 = \$8.51$$

Since the stock trades at \$24.34, we could pay a premium of up to \$12.33 to acquire the firm. ■

RELATIVE VALUATION

In discounted cash flow valuation, the objective is to find the value of assets given their cash flow, growth, and risk characteristics. In relative valuation, the objective is to value assets based on how similar assets are currently priced in the market. In

---

[35] You may wonder why the dollar debt does not change even though the firm is moving to a 30% debt ratio. In reality, it will increase, but the number of shares will decrease when Disney recapitalizes. The net effect is that the value per share will be close to our estimated value.

this section, we consider why and how asset prices have to be standardized before being compared to similar assets, and how to control for differences across comparable firms.

Standardized Values and Multiples

To compare the values of similar assets in the market, we need to standardize the values in some way. They can be standardized relative to the earnings they generate, to the book value or replacement value of the assets themselves, or to the revenues that they generate. We discuss each method next.

1. Earnings Multiples

One of the more intuitive ways to think of the value of any asset is as a multiple of the earnings it generates. When buying a stock, it is common to look at the price paid as a multiple of the earnings per share generated by the company. This *price/earnings ratio* can be estimated using earnings per share over the last four quarters, called a *trailing PE*, or an expected earnings per share in the next financial year, called a *forward PE*. When buying a business, as opposed to just the equity in the business, it is common to examine the value of the firm, usually net of cash (enterprise value), as a multiple of the operating income or the earnings before interest, taxes, depreciation, and amortization (EBITDA). To a buyer of the equity or the firm, a lower multiple is better than a higher one, but these multiples will be affected by the growth potential and risk of the business being acquired.

2. Book Value or Replacement Value Multiples

Although markets provide one estimate of the value of a business, accountants often provide a very different estimate. The accounting estimate of book value is determined by accounting rules and is heavily influenced by the original price paid for the asset and any accounting adjustments (such as depreciation) made since that time. Investors often look at the relationship between the market's assessment of the value of equity and the book value of equity (or net worth) as a measure of how over- or undervalued a stock is; the *price/book value* ratio that emerges can vary widely across industries, depending again on the growth potential and the quality of the investments in each. When valuing businesses, we estimate this ratio using the value of the firm and the book value of all capital (rather than just the equity). For those who believe that book value is not a good measure of the true value of the assets, an alternative is to use the replacement cost of the assets; the ratio of the value of the firm to replacement cost is called the Q Ratio.

3. Revenue Multiples

Both earnings and book value are accounting measures and are determined by accounting rules and principles. An alternative that is far less affected by these factors, is to use the ratio of the value of an asset to the revenues it generates. For equity investors, this ratio is the *price/sales ratio (PS)*, where the market value of equity is divided by the revenues generated by the firm. For firm value, this ratio can be modified as the *value/sales ratio (VS)*, where the numerator becomes the value of the firm. This ratio again varies widely across sectors, largely as a function of the profit margins in each. The advantage of using revenue multiples, however, is that it becomes far easier to compare firms in different markets, with different accounting systems at work, than it is to compare earnings or book value multiples.

Determinants of Multiples

One reason commonly given for the use of these multiples to value equity and firms is that they require far fewer assumptions than discounted cash flow valuation does. We believe this is a misconception. The difference between discounted cash flow valuation and relative valuation is that the assumptions we make are explicit in the former and remain implicit in the latter. It is important that we know what the variables are that cause multiples to change, because these are the variables we have to control for when comparing these multiples across firms.

To look under the hood, so to speak, of equity and firm value multiples, we will go back to fairly simple discounted cash flow models for equity and firm value and use them to derive our multiples. Thus, the simplest discounted cash flow model for equity, which is a stable growth dividend discount model, would suggest that the value of equity is:

$$\text{Value of equity} = P_0 = \frac{\text{DPS}_1}{k_e - g_n}$$

where DPS_1 is the expected dividend in the next year, k_e is the cost of equity, and g_n is the expected stable growth rate. Dividing both sides by the earnings, we obtain the discounted cash flow equation specifying the PE ratio for a stable growth firm:

$$\frac{P_0}{\text{EPS}_0} = \text{PE} = \frac{\text{Payout ratio} * (1 + g_n)}{k_e - g_n}$$

Dividing both sides by the book value of equity, we can estimate the price/book value ratio for a stable-growth firm:

$$\frac{P_0}{\text{BV}_0} = \text{PBV} = \frac{\text{ROE} * \text{Payout ratio} * (1 + g_n)}{k_e - g_n}$$

Dividing by the sales per share, the price/sales ratio for a stable-growth firm can be estimated as a function of its profit margin, payout ratio, profit margin, and expected growth.

$$\frac{P_0}{\text{Sales}_0} = \text{PS} = \frac{\text{Net profit margin} * \text{Payout ratio} * (1 + g_n)}{k_e - g_n}$$

We can do a similar analysis from the perspective of firm valuation.[36] The value of a firm in stable growth can be written as

$$\text{Value of firm} = V_0 = \frac{\text{FCFF}_1}{k_c - g_n}$$

---

[36]In practice, cash and marketable securities are subtracted from firm value to arrive at what is called enterprise value. All the multiples in the following section can be written in terms of enterprise value, and the determinants remain unchanged.

where k_c is the cost of capital. Dividing both sides by the expected FCFF yields the value/FCFF multiple for a stable-growth firm:

$$\frac{V_0}{\text{FCFF}_1} = \frac{1}{k_c - g_n}$$

Because the FCFF is the after-tax operating income netted against the net capital expenditures and working capital needs of the firm, the multiples of EBIT, after-tax EBIT, and EBITDA can also be estimated similarly. The value/EBITDA multiple, for instance, can be written as follows:

$$\frac{\text{Value}}{\text{EBITDA}} = \frac{(1-t)}{k_c - g} + \frac{\text{Depr}(t)/\text{EBITDA}}{k_c - g} - \frac{\text{CEx}/\text{EBITDA}}{k_c - g}$$
$$- \frac{\Delta\text{Working capital}/\text{EBITDA}}{k_c - g}$$

The point of this analysis is not to suggest that we go back to using discounted cash flow valuation, but to understand the variables that may cause these multiples to vary across firms in the same sector. If we ignore these variables, we might conclude that a stock with a PE of 8 is cheaper than one with a PE of 12, when the true reason may be that the latter has higher expected growth; or we might decide that a stock with a P/BV ratio of 0.7 is cheaper than one with a P/BV ratio of 1.5, when the true reason may be that the latter has a much higher return on equity. Table 12.10 lists the multiples that are widely used and the variables that determine each; the variable that (in our view) is the most significant determinant is highlighted for each multiple. This variable is what we would call the *companion variable* for this multiple, that is, the one variable we need to know to use this multiple to find under or overvalued assets.

 eqmult.xls: This spreadsheet allows you to estimate the equity multiples for a firm, given its fundamentals.

 firmmult.xls: This spreadsheet allows you to estimate the firm value multiples for a firm, given its fundamentals.

Table 12.10 MULTIPLES AND COMPANION VARIABLES (IN ITALIC)	
Multiple	**Determining Variables**
Price/earnings	*Growth*, payout, risk
Price/book value	Growth, payout, risk, *ROE*
Price/sales	Growth, payout, risk, *net margin*
Value/EBIT	
Value/EBIT $(1-t)$	Growth, *reinvestment needs*, leverage, risk
Value/EBITDA	
Value/sales	Growth, reinvestment needs, leverage, risk, *operating margin*
Value/book capital	Growth, leverage, risk, *ROC*

The Use of Comparable Firms

When we use multiples, we tend to use them in conjunction with comparable firms to determine the value of a firm or its equity. This analysis begins with two choices—the multiple that will be used in the analysis, and the group of firms that will make up the comparable firms. The multiple is computed for each of the comparable firms, and the average is computed. To evaluate an individual firm, we then compare its multiple to the average computed; if it is significantly different, we make a subjective judgment about whether the firm's individual characteristics (growth, risk, or cash flows) may explain the difference. Thus, a firm may have a PE ratio of 22 in a sector where the average PE is only 15, but the analyst may conclude that this difference can be justified because the firm has higher growth potential than the average firm in the industry. In the analysts' judgment, if the difference on the multiple cannot be explained by the variables listed in Table 12.10, the firm will be viewed as overvalued (if its multiple is higher than the average) or undervalued (if its multiple is lower than the average). Choosing comparable firms and adequately controlling for differences across these comparable firms then become critical steps in this process. In this section, we consider both decisions.

1. Choosing Comparables

The first step in relative valuation is usually the selection of comparable firms. A comparable firm is one with cash flows, growth potential, and risk similar to the firm being valued. It would be ideal if we could value a firm by looking at how an exactly identical firm—in terms of risk, growth, and cash flows—is priced. In most analyses, however, analysts define comparable firms as being other firms in the same business or businesses. If there are enough firms in the industry to allow for it, this list is pruned further using other criteria; for instance, only firms of similar size may be considered. The implicit assumption being made here is that firms in the same sector have similar risk, growth, and cash flow profiles and therefore can be compared with much more legitimacy.

   This approach becomes more difficult to apply when there are relatively few firms in a sector. In most markets outside the United States, the number of publicly traded firms in a particular sector is small, especially if the sector is defined narrowly. It is also difficult to find comparable firms if differences in risk, growth, and cash flow profiles across firms within a sector are large. Thus, there may be hundreds of computer software companies listed in the United States, but the differences across these firms are also large. The tradeoff, therefore, is simple. Defining a industry more broadly increases the number of comparable firms, but it also results in a more diverse group.

2. Controlling for Differences across Firms

In Table 12.10, we listed the variables that determined each multiple. Because it is impossible to find firms identical to the one being valued, we have to find ways of controlling for differences across firms on these variables. The process of controlling for the variables can range from very simple approaches that modify the multiples to take into account differences on one key variable to more complex approaches that allow for differences on more than one variable.

a. Simple Adjustments

Let's start with the simple approaches. In this case, we modify the multiple to take into account the most important variable determining it. Thus, the PE ratio is divided by the expected growth rate in earnings per share (EPS) for a company to determine a growth-adjusted PE ratio or the *PEG ratio*. Similarly, the PBV ratio is divided by the ROE to find a *value ratio*. These modified ratios are then compared across companies in a sector. The implicit assumption we make is that these firms are comparable on all the other measures of value, besides the one being controlled for.

ILLUSTRATION 12.15 Comparing PE Ratios and Growth Rates across Firms— Entertainment Companies

To value Disney, we look at the PE ratios and expected growth rates in EPS over the next five years, based on consensus estimates from analysts, for all entertainment companies where data is available on PE ratios and analyst estimates of expected growth in earnings over the next five years. Table 12.11 lists the firms and PE ratios.

At 9.4 times forward earnings and 9.45 times current earnings, Disney looks overvalued relative to the median values for the sector. It is true that it looks cheap when compared to the average values, but those averages are skewed by a few outliers.

Table 12.11 ENTERTAINMENT FIRM PE RATIOS AND GROWTH RATES, 2009

	Current PE	Trailing PE	Forward PE	Expected Growth in EPS, Next 5 Years	PEG
Belo Corp. "A"	1.56	2.60	1.88	1.50%	1.04
CBS Corp. "B"	3.76	4.23	5.93	4.50%	0.84
Central European Media Enterps	9.10	5.69	5.58	9.78%	0.93
CTC Media Inc	5.26	4.18	4.44	6.55%	0.80
Cumulus Media Inc	20.41	4.89	5.53	12.00%	1.70
Disney (Walt)	10.24	9.40	9.45	14.50%	0.71
DreamWorks Animation	9.37	10.17	12.26	14.50%	0.65
Global Traffic Network Inc	62.00	39.04	32.44	21.40%	2.90
Lin TV Corp.	4.22		1.43	8.00%	0.53
News Corp.	6.74	7.12	11.98	14.00%	0.48
Playboy Enterprises "B"	15.81		30.86	42.50%	0.37
RC2 Corp	7.23	22.00	6.93	10.50%	0.69
Regal Entertainment Group	13.87		11.74	8.00%	1.73
Rentrak Corp	25.35	29.15	35.73	50.00%	0.51
Saga Communic. "A"	2.21	2.29	2.76	8.00%	0.28
Sinclair Broadcast	12.36	4.84	9.39	15.00%	0.82
Time Warner	8.42	9.35	8.98	6.00%	1.40
Viacom Inc. "B"	6.69	6.69	7.72	12.00%	0.56
World Wrestling Ent.	14.39	14.06	12.18	15.00%	0.96
Median	9.10	6.90	8.98	12.00%	0.80
Average	12.58	10.98	11.43	14.41%	0.94

Source: Value Line.

In this valuation, we assume that Disney has a growth rate similar to the average for the sector. One way of bringing growth into the comparison is to compute the PEG ratio, which is reported in the last column. On this measure, Disney looks more undervalued, with a PEG ratio of 0.71, below both the median (0.8) and the average (0.94) for the sector. Although this may seem like an easy adjustment to resolve the problem of differences across firms, the conclusion holds only if these firms are of equivalent risk. Implicitly, this approach assumes a linear relationship between growth rates and PE.[37]

12.11 UNDERLYING ASSUMPTIONS IN COMPARABLE VALUATION

Assume that you are reading an equity research report in which a buy recommendation for a company is being based on the fact that its PE ratio is lower than the average for the industry. Implicitly, what is the underlying assumption or assumptions being made by the analyst?

a.   The sector itself is, on average, fairly priced.

b.   The earnings of the firms in the group are being measured consistently.

c.   The firms in the group are all of equivalent risk.

d.   The firms in the group are all at the same stage in the growth cycle.

e.   The firms in the group have similar cash flow patterns.

All of the above.

pe.xls: There is a data set online that summarizes PE ratios and PEG ratios by industry group in the United States for the most recent quarter.

b. Adjusting for More Than One Variable

When firms differ on more than one variable, it becomes difficult to modify the multiples to account for the differences across firms. We can run regressions of the multiples against the variables and then use these regressions to find predicted values for each firm. This approach works reasonably well when the number of comparable firms is large and the relationship between the multiple and the variables is stable. When these conditions do not hold, a few outliers can cause the coefficients to change dramatically and make the predictions much less reliable.

ILLUSTRATION 12.16   Price to Book Value Ratios and Return on Equity—European Banks
Table 12.12 lists the price/book value ratios of European banks and reports on their returns on equity and risk levels (measured using the stock beta over the previous five years).

Trading at 0.41 times book equity, Deutsche looks cheap relative to the rest of the sector. However, part of the reason for this may be its low return on equity in 2008 (5.48%) and high beta (1.61). Because these firms differ on both risk and return on equity, we run a regression of PBV ratios on both variables:

$$PBV = 1.03 + 1.54\,ROE - 0.40\,Beta \quad R^2 = 58.31\%$$
$$(3.79)\ (2.26)\qquad (2.18)$$

---

[37]Put another way, we are assuming that as growth doubles, the PE ratio will also double.

Table 12.12 EUROPEAN BANKS: PRICE TO BOOK VALUE RATIO, 2009

	P/Book Equity	Beta	ROE
Royal Bank of Scotland Group plc	0.24	1.77	−15.37%
Deutsche Bank AG	0.41	1.61	5.48%
UniCredito Italiano S.p.A. (CM:UCG)	0.44	1.38	7.15%
Credit Agricole SA (ENXTPA:ACA)	0.44	1.16	1.13%
Barclays plc (LSE:BARC)	0.49	1.32	15.71%
Lloyds TSB Group plc (LSE:LLOY)	0.52	1.02	21.53%
KBC Group NV (ENXTBR:KBC)	0.54	1.53	5.96%
Banca Monte dei Paschi di Siena SpA (CM:BMPS)	0.58	1.37	9.59%
Unione di Banche Italiane Scpa (CM:UBI)	0.62	1.12	8.54%
Intesa Sanpaolo SpA (CM:ISP)	0.67	0.99	8.43%
Nordea Bank AB (OM:NDA SEK)	0.81	1.17	16.25%
Credit Suisse Group (VIRTX:CSGN)	0.84	1.07	14.24%
HSBC Holdings plc (LSE:HSBA)	0.9	0.56	12.14%
UBS AG (VIRTX:UBSN)	0.99	1.31	12.93%
Svenska Handelsbanken AB (OM:SHB A)	1.02	0.72	19.58%
National Bank of Greece SA (ATSE:ETE)	1.02	1.09	21.62%
Banco Santander, S.A. (CATS:SAN)	1.03	1.23	17.52%
Banco Popular Espanol SA (CATS:POP)	1.14	0.5	19.26%
Banco Bilbao Vizcaya Argentaria (CATS:BBVA)	1.24	0.85	22.30%
Standard Chartered PLC (LSE:STAN)	1.31	0.85	16.18%
Median	**0.74**	**1.14**	**0.13585**
Average	**0.7625**	**1.131**	**0.120085**

Source: Capital IQ.

Firms with higher return on equity and lower standard deviations trade at much higher price to book ratios. The numbers in parentheses are *t*-statistics and suggest that the relationships between PBV ratios and both variables in the regression are statistically significant. The R^2 indicates the percentage of the differences in PBV ratios that is explained by the independent variables. Finally, the regression itself can be used to get predicted PBV ratios for the companies in the list.[38] Thus, the predicted PBV ratio for Deutsche Bank, based on its return on equity of 5.48% and its beta of 1.61, would be 0.47.

$$\text{Predicted PBV}_{\text{Deutsche Bank}} = 1.03 + 1.54(0.0548) - 0.40(1.61) = 0.47$$

Because the actual PBV ratio for Deutsche Bank at the time of the analysis was 0.41, this would suggest that the stock is trading close to its fundamentals, given how other banks are being priced.

pbv.xls: There is a data set online that summarizes price-to-book ratios and returns on equity by industry group in the United States for the most recent quarter.

---

[38] Both approaches described assume that the relationship between a multiple and the variables driving value are linear. Because this is not always true, we might have to run nonlinear versions of these regressions.

ps.xls: There is a data set online that summarizes price to sales ratios and margins by industry group in the United States for the most recent quarter.

3. Expanding the Range of Comparable Firms

Searching for comparable firms within the sector in which a firm operates is fairly restrictive, especially when there are relatively few firms in the sector, or when a firm operates in more than one sector. Because the definition of a comparable firm is not one that is in the same business but one that has the same growth, risk, and cash flow characteristics as the firm being analyzed, we need not restrict our choice of comparable firms to those in the same industry. A software firm should be comparable to an automobile firm, if we can control for differences in the fundamentals.

The regression introduced in the previous section allows us to control for differences on those variables that we believe cause multiples to vary across firms. Based on the variables listed in Table 12.10, we should be able to regress multiples against the variables that should affect them. It is, however, possible that the proxies that we use for risk (beta), growth (expected growth rate), and cash flow (payout) are imperfect, and that the relationship may not be linear. To deal with these limitations, we can add more variables to the regression—for example, the size of the firm may operate as a good proxy for risk—and use transformations of the variables to allow for nonlinear relationships.

We ran these regressions for multiples across publicly listed firms in the United States in January 2009 against analyst estimates of expected growth in earnings per share and other financial indicators from the most recent year.[39] The sample, which had about 7,000 firms in it, yielded the regressions reported in Table 12.13.

The first advantage of this approach over the "subjective" comparison across firms in the same sector is that it does quantify, based on actual market data, the degree to which higher growth or risk should affect the multiples. Second, by looking at all firms in the market, this approach allows us to make more meaningful comparisons of firms that operate in industries with relatively few firms. Third, it allows us to examine whether all firms in an industry are under- or overvalued by estimating their values relative to other firms in the market.

ILLUSTRATION 12.17   Applying Market Regression to Estimate Multiples—Disney

We will use the results of the market regression just summarized to estimate the appropriate value for Disney. Consider the regression for the PE ratio:

$$PE = 7.62 + 77.98 g_{EPS} + 7.67 \text{ Payout} - 5.37 \text{ beta}$$

The corresponding values for Disney are as follows:

$$\text{Expected growth rate} = 14.5\% \, (\text{analyst consensus estimate for EPS growth})$$
$$\text{Payout ratio} = 15.35\%$$
$$\text{Beta} = 0.9011$$

The estimated price earnings ratio for Disney is

$$PE = 7.62 + 77.98(0.145) + 7.67(0.1535) - 5.37(0.90) = 15.27$$

---

[39]We ran the regression both with intercepts and without intercepts. If the intercept is negative, we report the regression without the intercept.

Table 12.13   MARKET-WIDE REGRESSIONS OF MULTIPLES: U.S. COMPANIES, JANUARY 2009 (T-STATISTICS IN BRACKETS BELOW COEFFICIENTS)

Regression	R^2
$PE = 7.62 + 77.98\, g_{EPS} + 7.67\ \text{payout} - 5.37\ \text{beta}$ (8.77) (26.71) (13.09) (7.21)	28.6%
$PBV = 1.28 + 6.72\, g_{EPS} + 0.33\ \text{payout} - 1.65\ \text{beta} + 8.67\ ROE$ (10.09) (15.85) (4.95) (11.70) (38.48)	68.3%
$PS = 0.29 + 4.32\, g_{EPS} + 0.31\ \text{payout} - 0.86\ \text{beta} + 11.42\ \text{net margin}$ (2.48) (9.52) (4.58) (8.60) (35.72)	62.3%
EV/Invested capital $= 1.10 + 3.99\, g + 5.06\ ROIC - 1.35\ (\text{Debt/Capital})$ (10.23) (6.60) (20.59) (10.1)	50.1%
EV/Sales $= 1.72 + 1.94\, g + 5.58\ \text{operating margin} - 4.87\ \text{tax rate}$ (16.46) (3.32) (29.00) (18.80)	50.3%
EV/EBITDA $= 6.68 + 25.34\, g - 7.99\ \text{tax rate} - 1.59\ (\text{Debt/Capital}) - 1.837\ RIR$ (18.58) (12.35) (9.78) (3.84) (1.94)	19.3%

g_{EPS} = Expected growth rate in EPS for next five years (analyst estimates)
g = Expected growth rate in revenues for next years (if not available, use g_{EPS})
Payout = Dividends/Earnings
ROIC = Return on capital = EBIT (1 − Tax rate)/Invested capital
Invested capital = Book value of equity + Book value of debt − Cash
ROE = Net income/Book value of equity
Tax rate = Effective tax rate
Debt/Capital = Debt/(Market value of equity + Debt)
RIR = Reinvestment rate = (Cap ex − Depreciation + Chg in WC)/EBIT (1 − t)

Because Disney trades at an actual PE ratio of 9.45, it looks significantly undervalued (by almost 40%), relative to the market.

 multregr.xls: This data set summarizes the latest regression of multiples against fundamentals for the United States for the most recent quarter.

Equity as an Option

In most publicly traded firms, equity has two features. The first is that the equity investors run the firm and can choose to liquidate its assets and pay off other claim holders at any time. The second is that the liability of equity investors in some private firms, and almost all publicly traded firms, is restricted to their equity investments in these firms. This combination of the option to liquidate and limited liability allows equity to have the features of a call option. In firms with substantial debt and a significant potential for bankruptcy, the option value of equity may be in excess of the discounted cash flow value of equity.

The Payoff on Equity as an Option

The equity in a firm is a residual claim—that is, equity holders lay claim to all cash flows left after other financial claimholders (debt, preferred stock, etc.) have been satisfied. If a firm is liquidated, the same principle applies; equity investors receive the cash that is left in the firm after all outstanding debt and other financial claims have been paid off. With limited liability, if the value of the firm is less than the value of the outstanding debt, equity investors cannot lose more than their investment in the firm. The payoff to equity investors on liquidation can therefore be written as

$$\text{Payoff to equity on liquidation} \quad \begin{aligned} &= V - D & \text{if } V > D \\ &= 0 & \text{if } V \le D \end{aligned}$$

where

$V = $ Liquidation value of the firm

$D = $ Face value of the outstanding debt and other external claims

Equity can thus be viewed as a call option on the assets of the firm such that exercising the option requires that the firm be liquidated and that the face value of the debt (which corresponds to the exercise price) be paid off. The firm is the underlying asset, and the option expires when the debt comes due. The payoffs are shown in Figure 12.7:

Figure 12.7   Payoff on Equity as Option on a Firm

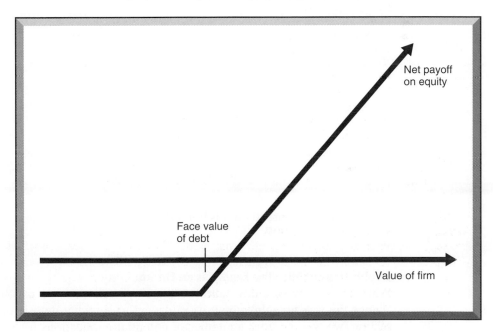

ILLUSTRATION 12.18   Valuing Equity as an Option

Assume that we are valuing the equity in a firm whose assets are currently valued at $100 million; the standard deviation in this asset value is 40%. The face value of debt is $80 million (it is zero-coupon debt with ten years left to maturity). The ten-year treasury bond rate is 10%. We can value equity as a call option on the firm using the following inputs for the option pricing model.

$$\text{Value of the underlying asset} = S = \text{Value of the firm} = \$100 \text{ million}$$
$$\text{Exercise price} = K = \text{Face value of outstanding debt} = \$80 \text{ million}$$
$$\text{Life of the option} = t = \text{Life of zero-coupon debt} = 10 \text{ years}$$
$$\text{Variance in the value of the underlying asset} = \sigma^2$$
$$= \text{Variance in firm value} = 0.16$$
$$\text{Riskless rate} = r = \text{Treasury bond rate corresponding to option life} = 10\%$$

Based upon these inputs, the Black–Scholes model provides the following value for the call.

$$d_1 = 1.5994 \qquad\qquad N(d_1) = 0.9451$$
$$d_2 = 0.3345 \qquad\qquad N(d_2) = 0.6310$$
$$\text{Value of the call} = 100(0.9451) - 80e^{-(0.10)(10)}(0.6310) = \$75.94 \text{ million}$$

Since the call value represents the value of equity and the firm value is $100 million, the estimated value of the outstanding debt can be calculated.

$$\text{Value of the outstanding debt} = \$100 - \$75.94 = \$24.06 \text{ million}$$

Since the debt is a ten-year zero-coupon bond, the market interest rate on the bond can be calculated.

$$\text{Interest rate on debt} = \left(\frac{\$80}{\$24.06}\right)^{\frac{1}{10}} - 1 = 12.77\%$$

Thus, the default spread on this bond should be 2.77%.

Implications of Viewing Equity as an Option

When the equity in a firm takes on the characteristics of a call option, we have to change the way we think about its value and about what determines its value. In this section, we will consider a number of potential implications for equity investors and bondholders in the firm.

When Will Equity Be Worthless?

In discounted cash flow valuation, we argue that equity is worthless if what we own (the value of the assets of the firm) is less than what we owe. The first implication of viewing equity as a call option is that equity will have value, even if the value of the firm falls well below the face value of the outstanding debt. While the firm will be viewed as troubled by investors, accountants, and analysts, its equity is not worthless. In fact, just as deep out-of-the-money traded call options command value because of the possibility that the value of the underlying asset may increase above the strike price in the remaining lifetime of the option, equity commands value because of the time premium on the option (the time until the bonds mature and come due) and the possibility that the value of the assets may increase above the face value of the bonds before they come due.

ILLUSTRATION 12.19   Firm Value and Equity Value

Revisiting the preceding example, assume that the value of the firm drops to $50 million, below the face value of the outstanding debt ($80 million). Assume that all the other inputs remain unchanged. The parameters of equity as a call option are as follows:

$$\text{Value of the underlying asset} = S = \text{Value of the firm} = \$50 \text{ million}$$
$$\text{Exercise price} = K = \text{Face value of outstanding debt} = \$80 \text{ million}$$
$$\text{Life of the option} = t = \text{Life of zero-coupon debt} = 10 \text{ years}$$
$$\text{Variance in the value of the underlying asset} = \sigma^2$$
$$= \text{Variance in firm value} = 0.16$$
$$\text{Riskless rate} = r = \text{Treasury bond rate corresponding to option life} = 10\%$$

Based upon these inputs, the Black–Scholes model provides the following value for the call.

$$d_1 = 1.0515 \qquad\qquad N(d_1) = 0.8534$$
$$d_2 = -0.2135 \qquad\qquad N(d_2) = 0.4155$$
$$\text{Value of the call (equity)} = 50(0.8534) - 80 \exp^{(-0.10)(10)}(0.4155) = \$30.44 \text{ million}$$
$$\text{Value of the bond} = \$50 - \$30.44 = \$19.56 \text{ million}$$

As we can see, the equity in this firm retains value, because of the option characteristics of equity. In fact, equity continues to have value in this example even if the firm value drops to $10 million or below.

Increasing Risk Can Increase Equity Value

In traditional discounted cash flow valuation, higher risk almost always translates into lower value for equity investors. When equity takes on the characteristics of a call option, we should not expect this relationship to continue to hold. Risk can become our ally when we are equity investors in a troubled, highly levered firm. In essence, we have little to lose and much to gain from swings in firm value.

ILLUSTRATION 12.20   Equity Value and Volatility

Let us revisit the valuation in Illustration 12.8. The value of the equity is a function of the variance in firm value, which we assumed to be 40%. If we change this variance, holding all else constant, the value of the equity will change as evidenced in Figure 12.8.

Figure 12.8   Equity Value and Standard Deviation in Firm Value

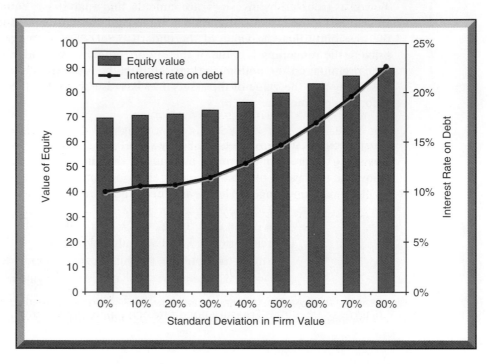

Note that the value of equity increases as the standard deviation increases if we hold firm value constant. The interest rate on debt also increases as the standard deviation increases.

Probability of Default and Default Spreads

One of the more interesting pieces of output from the option pricing model is the risk-neutral probability of default that we can obtain for the firm. In the Black–Scholes model, we can estimate this value from $N(d2)$, which is the risk-neutral probability that $S > K$, which in this model is the probability that the value of the firm's asset will exceed the face value of the debt.

$$\text{Risk-neutral probability of default} = 1 - N(d2)$$

In addition, the interest rate from the debt allows us to estimate the appropriate default spread to charge on bonds.

You can see the potential in applying this model to bank loan portfolios both to extract the probability of default and to measure whether you are charging an interest rate that is high enough on the debt. In fact, there are commercial services that use fairly sophisticated option-pricing models to estimate both values for firms.

ILLUSTRATION 12.21   Probabilities of Default and Default Spreads

We return to Illustration 12.8 and estimate the probability of default as $N(d2)$ and the default spread, measured as the difference between the interest rate on a firm's debt and the risk-free rate, as a function of the variance. These values are graphed in Figure 12.9.

Note that the probability of default climbs very quickly as the standard deviation in firm value increases—and the default spread follows it along.

Estimating the Value of Equity as an Option

The examples we have used thus far to illustrate the application of option pricing to value equity have included some simplifying assumptions. Among them are the following:

- There are only two claimholders in the firm—debt and equity.
- There is only one issue of debt outstanding, and it can be retired at face value.
- The debt has a zero-coupon and no special features (convertibility, put clauses, etc.).
- The value of the firm and the variance in that value can be estimated.

Each of these assumptions is made for a reason. First, by restricting the claimholders to just debt and equity, we make the problem more tractable; introducing other

Figure 12.9   Risk Neutral Probability of Default and Default Spreads

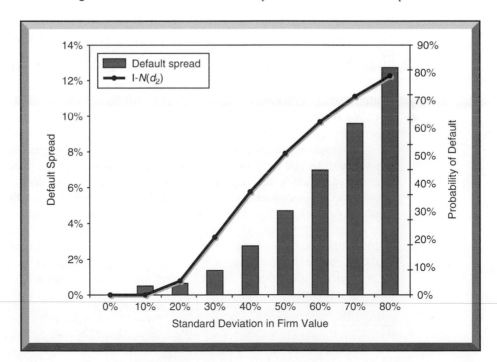

claimholders such as preferred stock makes it more difficult to arrive at a result (although not impossible). Second, by assuming only one zero-coupon debt issue that can be retired at face value any time prior to maturity, we align the features of the debt more closely to the features of the strike price on a standard option. Third, if the debt is coupon debt, or more than one debt issue is outstanding, the equity investors can be forced to exercise (liquidate the firm) at these earlier coupon dates if they do not have the cash flows to meet their coupon obligations.

Finally, knowing the value of the firm and the variance in that value makes the option pricing possible, but it also raises an interesting question about the usefulness of option pricing in equity valuation. If the bonds of the firm are publicly traded, the market value of the debt can be subtracted from the value of the firm to obtain the value of equity much more directly. The option pricing approach does have its advantages, however. Specifically, when the debt of a firm is not publicly traded, option pricing theory can provide an estimate of value for the equity in the firm. Even when the debt is publicly traded, the bonds may not be correctly valued, and the option pricing framework can be useful in evaluating the values of debt and equity. Finally, relating the values of debt and equity to the variance in firm value provides some insight into the redistributive effects of actions taken by the firm.

Inputs for Valuing Equity as an Option
Since most firms do not fall into the neat framework developed above (such as having only one zero-coupon bond outstanding), we have to make some compromises to use this model in valuation.

Value of the Firm
We can obtain the value of the firm in one of four ways. In the first, we cumulate the market values of outstanding debt and equity, assuming that all debt and equity are traded, to obtain firm value. The option pricing model then reallocates the firm value between debt and equity. This approach, while simple, is internally inconsistent. We start with one set of market values for debt and equity and, using the option pricing model, end up with entirely different values for each.

In the second, we estimate the market values of the assets of the firm by discounting expected cash flows at the cost of capital. The one consideration that we need to keep in mind is that the value of the firm in an option pricing model should be the value obtained on liquidation. This may be less than the total firm value, which includes expected future investments, and it may also be reduced to reflect the cost of liquidation. If we estimate the firm value using a discounted cash flow model, then this would suggest that only existing investments[40] should be considered while estimating firm value.

In the third approach, we estimate a multiple of revenues or EBITDA by looking at healthy firms in the same business and apply this multiple to the revenues or EBITDA of the firm we are valuing. Implicitly, we are assuming that a potential buyer, in the event of liquidation, will pay this value.

---

[40]Technically, this can be done by putting the firm into stable growth and valuing it as a stable growth firm, where reinvestments are used to either preserve or augment existing assets.

We can use the fourth approach for firms that have separable assets that are individually traded. Here, we cumulate the value of the market values of the assets to arrive at firm value. For example, we can value a troubled real estate firm that owns five properties by valuing each property separately and then aggregating the values.

Variance in Firm value

We can obtain the variance in firm value directly if both stocks and bonds in the firm are traded. Defining σ_e^2 as the variance in the stock price and σ_d^2 as the variance in the bond price, w_e as the market-value weight of equity and w_d as the market-value weight of debt, we can write the variance in firm value as[41]

$$\sigma_{firm}^2 = w_e^2\,\sigma_e^2 + w_d^2\,\sigma_d^2 + 2w_e\,w_d\,\rho_{ed}\,\sigma_e\,\sigma_d$$

where ρ_{ed} is the correlation between the stock and the bond prices. When the bonds of the firm are not traded, we can use the variance of similarly rated bonds as the estimate of σ_d^2 and the correlation between similarly rated bonds and the firm's stock as the estimate of ρ_{ed}.

When companies get into financial trouble, this approach can yield misleading results as both its stock prices and its bond prices become more volatile. An alternative that often yields more reliable estimates is to use the average variance in firm value for other firms in the sector. Thus, the value of equity in a deeply troubled steel company can be estimated using the average variance in firm value of all traded steel companies.

Maturity of the Debt

Most firms have more than one debt issue on their books, and much of the debt comes with coupons. Since the option pricing model allows for only one input for the time to expiration, we have to convert these multiple bonds issues and coupon payments into one equivalent zero-coupon bond.

- One solution, which takes into account both the coupon payments and the maturity of the bonds, is to estimate the duration of each debt issue and calculate a face value–weighted average of the durations of the different issues. This value-weighted duration is then used as a measure of the time to expiration of the option.

- An approximation is to use the face-value weighted maturity of the debt as the maturity of the zero-coupon bond in the option pricing model.

Face Value of Debt

When a distressed firm has multiple debt issues outstanding, we have three choices when it comes to what we use as the face value of debt:

1. We could add up the principal due on all of the debt of the firm and consider it to be the face value of the hypothetical zero-coupon bond that we assume that the firm has issued. The limitation of this approach is that it will understate what the firm will truly have to pay out over the life of the debt, since there will be coupon payments and interest payments during the period.

---

[41] This is an extension of the variance formula for a two-asset portfolio.

2. At the other extreme, we could add the expected interest and coupon payments that will come due on the debt to the principal payments to come up with a cumulated face value of debt. Since the interest payments occur in the near years and the principal payments are due only when the debt comes due, we are mixing cash flows up at different points in time when we do this. This is, however, the simplest approach to dealing with intermediate interest payments coming due.

3. We can consider only the principal due on the debt as the face value of the debt, and the interest payments each year, specified as a percent of firm value, can take the place of the dividend yield in the option pricing model. In effect, each year that the firm remains in existence, we would expect to see the value of the firm decline by the expected payments on the debt.

ILLUSTRATION 12.22   Valuing Equity as an Option—Aracruz, 2009

For Aracruz, 2008 was a very bad year, with losses from derivatives in the billions leading the firm to the brink of disaster. In June 2009, the firm owed in excess of R\$9.8 billion in debt and had operating income of only R\$574 million. Even if we assume that the firm reverts back to its average profitability between 2003 and 2007, the firm will generate pretax operating income of only R\$1.007 billion (see Chapter 8). Assuming a perpetual growth rate of 7% growth rate (in nominal R\$) and a return on capital of 15% and using the cost of capital of 18.37% (also in nominal R\$, estimated in Chapter 4) allow us to estimate the value of the operating assets:

$$\text{Value of operating assets} = \frac{\text{EBIT}(1-t)(1-\frac{g}{ROC})(1+g)}{(\text{Cost of capital} - g)}$$

$$= \frac{1007(1-0.34)\left(1-\frac{0.07}{0.15}\right)(1.07)}{(0.1837-0.07)} = \text{R\$5,807 million}$$

Since this is well below the face value of the debt, it would be difficult to justify a positive value for equity, using an intrinsic valuation model.

We can try to estimate the value of Aracruz, as an equity option, assuming that the debt has a weighted average duration of three years and using the industry average standard deviation of 34% as the standard deviation in firm value.[42] In summary, the inputs to the option pricing model are as follows:

$$\text{Value of the underlying asset} = S = \text{Value of the firm} = \text{R\$5,807 million}$$

$$\text{Exercise price} = K = \text{Face value of outstanding debt} = \text{R\$9,835 million}$$

$$\text{Life of the option} = t = \text{Weighted average duration of debt} = 3 \text{ years}$$
$$\text{Variance in the value of the underlying asset} = \sigma^2$$
$$= \text{Variance in firm value} = (0.34)^2 = 0.115$$
$$\text{Risk less rate} = r = \text{Risk free corresponding to option life} = 6.5\%$$

---

[42] This is the industry average for firm value variances of paper and pulp companies.

Based upon these inputs, we estimate the following value for the call:

$$d_1 = 0.2691 \qquad\qquad N(d_1) = 0.3939$$
$$d_2 = -0.8580 \qquad\qquad N(d_2) = 0.1954$$
$$\text{Value of the call} = 5,807(0.3939) - 9,835e^{(-0.065)(3)}(0.1954) = \text{R\$706 million}$$

If we treat this as the value of equity, it yields a value per share of R\$1.20 a share, which while much lower than the stock price of R\$15.14 per share, is still greater than the value of zero we would have estimated with an intrinsic valuation model.

The option pricing framework, in addition to yielding a value for Aracruz equity, yields some valuable insight into the drivers of value for this equity. While it is certainly important that the firm try to bring costs under control and increase operating margins, the two most critical variables determining equity value are the duration of the debt and the variance in firm value. Any action that increases (decreases) the debt duration will have a positive (negative) effect on equity value. Thus, the results of debt renegotiation talks that were ongoing at the time of this analysis could have a significant effect on value.

RECONCILING DIFFERENT VALUATIONS

The standard approaches to valuation—discounted cash flow valuation and relative valuation—yield different values for Disney.[43] In fact, Disney is undervalued using a discounted cash flow model but is closer to being fairly valued using relative valuation models. Even within relative valuation, we arrive at different estimates of value, depending on which multiple we use and the firms on which we based the relative valuation.

The differences in value between discounted cash flow valuation and relative valuation come from different views of market efficiency—or, put more precisely, market inefficiency. In discounted cash flow valuation, we assume that markets make mistakes, that they correct these mistakes over time, and that these mistakes can often occur across entire sectors or even the entire market. In relative valuation, we assume that although markets make mistakes on individual stocks, they are correct on average. In other words, when we value Disney relative to other entertainment companies, we are assuming that the market has priced these companies correctly, on average, even though it might have made mistakes in pricing each of them individually. Thus, a stock may be overvalued on a discounted cash flow basis but undervalued on a relative basis, if the firms used in the relative valuation are all overpriced by the market. The reverse would occur if an entire sector or market were underpriced.

To conclude, we suggest the following broad guidelines on gauging value using different approaches:

- Discounted cash flow models are built on the implicit assumption of long time horizons, giving markets time to correct their errors.

- When using relative valuation, it is dangerous to base valuations on multiples where the differences across firms cannot be explained well using financial

---

[43]S. Kaplan and R. Ruback, "The Valuation of Cash Flow Forecasts: An Empirical Analysis," *Journal of Finance* 50:1059–1093. They examine valuations in acquisitions and find that discounted cash flow models better explain prices paid than relative valuation models do.

fundamentals—growth, risk, and cash flow patterns. One of the advantages of using the regression approach described in the later part of this chapter is that the R^2 and t-statistics from the regressions yield a tangible estimate of the strength (or weakness) of this relationship.

12.12 VALUING AN IPO

If you were an investment banker pricing an IPO, would you primarily use discounted cash flow valuation, relative valuation, or a combination of the two?

a. Relative valuation, because the buyers of the IPO will look at comparables
b. Discounted cash flow valuation, because it reflects intrinsic value
c. The higher of the two values, because it is my job to get the highest price I can for my client
d. None of the above

Explain.

CONCLUSION

There are three basic approaches to valuation. The first is discounted cash flow valuation, in which the value of any asset is estimated by computing the present value of the expected cash flows on it. The actual process of estimation, in either case, generally requires four inputs:

1. The length of the period for which a firm or asset can be expected to generate growth greater than the stable growth rate (which is constrained to be close to the growth rate of the economy in which the firm operates)
2. The cash flows during the high-growth period
3. The terminal value at the end of the high-growth period
4. A discount rate

The expected growth potential will vary across firms: some firms are already growing at a stable growth rate, and for others it is expected, at least, that high growth will last for some period into the future. We can value the operating assets of a firm by discounting cash flows before debt payments but after reinvestment at the cost of capital. Adding the value of cash and nonoperating assets give us firm value, and subtracting debt yields the value of equity. We can also value equity directly by discounting cash flows after debt payments and reinvestment needs at the cost of equity.

The second approach to valuation is relative valuation, where the value of any asset is estimated by looking at how similar assets are priced in the market. The key steps in this approach are defining comparable firms or assets and choosing a standardized measure of value (usually value as a multiple of earnings, cash flows, or book value) to compare the firms. To compare multiples across companies, we have to control for differences in growth, risk, and cash flows, just as we would have in discounted cash flow valuation.

In the final approach to valuation, we assume that equity investors own the option to liquidate the firm's assets and claim the difference between asset value and debt outstanding for themselves. This approach works for highly levered and distressed firms and is the only one where equity value increases as risk increases.

LIVE CASE STUDY

VALUATION

Objective: To value your firm, based on its existing management, and your expectations for the future.

<table>
<tr><td>Key Questions</td><td>

- What type of cash flow (dividends, FCFE, or FCFF) would you choose to discount for this firm?
- What growth pattern would you pick for this firm? How long will high growth and excess returns last?
- When will your firm be in stable growth, and what will your firm look like when it reaches stable growth?
- What is your estimate of value of equity in this firm? How does this compare to the market value?
</td></tr>
<tr><td>Framework for Analysis</td><td>

1. Cash Flow Estimation
- What is this firm's accounting operating income? Would you adjust it for your valuation?
- What is your firm's effective tax rate? What is its marginal tax rate? Which would you use in your valuation?
- How much did your firm reinvest last year in internal investments, acquisitions, R&D, and working capital?

2. Growth Pattern Choice
- How fast have this company's earnings grown historically?
- How quickly do analysts expect this company's earnings to grow in the future?
- What do the fundamentals suggest about earnings growth at this company? (How much is being reinvested, and at what rate of return?)
- If there is anticipated high growth with excess returns, what are the barriers to entry that will allow these excess returns to continue (and for how long)?

3. Valuation
- What is the value of the operating assets of the firm, based on a discounted cash flow model?
- Does the firm have cash and nonoperating assets, and what are their values?
- Are there equity options outstanding (management options, convertible bonds)? If so, how much are they worth? If not, why not?
- What is the value of equity per share?

4. Relative Valuation
- What multiple would you use to value the firm or its equity?
</td></tr>
</table>

- What industry does the firm belong to, and what are the comparable firms?
- How does your firm's valuation (in multiple terms) compare to those of the other firms in the industry?
- What value would you assign your firm (or its equity), given how comparable firms are valued?

Getting Information for Valuation

Most of the information that you need for valuation comes from your current or past financial statements. You will also need a beta and a debt ratio (see the risk and return section for both) to estimate the FCFE. You can get analyst estimates of growth in several sources, including Zack's and I/B/E/S.

Online sources of information
www.stern.nyu.edu/~adamodar/cfin2E/project/data.htm

PROBLEMS AND QUESTIONS

In the problems below, you can use a risk premium of 5.5% and a tax rate of 40% if none is specified.

1. Vernon Enterprises has current after-tax operating income of $100 million and a cost of capital of 10%. The firm earns a return on capital equal to its cost of capital.
   a. Assume that the firm is in stable growth, growing 5% a year forever; estimate the firm's reinvestment rate.
   b. Given this reinvestment rate, estimate the value of the firm.
   c. What is the value of the firm, if you assume a zero reinvestment rate and no growth?

2. Assume in the previous question with Vernon Enterprises that the firm will earn a return on capital of 15% in perpetuity.
   a. Assume that the firm is in stable growth, growing 5% a year forever; estimate the firm's reinvestment rate.
   b. Given this reinvestment rate, estimate the value of the firm.

3. Cello is a manufacturer of pianos. It earned an after-tax return on capital of 10% last year and expects to maintain this next year. If the current year's after-tax operating income is $100 million and the firm reinvests 50% of this income back, estimate the FCFF next year. (After-tax operating income = EBIT $(1 − t)$.)

4. Cell Phone is a cellular firm that reported net income of $50 million in the most recent financial year. The firm had $1 billion in debt, on which it reported interest expenses of $100 million in the most recent financial year. The firm had depreciation of $100 million for the year, and capital expenditures were 200% of depreciation. The firm has a cost of capital of 11%. Assuming that there is no working capital requirement, and using a constant growth rate of 4% in perpetuity, estimate the value of the firm.

5. Netsoft is a company that manufactures networking software. In the current year, the firm reported operating earnings, before interest and taxes, of $200 million (operating earnings does not include interest income), and these earnings are expected to grow 4% a year in perpetuity. In addition, the firm has a cash balance of $250 million on which it earned interest income of $20 million. The unlevered beta for other networking software firm is 1.2, and these firms have on average cash balances of 10% of firm value. If Netsoft has a debt ratio of 15%, a tax rate of 40%, a return on capital of 10% on operating assets, and a cost of debt of 10%, estimate the value of the firm. (The risk-free rate is 6%, and you can assume a market risk premium of 5.5%.)

6. Gemco Jewelers earned $5 million in after-tax operating income in the most recent year. The firm also had capital expenditures of $4 million and depreciation of $2 million during the year, and the noncash working capital at the end of the year was $10 million.
   a. Assuming that the firm's operating income will grow 20% next year, and that all other items (capital expenditures, depreciation, and noncash working capital) will grow at the same rate, estimate the FCFF next year.
   b. If the firm can grow at 20% for the next five years, estimate the present value of the FCFF over that period. You can assume a cost of capital of 12%.
   c. After year 5, the firm's capital expenditures will decline to 125% of revenues, and the growth rate will drop to 5% (in both operating income and noncash working capital). In addition, the cost of capital will decline to 10%. Estimate the terminal value of the firm at the end of year 5.
   d. Estimate the total value of the operating assets of the firm.

7. Now assume that Gemco Jewelers has $10 million in cash and nonoperating assets and that the firm has $15 million in outstanding debt.
   a. Estimate the value of equity in the firm.
   b. If the firm has 5 million shares outstanding, estimate the value of equity per share.
   c. How would your answer to b change if you learn that the firm has 1 million options outstanding, with an exercise price of $5 and five years to maturity? (The estimated value per option is $7.)

8. Union Pacific Railroad reported net income of $770 million after interest expenses of $320 million

in a recent financial year. (The corporate tax rate was 36%.) It reported depreciation of $960 million in that year, and capital spending was $1.2 billion. The firm also had $4 billion in debt outstanding on the books, was rated AA (carrying a yield to maturity of 8%), and was trading at par (up from $3.8 billion at the end of the previous year). The beta of the stock is 1.05, and there were 200 million shares outstanding (trading at $60 per share), with a book value of $5 billion. Union Pacific paid 40% of its earnings as dividends, and working capital requirements are negligible. (The Treasury bond rate is 7%.)

   a. Estimate the FCFF for the most recent financial year.

   b. Estimate the value of the firm now.

   c. Estimate the value of equity and the value per share now.

9. Lockheed, one of the largest defense contractors in the United States, reported EBITDA of $1,290 million in a recent financial year prior to interest expenses of $215 million and depreciation charges of $400 million. Capital expenditures amounted to $450 million during the year, and working capital was 7% of revenues (which were $13,500 million). The firm had debt outstanding of $3.068 billion (in book value terms) trading at a market value of $3.2 billion and yielding a pretax interest rate of 8%. There were 62 million shares outstanding trading at $64 per share, and the most recent beta is 1.10. The tax rate for the firm is 40%. (The Treasury bond rate is 7%.) The firm expects revenues, earnings, capital expenditures, and depreciation to grow at 9.5% a year for the next five years, after which the growth rate is expected to drop to 4%. (Even though this is unrealistic, you can assume that capital spending will offset depreciation in the stable-growth period.) The company also plans to lower its debt/equity ratio to 50% for the steady state (which will result in the pretax interest rate dropping to 7.5%).

   a. Estimate the value of the firm.

   b. Estimate the value of the equity in the firm and the value per share.

10. In the face of disappointing earnings results and increasingly assertive institutional stockholders, Eastman Kodak was considering the sale of its health division, which earned $560 million in EBIT in the most recent year on revenues of $5.285 billion. The expected growth in earnings was expected to moderate to 6% for the next five years, and to 4% after that. Capital expenditures in the health division amounted to $420 million in the most recent year, whereas depreciation was $350 million. Both are expected to grow 4% a year in the long run. Working capital requirements are negligible. The average beta of firms competing with Eastman Kodak's health division is 1.15. Although Eastman Kodak has a debt ratio (D/[D + E]) of 50%, the health division can sustain a debt ratio (D/[D + E]) of only 20%, which is similar to the average debt ratio of firms competing in the health sector. At this level of debt, the health division can expect to pay 7.5% on its debt, before taxes. (The tax rate is 40%, and the Treasury bond rate is 7%.)

   a. Estimate the cost of capital for the division.

   b. Estimate the value of the division.

11. You have been asked to value Alcoa and have come up with the following inputs.

- The stock has a beta of 0.90, estimated over the last five years. During this period, the firm had an average debt/equity ratio of 20% and an average cash balance of 15%.

- The firm's current market value of equity is 1.6 billion and its current market value of debt is $800 million. The current cash balance is $500 million.

- The firm earned earnings before interest and taxes of $450 million, which includes the interest income on the current cash balance of $50 million. The firm's tax rate is 40%.

- The firm is in stable growth, and its earnings from operations are expected to grow 5% a year. The net capital expenditures next year are expected to be $90 million.

Estimate the value of the noncash assets of the firm, its total value, and the value of its equity.

12. You are analyzing a valuation done on a stable firm by a well-known analyst. Based on the expected FCFF next year of $30 million, and an expected growth rate of 5%, the analyst has estimated a value of $750 million. However, he has made the mistake of using the book values of debt and equity in his calculation. Although you do not know the book value weights he used, you know that the firm has a cost of equity of 12% and an after-tax cost of debt of 6%. You also know that the market

value of equity is three times the book value of equity, and that the market value of debt is equal to the book value of debt. Estimate the correct value for the firm.

13. You have been asked to value Office Help, a private firm providing office support services in the New York area.

- The firm reported pretax operating income of $10 million in its most recent financial year on revenues of $100 million. In the most recent financial year, you note that the owners of the business did not pay themselves a salary. You believe that a fair salary for their services would be $1.5 million a year.

- The cost of capital for comparable firms that are publicly traded is 9%. (You can assume that this firm will have similar leverage and cost of capital.)

- The firm is in stable growth and expects to grow 5% a year in perpetuity. The tax rate is 40%.

The average illiquidity discount applied to private firms is 30%, but you have run a regression and arrived at the following estimate for the discount:

$$\text{Illiquidity discount} = 0.30 - 0.04$$
$$(\ln [\text{Revenues in millions}])$$

Estimate the value of Office Help for sale in a private transaction (to an individual).

14. National City, a bank holding company, reported earnings per share of $2.40 and paid dividends per share of $1.06. The earnings had grown 7.5% a year over the prior five years and were expected to grow 5% a year in the long run. The stock had a beta of 1.05 and traded for ten times earnings. The Treasury bond rate was 7%.

a. Estimate the P/E ratio for National City.

b. What long-term growth rate is implied in the firm's current PE ratio?

15. The following were the P/E ratios of firms in the aerospace/defense industry with additional data on expected growth and risk:

a. Estimate the average and median P/E ratios. What, if anything, would these averages tell you?

b. An analyst concludes that Thiokol is undervalued because its P/E ratio is lower than the industry average. Under what conditions is

this statement true? Would you agree with it in this case?

c. Using the PEG ratio, assess whether Thiokol is undervalued. What are you assuming about the relationship between value and growth when you use PEG ratios?

d. Using a regression, control for differences across firms on risk, growth, and payout. Specify how you would use this regression to spot under- and overvalued stocks. What are the limitations of this approach?

	P/E Ratio	Expected Growth	Beta	Payout
Boeing	17.3	3.5%	1.10	28%
General Dynamics	15.5	11.5%	1.25	40%
General Motors–Hughes	16.5	13.0%	0.85	41%
Grumman	11.4	10.5%	0.80	37%
Lockheed	10.2	9.5%	0.85	37%
Logicon	12.4	14.0%	0.85	11%
Loral	13.3	16.5%	0.75	23%
Martin Marietta	11.0	8.0%	0.85	22%
McDonnell Douglas	22.6	13.0%	1.15	37%
Northrop	9.5	9.0%	1.05	47%
Raytheon	12.1	9.5%	0.75	28%
Rockwell	13.9	11.5%	1.00	38%
Thiokol	8.7	5.5%	0.95	15%
United Industrial	10.4	4.5%	0.70	50%

16. NCH, which markets cleaning chemicals, insecticides, and other products, paid dividends of $2.00 per share on earnings of $4.00 per share. The book value of equity per share was $40.00, and earnings are expected to grow 5% a year in the long term. The stock has a beta of 0.85, and sells for $60 per share. The Treasury bond rate is 7%.

a. Based on these inputs, estimate the price/book value ratio for NCH.

b. How much would the return on equity have to increase to justify the price/book value ratio at which NCH sells for currently?

17. You are trying to estimate a price per share on an IPO of a company involved in environmental waste disposal. The company has a book value per share of $20 and earned $3.50 per share in the most recent time period. Although it does not

pay dividends, the capital expenditures per share were $2.50 higher than depreciation per share in the most recent period, and the firm uses no debt financing. Analysts project that earnings for the company will grow 25% a year for the next five years. You have data on other companies in the environment waste disposal business:

	Price	BV/ Share	EPS	DPS	Beta	Exp. Growth
Air & Water	$9.60	$8.48	$0.40	$0.00	1.65	10.5%
Allwaste	$5.40	$3.10	$0.25	$0.00	1.10	18.5%
Browning Ferris	$29.00	$11.50	$1.45	$0.68	1.25	11.0%
Chemical Waste	$9.40	$3.75	$0.45	$0.15	1.15	2.5%
Groundwater	$15.00	$14.45	$0.65	$0.00	1.00	3.0%
Int'l Tech.	$3.30	$3.35	$0.16	$0.00	1.10	11.0%
Ionics	$48.00	$31.00	$2.20	$0.00	1.00	14.5%
Laidlaw	$6.30	$5.85	$0.40	$0.12	1.15	8.5%
OHM	$16.00	$5.65	$0.60	$0.00	1.15	9.5%
Rollins	$5.10	$3.65	$0.05	$0.00	1.30	1.0%
Safety-Kleen	$14.00	$9.25	$0.80	$0.36	1.15	6.5%

The average debt/equity ratio of these firms is 20%, and the tax rate is 40%.

a. Estimate the average price/book value ratio for these comparable firms. Would you use this average P/BV ratio to price the IPO?

b. What subjective adjustments would you make to the price/book value ratio for this firm, and why?

18. Longs Drug, a large U.S. drugstore chain operating primarily in northern California, had sales per share of $122 on which it reported earnings per share of $2.45 and paid a dividend per share of $1.12. The company is expected to grow 6% in the long run, and has a beta of 0.90. The current Treasury bond rate is 7%.

a. Estimate the appropriate price/sales multiple for Longs Drug.

b. The stock is currently trading for $34 per share. Assuming the growth rate is estimated correctly, what would the profit margin need to be to justify this price per share?

19. You have been asked to assess whether Walgreen's, a drugstore chain, is correctly priced relative to its competitors in the drugstore industry. The following are the price/sales ratios, profit margins, and other relative details of the firms in the drugstore industry.

	P/S Ratio	Profit Margin	Payout	Expected Growth	Beta
Arbor Drugs	0.42	3.40%	18%	14.0%	1.05
Big B	0.30	1.90%	14%	23.5%	0.70
Drug Emporium	0.10	0.60%	0%	27.5%	0.90
Fay's	0.15	1.30%	37%	11.5%	0.90
Genovese	0.18	1.70%	26%	10.5%	0.80
Longs Drug	0.30	2.00%	46%	6.0%	0.90
Perry Drugs	0.12	1.30%	0%	12.5%	1.10
Rite-Aid	0.33	3.20%	37%	10.5%	0.90
Walgreen's	0.60	2.70%	31%	13.5%	1.15

Based entirely on a subjective analysis, do you think that Walgreen's is overpriced because its price/sales ratio is the highest in the industry? If not, how would you rationalize its value?

20. Time Warner is considering a sale of its publishing division. The division had earnings EBITDA of $550 million in the most recent year (depreciation was $150 million), growing at an estimated 5% a year (you can assume that depreciation grows at the same rate). The return on capital in the division is 15%, and the corporate tax rate is 40%. If the cost of capital for the division is 9%, estimate the following:

a. Value/FCFF multiple

b. Value/EBIT multiple

c. Value/EBITDA multiple

APPENDIX 1

BASIC STATISTICS

The problem that we face in financial analysis today is not having too little information, but having too much. Making sense of large amounts of often contradictory information is part of what we are called on to do when analyzing companies. Basic statistics can make this job easier. In this appendix, we consider the most fundamental tools available in data analysis.

SUMMARIZING DATA

Large amounts of data are often compressed into more easily assimilated summaries that provide the user with a sense of the content without overwhelming him or her with too many numbers. There a number of ways data can be presented. We will consider two here—one is to present the data in a distribution, and the other is to provide summary statistics that capture key aspects of the data.

Data Distributions

When presented with thousands of pieces of information, you can break the numbers down into individual values (or ranges of values) and indicate the number of individual data items that take on each value or range of values. This is called a *frequency distribution*. If the data can only take on specific values, as is the case when we record the number of goals scored in a soccer game, you get a *discrete distribution*. When the data can take on any value within the range, as is the case with income or market capitalization, it is called a *continuous distribution*.

The advantages of presenting the data in a distribution are twofold. For one thing, you can summarize even the largest data sets into one distribution and get a measure of what values occur most frequently and the range of high and low values. The second is that the distribution can resemble one of the many common ones about which we know a great deal in statistics. Consider, for instance, the distribution that we tend to draw on the most in analysis: the normal distribution, illustrated in Figure A1.1.

A normal distribution is symmetric; it has a peak centered around the middle of the distribution and tails that are not fat and that stretch to include infinite positive or negative values. Not all distributions are symmetric, though. Some are weighted toward extreme positive values (positively skewed), and some toward extreme negative values (negatively skewed). Figure A1.2 illustrates positively and negatively skewed distributions.

Summary Statistics

The simplest way to measure the key characteristics of a data set is to estimate the summary statistics for the data. For a data series, $X_1, X_2, X_3, \ldots X_n$, where n is the

Figure A1.1   Normal Distribution

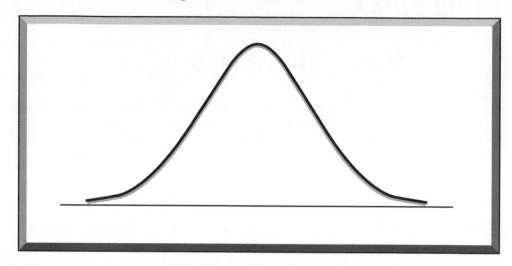

Figure A1.2   Skewed Distributions

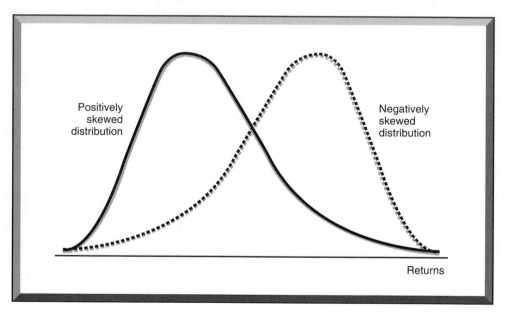

number of observations in the series, the most widely used summary statistics are as follows:

- The mean (μ), which is the average of all of the observations in the data series.

$$Mean = \mu_X = \frac{\sum\limits_{j=1}^{j=n} X_j}{n}$$

- The median, which is the midpoint of the series; half the data in the series is higher than the median, and half is lower.
- The variance, which is a measure of the spread in the distribution around the mean and is calculated by first summing up the squared deviations from the mean, and then dividing by either the number of observations (if the data represent the entire population) or by this number, reduced by 1 (if the data represent a sample).

$$\text{Variance} = \sigma_X^2 = \frac{\sum_{j=1}^{j=n} (X_j - \mu_x)^2}{n-1}$$

The standard deviation is the square root of the variance.

The mean and the standard deviation are the called the first two moments of any data distribution. A normal distribution can be entirely described by just these two moments; in other words, the mean and the standard deviation of a normal distribution suffice to characterize it completely. If a distribution is not symmetric, the skewness is the third moment that describes both the direction and the magnitude of the asymmetry, and the kurtosis (the fourth moment) measures the fatness of the tails of the distribution relative to a normal distribution.

LOOKING FOR RELATIONSHIPS IN THE DATA

When there are two series of data, there are a number of statistical measures that can be used to capture how the series move together over time.

Correlations and Covariances

The two most widely used measures of how two variables move together (or do not) are the correlation and the covariance. For two data series $X(X_1, X_2,)$ and $Y(Y, Y \ldots)$, the covariance provides a measure of the degree to which they move together and is estimated by taking the product of the deviations from the mean for each variable in each period.

$$\text{Covariance} = \sigma_{XY} = \frac{\sum_{j=1}^{j=n} (X_j - \mu_X)(Y_j - \mu_Y)}{n-1}$$

The sign on the covariance indicates the type of relationship the two variables have. A positive sign indicates that they move together, and a negative sign that they move in opposite directions. Although the covariance increases with the strength of the relationship, it is still relatively difficult to draw judgments on the strength of the relationship between two variables by looking at the covariance, because it is not standardized.

The correlation is the standardized measure of the relationship between two variables. It can be computed from the covariance:

$$\text{Correlation} = \rho_{XY} = \sigma_{XY}/\sigma_X\sigma_Y = \frac{\sum\limits_{j=1}^{j=n}(X_j - \mu_X)(Y_j - \mu_Y)}{\sqrt{\sum\limits_{j=1}^{j=n}(X_j - \mu_X)^2}\sqrt{\sum\limits_{j=1}^{j=n}(Y_j - \mu_Y)^2}}$$

The correlation can never be greater than 1 or less than -1. A correlation close to 0 indicates that the two variables are unrelated. A positive correlation indicates that the two variables move together, and the relationship is stronger as the correlation gets closer to 1. A negative correlation indicates the two variables move in opposite directions, and the relationship gets stronger as the correlation gets closer to -1. Two variables that are perfectly positively correlated ($\rho_{XY} = 1$) essentially move in perfect proportion in the same direction, whereas two variables that are perfectly negatively correlated move in perfect proportion in opposite directions.

Regressions

A simple *regression* is an extension of the correlation/covariance concept. It attempts to explain one variable (the dependent variable) using the other variable (the independent variable).

Scatter Plots and Regression Lines

Keeping with statistical tradition, let Y be the dependent variable and X be the independent variable. If the two variables are plotted against each other with each pair of observations representing a point on the graph, you have a scatter plot, with Y on the vertical axis and X on the horizontal axis. Figure A1.3 illustrates a scatter plot.

In a regression, we attempt to fit a straight line through the points that best fit the data. In its simplest form, this is accomplished by finding a line that minimizes the sum of the squared deviations of the points from the line. Consequently, it is called an *ordinary least squares* (OLS) regression. When such a line is fit, two parameters emerge—one is the point at which the line cuts through the Y-axis, called the intercept of the regression, and the other is the slope of the regression line:

$$Y = a + bX$$

The slope (b) of the regression measures both the direction and the magnitude of the relationship between the dependent variable (Y) and the independent variable (X). When the two variables are positively correlated, the slope will also be positive, whereas when the two variables are negatively correlated, the slope will be negative. The magnitude of the slope of the regression can be read as follows: for every unit increase in the dependent variable (X), the independent variable will change by b (slope).

Estimating Regression Parameters

Although there are statistical packages that allow us to input data and get the regression parameters as output, it is worth looking at how they are estimated in the first place. The

Figure A1.3   Scatter Plot of Y versus X

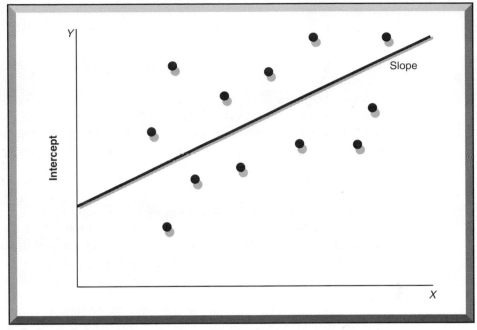

Scatter Plot

slope of the regression line is a logical extension of the covariance concept introduced in the last section. In fact, the slope is estimated using the covariance:

$$\text{Slope of the regression} = b = \frac{\text{Covariance}_{YX}}{\text{Variance of } X} = \frac{\sigma_{YX}}{\sigma_X^2}$$

The intercept (a) of the regression can be read in a number of ways. One interpretation is that it is the value that Y will have when X is 0. Another is more straightforward and is based on how it is calculated. It is the difference between the average value of Y and the slope-adjusted value of X.

$$\text{Intercept of the regression} = a = \mu_Y - b^* \, (\mu_X)$$

Regression parameters are always estimated with some error or statistical noise, partly because the relationship between the variables is not perfect, and partly because we estimate them from samples of data. This noise is captured in a couple of statistics. One is the R^2 of the regression, which measures the proportion of the variability in the dependent variable (Y) that is explained by the independent variable (X). It is also a direct function of the correlation between the variables:

$$R\text{ - squared of the regression} = \text{Correlation}_{YX}^2 = \rho_{YX}^2 = \frac{b^2 \sigma_X^2}{\sigma_Y^2}$$

An R^2 value close to 1 indicates a strong relationship between the two variables, although the relationship may be either positive or negative. Another measure of noise in a regression is the standard error, which measures the "spread" around each of the two parameters estimated—the intercept and the slope. Each parameter has an associated standard error, which is calculated from the data:

$$\text{Standard error of intercept} = \text{SE}_a = \sqrt{\frac{\left(\sum_{j=1}^{j=n} X_j^2\right)\left(\sum_{j=1}^{j=n} (Y_j - bX_j)^2\right)}{(n-1)\sum_{j=1}^{j=n} (X_j - \mu_X)^2}}$$

$$\text{Standard error of slope} = \text{SE}_b = \sqrt{\frac{\left(\sum_{j=1}^{j=n} (Y_j - bX_j)^2\right)}{(n-1)\sum_{j=1}^{j=n} (X_j - \mu_X)^2}}$$

If we make the additional assumption that the intercept and slope estimates are normally distributed, the parameter estimate and the standard error can be combined to get a t-statistic that measures whether the relationship is statistically significant.

$$t\text{-Statistic for Intercept} = a/\text{SE}_a$$
$$t\text{-Statistic for slope} = b/\text{SE}_b$$

For samples with more than 120 observations, a t-statistic greater than 1.95 indicates that the variable is significantly different from 0 with 95% certainty, whereas a statistic greater than 2.33 indicates the same with 99% certainty. For smaller samples, the t-statistic has to be larger to have statistical significance.[1]

Using Regressions

Although regressions mirror correlation coefficients and covariances in showing the strength of the relationship between two variables, they also serve another useful purpose. The regression equation described in the last section can be used to estimate predicted values for the dependent variable, based on assumed or actual values for the independent variable. In other words, for any given Y, we can estimate what X should be:

$$X = a + b(Y)$$

How good are these predictions? That will depend entirely on the strength of the relationship measured in the regression. When the independent variable explains a high proportion of the variation in the dependent variable (R^2 is high), the predictions will be precise. When the R^2 is low, the predictions will have a much wider range.

From Simple to Multiple Regressions

The regression that measures the relationship between two variables becomes a multiple regression when it is extended to include more than one independent variables ($X1$, $X2$, $X3$, $X4\ldots$) in trying to explain the dependent variable Y. Although the

---

[1]The actual values that t-statistics need to take can be found in a table for the t distribution, which can be found in any standard statistics book or software package).

graphical presentation becomes more difficult, the multiple regression yields output that is an extension of the simple regression.

$$Y = a + bX1 + cX2 + dX3 + eX4$$

The R^2 still measures the strength of the relationship, but an additional R^2 statistic called the adjusted R^2 is computed to counter the bias that will induce the R^2 to keep increasing as more independent variables are added to the regression. If there are k independent variables in the regression, the adjusted R^2 is computed as follows:

$$R\text{squared} = \frac{\left(\sum_{j=1}^{j=n} (Y_j - bX_j)^2\right)}{n - 1}$$

$$\text{Adjusted} R\text{squared} = \frac{\left(\sum_{j=1}^{j=n} (Y_j - bX_j)^2\right)}{n - k}$$

Multiple regressions are powerful tools that allow us to examine the determinants of any variable.

Regression Assumptions and Constraints

Both the simple and multiple regressions described in this section also assume linear relationships between the dependent and independent variables. If the relationship is not linear, we have two choices. One is to transform the variables by taking the square, square root, or natural log (for example) of the values and hope that the relationship between the transformed variables is more linear. The other is to run nonlinear regressions that attempt to fit a curve (rather than a straight line) through the data.

There are implicit statistical assumptions behind every multiple regression, and we ignore them at our own peril. For the coefficients on the individual independent variables to make sense, the independent variables needs to be uncorrelated with each other, a condition that is often difficult to meet. When independent variables are correlated with each other, the statistical hazard that is created is called *multicollinearity*. In its presence, the coefficients on independent variables can take on unexpected signs (positive instead of negative, for instance) and unpredictable values. There are simple diagnostic statistics that allow us to measure how far the data may be deviating from our ideal.

CONCLUSION

In the course of trying to make sense of large amounts of contradictory data, there are useful statistical tools on which we can draw. Although we have looked at the only most basic ones in this appendix, there are far more sophisticated and powerful tools available.

APPENDIX 2

FINANCIAL STATEMENTS

Financial statements provide the fundamental information that we use to analyze and answer valuation questions. Therefore, it is important that we understand the principles governing these statements by looking at three questions:

- How valuable are the assets of a firm? Assets can come in several forms: those with long lives, such as land and buildings; those with shorter lives, such inventory; and intangible assets that still produce revenues for the firm, such as patents and trademarks.
- How did the firm raise the funds to finance these assets? In acquiring them, firms can use the funds of the owners (equity) or borrowed money (debt), and the mix is likely to change as the assets age.
- How profitable are these assets? A good investment, we argued, is one that makes a return greater than the hurdle rate. To evaluate whether the investments that a firm has already made are good, we need to estimate the returns being made on these investments.

We will look at the way accountants would answer these questions and why the answers might be different when doing financial analysis. Some of these differences can be traced to the differences in objectives—accountants try to measure the current standing and immediate past performance of a firm, whereas financial analysis is much more forward-looking.

THE BASIC ACCOUNTING STATEMENTS

There are three basic accounting statements that summarize information about a firm. The first is the *balance sheet*, shown in Figure A2.1, which summarizes the assets owned by a firm, the value of these assets, and the mix of financing, debt, and equity used to finance these assets at a point in time.

The next is the *income statement*, shown in Figure A2.2, which provides information on the revenues and expenses of the firm and the resulting income made during a period. The period can be a quarter (if it is a quarterly income statement) or a year (if it is an annual report).

Finally, there is the *statement of cash flows*, shown in Figure A2.3, which specifies the sources and uses of cash of the firm from operating, investing, and financing activities during a period.

The statement of cash flows can be viewed as an attempt to explain how much the cash flows during a period were, and why the cash balance changed during the period.

Figure A2.1   The Balance Sheet

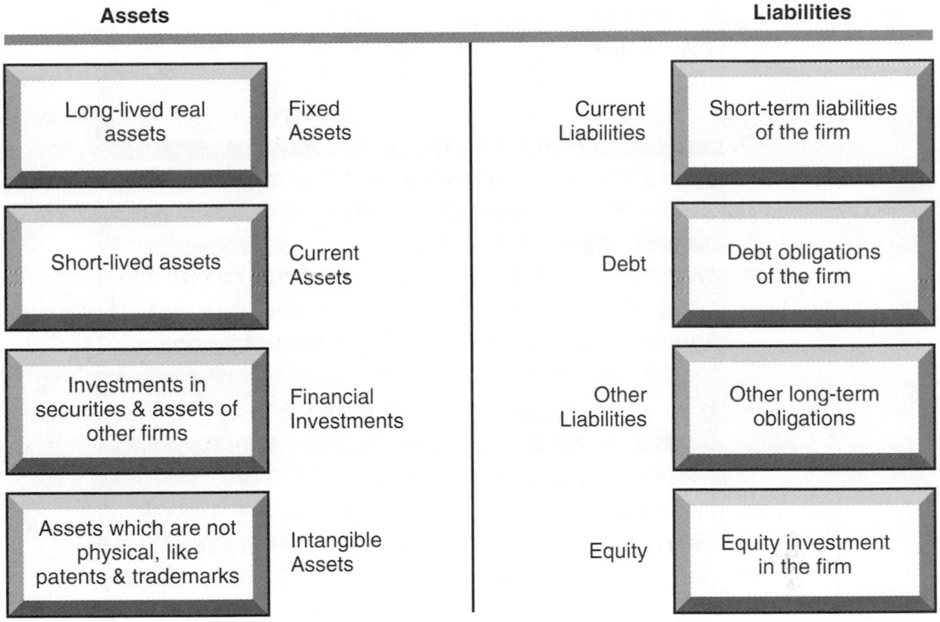

Assets		Liabilities	
Long-lived real assets	Fixed Assets	Current Liabilities	Short-term liabilities of the firm
Short-lived assets	Current Assets	Debt	Debt obligations of the firm
Investments in securities & assets of other firms	Financial Investments	Other Liabilities	Other long-term obligations
Assets which are not physical, like patents & trademarks	Intangible Assets	Equity	Equity investment in the firm

ASSET MEASUREMENT AND VALUATION

When analyzing any firm, we would like to know the types of assets that it owns, the values of these assets, and the degree of uncertainty about these values. Accounting statements do a reasonably good job of categorizing the assets owned by a firm, a partial job of assessing the values of these assets, and a poor job of reporting uncertainty about asset values. In this section, we will begin by looking at the accounting principles underlying asset categorization and measurement and the limitations of financial statements in providing relevant information about assets.

Accounting Principles Underlying Asset Measurement

The accounting view of asset value is to a great extent grounded in the notion of *historical cost*, which is the original cost of the asset, adjusted upward for improvements made to the asset since purchase and downward for loss in value associated with the aging of the asset. This historical cost is called the *book value*. Although the generally accepted accounting principles for valuing an asset vary across different kinds of assets, three principles underlie the way assets are valued in accounting statements.

1. *An abiding belief in book value as the best estimate of value:*   Accounting estimates of asset value begin with the book value. Unless a substantial reason is

Figure A2.2   Income Statement

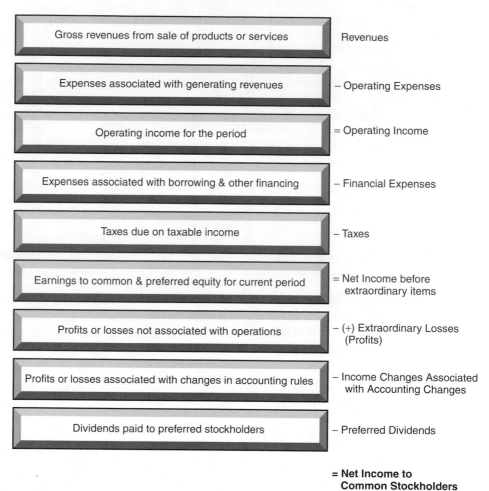

given to do otherwise, accountants view the historical cost as the best estimate of the value of an asset.

2. *A distrust of market or estimated value:*   When a current market value exists for an asset that is different from the book value, accounting convention seems to view it with suspicion. The market price of an asset is often viewed as both much too volatile and too easily manipulated to be used as an estimate of value for an asset. This suspicion runs even deeper when values are estimated for an asset based on expected future cash flows.

3. *A preference for underestimating value rather than overestimating it:*   When there is more than one approach to valuing an asset, accounting convention takes the view that the more conservative (lower) estimate of value should be used rather than the less conservative (higher) estimate of value.

Figure A2.3   Statement of Cash Flows

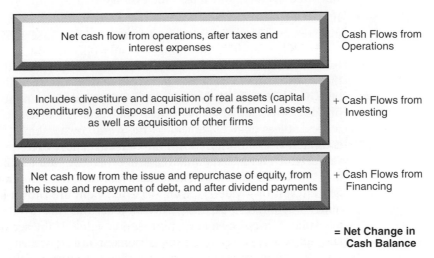

Measuring Asset Value

The financial statement in which accountants summarize and report asset value is the balance sheet. To examine how asset value is measured, let us begin with the way assets are categorized in the balance sheet.

- First, there are the *fixed assets*, which include the long-term assets of the firm, such as plant, equipment, land, and buildings. Generally accepted accounting principles (GAAPs) in the United States require the valuation of fixed assets at historical cost, adjusted for any estimated gain and loss in value from improvements and the aging, respectively, of these assets. Although in theory the adjustments for aging should reflect the loss of earning power of the asset as it ages, in practice they are much more a product of accounting rules and convention. These adjustments are called *depreciation*. Depreciation methods can be categorized, very broadly, into straight-line (where the loss in asset value is assumed to be the same every year over its lifetime) and accelerated (where the asset loses more value in the earlier years and less in the later years).

- Next, we have the short-term assets of the firm, including inventory (such as raw materials, works in progress, and finished goods), receivables (summarizing moneys owed to the firm), and cash; these are categorized as *current assets*. It is in this category accountants are most amenable to the use of market value. Accounts receivable are generally recorded as the amount owed to the firm based on the billing at the time of the credit sale. The only major valuation and accounting issue is when the firm has to recognize accounts receivable that are not collectible. There is some discretion allowed to firms in the valuation of inventory, with three commonly used approaches—first-in, first-out (FIFO), where the inventory is valued based upon the cost of material bought latest in the year; last-in, first-out (LIFO), where inventory is valued based upon the cost of material bought earliest in the year; and weighted average, which uses the average cost over the year.

- In the category of *investments and marketable securities*, accountants consider investments made by firms in the securities or assets of other firms and other marketable securities, including Treasury bills or bonds. The way these assets are valued depends on the way the investment is categorized and the motive behind the investment. In general, an investment in the securities of another firm can be categorized as a minority, passive investment; a minority, active investment; or a majority, active investment. If the securities or assets owned in another firm represent less than 20 percent of the overall ownership of that firm, an investment is treated as a minority, passive investment. These investments have an acquisition value, which represents what the firm originally paid for the securities, and often a market value. For investments held to maturity, the valuation is at acquisition value, and interest or dividends from this investment are shown in the income statement under net interest expenses. Investments that are available for sale or trading investments are shown at current market value. If the securities or assets owned in another firm represent between 20 percent and 50 percent of the overall ownership of that firm, an investment is treated as a minority, active investment. Although these investments have an initial acquisition value, a proportional share (based on ownership proportion) of the net income and losses made by the firm in which the investment was made, is used to adjust the acquisition cost. In addition, the dividends received from the investment reduce the acquisition cost. This approach to valuing investments is called the equity approach. If the securities or assets owned in another firm represent more than 50 percent of the overall ownership of that firm, an investment is treated as a majority, active investment.[1] In this case, the investment is no longer shown as a financial investment but is replaced by the assets and liabilities of the firm in which the investment was made. This approach leads to a consolidation of the balance sheets of the two firms, where the assets and liabilities of the two firms are merged and presented as one balance sheet. The share of the equity in the subsidiary that is owned by other investors is shown as a minority interest on the liability side of the balance sheet.

- Finally, we have what are loosely categorized as *intangible assets*. These include patents and trademarks that presumably will create future earnings and cash flows and also uniquely accounting assets, such as goodwill, that arise because of acquisitions made by the firm. Patents and trademarks are valued differently depending on whether they are generated internally or acquired. When patents and trademarks are generated from internal sources, such as research, the costs incurred in developing the asset are expensed in that period, even though the asset might have a life of several accounting periods. Thus, the intangible asset is not usually valued in the balance sheet of the firm. In contrast, when an intangible asset is acquired from an external party, it is treated as an asset. When a firm acquires another firm, the purchase price is first allocated to tangible assets and then allocated to any intangible assets, such as patents or trade names. Any residual

---

[1]Firms have evaded the requirements of consolidation by keeping their share of ownership in other firms below 50%.

becomes goodwill. Although until recently, accounting standards in the United States gave firms latitude in how they dealt with goodwill, the current requirement is much more stringent. All firms that do acquisitions and pay more than book value have to record goodwill as assets, and this goodwill has to be written off if the accountants deem it to be impaired.[2]

MEASURING FINANCING MIX

The second set of questions that we would like to answer (and would like accounting statements to shed some light on) relates to the current value and subsequently the mixture of debt and equity used by the firm. The bulk of the information about these questions is provided on the liability side of the balance sheet and the footnotes.

Accounting Principles Underlying Liability and Equity Measurement

Just as with the measurement of asset value, the accounting categorization of liabilities and equity is governed by a set of fairly rigid principles. The first is a *strict categorization of financing into either a liability or equity* based on the nature of the obligation. For an obligation to be recognized as a liability, it must meet three requirements:

1. It must be expected to lead to a future cash outflow or the loss of a future cash inflow at some specified or determinable date.

2. The firm cannot avoid the obligation.

3. The transaction giving rise to the obligation has happened already.

In keeping with the earlier principle of conservatism in estimating asset value, accountants recognize as liabilities only cash flow obligations that cannot be avoided.

The second principle is that the value of both liabilities and equity in a firm are *better estimated using historical costs* with accounting adjustments, rather than with expected future cash flows or market value. The process by which accountants measure the value of liabilities and equities is inextricably linked to the way they value assets. Because assets are primarily valued at historical cost or at book value, both debt and equity also get measured primarily at book value. In what follows, we will examine the accounting measurement of both liabilities and equity.

Measuring the Value of Liabilities

Accountants categorize liabilities into current liabilities, long-term debt, and long-term liabilities that are neither debt nor equity; the last category includes leases, underfunded pension and health care obligations, and deferred taxes.

- *Current liabilities* include all obligations that the firm has coming due in the next accounting period. These generally include accounts payable (representing

---

[2]To make this judgment, accountants have to value the acquired company at regular intervals and compare the value that they get to the price paid. If the value is substantially lower than the price, the company has to write off an equivalent portion of the goodwill.

credit received from suppliers and other vendors to the firm), short-term borrowing (representing short-term loans taken to finance the operations or current asset needs of the business), and the short-term portion of long-term borrowing (representing the portion of the long-term debt or bonds that is coming due in the next year). As with current assets, these items are usually recorded at close to their current market value. *Long-term debt* for firms can take one of two forms: a long-term loan from a bank or other financial institution, or a long-term bond issued to financial markets (in which case the creditors are the investors in the bond). Accountants measure the value of long-term debt by looking at the present value of payments due on the loan or bond at the time of the borrowing. For bank loans, this will be equal to the nominal value of the loan. With bonds, however, there are three possibilities. When bonds are issued at par value, for instance, the value of the long-term debt is generally measured in terms of the nominal obligation created in terms of principal (face value) due on the borrowing. When bonds are issued at a premium or a discount on par value, the bonds are recorded at the issue price, but the premium or discount to the face value is amortized over the life of the bond. In all these cases, the book value of debt is unaffected by changes in interest rates during the life of the loan or bond..

- *Lease obligations* include obligations to lessors on assets that firms have leased. There are two ways of accounting for leases. In an operating lease, the lessor (or owner) transfers only the right to use the property to the lessee. At the end of the lease period, the lessee returns the property to the lessor. Because the lessee does not assume the risk of ownership, the lease expense is treated as an operating expense in the income statement, and the lease does not affect the balance sheet. In a capital lease, the lessee assumes some of the risks of ownership and enjoys some of the benefits. Consequently, the lease, when signed, is recognized both as an asset and as a liability (for the lease payments) on the balance sheet. The firm gets to claim depreciation each year on the asset and also deducts the interest expense component of the lease payment each year.

- In *a pension plan*, the firm agrees to provide certain benefits to its employees, either by specifying a "defined contribution" (wherein a fixed contribution is made to the plan each year by the employer, without any promises as to the benefits to be delivered in the plan) or a "defined benefit" (wherein the employer promises to pay a certain benefit to the employee). In the latter case, the employer has to put sufficient money into the plan each period to meet the defined benefits. A pension fund whose assets exceed its liabilities is an overfunded plan, whereas one whose assets are less than its liabilities is an underfunded plan, and disclosures to that effect have to be included in financial statements, generally in the footnotes.

- Firms often use different methods of accounting for tax and financial reporting purposes, leading to a question of how tax liabilities should be reported. Because accelerated depreciation and favorable inventory valuation methods for tax accounting purposes lead to a deferral of taxes, the taxes on the income reported in the financial statements will generally be much greater than the actual tax paid. The same principles of matching expenses to income that underlie accrual accounting require that the *deferred income tax* be recognized in the financial statements, as a liability (if the firm underpaid taxes) or as an asset (if the firm overpaid taxes).

Measuring the Value of Equity

The accounting measure of equity is a historical cost measure. The value of equity shown on the balance sheet reflects the original proceeds received by the firm when it issued the equity, augmented by any earnings since then (or reduced by losses, if any) and reduced by any dividends paid out during the period. A sustained period of negative earnings can make the book value of equity negative. In addition, any unrealized gain or loss in marketable securities that are classified as available-for-sale is shown as an increase or decrease in the book value of equity in the balance sheet.

When companies buy back stock for short periods with the intent of reissuing the stock or using it to cover option exercises, they are allowed to show the repurchased stock as *treasury stock*, which reduces the book value of equity. Firms are not allowed to keep treasury stock on the books for extended periods and have to reduce their book value of equity by the value of repurchased stock in the case of actions such as stock buybacks. Because these buybacks occur at the current market price, they can result in significant reductions in the book value of equity.

Accounting rules still do not seem to have come to grips with the effect of warrants and equity options (such as those granted by many firms to management) on the book value of equity. If warrants are issued to financial markets, the proceeds from this issue will show up as part of the book value of equity. In the far more prevalent case, where options are given or granted to management, there is no effect on the book value of equity. When the options are exercised, the cash inflows do ultimately show up in the book value of equity, and there is a corresponding increase in the number of shares outstanding. The same point can be made about convertible bonds, which are treated as debt until conversion, when they become part of equity.

As a final point on equity, accounting rules still seem to consider preferred stock, with its fixed dividend, as equity or near equity, largely because of the fact that preferred dividends can be deferred or accumulated without the risk of default. Preferred stock is valued on the balance sheet at its original issue price, with any accumulated unpaid dividends added on. To the extent that there can still be a loss of control in the firm (as opposed to bankruptcy), we would argue that preferred stock shares almost as many characteristics with unsecured debt as it does with equity.

MEASURING EARNINGS AND PROFITABILITY

How profitable is a firm? What did it earn on the assets in which it invested? These are the fundamental questions we would like financial statements to answer. Accountants use the income statement to provide information about a firm's operating activities over a specific time period. In terms of our description of the firm, the income statement is designed to measure the earnings from assets in place.

Accounting Principles Underlying Measurement of Earnings and Profitability

Two primary principles underlie the measurement of accounting earnings and profitability. The first is the principle of accrual accounting. In accrual accounting, the revenue from selling a good or service is recognized in the period in which the good is sold or the service is performed (in whole or substantially). A corresponding effort is made on the expense side to match expenses to revenues.[3] This is in contrast to cash accounting, wherein revenues are recognized when payment is received and expenses are recorded when they are paid.

The second principle is the categorization of expenses into operating, financing, and capital expenses. Operating expenses are expenses that, at least in theory, provide benefits only for the current period; the cost of labor and materials expended to create products that are sold in the current period is a good example. Financing expenses are expenses arising from the nonequity financing used to raise capital for the business; the most common example is interest expenses. Capital expenses are expected to generate benefits over multiple periods; for instance, the cost of buying land and buildings is treated as a capital expense.

Operating expenses are subtracted from revenues in the current period to arrive at a measure of operating earnings from the firm. Financing expenses are subtracted from operating earnings to estimate earnings to equity investors or net income. Capital expenses are written off over their useful life (in terms of generating benefits) as depreciation or amortization.

Measuring Accounting Earnings and Profitability

Because income can be generated from a number of different sources, accounting principles require that income statements be classified into four sections: income from continuing operations, income from discontinued operations, extraordinary gains or losses, and adjustments for changes in accounting principles.

Accounting principles require publicly traded companies to use accrual accounting to record earnings from continuing operations. Although accrual accounting is straightforward in firms that produce goods and sell them, there are special cases in which accrual accounting can be complicated by the nature of the product or service being offered. For instance, firms that enter into long-term contracts with their customers, for instance, are allowed to recognize revenue on the basis of the percentage of the contract that is completed. As the revenue is recognized on a percentage of completion basis, a corresponding proportion of the expense is also recognized. When there is considerable uncertainty about the capacity of the buyer of a good or service to pay for a service, the firm providing the good or service may recognize the income only when it collects portions of the selling price under the installment method.

Operating expenses should reflect only those expenses that create revenues in the current period. In practice, however, a number of expenses are classified as operating expenses that do not meet this test. The first is depreciation and amortization. Although the notion that capital expenditures should be written off over multiple periods is reasonable, the accounting depreciation that is computed on the original historical cost often bears little resemblance to the actual economic depreciation. The second expense is research and development expenses, which accounting standards in the United States classify as operating expenses but which clearly provide benefits over multiple periods. The rationale used for this classification is that the benefits cannot be counted on or easily quantified. The third is operating lease expenses, which are closer to being financial than operating expenses.

---

[3]If a cost (such as an administrative cost) cannot be easily linked with a particular revenues, it is usually recognized as an expense in the period in which it is consumed.

Much of financial analysis is built around the expected future earnings of a firm, and many of these forecasts start with the current earnings. It is therefore important that we know how much of these earnings come from the ongoing operations of the firm, and how much can be attributed to unusual or extraordinary events that are unlikely to recur on a regular basis. Nonrecurring items include the following:

- *Unusual or infrequent items*, such as gains or losses from the divestiture of an asset or division and writeoffs or restructuring costs. Companies sometimes include such items as part of operating expenses. As an example, in 1997 Boeing took a writeoff of $1,400 million to adjust the value of assets it acquired in its acquisition of McDonnell Douglas, and it showed this as part of operating expenses.

- *Extraordinary items*, which are defined as events that are unusual in nature, infrequent in occurrence, and material in impact. Examples include the accounting gain associated with refinancing high-coupon debt with lower-coupon debt and gains or losses from marketable securities that are held by the firm.

- *Losses associated with discontinued operations*, which measure both the loss from the phase-out period and the estimated loss on the sale of the operations. To qualify, however, the operations have to be separable from the firm.

- *Gains or losses associated with accounting changes*, which measure earnings changes created by accounting changes made voluntarily by the firm (such as a change in inventory valuation and change in reporting period) and accounting changes mandated by new accounting standards.

Measures of Profitability

Although the income statement allows us to estimate how profitable a firm is in absolute terms, it is just as important that we gauge the profitability of the firm in comparison terms or percentage returns. The simplest and most useful gauge of profitability is relative to the capital employed to get a rate of return on investment. This can be done either from the viewpoint of just the equity investors or by looking at the entire firm.

I. Return on Assets (ROA) and Return on Capital (ROC)

The *return on assets* (ROA) of a firm measures its operating efficiency in generating profits from its assets prior to the effects of financing.

$$\text{ROA} = \frac{\text{EBIT}(1 - \text{Tax rate})}{\text{Total assets}}$$

Earnings before interest and taxes (EBIT) is the accounting measure of operating income from the income statement, and total assets refers to the assets as measured using accounting rules—that is, using book value for most assets. Alternatively, ROA can be written as

$$\text{ROA} = \frac{\text{Net income} + \text{Interest expenses}(1 - \text{Tax rate})}{\text{Total assets}}$$

By separating the financing effects from the operating effects, the ROA provides a cleaner measure of the true return on these assets.

ROA can also be computed on a pretax basis with no loss of generality, by using the EBIT and not adjusting for taxes:

$$\text{Pre-tax ROA} = \frac{\text{EBIT}}{\text{Total assets}}$$

This measure is useful if the firm or division is being evaluated for purchase by an acquirer with a different tax rate or structure.

A more useful measure of return relates the operating income to the capital invested in the firm, where capital is defined as the sum of the book value of debt and equity, net of cash and marketable securities. This is the *return on capital* (ROC). When a substantial portion of the liabilities is either current (such as accounts payable) or non–interest-bearing, this approach provides a better measure of the true return earned on capital employed in the business.

$$\text{After-tax ROC} = \frac{\text{EBIT}(1 - t)}{\text{BV of debt} + \text{BV of equity} - \text{Cash}}$$
$$\text{Pre-tax ROC} = \frac{\text{EBIT}}{\text{BV of debt} + \text{BV of equity} - \text{Cash}}$$

The ROC of a firm can be written as a function of its operating profit margin and its capital turnover ratio:

$$\text{After-tax ROC} = \frac{\text{EBIT}(1 - t)}{\text{BV of capital}} = \frac{\text{EBIT}(1 - t)}{\text{Sales}} \times \frac{\text{Sales}}{\text{BV of capital}}$$
$$= \text{After-tax operating margin} * \text{Capital turnover ratio}$$
$$\text{Pre-tax ROC} = \text{Pre-tax operating margin} * \text{Capital turnover ratio}$$

Thus, a firm can arrive at a high ROC by either increasing its profit margin or more efficiently using its capital to increase sales. There are likely to be competitive and technological constraints on increasing sales, but firms still have some freedom within these constraints to choose the mix of profit margin and capital turnover that maximizes their ROC. The return on capital varies widely across firms in different businesses, largely as a consequence of differences in profit margins and capital turnover ratios.

II. Return on Equity

Although ROC measures the profitability of the overall firm, the *return on equity* (ROE) examines profitability from the perspective of the equity investor by relating profits to the equity investor (net profit after taxes and interest expenses) to the book value of the equity investment.

$$\text{ROE} = \frac{\text{Net income}}{\text{Book value of common equity}}$$

Because preferred stockholders have a different type of claim on the firm than common stockholders, the net income should be estimated after preferred dividends, and the book value of common equity should not include the book value of preferred stock.

SUMMARY

Financial statements remain the primary source of information for most investors and analysts. There are differences, however, in how accounting and financial analysis approach answering a number of key questions about the firm.

The first question that we examined related to the nature and the value of the assets owned by a firm. The focus in accounting statements on the original price of assets in place (book value) in accounting statements can lead to significant differences between the stated value of these assets and their market value. With growth assets, accounting rules result in low or no values for assets generated by internal research.

The second issue that we examined was the measurement of profitability. The two principles that seem to govern how profits are measured are accrual accounting and the categorization of expenses into operating, financing, and capital expenses. Operating and financing expenses are shown in income statements. Capital expenditures take the form of depreciation and amortization and are spread over several time periods. Accounting standards miscategorize operating leases and R&D expenses as operating expenses, when the former should be categorized as financing expenses and the latter as capital expenses.

APPENDIX 3

TIME VALUE OF MONEY

The simplest tools in finance are often the most powerful. *Present value* is a concept that is intuitively appealing and simple to compute and that has a wide range of applications. It is useful in decision making ranging from simple personal decisions (buying a house, saving for a child's education, estimating income in retirement) to more complex corporate financial decisions (picking projects in which to invest, as well as the right financing mix for these projects).

TIMELINES AND NOTATION

Dealing with cash flows that are at different points in time is made easier using a timeline that shows both the timing and the amount of each cash flow in a stream. Thus a cash flow stream of $100 at the end of each of the next four years can be depicted on a timeline like the one depicted in Figure A3.1.

In the figure, 0 refers to right now. A cash flow that occurs at time 0 is therefore already in present value terms and does not need to be adjusted for time value. A distinction must be made here between a *period* of time and a *point* in time. The portion of the timeline between 0 and 1 refers to period 1, which in this example is the first year. The cash flow that occurs at the point in time 1 refers to the cash flow that occurs at the end of period 1. Finally, the discount rate, which is 10% in this example, is specified for each period on the timeline and may be different for each period. Had the cash flows been at the beginning of each year instead of at the end of each year, the timeline would have been redrawn as it appears in Figure A3.2.

Note that in present value terms, a cash flow that occurs at the beginning of year 2 is the equivalent of a cash flow that occurs at the end of year 1.

Cash flows can be either positive or negative; positive cash flows are called cash inflows and negative cash flows are called cash outflows. For notational purposes, we will assume the following for the chapter that follows:

Figure A3.1 A Time line for Cash Flows: $100 in Cash Flows Received at the End of Each of Next 4 years

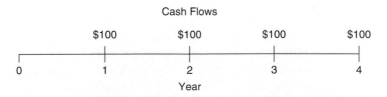

694

Figure A3.2   A Time line for Cash Flows: $100 in Cash Received at the Beginning of Each Year for Next 4 years

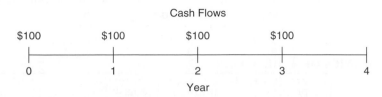

Notation	Stands For
PV	Present value
FV	Future value
CF_t	Cash flow at the end of period t
A	Annuity: constant cash flows over several periods
r	Discount rate
g	Expected growth rate in cash flows
n	Number of years over which cash flows are received or paid

THE INTUITIVE BASIS FOR PRESENT VALUE

There are three reasons why a cash flow in the future is worth less than a similar cash flow today.

1. ***Individuals prefer present consumption to future consumption.***   People would have to be offered more in the future to give up present consumption. If the preference for current consumption is strong, individuals will have to be offered much more in terms of future consumption to give up current consumption, a tradeoff that is captured by a high "real" rate of return or discount rate. Conversely, when the preference for current consumption is weaker, individuals will settle for much less in terms of future consumption and, by extension, a low real rate of return or discount rate.

2. ***When there is monetary inflation, the value of currency decreases over time.*** The greater the inflation, the greater the difference in value between a nominal cash flow today and the same cash flow in the future.

3. ***A promised cash flow might not be delivered for a number of reasons:***   The promisor might default on the payment, the promisee might not be around to receive payment, or some other contingency might intervene to prevent the promised payment or to reduce it. Any uncertainty (risk) associated with the cash flow in the future reduces the value of the cash flow.

The process by which future cash flows are adjusted to reflect these factors is called discounting, and the magnitude of these factors is reflected in the discount rate. The discount rate can be viewed as a composite of the expected real return (reflecting consumption preferences in the aggregate over the investing population), the expected inflation rate (to capture the deterioration in the purchasing power of the cash flow), and the uncertainty associated with the cash flow.

THE MECHANICS OF TIME VALUE

The process of discounting future cash flows converts them into cash flows in present value terms. Conversely, the process of compounding converts present cash flows into future cash flows. There are five types of cash flows—simple cash flows, annuities, growing annuities, perpetuities, and growing perpetuities—which we discuss next.

Simple Cash Flows

A simple cash flow is a single cash flow in a specified future time period; it can be depicted on a timeline as in Figure A3.3.

Figure A3.3   Present Value of a Cash Flow

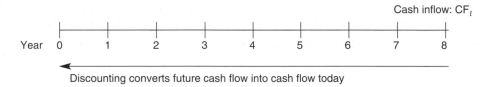

where $CF_t =$ the cash flow at time t.

This cash flow can be discounted back to the present using a discount rate that reflects the uncertainty of the cash flow. Concurrently, cash flows in the present can be compounded to arrive at an expected future cash flow.

Discounting a Simple Cash Flow

Discounting a cash flow converts it into present value dollars and enables the user to do several things. First, once cash flows are converted into present value dollars, they can be aggregated and compared. Second, if present values are estimated correctly, the user should be indifferent between the future cash flow and the present value of that cash flow. The present value of a cash flow can be written as follows:

$$\text{Present value of simple cash flow} = \frac{CF_t}{(1+r)^t}$$

where $r =$ discount rate.

Other things remaining equal, the present value of a cash flow will decrease as the discount rate increases and continue to decrease the further into the future the cash flow occurs.

To illustrate this concept, assume that you own are currently leasing your office space and expect to make a lump-sum payment to the owner of the real estate of

Figure A3.4   Present Value of $500,000 in 10 Years

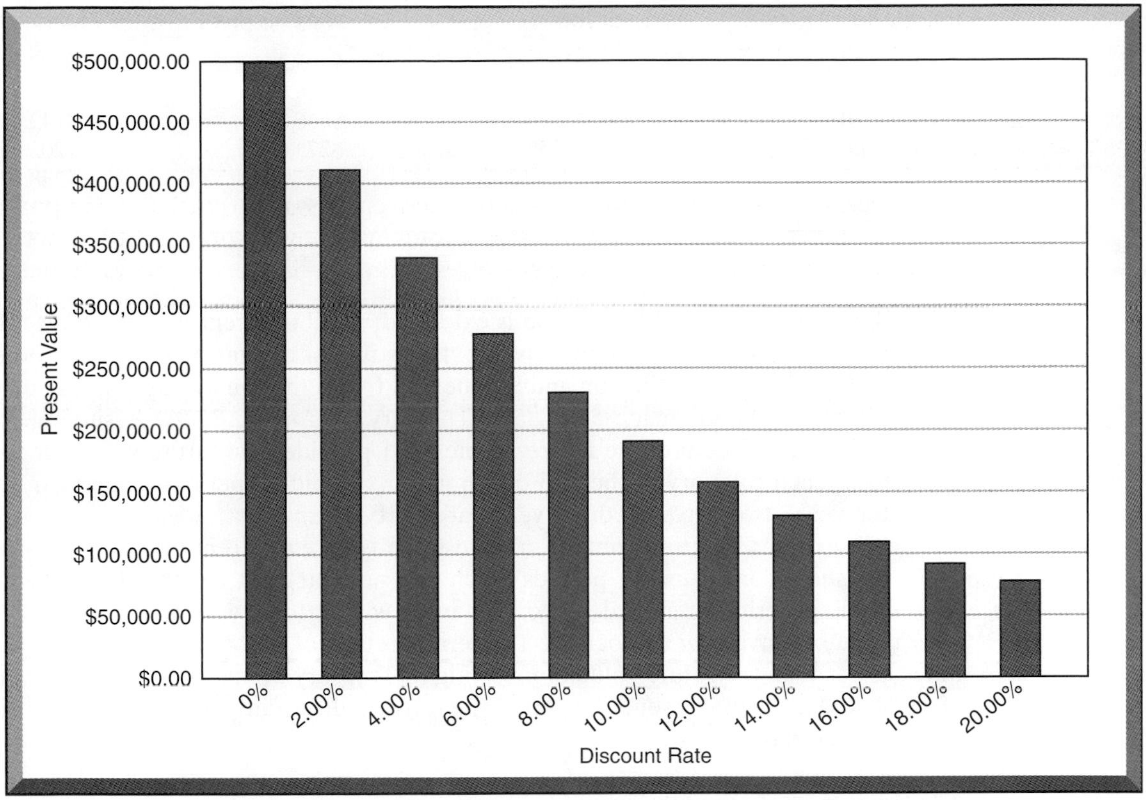

$500,000 ten years from now. Assume that an appropriate discount rate for this cash flow is 10%. The present value of this cash flow can then be estimated:

$$\text{Present value of payment} = \frac{\$500,000}{(1.10)^{10}} = \$192,772$$

This present value is a decreasing function of the discount rate, as illustrated in Figure A3.4.

Compounding a Cash Flow

Current cash flows can be moved to the future by compounding the cash flow at the appropriate discount rate.

$$\text{Future value of simple cash flow} = \text{CF}_0(1 + r)^t$$

where

$$CF_0 = \text{cash flow now}$$
$$r = \text{discount rate}$$

Again, the compounding effect increases with both the discount rate and the compounding period.

Table A3.1	Future Values of Investments—Asset Classes		
Holding Period (Years)	**Stocks**	**Treasury Bonds**	**Treasury Bills**
1	$112.40	$105.20	$103.60
5	$179.40	$128.85	$119.34
10	$321.86	$166.02	$142.43
20	$1,035.92	$275.62	$202.86
30	$3,334.18	$457.59	$288.93
40	$10,731.30	$759.68	$411.52

As the length of the holding period is extended, small differences in discount rates can lead to large differences in future value. In a study of returns on stocks and bonds between 1926 and 1997, Ibbotson and Sinquefield found that on average, stocks made 12.4%, Treasury bonds made 5.2%, and Treasury bills made 3.6%. Assuming that these returns continue into the future, Table A3.1 provides the future values of $100 invested in each category at the end of a number of holding periods—one year, five years, ten years, twenty years, thirty years, and forty years.[1]

The differences in future value from investing at these different rates of return are small for short compounding periods (such as one year) but become larger as the compounding period is extended. For instance, with a forty-year time horizon, the future value of investing in stocks at an average return of 12.4% is more than twelve times larger than the future value of investing in Treasury bonds at an average return of 5.2%, and more than twenty-five times the future value of investing in Treasury bills at an average return of 3.6%.

The Frequency of Discounting and Compounding
The frequency of compounding affects both the future and present values of cash flows. In the examples just discussed, the cash flows were assumed to be discounted and compounded annually—that is, interest payments and income were computed at the end of each year, based on the balance at the beginning of the year. In some cases, however, the interest may be computed more frequently, such as on a monthly or semiannual basis. In these cases, the present and future values may be very different from those computed on an annual basis; the stated interest rate on an annual basis can deviate significantly from the effective or true interest rate. The effective interest rate can be computed as follows:

$$\text{Effective interest rate} = \left(1 + \frac{\text{Stated annual interest rate}}{n}\right)^n - 1$$

where n = number of compounding periods during the year (2 = semiannual; 12 = monthly). For instance, a 10% annual interest rate, if there is semiannual compounding, works out to an effective interest rate of

$$\text{Effective interest rate} = 1.05^2 - 1 = 0.10125, \text{ or } 10.125\%$$

---

[1] See *Stocks, Bonds, Bills and Inflation Yearbook* (Chicago: Ibbotson Associates, 1998).

Table A3.2 Effect of Compounding Frequency on Effective Interest Rates

Frequency	Rate	t (Days)	Formula	Effective Annual Rate
Annual	10%	1	0.10	10%
Semiannual	10%	2	$(1 + 0.10/2)^2 - 1$	10.25%
Monthly	10%	12	$(1 + 0.10/12)^{12} - 1$	10.47%
Daily	10%	365	$(1 + 0.10/365)^{365} - 1$	10.5156%
Continuous	10%		$\exp^{0.10} - 1$	10.5171%

As compounding becomes continuous, the effective interest rate can be computed as follows

$$\text{Effective interest rate} = \exp^r - 1$$

where

$$\exp = \text{exponential function}$$
$$r = \text{stated annual interest rate}$$

Table A3.2 provides the effective rates as a function of the compounding frequency.

As you can see, compounding becomes more frequent, the effective rate increases, and the present value of future cash flows decreases.

Annuities

An *annuity* is a constant cash flow that occurs at regular intervals for a fixed period of time. Defining A to be the annuity, the timeline for an annuity may be drawn as follows:

An annuity can occur at the end of each period—as in this timeline—or at the beginning of each period.

I. Present Value of an End-of-the-Period Annuity

The present value of an annuity can be calculated by taking each cash flow and discounting it back to the present, and then adding up the present values. Alternatively, a formula can be used in the calculation. In the case of annuities that occur at the end of each period, this formula can be written as

$$PV \text{ of an annuity} = PV(A,r,n) = A \left[\frac{1 - \dfrac{1}{(1+r)^n}}{r} \right]$$

where

$$A = \text{annuity}$$
$$r = \text{discount rate}$$
$$n = \text{number of years}$$

Accordingly, the notation we will use in the rest of this book for the present value of an annuity will be PV(A, r, n).

To illustrate, assume again that you are have a choice of buying a copier for (1) $10,000 cash down or (2) $3,000 a year, at the end of each year, for five years. If the opportunity cost is 12%, which would you rather do?

$$PV \text{ of } \$3000 \text{ each year for next 5 years} = \$3000 \left[\frac{1 - \dfrac{1}{(1.12)^5}}{0.12} \right] = \$10,814$$

The present value of the installment payments exceeds the cash-down price; therefore, you would want to pay the $10,000 in cash now.

Alternatively, the present value could have been estimated by discounting each of the cash flows back to the present and aggregating the present values as illustrated in Figure A3.5.

II. Amortization Factors: Annuities Given Present Values

In some cases, the present value of the cash flows is known, and the annuity needs to be estimated. This is often the case with home and automobile loans, for example, where the borrower receives the loan today and pays it back in equal monthly installments over an extended period of time. This process of finding an annuity when the present value is known is examined here:

$$\text{Annuity given present value} = A(PV, r, n) = PV \left[\frac{r}{1 - \dfrac{1}{(1+r)^n}} \right]$$

Suppose you are trying to borrow $200,000 to buy a house with a conventional thirty-year mortgage with monthly payments. The annual percentage rate on the loan is 8%.

Figure A3.5 Payment of $3000 at the End of Each of Next 5 Years

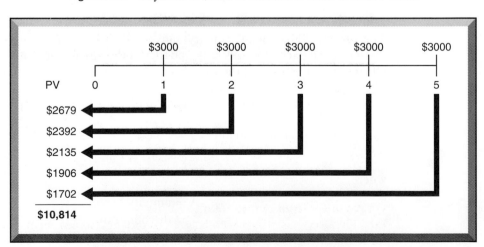

The monthly payments on this loan can be estimated using the annuity due formula:

$$\text{Monthly interest rate on loan} = \text{APR}/12 = 0.08/12 = 0.0067$$

$$\text{Monthly payment on mortgage} = \$200{,}000 \left[\frac{0.0067}{1 - \dfrac{1}{(1.0067)^{360}}} \right] = \$1473.11$$

This monthly payment is an increasing function of interest rates. When interest rates drop, homeowners usually have a choice of refinancing, although there is an up-front cost to doing so.

III. Future Value of End-of-the-Period Annuities

In some cases, an individual may plan to set aside a fixed annuity each period for a number of periods and will want to know how much he or she will have at the end of the period. The future value of an end-of-the-period annuity can be calculated as follows:

$$FV \text{ of an annuity} = \text{FV}(A, r, n) = A \left[\frac{(1+r)^n - 1}{r} \right]$$

Thus, the notation we will use throughout this book for the future value of an annuity will be $\text{FV}(A, r, n)$.

Individual retirement accounts (IRAs) allow some taxpayers to set aside up to $2,000 a year for retirement and exempt the income earned on these accounts from taxation. If an individual starts setting aside money in an IRA early in his or her working life, the value at retirement can be substantially higher than the nominal amount actually put in. For instance, assume that this individual sets aside $2,000 at the end of every year, starting when she is twenty-five years old, for an expected retirement at the age of sixty-five, and that she expects to make 8% a year on her investments. The expected value of the account on her retirement date can be estimated as follows:

$$\text{Expected value of IRA set aside at 65} = \$2{,}000 \left[\frac{(1.08)^{40} - 1}{0.08} \right] = \$518{,}113$$

The tax exemption adds substantially to the value, because it allows the investor to keep the pretax return of 8% made on the IRA investment. If the income had been taxed at, say, 40%, the after-tax return would have dropped to 4.8%, resulting in a much lower expected value:

$$\text{Expected value of IRA set aside at 65 if taxed} = \$2{,}000 \left[\frac{(1.048)^{40} - 1}{0.048} \right]$$
$$= \$230{,}127$$

As you can see, the available funds at retirement drops by more than 55% as a consequence of the loss of the tax exemption.

IV. Annuity Given Future Value

Individuals or businesses who have a fixed obligation to meet or a target to meet (in terms of savings) some time in the future need to know how much they should set aside each period to reach this target. If you are given the future value and are looking for an annuity—A(FV, r, n) in terms of notation:

$$\text{Annuity given future value} = A(FV, r, n) = FV\left[\frac{r}{(1+r)^n - 1}\right]$$

In any *balloon payment loan*, only interest payments are made during the life of the loan, and the principal is paid at the end of the period. Companies that borrow money using balloon payment loans or conventional bonds (which share the same features) often set aside money in sinking funds during the life of the loan to ensure that they have enough at maturity to pay the principal on the loan or the face value of the bonds. Thus, a company with bonds with a face value of $100 million coming due in ten years would need to set aside the following amount each year (assuming an interest rate of 8%):

$$\text{Sinking fund provision each year} = \$100,000,000\left[\frac{0.08}{(1.08)^{10} - 1}\right] = \$6,902,950$$

The company would need to set aside $6.9 million at the end of each year to ensure that there are enough funds ($10 million) to retire the bonds at maturity.

V. Effect of Annuities at the Beginning of Each Year

The annuities considered thus far in this appendix are end-of-the-period cash flows. Both the present and future values will be affected if the cash flows occur at the beginning of each period instead of the end. To illustrate this effect, consider an annuity of $100 at the end of each year for the next four years, with a discount rate of 10%.

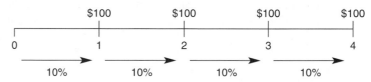

Contrast this with an annuity of $100 at the beginning of each year for the next four years, with the same discount rate.

Because the first of these annuities occurs right now and the remaining cash flows take the form of an end-of-the-period annuity over three years, the present value of this annuity can be written as follows:

$$PV\text{ of }\$100\text{ at beginning of each of next 4 years} = \$100 + \$100\left[\frac{1 - \dfrac{1}{(1.10)^3}}{0.10}\right]$$

In general, the present value of a beginning-of-the-period annuity over n years can be written as follows:

$$PV \text{ of beginning of period annuities over n years} = A + A \left[\frac{1 - \dfrac{1}{(1+r)^{n-1}}}{r} \right]$$

This present value will be higher than the present value of an equivalent annuity at the end of each period.

The future value of a beginning-of-the-period annuity typically can be estimated by allowing for one additional period of compounding for each cash flow:

$$FV \text{ of a beginning-of-the-period annuity} = A(1+r) \left[\frac{(1+r)^n - 1}{r} \right]$$

This future value will be higher than the future value of an equivalent annuity at the end of each period.

Consider again the example of an individual who sets aside $2,000 at the end of each year for the next forty years in an IRA account at 8%. The future value of these deposits amounted to $518,113 at the end of year 40. If the deposits had been made at the beginning of each year instead of the end, the future value would have been higher:

$$\text{Expected value of IRA (beginning of year)} = \$2,000(1.08) \left[\frac{(1.08)^{40} - 1}{0.08} \right]$$
$$= \$559,562$$

As you can see, the gains from making payments at the beginning of each period can be substantial.

Growing Annuities

A *growing annuity* is a cash flow that grows at a constant rate for a specified period of time. If A is the current cash flow and g is the expected growth rate, the timeline for a growing annuity appears as follows:

Note that to qualify as a growing annuity, the growth rate in each period has to be the same as the growth rate in the prior period.

In most cases, the present value of a growing annuity can be estimated by using the following formula:

$$PV \text{ of a growing annuity} = A(1+g) \left[\frac{1 - \dfrac{(1+g)^n}{(1+r)^n}}{r - g} \right]$$

The present value of a growing annuity can be estimated in all cases but one—when the growth rate is equal to the discount rate. In that case, the present value is equal to the nominal sums of the annuities over the period, without the growth effect.

$$PV \text{ of a growing annuity for } n \text{ years (when } r = g) = nA$$

Note also that this formulation works even when the growth rate is greater than the discount rate.[2]

To illustrate a growing annuity, suppose you have the rights to a gold mine for the next twenty years, over which time you plan to extract 5,000 ounces of gold every year. The current price per ounce is $300 and is expected to increase 3% a year. The appropriate discount rate is 10%. The present value of the gold that will be extracted from this mine can be estimated as follows:

$$PV \text{ of extracted gold} = \$300 * 5000 * (1.03) \left[\frac{1 - \dfrac{(1.03)^{20}}{(1.10)^{20}}}{0.10 - 0.03} \right] = \$16,145,980$$

The present value of the gold expected to be extracted from this mine is $16.146 million; it is an increasing function of the expected growth rate in gold prices. Figure A3.6 illustrates the present value as a function of the expected growth rate.

Perpetuities

A *perpetuity* is a constant cash flow at regular intervals forever. The present value of a perpetuity can be written as

$$PV \text{ of perpetuity} = \frac{A}{r}$$

where A is the perpetuity. The most common example offered for a perpetuity is a console bond. A console bond is a bond that has no maturity and pays a fixed coupon. Assume that you have a 6% coupon console bond. The value of this bond, if the interest rate is 9%, is as follows:

$$\text{Value of console bond} = \$60/0.09 = \$667$$

The value of a console bond will be equal to its face value (which is usually $1,000) only if the coupon rate is equal to the interest rate.

Growing Perpetuities

A *growing perpetuity* is a cash flow that is expected to grow at a constant rate forever. The present value of a growing perpetuity can be written as

$$PV \text{ of growing perpetuity} = \frac{CF_1}{(r - g)}$$

where CF_1 is the expected cash flow next year, g is the constant growth rate, and r is the discount rate. Although a growing perpetuity and a growing annuity share several features, the fact that a growing perpetuity lasts forever puts constraints on the growth rate. It has to be less than the discount rate for this formula to work.

---

[2]Both the denominator and the numerator in the formula will be negative, yielding a positive present value.

Figure A3.6   Present Value of Extracted Gold as a Function of Growth Rate

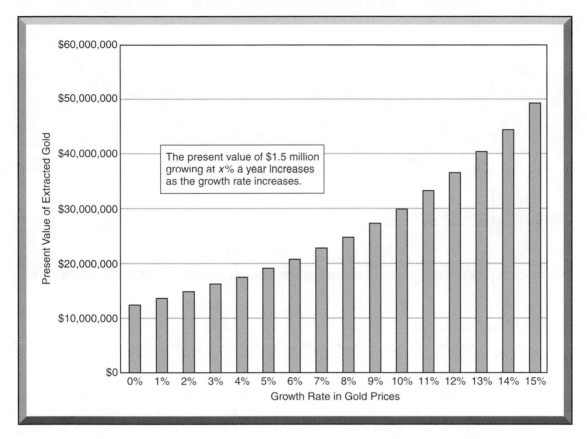

Growing perpetuities are especially useful when valuing equity in publicly traded firms, because they could potentially have perpetual lives. Consider a simple example. In 1992, Southwestern Bell paid dividends per share of $2.73. Its earnings and dividends had grown at 6% a year between 1988 and 1992 and were expected to grow at the same rate in the long run. The rate of return required by investors on stocks of equivalent risk was 12.23%. With these inputs, we can value the stock using a perpetual growth model:

$$\text{Value of stock} = \$2.73 * 1.06/(0.1223 - 0.06) = \$46.45$$

As an aside, the stock was actually trading at $70 per share. This price could be justified by using a higher growth rate. The value of the stock is graphed in Figure A3.7 as a function of the expectedgrowth rate.

The growth rate would have to be approximately 8% to justify a price of $70. This growth rate is often referred to as an *implied growth rate*.

Figure A3.7   Southwestern Bell: Value versus Expected Growth

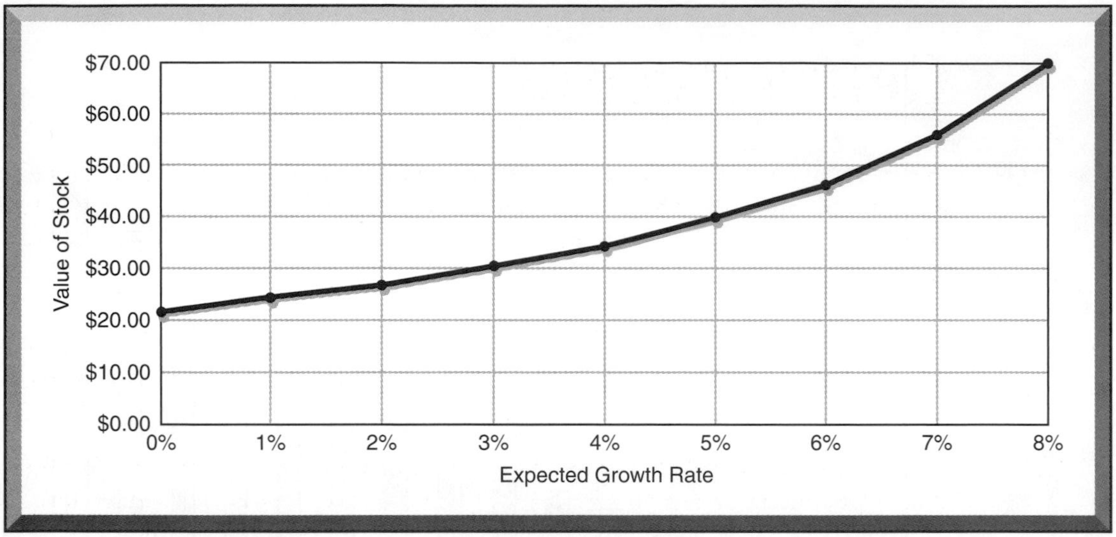

CONCLUSION

Present value remains one of the simplest and most powerful techniques in finance, providing a wide range of applications in both personal and business decisions. Cash flow can be moved back to present value terms by discounting and can be moved forward by compounding. The discount rate at which the discounting and compounding are done reflects three factors: (1) the preference for current consumption, (2) expected inflation, and (3) the uncertainty associated with the cash flows being discounted.

In this appendix, we explored approaches to estimating the present value of five types of cash flows: simple cash flows, annuities, growing annuities, perpetuities, and growing perpetuities.

APPENDIX 4

OPTION PRICING

In general, the value of any asset is the present value of the expected cash flows on that asset. In this appendix, we will consider an exception to that rule when we will look at assets with two specific characteristics:

1. They derive their value from the values of other assets.
2. The cash flows on the assets are contingent on the occurrence of specific events.

These assets are called options, and the present value of the expected cash flows on them will understate their true value. We will describe the cash flow characteristics of options, consider the factors that determine their value, and examine how best to value them.

Cash Flows on Options

There are two types of options. A *call option* gives the buyer of the option the right to buy the underlying asset at a fixed price, whereas a *put option* gives the buyer the right to sell the underlying asset at a fixed price. In both cases, the fixed price at which the underlying asset can be bought or sold is called the *strike* or *exercise price*.

To look at the payoffs on an option, consider first the case of a call option. When you acquire the right to buy an asset at a fixed price, you want the price of the asset to increase above that fixed price. If it does, you make a profit, because you can buy at the fixed price and then sell at the much higher price; this profit has to be netted against the cost initially paid for the option. However, if the price of the asset decreases below the strike price, it does not make sense to exercise your right to buy it at a higher price. In this scenario, you lose what you originally paid for the option. Figure A4.1 summarizes the cash payoff at expiration to the buyer of a call option.

With a put option, you get the right to sell at a fixed price, so you want the price of the asset to decrease below the exercise price. If it does, you buy the asset at the current price and then sell it back at the exercise price, claiming the difference as a gross profit. When the initial cost of buying the option is netted against the gross profit, you arrive at an estimate of the net profit. If the value of the asset rises above the exercise price, you will not exercise the right to sell at a lower price. Instead, the option will be allowed to expire without being exercised, resulting in a net loss of the original price paid for the put option. Figure A4.2 summarizes the net payoff on buying a put option.

With both call and put options, the potential for profit to the buyer is significant, but the potential for loss is limited to the price paid for the option.

Figure A4.1   Payoff on Call Option

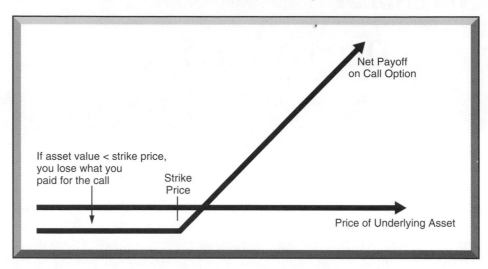

Figure A4.2   Payoff on Put Option

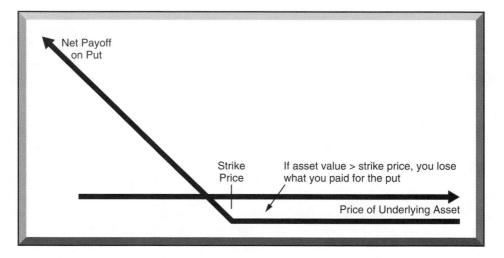

Determinants of Option Value

What is it that determines the value of an option? At one level, options have expected cash flows just like all other assets, which may seem like good candidates for discounted cash flow valuation. The two key characteristics of options—that they derive their value from some other traded asset, and that their cash flows are contingent on the occurrence of a specific event—does suggest an easier alternative. We can create a portfolio that has the same cash flows as the option being valued by combining a position in the underlying asset with borrowing or lending. This portfolio is called a *replicating portfolio* and should cost the same amount as the option. The principle that two assets (the option and the replicating portfolio) with identical cash flows cannot sell at different prices is called the *arbitrage principle*.

The Binomial Model

The simplest model for illustrating the replicating portfolio and arbitrage principles on which option pricing is based is the binomial model. The *binomial option pricing model* is based on a simple formulation for the asset price process in which the asset, in any time period, can move to one of two possible prices. The general formulation of a stock price process that follows the binomial is shown in Figure A4.3.

In this figure, S is the current stock price; the price moves up to Su with probability p and down to Sd with probability $1-p$ in any time period. For instance, if the stock price today is $100, u is 1.1, and d is 0.9, then the stock price in the next period can either be $110 (if u is the outcome) or $90 (if d is the outcome).

The objective in creating a replicating portfolio is to use a combination of risk-free borrowing/lending and the underlying asset to create the same cash flows as the option being valued. In the case of the general formulation, where stock prices can either move up to Su or down to Sd in any time period, the replicating portfolio for a call with a given strike price will involve borrowing $B and acquiring Δ of the underlying asset. Of course, this formulation is of no use if we cannot determine how much we need to borrow and what Δ is. There is a way, however, of identifying both variables. To do this, note that the value of this position has to be same as the value of the call, no matter what the stock price does. Let us assume that the value of the call is C_u if the stock price goes to Su, and C_d if the stock price goes down to Sd. If we had borrowed $B and bought Δ shares of stock with the money, the value of this position under the two scenarios would have been as follows.

Figure A4.3 General Formulation for Binomial Price Path

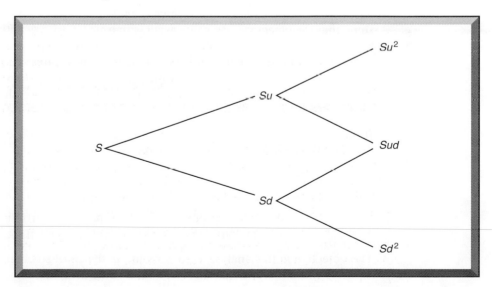

	Value of Position	Value of Call
If stock price goes up to Su	$\Delta Su - \$B(1 + r)$	C_u
If stock price goes down to Sd	$\Delta Sd - \$B(1 + r)$	C_d

Note that in either case, we have to pay back the borrowing with interest. Because the position has to have the same cash flows as the call, we get

$$\Delta Su - \$B(1 + r) = C_u$$
$$\Delta Sd - \$B(1 + r) = C_d$$

Solving for Δ, we get

$$\Delta = \text{Number of units of the underlying asset bought} = (C_u - C_d)/(Su - Sd)$$

where

$$C_u = \text{Value of the call if the stock price is } Su \text{ and}$$
$$C_d = \text{Value of the call if the stock price is } Sd.$$

When there are multiple periods involved, we have to begin with the last period, where we know what the cash flows on the call will be, solve for the replicating portfolio, and then estimate how much it would cost us to create this portfolio. We use this value as the estimated value of the call and estimate the replicating portfolio in the previous period. We continue to do this until we get to the present. The replicating portfolio we obtain for the present can be priced to yield a current value for the call.

$$\text{Value of the call} = \text{Current value of underlying asset} * \text{Option delta} - \text{Borrowing needed to replicate the option}$$

ILLUSTRATION A4.1   An Example of Binomial Valuation

Assume that the objective is to value a call with a strike price of $50, which is expected to expire in two time periods, on an underlying asset whose price is currently $50, and expected to follow a binomial process. Figure A4.4 illustrates the path of underlying asset prices and the value of the call (with a strike price of 50) at the expiration.

Note that because the call has a strike price of $50, the gross cash flows at expiration are as follows:

If the stock price moves to $100: Cash flow on call = $100 − $50 = $50
If the stock price moves to $50: Cash flow on call = $50 − $50 = $0
If the stock price moves to $25: Cash flow on call = $0 (option is not exercised)

Now assume that the interest rate is 11%. In addition, define

$$\Delta = \text{Number of shares in the replicating portfolio}$$
$$B = \text{Dollars of borrowing in replicating portfolio}$$

The objective in this analysis is to combine Δ shares of stock and $B of borrowing to replicate the cash flows from the call with a strike price of $50.

Figure A4.4   Binomial Price Path

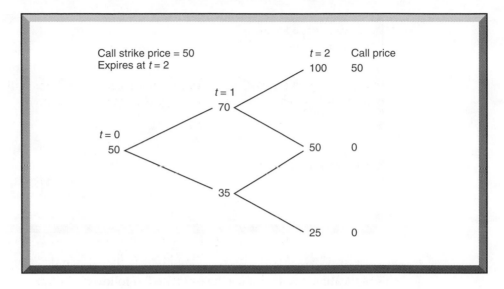

Call strike price = 50
Expires at $t = 2$

	$t = 2$	Call price
	100	50
$t = 1$ 70		
$t = 0$ 50	50	0
	35	
	25	0

Figure A4.5   Replicating Portfolios When Price Is $ 70

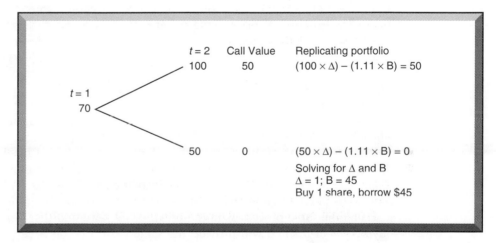

	$t = 2$	Call Value	Replicating portfolio
	100	50	$(100 \times \Delta) - (1.11 \times B) = 50$
$t = 1$ 70			
	50	0	$(50 \times \Delta) - (1.11 \times B) = 0$
			Solving for Δ and B $\Delta = 1$; B = 45 Buy 1 share, borrow $45

The first step in doing this is to start with the last period and work backward. Consider, for instance, one possible outcome at $t = 1$. The stock price has jumped to $70 and is poised to change again, either to $100 or $50. We know the cash flows on the call under either scenario, and we also have a replicating portfolio composed of Δ shares of the underlying stock and $B of borrowing. Writing out the cash flows on the replicating portfolio under both scenarios (stock price of $100 and $50), we get the replicating portfolios in Figure A4.5:

In other words, if the stock price is $70 at $t = 1$, borrowing $45 and buying one share of the stock will give the same cash flows as buying the call. The value of the call

Figure A4.6   Replicating Portfolio When Price Is $35

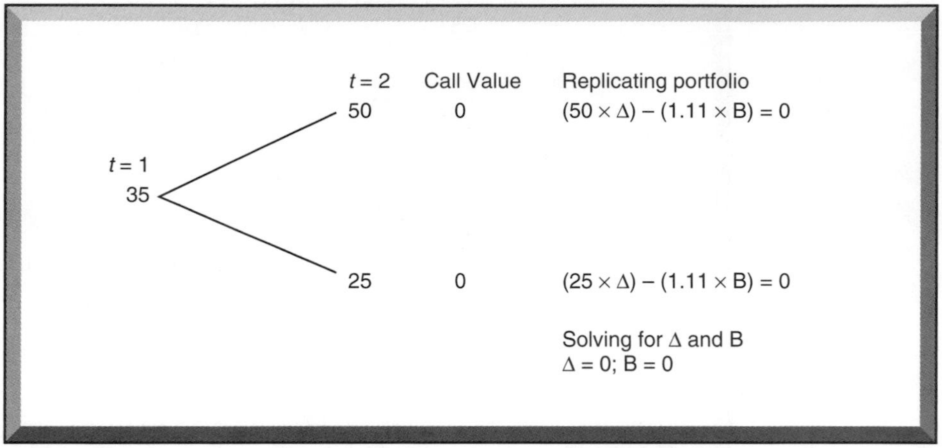

at $t = 1$, if the stock price is $70, should thus be the cash flow associated with creating this replicating position; it can be estimated as follows:

$$70\Delta - B = 70 - 45 = 25$$

The cost of creating this position is only $25, because $45 of the $70 is borrowed. This should also be the price of the call at $t = 1$ if the stock price is $70.

Consider now the other possible outcome at $t = 1$ where the stock price is $35 and is poised to jump to either $50 or $25. Here again, the cash flows on the call can be estimated, as can the cash flows on the replicating portfolio composed of Δ shares of stock and $B of borrowing. Figure A4.6 illustrates the replicating portfolio.

Because the call is worth nothing under either scenario, the replicating portfolio also is empty. The cash flow associated with creating this position is obviously zero, which becomes the value of the call at $t = 1$ if the stock price is $35.

We now have the value of the call under both outcomes at $t = 1$; it is worth $25 if the stock price goes to $70 and $0 if it goes to $35. We now move back to today ($t = 0$) and look at the cash flows on the replicating portfolio. Figure A4.7 summarizes the replicating portfolios as viewed from today.

Using the same process as in the previous step, we find that borrowing $22.50 and buying 5/7 of a share will provide the same cash flows as a call with a strike price of $50. The cost to the investor of borrowing $22.5 and buying 5/7 of a share at the current stock price of $50 yields:

$$\text{Cost of replicating position} = 5/7 * \$50 - \$22.5 = \$13.20$$

This should also be the value of the call.

The Black–Scholes Model

While the binomial model provides an intuitive feel for the determinants of option value, it requires a large number of inputs in terms of expected future prices at each node. As we make time periods shorter in the binomial model, we can make one of

Figure A4.7 Replicating Portfolios for Call Value

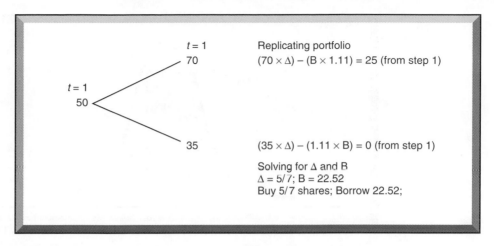

two assumptions about asset prices. We can assume that price changes become smaller as periods get shorter; this leads to price changes becoming infinitesimally small as time periods approach zero, leading to a **continuous price process**. Alternatively, we can assume that price changes stay large even as the period gets shorter; this leads to a **jump price process**, wherein prices can jump in any period.[1] When the price process is continuous, the binomial model for pricing options converges on the Black–Scholes model. The model, named after its creators, Fischer Black and Myron Scholes, allows us to estimate the value of any option using a small number of inputs and has been shown to be remarkably robust in valuing many listed options.[2]

The Model

While the derivation of the Black–Scholes model is far too complicated to present here, it is also based upon the idea of creating a portfolio of the underlying asset and the riskless asset with the same cash flows, and hence the same cost as the option being valued. The value of a call option in the Black–Scholes model can be written as a function of the five variables:

$$S = \text{Current value of the underlying asset}$$
$$K = \text{Strike price of the option}$$
$$t = \text{Life to expiration of the option}$$
$$r = \text{Riskless interest rate corresponding to the life of the option}$$
$$\sigma^2 = \text{Variance in the ln(value)of the underlying asset}$$

The value of a call is then

$$\text{Value of call} = SN(d_1) - Ke^{-rt}N(d_2)$$

---

[1]While we do not consider jump process option pricing models in this appendix, they do exist but are not widely used because of the difficulties we face in estimating jump process parameters.

[2]See F. Black and M. Scholes, "The Valuation of Option Contracts and a Test of Market Efficiency," *Journal of Finance* 27:399–417.

Figure A4.8   Cumulative Normal Distribution

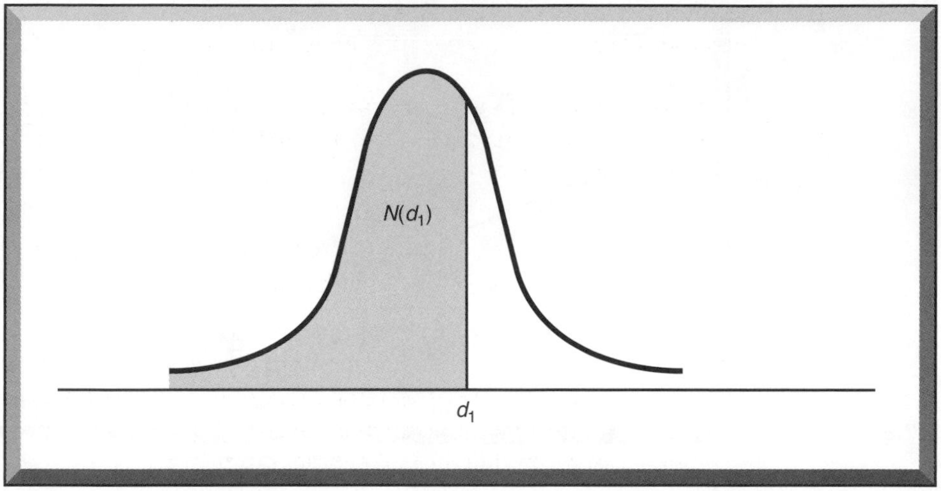

where

$$d_1 = \frac{\ln\left(\frac{S}{K}\right) + \left(r + \frac{\sigma^2}{2}\right)t}{\sigma\sqrt{t}}$$

$$d_2 = d_1 - \sigma\sqrt{t}$$

Note that e^{-rt} is the present value factor and reflects the fact that the exercise price on the call option does not have to be paid until expiration. $N(d_1)$ and $N(d_2)$ are probabilities, estimated by using a cumulative standardized normal distribution and the values of d_1 and d_2 obtained for an option. The cumulative distribution is shown in Figure A4.8:

In approximate terms, these probabilities yield the likelihood that an option will generate positive cash flows for its owner at exercise—i.e., when $S > K$ in the case of a call option and when $K > S$ in the case of a put option. The portfolio that replicates the call option is created by buying $N(d_1)$ units of the underlying asset, and borrowing $Ke^{-rt}N(d_2)$. The portfolio will have the same cash flows as the call option and thus the same value as the option. $N(d_1)$, which is the number of units of the underlying asset that are needed to create the replicating portfolio, is called the **option delta**.

Model Limitations and Fixes
The Black–Scholes model was designed to value options that can be exercised only at maturity, and on underlying assets that do not pay dividends. In addition, options are valued based upon the assumption that option exercise does not affect the value of the underlying asset. In practice, assets do pay dividends, options sometimes get exercised early, and exercising an option can affect the value of the underlying asset. While they are not perfect, adjustments do provide partial corrections to the Black–Scholes model.

Dividends The payment of a dividend reduces the stock price; note that on the ex-dividend day, the stock price generally declines. Consequently, call options will become less valuable and put options more valuable as expected dividend payments increase. There are two ways of dealing with dividends in the Black–Scholes:

1. **Short-Term Options:** One approach to dealing with dividends is to estimate the present value of expected dividends that will be paid by the underlying asset during the option life and subtract it from the current value of the asset to use as S in the model.

   Modified stock price = Current stock price − Present value of expected dividends during the life of the option

2. **Long-Term Options:** Since it becomes impractical to estimate the present value of dividends as the option life becomes longer, we suggest an alternate approach. If the dividend yield (y = dividends/current value of the asset) on the underlying asset is expected to remain unchanged during the life of the option, the Black–Scholes model can be modified to take dividends into account.

$$C = Se^{-yt}N(d_1) - Ke^{-rt}N(d_2)$$

where

$$d_1 = \frac{\ln\left(\frac{S}{K}\right) + \left(r - y + \frac{\sigma^2}{2}\right)t}{\sigma\sqrt{t}}$$

$$d_2 = d_1 - \sigma\sqrt{t}$$

From an intuitive standpoint, the adjustments have two effects. First, the value of the asset is discounted back to the present at the dividend yield to take into account the expected drop in asset value resulting from dividend payments. Second, the interest rate is offset by the dividend yield to reflect the lower carrying cost from holding the asset (in the replicating portfolio). The net effect will be a reduction in the value of calls estimated using this model.

Early Exercise The Black–Scholes model was designed to value options that can be exercised only at expiration. Options with this characteristic are called **European options**. In contrast, most options that we encounter in practice can be exercised any time until expiration. These options are called **American options**. The possibility of early exercise makes American options more valuable than otherwise similar European options; it also makes them more difficult to value. In general, though, with traded options, it is almost always better to sell the option to someone else rather than exercise early, since options have a time premium—i.e., they sell for more than their exercise value. There are two exceptions. One occurs when the underlying asset pays large dividends, thus reducing the expected value of the asset. In this case, call options may be exercised *just before an ex-dividend* date, if the time premium on the options is less than the expected decline in asset value as a consequence of the dividend payment. The other exception arises when an investor holds both the underlying asset and *deep in-the-money puts*—i.e., puts with strike prices well above the current price of the underlying asset—on that asset when interest rates are high. In this case, the time premium on the put may be less than the potential gain from exercising the put early and earning interest on the exercise price.

There are two basic ways of dealing with the possibility of early exercise. One is to continue to use the unadjusted Black–Scholes model and regard the resulting value as a floor or conservative estimate of the true value. The other is to try to adjust the value of the option for the possibility of early exercise. There are two approaches for doing so. One uses the Black–Scholes to value the option to each potential exercise date. With options on stocks, this basically requires that we value options to each ex-dividend day and choose the maximum of the estimated call values. The second approach is to use a modified version of the binomial model to consider the possibility of early exercise. In this version, the up and down movements for asset prices in each period can be estimated from the variance and the length of each period.[3]

The Impact of Exercise on the Value of the Underlying Asset   The Black–Scholes model is based upon the assumption that exercising an option does not affect the value of the underlying asset. This may be true for listed options on stocks, but it is not true for some types of options. For instance, the exercise of warrants increases the number of shares outstanding and brings fresh cash into the firm, both of which will affect the stock price.[4] The expected negative impact (dilution) of exercise will decrease the value of warrants compared to otherwise similar call options. The adjustment for dilution in the Black–Scholes to the stock price is fairly simple. The stock price is adjusted for the expected dilution from the exercise of the options. In the case of warrants, for instance,

$$\text{Dilution-adjusted } S = \frac{Sn_S + Wn_W}{n_S + n_W}$$

where

$$S = \text{Current value of the stock}$$
$$n_w = \text{Number of warrants outstanding}$$
$$W = \text{Value of warrants outstanding}$$
$$ns = \text{Number of shares outstanding}$$

When the warrants are exercised, the number of shares outstanding will increase, reducing the stock price. The numerator reflects the market value of equity, including both stocks and warrants outstanding. The reduction in S will reduce the value of the call option.

---

[3]To illustrate, if σ^2 is the variance in ln(stock prices), the up and down movements in the binomial can be estimated as follows:

$$u = e^{\left[\left(r - \frac{\sigma^2}{2}\right)\left(\frac{T}{m}\right) + \sqrt{\frac{\sigma^2 T}{m}}\right]}$$

$$d = e^{\left[\left(r - \frac{\sigma^2}{2}\right)\left(\frac{T}{m}\right) - \sqrt{\frac{\sigma^2 T}{m}}\right]}$$

where u and d are the up and down movements per unit time for the binomial, T is the life of the option, and m is the number of periods within that lifetime.

[4]Warrants are call options issued by firms, either as part of management compensation contracts or to raise equity. We will discuss them in Chapter 16.

There is an element of circularity in this analysis, since the value of the warrant is needed to estimate the dilution-adjusted S and the dilution-adjusted S is needed to estimate the value of the warrant. This problem can be resolved by starting the process off with an assumed value for the warrant (say, the exercise value or the current market price of the warrant). This will yield a value for the warrant, and this estimated value can then be used as an input to reestimate the warrant's value until there is convergence.

CONCLUSION

An option is an asset with payoffs that are contingent on the value of an underlying asset. A call option provides its holder with the right to buy the underlying asset at a fixed price, whereas a put option provides its holder with the right to sell at a fixed price, any time before the expiration of the option. The value of an option is determined by six variables: the current value of the underlying asset, the variance in this value, the strike price, the life of the option, the riskless interest rate, and the expected dividends on the asset. This is illustrated in both the binomial and Black–Scholes models, which value options by creating replicating portfolios composed of the underlying asset and riskless lending or borrowing.

Glossary

(For a more complete listing, check online on the website for the book)

Arbitrage: An investment opportunity with no risk that earns a return higher than the riskless rate.

Assets in Place: The assets already owned by a firm, or projects that it has already taken.

Bankruptcy Costs: The costs associated with going bankrupt. It includes both direct costs (from going bankrupt) and indirect costs (arising from the perception that a firm may go bankrupt).

Beta: The beta of any investment in the CAPM is a standardized measure of the risk that it adds to the market portfolio.

Bond Covenants: Covenants are restrictions built into contractual agreements. The most common reference in corporate finance to covenants is in bond agreements, and they represent restrictions placed by lenders on investment, financing, and dividend decisions made by the firm.

Book-to-Market Ratio: This is the ratio of the book value of equity to the market value of equity.

Capital Rationing: The scenario where the firm does not have sufficient funds—either on hand or in terms of access to markets—to take on all of the good projects it might have.

Commodity-Linked Bonds: Bonds in which the interest and/or the principal payments are linked to the price of the commodity. In most cases, the payments will increase or decrease with the price of the commodity.

Comparable (Firm): A firm similar to the firm being analyzed in terms of underlying characteristics in risk, growth, and cash flow patterns. The conventional definition of a comparable firm is one that is the same business as the one being analyzed, and of similar size.

Competitive Risk: The unanticipated effect on the cash flows in a project of competitor actions, whether positive or negative.

Contingent Value Rights: A contingent value right provides the holder with the right to sell a share of stock in the underlying company at a fixed price during the life of the right.

Convertible Debt: Debt that can be converted into equity at a rate that is specified as part of the debt agreement (conversion rate).

Cyclical Firm: A firm whose revenues and operating income tend to move strongly with the economy—up when the economy is doing well, and down during recessions.

Default Risk: The risk that a firm will fail to make obligated debt payments, such as interest expenses or principal payments.

Diversification: The process of holding many investments in a portfolio, either across the same asset class (e.g. stocks) or across asset classes (real estate, bonds, etc.).

Double Taxation: When the same income gets taxed twice—once at the entity level, and once at the individual level. Thus, dividends, which are paid out of after-tax corporate profits, are double-taxed when individuals have to pay taxes on them as well.

Factor Analysis: A statistical technique in which past data is analyzed with the intent of extracting common factors that might have affected the data.

Financial Flexibility: The capacity of firms to meet any unforeseen contingencies that may arise (such as recessions and sales downturns) and take advantage of unanticipated opportunities (such as great projects), using funds on hand and any excess debt capacity that they might have nurtured.

Free Cash Flows (Jensen's): The free cash flows referred to here are the operating cash flows after taxes but before discretionary capital expenditures.

Golden Parachute: A golden parachute refers to a contractual clause in a management contract that allows the manager to be paid a specified sum of money in the event control of the firm changes, usually in the context of a hostile takeover.

Greenmail: Greenmail refers to the purchase of a potential hostile acquirer's stake in a business at a premium over the price paid for that stake by the target company.

Hurdle Rate: A hurdle rate is a minimum acceptable rate of return for investing resources in a new investment.

Hurdle Rate: The minimum acceptable rate of return that a firm will accept for taking a given project.

Hybrid Security: Any security that shares some of the characteristics of debt and some characteristics of equity.

Industry-Specific Risk: Unanticipated effects on project cash flows of industry-wide shifts in technology or changes in laws, or in the price of a commodity.

Internal Rate of Return (IRR): The rate of return earned by the project based on cash flows, allowing for the time value of money.

International Risk: The additional uncertainty created in cash flows of projects by unanticipated changes in exchange rates and by political risk in foreign markets.

Investment Grade Bonds: An investment grade bond has a rating greater than BBB. Some institutional investors, such as pension funds, are constrained from holding bonds with lower ratings.

Jensen's Alpha: This is the difference between the actual return on an asset and the return you would have expected it to make during a past period, given what the market did and the asset's beta.

Leveraged Recapitalization: In a leveraged recapitalization, a firm borrows money and either buys back stock or pays a dividend, thus increasing its debt ratio substantially.

Market Risk: Market risk refers to the unanticipated changes in project cash flows created by changes in interest rates, inflation rates, and the economy that affect all firms, though to differing degrees.

Modified Internal Rate of Return (MIRR): The IRR computed on the assumption that intermediate cash flows are reinvested at the hurdle rate.

Mutually Exclusive Projects: A group of projects is said to be mutually exclusive when acceptance of one of the projects implies that the rest have to be rejected.

Net Present Value (NPV): The sum of the present values of the expected cash flows on the project, net of the initial investment.

NPV Profile: This measures the sensitivity of the NPV to changes in the discount rate.

Operating Leverage: A measure of the proportion of the operating expenses of a company that are fixed costs.

Opportunity Cost: The cost assigned to a project resource that is already owned by the firm. It is based on the next best alternative use.

Payback: The length of time it will take for nominal cash flows from the project to cover the initial investment.

Poison Pill: A security or a provision that is triggered by the hostile acquisition of the firm, resulting in a large cost to the acquirer.

Preferred Stock: A hybrid security. Like debt, it has a promised payment (the preferred dividend) in each period. Like equity, its cash flows are not tax-deductible, and it has an infinite life.

Product Cannibalization: Sales generated by one product that come at the expense of other products manufactured by the same firm.

Project Risk: Risk that affects only the project under consideration and that may arise from factors specific to the project or estimation error.

Project Synergy: The increase in cash flows that accrue to other projects as a consequence of the project under consideration.

Public and Private Information: Public information refers to any information that is available to the investing public, whereas private information is restricted to only insiders or a few investors in the firm.

R Squared (R^2): The R squared measures the proportion of the variability of a dependent variable that is explained by an independent variable or variables in a regression.

Real Option: An option on a nontraded asset, such as an investment project or a gold mine.

Riskless Asset: A riskless asset is one for which the actual return is always equal to the expected return.

Salvage Value: The estimated liquidation value of the assets invested in the projects at the end of the project life.

Synergy: The additional value created by bringing together two entities and pooling their strengths. In the context of a merger, synergy is the difference between the value of the merged firm and sum of the values of the firms operating independently.

Unanticipated Inflation: This is the difference between actual inflation and expected inflation.

Variance in Returns: This is a measure of the squared difference between the actual returns and the expected returns on an investment.

Venture Capital: Equity capital provided to a private firm by investors, in exchange for a share of the ownership of the\break firm.

Warrant: A security issued by a company that provides the holder with the right to buy a share of stock in the company at a fixed price during the life of the warrant.

INDEX